Econometric Analysis

ECONOMETRIC ANALYSIS

William H. Greene
NEW YORK UNIVERSITY

MACMILLAN PUBLISHING COMPANY
New York

COLLIER MACMILLAN PUBLISHERS
London

Macmillan Publishing Company
866 Third Avenue, New York, New York 10022

Collier Macmillan Canada, Inc.

Library of Congress Cataloging in Publication Data

Greene, William H. (date)
    Econometric analysis/William H. Greene.
        p.   cm.
    Includes index.
    ISBN 0-02-346390-2
    1. Econometrics.   I. Title.
HB139.G74 1990
330'.028—dc19
                                                        88-23400
                                                            CIP

Printing: 1 2 3 4 5 6 7 8   Year: 0 1 2 3 4 5 6 7 8 9

BOOK TEAM

Acquisition Editor: *Kenneth MacLeod*
Production Supervisor: *Elaine Wetterau*
Production Manager: *Nicholas Sklitsis*
Text Designer: *Patricia Smythe*
Cover Designer: *Patricia Smythe*
Cover illustration: *Leslie Bakshi*
Illustrations: *ECL Art Associates*
This book was set in Times Roman by Polyglot, printed by Quinn Woodbine, and bound by Quinn Woodbine. The cover was printed by Phoenix Color Corp.

Preface

This book is intended for a one-year graduate course in econometrics. The prerequisites for that course include calculus, statistics, and an introduction to econometrics at the level of, say, Gujarati's *Basic Econometrics* (McGraw-Hill, 1988) or Maddala's *Introduction to Econometrics* (Macmillan, 1988). I have included in Chapters 2 through 4 self-contained summaries of the matrix algebra and statistical theory used later in the book. The remainder of the book is intended to provide an up-to-date summary of econometric methods. This includes the traditional treatment of multiple linear regression as well as, for example, more recent developments in hypothesis testing including Lagrange multiplier tests, specification tests, microeconometrics, the analysis of panel data, and limited dependent variables.

Although the coverage of this book is comprehensive, there is one omission that will be readily apparent. I admit at the outset a rather limited treatment of time-series analysis and ARIMA modeling. I hope that time-series enthusiasts will not feel shortchanged. It is impossible to do justice to this topic in a single chapter of any book. Since there are book-length treatments at every level, there is no shortage of material for students to read. Some may also find missing one or more particular subjects that have some appeal for them. For example, I have not discussed models of rational expectations or the new work on duration models (too advanced). Also, I suppose that there is more to be said on the subject of aggregation. But the book is long as it is, and enough is enough.

I have attempted to keep the mathematical level consistent throughout. This has meant liberal use of matrix algebra—one simply cannot talk one's way through three-stage least squares—but has required relatively little advanced distribution theory. Still, purists might prefer more in the way of detailed mathematical proofs. I give formal proofs only when they are particularly revealing about some underlying principle that will reappear in other contexts or provide students with a useful tool for their work. White's proof of the limiting distribution of the Wald statistic in Chapter 10 is an example. In contrast, a proof of the central limit theorem, while obviously of great utility on its own, is a one-shot deal. For those who are teaching at a relatively high level and who desire more of the theorem/proof format, I would suggest Peter Schmidt's *Econometrics* (Marcel Dekker, 1976) as a very handy adjunct.

One feature that distinguishes this work from its predecessors is its greater attention to nonlinear models, including full chapters on nonlinear regression and nonlinear optimization. Computer software now in wide use has made estimation of nonlinear models as simple as estimation of linear ones, and the recent literature reflects that progression. The purpose of these chapters is to bring the textbook treatment up to the level of common practice. I have also included two long chapters on limited dependent-variable models. These models are becoming ever more common in the applied literature. I have written these chapters because there is no other source that presents these topics at a level elementary enough to initiate the newcomer but complete enough to enable a diligent student to use the information to undertake a serious piece of empirical analysis.

Finally, the reader will note an occasional discussion of the computational aspects of some econometric methods. It is now generally accepted that training in econometrics must include some exposure to the mechanics of computation. This, it seems to me, should be self-evident. Computers and computer software have come a long way from the days when one trudged across campus in the snow to hand a deck of cards to the operator of a hostile mainframe (only to find out the next day that the entire job had aborted because of a comma punched in the wrong column). The greatest advance has been the appearance of microcomputers, which have changed both teaching and research. One now has on a desktop as much computing power as was once contained in a room-sized mainframe. What this means for teaching is that students can be given realistic data sets and challenging empirical analyses as routinely as theoretical exercises. To this end, I have included in this book a large number of data sets, many of which have been used in studies already in the literature. In addition, the appendix to Chapter 19 contains a yearly data set on a number of macroeconomic variables. (Quarterly data are available from the same sources.) These could be used, for example, to update Klein's model I or, for the more ambitious, to estimate a new model.

There are many computer programs that students can use in an econometrics course. Their most important features are ease of use and flexibility; the same program can easily be used for many different types of analyses. (Every worked example in this book was computed with the same program, ET.) A partial list of the general econometrics programs now in use is as follows:

ET*	Professor William Greene, Stern School of Business, New York University (general econometrics, Tobit, probit, matrix algebra)
GAUSS*	Aptech Systems, Kent, Washington (matrix programming language, maximum likelihood)
LIMDEP	W. Greene (limited and qualitative dependent variables and general econometrics)
MicroTSP*	Quantitative Micro Software, Irvine, California (forecasting and time-series models, nonlinear regression)
RATS	VAR Econometrics, Minneapolis, Minnesota (regression analysis of time series)
SAS	SAS Institute, Cary, North Carolina (general econometrics and modeling)
SHAZAM	Professor Ken White, University of British Columbia (general econometrics, multiple-equations models, Tobit, probit)
SORITEC	Sorites Group, Springfield, Virginia (large-scale multiple-equation modeling)
SPSS	SPSS, Inc., Chicago, Illinois (general statistical analysis for social scientists)
SST	Dubin Rivers Research, Pasadena, California (regression, maximum likelihood, limited dependent variables)
TSP	TSP International, Palo Alto, California (general econometrics, linear and nonlinear multiple-equation models, time-series analysis)

Most of these programs are available in both mainframe and microcomputer versions. Those marked with an asterisk were written especially for personal computers. All are general-purpose programs. Their primary differences (apart from price) are their range of techniques (suggested in the listing), the amount of programming required of the user, and the level of difficulty of command entry. For the last of these, programs vary from those with commands that are very low level, such as Gauss which is a programming language, to those that use powerful single commands to invoke large processors that automate many complex computations, such as TSP's LSQ procedures. Since the tastes and needs of users will vary, prospective users should contact the authors for information about the programs. Journals such as *The American Statistician* also publish reviews of particular programs. Finally, a clearing house for information about software is the Economic and Social Research Council Centre in Economic Computing at the London School of Economics.

It is a pleasure to express my appreciation to those who have influenced this work (some inadvertently). I would add my name to the long list of practitioners, teachers, and authors who have thanked Arthur Goldberger for his contribution to their education. Dennis Aigner and Laurits Christensen were also influential in shaping my views on econometrics. The number of students and colleagues whose input has helped produce what you find here is far too large to allow me to thank them individually. I do owe a debt to Aline Quester, whose persistent questioning and encouragement strongly influenced Chapters 20 and 21, and to David Hensher and Donald Waldman, who allowed me to cite their unpublished work in these chapters.

This book has benefited at several stages from the careful reading of many reviewers, including Badi H. Baltagi, University of Houston; Leonard A. Carlson, Emory University; Michael Ellis, Wesleyan University; K. Rao Kadiyala, Purdue University; Edward J. Mathis, Villanova University; Thad Mirer, State University of New York at Albany; Peter J. Schmidt, Michigan State University; Terry G. Seaks, University of North Carolina at Greensboro; Donald Snyder, California State University, Los Angeles; Houston H. Stokes, University of Illinois at Chicago; Mark Watson, Harvard University; and Kenneth D. West, Princeton University. I owe special thanks to Terry Seaks, whose painstaking review went far beyond the call of duty. I owe my greatest debt to my wife Lynne, who has tolerated with good humor and even encouraged this demanding intrusion into her life for over three years, and to my daughters Lesley, Allison, and Elizabeth.

W. H. G.

Contents

Part II   The Classical Regression Model

Part III   The Generalized Regression Model

Chapter 13   Nonspherical Disturbances   381

Chapter 14   Heteroscedasticity   397

Chapter 18   Models of Economic Time Series   543

Chapter 19   Simultaneous-Equations Models   591

Chapter 20   Models with Discrete Dependent Variables   661

Chapter 21   Limited Dependent Variable Models   715

Econometric Analysis

Chapter 1
Introduction

1.1. Econometrics

In the first issue of *Econometrica*, the Econometric Society stated that

> its main object shall be to promote studies that aim at a unification of the theoretical-quantitative and the empirical-quantitative approach to economic problems and that are penetrated by constructive and rigorous thinking similar to that which has come to dominate the natural sciences.
>
> But there are several aspects of the quantitative approach to economics, and no single one of these aspects, taken by itself, should be confounded with econometrics. Thus, econometrics is by no means the same as economic statistics. Nor is it identical with what we call general economic theory, although a considerable portion of this theory has a definitely quantitative character. Nor should econometrics be taken as synonomous [sic] with the application of mathematics to economics. Experience has shown that each of these three view-points, that of statistics, economic theory, and mathematics, is a necessary, but not by itself a sufficient, condition for a real understanding of the quantitative relations in modern economic life. It is the *unification* of all three that is powerful. And it is this unification that constitutes econometrics.[1]

Frisch and his society responded to an unprecedented accumulation of statistical information. They saw a need to establish a body of principles that could organize what would otherwise become a bewildering mass of data. Neither the pillars nor the objectives of econometrics have changed in the half century since this editorial appeared. Econometrics is the field of economics that concerns itself with the application of mathematical statistics and the tools of statistical inference to the empirical measurement of relationships postulated by economic theory.

1.2. Econometric Modeling

Economic theory is typically crisp and unambiguous. Models of demand, production, and aggregate consumption all postulate precise, *deterministic* relationships. Dependent and

---

[1] Frish (1933).

independent variables are identified, a functional form is specified, and, in most cases, at least a qualitative statement is made about effects that occur when independent variables in the model change. Of course, the model is only a simplification of reality. It will include the salient features of the relationship that interests us, but will leave unaccounted for influences that might well be present but are, for our purposes, unimportant. Naturally, people may differ on just how minimal some influences really are, and in the end, this may be yet another empirical question. Still, only the most optimistic analyst would expect to find an exact correspondence between his or her model and its real-world counterpart.

No model could hope to encompass the myriad essentially random aspects of economic life. For example, no matter how elegant or complete a model of production might be, it has no way of coping with the possibility that a snowy day might necessitate a plant closing and show up as an outlier in an otherwise immaculately constructed body of data on production costs. It is thus necessary to incorporate stochastic elements in our empirical models. As a consequence, observations on the dependent variable will display variation attributable not only to differences in variables we have explicitly accounted for, but also to the randomness of human behavior and the interaction of countless minor influences that we have not. Now it is understood that the introduction of a random "disturbance" into a deterministic model is not intended merely to paper over its inadequacies. It is essential to examine the results of the study, in a sort of post mortem, to ensure that the allegedly random, unexplained factor is truly unexplainable. If it is not, the model is, in fact, inadequate. To pursue our example, ignoring (or being unaware of) a snowstorm is one thing; neglecting regional differences in the unit prices of the factors of production is quite another. Without such omissions the stochastic element endows the model with its statistical properties. Observations on the variable(s) under study are thus taken to be the outcomes of a random process. With a sufficiently detailed stochastic structure and adequate data, our analysis will become a matter of deducing the properties of a probability distribution. The tools and methods of mathematical statistics will provide the operating principles.

A model (or theory) can never truly be confirmed unless it is made so broad as to exclude every other possibility. But we may subject it to ever more rigorous scrutiny and, in the face of contradictory evidence, refute it. A deterministic theory will be invalidated by a single errant observation. The introduction of stochastic elements into the model changes it from an exact statement to a probabilistic description about expected outcomes and carries with it an important implication. Only a preponderance of contradictory evidence can convincingly invalidate the probabilistic model, and what constitutes a "preponderance of evidence" is a matter of interpretation. Thus, the probabilistic model is both less precise and, perhaps not necessarily to the good, more robust.

The role of theory in econometrics cannot be overstated. The belief that we may scrutinize a set of nonexperimental data and expect some complex truth to be revealed to us if we only spend enough time manipulating the numbers is hopelessly optimistic. In an experimental setting, we are free to choose the values of the stimuli and move them in whatever way we wish to elicit a change in the response variable. What remains is only to quantify the observed relationship. In the realm of economics, we are only passive observers of the economy. The notion of a controlled experiment is almost unheard of. At best, we can expect to sample observations from a large population and to assume that the conditions needed to employ our tools of statistical inference are met. Theory plays the role of organizer of the data. With no theoretical basis, the result of the exercise is most likely to be an ambiguous catalog of possibilities.

The theorist has another advantage over the rank empiricist whether the objective is to forecast, control, or explain. To consider a widely cited example, the atheoretical forecasting models that are alleged to (and occasionally do) outperform their econometric counterparts rest on a slim reed. The forecasters who use them have no basis on which to pin their hope that the forecasting equations will perform well for yet one more period, other than that they did so in the past. *Je ne sais quoi.* They must hope for yet another favorable draw from the data-generating mechanism. Armed with a theoretical structure that has withstood serious empirical scrutiny, the theory-based modeler can at least justify the claim that, barring some fundamental change in the economy, the model will perform as well as it did in the past. The disadvantage of the empiricist in attempting to use his or her data to formulate a control mechanism is yet more stark, and, of course, the futility of attempting blindly to coerce a mass of data to explain how the economy operates is obvious. It is this reliance on an underlying theory to explain the data in hand that gives econometrics its unique flavor.

The process of econometric analysis departs from the specification of a theoretical relationship. We initially proceed on the optimistic assumption that we can obtain precise measurements on all of the variables in our correctly specified model. If the ideal conditions are met at every step, the subsequent analysis will probably be routine. Unfortunately, they rarely are. Some of the difficulties one can expect to encounter are the following:

1. The data may be badly measured or may correspond only vaguely to the variables in the model. "The interest rate" is one example.
2. Some of the variables may be inherently unmeasurable. "Expectations" are a case in point.
3. The theory may make only a rough guess as to the correct functional form, if it makes any at all, and we may be forced to choose from an embarrassingly long menu of possibilities.
4. The assumed stochastic properties of the random terms in the model may be demonstrably violated. This may call into question the methods of estimation and inference procedures we have used.
5. Some relevant variables may be missing from the model.

And so on. The ensuing steps of the analysis consist of coping with these problems and attempting to cull whatever information is likely to be present in such obviously imperfect data. The methodology is that of mathematical statistics and econometric theory. The product is an econometric model.

1.3.   *Theoretical and Applied Econometrics*

A distinction is usually made between theoretical and applied econometrics. A rough line can be drawn between the development of techniques and the application of those techniques in a particular setting. Theorists also analyze the consequences of applying particular methods when the assumptions that justify them are not met. But the distinction is often artificial. It is common for new techniques to be developed in the field, in response to a particular problem in a specific study, rather than in the laboratory.[2] This book is oriented to techniques that are usable (and used) in the field. Still, the emphasis is on methods, rather than on specific results.[3] The numerous examples are presented to illustrate techniques rather than to

---

[2] In the abstract, there is an intellectual appeal to a technique that is developed in order to solve a particular problem, as opposed to one that is devised, and then sent off to find a problem to solve.
[3] There are a number of excellent works devoted to applied econometrics, among them Bridge (1971), Desai (1976), and Berndt (1990).

produce new empirical evidence. In a few instances, we have attempted to replicate (sometimes without success) earlier studies, while in others we have repeated studies already in the literature with more recent data. The interested reader may wish to extend these studies with newer or different data sets.

1.4.   *Plan of the Book*

This book is organized into four parts.

Part I consists of three chapters that survey the tools used in econometrics: Chapter 2 on matrix algebra, Chapter 3 on probability and distribution theory, and Chapter 4 on statistical inference. Since it is assumed that the reader has some previous training in each of these topics, these summaries are fairly brief and are included primarily for those who desire a refresher or a convenient reference.

Part II develops the classical regression model. Chapters 5, 6, and 7 present the basic results of the classical linear regression model. Chapter 8 discusses extensions of the classical model that show, among other things, that the linear model is not nearly so restrictive as its appearance might suggest. Chapter 9, on multicollinearity, measurement error, and missing data, raises some issues that impede the simple mechanical application of the theoretical model to real-world data. Chapters 10, 11, and 12 present somewhat more advanced topics. The large sample results used throughout the subsequent chapters are discussed in Chapter 10. Chapter 11 is devoted to nonlinear regression models. Chapter 12 introduces some of the technical aspects of nonlinear optimization.

Part III is devoted to the generalized regression model. From Chapter 13 on, the restrictions of the classical model are progressively relaxed. Chapter 13 presents some general theoretical results for the model. These principles are then used in two standard applications: heteroscedasticity in Chapter 14 and autocorrelation in Chapter 15. The combination of these two phenomena is discussed in Chapter 16 under the heading "Cross-Section–Time Series Data."

Part IV contains several chapters on more or less advanced topics in econometrics. (I hesitate to use that term, since most of the methods discussed there are, in fact, widely used by practitioners throughout the profession. Perhaps *further* topics would be a better name.) Chapter 17 discusses the multivariate regression model and the estimation of systems of demand equations. Chapter 18 presents topics in time series analysis and distributed lag models. Chapter 19 discusses simultaneous equations models. Interest in this topic, is marked by an ebb and flow. Empirical applications of simultaneous equations models as envisioned by the Cowles Commission have received progressively less emphasis and far less attention in the applied econometrics literature in recent years. Interestingly enough, theoretical research on the topic continues unabated and regularly produces important insights, which are often more useful in other frameworks. Chapters 20 and 21 present two relatively new areas in econometrics: models with discrete dependent variables and limited dependent variable models.

References

Berndt, E., *The Practice of Econometrics*, Reading, Mass.: Addison-Wesley, 1990.

Bridge, J., *Applied Econometrics*, Amsterdam: North Holland, 1971.

Desai, M., *Applied Econometrics*, New York: McGraw-Hill, 1976.

Frisch, R., Editorial, *Econometrica*, 1, 1, 1933, pp. 1–4.

Part I

Tools

Chapter 2
Matrix Algebra

2.1. Introduction

This is the first of three chapters devoted to mathematical and statistical tools used in econometrics. This chapter presents most of the matrix results used in this book; the few additional results that become necessary later on will be developed in passing. By using matrix algebra, the fundamental results in econometrics can be presented in an elegant, compact, and uncluttered format. But, more important, we find that many diverse and seemingly complex results have a common structure and a surprising simplicity. The set of theorems and techniques we require are collected here, in one place, so that later in the book we can use them without interrupting the discussion to derive them. For those students who have not used matrix algebra for a while (or have not yet encountered the subject), this chapter also provides a reasonably concise summary.[1]

2.2. Some Terminology

A **matrix** is a rectangular array of numbers, denoted

$$\mathbf{A} = [a_{ik}] \qquad \text{or} \qquad [\mathbf{A}]_{ik}$$

$$= \begin{bmatrix} a_{11} & a_{12} & \cdots & a_{1K} \\ a_{21} & a_{22} & \cdots & a_{2K} \\ & & \vdots & \\ a_{n1} & a_{n2} & \cdots & a_{nK} \end{bmatrix}. \tag{2-1}$$

Note, in the first line, how the typical element is used to denote the matrix. A subscripted element of a matrix is always read as $a_{\text{row, column}}$. An example is given in Table 2.1. In these data, the rows are identified with years and the columns with particular variables.

A **vector** is an ordered set of numbers arranged either in a row or a column. In view of the preceding, a **row vector** is also a matrix with one row, while a **column vector** is a matrix with

---

[1] For a more complete description of the topic, some sources to consider are Dhrymes (1974), Bellman (1970), Hadley (1961), Strang (1976), and, for a large collection of useful results, Rao (1965).

Table 2.1

		Column			
	1	2	3	4	5
Row	Year	Consumption (billions of dollars)	GNP (billions of dollars)	GNP Deflator	Discount Rate (N.Y. Fed., avg.)
1	1972	737.1	1185.9	1.0000	4.50
2	1973	812.0	1326.4	1.0575	6.44
3	1974	808.1	1434.2	1.1508	7.83
4	1975	976.4	1549.2	1.2579	6.25
5	1976	1084.3	1718.0	1.3234	5.50
6	1977	1204.4	1918.3	1.4005	5.46
7	1978	1346.5	2163.9	1.5042	7.46
8	1979	1507.2	2417.8	1.6342	10.28
9	1980	1667.2	2633.1	1.7864	11.77

Source: Data are from the *Economic Report of the President*, Government Printing Office, Washington, D.C., 1983.

one column. Thus, the five variables observed for 1972 constitute a row vector, while the time series of values for consumption is a column vector.

A matrix can also be viewed as a set of column vectors, which would be a natural interpretation of the sample data set, or, of course, as a set of row vectors.[2] The **dimensions** of a matrix are the numbers of rows and columns it contains. "**A** is an $n \times K$ matrix" (read "n by K") will always mean that **A** has n rows and K columns. If n equals K, then **A** is a **square matrix**. There are several particular types of square matrices that occur frequently in econometrics.

1. A **triangular matrix** is one that has only zeros either above or below the main diagonal. If the zeroes are above the diagonal, the matrix is lower triangular.
2. A **symmetric matrix**, **A**, is one in which $a_{ik} = a_{ki}$ for all i and k.

For example,

$$A = \begin{bmatrix} 1 & 3 & 7 \\ 3 & 5 & 2 \\ 7 & 2 & 1 \end{bmatrix}.$$

3. A **diagonal matrix** is a square matrix whose only nonzero elements appear on the main diagonal, moving from upper left to lower right.
4. A **scalar matrix** is a diagonal matrix with the same value in all diagonal elements.
5. An **identity matrix** is a scalar matrix with ones on the diagonal. This is always denoted **I**. A subscript is sometimes included to indicate its size, or **order**. For example,

$$I_3 = \begin{bmatrix} 1 & 0 & 0 \\ 0 & 1 & 0 \\ 0 & 0 & 1 \end{bmatrix}. \tag{2-2}$$

[2] Henceforth, we shall denote a matrix by a bold-faced capital letter, as in (2–1), and a vector as a bold-faced lowercase letter, as in **a**. Unless otherwise noted, a vector will always be assumed to be a *column vector*.

2.3. *Algebraic Manipulation of Matrices*

Matrices provide a convenient way of collecting sets of equations and equations involving sums of values. This section outlines some of the basic arithmetic operations of matrix algebra.

2.3.1. Equality of Matrices

Matrices (or vectors) **A** and **B** are equal if and only if they have the same dimensions and each element of **A** equals the corresponding element of **B**.

$$\mathbf{A} = \mathbf{B} \text{ if and only if } a_{ik} = b_{ik} \text{ for all } i \text{ and } k.$$

2.3.2. Transposition

The **transpose** of a matrix **A**, denoted **A**′, is obtained by creating the matrix whose kth row is the kth column of the original matrix. Thus, if **B** = **A**′, each column of **A** will appear as the corresponding row of **B**. If **A** is $n \times K$, **A**′ is $K \times n$. For example,

$$\mathbf{A} = \begin{bmatrix} 1 & 2 & 3 \\ 5 & 1 & 5 \\ 6 & 4 & 5 \\ 3 & 1 & 4 \end{bmatrix}, \qquad \mathbf{A}' = \begin{bmatrix} 1 & 5 & 6 & 3 \\ 2 & 1 & 4 & 1 \\ 3 & 5 & 5 & 4 \end{bmatrix}.$$

An equivalent definition of the transpose of a matrix is

$$\mathbf{B} = \mathbf{A}' \Leftrightarrow b_{ik} = a_{ki} \qquad \text{for all } i \text{ and } k. \tag{2-3}$$

The definition of a symmetric matrix implies that

$$\text{if } \mathbf{A} \text{ is symmetric, } \mathbf{A} = \mathbf{A}'. \tag{2-4}$$

For any **A**,

$$(\mathbf{A}')' = \mathbf{A}. \tag{2-5}$$

Finally, the transpose of a column vector, **a**, is a row vector:

$$\mathbf{a}' = \begin{bmatrix} a_1 & a_2 & \cdots & a_n \end{bmatrix}.$$

2.3.3. Matrix Addition

The operation of addition is extended to matrices by defining

$$\mathbf{C} = \mathbf{A} + \mathbf{B} = [a_{ik} + b_{ik}]. \tag{2-6}$$

Matrices cannot be added unless they have the same dimensions, in which case they are said to be **conformable** for addition. A **zero matrix** or **null matrix** is one whose elements are all zero. In the addition of matrices, it plays the same role as the scalar 0 in scalar addition, that is,

$$\mathbf{A} + \mathbf{0} = \mathbf{A}. \tag{2-7}$$

We also extend the operation of subtraction to matrices precisely as if they were scalars by performing the operation element by element. Thus,

$$\mathbf{A} - \mathbf{B} = [a_{ik} - b_{ik}]. \tag{2-8}$$

It follows that matrix addition is commutative

$$A + B = B + A \tag{2-9}$$

and associative

$$(A + B) + C = A + (B + C) \tag{2-10}$$

and that

$$(A + B)' = A' + B'. \tag{2-11}$$

2.3.4.   Matrix Multiplication

Matrices are multiplied by using the **inner product**. The inner product (or **dot product**) of two vectors, **a** and **b**, is a scalar, and is written

$$a'b = a_1 b_1 + a_2 b_2 + \cdots + a_n b_n. \tag{2-12}$$

Note that the inner product is written as the transpose of vector **a** times vector **b**, a row vector times a column vector. For example,

$$a'b = \begin{bmatrix} 1 & 3 & 4 \end{bmatrix} \begin{bmatrix} 3 \\ 8 \\ 2 \end{bmatrix} = 1(3) + 3(8) + 4(2) = 35.$$

In (2–12), each term $a_j b_j$ equals $b_j a_j$; hence

$$a'b = b'a. \tag{2-13}$$

For an $n \times K$ matrix **A** and a $K \times T$ matrix **B**, the product matrix

$$C = AB \tag{2-14}$$

is an $n \times T$ matrix whose ikth element is the inner product of row i of **A** and column k of **B**;

$$C = AB \Rightarrow c_{ik} = \tilde{a}_i' b_k. \tag{2-15}$$

[In (2–15) we have defined a notation for a row vector from **A**.] In order to multiply two matrices, the number of columns in the first must be the same as the number of rows in the second, in which case, they are **conformable** for multiplication.[3] For example,

$$
\begin{aligned}
AB &= \begin{bmatrix} 1 & 3 & 2 \\ 4 & 5 & -1 \end{bmatrix} \begin{bmatrix} 2 & 4 \\ 1 & 6 \\ 0 & 5 \end{bmatrix} \\
&= \begin{bmatrix} 1(2) + 3(1) + 2(0) & 1(4) + 3(6) + 2(5) \\ 4(2) + 5(1) + (-1)(0) & 4(4) + 5(6) + (-1)(5) \end{bmatrix} \\
&= \begin{bmatrix} 5 & 32 \\ 13 & 41 \end{bmatrix}.
\end{aligned}
$$

---

[3] A simple way to check the conformability of two matrices for multiplication is to write down the dimensions of the operation, for example, $(n \times K)$ times $(K \times T)$. The inner dimensions must be equal; the result has dimensions equal to the outer values.

Multiplication of matrices is generally not commutative. For example, in the preceding calculation, $\mathbf{AB}$ is a 2×2 matrix, while

$$\mathbf{BA} = \begin{bmatrix} 2(1) + 4(4) & 2(3) + 4(5) & 2(2) + 4(-1) \\ 1(1) + 6(4) & 1(3) + 6(5) & 1(2) + 6(-1) \\ 0(1) + 5(4) & 0(3) + 5(5) & 0(2) + 5(-1) \end{bmatrix}$$

$$= \begin{bmatrix} 18 & 26 & 0 \\ 25 & 33 & -4 \\ 20 & 25 & -5 \end{bmatrix}.$$

In other cases, $\mathbf{AB}$ may exist, but $\mathbf{BA}$ may be undefined or, if it does exist, may have different dimensions, as in the preceding example. However, in general, even if $\mathbf{AB}$ and $\mathbf{BA}$ do have the same dimensions, they will not be equal. In view of this, we define **premultiplication** and **postmultiplication** of matrices. In the product $\mathbf{AB}$, $\mathbf{B}$ is *premultiplied* by $\mathbf{A}$, while $\mathbf{A}$ is *postmultiplied* by $\mathbf{B}$.

The product of a matrix and a vector is written

$$\mathbf{c} = \mathbf{Ab}.$$

The number of elements in $\mathbf{b}$ must equal the number of columns in $\mathbf{A}$; the result is a vector with a number of elements equal to the number of rows in $\mathbf{A}$. For example,

$$\begin{bmatrix} 5 \\ 4 \\ 1 \end{bmatrix} = \begin{bmatrix} 4 & 2 & 1 \\ 2 & 6 & 1 \\ 1 & 1 & 0 \end{bmatrix} \begin{bmatrix} a \\ b \\ c \end{bmatrix}.$$

We can interpret this in two ways. First, it is a compact way of writing the three equations

$$5 = 4a + 2b + 1c,$$

$$4 = 2a + 6b + 1c,$$

$$1 = 1a + 1b + 0c.$$

Second, by writing the set of equations as

$$\begin{bmatrix} 5 \\ 4 \\ 1 \end{bmatrix} = a \begin{bmatrix} 4 \\ 2 \\ 1 \end{bmatrix} + b \begin{bmatrix} 2 \\ 6 \\ 1 \end{bmatrix} + c \begin{bmatrix} 1 \\ 1 \\ 0 \end{bmatrix},$$

we see that the right-hand side is a **linear combination** of the columns of the matrix where the coefficients are the elements of the vector. For the general case,

$$\mathbf{c} = \mathbf{Ab}$$

$$= b_1 \mathbf{a}_1 + b_2 \mathbf{a}_2 + \cdots + b_K \mathbf{a}_K. \qquad (2-16)$$

In the calculation of a matrix product $\mathbf{C} = \mathbf{AB}$, each column of $\mathbf{C}$ is a linear combination of the columns of $\mathbf{A}$, where the coefficients are the elements in the corresponding column of $\mathbf{B}$. That is,

$$\mathbf{C} = \mathbf{AB} \Leftrightarrow \mathbf{c}_k = \mathbf{Ab}_k. \qquad (2-17)$$

Let $\mathbf{e}_k$ be a column vector that has 0s everywhere except for a 1 in the kth position. Then $\mathbf{Ae}_k$ is a linear combination of the columns of $\mathbf{A}$ in which the coefficient on every column but the kth is 0, while that on the kth is 1. The result is

$$\mathbf{a}_k = \mathbf{A}\mathbf{e}_k. \tag{2–18}$$

Combining this result with (2–17) produces

$$(\mathbf{a}_1 \quad \mathbf{a}_2 \quad \cdots \quad \mathbf{a}_n) = \mathbf{A}(\mathbf{e}_1 \quad \mathbf{e}_2 \quad \cdots \quad \mathbf{e}_n)$$

$$= \mathbf{A}\begin{bmatrix} 1 & 0 & 0 & \cdots & 0 \\ 0 & 1 & 0 & \cdots & 0 \\ & & & \vdots & \\ 0 & 0 & 0 & \cdots & 1 \end{bmatrix} \tag{2–19}$$

$$= \mathbf{AI} = \mathbf{A}.$$

In connection with matrix multiplication, the identity matrix is analogous to the scalar 1. For any matrix or vector, $\mathbf{A}$, $\mathbf{AI} = \mathbf{A}$. In addition, $\mathbf{IA} = \mathbf{A}$, though if $\mathbf{A}$ is not a square matrix, the two identity matrices are of different orders.

A conformable matrix of zeros produces the expected result; $\mathbf{A0} = \mathbf{0}$, although the dimensions of the result depend on the dimensions of the zero matrix.

Some general rules for matrix multiplication are as follows:

$$\text{(Associative law)} \quad (\mathbf{AB})\mathbf{C} = \mathbf{A}(\mathbf{BC}), \tag{2–20}$$

$$\text{(Distributive law)} \quad \mathbf{A}(\mathbf{B} + \mathbf{C}) = \mathbf{AB} + \mathbf{AC}. \tag{2–21}$$

(Note the order of multiplication of the matrices in the second rule: $\mathbf{BA}$ and $\mathbf{CA}$ may not be defined.)

$$\text{(Transpose of a product)} \quad (\mathbf{AB})' = \mathbf{B}'\mathbf{A}'. \tag{2–22}$$

By direct extension,

$$(\mathbf{ABC})' = \mathbf{C}'\mathbf{B}'\mathbf{A}'. \tag{2–23}$$

Finally, **scalar multiplication** of a matrix is the operation of multiplying every element of the matrix by a given scalar. For scalar c and matrix $\mathbf{A}$,

$$c\mathbf{A} = [ca_{ik}]. \tag{2–24}$$

2.3.5. Sums of Values

Matrices and vectors provide a particularly convenient way to represent sums of values. A useful device is the vector $\mathbf{i}$, which contains a column of 1s. The sum of the elements in any vector $\mathbf{x}$ is

$$\sum_{i=1}^{n} x_i = x_1 + x_2 + \cdots + x_n = \mathbf{i}'\mathbf{x}. \tag{2–25}$$

If all elements in $\mathbf{x}$ are equal to the same constant, a, then $\mathbf{x} = a\mathbf{i}$ and

$$\sum_i x_i = \mathbf{i}'(a\mathbf{i}) = a(\mathbf{i}'\mathbf{i}) = na. \tag{2–26}$$

For any constant, a, and vector, $\mathbf{x}$,

$$\sum_i ax_i = a\sum_i x_i = a\mathbf{i}'\mathbf{x}. \tag{2–27}$$

If $a = 1/n$, we obtain the arithmetic mean,

$$\bar{x} = \frac{1}{n}\sum_i x_i = \frac{1}{n}\mathbf{i}'\mathbf{x},$$

(2–28)

from which it follows that

$$\sum_i x_i = \mathbf{i}'\mathbf{x} = n\bar{x}.$$

Sums of squares and cross products are obtained easily with the inner product operation. The sum of squares of the elements in a vector $\mathbf{x}$ is

$$\sum_i x_i^2 = \mathbf{x}'\mathbf{x};$$

(2–29)

the sum of the products of the elements in vectors $\mathbf{x}$ and $\mathbf{y}$ is

$$\sum_i x_i y_i = \mathbf{x}'\mathbf{y}.$$

(2–30)

By the definition of matrix multiplication,

$$[\mathbf{X}'\mathbf{X}]_{ij} = [\mathbf{x}_i'\mathbf{x}_j]$$

(2–31)

is the inner product of the ith and jth columns of $\mathbf{X}$. Thus, for example, for the data set given in the introduction, if we define $\mathbf{X}$ as the 9×3 matrix containing (year, consumption, GNP), then

$$[\mathbf{X}'\mathbf{X}]_{23} = \sum_{i=1}^{9} \text{consumption}_i \text{GNP}_i$$

$$= 737.1(1185.9) + \cdots + 1667.2(2633.1) = 19{,}743{,}711.34.$$

If $\mathbf{X}$ is $n \times K$,

$$\mathbf{X}'\mathbf{X} = \sum_{i=1}^{n} \tilde{\mathbf{x}}_i \tilde{\mathbf{x}}_i',$$

where $\tilde{\mathbf{x}}_i$ is the transpose of the ith row of $\mathbf{X}$. This form shows that the $K \times K$ matrix $\mathbf{X}'\mathbf{X}$ is the sum of n $K \times K$ matrices, each formed from a single row (year) of $\mathbf{X}$. For the example given earlier, this is the sum of nine 3×3 matrices, each formed from one row (year) of the original data matrix. Suppose that $\mathbf{X}'\mathbf{X}$ for the nine years of data was already in hand, and a tenth year of data was obtained. The matrix of sums of squares and cross products can be updated just by adding a 3×3 matrix to the $\mathbf{X}'\mathbf{X}$ already computed.

2.3.6.   A Useful Idempotent Matrix

A fundamental matrix in statistics is the one that is used to transform data to deviations from their mean. First,

$$\mathbf{i}\bar{x} = \mathbf{i}\frac{1}{n}\mathbf{i}'\mathbf{x}$$

$$= \begin{bmatrix} \bar{x} \\ \bar{x} \\ \vdots \\ \bar{x} \end{bmatrix} = \frac{1}{n}\mathbf{i}\mathbf{i}'\mathbf{x}.$$

(2–32)

The matrix $(1/n)\mathbf{ii}'$ is an $n \times n$ matrix with every element equal to $1/n$. The set of values in deviations form is thus

$$\begin{bmatrix} x_1 - \bar{x} \\ x_2 - \bar{x} \\ \vdots \\ x_n - \bar{x} \end{bmatrix} = [\mathbf{x} - \mathbf{i}\bar{x}] = \left[\mathbf{x} - \frac{1}{n}\mathbf{ii}'\mathbf{x} \right]. \tag{2-33}$$

Since $\mathbf{x} = \mathbf{Ix}$,

$$\left[\mathbf{x} - \frac{1}{n}\mathbf{ii}'\mathbf{x} \right] = \left[\mathbf{Ix} - \frac{1}{n}\mathbf{ii}'\mathbf{x} \right]$$

$$= \left[\mathbf{I} - \frac{1}{n}\mathbf{ii}' \right]\mathbf{x} \tag{2-34}$$

$$= \mathbf{M}^0\mathbf{x}.$$

Henceforth, the symbol $\mathbf{M}^0$ will be used only for this matrix. Its diagonal elements are all $1 - 1/n$, and its off-diagonal elements are $-1/n$.

The matrix $\mathbf{M}^0$ is primarily useful in computing sums of squared deviations. Some computations are simplified by the result

$$\mathbf{M}^0\mathbf{i} = \left[\mathbf{I} - \frac{1}{n}\mathbf{ii}' \right]\mathbf{i}$$

$$= \mathbf{i} - \frac{1}{n}\mathbf{i}(\mathbf{i}'\mathbf{i})$$

$$= \mathbf{0}.$$

This implies that $\mathbf{i}'\mathbf{M}^0 = \mathbf{0}'$. The sum of deviations about the mean is then

$$\sum_i (x_i - \bar{x}) = \mathbf{i}'[\mathbf{M}^0\mathbf{x}] = \mathbf{0}'\mathbf{x} = 0. \tag{2-35}$$

For a single variable, $\mathbf{x}$, the sum of squared deviations about the mean is

$$\sum_i (x_i - \bar{x})^2 = \sum_i [x_i^2 - 2\bar{x}x_i + \bar{x}^2]$$

$$= \sum_i x_i^2 - n\bar{x}^2. \tag{2-36}$$

In matrix terms,

$$\sum_i (x_i - \bar{x})^2 = (\mathbf{x} - \bar{x}\mathbf{i})'(\mathbf{x} - \bar{x}\mathbf{i})$$

$$= (\mathbf{M}^0\mathbf{x})'(\mathbf{M}^0\mathbf{x})$$

$$= \mathbf{x}'\mathbf{M}^{0'}\mathbf{M}^0\mathbf{x}.$$

Two properties of $\mathbf{M}^0$ are useful at this point. First, since all off-diagonal elements of $\mathbf{M}^0$ equal $-1/n$, $\mathbf{M}^0$ is symmetric. Second, as can easily be verified by multiplication, $\mathbf{M}^0$ is equal to its square; $\mathbf{M}^0\mathbf{M}^0 = \mathbf{M}^0$.

Definition. An idempotent matrix is one that is equal to its square. If $\mathbf{M}$ is a symmetric idempotent matrix—most of the idempotent matrices we shall encounter are—then $\mathbf{M}'\mathbf{M} = \mathbf{M}$.

Thus, $\mathbf{M}^0$ is an idempotent matrix. Combining these, we obtain

$$\sum_i (x_i - \bar{x})^2 = \mathbf{x}'\mathbf{M}^0\mathbf{x}. \tag{2-37}$$

Consider constructing a matrix of sums of squares and cross products in deviations from the column means. For two vectors $\mathbf{x}$ and $\mathbf{y}$,

$$\sum_i (x_i - \bar{x})(y_i - \bar{y}) = (\mathbf{M}^0\mathbf{x})'(\mathbf{M}^0\mathbf{y}), \tag{2-38}$$

so,

$$\begin{bmatrix} \Sigma_i(x_i - \bar{x})^2 & \Sigma_i(x_i - \bar{x})(y_i - \bar{y}) \\ \Sigma_i(y_i - \bar{y})(x_i - \bar{x}) & \Sigma_i(y_i - \bar{y})^2 \end{bmatrix} = \begin{bmatrix} \mathbf{x}'\mathbf{M}^0\mathbf{x} & \mathbf{x}'\mathbf{M}^0\mathbf{y} \\ \mathbf{y}'\mathbf{M}^0\mathbf{x} & \mathbf{y}'\mathbf{M}^0\mathbf{y} \end{bmatrix}. \tag{2-39}$$

If we put the two column vectors, $\mathbf{x}$ and $\mathbf{y}$, in an $n \times 2$ matrix $\mathbf{Z} = [\mathbf{x}, \mathbf{y}]$, then $\mathbf{M}^0\mathbf{Z}$ is the $n \times 2$ matrix in which the two columns of data are in mean deviation form. Then

$$(\mathbf{M}^0\mathbf{Z})'(\mathbf{M}^0\mathbf{Z}) = \mathbf{Z}'\mathbf{M}^0\mathbf{M}^0\mathbf{Z} = \mathbf{Z}'\mathbf{M}^0\mathbf{Z}.$$

2.4. Geometry of Matrices

Matrix algebra is extremely useful in the formulation and solution of sets of linear equations. At the same time, the algebraic results have a geometrical basis that is very helpful in understanding the calculations. Before developing the mathematical results, it will be useful to digress to a geometric treatment of matrices and vectors.

2.4.1. Vector Spaces

The K elements of a column vector

$$\mathbf{a} = \begin{bmatrix} a_1 \\ a_2 \\ a_3 \\ \vdots \\ a_K \end{bmatrix}$$

can be viewed as the coordinates of a point in a K-dimensional space, as shown in Figure 2.1 for two dimensions, or as the definition of the line segment connecting the origin and this point.

Two basic operations are defined for vectors, **scalar multiplication** and **addition**. A scalar multiple of a vector, $\mathbf{a}$, is another vector, say $\mathbf{a}^*$, whose coordinates are the scalar multiple of $\mathbf{a}$'s coordinates. Thus, in Figure 2.1,

$$\mathbf{a} = \begin{bmatrix} 1 \\ 2 \end{bmatrix}, \quad \mathbf{a}^* = 2\mathbf{a} = \begin{bmatrix} 2 \\ 4 \end{bmatrix}, \quad \text{and} \quad \mathbf{a}^{**} = -\tfrac{1}{2}\mathbf{a} = \begin{bmatrix} -\tfrac{1}{2} \\ -1 \end{bmatrix}.$$

The set of all possible scalar multiples of $\mathbf{a}$ is the line through $\mathbf{0}$ and $\mathbf{a}$. Any scalar multiple of $\mathbf{a}$ is a segment of this line. The sum of two vectors, $\mathbf{a}$ and $\mathbf{b}$, is a third vector whose coordinates are the sums of the corresponding coordinates of $\mathbf{a}$ and $\mathbf{b}$. For example,

$$\mathbf{c} = \mathbf{a} + \mathbf{b} = \begin{bmatrix} 1 \\ 2 \end{bmatrix} + \begin{bmatrix} 2 \\ 1 \end{bmatrix} = \begin{bmatrix} 3 \\ 3 \end{bmatrix}.$$

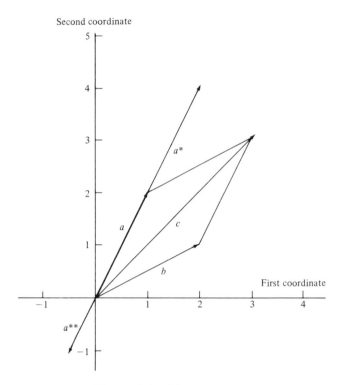

Figure 2.1   Vector space.

Geometrically, **c** is obtained by moving in the distance and direction defined by **b** from the tip of **a** or, because addition is commutative, from the tip of **b** in the distance and direction of **a**. This is a geometric interpretation of the operations of scalar multiplication and addition of matrices applied to vectors.

The two-dimensional plane is the set of all vectors with two real-valued coordinates. We label this set $\mathbb{R}^2$. It has two important properties.

   1. $\mathbb{R}^2$ is *closed under scalar multiplication*; every scalar multiple of a vector in the plane is also in the plane.

   2. $\mathbb{R}^2$ is *closed under addition*; the sum of any two vectors is always a vector in the plane.

Definition. A **vector space** is any set of vectors that is closed under scalar multiplication and addition.

Another example is the set of all real numbers, that is $\mathbb{R}^1$, the set of vectors with one real element. In general, that set of K-element vectors all of whose elements are real numbers is a K-dimensional vector space, denoted $\mathbb{R}^K$. The preceding examples are drawn in $\mathbb{R}^2$.[4]

2.4.2.   Linear Combinations of Vectors and Basis Vectors

In Figure 2.2, $\mathbf{c} = \mathbf{a} + \mathbf{b}$ and $\mathbf{d} = \mathbf{a}^* + \mathbf{b}$. But since $\mathbf{a}^* = 2\mathbf{a}$, $\mathbf{d} = 2\mathbf{a} + \mathbf{b}$. Also, $\mathbf{e} = \mathbf{a} + 2\mathbf{b}$ and $\mathbf{f} = \mathbf{b} + (-\mathbf{a}) = \mathbf{b} - \mathbf{a}$. As this exercise suggests, any vector in $\mathbb{R}^2$ could be obtained as a **linear combination** of **a** and **b**.

---

[4] The definition extends to $\mathscr{C}^K$, the set of vectors whose elements are complex pairs. We shall not require complex vectors in this book.

Definition. A set of vectors in a vector space is a **basis** for that vector space if any vector in the vector space can be written as a linear combination of them.

As is clear from Figure 2.2, any pair of two-element vectors, including **a** and **b**, that point in different directions will form a basis for $\mathbb{R}^2$. Consider an arbitrary set of vectors in $\mathbb{R}^2$, **a**, **b**, and **c**. If **a** and **b** are a basis, we can find numbers α_1 and α_2 such that $\mathbf{c} = \alpha_1 \mathbf{a} + \alpha_2 \mathbf{b}$. Let

$$\mathbf{a} = \begin{bmatrix} a_1 \\ a_2 \end{bmatrix}, \qquad \mathbf{b} = \begin{bmatrix} b_1 \\ b_2 \end{bmatrix}, \qquad \text{and} \qquad \mathbf{c} = \begin{bmatrix} c_1 \\ c_2 \end{bmatrix}.$$

Then

$$\begin{aligned} c_1 &= \alpha_1 a_1 + \alpha_2 b_1, \\ c_2 &= \alpha_1 a_2 + \alpha_2 b_2. \end{aligned} \tag{2-40}$$

The solutions to this pair of equations are

$$\begin{aligned} \alpha_1 &= \frac{b_2 c_1 - a_2 c_2}{a_1 b_2 - b_1 a_2}, \\[2mm] \alpha_2 &= \frac{a_1 c_2 - b_1 c_1}{a_1 b_2 - b_1 a_2}. \end{aligned} \tag{2-41}$$

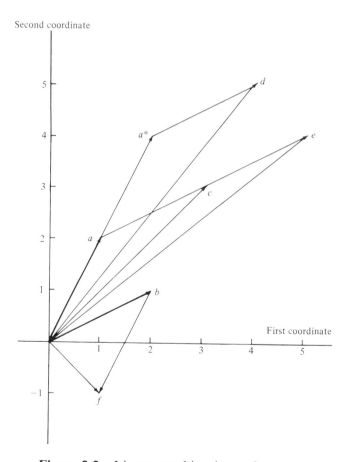

Figure 2.2   Linear combinations of vectors.

This gives a unique solution unless $(a_1 b_2 - b_1 a_2) = 0$. If $(a_1 b_2 - b_1 a_2) = 0$, then $a_1/a_2 = b_1/b_2$, which means that **b** is just a multiple of **a**. This returns us to our original condition, that **a** and **b** point in different directions. The implication is that if **a** and **b** are any pair of vectors for which the denominator in (2–41) is not zero, then any other vector, **c**, can be formed as a *unique* linear combination of **a** and **b**. The basis of a vector space is not unique, since any set of vectors that satisfy the definition will do. But for any particular basis, there is only one linear combination of them that will produce another particular vector in the vector space.

2.4.3.   Linear Dependence

As the preceding should suggest, K vectors are required to form a basis for $\mathbb{R}^K$. Although the basis for a vector space is not unique, not every set of K vectors will suffice. In Figure 2.2, **a** and **b** form a basis for $\mathbb{R}^2$, but **a** and **a*** do not. The difference between these two pairs is that **a** and **b** are linearly independent while **a** and **a*** are linearly dependent.

> **Definition.** A set of vectors is **linearly dependent** if any one of the vectors in the set can be written as a linear combination of the others.

Since **a*** is a multiple of **a**, **a** and **a*** are linearly dependent. For another example, if

$$a = \begin{bmatrix} 1 \\ 2 \end{bmatrix}, \qquad b = \begin{bmatrix} 3 \\ 3 \end{bmatrix}, \qquad c = \begin{bmatrix} 10 \\ 14 \end{bmatrix},$$

then

$$2a + b - (\tfrac{1}{2})c = 0,$$

so **a**, **b**, and **c** are linearly dependent. However, any of the three possible pairs of them are linearly independent.

> **Definition.** A set of vectors is **linearly independent** if and only if the only solution to
>
> $$\alpha_1 a_1 + \alpha_2 a_2 + \cdots + \alpha_K a_K = 0$$

is

$$\alpha_1 = \alpha_2 = \cdots = \alpha_K = 0.$$

The preceding implies the following equivalent definition of a basis:

> **Definition.** A basis for a vector space of K dimensions is any set of K linearly independent vectors in that space.

Since any $K + 1$st vector can be written as a linear combination of the K basis vectors, it follows that any set of more than K vectors in $\mathbb{R}^K$ must be linearly dependent.

2.4.4.   Subspaces

> **Definition.** The set of all linear combinations of a set of vectors is the vector space that is **spanned** by those vectors.

For example, by definition, the space spanned by a basis for $\mathbb{R}^K$ is $\mathbb{R}^K$. An implication of this is that if **a** and **b** are a basis for $\mathbb{R}^2$ and **c** is another vector in $\mathbb{R}^2$, the space spanned by $[a, b, c]$ is, again, $\mathbb{R}^2$. Of course, **c** is superfluous. Nonetheless, any vector in $\mathbb{R}^2$ can be expressed as a linear combination of **a**, **b**, and **c**. (The linear combination will not be unique. Suppose, for example, that **a** and **c** are also a basis for $\mathbb{R}^2$.)

Consider the set of three coordinate vectors whose third element is zero. In particular,

$$\mathbf{a}' = [a_1, \quad a_2, \quad 0] \qquad \text{and} \qquad \mathbf{b}' = [b_1, \quad b_2, \quad 0].$$

Vectors $\mathbf{a}$ and $\mathbf{b}$ do not span the three-dimensional space $\mathbb{R}^3$. Every linear combination of $\mathbf{a}$ and $\mathbf{b}$ has a third coordinate equal to zero, so, for instance, $\mathbf{c}' = [1, 2, 3]$ could not be written as a linear combination of $\mathbf{a}$ and $\mathbf{b}$. However, if $(a_1 b_2 - a_2 b_1)$ is not equal to zero [see (2–41)], then *any vector whose third element is zero can be expressed as a linear combination of* $\mathbf{a}$ *and* $\mathbf{b}$. So, while $\mathbf{a}$ and $\mathbf{b}$ do not span $\mathbb{R}^3$, they do span something, the set of vectors in $\mathbb{R}^3$ whose third element is zero. This is a plane (the "floor" of the box in a three-dimensional figure). This plane in $\mathbb{R}^3$ is a **subspace**, in this instance, a two-dimensional subspace. Note that *it is not* $\mathbb{R}^2$. It is the set of vectors in $\mathbb{R}^3$ whose third coordinate is 0. Any plane in $\mathbb{R}^3$, regardless of how it is oriented, forms a two-dimensional subspace. Any two independent vectors that lie in that subspace will span it. But without a third vector that points in some other direction, we cannot span any more of $\mathbb{R}^3$ than this two-dimensional part of it. By the same logic, any line in $\mathbb{R}^3$ is a one-dimensional subspace, in this case, the set of all vectors in $\mathbb{R}^3$ whose coordinates are multiples of those of the vector that define the line. A subspace is a vector space in all of the respects in which we have defined it. We emphasize that it is *not* a vector space of lower dimension. For example, $\mathbb{R}^2$ is not a subspace of $\mathbb{R}^3$. The essential difference is the number of dimensions in the vectors. The vectors in $\mathbb{R}^3$ that form a two-dimensional subspace are still three-element vectors; they all just happen to lie in the same plane.

The space spanned by a set of vectors in $\mathbb{R}^K$ has at most K dimensions. If this space has fewer than K dimensions, it is a subspace, or **hyperplane**. But the important point in the preceding discussion is that *every set of vectors spans some space*; it may be the entire space in which the vectors reside, or some subspace of it.

2.4.5.   Rank of a Matrix

We view a matrix as a set of column vectors. The number of columns in the matrix equals the number of vectors in the set, and the number of rows equals the number of coordinates in each column vector.

Definition. The **column space** of a matrix is the vector space that is spanned by its column vectors.

If the matrix contains K rows, its column space might have K dimensions. But, as we have seen, it might have fewer dimensions; the column vectors might be linearly dependent, or there might be fewer than K of them. Consider the matrix

$$\mathbf{A} = \begin{bmatrix} 1 & 5 & 6 \\ 2 & 6 & 8 \\ 7 & 1 & 8 \end{bmatrix}.$$

It contains three vectors from $\mathbb{R}^3$, but the third is the sum of the first two, so the column space of this matrix cannot have three dimensions. Nor does it have only one, since the three columns are not all scalar multiples of one another. Hence it has two, and the column space of this matrix is a two-dimensional subspace of $\mathbb{R}^3$.

Definition. The **column rank** of a matrix is the dimension of the vector space that is spanned by its columns.

It follows that the column rank of a matrix is equal to the largest number of linearly independent column vectors it contains. The column rank of $\mathbf{A}$ is 2. For another specific example, consider

$$\mathbf{B} = \begin{bmatrix} 1 & 2 & 3 \\ 5 & 1 & 5 \\ 6 & 4 & 5 \\ 3 & 1 & 4 \end{bmatrix}.$$

It can be shown (we shall see how later) that this matrix has a column rank equal to 3. Since each column of **B** is a vector in $\mathbb{R}^4$, the column space of **B** is a three-dimensional subspace of $\mathbb{R}^4$.

Consider, instead, the set of vectors obtained by using the *rows* of **B** instead of the columns. The new matrix would be

$$\mathbf{C} = \begin{bmatrix} 1 & 5 & 6 & 3 \\ 2 & 1 & 4 & 1 \\ 3 & 5 & 5 & 4 \end{bmatrix}.$$

This matrix is composed of four column vectors from $\mathbb{R}^3$. (Note that **C** is **B**′.) The column space of **C** is at most $\mathbb{R}^3$, since four vectors in $\mathbb{R}^3$ must be linearly dependent. In fact, the column space of **C** *is* $\mathbb{R}^3$. Although this is not the same as the column space of **B**, it does have the same dimension. Thus, the column rank of **C** and the column rank of **B** are the same. But the columns of **C** are the rows of **B**. Thus, the column rank of **C** equals the **row rank** of **B**. The fact that the column and row ranks of **B** were the same was not a coincidence. The general results (which are equivalent) are

1. The **column rank** and **row rank** of a matrix are equal.
2. The **row space** and **column space** of a matrix have the same dimension. $\qquad$ (2–42)

The two propositions hold regardless of the actual row and column rank. If the column rank of a matrix happens to equal the number of columns it contains, the matrix is said to have **full column rank**. **Full row rank** is defined likewise. Since the row and column ranks of a matrix are always equal, we can speak unambiguously of the **rank of a matrix**. For either the row rank or the column rank (and, at this point, we shall drop the distinction),

$$\text{rank}(\mathbf{A}) = \text{rank}(\mathbf{A}') \le \min(\#\text{rows}, \#\text{columns}). \qquad (2–43)$$

In most contexts, we shall be interested in the columns of the matrices we manipulate. We shall use the term **full rank** to describe a matrix whose rank is equal to the number of columns it contains.

Of particular interest will be the distinction between **full rank** and **short rank matrices**. The distinction turns on the solutions to $\mathbf{Ax} = \mathbf{0}$. If a nonzero **x** for which $\mathbf{Ax} = \mathbf{0}$ exists, **A** does not have full rank. Equivalently, if the nonzero **x** exists, the columns of **A** are linearly dependent, and at least one of them can be expressed as a linear combination of the others. For example, a nonzero set of solutions to

$$\begin{bmatrix} 1 & 3 & 10 \\ 2 & 3 & 14 \end{bmatrix} \begin{bmatrix} x_1 \\ x_2 \\ x_3 \end{bmatrix} = \begin{bmatrix} 0 \\ 0 \end{bmatrix}$$

is any multiple of $\mathbf{x}' = (2, 1, -\frac{1}{2})$.

In a product matrix, $\mathbf{C} = \mathbf{AB}$, every column of **C** is a linear combination of the columns of **A**, so each column of **C** is in the column space of **A**. It is possible that the set of columns in

C could span this space, but it is not possible for them to span a higher dimensional space. At best, they could be a full set of linearly independent vectors in **A**'s column space. We conclude that the column rank of **C** could not be greater than that of **A**. Now, apply the same logic to the rows of **C**, which are all linear combinations of the rows of **B**. For the same reason that the column rank of **C** cannot exceed the column rank of **A**, the row rank of **C** cannot exceed the row rank of **B**. Since row and column ranks are always equal, we conclude that

$$\text{rank}(\mathbf{AB}) \le \min(\text{rank}(\mathbf{A}), \text{rank}(\mathbf{B})). \qquad (2\text{--}44)$$

A useful corollary of (2–44) is

If **A** is $M \times n$ and **B** is a square matrix of rank n, $\text{rank}(\mathbf{AB}) = \text{rank}(\mathbf{A})$.   (2–45)

The proof is left as an exercise.

Another application that plays a central role in the development of regression analysis is, for any **A**,

$$\text{Rank}(\mathbf{A}) = \text{rank}(\mathbf{A'A}) = \text{rank}(\mathbf{AA'}). \qquad (2\text{--}46)$$

2.4.6.   Determinant of a Matrix

The vectors of the matrix

$$\mathbf{A} = [\mathbf{a}, \mathbf{b}]$$

$$= \begin{bmatrix} 4 & 2 \\ 1 & 3 \end{bmatrix}$$

are shown in Figure 2.3. The area of the parallelogram formed by the columns of **A** can be obtained by manipulating congruent triangles. The result is $4(3) - 1(2) = 10$. This area is the

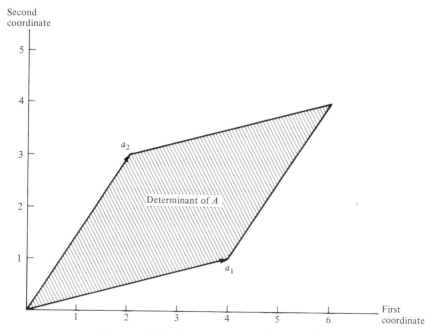

Figure 2.3   Determinant of a matrix.

determinant of **A**.[5] If the columns of **A** were linearly dependent, that is, if one were a scalar multiple of the other, the two vectors would lie on the same line. The "parallelogram" would collapse to a line and would have zero area. This implies that *if the columns of a matrix are linearly dependent, its determinant is zero.* Recalling our earlier discussion of linear dependence in $\mathbb{R}^2$, we see that this is the case of $(a_1b_2 - a_2b_1) = 0$ in (2–41). (The determinant of **A** is, in fact, $a_1b_2 - a_2b_1$.)

Consider the same exercise in $\mathbb{R}^3$. If we complete the parallelograms in all dimensions for a set of three-dimensional vectors, we shall form a solid, that is, a parallelotope. The determinant will be the volume of this solid. But if the columns of the matrix are linearly dependent, the columns will all lie in the same plane (or on the same line). The "solid" thus formed will collapse to a plane or a line and will have no volume; again, the determinant will be zero. This general result carries over to higher dimensions as well.

Proposition. The determinant of a matrix is nonzero if and only if it has full rank.

Full rank and short rank matrices can be distinguished by whether their determinants are nonzero or not. There are some settings in which the value of the determinant is also of interest, so we now consider some algebraic results.

It is most convenient to begin with a diagonal matrix,

$$\mathbf{D} = \begin{bmatrix} d_1 & 0 & 0 & \cdots & 0 \\ 0 & d_2 & 0 & \cdots & 0 \\ & & & \vdots & \\ 0 & 0 & 0 & \cdots & d_K \end{bmatrix}.$$

The column vectors of **D** define a "box" in $\mathbb{R}^K$ whose sides are all at right angles to one another.[6] Its "volume," or determinant, is simply the product of the lengths of the sides, which we denote

$$|\mathbf{D}| = d_1 d_2 \cdots d_K = \prod_{i=1}^{K} d_i. \tag{2–47}$$

A special case is the identity matrix, which has, regardless of K, $|\mathbf{I}_K| = 1$. Multiplying **D** by a scalar, c, is equivalent to multiplying the length of each side of the box by c, which would multiply its volume by c^K. Thus,

$$|c\mathbf{D}| = c^K|\mathbf{D}|. \tag{2–48}$$

Continuing with this admittedly special case, we suppose that only one column of **D** is multiplied by c. In two dimensions, this would make the box wider, but not higher, or vice versa. Hence, the "volume" (area) would also be multiplied by c. Now suppose that each side of the box were multiplied by a different c, the first by c_1, the second by c_2, and so on. The volume would, by an obvious extension, now be $c_1 c_2 \cdots c_K|\mathbf{D}|$. The matrix with columns defined by $[c_1\mathbf{d}_1, c_2\mathbf{d}_2, \ldots]$ is just **DC**, where **C** is a diagonal matrix with c_i as its ith diagonal element. The computation just described is, therefore,

$$|\mathbf{DC}| = |\mathbf{D}| \cdot |\mathbf{C}|. \tag{2–49}$$

---

[5] Strictly speaking, the area is the absolute value of the determinant. Since we are concerned with geometric results at this point, we shall neglect the sign. Later, in an algebraic context, the sign of the determinant will be important. Note that *the determinant is defined only for square matrices.*

[6] Each column vector defines a segment on one of the axes, and all are orthogonal.

(The determinant of C is the product of the c_i's since C, like D, is a diagonal matrix.) Note, in particular, what happens to the whole thing if one of the c_i's is zero.

Thus far, we have considered only diagonal matrices. We now consider the general case. The absolute value of a determinant is still the volume of the parallelotope built up from the columns of the matrix. We have already seen the result for 2×2 matrices:

$$\begin{vmatrix} a & c \\ b & d \end{vmatrix} = (ad - bc). \qquad (2-50)$$

Notice that it is a function of all of the elements of the matrix. This will be true, in general. For more than two dimensions, the determinant can be obtained by using an **expansion by cofactors**. Using *any* row, say i, we obtain

$$|\mathbf{A}| = \sum_{j=1}^{K} a_{ij}(-1)^{i+j}|\mathbf{A}_{ij}|, \qquad (2-51)$$

where $\mathbf{A}_{ij}$ is the matrix obtained from $\mathbf{A}$ by deleting row i and column j. The determinant of $\mathbf{A}_{ij}$ is called a **minor** of $\mathbf{A}$.[7] When the correct sign, $(-1)^{i+j}$, is added, it becomes a **cofactor**. This operation can be done using any column as well. For example, a 4×4 determinant becomes a sum of four 3×3's, while a 5×5 is a sum of five 4×4's, each of which is a sum of four 3×3's, and so on. Obviously, it is a good idea, if possible, to base (2-51) on a row or column with many zeros in it. In practice, this rapidly becomes a heavy burden. It is unlikely, though, that you will ever calculate any determinants over 3×3 without a computer. You might, however, compute a 3×3 on occasion; if so, the following shortcut will prove useful:

$$\begin{vmatrix} a_{11} & a_{12} & a_{13} \\ a_{21} & a_{22} & a_{23} \\ a_{31} & a_{32} & a_{33} \end{vmatrix} = a_{11}a_{22}a_{33} + a_{12}a_{23}a_{31} + a_{13}a_{32}a_{21} \\ - a_{31}a_{22}a_{13} - a_{21}a_{12}a_{33} - a_{11}a_{23}a_{32}.$$

Although (2-48) and (2-49) were given for diagonal matrices, they hold for general matrices C and D. One special case of (2-48) to note is that of $c = -1$. Multiplying a matrix by -1 does not necessarily change the sign of its determinant. It does so only if the order of the matrix is odd. By using the expansion by cofactors formula, an additional result can be shown:

$$|\mathbf{A}| = |\mathbf{A}'|. \qquad (2-52)$$

2.4.7. A Least Squares Problem

Given a vector, y, and a matrix, X, we are interested in expressing y as a linear combination of the columns of X. There are two possibilities. If y lies in the column space of X, we shall be able to find a b such that

$$y = Xb. \qquad (2-53)$$

Figure 2.4 illustrates such a case for three dimensions in which the two columns of X both have a third coordinate equal to zero. Only y's whose third coordinate is zero, such as y^0 in the figure, can be expressed as Xb for some b. For the general case, assuming that y is, indeed, in the column space of X, we can find the coefficients b by solving the set of equations in (2-53). Procedures for doing so are discussed in the next section.

---

[7] If i equals j, the determinant is a **principal minor**.

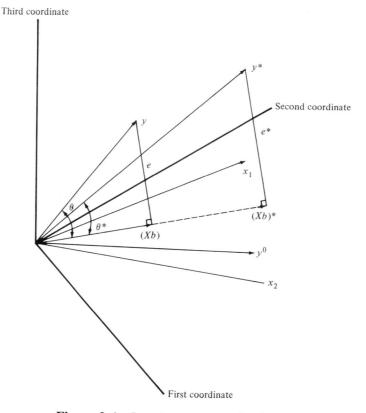

Third coordinate

Figure 2.4   Least squares projections.

Suppose, however, that **y** is not in the column space of **X**. In the context of our example, suppose that **y**'s third component is not zero. Then there is no **b** such that (2–53) holds. We can, however, write

$$\mathbf{y} = \mathbf{Xb} + \mathbf{e}, \tag{2–54}$$

where **e** is the difference between **y** and **Xb**. By this construction, we find an **Xb** that is in the column space of **X**, and **e** is the difference, or "residual." The figure shows two examples, **y** and **y***. For the present, we consider only **y**. We are interested in finding the **b** such that **y** is as close as possible to **Xb** in the sense that **e** is as short as possible.

Definition. The length, or **norm**, of a vector **e** is

$$\|\mathbf{e}\| = \sqrt{\mathbf{e}'\mathbf{e}}.$$

The problem is to find the **b** for which

$$\|\mathbf{e}\| = \|\mathbf{y} - \mathbf{Xb}\|$$

is as small as possible. The solution is that **b** that makes **e** perpendicular, or orthogonal, to **Xb**.

Definition. Two vectors, **a** and **b**, are **orthogonal**, written **a** ⊥ **b**, if and only if

$$\mathbf{a}'\mathbf{b} = \mathbf{b}'\mathbf{a} = 0. \tag{2–55}$$

Returning once again to our fitting problem, we find that the **b** we seek is that for which

$$\mathbf{e} \perp \mathbf{Xb}.$$

Expanding this set of equations gives the requirement

$$(\mathbf{Xb})'\mathbf{e} = \mathbf{0}$$

$$= \mathbf{b}'\mathbf{X}'\mathbf{y} - \mathbf{b}'\mathbf{X}'\mathbf{Xb}$$

$$= \mathbf{b}'[\mathbf{X}'\mathbf{y} - \mathbf{X}'\mathbf{Xb}]$$

or, since **b** is not **0**, the set of equations

$$\mathbf{X}'\mathbf{y} = \mathbf{X}'\mathbf{Xb}.$$

The means of solving such a set of equations is the subject of the next section.

In Figure 2.4, the linear combination **Xb** is called the **projection** of **y** into the space of **X**. The figure is drawn so that although **y** and **y*** are different, they have the same projection. The question we wish to pursue here is, which vector, **y** or **y***, is closer to its projection in the space of **X**? Superficially, it would appear that **y** is closer, since **e** is shorter than **e***. However, **y*** is much more nearly parallel to its projection than **y**; the only reason that its residual vector is longer is that **y*** is so long compared to **y**. A measure of comparison that would be unaffected by the length of the vectors is the angle between the vector and its projection. By this measure, θ* is considerably smaller than θ, which would reverse the earlier conclusion.

Theorem. The angle θ between two vectors, **a** and **b**, satisfies

$$\cos \theta = \frac{\mathbf{a}'\mathbf{b}}{\|\mathbf{a}\| \cdot \|\mathbf{b}\|}.$$

The two vectors in the calculation would be **y** or **y*** and **Xb**. A zero cosine implies that the vectors are orthogonal. If the cosine is one, the angle is zero, which means that the vectors are the same. (They would be if **y** were in the column space of **X**.) By dividing by the lengths, we automatically compensate for the length of **y**. By this measure, we would find that **y*** is closer to its projection than **y**.

2.5.   *Solution of a System of Equations*

Consider the set of n linear equations

$$\mathbf{Ax} = \mathbf{b}, \tag{2-56}$$

in which the K elements of **x** constitute the unknowns. **A** is a known matrix of coefficients, and **b** is a specified vector of values. We are interested in knowing whether a solution exists; if so, how to obtain it; and, lastly, if it does exist, whether it is unique.

2.5.1.   Systems of Linear Equations

For most of our applications, we shall consider only square systems of equations, that is, those in which **A** is a square matrix. In what follows, therefore, we take n to equal K. Since the number of rows in **A** is the number of equations, while the number of columns in **A** is the number of variables, this is the familiar case of "n equations in n unknowns." There are two types of systems:

(1) Homogeneous system: $\mathbf{Ax} = \mathbf{0}$.

By definition, a nonzero solution to such a system will exist if and only if $\mathbf{A}$ does not have full rank. If so, then for at least one column of $\mathbf{A}$, we can write the preceding as

$$\mathbf{a}_j = -\sum_{i \neq j} \frac{x_i}{x_j} \mathbf{a}_i.$$

This means, as we know, that the columns of $\mathbf{A}$ are linearly dependent and that $|\mathbf{A}| = 0$.

(2) Nonhomogeneous system: $\mathbf{Ax} = \mathbf{b}$.

The vector $\mathbf{b}$ is chosen arbitrarily and is to be expressed as a linear combination of the columns of $\mathbf{A}$. Since $\mathbf{b}$ has K elements, this will be possible only if the columns of $\mathbf{A}$ span the entire K-dimensional space, $\mathbb{R}^K$.[8] Equivalently, we shall require that the columns of $\mathbf{A}$ be linearly independent, or that $|\mathbf{A}|$ not be equal to zero.

2.5.2. Inverse Matrices

To solve the system $\mathbf{Ax} = \mathbf{b}$ for $\mathbf{x}$, something akin to division by a matrix is called for. Suppose we could find a square matrix, $\mathbf{B}$, such that $\mathbf{BA} = \mathbf{I}$. If the equation system is premultiplied by this $\mathbf{B}$, the following would be obtained:

$$\mathbf{BAx} = \mathbf{Ix} = \mathbf{x} = \mathbf{Bb}. \tag{2–57}$$

If the matrix $\mathbf{B}$ exists, it is the **inverse** of $\mathbf{A}$, denoted

$$\mathbf{B} = \mathbf{A}^{-1}.$$

From the definition,

$$\mathbf{A}^{-1}\mathbf{A} = \mathbf{I}.$$

In addition, by premultiplying by $\mathbf{A}$ and postmultiplying by $\mathbf{A}^{-1}$, then canceling terms, we find

$$\mathbf{AA}^{-1} = \mathbf{I}$$

as well.

If the inverse exists, it must be unique. Suppose that it is not, and that $\mathbf{C}$ is a different inverse of $\mathbf{A}$. Then $\mathbf{CAB} = \mathbf{CAB}$, but $(\mathbf{CA})\mathbf{B} = \mathbf{IB} = \mathbf{B}$ and $\mathbf{C}(\mathbf{AB}) = \mathbf{C}$, which would be a contradiction if $\mathbf{C}$ did not equal $\mathbf{B}$. Since, by (2–57), the solution is $\mathbf{x} = \mathbf{A}^{-1}\mathbf{b}$, the solution to the equation system is unique as well.

We now consider the calculation of the inverse matrix. For a 2×2 matrix,

$$\mathbf{AB} = \mathbf{I}$$

implies

$$\begin{bmatrix} a_{11} & a_{12} \\ a_{21} & a_{22} \end{bmatrix} \begin{bmatrix} b_{11} & b_{12} \\ b_{21} & b_{22} \end{bmatrix} = \begin{bmatrix} 1 & 0 \\ 0 & 1 \end{bmatrix}$$

---

[8] If $\mathbf{A}$ does not have full rank, the nonhomogeneous system will have solutions for *some* vectors, $\mathbf{b}$, namely, any $\mathbf{b}$ in the column space of $\mathbf{A}$. But we are interested in the case in which there are solutions for *all* nonzero vectors, $\mathbf{b}$, which requires $\mathbf{A}$ to have full rank.

or

$$a_{11}b_{11} + a_{12}b_{21} = 1$$

$$a_{11}b_{12} + a_{12}b_{22} = 0$$

$$a_{21}b_{11} + a_{22}b_{21} = 0$$

$$a_{21}b_{12} + a_{22}b_{22} = 1.$$

The solutions are

$$\begin{bmatrix} b_{11} & b_{12} \\ b_{21} & b_{22} \end{bmatrix} = \frac{1}{a_{11}a_{22} - a_{12}a_{21}} \begin{bmatrix} a_{22} & -a_{21} \\ -a_{12} & a_{11} \end{bmatrix} \tag{2-58}$$

$$= \frac{1}{|\mathbf{A}|} \begin{bmatrix} a_{22} & -a_{21} \\ -a_{12} & a_{22} \end{bmatrix}.$$

Notice the presence of the reciprocal of $|\mathbf{A}|$ in $\mathbf{A}^{-1}$. This is not specific to the 2×2 case. We infer from it that if the determinant is zero, the inverse does not exist.

Definition. A matrix whose inverse exists is **nonsingular**.

The simplest inverse matrix to compute is that of a diagonal matrix. If

$$\mathbf{D} = \begin{bmatrix} d_1 & 0 & 0 & \cdots & 0 \\ 0 & d_2 & 0 & \cdots & 0 \\ & & \vdots & & \\ 0 & 0 & 0 & & d_K \end{bmatrix}, \quad \mathbf{D}^{-1} = \begin{bmatrix} 1/d_1 & 0 & 0 & \cdots & 0 \\ 0 & 1/d_2 & 0 & \cdots & 0 \\ & & \vdots & & \\ 0 & 0 & 0 & \cdots & 1/d_K \end{bmatrix},$$

which shows, incidentally, that $\mathbf{I}^{-1} = \mathbf{I}$.

We shall use a^{ij} to indicate the ijth element of $\mathbf{A}^{-1}$. The general formula for computing an inverse matrix is

$$a^{ij} = \frac{|\mathbf{C}_{ji}|}{|\mathbf{A}|}, \tag{2-59}$$

where $|\mathbf{C}_{ji}|$ is the jith cofactor of $\mathbf{A}$. It follows, therefore, that for $\mathbf{A}$ to be nonsingular, $|\mathbf{A}|$ must be nonzero. Notice the reversal of the subscripts. For anything larger than a 3×3 matrix, (2–59) represents a formidable computation. But that is why we have computers.

Some computational results involving inverses are[9]

$$|\mathbf{A}^{-1}| = \frac{1}{|\mathbf{A}|}, \tag{2-60}$$

$$(\mathbf{A}^{-1})^{-1} = \mathbf{A}, \tag{2-61}$$

$$(\mathbf{A}^{-1})' = (\mathbf{A}')^{-1}. \tag{2-62}$$

If $\mathbf{A}$ is symmetric, $\mathbf{A}^{-1}$ is symmetric. $\tag{2-63}$

When both inverse matrices exist,

$$(\mathbf{AB})^{-1} = \mathbf{B}^{-1}\mathbf{A}^{-1}. \tag{2-64}$$

---

[9] The proofs of most of these results are obvious and are left as exercises.

Note the condition preceding (2–64). It may be that **AB** is a square, nonsingular matrix when neither **A** nor **B** are even square. (Consider, for example, **A′A**.) Extending (2–64), we have

$$(\mathbf{ABC})^{-1} = \mathbf{C}^{-1}(\mathbf{AB})^{-1} = \mathbf{C}^{-1}\mathbf{B}^{-1}\mathbf{A}^{-1}. \tag{2-65}$$

Recall that for a data matrix **X**, **X′X** is the sum of the *outer products* of the rows **X**. Suppose we have already computed $\mathbf{S} = (\mathbf{X'X})^{-1}$ for a number of years of data, such as those given at the beginning of this chapter. The following result, which is called an **updating formula**, shows how to compute the new **S** that would result when a new row is added to **X**:

$$[\mathbf{A} \pm \mathbf{bb'}]^{-1} = \mathbf{A}^{-1} \mp \left[\frac{1}{1 + \mathbf{b'A}^{-1}\mathbf{b}} \right] \mathbf{A}^{-1}\mathbf{bb'A}^{-1}. \tag{2-66}$$

Note the reversal of the sign in the inverse. Two more general forms of (2–66) that are occasionally useful are

$$[\mathbf{A} \pm \mathbf{bc'}]^{-1} = \mathbf{A}^{-1} \mp \left[\frac{1}{1 + \mathbf{c'A}^{-1}\mathbf{b}} \right] \mathbf{A}^{-1}\mathbf{bc'A}^{-1}, \tag{2-66'}$$

$$[\mathbf{A} \pm \mathbf{BCB'}]^{-1} = \mathbf{A}^{-1} \mp \mathbf{A}^{-1}\mathbf{B}[\mathbf{C}^{-1} + \mathbf{B'A}^{-1}\mathbf{B}]^{-1}\mathbf{B'A}^{-1}. \tag{2-66''}$$

2.5.3. Nonhomogeneous Systems of Equations

For the nonhomogeneous system,

$$\mathbf{Ax} = \mathbf{b},$$

if **A** is nonsingular, the unique solution is[10]

$$\mathbf{x} = \mathbf{A}^{-1}\mathbf{b}.$$

2.6. *Partitioned Matrices*

In formulating the elements of a matrix—for example, in structuring sets of equations—it is sometimes useful to group some of the elements in **submatrices**. For example, we might write

$$\mathbf{A} = \begin{bmatrix} 1 & 4 & 5 \\ 2 & 9 & 3 \\ \hline 8 & 9 & 6 \end{bmatrix}$$

$$= \begin{bmatrix} \mathbf{A}_{11} & \mathbf{A}_{12} \\ \mathbf{A}_{21} & \mathbf{A}_{22} \end{bmatrix}.$$

A is a **partitioned matrix**. The subscripts of the submatrices are defined in the same fashion as those for the elements of a matrix. A common special case is the **block diagonal matrix**,

$$\mathbf{A} = \begin{bmatrix} \mathbf{A}_{11} & \mathbf{0} \\ \mathbf{0} & \mathbf{A}_{22} \end{bmatrix},$$

where $\mathbf{A}_{11}$ and $\mathbf{A}_{22}$ are square matrices.

---

[10] Computationally, there are simpler (albeit equivalent) ways of obtaining **x** that do not require explicit computation of $\mathbf{A}^{-1}$. See Johnston (1984, pp. 138–140) or Strang (1976).

2.6.1. Addition and Multiplication of Partitioned Matrices

Addition and multiplication extend to partitioned matrices. For conformably partitioned matrices **A** and **B**,

$$\mathbf{A} + \mathbf{B} = \begin{bmatrix} \mathbf{A}_{11} + \mathbf{B}_{11} & \mathbf{A}_{12} + \mathbf{B}_{12} \\ \mathbf{A}_{21} + \mathbf{B}_{21} & \mathbf{A}_{22} + \mathbf{B}_{22} \end{bmatrix} \tag{2-67}$$

and

$$\begin{aligned} \mathbf{AB} &= \begin{bmatrix} \mathbf{A}_{11} & \mathbf{A}_{12} \\ \mathbf{A}_{21} & \mathbf{A}_{22} \end{bmatrix} \begin{bmatrix} \mathbf{B}_{11} & \mathbf{B}_{12} \\ \mathbf{B}_{21} & \mathbf{B}_{22} \end{bmatrix} \\ &= \begin{bmatrix} \mathbf{A}_{11}\mathbf{B}_{11} + \mathbf{A}_{12}\mathbf{B}_{21} & \mathbf{A}_{11}\mathbf{B}_{12} + \mathbf{A}_{12}\mathbf{B}_{22} \\ \mathbf{A}_{21}\mathbf{B}_{11} + \mathbf{A}_{22}\mathbf{B}_{21} & \mathbf{A}_{21}\mathbf{B}_{12} + \mathbf{A}_{21}\mathbf{B}_{22} \end{bmatrix}. \end{aligned} \tag{2-68}$$

In all of these, the matrices must be conformable for the operations involved. With respect to addition, the dimensions of $\mathbf{A}_{ij}$ and $\mathbf{B}_{ij}$ must be the same. For multiplication, the number of columns in $\mathbf{A}_{ij}$ must equal the number of rows in $\mathbf{B}_{jk}$ for all pairs i and j. That is, all of the necessary matrix products of the submatrices must be defined.

Two cases frequently encountered are of the form

$$\begin{bmatrix} \mathbf{A}_1 \\ \mathbf{A}_2 \end{bmatrix}' \begin{bmatrix} \mathbf{A}_1 \\ \mathbf{A}_2 \end{bmatrix} = [\mathbf{A}_1' \mathbf{A}_2'] \begin{bmatrix} \mathbf{A}_1 \\ \mathbf{A}_2 \end{bmatrix}$$

$$= [\mathbf{A}_1' \mathbf{A}_1 + \mathbf{A}_2' \mathbf{A}_2] \tag{2-69}$$

and

$$\begin{bmatrix} \mathbf{A}_{11} & \mathbf{0} \\ \mathbf{0} & \mathbf{A}_{22} \end{bmatrix}' \begin{bmatrix} \mathbf{A}_{11} & \mathbf{0} \\ \mathbf{0} & \mathbf{A}_{22} \end{bmatrix} = \begin{bmatrix} \mathbf{A}_{11}'\mathbf{A}_{11} & \mathbf{0} \\ \mathbf{0} & \mathbf{A}_{22}'\mathbf{A}_{22} \end{bmatrix}. \tag{2-70}$$

2.6.2. Determinants of Partitioned Matrices

The determinant of a block diagonal matrix is obtained analogously to that of a diagonal matrix.

$$\begin{vmatrix} \mathbf{A}_{11} & \mathbf{0} \\ \mathbf{0} & \mathbf{A}_{22} \end{vmatrix} = |\mathbf{A}_{11}| \cdot |\mathbf{A}_{22}|. \tag{2-71}$$

The result for a general 2×2 matrix is

$$\begin{vmatrix} \mathbf{A}_{11} & \mathbf{A}_{12} \\ \mathbf{A}_{21} & \mathbf{A}_{22} \end{vmatrix} = |\mathbf{A}_{22}| \cdot |\mathbf{A}_{11} - \mathbf{A}_{12}\mathbf{A}_{22}^{-1}\mathbf{A}_{21}| \tag{2-72}$$

$$= |\mathbf{A}_{11}| \cdot |\mathbf{A}_{22} - \mathbf{A}_{21}\mathbf{A}_{11}^{-1}\mathbf{A}_{12}|.$$

The result for matrices larger than 2×2 is extremely cumbersome but will not be necessary for our work.

2.6.3. Inverses of Partitioned Matrices

The inverse of a block diagonal matrix is

$$\begin{bmatrix} \mathbf{A}_{11} & \mathbf{0} \\ \mathbf{0} & \mathbf{A}_{22} \end{bmatrix}^{-1} = \begin{bmatrix} \mathbf{A}_{11}^{-1} & \mathbf{0} \\ \mathbf{0} & \mathbf{A}_{22}^{-1} \end{bmatrix}, \tag{2-73}$$

which can be verified by direct multiplication.

For the general 2×2 partitioned matrix, one form of the **partitioned inverse** is

$$\begin{bmatrix} A_{11} & A_{12} \\ A_{21} & A_{22} \end{bmatrix} = \begin{bmatrix} A_{11}^{-1}(I + A_{12}F_2A_{21}A_{11}^{-1}) & -A_{11}^{-1}A_{12}F_2 \\ -F_2A_{21}A_{11}^{-1} & F_2 \end{bmatrix}, \qquad (2-74)$$

where

$$F_2 = (A_{22} - A_{21}A_{11}^{-1}A_{12})^{-1}.$$

This can be checked most easily by postmultiplying A by the inverse. In view of the symmetry of the calculation, the upper left block could also be written as

$$F_1 = (A_{11} - A_{12}A_{22}^{-1}A_{21})^{-1}.$$

2.6.4.   Deviations from Means

A useful application of the preceding is the following calculation: Suppose that we begin with a column vector of n values, x, and let

$$A = \begin{bmatrix} n & \Sigma_i x_i \\ \Sigma_i x_i & \Sigma_i x_i^2 \end{bmatrix}$$

$$= \begin{bmatrix} i'i & i'x \\ x'i & x'x \end{bmatrix}.$$

We are interested in the lower right-hand element of A^{-1}. Upon using the definition of F_2 in (2-75), this will be

$$F_2 = [x'x - (x'i)(i'i)^{-1}(i'x)]^{-1}$$

$$= \left\{ x'\left[Ix - i\left(\frac{1}{n}\right)i'x \right] \right\}^{-1}$$

$$= \left\{ x'\left[I - \left(\frac{1}{n}\right)ii' \right]x \right\}^{-1}$$

$$= [x'M^0x]^{-1}.$$

Therefore, the lower right-hand value in the inverse matrix is

$$(x'M^0x)^{-1} = \frac{1}{\Sigma_i(x_i - \bar{x})^2}.$$

Now, suppose that instead of only a single column, x were X, a matrix with several columns. We seek the lower right block of $[Z'Z]^{-1}$. The analogous result is

$$(Z'Z)^{22} = [X'X - X'i(i'i)^{-1}i'X]^{-1}$$

$$= [X'M^0X]^{-1},$$

which implies that the $K \times K$ matrix in the lower right of $(Z'Z)^{-1}$ is the inverse of the $K \times K$ *matrix whose jkth element is* $\Sigma_i(x_{ij} - \bar{x}_j)(x_{ik} - \bar{x}_k)$. Thus, when a data matrix contains a column of 1s, the elements of the inverse of the matrix of sums of squares and cross products will be computed from the original data in the form of deviations from the respective column means.

2.6.5. Kronecker Products

A calculation that helps to condense the notation when dealing with sets of regression models is the **Kronecker product**. For general matrices **A** and **B**,

$$\mathbf{A} \otimes \mathbf{B} = \begin{bmatrix} a_{11}\mathbf{B} & a_{12}\mathbf{B} & \cdots & a_{1K}\mathbf{B} \\ a_{21}\mathbf{B} & a_{22}\mathbf{B} & \cdots & a_{2K}\mathbf{B} \\ & & \vdots & \\ a_{n1}\mathbf{B} & \mathbf{a}_{n2}\mathbf{B} & \cdots & a_{nK}\mathbf{B} \end{bmatrix}. \tag{2-75}$$

For example,

$$\begin{bmatrix} 3 & 0 \\ 5 & 2 \end{bmatrix} \otimes \begin{bmatrix} 1 & 4 \\ 4 & 7 \end{bmatrix} = \begin{bmatrix} 3\begin{bmatrix} 1 & 4 \\ 4 & 7 \end{bmatrix} & 0\begin{bmatrix} 1 & 4 \\ 4 & 7 \end{bmatrix} \\ 5\begin{bmatrix} 1 & 4 \\ 4 & 7 \end{bmatrix} & 2\begin{bmatrix} 1 & 4 \\ 4 & 7 \end{bmatrix} \end{bmatrix}.$$

Notice that there is no requirement for conformability in this operation. The Kronecker product can be computed for any pair of matrices. If **A** is $K \times L$ and **B** is $m \times n$, then $\mathbf{A} \otimes \mathbf{B}$ is $(Km) \times (Ln)$.

For the Kronecker product,

$$[\mathbf{A} \otimes \mathbf{B}]^{-1} = [\mathbf{A}^{-1} \otimes \mathbf{B}^{-1}], \tag{2-76}$$

which can be verified by direct multiplication. If **A** is $M \times M$ and **B** is $n \times n$, then

$$|\mathbf{A} \otimes \mathbf{B}| = |\mathbf{A}|^M |\mathbf{B}|^n$$

and (see Section 2.7.7)

$$\text{Trace } (\mathbf{A} \otimes \mathbf{B}) = tr(\mathbf{A})tr(\mathbf{B}).$$

2.7. Characteristic Roots and Vectors

A useful set of results for analyzing a square matrix, **A**, arises from the solutions to the set of equations

$$\mathbf{Ac} = \lambda\mathbf{c}. \tag{2-77}$$

The pairs of solutions are the **characteristic vectors**, **c**, and characteristic roots, λ. If **c** is any solution vector, $k\mathbf{c}$ is also for any value of k. To remove the indeterminacy, **c** is **normalized** so that

$$\mathbf{c}'\mathbf{c} = 1.$$

The solution then consists of λ and the $n - 1$ unknown elements in **c**.

2.7.1. The Characteristic Equation

Solving (2–77) can, in principle, proceed as follows: First, (2–77) implies that

$$\mathbf{Ac} = \lambda\mathbf{Ic}$$

or that

$$(\mathbf{A} - \lambda\mathbf{I})\mathbf{c} = \mathbf{0}.$$

This is a homogeneous system that has a nonzero solution only if the matrix $(\mathbf{A} - \lambda\mathbf{I})$ is singular or has a zero determinant. Therefore, if λ is a solution,

$$|\mathbf{A} - \lambda\mathbf{I}| = \mathbf{0}. \tag{2-78}$$

This polynomial in λ is the **characteristic equation** of $\mathbf{A}$. For example, if

$$\mathbf{A} = \begin{bmatrix} 5 & 1 \\ 2 & 4 \end{bmatrix},$$

then

$$\begin{aligned} |\mathbf{A} - \lambda\mathbf{I}| &= \begin{vmatrix} 5 - \lambda & 1 \\ 2 & 4 - \lambda \end{vmatrix} \\ &= (5 - \lambda)(4 - \lambda) - 2(1) \\ &= \lambda^2 - 9\lambda + 18. \end{aligned}$$

The two solutions are $\lambda = 6$ and $\lambda = 3$.

In solving the characteristic equation, there is no guarantee that the characteristic roots will be real. In the preceding example, if the 2 in the lower right-hand corner of the matrix were -2 instead, the solution would be a pair of complex values. The same problem can emerge in the general $n \times n$ case. The characteristic roots of a symmetric matrix are real, however.[11] This result will be convenient, as our applications will only involve the characteristic roots and vectors of symmetric matrices. Henceforth, in our treatment of characteristic roots and vectors, we shall assume that the matrices are symmetric.

For an $n \times n$ matrix, the characteristic equation is an nth-order polynomial in λ. Its solutions may be n distinct values, as in the preceding example, may contain repeated values of λ, as in

$$\begin{vmatrix} 2 - \lambda & 6 \\ 6 & 2 - \lambda \end{vmatrix} = 0 = (2 - \lambda)^2 - 36$$

$$\Rightarrow \lambda_1 = \lambda_2 = 8,$$

and may, as well, contain some zeros, as in

$$\begin{vmatrix} 1 - \lambda & 2 \\ 2 & 4 - \lambda \end{vmatrix} = \lambda^2 - 5\lambda = 0$$

$$\Rightarrow \lambda_1 = 5 \quad \text{and} \quad \lambda_2 = 0.$$

2.7.2.   Characteristic Vectors

With λ in hand, the characteristic vectors are derived from the original problem,

$$\mathbf{Ac} = \lambda\mathbf{c}$$

or

$$(\mathbf{A} - \lambda\mathbf{I})\mathbf{c} = \mathbf{0}.$$

For the first example, we have

$$\begin{bmatrix} 5 - \lambda & 1 \\ 2 & 4 - \lambda \end{bmatrix} \begin{bmatrix} c_1 \\ c_2 \end{bmatrix} = \begin{bmatrix} 0 \\ 0 \end{bmatrix}. \tag{2-79}$$

---

[11] A proof may be found in Theil (1971).

The two values for λ are 6 and 3. Inserting these values in $(2-41)$ yields

1. For $\lambda = 6$, $-c_1 + c_2 = 0$ and $2c_1 - 2c_2 = 0$, or $c_1 = c_2$.
2. For $\lambda = 3$, $2c_1 + c_2 = 0$ and $2c_1 + c_2 = 0$, or $c_1 = (-\frac{1}{2})c_2$.

Neither pair determines the values of c_1 and c_2. But this was to be expected; it was the reason $c'c = 1$ was specified at the outset. So, for example, if $\lambda = 6$, any vector c with equal elements will satisfy $(2-79)$. However, the additional equation $c'c = 1$ produces complete solutions for both vectors:

1. For $\lambda = 6$, $c = \begin{bmatrix} 1/\sqrt{2} \\ 1/\sqrt{2} \end{bmatrix}$.

2. For $\lambda = 3$, $c = \begin{bmatrix} 1/\sqrt{5} \\ -2/\sqrt{5} \end{bmatrix}$.

These are the only vectors that satisfy both $(2-79)$ and $c'c = 1$.

2.7.3. General Results for Characteristic Roots and Vectors

A $K \times K$ symmetric matrix has K distinct characteristic vectors, $c_1, c_2, \ldots, c_K$. The corresponding characteristic roots, $\lambda_1, \lambda_2, \ldots, \lambda_K$, while real, need not be distinct. The characteristic vectors of a symmetric matrix are orthogonal.[12] This implies that for every $i \neq j$, $c_i'c_j = 0$.[13] It is convenient to collect the K-characteristic vectors in a $K \times K$ matrix whose ith column is the c_i corresponding to λ_i,

$$C = [c_1 \quad c_2 \quad \cdots \quad c_K],$$

and the K-characteristic roots in the same order, in a diagonal matrix,

$$\Lambda = \begin{bmatrix} \lambda_1 & 0 & 0 & \cdots & 0 \\ 0 & \lambda_2 & 0 & \cdots & 0 \\ & & \vdots & & \\ 0 & 0 & 0 & \cdots & \lambda_K \end{bmatrix}.$$

Then, the full set of equations,

$$Ac_i = \lambda_i c_i,$$

is contained in

$$AC = C\Lambda. \tag{2-80}$$

Since the vectors are orthogonal and $c_i'c_i = 1$, we have

$$C'C = \begin{bmatrix} c_1'c_1 & c_1'c_2 & \cdots & c_1'c_K \\ c_2'c_1 & c_2'c_2 & \cdots & c_2'c_K \\ & & \vdots & \\ c_K'c_1 & c_K'c_2 & \cdots & c_K'c_K \end{bmatrix} \tag{2-81}$$

$$= I.$$

---

[12] For proofs of these propositions, see Hadley (1961) or Strang (1976).
[13] This is not true if the matrix is not symmetric. For instance, it does not hold for the characteristic vectors computed in the first example.

Result (2–81) implies that

$$\mathbf{C}' = \mathbf{C}^{-1}. \tag{2-82}$$

Consequently,

$$\mathbf{CC}' = \mathbf{CC}^{-1} = \mathbf{I} \tag{2-83}$$

as well; the rows of $\mathbf{C}$ are also orthogonal.

2.7.4. Diagonalization of a Matrix

By premultiplying (2–80) by $\mathbf{C}'$ and using (2–81), we obtain the **diagonalization** of $\mathbf{A}$;

$$\mathbf{C}'\mathbf{AC} = \mathbf{C}'\mathbf{C}\Lambda = \mathbf{I}\Lambda = \Lambda. \tag{2-84}$$

2.7.5. Rank of a Matrix

The diagonalization theorem enables us to obtain the rank of a matrix very easily.[14] For any matrix $\mathbf{A}$ and any nonsingular matrices $\mathbf{B}$ and $\mathbf{C}$, the rank of $\mathbf{BAC}$ is equal to the rank of $\mathbf{A}$. Since $\mathbf{C}'$ and $\mathbf{C}$ are nonsingular, we use them to apply the theorem to (2–84). By an obvious substitution, we have

$$\text{Rank}(\mathbf{A}) = \text{rank}(\Lambda).$$

Finding the rank of Λ is trivial. Since Λ is a diagonal matrix, its rank is just the number of nonzero values on its diagonal. The general result, then, is the following:

> The rank of a symmetric matrix is the number of nonzero characteristic roots it contains. (2-85)

It would appear that this simple rule will not be useful if $\mathbf{A}$ is not square. But recall that

$$\text{Rank}(\mathbf{A}) = \text{rank}(\mathbf{A}'\mathbf{A}).$$

Since $\mathbf{A}'\mathbf{A}$ is always square, we can use it instead of $\mathbf{A}$. Indeed, we can use it even if $\mathbf{A}$ is square, which leads to a fully general result:

> The rank of *any* matrix, $\mathbf{A}$, equals the number of nonzero characteristic roots in $\mathbf{A}'\mathbf{A}$. (2-86)

This result is useful because it provides a simple way to find the rank of a nonsymmetric matrix. Computationally, finding the characteristic roots of nonsymmetric matrices is rather difficult and involves complex arithmetic. But symmetric matrices, because of their real roots, are much simpler to analyze.

Since the row rank and column rank of a matrix are equal, we should be able to apply (2–86) to $\mathbf{AA}'$ as well. This requires, however, an additional result:

> The nonzero characteristic roots of $\mathbf{AA}'$ are the same as those of $\mathbf{A}'\mathbf{A}$. (2-87)

The proof is left as an exercise. A useful special case for you to examine is the characteristic roots of $\mathbf{aa}'$ and $\mathbf{a}'\mathbf{a}$, where $\mathbf{a}$ is an $n \times 1$ vector.

---

[14] Recall that when we last considered this problem, we had to try to identify the largest set of linearly independent columns. This might be hopelessly cumbersome if $\mathbf{A}$ has, say, 20 columns, which would be common in regression analysis.

If a characteristic root of a matrix is zero, then we have $\mathbf{Ac} = \mathbf{0}$. This means that if the matrix has a zero root, it must be singular. Otherwise, no nonzero $\mathbf{c}$ would exist. In general, therefore, a matrix is singular, that is, it does not have full rank if and only if it has at least one zero root.

2.7.6. Condition Number of a Matrix

As the preceding might suggest, there is a discrete difference between full rank and short rank matrices. However, in analyzing data matrices such as the one in Section 2.2, we shall often encounter cases in which a matrix is not quite short ranked, as it has all nonzero roots, but it is close. That is, by some measure, we can come very close to being able to write one column as a linear combination of the others. This is an important case; we shall examine it at length in our discussion of multicollinearity. Our definitions of rank and determinant will fail to indicate this possibility, but an alternative measure, the **condition number**, is designed for that purpose. Formally, the condition number for a square matrix, $\mathbf{A}$, is

$$\gamma = \left[\frac{\text{maximum root}}{\text{minimum root}}\right]^{1/2}.$$

For nonsquare matrices, $\mathbf{X}$, such as the data matrix in the example, we use $\mathbf{A} = \mathbf{X}'\mathbf{X}$. As a further refinement, because the characteristic roots are affected by the scaling of the columns of $\mathbf{X}$, we scale the columns to have length 1 by dividing each column by the square root of its norm. For the $\mathbf{X}$ in Section 2.2, the largest characteristic root of $\mathbf{A}$ is 4.953 and the smallest is 0.0001543. Therefore, the condition number is 178.67, which is extremely large. (Values larger than 20 are large.) The fact that the smallest root is close to zero compared to the largest means that this matrix is nearly singular. Matrices with large condition numbers are difficult to invert accurately.

2.7.7. Trace of a Matrix

The **trace** of a square matrix is the sum of its diagonal elements;

$$tr(\mathbf{A}) = \sum_i a_{ii}. \tag{2-88}$$

Some easily proven results are

$$tr(c\mathbf{A}) = c(tr(\mathbf{A})), \tag{2-89}$$

$$tr(\mathbf{A}') = tr(\mathbf{A}), \tag{2-90}$$

$$tr(\mathbf{A} + \mathbf{B}) = tr(\mathbf{A}) + tr(\mathbf{B}), \tag{2-91}$$

and

$$tr(\mathbf{I}_K) = K. \tag{2-92}$$

A particularly useful result is the trace of a product matrix;

$$tr(\mathbf{AB}) = tr(\mathbf{BA}). \tag{2-93}$$

See, for example, the two product matrices after (2–15). Two useful applications of (2–93) are

$$\mathbf{a}'\mathbf{a} = tr(\mathbf{a}'\mathbf{a}) = tr(\mathbf{aa}')$$

and

$$tr(\mathbf{A}'\mathbf{A}) = \sum_i \mathbf{a}_i'\mathbf{a}_i = \sum_i \sum_j a_{ij}^2.$$

The permutation rule can be extended to any *cyclic* permutation in a product;

$$tr(\mathbf{ABCD}) = tr(\mathbf{BCDA}) = tr(\mathbf{CDAB}) = tr(\mathbf{DABC}). \qquad (2-94)$$

By using (2–84), we obtain

$$tr(\mathbf{C'AC}) = tr(\mathbf{ACC'}) = tr(\mathbf{AI})$$
$$= tr(\mathbf{A}) = tr(\mathbf{\Lambda}). \qquad (2-95)$$

Since $\mathbf{\Lambda}$ is diagonal with the roots of $\mathbf{A}$ on its diagonal, the general result is

> The trace of a matrix equals the sum of its characteristic roots. $\qquad (2-96)$

2.7.8.   Determinant of a Matrix

Recalling how tedious the calculation of a determinant promised to be, we find that the following is particularly useful. Since

$$\mathbf{C'AC} = \mathbf{\Lambda},$$

$$|\mathbf{C'AC}| = |\mathbf{\Lambda}|.$$

Using a number of earlier results, we have

$$|\mathbf{C'AC}| = |\mathbf{C'}| \cdot |\mathbf{A}| \cdot |\mathbf{C}| = |\mathbf{C'}| \cdot |\mathbf{C}| \cdot |\mathbf{A}| = |\mathbf{C'C}| \cdot |\mathbf{A}|$$
$$= |\mathbf{I}| \cdot |\mathbf{A}| = 1 \cdot |\mathbf{A}|$$
$$= |\mathbf{A}|$$
$$= |\mathbf{\Lambda}|.$$

Since $|\mathbf{\Lambda}|$ is just the product of its diagonal elements,

> The determinant of a matrix equals the product of its characteristic roots. $\qquad (2-97)$

Notice that we get the expected result if any of these roots is zero. Since the determinant is the product of the roots, it follows that a matrix is singular if and only if its determinant is zero, and, in turn, if and only if it has at least one zero characteristic root.

2.7.9.   Spectral Decomposition of a Matrix

Starting once more with $\mathbf{AC} = \mathbf{C\Lambda}$, we have $\mathbf{ACC'} = \mathbf{C\Lambda C'}$, or

$$\mathbf{A} = \mathbf{C\Lambda C'}. \qquad (2-98)$$

This is called the **spectral** or **eigenvalue decomposition** of matrix $\mathbf{A}$. We can write this as a sum of outer products:

$$\mathbf{A} = \sum_{i=1}^{N} \lambda_i \mathbf{c}_i \mathbf{c}_i'. \qquad (2-99)$$

2.7.10.   Powers of a Matrix

We often use expressions involving powers of matrices, such as $\mathbf{AA} = \mathbf{A}^2$. For positive-integer powers, this can be computed by repeated multiplication. But this does not show how to handle a problem such as finding a $\mathbf{B}$ such that $\mathbf{B}^2 = \mathbf{A}$, that is, the square root of a matrix. The characteristic roots and vectors provide a simple solution.

Consider, first,

$$\mathbf{AA} = \mathbf{A}^2$$
$$= (\mathbf{CAC'})(\mathbf{CAC'}) = \mathbf{CAC'CAC'} \tag{2-100}$$
$$= \mathbf{CAIAC'} = \mathbf{CAAC'} = \mathbf{CA^2C'}.$$

Two results follow immediately. Since $\mathbf{A}^2$ is a diagonal matrix whose nonzero elements are the squares of those in $\mathbf{A}$, this implies the following:

> For any symmetric matrix, the characteristic
> roots of $\mathbf{A}^2$ are the squares of those of $\mathbf{A}$ and $\tag{2-101}$
> the characteristic vectors are the same.

The proof is immediately obtained by observing that the last line in (2–100) is the eigenvalue decomposition of the matrix $\mathbf{B} = \mathbf{AA}$. Since $\mathbf{A}^3 = \mathbf{AA}^2$, and so on, (2–101) extends to any positive integer. By convention, for any $\mathbf{A}$, $\mathbf{A}^0 = \mathbf{I}$. Thus, for any symmetric matrix, $\mathbf{A}$, $\mathbf{A}^K = \mathbf{CA}^K\mathbf{C'}$, $K = 0, 1, \ldots$. Hence the characteristic roots of $\mathbf{A}^K$ are λ^K, while the characteristic vectors are the same as those of $\mathbf{A}$. If $\mathbf{A}$ is nonsingular, so that all of its roots, λ_i, are nonzero, this can be extended to negative powers as well. If $\mathbf{A}^{-1}$ exists, then

$$\mathbf{A}^{-1} = (\mathbf{CAC'})^{-1}$$
$$= (\mathbf{C'})^{-1}\mathbf{A}^{-1}\mathbf{C}^{-1} \tag{2-102}$$
$$= \mathbf{CA}^{-1}\mathbf{C'},$$

where we have used the earlier result, $\mathbf{C'} = \mathbf{C}^{-1}$. If $\mathbf{A}^{-1}$ exists, the characteristic roots of $\mathbf{A}^{-1}$ are the reciprocals of those of $\mathbf{A}$ and the characteristic vectors are the same. By extending the notion of repeated multiplication,

> For any *nonsingular* symmetric matrix, $\mathbf{A}$,
> $\mathbf{A}^K = \mathbf{CA}^K\mathbf{C'}$, $K = \cdots, -2, -1, 0, 1, 2, \ldots$. $\tag{2-103}$

We now turn to the general problem of how to compute the square root of a matrix. In the scalar case, the value would have to be nonnegative. The matrix analog to this requirement is that all of the characteristic roots are nonnegative. Consider, then, the candidate,

$$\mathbf{A}^{1/2} = \mathbf{CA}^{1/2}\mathbf{C'}$$

$$= \mathbf{C}\begin{bmatrix} \sqrt{\lambda_1} & 0 & \cdots & 0 \\ 0 & \sqrt{\lambda_2} & \cdots & 0 \\ & & \vdots & \\ 0 & 0 & \cdots & \sqrt{\lambda_N} \end{bmatrix}\mathbf{C'}. \tag{2-104}$$

This satisfies the requirement for a square root, since

$$\mathbf{A}^{1/2}\mathbf{A}^{1/2} = \mathbf{CA}^{1/2}\mathbf{C'CA}^{1/2}\mathbf{C'} = \mathbf{CAC'}$$
$$= \mathbf{A}.$$

If we continue in this fashion, we can define the powers of a matrix more generally, still assuming that all of the characteristic roots are nonnegative. For example, $\mathbf{A}^{1/3} = \mathbf{CA}^{1/3}\mathbf{C'}$. If all of the roots are strictly positive, we can go one step further and extend the result to any real power. For reasons that will be made clear in the next section, we say that a matrix with positive characteristic roots is **positive definite**. It is the matrix analog to a positive number.

$$\text{For a } positive \text{ } definite \text{ } matrix, \mathbf{A}, \mathbf{A}^r = \mathbf{C}\mathbf{\Lambda}^r\mathbf{C}' \qquad (2-105)$$

for any real number, r. The characteristic roots of $\mathbf{A}^r$ are the rth power of those of $\mathbf{A}$, and the characteristic vectors are the same.

If $\mathbf{A}$ is only **nonnegative definite**, that is, has roots that are either zero or positive, (2–105) holds only for nonnegative r.

2.7.11. Idempotent Matrices

Idempotent matrices are ones that are equal to their squares. [See (2–37).] In view of their importance in econometrics, we collect a few results related to idempotent matrices at this point. First, (2–101) implies that if λ is a characteristic root of an idempotent matrix, $\lambda = \lambda^K$ for all nonnegative integers K. As such, if $\mathbf{A}$ is a symmetric idempotent matrix, all of its roots are 1 or 0. Assume that all of the roots of $\mathbf{A}$ are 1. Then $\mathbf{\Lambda} = \mathbf{I}$, and $\mathbf{A} = \mathbf{C}\mathbf{\Lambda}\mathbf{C}' = \mathbf{C}\mathbf{I}\mathbf{C}' = \mathbf{C}\mathbf{C}' = \mathbf{I}$. If the roots are not all 1, one or more are 0. Consequently, we have the following results for symmetric idempotent matrices.[15]

$$\begin{array}{ll}\text{The only full rank, symmetric idempotent matrix is} & (2-106)\\ \text{the identity matrix, } \mathbf{I}.\end{array}$$

$$\begin{array}{ll}\text{All symmetric idempotent matrices except the} & (2-107)\\ \text{identity matrix are singular.}\end{array}$$

The final result on idempotent matrices is obtained by observing that the count of the nonzero roots of $\mathbf{A}$ is also equal to their sum. Hence

$$\text{The rank of a symmetric idempotent matrix is equal to its trace.} \qquad (2-108)$$

2.7.12. Factoring a Matrix

In some applications, we shall require an alternative representation of a matrix. In particular, we seek a $\mathbf{P}$ such that

$$\mathbf{P}'\mathbf{P} = \mathbf{A}^{-1}.$$

One choice is

$$\mathbf{P} = \mathbf{\Lambda}^{-1/2}\mathbf{C}',$$

whence

$$\mathbf{P}'\mathbf{P} = (\mathbf{C}')'(\mathbf{\Lambda}^{-1/2})'\mathbf{\Lambda}^{-1/2}\mathbf{C}'$$
$$= \mathbf{C}\mathbf{\Lambda}^{-1}\mathbf{C}'$$

as desired.[16]

The **Cholesky factorization** of a symmetric positive definite matrix is an alternative representation that is useful in regression analysis. Any symmetric positive definite matrix, $\mathbf{A}$, may be written as the product of a **lower triangular** matrix, $\mathbf{L}$, and its transpose (which is an

---

[15] Not all idempotent matrices are symmetric. However, we shall not encounter any asymmetric ones in our work.

[16] We say that this is the easiest choice because if $\mathbf{A}$ is symmetric, as it will be in all of our applications, there are other candidates. You can easily verify that $\mathbf{C}\mathbf{\Lambda}^{-1/2}\mathbf{C}' = \mathbf{A}^{-1/2}$ works as well.

upper triangular matrix), $L' = U$. Thus, $A = LU$. This is the Cholesky decomposition of A. The usefulness of this formulation arises when the inverse of A is required. Once L is computed, finding $A^{-1} = U^{-1}L^{-1}$ is also straightforward, as well as extremely fast and accurate. Most recently developed econometric software uses this technique for inverting positive definite matrices.

2.7.13.   The Generalized Inverse of a Matrix

The inverse matrix is fundamental in econometrics. Although we shall not require them much in our treatment in this book, there are more general forms of inverse matrices than we have considered thus far. A generalized inverse of a matrix, A, is another matrix, A^+, that satisfies the following requirements:

1. $AA^+A = A$.
2. $A^+AA^+ = A^+$.
3. A^+A is symmetric.
4. AA^+ is symmetric.

A unique A^+ can be found for any matrix, whether A is singular or not, or even if A is not square.[17] The unique matrix that satisfies all four requirements is called the **Moore–Penrose inverse** or **pseudoinverse** of A. If A happens to be square and nonsingular, the generalized inverse will be the familiar ordinary inverse. But if A^{-1} does not exist, A^+ can still be computed.

An important special case is the overdetermined system of equations

$$Ab = y,$$

where A has n rows, $K < n$ columns, and column rank equal to $R \le K$. Suppose that R equals K, so that $(A'A)^{-1}$ exists. Then the Moore–Penrose inverse of A is

$$A^+ = (A'A)^{-1}A',$$

which can be verified by multiplication. A solution to the system of equations can be written

$$b = A^+y.$$

Readers familiar with regression will recognize this as the least squares solution.

Now suppose that A does not have full rank. The previous solution cannot be computed. However, an alternative solution can be obtained. We continue to use the matrix $A'A$. In the spectral decomposition of Section 7.8, if A has rank R, there are R terms in the summation in (2–99). In (2–102), the spectral decomposition using the reciprocals of the characteristic roots is used to compute the inverse. To compute the Moore–Penrose inverse, we apply this calculation to $A'A$, using only the nonzero roots, then postmultiply the result by A'. Let C_1 be the R characteristic vectors corresponding to the nonzero roots, which we array in the diagonal matrix, Λ_1. Then the Moore–Penrose inverse is

$$A^+ = C_1\Lambda_1^{-1}C_1'A',$$

which is very similar to the previous solution.

If A is a square matrix with rank $R \le K$, the Moore–Penrose inverse is computed precisely as in the previous equation without postmultiplying by A'. Thus, for a square

---

[17] A proof of uniqueness, with several other results, may be found in Theil (1983).

symmetric matrix, **A**,

$$\mathbf{A}^+ = \mathbf{C}_1 \mathbf{\Lambda}_1^{-1} \mathbf{C}_1',$$

where $\mathbf{\Lambda}_1$ is a diagonal matrix containing the reciprocals of the *nonzero* roots of **A**.

2.8. *Quadratic Forms and Definite Matrices*

Many optimization problems involve double sums of the form

$$q = \sum_{i=1}^{n} \sum_{j=1}^{n} x_i x_j a_{ij}. \tag{2-109}$$

This **quadratic form** can be written

$$q = \mathbf{x}'\mathbf{A}\mathbf{x},$$

where **A** is a symmetric matrix. In general, q may be positive, negative, or zero; it depends on **A** and **x**. However, there are some matrices for which q will be positive regardless of **x**, and others for which q will always be negative (or nonnegative or nonpositive). For a given matrix, **A**,

1. If $\mathbf{x}'\mathbf{A}\mathbf{x} > (<)0$ for all **x**, then **A** is **positive (negative) definite**.
2. If $\mathbf{x}'\mathbf{A}\mathbf{x} \geq (\leq 0)$ for all **x**, then **A** is **nonnegative definite** or **positive semidefinite** (nonpositive definite).

It might seem that it would be impossible to check a matrix for definiteness, since **x** can be chosen arbitrarily. But we have already used the set of results necessary to do so. Recall that a symmetric matrix can be decomposed into

$$\mathbf{A} = \mathbf{C}\mathbf{\Lambda}\mathbf{C}'.$$

Therefore, the quadratic form can be written as

$$\mathbf{x}'\mathbf{A}\mathbf{x} = \mathbf{x}'\mathbf{C}\mathbf{\Lambda}\mathbf{C}'\mathbf{x}.$$

Let $\mathbf{y} = \mathbf{C}'\mathbf{x}$. Then

$$\mathbf{x}'\mathbf{A}\mathbf{x} = \mathbf{y}'\mathbf{\Lambda}\mathbf{y}$$

$$= \sum_{i=1}^{n} \lambda_i y_i^2. \tag{2-110}$$

To take the obvious case, if λ_i is positive for all i, then regardless of **y**, that is, regardless of **x**, q will be positive. This was the case identified earlier as a positive definite matrix. Continuing this line of reasoning, if all of the characteristic roots of **A** are negative, we find that **A** is **negative definite**. If some of the roots are zero, then **A** is **nonnegative definite** if the remainder are positive and **nonpositive definite** if they are negative. If **A** has both negative and positive roots, then **A** is **indefinite**. (The preceding give, in each case, the "if" part of the theorem. To establish the "only if" part, assume that the condition on the roots does not hold. This must lead to a contradiction. For example, if some λ can be negative, then $\mathbf{y}'\mathbf{\Lambda}\mathbf{y}$ could be negative for some **y**, so **A** cannot be positive definite.)

2.8.1.   Nonnegative Definite Matrices

A case of particular interest is that of nonnegative definite matrices. The previous theorem implies a number of related results.

$$\text{If } \mathbf{A} \text{ is nonnegative definite, then } |\mathbf{A}| \geq 0. \tag{2–111}$$

The proof follows immediately from the fact that the determinant is the product of the roots. The converse, however, is not true. For example, a 2×2 matrix with two negative roots is clearly not positive definite, but it does have a positive determinant.

$$\text{If } \mathbf{A} \text{ is positive definite, so is } \mathbf{A}^{-1}. \tag{2–112}$$

Proof: The roots are the reciprocals of those of $\mathbf{A}$, which are, therefore, positive.

$$\text{The identity matrix, } \mathbf{I}, \text{ is positive definite.} \tag{2–113}$$

Proof: $\mathbf{x}'\mathbf{Ix} = \mathbf{x}'\mathbf{x} > 0$ if $\mathbf{x} \neq \mathbf{0}$.

A very important result for regression analysis is

$$\text{If } \mathbf{A} \text{ is } n \times K \text{ with full rank and } n > K, \text{ then } \mathbf{A}'\mathbf{A} \text{ is} \\ \text{positive definite and } \mathbf{AA}' \text{ is nonnegative definite.} \tag{2–114}$$

Proof: By assumption, $\mathbf{Ax} \neq \mathbf{0}$. So $\mathbf{x}'\mathbf{A}'\mathbf{Ax} = (\mathbf{Ax})'(\mathbf{Ax}) = \mathbf{y}'\mathbf{y} = \sum_i y_i^2 > 0$.

A similar proof establishes the nonnegative definiteness of $\mathbf{AA}'$. The difference in the latter case is that because $\mathbf{A}$ has more rows than columns, there is an $\mathbf{x}$ such that $\mathbf{A}'\mathbf{x} = \mathbf{0}$. Thus, in the proof, we only have $\mathbf{y}'\mathbf{y} \geq 0$. The case in which $\mathbf{A}$ does not have full column rank is the same as that of $\mathbf{AA}'$.

$$\text{If } \mathbf{A} \text{ is positive definite and } \mathbf{B} \text{ is a nonsingular matrix,} \\ \text{then } \mathbf{B}'\mathbf{AB} \text{ is positive definite.} \tag{2–115}$$

Proof: $\mathbf{x}'\mathbf{B}'\mathbf{ABx} = \mathbf{y}'\mathbf{Ay} > 0$, where $\mathbf{y} = \mathbf{Bx}$. But, $\mathbf{y}$ cannot be $\mathbf{0}$ because $\mathbf{B}$ is nonsingular.

Note, finally, that for $\mathbf{A}$ to be negative definite, all of $\mathbf{A}$'s characteristic roots must be negative. But, in this case, $|\mathbf{A}|$ is positive if $\mathbf{A}$ is of even order and negative if $\mathbf{A}$ is of odd order.

2.8.2   Idempotent Quadratic Forms

Quadratic forms in idempotent matrices play an important role in the distributions of many test statistics. As such, we shall encounter them fairly often. There are two central results that will be of interest.

$$\text{Every symmetric idempotent matrix is nonnegative definite.} \tag{2–116}$$

Proof: All roots are 1 or 0; hence, the matrix is nonnegative definite by definition.

Combining this with some earlier results yields a result used in determining the sampling distribution of most of the standard test statistics.

If **A** is symmetric and independent, $n \times n$ with rank J, then every quadratic form in **A** can be written

(2–117)

$$\mathbf{x}'\mathbf{A}\mathbf{x} = \sum_{i=1}^{J} y_i^2.$$

Proof: This is (2–110) with $\lambda = 1$ or 0.

2.8.3. Ranking Matrices

It is not obvious how one can compare two matrices. As a starting point, of course, the matrices must be of the same dimensions. A useful, although not always conclusive, comparison is based on

$$d = \mathbf{x}'\mathbf{A}\mathbf{x} - \mathbf{x}'\mathbf{B}\mathbf{x}.$$

If this is always positive, regardless of the choice of **x**, then, at least by this criterion, we could say that

$$\mathbf{A} > \mathbf{B}.$$

(2–118)

The reverse would apply if d is always negative. For some matrices, the result might be ambiguous. It follows from the definition that

$$d > 0 \text{ implies that } \mathbf{A} - \mathbf{B} \text{ is positive definite,}$$

as

$$d = \mathbf{x}'(\mathbf{A} - \mathbf{B})\mathbf{x}.$$

For example,

$$\mathbf{A} = \begin{bmatrix} 3 & -1 \\ -1 & 49 \end{bmatrix} \quad \text{and} \quad \mathbf{B} = \begin{bmatrix} 2 & 5 \\ 5 & 13 \end{bmatrix}.$$

Is $\mathbf{A} > \mathbf{B}$?

$$\mathbf{A} - \mathbf{B} = \begin{bmatrix} 1 & -6 \\ -6 & 36 \end{bmatrix}.$$

The characteristic roots of this rank 1 matrix are 37 and 0. Therefore, $\mathbf{A} - \mathbf{B}$ is nonnegative definite. For this **A** and **B**, a quadratic form in **A** will always be at least as large as the one in **B** that uses the same **x**.

A particular case of the general result is

If **A** is positive definite and **B** is nonnegative definite, then $\mathbf{A} + \mathbf{B} > \mathbf{A}$.

(2–119)

Consider, for example, the "updating formula" introduced in (2–66). This uses a matrix

$$\mathbf{A} = \mathbf{B}'\mathbf{B} + \mathbf{b}\mathbf{b}' > \mathbf{B}'\mathbf{B}.^{[18]}$$

Finally, in comparing matrices, it may be more convenient to compare their inverses. The result analogous to a familiar scalar result is

If $\mathbf{A} > \mathbf{B}$, then $\mathbf{B}^{-1} > \mathbf{A}^{-1}$.

(2–120)

---

[18] The earlier example is constructed using this result.

2.9.   Calculus and Matrix Algebra

Many problems in econometrics involve the extension of some familiar results from calculus to a multivariable setting. Examples include the formulation of approximating functions, maximization or minimization of a function of many variables, and the analysis of transformations from one set of variables to another. This section presents the basic set of results used later in the book in the discussion of these problems.[19] Each of the three parts begins with the basic result from the univariate calculus and then proceeds to the extension to the multivariate case.

2.9.1.   Differentiation and the Taylor Series

A variable, y, is a function of another variable, x, written

$$y = f(x), \qquad y = g(x), \qquad y = y(x), \qquad \text{and so on}$$

if each value of x is associated with a single value of y. In this relationship, y and x are sometimes labeled the **dependent variable** and the **independent variable**, respectively. Assuming that the function $f(x)$ is continuous and differentiable, we obtain the following derivatives:

$$f'(x) = \frac{dy}{dx},$$

$$f''(x) = \frac{d^2 y}{dx^2},$$

and so on.

A frequent use of the derivatives of $f(x)$ is in the **Taylor series approximation**. A Taylor series is a polynomial approximation to $f(x)$. Letting x^0 be an arbitrarily chosen expansion point,

$$f(x) \simeq f(x^0) + \sum_{i=1}^{P} \frac{1}{i!} \frac{d^i f(x)}{dx^i}\bigg|_{x=x^0} \cdot (x - x^0)^i. \tag{2-121}$$

The choice of the number of terms is arbitrary; the more that are used, the more accurate will be the approximation. The approximations used most frequently in econometrics are the **linear approximation**,

$$f(x) \simeq [f(x^0) - f'(x^0)x^0] + f'(x^0)x$$
$$= \beta_1 + \beta_2 x \tag{2-122}$$

and the **quadratic approximation**,

$$f(x) \simeq [f^0 - f'^0 x^0 + \tfrac{1}{2} f''^0 (x^0)^2] + [f'^0 - f''^0 x^0]x + \tfrac{1}{2} f''^0 x^2$$
$$= \beta_1 + \beta_2 x + \beta_3 x^2, \tag{2-123}$$

where the superscript indicates that the function is evaluated at x^0.

We can regard a function $y = f(x_1, x_2, \ldots, x_n)$ as a **scalar-valued function** of a vector,

---

[19] For a complete exposition, see Magnus and Neudecker (1988).

that is, $y = f(\mathbf{x})$. The vector of partial derivatives, or **gradient vector** (or simply gradient) is

$$\frac{\partial f(\mathbf{x})}{\partial \mathbf{x}} = \begin{bmatrix} \partial y/\partial x_1 \\ \partial y/\partial x_2 \\ \vdots \\ \partial y/\partial x_n \end{bmatrix} = \begin{bmatrix} f_1 \\ f_2 \\ \vdots \\ f_n \end{bmatrix}. \tag{2-124}$$

The vector $\mathbf{g}(\mathbf{x})$ or $\mathbf{g}$ is used to represent the gradient vector. Notice that it is a column vector. The shape of the derivative is determined by the denominator of the derivative.

A **second derivatives matrix** or **Hessian matrix** is computed as

$$\mathbf{H} = \begin{bmatrix} \partial^2 y/\partial x_1 \partial x_1 & \partial^2 y/\partial x_1 \partial x_2 & \cdots & \partial^2 y/\partial x_1 \partial x_n \\ \partial^2 y/\partial x_2 \partial x_1 & \partial^2 y/\partial x_2 \partial x_2 & \cdots & \partial^2 y/\partial x_2 \partial x_n \\ \vdots & \vdots & \vdots & \vdots \\ \partial^2 y/\partial x_n \partial x_1 & \partial^2 y/\partial x_n \partial x_2 & \cdots & \partial^2 y/\partial x_n \partial x_n \end{bmatrix} \tag{2-125}$$

$$= [f_{ij}].$$

In general, $\mathbf{H}$ is a square, symmetric matrix. Each row and column of $\mathbf{H}$ is the derivative of the gradient vector with respect to one of the variables. Therefore,

$$\mathbf{H} = \frac{\partial[\partial y/\partial \mathbf{x}]}{\partial x_1} \quad \frac{\partial[\partial y/\partial \mathbf{x}]}{\partial x_2} \quad \cdots \quad \frac{\partial[\partial y/\partial \mathbf{x}]}{\partial x_n}$$

$$= \frac{\partial[\partial y/\partial \mathbf{x}]}{\partial(x_1 \quad x_2 \quad \cdots \quad x_n)}$$

$$= \frac{\partial[\partial y/\partial \mathbf{x}]}{\partial \mathbf{x}'}$$

$$= \frac{\partial^2 y}{\partial \mathbf{x} \partial \mathbf{x}'}.$$

The first-order, or linear Taylor series, approximation is

$$y \simeq f(\mathbf{x}^0) + \sum_i f_i(\mathbf{x}^0)(x_i - x_i^0)$$

$$= f(\mathbf{x}^0) + \left[\frac{\partial f(\mathbf{x}^0)}{\partial \mathbf{x}^0}\right]'(\mathbf{x} - \mathbf{x}^0)$$

$$= f(\mathbf{x}^0) + \mathbf{g}(\mathbf{x}^0)'(\mathbf{x} - \mathbf{x}^0) \tag{2-126}$$

$$= [f(\mathbf{x}^0) - \mathbf{g}(\mathbf{x}^0)'\mathbf{x}^0] + \mathbf{g}(\mathbf{x}^0)'\mathbf{x}$$

$$= [f^0 - \mathbf{g}^{0'}\mathbf{x}^0] + \mathbf{g}^{0'}\mathbf{x}$$

$$= \beta_1 + \boldsymbol{\beta}_2'\mathbf{x}.$$

The second-order, or quadratic, approximation adds the second-order terms in the approximation,

$$\tfrac{1}{2}\sum_i \sum_j f_{ij}^0(x_i - x_i^0)(x_j - x_j^0) = \tfrac{1}{2}(\mathbf{x} - \mathbf{x}^0)'\mathbf{H}(\mathbf{x} - \mathbf{x}^0)$$

to the preceding one. Collecting terms in the same manner as in (2-126), we have

$$y \simeq \beta_1 + \boldsymbol{\beta}_2'\mathbf{x} + \tfrac{1}{2}\mathbf{x}'\boldsymbol{\Gamma}_3\mathbf{x}, \tag{2-127}$$

where

$$\beta_1 = f^0 - \mathbf{g}^{0\prime}\mathbf{x}^0 + \tfrac{1}{2}\mathbf{x}^{0\prime}\mathbf{H}^0\mathbf{x}^0,$$
$$\beta_2 = -\mathbf{g}^0 + \mathbf{H}^0\mathbf{x}^0,$$

and

$$\Gamma_3 = \mathbf{H}^0.$$

A linear function can be written

$$y = \mathbf{a}'\mathbf{x} = \mathbf{x}'\mathbf{a} = \sum_i a_i x_i.$$

Hence

$$\frac{\partial(\mathbf{a}'\mathbf{x})}{\partial\mathbf{x}} = \mathbf{a}. \qquad (2\text{-}128)$$

Note, in particular, that $\partial(\mathbf{a}'\mathbf{x})/\partial\mathbf{x} = \mathbf{a}$, not $\mathbf{a}'$. In a set of linear functions,

$$y = \mathbf{A}\mathbf{x},$$

each element y_i of $\mathbf{y}$ is

$$y_i = \mathbf{a}_i\mathbf{x},$$

where $\mathbf{a}_i$ is the ith row of $\mathbf{A}$. Therefore,

$$\frac{\partial y_i}{\partial\mathbf{x}} = \mathbf{a}_i'$$

$$= \text{the transpose of the } i\text{th row of } \mathbf{A}$$

and

$$\begin{bmatrix} \partial y_1/\partial\mathbf{x}' \\ \partial y_2/\partial\mathbf{x}' \\ \vdots \\ \partial y_n/\partial\mathbf{x}' \end{bmatrix} = \begin{bmatrix} \mathbf{a}_1 \\ \mathbf{a}_2 \\ \vdots \\ \mathbf{a}_n \end{bmatrix}.$$

Collecting all terms, we find that $\partial\mathbf{A}\mathbf{x}/\partial\mathbf{x}' = \mathbf{A}$, while the more familiar form will be

$$\frac{\partial\mathbf{A}\mathbf{x}}{\partial\mathbf{x}} = \mathbf{A}'. \qquad (2\text{-}129)$$

A quadratic form is written

$$\mathbf{x}'\mathbf{A}\mathbf{x} = \sum_i \sum_j x_i x_j a_{ij}. \qquad (2\text{-}130)$$

For example,

$$\mathbf{A} = \begin{bmatrix} 1 & 3 \\ 3 & 4 \end{bmatrix},$$

so that

$$\mathbf{x}'\mathbf{A}\mathbf{x} = 1x_1^2 + 4x_2^2 + 6x_1 x_2.$$

Then

$$\frac{\partial \mathbf{x}'\mathbf{A}\mathbf{x}}{\partial \mathbf{x}} = \begin{bmatrix} 2x_1 + 6x_2 \\ 6x_1 + 8x_2 \end{bmatrix}$$

$$= \begin{bmatrix} 2 & 6 \\ 6 & 8 \end{bmatrix} \begin{bmatrix} x_1 \\ x_2 \end{bmatrix} = 2\mathbf{A}\mathbf{x}, \qquad (2-131)$$

which is the general result when $\mathbf{A}$ is a symmetric matrix. If $\mathbf{A}$ is not symmetric, then

$$\frac{\partial(\mathbf{x}'\mathbf{A}\mathbf{x})}{\partial \mathbf{x}} = (\mathbf{A} + \mathbf{A}')\mathbf{x}. \qquad (2-132)$$

Referring to the preceding double summation, we find that for each term, the coefficient on a_{ij} is $x_i x_j$. Therefore,

$$\frac{\partial(\mathbf{x}'\mathbf{A}\mathbf{x})}{\partial a_{ij}} = x_i x_j.$$

The square matrix whose ijth element is $x_i x_j$ is $\mathbf{x}\mathbf{x}'$, so

$$\frac{\partial(\mathbf{x}'\mathbf{A}\mathbf{x})}{\partial \mathbf{A}} = \mathbf{x}\mathbf{x}'. \qquad (2-133)$$

Derivatives involving determinants appear in maximum likelihood estimation. From the cofactor expansion in (2–53),

$$\frac{\partial|\mathbf{A}|}{\partial \mathbf{A}_{ij}} = (-1)^{i+j}|\mathbf{C}_{ij}|,$$

where $|\mathbf{C}_{ij}|$ is the ijth cofactor in $\mathbf{A}$. The inverse of $\mathbf{A}$ can be computed using

$$\mathbf{A}_{ij}^{-1} = \frac{(-1)^{i+j}|\mathbf{C}_{ji}|}{|\mathbf{A}|},$$

—note the reversal of the subscripts—which implies that

$$\frac{\partial \ln|\mathbf{A}|}{\partial \mathbf{A}_{ij}} = \frac{(-1)^{i+j}|\mathbf{C}_{ij}|}{|\mathbf{A}|}$$

or, collecting terms,

$$\frac{\partial \ln|\mathbf{A}|}{\partial \mathbf{A}} = \mathbf{A}^{-1'}.$$

Since the matrices for which we shall make this calculation will be symmetric in our applications, the transposition will be unnecessary.

2.9.2. Optimization

Many problems involve finding the x where $f(x)$ is maximized or minimized. Since $f'(x)$ is the slope of $f(x)$, either optimum must occur where $f'(x) = 0$. Otherwise, the function will be increasing or decreasing at x. This implies the **first-order** or

necessary condition for an optimum:

$$\frac{dy}{dx} = 0. \qquad (2-134)$$

The same condition is necessary for both a maximum and a minimum. For a maximum, the function must be concave; for a minimum, it must be convex. This leads to a

sufficient condition for an optimum:

$$\text{For a maximum, } \frac{d^2y}{dx^2} < 0;$$

$$\text{For a minimum, } \frac{d^2y}{dx^2} > 0.$$

(2–135)

Some functions, such as the sine and cosine functions, have many **local optima**, that is, many minima and maxima. A function such as $\sin x/|x|$, which is a damped sine wave, does as well but differs in that although it has many local maxima, it has one, at $x = 0$, at which $f(x)$ is greater than it is at any other point. Thus, $x = 0$ is the **global maximum**, while the other maxima are only **local maxima**. Certain functions, such as quadratic, have only a single optimum. These functions are **globally concave** if the optimum is a maximum and **globally convex** if it is a minimum.

For maximizing or minimizing a function of several variables, the first-order conditions are

$$\frac{\partial f(\mathbf{x})}{\partial \mathbf{x}} = \mathbf{0}.$$

(2–136)

This is interpreted in the same manner as the necessary condition in the univariate case. At the optimum, it must be true that no small change in any variable leads to an improvement in the function value. In the single-variable case, d^2y/dx^2 must be positive for a minimum and negative for a maximum. In the multivariate case, we attach a similar condition to the second derivatives matrix of the objective function. In particular, the second-order conditions for an optimum are that at the optimizing value,

$$\mathbf{H} = \frac{\partial^2 f(\mathbf{x})}{\partial \mathbf{x} \partial \mathbf{x}'}$$

(2–137)

must be positive definite for a minimum and negative definite for a maximum.

In a single-variable problem, the second-order condition can usually be verified by inspection. This will not generally be true in the multivariate case. As discussed earlier, checking the definiteness of a matrix is, in general, a relatively difficult problem. For most of the problems encountered in econometrics, however, the second-order condition will be implied by the structure of the problem. That is, the matrix $\mathbf{H}$ will usually be of such a form that it is always definite.

For an example of the preceding, consider the problem

$$\text{Maximize}_\mathbf{x} \ R = \mathbf{a}'\mathbf{x} - \mathbf{x}'\mathbf{A}\mathbf{x},$$

where

$$\mathbf{a}' = (5 \quad 4 \quad 2)$$

and

$$\mathbf{A} = \begin{bmatrix} 2 & 1 & 3 \\ 1 & 3 & 2 \\ 3 & 2 & 5 \end{bmatrix}.$$

Using some now familiar results, we obtain

$$\frac{\partial R}{\partial \mathbf{x}} = \mathbf{a} - 2\mathbf{A}\mathbf{x}$$

$$= \begin{bmatrix} 5 \\ 4 \\ 2 \end{bmatrix} - \begin{bmatrix} 4 & 2 & 6 \\ 2 & 6 & 4 \\ 6 & 4 & 10 \end{bmatrix} \begin{bmatrix} x_1 \\ x_2 \\ x_3 \end{bmatrix} = \mathbf{0}. \tag{2-138}$$

The solutions are

$$\begin{bmatrix} x_1 \\ x_2 \\ x_3 \end{bmatrix} = \begin{bmatrix} 4 & 2 & 6 \\ 2 & 6 & 4 \\ 6 & 4 & 10 \end{bmatrix}^{-1} \begin{bmatrix} 5 \\ 4 \\ 2 \end{bmatrix} = \begin{bmatrix} 11.25 \\ 1.75 \\ -7.25 \end{bmatrix}.$$

The sufficient condition is that

$$\frac{\partial^2 R(\mathbf{x})}{\partial \mathbf{x} \partial \mathbf{x}'} = -2A = \begin{bmatrix} -4 & -2 & -6 \\ -2 & -6 & -4 \\ -6 & -4 & -10 \end{bmatrix} \tag{2-139}$$

must be negative definite. The three characteristic roots of this matrix are -15.776, -4, and -0.25403. Since all three roots are negative, the matrix is negative definite, as required.

In the preceding, it was necessary to compute the characteristic roots of the Hessian to verify the sufficient condition. For a general matrix of order larger than 2, this will normally require a computer. However, suppose that $\mathbf{A}$ is of the form

$$\mathbf{A} = \mathbf{B}'\mathbf{B},$$

where $\mathbf{B}$ is some known matrix. Then, as shown earlier, we know that $\mathbf{A}$ will always be positive definite (assuming that $\mathbf{B}$ has full rank). It is not necessary to calculate the characteristic roots of $\mathbf{A}$ to verify the sufficient conditions.

2.9.3. Constrained Optimization

It is often necessary to solve an optimization problem subject to some constraints on the solution. One method is merely to "solve out" the constraints. For example, in the maximization problem considered earlier, suppose that the constraint $x_1 = x_2 - x_3$ is imposed on the solution. For a single constraint such as this one, it is possible merely to substitute the right-hand side of this equation for x_1 in the objective function and solve the resulting problem as a function of the remaining two variables. However, for more general constraints, or when there is more than one constraint, the method of Lagrange multipliers provides a more straightforward method of solving the problem. We

$$\text{Maximize}_{\mathbf{x}} \ f(\mathbf{x}) \text{ subject to } c_1(\mathbf{x}) = 0$$

$$c_2(\mathbf{x}) = 0$$

$$\vdots \tag{2-140}$$

$$c_J(\mathbf{x}) = 0.$$

The Lagrangean formulation is

$$\text{Maximize}_{\mathbf{x}, \lambda} \ L^*(\mathbf{x}, \lambda) = f(\mathbf{x}) + \sum_{j=1}^{J} \lambda_j c_j(\mathbf{x}), \tag{2-141}$$

where $c_1(\cdot), \ldots, c_J(\cdot)$ are the J constraints and λ_j are the Lagrange multipliers. Define a vector of Lagrange multipliers, λ, and arrange the constraints in a vector, $\mathbf{c}(\mathbf{x})$. Then the Lagrangean formula is

$$L^*(\mathbf{x}, \lambda) = f(\mathbf{x}) + \lambda' \mathbf{c}(\mathbf{x}). \tag{2-142}$$

The first-order conditions are

$$\frac{\partial L^*}{\partial \mathbf{x}} = \frac{\partial f(\mathbf{x})}{\partial \mathbf{x}} + \frac{\partial \lambda' \mathbf{c}(\mathbf{x})}{\partial \mathbf{x}} = \mathbf{0}(n \times 1)$$

$$\frac{\partial L^*}{\partial \lambda} = \mathbf{c}(\mathbf{x}) = \mathbf{0}(J \times 1). \tag{2-143}$$

The second term in $\partial L^*/\partial \mathbf{x}$ is

$$\frac{\partial \lambda' \mathbf{c}(\mathbf{x})}{\partial \mathbf{x}} = \frac{\partial \mathbf{c}(\mathbf{x})' \lambda}{\partial \mathbf{x}}$$

$$= \left[\frac{\partial \mathbf{c}(\mathbf{x})'}{\partial \mathbf{x}} \right] \lambda \tag{2-144}$$

$$= \mathbf{C}' \lambda,$$

where $\mathbf{C}$ is the derivatives of the constraints with respect to $\mathbf{x}$. The jth row of the $J \times n$ matrix $\mathbf{C}$ is the vector of derivatives of the jth constraint, $c_j(\mathbf{x})$, with respect to $\mathbf{x}'$. Upon collecting terms, the first-order conditions are

$$\frac{\partial L^*}{\partial \mathbf{x}} = \frac{\partial f(\mathbf{x})}{\partial \mathbf{x}} + \mathbf{C}' \lambda = \mathbf{0}$$

$$\frac{\partial L^*}{\partial \lambda} = \mathbf{c}(\mathbf{x}) = \mathbf{0}. \tag{2-145}$$

The second-order conditions for a maximum or minimum when there are constraints still require the Hessian to be definite, but only for the admissable values of $\mathbf{x}$, that is, only those that satisfy the constraints. Since we shall only be analyzing problems in which the Hessian is definite for all values of $\mathbf{x}$, it will not be necessary to deal with this condition.

There is one very important aspect of the constrained solution to consider. In the unconstrained solution, we have $\partial f(\mathbf{x})/\partial \mathbf{x} = \mathbf{0}$. From (2–145), we obtain for a constrained solution,

$$\frac{\partial f(\mathbf{x})}{\partial \mathbf{x}} = -\mathbf{C}' \lambda,$$

which will not equal $\mathbf{0}$ unless $\lambda = \mathbf{0}$. This has two important implications.

1. The constrained solution *must* be inferior to the unconstrained solution. This is implied by the nonzero gradient at the constrained solution.
2. If the Lagrange multipliers are zero, then the constrained solution will equal the unconstrained solution.

To continue the example begun earlier, suppose that we add the following conditions:

$$x_1 - x_2 + x_3 = 0,$$

$$x_1 + x_2 + x_3 = 0.$$

To put this in the format of the general problem, write the constraints as

$$c(x) = Cx = 0,$$

where

$$C = \begin{bmatrix} 1 & -1 & 1 \\ 1 & 1 & 1 \end{bmatrix}.$$

The Lagrangean problem is

$$R^*(x, \lambda) = a'x - x'Ax + \lambda'Cx.$$

Note the dimensions and arrangement of the various parts. In particular, C is a 2×3 matrix, with one row for each constraint and one column for each variable in the objective function. The vector of Lagrange multipliers thus has two elements, one for each constraint. The first-order conditions are

$$a - 2Ax + C'\lambda = 0 \qquad \text{(three equations)}$$

and

$$Cx = 0 \qquad \text{(two equations).} \tag{2-146}$$

These may be combined in the single equation

$$\begin{bmatrix} -2A & C' \\ C & 0 \end{bmatrix} \begin{bmatrix} x \\ \lambda \end{bmatrix} = \begin{bmatrix} -a \\ 0 \end{bmatrix}.$$

Using the partitioned inverse of (2–75) produces the solution

$$\lambda = -[CA^{-1}C']^{-1}CA^{-1}a \tag{2-147}$$

and

$$x = 2A^{-1}[I - C'(CA^{-1}C')^{-1}CA^{-1}]a. \tag{2-148}$$

The two results, (2–147) and (2–148), yield analytic solutions for λ and x. For the specific matrices and vectors of the example, these are $\lambda = [-0.5 \quad -7.5]'$ and the constrained solution vector is $x^* = [1.5 \quad 0 \quad -1.5]'$. Note that in computing the solution to this sort of problem, it is not necessary to use the rather cumbersome form of (2–148). Once λ is obtained from (2–147), the solution can be inserted in (2–146) for a much simpler computation. The solution

$$x = 2A^{-1}a + 2A^{-1}C'\lambda$$

suggests a useful result for the constrained optimum:

$$\text{Constrained solution} = \text{unconstrained solution} - [2A]^{-1}C'\lambda. \tag{2-149}$$

Finally, inserting the two solutions in the original function, we find that $R = 24.375$ and $R^* = 2.25$, which illustrates again that the constrained solution (in this *maximization* problem) is inferior to the unconstrained solution.

2.9.4. Transformations

If a function is strictly monotonic, then it is **one-to-one**. Each y is associated with exactly one value of x, and vice versa. In this case, an **inverse function** exists, which expresses x as a function of y, written

$$y = f(x) \quad \text{and} \quad x = f^{-1}(y). \tag{2-150}$$

An example is the inverse relationship between the log and the exponential functions. The slope of the inverse function,

$$\frac{dx}{dy} = \frac{df^{-1}(y)}{dy} = f^{-1\prime}(y) \tag{2-151}$$

is the **Jacobian** of the transformation from x to y. For example, if

$$y = a + bx, \tag{2-152}$$

then

$$x = -\frac{a}{b} + \left(\frac{1}{b}\right)y \tag{2-153}$$

is the inverse transformation and

$$J = \frac{dx}{dy} = \frac{1}{b}. \tag{2-154}$$

Looking ahead to the statistical application of this concept, we observe that if $y = f(x)$ were *vertical*, then this would no longer be a functional relationship. The same x would be associated with more than one value of y. In this case, at this value of x, we would find that $J = 0$, indicating a singularity in the function. This is of particular significance in probability distribution theory.

If $\mathbf{y}$ is a column vector of functions, $\mathbf{y} = \mathbf{f}(\mathbf{x})$,

$$\mathbf{J} = \frac{\partial \mathbf{x}}{\partial \mathbf{y}}$$

$$= \begin{bmatrix} \partial x_1/\partial y_1 & \partial x_1/\partial y_2 & \cdots & \partial x_1/\partial y_n \\ \partial x_2/\partial y_1 & \partial x_2/\partial y_2 & \cdots & \partial x_2/\partial y_n \\ & & \vdots & \\ \partial x_n/\partial y_1 & \partial x_n/\partial y_2 & \cdots & \partial x_n/\partial y_n \end{bmatrix}. \tag{2-155}$$

Consider the set of linear functions $\mathbf{y} = \mathbf{Ax} = \mathbf{f}(\mathbf{x})$. The inverse transformation is $\mathbf{x} = \mathbf{f}^{-1}(\mathbf{y})$, which will be either

$$\mathbf{x} = \mathbf{A}^{-1}\mathbf{y}$$

if $\mathbf{A}$ is nonsingular or

$$\mathbf{x} = \mathbf{0}$$

if $\mathbf{A}$ is singular. Let $\mathbf{J}$ be the matrix of partial derivatives of the inverse functions;

$$\mathbf{J} = \left[\frac{\partial x_i}{\partial y_j}\right]. \tag{2-156}$$

The absolute value of the determinant of $\mathbf{J}$,

$$\|\mathbf{J}\| = \left|\frac{\partial \mathbf{x}}{\partial \mathbf{y'}}\right|, \tag{2-157}$$

is the **Jacobian** of the transformation from x to y. In the nonsingular case,

$$|\mathbf{J}| = |\mathbf{A}^{-1}| = \frac{1}{|\mathbf{A}|}. \qquad (2-158)$$

In the singular case, all of the partial derivatives will be zero, as will be the Jacobian. In this instance, a zero Jacobian implies that $\mathbf{A}$ is singular, or equivalently, that the transformations from x to y are functionally dependent. The singular case is analogous to the single-variable case.

Clearly, if the vector x is given, then $y = \mathbf{A}x$ can be computed from x. Whether x can be deduced from y is another question. Evidently, it depends on the Jacobian. If the Jacobian is not zero, then the inverse transformations exist, and we can obtain x. If not, then we cannot obtain x.

Exercises

1. For the matrices

$$\mathbf{A} = \begin{bmatrix} 1 & 3 & 3 \\ 2 & 4 & 1 \end{bmatrix}, \qquad \mathbf{B} = \begin{bmatrix} 2 & 4 \\ 1 & 5 \\ 6 & 2 \end{bmatrix},$$

compute $\mathbf{AB}$, $\mathbf{A'B'}$, and $\mathbf{BA}$.

2. Prove that $tr(\mathbf{AB}) = tr(\mathbf{BA})$, where $\mathbf{A}$ and $\mathbf{B}$ are any two matrices that are conformable for both multiplications. They need not be square.

3. Prove that $tr(\mathbf{A'A}) = \sum_i \sum_j a_{ij}^2$.

4. Expand the matrix product

$$\mathbf{X} = ([\mathbf{AB} + (\mathbf{CD})'][(\mathbf{EF})^{-1} + \mathbf{GH}])'.$$

Assume that all matrices are square and $\mathbf{E}$ and $\mathbf{F}$ are nonsingular.

5. Prove that for n $K \times 1$ column vectors x_i, $i = 1,\ldots,n$, and some nonzero vector $\mathbf{a}$,

$$\sum_i (x_i - \mathbf{a})(x_i - \mathbf{a})' = \mathbf{X'M^0X} + n(\bar{x} - \mathbf{a})(\bar{x} - \mathbf{a})',$$

where the ith row of $\mathbf{X}$ is x_i' and $\mathbf{M}^0$ is defined in (2-34).

6. Let $\mathbf{A}$ be any square matrix whose columns are $[\mathbf{a}_1, \mathbf{a}_2, \ldots, \mathbf{a}_M]$, and let $\mathbf{B}$ be any rearrangement of the columns of the $M \times M$ identity matrix. What operation is performed by the multiplication $\mathbf{AB}$? By the multiplication $\mathbf{BA}$?

7. Consider the 3×3 case of the matrix $\mathbf{B}$ in the previous problem. For example,

$$\mathbf{B} = \begin{bmatrix} 0 & 1 & 0 \\ 0 & 0 & 1 \\ 1 & 0 & 0 \end{bmatrix}.$$

Compute $\mathbf{B}^2$ and $\mathbf{B}^3$. Repeat for a 4×4 matrix. Can you generalize your finding?

8. Calculate $|\mathbf{A}|$, $tr(\mathbf{A})$, and $\mathbf{A}^{-1}$ for

$$\mathbf{A} = \begin{bmatrix} 1 & 4 & 7 \\ 3 & 2 & 5 \\ 5 & 2 & 8 \end{bmatrix}.$$

9. Obtain the *Cholesky decomposition* of the matrix

$$A = \begin{bmatrix} 25 & 7 \\ 7 & 13 \end{bmatrix}.$$

Recall that the Cholesky decomposition of a matrix, A, is the matrix product $LU = A$, where L is a lower triangular matrix and $U = L'$.

10. A symmetric positive definite matrix, A, can also be written as $A = UL$, where U is an upper triangular matrix and $L = U'$. This is not the Cholesky decomposition, however. Obtain this decomposition of the matrix in Exercise 9. (This result is used in Section 19.4.1a.)

11. What operation is performed by postmultiplying a matrix by a diagonal matrix? What about premultiplication?

12. Are the following quadratic forms positive for all values of x?

(a) $y = x_1^2 - 28x_1x_2 + (11x_2)^2$.

(b) $y = 5x_1^2 + x_2^2 + 7x_3^2 + 4x_1x_2 + 6x_1x_3 + 8x_2x_3$.

13. Prove that $tr(A \otimes B) = tr(A)\,tr(B)$.

14. A matrix, A, is **nilpotent** if $\lim_{K \to \infty} A^K = 0$. Prove that a necessary and sufficient condition for a symmetric matrix to be nilpotent is that all of its characteristic roots be less than 1 in absolute value. (For an application, see Section 19.6.2.)

15. Compute the characteristic roots of

$$A = \begin{bmatrix} 2 & 4 & 3 \\ 4 & 8 & 6 \\ 3 & 6 & 5 \end{bmatrix}.$$

16. Suppose that $A = A(z)$, where z is a scalar. What is $\partial(x'Ax)/\partial z$? Suppose that each element of x is also a function of z. Once again, what is $\partial(x'Ax)/\partial z$?

17. Show that the solutions to the determinantal equations

$$|B - \lambda A| = 0 \quad \text{and} \quad |A^{-1}B - \lambda I| = 0$$

are the same. How do the solutions to this equation relate to those of the equation $|B^{-1}A - \mu I| = 0$? (For an application of the first of these equations, see Section 19.4.4d.)

18. Using matrix A in Exercise 9, find the vector x that minimizes $y = x'Ax + 2x_1 + 3x_2 - 10$. What is the value of y at the minimum? Now minimize y subject to the constraint $x_1 + x_2 = 1$. Compare the two solutions.

19. What is the Jacobian for the following transformations?

$$y_1 = \ln\left(\frac{x_1}{x_2}\right),$$

$$y_2 = x_1 - x_2 + x_3,$$

and

$$y_3 = x_1 x_2 x_3.$$

20. Prove that exchanging two columns of a square matrix reverses the sign of its determinant. (**Hint:** Use a permutation matrix. See Exercise 6.)

21. Suppose that $\mathbf{x} = \mathbf{x}(z)$, where z is a scalar. What is

$$\frac{\partial[\mathbf{x}'\mathbf{Ax}/\mathbf{x}'\mathbf{Bx}]}{\partial z}?$$

22. Suppose that $\mathbf{y}$ is an $N \times 1$ vector and $\mathbf{X}$ is an $N \times K$ matrix. The projection of $\mathbf{y}$ into the column space of $\mathbf{X}$ is defined earlier after (2–55), $\hat{\mathbf{y}} = \mathbf{Xb}$. Now consider the projection of $\mathbf{y}^* = c\mathbf{y}$ into the column space of $\mathbf{X}^* = \mathbf{XP}$, where c is a scalar and $\mathbf{P}$ is a nonsingular $K \times K$ matrix. Find the projection of $\mathbf{y}^*$ into the column space of $\mathbf{X}^*$. Prove that the cosine of the angle between $\mathbf{y}^*$ and its projection into the column space of $\mathbf{X}^*$ is the same as that between $\mathbf{y}$ and its projection into the column space of $\mathbf{X}$. How do you interpret this result?

23. For the matrix

$$\mathbf{X}' = \begin{bmatrix} 1 & 1 & 1 & 1 \\ 4 & -2 & 3 & -5 \end{bmatrix}$$

compute $\mathbf{P} = \mathbf{X}(\mathbf{X}'\mathbf{X})^{-1}\mathbf{X}'$ and $\mathbf{M} = (\mathbf{I} - \mathbf{P})$. Verify that $\mathbf{MP} = \mathbf{0}$. Let

$$\mathbf{Q} = \begin{bmatrix} 1 & 3 \\ 2 & 8 \end{bmatrix}.$$

(Hint: Show that $\mathbf{M}$ and $\mathbf{P}$ are idempotent.)

(a) Compute $\mathbf{P}$ and $\mathbf{M}$ based on $\mathbf{XQ}$ instead of $\mathbf{X}$.

(b) What are the characteristic roots of $\mathbf{M}$ and $\mathbf{P}$?

24. Suppose that $\mathbf{A}$ is an $n \times n$ matrix of the form

$$\mathbf{A} = (1 - \rho)\mathbf{I} + \rho\mathbf{ii}',$$

where $\mathbf{i}$ is a column of 1s and $0 < \rho < 1$. Write the format of $\mathbf{A}$ explicitly for $N = 4$. Find all of the characteristic roots and vectors of $\mathbf{A}$. (Hint: There are only two distinct characteristic roots, which occur with multiplicity 1 and $n - 1$. Every $\mathbf{c}$ of a certain type is a characteristic vector of $\mathbf{A}$.) For an application that uses a matrix of this type, see Section 16.4.3 on the random effects model.

25. Find the inverse of the matrix in the previous problem. [Hint: Use (2–66).]

26. Prove that every matrix in the sequence of matrices

$$\mathbf{H}_{i+1} = \mathbf{H}_i + \mathbf{d}_i\mathbf{d}_i',$$

where

$$\mathbf{H}_0 = \mathbf{I}$$

is positive definite. For an application, see Section 12.5.5. For an extension, prove that every matrix in the sequence of matrices defined in (12–29) is positive definite if $\mathbf{H}_0 = \mathbf{I}$.

27. What is the inverse matrix of

$$\mathbf{P} = \begin{bmatrix} \cos(x) & \sin(x) \\ -\sin(x) & \cos(x) \end{bmatrix}.$$

What are the characteristic roots of $\mathbf{P}$?

28. (This requires a computer.) For the $\mathbf{X}'\mathbf{X}$ matrix at the end of Section 6.3.2,

    (a) Compute the characteristic roots of $\mathbf{X}'\mathbf{X}$.

    (b) Compute the condition number of $\mathbf{X}'\mathbf{X}$. (Do not forget to scale the columns of the matrix, so that the diagonal elements are 1.)

References

Bellman, R., *Introduction to Matrix Analysis*, New York: McGraw-Hill, 1970.

Dhrymes, P., *Mathematics for Econometrics*, New York: Springer Verlag, 1974.

Hadley, G., *Linear Algebra*, Reading, Mass.: Addison-Wesley, 1961.

Johnston, J., *Econometric Methods*, New York: McGraw-Hill, 1984, pp. 138–140.

Magnus, J., and H. Neudecker, *Matrix Differential Calculus*, New York: Wiley, 1988.

Rao, C. R., *Linear Statistical Inference and Its Applications*, New York: Wiley, 1965.

Strang, G., *Linear Algebra and Its Application*, New York: Academic Press, 1976.

Theil, H., *Principles of Econometrics*, New York. Wiley, 1971.

Theil, H., "Linear Algebra and Matrix Methods in Econometrics," in Z. Griliches and M. Intrilligator, eds., *Handbook of Econometrics*, Vol. 1, Amsterdam: North Holland, 1983.

Chapter 3

Probability and Distribution Theory

3.1. Introduction

This chapter reviews the distribution theory used later in the book. Since a previous course in statistics is assumed, most of the results will be stated without proof. The more advanced results in the later sections will be developed in greater detail.

3.2. Random Variables

We view our observation on some aspect of the economy as the **outcome** of a random experiment. The outcomes of the experiment are assigned unique numeric values. The assignment is one-to-one; each outcome gets one value, and no two distinct outcomes receive the same value. This outcome variable, X, is a **random variable** because, until the experiment is performed, it is uncertain what value X will take. Probabilities are associated with outcomes to quantify this uncertainty. We usually use capital letters for the "name" of a random variable and lowercase letters for the values it takes. Thus, the probability that X takes a particular value, x, might be denoted $\text{Prob}(X = x)$.

A random variable is **discrete** if the set of outcomes is either finite in number or countably infinite. The random variable is **continuous** if the set of outcomes is infinitely divisible and, hence, not countable. These definitions will correspond to the sorts of data we observe in practice. Counts of occurrences will provide observations on discrete random variables, while measurements such as time or income will give observations on continuous random variables.

3.2.1. Probability Distributions

A listing of the values, x, taken by a random variable, X, and their associated probabilities is a **probability distribution**, $f(x)$. For a discrete random variable,

$$f(x) = \text{Prob}(X = x).$$ (3–1)

The axioms of probability require that

1. $0 \leq \text{Prob}(x) \leq 1$.

2. $\sum_x f(x_i) = 1.$ (3–2)

EXAMPLE 3.1. $X =$ number of customers to arrive at a teller's window at a bank in a randomly chosen time span of given length. A frequently used model is the **Poisson distribution**:

$$f(x) = \frac{e^{-\lambda}\lambda^x}{x!}, \qquad x = 0, 1, 2, \ldots, \tag{3-3}$$

where λ is the average number of persons to arrive in a given time span. Note that regardless of the value of λ, the probability model is, in fact, at odds with the physical phenomenon being described. The number of persons must, of course, be finite. But, for large values of x, the probabilities assigned by this model become arbitrarily small.

For the continuous case, the probability associated with any particular point is zero, and we can only assign positive probabilities to intervals in the range of x. The **probability distribution function (pdf)** is defined so that $f(x) \geq 0$ and

$$1. \; \text{Prob}(a \leq x \leq b) = \int_a^b f(x)\,dx \geq 0. \tag{3-4}$$

This is the area under $f(x)$ in the range from a to b. For a continuous variable,

$$2. \; \int_{-\infty}^{+\infty} f(x)\,dx = 1. \tag{3-5}$$

If the range of x is not infinite, it is understood that $f(x) = 0$ anywhere outside the appropriate range. Since the probability associated with any individual point is 0,

$$\text{Prob}(a \leq x \leq b) = \text{Prob}(a \leq x < b)$$
$$= \text{Prob}(a < x \leq b)$$
$$= \text{Prob}(a < x < b).$$

3.2.2. Cumulative Distribution Function

For any random variable x, the probability that x is less than or equal to a is denoted $F(a)$. $F(x)$ is the **cumulative distribution function (cdf)**. For a discrete random variable,

$$F(x) = \sum_{X \leq x} f(x)$$
$$= \text{Prob}(X \leq x). \tag{3-6}$$

In view of the definition of $f(x)$,

$$f(x_i) = F(x_i) - F(x_{i-1}). \tag{3-7}$$

For a continuous random variable

$$F(x) = \int_{-\infty}^{x} f(t)\,dt \tag{3-8}$$

and

$$f(x) = \frac{dF(x)}{dx}. \tag{3-9}$$

In both the continuous and discrete cases, $F(x)$ must satisfy the following properties:

1. $0 \leq F(x) \leq 1$.
2. If $x > y$, $F(x) \geq F(y)$.

3. $F(+\infty) = 1$.
4. $F(-\infty) = 0$.

From the definition of the cdf,

$$\text{Prob}(a \leq x \leq b) = F(b) - F(a). \tag{3-10}$$

Any valid pdf will imply a valid cdf, so there is no need to verify these conditions separately.

3.3. Expectations of a Random Variable

Definition. The **mean**, or **expected value**, of a random variable is

$$E[x] = \begin{cases} \sum_x xf(x) & \text{if } x \text{ is discrete,} \\ \int_x xf(x)\,dx & \text{if } x \text{ is continuous.} \end{cases} \tag{3-11}$$

(The notation $\sum_x$ or $\int_x$, used henceforth, means the sum or integral over the entire range of values of x.) The mean is usually denoted μ. It is a weighted average of the values taken by x, where the weights are the respective probabilities. It is not necessarily a value actually taken by the random variable. For example, the expected number of heads in one toss of a coin is $\frac{1}{2}$.

Other **measures of central tendency** are the **median**, which is the value that is exceeded by the random variable with probability one-half, and the **mode**, which is the value of x at which $f(x)$ takes its maximum. The first of these measures is more frequently used. Loosely speaking, the median corresponds more closely than the mean to the middle of a distribution. It is unaffected by extreme values. In the discrete case, the modal value of x has the highest probability of occurring.

Let $g(x)$ be a function of x. The function that gives the expected value of $g(x)$ is denoted

$$E[g(x)] = \begin{cases} \sum_i g(x_i)\,\text{Prob}(X = x_i) & \text{if } X \text{ is discrete,} \\ \int_{-\infty}^{+\infty} g(x)f(x)\,dx & \text{if } X \text{ is continuous.} \end{cases} \tag{3-12}$$

An important case is $g(x) = a + bx$ for constants a and b:

$$E[a + bx] = a + bE[x].$$

One important case is the expected value of a constant, a, which is just a.

Definition. The **variance** of a random variable is

$$\text{Var}[x] = E[(x - \mu)^2]$$

$$= \begin{cases} \sum_x (x - \mu)^2 f(x) & \text{if } x \text{ is discrete,} \\ \int_x (x - \mu)^2 f(x)\,dx & \text{if } x \text{ is continuous.} \end{cases} \tag{3-13}$$

$\text{Var}[x]$, which must be positive, is usually denoted σ^2. This is a measure of the dispersion of a distribution. Computation of the variance is simplified by using the following important result:

$$\text{Var}[x] = E[x^2] - \mu^2. \tag{3-14}$$

A convenient corollary to (3–14) is

$$E[x^2] = \sigma^2 + \mu^2. \tag{3-15}$$

By inserting $y = a + bx$ in (3–13) and expanding, we find that

$$\text{Var}[a + bx] = b^2 \, \text{Var}[x], \tag{3-16}$$

which implies, for any constant, a, that

$$\text{Var}[a] = 0. \tag{3-17}$$

To describe a distribution, we usually use σ, the positive square root, which is the **standard deviation** of x. The standard deviation can be interpreted as having the same units of measurement as x and μ. For any random variable x and any positive constant k, the **Chebyshev inequality** states that

$$\text{Prob}(\mu - k\sigma \leq x \leq \mu + k\sigma) \geq 1 - \frac{1}{k^2}. \tag{3-18}$$

[A proof appears in Goldberger (1964).]
    Two other measures often used to describe a probability distribution are

$$\text{Skewness} = E[(x - \mu)^3]$$

and

$$\text{Kurtosis} = E[(x - \mu)^4].$$

Skewness is a measure of the asymmetry of a distribution. For symmetric distributions,

$$f(x - \mu) = f(x + \mu)$$

and

$$\text{Skewness} = 0.$$

For asymmetric distributions, the skewness will be negative if the "long tail" is in the positive direction. Kurtosis is a measure of the thickness of the tails of the distribution. A shorthand expression for other "moments" is

$$\mu_r = E[(x - \mu)^r].$$

Since μ_r tends to explode as r grows, the normalized measure, μ_r/σ^r, is often used for description. Two common measures are

$$\text{Skewness coefficient} = \frac{\mu_3}{\sigma^3}$$

and

$$\text{Degree of excess} = \frac{\mu_4}{\sigma^4} - 3.$$

The second is based on the normal distribution, which has excess of zero.

For any two functions $g_1(x)$ and $g_2(x)$,

$$E[g_1(x) + g_2(x)] = E[g_1(x)] + E[g_2(x)].$$ (3–19)

For the general case of a possibly nonlinear $g(x)$,

$$E[g(x)] = \int_x g(x)f(x)\,dx$$ (3–20)

and

$$\text{Var}[g(x)] = \int_x (g(x) - E[g(x)])^2 f(x)\,dx.$$ (3–21)

(For convenience, we shall omit the equivalent definitions for discrete variables in the following discussion and use the integral to mean either integration or summation, whichever is appropriate.)

A device used to approximate $E[g(x)]$ and $\text{Var}[g(x)]$ is the linear Taylor series approximation:

$$g(x) \simeq [g(x^0) - g'(x^0)x^0] + g'(x^0)x$$

$$= \beta_1 + \beta_2 x$$ (3–22)

$$= g^*(x).$$

If the approximation is reasonably accurate, the mean and variance of $g^*(x)$ will be approximately equal to the mean and variance of $g(x)$. A natural choice for the expansion point is $x^0 = \mu = E(x)$. Inserting this in (3–22) gives

$$g(x) \simeq [g(\mu) - g'(\mu)\mu] + g'(\mu)x,$$ (3–23)

so that

$$E[g(x)] \simeq g(\mu)$$ (3–24)

and

$$\text{Var}[g(x)] \simeq [g'(\mu)]^2 \text{Var}[x].$$ (3–25)

3.4. *Some Specific Probability Distributions*

Certain experimental situations give rise naturally to specific probability distributions. In the majority of cases in economics, however, the distributions used are merely models of the observed phenomena. Although the normal distribution, which we shall discuss at length, is the mainstay of econometric research, economists have used a wide variety of other distributions. A few are discussed here.[1]

3.4.1. The Normal Distribution

The general form of a normal distribution with mean μ and standard deviation σ is

$$f(x\,|\,\mu, \sigma) = \frac{1}{\sqrt{2\pi}\,\sigma} e^{-(x-\mu)^2/2\sigma^2}.$$ (3–26)

[1] A much more complete listing appears in Maddala (1977, Chapters 3 and 18) and in most mathematical statistics textbooks.

This is usually denoted $x \sim N[\mu, \sigma^2]$. The standard notation $x \sim f(x)$ is used to state that "x has probability distribution $f(x)$." Among the most useful properties of the normal distribution is its preservation under linear transformation.

$$\text{If } x \sim N[\mu, \sigma^2], (a + bx) \sim N[a + b\mu, b^2\sigma^2]. \tag{3-27}$$

One particularly convenient transformation is $a = -\mu/\sigma$ and $b = 1/\sigma$. The resulting variable,

$$z = \frac{x - \mu}{\sigma},$$

has the **standard normal distribution**, denoted $N[0, 1]$, with density

$$\phi(z) = \frac{1}{\sqrt{2\pi}} e^{-z^2/2}. \tag{3-28}$$

The specific notation, $\phi(z)$, is often used for this distribution and $\Phi(z)$ for its cdf.

Tables of the standard normal cdf appear in most statistics and econometrics textbooks. Because the form of the distribution does not change under a linear transformation, it is not necessary to tabulate the distribution for other values of μ and σ. For any normally distributed variable,

$$\text{Prob}(a < x < b) = \text{Prob}\left(\frac{a - \mu}{\sigma} < \frac{x - \mu}{\sigma} < \frac{b - \mu}{\sigma}\right), \tag{3-29}$$

which can always be read from a table of the standard normal distribution. In addition, because the distribution is symmetric, $\Phi(-z) = 1 - \Phi(z)$. Hence, it is not necessary to tabulate both the negative and positive halves of the distribution.

3.4.2.   The Chi-Squared, t, and F Distributions

The chi-squared, t, and F distributions are derived from the normal distribution. They arise in econometrics as sums of n or n_1 and n_2 other variables. These three distributions have associated with them one or two "degrees of freedom" parameters, which, for our purposes, will be the number of variables in the relevant sum.

The first of the essential results is

If $z \sim N[0, 1]$, $x = z^2 \sim$ chi-squared[1], that is,
chi-squared with one degree of freedom, denoted   (3-30)

$$z^2 \sim \chi^2[1].$$

This is a skewed distribution with mean 1 and variance 2. The second is

If $X_1, \ldots, X_n$ are n *independent* chi-squared[1]
variables, then $\Sigma_i X_i \sim$ chi-squared[n].   (3-31)

The mean and variance of a chi-squared variable with n degrees of freedom are n and $2n$, respectively. A number of useful corollaries can be derived using (3-30) and (3-31).

If z_i, $i = 1, \ldots, n$ are independent $N[0, 1]$ variables,

$$\sum_{i=1}^{n} z_i^2 \sim \chi^2[n]. \tag{3-32}$$

If $z_i, i = 1, \ldots, n$ are independent $N[0, \sigma^2]$ variables,

$$\sum_{i=1}^{n} \left(\frac{z_i}{\sigma}\right)^2 \sim \chi^2[n]. \tag{3-33}$$

If x_1 and x_2 are independent chi-squared variables with n_1 and n_2 degrees of freedom, respectively,

$$x_1 + x_2 \sim \chi^2[n_1 + n_2]. \tag{3-34}$$

This can be generalized to the sum of an arbitrary number of independent chi-squared variables.

Unlike the normal distribution, a separate table is required for the chi-squared distribution for each value of n. Typically, only a few percentage points of the distribution are tabulated for each n. The table in the appendix of this book gives upper (right) tail areas for a number of values.

If x_1 and x_2 are two independent chi-squared variables with degrees of freedom parameters n_1 and n_2, respectively, the ratio

$$F[n_1, n_2] = \frac{x_1/n_1}{x_2/n_2} \tag{3-35}$$

has the **F distribution**. The two degrees of freedom parameters n_1 and n_2 are the numerator and denominator degrees of freedom, respectively. Tables of the F distribution must be computed for each pair of values of (n_1, n_2). As such, only one or two specific values, such as the 95 percent and 99 percent upper tail values, are tabulated in most cases.

If z is an $N[0, 1]$ variable and x is $\chi^2[n]$, and is independent of z, the ratio

$$t[n] = \frac{z}{\sqrt{x/n}} \tag{3-36}$$

is distributed as t with n degrees of freedom. The t distribution has the same shape as the normal distribution but has thicker tails.[2] This distribution is tabulated in the same manner as the chi-squared distribution, with several specific cutoff points corresponding to specified tail areas for various values of the degrees of freedom parameter.

Comparing (3–35) with $n_1 = 1$ and (3–36), we see the useful relationship between the t and F distributions:

$$\text{If } t \sim t[n], t^2 \sim F[1, n].$$

3.4.3. Distributions with Large Degrees of Freedom

The chi-squared, t, and F distributions usually arise as sums of sample observations. The degrees of freedom parameter in each case equals the number of observations. We often deal with larger degrees of freedom than are shown in the tables. Thus, the standard tables are often inadequate. However, in all cases, there are **limiting distributions** that we can use when the degrees of freedom parameter grows large. The simplest case is the t distribution. The t distribution with infinite degrees of freedom is equivalent to the standard normal distribution. Beyond about 100 degrees of freedom, they are almost indistinguishable.

---

[2] The special case of $t[1]$, which is the ratio of two standard normal variables, is the Cauchy distribution.

For degrees of freedom greater than 30, a commonly used approximation for the distribution of the chi-squared variable, x, is

$$z = \sqrt{2x} - \sqrt{2n - 1}, \tag{3-37}$$

which is approximately standard normally distributed. Thus,

$$\text{Prob}(\chi^2[n] < a) \simeq P(z < \sqrt{2a} - \sqrt{2n - 1}).$$

EXAMPLE 3.2.   If x is chi-squared with 70 degrees of freedom,

$$\text{Prob}(x < 85) \simeq \text{Prob}(z < \sqrt{170} - \sqrt{139})$$

$$= \text{Prob}(z < 1.249) = 0.8942.$$

The correct value from the chi-squared distribution is 0.89409.

As used in econometrics, the F distribution with a large-denominator degrees of freedom is common. As n_2 becomes infinite, the denominator of F converges identically to 1, so we can treat the variable

$$x = n_1 F \tag{3-38}$$

as a chi-squared variable with n_1 degrees of freedom. Since the numerator degrees of freedom will typically be small, this approximation will suffice for the types of applications we are likely to encounter.[3] If not, the approximation given earlier for the chi-squared distribution can be applied to $n_1 F$.

3.4.4. Size Distributions—The Lognormal Distribution

In modeling size distributions, such as the distribution of firm sizes in an industry or the distribution of income in a country, the lognormal distribution has been particularly useful:[4]

$$f(x) = \frac{1}{\sqrt{2\pi}\,\sigma x} e^{-[(\ln x - \mu)^2]/2\sigma^2}, \qquad x \geq 0.$$

A lognormal variable has a mean equal to $e^{\mu + \sigma^2/2}$ and a variance equal to $e^{2\mu + \sigma^2}(e^{\sigma^2} - 1)$. If $y \sim \text{lognormal}[\mu, \sigma^2]$, $\ln y \sim N[\mu, \sigma^2]$.

3.4.5. The Gamma Distribution

The **gamma distribution** has been used in a variety of settings, including the study of income distribution and[5] production functions.[6] The general form of the distribution is

$$f(x) = \frac{\lambda^P}{\Gamma(P)} e^{-\lambda x} x^{P-1}, \qquad x \geq 0. \tag{3-39}$$

Many familiar distributions are special cases, including the exponential ($P = 1$) and chi-squared ($\lambda = 1/2$, $P = n/2$). The mean is P/λ and the variance is P/λ^2.

3.4.6. The Beta Distribution

Distributions are often chosen on the basis of the range within which the random variable is constrained to vary. The lognormal distribution, for example, is sometimes used to

---

[3] See Johnson and Kotz (1970) for other approximations.
[4] A study of applications of the lognormal distribution appears in Aitchison and Brown (1969).
[5] Salem and Mount (1974).
[6] Greene (1980).

model a variable that is always nonnegative. For a variable constrained between 0 and $c > 0$, the **beta distribution** has proved useful. Its density is

$$f(x) = \frac{\Gamma(\alpha + \beta)}{\Gamma(\alpha)\Gamma(\beta)} \left(\frac{x}{c}\right)^{\alpha-1} \left(1 - \frac{x}{c}\right)^{\beta-1} \left(\frac{1}{c}\right). \tag{3-40}$$

This functional form is extremely flexible in the shapes it will accommodate. It is symmetric if $\alpha = \beta$, asymmetric otherwise, and can be hump-shaped or U-shaped. The mean is $\alpha/(\alpha + \beta)$ and the variance is $\alpha\beta/(\alpha + \beta)^2$. The beta distribution has been applied in the study of labor force participation rates.[7]

3.5. The Distribution of a Function of a Random Variable

We considered finding the expected value of a function of a random variable. It is fairly common to analyze the random variable, itself, which results when we compute a function of some random variable. There are three types of transformations to consider. One discrete random variable may be transformed into another; a continuous variable may be transformed into a discrete one; and one continuous variable may be transformed into another.

The simplest case is the first one. The probabilities associated with the new variable are computed according to the laws of probability. If y is derived from x and the function is one to one, then the probability that $Y = y(x)$ equals the probability that $X = x$. If several values of x yield the same value of y, then $\text{Prob}(Y = y)$ is the sum of the corresponding probabilities for x.

The second type of transformation is illustrated by the way individual data on income are typically obtained in a survey. Income in the population can be expected to be distributed according to some skewed, continuous distribution such as the one shown in Figure 3.1.

Data are normally reported categorically, as shown in the lower part of the figure. Thus, the random variable corresponding to observed income is a discrete transformation of the actual underlying continuous random variable. Suppose, for example, that the transformed variable, y, is the mean income in the respective interval. Then,

$$\text{Prob}(Y = \mu_1) = P(-\infty < X \le a),$$

$$\text{Prob}(Y = \mu_2) = P(a < X \le b),$$

$$\text{Prob}(Y = \mu_3) = P(b < X \le c),$$

and so on, which illustrates the general procedure.

If x is a continuous random variable with pdf $f_x(x)$ and $y = g(x)$ is a continuous function of x, the density of y is obtained by using the change of variable technique to find the cdf of y.

$$\text{Prob}(y \le b) = \int_{-\infty}^{b} f_x(g^{-1}(y))|g^{-1\prime}(y)| \, dy.$$

This can now be written as

$$\text{Prob}(y \le b) = \int_{-\infty}^{b} f_y(y) \, dy.$$

---

[7] Heckman and Willis (1975).

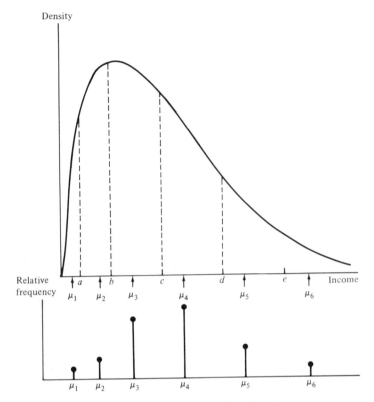

Figure 3.1 Censored distribution.

Hence

$$f_y(y) = f_x(g^{-1}(y))|g^{-1'}(y)|. \qquad (3\text{--}41)$$

To avoid the possibility of a negative pdf if $g(x)$ is decreasing, we use the absolute value of the derivative in the previous expression. The term $|g^{-1'}(y)|$ is the Jacobian of the transformation from x to y. The Jacobian must be nonzero for the density of y to be nonzero. In words, the probabilities associated with intervals in the range of y must be associated with intervals in the range of x. If the Jacobian is zero, the function $y = g(x)$ is vertical, and hence all values of y in the given range are associated with the same value of x. This single point must have probability zero.

EXAMPLE 3.3. If $x \sim N[\mu, \sigma^2]$, what is the distribution of $y = x/\sigma - \mu/\sigma$?

$$y = \frac{x}{\sigma} - \frac{\mu}{\sigma} \Rightarrow x = \sigma y + \mu \Rightarrow f^{-1'}(y) = \frac{dx}{dy} = \sigma.$$

Thus,

$$f_y(y) = \frac{1}{\sqrt{2\pi}\,\sigma} e^{-[(\sigma y + \mu) - \mu]^2/2\sigma^2}|\sigma| = \frac{1}{\sqrt{2\pi}} e^{-y^2/2},$$

which is the density of a normally distributed variable with mean 0 and standard deviation 1.

3.6. *Joint Distributions*

The **joint density function** for two random variables, X and Y, denoted $f(x, y)$, is defined so that

$$\text{Prob}(a \le x \le b, c \le y \le d) = \int_a^b \int_c^d f(x, y)\, dy\, dx$$

or

$$(3\text{–}42)$$

$$= \sum_{a \le x \le b} \sum_{c \le x \le d} f(x, y).$$

The counterparts of the requirements for a univariate probability density are

$$f(x, y) \ge 0$$

and

$$\sum_x \sum_y f(x, y) = 1 \qquad \text{if } x \text{ and } y \text{ are discrete,}$$

$$(3\text{–}43)$$

$$\int_x \int_y f(x, y)\, dy\, dx = 1 \qquad \text{if } x \text{ and } y \text{ are continuous.}$$

The cumulative probability is likewise the probability of a joint event:

$$F(x, y) = \text{Prob}(X \le x, Y \le y)$$

$$= \begin{cases} \displaystyle\sum_{X \le x} \sum_{Y \le y} f(x, y) & \text{in the discrete case,} \\[2ex] \displaystyle\int_{-\infty}^x \int_{-\infty}^y f(t, s)\, ds\, dt & \text{in the continuous case.} \end{cases}$$

$$(3\text{–}44)$$

3.6.1. **Marginal Distributions**

A **marginal probability density** or marginal probability distribution is defined with respect to an individual variable. To obtain the marginal distributions from the joint density, it is necessary to sum or integrate out the other variable:

$$f_x(x) = \begin{cases} \displaystyle\int_y f(x, y)\, dy & \text{if } y \text{ is continuous,} \\[2ex] \displaystyle\sum_y f(x, y) & \text{if } y \text{ is discrete,} \end{cases}$$

$$(3\text{–}45)$$

and similarly for $f_y(y)$.

Two random variables are **statistically independent** if and only if their joint density is the product of the marginal densities:

$$f(x, y) = f_x(x) f_y(y) \Leftrightarrow x \text{ and } y \text{ are independent.}$$

$$(3\text{–}46)$$

If (and only if) x and y are independent, then the cdf factors as well as the pdf;

$$F(x, y) = F_x(x) F_y(y)$$

or

$$(3\text{–}47)$$

$$\text{Prob}(X \le x, Y \le y) = \text{Prob}(X \le x)\, \text{Prob}(Y \le y).$$

3.6.2. Expectations in a Joint Distribution

The means, variances, and higher moments of the variables in a joint distribution are defined with respect to the marginal distributions. For the mean of x in a discrete distribution,

$$E[x] = \sum_x x f_x(x)$$

$$= \sum_x x \left[\sum_y f(x, y) \right] \tag{3-48}$$

$$= \sum_x \sum_y x f(x, y).$$

The means of the variables in a continuous distribution are defined likewise, using integration instead of summing:

$$E[x] = \int_x x f_x(x)\, dx.$$

$$= \int_x \int_y x f(x, y)\, dy\, dx. \tag{3-49}$$

Variances are computed in the same manner:

$$\text{Var}[x] = \sum_x (x - E[x])^2 f_x(x)$$

$$= \sum_x \sum_y (x - E[x])^2 f(x, y). \tag{3-50}$$

3.6.3. Covariance and Correlation

For any function $g(x, y)$,

$$E[g(x, y)] = \sum_x \sum_y g(x, y) f(x, y)$$

$$\tag{3-51}$$

or

$$\int_x \int_y g(x, y) f(x, y)\, dy\, dx.$$

The **covariance** of x and y is a special case:

$$\text{Cov}[x, y] = E[(x - \mu_x)(y - \mu_y)]$$

$$= E[xy] - \mu_x \mu_y \tag{3-52}$$

$$= \sigma_{xy}.$$

If x and y are independent, $f(x, y) = f_x(x) f_y(y)$ and

$$\sigma_{xy} = \sum_x \sum_y f_x(x) f_y(y)(x - \mu_x)(y - \mu_y)$$

$$= \sum_x [x - \mu_x] f_x(x) \sum_y [y - \mu_y] f_y(y)$$

$$= E[x - \mu_x] E[y - \mu_y]$$

$$= 0.$$

The sign of the covariance will indicate the direction of covariation of X and Y. However, its magnitude depends on the scales of measurement. In view of this, a preferable measure is the **correlation coefficient**:

$$r[x, y] = \rho_{xy}$$

$$= \frac{\sigma_{xy}}{\sigma_x \sigma_y}, \tag{3-53}$$

where σ_x and σ_y are the standard deviations of x and y, respectively. The correlation coefficient has the same sign as the covariance but is always between -1 and 1, and is thus unaffected by any scaling of the variables.

Variables that are uncorrelated are not necessarily independent. For example, in the discrete distribution $f(-1, 1) = f(0, 0) = f(1, 1) = \frac{1}{3}$, the correlation is zero, but $f(1, 1)$ does not equal $f_x(1) f_y(1) = (\frac{1}{3})(\frac{2}{3})$. An important exception is the joint normal distribution discussed subsequently, in which lack of correlation does imply independence.

Some general results regarding expectations in a joint distribution, which can be verified by applying the appropriate definition, are

$$E[ax + by + c] = aE[x] + bE[y] + c, \tag{3-54}$$

$$\text{Var}[ax + by + c] = a^2 \, \text{Var}[x] + b^2 \, \text{Var}[y] + 2ab \, \text{Cov}[x, y]$$

$$= \text{Var}[ax + by], \tag{3-55}$$

and

$$\text{Cov}[ax + by, cx + dy] = ac \, \text{Var}[x] + bd \, \text{Var}[y] + (ad + bc) \, \text{Cov}[x, y]. \tag{3-56}$$

If X and Y are uncorrelated,

$$\text{Var}[x + y] = \text{Var}[x - y]$$

$$= \text{Var}[x] + \text{Var}[y]. \tag{3-57}$$

For any two functions, $g_1(x)$ and $g_2(y)$, if x and y are independent,

$$E[g_1(x)g_2(y)] = E[g_1(x)]E[g_2(y)]. \tag{3-58}$$

3.7. *Conditioning in a Bivariate Distribution*

Conditioning and the use of conditional distributions play a pivotal role in econometric modeling. We consider some general results for a bivariate distribution. (All of these results will carry over directly to the multivariate case.)

In a bivariate distribution, there is a **conditional distribution** over y for each value of x. The conditional densities are

$$f(y \mid x) = \frac{f(x, y)}{f_x(x)}$$

and

$$f(x \mid y) = \frac{f(x, y)}{f_y(y)}. \tag{3-59}$$

It follows from (3–46) that

$$\text{If } x \text{ and } y \text{ are independent,}$$
$$f(y|x) = f_y(y) \text{ and } f(x|y) = f_x(x). \tag{3–60}$$

The interpretation is that if the variables are independent, the probabilities of events relating to one variable are unrelated to the other. The definition of conditional densities implies the important result

$$f(x, y) = f(y|x)f_x(x)$$
$$= f(x|y)f_y(y). \tag{3–61}$$

3.7.1.   Regression—The Conditional Mean

A **conditional mean** is the mean of the conditional distribution and is defined by

$$E[y|x] = \begin{cases} \int_y yf(y|x)\,dy & \text{if } y \text{ is continuous,} \\ \sum_y yf(y|x) & \text{if } y \text{ is discrete.} \end{cases} \tag{3–62}$$

The conditional mean function $E[y|x]$ is called the **regression of y on x.**

EXAMPLE 3.4.   Consider the conditional distribution:

$$f(y|x) = \frac{1}{\alpha + \beta x} e^{-y/(\alpha + \beta x)}, \qquad y \geq 0, \qquad 0 \leq x \leq 1.$$

Note that the conditional density of y is a function of x. The conditional mean can be derived directly by integration or by noting that this is an exponential distribution with $\lambda = 1/(\alpha + \beta x)$. The mean of an exponential distribution with parameter λ is $1/\lambda$. Therefore,

$$E[y|x] = \alpha + \beta x.$$

A random variable may always be written as

$$y = E[y|x] + (y - E[y|x])$$
$$= E[y|x] + \varepsilon.$$

EXAMPLE 3.5.   In a recent study, Hausman et al. (1984) suggest that the Poisson distribution (see Example 3.1) is a reasonable model for the distribution of patents granted to firms in any given year:

$$f(P) = \frac{\lambda^P e^{-\lambda}}{P!}, \qquad P = 0, 1, 2, \ldots.$$

However, it is known that the more spent on research and development (R&D), the greater, on average, is the number of patents received. This interaction should affect the distribution of P. How R&D is distributed across firms is a side issue that may or may not be of any interest. But we are interested in how R&D and the average number of patents interact. Since the mean value of patents received is λ, suppose we make the preceding a conditional distribution, and specify that

$$\lambda = \alpha + \beta R = E[P|R].$$

We would expect β to be positive. Thus,

$$f(P\,|\,R) = \frac{(\alpha + \beta R)^P e^{-(\alpha + \beta R)P}}{P!},$$

which captures the effect we sought. The observation of a large number of patents may reflect a high value from the Poisson process or may follow from an unusually high value of R&D.

3.7.2. Conditional Variance

A conditional variance is the variance of the conditional distribution:

$$\begin{aligned}\mathrm{Var}[y\,|\,x] &= E[(y - E[y\,|\,x])^2\,|\,x]\\ &= \int_y (y - E[y\,|\,x])^2 f(y\,|\,x)\,dy\end{aligned} \qquad (3\text{--}63)$$

or

$$\sum_y (y - E[y\,|\,x])^2 f(y\,|\,x).$$

The computation can be simplified by using

$$\mathrm{Var}[y\,|\,x] = E[y^2\,|\,x] - (E[y\,|\,x])^2. \qquad (3\text{--}64)$$

EXAMPLE 3.6. The Poisson distribution of Example 3.5 illustrates a pitfall that occasionally arises in specifying an econometric model. In a Poisson distribution, the mean is equal to the variance. We have not ruled out the possibility that $\alpha + \beta R$ could be negative for some values of α and β. Not only is this an invalid parameter for the Poisson distribution in any event, but beyond this, it allows a negative variance. This is a common error of specification.[8]

The conditional variance is called the **scedastic function**, and, like the regression, is generally a function of x. Unlike the conditional mean function, however, it is common for the conditional variance not to vary with x. We shall examine a particular case. This does not imply, however, that $\mathrm{Var}[y\,|\,x]$ equals $\mathrm{Var}[y]$, which will usually not be the case. It implies only that the conditional variance is a constant. The case in which the conditional variance does not vary with x is called **homoscedasticity** (same variance).

3.7.3. Relationships Among Marginal and Conditional Moments

Some useful results for the moments of a conditional distribution are as follows:

$$E[y] = E_x[E[y\,|\,x]]. \qquad (3\text{--}65)$$

The notation $E_x[\cdot]$ indicates the expectation over the values of x. This is sometimes labeled the **law of iterated expectations**.

EXAMPLE 3.7. In the distribution of Example 3.4, assume that x is uniformly distributed between 0 and 1. Then the marginal distribution of x is $f(x) = 1$ and the joint distribution is

$$f(x, y) = f(y\,|\,x)f(x).$$

---

[8] Maddala (1983, p. 51) gives an alternative Poisson regression model, some discussion, and further references.

Then

$$E[y] = \int_0^\infty \int_0^1 y\left(\frac{1}{\alpha + \beta x}\right) e^{-y/(\alpha + \beta x)} \, dx \, dy.$$

But $E[y\,|\,x] = \alpha + \beta x$, so

$$
\begin{aligned}
E[y] &= E_x[E[y\,|\,x]] \\
&= E[\alpha + \beta x] \\
&= \alpha + \beta E[x].
\end{aligned}
$$

(3–66)

Since x has a uniform distribution between 0 and 1, $E[x] = \frac{1}{2}$. Therefore,

$$E[y] = \alpha + \beta(\tfrac{1}{2}).$$

In any bivariate distribution,

$$
\begin{aligned}
\text{Cov}[x, y] &= \text{Cov}[x, E[y\,|\,x]] \\
&= \int_x (x - E[x])E[y\,|\,x]f_x(x)\,dx.
\end{aligned}
$$

EXAMPLE 3.8.   To continue Example 3.7,

$$\text{Cov}[x, y] = \int_0^\infty \int_0^1 \frac{(x - \frac{1}{2})[y - (\alpha + (\beta/2))]}{\alpha + \beta x} e^{-y/(\alpha + \beta x)} \, dx \, dy,$$

which can, in principle, be computed directly. However,

$$
\begin{aligned}
\text{Cov}[x, y] &= \text{Cov}[x, E[y\,|\,x]] \\
&= \text{Cov}[x, \alpha + \beta x] \\
&= \beta \,\text{Var}[x] = \beta(\tfrac{1}{12}).
\end{aligned}
$$

(3–67)

The preceding examples provide an additional result for the special case in which the conditional mean function is linear in x.

Moments in a Linear Regression

If $E[y\,|\,x] = \alpha + \beta x$,

$$\alpha = E[y] - \beta E[x]$$

(3–68)

and

$$\beta = \frac{\text{Cov}[x, y]}{\text{Var}[x]}.$$

(3–69)

The proof follows immediately from (3–66) and (3–67).
The following also appears in various forms in regression analysis:

Decomposition of Variance

$$\text{Var}[y] = \text{Var}_x[E[y\,|\,x]] + E_x[\text{Var}[y\,|\,x]].$$

(3–70)

The notation $\text{Var}_x[\cdot]$ indicates the variance over the distribution of x. This states that in a bivariate distribution, the variance of y decomposes into the variance of the conditional mean function plus the expected variance around the conditional mean.

EXAMPLE 3.9. The variance of y in Example 3.4 remains to be derived. As before, the direct integration of the joint distribution is somewhat difficult. However,

$$\text{Var}_x[E[y|x]] = \text{Var}[\alpha + \beta x] = \beta^2 \, \text{Var}[x]$$

$$= \frac{\beta^2}{12}$$

and

$$E_x[\text{Var}[y|x]] = E[[\alpha + \beta x]^2]$$

$$= \alpha^2 + \beta^2 E[x^2] + 2\alpha\beta E[x]$$

$$= \alpha^2 + \beta^2(\tfrac{1}{3}) + 2\alpha\beta(\tfrac{1}{2}).$$

The unconditional variance is the sum of the two parts:

$$\text{Var}[y] = \alpha(1 + \beta) + \frac{5\beta^2}{12}.$$

By rearranging (3–70), we obtain the following important result.

Residual Variance in a Regression

$$E_x[\text{Var}[y|x]] = \text{Var}[y] - \text{Var}_x[E[y|x]]. \tag{3–71}$$

On average, conditioning reduces the variance of the variable subject to the conditioning. For example, if y is homoscedastic, we have the unambiguous result that the variance of the conditional distribution(s) is less than or equal to the unconditional variance of y.

EXAMPLE 3.10. For the patents–R&D relationship in Example 3.5, suppose that R&D is a constant fraction of firm size and that firm sizes have a lognormal distribution. Then R&D will have a lognormal distribution as well. The density, mean, and variance of this distribution are given in Section 3.5. Assume that $\mu = 0$ and $\sigma = 1$. Then

$$E[R] = \sqrt{e} = 1.65 \quad \text{and} \quad \text{Var}[R] = 4.65.$$

Assume, as well, that $\alpha = 1$ and $\beta = 2$. Then

$$E[P|R] = 1 + 2R,$$

$$E[P] = 1 + 2E[R] = 4.30,$$

$$\text{Var}_R[E[P|R]] = 4 \, \text{Var}[R] = 18.6,$$

$$\text{Var}[P|R] = 1 + 2R,$$

$$E_R[\text{Var}[P|R]] = 4.30,$$

$$\text{Var}(P) = 18.6 + 4.30 = 22.9.$$

Note that $\text{Var}[P]$ is substantially greater than $E[\text{Var}[P|R]]$.

3.7.4. The Analysis of Variance

The variance decomposition result implies that in a bivariate distribution, variation in y arises from two sources:

1. Variation due to the fact that $E[y|x]$ varies with x:

$$\textbf{Regression variance} = \text{Var}_x[E[y|x]]. \tag{3–72}$$

2. Variation that arises because, in each conditional distribution, y varies around the conditional mean:

$$\text{Residual variance} = E_x[\text{Var}[y \,|\, x]]. \tag{3-73}$$

Thus,

$$\text{Var}[y] = \text{regression variance} + \text{residual variance}. \tag{3-74}$$

In analyzing a regression, we shall usually be interested in which of these two parts is the larger one in the **total variance**, $\text{Var}[y]$. For example, in the patents–R&D relationship, which explains more of the variance in the number of patents received, variation in the amount of R&D (regression variance) or random variation in patents received within the Poisson distribution (residual variance)? An obvious measure is the ratio

$$\textbf{Coefficient of determination} = \frac{\text{regression variance}}{\text{total variance}}. \tag{3-75}$$

EXAMPLE 3.11. For the decomposition in Example 3.10,

$$\text{Coefficient of determination} = \frac{18.6}{22.9} = 0.812.$$

In the setting of a linear regression, (3–75) arises from another relationship that emphasizes the interpretation of the correlation coefficient.

If $E[y \,|\, x] = \alpha + \beta x$, then

$$\text{Coefficient of determination} = \text{COD} = \rho^2, \tag{3-76}$$

where ρ^2 is the squared correlation between x and y. We conclude that the correlation coefficient (squared) is a measure of the proportion of the variance of y accounted for by variation in the mean of y given x. It is in this sense that correlation can be interpreted as a **measure of linear association** between two variables.

3.8. The Bivariate Normal Distribution

A bivariate distribution that embodies many of the features described earlier (and numerous others) is the bivariate normal. This is the joint distribution of two normally distributed variables. The density is

$$f(x, y) = \frac{1}{2\pi\sigma_x\sigma_y\sqrt{1 - \rho^2}} e^{-(\varepsilon_x^2 + \varepsilon_y^2 - 2\rho\varepsilon_x\varepsilon_y)/(2(1 - \rho^2))}$$

$$\varepsilon_x = \frac{x - \mu_x}{\sigma_x} \tag{3-77}$$

$$\varepsilon_y = \frac{y - \mu_y}{\sigma_y}.$$

The parameters μ_x, σ_x, μ_y, and σ_y are the means and standard deviations of the marginal distributions of x and y, respectively. The additional parameter, ρ, is the correlation between x and y. The covariance is

$$\sigma_{xy} = \rho\sigma_x\sigma_y. \tag{3-78}$$

The density is defined only if ρ is not 1 or -1. This, in turn, requires that the two variables not be linearly related.

If x and y have a bivariate normal distribution, denoted

$$(x, y) \sim N_2[\mu_x, \mu_y, \sigma_x^2, \sigma_y^2, \rho],$$

1. the marginal distributions are normal;

$$
\begin{aligned}
f_x(x) &= N[\mu_x, \sigma_x^2] \\
f_y(y) &= N[\mu_y, \sigma_y^2],
\end{aligned}
\tag{3-79}
$$

2. the conditional distributions are normal;

$$
f(y \mid x) = N[\alpha + \beta x, \sigma_y^2(1 - \rho^2)]
$$
$$
\alpha = \mu_y - \beta\mu_x
$$
$$
\beta = \frac{\sigma_{xy}}{\sigma_x^2},
\tag{3-80}
$$

and likewise for $f(x \mid y)$; and

3. x and y are independent if and only if $\rho = 0$. The density factors into the product of the two marginal normal distributions if $\rho = 0$.

Two things to note about the conditional distributions beyond their normality are their linear regression functions and their constant conditional variances. The conditional variance is less than the unconditional variance, which is consistent with the results of the previous section.

3.9. *Multivariate Distributions*

The extension of the results for bivariate distributions to more than two variables is direct. It is made much more convenient by using matrices and vectors. The term **random vector** applies to a vector whose elements are random variables. The joint density is $f(\mathbf{x})$, while the cdf is

$$
F(\mathbf{x}) = \int_{-\infty}^{x_n} \int_{-\infty}^{x_{n-1}} \cdots \int_{-\infty}^{x_1} f(\mathbf{x}) \, dx_1 \cdots dx_{n-1} \, dx_n.
\tag{3-81}
$$

Note that the cdf is an n-fold integral. The marginal distribution of any one (or more) of the n variables is obtained by integrating or summing over the other variables.

3.9.1. **Moments**

The expected value of a vector or matrix is the vector or matrix of expected values. A mean vector is defined as

$$
\mu = \begin{bmatrix} \mu_1 \\ \mu_2 \\ \vdots \\ \mu_n \end{bmatrix} = \begin{bmatrix} E[x_1] \\ E[x_2] \\ \vdots \\ E[x_n] \end{bmatrix} = E[\mathbf{x}].
\tag{3-82}
$$

Define the matrix

$$(\mathbf{x} - \boldsymbol{\mu})(\mathbf{x} - \boldsymbol{\mu})' = \begin{bmatrix} (x_1 - \mu_1)(x_1 - \mu_1) & (x_1 - \mu_1)(x_2 - \mu_2) & \cdots & (x_1 - \mu_1)(x_n - \mu_n) \\ (x_2 - \mu_2)(x_1 - \mu_1) & (x_2 - \mu_2)(x_2 - \mu_2) & \cdots & (x_2 - \mu_2)(x_n - \mu_n) \\ \vdots & & & \\ (x_n - \mu_n)(x_1 - \mu_1) & (x_n - \mu_n)(x_2 - \mu_2) & \cdots & (x_n - \mu_n)(x_n - \mu_n) \end{bmatrix}.$$

The expected value of each element in the matrix is the covariance of the two variables in the product. (The covariance of a variable with itself is its variance.) Thus,

$$E[(\mathbf{x} - \boldsymbol{\mu})(\mathbf{x} - \boldsymbol{\mu})'] = \Sigma$$

$$= \begin{bmatrix} \sigma_{11} & \sigma_{12} & \cdots & \sigma_{1n} \\ \sigma_{21} & \sigma_{22} & \cdots & \sigma_{2n} \\ \vdots & \vdots & & \\ \sigma_{n1} & \sigma_{n2} & \cdots & \sigma_{nn} \end{bmatrix} \qquad (3\text{–}83)$$

$$= E[\mathbf{x}\mathbf{x}'] - \boldsymbol{\mu}\boldsymbol{\mu}',$$

which is the **covariance matrix** of the random vector $\mathbf{x}$. Henceforth, we shall denote the covariance matrix of a random vector in boldface, as in

$$\text{Var}[\mathbf{x}] = \Sigma.$$

By dividing σ_{ij} by $\sigma_i \sigma_j$, we obtain the **correlation matrix**:

$$\mathbf{R} = \begin{bmatrix} 1 & \rho_{12} & \rho_{13} & \cdots & \rho_{1n} \\ \rho_{21} & 1 & \rho_{23} & \cdots & \rho_{2n} \\ \vdots & \vdots & \vdots & & \vdots \\ \rho_{n1} & \rho_{n2} & \rho_{n3} & \cdots & 1 \end{bmatrix}.$$

3.9.2. Sets of Linear Functions

Our earlier results for the mean and variance of a linear function can be extended directly to the multivariate case. For the mean,

$$E[a_1 x_1 + a_2 x_2 + \cdots + a_n x_n] = E[\mathbf{a}'\mathbf{x}]$$

$$= a_1 E[x_1] + a_2 E[x_2] + \cdots + a_n E[x_n]$$

$$= a_1 \mu_1 + a_2 \mu_2 + \cdots + a_n \mu_n \qquad (3\text{–}84)$$

$$= \mathbf{a}'\boldsymbol{\mu}.$$

For the variance,

$$\text{Var}[\mathbf{a}'\mathbf{x}] = E[(\mathbf{a}'\mathbf{x} - E[\mathbf{a}'\mathbf{x}])^2]$$

$$= E[\{\mathbf{a}'(\mathbf{x} - E[\mathbf{x}])\}^2]$$

$$= E[\mathbf{a}'(\mathbf{x} - \boldsymbol{\mu})(\mathbf{x} - \boldsymbol{\mu})'\mathbf{a}]$$

as $E[\mathbf{x}] = \boldsymbol{\mu}$ and $\mathbf{a}'(\mathbf{x} - \boldsymbol{\mu}) = (\mathbf{x} - \boldsymbol{\mu})'\mathbf{a}$. Since $\mathbf{a}$ is a vector of constants,

$$\text{Var}[\mathbf{a}'\mathbf{x}] = \mathbf{a}'E[(\mathbf{x} - \boldsymbol{\mu})(\mathbf{x} - \boldsymbol{\mu})']\mathbf{a}$$

$$= \mathbf{a}'\Sigma\mathbf{a} \qquad (3\text{–}85)$$

$$= \Sigma_i \Sigma_j a_i a_j \sigma_{ij}.$$

Since it is the expected value of a square, we know that a variance cannot be negative. As such, the preceding quadratic form is nonnegative, and the symmetric matrix, Σ, must be nonnegative definite.

In the set of linear functions $y = Ax$, the ith element of y is $y_i = a_i x$, where a_i is the ith row of A. Therefore,

$$E[y_i] = a_i' \mu.$$

Collecting the results in a vector, we have

$$E[Ax] = A\mu. \tag{3-86}$$

For two row vectors, a_i and a_j,

$$Cov[a_i x, a_j x] = a_i \Sigma a_j'.$$

Since $a_i \Sigma a_j'$ is the ijth element of $A\Sigma A'$,

$$Var[Ax] = A\Sigma A'. \tag{3-87}$$

This will be either nonnegative definite or positive definite, depending on the column rank of A.

3.9.3. Nonlinear Functions

Consider a set of possibly nonlinear functions of x, $y = g(x)$. Each element of y can be approximated with a linear Taylor series. Let j_i be the row vector of partial derivatives of the ith function with respect to the n elements of x:

$$j_i = \frac{\partial g_i(x)}{\partial x'} = \frac{\partial y_i}{\partial x'}. \tag{3-88}$$

Then, proceeding in the now familiar way, we use μ, the mean vector of x, as the expansion point, so that j_i is the row vector of partial derivatives evaluated at μ. Thus,

$$g_i(x) \simeq g_i(\mu) + j_i(x - \mu). \tag{3-89}$$

From this we obtain

$$E[g_i(x)] \simeq g_i(\mu), \tag{3-90}$$

$$Var[g_i(x)] \simeq j_i \Sigma j_i', \tag{3-91}$$

and

$$Cov[g_i(x), g_j(x)] \simeq j_i \Sigma j_j'. \tag{3-92}$$

These can be collected in a convenient form by arranging the row vectors j_i in a matrix J. Then, corresponding to the preceding equations, we have

$$E[g(x)] \simeq g(\mu) \tag{3-93}$$

$$Var[g(x)] \simeq J\Sigma J'. \tag{3-94}$$

The matrix J in the last preceding line is $\partial y / \partial x'$.

3.10. *The Multivariate Normal Distribution*

The foundation of most multivariate analysis in econometrics is the multivariate normal distribution. Let the vector $(x_1, x_2, \ldots, x_n)' = \mathbf{x}$ be the set of n random variables, $\boldsymbol{\mu}$ their mean vector, and $\boldsymbol{\Sigma}$ their covariance matrix. The general form of the joint density is

$$f(\mathbf{x}) = (2\pi)^{-n/2} |\boldsymbol{\Sigma}|^{-1/2} e^{-1/2(\mathbf{x}-\boldsymbol{\mu})'\boldsymbol{\Sigma}^{-1}(\mathbf{x}-\boldsymbol{\mu})}. \tag{3-95}$$

If $\mathbf{R}$ is the correlation matrix of the variables and $R_{ij} = \sigma_{ij}/(\sigma_i \sigma_j)$,

$$f(\mathbf{x}) = (2\pi)^{-n/2} (\sigma_1 \sigma_2 \cdots \sigma_n)^{-1} |\mathbf{R}|^{-1/2} e^{-1/2\boldsymbol{\varepsilon}'\mathbf{R}^{-1}\boldsymbol{\varepsilon}}, \tag{3-96}$$

where $\varepsilon_i = (x_i - \mu_i)/\sigma_i$.[9]

Two special cases are of interest. If all of the variables are uncorrelated, $\rho_{ij} = 0$ for $i \neq j$. Thus, $\mathbf{R} = \mathbf{I}$ and the density becomes

$$f(\mathbf{x}) = (2\pi)^{-n/2} (\sigma_1 \sigma_2 \cdots \sigma_n)^{-1} e^{-\boldsymbol{\varepsilon}'\boldsymbol{\varepsilon}/2}$$
$$= f(x_1) f(x_2) \cdots. \tag{3-97}$$

As in the bivariate case, if normally distributed variables are uncorrelated, they are independent. If $\sigma_i = \sigma$ and $\boldsymbol{\mu} = \mathbf{0}$, $x_i \sim N[0, \sigma^2]$, $\varepsilon_i = x_i/\sigma$, and the density becomes

$$f(\mathbf{x}) = (2\pi)^{-n/2} (\sigma^2)^{-n/2} e^{-\mathbf{x}'\mathbf{x}/2\sigma^2}. \tag{3-98}$$

Finally, if $\sigma = 1$,

$$f(\mathbf{x}) = (2\pi)^{-n/2} e^{-\mathbf{x}'\mathbf{x}/2}. \tag{3-99}$$

This is the multivariate standard normal, or spherical normal distribution.

3.10.1. Marginal and Conditional Distributions

Let $\mathbf{x}_1$ be any subset of the variables, including a single variable, and let $\mathbf{x}_2$ be the remaining variables. Partition $\boldsymbol{\mu}$ and $\boldsymbol{\Sigma}$ likewise, so that

$$\boldsymbol{\mu} = \begin{bmatrix} \mu_1 \\ \mu_2 \end{bmatrix} \quad \text{and} \quad \boldsymbol{\Sigma} = \begin{bmatrix} \Sigma_{11} & \Sigma_{12} \\ \Sigma_{21} & \Sigma_{22} \end{bmatrix}.$$

Then, the marginal distributions are also normal. In particular,

$$\mathbf{x}_1 \sim N(\boldsymbol{\mu}_1, \Sigma_{11}) \tag{3-100}$$

and

$$\mathbf{x}_2 \sim N(\boldsymbol{\mu}_2, \Sigma_{22}). \tag{3-101}$$

The conditional distribution of $\mathbf{x}_1$ given $\mathbf{x}_2$ is normal as well:

$$\mathbf{x}_1 | \mathbf{x}_2 \sim N(\boldsymbol{\mu}_{1.2}, \Sigma_{11.2}), \tag{3-102}$$

where

$$\boldsymbol{\mu}_{1.2} = \boldsymbol{\mu}_1 + \Sigma_{12} \Sigma_{22}^{-1} (\mathbf{x}_2 - \boldsymbol{\mu}_2) \tag{3-102a}$$

$$\Sigma_{11.2} = \Sigma_{11} - \Sigma_{12} \Sigma_{22}^{-1} \Sigma_{21}. \tag{3-102b}$$

---

[9] This result is obtained by constructing $\boldsymbol{\Delta}$, the diagonal matrix with σ_i as its ith diagonal element. Then, $\mathbf{R} = \boldsymbol{\Delta}^{-1} \boldsymbol{\Sigma} \boldsymbol{\Delta}^{-1}$, which implies that $\boldsymbol{\Sigma}^{-1} = \boldsymbol{\Delta}^{-1} \mathbf{R}^{-1} \boldsymbol{\Delta}^{-1}$. Inserting this in (3–95) yields (3–96). Note that the ith element of $\boldsymbol{\Delta}^{-1}(\mathbf{x} - \boldsymbol{\mu})$ is $(x_i - \mu_i)/\sigma_i$.

Proof: We partition μ and Σ as above just shown, and insert the parts in (3–102). To construct the density, we require the partitioning of the determinant,

$$|\Sigma| = |\Sigma_{22}||\Sigma_{11} - \Sigma_{12}\Sigma_{22}^{-1}\Sigma_{21}|,$$

and the inverse,

$$\begin{bmatrix} \Sigma_{11} & \Sigma_{12} \\ \Sigma_{21} & \Sigma_{22} \end{bmatrix}^{-1} = \begin{bmatrix} \Sigma_{11.2}^{-1} & -\Sigma_{11.2}^{-1}\mathbf{B} \\ -\mathbf{B}'\Sigma_{11.2}^{-1} & \Sigma_{22}^{-1} + \mathbf{B}'\Sigma_{11.2}^{-1}\mathbf{B} \end{bmatrix}.$$

For simplicity, we let

$$\mathbf{B} = \Sigma_{12}\Sigma_{22}^{-1}.$$

Inserting these in (3–101) and collecting terms produces the joint density as a product of two terms:

$$f(\mathbf{x}_1, \mathbf{x}_2) = f_{1.2}(\mathbf{x}_1 \mid \mathbf{x}_2)f_2(\mathbf{x}_2).$$

The first of these is a normal distribution with mean $\mu_{1.2}$ and variance $\Sigma_{11.2}$, while the second is the marginal distribution of $\mathbf{x}_2$. The conditional mean vector is a linear function of the unconditional mean and the conditioning variables, and the conditional variance matrix is constant and is smaller (in the sense discussed in Chapter 2) than the unconditional variance matrix. Notice that the conditional variance matrix is the inverse of the upper left block of Σ^{-1}. (That is, this is of the form shown in Chapter 2 for the partitioned inverse of a matrix.) An important special case is that in which $\mathbf{x}_1$ is a single variable, y, and $\mathbf{x}_2$ is K variables. Then the conditional distribution is that in (3–80) with $\beta = \Sigma_{xx}^{-1}\sigma_{xy}$.

3.10.2. Linear Functions of a Normal Vector

Any linear function of a normal vector is also normally distributed. The mean vector and covariance matrix of $\mathbf{Ax}$, where $\mathbf{x}$ is normally distributed, follow the general pattern given earlier. Thus,

$$\text{If } \mathbf{x} \sim N[\mu, \Sigma], \mathbf{Ax} + \mathbf{b} \sim N[\mathbf{A}\mu + \mathbf{b}, \mathbf{A}\Sigma\mathbf{A}'], \qquad (3\text{–}103)$$

assuming that $\mathbf{A}$ has full rank. If $\mathbf{A}$ does not have full rank, $\mathbf{A}\Sigma\mathbf{A}'$ is singular and the density does not exist. Nonetheless, even in this case, the individual elements of $\mathbf{Ax}$ will still be normally distributed.

3.10.3. Quadratic Forms in a Standard Normal Vector

The earlier discussion of the chi-squared distribution gives the distribution of $\mathbf{x}'\mathbf{x}$ if $\mathbf{x}$ has a standard normal distribution. In Chapter 2, we saw that

$$\mathbf{x}'\mathbf{x} = \sum_i x_i^2 = \sum_i (x_i - \bar{x})^2 + n\bar{x}^2. \qquad (3\text{–}104)$$

We know from (3–32) that $\mathbf{x}'\mathbf{x}$ has a chi-squared distribution. It seems natural, therefore, to invoke (3–34) for the two parts on the right-hand side of (3–104). However, it is not yet obvious that either of the two terms has a chi-squared distribution or that the two terms are independent, as required. To show these conditions, it is necessary to derive the distributions of **idempotent quadratic forms** and to show when they are independent.

To begin, the second term is the square of $(\sqrt{n})\bar{x}$, which can easily be shown to have a standard normal distribution. Thus, the second term is the square of a standard normal variable and has chi-squared distribution with one degree of freedom. But the first term is the sum of n nonindependent variables, and it remains to be shown that the two terms are independent.

3.10.3a. *Idempotent Quadratic Forms*

A particular case of (3–103) is

> If $x \sim N(0,I)$ and C is a square matrix
> such that $C'C = I$, then $C'x \sim N[0,I]$.

Consider, then, a quadratic form in a standard normal vector, x:

$$q = x'Ax. \tag{3-105}$$

Let the characteristic roots and vectors of A be arranged in a diagonal matrix, Λ, and an orthogonal matrix, C, as in Chapter 2. Then

$$q = x'C\Lambda C'x. \tag{3-106}$$

By definition, C satisfies the requirement that $C'C = I$. Thus, the vector $y = C'x$ has a standard normal distribution. Consequently,

$$\begin{aligned} q &= y'\Lambda y \\ &= \sum_i \lambda_i y_i^2. \end{aligned} \tag{3-107}$$

If λ_i is always 1 or 0,

$$q = \sum_j y_j^2, \tag{3-108}$$

which has a chi-squared distribution. The sum is taken over the $j = 1,\ldots,J$ elements associated with the roots that are equal to 1. A matrix whose characteristic roots are all 0 or 1 is idempotent. Therefore, we have proved the result that

> If $x \sim N(0,I)$ and A is idempotent, then $x'Ax$ has a chi-squared distribution
> with degrees of freedom equal to the number of unit roots of A.

The rank of a matrix is equal to the number of nonzero characteristic roots it has. Therefore, the degrees of freedom in the preceding chi-squared distribution equals J, the rank of A.
We can apply this result directly to the earlier sum of squares. The first term is

$$\sum_i (x_i - \bar{x})^2 = x'M^0x,$$

where M^0 was defined in Chapter 2 as the matrix that transforms data to mean deviation form:

$$M^0 = \left[I - \frac{1}{n}ii' \right].$$

Since M^0 is idempotent, the sum of squared deviations from the mean has a chi-squared distribution. The degrees of freedom equals the rank of M^0, which is not obvious except for the useful result in (2–108), that

The rank of an idempotent matrix is equal to its trace. (3–109)

Each diagonal element of $\mathbf{M}^0$ is $1 - (1/n)$; hence, the trace is $n(1 - (1/n)) = n - 1$. Therefore,

$$\text{If } \mathbf{x} \sim N[\mathbf{0}, \mathbf{I}], \sum_i (x_i - \bar{x})^2 \sim \chi^2[n - 1]. \tag{3-110}$$

We have already shown that the second term in (3–110) has a chi-squared distribution with one degree of freedom. It is instructive to set this up as a quadratic form:

$$n\bar{x}^2 = \mathbf{x}' \left[\frac{1}{n} \mathbf{ii}' \right] \mathbf{x}$$

$$= \mathbf{x}'[\mathbf{jj}']\mathbf{x}. \tag{3-111}$$

where

$$\mathbf{j} = \left(\frac{1}{\sqrt{n}} \right) \mathbf{i}.$$

The matrix in brackets is the outer product of a nonzero vector, which always has rank one. You can verify that it is idempotent by multiplication. Thus, $\mathbf{x}'\mathbf{x}$ is the sum of two chi-squared variables, one with $n - 1$ degrees of freedom and the other with one. It is now necessary to show that the two terms are independent.

3.10.3b.   Independence of Idempotent Quadratic Forms

As before, we show the result for the general case and then specialize it for the example. The general result is

> If $\mathbf{x} \sim N[\mathbf{0}, \mathbf{I}]$ and $\mathbf{x}'\mathbf{A}\mathbf{x}$ and $\mathbf{x}'\mathbf{B}\mathbf{x}$ are two idempotent quadratic forms in $\mathbf{x}$, $\mathbf{x}'\mathbf{A}\mathbf{x}$ and $\mathbf{x}'\mathbf{B}\mathbf{x}$ are independent if $\mathbf{AB} = \mathbf{0}$. $\tag{3-112}$

Since both $\mathbf{A}$ and $\mathbf{B}$ are symmetric and idempotent, $\mathbf{A} = \mathbf{A}'\mathbf{A}$ and $\mathbf{B} = \mathbf{B}'\mathbf{B}$. The quadratic forms are therefore

$$\mathbf{x}'\mathbf{A}\mathbf{x} = \mathbf{x}'\mathbf{A}'\mathbf{A}\mathbf{x} = \mathbf{x}_1'\mathbf{x}_1 \qquad \text{where } \mathbf{x}_1 = \mathbf{A}\mathbf{x}$$

and

$$\mathbf{x}'\mathbf{B}\mathbf{x} = \mathbf{x}_2'\mathbf{x}_2 \qquad \text{where } \mathbf{x}_2 = \mathbf{B}\mathbf{x}. \tag{3-113}$$

Both vectors have zero mean vectors, so the covariance matrix of $\mathbf{x}_1$ and $\mathbf{x}_2$ is

$$E(\mathbf{x}_1\mathbf{x}_2') = \mathbf{AIB}' = \mathbf{AB} = \mathbf{0}.$$

Since $\mathbf{Ax}$ and $\mathbf{Bx}$ are linear functions of a normal vector, they are, in turn, normally distributed. Their zero covariance matrix implies that they are statistically independent. This establishes the independence of the two quadratic forms. For the case of $\mathbf{x}'\mathbf{x}$, the two matrices are $\mathbf{M}^0$ and $[\mathbf{I} - \mathbf{M}^0]$. You can show that $\mathbf{M}^0[\mathbf{I} - \mathbf{M}^0] = \mathbf{0}$ just by multiplying it out.

3.10.4.   The *F* Distribution

The normal family of distributions (chi-squared, F, and t) can all be derived as functions of idempotent quadratic forms in a standard normal vector. The F distribution is the ratio of two independent chi-squared variables, each divided by its respective degrees of freedom. Let $\mathbf{A}$ and $\mathbf{B}$ be two idempotent matrices with ranks r_a and r_b, and let $\mathbf{AB} = \mathbf{0}$. Then

$$\frac{\mathbf{x}'\mathbf{A}\mathbf{x}/r_a}{\mathbf{x}'\mathbf{B}\mathbf{x}/r_b} \sim F[r_a, r_b]. \tag{3-114}$$

If $\text{Var}[\mathbf{x}] = \sigma^2 \mathbf{I}$ instead, this is modified to

$$\frac{(\mathbf{x}'\mathbf{Ax}/\sigma^2)/r_a}{(\mathbf{x}'\mathbf{Bx}/\sigma^2)/r_b} \sim F[r_a, r_b]. \qquad (3\text{–}115)$$

3.10.5.   A Full Rank Quadratic Form

Finally, consider the general case,

$$\mathbf{x} \sim N[\boldsymbol{\mu}, \boldsymbol{\Sigma}].$$

We are interested in the distribution of

$$q = (\mathbf{x} - \boldsymbol{\mu})'\boldsymbol{\Sigma}^{-1}(\mathbf{x} - \boldsymbol{\mu}). \qquad (3\text{–}116)$$

First, the vector can be written as $\mathbf{z} = \mathbf{x} - \boldsymbol{\mu}$, and $\boldsymbol{\Sigma}$ is the variance matrix of $\mathbf{z}$ as well as of $\mathbf{x}$. Therefore, we seek the distribution of

$$q = \mathbf{z}'\boldsymbol{\Sigma}^{-1}\mathbf{z} = \mathbf{z}'(\text{Var}[\mathbf{z}])^{-1}\mathbf{z}, \qquad (3\text{–}117)$$

where $\mathbf{z}$ is normally distributed with mean $\mathbf{0}$. This is a quadratic form, but not necessarily in an idempotent matrix.[10] Since $\boldsymbol{\Sigma}$ is positive definite, it has a square root. Define the symmetric matrix, $\boldsymbol{\Sigma}^{1/2}$, so that $\boldsymbol{\Sigma}^{1/2}\boldsymbol{\Sigma}^{1/2} = \boldsymbol{\Sigma}$. Then

$$\boldsymbol{\Sigma}^{-1} = \boldsymbol{\Sigma}^{-1/2}\boldsymbol{\Sigma}^{-1/2}$$

and

$$\begin{aligned}
\mathbf{z}'\boldsymbol{\Sigma}^{-1}\mathbf{z} &= \mathbf{z}'\boldsymbol{\Sigma}^{-1/2'}\boldsymbol{\Sigma}^{-1/2}\mathbf{z} \\
&= (\boldsymbol{\Sigma}^{-1/2}\mathbf{z})'(\boldsymbol{\Sigma}^{-1/2}\mathbf{z}) \\
&= \mathbf{w}'\mathbf{w}.
\end{aligned}$$

Now $\mathbf{w} = \mathbf{Az}$, so

$$E(\mathbf{w}) = \mathbf{A}E[\mathbf{z}] = \mathbf{0}$$

and

$$\text{Var}[\mathbf{w}] = \mathbf{A}\boldsymbol{\Sigma}\mathbf{A}' = \boldsymbol{\Sigma}^{-1/2}\boldsymbol{\Sigma}\boldsymbol{\Sigma}^{-1/2} = \boldsymbol{\Sigma}^0 = \mathbf{I}.$$

This provides two results:

1. If $\mathbf{x} \sim N[\boldsymbol{\mu}, \boldsymbol{\Sigma}]$,   then $\boldsymbol{\Sigma}^{-1/2}(\mathbf{x} - \boldsymbol{\mu}) \sim N[\mathbf{0}, \mathbf{I}]$.

The obvious special case is that in which $\mathbf{x}$ has only one variable, so that the transformation is just $(x - \mu)/\sigma$. Combining this with the earlier results concerning the sum of squares of standard normals, we have:

2. If $\mathbf{x} \sim N[\boldsymbol{\mu}, \boldsymbol{\Sigma}]$,   then $(\mathbf{x} - \boldsymbol{\mu})'\boldsymbol{\Sigma}^{-1}(\mathbf{x} - \boldsymbol{\mu}) \sim \chi^2[n]$.

3.10.6.   Independence of a Linear and a Quadratic Form

The t distribution is used in many forms of hypothesis tests. In some situations, it arises as the ratio of a linear to a quadratic form in a normal vector. To establish the distribution of

---

[10] It will be idempotent only in the special case of $\boldsymbol{\Sigma} = \mathbf{I}$.

these statistics, we use the following result:

> A linear function, $\mathbf{Lx}$, and an idempotent quadratic form, $\mathbf{x'Ax}$, in a standard normal vector are statistically independent if $\mathbf{LA} = \mathbf{0}$.

The proof follows the same logic as that for two quadratic forms. Write $\mathbf{x'Ax}$ as $\mathbf{x'A'Ax} = (\mathbf{Ax})'(\mathbf{Ax})$. The covariance matrix of the variables $\mathbf{Lx}$ and $\mathbf{Ax}$ is $\mathbf{LA} = \mathbf{0}$, which establishes the independence of these two random vectors. The independence of the linear function and the quadratic form follows immediately.

The t distribution is defined as the ratio of a standard normal variable to the square root of a chi-squared variable divided by its degrees of freedom:

$$t[J] = \frac{N[0,1]}{\{\chi^2[J]/J\}^{1/2}}.$$

A particular case is

$$t[n-1] = \frac{\sqrt{n}\,\bar{x}}{[(\sum_i(x_i - \bar{x})^2)/(n-1)]^{1/2}}$$

$$= \frac{\sqrt{n}\,\bar{x}}{s},$$

where s is the standard deviation of the values in $\mathbf{x}$. The distribution of the two variables in $t[n-1]$ was shown earlier; we need only show that they are independent. But

$$\sqrt{n}\,\bar{x} = \frac{1}{\sqrt{n}}\mathbf{i'x} = \mathbf{j'x}$$

and

$$s^2 = \frac{\mathbf{x'M^0 x}}{n-1}.$$

It suffices to show that $\mathbf{M^0 j} = \mathbf{0}$, which follows from

$$\mathbf{M^0 i} = [\mathbf{I} - \mathbf{i}(\mathbf{i'i})^{-1}\mathbf{i'}]\mathbf{i}$$

$$= \mathbf{i} - \mathbf{i}(\mathbf{i'i})^{-1}(\mathbf{i'i})$$

$$= \mathbf{0}.$$

Exercises

1. How many different five-card poker hands can be dealt from a deck of 52 cards?

2. Compute the probability of being dealt four of a kind in a poker hand.

3. Suppose that a lottery ticket costs $1 per play. The game is played by drawing six numbers without replacement from the numbers 1 to 48. If you guess all six numbers, you win the prize. Now suppose that N = the number of tickets sold and P = the size of the prize. N and P are related by

$$N = 5 + 1.2P,$$

$$P = 1 + 0.4N.$$

N and P are in millions. What is the expected value of a ticket in this game? (Don't forget that you may have to share the prize with other winners.)

4. If x has a normal distribution with mean 1 and standard deviation 3, what are the following?

(a) $\text{Prob}[|x| > 2]$.

(b) $\text{Prob}[x > -1 \,|\, x < 1.5]$.

5. Approximately what is the probability that a random variable with chi-squared distribution with 264 degrees of freedom is less than 297?

6. *Chebychev inequality:* For the following two probability distributions, find the lower limit of the probability of the indicated event, using the Chebychev inequality (3–18), and the exact probability, using the appropriate table:

(a) $x \sim \text{normal}(0, 3)$ and $-4 < x < 4$.

(b) $x \sim$ chi-squared, eight degrees of freedom, $0 < x < 16$.

7. Given the following joint probability distribution

		\multicolumn{3}{c}{X}
		0	1	2
Y	0	0.05	0.1	0.03
	1	0.21	0.11	0.19
	2	0.08	0.15	0.08

(a) Compute the following probabilities:

$$\text{Prob}[Y < 2],$$

$$\text{Prob}[Y < 2, X > 0],$$

$$\text{Prob}[Y = 1, X \geq 1].$$

(b) Find the marginal distributions of X and Y.

(c) Calculate $E[X]$, $E[Y]$, $\text{Var}[X]$, $\text{Var}[Y]$, $\text{Cov}[X, Y]$, and $E[X^2 Y^3]$.

(d) Calculate $\text{Cov}[Y, X^2]$.

(e) What is the conditional distribution of Y given $X = 2$? What is the conditional distribution of X given $Y > 0$?

(f) Find $E[Y|X]$ and $\text{Var}[Y|X]$. Obtain the two parts of the variance decomposition

$$\text{Var}[Y] = E_x[\text{Var}[Y|X]] + \text{Var}_x[E[Y|X]].$$

8. *Minimum mean-squared error predictor:* For the joint distribution in Problem 7, compute $E[y - E[y|x]]^2$. Now find the a and b that minimize the function $E[y - a - bx]^2$. Given the solutions, verify that

$$E[y - E[y|x]]^2 \leq E[y - a - bx]^2.$$

The result is fundamental in least squares theory. Verify that the a and b that you found satisfy (3–68) and (3–69).

9. Suppose that x has an exponential distribution,

$$f(x) = \theta e^{-\theta x}, \qquad x \geq 0.$$

(For an application, see Examples 3.7 and 3.9.) Find the mean, variance, skewness, and kurtosis of x. [**Hints:** The latter two are defined in Section 3.3. The gamma integral in the appendix to this chapter will be useful for finding the raw moments.]

10. For the random variable in the previous exercise, what is the probability distribution of the random variable $y = e^{-x}$? What is $E[y]$? Prove that the distribution of this y is a special case of the beta distribution in (3–40).

11. If the probability density of y is $\alpha y^2(1 - y)^3$ for y between 0 and 1, what is α? What is the probability that y is between 0.25 and 0.75?

12. Suppose that x has the discrete probability distribution

$$X \quad 1 \quad 2 \quad 3 \quad 4$$

$$\text{Prob}[X = x] \quad 0.1 \quad 0.2 \quad 0.4 \quad 0.3$$

Find the exact mean and variance of X. Now suppose that $Y = 1/X$. Find the exact mean and variance of Y. Find the mean and variance of the linear and quadratic approximations to $Y = f(X)$. Are the mean and variance of the quadratic approximation closer to the true mean than those of the linear approximation?

13. *Interpolation in the chi-squared table:* In order to find a percentage point in the chi-squared table that is between two values, we interpolate linearly between the *reciprocals* of the degrees of freedom. The chi-squared distribution is defined for noninteger values of the degrees of freedom parameter [see (3–39)], but your table does not contain critical values for noninteger values. Using linear interpolation, find the 99 percent critical value for a chi-squared variable with degrees of freedom parameter 11.3. (For an application of this calculation, see Section 8.5.1 and Example 8.7.)

14. Suppose that x has a standard normal distribution. What is the pdf of the following random variable?

$$y = \frac{1}{\sqrt{2\pi}} e^{-x^2/2}.$$

[**Hints:** You know the distribution of $z = x^2$ from (3–30). The density of this z is given in (3–39). Solve the problem in terms of $y = g(z)$.]

15. *The fundamental probability transformation:* Suppose that the continuous random variable x has cumulative distribution $F(x)$. What is the probability distribution of the random variable $y = F(x)$? (**Observation:** This result forms the basis of the simulation of draws from many continuous distributions.)

16. *Random number generators:* Suppose that x is distributed uniformly between 0 and 1, so $f(x) = 1, 0 \le x \le 1$. Let θ be some positive constant. What is the pdf of $y = -(1/\theta)\ln x$. (**Hint:** See Section 3.5.) Does this suggest a means of simulating draws from this distribution if one has a random number generator that will produce draws from the uniform distribution? To continue, suggest a means of simulating draws from a logistic distribution, $f(x) = e^x/(1 + e^x)$.

17. Suppose that x_1 and x_2 are distributed as independent standard normal. What is the joint distribution of $y_1 = 2 + 3x_1 + 2x_2$ and $y_2 = 4 + 5x_1$? Suppose that you were able to obtain two samples of observations from independent standard normal distributions. How would you obtain a sample from the bivariate normal distribution with means 1 and 2, variances 4 and 9, and covariance 3?

18. The density of the standard normal distribution, denoted $\phi(x)$, is given in (3–26). The function based on the ith derivative of the density given by

$$H_i = \frac{(-1)^i d^i \phi(x)/dx^i}{\phi(x)}, \qquad i = 0, 1, 2, \ldots$$

is called a *hermite polynomial*. By definition, $H_0 = 1$.

(a) Find the next three hermite polynomials.

(b) A useful device in this context is the differential equation

$$\frac{d^r \phi(x)}{dx^r} + \frac{x d^{r-1} \phi(x)}{dx^{r-1}} + \frac{(r-1) d^{r-2} \phi(x)}{dx^{r-2}} = 0.$$

Use this result and the results of part (a) to find H_4 and H_5.

19. *Continuation: orthogonal polynomials:* The hermite polynomials are orthogonal if x has a standard normal distribution. That is, $E[H_i H_j] = 0$. Prove this for the H_1, H_2, and H_3 that you just obtained.

20. If x and y have means μ_x and μ_y, variances σ_x^2 and σ_y^2, and covariance σ_{xy}, what is the covariance matrix of the two random variables $f_1 = x/y$ and $f_2 = xy$?

21. *Factorial moments:* For finding the moments of a distribution such as the Poisson, a useful device is the factorial moment. (The Poisson distribution is given in Example 3.1.) The density is

$$f(x) = \frac{e^{-\lambda} \lambda^x}{x!}, \qquad x = 0, 1, 2, \ldots.$$

To find the mean, we can use

$$E[x] = \sum_{x=0}^{\infty} x f(x) = \sum_{x=0}^{\infty} \frac{x e^{-\lambda} \lambda^x}{x!}$$

$$= \lambda \sum_{x=1}^{\infty} \frac{e^{-\lambda} \lambda^{x-1}}{(x-1)!}$$

$$= \lambda \sum_{y=0}^{\infty} \frac{e^{-\lambda} \lambda^y}{y!}$$

$$= \lambda,$$

since the probabilities sum to 1. To find the variance, we can extend this method by finding $E[x(x-1)]$, and likewise for other moments. Use this method to find the variance and third central moment of the Poisson distribution. (Note that this device is used to transform the factorial in the denominator in the probability.)

22. If x has a normal distribution with mean μ and standard deviation σ, what is the probability distribution of $y = e^x$?

23. If y has a lognormal distribution, what is the probability distribution of y^2?

24. Suppose that y, x_1, and x_2 have a joint normal distribution with parameters

$$\mu' = [1, \quad 2, \quad 4]$$

and covariance matrix

$$\Sigma = \begin{bmatrix} 2 & 3 & 1 \\ 3 & 5 & 2 \\ 1 & 2 & 6 \end{bmatrix}.$$

(a) Compute the intercept and slope in the function $E[y|x_1]$, $\text{Var}[y|x_1]$ and the coefficient of determination in this regression. (**Hint:** See Section 3.10.1.)

(b) Compute the intercept and slopes in the conditional mean function, $E[y|x_1, x_2]$. What is $E[y|x_1 = 2.5, x_2 = 3.3]$? What is $\text{Var}[y|x_1 = 2.5, x_2 = 3.3]$?

25. What is the density of $y = 1/x$ if x has a chi-squared distribution?

26. *Probability Generating Function:* For a discrete random variable, x, the function

$$E[t^x] = \sum_{x=0}^{\infty} t^x \text{Prob}[X = x]$$

is called the **probability generating function** because in the function the coefficient on t^i is $\text{Prob}[X = i]$. Suppose that x is the number of the repetitions of an experiment with probability π of success upon which the first success occurs. The density of x is the **geometric distribution**:

$$\text{Prob}[X = x] = (1 - \pi)^{x-1}\pi.$$

What is the probability generating function?

27. *Moment generating function:* For the random variable X with pdf $f(x)$, if the function

$$M(t) = E[e^{tx}]$$

exists, it is the moment generating function (MGF). Assuming that the function exists, it can be shown that

$$\frac{d^r M(t)}{dt^r}\bigg|_{t=0} = E[x^r].$$

Find the MGFs for

(a) The exponential distribution of Problem 9.

(b) The Poisson distribution of Problem 21.

The moment generating function need not exist for some values of t. We are interested in convergence of the Taylor series expansion in the neighborhood of $t = 0$, so the nonconvergence need not be a problem. But for some distributions, such as $f(x) = \exp(-x^2)$, the moment generating function does not exist for any t. A companion function for which convergence is not a problem is the **characteristic function**, $E[\exp(itx)]$, where $i^2 = -1$. We shall not require the characteristic function in this book, but it is an important tool in more advanced treatments, for example, in proofs of variants of the central limit theorem.

28. *Moment generating function for a sum of variables:* When it exists, the moment generating function has a one-to-one correspondence with the distribution. Thus, for example, if we begin with some random variable and find that a transformation of it has a particular familiar MGF, we may infer that the function of the random variable has the distribution associated with that MGF. A useful application is the following:

If x and y are independent, the MGF of $x + y$ is $M_x(t)M_y(t)$.

(a) Use this result to prove that the sum of Poisson random variables has a Poisson distribution.

(b) Use this result to prove that the sum of chi-squared variables has a chi-squared distribution. [*Note:* you must first find the MGF for a chi-squared variate. The density is given in (3–39).]

(c) The MGF for the standard normal distribution is

$$M_z = e^{-t^2/2}.$$

Find the MGF for the $N[\mu, \sigma^2]$ distribution; then find the distribution of a sum of normally distributed variables.

An interesting related problem is the **problem of moments**. A distribution, $f(x)$, implies a sequence of moments, $E[x^r], r = 1, 2, \ldots$ Does the converse hold? That is, does the sequence of moments imply the distribution? It does if the moment generating function exists, but not necessarily otherwise. For discussion, see M. Kendall and A. Stuart, *The Advanced Theory of Statistics*, Vol. 1, London: Griffin, 1969.

Appendix: Integration—The Gamma Function

For any positive constant, p, the gamma function is

$$\Gamma(p) = \int_0^\infty t^{p-1} e^{-t} \, dt.$$

For an integer p,

$$\Gamma(p) = (p-1)!, \qquad p = 1, 2, \ldots,$$

which follows from the recursion

$$\Gamma(p) = (p-1)\Gamma(p-1).$$

For p greater than 1, the gamma function may be regarded as a generalization of the factorial operation for noninteger values of p. In addition,

$$\Gamma(\tfrac{1}{2}) = \sqrt{\pi}.$$

For integer values of p,

$$\Gamma(p + \tfrac{1}{2}) = (p - \tfrac{1}{2})\Gamma(p - \tfrac{1}{2}).$$

For positive constants a, p, and c,

$$\int_0^\infty x^{p-1} e^{-ax^c} \, dx = \int_0^\infty x^{-(p+1)} e^{-a/x^c} \, dx = \left(\frac{1}{c}\right) a^{-p/c} \Gamma\left(\frac{p}{c}\right).$$

The derivatives of the gamma function are

$$\frac{d^r \Gamma(p)}{dp^r} = \int_0^\infty (\ln p)^r x^{p-1} e^{-x} \, dx.$$

For values of p that are not multiples of 0.5, the gamma function must be numerically approximated. The derivatives must be approximated for all values of p.

References

Abramovitz, M., and I. Stegun, *Handbook of Mathematical Functions*, New York: Dover Press, 1977.

Aitchison, J., and J. Brown, *The Lognormal Distribution with Special Reference to Its Uses in Economics*, New York: Cambridge University Press, 1969.

Goldberger, A. S., *Econometric Theory*, New York: Wiley, 1964.

Greene, W., "Maximum Likelihood Estimation of Econometric Frontier Functions," *Journal of Econometrics*, 13, 1980, pp. 27–56.

Hausman, J., B. Hall, and Z. Griliches, "Economic Models for Count Data with an Application to the Patents–R&D Relationship," *Econometrica*, 52, 1984, 909–938.

Heckman, J., and R. Willis, "A Beta-Logistic Model for the Analysis of Sequential Labor Force Participation by Married Women," National Bureau of Economic Research Working Paper No. 112, November 1975.

Johnson, N., and S. Kotz, *Distributions in Statistics, Continuous Univariate Distributions-2*, New York: Wiley, 1970.

Kendall, M., and A. Stuart, *The Advanced Theory of Statistics, Vol. 1: Distribution Theory*, London: Griffin, 1969.

Maddala, G. S., *Econometrics*, New York: McGraw-Hill, 1977.

Maddala, G. S., *Limited Dependent and Qualitative Variables in Econometrics*, Cambridge: Cambridge University Press, 1983.

Salem, D., and T. Mount, "A Convenient Descriptive Model of the Income Distribution," *Econometrica*, 42, 6, 1974, pp. 1115–1128.

Zellner, A., "Statistical Theory and Econometrics," in Z., Griliches and M., Intrilligator, eds., *Handbook of Econometrics*, Amsterdam: North Holland, 1983.

Chapter 4

Statistical Inference

4.1. Introduction

The probability distributions discussed in Chapter 3 serve as models for the underlying processes that produce our observed data. The goal of statistical inference in econometrics is to use the principles of mathematical statistics to combine these theoretical distributions and the observed data into an empirical model of the economy. This analysis takes place in one of two frameworks, Bayesian or classical. The overwhelming majority of empirical study in econometrics has been done in the classical framework. Our focus, therefore, will be on classical methods of inference. Bayesian methods will be discussed briefly in Chapter 6.[1]

4.2. Samples and Sampling Distributions

The classical theory of statistical inference centers on rules for using the sampled data effectively. These rules, in turn, are based on the properties of samples and sampling distributions.

4.2.1. Random Sampling

A sample of n observations on one or more variables, denoted $x_1, x_2, \ldots, x_n$ is a **random sample** if the n observations are drawn independently from the same population, or probability distribution, $f(x_i, \theta)$. The sample may be univariate if x_i is a single random variable or multivariate if each observation contains several variables. The vector θ contains one or more unknown parameters. Data are generally drawn in one of two settings. A **cross section** is a sample of a number of observational units all drawn at the same point in time. A **time series** is a set of observations drawn on the same observational unit at a number of (usually evenly spaced) points in time. Many recent studies have been based on time-series cross sections, which generally consist of the same cross section observed at several points in time. Since the typical data set of this sort consists of a large number of cross-sectional units

---

[1] An excellent reference is Leamer (1978). A summary of the results as they apply to econometrics is contained in Zellner (1971).

observed at a few points in time, the common term **panel data set** is usually more fitting for this sort of study.

4.2.2.   Descriptive Statistics

Before attempting to estimate parameters of a population or fit models to data, we normally examine the data themselves. One place to begin is with a **scatter diagram**, which is useful in a bivariate sample if the sample contains a reasonable number of observations. Figure 4.1 gives an example for a small data set. However, in most cases, and particularly if the number of observations in the sample is large, we shall use some summary statistics to describe the sample data. Of most interest are measures of **location**, that is, the center of the data, and **scale**, or the dispersion of the data. If the sample contains data on more than one variable, we are also interested in measures of association among the variables.

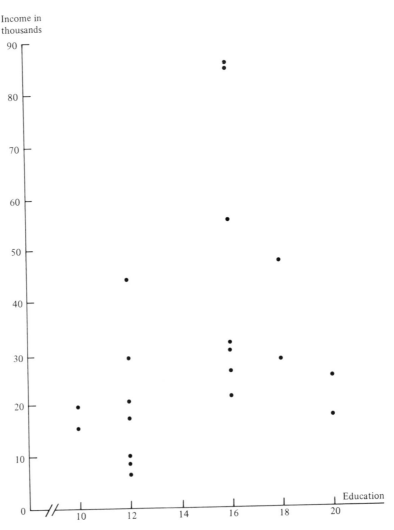

Figure 4.1   Scatter diagram.

A few measures of central tendency are as follows:

Mean: $\bar{x} = \dfrac{\sum_i x_i}{n}$.

Median: M = the middle ranked observation.

Sample midrange: midrange $= \dfrac{\text{maximum} - \text{minimum}}{2}$. (4–1)

The dispersion of the sample observations is usually measured by the

Standard deviation: $s_x = \left[\dfrac{\sum_i (x_i - \bar{x})^2}{n-1} \right]^{1/2}$. (4–2)

Other measures, such as the average absolute deviation from the sample mean, are used as well, though less frequently. If the sample is a multivariate one, the degree of linear association among the variables can be measured by the pairwise measures

Covariance: $s_{xy} = \dfrac{\sum_i (x_i - \bar{x})(y_i - \bar{y})}{n-1}$

and (4–3)

Correlation: $r_{xy} = \dfrac{s_{xy}}{s_x s_y}$.

If the sample contains data on several variables, it is sometimes convenient to arrange the covariances or correlations in a

Covariance matrix: $S = [s_{ij}]$

or [4–4]

Correlation matrix: $R = [r_{ij}]$.

Some useful algebraic results for any two variables, (x_i, y_i), $i = 1, \ldots, n$, and constants, a and b, are

$$s_x^2 = \frac{\sum_i x_i^2 - n\bar{x}^2}{n-1},$$ (4–5)

$$s_{xy} = \frac{\sum_i x_i y_i - n\bar{x}\bar{y}}{n-1},$$ (4–6)

$$-1 \le r_{xy} \le 1,$$

$$r_{ax,by} = \frac{ab}{|ab|} r_{xy} \qquad \text{for } a, b \ne 0,$$ (4–7)

$$s_{ax} = |a| s_x,$$

$$s_{ax,by} = ab s_{xy}.$$ (4–8)

Note that these algebraic results parallel the theoretical results for bivariate probability distributions.

Table 4.1   Observations on Income and Education

Observation	Income	Education	Observation	Income	Education
1	20.5	12	11	55.8	16
2	31.5	16	12	25.2	20
3	47.7	18	13	29.0	12
4	26.2	16	14	85.5	16
5	44.0	12	15	15.1	10
6	8.28	12	16	28.5	18
7	30.8	16	17	21.4	16
8	17.2	12	18	17.7	20
9	19.9	10	19	6.42	12
10	9.96	12	20	84.9	16

I = income in thousands; E = education in years.

EXAMPLE 4.1   Table 4.1 is a (hypothetical) sample of observations on income and education:

A scatter diagram appears in Figure 4.1. It suggests a weak positive association between income and education in these data.

Means:

$$\bar{I} = \tfrac{1}{20}(20.5 + \cdots + 84.9) = 31.28,$$

$$\bar{E} = \tfrac{1}{20}(12 + \cdots + 16) = 14.6.$$

Standard deviations:

$$s_I = \sqrt{\tfrac{1}{19}[(20.5 - 3.28)^2 + \cdots + (84.9 - 31.28)^2]} = 22.37,$$

$$s_E = \sqrt{\tfrac{1}{19}[(12 - 14.6)^2 + \cdots + (16 - 14.6)^2]} = 3.119.$$

Covariance:

$$\tfrac{1}{19}(20.5(12) + \cdots + 84.9(16) - 20(31.28)(14.6)) = 23.59.$$

Correlation:

$$\frac{23.59}{(22.37)(3.19)} = 0.338.$$

The positive correlation is consistent with our observation of the scatter diagram.

4.2.3. Sampling Distributions

The measures described in the previous section summarize the data in a random sample. Each measure has a counterpart in the population, that is, the distribution from which the data were drawn. Sample quantities such as the means and the correlation coefficient correspond to population expectations, while the values in Table 4.2 parallel the population pdf and cdf. In the setting of a random sample, we expect these quantities to mimic the population, though not perfectly. The precise manner in which these quantities reflect the population values defines the sampling distribution of a sample statistic.

Definition. A statistic is any function computed from the data in a sample.

Table 4.2 Income Distribution

Range	Relative Frequency	Cumulative Frequency
< 10,000	0.15	0.15
10,000–25,000	0.30	0.45
25,000–50,000	0.40	0.85
> 50,000	0.15	1.00

If another sample were drawn under identical conditions, different values would be obtained for the observations, as each one is a random variable. Consequently, the statistic is also a random variable with a probability distribution called a **sampling distribution**. For example, the following shows an exact result for the sampling behavior of a widely used statistic:

Theorem 4.1. Sampling Distribution of the Sample Mean. If $x_1, \ldots, x_n$ are a random sample from a population with mean μ and variance σ^2, then $\bar{x}$ is a random variable with mean μ and variance σ^2/n.

Proof: $\bar{x} = (1/n)\sum_i x_i$. $E[\bar{x}] = (1/n)\sum_i \mu = \mu$. The observations are independent, so $\text{Var}[\bar{x}] = (1/n)^2 \text{Var}[\sum_i x_i] = (1/n^2)\sum_i \sigma^2 = \sigma^2/n$.

Notice that the fundamental result in Theorem 4.1 does not assume a distribution for x_i.

EXAMPLE 4.2. Figure 4.2 shows a frequency plot of the means of 1000 random samples of four observations drawn from a chi-squared distribution with one degree of freedom, which has mean 1 and variance 2.

We are often interested in how a statistic behaves in a large sample or as the sample size increases. The following illustrates one such case.

EXAMPLE 4.3. If $x_1, \ldots, x_n$ are a random sample from an exponential distribution with $f(x) = \theta e^{-\theta x}$, the sampling distribution of the sample minimum in a sample of n observations, denoted $x_{(1)}$, is

$$f(x_{(1)}) = (n\theta)e^{-(n\theta)x_{(1)}}.$$

The proof is considered in the exercises. Since $E[x] = 1/\theta$ and $\text{Var}[x] = 1/\theta^2$, by analogy $E[x_{(1)}] = 1/(n\theta)$ and $\text{Var}[x_{(1)}] = 1/(n\theta)^2$. Thus, in increasingly larger samples, the minimum will be arbitrarily close to 0. (The Chebyshev inequality in Theorem 4.2 can be used to prove this intuitively appealing result.)

Sampling distributions are used to make inferences about the population. To consider a perhaps obvious example, since the sampling distribution of the mean of a set of normally distributed observations has mean μ, the sample mean is a natural candidate for an estimate of μ. The observation that the sample "mimics" the population is a statement about the sampling distributions of the sample statistics. Consider, for example, the sample data collected in Figure 4.2. The sample mean of four observations clearly has a sampling distribution, which appears to have a mean roughly equal to the population mean. This is the departure point for our theory of parameter estimation.

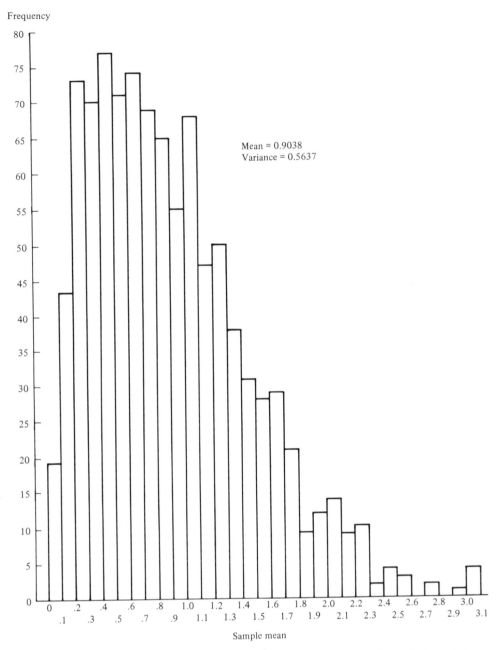

Figure 4.2 Sampling distribution of means of 1000 samples of size 4 from chi-squared (1).

4.3. *Point Estimation of Parameters*

Our objective is to use the sample data to infer the value of a parameter or set of parameters, which we denote θ. A **point estimate** is a statistic computed from a sample that gives a single value for θ. The **standard error** of the estimate is the standard deviation of the sampling distribution of the statistic; the square of this quantity is the **sampling variance**. An **interval estimate** is a range of values that will contain the true parameter with a preassigned probability. There will be a connection between the two types of estimates; generally, if $\hat{\theta}$ is the point estimate, the interval estimate will be $\hat{\theta} \pm$ a measure of sampling error.

An **estimator** is a rule or strategy for using the data to estimate the parameter. It is defined before the data are drawn. Obviously, some estimators are better than others. To take a simple example, your intuition should convince you that the sample mean would be a better estimator of the population mean than the sample minimum; the minimum is almost certain to underestimate the mean. Nonetheless, the minimum is not entirely without virtue; it is easy to compute, and ease of computation is occasionally a relevant criterion. The search for good estimators constitutes much of econometrics. Estimators are compared on the basis of a variety of attributes. **Finite sample properties** of estimators are those attributes that can be compared regardless of the sample size. Some estimation problems involve characteristics that are not known in finite samples. In these instances, estimators are compared on the basis of their large sample, or **asymptotic properties**. We consider these in turn.

4.3.1. **Estimation in a Finite Sample**

The following are some finite sample estimation criteria for estimating a single parameter. The extensions to the multiparameter case are direct. We shall consider them in passing where necessary.

Definition. An estimator of a parameter, θ, is **unbiased** if the mean of its sampling distribution is θ. Formally,

$$E[\hat{\theta}] = \theta$$

or

$$E[\hat{\theta} - \theta] = \text{Bias}[\hat{\theta} \mid \theta] = 0$$

implies that $\hat{\theta}$ is unbiased. Note that this implies that the expected sampling error is zero. If θ is a vector of parameters, the estimator is unbiased if the expected value of every element of $\hat{\theta}$ equals the corresponding element of θ.

If samples of size n are drawn repeatedly and $\hat{\theta}$ is computed for each one, the average value of these estimates will tend to equal θ. For example, the average of the 1000 sample means underlying Figure 4.2 is 0.9038, which is reasonably close to the population mean of 1. The sample minimum is clearly a biased estimator of the mean; it will almost always underestimate the mean, so it will do so on average as well.

Unbiasedness is a desirable attribute, but it is rarely used by itself as an estimation criterion. One reason is that there are many unbiased estimators that are obviously poor uses of the data. For example, in a sample of size n, the first observation drawn is an unbiased estimator of the mean that clearly wastes a great deal of information. A second criterion used to choose among unbiased estimators is efficiency.

Definition. An unbiased estimator $\hat{\theta}_1$ is more **efficient** than $\hat{\theta}_2$ if the variance of the sampling distribution of $\hat{\theta}_1$ is less than that of $\hat{\theta}_2$. That is,

$$\text{Var}[\hat{\theta}_1] < \text{Var}[\hat{\theta}_2].$$

In the multiparameter case, the comparison is based on the covariance matrices of the two estimators; $\hat{\theta}_1$ is more efficient than $\hat{\theta}_2$ if $\text{Var}[\hat{\theta}_2] - \text{Var}[\hat{\theta}_1]$ is a nonnegative definite matrix.

By this criterion, the sample mean is obviously to be preferred to the first observation as an estimator of the population mean. If σ^2 is the population variance,

$$\text{Var}[x_1] = \sigma^2 > \text{Var}[\bar{x}] = \frac{\sigma^2}{n}.$$

In discussing efficiency, we have restricted the discussion to unbiased estimators. Clearly, there are biased estimators that have smaller variances than the unbiased ones we have considered. Any constant has a variance of zero. Of course, using a constant as an estimator is not likely to be an effective use of the sample data. However, focusing on unbiasedness may still preclude a *tolerably* biased estimator with a much smaller variance. A criterion that recognizes this possible tradeoff is the mean-squared error.

Definition. The **mean-squared error** of an estimator is

$$\begin{aligned}
\text{MSE}[\hat{\theta}] &= E[(\hat{\theta} - \theta)^2] \\
&= \text{Var}[\hat{\theta}] + (\text{Bias}[\hat{\theta}])^2 \qquad \text{if } \theta \text{ is a scalar} \qquad (4\text{--}9) \\
&= \text{Var}[\hat{\theta}] + \text{Bias}[\hat{\theta}]\,\text{Bias}[\hat{\theta}]' \qquad \text{if } \theta \text{ is a vector.}
\end{aligned}$$

Figure 4.3 illustrates the effect. On average, the second estimator will be closer to the true parameter than the first, even though it is slightly biased.

EXAMPLE 4.4.   In sampling from a normal distribution, the most frequently used estimator for σ^2 is

$$s^2 = \frac{\sum_i (x_i - \bar{x})^2}{n - 1}.$$

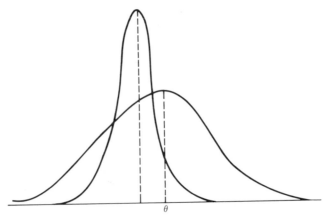

Figure 4.3   Sampling distributions.

It is straightforward to show that s^2 is unbiased, so

$$\text{Var}[s^2] = \frac{2\sigma^4}{n-1} = \text{MSE}[s^2].$$

(A proof is based on the distribution of the idempotent quadratic form $(\mathbf{x} - \mathbf{i}\mu)'\mathbf{M}^0(\mathbf{x} - \mathbf{i}\mu)$, which we discussed in Chapter 3.) A less frequently used estimator is

$$\hat{\sigma}^2 = \frac{\sum_i(x_i - \bar{x})^2}{n} = \frac{(n-1)s^2}{n}.$$

This estimator is slightly biased downward:

$$E[\hat{\sigma}^2] = \frac{(n-1)E(s^2)}{n} = \frac{(n-1)\sigma^2}{n},$$

so its bias is

$$E[\hat{\sigma}^2 - \sigma^2] = \text{Bias}[\hat{\sigma}^2] = \frac{-1}{n}\sigma^2.$$

But it has a smaller variance than s^2:

$$\text{Var}[\hat{\sigma}^2] = \left[\frac{n-1}{n}\right]^2 \frac{2\sigma^4}{n} < \text{Var}[s^2].$$

To compare the two estimators, we can use the difference in their mean-squared errors:

$$\text{MSE}[\hat{\sigma}^2] - \text{MSE}[s^2] = \sigma^4 \left[\frac{2n-1}{n^2} - \frac{2}{n-1}\right] < 0.$$

The biased estimator is a bit more precise. The difference will obviously be negligible in a large sample, but, for example, it is about 10 percent in a sample of 16.

Which of these criteria should be used in a given situation depends on the particulars of that setting and our objectives in the study.

EXAMPLE 4.5. In a **decision theoretic** setting, the purpose of estimating the parameter is to use the data to formulate a decision. The decision depends on the estimated parameter and will be erroneous if $\hat{\theta}$ does not equal the true parameter. The cost of the decision, or **loss**, will depend on the estimate and the true value of θ. Since $\hat{\theta}$ is random, so is the loss. Suppose that the cost associated with a decision is proportional to the square of the difference between the estimate and the true parameter. To minimize the expected loss, we would choose the estimator with the minimum mean-squared error.

Unfortunately, the MSE criterion is rarely operational; minimum mean-squared error estimators, when they exist at all, usually depend upon unknown parameters. Thus, we are usually less demanding. A commonly used criterion is **minimum variance unbiasedness**.

4.3.2. Efficient Unbiased Estimation

In a random sample of n observations, the density of each observation is $f(x_i, \theta)$. Since the n observations are independent, their joint density is

$$f(x_1, x_2, \ldots, x_n, \theta) = f(x_1, \theta)f(x_2, \theta)\cdots f(x_n, \theta)$$

$$= \Pi_{i=1}^n f(x_i, \theta) = L(\theta \mid x_1, x_2, \ldots, x_n). \qquad (4\text{--}10)$$

The function $L(\theta|\mathbf{x})$ is the **likelihood function** for θ given the data, $\mathbf{x}$. It is frequently abbreviated to $L(\theta)$. Where no ambiguity can arise, we shall abbreviate it further to L.

EXAMPLE 4.6. If $x_1,\dots,x_n$ are a sample of n observations from an exponential distribution with parameter θ,

$$L(\theta) = \Pi_i \theta e^{-\theta x_i}$$

$$= \theta^n e^{-\theta \Sigma_i x_i}.$$

EXAMPLE 4.7. If $x_1,\dots,x_n$ are a sample of n observations from a normal distribution with mean μ and standard deviation σ,

$$L(\mu,\sigma) = \Pi_i (2\pi\sigma^2)^{-1/2} e^{[-(1/2\sigma^2)(x_i-\mu)^2]}. \tag{4-11}$$

$$= (2\pi\sigma^2)^{-n/2} e^{[-(1/2\sigma^2)\Sigma_i(x_i-\mu)^2]}.$$

The likelihood function is the cornerstone for most of our theory of parameter estimation. An important result for efficient estimation is the following:

Cramér–Rao Lower Bound. Assuming that the density of x satisfies certain regularity conditions,[2] the variance of an unbiased estimator of a parameter, θ, will always be at least as large as

$$[I(\theta)]^{-1} = \left(-E\left[\frac{\partial^2 \ln L(\theta)}{\partial\theta^2}\right]\right)^{-1} \tag{4-12}$$

$$= (E[\partial \ln L(\theta)/\partial\theta)^2])^{-1}.$$

The quantity $I(\theta)$ *is the* **information number** for the sample.

In some cases, the second derivative of the log likelihood is a constant, so the Cramér–Rao bound is simple to obtain. For instance, in sampling from an exponential distribution, from Example 4.6,

$$\ln L = n \ln \theta - \theta \sum_i x_i,$$

$$\frac{\partial \ln L}{\partial\theta} = \frac{n}{\theta} - \sum_i x_i,$$

$$\frac{\partial^2 \ln L}{\partial\theta^2} = -\frac{n}{\theta^2}.$$

Therefore, the variance bound is

$$[I(\theta)]^{-1} = \frac{\theta^2}{n}.$$

In most situations, the second derivative is a random variable with a distribution of its own. The following examples show two such cases.

EXAMPLE 4.8. For the Poisson distribution,

$$f(x) = \frac{e^{-\theta}\theta^x}{x!},$$

---

[2] A discussion of these conditions can be found in Theil (1971, Chapter 8). They are rarely violated in the models analyzed by econometricians. For a case in which they are, see Greene (1980).

$$\ln L = -n\theta + \left(\sum_i x_i\right) \ln \theta - \sum_i \ln(x_i!),$$

$$\frac{\partial \ln L}{\partial \theta} = -n + \frac{\sum_i x_i}{\theta},$$

$$\frac{\partial^2 \ln L}{\partial \theta^2} = -\frac{\sum_i x_i}{\theta^2}.$$

The sum of n identical Poisson variables has a Poisson distribution. We have seen that the actual distribution of the first derivative will be that of a linear function of a Poisson distributed variable. Since

$$E\left[\sum_i x_i\right] = nE[x_i] = n\theta,$$

the variance bound for the Poisson distribution is

$$[I(\theta)]^{-1} = \frac{\theta}{n}.$$

Consider, finally, a multivariate case. If $\boldsymbol{\theta}$ is a vector of parameters, $\mathbf{I}(\boldsymbol{\theta})$ is the **information matrix**. The Cramér–Rao theorem states that the variance matrix of any unbiased estimator will exceed

$$[\mathbf{I}(\boldsymbol{\theta})]^{-1} = \left\{ -E\left[\frac{\partial^2 \ln L(\boldsymbol{\theta})}{\partial \boldsymbol{\theta} \partial \boldsymbol{\theta}'}\right] \right\}^{-1}$$

$$= \left\{ E\left[\left(\frac{\partial \ln L(\boldsymbol{\theta})}{\partial \boldsymbol{\theta}}\right)\left(\frac{\partial \ln L(\boldsymbol{\theta})}{\partial \boldsymbol{\theta}'}\right)\right] \right\}^{-1}$$

by a nonnegative definite matrix.

EXAMPLE 4.9. For random sampling from a normal distribution, the log-likelihood and its derivatives are

$$\ln L(\mu, \sigma^2) = -\frac{n}{2}\ln(2\pi) - \frac{n}{2}\ln \sigma^2 - \frac{1}{2\sigma^2}\sum_i (x_i - \mu)^2,$$

$$\frac{\partial \ln L}{\partial \mu} = \frac{1}{\sigma^2}\sum_i (x_i - \mu),$$

$$\frac{\partial \ln L}{\partial \sigma^2} = -\frac{n}{2\sigma^2} + \frac{1}{2\sigma^4}\sum_i (x_i - \mu)^2, \tag{4-13}$$

$$\frac{\partial^2 \ln L}{\partial \mu^2} = -\frac{n}{\sigma^2},$$

$$\frac{\partial^2 \ln L}{\partial (\sigma^2)^2} = \frac{n}{2\sigma^4} - \frac{1}{\sigma^6}\sum_i (x_i - \mu)^2,$$

$$\frac{\partial^2 \ln L}{\partial \mu \partial \sigma^2} = -\frac{1}{\sigma^4}\sum_i (x_i - \mu).$$

The information matrix contains the negatives of the expected values of the second derivatives:

$$\mathbf{I}(\mu, \sigma^2) = \begin{bmatrix} n/\sigma^2 & 0 \\ 0 & n/2\sigma^4 \end{bmatrix}.$$

Inverting this, we obtain the variance bound for unbiased estimation of μ and σ^2 of a normal distribution:

$$[\mathbf{I}(\mu, \sigma^2)]^{-1} = \begin{bmatrix} \sigma^2/n & 0 \\ 0 & 2\sigma^4/n \end{bmatrix}. \tag{4-14}$$

The normal distribution is somewhat unusual in its diagonal information matrix.

If $\hat{\mu}$ and $\hat{\sigma}^2$ are any pair of unbiased estimators for μ and σ^2, and $\mathbf{V}$ is their 2×2 covariance matrix, then $\mathbf{V} - [\mathbf{I}(\mu, \sigma^2)]^{-1}$ is a nonnegative definite matrix. Consider the two unbiased estimators

$$\hat{\mu} = \bar{x} = \frac{1}{n}\mathbf{i}'\mathbf{x},$$

$$\hat{\sigma}^2 = s^2 = \frac{\sum_i (x_i - \bar{x})^2}{n-1} = \frac{\mathbf{x}'\mathbf{M}^0\mathbf{x}}{n-1}.$$

The mean and variance of $\bar{x}$ were given in Theorem 4.1. The independence $\bar{x}$ and s^2 was shown in Chapter 3. Thus, their covariance is 0. Therefore,

$$\mathrm{Var}[\bar{x}, s^2] - [\mathbf{I}(\mu, \sigma^2)]^{-1} = \begin{bmatrix} \sigma^2/n & 0 \\ 0 & 2\sigma^4/(n-1) \end{bmatrix} - \begin{bmatrix} \sigma^2/n & 0 \\ 0 & 2\sigma^4/n \end{bmatrix}$$

$$= \begin{bmatrix} 0 & 0 \\ 0 & 2\sigma^4/(n(n-1)) \end{bmatrix}, \tag{4-15}$$

which is a nonnegative definite matrix. Note that the mean attains the variance bound, while the variance estimator does not.

In most settings, there are numerous estimators available for the parameters of a distribution. The usefulness of the Cramér–Rao bound is that if one of these is known to attain the variance bound, there is no need to consider any other in order to seek a more efficient estimator. Regarding the use of the variance bound, we emphasize that if an unbiased estimator attains it, that estimator is efficient. However, if a given estimator does not attain the variance bound, we do not know, except in a few special cases, whether this estimator is efficient or not. It may be that no unbiased estimator can attain the Cramér–Rao bound, which can leave the question of whether a given unbiased estimator is efficient or not unanswered.

We note, finally, that in some cases we further restrict the set of estimators to linear functions of the data.

Definition. An estimator is **minimum variance linear unbiased (MVLUE)** or **best linear unbiased (BLUE)** if it is a linear function of the data and has minimum variance among linear unbiased estimators.

In a few instances, such as the normal mean, there will be an efficient linear unbiased estimator; $\bar{x}$ is efficient among all unbiased estimators, both linear and nonlinear. In other cases, such as the normal variance, there is no linear unbiased estimator. This criterion is useful because we can sometimes find an MVLU estimator without having to specify the distribution at all. Thus, by limiting ourselves to a somewhat restricted class of estimators, we free ourselves from having to assume a particular distribution.

4.4. *Large-Sample Distribution Theory*[3]

In most cases, whether an estimator is exactly unbiased, or what its exact sampling variance is in samples of a given size, will be unknown. But we may be able to obtain approximate results about the behavior of the distribution of an estimator as the sample becomes large. For example, it is well known that the distribution of the mean of a sample tends to approximate normality as the sample size grows, regardless of the distribution of the individual observations. Knowledge about the limiting behavior of the distribution of an estimator can be used to infer an approximate distribution for the estimator in a finite sample. In order to describe how this is done, it is necessary, first, to present some results on convergence of random variables.

4.4.1. Convergence in Probability

Limiting arguments in this discussion will be with respect to the sample size, n. Let x_n be a random variable indexed by the size of a sample.

Definition. x_n **converges in probability** to a constant, c, if $\lim_{n \to \infty} \text{Prob}(|x_n - c| > \varepsilon) = 0$ for any positive ε.

Convergence in probability implies that the values that the variable may take that are not close to c become increasingly unlikely. To consider a well-known example, suppose that the random variable x_n takes two values, 0 and n, with probabilities $1 - (1/n)$ and $(1/n)$, respectively. As n increases, the second point will become ever more remote from any constant but, at the same time, will become increasingly less probable. In this example, x_n converges in probability to 0. The crux of this form of convergence is that all of the probability of the distribution becomes concentrated at points close to c. If x_n converges in probability to c, we write

$$\text{plim } x_n = c. \tag{4-16}$$

A special case of convergence in probability is **convergence in mean square** or **convergence in quadratic mean**.

Theorem 4.2. If x_n has mean μ_n and variance σ_n^2 such that the ordinary limits of μ_n and σ_n^2 are c and 0, respectively,

$$\text{plim } x_n = c.$$

The **Chebyshev inequality** states that for *any* random variable,

$$\text{Prob}(|x_n - \mu_n| > \varepsilon) \le \frac{\sigma_n^2}{\varepsilon^2}. \tag{4-17}$$

---

[3] An up-to-date summary of many recent developments in large-sample theory appears in White (1984).

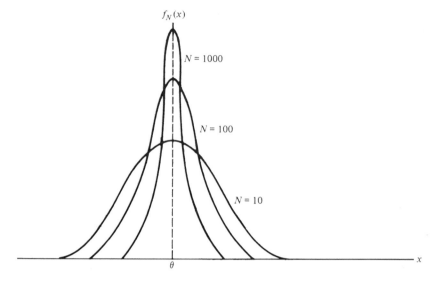

Figure 4.4   Quadratic convergence to a constant, θ.

Taking the limits of μ_n and σ_n^2 in this expression, we see that if

$$\lim_{n \to \infty} E[x_n] = c \quad \text{and} \quad \lim_{n \to \infty} \text{Var}[x_n] = 0,$$

then   (4–18)

$$\text{plim } x_n = c.$$

As we have shown, convergence in mean square implies convergence in probability. Mean-square convergence implies that the distribution of x_n collapses to a spike at plim x_n, as shown in Figure 4.4.

EXAMPLE 4.10.   As noted in Example 4.3, in sampling from an exponential distribution, for the sample minimum, $x_{(1)}$,

$$\lim_{n \to \infty} E[x_{(1)}] = \lim_{n \to \infty} \frac{1}{n\theta} = 0,$$

$$\lim_{n \to \infty} \text{Var}[x_{(1)}] = \lim_{n \to \infty} \frac{1}{(n\theta)^2} = 0.$$

Therefore,

$$\text{plim } x_{(1)} = 0.$$

Note, in particular, that the variance is divided by n^2. Thus, this estimator converges very rapidly to 0.

Convergence in probability does not imply convergence in mean square. Consider the simple example given earlier in which x_n equals either 0 or n with probabilities $1 - (1/n)$ and $(1/n)$. The exact expected value of x_n is 1 for all n, which is not the probability limit. Indeed, if we let $\text{Prob}(x_n = n^2) = (1/n)$ instead, the mean of the distribution explodes, but the probability limit is still zero. Again, the point $x_n = n^2$ becomes ever more extreme but, at the same time, becomes ever less likely. The conditions for convergence in mean square are usually easier to verify than those for the more general form. Fortunately, we shall rarely encounter circumstances in which it will be necessary to show convergence in probability in which we cannot rely upon convergence in mean square. Our most frequent use of this concept will be in formulating consistent estimators.

Definition. An estimator $\hat{\theta}$ of a parameter θ is a **consistent** estimator of θ if and only if

$$\text{plim } \hat{\theta} = \theta. \tag{4-19}$$

Theorem 4.3. The mean of a random sample from *any* population with finite mean μ and finite variance σ^2 is a consistent estimator of μ.

Proof: $E[\bar{x}] = \mu$ and $\text{Var}[\bar{x}] = \sigma^2/n$. Therefore, $\bar{x}$ converges in mean square to μ or $\text{plim } \bar{x} = \mu$.

This theorem is broader than it might appear at first.

Corollary. In random sampling, for any function $g(x)$, if $E[g(x)]$ and $\text{Var}[g(x)]$ are finite constants,

$$\text{plim } \frac{1}{n} \sum_i g(x_i) = E[g(x)]. \tag{4-20}$$

The proof follows from Theorem 4.3 by defining $y_i = g(x_i)$. The result is useful in estimation in view of the fact that $E[(1/n)\sum_i g(x_i)]$ will usually not equal $E[g(x)]$.

EXAMPLE 4.11.   In sampling from a normal distribution with mean μ and variance 1,

$$E[e^x] = e^{\mu + 1/2} \quad \text{and} \quad \text{Var}[e^x] = e^{2\mu + 2} - e^{2\mu + 1}.$$

Hence,

$$\text{plim } \frac{1}{n} \sum_i e^{x_i} = e^{\mu + 1/2}.$$

A particularly convenient result is the

Slutsky theorem. For a continuous function $g(x_n)$,

$$\text{plim } g(x_n) = g(\text{plim } x_n). \tag{4-21}$$

The generalization to a function of several random variables is direct, as illustrated in the next example.

EXAMPLE 4.12.   In random sampling from a population with mean μ and variance σ^2, the exact expected value of $\bar{x}^2/s^2$ will be difficult, if not impossible, to derive. But, by the Slutsky theorem,

$$\text{plim } \frac{\bar{x}^2}{s^2} = \frac{\mu^2}{\sigma^2}.$$

If $\text{plim } x_n = c$ and $\text{plim } y_n = d$, a few implications of the Slutsky theorem are as follows:

$$\text{plim}(x_n + y_n) = c + d, \tag{4-22}$$

$$\text{plim } x_n y_n = cd, \tag{4-23}$$

$$\text{plim } \frac{x_n}{y_n} = \frac{c}{d} \quad \text{as long as } d \neq 0, \tag{4-24}$$

and so on. The Slutsky theorem applies to functions of random vectors and matrices as well. For example, suppose that $\mathbf{W}$ is a random matrix (i.e., a matrix whose elements are random variables). Then,

$$\text{If plim } \mathbf{W} = \Omega, \text{ plim } \mathbf{W}^{-1} = \Omega^{-1}. \tag{4–25}$$

Also,

$$\text{If plim } \mathbf{X} = \mathbf{A} \text{ and plim } \mathbf{Y} = \mathbf{B}, \text{ plim } \mathbf{XY} = \mathbf{AB}. \tag{4–26}$$

4.4.2. Convergence in Distribution—Limiting Distributions

A second form of convergence is **convergence in distribution**. Let x_n be a sequence of random variables indexed by the sample size, and assume that x_n has cdf $F_n(x)$.

Definition. x_n converges in distribution to a random variable x with cdf $F(x)$ if $\lim_{n \to \infty} |F_n(x) - F(x)| = 0$ at all continuity points of $F(x)$.

Note that this is a statement about the probability distribution associated with x_n; it does not imply that x_n converges at all. To take a trivial example, suppose that the exact distribution of the random variable x_n is

$$\text{Prob}(x_n = 1) = \frac{1}{2} + \frac{1}{n+1},$$

$$\text{Prob}(x_n = 2) = \frac{1}{2} - \frac{1}{n+1}.$$

As n increases without bound, the two probabilities converge to $\frac{1}{2}$, but x_n obviously does not converge to a constant.

Definition. If x_n converges in distribution to x, where $F(x)$ is the cdf of x, then $F(x)$ is the **limiting distribution** of x. This is written

$$x_n \xrightarrow{d} x.$$

The limiting distribution is often given in terms of the pdf, or simply the parametric family. For example, "the limiting distribution of x_n is standard normal."

EXAMPLE 4.13.   Consider a sample of size n from a standard normal distribution. A familiar inference problem is the test of the hypothesis that the population mean is zero. The test statistic usually used is the t statistic:

$$t_{n-1} = \frac{\bar{x}}{s/\sqrt{n}},$$

where

$$s^2 = \frac{\sum_i (x_i - \bar{x})^2}{n-1}.$$

The exact distribution of the random variable t_{n-1} is t with $n-1$ degrees of freedom. The density is different for every n:

$$f(t_{n-1}) = \frac{\Gamma(n/2)}{\Gamma((n-1)/2)} ((n-1)\pi)^{-1/2} \left[1 + \frac{t_{n-1}^2}{n-1} \right]^{-n/2} \tag{4–27}$$

as is the cdf, $F_n(t) = \int_{-\infty}^t f_n(x)\,dx$. This distribution has mean 0 and variance $(n-1)/(n-3)$.

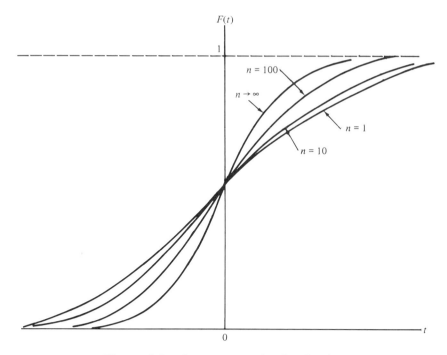

Figure 4.5   Convergence in distribution.

As discussed earlier, as n grows to infinity, t_{n-1} converges to the standard normal, which is written

$$t_{n-1} \xrightarrow{d} N[0,1].$$

Figure 4.5 shows the cdf of this random variable for several values of n.

Definition. The **limiting mean** and **variance** of a random variable are the mean and variance of the limiting distribution, assuming that the limiting distribution and its moments exist.

For the random variable with t distribution, the exact mean and variance are 0 and $n/(n-2)$, while the limiting mean and variance are 0 and 1. The example might suggest that the moments of the limiting distribution are the ordinary limits of the moments of the finite sample distributions. This is almost always true. However, it need not be the case. It is possible to construct examples in which the exact moments do not even exist, even though the moments of the limiting distribution are well defined.[4] Even in such cases, we can usually derive the mean and variance of the limiting distribution.

Limiting distributions, like probability limits, can greatly simplify the analysis of a problem. Some results that combine the two concepts are as follows:[5]

1. If $x_n \xrightarrow{d} x$ and $\text{plim } y_n = c$,

$$x_n y_n \xrightarrow{d} cx, \tag{4-28}$$

[4] See, for example, Maddala (1977, p. 150).
[5] For proofs and further discussion, see, for example, Greenberg and Webster (1983).

which means that the limiting distribution of $x_n y_n$ is the distribution of cx:

$$x_n + y_n \xrightarrow{d} x + c, \tag{4-29}$$

$$\frac{x_n}{y_n} \xrightarrow{d} \frac{x}{c} \quad \text{if } c \neq 0. \tag{4-30}$$

2. If $x_n \xrightarrow{d} x$ and $g(x_n)$ is a continuous function,

$$g(x_n) \xrightarrow{d} g(x). \tag{4-31}$$

The second of these results is analogous to the Slutsky theorem for probability limits. For an example, consider the t_n random variable discussed earlier. The *exact* distribution of t_n^2 is $F[1, n-1]$. But as n increases, t_n converges to a standard normal variable. According to the previous result, the limiting distribution of t_n^2 will be that of the square of a standard normal, which is chi-squared with one degree of freedom. We conclude, therefore, that

$$F[1, n] \xrightarrow{d} \text{chi-squared}(1). \tag{4-32}$$

We encountered this result in our earlier discussion of limiting forms of the standard normal family of distributions.

3. A result that combines convergence in distribution and in probability is

> If y_n has a limiting distribution and $\text{plim}(x_n - y_n) = 0$,
> then x_n has the same limiting distribution as y_n.

It may be possible to establish this property by using mean-square convergence.[6]

We are ultimately interested in finding a way to describe the statistical properties of estimators when their exact distributions are unknown. The concepts of consistency and convergence in probability are obviously important. But the theory of limiting distributions given earlier is not yet adequate. We rarely deal with estimators that are not consistent for something, though perhaps not always the parameter we are trying to estimate. As such, if

$$\text{plim } \hat{\theta}_n = \theta, \quad \text{then} \quad \hat{\theta}_n \xrightarrow{d} \theta.$$

That is, the limiting distribution of $\hat{\theta}_n$ is a spike. This is not very informative, nor is it at all what we have in mind when we speak of the statistical properties of an estimator. (To endow our finite sample estimator, $\hat{\theta}_n$, with the zero sampling variance of the spike at θ would be optimistic in the extreme.)

As an intermediate step, then, to a more reasonable description of the statistical properties of an estimator, we use a **stabilizing transformation** of the random variable to one that does have a well-defined limiting distribution. To jump to the most common application, whereas

$$\text{plim } \hat{\theta}_n = \theta,$$

we often find that

$$z = \sqrt{n}(\hat{\theta} - \theta) \xrightarrow{d} f(z),$$

where $f(z)$ is a well-defined distribution with a mean and a positive variance. The single most important theorem in econometrics provides an application of this proposition.

---

[6] Lucid discussion of this topic may be found in Greenberg and Webster (1983, pp. 12–13).

Central limit theorem. If $x_1, \ldots, x_n$ are a random sample from any probability distribution with finite mean μ and finite variance σ^2, and $\bar{x}_n = (1/n)\sum_i x_i$,

$$\sqrt{n}(\bar{x}_n - \mu) \xrightarrow{d} N[0, \sigma^2].$$

Notice that the central limit theorem holds regardless of the form of the parent distribution. For a striking example, return to Figure 4.2. The distribution from which the data were drawn in that example has the same shape as the chi-squared distribution shown in Figure 3.1. This is far removed from the normal distribution. However, in samples of only four observations, the force of the central limit theorem is clearly visible in the sampling distribution of the means.

The preceding is one of many forms of this extremely powerful result.[7] For our purposes, an important extension allows us to relax the assumption of equal variances. Let μ be the common mean of the x's, but suppose that they are drawn from distributions with different positive variances. Let

$$\bar{\sigma}_n^2 = \frac{1}{n}(\sigma_1^2 + \sigma_2^2 + \cdots).$$

As long as no single term dominates the average variance and the average converges to a finite constant,[8]

$$\sqrt{n}(\bar{x}_n - \mu) \xrightarrow{d} N[0, \bar{\sigma}^2] \qquad \text{where} \qquad \bar{\sigma}^2 = \lim_{n \to \infty} \bar{\sigma}_n^2.$$

In practical terms, the theorem states that sums of random variables, regardless of their form, will tend to be normally distributed. Since nearly all of the estimators we construct in econometrics fall under the purview of the central limit theorem, it is obviously an important result.

4.4.3. Asymptotic Distributions

The theory of limiting distributions is only a means to an end. We are interested in the behavior of the estimators, themselves. The limiting distributions obtained through the central limit theorem all involve unknown parameters, generally the ones we are trying to estimate. Moreover, our samples are always finite. Thus, we depart from the limit distributions to derive the asymptotic distributions of the estimators.

Definition. An **asymptotic distribution** is a distribution that is used to approximate the true finite sample distribution of a random variable.

By far the most common means of formulating an asymptotic distribution (at least by econometricians) is to construct it from the known limiting distribution of a function of the random variable. If

$$\frac{\sqrt{n}(\bar{x}_n - \mu)}{\sigma} \xrightarrow{d} N[0, 1], \tag{4-33}$$

then approximately, or asymptotically,

$$\bar{x}_n \sim N\left[\mu, \frac{\sigma^2}{n}\right],$$

---

[7] See, for example, Greenberg and Webster (1983).
[8] The result also requires that the third moment of x_i be finite. See Greenberg and Webster (1983).

Figure 4.6   True versus asymptotic distribution.

which we write

$$\bar{x}_n \xrightarrow{a} N\left[\mu, \frac{\sigma^2}{n}\right].$$ (4–34)

The statement that $\bar{x}_n$ is asymptotically normally distributed with mean μ and variance σ^2/n says only that this normal distribution provides an approximation to the true distribution, not that the true distribution is exactly normal.

   EXAMPLE 4.14.   In sampling from an exponential distribution with parameter θ, the *exact* distribution of $\bar{x}$ is that of $\theta/(2n)$ times a chi-squared variable with $2n$ degrees of freedom. The *asymptotic* distribution is $N[\theta, \theta^2/n]$. The exact and asymptotic distributions are shown in Figure 4.6 for the case of $\theta = 1$ and $n = 16$.

   Extending the definition, suppose that $\hat{\theta}$ is an estimate of the parameter vector θ. The asymptotic distribution of the vector $\hat{\theta}$ is obtained from the limiting distribution:

$$\sqrt{n}(\hat{\theta} - \theta) \xrightarrow{d} N[\mathbf{0}, \mathbf{V}]$$ (4–35)

implies that

$$\hat{\theta} \xrightarrow{a} N\left[\theta, \frac{1}{n}\mathbf{V}\right].$$ (4–36)

This is read "$\hat{\theta}$ is asymptotically normally distributed, with mean vector θ and covariance matrix $(1/n)\mathbf{V}$." The covariance matrix of the asymptotic distribution is the **asymptotic** covariance matrix and is denoted

$$\text{Asy. Var}[\hat{\theta}] = \frac{1}{n}\mathbf{V}.$$

Note, once again, the logic used to reach the result; (4–35) holds exactly as $n \to \infty$. We assume that it holds approximately for finite n, which leads to (4–36).

Definition. An estimator $\hat{\theta}$ is **asymptotically normal** if (4–35) holds. The estimator is **asymptotically efficient** if the variance matrix of any other consistent, asymptotically normally distributed estimator exceeds $(1/n)\mathbf{V}$ by a nonnegative definite matrix.

For most estimation problems, these are the criteria used to choose an estimator.

EXAMPLE 4.15.   In sampling from a normal distribution with mean μ and variance σ^2, both the mean and the median of the sample are consistent estimators of μ. Since the limiting distributions of both estimators are spikes at μ, they can only be compared on the basis of their asymptotic properties. The necessary results are

$$\bar{x} \xrightarrow{a} N\left[\mu, \frac{\sigma^2}{n}\right] \quad \text{and} \quad M \xrightarrow{a} N\left[\mu, \frac{\pi\sigma^2}{2n}\right].$$

Therefore, the mean is more efficient by a factor of $\pi/2$.

4.4.4. Asymptotic Distribution of a Nonlinear Function

At several points in Chapter 3, we used a linear Taylor series approximation to analyze the distribution and moments of a random variable. We are now able to justify this usage.

Theorem 4.4. If $\sqrt{n}(\hat{\theta} - \theta) \xrightarrow{d} N[0, \sigma^2]$, and if $g(\theta)$ is a continuous function,

$$\sqrt{n}(g(\hat{\theta}) - g(\theta)) \xrightarrow{d} N[0, \{g'(\theta)\}^2\sigma^2]$$

and

(4–37)

$$g(\hat{\theta}) \xrightarrow{a} N\left[g(\theta), \frac{\{g'(\theta)\}^2\sigma^2}{n}\right].$$

Notice that the mean and variance of the asymptotic distribution are the mean and variance of the linear approximation:

$$g(\hat{\theta}) \simeq g(\theta) + g'(\theta)(\hat{\theta} - \theta).$$

(4–38)

The generalization to a multivariate setting is direct, as the following example illustrates.

EXAMPLE 4.16.   Suppose that b and t are estimates of parameters β and θ, such that

$$\begin{bmatrix} b \\ t \end{bmatrix} \xrightarrow{a} N\left[\begin{bmatrix} \beta \\ \theta \end{bmatrix}, \begin{bmatrix} \sigma_{\beta\beta} & \sigma_{\beta\theta} \\ \sigma_{\theta\beta} & \sigma_{\theta\theta} \end{bmatrix}\right].$$

Find the asymptotic distribution of $c = b/(1 - t)$. Let $\gamma = \beta/(1 - \theta)$. By the Slutsky theorem, c is consistent for γ. We shall require

$$\frac{\partial\gamma}{\partial\beta} = \frac{1}{1 - \theta} = \gamma_\beta$$

and

$$\frac{\partial \gamma}{\partial \theta} = \frac{\beta}{(1 - \theta)^2} = \gamma_\theta.$$

Let Σ be the 2×2 asymptotic covariance matrix given previously. Then, the asymptotic variance of c is

$$(\gamma_\beta \quad \gamma_\theta)\Sigma \begin{bmatrix} \gamma_\beta \\ \gamma_\theta \end{bmatrix} = \gamma_\beta^2 \sigma_{\beta\beta} + \gamma_\theta^2 \sigma_{\theta\theta} + 2\gamma_\beta \gamma_\theta \sigma_{\beta\theta}.$$

This is the variance of the linear approximation:

$$\hat{\gamma} \simeq \gamma + \gamma_\beta(b - \beta) + \gamma_\theta(t - \theta).$$

4.4.5. Asymptotic Expectations

The asymptotic mean and variance of a random variable are usually the mean and variance of the asymptotic distribution. Thus, for an estimator with the limiting distribution defined in

$$\sqrt{n}(\hat{\theta} - \theta) \xrightarrow{d} N[0, V],$$

the asymptotic expectation is θ and the asymptotic variance is $(1/n)V$. This implies, among other things, that the estimator is "asymptotically unbiased."

At the risk of clouding the issue a bit, it is necessary to reconsider one aspect of the previous description. We have deliberately avoided the use of consistency in spite of the fact that, in most instances, that is what we have in mind. The description thus far might suggest that consistency and asymptotic unbiasedness are the same. Unfortunately (because it is a source of some confusion), they are not. They are if the estimator is consistent and asymptotically normally distributed, or CAN, as would be obvious from the earlier definition. However, they may differ in other settings. There are at least three possible definitions of asymptotic unbiasedness:

1. The mean of the limiting distribution of $\sqrt{n}(\hat{\theta} - \theta)$ is 0.
2. $\text{Lim}_{n \to \infty} E[\hat{\theta}] = \theta.$
3. $\text{Plim } \hat{\theta} = \theta.$

In most cases encountered in practice, the estimator in hand will have all three properties, so there is no ambiguity. However, it is not difficult to construct cases in which the left-hand sides of all three definitions are different.[9] There is no general agreement among authors as to the precise meaning of asymptotic unbiasedness, perhaps because the term is misleading at the outset; *asymptotic* refers to an approximation, while *unbiasedness* is an exact result.[10] Nonetheless, the majority view seems to be that (2), is the proper definition of asymptotic unbiasedness.[11] Note, though, that this definition relies upon quantities that are generally unknown and that may not exist.

[9] See, for example, Maddala (1977, p. 150).
[10] See, for example, Theil (1971, p. 377).
[11] Many studies of estimators analyze the "asymptotic bias" of, say, $\hat{\theta}$ as an estimator of a parameter, θ. In most cases, the quantity of interest is actually $\text{plim}[\hat{\theta} - \theta]$. See, for example, Greene (1980) and another example in Johnston (1984, p. 312).

A similar problem arises in the definition of the asymptotic variance of an estimator. One common definition is

$$\text{Asy. Var}[\hat{\theta}] = \frac{1}{n} \lim_{n \to \infty} E\left[\left\{\sqrt{n}\left(\hat{\theta} - \lim_{n \to \infty} E[\hat{\theta}]\right)\right\}^2\right],\qquad(4\text{--}39)$$

which is based on the exact mean and variance.[12] This is a **leading term approximation**, and it will be sufficient for nearly all applications. Note, however, that like definition (2) of asymptotic unbiasedness, it relies on unknown and possibly nonexistent quantities.

EXAMPLE 4.17.   In any population, the exact expected value and variance of the variance estimator

$$m_2 = \frac{1}{n} \sum_i (x_i - \mu)^2 \qquad(4\text{--}40)$$

are

$$E[m_2] = \frac{(n-1)\sigma^2}{n} \qquad(4\text{--}41)$$

and

$$\text{Var}[m_2] = \frac{\mu_4 - \sigma^4}{n} - \frac{2(\mu_4 - 2\sigma^4)}{n^2} + \frac{\mu_4 - 3\sigma^4}{n^3}, \qquad(4\text{--}42)$$

where

$$\mu_4 = E[(x - \mu)^4].^{[13]}$$

The leading term approximation would be

$$\text{Asy. Var}[m_2] = \frac{\mu_4 - \sigma^4}{n}.$$

The formal definition given in (4–39) is adequate if the exact variance is "of order $1/n$."

Definition: c_n is of order $1/n$, denoted $O(1/n)$, if plim nc_n is a nonzero constant.

Definition: c_n is of order less than $1/n$, denoted $o(1/n)$, if plim nc_n equals 0.

For example, the variance of the sample minimum in Example 4.3 is $o(1/n)$ because n times this variance still converges to zero. But we have already encountered an ordinary situation in which this approximation is inadequate. In sampling from an exponential distribution, the variance of the sample minimum is $O(1/n^2)$. If we use the definition just given, the asymptotic variance is 0, which would be a poor approximation to the variance in a finite sample.

The point of this discussion is to emphasize the need for care and precision in formulating asymptotic distributions. The central limit theorem and the surrounding results allow the simple formulation of the correct asymptotic distribution in the vast majority of cases encountered in econometrics. However, there are relatively common situations, particularly in theoretical econometrics, in which some caution is warranted.

---

[12] Kmenta (1986, p. 165).
[13] A proof appears in Goldberger (1964, pp. 97–99).

4.4.6. Consistent Estimation

There are some situations in which all we require is a consistent estimator of some parameter; efficiency is secondary. Examples are the correlation coefficient in the $AR(1)$ regression model, the disturbance covariance matrix in a multiple equation model, the correlation coefficient in the sample selection model, and the disturbance variances in some heteroscedastic regressions.

A technique used in many such cases is the **method of moments**. The principle of this method is as follows: As suggested by the preceding, in random sampling a sample statistic will converge in probability to some constant. For example, $(1/n)\sum_i x_i^2$ will converge in mean square to the variance plus the squared mean of the distribution of x. This quantity will, in turn, be a function of the unknown parameters of the distribution. To estimate M parameters, $\theta_1, \ldots, \theta_M$, we compute M statistics from the sampled data, $m_1, \ldots, m_M$, whose probability limits are known functions of the parameters. These M moments are equated to these functions, and the functions are inverted to express the parameters as functions of the moments. The Slutsky theorem guarantees that these estimates will be consistent.[14]

EXAMPLE 4.18.   In sampling from $N[\mu, \sigma^2]$,

$$\text{plim}\frac{1}{n}\sum_i x_i = \text{plim } m_1' = \mu$$

and

$$\text{plim}\frac{1}{n}\sum_i x_i^2 = \text{plim } m_2' = \sigma^2 + \mu^2.$$

(A standard notation for $(1/n)\sum_i x_i^r$ is m_r'.) Equating the right- and left-hand sides of the probability limits, we obtain

$$\hat{\mu} = m_1'$$

and

$$\hat{\sigma}^2 = m_2' - m_1'^2.$$

Note that the estimator of σ^2 is biased, though both estimators are consistent.

EXAMPLE 4.19.   In sampling from a gamma distribution (see Section 13.5.5),

$$f(x) = \frac{\lambda^P}{\Gamma(P)}e^{-\lambda x}x^{P-1},$$

$$\text{plim}\frac{1}{n}\sum_i x_i = \frac{P}{\lambda},$$

$$\text{plim}\frac{1}{n}\sum_i x_i^2 = \frac{P(P+1)}{\lambda^2},$$

$$\text{plim}\frac{1}{n}\sum_i \ln(x_i) = \frac{d\ln\Gamma(P)}{dP},$$

---

[14] An interesting application of the technique appears in Quandt and Ramsey (1978) and the accompanying comments and rejoinder.

and

$$\text{plim}\frac{1}{n}\sum_i\left(\frac{1}{x_i}\right)=\frac{\lambda}{(P-1)}.$$

Any pair of these equations could be used to estimate λ and P.

In most cases in which it is available, the method of moments is extremely simple to use. However, it is rarely efficient; it is minimum variance only in those cases in which the moment estimates are functions of sufficient statistics.[15]

4.5. Efficient Estimation—Maximum Likelihood

The principle of **maximum likelihood** provides a means of choosing an asymptotically efficient estimator for a parameter or a set of parameters. The logic of the technique is best illustrated in the setting of a discrete distribution. Consider a random sample of 10 observations from a Poisson distribution: 5, 0, 1, 1, 0, 3, 2, 3, 4, and 1. The density for each observation is

$$f(x_i,\theta)=\frac{e^{-\theta}\theta^{x_i}}{x_i!}.$$

Since the observations are independent, their joint density, which was identified earlier as the **likelihood** for the sample, is

$$f(x_1,x_2,\ldots,x_{10}\,|\,\theta)=\Pi_{i=1}^{10}f(x_i,\theta)$$
$$=\frac{e^{-10\theta}\theta^{\Sigma_i x_i}}{\Pi x_i!}$$
$$=\frac{e^{-10\theta}\theta^{20}}{207,360}.$$

The last line gives the probability of observing *this particular sample*, assuming that a Poisson distribution with as yet unknown parameter θ generated the data. What value of θ would make this sample most probable? Figure 4.7 plots this function for various values of θ. It has a single mode at $\theta=2$, which would be the maximum likelihood estimate of θ.

Consider maximizing the function directly. Since the log function is monotonically increasing and easier to work with, we usually maximize $\ln L(\theta)=\mathscr{L}(\theta)$ instead:

$$\ln L(\theta)=-10\theta+20\ln\theta-12.242,$$
$$\frac{d\ln L(\theta)}{d\theta}=-10+\frac{20}{\theta}=0\Rightarrow\hat{\theta}=2,$$

and

$$\frac{d^2\ln L(\theta)}{d\theta^2}=\frac{-20}{\theta^2}<0\Rightarrow\text{ this is a maximum.}$$

[15] See Kendall and Stuart (1961, pp. 1–29) for a discussion of sufficient statistics.

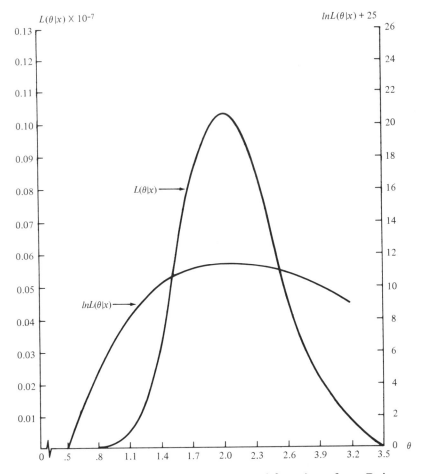

Figure 4.7   Likelihood and loglikelihood functions for a Poisson distribution.

Of course, the solution is the same as before. Figure 4.7 also plots the log of L to illustrate the result.

In a continuous distribution, the analogy to the probability of observing the given sample is not exact, since a particular sample has probability zero. However, the principle is the same for either. The joint density of the n observations, which may be univariate (x_i) or multivariate ($\mathbf{x}_i$), is the product of the individual densities. This joint density is the **likelihood function**, defined as a function of the unknown parameter vector, $\boldsymbol{\theta}$:

$$f(\mathbf{x}_1, \ldots, \mathbf{x}_n, \boldsymbol{\theta}) = \Pi_i f(\mathbf{x}_i, \boldsymbol{\theta})$$
$$= L(\boldsymbol{\theta} \mid \mathbf{X}),$$

(4–43)

where $\mathbf{X}$ is used to indicate the sample data. It is usually simpler to work with the log of the likelihood function;

$$\ln L(\boldsymbol{\theta} \mid \mathbf{X}) = \sum_i \ln f(\mathbf{x}_i, \boldsymbol{\theta}).$$

(4–44)

The values of the parameters that maximize this function are the **maximum likelihood estimates**, generally denoted $\hat{\theta}$. Since the logarithm is a monotonic function, the values that maximize L are the same as those that maximize $\ln L$. The likelihood function and its logarithm, evaluated at $\hat{\theta}$, are usually denoted $\hat{L}$ and $\ln \hat{L}$, respectively. The necessary condition for maximizing $\ln L(\theta)$ is

$$\frac{\partial \ln L(\theta)}{\partial \theta} = 0, \tag{4-45}$$

which is called the **likelihood equation**.

EXAMPLE 4.20.   In sampling from a Poisson population,

$$\ln L(\theta) = -n\theta + (\ln \theta) \sum_i x_i - \sum_i \ln(x_i!),$$

$$\frac{d \ln L(\theta)}{d\theta} = -n + \frac{1}{\theta} \sum_i x_i = 0 \Rightarrow \hat{\theta} = \bar{x}.$$

EXAMPLE 4.21.   In sampling from a normal distribution with mean μ and variance σ^2, the log-likelihood function and the likelihood equations for μ and σ^2 are

$$\ln L(\mu, \sigma^2) = -\frac{n}{2}\ln(2\pi) - \frac{n}{2}\ln \sigma^2 - \frac{1}{2}\sum_i \left[\frac{(x_i - \mu)^2}{\sigma^2}\right], \tag{4-46}$$

$$\frac{\partial \ln L}{\partial \mu} = \frac{1}{\sigma^2}\sum_i (x_i - \mu) = 0, \tag{4-47}$$

and

$$\frac{\partial \ln L}{\partial \sigma^2} = -\frac{n}{2\sigma^2} + \frac{1}{2\sigma^4}\sum_i (x_i - \mu)^2 = 0. \tag{4-48}$$

To solve the likelihood equations, multiply (4–47) by σ^2 and solve for $\hat{\mu}$; then insert this solution in (4–48) and solve for σ^2. The solutions are

$$\hat{\mu} = \frac{1}{n}\sum_i x_i = \bar{x}$$

and $\tag{4-49}$

$$\hat{\sigma}^2 = \frac{1}{n}\sum_i (x_i - \bar{x})^2.$$

EXAMPLE 4.22. Multivariate Normal Mean Vector.   Consider, finally, sampling from a multivariate normal distribution with mean vector $\boldsymbol{\mu} = (\mu_1, \mu_2, \ldots, \mu_M)$ and variance matrix $\sigma^2 \mathbf{I}$. (The M random variables each have a different mean but a common variance, σ^2, and they are uncorrelated.) The sample consists of n multivariate observations, $\mathbf{x}_1, \ldots, \mathbf{x}_n$. The density for each observation, from (3–95), is

$$f(\mathbf{x}_i) = (2\pi)^{-M/2}|\sigma^2 \mathbf{I}|^{-1/2}e^{-1/2(\mathbf{x}_i - \boldsymbol{\mu})'[\sigma^2 \mathbf{I}]^{-1}(\mathbf{x}_i - \boldsymbol{\mu})}$$

$$= (2\pi)^{-M/2}(\sigma^2)^{-M/2}e^{-1/2\sigma^2(\mathbf{x}_i - \boldsymbol{\mu})'(\mathbf{x}_i - \boldsymbol{\mu})}.$$

Taking logs and summing over the sample gives the log likelihood for n observations:

$$\ln L = -\frac{nM}{2}\ln(2\pi) - \frac{nM}{2}\ln \sigma^2 - \frac{1}{2\sigma^2}\sum_i (\mathbf{x}_i - \boldsymbol{\mu})'(\mathbf{x}_i - \boldsymbol{\mu}).$$

To obtain the maximum likelihood estimators, we require

$$\frac{\partial \ln L}{\partial \mu} = \frac{1}{\sigma^2} \sum_i (\mathbf{x}_i - \mu) = \mathbf{0}$$

and

$$\frac{\partial \ln L}{\partial \sigma^2} = -\frac{nM}{2\sigma^2} - \frac{1}{2\sigma^4} \sum_i (\mathbf{x}_i - \mu)'(\mathbf{x}_i - \mu).$$

Solving the first set of equations gives, as might be expected,

$$\hat{\mu}_i = \bar{x}_i.$$

Inserting this solution in the second condition gives

$$\hat{\sigma} = \frac{\sum_i \sum_j (x_{ij} - \bar{x}_j)^2}{nM}.$$

4.5.1. Properties of Maximum Likelihood Estimators

Maximum likelihood estimators are most attractive because of their large-sample or asymptotic properties. If we assume that the regularity conditions stated earlier are met by $f(\mathbf{x}, \theta)$,[16] the maximum likelihood estimator will have the following **asymptotic properties**:

1. It is consistent:[17]

$$\text{plim } \hat{\theta}_{\text{ML}} = \theta.$$

2. It is asymptotically normally distributed:[18]

$$\hat{\theta} \xrightarrow{a} N[\theta, \{\mathbf{I}(\theta)\}^{-1}].$$

3. It is asymptotically efficient and achieves the Cramér–Rao lower bound for consistent estimators:

$$\text{Asy. Var}[\hat{\theta}_{\text{ML}}] = -\left\{ E\left[\frac{\partial^2 \ln L(\theta)}{\partial \theta \partial \theta'} \right] \right\}^{-1}$$

$$= \left\{ E\left[\left(\frac{\partial \ln L(\theta)}{\partial \theta} \right)\left(\frac{\partial \ln L(\theta)}{\partial \theta'} \right) \right] \right\}^{-1}.$$

These three properties explain the prevalence of the maximum likelihood technique in econometrics. The second one greatly facilitates hypothesis testing and the construction of interval estimates. The third one is a particularly powerful result. The MLE has the minimum variance achievable by a consistent estimator. It is important to note, however, that these are asymptotic properties. The finite sample properties of the MLE are usually unknown. When they are known, we sometimes find that the MLE is not the best estimator in a small sample.

EXAMPLE 4.23. For the likelihood function in Example 4.22, the second derivatives are

$$\frac{\partial^2 \ln L}{\partial \mu \partial \mu'} = -\frac{n}{\sigma^2} \mathbf{I},$$

---

[16] Discussions of these conditions can be found in Theil (1971) and Greenberg and Webster (1983).

[17] It may, however, be biased. For example, the MLE of σ^2 in a normal distribution is biased downward. See (4–49) and Example 4.4.

[18] A proof of this, which is based on the central limit theorem, may be found in Theil (1971) or in Norden (1972). Another extensive source on the theory of maximum likelihood estimation is Kendall and Stuart (1961).

$$\frac{\partial^2 \ln L}{\partial (\sigma^2)^2} = \frac{nM}{2\sigma^4} + \frac{1}{\sigma^6} \sum_i (\mathbf{x}_i - \boldsymbol{\mu})'(\mathbf{x}_i - \boldsymbol{\mu}),$$

$$\frac{\partial^2 \ln L}{\partial \boldsymbol{\mu} \partial \sigma^2} = -\frac{1}{\sigma^4} \sum_i (\mathbf{x}_i - \boldsymbol{\mu}).$$

For the asymptotic variance of the maximum likelihood estimator, we need the expectations of these derivatives. The first is nonstochastic, and the third has expectation $\mathbf{0}$, as $E[\mathbf{x}_i] = \boldsymbol{\mu}$. That leaves the second, which you can verify has expectation $-nM/(2\sigma^4)$ because each of the n terms $(\mathbf{x}_i - \boldsymbol{\mu})'(\mathbf{x}_i - \boldsymbol{\mu})$ has expected value $M\sigma^2$. Collecting these in the information matrix, reversing the sign, and inverting the matrix gives the asymptotic covariance matrix for the maximum likelihood estimators:

$$\left\{ -E\left[\frac{\partial^2 \ln L}{\partial \boldsymbol{\theta} \partial \boldsymbol{\theta}'}\right]\right\}^{-1} = \begin{bmatrix} \sigma^2 \mathbf{I}/n & \mathbf{0} \\ \mathbf{0}' & 2\sigma^4/(nM) \end{bmatrix}.$$

The asymptotic covariance matrix for estimating a single mean and the variance of a normal distribution is given in (4–14) in Example 4.9. Notice that the preceding expression is analogous for the means but differs in the divisor for the variance. In this case, instead of one estimator of σ^2, we have M, which explains the difference.

Finally, maximum likelihood estimators have a very useful feature.

Invariance. If $\hat{\boldsymbol{\theta}}_{\text{ML}}$ is the maximum likelihood estimate of $\boldsymbol{\theta}$ and if $g(\boldsymbol{\theta})$ is a continuous function, the maximum likelihood estimate of $g(\boldsymbol{\theta})$ is $g(\hat{\boldsymbol{\theta}}_{\text{ML}})$.

For the asymptotic distribution of $g(\hat{\boldsymbol{\theta}})$, we refer to our earlier general set of results. The invariance property has two useful practical implications. First, if estimates have already been obtained for a set of parameters, and estimates are desired for a function of them, there is no need to reestimate the model. For example, to estimate σ from a normal distribution, we may simply use the square root of $\hat{\sigma}^2$. Second, the invariance principle implies that we are free to **reparameterize** a likelihood function in any way we like, which may simplify estimation.

4.5.2. Estimating the Variance of the Maximum Likelihood Estimate

The asymptotic covariance matrix of the maximum likelihood estimate is a matrix of parameters that must be estimated. (That is, it is a function of $\boldsymbol{\theta}$ that is being estimated.) If the form of the expected values of the second derivatives of the log likelihood is known,

$$[\mathbf{I}(\boldsymbol{\theta})]^{-1} = \left\{ -E\left[\frac{\partial^2 \ln L(\boldsymbol{\theta})}{\partial \boldsymbol{\theta} \partial \boldsymbol{\theta}'}\right]\right\}^{-1} \tag{4–50}$$

can be evaluated at $\hat{\boldsymbol{\theta}}$ to estimate the variance matrix for the MLE. This estimator will rarely be available. The second derivatives of the log likelihood will almost always be complicated nonlinear functions of the data, whose exact expected values will be unknown. There are, however, two alternatives. A second estimator is

$$[\hat{\mathbf{I}}(\hat{\boldsymbol{\theta}})]^{-1} = \left(\frac{-\partial^2 \ln L(\hat{\boldsymbol{\theta}})}{\partial \hat{\boldsymbol{\theta}} \partial \hat{\boldsymbol{\theta}}'}\right)^{-1}. \tag{4–51}$$

This is computed simply by evaluating the actual (not expected) second derivatives matrix of the log-likelihood function at the maximum likelihood estimates. It is straightforward to show that this amounts to estimating the expected second derivatives of the density with the sample mean of this quantity. Result (4–20) can be used to justify the computation. The only shortcoming of this estimator is that the second derivatives can be complicated to derive and program for a computer. A third estimator based on the result that the expected second derivatives matrix is the variance matrix of the first derivatives vector[19] is

$$[\hat{\mathbf{I}}(\hat{\theta})]^{-1} = \left[\sum_i \hat{\mathbf{g}}_i \hat{\mathbf{g}}_i' \right]^{-1}, \tag{4-52}$$

where

$$\hat{\mathbf{g}}_i = \frac{\partial \ln f(\mathbf{x}_i, \hat{\theta})}{\partial \hat{\theta}}.$$

For a single parameter, this is just the reciprocal of the sum of squares of the first derivatives. This estimator is extremely convenient, in most cases, because it does not require any computations beyond those required to solve the likelihood equation.[20]

EXAMPLE 4.24.   The sample data in Table 4.1 are generated by a model of the form

$$f(y_i, \beta) = \frac{1}{\beta + x_i} e^{-y_i/(\beta + x_i)},$$

where $y = $ income and $x = $ education. To find the maximum likelihood estimate of β, we maximize

$$\ln L(\beta) = -\sum_i \ln(\beta + x_i) - \sum_i \frac{y_i}{\beta + x_i}.$$

The likelihood equation is

$$\frac{\partial \ln L(\beta)}{\partial \beta} = -\sum_i \frac{1}{\beta + x_i} + \sum_i \frac{y_i}{(\beta + x_i)^2} = 0, \tag{4-53}$$

which has the solution $\hat{\beta} = 15.60275$. To compute the asymptotic variance of the MLE, we require

$$\frac{\partial^2 \ln L(\beta)}{\partial \beta^2} = \sum_i \frac{1}{(\beta + x_i)^2} - 2\sum_i \frac{y_i}{(\beta + x_i)^3}. \tag{4-54}$$

Since $E(y_i) = \beta + x_i$ is known, the exact form of the expected value in (4–54) is known. Inserting $\beta + x_i$ for y_i in (4–54) and taking the reciprocal yields the first variance estimate, 44.255. Simply inserting $\hat{\beta} = 15.60275$ in (4–54) and taking the reciprocal gives the second estimate, 46.164. Finally, by computing the reciprocal of the sum of squares of first derivatives of the densities evaluated at $\hat{\beta}$,

$$[\hat{\mathbf{I}}(\hat{\beta})]^{-1} = \frac{1}{\sum_i [-1/(\hat{\beta} + x_i) + y_i/(\hat{\beta} + x_i)^2]^2},$$

we obtain the Berndt et al. estimate, 100.512.

None of the three estimators given previously is preferable to the others on statistical grounds; all are asymptotically equivalent. In most cases, the third will be easiest to compute. One caution is in order. As the example illustrates, they can give different results in a finite

[19] See, for example, Theil (1971, Chapter 8).
[20] It appears to have been advocated first in the econometrics literature in Berndt et al. (1974).

sample. This is an unavoidable finite sample problem that can, in some cases, lead to different statistical conclusions. The example is a case in point. Using the usual procedures, we would reject the hypothesis that $\beta = 0$ if either of the first two variance estimators were used, but not if the third were used.

4.6. *Interval Estimation*

Regardless of the properties of an estimator, the estimate obtained will vary from sample to sample, and there is some probability that it will be quite erroneous. A point estimate will not provide any information on the likely range of error. The logic behind an **interval estimate** is that we use the sample data to construct an interval, [lower(**X**), upper(**X**)], such that we can expect this interval to contain the true parameter in some specified proportion of samples, or equivalently, with some desired level of confidence. Clearly, the wider the interval, the more confident we can be that it will, in any given sample, contain the parameter being estimated.

The theory of interval estimation is based on a **pivotal quantity**, which is a function of both the parameter and a point estimate that has a known distribution. Consider the following examples.

EXAMPLE 4.25. In sampling from a normal distribution with mean μ and standard deviation σ,

$$z = \frac{\sqrt{n}(\bar{x} - \mu)}{s} \sim t[n - 1], \tag{4-55}$$

$$c = \frac{(n - 1)s^2}{\sigma^2} \sim \chi^2[n - 1]. \tag{4-56}$$

Given the pivotal quantity, we can make probability statements about events involving the parameter and the estimate. Let $p(g, \theta)$ be the constructed random variable, for example, z or c. Given a prespecified **confidence level**, $1 - \alpha$, we can state that

$$\text{Prob}(\text{lower} < p(g, \theta) < \text{upper}) = 1 - \alpha, \tag{4-57}$$

where lower and upper are obtained from the appropriate table. This statement is then manipulated to make equivalent statements about the endpoints of the intervals. For example, the following statements are equivalent:

$$\text{Prob}\left[-Z < \frac{\sqrt{n}(\bar{x} - \mu)}{s} < Z \right] = 1 - \alpha,$$

$$\text{Prob}\left[\bar{x} - \frac{Zs}{\sqrt{n}} < \mu < \bar{x} + \frac{Zs}{\sqrt{n}} \right] = 1 - \alpha.$$

Note that the second of these is a statement about the interval, not the parameter; that is, it is the interval that is random, not the parameter. We attach a probability, or $100(1 - \alpha)$ percent confidence level, to the interval itself; in repeated sampling, an interval constructed in this fashion will contain the true parameter $100(1 - \alpha)$ percent of the time.

In general, the interval constructed by this method will be of the form

$$\text{Lower}(\mathbf{X}) = \hat{\theta} - e_1,$$

$$\text{Upper}(\mathbf{X}) = \hat{\theta} + e_2,$$

where **X** is the sample data, e_1 and e_2 are sampling errors, and $\hat{\theta}$ is a point estimate of θ. It is clear from the preceding example that if the sampling distribution of the pivotal quantity is either t or standard normal, which will be true in the vast majority of cases we encounter in practice, then the confidence interval will be

$$\hat{\theta} \pm C_{(1-\alpha)/2}[\mathrm{se}(\hat{\theta})], \qquad (4-58)$$

where se$(\cdot)$ is the (known or estimated) standard error of the parameter estimate and $C_{(1-\alpha)/2}$ is the value from the t or standard normal distribution that is exceeded with probability $(1 - \alpha)/2$. The usual values for α are 0.10, 0.05, or 0.01.

EXAMPLE 4.26.   In a sample of 25,

$$\bar{x} = 1.63 \qquad \text{and} \qquad s = 0.51.$$

Construct a 95 percent confidence interval for μ. Assuming that the sample of 25 is from a normal distribution,

$$\mathrm{Prob}\left(-2.064 < \frac{5(\bar{x} - \mu)}{s} < 2.064\right) = 0.95,$$

where 2.064 is the critical value from a t distribution with 24 degrees of freedom. Thus, the confidence interval is

$$1.63 \pm \frac{2.064(0.51)}{5} \qquad \text{or} \qquad [1.4195, \ 1.8405].$$

Remark.   Had the parent distribution not been specified, it would have been natural to use the standard normal distribution instead, perhaps relying on the central limit theorem. But a sample size of 25 is small enough that the more conservative t distribution might still be preferable.

The theory does not prescribe exactly how to choose the endpoints for the confidence interval. An obvious criterion is to minimize the width of the interval. If the sampling distribution is symmetric, the symmetric interval is the best one. If the sampling distribution is not symmetric, however, this procedure will not be optimal.

EXAMPLE 4.27.   The chi-squared distribution is used to construct a confidence interval for the variance of a normal distribution. Using the data from the previous example, we find that the usual procedure would use

$$\mathrm{Prob}\left(12.4 < \frac{24s^2}{\sigma^2} < 39.4\right) = 0.95,$$

where 12.4 and 39.4 are the 0.025 and 0.975 cutoff points from the chi-squared(24) distribution. This leads to the 95 percent confidence interval $[0.1581, 0.5032]$. By making use of the asymmetry of the distribution, a narrower interval can be constructed. Allocating 4 percent to the left-hand tail and 1 percent to the right instead of 2.5 percent to each, the two cutoff points are 13.4 and 42.9, and the resulting 95 percent confidence interval is $[0.1455, 0.4659]$.[21]

Finally, the confidence interval can be manipulated in an obvious fashion to obtain a confidence interval for a function of a parameter. For example, based on the preceding, a 95 percent confidence interval for σ would be $[\sqrt{0.1581}, \sqrt{0.5032}] = [0.3976, 0.7094]$.

---

[21] Formal conditions for finding the narrowest interval are considered in Exercise 18.

4.7. *Hypothesis Testing*

The second major group of statistical inference procedures is hypothesis tests. The classical testing procedures are based on constructing a statistic from a random sample that will enable the analyst to decide, with reasonable confidence, whether or not the data in the sample would have been generated by a hypothesized population. The formal procedure involves a statement of the hypothesis, usually in terms of a "null" or maintained hypothesis and an alternative, conventionally denoted H_0 and H_1, respectively. The procedure itself is a rule, stated in terms of the data, that dictates whether the null hypothesis should be rejected or not. For example, the hypothesis might state that a parameter is equal to a specified value. The decision rule might state that the hypothesis should be rejected if a sample estimate of that parameter is too far away from that value (where "far" remains to be defined). More generally, the classical, or Neyman–Pearson, methodology involves partitioning the sample space into two regions. If the observed data (i.e., the test statistic) fall in the **rejection region** (sometimes called the **critical region**), the null hypothesis is rejected; if they fall in the **acceptance region**, it is not.

4.7.1. Testing Procedures

Since the sample is random, the test statistic, however defined, is also random. The same test procedure can lead to different conclusions in different samples. As such, there are two ways such a procedure can be in error:

1. **Type I error.** The procedure may lead to rejection of the null hypothesis when it is true.

2. **Type II error.** The procedure may fail to reject the null hypothesis when it is false.

To continue the previous example, there is some probability that the estimate of the parameter will be quite far from the hypothesized value, even if the hypothesis is true. This might cause a type I error.

Definition. The probability of a type I error is the **size** of the test. This is conventionally denoted α and $(1 - \alpha)$ is usually called the **significance level**.

The size of the test is under the control of the analyst. It can be changed just by changing the decision rule. Indeed, the type I error could be eliminated altogether just by making the rejection region very small. But this would come at a cost. By eliminating the probability of a type I error, that is, by making it unlikely that the hypothesis is rejected, we must increase the probability of a type II error. Ideally, we would like both probabilities to be as small as possible. However, it is clear that there is a tradeoff between the two. The best we can hope for is that for a given probability of type I error, the procedure we choose will have as small a probability of type II error as possible.

Definition. The **power** of a test is the probability that it will correctly lead to rejection of a false null hypothesis:

$$\text{Power} = 1 - \beta = 1 - \text{Prob(type II error)}. \tag{4-59}$$

For a given significance level, $(1 - \alpha)$, we would like β to be as small as possible. Since β is defined in terms of the alternative hypothesis, it depends on the true value of the parameter.

EXAMPLE 4.28. For testing $H_0: \mu = \mu^0$ in a normal distribution with known variance, σ^2, the decision rule is to reject the hypothesis if the absolute value of the z statistic,

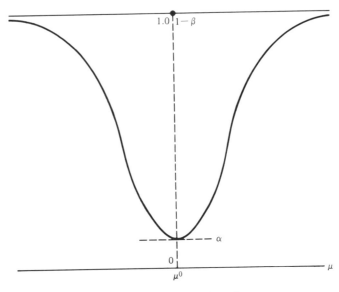

Figure 4.8   Power function for a test.

$\sqrt{n}(\bar{x} - \mu^0)/\sigma$, exceeds the predetermined critical value. For a test at the 95 percent signif-icance level, we set the critical value at 1.96. The power of the test is, therefore, the probabil-ity that the absolute value of the test statistic will exceed 1.96 given that the true value of μ is, in fact, not μ^0. This depends on the alternative value of μ, as shown in Figure 4.8. Notice that for this test the power is equal to the size at the point where μ equals μ^0. As might be expected, the test becomes more powerful the farther the true mean is from the hypothesized value.

Hypothesis tests, like estimators, can be compared using a number of criteria.

Definition. A test is **most powerful** if it has greater power than any other test of the same size.

This is a very strong requirement. Since the power depends on the alternative hypothesis, we might require that the test be **uniformly most powerful (UMP)**, that is, have greater power than any other test of the same size for all admissable values of the parameter. There are few situations in which a UMP test is available. We usually must be less stringent in our requirements. Nonetheless, the criteria for comparing hypothesis testing procedures are generally based on their respective power functions. A common and very modest re-quirement is that the test be unbiased.

Definition. A test is **unbiased** if its power $(1 - \beta)$ is greater than its size α for all values of the parameter.

If a test is **biased**, then for some values of the parameter, we are more likely to accept the null hypothesis when it is false than when it is true.

The use of the term *unbiased* here is unrelated to the concept of an unbiased estimator. Fortunately, there is little chance of confusion. However, tests and estimators are clearly connected. The following criterion derives, in general, from the corresponding attribute of a parameter estimate.

Definition. A test is **consistent** if its power goes to one as the sample size grows to infinity.

EXAMPLE 4.29.   A confidence interval for the mean of a normal distribution is $\bar{x} \pm t_{(1-\alpha)/2}(s/\sqrt{n})$, where $\bar{x}$ and s are the usual consistent estimators for μ and σ, n is the sample size, and $t_{(1-\alpha)/2}$ is the correct critical value from the t distribution with $n-1$ degrees of freedom. For testing $H_0: \mu = \mu_0$ versus $H_1: \mu \neq \mu_0$, let the procedure be to reject H_0 if the confidence interval does not contain μ_0. Since $\bar{x}$ is consistent for μ, if H_0 is false, as $n \to \infty$, this will be discernible with probability 1, as $\bar{x}$ will be arbitrarily close to the true μ. Therefore, this test is consistent.

As a general rule, a test will be consistent if it is based on a consistent estimate of the parameter.

4.7.2.   Tests Based on Confidence Intervals

There is an obvious link between interval estimation and the sorts of hypothesis tests we have been discussing here. The confidence interval gives a range of plausible values for the parameter. Therefore, it stands to reason that if a hypothesized value of the parameter does not fall in this range of plausible values, the data are not consistent with the hypothesis, and it should be rejected. Consider, then, testing

$$H_0: \theta = \theta_0,$$

$$H_1: \theta \neq \theta_0.$$

We form a confidence interval based on $\hat{\theta}$ as described earlier;

$$\hat{\theta} - C_{(1-\alpha)/2}[\text{se}(\hat{\theta})] < \theta < \hat{\theta} + C_{(1-\alpha)/2}[\text{se}(\hat{\theta})].$$

H_0 is rejected if θ_0 exceeds the upper limit or is less than the lower limit. Equivalently, H_0 is rejected if

$$\left| \frac{(\hat{\theta} - \theta_0)}{\text{se}(\hat{\theta})} \right| > C_{(1-\alpha)/2}.$$

In words, the hypothesis is rejected if the estimate is too far from θ_0, where the distance is measured in standard error units. The critical value is taken from the t or standard normal distribution, whichever is appropriate.

EXAMPLE 4.30.   For the results in Example 4.26, test $H_0: \mu = 1.98$ versus $H_1: \mu \neq 1.98$, assuming sampling from a normal distribution.

$$t = \left| \frac{(\bar{x} - 1.98)}{(s/\sqrt{n})} \right| = \left| \frac{(1.63 - 1.98)}{0.102} \right| = 3.43.$$

The 95 percent critical value for $t(24)$ is 2.064. Therefore, reject H_0. If the critical value from the standard normal table of 1.96 is used instead, the same result is obtained.

If the test is one-sided, as in

$$H_0: \theta > \theta_0,$$

$$H_1: \theta \leq \theta_0,$$

the critical region must be adjusted. Thus, for this test, H_0 will be rejected if a point estimate of θ falls sufficiently below θ_0. (One-sided tests can be set up by departing from the decision criterion "What sample results are inconsistent with the hypothesis?".)

EXAMPLE 4.31.   A sample of 25 from a normal distribution yields $\bar{x} = 1.63$ and $s = 0.51$. Test

$$H_0: \mu < 1.5,$$
$$H_1: \mu \geq 1.5.$$

Obviously, no observed $\bar{x}$ less than or equal to 1.5 will lead to rejection of H_0. Using the borderline value of 1.5 for μ, we obtain

$$\text{Prob}\left[\frac{\sqrt{n}(\bar{x} - 1.5)}{s} > \frac{5(1.63 - 1.5)}{0.51}\right] = \text{Prob}[t_{24} > 1.27].$$

This is approximately 0.11. This is not unlikely by the usual standards. Hence, at a significance level of 0.89, we would not reject the hypothesis.

4.7.3. Three Asymptotically Equivalent Test Procedures

The next several sections will discuss the most commonly used test procedures—the likelihood ratio, Wald, and Lagrange multiplier tests. We consider maximum likelihood estimation of a parameter, θ, and a test of the hypothesis $H_0: c(\theta) = 0$. The logic of the tests can be seen in Figure 4.9.[22] The figure plots the log-likelihood function, $\ln L(\theta)$, its derivative with respect to θ, $d\ln L(\theta)/d\theta$, and the constraint, $c(\theta)$. There are three approaches to testing the hypothesis suggested in the figure:

Likelihood ratio test.   If the restriction, $c(\theta) = 0$, is valid, imposing it should not lead to a large reduction in the log-likelihood function. Therefore, we base the test on the difference, $\ln L - \ln L_R$, where L is the value of the likelihood function at the unconstrained value of θ and L_R is the value of the likelihood function at the restricted estimate.

Wald test.   If the restriction is valid, $c(\hat{\theta}_{MLE})$ should be close to zero, since the MLE is consistent. Therefore, the test is based on $c(\hat{\theta}_{MLE})$. We reject the hypothesis if this is significantly different from zero.

Lagrange multiplier test.   If the restriction is valid, the restricted estimator should be near the point that maximizes the log-likelihood. Therefore, the slope of the log-likelihood function should be near zero at the restricted estimator. The test is based on the slope of the log likelihood at the point where the function is maximized subject to the restriction.

These three tests are asymptotically equivalent, but they can behave rather differently in a small sample. Unfortunately, their small-sample properties are unknown, except in a few special cases. As a consequence, the choice among them is typically made on the basis of ease of computation. The likelihood ratio test requires calculation of both restricted and unrestricted estimators. If both are simple to compute, this will be a convenient way to proceed. The Wald test requires only the unrestricted estimator, and the Lagrange multiplier test requires only the restricted estimator. In some problems, one of these estimators may be much easier to compute than the other. For example, a linear model is simple to estimate but becomes nonlinear and cumbersome if a nonlinear constraint is imposed. In this case, the

---

[22] See Buse (1982).

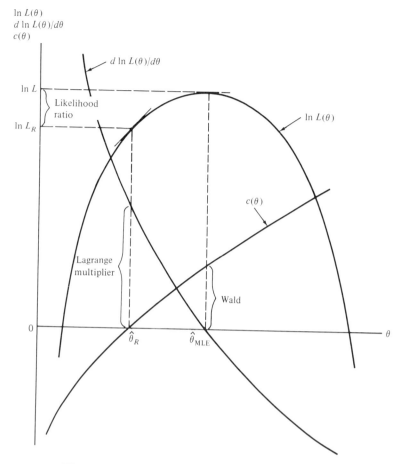

Figure 4.9 Three bases for hypothesis tests.

Wald statistic would be preferable. Alternatively, restrictions sometimes amount to the removal of nonlinearities, which would make the Lagrange multiplier test the simpler procedure.

4.7.3a. The Likelihood Ratio Test

Let θ be a vector of parameters to be estimated, and let H_0 specify some sort of restriction on these parameters. Let $\hat{\theta}_U$ be the maximum likelihood estimate of θ obtained without regard to the constraints, and let θ_R be the constrained maximum likelihood estimator. If $\hat{L}_U$ and $\hat{L}_R$ are the likelihood functions evaluated at these two estimates, then the **likelihood ratio** is

$$\lambda = \frac{\hat{L}_R}{\hat{L}_U}. \tag{4-60}$$

This function must be between 0 and 1. Both likelihoods are positive, and $\hat{L}_R$ cannot be larger than $\hat{L}_U$. (A restricted optimum is never superior to an unrestricted one.) If λ is too small, doubt is cast on the restrictions.

An example from a discrete distribution helps to fix these ideas. In estimating from a sample of 10 from a Poisson distribution at the beginning of Section 4.5, we found the MLE of the parameter θ to be 2. At this value, the likelihood, which is the probability of observing the sample we did, is 0.104×10^{-8}. Are these data consistent with H_0 $\theta = 1.8$? $L_R = 0.0936 \times 10^{-8}$, which is, as expected, smaller. This particular sample is somewhat less probable under the hypothesis.

The formal test procedure is based on the following result:

Definition: Likelihood ratio test statistic: Under regularity, the large sample distribution of $-2 \ln \lambda$ is chi-squared, with degrees of freedom equal to the number of restrictions imposed.

The null hypothesis is rejected if this value exceeds the appropriate critical value from the chi-squared tables. Thus, for the Poisson example,

$$-2 \ln \lambda = -2 \ln \left(\frac{0.0936}{0.104} \right) = 0.21072.$$

This chi-squared statistic with one degree of freedom is not significant at any conventional level, so we would not reject the hypothesis that $\theta = 1.8$ on the basis of this test.[23]

Before considering some other test procedures, a few comments about this test statistic are in order. It is tempting to use the likelihood ratio test to test a simple null hypothesis against a simple alternative. For example, we might be interested in the Poisson setting in testing H_0: $\theta = 1.8$ against H_1: $\theta = 2.2$. Unfortunately, the test cannot be used in this fashion. The degrees of freedom of the chi-squared statistic for the likelihood ratio test equals the reduction in the number of dimensions in the parameter space that results from imposing the restrictions. In testing a single null hypothesis against a single alternative, this is zero.[24] Second, one sometimes encounters an attempt to test one distributional assumption against another with a likelihood ratio test; for example, a certain model will be estimated assuming a normal distribution and then assuming a t distribution. The ratio of the two likelihoods is then compared to determine which distribution is preferred. This is also inappropriate. The parameter spaces, and hence the likelihood functions of the two cases, are unrelated. The calculation does make some sense in a Bayesian setting, in which it is related to the posterior odds ratio. This is one of a number of cases in which the Bayesian approach is more flexible than the classical method. In the classical method, some progress has been made in testing distributional assumptions; see, for example, the tests of normality discussed in Chapter 10.

4.7.3b.   The Wald Test

A practical shortcoming of the likelihood ratio test is that it requires estimation of both the restricted and unrestricted parameter vectors. In complex models, one or the other of these estimates may be very difficult to compute. It would be unfortunate if this precluded testing of the hypothesis. Fortunately, there are two alternative testing procedures, the Wald test and the Lagrange multiplier test, which circumvent this problem. Both tests are based on an estimator that is asymptotically normally distributed.

These two tests are based on the distribution of the full rank quadratic form considered at the end of the previous chapter. Specifically,

$$\text{If } \mathbf{x} \sim N_J[\boldsymbol{\mu}, \boldsymbol{\Sigma}], (\mathbf{x} - \boldsymbol{\mu})'\boldsymbol{\Sigma}^{-1}(\mathbf{x} - \boldsymbol{\mu}) \sim \text{chi-squared}[J]. \tag{4-61}$$

---

[23] Of course, our use of the large-sample result in a sample of 10 might be questionable.
[24] Note that because both likelihoods are restricted in this instance, there is nothing to prevent $-2 \ln \lambda$ from being negative.

In the setting of a hypothesis test, under the hypothesis that $E(\mathbf{x}) = \mu$, the quadratic form has the chi-squared distribution. However, if the hypothesis that $E(\mathbf{x}) = \mu$ is false, the quadratic form just given will, on average, be larger than it would be if the hypothesis were true.[25] This condition forms the basis for the test statistics discussed in this and the next section.

Let $\hat{\theta}$ be the vector of parameter estimates obtained without restrictions. We hypothesize a set of restrictions

$$H_0: \mathbf{c}(\theta) = \mathbf{q}.$$

If the restrictions are valid, then at least approximately, $\hat{\theta}$ should satisfy them. However, if the hypothesis is erroneous, $\mathbf{c}(\hat{\theta}) - \mathbf{q}$ should be farther from $\mathbf{0}$ than would be explained by sampling variability alone. The device we use to formalize this notion is the Wald test.

Definition. Wald test statistic:

$$W = (\mathbf{c}(\hat{\theta}) - \mathbf{q})'(\text{Var}[\mathbf{c}(\hat{\theta}) - \mathbf{q}])^{-1}(\mathbf{c}(\hat{\theta}) - \mathbf{q}). \tag{4-62}$$

Under H_0, W has a chi-squared distribution with degrees of freedom equal to the number of restrictions (i.e., the number of equations in $\mathbf{c}(\theta) = \mathbf{q}$).

This test is analogous to the chi-squared statistic in (4-61) if $\mathbf{c}(\hat{\theta}) - \mathbf{q}$ is normally distributed, with a hypothesized mean of $\mathbf{0}$. A large value of W leads to rejection of the hypothesis. Note, finally, that W only requires computation of the unrestricted model. One must still compute the variance matrix appearing in the preceding quadratic form. This is the variance of a possibly nonlinear function, which we treated earlier.

$$\text{Var}[\mathbf{c}(\hat{\theta}) - \mathbf{r}] = \mathbf{C}\,\text{Var}[\hat{\theta}]\mathbf{C}',$$

$$\mathbf{C} = \left[\frac{\partial \mathbf{c}(\hat{\theta})}{\partial \hat{\theta}'}\right]. \tag{4-63}$$

That is, $\mathbf{C}$ is the $J \times K$ matrix whose jth row is the derivatives of the jth constraint with respect to the K elements of θ. A common application occurs in testing a set of linear restrictions.

For testing a set of linear restrictions, $\mathbf{R}\theta = \mathbf{q}$, the Wald test would be based on

$$H_0: \mathbf{c}(\theta) - \mathbf{q} = \mathbf{R}\theta - \mathbf{q} = \mathbf{0},$$

$$\mathbf{C} = \left[\frac{\partial \mathbf{c}(\hat{\theta})}{\partial \hat{\theta}'}\right] = \mathbf{R}, \tag{4-64}$$

$$\text{Var}[(\hat{\theta}) - \mathbf{q}] = \mathbf{R}\,\text{Var}[\hat{\theta}]\mathbf{R}'$$

and

$$W = [\mathbf{R}\hat{\theta} - \mathbf{q}]'[\mathbf{R}\,\text{Var}(\hat{\theta})\mathbf{R}']^{-1}[\mathbf{R}\hat{\theta} - \mathbf{q}].$$

The degrees of freedom is the number of rows in $\mathbf{R}$.

EXAMPLE 4.32. If $\mathbf{c}(\theta) - \mathbf{q}$ is a single restriction, the Wald test will be the same as the test based on the confidence interval previously developed. If the test is

$$H_0: \theta = \theta_0 \quad \text{vs.} \quad H_1: \theta \neq \theta_0,$$

[25] If the mean is not μ, the statistic in (4-61) will have a **noncentral chi-squared distribution**. This distribution has the same basic shape as the central chi-squared distribution, with the same degrees of freedom, but lies to the right of it. Thus, a random draw from the noncentral distribution will tend, on average, to be larger than a random observation from the central distribution.

then the earlier test is based on

$$z = \frac{|\hat{\theta} - \theta_0|}{s(\hat{\theta})}, \qquad (4\text{--}65)$$

where s is the estimated asymptotic standard error. The test statistic is compared to the appropriate value from the standard normal table. The Wald test will be based on

$$W = [(\hat{\theta} - \theta_0) - 0](\text{Var}[(\hat{\theta} - \theta_0) - 0])^{-1}[(\hat{\theta} - \theta_0) - 0]$$

$$= \frac{(\hat{\theta} - \theta_0)^2}{\text{Var}[\hat{\theta}]} \qquad (4\text{--}66)$$

$$= z^2.$$

Here W has a chi-squared distribution with one degree of freedom, which is, of course, the distribution of the square of the standard normal test statistic in (4–65).

EXAMPLE 4.33. Testing a Hypothesis About a Mean.   For sampling from a normal distribution, the Wald statistic for testing the hypothesis that the mean takes a particular value is simply the square of the t statistic in Example 4.30 or the t ratio, which uses s^2 instead of σ^2 if σ^2 is unknown. Consider the multivariate example in Example 4.22, in which we obtained the maximum likelihood estimate of a vector of means. Suppose that we wished to test the hypothesis that the means of the M distributions were all equal. There are two cases to consider. First, we might have a particular value, μ^0, in mind. Using the results from that example and the variance matrix we derived in Example 4.23, we find that the Wald statistic would be

$$W = (\bar{\mathbf{x}} - \mu^0 \mathbf{i})' \left(\frac{s^2}{n} \mathbf{I} \right)^{-1} (\bar{\mathbf{x}} - \mu^0 \mathbf{i})$$

$$= \frac{n}{s^2} (\bar{\mathbf{x}} - \mu^0 \mathbf{i})' (\bar{\mathbf{x}} - \mu^0 \mathbf{i}).$$

where $\bar{\mathbf{x}}$ is the vector of sample means. This statistic would be asymptotically distributed as chi-squared with M degrees of freedom. A slightly less restrictive hypothesis is that the means are equal, but we do not have a specific value in mind. This imposes only $M - 1$ restrictions. The statistic is the same one, except that μ^0 must be replaced with a consistent estimator of the common mean, for which we can use $\bar{\bar{x}} = (1/(nM))\Sigma_i\Sigma_j x_{ij}$.

To summarize, then, the Wald test is based on measuring the extent to which the unrestricted estimates fail to satisfy the hypothesized restrictions.

4.7.3c.   The Lagrange Multiplier Test

The second test procedure is the **Lagrange Multiplier (LM)** or **efficient score** test. It is based on the restricted model instead of the unrestricted model. Suppose that we maximize the log-likelihood subject to the set of constraints $c(\theta) - q = 0$. Let λ be a vector of Lagrange multipliers. The necessary conditions for maximizing the Lagrangean function, $\ln L^*$, are

$$\frac{\partial \ln L^*}{\partial \theta} = \frac{\partial \ln L(\theta)}{\partial \theta} + C'\lambda = 0,$$

$$\frac{\partial \ln L^*}{\partial \lambda} = 0, \qquad (4\text{--}67)$$

where $\mathbf{C}'$ is the transpose of the matrix in the second line of(4–63). If the restrictions are valid, imposing them will not lead to a significant difference in the maximized value of the likelihood function. In the first-order conditions, this will mean that the second term in the derivative vector will be small. In particular, λ will be small. We could test this directly; that is, test $H_0: \lambda = \mathbf{0}$, which leads to the Lagrange multiplier test. However, there is an equivalent simpler formulation. At the restricted maximum, the derivatives of the unrestricted log likelihood are

$$\frac{\partial \ln L(\theta)}{\partial \theta} = -\mathbf{C}'\lambda. \tag{4–68}$$

If the restrictions are valid, at least within the range of sampling variability,

$$\frac{\partial \ln L(\hat{\theta}_R)}{\partial \hat{\theta}_R} \simeq \mathbf{0}.$$

That is, the derivatives of the log likelihood evaluated at the **restricted** parameter vector will be approximately zero. The vector of first derivatives of the log likelihood is the vector of **efficient scores**. Since the test is based on this vector, it is called the **score test** as well as the Lagrange multiplier test. The variance of the first derivative vector is the information matrix, which we have used to compute the asymptotic variance matrix of the MLE. Therefore, the test statistic, based on reasoning analogous to that behind the Wald test statistic, is

Definition. Lagrange multiplier test statistic:

$$\mathrm{LM} = \left(\frac{\partial \ln L(\hat{\theta}_R)}{\partial \hat{\theta}_R}\right)' [I(\hat{\theta}_R)]^{-1} \left(\frac{\partial \ln L(\hat{\theta}_R)}{\partial \hat{\theta}_R}\right). \tag{4–69}$$

LM has a chi-squared distribution with degrees of freedom equal to the number of restrictions. All terms are computed at the restricted estimator.

4.7.4. An Example of the Test Procedures

Consider, again, the data in Table 4.1. In Example 4.24, the parameter β in the model

$$f(y_i, \beta) = \frac{1}{(\beta + x_i)} e^{[-y_i/(\beta + x_i)]} \tag{4–70}$$

was estimated by maximum likelihood. This exponential density is a restricted form of the more general gamma distribution:

$$f(y_i, \beta, \rho) = \frac{(\beta + x_i)^{-\rho}}{\Gamma(\rho)} y_i^{\rho-1} e^{-y_i/(\beta + x_i)}. \tag{4–71}$$

The restriction is $\rho = 1.$[26] We consider testing

$$H_0: \rho = 1 \qquad \text{versus} \qquad H_1: \rho \neq 1,$$

using the various procedures developed previously.

[26] The gamma function, $\Gamma(\rho)$, and the gamma distribution are described in Chapter 3 and the appendix to Chapter 3.

The log likelihood and its derivatives are

(a) $\ln L(\beta, \rho) = -\rho \sum_i \ln(\beta + x_i) - n \ln \Gamma(\rho) - \sum_i \dfrac{y_i}{\beta + x_i} + (\rho - 1) \sum_i \ln y_i,$

(b) $\dfrac{\partial \ln L}{\partial \beta} = -\rho \sum_i \dfrac{1}{\beta + x_i} + \sum_i \dfrac{y_i}{(\beta + x_i)^2},$

(c) $\dfrac{\partial \ln L}{\partial \rho} = -\sum_i \ln(\beta + x_i) - \dfrac{n \Gamma'(\rho)}{\Gamma(\rho)} + \sum_i \ln y_i,$ (4-72)

(d) $\dfrac{\partial^2 \ln L}{\partial \beta^2} = \rho \sum_i \dfrac{1}{(\beta + x_i)^2} - 2 \sum_i \dfrac{y_i}{(\beta + x_i)^3},$

(e) $\dfrac{\partial^2 \ln L}{\partial \rho^2} = -\dfrac{n[\Gamma(\rho) \Gamma''(\rho) - \Gamma'(\rho)^2]}{\Gamma(\rho)^2},$

(f) $\dfrac{\partial^2 \ln L}{\partial \beta \partial \rho} = -\sum_i \dfrac{1}{\beta + x_i}.$

Maximum likelihood estimates are obtained by equating the two first derivatives to zero, with and without the restriction. The results are shown in Table 4.3.

CONFIDENCE INTERVAL TEST.   A 95 percent confidence interval for ρ based on the unrestricted estimates is

$$3.151 \pm 1.96\sqrt{0.6625} = [1.556, \quad 4.746].$$

This does not contain $\rho = 1$; therefore, the hypothesis is rejected.

Table 4.3   Maximum Likelihood Estimates

Quantity	Unrestricted	Restricted
β	-4.719	15.603
ρ	3.151	1.000
$\ln \hat{L}$	-82.916	-88.436
$\dfrac{\partial \ln \hat{L}}{\partial \hat{\beta}}$	0.000	0.000
$\dfrac{\partial \ln \hat{L}}{\partial \hat{\rho}}$	0.000	7.914
$\dfrac{\partial^2 \ln \hat{L}}{\partial \hat{\beta}^2}$	-0.8534	-0.02166
$\dfrac{\partial^2 \ln \hat{L}}{\partial \hat{\rho}^2}$	-7.436	-32.894
$\dfrac{\partial^2 \ln \hat{L}}{\partial \hat{\beta} \partial \hat{\rho}}$	-2.242	-0.6689
$\text{Vâr}(\hat{\beta})$	5.773	46.164
$\text{Vâr}(\hat{\rho})$	0.6625	0.000
$\text{Côv}(\hat{\beta}, \hat{\rho})$	-1.746	0.000

LIKELIHOOD RATIO TEST.   The likelihood ratio test statistic is

$$\lambda = -2[-88.436 - (-82.916)] = 11.04.$$

The table value for the test, with one degree of freedom, is 3.842. The hypothesis is again rejected.

WALD TEST.   The Wald test is based on the unrestricted estimates. For this restriction,

$$c(\theta) - q = \rho - 1,$$

$$\frac{dc(\hat{\rho})}{d\hat{\rho}} = 1,$$

$$\text{Vâr}[c(\hat{\rho}) - q] = \text{Vâr}[\hat{\rho}] = 0.6625,$$

$$W = (3.151 - 1)[0.6625]^{-1}(3.151 - 1) = 6.984.$$

The critical value is the same as the previous one; hence, H_0 is again rejected. Note that the Wald test statistic is the square of the corresponding test statistic that would be used in the confidence interval test:

$$\frac{|3.151 - 1|}{\sqrt{0.6625}} = 2.626.$$

LAGRANGE MULTIPLIER TEST.   The Lagrange multiplier test is based on the restricted estimates:

$$LM = [0.000 \quad 7.914] \begin{bmatrix} 0.02166 & 0.6689 \\ 0.6689 & 32.89 \end{bmatrix}^{-1} \begin{bmatrix} 0.000 \\ 7.914 \end{bmatrix} = 5.120.$$

The conclusion is the same as before.

    Note that the latter three test statistics have substantially different values. It is possible to reach different conclusions depending upon which one is used. For example, if the test had been carried out at the 1 percent significance level instead of the 5 percent level, the critical value from the chi-squared table would be 6.635. The hypothesis would then have been rejected if the test were based on the likelihood ratio or the Wald test statistics, but not if it were based on the LM statistic. Asymptotically, all three tests are equivalent. However, in a finite sample, differences such as these are to be expected, particularly in a small sample such as ours.[27] Unfortunately, there is no clear rule for how to proceed in such a case. Its possibility, however, does highlight the problem of relying upon a particular significance level and drawing a firm reject/accept conclusion based on sample evidence.

Exercises

1. The following sample is drawn from a normal distribution with mean μ and standard deviation σ:

$$x = 1.3, \quad 2.1, \quad 0.4, \quad 1.3, \quad 0.5, \quad 0.2, \quad 1.8, \quad 2.5, \quad 1.9, \quad 3.2.$$

Compute the mean, median, variance, and standard deviation of the sample.

[27] For further discussion of this problem, see Berndt and Savin (1977).

2. Using the data in the previous example, test the following hypotheses:

$$\mu > 2.$$

$$\mu < 0.7.$$

$$\sigma^2 = 0.5.$$

Using a likelihood ratio test, test the following hypothesis:

$$\mu = 1.8, \qquad \sigma^2 = 0.8.$$

3. Suppose that the following sample is drawn from a normal distribution with mean μ and standard deviation σ:

$$y = 3.1, \quad -0.1, \quad 0.3, \quad 1.4, \quad 2.9, \quad 0.3, \quad 2.2, \quad 1.5, \quad 4.2, \quad 0.4.$$

Test the hypothesis that the mean of the distribution that produced these data is the same as the one that produced the data in Exercise 1. Test the hypothesis, assuming that the variances are the same. Test the hypothesis that the variances are the same, using an F test and using a likelihood ratio test. (Do not assume that the means are the same.)

4. A common method of simulating random draws from the standard normal distribution is to compute the sum of 12 draws from the uniform $[0, 1]$ distribution and subtract 6. Can you justify this procedure?

5. Using the data in Exercise 1, form confidence intervals for the mean and standard deviation.

6. Based on a sample of 65 observations from a normal distribution, you obtain a *median* of 34 and a standard deviation of 13.3. Form a confidence interval for the mean. (**Hint:** Use the asymptotic distribution; see Example 4.15.) Compare your confidence interval to the one you would have obtained had the estimate of 34 been the sample mean instead of the sample median.

7. The random variable x has a continuous distribution $f(x)$ and a cumulative distribution function $F(x)$. What is the probability distribution of the sample maximum? (**Hint:** In a random sample of n observations, $x_1, x_2, \ldots, x_n$, if z is the maximum, every observation in the sample is less than or equal to z. Use the cdf.)

8. Assume that the distribution of x is

$$f(x) = \frac{1}{\theta}, \qquad 0 \le x \le \theta.$$

In random sampling from this distribution, prove that the sample maximum is a consistent estimator of θ. *Note:* You can prove that the maximum is the maximum likelihood estimator of θ. But the usual properties do not apply here. Why not? (**Hint:** Attempt to verify that the expected first derivative of the log likelihood with respect to θ is zero.)

9. In random sampling from the exponential distribution,

$$f(x) = \frac{1}{\theta} e^{-x/\theta}, \qquad x \ge 0, \qquad \theta > 0,$$

find the maximum likelihood estimator of θ and obtain the asymptotic distribution of this estimator.

10. Suppose that in a sample of 500 observations from a normal distribution with mean μ and standard deviation σ, you are told that 35 percent of the observations are less than 2.1 and 55 percent are less than 3.6. Estimate μ and σ.

11. For random sampling from a normal distribution with nonzero mean μ and standard deviation σ, find the asymptotic joint distribution of the maximum likelihood estimators of σ/μ and μ^2/σ^2.

12. The random variable x has the following distribution:

$$f(x) = \frac{e^{-\lambda}\lambda^x}{x!}, \qquad x = 0, 1, 2, \dots.$$

The following random sample is drawn:

$$1, \quad 1, \quad 4, \quad 2, \quad 0, \quad 0, \quad 3, \quad 2, \quad 3, \quad 5, \quad 1, \quad 2, \quad 1, \quad 0, \quad 0.$$

Carry out a Wald test of the hypothesis that $\lambda = 2$.

13. Based on random sampling of 16 observations from the exponential distribution of Exercise 9, we wish to test the hypothesis that $\theta = 1$. We will reject the hypothesis if $\bar{x}$ is greater than 1.2 or less than 0.8. We are interested in the power of this test.

(a) Using the asymptotic distribution of $\bar{x}$, graph the asymptotic approximation to the true power function.

(b) Using the result discussed in Example 4.14, describe how to obtain the true power function for this test.

14. *Testing for normality.* One method that has been suggested for testing whether the distribution underlying a sample is normal is to refer the statistic

$$L = n\left[\frac{\text{skewness}^2}{6} + \frac{(\text{kurtosis} - 3)^2}{24}\right]$$

to the chi-squared distribution with two degrees of freedom. Using the data in Exercise 1, carry out the test. (**Hint:** To compute the statistic, use the sample estimates of the coefficients defined in Section 3.3.)

15. *Mixture distribution.* Suppose that the joint distribution of the two random variables x and y is

$$f(x, y) = \frac{\theta e^{-(\beta + \theta)y}(\beta y)^x}{x!} \qquad \beta, \theta > 0, \qquad y \ge 0, \qquad x = 0, 1, 2, \dots.$$

(a) Find the maximum likelihood estimators of β and θ and their asymptotic joint distribution.

(b) Find the maximum likelihood estimator of $\theta/(\beta + \theta)$ and its asymptotic distribution.

(c) Prove that $f(x)$ is of the form

$$f(x) = \gamma(1 - \gamma)^x, \qquad x = 0, 1, 2, \dots.$$

Then find the maximum likelihood estimator of γ and its asymptotic distribution.

(d) Prove that $f(y\mid x)$ is of the form

$$\frac{\lambda e^{-\lambda y}(\lambda y)^x}{x!}.$$

Prove that $f(y \mid x)$ integrates to 1. Find the maximum likelihood estimator of λ and its asymptotic distribution. (**Hint:**   In the conditional distribution, just carry the x's along as constants.)

(e) Prove that

$$f(y) = \theta e^{-\theta y}.$$

Then find the maximum likelihood estimator of θ and its asymptotic variance.

(f) Prove that

$$f(x \mid y) = \frac{e^{-\beta y}(\beta y)^x}{x!}.$$

Based on this distribution, what is the maximum likelihood estimator of β?

16. Suppose that x has the Weibull distribution:

$$f(x) = \alpha \beta x^{\beta-1} e^{-\alpha x^\beta}, \qquad x > 0, \qquad \alpha, \beta > 0.$$

(a) Obtain the log-likelihood function for a random sample of n observations.

(b) Obtain the likelihood equations for maximum likelihood estimation of α and β. Note that the first provides an explicit solution for α in terms of the data and β. But after inserting this in the second, we obtain only an implicit solution for β. How would you obtain the maximum likelihood estimators?

(c) Obtain the second derivatives matrix of the log likelihood with respect to α and β. The exact expectations of the elements involving β include the derivatives of the gamma function and are quite messy analytically. Of course, your exact result provides an empirical estimator. How would you estimate the asymptotic covariance matrix for your estimators in part (b)?

(d) Prove that $\alpha\beta \mathrm{Cov}(\ln x, x^\beta) = 1$. (**Hint:**   Use the fact that the expected first derivatives of the log-likelihood function are zero.)

17. The following data were generated by the Weibull distribution of the previous exercise:

1.3043	0.49254	1.2742	1.4019	0.32556	0.29965	0.26423
1.0878	1.9461	0.47615	3.6454	0.15344	1.2357	0.96381
0.33453	1.1227	2.0296	1.2797	0.96080	2.0070	

(a) Obtain the maximum likelihood estimates of α and β, and give the asymptotic covariance matrix for the estimates.

(b) Carry out a Wald test of the hypothesis that $\beta = 1$.

(c) Obtain the maximum likelihood estimate of α under the hypothesis that $\beta = 1$.

(d) Using the results of parts (a) and (c), carry out a likelihood ratio test of the hypothesis that $\beta = 1$.

(e) Carry out a Lagrange multiplier test of the hypothesis that $\beta = 1$.

18. We consider forming a confidence interval for the variance of a normal distribution. As shown in Example 4.27, the interval is formed by finding c_{lower} and c_{upper} such that

$$\mathrm{Prob}[c_{\text{lower}} < \chi^2[n-1] < c_{\text{upper}}] = 1 - \alpha.$$

The endpoints of the confidence interval are then $(n-1)s^2/c_{\text{upper}}$ and $(n-1)s^2/c_{\text{lower}}$. How do we find the narrowest interval? Consider simply minimizing the width of the interval $c_{upper} - c_{lower}$, subject to the constraint that the probability contained in the interval is $(1 - \alpha)$. Prove that for symmetric and asymmetric distributions alike, the narrowest interval will be such that the density is the same at the two endpoints.

References

Berndt, E., B. Hall, R. Hall, and J. Hausman, "Estimation and Inference in Nonlinear Structural Models," *Annals of Economic and Social Measurement*, Vols. 3/4, 1974, pp. 653–665.

Berndt, E., and E. Savin, "Conflict Among Criteria for Testing Hypotheses in the Multivariate Linear Regression Model," *Econometrica*, 48, 1977, pp. 1263–1278.

Buse, A., "The Likelihood Ratio, Wald, and Lagrange Multiplier Tests: An Expository Note," *American Statistician*, 36, 1982, pp. 153–157.

Goldberger, A., *Econometric Theory*, New York: Wiley, 1964.

Greenberg, E., and C. Webster, *Advanced Econometrics: A Bridge to the Literature*, New York: Wiley, 1983.

Greene, W., "Maximum Likelihood Estimation of Econometric Frontier Functions," *Journal of Econometrics*, 13, 1980, pp. 27–56.

Greene, W., "On the Asymptotic Bias of the Ordinary Least Squares Estimator of the Tobit Model," *Econometrica*, 1980, pp. 505–513.

Hansen, L., "Large Sample Properties of Generalized Method of Moments Estimators," *Econometrica*, 50, 1982, pp. 1029–1054.

Johnston, J., *Econometric Methods*, New York: McGraw-Hill, 1984.

Judge, G., R. Hill, W. Griffiths, T. Lee, and H. Lutkepol, *An Introduction to the Theory and Practice of Econometrics*, New York: Wiley, 1982.

Kendall, M., and A. Stuart, *The Advanced Theory of Statistics*, Vol. 2, London: Griffin, 1961, pp. 1–29.

Kmenta, J., *Elements of Econometrics*, New York: Macmillan, 1986.

Leamer, E. E., *Specification Searches: Ad Hoc Inferences with Nonexperimental Data*, New York: Wiley, 1978.

Maddala, G. S., *Econometrics*, New York: McGraw-Hill, 1977.

Mood, A., F. Graybill, and D. Boes, *Introduction to the Theory of Statistics*, New York: McGraw-Hill, 1974.

Norden, R. H., "A Survey of Maximum Likelihood Estimation," *Review of the International Statistical Institute*, 41, 1972, pp. 329–354.

Olsen, R., "A Note on the Uniqueness of the Maximum Likelihood Estimator in the Tobit Model," *Econometrica*, 46, 1978, pp. 1211–1215.

Quandt, R., and J. B. Ramsey, "Estimating Mixtures of Normal Distributions and Switching Regressions," *Journal of the American Statistical Association*, 73, 1978, pp. 730–738.

Theil, H., *Principles of Econometrics*, New York: Wiley, 1971.

White, H., "Maximum Likelihood Estimation of Misspecified Models," *Econometrica*, 53, 1982, pp. 1–16.

White, H., *Asymptotic Theory for Econometricians*, New York: Academic Press, 1984.

Zellner, A., *Introduction to Bayesian Inference in Econometrics*, New York: Wiley, 1971.

Part II

The Classical Regression Model

Chapter 5

The Classical Linear Regression Model

5.1. Introduction

An econometric study begins with a set of theoretical propositions about some aspect of the economy. The theory specifies a set of relationships among variables. Familiar examples are demand equations, production functions, and macroeconomic models. The empirical investigation provides estimates of unknown parameters in the model, such as elasticities or the marginal propensity to consume, and often attempts to measure the validity of the propositions against the behavior of observable data. This and the next several chapters develop a number of techniques used in this context. We begin with the simplest case of a linear equation linking two variables. Subsequent chapters are devoted to more elaborate specifications and to various complications that arise in the application of these techniques.

5.2. Specifying the Regression Model—An Example

Consider the following propositions from Keynes's (1936) *General Theory*:

> We shall therefore define what we shall call the propensity to consume as the functional relationship X between Y, a given level of income and C the expenditure on consumption out of that level of income, so that $C = X(Y)$.
>
> The amount that the community spends on consumption depends (i) partly on the amount of its income, (ii) partly on other objective attendant circumstances, and (iii) partly on the subjective needs and the psychological propensities and habits of the individuals composing it....
>
> The fundamental psychological law upon which we are entitled to depend with great confidence, both a priori from our knowledge of human nature and from the detailed facts of experience, is that men are disposed, as a rule and on the average, to increase their consumption as their income increases, but not by as much as the increase in their income.[1] That is... dC/dY is positive and less than unity.
>
> But, apart from short-period changes in the level of income, it is also obvious that a higher absolute level of income will tend as a rule to widen the gap between income and consumption.... These reasons will lead, as a rule, to a greater proportion of income being saved as real income increases.

---

[1] Modern economists are rarely this confident about their theories.

The theory posits a stable relationship between consumption and income:

$$C = f(Y)$$

and claims in the third paragraph that the marginal propensity to consume (MPC) is between 0 and 1:

$$0 < \frac{dC}{dY} < 1.$$

The final paragraph asserts that the average propensity to consume (APC), that is, the ratio of consumption to income, falls as income rises, or

$$\frac{d(\text{APC})}{dY} = \frac{d(C/Y)}{dY} = \frac{(\text{MPC} - \text{APC})}{Y} < 0.$$

It follows that MPC < APC. The most common formulation of the consumption function is a linear relationship

$$C = \alpha + \beta Y \tag{5-1}$$

that satisfies Keynes's "laws" if β lies between 0 and 1 and α is greater than 0.[2]

These theoretical results provide the basis for an empirical study. In particular, given an appropriate data set, we could investigate whether the linear function just given is a satisfactory description of the relation between consumption and income, and, if so, whether α is positive and β is between 0 and 1.

Figure 5.1 and Table 5.1 present aggregate consumption and personal income in constant dollars for the U.S. economy for the 10 years 1970–1979.

It is apparent from the figure that, at least superficially, the data are consistent with the theory. But the linear function is only approximate; in fact, it is unlikely that consumption and income can be connected by any simple relationship. The **deterministic** relationship in (5–1) is clearly inadequate. (Recall the list of three explanations in the second paragraph of the excerpt.) The model is intended only to represent the salient features of this part of the economy. We are not so ambitious as to attempt to capture every influence in our relationship, but only those that are substantial enough to model directly.

Our next step is to incorporate in the model the inherent randomness in its real-world counterpart. Thus, we write

$$C = f(Y, \varepsilon),$$

where ε is the stochastic element. It is important not to view the disturbance ε as a catchall for the inadequacies of the model. For example, Figure 5.2 shows the same measured variables as 5.1 for the years 1940 to 1950. The same moderate lack of fit appears. But for the years 1942–1945, something is obviously missing. These differences are not the result of random variation; 1942–1945 were years of wartime rationing, which prevented consumption from rising to rates historically consistent with these levels of income. This fact would be incorporated in the model if one intended to apply it to this earlier period. It remains to establish how the stochastic element will be incorporated in the regression equation. The most frequent approach is to assume that it is *additive*. Thus, we recast the equation in **stochastic** terms:

$$C = \alpha + \beta Y + \varepsilon, \tag{5-2}$$

where ε is a random **disturbance**.

---

[2] For analysis of nonlinear models, see Chapter 11 and, for example, Husby (1971).

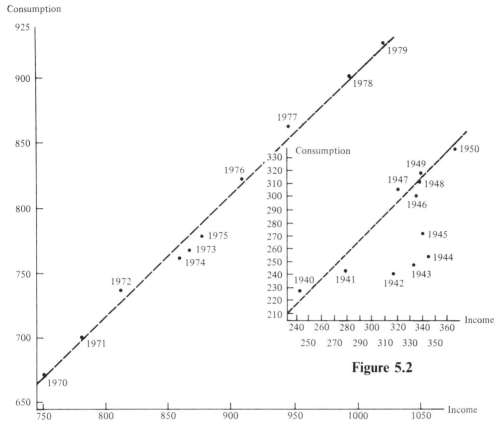

Figures 5.1 and 5.2   Consumption function.

Table 5.1.   Disposable Personal Income and Personal Consumption Expenditures in 1972 Dollars (billions of dollars)

Year	Disposable Income	Personal Consumption
1970	751.6	672.1
1971	779.2	696.8
1972	810.3	737.1
1973	864.7	767.9
1974	857.5	762.8
1975	874.9	779.4
1976	906.8	823.1
1977	942.9	864.3
1978	988.8	903.2
1979	1015.7	927.6

Source: Data are from the *Economic Report of the President,* Government Printing Office, Washington, D.C., 1984.

Equation (5–2) is the empirical counterpart to the theoretical model in (5–1). The disturbance (so named because it "disturbs" an otherwise stable relationship) arises for several reasons. The primary reason is that we cannot hope to capture every influence on consumption, such as expectations, seasonal factors, fads, and all of the inherent randomness in human behavior, in a model, no matter how elaborate. The net effect, which can be positive or negative, of these omitted factors is captured in the disturbance. There are many other contributors to the disturbance in an empirical model. Probably the most significant is errors of measurement. It is easy to theorize about the relationships among precisely defined variables; it is quite another to obtain accurate measures of these variables. For example, the difficulty of obtaining reasonable measures of profits, interest rates, capital stocks, or, worse yet, flows of services from capital stocks is a recurrent theme in the empirical literature. At the extreme, there may be no observable counterpart to the theoretical variable. The literature on the permanent income model of consumption provides an interesting example.[3]

We assume that each observation in our sample, (C_i, Y_i), $i = 1, \ldots, n$, is generated by an underlying process described by

$$C_i = \alpha + \beta Y_i + \varepsilon_i, \qquad i = 1, \ldots, n. \tag{5–3}$$

Observed consumption is the sum of two parts, a deterministic part, $\alpha + \beta Y$, and the random component, ε. Our objective is to estimate the unknown parameters of the model, use the data to study the validity of the theoretical propositions, and perhaps use the estimated model to predict the value of consumption. How we proceed from here depends crucially on what we assume about the stochastic process that has led to our observation of the data in hand.

5.3. *The Assumptions of the Linear Regression Model*

In general terms, the model to be estimated is of the form

$$y_i = \alpha + \beta x_i + \varepsilon_i, \qquad i = 1, \ldots, n, \tag{5–4}$$

where y is the **dependent** or explained variable, x is the **independent** or explanatory variable, and i indexes the n sample observations. This is commonly called the **population linear regression equation** of y on x. In this setting, y is the **regressand** and x is the **regressor**.

The basic set of assumptions that comprise the **classical linear regression model** are as follows:

1. *Functional form:* $y_i = \alpha + \beta x_i + \varepsilon_i, i = 1, \ldots, n.$
2. *Zero mean of the disturbance:* $E[\varepsilon_i] = 0$ for all i.
3. *Homoscedasticity:* $\text{Var}[\varepsilon_i] = \sigma^2$, a constant, for all i.
4. *Nonautocorrelation:* $\text{Cov}[\varepsilon_i, \varepsilon_j] = 0$ if $i \neq j$.
5. *Uncorrelatedness of regressor and disturbance:* $\text{Cov}[x_i, \varepsilon_j] = 0$ for all i and j.

Figure 5.3 summarizes these assumptions. The disturbance is assumed to be the sum of many small, individually unimportant effects, some positive and others negative. Thus, it is common to appeal to the central limit theorem and add an additional assumption to the list:

6. *Normality:* $\varepsilon_i \sim N[0, \sigma^2]$.

---

[3] See, for example, Friedman (1957).

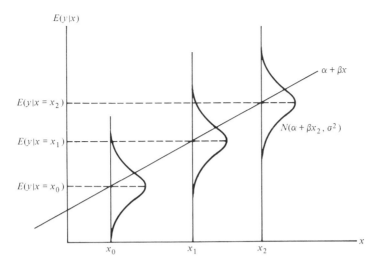

Figure 5.3   The classical regression model.

If the disturbances are normally distributed, then assumption 4 implies that they are independent as well. The normality assumption is useful for making exact statements about the behavior of estimators and hypothesis testing procedures, but it is worth noting that many of the results we shall obtain in this chapter require only assumptions 1–5.

5.3.1.   Functional Form and Nonlinear Models

For the present, we shall focus on the deterministic part of (5–4), $\alpha + \beta x$. The stochastic element is reconsidered in the next section. Linearity of the regression model implies that apart from the random disturbances, the observations on x and y will be scattered about a straight line in the $x-y$ plane. The linearity assumption is not so narrow as it might at first appear. In the regression context, *linearity* refers to the manner in which the parameters enter the equation, not necessarily to the relationship between variables x and y. For example, only the first of the four relations shown in Figure 5.4 is linear in the familiar sense. However, by letting z equal e^x, $R = (1/x)$, and $q = \ln x$, we obtain

$$y = a + bx, \; y = a + bz, \; y = a + bR, \; y = a + bq,$$

all of which are linear by the definition we shall use here. The variety of functional forms that can be transformed to linearity is substantial. All that is required is that we be able to specify the model as a linear relationship between y and x or some functions of them. In the examples, only x has been transformed, but y could have been as well, and there are many other functions that could have been used.

A commonly used functional form is the **log-linear** model:

$$y = Ax^\beta.$$

In logs,

$$\ln y = \alpha + \beta \ln x.$$

This is also known as the *constant elasticity form*, as in this equation, the elasticity of y with

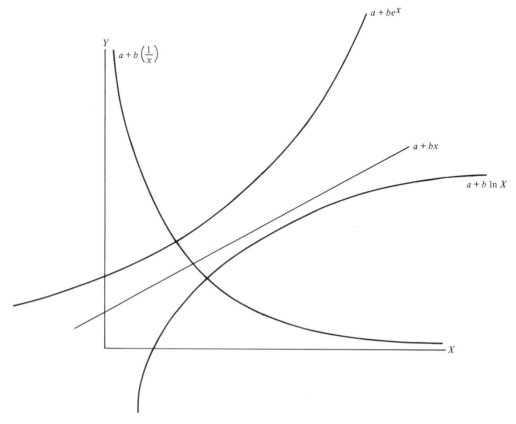

Figure 5.4   Linear models.

respect to changes in x is

$$\eta = \frac{(dy/y)}{(dx/x)} = \frac{d\ln y}{d\ln x} = \beta,$$

which does not vary with x. In contrast, the elasticity in the linear model is

$$\eta = \left(\frac{dy}{dx} \middle/ \frac{y}{x}\right) = \left(\frac{x}{(\alpha + \beta x)}\right)\left(\frac{dy}{dx}\right)$$

$$= \frac{\beta x}{(\alpha + \beta x)}.$$

The log-linear model is often used in the estimation of demand equations and production functions. Different values of β produce widely varying functions, as shown in Figure 5.5. Other variations of the general form

$$f(y_i) = \alpha + \beta g(x_i) + \varepsilon_i$$

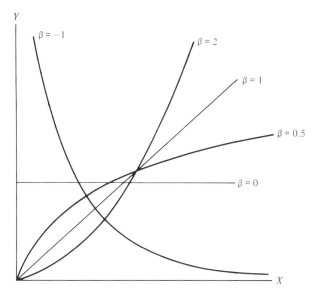

Figure 5.5   Forms of $Y = AX^\beta$.

will allow a tremendous variety of functional forms, all of which fit into our definition of a linear model. The Box–Cox model, discussed in Chapter 11, is a notable example. In spite of its great flexibility, the linear model does not include all of the situations we encounter in practice. For example, there is no transformation that will reduce

$$y = \alpha + \frac{1}{\beta + x}$$

to linearity. The methods we consider in this chapter are not appropriate for estimating the parameters of such a model. However, relatively straightforward techniques have been developed for inherently nonlinear models. We shall treat them in detail in Chapters 11 and 12.

5.3.2.   The Regressor

It is common to assume that x_i is nonstochastic, as it would be in an experimental situation. Here the analyst chooses the values of the regressor x_i and then observes y_i. This would apply, for example, in an agricultural experiment in which y_i is yield and x_i is fertilizer concentration. As a point of departure, we will make that assumption here.

7. *Nonstochastic regressor:* The value of x_i is a known constant in the probability distribution of y_i.

The implication is that each value of y_i is a realization from a probability distribution with mean

$$E[y_i \,|\, x_i] = E[\alpha + \beta x_i + \varepsilon_i] = \alpha + \beta x_i + E[\varepsilon_i] = \alpha + \beta x_i$$

and variance

$$\text{Var}[y_i \,|\, x_i] = \text{Var}[\alpha + \beta x_i + \varepsilon_i] = \text{Var}[\varepsilon_i] = \sigma^2.$$

In addition, it is necessary to assume that for any n greater than 1,

$$\left(\frac{1}{n}\right)S_{xx} = \left(\frac{1}{n}\right)\sum_i (x_i - \bar{x})^2$$

is a finite positive number. This assumption is known as an **identification condition**. If there is no variation in x_i, all of our observations will lie on a vertical line, for example, above x_2 in Figure 5.3. This does not invalidate the other assumptions of the model; presumably, it is a flaw in the data set. But if all of our observations lie on a vertical line, our **observed data** will not permit us to infer anything about the regression, $\alpha + \beta x$.

The assumption of a nonstochastic regressor at this point is largely a convenience. With it, we shall be able to use the results of elementary statistics to obtain our results, as we did in deriving $\text{Var}[y_i]$. However, social scientists are rarely able to analyze experimental data, and relatively few of their models are built around nonrandom regressors. Clearly, for example, in the consumption function, it would be difficult to defend such an asymmetric treatment of aggregate consumption and aggregate income. Since some of our results rely on the assumption that x_i is a known constant, it is important to consider the implications of a random regressor.

If x is taken to be a random variable, Assumption 1 becomes a statement about the joint distribution of y and x. The development of Section 3.7 would apply. It is common in social science research to take the alternative view that the observations on x are "fixed in repeated samples," which is equivalent to doing the statistical analysis **conditionally** on the sample we have observed. Thus, we would only assume that the regression model and its assumptions apply to the particular set of x's we have observed. This treatment allows us to disregard the ultimate source of variation in x and concentrate on the relationship between y and x. The precise nature of the regressor and how we view the sampling process will be a major determinant of our derivation of the statistical properties of our estimators and test statistics. As we shall see in Chapter 10, we can relax the assumption of fixed regressors at almost no cost. In the end, the crucial assumption is Assumption 5, the uncorrelatedness of x and ε.

5.3.3. The Disturbance

The assumption of linearity of the regression model includes the additive disturbance. For the regression to be linear in the sense described here, it must be of the form

$$y = \alpha + \beta x + \varepsilon$$

either in the original variables or after some suitable transformation. For example, the model

$$y = Ax^\beta e^\varepsilon$$

is linear, while

$$y = Ax^\beta + \varepsilon$$

is not. The observed dependent variable is thus the sum of two components, a nonstochastic element, $\alpha + \beta x$, and a random variable, ε. It is worth emphasizing that neither of the two parts is directly observed because α and β are unknown.

The assumption of a zero mean for the disturbance,

$$E[\varepsilon_i] = 0 \qquad \text{for all } i, \tag{5-5}$$

is natural. Since ε is usually viewed as the sum of many individual effects, the sign of each of which is unknown, there is no reason to expect any other value. Arguably, if we have reason to specify that the mean of the disturbance is something other than zero, we shall build it into the systematic part of our regression, leaving in the disturbance only the unknown part of ε.[4]

Each disturbance is a realization of a random variable with a continuous probability distribution. We assume at this point that these all have the same variance:

$$\text{Var}[\varepsilon_i] = \sigma^2 \qquad \text{for all } i. \tag{5-6}$$

This is termed **homoscedasticity**. Consider a model that describes the profits of firms in an industry as a function of, say, size. Even accounting for size, measured in dollar terms, the profits of large firms will exhibit much greater variation than those of smaller firms. The homoscedasticity assumption would be inappropriate here. Also, survey data on household expenditure patterns often display marked heteroscedasticity, even after accounting for income and household size. In contrast, the data in Figure 5.1 appear consistent with this assumption; the variance of consumption does not appear to be changing over time or with different values of income.

The random components of the observations are assumed to be uncorrelated:

$$E[\varepsilon_i \varepsilon_j] = 0 \qquad \text{for all pairs } i \text{ and } j. \tag{5-7}$$

This is also called **nonautocorrelation**. This does not necessarily imply that they are independent, although we will commonly make this assumption as well. It does follow when we assume that the disturbances are normally distributed.

In Figure 5.1, there is some suggestion that the observations might not be truly independent across observations. Although the number of observations is limited, it does appear that, on average, each disturbance tends to be followed by one with the same sign. This "inertia" is precisely what is meant by autocorrelation, and it is assumed away at this point. Methods of handling autocorrelation in economic data occupy a large proportion of the literature and will be treated at length in Chapter 15.

It is convenient to assume that the disturbances are independent and **normally distributed**, with zero mean and constant variance. This will enable us to obtain several exact statistical results. In view of our description of the source of ε, the conditions of the central limit theorem will generally apply, at least approximately, and the normality assumption will be reasonable in most settings. Later, it will be possible to relax this assumption and retain most of the statistical results we obtain here.

5.4.   *Least Squares*

Our data are assumed to be produced by the stochastic relation

$$y_i = \alpha + \beta x_i + \varepsilon_i = E[y_i \mid x_i] + \varepsilon_i. \tag{5-8}$$

The unknown parameters of this line are the objects of estimation. It is necessary to distinguish between population quantities, such as α and β, and our sample estimates of them, denoted a and b. The population regression is $E[y_i] = \alpha + \beta x_i$, while our estimate of $E[y_i]$ is denoted

$$\hat{y}_i = a + bx_i.$$

---

[4] Suppose that the mean of ε is μ. Then $\alpha + \beta x + \varepsilon$ is the same as $(\alpha + \mu) + \beta x + (\varepsilon - \mu)$. Letting $\alpha' = \alpha + \mu$ and $\varepsilon' = \varepsilon - \mu$ produces the original model. For an application, see the discussion of frontier production functions in Chapter 10.

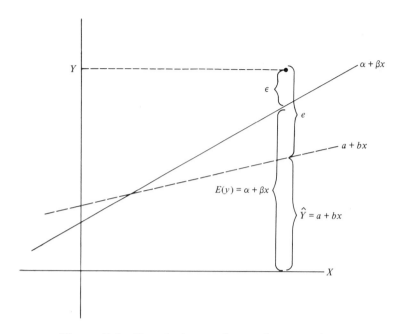

Figure 5.6   Population and sample regression.

The disturbance with any data point is

$$\varepsilon_i = y_i - \alpha - \beta x_i.$$

For any values of a and b, we shall estimate ε_i with a **residual**,

$$e_i = y_i - a - bx_i.$$

From the definitions,

$$y_i = \alpha + \beta x_i + \varepsilon_i$$
$$= a + bx_i + e_i.$$

These are summarized in Figure 5.6.

5.4.1.   The Least Squares Coefficients

The population quantities α and β are unknown parameters of the probability distribution of y_i whose values we hope to estimate with our sample data. This is, of course, a problem of statistical inference. It is instructive, however, to begin by considering the purely algebraic problem of choosing an a and a b so that the fitted line, $a + bx$, is close to the data points. The scatter of points in Figure 5.1 provides a good illustration. The measure of closeness constitutes a **fitting criterion**. Although numerous candidates have been suggested, the one used most frequently is **least squares**.[5]

For any pair of values, a and b, the **sum of squared residuals** is

$$\sum_i e_i^2 = \sum_i (y_i - a - bx_i)^2. \qquad (5\text{--}9)$$

---

[5] We shall have to establish that the practical criterion of fitting the line as closely as possible to the data by least squares leads to estimates with good statistical properties. This makes intuitive sense and is, indeed, the case.

The least squares coefficients are the values of a and b that minimize this fitting criterion. The first-order conditions for a minimum are

$$\frac{\partial(\sum_i e_i^2)}{\partial a} = \sum_i 2(y_i - a - bx_i)(-1)$$
$$= -2\sum_i (y_i - a - bx_i) = 0,$$

$(5\text{--}10)$

or, equivalently,

$$\sum_i e_i = 0$$

and

$$\frac{\partial(\sum_i e_i^2)}{\partial b} = \sum_i 2(y_i - a - bx_i)(-x_i) = 0$$
$$= -2\sum_i x_i(y_i - a - bx_i) = 0,$$

$(5\text{--}11)$

which implies that

$$\sum_i x_i e_i = 0.$$

Expanding these and collecting terms yields the **normal equations**

$$\sum_i y_i = na + \left(\sum_i x_i\right)b,$$

$(5\text{--}12)$

$$\sum_i x_i y_i = \left(\sum_i x_i\right)a + \left(\sum_i x_i^2\right)b.$$

$(5\text{--}13)$

To obtain a solution, we first divide (5–12) by n. The immediate result is

$$\bar{y} = a + b\bar{x}.$$

The least squares regression line passes through the point of means. (If there is no intercept term, this will not be true. This is considered in the exercises.) Now isolate a:

$$a = \bar{y} - b\bar{x}.$$

$(5\text{--}14)$

With a in hand, we can solve (5–13) for b. First, $\sum_i x_i = n\bar{x}$. Insert this and (5–14) in (5–13) and rearrange the terms:

$$\sum_i x_i y_i - n\overline{xy} = b\left(\sum_i x_i^2 - n\bar{x}^2\right)$$

or

$$b = \frac{(\sum_i x_i y_i - n\overline{xy})}{(\sum_i x_i^2 - n\bar{x}^2)}$$
$$= \frac{\sum_i (x_i - \bar{x})(y_i - \bar{y})}{\sum_i (x_i - \bar{x})^2}.$$

$(5\text{--}15)$

The solution is given only in terms of the sample means, sums of squares, and cross products, so b may be computed independently of a. Once this explicit solution for b is computed, the value of a may be obtained from (5–14).

EXAMPLE 5.1.   For the consumption data in Figure 5.1, the **normal equations** are

$$7934.3 \quad = \quad 10a + \quad 8792.4b,$$
$$7041953.27 = 8792.4a + 7797822.22b.$$

The solutions are

$$a = -67.5806 \quad \text{and} \quad b = 0.979267.$$

(This is the line plotted in Figure 5.1.)

It remains to verify that we have, indeed, found a minimum of the sum of squared residuals. The matrix of second derivatives with respect to a and b is

$$\begin{bmatrix} \partial^2(\sum_i e_i^2)/\partial a^2 & \partial^2(\sum_i e_i^2)/\partial a \partial b \\ \partial^2(\sum_i e_i^2)/\partial b \partial a & \partial^2(\sum_i e_i^2)/\partial b^2 \end{bmatrix} = \begin{bmatrix} 2n & 2\sum_i x_i \\ 2\sum_i x_i & 2\sum_i x_i^2 \end{bmatrix}.$$

We must show that this matrix is positive definite. The two diagonal elements are obviously positive, so it is only necessary to verify that the determinant is positive. This is $(4n)\sum_i x_i^2 - 4(\sum_i x_i)^2$. But $\sum_i x_i = n\bar{x}$, so the determinant is

$$4n\left(\sum_i x_i^2 - n\bar{x}^2\right) = 4n\left(\sum_i (x_i - \bar{x})^2\right),$$

which is positive. Thus, a and b are the minimizers of the sum of squares.[6] It is worth noting that the second derivatives do not involve a and b. The Hessian is *always* positive definite. This means that the sum of squared residuals is strictly concave in a and b, and *any* values that satisfy the first-order conditions are minimizers. But only one pair of values does so.

5.4.2.   Evaluating the Fit of the Regression

The original fitting criterion, the sum of squared residuals, also provides a measure of the fit of the regression line to the data. Unfortunately, as can easily be verified, the sum of squared residuals can be scaled arbitrarily just by multiplying the values of y by the desired scale factor. Since the fitted values from the regression are based on the values of x, we might ask, instead, whether variation in x is a good predictor of variation in y. Figure 5.7 shows several possible cases. The measure of fit described here embodies both of these considerations.

Variation of the dependent variable is defined in terms of deviations from its mean $(y_i - \bar{y})$. The *total variation* in y is the sum of squared deviations:

$$\text{SST} = \sum_i (y_i - \bar{y})^2.$$

(The squares are used because the sum of deviations is always zero.) In terms of the regression equation, we may write

$$y_i = \hat{y}_i + e_i$$
$$= a + bx_i + e_i$$
$$= \bar{y} - b\bar{x} + bx_i + e_i.$$

---

[6] The second-order condition fails if $\sum_i (x_i - \bar{x})^2$ is zero. But this is the case in which all of the values of x are the same. This was ruled out earlier.

Figure 5.7   Sample data.

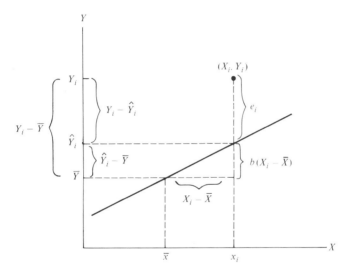

Figure 5.8   Decomposition of y_i.

Subtracting $\bar{y}$ from both sides gives

$$(y_i - \bar{y}) = \hat{y} - \bar{y} + e_i = b(x_i - \bar{x}) + e_i. \tag{5-16}$$

Figure 5.8 illustrates the computation. Intuitively, the regression would appear to fit well if the deviations of y from its mean are more largely accounted for by deviations of x from its mean than by the residuals. However, since both terms in (5–16) sum to zero, we use the sums of squares instead. It follows from (5–10) and (5–11) that the cross-product term in the sum of squares of the deviations in (5–16) is zero, and

$$\sum_i (y_i - \bar{y})^2 = \sum_i (\hat{y}_i - \bar{y})^2 + \sum_i e_i^2 \tag{5-17}$$

$$= b^2 \sum_i (x_i - \bar{x})^2 + \sum_i e_i^2.$$

We write this as

Total sum of squares = explained sum of squares + residual sum of squares   (5–18)

or

$$SST = SSR + SSE.$$

Equation (5–17) shows two ways to compute the explained sum of squares. Returning to the original question, we can obtain a measure of how well the regression line fits the data by using the

$$\text{Coefficient of determination} = \frac{SSR}{SST}. \qquad (5–19)$$

As we have shown, this must be between 0 and 1. It is denoted R^2. It takes the value of zero if the regression is a horizontal line. In this case, the predicted values of y are always $\bar{y}$, so deviations of x from its mean do not translate into different predictions for y. As such, x has no explanatory power. The other extreme, R^2 equals 1, occurs if the values of x and y all lie on a straight line, so that the residuals are zero. If all of the values of y_i lie on a horizontal line, so that there is no variation in y to explain, R^2 has no meaning and cannot be computed.

There are some useful shortcuts for the computation of this **variance decomposition**. For convenience, define the sample quantities

$$S_{xx} = \sum_i (x_i - \bar{x})^2, \qquad\qquad S_x = \sqrt{S_{xx}},$$

$$S_{yy} = \sum_i (y_i - \bar{y})^2, \qquad\qquad S_y = \sqrt{S_{yy}},$$

and

$$S_{xy} = \sum_i (x_i - \bar{x})(y_i - \bar{y}).$$

The sample correlation between x and y is $r_{xy} = S_{xy}/(S_x S_y)$. By using $b = S_{xy}/S_{xx}$, we obtain $r_{xy} = b(S_x/S_y)$, which shows that the slope of the regression has the same sign as the correlation between x and y. Therefore,

$$R^2 = \frac{SSR}{SST} = \frac{b^2 S_{xx}}{S_{yy}} = r_{xy}^2. \qquad (5–20)$$

A result that will be useful in cases in which we have more than one explanatory variable is obtained by computing the squared correlation between the actual and fitted values of y:

$$r_{xy}^2 = \frac{[\sum_i (\hat{y}_i - \bar{y})(y_i - \bar{y})]^2}{[SSR \; S_{yy}]}.$$

But $(\hat{y}_i - \bar{y}) = b(x_i - \bar{x})$. So, the numerator is $b^2 S_{xy}^2$ and the denominator is $b^2 S_{xx} S_{yy}$. Collecting terms, we have shown that the coefficient of determination is the squared correlation between the actual and fitted values of the dependent variable. This further justifies our use of R^2 as a measure of goodness of fit of the regression model.

EXAMPLE 5.2.   Continuing the example of the consumption function, where C is consumption and Y is income, we find that

Table 5.2.   Analysis of Variance Table

Source of Variation	Variation	Degrees of Freedom	Mean Square
Regression	$SSR = b^2 S_{xx}$	1	$\dfrac{SSR}{1}$
Residual	$SSE = \Sigma_i e_i^2$	$n-2$	$\dfrac{SSE}{(n-2)}$
Total	S_{yy}	$n-1$	$\dfrac{S_{yy}}{(n-1)}$

$$F[1, n-2] = \frac{(SSR/1)}{(SSE/(n-2))}$$

$$\bar{C} = 793.43, \qquad \bar{Y} = 879.24,$$

$$S_{CC} = 64972.12, \qquad S_{YY} = 67192.44,$$

$$S_{YC} = 65799.34.$$

The components of the total sum of squares are

$$\text{Total sum of squares} = 64972.12$$

$$\text{Regression sum of squares} = 64435.13$$

$$\text{Residual sum of squares} = 537.00$$

$$R^2 = \frac{64435.13}{64972.12} = 0.99173.$$

Apparently (as can be seen in Figure 5.1), the regression provides quite a good fit.

The value of R^2 we obtained for the consumption function seems high in an absolute sense. Is it? Unfortunately, there is no absolute basis for comparison. In fact, in using aggregate time-series data, coefficients of determination this high are routine. In terms of the values one normally encounters in cross sections, an R^2 of 0.5 is relatively high. Still, it is

Table 5.3.   Analysis of Variance Table for the Data in Example 5.6

Source of Variation	Variation	Degrees of Freedom	Mean Square
Regression	64435.13	1	64435.13
Residual	537.00	8	67.124
Total	64972.12	9	7219.12

$$F[1,8] = \frac{64435.13}{67.124} = 959.94$$

much lower than the one obtained for the consumption function. Coefficients of determination in cross sections of individual data as high as 0.2 are sometimes noteworthy. The point of this discussion is that whether a regression line provides a good fit to a body of data depends on the setting.

Little can be said about the relative quality of fits of regression lines in different contexts. One must be careful, however, even in a single context, to be sure to use the same basis for comparison for competing models. Usually, this concerns how the dependent variable is computed. For example, a perennial question concerns whether a linear or log-linear model fits the data better. Unfortunately, the question cannot be answered with a direct comparison. An R^2 for the linear regression model is different from an R^2 for the log-linear model. Variation in y is different from variation in $\ln y$. To continue the example, the R^2 in the regression of $\ln C$ on $\ln y$ is 0.99154, which suggests that (albeit only trivially) the linear model fits slightly better. However, it is often useful to compute an analog to the usual R^2 that can (save for the following caveat) be used to compare models:

$$R^2 = 1 - \frac{\sum_i e_i^2}{S_{yy}}.$$

The residuals can be computed as $y_i - \hat{y}_i$ from any model. To continue the example, if we compute the predicted values from the log-linear model, and then use for the fitted values

$$\hat{C} = e^{\widehat{\ln C}},$$

the R^2 for this "regression," computed as previously, is 0.991956, which is a slight improvement over the linear model.

It is worth emphasizing that R^2 is a measure of *linear* association between x and y. For example, the third panel of Figure 5.7 shows data that might arise from the model

$$y_i = \alpha + \beta(x_i - c)^2 + \varepsilon_i.$$

(The constant, c, allows x to be distributed about some value other than zero.) The relationship between y and x in this model is nonlinear, and a linear regression would find no fit.

A final word of caution is in order. The interpretation of R^2 as a proportion of variation explained is dependent on the use of least squares to compute the fitted values. It is always correct to write

$$y_i - \bar{y} = \hat{y} - \bar{y} + e_i.$$

However, in computing the sum of squares on the two sides, the cross-product term vanishes only if least squares is used to compute the fitted values and if the model contains a constant term.[7] Thus, in our previous example, it is not unambiguous that the log-linear model fits better; the cross-product term has been ignored in computing R^2 for the log-linear model. Thus, it is only in the case of least squares applied to a linear equation that R^2 can be interpreted as the proportion of variation in y explained by variation in x.

---

[7] An analogous computation can be done without computing deviations from means if the regression does not contain a constant term. However, other purely algebraic artifacts will crop up in regressions without a constant. For example, the value of R^2 will change when the same constant is added to each observation on y, but it is obvious that nothing fundamental has changed in the regression relationship. One should be wary (even skeptical) in the calculation and interpretation of fit measures for regressions without constant terms.

5.5. *Statistical Properties of the Least Squares Estimator*

The preceding discussion treated the fitting of the regression to the data as a purely algebraic problem. We can now treat the results as parameter estimates and assess the virtues of least squares on a statistical basis. There are other candidates for estimating α and β. We might, for example, just find the slope of the line between the points with the largest and smallest values of x or (which would be more difficult) find the a and b that minimize the sum of absolute values of the residuals. The question of which estimator to choose is usually based on the statistical properties of the candidates, such as unbiasedness, efficiency, and precision.[8] These, in turn, frequently depend on the particular distribution that we assume produced the data. It is interesting that a number of desirable properties can be obtained for the least squares estimator without even specifying a particular distribution for the disturbances in the regression.

Recall that the statistical model underlying the observed data is

$$y_i = \alpha + \beta x_i + \varepsilon_i.$$

The least squares estimator of β is

$$b = \frac{S_{xy}}{S_{xx}} = \frac{\sum_i (x_i - \bar{x}) y_i}{S_{xx}}$$

$$= \sum_i c_i y_i. \tag{5-21}$$

The weight in the sum

$$c_i = \frac{(x_i - \bar{x})}{S_{xx}}$$

is a function of only $x_1, \ldots, x_n$. Inserting $y_i = \alpha + \beta x_i$ in (5–21), we obtain

$$b = \frac{\sum_i (x_i - \bar{x})(\alpha + \beta x_i + \varepsilon_i)}{S_{xx}}$$

$$= \frac{\alpha \sum_i (x_i - \bar{x})}{S_{xx}} + \frac{\beta \sum_i (x_i - \bar{x}) x_i}{S_{xx}} + \frac{\sum_i (x_i - \bar{x}) \varepsilon_i}{S_{xx}} \tag{5-22}$$

$$= \beta + \sum_i c_i \varepsilon_i$$

because $S_{xx} = \sum_i (x_i - \bar{x})^2 = \sum_i (x_i - \bar{x}) x_i$ and $\sum_i (x_i - \bar{x}) = 0$. Therefore,

$$E[b] = \beta + E\left[\sum_i c_i \varepsilon_i\right] \tag{5-23}$$

$$= \beta,$$

since $E[\varepsilon_i] = 0$. *Regardless of the distribution of* ε, *under our other assumptions,* b *is an unbiased estimator of* β. The sampling variance of b is derived by using (5–23).

$$\text{Var}[b] = \text{Var}[b - \beta] = \text{Var}\left[\sum_i c_i \varepsilon_i\right].$$

---

[8] See Section 4.3.

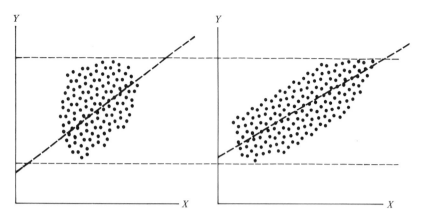

Figure 5.9   Effect of increased variation in X given the same variation in Y.

Assumption 4 implies that the covariance terms in the variance of this sum are zero, which leaves

$$\text{Var}[b] = \sum_i \text{Var}[c_i \varepsilon_i] = \sum_i \sigma^2 c_i^2 = \frac{\sigma^2}{S_{xx}}. \tag{5-24}$$

Note, in particular, the denominator of the variance of b. The greater the variation in x, the smaller this variance will be. For example, consider the problem of estimating the slopes of the two regressions in Figure 5.9. Obviously, a more precise result will be obtained for the data in panel 2 of the figure. This does not necessarily argue that one should always attempt, if possible, to maximize the variation in x. The greater the range of variation we consider, the more likely it becomes that our assumption of linearity of the regression becomes suspect. This notwithstanding, greater variation in the explanatory variable is to be preferred.

By similar reasoning, we can write the least squares intercept, a, as

$$a = \bar{y} - b\bar{x}$$

$$= \frac{1}{n} \sum_i y_i - b\bar{x}$$

$$= \frac{1}{n} \sum_i (\alpha + \beta x_i + \varepsilon_i) - b\bar{x}.$$

Collecting terms, we have

$$a - \alpha = \sum_i d_i \varepsilon_i,$$

where

$$d_i = \left(\frac{1}{n} - \bar{x} c_i \right).$$

Therefore, since each term in the sum has expectation 0, a is also unbiased. The sampling variance of a is the variance of $\sum_i d_i \varepsilon_i$, which by independence is

$$\text{Var}[a] = \sum_i \sigma^2 d_i^2 = \sigma^2 \left(\frac{1}{n} + \bar{x}^2 \sum_i c_i^2 \right) \tag{5-25}$$

(The latter result is obtained by squaring the term in parentheses and using the result that $\sum_i c_i = 0$.) From the earlier results,

$$\text{Var}[a] = \sigma^2 \left[\frac{1}{n} + \frac{\bar{x}^2}{S_{xx}} \right].$$

The covariance of the two estimators is

$$\text{Cov}[a, b] = E(a - \alpha)(b - \beta) = E\left[\left(\sum_i d_i \varepsilon_i \right) \left(\sum_i c_i \varepsilon_i \right) \right]$$

$$= \sigma^2 \sum_i c_i d_i \tag{5-26}$$

$$= \frac{-\bar{x}\sigma^2}{S_{xx}}.$$

Both a and b are of the form $\sum_i w_i y_i$; thus, they are **linear** estimators. The preceding gives the sampling mean and variance of both and establishes that they are unbiased. As noted, there are other ways one might use the data to estimate α and β. However, in the context of **linear unbiased estimators**, no estimator has a smaller sampling variance than least squares. This is the **Gauss–Markov theorem**, which we shall prove for the slope estimator. The proof for the intercept is left as an exercise. Recall that the least squares slope is $b = \sum c_i y_i$. Let a competing estimator be

$$b' = \sum_i q_i y_i = \alpha \sum_i q_i + \beta \sum_i q_i x_i + \sum_i q_i \varepsilon_i.$$

Taking expectations on both sides of the equation, we see that for b' to be unbiased, we must have $\sum_i q_i = 0$ and $\sum_i q_i x_i = 1$. (You should verify that these are true for c_i.) Thus, $b' = \beta + \sum_i q_i \varepsilon_i$. The variance of b' is

$$\text{Var}[b'] = \sigma^2 \sum_i q_i^2.$$

Let $v_i = q_i - c_i$. Then $q_i = c_i + v_i$ and

$$\text{Var}[b'] = \sigma^2 \sum_i (c_i + v_i)^2$$

$$= \sigma^2 \left(\sum_i c_i^2 + \sum_i v_i^2 + 2\sum_i c_i v_i \right).$$

But $\sum c_i v_i = 0$. This leaves only the two sums of squares in the variance of b', which means that $\text{Var}[b']$ must be greater than $\text{Var}[b]$. A similar proof establishes the result for a.

The Gauss–Markov theorem is a powerful result. It is remarkable that we are able to establish such a strong result for least squares without any assumption about the disturbances beyond their zero mean, independence, and constant variance. Note, in particular, that we have not used the assumption of normality in the proof. This follows because we have restricted ourselves to a relatively small class of estimators, namely, those that are both linear and unbiased. There may be (indeed, we know that there are) more precise estimators than least squares in the broader classes that allow for small amounts of bias or, possibly in some settings, nonlinear estimators.

When the assumption of normally distributed disturbances is added to the preceding, we obtain a complete result for the distributions of the estimators. Because they are linear functions of normally distributed variables, a and b are also normally distributed, with the means and variances derived earlier. To summarize, under the assumption of normality,

$$\begin{bmatrix} a \\ b \end{bmatrix} \sim N\left[\begin{bmatrix} \alpha \\ \beta \end{bmatrix}, \quad \sigma^2\begin{bmatrix} 1/n + \bar{x}^2/S_{xx} & -\bar{x}/S_{xx} \\ -\bar{x}/S_{xx} & 1/S_{xx} \end{bmatrix}\right]. \tag{5-27}$$

We obtained the Gauss–Markov result as a characterization of the least squares estimator. That is, we began with a particular estimator in mind and assessed its statistical properties. An alternative approach would have been to pose the general problem of finding the estimator with the smallest variance, subject to the constraint that it be linear and unbiased. Of course, we would have been led, once again, to least squares. Suppose that we drop the assumption of linearity and seek only the minimum variance unbiased estimator? This is a far more difficult problem that requires us to specify a particular distribution for the disturbance. Under normality, linearity is, in fact, superfluous. The least squares estimator has minimum variance among *all* unbiased estimators. However, as we shall show in Chapter 9, there *are* biased estimators with smaller *mean squared errors* than least squares.[9] If we drop the assumption of normality, many of these results no longer hold. The Gauss–Markov theorem is intact, but without normality, the class of **linear unbiased** estimators becomes a bit restrictive. Other "robust" estimators, which may outperform least squares in some circumstances, have been proposed. The conclusion is that least squares is a powerful technique that produces an estimator with desirable statistical properties in many cases. However, in more general cases than we consider here, the field is much broader and there is room for other estimators to compete quite favorably with least squares.

5.6. Statistical Inference

The preceding section presented the exact sampling distribution of the least squares estimators, a and b, under two specific assumptions: that the disturbances are normally distributed and that the sample $x_1, \ldots, x_n$ may be taken as fixed and nonstochastic (or fixed in repeated samples). The usual procedures in parameter estimation will involve forming confidence intervals and testing hypotheses about the values of α and β. In order to do so, we need estimates of the true sampling variances of the parameters, which will require an estimate of the unknown σ^2.

5.6.1. Estimating the Sampling Distribution

Since σ^2 is the expected value of ε^2 and e_i is an estimate of ε_i,

$$\hat{\sigma}^2 = \frac{1}{n}\sum_i e_i^2 \tag{5-28}$$

would seem to be a natural estimator. However, by writing $e_i = y_i - a - bx_i$, and substituting $y_i = a + bx_i + e_i$ and $a = \bar{y} - b\bar{x}$, we obtain

$$e_i = \varepsilon_i - \bar{\varepsilon} - (x_i - \bar{x})(b - \beta)$$

$$= \varepsilon_i - \bar{\varepsilon} - (x_i - \bar{x})\left(\sum_j c_j \varepsilon_j\right). \tag{5-29}$$

---

[9] See Judge et al. (1985) for an extensive discussion.

Our estimate of an individual disturbance, ε_i, is distorted by two elements: the sample average of all the disturbances and an effect that we can attribute to the fact that β is not estimated perfectly. Recall that all disturbances are independent, so $E(\varepsilon_i \varepsilon_j) = 0$ if $i \neq j$. Now we square both sides of (5–29) and take expected values, which yields

$$E[e_i^2] = \sigma^2 + \frac{\sigma^2}{n} + \sigma^2 (x_i - \bar{x}) \left(\sum_j c_j^2 \right) - \frac{2\sigma^2}{n} - 2\sigma^2 (x_i - \bar{x}) c_i + 2\sigma^2 (x_i - \bar{x}) \left(\sum_j c_j \right).$$

In summing these terms, we use $\sum_i c_i = 0$, $\sum_i (x_i - \bar{x}) c_i = 1$, and $\sum_i c_i^2 = 1/S_{xx}$. Collecting terms, we have

$$E\left[\sum_i e_i^2 \right] = (n-2)\sigma^2.$$

This implies that an unbiased estimator of σ^2 is

$$s^2 = \frac{\sum_i e_i^2}{(n-2)}. \tag{5–30}$$

Thus, we can obtain an estimate of the sampling variance of b with

$$\text{Est. Var}[b] = \frac{s^2}{S_{xx}}.$$

(Henceforth, we shall use the notation Est. Var[·] to indicate a sample estimate of the sampling variance of an estimator.) The square root of this quantity,

$$s_b = \frac{s}{\sqrt{S_{xx}}},$$

is the "standard error" of the estimate, b. This is often denoted simply "the standard error of b."

Based on (5–27), the exact distribution of

$$z = \frac{(b - \beta)}{\sqrt{\sigma^2 / S_{xx}}} \tag{5–31}$$

is standard normal. We defer until Chapter 6 (where it will be much simpler, using the tools of matrix algebra) a proof of the following:

$$\frac{(n-2)s^2}{\sigma^2} \sim \text{chi-squared}[n-2], \tag{5–32}$$

which is independent of b (and z). Consider, then, replacing the unknown value of σ^2 in (5–31) with s^2, our unbiased estimate. The result,

$$t = \frac{(b - \beta)}{\sqrt{s^2 / S_{xx}}},$$

is the ratio of a standard normal variable to the square root of a chi-squared variate divided by its degrees of freedom, which has a t distribution with $(n-2)$ degrees of freedom. Thus, the ratio

$$\frac{b - \beta}{s_b} \sim t[n-2] \tag{5–33}$$

can form the basis of statistical inference.

5.6.2. Testing a Hypothesis About β

A confidence interval for β would be based on (5–31). In particular, we could say that

$$\text{Prob}[b - t_{\lambda/2}s_b \le \beta \le b + t_{\lambda/2}s_b] = 1 - \lambda,$$

where λ is the desired level of confidence and $t_{\lambda/2}$ is the appropriate critical value from the t distribution with $(n - 2)$ degrees of freedom. A confidence interval for α would be constructed likewise, using a and its estimated variance.

EXAMPLE 5.3.   In the earlier regression, we obtained

$$a = -67.5806 \quad \text{and} \quad b = 0.9793.$$

To compute the standard errors, we need

$$s^2 = \frac{537.00}{8} = 67.125,$$

$$S_{xx} = 67192.45,$$

and

$$\bar{x} = 879.24.$$

Inserting these in (5–24) and (5–25), using s^2 instead of σ^2, the estimated variances are

$$\text{Est. Var}[a] = 778.96 \quad \text{or} \quad s_a = 27.91$$

and

$$\text{Est. Var}[b] = 0.0009992 \quad \text{or} \quad s_b = 0.03161.$$

For a t distribution with $n - 2 = 8$ degrees of freedom, the 95 percent critical value is 2.306. Therefore, 95 percent confidence intervals for α and β are

$$-67.5806 \pm 2.306(27.91) \quad \text{or} \quad -131.94 \text{ to } -3.22 \text{ for } \alpha$$

and

$$0.9793 \pm 2.306(0.03161) \quad \text{or} \quad 0.90641 \text{ to } 1.0522 \text{ for } \beta.$$

We can also form a confidence interval for the disturbance variance, σ^2. Using (5–32) and the same reasoning we used previously, we find that a 95 percent confidence interval for σ^2 would be

$$\frac{(n - 2)s^2}{\chi^2_{0.975}} \quad \text{to} \quad \frac{(n - 2)s^2}{\chi^2_{0.025}}. \tag{5–34}$$

EXAMPLE 5.4.   Continuing the previous example, we obtain a confidence interval for σ^2 that would be based on the chi-squared distribution with $(10 - 2) = 8$ degrees of freedom. The appropriate critical values are 2.18 and 15.5, so that the interval is

$$(10 - 2)\frac{67.125}{15.5} < \sigma^2 < (10 - 2)\frac{67.125}{2.18}$$

or

$$34.645 < \sigma^2 < 246.33.$$

This might seem to be rather wide. However, we are usually more interested in the standard deviation rather than the variance of ε. A 95 percent confidence interval for σ, based on these same results, would be 5.89 to 15.69.[10]

A related procedure is to test whether the parameter takes a given value. To test the hypothesis

$$H_0: \beta = \beta^0 \qquad \text{versus} \qquad H_1: \beta \neq \beta^0,$$

the simplest procedure is to appeal to our confidence interval. The confidence interval gives a set of plausible values of β, given our sample data. If this set does not include β^0, the null hypothesis should be rejected. Formally, under the null hypothesis, the ratio

$$t = \frac{(b - \beta^0)}{s_b} \qquad\qquad (5-35)$$

has a t distribution with $(n - 2)$ degrees of freedom, which has a mean of zero. Extreme values of this ratio, in either tail of the distribution, cast doubt on the hypothesis. Thus, in general, we reject H_0 if

$$\frac{|b - \beta^0|}{s_b} \geq t_{\lambda/2},$$

where $t_{\lambda/2}$ is the $100(1 - \lambda)$ percent critical value from the t distribution with $(n - 2)$ degrees of freedom. For a one-sided test, we adjust the critical region and use the t_{λ} critical point from the distribution. Again, values of the sample estimate that are greatly inconsistent with the hypothesis cast doubt upon it.

EXAMPLE 5.5.   Recall Keynes's fundamental principle that the marginal propensity to consume is less than 1. Are the data consistent with the hypothesis that β is less than 1? Consider testing the alternative,

$$H_0: \beta \geq 1 \qquad \text{versus} \qquad H_1: \beta < 1.$$

The appropriate test statistic is

$$t = \frac{(0.9793 - 1)}{0.03161} = -0.655.$$

This is well above the 0.05 critical point of -2.306. We conclude that H_0 should not be rejected. The data are consistent with the hypothesis that $\beta \geq 1$. They are also consistent with the hypothesis that $\beta < 1$ (i.e., the estimate is not *significantly* different from 1).

A common test is whether a parameter, β, is significantly different from zero. The appropriate test statistic,

$$t = \frac{b}{s_b}, \qquad\qquad (5-36)$$

is presented as standard output with the other results by most computer programs. The test is done in the usual way. This is usually labeled the *t ratio* for the estimate, b. If $|b/s_b| > t_{\lambda/2}$, the hypothesis is rejected and the coefficient is said to be "statistically significant." The value of 1.96, which would apply for the 95 percent significance level in a large sample, is often used as a benchmark value when a table of critical values is not immediately available.

---

[10] It is also not the narrowest possible confidence interval for σ^2 because of the asymmetry of the chi-squared distribution. See Exercise 18 in Chapter 4.

5.6.3.   Tests Based on the Fit of the Regression

A different type of hypothesis test focuses on the fit of the regression. Recall that the least squares value of b was chosen to minimize the sum of squared deviations. Since $R^2 = 1 - SSE/S_{yy}$, it follows that the value of b is chosen to maximize R^2. One might ask whether choosing some other value for the slope of the line leads to a significant loss of fit. For example, for the consumption function, one might be interested in whether a value of 0.8 as opposed to the least squares value of 0.9793 leads to a substantially worse fit (see Figure 5.10).

It is clear that if b equals zero, R^2 equals zero as well.[11] Thus, the t ratio in (5–36) can be construed as a test of whether choosing $b = 0$ would lead to a significant loss of fit. Formally, consider the square of the t ratio in (5–36):

$$t^2 = \frac{b^2 S_{xx}}{s^2} = \frac{(S_{xy}^2/S_{xx}^2)S_{xx}}{S_{yy}(1 - R^2)/(n - 2)}$$

$$= \frac{R^2/1}{(1 - R^2)/(n - 2)}$$

$$= F[1, n - 2].$$

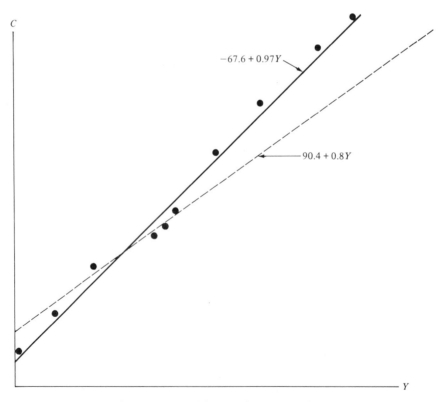

Figure 5.10   Alternative regressions.

[11] A horizontal line provides no fit to the data.

(The division by one in the numerator is included to maintain consistency with several results that we will derive later.) The square of a variable with a t distribution with $(n - 2)$ degrees of freedom has an F distribution with one and $(n - 2)$ degrees of freedom.[12] Thus, this provides an alternative test of the hypothesis that $\beta = 0$.

EXAMPLE 5.6.   In the consumption function, the t ratio for testing

$$H_0: \beta = 0$$

is $0.97927/0.031608$, or 30.982. (This is, of course, significant by any standard.) The F ratio for the same hypothesis is

$$F(1, 8) = \frac{[0.991735/1]}{[(1 - 0.991735)/8]} = 959.93.$$

This equals the square of the t ratio. The critical value from the table of $F -$ ratios is $5.32 = 2.306^2$, as expected.

A convenient way to summarize these calculations is the **analysis of variance table**. The general form of this table for a simple regression is as shown in Table 5.2.

EXAMPLE 5.7.   For the data of the previous example, the analysis of variance table would be as shown in Table 5.3.

The two tests we have considered are equivalent. Not only is the F statistic shown in the table of Example 5.7 equal to the square of the t ratio (that is how it was derived), but the critical values of F and t in the tables have the same relationship. If the t ratio is large in absolute value, the F statistic will be large as well.

Consider, then, how the fit of the line to our data changes if we use, say, b_* for the slope rather than b, the least squares value. If we use a different slope, a different intercept will result as well; that is, if we minimize

$$\sum_i e_{i*}^2 = \sum (y_i - a_* - b_* x_i)^2 \tag{5-37}$$

with respect to a_* with the given value of b_*, the result is

$$a_* = \bar{y} - b_* \bar{x}.$$

The resulting sum of squares when we use a_* and b_* is given in (5–37). Using a well-known trick, we first note that we can write

$$a_* = a + (b - b_*)\bar{x},$$

where a is the original least squares value given in (5–14). Now

$$\begin{aligned} \sum_i e_{i*}^2 &= \sum_i [y_i - a - (b - b_*)\bar{x} - bx_i + bx_i - b_* x_i]^2 \\ &= \sum_i [e_i + (b - b_*)(x_i - \bar{x})]^2 \tag{5-38} \\ &= \sum_i e_i^2 + (b - b_*)^2 S_{xx}, \end{aligned}$$

where e_i is the original least squares residual. This new sum of squares is larger than the one that uses b. We define R_*^2 to be the coefficient of determination when we use this alternative

---

[12] See Section 3.4.2.

estimate:

$$R_*^2 = 1 - \frac{\sum_i e_{i*}^2}{S_{yy}}.$$

From before, $R^2 = 1 - (\sum_i e_i^2)/S_{yy}$. Therefore, the difference between these two values is

$$R^2 - R_*^2 = \frac{(b - b_*)^2 S_{xx}}{S_{yy}},$$

which is, of course, positive.

The alternative regression line will not fit as well as the least squares regression line. To test this statistically, recall that the earlier test of $H_0: \beta = \beta^0$ was based on the test statistic

$$t(n - 2) = \left| \frac{(b - \beta_0)}{s_b} \right|.$$

Suppose that we use b_* for β^0. Squaring this and inserting the previous result, we have

$$\begin{aligned} t^2 &= \frac{(b - b_*)^2 S_{xx}/S_{yy}}{(1 - R^2)/(n - 2)} \\ &= \frac{(R^2 - R_*^2)/1}{(1 - R^2)/(n - 2)}. \end{aligned} \tag{5-39}$$

Thus, the test statistic is based on the difference in the two coefficients of determination. Again, the test is precisely equivalent to the earlier t test. The test statistic is just the square of the t statistic (by definition) and the critical value used as the benchmark will be the square of the t value found in the tables.

The preceding has shown that we may test a hypothesis about the slope in our regression from either of two points of view. Our first test, the t test, is based on the difference between our least squares estimate of a parameter and a hypothesized value. The principle involved is that if the hypothesis is correct, the least squares estimate will satisfy it within the range of sampling variation (i.e., we measure the distance of b from β_0 in standard error units). The second equivalent test is based on the principle that if a hypothesis is correct, assuming it is true will not significantly degrade the fit of the regression to our data. It is thus based on the difference between a measure of goodness of fit computed for the least squares value and for our hypothesized value.

5.7. Prediction

Aside from the estimation of parameters, the most common use of regression is for prediction. Suppose that x^0 is a known value of the regressor, and we are interested in predicting y^0, the value of y associated with x^0. At the outset, we must reconcile ourselves to at least two sources of error. We shall attempt to predict the true value of y^0:

$$y^0 = \alpha + \beta x^0 + \varepsilon^0.$$

Since we have only our sample estimates of α and β, one source of error will be the sampling error in our parameter estimates. But regardless of the precision of our parameter estimates, we will never be able to forecast ε^0 perfectly. The forecast will be

$$\hat{y}^0 = a + bx^0. \tag{5-40}$$

The prediction error is

$$e^0 = y^0 - \hat{y}^0$$
$$= \alpha + \beta x^0 + \varepsilon^0 - a - bx^0$$
$$= (\alpha - a) + (\beta - b)x^0 + \varepsilon^0.$$

By taking expectations on both sides, we see that $E(e^0) = 0$. Therefore, the least squares forecast is **unbiased** in the sense that the forecast error has a mean of zero. The variance of the prediction error is

$$\text{Var}[e^0] = \text{Var}[a] + (x^0)^2 \text{Var}[b] + 2x^0 \text{Cov}[a,b] + \text{Var}[\varepsilon^0]$$

$$= \sigma^2 \left[1 + \frac{1}{n} + \frac{\bar{x}^2}{S_{xx}} + \frac{(x^0)^2}{S_{xx}} - \frac{2\bar{x}x^0}{S_{xx}} \right] \qquad (5\text{-}41)$$

$$= \sigma^2 \left[1 + \frac{1}{n} + \frac{(x^0 - \bar{x})^2}{S_{xx}} \right].$$

By inserting the sample estimate of s^2 for σ^2, we can construct a **prediction interval** for y^0 in the same fashion as we did for the individual parameters. In particular, our forecast interval will be

$$(a + bx^0) \pm t_{\lambda/2} \sqrt{s^2 \left[1 + \frac{1}{n} + \frac{(x^0 - \bar{x})^2}{S_{xx}} \right]}. \qquad (5\text{-}42)$$

EXAMPLE 5.8.   Suppose, using the consumption data of Example 5.1, that 1980 disposable income were forecasted to be \$1030 billion. To compute a forecast interval, we require

$$a = -67.5806,$$
$$b = 0.9793,$$
$$s^2 = 67.125,$$
$$\bar{x} = 879.24,$$
$$S_{xx} = 67192.44,$$
$$n = 10.$$

The critical value from the t distribution is 2.306. Inserting these in (5–42) produces a forecast interval of

$$-67.5806 + 0.9793(1030) \pm 2.306(9.8256)$$

or

$$941.1 \pm 22.658^{13}.$$

Figure 5.11 shows the computation for the data we have been using in our example of the consumption function. There are two important features of the prediction interval. First, note that its width is a function of $(x^0 - \bar{x})^2$. Thus, the farther x^0 is from $\bar{x}$, the wider will be the forecast interval. This reflects the intuitively appealing result that forecasting is more difficult the further we go outside the range of our experience (in either direction). Second,

---

[13] The actual outcomes were disposable income of \$1021.6 billion and consumption of \$931.8 billion. Based on knowledge of the figure of 1021.6, our forecast of consumption would have been 932.9, with an ex post forecast error of 0.12 percent.

Figure 5.11   Forecast intervals.

note that the forecast variance in (5–41) is composed of three parts. The second and third become progressively smaller as we accumulate more data (i.e., as n increases). But the first term, σ^2, is constant, which implies that no matter how much data we have, we can never predict perfectly.

EXAMPLE 5.9. Prediction with a Log-Linear Model.   If the regression model is

$$y = \alpha x^\beta e^\varepsilon,$$

the results of this section apply to predictions of

$$\ln y = \alpha' + \beta \ln x + \varepsilon.$$

It is natural to use

$$\hat{y} = e^{\widehat{\ln y}}$$

and just exponentiate the surrounding confidence limits. But if $\ln y$ has a normal distribution with mean μ, y has a lognormal distribution with mean

$$E[y] = e^\mu e^{\sigma^2/2}$$

and *median*

$$\text{Med}[y] = e^\mu.$$

So, our forecast estimates the median, which is less than the mean because the distribution is skewed to the right. We do have a proper confidence interval for the median if that is what is desired. One simple approach is just to scale the estimate of $E[y]$, as well as the confidence limits by $e^{\hat{\sigma}^2/2}$, where $\hat{\sigma}^2$ is the estimated forecast variance. Further refinements are suggested by Dadkah (1984).

Exercises

1. Production data for 22 firms in a certain industry produce the following, where $y = \ln$ output and $x = \ln$ labor hours input:

$$\bar{y} = 20 \qquad \sum_i (y_i - \bar{y})^2 = 100,$$

$$\bar{x} = 10 \qquad \sum_i (x_i - \bar{x})^2 = 60$$

$$\sum_i (x_i - \bar{x})(y_i - \bar{y}) = 30.$$

(a) Compute the least squares estimates of α and β in the model

$$y = \alpha + \beta x + \varepsilon.$$

(b) Test the hypothesis that $\beta = 1$.

(c) Form a 99 percent confidence interval for σ^2, the variance of ε.

2. Data from a different industry are used to obtain the following estimated regression:

$$\hat{y} = 25 + 0.4x, \qquad R^2 = 0.2, \ \bar{y} = 35, \ n = 12,$$

$$\sum_i (x_i - \bar{x})^2 = 100.$$

Test the hypothesis that the slopes are the same in this regression and the one in the previous problem, assuming that the disturbance variances are the same. [**Hint:** For independent samples, there are two approaches. If it can be assumed that the disturbance variances in the two models are equal, the two samples can be pooled to estimate the common σ^2. Determine the pooled moments by manipulating the previous results. Then the statistic $(b_1 - b_2)/\{s^2[(1/(\mathbf{x}_1'\mathbf{M}^0\mathbf{x}_1)) + (1/(\mathbf{x}_2'\mathbf{M}^0\mathbf{x}_2))]\}^{1/2}$ may be referred to the t distribution with $n_1 + n_2 - 4$ degrees of freedom. If the assumption of equal variances is untenable, the statistic $(b_1 - b_2)/\{\text{Est. Var}[b_1] + \text{Est. Var}[b_2]\}^{1/2}$ will be approximately distributed as standard normal. Carry out the test, using both methods.]

3. Suppose you have two independent unbiased estimators of the same parameter, θ, say $\hat{\theta}_1$ and $\hat{\theta}_2$, with different variances, v_1 and v_2. What linear combination, $\hat{\theta} = c_1\hat{\theta}_1 + c_2\hat{\theta}_2$, is the minimum variance unbiased estimator of θ? Use your result to compute the minimum variance unbiased estimator of the common slope in the two regressions in Exercises 1 and 2.

4. For the data in Exercise 1, what is the R^2 in the regression of y on x? Now suppose that the regression is fit without a constant term and the computer program computes the R^2, using

$$R^2 = 1 - \frac{\mathbf{e}'\mathbf{e}}{\sum_i (y_i - \bar{y})^2}.$$

What value will be reported? What if it uses

$$R^2 = \frac{b^2 \sum_i (x_i - \bar{x})^2}{\sum_i (y_i - \bar{y})^2}$$

instead? What value will be reported? What is the appropriate value to report?

5. We are interested in studying salary differences between two professions. Our sample consists of 60 individuals from profession A and 40 from profession B. The average

salary in B is 1. The average salary in the entire sample is 0.85. If we compute a least squares regression of salaries on a constant and a variable that is simply 0 for all individuals in A and 1 for those in B, what will be the constant and the slope? If the standard deviations of the two samples are 0.2 for profession A and 0.3 for profession B, what are the estimates of the variances and covariance of the two estimates? What is the R^2 in the regression? (For further applications, see Section 8.2.)

6. Suppose that a regression of the balance of trade with a particular country gives results

$$Y = 100000 + 0.6X + e, \qquad R^2 = 0.4,$$

using yearly observations quoted in 1972 dollars. Suppose that the figures were rescaled to 1982 dollars by multiplying by 0.74. What would have been obtained for the constant and slope? Based on the previous figures, would you be able to determine the least squares results if the figures were quoted in the currency of the other country instead if you knew the exchange rates?

7. Three variables, N, D, and Y, all have zero means and unit variances. A fourth variable is $C = N + D$. In the regression of C on Y, the slope is 0.8. In the regression of C on N, the slope is 0.5. In the regression of D on Y, the slope is 0.4. What is the sum of squared residuals in the regression of C on D? There are 21 observations, and all moments are computed using $1/(n-1)$ as the divisor.

8. Prove that the least squares intercept estimator in the classical regression model is the minimum variance linear unbiased estimator.

9. Suppose that the data for a regression are given in terms of deviations from the sample means. What is the expected value of the slope in the regression of $(y_i - \bar{y})$ on $(x_i - \bar{x})$ if it is computed without a constant term? Suppose that only the data on x are in mean deviation form. Now what is the expected value of the slope estimator? Finally, suppose that only y is in mean deviation form. What is the expected value of the slope estimator in the regression of the centered y's on the uncentered x's, assuming that the true value of the intercept is not zero.?

10. Consider the simple regression

$$y_i = \beta x_i + \varepsilon_i.$$

(a) What is the minimum mean squared error linear estimator of β? [**Hint:** Let the estimator be $\hat{\beta} = c'y$. Choose c to minimize $\text{Var}[\beta] + (E[\hat{\beta} - \beta])^2$. The answer is a function of the unknown parameters.]

(b) For the estimator in part (a), show that the ratio of the mean squared error of $\hat{\beta}$ to that of the ordinary least squares estimator, b, is

$$\frac{\text{MSE}[\hat{\beta}]}{\text{MSE}[b]} = \frac{\tau^2}{(1 + \tau^2)},$$

where

$$\tau^2 = \frac{\beta^2}{\sigma^2/x'x}.$$

Note that τ is the square of the population analog to the t ratio for testing the hypothesis that $\beta = 0$, which is given in (5–33). How do you interpret the behavior of this ratio as $\tau \to \infty$? (For some further discussion of this result and some related issues, see Section 8.5.)

11. Suppose that the classical regression model applies, but the true value of the constant is zero. Compare the variance of the least squares slope estimator computed without a constant term to that of the estimator computed with an unnecessary constant term.

12. The next year's data for the consumption data given in Table 5.1 appear in a footnote to Example 5.8. Reestimate the regression with this new information; then use the updated regression to compute a 95 percent forecast interval for 1981 consumption, assuming that disposable income is forecasted to be $1037.4 billion.

13. Suppose that the regression model is

$$y_i = \alpha + \beta x_i + \varepsilon_i,$$

$$f(\varepsilon_i) = \left(\frac{1}{\lambda}\right) e^{-\varepsilon_i/\lambda}, \qquad \varepsilon_i \geq 0.$$

This is rather a peculiar model in that all of the disturbances are assumed to be positive. Note that the disturbances have $E[\varepsilon_i] = \lambda$. Show that the least squares constant term is unbiased but that the intercept is biased. (This is an example of a "frontier function." Applications and discussion of some related issues appear in Sections 10.5.3–10.5.4.)

14. For the regression model without a constant term in Exercise 10, prove that the estimator $\bar{y}/\bar{x}$ is unbiased and show that its variance is greater than that of the ordinary least squares estimator.

15. As a profit-maximizing monopolist, you face the demand curve

$$Q = \alpha + \beta P + \varepsilon.$$

In the past, you have set the following prices and sold the accompanying quantities:

Q	3	3	7	6	10	15	16	13	9	15	9	15	12	18	21,
P	18	16	17	12	15	15	4	13	11	6	8	10	7	7	7.

Suppose that your marginal cost is 10. Based on the least squares regression, compute a 95 percent confidence interval for the profit-maximizing output.

16. For the bivariate distribution in Exercise 15 of Chapter 4, it is shown (claimed) in part (f) that

$$f(x|y) = \frac{e^{-\beta y}(\beta y)^x}{x!}.$$

It follows that

$$E[x|y] = \beta y.$$

(a) Does this suggest an alternative estimator for β to the maximum likelihood estimator of part (a) of that exercise?

(b) It can also be shown (can you do it?) that in the conditional distribution in part (d),

$$E[y|x] = \alpha x \qquad \text{where} \qquad \alpha = \frac{1}{\beta + \theta}.$$

Does this suggest an alternative estimator to the maximum likelihood estimator of α implied by part (a) of that exercise? What is the MLE of α for that bivariate distribution? What is its asymptotic distribution?

References

Dadkah, K. M., "Confidence Interval Predictions for Logarithmic Models," *Review of Economics and Statistics*, 77, 1984, pp. 527–528.

Friedman, M., *A Theory of the Consumption Function*, Chicago: National Bureau of Economic Research, 1957.

Husby, R., "A Nonlinear Consumption Function Estimated from Time Series and Cross Section Data," *Review of Economics and Statistics*, 53, 1971, pp. 211–216.

Judge, G., C. Hill, W. Griffiths, T. Lee, and H. Lutkepohl, *The Theory and Practice of Econometrics*, New York: Wiley, 1985.

Keynes, J. M., *The General Theory of Employment, Interest, and Money*, Orlando, Fla.: Harcourt Brace Jovanovich, 1936.

Maddala, G., *Econometrics*, New York: McGraw-Hill, 1977.

Chapter 6
Multiple Regression

6.1. Introduction

The regression model developed in Chapter 5 is flexible enough to accommodate a variety of settings. But it is inadequate when we can identify more than one independent influence on the dependent variable. The **multiple regression model** allows us to study the relationship between a dependent variable and several independent variables.

    EXAMPLE 6.1. A number of recent studies have analyzed the relationship between income and education. We would expect, on average, higher levels of education to be associated with higher incomes. However, the simple regression model

$$\text{Income} = \beta_1 + \beta_2 \text{education} + \varepsilon$$

neglects the fact that most people have a higher income when they are older than when they are young, regardless of their education. This means that β_2 will overstate the marginal impact of education. If age and education are positively correlated, it will associate all of the observed increases in income with increases in education. A better specification would account for the effect of age, as in

$$\text{Income} = \beta_1 + \beta_2 \text{education} + \beta_3 \text{age} + \varepsilon.$$

It is often observed that income tends to rise less rapidly in the later earning years than in the early ones. To accommodate this possibility, we might extend the model to

$$\text{Income} = \beta_1 + \beta_2 \text{education} + \beta_3 \text{age} + \beta_4 \text{age}^2 + \varepsilon.$$

We would expect β_3 to be positive and β_4 to be negative.

6.2. Assumptions of the Linear Model

The general form of the multiple linear regression model is

$$y_i = \beta_1 x_{i1} + \beta_2 x_{i2} + \cdots + \beta_K x_{iK} + \varepsilon_i. \tag{6-1}$$

The nature and sources of the disturbance were discussed in Chapter 5. The only difference here is the number of right-hand variables in the model. The model is linear in the variables x_k

and has an additive disturbance. (Of course, this does not restrict us to simple linear equations, however. Consider, for instance, the quadratic function of age in the model discussed in the Introduction.)

Let the column vector x_k be the n observations on variable $x_k, k = 1, \ldots, K$ and assemble these data in an $n \times K$ data matrix, X. In most contexts, the first column of X is assumed to be a column of ones, so that β_1 is the constant term in the model. Finally, let y be the n observations, $y_1, \ldots, y_n$. The model can now be written

$$y = x_1\beta_1 + \cdots + x_K\beta_K + \varepsilon \tag{6-2}$$

or

$$1. \ y = X\beta + \varepsilon. \tag{6-3}$$

As before, our primary interest is in estimation and inference about the parameter vector β. Note that the simple regression model of Chapter 5 is a special case in which X has only two columns. As before, we assume that X is a matrix of known constants. The more general case of stochastic regressors is considered in Chapter 10.

It is convenient to reformulate our earlier assumptions about the disturbance in matrix notation.

$$E[\varepsilon_i] = 0$$

or

$$2. \ E[\varepsilon] = \begin{bmatrix} E[\varepsilon_1] \\ E[\varepsilon_2] \\ \vdots \\ E[\varepsilon_n] \end{bmatrix} = 0, \tag{6-4}$$

which implies that

$$E[y] = X\beta.$$

The assumptions of constant variance, or homoscedasticity, and uncorrelatedness across observations imply that

$$E[\varepsilon\varepsilon'] = \begin{bmatrix} E[\varepsilon_1\varepsilon_1] & E[\varepsilon_1\varepsilon_2] & \cdots & E[\varepsilon_1\varepsilon_n] \\ E[\varepsilon_2\varepsilon_1] & E[\varepsilon_2\varepsilon_2] & \cdots & E[\varepsilon_2\varepsilon_n] \\ \vdots & \vdots & \vdots & \vdots \\ E[\varepsilon_n\varepsilon_1] & E[\varepsilon_n\varepsilon_2] & \cdots & E[\varepsilon_n\varepsilon_n] \end{bmatrix}$$

$$= \begin{bmatrix} \sigma^2 & 0 & \cdots & 0 \\ 0 & \sigma^2 & \cdots & 0 \\ & & \vdots & \\ 0 & 0 & \cdots & \sigma^2 \end{bmatrix}. \tag{6-5}$$

$$3. \ E[\varepsilon\varepsilon'] = \sigma^2 I.$$

We shall maintain the assumption that the disturbances are independently and identically normally distributed:

$$4. \ \varepsilon \sim N[0, \sigma^2 I]. \tag{6-6}$$

The assumption of normality of the disturbances is not always necessary to obtain the statistical results we use in multiple regression analysis. However, except in those cases in which some alternative distribution is explicitly assumed,[1] the normality assumption is probably quite reasonable.[2]

Another very important assumption must be made about the regressors. We assume that there are no exact linear relationships among the variables.

$$5. \ \text{Rank}(\mathbf{X}) = K, \tag{6-7}$$

which means that $\mathbf{X}$ has full column rank; the columns of $\mathbf{X}$ are linearly independent. The counterpart in the simple model of the previous chapter was the assumption that $\sum_i (x_i - \bar{x})^2$ is different from zero. If not, all values are the same and the second column of $\mathbf{X}$ is a multiple of the first. Among other things, this implies that we must have at least K observations. To see the need for this assumption, consider an example.

EXAMPLE 6.2. Suppose that a cross-section model specifies $C = \beta_1 + \beta_2 \text{nonlabor}$ income $+ \beta_3 \text{salary} + \beta_4 \text{income} + \varepsilon$, where income is exactly equal to salary plus nonlabor income. Clearly, there is an exact linear dependency in the model. Now let

$$\beta'_2 = \beta_2 + a,$$
$$\beta'_3 = \beta_3 + a,$$

and

$$\beta'_4 = \beta_4 - a,$$

where a is any number. Then the exact same value appears on the right-hand side if we substitute β'_2, β'_3, and β'_4 for β_2, β_3, and β_4. Obviously, there is no way to estimate the parameters of this model. As we shall see later, there are certain functions of the parameters that can be estimated in a case such as this. For instance, regardless of the value of a,

$$\beta_2 + \beta_4 = \beta'_2 + \beta'_4$$

and

$$\beta_3 + \beta_4 = \beta'_3 + \beta'_4.$$

We should be able to estimate a model that is a function of $\gamma_1 = \beta_2 + \beta_4$ and $\gamma_2 = \beta_3 + \beta_4$. By substituting income = nonlabor income + salary in the previous equation, we obtain precisely

$$C = \beta_1 + \gamma_1 \text{nonlabor income} + \gamma_2 \text{salary} + \varepsilon.$$

6.3. Least Squares Regression

As before, we consider the most common method of estimating the parameters of the linear regression model, least squares.

6.3.1. The Least Squares Coefficient Vector

The least squares coefficient vector minimizes the sum of squared residuals:

$$\sum_i \tilde{\varepsilon}_i^2 = \sum_i (y_i - \mathbf{x}'_i \tilde{\boldsymbol{\beta}})^2, \tag{6-8}$$

---

[1] See, for example, Aigner et al. (1977) and Chapter 10.
[2] As a practical matter, the loss of generality in making this assumption is sometimes exaggerated.

where $\tilde{\beta}$ is the arbitrary choice for the coefficient vector. The minimization problem, then, is to choose $\tilde{\beta}$ to

$$\text{Minimize }_{\tilde{\beta}} S(\tilde{\beta}) = \tilde{\varepsilon}'\tilde{\varepsilon} = (\mathbf{y} - \mathbf{X}\tilde{\beta})'(\mathbf{y} - \mathbf{X}\tilde{\beta}). \tag{6-9}$$

Expanding this, we have

$$\tilde{\varepsilon}'\tilde{\varepsilon} = \mathbf{y}'\mathbf{y} - \tilde{\beta}'\mathbf{X}'\mathbf{y} - \mathbf{y}'\mathbf{X}\tilde{\beta} + \tilde{\beta}'\mathbf{X}'\mathbf{X}\tilde{\beta}$$

$$\tag{6-10}$$

or

$$S(\tilde{\beta}) = \mathbf{y}'\mathbf{y} - 2\tilde{\beta}'\mathbf{X}'\mathbf{y} + \tilde{\beta}'\mathbf{X}'\mathbf{X}\tilde{\beta}.$$

The necessary condition for a minimum is

$$\frac{\partial S(\tilde{\beta})}{\partial \tilde{\beta}} = -2\mathbf{X}'\mathbf{y} + 2\mathbf{X}'\mathbf{X}\tilde{\beta} = \mathbf{0}. \tag{6-11}$$

Let $\mathbf{b}$ be the solution. Then $\mathbf{b}$ satisfies the normal equations

$$\mathbf{X}'\mathbf{X}\mathbf{b} = \mathbf{X}'\mathbf{y}.$$

These are the least squares normal equations that we analyzed earlier. Assuming that the inverse of $(\mathbf{X}'\mathbf{X})$ exists, which follows from the full rank assumption,[3] we find that the solution is

$$\mathbf{b} = (\mathbf{X}'\mathbf{X})^{-1}\mathbf{X}'\mathbf{y}. \tag{6-12}$$

In order to verify that this is indeed a minimum, we require

$$\frac{\partial^2 S(\mathbf{b})}{\partial \mathbf{b} \partial \mathbf{b}'} = 2\mathbf{X}'\mathbf{X} \tag{6-13}$$

to be a positive definite matrix. Let $q = \mathbf{c}'\mathbf{X}'\mathbf{X}\mathbf{c}$ for some arbitrary vector, $\mathbf{c}$. Then

$$q = \mathbf{v}'\mathbf{v} = \sum_i v_i^2, \qquad \text{where } \mathbf{v} = \mathbf{X}\mathbf{c}.$$

Unless every element of $\mathbf{v}$ is zero, q is positive. But if $\mathbf{v}$ could be zero, $\mathbf{v}$ would be a linear combination of the columns of $\mathbf{X}$ that equals $\mathbf{0}$. This contradicts the assumption that $\mathbf{X}$ has full rank.

6.3.2. Some Examples

EXAMPLE 6.3.   To illustrate the computations, we consider an example based on recent macroeconomic data (see Table 6.1).

In order to estimate an investment equation, we first convert the Investment and GNP series to real terms by dividing them by the CPI[4] and then scale the two series so that they are measured in trillions of dollars. The other variables in the regression are a time trend $(1, 2, \ldots)$, the interest rate, and the rate of inflation, computed as the percentage change in the CPI.[5] These produce the data matrices listed in Table 6.2.

---

[3] The condition assumed in Chapter 5 that $\Sigma(x_i - \bar{x})^2$ is positive is the equivalent in the two-variable case.
[4] Arguably, one might choose a better deflator.
[5] The 1967 figure for the CPI is 79.06.

Table 6.1

Year	Nominal GNP	Nominal Investment	CPI	Interest Rate[a]
1968	873.4	133.3	82.54	5.16
1969	944.0	149.3	86.79	5.87
1970	992.7	144.2	91.45	5.95
1971	1077.6	166.4	96.01	4.88
1972	1185.9	195.0	100.00	4.50
1973	1326.4	229.8	105.75	6.44
1974	1434.2	228.7	115.08	7.83
1975	1549.2	206.1	125.79	6.25
1976	1718.0	257.9	132.34	5.50
1977	1918.3	324.1	140.05	5.46
1978	2163.9	386.6	150.42	7.46
1979	2417.8	423.0	163.42	10.28
1980	2633.1	402.3	178.64	11.77
1981	2937.7	471.5	195.51	13.42
1982	3057.5	421.9	207.23	11.02

Source: Data are from the *Economic Report of the President,* Government Printing Office, Washington, D.C., 1983.
[a] Average yearly discount rate at the New York Federal Reserve Bank.

Table 6.2

Real Investment (Y)	Constant (1)	Trend (T)	Real GNP (G)	Interest Rate (R)	Inflation Rate (P)
0.161	1	1	1.058	5.16	4.40
0.172	1	2	1.088	5.87	5.15
0.158	1	3	1.086	5.95	5.37
0.173	1	4	1.122	4.88	4.99
0.195	1	5	1.186	4.50	4.16
0.217	1	6	1.254	6.44	5.75
0.199	1	7	1.246	7.83	8.82
0.163	1	8	1.232	6.25	9.31
0.195	1	9	1.298	5.50	5.21
0.231	1	10	1.370	5.46	5.83
0.257	1	11	1.439	7.46	7.40
0.259	1	12	1.479	10.28	8.64
0.225	1	13	1.474	11.77	9.31
0.241	1	14	1.503	13.42	9.44
0.204	1	15	1.475	11.02	5.99

The Y column and X matrix are indicated in the table.

Consider first a simple regression of real investment on a constant, a time trend, and real GNP, which correspond to x_1, x_2, and x_3. The normal equations are

$$\begin{bmatrix} \sum_i x_{i1}x_{i1} & \sum_i x_{i1}x_{i2} & \sum_i x_{i1}x_{i3} \\ \sum_i x_{i2}x_{i1} & \sum_i x_{i2}x_{i2} & \sum_i x_{i2}x_{i3} \\ \sum_i x_{i3}x_{i1} & \sum_i x_{i3}x_{i2} & \sum_i x_{i3}x_{i3} \end{bmatrix} \begin{bmatrix} b_1 \\ b_2 \\ b_3 \end{bmatrix} = \begin{bmatrix} \sum_i x_{i1}y_i \\ \sum_i x_{i2}y_i \\ \sum_i x_{i3}y_i \end{bmatrix}.$$

Inserting the specific variables of the example, we have

$$b_1 n \quad + b_2 \sum T + b_3 \sum G = \sum Y,$$
$$b_1 \sum T + b_2 \sum T^2 + b_3 \sum TG = \sum TY,$$
$$b_1 \sum G + b_2 \sum TG + b_3 \sum G^2 = \sum GY.$$

A solution can be obtained by first dividing the first equation by n to obtain

$$b_1 = \bar{Y} - b_2 \bar{T} - b_3 \bar{G}.$$

Insert this in the second and third equations, and rearrange terms to yield a set of two equations:

$$b_2 \sum (T - \bar{T})^2 \quad + b_3 \sum (T - \bar{T})(G - \bar{G}) = \sum (T - \bar{T})(Y - \bar{Y}),$$
$$b_2 \sum (T - \bar{T})(G - \bar{G}) + b_3 \sum (G - \bar{G})^2 \quad = \sum (G - \bar{G})(Y - \bar{Y}).$$

This shows the nature of the solution for the slopes, which will be computed from the sums of squared deviations and cross products of the variables. Letting lowercase letters indicate variables measured as deviations from the sample means, we find that the least squares solutions for b_2 and b_3 are

$$b_2 = \frac{\sum ty \sum g^2 - \sum gy \sum tg}{\sum t^2 \sum g^2 - \left(\sum gt\right)^2},$$

$$b_3 = \frac{\sum gy \sum t^2 - \sum ty \sum tg}{\sum t^2 \sum g^2 - \left(\sum gt\right)^2}.$$

With these solutions in hand, the intercept can now be computed. The sample sums for the variables of this regression are

$\bar{Y} = 0.20333$	$\sum y^2 = 0.016353$	$\sum ty = 1.60400,$
$\bar{T} = 8$	$\sum t^2 = 280$	$\sum gy = 0.066196,$
$\bar{G} = 1.2873$	$\sum g^2 = 0.359609$	$\sum tg = 9.82000.$

Therefore, the least squares slopes and intercept in the regression of Y on a constant, T and G, are

$$b_1 = -0.5005639,$$
$$b_2 = -0.0171984,$$
$$b_3 = 0.653723.$$

The solution for the least squares slopes for the three-variable regression is presented in detail to highlight the computations involved. In particular, note that the results can be obtained by first obtaining the means and sample central moments, then solving the pair of equations for the slopes, and finally, obtaining the constant term.

Some additional insight is provided by manipulating the solution for, say b_3, the slope on GNP. Suppose that we just regressed investment on GNP, neglecting the time trend. At least some of the correlation we observe will be explainable by the fact that both investment and real GNP have an obvious time trend. (This is clear in the raw data in the preceding table.) The slope in this regression would be

$$b_{yg} = \frac{\sum gy}{\sum g^2} = 0.184078.$$

Now divide the preceding expression for b_3 by $\sum t^2 \sum g^2$. By manipulating it a bit and using the definition of the sample correlation between G and T, $r_{gt}^2 = (\sum gt)^2/(\sum g^2 \sum t^2)$, we obtain

$$b_{yg.t} = \frac{b_{yg}}{1 - r_{gt}^2} - \frac{b_{yt}b_{tg}}{1 - r_{gt}^2} = 0.653673.$$

(The notation used on the left-hand side is interpreted to mean the slope in the regression of y on g "in the presence of t.") The slope in the multiple regression embodies a correction to the slope in the simple regression that accounts for the influence of the additional variable, T, on both Y and G. For an explicit example of this effect, note what we get in the simple regression of real investment on a time trend: $b_{yt} = 1.604/280 = 0.057286$, a positive number that reflects the upward secular trend apparent in the preceding data. But in the multiple regression, after we account for the influence of GNP on real investment, the slope on the time trend, as we have seen, is -0.0171967, indicating instead a downward trend. This simple example illustrates the considerable danger of drawing conclusions from a badly specified regression model. The general result for a three-variable regression in which x_1 is a constant term is

$$b_{y2.3} = \frac{b_{y2} - b_{y3}b_{32}}{1 - r_{23}^2}. \tag{6-14}$$

It is clear from this expression that the magnitudes of $b_{y2.3}$ and b_{y2} can be quite different. They need not even have the same sign. The omission of important variables can be particularly serious.

As a final observation, note what becomes of $b_{yg.t}$ if r_{gt}^2 equals zero. The first term becomes b_{yg}, while the second becomes zero. (If G and T are not correlated, the slope in the regression of G on T, b_{gt}, is zero.) Therefore, we conclude the following:

> If the variables in a multiple regression are not correlated (i.e., are orthogonal), the multiple regression slopes are the same as the slopes in the individual simple regressions.

In practice, you will rarely compute a multiple regression by hand or with a calculator. Computers and easy-to-use software have greatly simplified the process. Still, it helps to see the nature of the calculations involved. For a regression with more than three variables, the calculations proceed along similar lines but are extremely cumbersome. The tools of matrix algebra rapidly become indispensable (as does a computer). Consider, for example, an enlarged model of investment that includes, in addition to the constant, time trend, and GNP, an interest rate and the rate of inflation. Least squares requires the simultaneous solution of five normal equations. Letting $\mathbf{X}$ and $\mathbf{y}$ denote the full data matrices shown previously, the normal equations are

$$(\mathbf{X'X})\mathbf{b} = \mathbf{X'y}$$

or

$$
\begin{bmatrix}
15.000 & 120.00 & 19.310 & 111.79 & 99.770 \\
120.000 & 1240.0 & 164.30 & 1035.9 & 875.60 \\
19.310 & 164.30 & 25.218 & 148.98 & 131.22 \\
111.79 & 1035.9 & 148.98 & 943.86 & 799.02 \\
99.770 & 875.60 & 131.22 & 799.02 & 716.67
\end{bmatrix}
\begin{bmatrix}
b_1 \\ b_2 \\ b_3 \\ b_4 \\ b_5
\end{bmatrix}
=
\begin{bmatrix}
3.0500 \\ 26.004 \\ 3.9926 \\ 23.521 \\ 20.732
\end{bmatrix}.
$$

The solution is

$$\mathbf{b} = (\mathbf{X}'\mathbf{X})^{-1}\mathbf{X}'\mathbf{y}$$

or

$$
\begin{bmatrix} b_1 \\ b_2 \\ b_3 \\ b_4 \\ b_5 \end{bmatrix} = \begin{bmatrix} -0.5090 \\ -0.0166 \\ 0.6704 \\ -0.0023 \\ -0.0001 \end{bmatrix}
$$

$$
= \begin{bmatrix}
67.41 & 2.270 & -66.77 & 0.1242 & -0.0711 \\
2.270 & 0.08624 & -2.257 & -0.0064 & -0.0009 \\
-66.77 & -2.257 & 67.09 & -0.1614 & -0.0506 \\
0.1242 & -0.0064 & -0.1614 & 0.03295 & -0.01665 \\
-.0711 & -0.0009 & -0.0506 & -0.01665 & 0.04028
\end{bmatrix}
\begin{bmatrix}
3.050 \\
26.004 \\
3.993 \\
23.521 \\
20.732
\end{bmatrix}.
$$

6.3.3. Some Algebraic Aspects of the Solution

As a prelude to some later results, it is useful to examine some algebraic aspects of the least squares solution. The normal equations are

$$\mathbf{X}'\mathbf{X}\mathbf{b} - \mathbf{X}'\mathbf{y} = \mathbf{X}'(\mathbf{y} - \mathbf{X}\mathbf{b}) = \mathbf{X}'\mathbf{e}$$

$$= \mathbf{0}.$$

This means that for every column $\mathbf{x}_k$ of $\mathbf{X}$,

$$\mathbf{x}_k'\mathbf{e} = 0.$$

In particular, if the first column of $\mathbf{X}$ is a column of ones, the least squares residuals sum to zero. Two implications of this are as follows:

1. The regression hyperplane passes through the point of means of the data. The first normal equation implies that

$$\bar{y} = \mathbf{b}'\bar{\mathbf{x}},$$

where $\bar{\mathbf{x}}$ is the vector of means of the regressors.

2. The mean of the fitted values from the regression equals the mean of the actual values. This follows from (1) because the fitted values are just

$$\hat{\mathbf{y}} = \mathbf{X}\mathbf{b}.$$

It is important to note that neither of these results need hold if the regression does not contain a constant term.

By definition, the vector of least squares residuals is

$$\mathbf{e} = \mathbf{y} - \mathbf{X}\mathbf{b}. \tag{6-15}$$

Inserting (6–12) for $\mathbf{b}$ gives

$$\mathbf{e} = \mathbf{y} - \mathbf{X}(\mathbf{X}'\mathbf{X})^{-1}\mathbf{X}'\mathbf{y}$$

$$= (\mathbf{I} - \mathbf{X}(\mathbf{X}'\mathbf{X})^{-1}\mathbf{X}')\mathbf{y} \tag{6-16}$$

$$= \mathbf{M}\mathbf{y}.$$

The $n \times n$ matrix, $\mathbf{M}$, is fundamental in regression analysis. You can easily show that $\mathbf{M}$ is both symmetric ($\mathbf{M} = \mathbf{M}'$) and idempotent ($\mathbf{M} = \mathbf{M}^2$). In view of (6–16), we can interpret $\mathbf{M}$ as a matrix that, when it premultiplies any vector $\mathbf{y}$, produces the vector of least squares residuals in the regression of $\mathbf{y}$ on $\mathbf{X}$. It follows immediately that

$$\mathbf{MX} = \mathbf{0}.$$

One way to interpret this result is that if $\mathbf{X}$ is regressed on $\mathbf{X}$, a perfect fit will result and the residuals will be zero.

Finally, (6–15) implies that

$$\mathbf{y} = \mathbf{Xb} + \mathbf{e},$$

which is the sample analog to (6–3). Our least squares results partition $\mathbf{y}$ into two parts, the fitted values, $\mathbf{y} = \mathbf{Xb}$, and the residuals, $\mathbf{e}$. We see from $\mathbf{MX} = \mathbf{0}$ that these two parts are orthogonal. Now, given (6–16),

$$\hat{\mathbf{y}} = \mathbf{y} - \mathbf{e} = [\mathbf{I} - \mathbf{M}]\mathbf{y} = \mathbf{Py}.$$

The matrix $\mathbf{P}$, which is also symmetric and idempotent, is a **projection matrix**. It is the matrix formed from $\mathbf{X}$ such that when a vector, $\mathbf{y}$, is premultiplied by $\mathbf{P}$, the result is the fitted values in the least squares regression of $\mathbf{y}$ on $\mathbf{X}$.[6] Given the earlier results,

$$\mathbf{PX} = \mathbf{X}$$

and

$$\mathbf{PM} = \mathbf{MP} = \mathbf{0}.$$

In manipulating equations involving least squares results, the following equivalent expressions for the sum of squared residuals are often useful:

$$\mathbf{e}'\mathbf{e} = \mathbf{y}'\mathbf{M}'\mathbf{My} = \mathbf{y}'\mathbf{My} = \mathbf{y}'\mathbf{e} = \mathbf{e}'\mathbf{y},$$

$$\mathbf{e}'\mathbf{e} = \mathbf{y}'\mathbf{y} - \mathbf{b}'\mathbf{X}'\mathbf{Xb},$$

and

$$\mathbf{e}'\mathbf{e} = \mathbf{y}'\mathbf{y} - \mathbf{b}'\mathbf{X}'\mathbf{y} = \mathbf{y}'\mathbf{y} - \mathbf{y}'\mathbf{Xb}.$$

(You should be able to verify these expressions.)

6.3.4. Partitioned Regression and Partial Regression

It is common to specify a multiple regression model when, in fact, interest centers on only one or a subset of the full set of variables. Consider, for example, the income equation discussed in the Introduction. Although we are primarily interested in the association of income and education, age is, of necessity, included in the model. We have already established that it would be erroneous to omit age from the equation. The question we consider here is what computations are involved in obtaining, in isolation, the coefficients of a subset of the variables in a multiple regression, for example, the coefficient of education in the aforementioned regression.

In general terms, suppose that the regression involves two sets of variables, $\mathbf{X}_1$ and $\mathbf{X}_2$. Thus,

$$\mathbf{y} = \mathbf{X}\boldsymbol{\beta} + \boldsymbol{\varepsilon} = \mathbf{X}_1\boldsymbol{\beta}_1 + \mathbf{X}_2\boldsymbol{\beta}_2 + \boldsymbol{\varepsilon}.$$

[6] It creates the projection of the vector $\mathbf{y}$ in the column space of $\mathbf{X}$. This is the problem analyzed in Section 2.4.7.

What is the algebraic solution for $\mathbf{b}_2$? The normal equations are

$$\begin{aligned}(1)\\(2)\end{aligned}\begin{bmatrix} \mathbf{X}_1'\mathbf{X}_1 & \mathbf{X}_1'\mathbf{X}_2 \\ \mathbf{X}_2'\mathbf{X}_1 & \mathbf{X}_2'\mathbf{X}_2 \end{bmatrix}\begin{bmatrix} \mathbf{b}_1 \\ \mathbf{b}_2 \end{bmatrix} = \begin{bmatrix} \mathbf{X}_1'\mathbf{y} \\ \mathbf{X}_2'\mathbf{y} \end{bmatrix}.$$

A solution can be obtained by using the partitioned inverse matrix of Section 2.6.3 in the result

$$\begin{bmatrix} \mathbf{X}_1'\mathbf{X}_1 & \mathbf{X}_1'\mathbf{X}_2 \\ \mathbf{X}_2'\mathbf{X}_1 & \mathbf{X}_2'\mathbf{X}_2 \end{bmatrix}^{-1}\begin{bmatrix} \mathbf{X}_1'\mathbf{y} \\ \mathbf{X}_2'\mathbf{y} \end{bmatrix} = \begin{bmatrix} \mathbf{b}_1 \\ \mathbf{b}_2 \end{bmatrix}.$$

Alternatively, (1) and (2) can be manipulated directly to solve for $\mathbf{b}_2$. We first solve (1) for $\mathbf{b}_1$:

$$\begin{aligned} \mathbf{b}_1 &= (\mathbf{X}_1'\mathbf{X}_1)^{-1}\mathbf{X}_1'\mathbf{y} - (\mathbf{X}_1'\mathbf{X}_1)^{-1}\mathbf{X}_1'\mathbf{X}_2\mathbf{b}_2 \\ &= (\mathbf{X}_1'\mathbf{X}_1)^{-1}\mathbf{X}_1'(\mathbf{y} - \mathbf{X}_2\mathbf{b}_2). \end{aligned} \tag{6-17}$$

(Note that this solution states that $\mathbf{b}_1$ is the set of coefficients in the regression of $\mathbf{y}$ on $\mathbf{X}_1$, minus a correction vector.) Then, inserting this in (2) produces

$$\mathbf{X}_2'\mathbf{X}_1(\mathbf{X}_1'\mathbf{X}_1)^{-1}\mathbf{X}_1'\mathbf{y} - \mathbf{X}_2'\mathbf{X}_1(\mathbf{X}_1'\mathbf{X}_1)^{-1}\mathbf{X}_1'\mathbf{X}_2\mathbf{b}_2 + \mathbf{X}_2'\mathbf{X}_2\mathbf{b}_2 = \mathbf{X}_2'\mathbf{y}.$$

After collecting terms,

$$\mathbf{X}_2'(\mathbf{I} - \mathbf{X}_1(\mathbf{X}_1'\mathbf{X}_1)^{-1}\mathbf{X}_1')\mathbf{X}_2\mathbf{b}_2 = \mathbf{X}_2'(\mathbf{I} - \mathbf{X}_1(\mathbf{X}_1'\mathbf{X}_1)^{-1}\mathbf{X}_1')\mathbf{y}.$$

The solution is

$$\begin{aligned} \mathbf{b}_2 &= (\mathbf{X}_2'(\mathbf{I} - \mathbf{X}_1(\mathbf{X}_1'\mathbf{X}_1)^{-1}\mathbf{X}_1')\mathbf{X}_2)^{-1}\mathbf{X}_2'(\mathbf{I} - \mathbf{X}_1(\mathbf{X}_1'\mathbf{X}_1)^{-1}\mathbf{X}_1')\mathbf{y} \\ &= (\mathbf{X}_2'\mathbf{M}_1\mathbf{X}_2)^{-1}(\mathbf{X}_2'\mathbf{M}_1\mathbf{y}). \end{aligned} \tag{6-18}$$

Notice that the matrix appearing in parentheses inside each set of square brackets is the "residual maker" discussed earlier, in this case for a regression on the columns of $\mathbf{X}_1$. Thus, $\mathbf{M}_1\mathbf{X}_2$ is a matrix of residuals; each column of $\mathbf{M}_1\mathbf{X}_2$ is a vector of residuals in the regression of the corresponding column of $\mathbf{X}_2$ on the variables in $\mathbf{X}_1$. By exploiting the fact that $\mathbf{M}_1$, like $\mathbf{M}$, is idempotent, we can rewrite (6-18) as

$$\mathbf{b}_2 = (\mathbf{X}_2^{*\prime}\mathbf{X}_2^*)^{-1}\mathbf{X}_2^{*\prime}\mathbf{y}^*,$$

where

$$\tag{6-19}$$

$$\mathbf{X}_2^* = \mathbf{M}_1\mathbf{X}_2 \quad \text{and} \quad \mathbf{y}^* = \mathbf{M}_1\mathbf{y}.$$

Therefore, $\mathbf{b}_2$ is the set of coefficients obtained when the residuals from a regression of $\mathbf{y}$ on $\mathbf{X}_1$ alone are regressed on the set of residuals obtained when each column of $\mathbf{X}_2$ is regressed on $\mathbf{X}_1$. This process is commonly called *partialing out* or *netting out* the effect of $\mathbf{X}_1$. It is partly for this reason that the coefficients in a multiple regression are often called the *partial regression coefficients*.

In terms of our first example, we could obtain the coefficient on education in the least squares regression by first regressing income and education on age (or age and age squared) and then using the residuals from these regressions in a simple regression. In a classic application of this latter observation, Frisch and Waugh (1933) noted that in a time series setting, the same results were obtained whether a regression was fitted with a time trend variable or the data were first "detrended" by netting out the effect of time, as noted earlier, and using just the detrended data in a simple regression.[7]

---

[7] Recall our earlier investment example.

6.3.5.   Partial Regression and Partial Correlation Coefficients

The use of multiple regression involves a conceptual experiment that we might not be able to carry out in practice, the *ceteris paribus* analysis familiar in economics. To pursue an example considered in the Introduction, a regression equation relating income to age and education enables us to do the conceptual experiment of comparing, for example, the incomes of two individuals of the same age with different education levels, *even if the sample contains no such pair of individuals*. It is this characteristic of the regression that is implied by the term *partial regression coefficients*. The way we obtain this result, as we have seen, is first to regress income and education on age and then to compute the residuals from this regression. By construction, age will not have any power in explaining variation in these residuals. Therefore, any correlation between income and education after this "purging" is independent of (or after netting out the effect of) age.

The same principle can be applied to the correlation between two variables. To continue our example, when we observe a correlation of, say, 0.7 between income and education in our sample, to what extent can we assume that this correlation is due to any direct relationship, as opposed to being due to the fact that as individuals become older, both income and education tend, on average, to rise? To find out, we would use a **partial correlation coefficient**, which is computed along the same lines as the partial regression coefficient. In the context of our example, the partial correlation coefficient between income and education, controlling for the effect of age, is obtained as follows:

1. $Y^* = $ the residuals in a regression of income on age.
2. $E^* = $ the residuals in a regression of education on age.
3. The partial correlation, r^*_{YE}, is the simple correlation between Y^* and E^*.

This might seem to be a formidable amount of computation. There is, however, a convenient shortcut. Once the multiple regression is computed, the t ratio in (6–31) for testing the hypothesis that the coefficient equals zero (e.g., the last column of the table in Example 6.5) can be used to compute

$$r^{*2}_{yi} = \frac{t_i^2}{(t_i^2 + \text{degrees of freedom})}. \tag{6–20}$$

EXAMPLE 6.4.   **Partial Correlations.**   For the data of Example 6.2, the simple correlations between investment and the regressors r_{yi}, and partial correlations (given the other variables), r^*_{yi}, between investment and the four regressors are listed in Table 6.3.

As is clear from the figures, there is no necessary relation between the gross and partial correlation coefficients. One thing worth noting is the signs of the coefficients. The signs of the partial correlation coefficients are the same as the signs of the respective regression coefficients, three of which are negative. All of the gross correlation coefficients are positive because of the latent "effect" of time.

Table 6.3

	Simple Correlation	Partial Correlation
Time	0.7496	−0.9360
GNP	0.8632	0.9680
Interest	0.5871	−0.5166
Inflation	0.4777	−0.0221

6.3.6.   Deviations from Means—Regression on a Constant

As an application of the results in the preceding section, consider the case in which X_1 is just the first column of X, the column of ones. The solution for b_2 in this case will then be the slopes in a regression with a constant term. Let i be the column of ones. The coefficient in a regression of any variable, z, on i is $[i'i]^{-1}i'z = \bar{z}$, the fitted values are $i\bar{z}$, and the residuals are $z_i - \bar{z}$. Therefore, when we apply this to our previous results, we find the following:

> The slopes in a multiple regression that contains a
> constant term are obtained by transforming the data
> to deviations from their means, then regressing the
> variable y in deviation form on the explanatory
> variables, also in deviation form.

(We obtained this result for a specific case, $K = 3$, earlier.)

Exercise. What happens in the preceding regression if we neglect to transform y to deviations from $\bar{y}$ before we compute the slopes?

Having obtained the coefficients on X_2, how can we recover the coefficients on X_1? One way, of course, is to repeat the exercise of the previous section while reversing the roles of X_1 and X_2. But there is an easier way. For the general case, the first of the two normal equations is

$$X_1'X_1b_1 + X_1'X_2b_2 = X_1'y.$$

We have already solved for b_2. Therefore, we can use this in a solution for b_1:

$$b_1 = (X_1'X_1)^{-1}X_1'y - (X_1'X_1)^{-1}X_1'X_2b_2 = (X_1'X_1)^{-1}X_1'(y - X_2b_2). \qquad (6-21)$$

If X_1 is just a column of ones, the first of these produces the result

$$b_1 = \bar{y} - \bar{x}_2b_2 - \cdots - \bar{x}_Kb_K, \qquad (6-22)$$

which we have seen before.

6.4.   *Statistical Properties of the Least Squares Estimator*

In Chapter 5, we showed that the least squares estimator was the best linear unbiased estimator of β under the classical assumptions. Since that model is just a special case of the one considered here, we should expect these results to carry over to this more general case. Insert (6–3) in (6–12) to obtain

$$b = (X'X)^{-1}X'(X\beta + \varepsilon) = \beta + (X'X)^{-1}X'\varepsilon. \qquad (6-23)$$

If X is nonstochastic, or if $E(X'\varepsilon) = 0$, the expected value of the second term in (6–23) is 0. The least squares estimator is, therefore, unbiased. Its variance matrix is

$$
\begin{aligned}
\text{Var}[b] &= E[(b - \beta)(b - \beta)'] \\
&= E[(X'X)^{-1}X'\varepsilon\varepsilon'X(X'X)^{-1}] \\
&= (X'X)^{-1}X'E[\varepsilon\varepsilon']X(X'X)^{-1} \qquad (6-24) \\
&= (X'X)^{-1}X'(\sigma^2I)X(X'X)^{-1} \\
&= \sigma^2(X'X)^{-1}.
\end{aligned}
$$

The Gauss–Markov theorem derived in Chapter 5 implies that for a special case $(K = 2)$, **b** is the most efficient linear unbiased estimator of β. We now give a more general proof of this fundamental result. Let $\tilde{\mathbf{b}} = \mathbf{C}\mathbf{y}$ be another linear unbiased estimator of β, where **C** is a $K \times n$ matrix. If $\tilde{\mathbf{b}}$ is unbiased,

$$E[\mathbf{C}\mathbf{y}] = E[\mathbf{C}\mathbf{X}\beta + \mathbf{C}\varepsilon] = \beta,$$

which implies that $\mathbf{C}\mathbf{X} = \mathbf{I}$. The variance matrix of $\tilde{\mathbf{b}}$ can be found by replacing $(\mathbf{X}'\mathbf{X})^{-1}\mathbf{X}'$ with **C** in (6–24); the result is

$$\mathrm{Var}[\tilde{\mathbf{b}}] = \sigma^2 \mathbf{C}\mathbf{C}'.$$

Now let $\mathbf{D} = \mathbf{C} - (\mathbf{X}'\mathbf{X})^{-1}\mathbf{X}'$.[8] Then

$$\mathrm{Var}[\tilde{\mathbf{b}}] = \sigma^2[(\mathbf{D} + (\mathbf{X}'\mathbf{X})^{-1}\mathbf{X}')(\mathbf{D} + (\mathbf{X}'\mathbf{X})^{-1}\mathbf{X}')'].$$

Before expanding this sum of four terms, we note that

$$\mathbf{C}\mathbf{X} = \mathbf{I} = \mathbf{D}\mathbf{X} + (\mathbf{X}'\mathbf{X})^{-1}(\mathbf{X}'\mathbf{X}).$$

Since the last preceding term is **I**, $\mathbf{D}\mathbf{X} = \mathbf{0}$. Therefore,

$$\mathrm{Var}[\tilde{\mathbf{b}}] = \sigma^2 \mathbf{D}\mathbf{D}' + \sigma^2(\mathbf{X}'\mathbf{X})^{-1}$$

$$= \mathrm{Var}[\mathbf{b}] + \sigma^2 \mathbf{D}\mathbf{D}'.$$

The variance matrix of $\tilde{\mathbf{b}}$ equals that of **b** plus a positive definite matrix.[9] Therefore, every quadratic form in $\mathrm{Var}[\tilde{\mathbf{b}}]$ is larger than the corresponding quadratic form in $V(\mathbf{b})$. This implies the

Gauss–Markov theorem.   For any vector of constants, **w**, the minimum variance linear unbiased estimator of $\mathbf{w}'\beta$ in the classical regression model is $\mathbf{w}'\mathbf{b}$, where **b** is the least squares estimator. The proof follows from the previous derivation, since the variance of $\mathbf{w}'\mathbf{b}$ is a quadratic form in $\mathrm{Var}[\mathbf{b}]$, and likewise for any $\tilde{\mathbf{b}}$.

This proves that each estimator, b_i, is the best linear unbiased estimator of β_i. (Let **w** be all zeros except for a one in the ith position.) However, the theorem is much broader than this, since the result also applies to every other linear combination of the elements of β.

6.5.   *Statistical Inference*

In (6–23), **b** is a linear function of the normally distributed disturbance, ε. Hence, we may use the results of Chapter 4 and the mean vector and variance matrix derived earlier to state that

$$\mathbf{b} \sim N[\beta, \sigma^2(\mathbf{X}'\mathbf{X})^{-1}]. \tag{6–25}$$

This is a multivariate normal distribution, so each element of **b** is normally distributed:

$$b_i \sim N[\beta_i, \sigma^2(\mathbf{X}'\mathbf{X})^{-1}_{ii}]. \tag{6–26}$$

Let S^{ii} be the ith diagonal element of $(\mathbf{X}'\mathbf{X})^{-1}$. Then

$$z_i = \frac{b_i - \beta_i}{\sqrt{\sigma^2 S^{ii}}} \tag{6–27}$$

---

[8] Thus, **Dy** is just $\tilde{\mathbf{b}} - \mathbf{b}$.
[9] A quadratic form in $\mathbf{D}\mathbf{D}'$ is $\mathbf{q}'\mathbf{D}\mathbf{D}'\mathbf{q} = \mathbf{z}'\mathbf{z} > 0$.

has a standard normal distribution. If σ^2 were known, statistical inference about β_i could be based on z_i. However, σ^2 remains to be estimated, so (6–27) is not usable.

The least squares residuals are

$$e = My = M[X\beta + \varepsilon]$$
$$= M\varepsilon,$$

as $MX = 0$. An estimator of σ^2 will be based on the sum of squared residuals:

$$e'e = \varepsilon'M\varepsilon.$$

The expected value of this quadratic form is

$$E[e'e] = E[\varepsilon'M\varepsilon]$$
$$= E[tr(\varepsilon'M\varepsilon)] = E[tr(M\varepsilon\varepsilon')]$$
$$= tr(ME[\varepsilon\varepsilon']) = tr(M\sigma^2I)$$
$$= \sigma^2 tr(M).$$

The trace of M is

$$tr[I_n - X(X'X)^{-1}X'] = tr(I_n) - tr((X'X)^{-1}X'X)$$
$$= tr(I_n) - tr(I_K) = n - K.$$

Therefore,

$$E[e'e] = (n - K)\sigma^2,$$

and an unbiased estimator of σ^2 is

$$s^2 = \frac{e'e}{n - K}. \tag{6–28}$$

The **standard error of the regression** is s, the square root of s^2. With s^2, we can then compute

$$\text{Est. Var}[b] = s^2(X'X)^{-1}.$$

By using s^2 instead of σ^2, we can derive a statistic to use in place of z_i in (6–27). The quantity

$$\frac{(n-K)s^2}{\sigma^2} = \frac{e'e}{\sigma^2} = \left(\frac{\varepsilon}{\sigma}\right)'M\left(\frac{\varepsilon}{\sigma}\right) \tag{6–29}$$

is an idempotent quadratic form in a standard normal vector (ε/σ). Therefore, it has a chi-squared distribution with $\text{rank}(M) = \text{trace}(M) = n - K$ degrees of freedom.[10] The chi-squared variable in (6–29) is independent of the standard normal variable in (6–27). To prove this, it suffices to show that

$$\frac{(b - \beta)}{\sigma} = (X'X)^{-1}X'\left(\frac{\varepsilon}{\sigma}\right) \tag{6–30}$$

is independent of $(n - K)s^2/\sigma^2$. In Section 3.10.6, we found that a sufficient condition for the independence of a linear form, Lx, and an idempotent quadratic form, $x'Ax$, in a standard

[10] This was proved in Section 3.10.3a.

normal vector, $\mathbf{x}$, is that $\mathbf{LA} = \mathbf{0}$. Letting ε/σ equal $\mathbf{x}$, we find that the requirement here would be that $(\mathbf{X'X})^{-1}\mathbf{X'M} = \mathbf{0}$. It does, as can be verified by multiplying it out. The general result is central in the derivation of many test statistics in regression analysis:

> If ε is normally distributed, the least squares coefficient estimator, $\mathbf{b}$, is statistically independent of the residual vector, $\mathbf{e}$, and, therefore, all functions of $\mathbf{e}$, including s^2.

Therefore, the ratio

$$t_i = \frac{(b_i - \beta_i)/\sqrt{\sigma^2 S^{ii}}}{\{[(n-K)s^2/\sigma^2]/(n-K)\}^{1/2}} \qquad (6-31)$$
$$= \frac{b_i - \beta_i}{\sqrt{s^2 S^{ii}}}$$

has a t distribution with $(n - K)$ degrees of freedom.[11] We can use t_i in the same fashion as in Chapter 5 to test hypotheses or form confidence intervals about the individual elements of β. For example, the t ratio for the test of the hypothesis that a coefficient equals zero is a standard part of the regression output of most computer programs.

EXAMPLE 6.5. To continue the earlier investment example, the matrix $(\mathbf{X'X})^{-1}$ for the five-variable regression has been given. The sum of squared residuals from that regression is 0.0004507, so the estimate of σ^2 is $s^2 = 0.0004507/(15 - 5) = 0.00004507$. Multiplying $(\mathbf{X'X})^{-1}$ by this yields the estimated covariance matrix for the least squares slopes shown in Table 6.4.

A summary of the regression results is presented in Table 6.5.

There are 15 observations and 5 coefficients, so the t statistics have 10 degrees of freedom. The 95 percent critical value for a t distribution with 10 degrees of freedom is 2.228. Thus, the individual hypotheses that the first 3 coefficients are zero are rejected. The last 2 are not significantly different from zero by this test. Testing a hypothesis about a particular value of a coefficient other than zero proceeds along the lines developed in Chapter 5. For example, are these data consistent with the hypothesis that each \$1 billion increase in GNP will be associated with an equal increase in investment? The t ratio for testing this hypothesis is $(0.67035 - 1)/0.0549 = -6.004$, which indicates that the slope on GNP is significantly less than one.

Table 6.4

Constant	Time	Real GNP	Interest	Inflation
0.00304				
0.000102	0.0000039			
−0.00301	−0.000102	0.00302		
0.0000056	−0.0000003	−0.000007	0.0000015	
−0.0000032	−0.00000004	−0.0000022	−0.0000008	0.0000018

[11] See (3–36) in Section 3.4.2. It is the ratio of a standard normal variable to the square root of a chi-squared variable divided by its degrees of freedom.

Table 6.5.   Regression Results for an
Investment Equation

Variable	Coefficient	Standard Error	t Ratio
Sum of squared residuals			0.0004507
Standard error of the regression			0.006713
Constant	−0.50907	0.0551	−9.23
Time	−0.01658	0.001972	−8.41
Real GNP	0.67038	0.05500	12.19
Interest	−0.00232	0.001219	1.91
Inflation	−0.00009	0.001347	−0.070

We shall often be interested in testing hypotheses involving more than one coefficient. We can use a test statistic similar to the one in (6–31). Suppose the hypothesis is

$$H_0: r_1\beta_1 + r_2\beta_2 + \cdots + r_K\beta_K = q.$$

(Usually some of the r's will be zero.) The sample estimate of the left-hand side is

$$r_1 b_1 + r_2 b_2 + \cdots + r_K b_K = \hat{q}.$$

If $\hat{q}$ differs significantly from q, we would conclude that the sample data are not consistent with the hypothesis. Consistent with (6–31), it is natural to base the test on

$$t = \frac{\hat{q} - q}{se(\hat{q})}. \tag{6–32}$$

We require an estimate of the standard error of $\hat{q}$. Since $\hat{q}$ is a linear function of $\mathbf{b}$ and we have an estimate of the variance matrix of $\mathbf{b}$, $s^2(\mathbf{X'X})^{-1}$, we can estimate the variance of $\hat{q}$ with

$$\text{Est. Var}[\hat{q}] = \mathbf{r}'[s^2(\mathbf{X'X})^{-1}]\mathbf{r}.$$

The denominator in (6–32) is the square root of this quantity.[12] In words, (6–32) is the distance between the hypothesized function of the true coefficients and the same function of our estimates of them. If the hypothesis is true, our estimates should reflect that fact, at least within the range of sampling variability. Thus, if the absolute value of the preceding t ratio is larger than the appropriate critical value, doubt is cast on the hypothesis.

EXAMPLE 6.6. Linear Combination of Coefficients.   In the preceding example, we might ask whether it is more appropriate to formulate the regression in terms of the real interest rate, rather than to treat the interest rate and the rate of inflation separately.[13] If investors were only interested in the real rate of interest, equal increases in interest rates and the rate of inflation would have no effect on investment. The hypothesis is

$$H_0: \beta_4 + \beta_5 = 0.$$

To form the appropriate test statistic, we require the standard error of $\hat{q} = b_4 + b_5$, which is

$$se(\hat{q}) = (0.15 \times 10^{-5} + 0.18 \times 10^{-5} + 2(-0.8 \times 10^{-6}))^{1/2} = 0.001303.$$

---

[12] This is a special case of the more general result to be proven, so we need not derive the distribution separately.
[13] Once again, the use of the CPI and, here, an ex post rate of inflation is questionable. We retain these variables purely for the sake of a reasonably uncomplicated example.

The t ratio for the test is, therefore,

$$t = \frac{(-0.00232 + (-0.00009))}{0.001303} = -1.848.$$

Using the same critical value as before, we conclude that the sum of the two coefficients is not significantly different from zero.

Finally, we consider a set of J linear restrictions of the form

$$H_0: \mathbf{R}\boldsymbol{\beta} = \mathbf{q}.$$

Each row of $\mathbf{R}$ is a single linear restriction on the coefficient vector. Typically, $\mathbf{R}$ will have only a few rows and numerous zeros in each row. Some examples are as follows.

1. One of the coefficients is zero; $\beta_j = 0$,

   $\mathbf{R} = [0 \quad 0 \quad \cdots \quad 1 \quad 0 \quad \cdots \quad 0]$ and $\mathbf{q} = 0$.

2. Two of the coefficients are equal; $\beta_i = \beta_j$,

   $\mathbf{R} = [0 \quad 0 \quad 1 \quad \cdots \quad -1 \quad \cdots \quad 0]$ and $\mathbf{q} = 0$.

3. A set of the coefficients sum to one; $\beta_2 + \beta_3 + \beta_4 = 1$,

   $\mathbf{R} = [0 \quad 1 \quad 1 \quad 1 \quad 0 \quad \cdots]$ and $\mathbf{q} = 1$.

4. A subset of the coefficients are all zero; $\beta_1 = 0$, $\beta_2 = 0$, and $\beta_3 = 0$,

$$\mathbf{R} = \begin{bmatrix} 1 & 0 & 0 & 0 & \cdots & 0 \\ 0 & 1 & 0 & 0 & \cdots & 0 \\ 0 & 0 & 1 & 0 & \cdots & 0 \end{bmatrix} \quad \text{and} \quad \mathbf{q} = \begin{bmatrix} 0 \\ 0 \\ 0 \end{bmatrix}$$

or, equivalently,

$$[\mathbf{I}:\mathbf{0}]\boldsymbol{\beta} = \mathbf{0}.$$

5. Several constraints hold simultaneously:

$$\beta_2 + \beta_3 = 1, \beta_4 + \beta_6 = 0, \text{ and } \beta_5 + \beta_6 = 0,$$

$$\begin{bmatrix} 0 & 1 & 1 & 0 & 0 & 0 \\ 0 & 0 & 0 & 1 & 0 & 1 \\ 0 & 0 & 0 & 0 & 1 & 1 \end{bmatrix} \begin{bmatrix} \beta_1 \\ \beta_2 \\ \beta_3 \\ \beta_4 \\ \beta_5 \\ \beta_6 \end{bmatrix} = \begin{bmatrix} 1 \\ 0 \\ 0 \end{bmatrix}.$$

Given the least squares estimator, $\mathbf{b}$, our interest centers on the "discrepancy," vector $\mathbf{d} = \mathbf{Rb} - \mathbf{q}$. It is unlikely that $\mathbf{d}$ will be exactly $\mathbf{0}$. The statistical question is whether the deviation of $\mathbf{d}$ from $\mathbf{0}$ can be attributed to sampling error or whether it is significant. Since $\mathbf{b}$ is normally distributed and $\mathbf{d}$ is a linear function of $\mathbf{b}$, $\mathbf{d}$ is also normally distributed. If the null hypothesis is true, $\mathbf{d}$ has mean vector $\mathbf{0}$ and variance

$$\text{Var}[\mathbf{d}] = \text{Var}[\mathbf{Rb} - \mathbf{q}] = \mathbf{R}\,\text{Var}[\mathbf{b}]\mathbf{R}' = \sigma^2 \mathbf{R}(\mathbf{X}'\mathbf{X})^{-1}\mathbf{R}'. \tag{6-33}$$

We can base a test of H_0 on the *Wald criterion*:

$$W = \chi^2(J) = \mathbf{d}'[\text{Var}(\mathbf{d})]^{-1}\mathbf{d}. \tag{6-34}$$

This has a chi-squared distribution with J degrees of freedom if the hypothesis is correct.[14] Intuitively, the larger is $\mathbf{d}$, that is, the worse is the failure of least squares to satisfy the restrictions, the larger will be the chi-squared statistic. Therefore, a large chi-squared value will weigh against the hypothesis.

The chi-squared statistic in (6-34) is not usable because of the unknown σ^2. We can derive a usable sample statistic similar to the t ratio in (6-31) by using s^2 instead of σ^2. Let

$$F = \frac{(\mathbf{Rb} - \mathbf{q})'[\sigma^2\mathbf{R}(\mathbf{X}'\mathbf{X})^{-1}\mathbf{R}']^{-1}(\mathbf{Rb} - \mathbf{q})/J}{[(n - K)s^2/\sigma^2]/(n - K)}. \tag{6-35}$$

The numerator is $(1/J)$ times W in (6-34). The denominator is $1/(n - K)$ times the idempotent quadratic form in (6-29). Therefore, F is the ratio of two chi-squared variates, each divided by its degrees of freedom. If they are independent, F is distributed as $F[J, (n - K)]$. We found earlier that $\mathbf{b}$ is distributed independently of s^2, so the condition is met. It is instructive, however, to verify it directly. By using (6-29) and the fact that $\mathbf{M}$ is idempotent, we may write F as

$$F = \frac{\{\mathbf{R}(\mathbf{b} - \beta)/\sigma\}'[\mathbf{R}(\mathbf{X}'\mathbf{X})^{-1}\mathbf{R}']^{-1}\{\mathbf{R}(\mathbf{b} - \beta)/\sigma\}/J}{[\mathbf{M}(\varepsilon/\sigma)]'[\mathbf{M}(\varepsilon/\sigma)]/(n - K)}. \tag{6-36}$$

If H_0 is true,

$$\frac{\mathbf{R}(\mathbf{b} - \beta)}{\sigma} = \mathbf{R}(\mathbf{X}'\mathbf{X})^{-1}\mathbf{X}'\left(\frac{\varepsilon}{\sigma}\right) = \mathbf{T}\left(\frac{\varepsilon}{\sigma}\right).$$

The F statistic is the ratio of two quadratic forms in (ε/σ). However, one of them is not idempotent, so the result of Section 3.10.4 does not apply. Nonetheless, since $\mathbf{M}(\varepsilon/\sigma)$ and $\mathbf{T}(\varepsilon/\sigma)$ are normally distributed and their covariance, $\mathbf{TM}$, is $\mathbf{0}$, the vectors of the quadratic forms are independent. The numerator and denominator of F are functions of independent random vectors and are, therefore, independent. This completes the proof.

Canceling the two appearances of σ^2 in (6-35) leaves the F statistic for testing a linear hypothesis:

$$\begin{aligned} F &= \frac{(\mathbf{Rb} - \mathbf{q})'[\mathbf{R}(\mathbf{X}'\mathbf{X})^{-1}\mathbf{R}']^{-1}(\mathbf{Rb} - \mathbf{q})/J}{\mathbf{e}'\mathbf{e}/(n - K)} \\ &= \frac{(\mathbf{Rb} - \mathbf{q})'[s^2\mathbf{R}(\mathbf{X}'\mathbf{X})^{-1}\mathbf{R}']^{-1}(\mathbf{Rb} - \mathbf{q})}{J}. \end{aligned} \tag{6-37}$$

EXAMPLE 6.7.   In the investment equation estimated earlier, consider a test of the joint hypothesis

$$\beta_2 = 0 \qquad \text{(there is no time trend)}$$

$$\beta_3 = 1 \qquad \text{(the marginal propensity to invest} = 1\text{)}$$

$$\beta_4 + \beta_5 = 0 \qquad \text{(investors consider the real interest rate)}$$

Then

$$\mathbf{R} = \begin{bmatrix} 0 & 1 & 0 & 0 & 0 \\ 0 & 0 & 1 & 0 & 0 \\ 0 & 0 & 0 & 1 & 1 \end{bmatrix} \qquad \text{and} \qquad \mathbf{q} = \begin{bmatrix} 0 \\ 1 \\ 0 \end{bmatrix}.$$

---

[14] This is an application of the "full rank quadratic form" of Section 3.10.5.

Based on the sample estimates, we obtain

$$\mathbf{Rb} - \mathbf{q} = \begin{bmatrix} -0.0166 \\ -0.3296 \\ -0.0024 \end{bmatrix}.$$

The covariance matrix was given in Example 6.5. Inserting these values in (6–37) yields

$$F = 1409.59.$$

The 5 percent critical value for $F(3, 10)$ from the table is 3.71. We conclude, therefore, that these data are not consistent with the hypothesis. This gives no hint as to which of the restrictions is particularly problematic. However, based on the individual test statistics, we would expect both the first and second hypotheses to be rejected.

A confidence interval for a single coefficient is based on a set of values for which the t ratio in (6–31) is less than a specified critical value. It is the set of values for which, at a given level of significance, we would not reject the hypothesis that β equals this value. In a multiple regression model, a joint confidence region for a set of coefficients would be the set of values for which the hypothesis that the set of true coefficients simultaneously equal these values would not be rejected. The test statistic is the F ratio in (6–37). For two coefficients, this would be

$$F[2, n - K] = \tfrac{1}{2}(\mathbf{b} - \boldsymbol{\beta})'(\text{Est. Var}[\mathbf{b}])^{-1}(\mathbf{b} - \boldsymbol{\beta}). \tag{6–38}$$

(For convenience, we assume that only the two coefficients of interest appear in the vectors in (6–38) and that the estimated variance matrix is a 2×2 submatrix of the full covariance matrix.) The set of values of β_1 and β_2 for which this quadratic form is less than a tabulated critical value form a joint confidence region for β_1 and β_2.

EXAMPLE 6.8. Joint Confidence Region. Figure 6.1 shows a confidence region for β_2 and β_3 for the investment equation. It is the set of values for which the quadratic form

$$\tfrac{1}{2}[(-0.1658 - \beta_1)(0.67038 - \beta_2)]\begin{bmatrix} 0.389E-05 & -0.102E-03 \\ -0.102E-03 & 0.302E-02 \end{bmatrix}^{-1}\begin{bmatrix} (-0.1658 - \beta_1) \\ (0.67038 - \beta_2) \end{bmatrix}$$

is less than or equal to the critical $F(2, 10)$ of 4.1. The individual confidence intervals for the coefficients are shown on the axes. Note how the interaction of the two coefficients affects the joint confidence region.

The calculation of the confidence ellipse can be a bit tedious. It can be shown that the simple rectangle formed by the two individual confidence intervals provides a confidence region with probability at least $1 - \alpha_1 - \alpha_2$.[15] Thus, for example, the rectangle in Figure 6.1 contains at least 90 percent of the probability in the estimate of the joint distribution of b_2 and b_3.

6.6. *Goodness of Fit and the Analysis of Variance*

Regression analysis is primarily used for two purposes: for estimating coefficients of interest and testing hypotheses about them, and for forecasting. For the second, we are interested in how well the regression model predicts movements in the dependent variable. The **coefficient**

---

[15] See Theil (1971, p. 132).

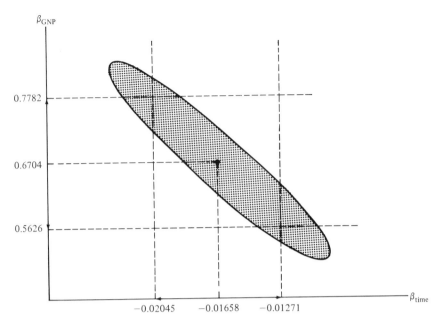

Figure 6.1   Joint confidence region.

of determination, R^2, is a measure of the fit of the model. Two equivalent ways to compute R^2 are

$$R^2 = 1 - \frac{e'e}{y'M^0y}$$

$$= 1 - \frac{\text{residual sum of squares}}{\text{total sum of squares}} \tag{6-39}$$

$$= \frac{\text{regression sum of squares}}{\text{total sum of squares}}$$

and

$$R^2 = \frac{[\sum(y - \bar{y})(\hat{y} - \hat{\bar{y}})]^2}{([\sum(y - \bar{y})^2][(\hat{y} - \hat{\bar{y}})^2])}.$$

The first of these methods measures the proportion of the total variation in **y** that is accounted for by variation in the regressors. The second is the squared correlation between the observed values of y and the predictions produced by the estimated regression equation.

If **X** contains a constant term, R^2 is constrained to lie between 0 and 1. We start from

$$y = Xb + e$$

and then put all variables in deviation form by writing

$$M^0y = M^0Xb + M^0e.$$

Note that the column of M^0X corresponding to the constant term is zero and, since the residuals already have mean zero, $M^0e = e$. Then

$$y'M^0y = b'X'M^0Xb + e'e,$$

Table 6.6. Analysis of Variance

Source		Degrees of Freedom	Mean Square
Regression	$b'X'y - n\bar{y}^2$	$K - 1$[16]	
Residual	$e'e$	$n - K$	s^2
Total	$y'y - n\bar{y}^2$	$n - 1$	S_{yy}

Table 6.7. Analysis of Variance for the Investment Equation

Source		Degrees of Freedom	Mean Square
Regression	0.0159023	4	0.003976
Residual	0.0004507	10	0.00004507
Total	0.016353	14	0.0011681
Therefore, R^2 is $0.0159023/0.016353 = 0.97244$.			

as $e'M^0X = e'X = 0$. Both terms on the right-hand side are positive. Dividing both sides by $y'M^0y$ and rearranging gives the result. We can summarize the calculation of R^2 in an analysis of variance table, which might appear as shown in Table 6.6.[16]

EXAMPLE 6.9. The analysis of variance table for the investment equation would appear as shown in Table 6.7.

There are two problems with the use of R^2 in analyzing goodness of fit. The first concerns the number of degrees of freedom used up in estimating the parameters. It can be shown algebraically that R^2 will never decrease when another variable is added to a regression equation. (The proof appears in Chapter 7.) It is tempting to exploit this fact by just adding variables to the model; R^2 will continue to rise to its limit of one.[17] In view of this, we sometimes report an *adjusted* (for degrees of freedom) R^2, which is computed as follows:[18]

$$\bar{R}^2 = 1 - \frac{e'e/(n - K)}{y'M^0y/(n - 1)}.$$

For computational purposes, the connection between R^2 and $\bar{R}^2$ is

$$\bar{R}^2 = 1 - \frac{n - 1}{n - K}(1 - R^2). \tag{6-40}$$

The essential point to observe about this measure is that it may decline when a variable is added to the set of independent variables. Indeed, $\bar{R}^2$ may even be negative. To consider an admittedly extreme case, suppose that x and y have a sample correlation of zero. Then the

[16] This assumes that there is a constant term in the equation.
[17] This comes at a cost, however. The parameter estimates become progressively less precise as we do so.
[18] This measure is sometimes advocated on the basis of the unbiasedness of the two quantities in the fraction. Since the ratio is not an unbiased estimator of any population quantity, it is difficult to justify the adjustment on this basis.

adjusted R^2 will be $-1/(n-2)$. Whether $\bar{R}^2$ rises or falls depends on whether the contribution of the new variable to the fit of the regression more than offsets the correction for the loss of an additional degree of freedom. The general result (the proof of which is left as an exercise) is as follows:

> In a multiple regression, $\bar{R}^2$ will fall (rise) if the variable x is deleted from the regression if the t ratio associated with this variable is greater (less) than one.

A second difficulty with R^2 concerns the constant term in the model. The proof that $0 < R^2 < 1$ requires $\mathbf{X}$ to contain a column of ones. If not, then (1) $\mathbf{M}^0\mathbf{e} \neq \mathbf{e}$ and (2) $\mathbf{e}'\mathbf{M}^0\mathbf{X} \neq \mathbf{0}$, and the third term in the preceding expansion will not drop out. Consequently, when we compute

$$R^2 = 1 - \frac{\mathbf{e}'\mathbf{e}}{\mathbf{y}'\mathbf{M}^0\mathbf{y}},$$

the result is unpredictable. It may be higher or lower than the same figure computed for the regression with a constant term included. It can even be negative. Computer packages differ on the computation of R^2. An alternative computation,

$$R^2 = \frac{\mathbf{b}'\mathbf{X}'\mathbf{y}}{\mathbf{y}'\mathbf{M}^0\mathbf{y}},$$

is equally problematic. Again, this calculation will differ from the one obtained with the constant term included; this time, R^2 may be larger than one.

This might suggest that we can produce a higher R^2 simply by choosing whether or not to include a constant term in the model. One ought not to view the inclusion of a constant as an option. Certain models specify that the equation should not contain an intercept. But estimating a model without a constant term amounts to imposing a linear restriction, that is, that the constant term is zero. Arbitrarily assuming that the intercept is zero is no less restrictive than arbitrarily imposing some other linear restriction on the coefficients.

6.7. Testing the Significance of the Regression

A hypothesis that is often tested is the significance of the regression equation as a whole. This is a joint test of the hypothesis that *all* of the coefficients except the constant term are zero. If all of the coefficients are zero, the multiple correlation is zero as well, so we can base a test of this hypothesis on the value of R^2. The central result needed to carry out the test was presented in Chapter 5. The statistic

$$F[K-1, n-K] = \frac{[R^2/(K-1)]}{[(1-R^2)/(n-K)]}$$

has an F distribution with $K-1$ and $n-K$ degrees of freedom. The logic of the test is that the F statistic is a measure of the loss of fit (namely, all of R^2) that results when we impose the restriction that all of the slopes are zero. If F is large, the hypothesis is rejected.

EXAMPLE 6.10.   The F ratio for testing the hypothesis that the four slopes in the investment equation are all zero is

$$F[4, 10] = \frac{0.97244/4}{(1 - 0.97244)/10} = 88.211,$$

which is far larger than the critical value of 3.48.

We might have expected the preceding result, given the substantial t ratios presented earlier. Unfortunately, this need not always be the case. Examples can be constructed in which the individual coefficients are statistically significant, while jointly they are not.[19] This can be regarded as a pathological case, but the opposite one, in which none of the coefficients are significantly different from zero while R^2 is highly significant, is relatively common. The problem is that the interaction among the variables may serve to obscure their individual contribution to the fit of the regression, while their joint effect may still be significant. We return to this point in our discussion of multicollinearity.

6.8.   Prediction

The results for forecasting in the multiple regression setting are essentially the same as those discussed in Chapter 5. Suppose that we wish to predict the value y^0 associated with a regressor vector $\mathbf{x}^0$. This would be

$$y^0 = \boldsymbol{\beta}'\mathbf{x}^0 + \varepsilon^0. \tag{6-41}$$

It follows from the Gauss–Markov theorem that

$$\hat{y}^0 = \mathbf{b}'\mathbf{x}^0$$

is the minimum variance linear unbiased estimator of $E[y^0]$. The forecast error is

$$e^0 = y^0 - \hat{y}^0 = (\boldsymbol{\beta} - \mathbf{b})'\mathbf{x}^0 + \varepsilon^0.$$

Using the results of Chapter 5, the forecast variance to be applied to this estimate is

$$\begin{aligned}
\text{Var}[e^0] &= \sigma^2 + \text{Var}[(\boldsymbol{\beta} - \mathbf{b})'\mathbf{x}^0] \\
&= \sigma^2 + \mathbf{x}^{0\prime}[\sigma^2(\mathbf{X}'\mathbf{X})^{-1}]\mathbf{x}^0.
\end{aligned} \tag{6-42}$$

If the regression contains a constant term, an equivalent expression is

$$\text{Var}[e^0] = \sigma^2 + \frac{\sigma^2}{n} + \sigma^2 \left\{ \sum_{i=2}^{K} \sum_{j=2}^{K} (x_i^0 - \bar{x}_i)(x_j^0 - \bar{x}_j)(\underline{\mathbf{X}}'\mathbf{M}^0\underline{\mathbf{X}})^{ij} \right\},$$

where $\underline{\mathbf{X}}$ is the last $K - 1$ columns of $\mathbf{X}$ not including the column of ones. This shows, as before, that the width of the interval depends on the distance of the elements of $\mathbf{x}^0$ from the center of the data.

The forecast variance can be estimated by using s^2 in place of σ^2. A confidence interval for y^0 would be formed using

$$\text{Forecast interval} = \hat{y}^0 \pm t_{\lambda/2}\text{se}(\hat{y}^0).$$

[19] See, Maddala (1977, pp. 123–124).

EXAMPLE 6.11. Suppose that we wish to forecast the 1983 value of real investment based on forecasts of (1) real GNP $= 1.6T$, (2) a discount rate of 10 percent, and (3) inflation of 4 percent, using the regression results in Example 6.5. The forecast is

$$(1, \quad 16, \quad 1.5, \quad 10, \quad 4)(-0.509, \quad -0.017, \quad 0.670, \quad -0.002, \quad -0.0001)' = 0.20764.$$

The estimated variance of this forecast is

$$s^2(1 + x^{0\prime}(X'X)^{-1}x^0) = 0.00010444.$$

Using the square root of this result, we obtain the forecast interval:

$$0.20764 \pm 2.228(0.01022) = \langle 0.1849, 0.2304 \rangle.$$

6.8.1. A Convenient Method of Computing the Forecasts

The preceding would suggest that two sets of computations are necessary in order to obtain the predictions (6–41) and the associated standard errors (6–42): first, the least squares estimates, and second, the forecasts and the forecast variances. Salkever (1976) has suggested a convenient method of combining the computations by using an expanded regression. Suppose that the estimation is based on n observations, and we desire to forecast n^0 observations:

$$y^0 = X^0\beta + \varepsilon^0.$$

We first construct an augmented regression:

$$\begin{bmatrix} y \\ 0 \end{bmatrix} = \begin{bmatrix} X & 0 \\ X^0 & -I \end{bmatrix}\begin{bmatrix} \beta \\ \gamma \end{bmatrix} + \begin{bmatrix} \varepsilon \\ \varepsilon^0 \end{bmatrix} \tag{6–43}$$

or

$$y^* = X^*\beta^* + \varepsilon^*.$$

In (6–43) there are n^0 new observations added and a set of n^0 new variables. Each column in the second part of X^* is a **dummy variable** that takes the value one only for that observation and zero for all others. (Note that the new parameter vector, γ, is y^0.)

Based on the expanded regression model, we obtain the following results:

1. The least squares regression of y^* on X^* produces the coefficient vector $[b, c]$, where b is the original OLS coefficient vector and c is the predictions for y^0.

    Proof:

    $$X^{*\prime}X^* = \begin{bmatrix} X'X + X^{0\prime}X^0 & -X^{0\prime} \\ -X^0 & I \end{bmatrix} \quad \text{and} \quad X^{*\prime}y^* = \begin{bmatrix} X'y \\ 0 \end{bmatrix}.$$

    Using the partitioned inverse formula from Chapter 2, we obtain

    $$(X^{*\prime}X^*)^{-1} = \begin{bmatrix} (X'X)^{-1} & (X'X)^{-1}X^{0\prime} \\ X^0(X'X)^{-1} & I + X^{0\prime}(X'X)^{-1}X^0 \end{bmatrix}.$$

    Postmultiplying $(X^{*\prime}X^*)^{-1}$ by $X^{*\prime}y^*$ produces the result.

2. The residuals from this regression are, for the first T observations, the original least squares residuals, and for the last T^0, zero. The first part is obvious, since the

coefficient vector is the same. Multiplying it out produces

$$\mathbf{y}^* - \mathbf{X}^*\mathbf{b}^* = \begin{bmatrix} \mathbf{e} \\ \mathbf{0} \end{bmatrix}.$$

3. The estimated covariance matrix for the expanded vector of coefficient estimates contains, in its upper left block, the covariance matrix for the least squares estimates of $\boldsymbol{\beta}$ and, in its lower right block, the covariance matrix for the forecasts.

Proof:

$$s^{2*} = \mathbf{e}^{*\prime}\mathbf{e}^* = \frac{\mathbf{e}'\mathbf{e} + \mathbf{0}'\mathbf{0}}{n + n^0 - (K + n^0)} = s^2.$$

Therefore,

$$s^{2*}(\mathbf{X}^{*\prime}\mathbf{X}^*)^{-1} = \begin{bmatrix} s^2(\mathbf{X}'\mathbf{X})^{-1} & * \\ * & s^2[\mathbf{I} + \mathbf{X}^{0\prime}(\mathbf{X}'\mathbf{X})^{-1}\mathbf{X}^0] \end{bmatrix},$$

where * indicates a submatrix for which we have no convenient interpretation. The upper matrix is familiar. The ith diagonal element of the lower matrix is

$$\text{Est. Var}[c_i] = \text{Est. Var}[\hat{y}_i^0] = s^2(1 + \mathbf{x}_i^{0\prime}(\mathbf{X}'\mathbf{X})^{-1}\mathbf{x}_i^0),$$

which is (6–42). This completes the proof.

These results imply that the standard computer output from this expanded regression will contain, in addition to the usual least squares results, the forecasts and estimated forecast variances or standard errors. One thing to note is that the R^2 in the expanded regression will be incorrect. The total sum of squares will be computed using an expanded $\mathbf{y}$ vector containing a set of zeros. It would be possible to patch this up by replacing the zeros in $\mathbf{y}^*$ with $\bar{y}$ from the original data, but then the lower subvector of the coefficient vector would no longer be the least squares predictions.

There is an interesting corollary that follows from (2). It is not uncommon for researchers to include a dummy variable in a regression to account for something that applies only to a single observation. For example, in time series studies, an occasional study includes a dummy variable that is one only in a single unusual year, such as the year of a major strike. The result in (2) shows clearly what the effect of this variable will be

> A dummy variable that takes the value one
> only for one observation has the effect of deleting
> that observation from the least squares computations.

6.8.2. Measuring the Accuracy of Forecasts

Various measures have been proposed for assessing the predictive accuracy of forecasting models.[20] Most of these measures are designed to evaluate ex post forecasts, that is, forecasts for which the exogenous variables do not have to be forecasted. Two that are based on the residuals from the forecasts are

$$\text{Root mean squared error} = \text{RMSE} = \sqrt{\frac{1}{n^0}\sum_i (y_i - \hat{y}_i)^2}$$

---

[20] See Theil (1961) and Fair (1984).

and

$$\text{Mean absolute error} = \text{MAE} = \frac{1}{n^0}\sum_i |y_i - \hat{y}_i|,$$

where n^0 is the number of periods being forecasted. These have an obvious scaling problem. Several that do not are based on the Theil U statistic:[21]

$$U = \sqrt{\frac{\frac{1}{n^0}\sum_i(y_i - \hat{y}_i)^2}{\frac{1}{n^0}\sum_i y_i^2}}.$$

This measure is related to R^2 but is not bounded by zero and one. Large values indicate a poor forecasting performance. An alternative is to compute the measure in terms of the changes in y

$$U_\Delta = \sqrt{\frac{\frac{1}{n^0}\sum_i(\Delta y_i - \Delta\hat{y}_i)^2}{\frac{1}{n^0}\sum_i(\Delta y_i)^2}},$$

where

$$\Delta y_i = y_i - y_{i-1}$$

or, in percentage changes,

$$\Delta y_i = \frac{(y_i - y_{i-1})}{y_{i-1}}.$$

These measures will reflect the model's ability to track turning points in the data.

EXAMPLE 6.12.   Most of the cyclical variation in the investment data we have analyzed is picked up by GNP. Consider a comparison of the predictions of two models, one that includes GNP and one that does not. For these two candidates, the data are listed in Table 6.8. The last of these is particularly pronounced. In a forecasting model, the ability to predict turning points is obviously important. The actual values and predictions from the two competing models presented are shown in Table 6.9.

Table 6.8

	With GNP	Without GNP
RMSE	0.005482	0.02183
MAE	0.004227	0.01692
U	0.02661	0.10559
U_Δ	0.31522	1.00956

Note: U_Δ is computed using the absolute rather than the percentage changes.

[21] Ibid.

Table 6.9

	1968	1969	1970	1971	1972	1973	1974	1975
Actual	0.161	0.172	0.158	0.173	0.195	0.217	0.199	0.163
With GNP	0.171	0.173	0.155	0.165	0.192	0.217	0.191	0.187
Without GNP	0.162	0.168	0.174	0.181	0.187	0.192	0.198	0.205

	1976	1977	1978	1979	1980	1981	1982
Actual	0.195	0.231	0.257	0.259	0.225	0.241	0.204
With GNP	0.199	0.230	0.255	0.259	0.234	0.234	0.205
Without GNP	0.210	0.216	0.222	0.226	0.231	0.236	0.243

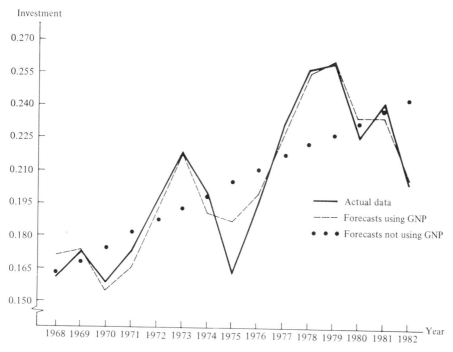

Figure 6.2   Model forecasts.

There were declines in real investment in 1970, 1973, 1974, 1980, and 1982. The model including GNP predicted all five turning points. The one omitting GNP missed all five. Figure 6.2 shows the effect.

6.9.   *Bayesian Estimation*

Proponents of the Bayesian methodology argue that the process of estimation is not one of deducing the values of fixed parameters, but rather of continually updating and sharpening our subjective beliefs about the state of the world. Assembled in the Bayesian methodology, these aspects of the theory come together in an intellectually appealing format.

The centerpiece of the Bayesian methodology is Bayes' theorem:

$$P(A \mid B) = \frac{P(B \mid A)P(A)}{P(B)}. \tag{6-44}$$

Paraphrased for our applications here, we should write this as

$$P(\text{parameters} \mid \text{data}) = \frac{P(\text{data} \mid \text{parameters})P(\text{parameters})}{P(\text{data})}. \tag{6-45}$$

In this setting, the data are viewed as constants whose distribution does not involve the parameters of interest. For the purpose of the study, we treat the data as only a fixed set of additional information to be used in updating our beliefs about the parameters. Thus, we write

$$P(\text{parameters} \mid \text{data}) \propto P(\text{data} \mid \text{parameters})P(\text{parameters}).$$

(The symbol $\propto$ means "is proportional to.") In the preceding, we have dropped the density of the data, so what remains is not a proper density until it is scaled by what will be an inessential proportionality constant. The first term is the joint distribution of the observed random variables, $\mathbf{y}$, given the parameters. As we shall analyze it here, this is the normal distribution we have used in all of our previous analysis. The second term is the "prior" beliefs of the analyst. The left-hand side is the "posterior" density of the parameters, given the current body of data, or our revised beliefs about the distribution of the parameters. The posterior is a mixture of the prior information and the "current information," that is, the data. Once obtained, this posterior density is available to be the prior density function when the next body of data or other usable information becomes available. The principle involved, which appears nowhere in the classical analysis, is one of continual accretion of knowledge about the parameters.

6.9.1. Bayesian Analysis of the Classical Regression Model

The complexity of the algebra involved in Bayesian analysis is extremely burdensome. However, for the classical regression model, many fairly straightforward results have been obtained. To provide some of the flavor of the techniques, we present the full derivation only for the simplest case. In the interest of brevity, and to avoid the burden of excessive algebra, we refer the reader to one of the several sources that present the full derivation of the more complex cases.[22]

The classical normal regression model we have analyzed thus far is constructed around the conditional distribution

$$f(\mathbf{y} \mid \boldsymbol{\beta}, \sigma, \mathbf{X}) = N(\mathbf{X}\boldsymbol{\beta}, \sigma^2 \mathbf{I}),$$
$$= (2\pi\sigma^2)^{-n/2} e^{-(1/(2\sigma^2))(\mathbf{y}-\mathbf{X}\boldsymbol{\beta})'(\mathbf{y}-\mathbf{X}\boldsymbol{\beta})}. \tag{6-46}$$

The departure point for the Bayesian analysis of this model is the specification of a prior distribution. This reflects the analyst's prior beliefs about the parameters of the model. One of two approaches is taken. If no prior information is known about the parameters, we can specify a "noninformative" prior that reflects that fact. We do this by specifying a flat prior for

---

[22] These include Judge et al. (1982 and 1985), Maddala (1977), and the canonical reference for econometricians, Zellner (1971).

the parameter in question:[23]

$$f(\text{parameter}) \propto \text{constant}.$$

The second possibility, an "informative prior," is treated in the next section.

To begin, we analyze the case in which σ is assumed to be known. This is obviously unrealistic, and we do so only to establish a point of departure. Using (6–45), we construct

$$f(\boldsymbol{\beta} \mid \mathbf{y}, \mathbf{X}, \sigma) = \frac{f(\mathbf{y} \mid \boldsymbol{\beta}, \sigma, \mathbf{X}) f(\boldsymbol{\beta} \mid \sigma, \mathbf{X})}{f(\mathbf{y})}$$

$$\propto f(\mathbf{y} \mid \boldsymbol{\beta}, \sigma, \mathbf{X}) f(\boldsymbol{\beta}),$$

assuming that the distribution of $\boldsymbol{\beta}$ does not depend on σ or $\mathbf{X}$. Since $f(\boldsymbol{\beta}) \propto$ a constant, this is the density in (6–46). By substituting

$$\mathbf{y} - \mathbf{X}\boldsymbol{\beta} = \mathbf{y} - \mathbf{X}\mathbf{b} - \mathbf{X}(\boldsymbol{\beta} - \mathbf{b}),$$

where $\mathbf{b} = (\mathbf{X}'\mathbf{X})^{-1}\mathbf{X}'\mathbf{y}$, we may write the exponent in (6–46) as

$$\left(\frac{-1}{2\sigma^2}\right)(\mathbf{y} - \mathbf{X}\mathbf{b})'(\mathbf{y} - \mathbf{X}\mathbf{b}) - \left(\frac{1}{2\sigma^2}\right)(\boldsymbol{\beta} - \mathbf{b})'\mathbf{X}'\mathbf{X}(\boldsymbol{\beta} - \mathbf{b})$$

$$= -\left(\frac{1}{2}\right)\left(\frac{vs^2}{\sigma^2}\right) - \left(\frac{1}{2}\right)(\boldsymbol{\beta} - \mathbf{b})'[\sigma^2(\mathbf{X}'\mathbf{X})^{-1}]^{-1}(\boldsymbol{\beta} - \mathbf{b}),$$

where v is the degrees of freedom, $n - K$, and $s^2 = \mathbf{e}'\mathbf{e}/v$. We may also write

$$(\sigma^2)^{-n/2} = \sigma^{-v}(\sigma^2)^{-K/2}$$

and

$$(2\pi)^{-n/2} = (2\pi)^{-v/2}(2\pi)^{-K/2}.$$

Using these three results, we can factor the density in (6–46) into two parts:

$$f(\boldsymbol{\beta} \mid \mathbf{y}, \mathbf{X}, \sigma) \quad \propto$$

$$h(\sigma) \times (2\pi\sigma^2)^{-K/2} e^{(-1/2)(\boldsymbol{\beta} - \mathbf{b})'[\sigma^2(\mathbf{X}'\mathbf{X})^{-1}]^{-1}(\boldsymbol{\beta} - \mathbf{b})}, \qquad (6\text{–}47)$$

where

$$h(\sigma) = \sigma^{-v}(2\pi)^{-v/2} e^{-(1/2)(vs^2/\sigma^2)}. \qquad (6\text{–}48)$$

For the present, we treat $h(\sigma)$ simply as a constant that involves σ, not as a probability density; (6–47) is *conditional* on σ. Since σ^2 and $\mathbf{X}'\mathbf{X}$ are being treated as known constants, we may multiply the latter part of (6–47) by $|\mathbf{X}'\mathbf{X}|^{-1/2}$, and since $h(\sigma)$ does not involve $\boldsymbol{\beta}$, drop it. (The density $f(\boldsymbol{\beta} \mid \mathbf{y}, \mathbf{X}, \sigma)$ is only *proportional* to the result we obtain here.) Moving σ^2 inside the K-order determinant, we obtain

$$f(\boldsymbol{\beta} \mid \mathbf{y}, \mathbf{X}, \sigma) \quad \propto$$

$$(2\pi)^{-K/2}|\sigma^2(\mathbf{X}'\mathbf{X})^{-1}|^{-1/2} e^{(-1/2)(\boldsymbol{\beta} - \mathbf{b})'[\sigma^2(\mathbf{X}'\mathbf{X})^{-1}]^{-1}(\boldsymbol{\beta} - \mathbf{b})}. \qquad (6\text{–}49)$$

---

[23] The fact that this "improper" density does not integrate to one is only a minor difficulty. Any constant of integration would ultimately drop out of the final result. See Zellner (1971, pp. 41–53) for a discussion of noninformative priors.

This is the density of the multivariate normal distribution with mean **b** and variance matrix $\sigma^2(\mathbf{X}'\mathbf{X})^{-1}$.

This is a familiar result, but it is interpreted very differently in this setting. First, we have combined our prior information about β (in this case, no information) and the sample information to obtain a posterior distribution. Thus, on the basis of the sample data in hand, we obtain a distribution for β with mean **b** and variance matrix $\sigma^2(\mathbf{X}'\mathbf{X})^{-1}$. There are two things to note. First, the result is dominated by the sample information, as it should be if there is no prior information. Second, in the absence of any prior information, the mean of the posterior distribution, which is our Bayesian point estimate, is the sampling theory estimator.

In order to generalize the preceding to an unknown σ, we specify a noninformative prior distribution for $\ln \sigma$ over the entire real line.[24] By the change of variable formula, if $f(\ln \sigma)$ is constant, $f(\sigma)$ is proportional to $1/\sigma$. Assuming that β and σ are independent, this gives the noninformative joint prior distribution:

$$f(\beta, \sigma) \quad \propto \quad \frac{1}{\sigma}.$$

We can obtain the joint posterior distribution for β and σ by using

$$f(\beta, \sigma \mid \mathbf{y}, \mathbf{X}) = f(\beta \mid \mathbf{y}, \mathbf{X}, \sigma)f(\sigma \mid \mathbf{y}, \mathbf{X})$$

$$= f(\beta \mid \mathbf{y}, \mathbf{X}, \sigma)f(\sigma) \tag{6-50}$$

$$\propto f(\beta \mid \mathbf{y}, \mathbf{X}, \sigma) \times \frac{1}{\sigma}.$$

Multiplying (6–49) by $1/\sigma$, therefore, gives the joint posterior for β and σ, given **y** and **X**. In order to obtain the marginal posterior distribution for β, it is now necessary to integrate σ out of the joint distribution (and vice versa to obtain the marginal distribution for σ.) Doing so for β produces what is known as a **multivariate t distribution**.[25] This is a generalization of the familiar univariate distribution we have used at various points. This distribution has a degrees of freedom parameter, $v = n - K$, mean **b**, and variance matrix $(v/(v-2))[s^2(\mathbf{X}'\mathbf{X})^{-1}]$. Each element of the K-element vector β has a marginal distribution that is the univariate t distribution with degrees of freedom $n - K$, mean b_k, and variance equal to the kth diagonal of the variance matrix given earlier. Once again, this is the same as our sampling theory result. The difference is a matter of interpretation. In the current context, the estimated distribution is for β and is centered at **b**.

The counterpart to a confidence interval in this setting is an interval of the posterior distribution that contains a specified probability. Clearly, it is desirable to have this interval be as narrow as possible. For a unimodal density, this corresponds to an interval within which the density function is higher than any points outside it, which justifies the term **highest posterior density (HPD) interval**. For the case we have analyzed, which involves a symmetric distribution, we would form the HPD interval for β around the least squares estimate, **b**, with terminal values taken from the standard t tables.

One might ask at this point, why bother? The Bayesian point estimates are identical to the sampling theory estimates, and the HPD interval for a parameter is exactly the same as the usual confidence interval. All that has changed is our interpretation of the results. This is,

---

[24] See Zellner (1971) for justification of this prior distribution.
[25] See, for example, Judge et al. (1985) for details.

however, exactly the way it should be. Remember that we entered this analysis with noninformative priors for β and σ. Therefore, the only information brought to bear on estimation is the sample data, and it would be pathological if anything other than the sampling theory estimates emerged at the end. The results do change when our prior brings data out of the sample information into the estimates.

6.9.2. Estimation with an Informative Prior Density

Once we leave the simple case of noninformative priors, matters become quite complicated, both at a practical level and, methodologically, in terms of just where the prior comes from. The integration of σ out of the joint posterior in (6–49) is complicated by itself. It is made much more so if the prior distribution of β is at all involved. Partly to offset these difficulties, we often use what is called a *conjugate prior*, which is one that has the same form as the conditional density and is, therefore, amenable to the integration needed to obtain the marginal distributions.[26]

Suppose that we assume that the prior beliefs about β may be summarized in a K-variate normal distribution with mean β^0 and variance matrix Σ^0. Once again, it is illuminating to begin with the case in which σ is assumed to be known. Proceeding in exactly the same fashion as before, we would obtain the following result: The posterior density of β conditioned on σ and the data will be normal with

$$E[\beta\,|\,\mathbf{y}, \mathbf{X}, \sigma] = \{\Sigma^{0-1} + [\sigma^2(\mathbf{X}'\mathbf{X})^{-1}]^{-1}\}^{-1}\{\Sigma^{0-1}\beta^0 + [\sigma^2(\mathbf{X}'\mathbf{X})^{-1}]^{-1}\mathbf{b}\}$$
$$= \mathbf{F}\beta^0 + (\mathbf{I} - \mathbf{F})\mathbf{b}, \tag{6–51}$$

where

$$\mathbf{F} = \{\Sigma^{0-1} + [\sigma^2(\mathbf{X}'\mathbf{X})^{-1}]^{-1}\}^{-1}\Sigma^{0-1}$$
$$= \{\mathrm{Var}[\beta^0]^{-1} + \mathrm{Var}[\mathbf{b}\,|\,\mathbf{y}, \mathbf{X}, \sigma]^{-1}\}^{-1}\,\mathrm{Var}[\beta^0]^{-1}.$$

This is a weighted average of the prior and the least squares estimates, where the weights are the inverses of the prior and the conditional covariance matrices. The smaller the variance of the estimator, the larger its weight, which makes sense. Also, still taking σ as known, we can write the variance of the posterior normal distribution as

$$\mathrm{Var}[\beta\,|\,\mathbf{y}, \mathbf{X}, \sigma] = \{\Sigma^{0-1} + [\sigma^2(\mathbf{X}'\mathbf{X})^{-1}]^{-1}\}^{-1}. \tag{6–52}$$

(Notice that the posterior variance combines the prior and conditional variances on the basis of their inverses.) We may interpret the noninformative prior as having infinite elements in Σ^0, which would reduce this to the earlier case.

Once again, it is necessary to account for the unknown σ. If our prior over σ is to be informative as well, the resulting distribution will be extremely cumbersome. A conjugate prior for β and σ that has been used is

$$f(\beta, \sigma) = f(\beta\,|\,\sigma)f(\sigma), \tag{6–53}$$

where $f(\beta\,|\,\sigma)$ is normal, with mean β^0 and variance $\sigma^2\mathbf{A}^{-1}$, and $f(\sigma)$ is of the form $h(\sigma)$ in (6–48).[27] This distribution is an *inverted gamma* distribution. It implies that $1/\sigma$ has a

---

[26] The idea that the prior can be specified arbitrarily in whatever form is mathematically convenient is very troubling in view of the fact that it is supposed to represent the accumulated prior belief about the parameter. On the other hand, it could be argued that the conjugate prior is the posterior of a previous analysis, which would justify its form.

[27] A constant of integration is needed to make it a proper prior, and instead of s^2, we would have a prior estimate of σ^2, that is, $\bar{\sigma}^2$.

gamma distribution.[28] The product in (6–53) produces what is called a *normal gamma* prior, which is the natural conjugate prior for this form of the model. By integrating out σ, we would obtain the prior marginal for β alone, which would be a multivariate t distribution. Combining (6–53) with (6–46) produces the joint posterior distribution for β and σ. Finally, the marginal posterior distribution for β is obtained by integrating out σ. It has been shown that this posterior distribution is multivariate t with

$$E[\beta \,|\, \mathbf{y}, \mathbf{X}] = \{\mathbf{\Sigma}^{0-1} + [\bar{s}^2(\mathbf{X}'\mathbf{X})^{-1}]^{-1}\}^{-1}\{\mathbf{\Sigma}^{0-1}\beta^0 + [\bar{s}^2(\mathbf{X}'\mathbf{X})^{-1}]^{-1}\mathbf{b}\} \qquad (6\text{–}54)$$

and

$$\mathrm{Var}[\beta \,|\, \mathbf{y}, \mathbf{X}] = \left(\frac{m}{(m-2)}\right)\{\mathbf{\Sigma}^{0-1} + [\bar{s}^2(\mathbf{X}'\mathbf{X})^{-1}]^{-1}\}^{-1}, \qquad (6\text{–}55)$$

where m is a degrees of freedom parameter

$$m = n - K + d \qquad (6\text{–}56)$$

and $\bar{s}^2$ is the Bayesian estimate of σ^2, the posterior mean of the distribution of σ.[29] The prior degrees of freedom, d, is a parameter of the prior distribution for σ that would have been determined at the outset. (See the following example.) Once again, it is clear that as the amount of data increases, the posterior density, and the estimates thereof, converge to the sampling theory results.

EXAMPLE 6.13. Bayesian Estimates of a Consumption Function. In Example 5.1, an estimate of the marginal propensity to consume is obtained using 10 observations from 1970 to 1979, with the following results:

Estimated MPC: 0.9793

Variance of b: $0.0316^2 = 0.0009989$

Degrees of freedom: $10 - 2 = 8$

Estimated σ: 8.192

A classical 95 percent confidence interval for β based on these estimates is $\langle 0.90641, 1.1251 \rangle$, as given earlier. Based on noninformative priors for β and σ, we would estimate the posterior density for β to be univariate t with eight degrees of freedom, with mean 0.9793 and variance $(8/6)0.0009989 = 0.0013319$. An HPD interval for β would coincide with the confidence interval.

An alternative estimate of β is obtained in Example 8.1, based on 11 observations from 1940 to 1950, with the following results:

Estimated MPC: 0.9596

Variance of b: $0.0895^2 = 0.0081025$

Degrees of freedom: $11 - 3 = 8$

Estimated σ: 9.0088

We take the earlier estimate and its estimated distribution as our prior for β and obtain a posterior density for β based on an informative prior instead. We assume for this exercise that

---

[28] See Maddala (1977, pp. 406–412) for details.
[29] This is a bit more complicated to compute. See Judge et al. (1985) for details.

σ may be taken as known at the sample value of 8.192. Then,

$$\bar{b} = \left\{ \frac{1}{0.0081025} + \frac{1}{0.0009989} \right\}^{-1} \left\{ \frac{0.9596}{0.0081025} + \frac{0.9793}{0.0009989} \right\}.$$

The weights in the average are 0.1109 and 0.8891, which gives an estimated posterior mean of 0.9771. The posterior variance is the inverse in brackets, which is 0.0008881. Since σ is assumed to be known, the posterior distribution is normal with this mean and variance. An HPD interval can be formed in the familiar fashion. Using the posterior standard deviation of 0.0298, we find that a 95 percent HPD interval for β is $0.9771 \pm 1.96(0.0298) = \langle 0.9187, 1.0355 \rangle$. Note that this is narrower than the earlier interval; this is the value of the prior information.

Exercises

1. Using the matrices of sums of squares and cross products immediately preceding Section 6.3.3, compute the coefficients in the multiple regression of real investment on a constant, real GNP, and the interest rate. The sum of squares of real investment is 0.63652. Compute R^2 and the estimate of the covariance matrix of the estimated slopes and constant term. Test the individual hypotheses that the two slopes are zero. Test the joint hypothesis that both slopes are zero.

2. The following matrix gives the slope in the simple regression of the column variable on the row variable:

$$\mathbf{A} = \begin{array}{c} \\ \\ \end{array} \begin{array}{ccc} y & x_1 & x_2 \\ \begin{bmatrix} 1 & 0.03 & 0.36 \\ 0.4 & 1 & 0.3 \\ 1.25 & 0.075 & 1 \end{bmatrix} & \begin{array}{c} y \\ x_1 \\ x_2 \end{array} \end{array}$$

For example, if y is regressed on x_1, the slope is 0.4, but if x_1 is regressed on y, the slope is 0.03. All variables have zero means, so the constant terms in all regressions are zero. What are the two slope coefficients in the multiple regression of y on x_1 and x_2?

3. Assuming that x_1 and x_2 have zero sample means and zero sample correlation, where is the inconsistency in the following results? (Estimated standard errors of the parameter estimates are given in parentheses.)

$$\hat{y} = 3 + 2x_1 + 1x_2, \qquad R^2 = 0.77$$

$$(0.25) \qquad (0.25) \qquad n = 23$$

Analysis of Variance

	Variation	Degrees of Freedom	Mean Square
Regression	68	2	34
Residual	20	20	1
Total	88	22	4

4. If the interest rate were added to the regression of investment on a constant, the time trend, and GNP that is given after Example 6.3, what would be its coefficient in the multiple regression? (**Hint:** You will find the necessary sums in the matrix you used for Exercise 1.)

5. For the regression in the previous problem, what is the new value of R^2 after you add the interest to the regression?

6. The following data relate to gasoline consumption in the United States in the years 1960 to 1986:

Year	G	P_g	Y	P_{nc}	P_{uc}	P_{pt}	P_d	P_n	P_s
1960	129.7	0.925	6036	1.045	0.836	0.810	0.444	0.331	0.302
1961	131.3	0.914	6113	1.045	0.869	0.846	0.448	0.335	0.307
1962	137.1	0.919	6271	1.041	0.948	0.874	0.457	0.338	0.314
1963	141.6	0.918	6378	1.035	0.960	0.885	0.463	0.343	0.320
1964	148.8	0.914	6727	1.032	1.001	0.901	0.470	0.347	0.325
1965	155.9	0.949	7027	1.009	0.994	0.919	0.471	0.353	0.332
1966	164.9	0.970	7280	0.991	0.970	0.952	0.475	0.366	0.342
1967	171.0	1.000	7513	1.000	1.000	1.000	0.483	0.375	0.353
1968	183.4	1.014	7728	1.028	1.028	1.046	0.501	0.390	0.368
1969	195.8	1.047	7891	1.044	1.031	1.127	0.514	0.409	0.386
1970	207.4	1.056	8134	1.076	1.043	1.285	0.527	0.427	0.407
1971	218.3	1.063	8322	1.120	1.102	1.377	0.547	0.442	0.431
1972	226.8	1.076	8562	1.110	1.105	1.434	0.555	0.458	0.451
1973	237.9	1.181	9042	1.111	1.176	1.448	0.566	0.497	0.474
1974	225.8	1.599	8867	1.175	1.226	1.480	0.604	0.572	0.513
1975	232.4	1.708	8944	1.276	1.464	1.586	0.659	0.615	0.556
1976	241.7	1.779	9175	1.357	1.679	1.742	0.695	0.638	0.598
1977	249.2	1.882	9381	1.429	1.828	1.824	0.727	0.671	0.648
1978	261.3	1.963	9735	1.538	1.865	1.878	0.769	0.719	0.698
1979	248.9	2.656	9829	1.660	2.010	2.003	0.821	0.800	0.756
1980	226.8	3.691	9722	1.793	2.081	2.516	0.892	0.894	0.839
1981	225.6	4.109	9769	1.902	2.569	3.120	0.957	0.969	0.926
1982	228.8	3.894	9725	1.976	2.964	3.460	1.000	1.000	1.000
1983	239.6	3.764	9930	2.026	3.297	3.626	1.041	1.021	1.062
1984	244.7	3.707	10421	2.085	3.757	3.852	1.038	1.050	1.117
1985	245.8	3.738	10563	2.152	3.797	4.028	1.045	1.075	1.173
1986	269.4	2.921	10780	2.240	3.632	4.264	1.053	1.069	1.224

The variables are

G = Total gasoline consumption, computed as current dollar expenditure divided by the price index

P_g = price index for gasoline

Y = per capita real disposable income

P_{nc} = price index for new cars

P_{uc} = price index for used cars

P_{pt} = price index for public transportation

P_d = aggregate price index for consumer durable goods

P_n = aggregate price index for consumer nondurable goods

P_s = aggregate price index for consumer services.

(All data are from the *Economic Report of the President: 1987*, Washington, D.C.: Council of Economic Advisors, 1987.)

(a) Compute the multiple regression of G on all of the other explanatory variables, including the time trend, and report all results. Do the signs of the estimates agree with your expectations?

(b) Test the hypothesis that at least in regard to demand for gasoline, consumers do not differentiate between changes in the prices of new and used cars.

(c) Estimate the own price elasticity of demand, the income elasticity, and the cross-price elasticity with respect to changes in the price of public transportation.

(d) Reestimate the regression in logarithms so that the coefficients are direct estimates of the elasticities. (Do not use the log of the time trend.) How do your estimates compare to the results in the previous question? Which specification do you prefer?

(e) Notice that the price indices for the automobile market are normalized to 1967, while the aggregate price indices are anchored at 1982. Does this discrepancy affect the results? How? If you were to renormalize the indices so that they were all 1.000 in 1982, how would your results change? Note that this would be an application of the principle in Exercise 12. What is the **P** matrix?

7. Suppose, for purposes of this exercise, that the variable Y in the previous exercise is total expenditure on consumer durables, nondurables, and services, rather than total income (which includes savings as well). Suppose, as well, that E_d, E_n, and E_s are the expenditures on the three categories. As defined,

$$Y = E_d + E_n + E_s.$$

Now consider the expenditure system

$$E_d = \alpha_d + \beta_d Y + \gamma_{dd} P_d + \gamma_{dn} P_n + \gamma_{ds} P_s + \varepsilon_s$$

$$E_n = \alpha_n + \beta_n Y + \gamma_{nd} P_d + \gamma_{nn} P_n + \gamma_{ns} P_s + \varepsilon_n$$

$$E_s = \alpha_s + \beta_s Y + \gamma_{sd} P_d + \gamma_{sn} P_n + \gamma_{ss} P_s + \varepsilon_s.$$

If all equations are estimated by ordinary least squares, prove that the sum of the income coefficients will be one and the other four column sums in the preceding model will be zero. (Some applications of demand systems such as this are discussed in Section 17.4.2.)

8. Prove the result in (6–20).

9. Prove that the adjusted R^2 in (6–40) rises (falls) when variable x_k is deleted from the regression if the square of the t ratio on x_k in the multiple regression is less (greater) than one.

10. Consider the multiple regression of **y** on K variables, **X**, and an additional variable, **z**. Prove that the true variance of the least squares estimator of the slopes on **X** is larger when **z** is included in the regression than when it is not. Does the same hold for the sample estimate of this covariance matrix? Why or why not?

11. An estimate of a Cobb–Douglas production function is given in the discussion preceding Example 7.1 in the next chapter. The basic equation is of the form

$$\ln Y = \alpha + \beta_k \ln K + \beta_l \ln L + \varepsilon.$$

We are interested in the issue of constant returns to scale, which is implied by $\beta_k + \beta_l = 1$. This hypothesis is tested in Example 7.2. For present purposes, construct a confidence region for these two parameters in the manner of Example 6.8. On the same figure, draw the line that represents the set of points for which $\beta_k + \beta_l = 1$.

12. Consider the least squares regression of y on K variables (and a constant), X. Consider an alternative set of regressors, $Z = XP$, where P is a nonsingular matrix. Thus, each column of Z is a mixture of some of the columns of X. Prove that the residual vectors in the regressions of y on X and Y on Z are identical. What relevance does this have to the question of changing the fit of a regression by changing the units of measurement of the independent variables?

13. Suppose b is the least squares coefficient vector in the regression of y on X and c is any other $K \times 1$ vector. Prove that the difference in the two sums of squared residuals is

$$(y - Xc)'(y - Xc) - (y - Xb)'(y - Xb) = (c - b)'X'X(c - b).$$

Prove that this difference is positive.

14. (Once again...) Suppose that you estimate a multiple regression first with and then without a constant. Whether the R^2 is higher in the second case than the first will depend in part on how it is computed. Upon using the (relatively) standard method,

$$R^2 = 1 - \frac{e'e}{y'M^0 y},$$

which regression will have a higher R^2? (**Hint:** Consider Exercise 13.)

15. In the least squares regression of y on a constant and X, in order to compute the regression coefficients on X, we can first transform y to deviations from the mean, $\bar{y}$, and transform each column of X to deviations from the respective column mean; second, we can regress the transformed y on the transformed X without a constant. Do we get the same result if we transform only y? What if we transform only X?

16. What is the result of the matrix product $M_1 M$, where M_1 is defined in (6–18) and M is defined in (6–16)?

17. Using the results of Example 6.5, compute a 95 percent forecast interval for real investment for 1983, assuming forecasts of 3100 for nominal GNP, 212 for the CPI, and 10.0 for the interest rate.

18. For the aforementioned study preceding Example 7.1, suppose that an earlier study had produced the following estimated production function:

$$\ln Q = 1.2 + 0.65 \ln L + 0.31 \ln K$$
$$(0.09) \qquad (0.16)$$

$$\text{Est. Cov.}[b_k, b_l] = 0.1$$

Using these estimates and the estimates of Example 7.1, form the Bayesian estimate of the posterior joint distribution, assuming a normal distribution for the prior. Assume that σ^2 is known.

References

Aigner, D., K. Lovell, and P. Schmidt, "Formulation and Estimation of Stochastic Frontier Production Models," *Journal of Econometrics*, 1977, 6, pp. 21–37.

Fair, R., *Specification and Analysis of Macroeconomic Models*, Cambridge, Mass.: Harvard University Press, 1984.

Feldstein, M., "The Error of Forecast in Econometric Models When the Forecast-Period Exogenous Variables Are Stochastic," *Econometrica*, 39, 1971, pp. 55–60.

Frisch, R., and F. Waugh, "Partial Time Regressions as Compared with Individual Trends," *Econometrica*, 1, 1933, pp. 387–401.

Judge, G., C. Hill, W. Griffiths, H. Lutkepohl, and T. Lee, *Introduction to the Theory and Practice of Econometrics*, New York: Wiley, 1982.

Judge, G., C. Hill, W. Griffiths, H. Lutkepohl, and T. Lee, *The Theory and Practice of Econometrics*, New York: Wiley, 1985.

Kloek, T., and Y. Haitovsky, eds., "Competing Statistical Paradigms in Econometrics," *Journal of Econometrics*, 37, 1, 1988, pp. 1–192.

Maddala, G., *Econometrics*, New York: McGraw-Hill, 1977.

Salkever, D., "The Use of Dummy Variables to Compute Predictions, Prediction Errors, and Confidence Intervals," *Journal of Econometrics*, 4, 1976, pp. 393–397.

Theil, H., *Economic Forecasts and Policy*, Amsterdam: North Holland, 1961.

Theil, H., *Principles of Econometrics*, New York: Wiley, 1971.

Zellner, A., *An Introduction to Bayesian Inference in Econometrics*, New York: Wiley, 1971.

Chapter 7

Hypothesis Tests with the Multiple Regression Model

7.1. *Introduction*

New and interesting techniques are constantly being developed by econometricians. Still, the classical multiple regression model remains by far the most useful tool in their kit. In this chapter, we examine some applications of hypothesis tests using the classical model. The basic statistical theory was developed in Section 6.5. This chapter also presents additional statistical results for some tests that do not fit into the framework of Chapter 6.

7.2. *Testing Restrictions*

The starting point for regression analysis is usually the estimation of parameters. In many cases, such as demand analysis, these estimates are useful in their own right. In others, we are interested in testing hypotheses as well. It is useful to depart at this point from a methodological proposition. Our approach to testing a hypothesis will be to formulate a statistical model that contains the hypothesis as a restriction on its parameters. A theory is said to have *testable implications* if it implies some testable restrictions on the model. Consider, for example, a simple model of investment,

$$\text{Investment} = \beta_1 + \beta_2 \text{interest} + \beta_3 \text{inflation} + \varepsilon,$$

which states that investors are sensitive to nominal interest rates and the rate of inflation. An alternative theory states that "investors care about real interest rates." But consider the alternative model,

$$\text{Investment} = \beta_1 + \beta_2(\text{interest-inflation}) + \beta_3 \text{inflation} + \varepsilon.$$

Although this new model does embody the theory, the equation still contains both nominal interest and inflation. The theory has no testable implication for our model. However, consider the stronger hypothesis, "investors care *only* about real interest rates." The resulting equation,

$$\text{Investment} = \beta_1 + \beta_2(\text{interest-inflation}) + \varepsilon,$$

is now restricted; in the context of the first one, the implication is that $\beta_2 + \beta_3 = 0$. The stronger statement implies something very specific about the parameters in the equation that may or may not be supported by the empirical evidence.

Chapter 6 presented the statistical results needed to test a hypothesis about one of the coefficients in the regression model. We also briefly considered the joint test that all of the slopes in the model are zero. Both of these are special cases of the general problem of testing linear restrictions on the coefficients. At the end of this section, we consider the still broader issue of nonlinear restrictions.

7.2.1. Two Approaches to Testing Hypotheses

Hypothesis testing can be approached from two viewpoints. First, having computed a set of parameter estimates, we can ask whether the estimates come reasonably close to satisfying the restrictions implied by the hypothesis. More formally, we can ascertain whether the failure of the estimates to satisfy the restrictions is simply the result of sampling error or is, instead, systematic. An alternative view of the testing procedure might proceed as follows: Suppose that we impose the restrictions implied by the theory. Since unrestricted least squares is, by definition, "least squares," this imposition must lead to a loss of fit. We can then ascertain whether this loss of fit results merely from sampling error or whether it is so large as to cast doubt on the validity of the restrictions. In order to analyze the second method, it is necessary to develop the technique of restricted least squares.

7.2.2. Testing a Set of Linear Restrictions

Beginning with the linear regression model,

$$\mathbf{y} = \mathbf{x}\boldsymbol{\beta} + \boldsymbol{\varepsilon}, \tag{7-1}$$

we consider a set of linear restrictions of the form

$$r_{11}\beta_1 + r_{12}\beta_2 + \cdots + r_{1K}\beta_K = q_1$$
$$r_{21}\beta_1 + r_{22}\beta_2 + \cdots + r_{2K}\beta_K = q_2$$
$$\vdots$$
$$r_{J1}\beta_1 + r_{J2}\beta_2 + \cdots + r_{JK}\beta_K = q_J.$$

These can be combined into the single equation

$$\mathbf{R}\boldsymbol{\beta} = \mathbf{q}. \tag{7-2}$$

Each row of $\mathbf{R}$ is the coefficients in one of the restrictions.[1] The matrix $\mathbf{R}$ has K columns to be conformable with $\boldsymbol{\beta}$, J rows for a total of J restrictions, and full row rank, so J must be less than or equal to K. The rows of R must be linearly independent. Although it does not violate the condition, the case of $J = K$ must also be ruled out.[2]

The restriction $\mathbf{R}\boldsymbol{\beta} = \mathbf{q}$ imposes J restrictions on K otherwise free parameters. This means that with the restrictions imposed, there are, in principle, only $K - J$ free parameters remaining. One way to view this is to partition $\mathbf{R}$ into two groups of columns, one with J and one with $K - J$, so that the first set are linearly independent. (There are many ways to do so; any one will do for the present.) Then, with $\boldsymbol{\beta}$ likewise partitioned and its elements reordered

---

[1] Several examples are given in Section 6.5.
[2] If the K slopes satisfy $J = K$ restrictions, $\mathbf{R}$ is square and nonsingular and $\boldsymbol{\beta} = \mathbf{R}^{-1}\mathbf{q}$. There is no estimation or inference problem.

in whatever way is needed, we may write

$$\mathbf{R}\boldsymbol{\beta} = \mathbf{R}_1\boldsymbol{\beta}_1 + \mathbf{R}_2\boldsymbol{\beta}_2 = \mathbf{q}.$$

If the J columns of $\mathbf{R}_1$ are independent,

$$\boldsymbol{\beta}_1 = \mathbf{R}_1^{-1}[\mathbf{q} - \mathbf{R}_2\boldsymbol{\beta}_2]. \tag{7-3}$$

The implication is that although $\boldsymbol{\beta}_2$ is free to vary, once $\boldsymbol{\beta}_2$ is determined, $\boldsymbol{\beta}_1$ is determined by (7-3). Thus, only the $K - \mathbf{J}$ elements of $\boldsymbol{\beta}_2$ are free parameters in the model.

The sample statistic used for testing

$$H_0: \mathbf{R}\boldsymbol{\beta} = \mathbf{q} \tag{7-4}$$

was derived in Section 6.5. To reiterate, we compare the test statistic

$$F[J, n - K] = \frac{(\mathbf{Rb} - \mathbf{q})'\{\mathbf{R}[s^2(\mathbf{X}'\mathbf{X})^{-1}]\mathbf{R}'\}^{-1}(\mathbf{Rb} - \mathbf{q})}{J} \tag{7-5}$$

to the critical value in the standard F table. A large value of F is evidence against the hypothesis.

7.2.3. Restricted Least Squares

Suppose, instead, that we explicitly impose the restrictions of the hypothesis in the regression. The restricted least squares estimator is obtained as the solution to

$$\text{Minimize}_{\tilde{\boldsymbol{\beta}}} S(\tilde{\boldsymbol{\beta}}) = (\mathbf{y} - \mathbf{X}\tilde{\boldsymbol{\beta}})'(\mathbf{y} - \mathbf{X}\tilde{\boldsymbol{\beta}}) \text{ subject to } \mathbf{R}\tilde{\boldsymbol{\beta}} = \mathbf{q}. \tag{7-6}$$

A Lagrangean solution for this problem can be written

$$\mathbf{b}_* = \text{Min}_{\tilde{\boldsymbol{\beta}}} S^*(\tilde{\boldsymbol{\beta}}) = (\mathbf{y} - \mathbf{X}\tilde{\boldsymbol{\beta}})'(\mathbf{y} - \mathbf{X}\tilde{\boldsymbol{\beta}}) + 2\boldsymbol{\lambda}'(\mathbf{R}\tilde{\boldsymbol{\beta}} - \mathbf{q}).[3] \tag{7-7}$$

The solution $\mathbf{b}_*$ and $\boldsymbol{\lambda}$ will satisfy the necessary conditions

$$\frac{\partial S^*}{\partial \mathbf{b}_*} = 2\mathbf{X}'(\mathbf{y} - \mathbf{X}\mathbf{b}_*) + 2\mathbf{R}'\boldsymbol{\lambda} = \mathbf{0}, \tag{7-8}$$

$$\frac{\partial S^*}{\partial \lambda} = 2(\mathbf{Rb}_* - \mathbf{q}) = \mathbf{0}. \tag{7-9}$$

The solutions can be obtained by first expanding (7-8) and solving for $\mathbf{b}_*$. (The solution for $\mathbf{b}_*$ is neater because of our use of 2λ in the original formulation.) By making the substitution $\mathbf{X}'\mathbf{y} = \mathbf{X}'\mathbf{X}\mathbf{b}$, where $\mathbf{b}$ is the unrestricted least squares coefficient vector, we can obtain a result for $\mathbf{b}_*$ in terms of $\mathbf{b}$,

$$\mathbf{b}_* = \mathbf{b} + (\mathbf{X}'\mathbf{X})^{-1}\mathbf{R}'\boldsymbol{\lambda}. \tag{7-10}$$

Now we multiply both sides of (7-10) by $\mathbf{R}$ and impose the restrictions $\mathbf{Rb}_* = \mathbf{q}$. This yields an explicit solution for $\boldsymbol{\lambda}$,

$$\boldsymbol{\lambda} = -[\mathbf{R}(\mathbf{X}'\mathbf{X})^{-1}\mathbf{R}']^{-1}(\mathbf{Rb} - \mathbf{q}), \tag{7-11}$$

which can be inserted back in (7-10) to provide the solution for $\mathbf{b}_*$,

$$\mathbf{b}_* = \mathbf{b} - (\mathbf{X}'\mathbf{X})^{-1}\mathbf{R}'[\mathbf{R}(\mathbf{X}'\mathbf{X})^{-1}\mathbf{R}']^{-1}(\mathbf{Rb} - \mathbf{q}). \tag{7-12}$$

---

[3] The value of λ will be obtained subsequently. Since λ is not restricted, we can formulate the constraint in terms of 2λ. It will be clear below why this is convenient.

Note that the solution for λ involves the discrepancy vector, $\mathbf{Rb} - \mathbf{q}$. If the unrestricted least squares estimator satisfied the restrictions, the Lagrangean multipliers would be zero and $\mathbf{b}_*$ would equal $\mathbf{b}$. Of course, this is unlikely. The constrained solution, $\mathbf{b}_*$, is equal to the unconstrained solution, $\mathbf{b}$, plus a term that accounts for the failure of the unrestricted solution to satisfy the constraints.

We know from several earlier results that the fit of the restricted least squares coefficients will be worse than that of the unrestricted solution. Let $\mathbf{e}_*$ equal $\mathbf{y} - \mathbf{Xb}_*$. Then, using a familiar device,

$$\mathbf{e}_* = \mathbf{y} - \mathbf{Xb} - \mathbf{X}(\mathbf{b}_* - \mathbf{b}) = \mathbf{e} - \mathbf{X}(\mathbf{b}_* - \mathbf{b}).$$

The new sum of squared deviations is

$$\mathbf{e}'_*\mathbf{e}_* = \mathbf{e}'\mathbf{e} + (\mathbf{b}_* - \mathbf{b})'\mathbf{X}'\mathbf{X}(\mathbf{b}_* - \mathbf{b}) \geq \mathbf{e}'\mathbf{e}.$$

(The middle term in the expansion involves $\mathbf{X}'\mathbf{e}$, which is zero.) As an alternative approach, then, we could base a test of the restrictions on the loss of fit, which is

$$\mathbf{e}'_*\mathbf{e}_* - \mathbf{e}'\mathbf{e} = (\mathbf{Rb} - \mathbf{q})'(\mathbf{R}(\mathbf{X}'\mathbf{X})^{-1}\mathbf{R}')^{-1}(\mathbf{Rb} - \mathbf{q}). \tag{7-13}$$

This appears in the numerator of the F statistic derived earlier. Inserting the remaining parts, we obtain an alternative form,

$$F[J, n - K] = \frac{(\mathbf{e}'_*\mathbf{e}_* - \mathbf{e}'\mathbf{e})/J}{\mathbf{e}'\mathbf{e}/(n - K)}. \tag{7-14}$$

Finally, by dividing the numerator and denominator of F by $\sum(y - \bar{y})^2$, we obtain a third form,

$$F[J, n - k] = \frac{(R^2 - R_*^2)/J}{(1 - R^2)/(n - K)}. \tag{7-15}$$

This form has some intuitive appeal in that the difference in the fits of the two models is directly incorporated in the test statistic. As an example of this approach, consider the earlier joint test that all of the slopes in the model are zero. This is the overall F ratio discussed in Section 67, where $R_*^2 = 0$.

7.2.4. Examples and Some General Procedures

The data in Table 7.1 have been used in several studies of production functions.[4]

Least squares regression of log output (value added) on a constant and the logs of labor and capital produce the estimates of a Cobb–Douglas production function shown in Table 7.2.

EXAMPLE 7.1.   For testing the hypothesis that the ith coefficient is equal to a particular value, $\mathbf{R}$ has a single row with a one in the ith position. Thus, $\mathbf{R}(\mathbf{X}'\mathbf{X})^{-1}\mathbf{R}'$ is the ith diagonal element of the inverse matrix, and $\mathbf{Rb} - \mathbf{q}$ is $(b_i - q)$. The F statistic is

$$F[1, n - K] = \frac{(b_i - q)^2}{\text{Var}[b_i]}, \tag{7-16}$$

---

[4] The data are statewide observations on SIC 33, the primary metals industry. They were originally constructed by Hildebrand and Liu (1957) and have subsequently been used by a number of authors, notably Aigner et al. (1977). The 28th data point used in the original study is incomplete; we have used only the remaining 27.

Table 7.1. Production Data for SIC 33: Primary Metals

Observation	Value Added	Labor	Capital
1	657.29	162.31	279.99
2	935.93	214.43	542.50
3	1110.65	186.44	721.51
4	1200.89	245.83	1,167.68
5	1052.68	211.40	811.77
6	3406.02	690.61	4,558.02
7	2427.89	452.79	3,069.91
8	4257.46	714.20	5,585.01
9	1625.19	320.54	1,618.75
10	1272.05	253.17	1,562.08
11	1004.45	236.44	662.04
12	598.87	140.73	875.37
13	853.10	145.04	1,696.98
14	1165.63	240.27	1,078.79
15	1917.55	536.73	2,109.34
16	9849.17	1564.83	13,989.55
17	1088.27	214.62	884.24
18	8095.63	1083.10	9,119.70
19	3175.39	521.74	5,686.99
20	1653.38	304.85	1,701.06
21	5159.31	835.69	5,206.36
22	3378.40	284.00	3,288.72
23	592.85	150.77	357.32
24	1601.98	259.91	2,031.93
25	2065.85	497.60	2,492.98
26	2293.87	275.20	1,711.74
27	745.67	137.00	768.59

Notes: Data are per establishment; labor is a measure of labor input; and capital is the gross value of plant and equipment. A scale factor used to normalize the capital figure in the original study has been omitted.

Table 7.2

Number of observations	27
Standard error of regression	0.18840
Sum of squared residuals	0.85163
R-squared	0.94346
Adjusted R-squared	0.93875

Variable	Coefficient	Std. Error	T ratio
Constant	1.171	0.3268	3.583
ln labor	0.6030	0.1260	4.787
ln capital	0.3757	0.0853	4.402

Estimated Covariance Matrix of the Estimates

	Constant	Labor	Capital
Constant	0.1068		
Labor	−0.01984	0.01586	
Capital	0.00189	−0.00961	0.00728

which is the square of the t statistic formulated in Chapter 6. For the preceding data, the hypothesis $H_0: \beta_2 = 1$ is rejected on the basis of an F statistic of

$$F(1, 24) = \frac{(0.6030 - 1)^2}{0.01586} = 9.937.$$

The 5 percent critical value from the F table is 5.99.

For testing a single linear restriction of the form

$$H_0: \mathbf{r}'\boldsymbol{\beta} = \mathbf{q},$$

the F statistic is

$$F[1, n - K] = \frac{(\sum r_i b_i - q)^2}{\sum_i \sum_j r_i r_j \text{Cov}[b_i, b_j]}. \tag{7-17}$$

If the number of coefficients is not large, this can easily be computed directly.

EXAMPLE 7.2. Constant Returns to Scale. The hypothesis that the two coefficients of the production function sum to one is equivalent to one of constant returns to scale. This is often tested in studies of production. For the preceding data,

$$F(1, 24) = \frac{(0.6030 + 0.3757 - 1)^2}{0.01586 + 0.00728 - 2(0.00961)}$$

$$= 0.1157.$$

This is substantially less than the critical value given earlier. We would not reject the hypothesis; the data are consistent with the hypothesis of constant returns to scale.

In most cases encountered in practice, it is possible to incorporate the restrictions of a hypothesis directly on the regression and estimate a restricted model.[5] For example, to impose the constraint $\beta_2 = 1$ on the model, we would write

$$\ln Y = \beta_1 + 1.0 \ln L + \beta_3 \ln K + \varepsilon$$

or

$$\ln Y - \ln L = \beta_1 + \beta_3 \ln K + \varepsilon.$$

Thus, the restricted model is estimated by regressing $\ln Y - \ln L$ on a constant and $\ln K$. Some care is needed if this regression is to be used to compute an F statistic. If the F-statistic is computed using the sum of squared residuals [i.e., using (7–14)], no problem will arise. However, if (7–15) is used instead, it may be necessary to account for the fact that the restricted regression has a different dependent variable from the unrestricted one. In the example just given, the dependent variable in the unrestricted regression is $\ln Y$, while in the restricted regression it is $\ln Y - \ln L$. The R^2 from the restricted regression is only 0.26979, which would imply an F statistic of 285.96, while the correct value is, as we saw earlier, 9.375. However, if we compute the appropriate R_*^2 using the correct denominator, its value is 0.94339 and the correct F value results.

For imposing a set of exclusion restrictions such as $\beta_i = 0$, for one or more coefficients, the obvious approach is simply to omit the variables from the regression and base the test on the sums of squared residuals from the restricted and unrestricted regressions.

---

[5] This is not the case when the restrictions are nonlinear. We consider this issue in Chapter 12.

EXAMPLE 7.3. **Translog Production Function.** A generalization of the Cobb–Douglas model used earlier is the *translog* model,[6] which is

$$\ln Y = \beta_1 + \beta_2 \ln L + \beta_3 \ln K + \beta_4 \frac{\ln^2 L}{2} + \beta_5 \frac{\ln^2 K}{2} + \beta_6 \ln L \ln K + \varepsilon.$$

As we shall analyze further in Chapter 17, this model differs from the Cobb–Douglas model in that it relaxes the Cobb–Douglas's assumption of a unitary elasticity of substitution. The Cobb–Douglas model is obtained by the restriction $\beta_4 = \beta_5 = \beta_6 = 0$. Thus, the restricted regression is simply the one we computed earlier. The results for the unrestricted regression are given in Table 7.3.

Table 7.3

Standard error of regression			0.17994
Sum of squared residuals			0.67993
R-squared			0.95486
Adjusted R-squared			0.94411

Variable	Coefficient	Standard Error	t Ratio
Constant	−0.944216	2.911	0.324
$\ln L$	3.61363	1.548	2.334
$\ln K$	−1.89311	1.016	−1.863
$\ln^2 L/2$	−0.96046	0.7074	−1.363
$\ln^2 K/2$	0.08530	0.2926	0.291
$\ln L \times \ln K$	0.31239	0.4389	0.712

The F statistic for the hypothesis of a Cobb–Douglas model is

$$F[3, 21] = \frac{(0.85163 - 0.67993)/3}{0.67993/21}$$

$$= 1.768.$$

The critical value from the F table is 6.59, so we would not reject the hypothesis that a Cobb–Douglas model is appropriate.

Note that the coefficient on $\ln K$ is now negative. We might conclude that the estimated output elasticity with respect to capital now has the wrong sign. However, this would be incorrect. In this expanded regression, the capital elasticity of output is

$$\frac{\partial \ln Y}{\partial \ln K} = \beta_3 + \beta_5 \ln K + \beta_6 \ln L.$$

If we insert the coefficient estimates and the mean values for $\ln K$ and $\ln L$ (not the logs of the means) of 7.44592 and 5.7637, respectively, the result is 0.5425, which is quite in line with our expectations and is fairly close to the value of 0.3757 obtained earlier. The estimated standard error for this linear combination of the least squares estimates is 0.1125, which likewise is reasonably close to the earlier estimate of 0.0854.

---

[6] Berndt and Christensen (1972).

The F statistic for testing the hypothesis that a subset, say β_2, of the coefficients are all zero is constructed using

$$\mathbf{R} = (\mathbf{0}:\mathbf{I}), \qquad \mathbf{q} = \mathbf{0},$$

and

$$J = K_2 = \text{the number of elements in } \beta_2.$$

The matrix $\mathbf{R(X'X)}^{-1}\mathbf{R'}$ is the $K_2 \times K_2$ lower right block of the full inverse matrix. Using our earlier results for partitioned inverses and the results of Section 6.3, we have

$$\mathbf{R(X'X)}^{-1}\mathbf{R'} = (\mathbf{X'_2 M_1 X_2})^{-1}$$

and

$$\mathbf{Rb} - \mathbf{q} = \mathbf{b_2}.$$

Inserting these in (7–13), we have the loss of fit that results when we drop a subset of the variables from the regression,

$$\mathbf{e'_* e_*} - \mathbf{e'e} = \mathbf{b'_2 X'_2 M_1 X_2 b_2}. \tag{7–18}$$

The procedure for computing the appropriate F statistic amounts simply to comparing the sums of squared deviations from the "short" and "long" regressions, which we saw earlier.

7.3. Tests of Structural Change

One of the more common applications of the F test is in tests of structural change.[7] In specifying a regression model, we assume that its assumptions apply to all of the observations in our sample. It is, however, straightforward to test the hypothesis that some or all of the regression coefficients are different in subsets of the data. To analyze a number of examples, we use the the *Longley data*, a data set that is widely used to calibrate regression programs.[8] (See Table 7.4.)

The dependent variable in the regression models will be employment, either total or in one of the two sectors given. The regressors will be a constant and the set of four variables listed at the left of the table. It will be convenient to label the three columns of employment $\mathbf{y}_t$, $\mathbf{y}_a$, and $\mathbf{y}_n$, and the matrix of regressors $[\mathbf{i} \ \mathbf{X}]$, where $\mathbf{i}$ is a column of ones.

7.3.1. Different Parameter Vectors

The preceding data span the years of the Korean conflict, which ended in 1953. Note the considerable change in the size of the armed forces during the period of this war. It is possible that the relationship between employment and the variables in $\mathbf{X}$ changed after the war. To test this as a hypothesis, we can proceed as follows: Denote the first 7 years of the data in $\mathbf{y}$ and $\mathbf{X}$ as $\mathbf{y}_1$ and $\mathbf{X}_1$. An unrestricted regression, which allows the coefficients to be different in

---

[7] This test is often labeled a *Chow test*, in reference to Chow (1960).
[8] These data are unusual in that the exact results of the least squares computation are known. They are from Longley (1967). Note that the total employment is not the sum of the two sectors given; several sectors from the original data set have been omitted.

Table 7.4.   The Longley Data

Year	GNP Deflator	GNP (mil.)	Armed Forces	Employment Total	Employment Agr.	Employment Nonagr.
1947	83.0	234,289	1590	60,323	8256	38,407
1948	88.5	259,426	1456	61,122	7960	39,241
1949	88.2	258,054	1616	60,171	8017	37,922
1950	89.5	284,599	1650	61,187	7497	39,196
1951	96.2	328,975	3099	63,221	7048	41,460
1952	98.1	346,999	3594	63,639	6792	42,216
1953	99.0	365,385	3547	64,989	6555	43,587
1954	100.0	363,112	3350	63,761	6495	42,271
1955	101.2	397,469	3048	66,019	6718	43,761
1956	104.6	419,180	2857	67,857	6572	45,131
1957	108.4	442,769	2798	68,169	6222	45,278
1958	110.8	444,546	2637	66,513	5844	43,530
1959	112.6	482,704	2552	68,655	5836	45,214
1960	114.2	502,601	2514	69,564	5723	45,850
1961	115.7	518,173	2572	69,331	5463	45,397
1962	116.9	554,894	2827	70,551	5190	46,652

the two periods, is

$$\begin{bmatrix} \mathbf{y}_1 \\ \mathbf{y}_2 \end{bmatrix} = \begin{bmatrix} \mathbf{X}_1 & \mathbf{0} \\ \mathbf{0} & \mathbf{X}_2 \end{bmatrix} \begin{bmatrix} \beta_1 \\ \beta_2 \end{bmatrix} + \begin{bmatrix} \varepsilon_1 \\ \varepsilon_2 \end{bmatrix}. \tag{7-19}$$

Denoting the data matrices as $\mathbf{y}$ and $\mathbf{X}$, we find that the unrestricted least squares estimator is

$$\mathbf{b} = (\mathbf{X}'\mathbf{X})^{-1}\mathbf{X}'\mathbf{y}$$

$$= \begin{bmatrix} \mathbf{X}_1'\mathbf{X}_1 & \mathbf{0} \\ \mathbf{0} & \mathbf{X}_2'\mathbf{X}_2 \end{bmatrix}^{-1} \begin{bmatrix} \mathbf{X}_1'\mathbf{y}_1 \\ \mathbf{X}_2'\mathbf{y}_2 \end{bmatrix} = \begin{bmatrix} \mathbf{b}_1 \\ \mathbf{b}_2 \end{bmatrix}, \tag{7-20}$$

which is least squares applied to the two equations separately. Therefore, the total sum of squared residuals from this regression will be the sum of the two residual sums of squares from the two separate regressions,

$$\mathbf{e}'\mathbf{e} = \mathbf{e}_1'\mathbf{e}_1 + \mathbf{e}_2'\mathbf{e}_2.$$

The restricted coefficient vector can be obtained in two ways. Formally, the restriction $\beta_1 = \beta_2$ is $\mathbf{R}\beta = \mathbf{q}$, where $\mathbf{R} = [\mathbf{I} - \mathbf{I}]$ and $\mathbf{q} = \mathbf{0}$. The general result given earlier can be applied directly. An easier way to proceed is to build the restriction directly into the model. If the two coefficient vectors are the same, (7-19) may be written

$$\begin{bmatrix} \mathbf{y}_1 \\ \mathbf{y}_2 \end{bmatrix} = \begin{bmatrix} \mathbf{X}_1 \\ \mathbf{X}_2 \end{bmatrix} \beta + \begin{bmatrix} \varepsilon_1 \\ \varepsilon_2 \end{bmatrix}$$

and the restricted estimator can be obtained simply by stacking the data and estimating a single regression. The residual sum of squares from this regression then forms the basis for the test.

EXAMPLE 7.4. Separate Regressions.   Using the data on total employment for this example, we obtain the three estimated regression equations shown in Table 7.5.

Table 7.5

Coefficients	1947–1962	1947–1953	1954–1962
Constant	1169090	1678148	3776130
Year	−576.464	−835.193	−1914.17
Deflator	−19.7681	−163.292	−42.4647
GNP	0.0643094	0.0948082	0.11233
Armed forces	−0.0101452	−0.246697	−2.57928
Standard error	667.328	415.457	298.187
Sum of squares	4,898,726	345,068	801,552

The F statistic for testing the restriction that the coefficients in the two equations are the same is

$$F(5,6) = \frac{(4,898,726 - 345,068 - 801,552)/5}{(345,068 + 801,552)/(7 + 9 - 10)} = 3.932.$$

The tabled critical value is 4.39 for 5 percent significance, so we would not reject the hypothesis that the coefficient vectors are the same in the two periods.

7.3.2.   Different Constant Terms

The general formulation previously suggested lends itself to many variations that allow a wide range of possible tests. Some important particular cases are suggested by our test data. We might consider the difference between employment in the agricultural and non-agricultural sectors. However, the figures for the two dependent variables are of a different order of magnitude. There are various ways to deal with this problem. One crude way would be to allow for different intercepts in the equations while stacking only the regressors in the restricted equation. Thus, the unrestricted equation is based on least squares regression of each category of employment on a constant and the four regressors, while the restricted regression is a pooled one with 32 observations. The restricted model has a regressor matrix of the form

$$X = \begin{bmatrix} i & 0 & W \\ 0 & i & W \end{bmatrix}.$$

The first two columns of X are **dummy variables** that indicate which sector the observation falls in. (This device was used in Section 6.8.1 in Salkever's formulation of the computation of least squares forecasts.)

EXAMPLE 7.5. Change in Slope Coefficients.   Using the 16 observations on the two dependent variables for the test, we obtain the data shown in Table 7.6.

The F statistic is

$$F[4,22] = \frac{(107,780,171 - 241,186 - 5,038,028)/4}{(241,186 + 5,038,028)/22}$$

$$= 106.79.$$

This is extremely large and leads to rejection of the hypothesis at any significance level.

Table 7.6

Coefficients	Agricultural	Nonagricultural	Pooled
Constant—agr.	201828	—	626192
Constant—nonagr.	—	1086740	662375
Year	−97.5838	−544.519	−321.051
Deflator	−40.5182	−23.3502	−31.9342
GNP	0.000513124	0.0534508	0.026982
Armed forces	−0.208122	0.764720	0.278299
Standard error	148.074	676.748	2036.024
Sum of squares	241,186	5,038,028	107,780,171

7.3.3. Change in a Subset of Coefficients

One factor that might have a strong influence in Example 7.5 is the clear secular trends in the dependent variables. In the cases of agricultural and nonagricultural employment, they are in opposite directions. It might have been more reasonable to allow both the constant term and the time trend (coefficient on "Year") to differ across the two equations. Once again, the unrestricted coefficient vector is the earlier one. The restricted coefficients are computed using a regressor matrix of the form

$$X = \begin{bmatrix} i & Year & 0 & 0 & W \\ 0 & 0 & i & Year & W \end{bmatrix}, \qquad (7-21)$$

where W contains (replicated for both data series) the last three columns of the original data matrix.

EXAMPLE 7.6. The F ratio that results from estimating the model in (7–21) is

$$F[3,22] = \frac{(11,917,648 - 5,279,214)/3}{5,279,214/22} = 9.221.$$

The critical value from the F table is 3.05, so we would still reject the hypothesis. However, the sample value is substantially reduced. Apparently, the difference in the secular trends accounted for much of the difference in the coefficient vectors.

7.3.4. Insufficient Observations

There are circumstances in which the data series are not long enough to estimate one or the other of the separate regressions for a test of structural change. For example, the data presented earlier on the armed forces series suggests that the major employment change, if there was one, occurred in 1951, not 1954. We might naturally consider the same test we did earlier, using the two subperiods 1947–1950 and 1951–1962. However, there are five parameters to estimate and only four observations in the first data set. Fisher (1970) has shown that in such a circumstance, a valid way to proceed is as follows:

1. Estimate the regression, using the full data set, and compute the restricted residual sum of squared residuals, $e'_* e_*$.
2. Use the longer (adequate) subperiod to estimate the regression, and compute the unrestricted sum of squares, $e'e$. This latter computation is done under the

assumption that with only $n_1 < K$ observations, we could obtain a perfect fit and thus contribute zero to the sum of squares.

3. The F statistic is then computed, using

$$F(n_1, n_1 + n_2 - K) = \frac{(e'_* e_* - e'e)/n_1}{e'e/(n_1 + n_2 - K)}. \tag{7-22}$$

Note that the numerator degrees of freedom is n_1, not K.[9] This test has been labeled the Chow *predictive test*, as it is equivalent to extending the restricted model to the shorter subperiod and basing the test on the prediction errors of the model in this period.

EXAMPLE 7.7. Inadequate Degrees of Freedom.   Using the total employment series as an example, we find that the F test for stability of the coefficients in the equation across the two subperiods is

$$F(4, 11) = \frac{(4{,}898{,}726 - 3{,}394{,}431)/4}{3{,}394{,}431/(4 + 12 - 5)} = 1.218.$$

This is not larger than the critical value of 3.36. Hence, the hypothesis of stability would not be rejected.

7.4. Tests of Structural Change with Unequal Variances

An important assumption made in using the Chow test is that the disturbance variance is the same in both (or all) regressions. In the restricted model, if this is not true, the first n_1 elements of ε have variance σ_1^2, while the next n_2 have variance σ_2^2, and so on. The restricted model is, therefore, heteroscedastic, and our results for the classical regression model no longer apply. As analyzed by Schmidt and Sickles (1977), Ohtani and Toyoda (1985), and Toyoda and Ohtani (1986), it is quite likely that we shall overestimate the significance level of our test statistic. (That is, we shall regard as large an F statistic that is actually less than the *appropriate* table value.) Precisely how severe this effect is going to be will depend on the data and the extent to which the variances differ, in ways that are not likely to be obvious.

There are direct ways to deal with this problem. Assuming that we can estimate both (all) of the separate regressions, we can examine our estimates of the disturbance variances. With these in hand, for instance, we can test directly for significant differences.[10] Without any significant difference, we can proceed as described. If, however, there is evidence to suggest that the variances actually are different, there are still simple and appropriate ways to carry out the analysis by explicitly estimating the model, accounting for the heteroscedasticity. This relies on some results that we develop more fully in Chapter 16, so we defer until that point a more complete discussion of the procedure.[11]

---

[9] One way to view this is that only $n_1 < K$ coefficients are needed to obtain this perfect fit.

[10] We consider this more fully in the discussion of the Goldfeld–Quandt test in Chapter 14.

[11] Since the initial test will have some probability of a type II error, there is that probability that we will fail to pick up an actual difference in the disturbance variances, and incorrectly estimate the model as if there were none. This potential is a contributor to *pretest bias* and is discussed more fully for this model in Toyoda and Ohtani (1986).

7.4.1. A Test That Is Valid in Large Samples

If the sample is reasonably large, we have a test that is valid whether or not the disturbance variances are the same. To set up the test, we shall use some general results presented in Chapter 4. Suppose that $\hat{\theta}_1$ and $\hat{\theta}_2$ are two normally distributed estimators of a parameter based on independent samples,[12] with variance matrices V_1 and V_2. Then, under the null hypothesis that the two estimates have the same expected value,

$$\hat{\theta}_1 - \hat{\theta}_2 \quad \text{has mean } 0 \text{ and variance } V_1 + V_2.$$

Thus, the Wald statistic,

$$W = (\hat{\theta}_1 - \hat{\theta}_2)'(V_1 + V_2)^{-1}(\hat{\theta}_1 - \hat{\theta}_2), \tag{7-23}$$

has a chi-squared distribution with K degrees of freedom. A test that the difference between the parameters is zero can be based on this statistic. It is straightforward to apply this to our test of common parameter vectors in our regressions. Large values of the statistic lead us to reject the hypothesis. What remains for us to resolve is whether it is valid to base such a test on *estimates* of V_1 and V_2. Looking ahead to our results in Chapter 14, the test is indeed valid in large samples, so we may use our least squares estimates of the two covariance matrices to compute W.

7.4.2. A Bounds Test for Small Samples

In a small or moderate-sized sample, the Wald test has the unfortunate property that the probability of a type I error is persistently larger than the critical level we use to carry it out. (That is, we shall too frequently reject the null hypothesis that the parameters are the same in the subsamples.) We should be using a larger critical value. Ohtani and Kobiyashi (1986) have devised a "bounds" test that gives a partial remedy for the problem.[13] The correct critical value to use for (7–23) depends on the particular data set in use. However, Ohtani and Kobiyashi (1986) show that for the various combinations of n_1, n_2, and K, the number of coefficients, there are constants c_l and c_u such that the appropriate critical value must be less than or equal to c_u and greater than or equal to c_l. Therefore, we may use the following test strategy:

1. Reject H_0 if $W > c_u$.
2. Do not reject H_0 if $W < c_l$.
3. Draw no conclusion if $c_l \leq W \leq c_u$.

The inconclusive region is, of course, a problem. Moreover, its power characteristics remain to be studied. Nonetheless, for small samples, this test may represent a considerable improvement over the usual chi-squared test.

EXAMPLE 7.8. Tests for Structural Change.   Using the Wald statistic instead of the Chow test used earlier to compare agricultural and nonagricutural employment, we obtain a chi-squared value of 10.999 with five degrees of freedom. In this case, because the regressions

---

[12] Without the required independence, this test and several similar ones will fail completely. The problem becomes a variant of the famous Behrens–Fisher problem.

[13] See also Kobiyashi (1986). An alternative, somewhat more cumbersome test is proposed by Jayatissa (1977). Further discussion is given in Thursby (1982).

have the same independent variables, the matrix is easy to compute:

$$(V_1 + V_2)^{-1} = \frac{1}{s_1^2 + s_2^2} X'X.$$

The critical value from the chi-squared table is 11.07. Thus, the Wald statistic, unlike the F statistic obtained earlier, is insignificant.

Sample sizes of 16 are clearly too small to expect good asymptotic behavior of the Wald test statistic. The 5 percent critical values from the Ohtani–Kobiyashi tables for n_1 and n_2 equal to 16 are as follows:

K	2	3	4	5	6
c_l	5.64	7.51	9.31	11.10	12.94
c_u	9.05	12.41	15.88	19.64	23.86
χ^2	5.99	7.81	9.49	11.07	12.59

(For comparison, the critical values from the chi-squared table are also given.) For our model here, with $K = 5$, the upper critical value is 19.64, which implies that our earlier conclusion based on the F test might be inappropriate.

7.5.   Alternative Tests of Model Stability

Example 7.7 shows a test of structural change based essentially on the model's ability to predict correctly outside the range of the observations used to estimate it. A similar logic underlies an alternative test of model stability proposed by Brown et al. (1975) based on **recursive residuals**. The technique is appropriate for time-series data, and might be used if one is uncertain about when a structural change might have taken place. The null hypothesis is that the coefficient vector, β, is the same in every period; the alternative is simply that it (or the disturbance variance) is not. The test is quite general in that it does not require a prior specification of when the structural change takes place. The cost, however, is that the power of the test is rather limited compared to that of the Chow test.[14]

Suppose that the sample contains a total of T observations.[15] The tth recursive residual is the ex post prediction error for y_t when the regression is estimated using only the first $t - 1$ observations:

$$e_t = y_t - x_t' b_{t-1},$$

where x_t is the vector of regressors associated with observation y_t and b_{t-1} is the least squares coefficients computed using the first $t - 1$ observations.[16] The forecast variance of this

[14] The test is frequently criticized on this basis. However, the Chow test is based on a rather definite piece of information, namely, when the structural change takes place. If this is not known or must be estimated, the advantage of the Chow test diminishes considerably.

[15] Since we are dealing explicitly with time-series data at this point, it is convenient to use T instead of n for the sample size and t instead of i to index observations.

[16] In principle, this requires the computation of $T - K$ regressions. The difficult part of the computation is $(X_t'X_t)^{-1}$. However, since $X_t'X_t = X_{t-1}'X_{t-1} + x_t x_t'$, the rank one updating formula of Section 2.5.2, equation (2–66) can be applied, beginning with an initial regression based on K observations. The result is useful and does provide insight into the calculation. [Discussion can be found in Johnston (1984, p. 387.)] However, using an electronic computer, it is unlikely that using the updating formula instead of actually computing the regression will save a noticeable amount of time. It is also possible, depending on how the accumulation is programmed, that this will introduce a new source of accumulated rounding error into the calculations. This may be a problem in a badly conditioned data set such as the Longley data used earlier.

residual is

$$\sigma_f^2 = \sigma^2[1 + \mathbf{x}_t'(\mathbf{X}_{t-1}'\mathbf{X}_{t-1})^{-1}\mathbf{x}_t]. \tag{7-24}$$

Let the tth scaled residual be

$$w_t = \frac{e_t}{\sqrt{[1 + \mathbf{x}_t'(\mathbf{X}_{t-1}'\mathbf{X}_{t-1})^{-1}\mathbf{x}_t]}}. \tag{7-25}$$

Under the hypothesis that the coefficients remain constant during the full sample period, $w_t \sim N(0, \sigma^2)$ and is independent of w_s for all $s \neq t$. Evidence that the distribution of w_t is changing over time weighs against the hypothesis of model stability.

Brown et al. suggest two tests based on w_t. The CUSUM test is based on the cumulated sum of the residuals:

$$W_t = \sum_{r=K+1}^{r=t} \frac{w_r}{\hat{\sigma}},$$

where

$$\hat{\sigma}^2 = \frac{1}{T-K} \sum_{r=K+1}^{T} (w_r - \bar{w})^2 \tag{7-26}$$

and

$$\bar{w} = \frac{1}{T-K} \sum_{r=K+1}^{r=T} w_r.$$

Under the null hypothesis, w_t has a mean of zero and a variance of approximately the number of residuals being summed (as each term has variance 1 and they are independent). The test is performed by plotting w_t against t. Confidence bounds for the sum are obtained by plotting the two lines that connect the points $(K, \pm a\sqrt{T-K})$ and $(T, \pm 3a\sqrt{T-K})$. Values of a that correspond to various significance levels can be found in their paper. Those corresponding to 95 percent and 99 percent are 0.948 and 1.143, respectively. The hypothesis is rejected if w_t strays outside the boundaries.

An alternative similar test is based on the squares of the residuals. The CUSUM-squared test uses

$$S_t = \frac{\sum_{r=K+1}^{r=t} w_r^2}{\sum_{r=K+1}^{r=T} w_r^2}. \tag{7-27}$$

Since the residuals are independent, each of the two terms is approximately a sum of chi-squared variables each with one degree of freedom. Therefore, $E[S_t]$ is approximately $(t-K)/(T-K)$. The test is carried out by constructing confidence bounds for $E[S_t]$ at the values of t and plotting S_t and these bounds against t. The appropriate bounds are $E(S) \pm c_0$, where c_0 depends on both $(T-K)$ and the significance level desired.[17] As before, if the cumulated sum strays outside the confidence bounds, doubt is cast on the hypothesis of parameter stability.

A related test proposed by Harvey and Collier (1977) is based directly on the mean. Under the hypothesis of model stability, $\bar{w}$ is normally distributed, with mean zero and

---

[17] Tables may be found in Harvey (1981) and Johnston (1984).

variance $\sigma^2/(T - K)$. The test is a familiar t test of the hypothesis that the mean of w_t is zero. The procedure uses

$$t[T - K - 1] = \frac{(\sqrt{T - K})\bar{w}}{s},$$ (7–28)

where

$$s^2 = \frac{1}{T - K - 1} \sum_{r=K+1}^{r=T} (w_r - \bar{w})^2.$$ (7–29)

The statistic is compared to the t distribution with $T - K - 1$ degrees of freedom.

EXAMPLE 7.9. Tests of Model Stability.   Example 11.4. presents estimates of a model of the demand for money, using aggregate U.S. data for 1966 through 1985. Applying the previous tests to the data given in the example, we find the evidence mixed on whether the underlying parameter vector is unchanged for the 20 years.

				CUSUM					
0	0	0	−0.203	0.180	0.348	0.293	0.263	0.608	1.45
2.02	2.23	2.33	2.82	3.67	4.43	6.47	9.05	10.42	11.64

				CUSUM-Squared					
0	0	0	0.000	0.003	0.0064	0.0067	0.0068	0.0192	0.0929
0.127	0.132	0.133	0.157	0.232	0.291	0.725	1.42	1.61	1.77

Figure 7.1 shows the CUSUM and CUSUM-squared tests based on these data. The CUSUM stays well within the boundaries, while the CUSUM-squared wanders outside for the last three observations. The Harvey–Collier test is based on

$$\bar{w} = 120.26$$

and

$$s = 132.08,$$

which gives

$$t[16] = 3.75.$$

This test agrees with the CUSUM-squared test in suggesting that the parameters are not constant across the full 20 years. The CUSUM and CUSUM-squared series suggest that the source of the instability, such as it is, is the last three observations. As a final check, we compute the Chow test of Example 7.7 for these three observations. The results are

$$F[3, 17] = \frac{(525,010 - 215,250)/3}{525,010/17} = 3.43.$$

This is slightly larger than the 95 percent critical value of 3.20. (The right tail area beyond this value is 0.04397.)

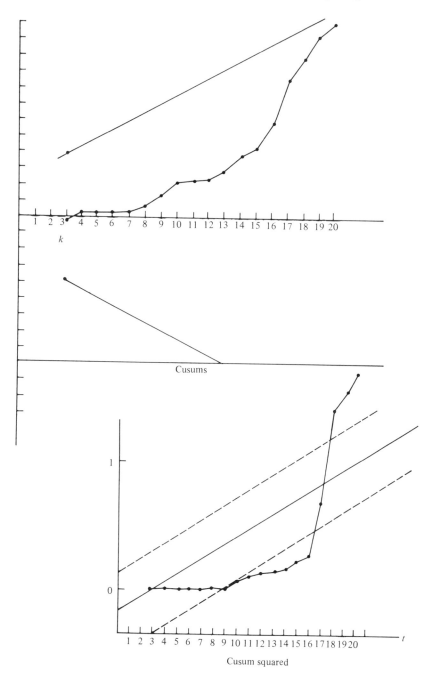

Figure 7.1   Cusum and cusum-squared tests.

7.6. *Testing a Nonlinear Restriction*

The preceding discussion has relied heavily on the linearity of the regression model. Most of the distributional results, for example, follow either from the normality of a linear function of normally distributed variables or from the F and chi-squared distributions derived from the normal distribution. When we analyze nonlinear functions of the parameters and nonlinear regression models, most of these exact distributional results no longer hold. We shall consider the appropriate "asymptotic" results in more detail in Chapter 10. However, there are some fairly straightforward results we can obtain now.

The general problem is that of testing a hypothesis that involves a nonlinear function of the regression coefficients:

$$H_0: f(\beta) = q.$$

We shall look at the case of a single restriction. However, the more general one, in which $\mathbf{f}(\beta) = \mathbf{q}$ is a set of restrictions, is a simple extension. The counterpart to the test statistic we used earlier would be

$$z = \frac{f(\hat{\beta}) - q}{\text{estimated standard error}} \tag{7-30}$$

or its square, which in the preceding were distributed as $t[n - K]$ and $F[1, n - K]$, respectively. The discrepancy in the numerator presents no difficulty. However, obtaining an estimate of the sampling variance of $f(\hat{\beta}) - q$ involves the variance of a nonlinear function of $\hat{\beta}$.

An approach that uses the large-sample properties of the estimates and provides an approximation to the variances we need is based on a linear Taylor series approximation. A linear Taylor series approximation to $f(\hat{\beta})$ around the true parameter vector, β, is

$$f(\hat{\beta}) \simeq f(\beta) + \left(\frac{\partial f(\beta)}{\partial \beta}\right)'(\hat{\beta} - \beta). \tag{7-31}$$

We must rely on consistency rather than unbiasedness here, since, in general, the expected value of a nonlinear function is not equal to the function of the expected value. Thus, in view of the approximation, and assuming that $\text{plim}(\hat{\beta}) = \beta$, we are justified in using $f(\hat{\beta})$ as an estimate of $f(\beta)$. (The relevant result is the Slutsky theorem.) Assuming that our use of this approximation is appropriate, the variance of the nonlinear function is approximately equal to the variance of the right-hand side, which is, then,

$$\text{Var}[f(\hat{\beta})] \simeq \mathbf{g}'\text{Var}[\hat{\beta} - \beta]\mathbf{g}$$

$$\mathbf{g} = \frac{\partial f(\beta)}{\partial \beta}. \tag{7-32}$$

The derivatives in the expression for the variance are functions of the unknown parameters. Since these are being estimated, we use our sample estimates in computing the derivatives. To estimate the variance of the estimator, we can use $s^2(\mathbf{X'X})^{-1}$, as is familiar. Lastly, we rely on results to be treated in more detail in Chapter 10 and use the standard normal distribution instead of the t distribution for the test statistic. Using our sample estimate, $\hat{f} = f(\hat{\beta})$ of $f(\mathbf{b})$, we can now test a hypothesis in the same fashion we did earlier.

EXAMPLE 7.10. **A Long-Run Marginal Propensity to Consume.**   A consumption function that has different short- and long-run marginal propensities to consume can be

Table 7.7

Year	Consumption	GNP	Year	Consumption	GNP
1963	522.67	832.57	1973	767.85	1254.28
1964	550.36	876.32	1974	771.72	1246.26
1965	578.81	929.40	1975	776.21	1231.58
1966	605.92	984.89	1976	819.93	1298.17
1967	620.16	1011.38	1977	859.98	1369.73
1968	650.47	1058.15	1978	895.16	1438.57
1969	670.35	1087.68	1979	922.29	1479.50
1970	679.83	1085.51	1980	933.27	1473.97
1971	700.14	1122.38	1981	942.77	1502.58
1972	737.10	1185.90	1982	951.60	1475.41

Table 7.8

R-squared			0.99758

Variable	Coefficient	Standard Error	t Ratio
Constant	−7.69575	11.44	−0.672
Real GNP	0.400147	0.06272	6.380
Cons. $(t-1)$	0.380728	0.09479	4.017

Estimated Covariance Matrix of Estimates

	Constant	Real GNP	Cons. $(t-1)$
Constant	130.972		
Real GNP	−0.43868	0.00393	
Cons. $(t-1)$	0.54959	−0.005590	0.00898

written in the form

$$C_t = \alpha + \beta Y_t + \gamma C_{t-1} + \varepsilon_t.$$

(This is a *distributed lag* model. We consider these models in more detail in Chapter 18.) In this model, the short-run marginal propensity to consume is β, while the long-run marginal propensity to consume is $\delta = \beta/(1 - \gamma)$. Consider testing the hypothesis that $\delta = 1$.[18]

The data in Table 7.7 are aggregate data on real consumption and GNP (deflated by the CPI) from the 1983 *Economic Report of the President.*

Least squares regression of consumption on a constant, GNP, and lagged consumption produced the following results (Table 7.8.).

The estimate of the long-run marginal propensity to consume is

$$d = \frac{b}{1-c} = \frac{0.400147}{(1-0.380728)} = 0.6461. \quad = f(\hat{\beta})$$

---

[18] The observant reader will notice that this is equivalent to $\beta = 1 - \gamma$, which is linear. However, it is instructive to pursue it as a nonlinear restriction.

To compute the estimated variance of d, we require

$$\frac{\partial \delta}{\partial \beta} = \frac{1}{1 - \gamma} = 1.6149,$$

$$\frac{\partial \delta}{\partial \gamma} = \frac{\beta}{(1 - \gamma)^2} = 1.0434$$

when evaluated at our estimates. The estimated variance is

$$\text{Est. Var}[\hat{\delta}] = 1.6149^2 (0.00393) + 1.0434^2 (0.00898) - 2(1.6149)(1.0434)0.0059$$

$$= 0.000143.$$

The square root is 0.01194. To test the hypothesis that the long-run marginal propensity to consume is greater than or equal to one, we would use

$$z = \frac{(0.6461 - 1)}{0.01194} = -29.64.$$

Because we are using a large-sample approximation, we refer this to a standard normal table instead of the usual t distribution. Obviously, the hypothesis should be rejected.[19]

The generalization to more than one function of the parameters proceeds along similar lines. Let $\mathbf{f}(\hat{\beta})$ be a set of J functions of the parameter vector. The estimate of the sampling covariance matrix of these functions is

$$\text{Est. Var}[\mathbf{f}] = \hat{\mathbf{G}}\{\text{Est. Var}[\hat{\beta}]\}\hat{\mathbf{G}}', \tag{7-33}$$

where $\hat{\mathbf{G}}$ is a $J \times K$ matrix of derivatives:

$$\hat{\mathbf{G}} = \frac{\partial \mathbf{f}(\hat{\beta})}{\partial \hat{\beta}'}. \tag{7-34}$$

(The jth row of $\mathbf{G}$ is the K derivatives of f_j with respect to the K elements of $\hat{\beta}$.) For example, the variance matrix for estimates of the short- and long-run marginal propensity to consume would be obtained using

$$\mathbf{G} = \begin{bmatrix} 0 & 1 & 0 \\ 0 & 1/(1 - \beta) & \beta/(1 - \gamma)^2 \end{bmatrix}.$$

The statistic, which in large samples has a chi-squared distribution with degrees of freedom equal to the number of restrictions, is

$$c = \mathbf{f}'\{\text{Est. Var}[\mathbf{f}]\}^{-1}\mathbf{f}. \tag{7-35}$$

Note that for a single restriction, this is the square of the statistic in (7-30).

The preceding analysis is based on the unrestricted least squares estimates. In the same way that we approached this problem before, we might have examined the loss of fit that results when the restrictions are imposed. But in this case, that would have involved fitting the regression subject to a set of nonlinear restrictions. Although straightforward in principle, this procedure is a bit more difficult in practice. It is taken up in Chapter 11.

---

[19] The t test of the equivalent restriction noted in the previous footnote produces a test statistic of -6.592, which also leads to rejection of the hypothesis.

7.7.   *An Asymptotically Valid Test for Nonnested Models*

The classical testing procedures that we have been using have been shown to be quite powerful for the types of hypotheses we have considered.[20] Although this is clearly desirable, the requirement that we be able to express the hypotheses in the form of restrictions on the model $y = X\beta + \varepsilon$,

$$H_0: R\beta = q,$$

versus

$$H_1: R\beta \neq q,$$

can be limiting. Two common exceptions are the general problem of determining which of two possible sets of regressors is more appropriate and whether a linear or log-linear model is more appropriate for a given analysis.

For the present, we restrict our attention to two competing linear models:

$$H_0: y = X\beta + \varepsilon_0 \qquad\qquad (7\text{--}36a)$$

and

$$H_1: y = Z\gamma + \varepsilon_1. \qquad\qquad (7\text{--}36b)$$

We shall consider nonlinear models (and the question of linear versus log-linear models) in Chapter 11.

Since H_1 cannot be written as a restriction on H_0, none of the procedures we have considered thus far are appropriate. One possibility is an artificial nesting of the two models. Let $\bar{X}$ be the set of variables in X that are not in Z, define $\bar{Z}$ likewise with respect to X, and let W be the variables that the models have in common. Then H_0 and H_1 can be combined in a "super model."

$$y = \overline{X}\beta + \overline{Z}\gamma + W\delta + \varepsilon.$$

In principle, H_1 is rejected if it is found that $\bar{\gamma} = 0$ by a conventional F test, while H_0 is rejected if it is found that $\bar{\beta} = 0$. There are two problems with this approach. First, δ remains a mixture of parts of β and γ, and it is not established by the F test that either of these parts is zero. Hence, this test does not really distinguish between H_0 and H_1; it distinguishes between H_1 and a hybrid model. Second, this compound model may have an extremely large number of regressors. In a time-series setting, the problem of collinearity may be severe.

The J test proposed by Davidson and MacKinnon (1981) is similar in spirit to the nesting strategy but overcomes its practical problems. An alternative to the preceding compound model is

$$y = (1 - \alpha)X\beta + \alpha(Z\gamma) + \varepsilon.$$

As written, a test of $\alpha = 0$ would be a test against H_1. The problem is that α cannot be estimated in this model. Davidson and MacKinnon's J test consists of estimating γ by a least squares regression and then regressing y on X and $Z\gamma$, the fitted values in this regression. A valid test, at least asymptotically, of H_1 is to test $H_0: \alpha = 0$. If H_0 is true,

$$\text{plim } \hat{\alpha} = 0.$$

---

[20] See, for example, Kendall and Stuart (1972, Chapter 27).

Asymptotically, the ratio

$$\frac{\hat{\alpha}}{\text{se}(\hat{\alpha})}$$

(i.e., the usual t ratio) is distributed as standard normal and may be referred to the standard tables to carry out the test. Unfortunately, in testing H_0 versus H_1 and vice versa, all four possibilities (reject both, neither, or either one of the two hypotheses) could occur. This is, however, a finite sample problem. Davidson and MacKinnon show that as $n \to \infty$, if H_1 is true, the probability that $\hat{\alpha}$ will differ significantly from zero approaches one.

EXAMPLE 7.11.   J Test for a Consumption Function.   Gaver and Geisel (1974) propose two forms of a consumption function:

$$H_0: C_t = \beta_1 + \beta_2 Y_t + \beta_3 Y_{t-1} + \varepsilon_{0t}$$

and

$$H_1: C_t = \gamma_1 + \gamma_2 Y_t + \gamma_3 C_{t-1} + \varepsilon_{1t}.$$

The first implies that consumption responds to changes in income over two periods, while the second implies that the effects of changes in income on consumption persist for many periods. (These models are examined further in Chapter 18.) Data on aggregate U.S. consumption and income are given in the previous example. Here we apply the J test to these data and the previous two specifications. First, the two models are estimated separately. The least squares regression of C on a constant, Y, lagged Y, and the fitted values from the second model produces an estimate of α of 2.74 with a t ratio of 5.21. Thus, H_0 should be rejected in favor of H_1. But reversing the roles of H_0 and H_1, we obtain an estimate of α of -2.70 with a t ratio of -3.55. Thus, H_1 is rejected as well.[21]

A related set of procedures based on the likelihood ratio test has been devised by Cox (1961 and 1962). The versions of the Cox test appropriate for the linear and nonlinear regression models have been derived by Pesaran (1974) and Pesaran and Deaton (1978). The latter present a test statistic for testing linear versus log-linear models that is extended in Aneuryn-Evans and Deaton (1980). Since, in the classical regression model, the least squares estimator is also the maximum likelihood estimator, it is perhaps not surprising that Davidson and MacKinnon (1981, p. 789) find that their test statistic is asymptotically equal to the negative of the Cox–Pesaran and Deaton statistic. The Cox statistic for testing the hypothesis that X is the correct set of regressors and Z is not is

$$c_{12} = \frac{n}{2}\ln\left[\frac{s_z^2}{s_x^2 + (1/n)\mathbf{b}'\mathbf{X}'\mathbf{M}_z\mathbf{Xb}}\right] \tag{7-37}$$

$$= \frac{n}{2}\ln\left[\frac{s_z^2}{s_{zx}^2}\right],$$

where $\mathbf{M}_z = \mathbf{I} - \mathbf{Z}(\mathbf{Z}'\mathbf{Z})^{-1}\mathbf{Z}'$ and $\mathbf{b} = (\mathbf{X}'\mathbf{X})^{-1}\mathbf{X}'\mathbf{Y}$.
The hypothesis is tested by taking

$$q = \frac{c_{12}}{(\text{Var}[c_{12}])^{1/2}} = \frac{c_{12}}{[(s_z^2/s_{zx}^2)\mathbf{b}'\mathbf{X}'\mathbf{M}_z\mathbf{M}_x\mathbf{M}_z\mathbf{Xb}]^{1/2}}, \tag{7-38}$$

---

[21] For related discussion of this possibility, see McAleer et al. (1982).

where $M_x = I - X(X'X)^{-1}X'$, into a standard normal table. A large value of q is evidence against the hypothesis. Although this involves a substantial amount of matrix algebra, there are several shortcuts that will simplify the result. First,

$$s_z^2 = \frac{e_z'e_z}{n} = \text{mean-squared residual in the regression of } y \text{ on } Z,$$

$$s_x^2 = \frac{e_x'e_x}{n} = \text{mean-squared residual in the regression of } y \text{ on } X,$$

$$Xb = \text{fitted values in the regression of } y \text{ on } X,$$

$$M_zXb = \text{residuals in a regression of } Xb \text{ on } Z,$$

$$b'X'M_zXb = \text{sum of squared residuals in the regression of } Xb \text{ on } Z,$$

$$s_{zx}^2 = s_x^2 + \frac{1}{n}b'X'M_zXb,$$

$$(b'X'M_z)M_x(M_zXb) = \text{sum of squared residuals in the regression of } M_zXb \text{ on } X.$$

Therefore, the Cox statistic can be computed simply by computing a set of least squares regressions.

EXAMPLE 7.12. Cox Test for a Consumption Function.   We continue the previous example by applying the Cox test to the data of Example 7.10. For purposes of the test, let

$$X = [i \quad y \quad y_{-1}] \qquad \text{and} \qquad Z = [i \quad y \quad c_{-1}].$$

Using the notation of (7–37) and (7–38), we find that

$$s_x^2 = 60.09631 \qquad \text{and} \qquad s_z^2 = 39.36133,$$

$$b'X'M_zXb = 46.630105 \qquad \text{and} \qquad b'X'M_zM_xM_zXb = 40.592986,$$

so that

$$s_{zx}^2 = 60.09631 + \frac{46.630105}{19} = 62.50527.$$

Thus,

$$c_{12} = \frac{19}{2}\ln\left(\frac{39.36133}{62.50527}\right) = -4.4003$$

and

$$\text{Est. Var}[c_{12}] = \frac{39.36133(40.592986)}{62.50527^2} = 0.40897$$

Thus, $q = -6.881$. On this basis, we reject the hypothesis that X is the correct set of regressors. Note, in the previous example, that we reached the same conclusion based on a t ratio of 5.21. As expected, the result has the opposite sign from the corresponding J statistic in the previous example. Now we reverse the roles of X and Z in our calculations. Letting d denote the least squares coefficients in the regression of consumption on Z, we find

$$d'Z'M_xZd = 97.63601 \qquad \text{and} \qquad d'Z'M_xM_zM_xZd = 84.99524,$$

so that

$$s_{xz}^2 = 39.36133 + \frac{97.63601}{19} = 44.50007.$$

Thus,

$$c_{12} = \left(\frac{19}{2}\right)\ln\left(\frac{60.09631}{44.50007}\right) = 2.8543$$

and

$$\text{Est. Var}[c_{12}] = \frac{60.09631(84.99524)}{44.50007^2} = 2.5794.$$

This produces a value of $q = 1.777$, which is considerably smaller (in absolute value) than its counterpart in the previous example, -3.55. Thus, since 1.777 is less than the 95 percent critical value of 1.96, we would not reject the hypothesis that $\mathbf{Z}$ is the preferred set of regressors.

The two approaches to nonnested models, Davidson and MacKinnon's J test and Cox's extension of the likelihood ratio test, have been analyzed in a large amount of recent research.[22]

Exercises

1. A multiple regression of y on a constant, x_1, and x_2 produces the following results:

$$y = 4 + 0.4x_1 + 0.9x_2, \qquad R^2 = \tfrac{8}{60},$$

$$\mathbf{e}'\mathbf{e} = 520, \qquad n = 29,$$

$$\mathbf{X}'\mathbf{X} = \begin{bmatrix} 29 & 0 & 0 \\ 0 & 50 & 10 \\ 0 & 10 & 80 \end{bmatrix}.$$

Test the hypothesis that the two slopes sum to one.

2. Using the results in Exercise 1, test the hypothesis that the slope on x_1 is zero by running the restricted regression and comparing the two sums of squared deviations.

3. The translog production function in Example 7.3 has constant returns to scale if

$$\frac{\partial \ln Y}{\partial \ln L} + \frac{\partial \ln Y}{\partial \ln K} = 1$$

for all values of K and L. (This model is analyzed in some detail in Chapter 17.)

(a) What restrictions on the coefficients produce constant returns to scale? How would you estimate the restricted model? A Cobb–Douglas production function with constant returns to scale is a restriction on the translog model with constant returns to scale. What is the restriction? How would you test the restriction as a hypothesis?

(b) Using the data given in Table 7.1, estimate the translog model subject to the restrictions of constant returns to scale and test the hypothesis. Carry out a test of the hypothesis of a Cobb–Douglas technology, assuming constant returns to scale.

---

[22] See, for example, two symposia in the *Journal of Econometrics* by White (1982 and 1983).

4. The gasoline data of Exercise 6 in Chapter 6 span the years of the oil embargo of 1973 and the tumultuous period thereafter. Did the market change sufficiently in 1973 that it is inappropriate to pool the data? The results of that example notwithstanding, regressions of G on a constant, P_g, Y, and P_{pt} produce the following residual sums of squares:

1960–1986	1960–1973	1974–1986
25025	313.26	996.86

(a) Carry out a Chow test of the hypothesis that the coefficient vectors are the same in the two subperiods. What are you assuming in making this test?

(b) An alternative hypothesis is that the year 1973 and the few (say, four) subsequent years that it took to return to normalcy in the market were aberrations. How would you test this hypothesis in the context of the full regression estimated in Exercise 6 of Chapter 6?

(c) Carry out the test in part (b).

5. Two samples of 50 observations each produce the following moment matrices (in each case, X is a constant and one variable):

	Sample 1	Sample 2
X'X	$\begin{bmatrix} 50 & 300 \\ 300 & 2100 \end{bmatrix}$	$\begin{bmatrix} 50 & 300 \\ 300 & 2100 \end{bmatrix}$
y'X	$\begin{bmatrix} 300 & 2000 \end{bmatrix}$	$\begin{bmatrix} 300 & 2200 \end{bmatrix}$
y'y	2100	2500

(a) Test the hypothesis that the same regression coefficients apply in both data sets, assuming that the disturbance variances are the same.

(b) Use a Wald test to test the hypothesis that the two coefficient vectors are the same without assuming that the disturbance variances are the same.

6. The regression model to be analyzed is

$$y = X_1\beta_1 + X_2\beta_2 + \varepsilon,$$

where X_1 and X_2 have K_1 and K_2 columns, respectively. The restriction is $\beta_2 = 0$.

(a) Using (7–12), prove that the restricted estimator is simply $[b_1, 0]$, where b_1 is the least squares coefficient vector in the regression of y on X_1.

(b) Prove that if the restriction is $\beta_2 = \beta_2^0$ for a nonzero β_2^0, the restricted estimator of β_1 is

$$b_{1_*} = (X_1'X_1)^{-1}X_1'(y - X_2\beta_2^0).$$

7. The expression for the restricted coefficient vector in (7–12) may be written in the form

$$b_* = [I - CR]b + w,$$

where **w** does not involve **b**. What is **C**? Show that covariance matrix of the restricted least squares estimator is

$$\sigma^2(\mathbf{X'X})^{-1} - \sigma^2(\mathbf{X'X})^{-1}\mathbf{R'}[\mathbf{R}(\mathbf{X'X})^{-1}\mathbf{R'}]^{-1}\mathbf{R}(\mathbf{X'X})^{-1}$$

and that this matrix may be written as

$$\text{Var}(\mathbf{b})[\{\text{Var}(\mathbf{b})\}^{-1} - \mathbf{R'}\{\text{Var}(\mathbf{Rb})\}^{-1}\mathbf{R}]\text{Var}(\mathbf{b}).$$

8. Prove the result that the restricted least squares estimator never has a larger variance matrix than the unrestricted least squares estimator.

9. Prove the result that the R^2 associated with a restricted least squares estimator is never larger than that associated with the unrestricted least squares estimator. Conclude that imposing restrictions never improves the fit of the regression.

10. What is the vector **w** in Exercise 7?

11. The Lagrange multiplier test of the hypothesis in (7–4) is equivalent to a Wald test of the hypothesis that $\lambda = \mathbf{0}$, where λ is defined in (7–11). Prove that

$$\chi^2 = \lambda'\{\text{Est. Var}[\lambda]^{-1}\}\lambda = (n - K)\left[\frac{\mathbf{e}'_*\mathbf{e}_*}{\mathbf{e}'\mathbf{e}} - 1\right].$$

Note that the fraction in brackets is the ratio of two estimators of σ^2. By virtue of (7–13) and the preceding discussion, we know that this is greater than one. [For some applications that reach a similar result, see (14–38) and especially Example 16.3 and (16–64).] Finally, prove that the earlier Lagrange multiplier statistic is simply JF, where J is the number of restrictions being tested and F is the conventional F statistic given in (7–14).

12. Use the Lagrange multiplier to test the hypothesis in Exercise 1.

13. Using the data and model of Exercise 6 in Chapter 6, carry out a test of the hypothesis that the three aggregate price indices are not significant determinants of the demand for gasoline.

14. Suppose that there are two competing models for the gasoline market of Exercise 6 in Chapter 6. Both models include the constant, time trend, price of gasoline, and income. Model 1 includes the three microeconomic price indices, P_{nc}, P_{uc}, and P_{pt}. Model 2 argues that these are just components of the broader categories. Thus, Model 2 includes P_d, P_n, and P_s instead. Use the J test to determine which theory is better. [**Hint:** The results of Exercise 6(a), Chapter 6, should give you an idea of what to expect.]

15. The model of Exercise 6, Chapter 6, may be written in logarithmic terms as

$$\ln G = \alpha + \beta_p \ln P_g + \beta_y \ln Y + \gamma_{nc} \ln P_{nc} + \gamma_{uc} \ln P_{uc} + \gamma_{pt} \ln P_{pt}$$
$$+ \beta_t \text{year} + \delta_d \ln P_d + \delta_n \ln P_n + \delta_s \ln P_s + \varepsilon.$$

Consider the hypothesis that the "micro" elasticities are a constant proportion of the elasticity with respect to their corresponding aggregate. Thus, for some positive θ (presumably between zero and one),

$$\gamma_{nc} = \theta\delta_d,$$
$$\gamma_{uc} = \theta\delta_d,$$
$$\gamma_{pt} = \theta\delta_s.$$

The first two imply the simple linear restriction $\gamma_{nc} = \gamma_{uc}$. By taking ratios, the first (or second) and third imply the nonlinear restriction

$$\frac{\gamma_{nc}}{\gamma_{pt}} = \frac{\delta_d}{\delta_s} \qquad \text{or} \qquad \gamma_{nc}\delta_s - \gamma_{pt}\delta_d = 0.$$

(a) Describe in detail how you would test the validity of the restriction.

(b) Using the data in Exercise 6, Chapter 6, test the restrictions separately and jointly.

16. Prove that under the hypothesis $\mathbf{R\beta} = \mathbf{q}$, the estimator

$$s_*^2 = \frac{(\mathbf{y} - \mathbf{Xb}_*)'(\mathbf{y} - \mathbf{Xb}_*)}{n - K + J},$$

where J is the number of restrictions, is unbiased for σ^2.

17. Show that in the multiple regression of $\mathbf{y}$ on a constant, $\mathbf{x}_1$, and $\mathbf{x}_2$, using $(7-3)$ to impose the restriction $\beta_1 + \beta_2 = 1$ leads to the regression of $\mathbf{y} - \mathbf{x}_1$ on a constant and $\mathbf{x}_2 - \mathbf{x}_1$.

References

Aigner, D., K. Lovell, and P. Schmidt, "Formulation and Estimation of Stochastic Frontier Production Function Models," *Journal of Econometrics*, 6, 1977, pp. 21–37.

Aneuryn-Evans, G., and A. Deaton, "Testing Linear Versus Logarithmic Regression Models," *Review of Economic Studies*, 47, 1980, pp. 275–291.

Berndt, E. R., and L. R. Christensen, "The Translog Function and the Substitution of Equipment, Structures, and Labor in U.S. Manufacturing," *Journal of Econometrics*, 1, 1972, pp. 81–114.

Brown, R., J. Durbin, and J. Evans, "Techniques for Testing the Constancy of Regression Relationships Over Time," *Journal of the Royal Statistical Society, Series B*, 37, 1975, pp. 149–192.

Chow, G., "Tests of Equality Between Sets of Coefficients in Two Linear Regressions," *Econometrica*, 28, 1960, pp. 591–605.

Cox, D. R., "Tests of Separate Families of Hypotheses," *Proceedings of the Fourth Berkeley Symposium on Mathematical Statistics and Probability*, Vol. 1, Berkeley: University of California Press, 1961.

Cox, D. R., "Further Results on Tests of Separate Families of Hypotheses," *Journal of the Royal Statistical Society, Series B*, 24, 1962, pp. 406–424.

Davidson, R., and J. MacKinnon, "Several Tests for Model Specification in the Presence of Alternative Hypotheses," *Econometrica*, 49, 3, 1981, pp. 781–793.

Fisher, F., "Tests of Equality Between Sets of Coefficients in Two Linear Regressions: An Expository Note," *Econometrica*, 28, 1970, pp. 361–366.

Gaver, K., and M. Geisel, "Discriminating Among Alternative Models: Bayesian and Non-Bayesian Methods," in P. Zarembka, ed., *Frontiers in Econometrics*, New York: Academic Press, 1974.

Harvey, A. C., *The Econometric Analysis of Time Series*, New York: Halsted Press, 1981.

Harvey, A. C., and G. Collier, "Testing for Functional Misspecification in Regression Analysis," *Journal of Econometrics*, 6, 1977, pp. 103–119.

Hildebrand, G., and T. Liu, *Manufacturing Production Functions in the United States*, Ithaca, N.Y.: Cornell University Press, 1957.

Jayatissa, W., "Tests of Equality Between Sets of Coefficients in Two Linear Regressions When Disturbance Variances Are Unequal," *Econometrica*, 45, 1977, pp. 1291–1292.

Kendall, M., and A. Stuart, *The Advanced Theory of Statistics*, Vol. 2, London: Griffin, 1972.

Kobiyashi, M., "A Bounds Test of Equality Between Sets of Coefficients in Two Linear Regressions When Disturbance Variances Are Unequal," *Journal of the American Statistical Association*, 81, 1986, pp. 510–514.

Longley, J. W., "An Appraisal of Least Squares Programs from the Point of the User," *Journal of the American Statistical Association*, 62, 1967, pp. 819–841.

McAleer, M., G. Fisher, and P. Volker, "Separate Misspecified Regressions and the U.S. Long-Run Demand for Money Function," *Review of Economics and Statistics*, 64, 1982, pp. 572–583.

Ohtani, K., and M. Kobiyashi, "A Bounds Test for Equality Between Sets of Coefficients in Two Linear Regression Models Under Heteroscedasticity," *Econometric Theory*, 2, 1986, pp. 220–231.

Ohtani, K., and T. Toyoda, "Small Sample Properties of Tests of Equality Between Sets of Coefficients in Two Linear Regressions under Heteroscedasticity," *International Economic Review*, 26, 1985, pp. 37–44.

Pesaran, H. "On the General Problem of Model Selection," *Review of Economic Studies*, 41, 1974, pp. 153–171.

Pesaran, H., and A. Deaton, "Testing Non-nested Nonlinear Regression Models," *Econometrica*, 46, 1978, pp. 677–694.

Schmidt, P., and R. Sickles, "Some Further Evidence on the Use of the Chow Test Under Heteroscedasticity," *Econometrica*, 45, 1977, pp. 1293–1298.

Thursby, J., "Misspecification, Heteroscedasticity, and the Chow and Goldfeld–Quandt Tests," *Review of Economics and Statistics*, 64, 1982, pp. 314–321.

Toyoda, T., "Use of the Chow Test Under Heteroscedasticity," *Econometrica*, 42, 1974, pp. 601–608.

Toyoda, T., and K. Ohtani, "Testing Equality Between Sets of Coefficients After a Preliminary Test for Equality of Disturbances in Two Linear Regressions," *Journal of Econometrics*, 31, 1, 1986, pp. 67–80.

White, H., ed., "Model Specification," *Journal of Econometrics*, 20, 1, 1982.

White, H., ed., "Non-Nested Models," *Journal of Econometrics*, 21, 1, 1983.

Chapter 8

Functional Form, Nonlinearity, and Specification

8.1. *Introduction*

In this chapter, we are concerned with the functional form of the regression model. There are many different types of functions that are "linear" by our definition. By using dummy variables and different arrangements of functions of variables, we can produce an impressive variety of models. Sections 2 and 3 of this chapter examine some of the devices used in constructing regression models. Sections 4 and 5 consider some questions concerning errors in the specification of the model and the dangers of using the same data both to estimate parameters and to determine what form the model will take.

8.2. *Dummy Variables*

One of the most useful devices in regression analysis is the binary, or *dummy*, variable. We have used it in two previous applications: in Section 6.8.1 in computing forecasts and in Chapter 7 in constructing Chow tests for structural change. In both cases, these variables were only computational devices. But binary variables are also a convenient means of building discrete shifts of the function into a regression model.

A comparison of the means of a variable in two groups might be formulated as follows:

$$\text{Group 1: } y_i = \mu + \varepsilon_i,$$

$$\text{Group 2: } y_i = \mu + \delta + \varepsilon_i.$$

The parameter δ is of particular interest. By defining the variable, d, as

$$d_i = 0 \text{ if group 1} \qquad \text{and} \qquad d_i = 1 \text{ if group 2,}[1]$$

these may be combined into the single equation

$$y_i = \mu + \delta d_i + \varepsilon_i.$$

---

[1] The choice of zero and one for the two values is purely for convenience. Any other two values could be used; however, the interpretation of the equation is simplest when we use zero and one.

If, for example, y_i is income and d_i indicates whether or not the individual attended college,

$$E[\text{income} \,|\, \text{did not attend college}] = \mu$$

and

$$E[\text{income} \,|\, \text{attended college}] = \mu + \delta.$$

In this model, δ is the difference between the average incomes of the two groups. A test of whether δ is zero is equivalent to a test that this difference is zero or that the means are the same. An alternative model is

$$y_i = \mu_N + \varepsilon_i \qquad \text{for those who did not attend college,}$$

and

$$y_i = \mu_C + \varepsilon_i \qquad \text{for those who attended college.}$$

By defining $h_i = 1$ if individual i did not attend college and $h_i = 0$ otherwise, so that h_i equals $1 - d_i$, we can combine these equations in

$$y_i = \mu_N h_i + \mu_C d_i + \varepsilon_i.$$

Of course, these are the same; in the first formulation,

$$\delta = \mu_C - \mu_N.$$

There is a difference in interpretation, however. A test of $\mu_N = 0$ or $\mu_C = 0$ makes little sense, but the test of $\delta = 0$ is equivalent to a test of $\mu_C = \mu_N$.[2]

Aside from the special nature of the independent variables, these are just multiple regression models that we can estimate by least squares. We arrange the observations so that the first n_1 are the individuals who did not attend college and the remaining n_2 are those who did. Denote by i_g a column of ones with n_g elements, either n_1 or n_2. Then the first model is

$$\mathbf{y} = \begin{bmatrix} i_1 & 0 \\ i_2 & i_2 \end{bmatrix} \begin{bmatrix} \mu \\ \delta \end{bmatrix} + \boldsymbol{\varepsilon}.$$

Least squares produces

$$\begin{bmatrix} m \\ d \end{bmatrix} = \begin{bmatrix} n_1 + n_2 & n_2 \\ n_2 & n_2 \end{bmatrix}^{-1} \begin{bmatrix} n_1 \bar{y}_1 + n_2 \bar{y}_2 \\ n_2 \bar{y}_2 \end{bmatrix} = \begin{bmatrix} \bar{y}_1 \\ \bar{y}_2 - \bar{y}_1 \end{bmatrix}.$$

For the second model,

$$\mathbf{y} = \begin{bmatrix} i_1 & 0 \\ 0 & i_2 \end{bmatrix} \begin{bmatrix} \mu_1 \\ \mu_2 \end{bmatrix} + \boldsymbol{\varepsilon}$$

and

$$\mathbf{m} = (\mathbf{X'X})^{-1}\mathbf{X'Y} = \begin{bmatrix} 1/n_1 & 0 \\ 0 & 1/n_2 \end{bmatrix} \begin{bmatrix} n_1 \bar{y}_1 \\ n_2 \bar{y}_2 \end{bmatrix} = \begin{bmatrix} \bar{y}_1 \\ \bar{y}_2 \end{bmatrix}.$$

The equation may be written either with an overall intercept and a dummy variable for the effect being analyzed or with no constant term and two dummy variables. What might

---

[2] See Suits (1984).

seem like a third possibility, an overall constant term and separate dummy variables for each group, leads to the *dummy variable trap*, a case of perfect collinearity. If the first model shown were written

$$\text{Income} = \mu + \delta_N h_i + \delta d_i + \varepsilon_i,$$

the matrix of independent variables would be

$$\mathbf{X} = \begin{bmatrix} \mathbf{i}_1 & \mathbf{i}_1 & \mathbf{0} \\ \mathbf{i}_2 & \mathbf{0} & \mathbf{i}_2 \end{bmatrix}.$$

The second and third columns sum to the first, which makes least squares estimation of the three parameters impossible.

8.2.1. Binary Variables in Regression

Dummy variables are most frequently used in regression equations that also contain other quantitative variables. Recall the consumption data discussed in Chapter 5 and shown in Figure 5.2. There are four data points, the years 1942–1945, that lie conspicuously below the regression line for the remaining data. Figure 8.1 suggests a means of treating this effect.

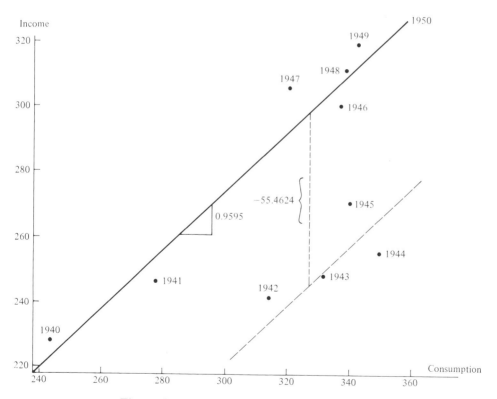

Figure 8.1 Dummy variable in regression.

EXAMPLE 8.1.   Consumption and income data for the years 1940 to 1950 are listed in Table 8.1. The regression model is

$$C_t = \beta_1 + \beta_2 x_t + \beta_3 W_t + \varepsilon_t,$$

where x_t is disposable income and W_t is the wartime dummy variable, which takes the value one in the years 1942–1945 and zero in the other years. (The subscript t is used here to indicate the observation at time t.) The regression results are given in Table 8.2. The regression results confirm that consumption during World War II was significantly below what would have been expected, given income.

Table 8.1   Consumption Expenditures (billions of 1972 dollars)

Year	Disposable Income	Personal Consumption
1940	244.0	229.9
1941	277.9	243.6
1942	317.5	241.1
1943	332.1	248.2
1944	343.6	255.2
1945	338.1	270.9
1946	332.7	301.0
1947	318.8	305.8
1948	335.8	312.2
1949	336.8	319.3
1950	362.8	337.3

Table 8.2

Number of observations			11
Standard error of regression			9.088
R-squared			0.95283

Variable	Coefficient	Standard Error	t Ratio (Sig. Lvl.)
Constant	−10.065	28.44	−0.354 (0.7326)
Y	0.959595	0.0895	10.724 (0.0001)
W	−55.4624	5.902	−9.397 (0.0001)

In more recent applications, researchers in many fields often study the effects of *treatments* on some kind of *response*. Examples include the effect of college on income, as in the preceding example, cross-sex differences in labor supply behavior and in salary structures in industries, and in pre- versus postregime shifts in macroeconomic models, to name but a few. These can all be formulated in regression models involving a single dummy variable:

$$y_i = \boldsymbol{\beta}' \mathbf{x}_i + \delta d_i + \varepsilon_i.$$

8.2.2. Several Categories

When there are several categories, a set of binary variables is necessary. Correcting for seasonal factors in macroeconomic data is a common application. Extending the device used earlier, we could write a consumption function for quarterly data as

$$C_t = \beta_1 + \beta_2 x_t + \delta_1 D_{t1} + \delta_2 D_{t2} + \delta_3 D_{t3} + \varepsilon_t,$$

where x_t is disposable income. Once again, to avoid the dummy variable trap, we drop the dummy variable for the fourth quarter. (Depending on the application, it might be preferable to have four separate dummy variables and drop the overall constant.) Any of the four quarters (or 12 months) can be used as the base period. The matrix of independent variables for this model is

$$\mathbf{X} = \begin{bmatrix} 1 & 0 & 0 & 0 & x_1 \\ 1 & 1 & 0 & 0 & x_2 \\ 1 & 0 & 1 & 0 & x_3 \\ 1 & 0 & 0 & 1 & x_4 \\ 1 & 0 & 0 & 0 & x_5 \\ \vdots & \vdots & \vdots & \vdots & \vdots \\ 1 & 0 & 0 & 1 & x_T \end{bmatrix}.$$

The preceding is a means of *deseasonalizing* the data. Consider the alternative formulation:

$$C_t = \beta x_t + \delta_1 D_{t1} + \delta_2 D_{t2} + \delta_3 D_{t3} + \delta_4 D_{t4} + \varepsilon_t. \qquad (8-1)$$

Using the results from Chapter 6 on partitioned regression, we know that the preceding multiple regression is equivalent to first regressing $\mathbf{C}$ and $\mathbf{x}$ on the four dummies and then using the residuals from these regressions in the subsequent regression of deseasonalized consumption on deseasonalized income. Clearly, deseasonalizing in this fashion prior to computing the simple regression of consumption on income is the same as including the set of dummy variables in the regression.

Finally, it might seem that an alternative to the dummy variable model is simply to have a *seasonal variable* taking the values 1, 2, and 3 for the second, third, and fourth quarters. This would be equivalent to assuming that the intercept shift is the same from each quarter to the next. The regression is

$$C_t = \beta_1 + \beta_2 x_t + \delta q_t + \varepsilon_t. \qquad (8-2)$$

The model is

$$C_t = \beta_1 + \beta_2 x_t + \delta + \varepsilon_t$$

in the first quarter,

$$C_t = \beta_1 + \beta_2 x_t + 2\delta + \varepsilon_t$$

in the second, and so on. This is a testable restriction on (8–1), but it is unlikely to be appropriate.

8.2.3. The Analysis of Variance

The *analysis of variance* provides another example of the use of a set of dummy variables. Consider, for instance, an analysis of statewide expenditure on education, and suppose that we have several years (T) of data for each of 50 (n) states.[3] Suppose that we are interested in whether the average expenditure differs across states. The traditional analysis of variance approach to this problem will be based on the following statistics, in which t indexes year and i indexes states:

$$\text{Grand mean} = \bar{\bar{y}} = \frac{1}{nT} \sum_i \sum_t y_{it},$$

$$\text{Group means} = \bar{y}_i = \frac{1}{T} \sum_t y_{it},$$

$$\text{Total variation} = \sum_i \sum_t (y_{it} - \bar{\bar{y}})^2, \tag{8-3}$$

$$\text{Within-groups variation} = \sum_i \left[\sum_t (y_{it} - \bar{y}_i)^2 \right],$$

$$\text{Between-groups variation} = \sum_i T(\bar{y}_i - \bar{\bar{y}})^2.$$

The hypothesis to be tested is that the mean expenditure is the same in every state:

$$H_0: \mu_1 = \mu_2 = \cdots = \mu_n = \mu.$$

Algebraically, it can easily be shown that

$$\text{Total variation} = \text{between groups} + \text{within groups.} \tag{8-4}$$

Inspection of the decomposition of the total variation suggests that the hypothesis will be based on the between-groups variation and whether this is a large proportion of the total. The between-groups variation will be large only if there are significant differences between the state means of expenditure. The proportion of the total variation accounted for by deviation of the group means from the grand mean is

$$R^2 = \frac{\text{between-groups variation}}{\text{total variation}}.$$

For testing the hypothesis that the means are all identical, we would use

$$F[n - 1, nT - n] = \frac{R^2/(n - 1)}{(1 - R^2)/(nT - n)},$$

which is distributed as F with $n - 1$ and $nT - n$ degrees of freedom. The larger is R^2 (or F), the less plausible is the hypothesis.

Consider formulating a regression for expenditure as

$$y_{it} = \mu + \delta_i + \varepsilon_{it}. \tag{8-5}$$

By defining 49 dummy variables and arbitrarily choosing one of the states to be the basis, analysis of this regression model becomes identical to the **one-way analysis of variance**. The R^2 is identical to the one given earlier, as is the F statistic for testing the hypothesis that the set of dummy variable coefficients are all zero. Proofs are left for the exercises.

---

[3] This is known as a *balanced design* in that there are the same number of observations for each state and in each period. Nothing in the analysis requires this, and we assume it just for the purpose of the illustration. This will also simplify some of the notation.

The **analysis of covariance** extends the preceding by adding one or more quantitative independent variables to the regression. For example, statewide average income might be a significant determinant of the amount spent on education. The corresponding regression equation is

$$y_{it} = \beta_1 + \beta_2 x_{it} + \cdots 49 \text{ dummies} + \varepsilon_{it}.$$

This is qualitatively the same as the consumption function with seasonal dummy variables. The primary difference is the much larger number of variables here. Computationally, the alternative formulation of the set of dummy variables without an overall constant term can simplify matters when there are a large number of categories.[4] Suppose that we write the regression with 50 individual statewide dummy variables and no overall constant, and there are 10 observations per state. The data matrices are

$$\mathbf{X} = \begin{bmatrix} \mathbf{i} & \mathbf{0} & \mathbf{0} & \cdots & \mathbf{0} & x_1 \\ \mathbf{0} & \mathbf{i} & \mathbf{0} & \cdots & \mathbf{0} & x_2 \\ \mathbf{0} & \mathbf{0} & \mathbf{i} & \cdots & \mathbf{0} & x_3 \\ & & & \vdots & & \\ \mathbf{0} & \mathbf{0} & \mathbf{0} & \cdots & \mathbf{i} & x_{50} \end{bmatrix} = [\mathbf{D} : \mathbf{x}].$$

The submatrix, **D**, has $50 \times 10 = 500$ rows and 50 columns. But it is not necessary to compute this large regression. Using the partitioned regressioned results, we can first regress **x** and **y** on the columns of **D** and then use the residuals from this regression. Since the columns of **D** are orthogonal, and consist only of ones and zeros, $\mathbf{D'D}$ is extremely simple, as are $\mathbf{D'w}$ and $\mathbf{D'y}$. In particular,

$$(\mathbf{D'D})^{-1} = \begin{bmatrix} 1/10 & 0 & 0 & 0 \\ 0 & 1/10 & 0 & 0 \\ & & \vdots & \\ 0 & 0 & 0 & 1/10 \end{bmatrix},$$

$$\mathbf{D'w} = \begin{bmatrix} 10\bar{x}_1 \\ 10\bar{x}_2 \\ \vdots \\ 10\bar{x}_{50} \end{bmatrix}, \quad \mathbf{D'y} = \begin{bmatrix} 10\bar{y}_1 \\ 10\bar{y}_2 \\ \vdots \\ 10\bar{y}_{50} \end{bmatrix}.$$

Therefore, $(\mathbf{D'D})^{-1}\mathbf{D'x}$ and $(\mathbf{D'D})^{-1}\mathbf{D'y}$ are just column vectors of state means, and the "residuals" from these regressions are the original data in deviations from their own statewide means. The regression coefficient on income is obtained by a simple regression (without a constant) of expenditure on income with the data centered about their respective state means. It is left as an exercise to prove that the coefficients on the dummy variables are the statewide means of the residuals $y_{it} - b_2 x_{it}$.

8.2.4. Several Groupings

The case in which several sets of dummy variables are needed is much the same as those we have already considered, with one important exception. In the previous example, suppose

---

[4] It is sometimes useful to reduce the size of a regression problem when the available computer software imposes constraints. This is especially true for some of the programs written for microcomputers that are designed for relatively small problems.

Table 8.3

Ship Type	Period Constructed			
	1960–1964	1965–1969	1970–1974	1975–1979
A	0	4	18	11
B	29	53	44	18
C	1	1	2	1
D	0	0	11	4
E	0	7	12	1

that we allowed the average expenditure to change over time, as well as across states. The regression would be

$$y_{it} = \mu + \delta_i + \theta_t + \varepsilon_{it}.$$

This is essentially the same as the earlier regression model. As before, it is necessary to drop one of the variables in the set of dummy variables to avoid the dummy variable trap. This is necessary even if the overall constant term is dropped. For our example, if the overall constant term is omitted and a total of 50 state dummies and 10 time dummies is retained, a problem of perfect multicollinearity remains; the sum of the 50 state dummies and the 10 time dummies are the same, that is, one. One of the variables in one of the sets must be omitted.

EXAMPLE 8.2. Analysis of Variance. The number of incidents of damage to a sample of ships, with the type of ship and the period when it was constructed,[5] is shown in Table 8.3. There are five types of ships and four different periods of construction. On inspection, it seems clear that the means will differ across ship types. Whether they will differ across periods is less clear. The regression results are as follows (we report only the regression coefficients):

Table 8.4

	Full Model	Time Effects	Type Effects	No Effects
Constant	3.4	6.0	8.25	10.85
B	27.75	0	27.75	0
C	−7.0	0	−7.0	0
D	−4.5	0	−4.5	0
E	−3.25	0	−3.25	0
65–69	7.0	7.0	0	0
70–74	11.4	11.4	0	0
75–79	1.0	1.0	0	0
R^2	0.84823	0.0986	0.74963	0
$e'e$	660.9	3925.2	1090.2	4354.5

[5] The data are from McCullagh and Nelder (1983, p. 137).

According to the full model, the expected number of incidents for a ship of the base type, A, built in the base period, 1960–1964, is 3.4. The other 19 predicted values follow from the previous results and are left as an exercise. The relevant test statistics for differences across ship type and year are as follows:

$$\text{Type: } F[4, 12] = \frac{(3925.2 - 660.9)/4}{660.9/12} = 14.82,$$

$$\text{Year: } F[3, 12] = \frac{(1090.3 - 660.9)/3}{660.9/12} = 2.60.$$

The 5 percent critical values from the F table with these degrees of freedom are 3.26 and 3.49, respectively, so we would conclude that the average number of incidents varies significantly across ship types but not across years.

8.2.5.   Threshold Effects

In most applications, we use dummy variables to account for purely qualitative factors, such as membership in a group, or to represent a particular time period. There are cases, however, in which the dummy variable(s) represent levels of some underlying factor that might have been measured directly if this were possible. For example, education is a case in which we typically observe certain thresholds rather than, say, years of education.[6] Suppose, for example, our interest is in a regression of the form

$$\text{Income} = \beta_1 + \beta_2 \text{Age} + \text{effect of education} + \varepsilon.$$

The data on education might consist of the highest level of education attained, for example, high school, undergraduate, masters, or Ph.D. An obviously unsatisfactory way to proceed is to use a variable, E, that is 0 for the first group, 1 for the second, 2 for the third, and 3 for the fourth, and write

$$\text{Income} = \beta_1 + \beta_2 \text{Age} + \beta_3 E + \varepsilon.$$

The difficulty with this approach is that it assumes that the increment in income at each threshold is the same; γ is the difference between income with a Ph.D. and a masters and between a masters and a bachelor's degree. This is unlikely and unduly restricts the regression. A more flexible model would use three (or four) binary variables, one for each level of education. Thus, we would write

$$\text{Income} = \beta_1 + \beta_2 \text{Age} + \delta_1 \text{BA} + \delta_2 \text{MA} + \delta_3 \text{PhD} + \varepsilon.$$

The correspondence between the coefficients and income for a given age is

$$\text{High school: Income} = \beta_1 + \beta_2 \text{Age},$$

$$\text{B.A.:} \qquad \text{Income} = \beta_1 + \beta_2 \text{Age} + \delta_1,$$

$$\text{M.A.:} \qquad \text{Income} = \beta_1 + \beta_2 \text{Age} + \delta_2,$$

$$\text{Ph.D.:} \qquad \text{Income} = \alpha_1 + \beta_2 \text{Age} + \delta_3.$$

The differences between, say, δ_3 and δ_2 and between δ_2 and δ_1 are of interest. Obviously, these are simple to compute. An alternative way to formulate the equation that reveals these

---

[6] Even this quantitative measure is only a crude measure of amount of education.

differences directly is to redefine the dummy variables to be 1 if the individual has the degree, rather than whether the degree is the highest degree obtained. Thus, for someone with a Ph.D., all three binary variables are 1, and so on. The independent variables appear as follows, where individuals with only a high school education are grouped first, and those with higher degrees are arranged in order below them:

$$\mathbf{X} = \begin{bmatrix} i & 0 & 0 & 0 & Age \\ i & i & 0 & 0 & Age \\ i & i & i & 0 & Age \\ i & i & i & i & Age \end{bmatrix}.$$

By defining the variables in this fashion, the regression is

High school: $Income = \alpha + \beta Age,$

B.A.: $Income = \alpha + \beta Age + \delta_1,$

M.A.: $Income = \alpha + \beta Age + \delta_1 + \delta_2,$

Ph.D.: $Income = \alpha + \beta Age + \delta_1 + \delta_2 + \delta_3.$

Instead of the difference between a Ph.D. and the base case, in this model δ_3 is the marginal value of the Ph.D. Of course, how equations with dummy variables are formulated is a matter of convenience. All of the results can be obtained from a basic equation.[7]

8.2.6. Interactions and Spline Regression

The tests of structural change analyzed earlier illustrate another common use of dummy variables. Recall that the data matrix for that model could be formulated as

$$\mathbf{X} = \begin{bmatrix} i & 0 & X_1 & 0 \\ i & i & X_2 & X_2 \end{bmatrix}.$$

If we let $\mathbf{d}$ be the second column of this matrix and $\mathbf{i}$ be a full column of ones, this data matrix is of the form

$$\mathbf{Z} = [\mathbf{i} \quad \mathbf{d} \quad \mathbf{X} \quad \mathbf{dX}].$$

The last column is just the product of the dummy variable and the other regressors. Consider, for example, a regression model that embodies the proposition that "not only are the salaries of college graduates higher than those of noncollege graduates at any given age, but they rise faster as the individuals grow older."[8] The regression would appear as in Figure 8.2 and could be written

$$S = \beta_1 + \beta_2 Age + \beta_3 d + \beta_4 dAge + \varepsilon.$$

Estimating the parameters is a straightforward application of multiple regression. It is simple to show (and we leave it as an exercise) that this is the same as computing two separate regressions. One ambiguity does arise in the estimation of the disturbance variance. If we

---

[7] See Suits (1984).
[8] The first of these propositions may, in fact, be inappropriate. In the earliest earning years, those who go to college are foregoing the income being earned by those of like age who are not in school.

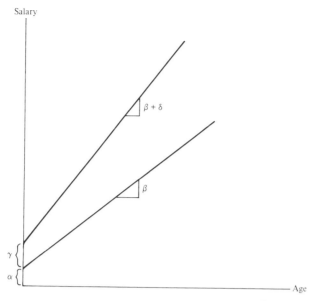

Figure 8.2   Shifting slope and intercept.

assume that the two groups have equal disturbance variances, then

$$E[\varepsilon^2 \mid d = 0] = \sigma^2$$

and

$$E[\varepsilon^2 \mid d = 1] = \sigma^2.$$

In this case, it is most efficient to pool the observations and estimate a single parameter. However, if the variances differ across groups, then pooling the observations will result in one biased estimate of both disturbance variances. In addition, the usual estimate of the variance matrix of the coefficients will be incorrect. In this instance, the proper approach is to disaggregate the data and use the subsamples separately.

   If one is examining income data for a large cross section of individuals of varying ages in a population, certain patterns with regard to some age thresholds will be clearly evident. In particular, throughout the range of values of age, income will be rising, but the slope might change at some distinct milestones, for example, at age 18, when the typical individual graduates from high school, and at age 22, when he or she graduates from college. The *time profile* of income for the typical individual in this population might appear as in Figure 8.3. Based on the discussion of the preceding paragraph, we could fit such a regression model just by dividing the sample into three subsamples. However, this would neglect the continuity of the preceding function; the result would appear more like the dotted figure than the continuous function we had in mind. Restricted regression, and what is known as a **spline** function, can be used to achieve the desired effect.[9]

---

[9] An important reference on this subject is Poirier (1984). An often cited application appears in Garber and Poirier (1974).

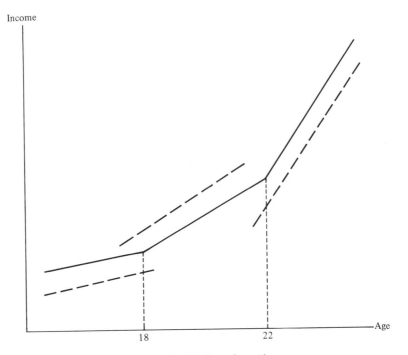

Figure 8.3   Spline function.

The function we wish to estimate is

$$\text{Income} = \alpha^0 + \beta^0 \text{Age} \quad \text{if Age} < 18,$$
$$\alpha^1 + \beta^1 \text{Age} \quad \text{if Age} \geq 18 \text{ and } \leq 22,$$
$$\alpha^2 + \beta^2 \text{Age} \quad \text{if Age} \geq 22.$$

The specific values for the thresholds, 18 and 22, are called *knots*. The function is simple enough to specify using dummy variables, as we have done. In particular, let

$$d_1 = 1 \text{ if Age} > t_1^*,$$
$$d_2 = 1 \text{ if Age} > t_2^*,$$

where $t_1^* = 18$ and $t_2^* = 22$. To combine all three equations, we use

$$\text{Income} = \beta_1 + \beta_2 \text{Age} + \gamma_1 d_1 + \delta_1 d_1 \text{Age} + \gamma_2 d_2 + \delta_2 d_2 \text{Age} + \varepsilon. \quad (8-6)$$

This is the dotted function in Figure 8.3. The slopes in the three segments are β_2, $\beta_2 + \delta_1$, and $\beta_2 + \delta_1 + \delta_2$. To make the figure continuous, we require that the segments join at the knots, that is,

$$\beta_1 + \beta_2 t_1^* = (\beta_1 + \gamma_1) + (\beta_2 + \delta_1) t_1^*$$

and

$$(\beta_1 + \gamma_1) + (\beta_2 + \delta_1) t_2^* = (\beta_1 + \gamma_1 + \gamma_2) + (\beta_2 + \delta_1 + \delta_2) t_2^*.$$

These are linear restrictions on the coefficients. Collecting terms, the first one is

$$\gamma_1 + \delta_1 t_1^* = 0 \qquad \text{or} \qquad \gamma_1 = -\delta_1 t_1^*.$$

Doing likewise for the second and inserting these in (8–6), we obtain

$$\text{Income} = \beta_1 + \beta_2 \text{Age} + \delta_1 d_1(\text{Age} - t_1^*) + \delta_2 d_2(\text{Age} - t_2^*).$$

It is worth noting that imposing these constraints amounts to no more than allowing the slope to be a free parameter and adjusting the intercepts up or down until the segments join at the knots. Constrained least squares estimates are obtainable by multiple regression, using the variables

$$x_1 = \text{age},$$

$$x_2 = \text{age} - 18 \text{ if age is} > 18 \text{ and } 0 \text{ otherwise},$$

and

$$x_3 = \text{age} - 22 \text{ if age is} > 22 \text{ and } 0 \text{ otherwise}.$$

We can test the hypothesis that the slope of the function is constant with the joint test of $\delta_1 = 0$ and $\delta_2 = 0$. Whether the individual tests, $\delta_1 = 0$ or $\delta_2 = 0$, are meaningful will depend on the context. In our example, the first of these is a test that graduating from high school (actually, reaching 18) does not carry with it any increase in the slope of the earnings function until age 22 is reached.

8.3. Nonlinearity in the Variables

It is useful at this point to write the linear regression model in a very general form: Let $\mathbf{z} = z_1, z_2, \ldots, z_L$ be a set of L independent variables; let $f_1, f_2, \ldots, f_K$ be K independent functions of $\mathbf{z}$; let $g(y)$ be an observable function of y; and retain the usual assumptions about the disturbance. The linear regression model is

$$g(y) = \beta_1 f_1(\mathbf{z}) + \beta_2 f_2(\mathbf{z}) + \cdots + \beta_K f_K(\mathbf{z}) + \varepsilon$$

$$= \beta_1 x_1 + \beta_2 x_2 + \cdots + \beta_K x_K + \varepsilon \qquad (8\text{–}7)$$

$$= \mathbf{x}'\boldsymbol{\beta} + \varepsilon.$$

By using logarithms, exponentials, reciprocals, transcendental functions, polynomials, products, ratios, and so on, this "linear" model can be tailored to any number of situations.

8.3.1. Functional Forms

A commonly used form of regression model is the log-linear model

$$y = \alpha \prod_k X_k^{\beta_k} e^{\varepsilon}$$

or

$$\ln y = \ln \alpha + \sum_k \beta_k \ln X_k + \varepsilon$$

$$= \beta_1 + \sum_k \beta_k x_k + \varepsilon.$$

In this model, the coefficients are elasticities:

$$\left(\frac{\partial y}{\partial x_k}\right)\left(\frac{x_k}{y}\right) = \frac{\partial \ln y}{\partial \ln X_k} = \beta_k. \tag{8-8}$$

This formulation is particularly useful in studies of demand and production.

A hybrid of the linear and log-linear models is the semilog equation

$$y = e^{\beta_1 + \beta_2 x + \varepsilon}$$

or

$$\ln y = \beta_1 + \beta_2 x + \varepsilon.$$

A common use of the semilog formulation is in exponential growth curves. If x is "time," t, then

$$\frac{d \ln y}{dt} = \beta_2$$

$$= \text{the average rate of growth of } y.$$

Macroeconomic models are often formulated with autonomous time trends. For example, aggregate models of productivity will usually include a trend variable, as in

$$\ln\left(\frac{Q}{L}\right)_t = \beta_1 + \beta_2 \ln\left(\frac{K}{L}\right)_t + \delta t + \varepsilon_t.$$

This provides an estimate of the "autonomous growth in productivity," usually attributed to technical change. In this equation, δ is the rate of growth of average product not attributable to increases in the use of capital.

Another useful formulation of the regression model is one with *interaction terms*. For example, a regression relating braking distance to speed and road wetness might be formulated as

$$D = \beta_1 + \beta_2 S + \beta_3 W + \beta_4 SW + \varepsilon.$$

In this model,

$$\frac{\partial E[D]}{\partial S} = \beta_2 + \beta_4 W$$

$$\frac{\partial E[D]}{\partial W} = \beta_3 + \beta_4 S,$$

which implies that the marginal effect of higher speed on braking distance is increased when the road is wetter (assuming that β_4 is positive). The translog production model in Example 7.3 is another example, in which the elasticity of output with respect to labor is

$$\frac{\partial E[\ln y]}{\partial \ln L} = \beta_2 + \beta_4 \ln L + \beta_6 \ln K.$$

Interactions between continuous variables and dummy variables were used at various points in the discussion of (8.2) and in the construction of spline regressions in Section 8.2.6.

A form of the linear model

$$y = \alpha + \beta g(x) + \varepsilon$$

that has appeared in a number of recent studies is the **Box–Cox transformation,**[10]

$$g^{(\lambda)}(x) = \frac{x^\lambda - 1}{\lambda}. \tag{8-9}$$

The linear model results if λ equals 1, while a log-linear or semilog model (depending on how y is measured) results if λ equals 0.[11] Other values of λ produce many different functional forms. For example, if λ equals -1, then the equation will involve the reciprocal of x. The Box–Cox model is a useful formulation that embodies many of the models we have considered as special cases. Of course, in itself, this is only a minor virtue; if λ is known, we merely insert the known value and obtain a model linear in the transformed variables. But except for the polar cases of λ equal to $-1, 0$, or 1, it is hard to conceive of situations in which a particular value would be specified a priori. By treating λ as an additional unknown parameter in the equation, we obtain a tremendous amount of flexibility.[12] The cost of doing so is that the model then becomes nonlinear in its parameters. We shall study the model in detail in Chapter 11.

In spite of their very complex functional forms, these models are intrinsically linear because they can be placed directly in the form of (8–7). As discussed in Chapter 5, the distinguishing feature of the linear model is not the relationship among the variables as such but the way the parameters enter the equation.

8.3.2. Identifying Nonlinearity

If the functional form is not known a priori, there are a few approaches that might help at least to identify any nonlinearity and to provide some information about it from the sample. For example, if the suspected nonlinearity is with respect to a single regressor in the equation, fitting a quadratic or cubic polynomial rather than a linear function may capture some of the intrinsic nonlinearity. By choosing several ranges for the regressor in question and allowing the slope of the function to be different in each range, a piecewise linear approximation to the nonlinear function can be fit.

EXAMPLE 8.3. Nonlinear Regression. In a celebrated study of the U.S. Electric Power Industry, Nerlove (1963) analyzed the production costs of 145 American electric generating companies. At the outset of the study, he fit a Cobb–Douglas cost function of the form

$$\log C = \beta_1 + \beta_q \log Q + \sum_k \beta_k \log P_k + \varepsilon, \tag{8-10}$$

where C is total cost, Q is output, and P_k is the unit price of the kth factor of production (k = labor, fuel, capital). (Nerlove did his calculations in common logarithms rather than natural logs, which we generally use here.) The underlying theory implies that $\sum_k \beta_k = 1$. This is imposed by regressing $\log C - \log P_F$ on a constant, $\log Q$, $\log P_L - \log P_F$, and $\log P_K - \log P_F$. This first set of results appears at the top of Table 8.5.

The implied total and average cost functions for these results are shown in Figure 8.4. The striking pattern of the residuals (sketched in the figure) and some thought about the

---

[10] See Box and Cox (1964) and Zarembka (1974). A survey of the properties of this model appears in Spitzer (1982b). Some further results on estimation appear in Spitzer (1982a).

[11] For λ equal to zero, L'Hospital's rule can be used to obtain the result of the transformation; $g^{(0)}(x) = [\lim_{\lambda \to 0} d(x^\lambda - 1)/d\lambda]/[\lim_{\lambda \to 0} d\lambda/d\lambda] = \ln x$.

[12] In principle, y could be modified by the Box–Cox transformation as well. However, some important issues of specification will arise. (That is, is the model linear or log-linear? What is the allowable range of the dependent variable?) We defer until Chapter 11 a detailed treatment of the Box–Cox transformation applied to the dependent variable.

Table 8.5. Cobb–Douglas Cost Function
(Standard Errors in Parentheses)

	$\log Q$	$\log P_L - \log P_F$	$\log P_K - \log P_F$	R^2
All firms	0.721	0.562	−0.003	0.931
	(0.175)	(0.198)	(0.192)	
Group 1	0.398	0.641	−0.093	0.512
	(0.079)	(0.691)	(0.669)	
Group 2	0.668	0.105	0.364	0.635
	(0.116)	(0.275)	(0.277)	
Group 3	0.931	0.408	0.249	0.571
	(0.198)	(0.199)	(0.189)	
Group 4	0.915	0.472	0.133	0.871
	(0.108)	(0.174)	(0.157)	
Group 5	1.045	0.604	−0.295	0.920
	(0.065)	(0.197)	(0.175)	

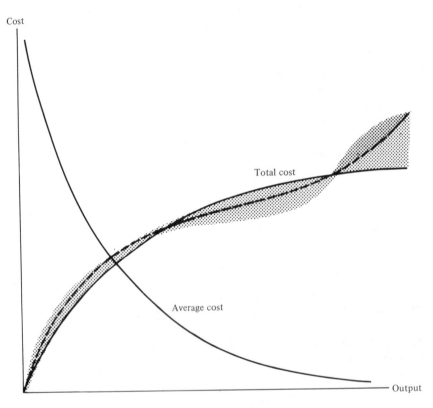

Figure 8.4 Cost functions.

Table 8.6. Log-Quadratic Cost Function
(Standard Errors in Parentheses)

	$\log Q$	$\log^2 Q$	$\log P_L - \log P_F$	$\log P_K - \log P_F$	R^2
All firms	0.151	0.117	0.498	0.062	0.958
	(0.062)	(0.012)	(0.161)	(0.151)	

implied form of production suggested that something was missing from the model.[13] In theory, the estimated model implies a continually declining average cost curve, which, in turn, implies pervasive economies of scale at all levels of output. This conflicts with the textbook notion of a **U**-shaped average cost curve and appears implausible for the data. Two approaches were used to analyze the model.[14]

By sorting his sample into five groups on the basis of output and fitting separate regressions to each group, Nerlove fit a piecewise linear model. (His was a bit more general than might have been necessary in that β_i was allowed to vary across the five groups.) The results are given in the lower rows of the table, where the firms in the successive groups are progressively larger. The results are persuasive that the (log)-linear cost function is inadequate. The output coefficient that rises toward and then crosses 1 is consistent with a **U**-shaped cost curve as surmised earlier. (See Exercise 3, Chapter 10.)

A second approach was to expand the cost function to include a quadratic term in log output. This corresponds to a much more general model (the dashed cost curve shown in Figure 8.4) and produced the results given in Table 8.6. Again, a simple t test strongly suggests that increased generality is called for.[15]

The preceding illustrates three useful tools in identifying and dealing with unspecified nonlinearity: analysis of residuals, the use of piecewise linear regression,[16] and the use of polynomials to approximate the unknown regression function.

8.3.3. Intrinsic Linearity and Identification

The log-linear model illustrates an intermediate case of a nonlinear regression model. The equation is intrinsically linear by our definition; by taking logs of

$$Y_i = \alpha X^{\beta_2} e^{\varepsilon_i},$$

we obtain

$$\ln Y_i = \ln \alpha + \beta_2 \ln X_i + \varepsilon_i \qquad (8\text{--}11)$$

or

$$y_i = \beta_1 + \beta_2 x_i + \varepsilon_i.$$

---

[13] A Durbin–Watson test of correlation among the residuals (see Chapter 15) revealed substantial autocorrelation. This is to be expected, given the pattern in the figure.

[14] A third approach based on a model of the production function appears in Example 11.5.

[15] Nerlove inadvertently measured economies of scale from this function as $1/(\beta_q + \delta \log Q)$, where β_q and δ are the coefficients on $\log Q$ and $\log^2 Q$. The correct expression would have been $1/[\partial \log C/\partial \log Q] = 1/[\beta_q + 2\delta \log Q]$. This slip was periodically rediscovered in several later papers.

[16] It might seem that a spline regression might be useful here. However, there is no theoretical basis for the choice of output knots. In fact, they were chosen simply to have 29 firms in each group.

Although this equation is linear in most respects, something has changed in that it is no longer linear in α. Written in terms of β_1, we obtain a fully linear model. However, this may not be the form of interest. Nothing is lost, of course, since β_1 is just ln α. If β_1 can be estimated, an obvious estimate of α is suggested.[17] This leads us to a second aspect of intrinsically linear models.

Maximum likelihood estimators have an invariance property. In the classical normal regression model, the maximum likelihood estimator of σ is the square root of the maximum likelihood estimator of σ^2. Under some conditions, least squares estimates have the same property. By exploiting this fact, we can broaden the definition of linearity and include some additional cases that might otherwise be quite complex.

> **Definition.** In the classical regression model, if the K parameters, $\beta_1, \beta_2, \ldots, \beta_K$ can be written as K one-to-one possibly nonlinear functions of a set of K underlying parameters, $\theta_1, \theta_2, \ldots, \theta_K$, then the model is intrinsically linear in θ.

The emphasis here is on "one-to-one." If the conditions are met, the model can be estimated in terms of the functions, $\beta_1, \ldots, \beta_K$, and the underlying parameters derived after these are estimated. The one-to-one correspondence is an *identification condition*. If the condition is met, the underlying parameters of the regression (θ) are said to be **exactly identified** in terms of the parameters of the linear model, β. An excellent example is provided by Kmenta (1986, p. 515).[18]

EXAMPLE 8.4. CES Production Function. The constant elasticity of substitution production function may be written

$$\ln Y_i = \ln \gamma - \frac{v}{\rho} \ln[\delta K^{-\rho} + (1 - \delta)L^{-\rho}] + \varepsilon. \qquad (8-12)$$

A Taylor series approximation to this function around the point $\rho = 0$ is

$$\ln Y = \ln \gamma + v\delta \ln K + v(1 - \delta)\ln L - \tfrac{1}{2}\rho v\delta[\ln K - \ln L]^2 + \varepsilon \qquad (8-13)$$

$$= \beta_1 + \beta_2 x_1 + \beta_3 x_2 + \beta_4 x_3 + \varepsilon, \qquad (8-14)$$

where $x_1 = \ln K$, $x_2 = \ln L$, $x_3 = \ln^2(K/L)$, and

$$\beta_1 = \ln \gamma \qquad\qquad \gamma = e^{\beta_1}$$

$$\beta_2 = v\delta \qquad\qquad \delta = \frac{\beta_2}{\beta_2 + \beta_3} \qquad (8-15)$$

$$\beta_3 = v(1 - \delta) \qquad\qquad v = \beta_2 + \beta_3$$

$$\beta_4 = -\frac{\rho v\delta(1 - \delta)}{2} \qquad \rho = -\frac{2\beta_4(\beta_2 + \beta_3)}{\beta_2 \beta_3}.$$

Estimates of $\beta_1, \beta_2, \beta_3$, and β_4 can be found by least squares. The estimates of γ, δ, v, and ρ obtained by the second column of (8–15) are the same as those we would obtain had we found the nonlinear least squares estimates of (8–13) directly. [As Kmenta shows, they are not the same as the nonlinear least squares estimates of (8–12) due to the use of the Taylor series approximation to get to (8–13).]

---

[17] See Example 10.1 for some related results.
[18] A second example appears in Example 11.5.

Some care is needed in using this result. Not all models of the form

$$y_i = \beta_1(\theta)x_1 + \beta_2(\theta)x_2 + \cdots + \beta_K(\theta)x_K + \varepsilon \qquad (8\text{--}16)$$

are intrinsically linear. Recall that the condition that the functions be one-to-one (i.e., that the parameters be exactly identified) was required. For example,

$$y_i = \alpha + \beta x_1 + \gamma x_2 + \beta\gamma x_3 + \varepsilon$$

is nonlinear. The reason is that if we write it in the form of (8–16), we fail to account for the condition that β_4 equals $\beta_2\beta_3$, which is a nonlinear restriction. In this model, the three parameters α, β, and γ are said to be **overidentified** in terms of the four parameters $\beta_1, \beta_2, \beta_3,$ and β_4. Unrestricted least squares estimates of β_2, β_3, and β_4 can be used to obtain two estimates of each of the underlying parameters, and there is no assurance that these will be the same.

8.4. Specification Analysis

Our analysis has been based on the assumption that the correct specification of the regression model is known to be

$$\mathbf{y} = \mathbf{X}\boldsymbol{\beta} + \boldsymbol{\varepsilon}.$$

There are numerous types of errors that one might make in the specification of the estimated equation. Perhaps the most common ones are the omission of relevant variables and the inclusion of superfluous variables.

8.4.1. Selection of Variables

Consider an initial model, which we assume contains a constant term and several independent variables:

$$\mathbf{y} = \mathbf{X}_1\boldsymbol{\beta}_1 + \boldsymbol{\varepsilon}. \qquad (8\text{--}17)$$

It is not unusual to begin with some formulation and then contemplate adding more variables to the model. As shown earlier, the effects of a new variable on the coefficients on $\mathbf{X}_1$ are uncertain. However, the effect on R^2 is unambiguous. The change in the residual sum of squares when a set of variables, $\mathbf{X}_2$, is added to the regression is

$$\mathbf{e}'_{1,2}\mathbf{e}_{1,2} = \mathbf{e}'_1\mathbf{e}_1 - \mathbf{b}'_2\mathbf{X}'_2\mathbf{M}_1\mathbf{X}_2\mathbf{b}_2,$$

where we use subscript 1 to indicate the regression based on (8–17) and 1, 2 to indicate the use of both $\mathbf{X}_1$ and $\mathbf{X}_2$. The coefficient vector $\mathbf{b}_2$ is the coefficients on $\mathbf{X}_2$ in the multiple regression of $\mathbf{y}$ on $\mathbf{X}_1$ and $\mathbf{X}_2$. [See (6–18) for definitions of $\mathbf{b}_2$ and $\mathbf{M}_1$.] Therefore,

$$R^2_{1,2} = 1 - \frac{\mathbf{e}'_1\mathbf{e}_1 - \mathbf{b}'_2\mathbf{X}'_2\mathbf{M}_1\mathbf{X}_2\mathbf{b}_2}{\mathbf{y}'\mathbf{M}^0\mathbf{y}}$$

$$= R^2_1 + \frac{\mathbf{b}'_2\mathbf{X}'_2\mathbf{M}_1\mathbf{X}_2\mathbf{b}_2}{\mathbf{y}'\mathbf{M}^0\mathbf{y}}.$$

This is greater than R^2_1 unless $\mathbf{b}_2$ equals zero. ($\mathbf{M}_1\mathbf{X}_2$ could not be zero unless $\mathbf{X}_2$ was a linear function of $\mathbf{X}_1$, in which case the regression could not be computed.) This can be manipulated a bit further to obtain

$$R_{1,2}^2 = R_1^2 + \frac{y'M_1y}{y'M^0y} \frac{b_2'X_2'M_1X_2b_2}{y'M_1y}.$$

But $y'M_1y = e_1'e_1$, so the first term in the product is $1 - R_1^2$. The second is the multiple correlation in the regression of M_1y on M_1X_2, or the **partial correlation** (after the effect of X_1 is removed) in the regression of y on X_2.[19] Collecting terms, we have

$$R_{1,2}^2 = R_1^2 + (1 - R_1^2)r_{y2.1}^2.$$

Clearly, it would be possible to push R^2 as high as desired just by adding regressors. It is this problem that motivates the use of

$$\bar{R}^2 = 1 - \frac{n-1}{n-K}(1 - R^2)$$

instead of R^2 as a method of choosing among alternative models.[20] Since $\bar{R}^2$ incorporates a penalty for reducing the degrees of freedom while still revealing an improvement in fit, one possibility is to choose the specification that maximizes $\bar{R}^2$. It can be shown that this is equivalent to minimizing the variance estimator, $e'e/(n-K)$. It has been suggested that the adjusted R-squared does not penalize the loss of degrees of freedom heavily enough.[21] Two alternatives that have been proposed for comparing models (which we index by j) are

$$\tilde{R}_j^2 = \frac{n+K_j}{n-K_j}(1 - R_j^2),$$

which minimizes Amemiya's *prediction criterion*,[22]

$$PC = \frac{e_j'e_j}{n-K_j}\left(1 + \frac{K_j}{n}\right),$$

and Akaike's (1973) information criterion,

$$AIC_j = \ln\left(\frac{e_j'e_j}{n}\right) + \frac{2K_j}{n}.$$

Although intuitively appealing, these measures are a bit unorthodox in that they have no basis in theory.[23] Perhaps a somewhat more palatable alternative is the method of stepwise regression.[24] This procedure evaluates each variable in turn on the basis of its significance level and accumulates the model by adding or deleting variables sequentially. At the second step, to say nothing of the latter steps of this procedure, the classical inference procedures break down. Suppose, for example (as is common), that the method is used to ensure that all of the variables ultimately included have F statistics (the square of the conventional t ratio) larger than one. It is hardly appropriate to call these F statistics and base inference on them as if they were drawn from an F distribution; it is known a priori that all of

---

[19] Partial correlation is discussed in Section 6.3.5.
[20] See Section 6.6.
[21] See, for example, Amemiya (1985, pp. 50–51).
[22] Ibid.
[23] There is a computer program that will automatically do the complete search among the 2^{K-1} specifications to find the maximum $\bar{R}^2$. In the interest of conserving resources, we leave the readers to their own devices to locate it.
[24] See Draper and Smith (1980) and Maddala (1977, pp. 124–127) for discussion.

them will be larger than one. For this reason, economists have tended to avoid stepwise regression methods.

The preceding creates a bit of a methodological dilemma for researchers using the classical procedures. On the one hand, there is a presumption that there is a "true model" known a priori. If so, orthodoxy dictates that the researcher will compute only a single regression and report the results. Of course, this is hardly likely, and in practice, some exploratory work is always necessary. There is, however, good reason to be skeptical of a "model" that is constructed entirely by mechanical means.

8.4.2.   Omission of Relevant Variables

Suppose that a correctly specified regression model would be

$$y = X_1\beta_1 + X_2\beta_2 + \varepsilon, \tag{8-18}$$

where the two parts of X have K_1 and K_2 columns, respectively. If we regress y on X_1 without including X_2, the estimator is

$$b_1 = (X_1'X_1)^{-1}X_1'y$$

$$= \beta_1 + (X_1'X_1)^{-1}X_1'X_2\beta_2 + (X_1'X_1)^{-1}X_1'\varepsilon. \tag{8-19}$$

Taking the expectation, we see that unless $X_1'X_2 = 0$, b_1 is biased:

$$E[b_1] = \beta_1 + P_{1.2}\beta_2, \tag{8-20}$$

where

$$P_{1.2} = (X_1'X_1)^{-1}X_1'X_2. \tag{8-21}$$

Each column of the $K_1 \times K_2$ matrix $P_{1.2}$ is the column of slopes in the least squares regression of the corresponding column of X_2 on the columns of X_1.

EXAMPLE 8.5. Omitted Variable.   If a demand equation is estimated without the relevant income variable, (8–20) shows how the estimated price elasticity will be biased. Letting b be the estimate, we obtain

$$E[b] = \beta + \frac{\text{Cov}[\text{price, income}]}{\text{Var}[\text{price}]}\gamma,$$

where γ is the income coefficient. In aggregate data, it is unclear whether the missing covariance would be positive or negative. However, the sign of the bias in b would be the same as this covariance, because $\text{Var}[\text{price}]$ and γ would be positive.

EXAMPLE 8.6. Forecasting with Omitted Variables.   Consider the simple regression of y on x_1 and x_2 without a constant term. If y is regressed only on x_1, what are the implications for forecasts of y obtained with this regression? We can apply the preceding result directly to obtain the expected value of the forecast. Inserting $E(b_1)$ in the expression, we have

$$E[\hat{y}^0] = E[b_1x_1^0] = \beta_1 + P_{1.2}\beta_2x_1^0,$$

while the true value is

$$y^0 = \beta_1x_1^0 + \beta_2x_2^0 + \varepsilon^0.$$

The forecast error is $e^0 = \hat{y}^0 - y^0$, which has expectation

$$E[e^0] = E[\varepsilon^0 + b_1x_1^0 + P_{1.2}b_2x_1^0 - b_1x_1^0 - b_2x_2^0]$$

$$= -\beta_2(x_2^0 - P_{1.2}x_1^0).$$

Depending on the nature of x_1 and x_2, the "regression"

$$\hat{x}_2 = P_{1.2} x_1 + \text{error}$$

might be purely descriptive. However, suppose that x_1 and x_2 have a joint distribution in which $E[x_2 | x_1]$ is a linear function of x_1. Then linear regression of x_2 on x_1 produces unbiased estimates of the slope and intercept (zero) of this function, and, as always, predictions from this regression will be unbiased. But this is exactly what appears earlier. The upshot is that, depending on the relationship between x_1 and x_2, leaving x_2 out of the regression may, in fact, not induce any biases in the forecasts. If a linear regression of x_2 on x_1 produces an "unbiased" forecast of x_2, the preceding forecast error has an expected value of zero. **Exercise**: Is this a free lunch? If not, where is the cost?

In this development, it is straightforward to deduce the directions of bias when there is a single included variable and one omitted variable. However, it is important to note that if more than one variable is included, the terms in the **omitted variable formula** involve multiple regression coefficients, which themselves have the sign of partial, not simple, correlations. For example, in the demand equation, if the price of a closely related product had been included as well, then the gross correlation between price and income would be insufficient to determine the direction of the bias in the price elasticity. What would be required would be the sign of the correlation between price and income net of the effect of the other price. This might not be obvious, and it would become even less so as more regressors were added to the equation.

The variance of $\mathbf{b}_1$ is that of the third term in (8–19), which is

$$\text{Var}[\mathbf{b}_1] = \sigma^2 (\mathbf{X}_1' \mathbf{X}_1)^{-1}. \tag{8-22}$$

If we had computed the correct regression, including $\mathbf{X}_2$, the slopes on $\mathbf{X}_1$ would have been unbiased and would have had a variance matrix equal to the upper right block of $\sigma^2 (\mathbf{X}'\mathbf{X})^{-1}$. This is

$$\text{Var}[\mathbf{b}_{1.2}] = \sigma^2 (\mathbf{X}_1' \mathbf{M}_2 \mathbf{X}_1)^{-1} \tag{8-23}$$

where

$$\mathbf{M}_2 = \mathbf{I} - \mathbf{X}_2 (\mathbf{X}_2' \mathbf{X}_2)^{-1} \mathbf{X}_2',$$

or

$$\text{Var}[\mathbf{b}_{1.2}] = \sigma^2 [\mathbf{X}_1' \mathbf{X}_1 - \mathbf{X}_1' \mathbf{X}_2 (\mathbf{X}_2' \mathbf{X}_2)^{-1} \mathbf{X}_2' \mathbf{X}_1]^{-1}.$$

We can compare the variance matrices of $\mathbf{b}_1$ and $\mathbf{b}_{1.2}$ more easily by comparing their inverses [see result (2–120)]:

$$\text{Var}[\mathbf{b}_{1.2}]^{-1} - \text{Var}[\mathbf{b}_1]^{-1} = \sigma^2 \mathbf{X}_1' \mathbf{X}_2 (\mathbf{X}_2' \mathbf{X}_2)^{-1} \mathbf{X}_2' \mathbf{X}_1,$$

which is positive definite. We conclude that although $\mathbf{b}_1$ is biased, it has a smaller variance than $\mathbf{b}_{1.2}$.

Suppose, for instance, that $\mathbf{X}_1$ and $\mathbf{X}_2$ are each a single column and that the variables are measured as deviations from their respective means. Then

$$\text{Var}[b_1] = \frac{\sigma^2}{s_{11}} \qquad \text{where } s_{11} = \sum (x_1 - \bar{x}_1)^2,$$

while

$$\text{Var}[b_{1.2}] = \sigma^2 (\mathbf{x}_1'\mathbf{x}_1 - \mathbf{x}_1'\mathbf{x}_2(\mathbf{x}_2'\mathbf{x}_2)^{-1}\mathbf{x}_2'\mathbf{x}_1)^{-1}$$

$$= \frac{\sigma^2}{s_{11}(1 - r_{12}^2)}, \qquad (8\text{--}24)$$

where

$$r_{12}^2 = \frac{(\mathbf{x}_1'\mathbf{x}_2)^2}{\mathbf{x}_1'\mathbf{x}_1 \mathbf{x}_2'\mathbf{x}_2}$$

is the squared sample correlation between $\mathbf{x}_1$ and $\mathbf{x}_2$. The more highly correlated are $\mathbf{x}_1$ and $\mathbf{x}_2$, the larger will be the variance of $b_{1.2}$ compared to that of b_1. Therefore, it is possible that b_1 is a more precise estimator based on the **mean-squared error** criterion.

For statistical inference, it would be necessary to estimate σ^2. Proceeding as usual, we would use

$$s^2 = \frac{\mathbf{e}_1'\mathbf{e}_1}{n - K_1}.$$

But,

$$\mathbf{e}_1 = \mathbf{M}_1 \mathbf{y} = \mathbf{M}_1(\mathbf{X}_1\boldsymbol{\beta}_1 + \mathbf{X}_2\boldsymbol{\beta}_2 + \boldsymbol{\varepsilon}) = \mathbf{M}_1\mathbf{X}_2\boldsymbol{\beta}_2 + \mathbf{M}_1\boldsymbol{\varepsilon}.$$

In order to find the expected value of $\mathbf{e}_1'\mathbf{e}_1$, we use the same approach we used in Chapter 6 and the fact that $E[\mathbf{X}_1'\boldsymbol{\varepsilon}] = \mathbf{0}$ to drop the middle term in the quadratic form. Thus,

$$E[\mathbf{e}_1'\mathbf{e}_1] = \boldsymbol{\beta}_2'\mathbf{X}_2'\mathbf{M}_1\mathbf{X}_2\boldsymbol{\beta}_2 + \sigma^2 Tr(\mathbf{M}_1)$$

$$= \boldsymbol{\beta}_2'\mathbf{X}_2'\mathbf{M}_1\mathbf{X}_2\boldsymbol{\beta}_2 + (n - K_1)\sigma^2. \qquad (8\text{--}25)$$

Consequently, s^2 is biased. Notice that the first term in the expectation is the population counterpart to the increase in the residual sum of squares that results when $\mathbf{X}_2$ is dropped from the regression. It is simple to show that the first preceding term is positive, so that s^2 is biased upward. Unfortunately, to take any account of this bias, we would require an estimate of $\boldsymbol{\beta}_2$.

The conclusion from this is that if we omit relevant variables from the regression, our estimates of both $\boldsymbol{\beta}_1$ and σ^2 are biased. It is possible for $\mathbf{b}_1$ to be more precise than $\mathbf{b}_{1.2}$. But even this should be of limited comfort. Since we cannot estimate σ^2, we cannot test hypotheses about $\mathbf{b}_1$. To make matters worse, even if we had an estimate of σ^2, we could only test hypotheses about $\boldsymbol{\beta}_1 + P_{1.2}\boldsymbol{\beta}_2$, which is unlikely to be of much interest. As a final observation, note that when the regressors are orthogonal, $(\mathbf{X}_1'\mathbf{X}_2) = \mathbf{0}$, the estimator in the short regression is unbiased. But the estimator of σ^2 is *still* biased upward, so we are still precluded from drawing valid inferences about $\boldsymbol{\beta}_1$. Of course, it is unlikely that in practice the regressors would be orthogonal. Omission of variables from the regression is a potentially quite serious problem.

8.4.3.   Inclusion of Irrelevant Variables

If the regression model is correctly given by

$$\mathbf{y} = \mathbf{X}_1\boldsymbol{\beta}_1 + \boldsymbol{\varepsilon} \qquad (8\text{--}26)$$

and we estimate it as if (8–18) were correct (i.e., we include some extra variables), it might seem that the same sorts of problems considered earlier would arise. In fact, this is not the case. We can view the omission of a set of relevant variables as equivalent to imposing an incorrect restriction on (8–18). In particular, omitting X_2 is equivalent to *incorrectly* estimating (8–18) subject to the restriction

$$\beta_2 = 0. \tag{8–27}$$

As we discovered, incorrectly imposing a restriction leads to a number of biases. Another way to view this error is to note that it amounts to incorporating incorrect information in our estimation. Suppose, however, that our error is simply a failure to use some information that *is correct*? It would seem that this would probably be less serious.

The inclusion of the irrelevant variables X_2 in the regression is equivalent to failing to impose (8–27) on (8–18) in estimation. However, (8–18) is not incorrect; it simply fails to incorporate (8–27). Therefore, we do not need to prove formally that the least squares estimator of β in (8–18) is unbiased *even given* (8–27); we have already proved it. We can assert on the basis of all of our earlier results that

$$E[b] = \begin{bmatrix} \beta_1 \\ \beta_2 \end{bmatrix} = \begin{bmatrix} \beta_1 \\ 0 \end{bmatrix}. \tag{8–28}$$

By the same reasoning, s^2 is also unbiased:

$$E\left[\frac{e'e}{n - K_1 - K_2}\right] = \sigma^2.$$

Then where is the problem? It would seem that one would generally want to "overfit" the model. From a theoretical standpoint, the difficulty with this view is that the failure to use correct information is always costly. In this instance, the cost is reduced precision of the estimates. As we have shown, the variance matrix in the short regression (omitting X_2) is always smaller than the variance matrix for the estimator obtained in the presence of the superfluous variables.[25] Consider again the single-variable comparison given earlier. If x_2 is highly correlated with x_1, incorrectly including it in the regression will greatly inflate the variance of the estimator.

8.4.4. Some General Results

In the regression setting of (8–17), a set of restrictions

$$R\beta - q = 0 \tag{8–29}$$

constitutes additional information that may or may not be correct. In general, the restricted least squares estimator is given by (8–31) and has

$$E[b_*] = \beta - W(R\beta - q)$$

and

$$\begin{aligned} \text{Var}[b_*] &= \sigma^2[(I - WR)(X'X)^{-1}(I - WR)'] \\ &= \sigma^2[(X'X)^{-1} - (X'X)^{-1}R'(R(X'X)^{-1}R')^{-1}R(X'X)^{-1}]. \end{aligned} \tag{8–30}$$

---

[25] There is no loss if $X_1'X_2 = 0$, which makes sense in terms of the information about X_1 contained in X_2 (here, none). However, this is not likely to occur in practice.

If the restrictions in (8–29) are, indeed, correct, $\mathbf{b}_*$ is unbiased. But whether they are or not, $\mathrm{Var}[\mathbf{b}_*]$ is smaller than $\mathrm{Var}[\mathbf{b}]$ in the sense defined in Section 2.8.3. We can interpret this as the value of the information contained in the restrictions. It is interesting to note that information about the parameters, good or bad, reduces the variance of the estimator. But since it may induce biases, its effect on their mean-squared errors is unclear.

8.5.   Biased Estimators and Pretest Estimators

Our focus on unbiased estimators parallels the general attraction among economists for them. However, it has been amply demonstrated that this approach will almost surely bypass estimators that though biased, are more precise in an expected squared error sense.[26] Indeed, the famous result of James and Stein (1961) shows that by a squared error loss criterion, there is always a feasible estimator that dominates least squares for every value of β.[27] From our point of view, the importance of this result will lie in how we can use information drawn from outside the sample data to sharpen our parameter estimates. At several points, we have invoked the general proposition that increased information, good or bad, reduces variance. However, we have also found that *incorrect* information will induce biases.[28] Here we shall explore further the possibility that when our out-of-sample information is sufficiently close to the truth, the induced bias will be offset by the improvement in the variance of the estimator in its expected squared error.

8.5.1.   The Mean-Squared-Error Test

Suppose that we incorporate a set of restrictions, $\mathbf{R}\beta = \mathbf{q}$, on the least squares estimator of β in the model $\mathbf{y} = \mathbf{X}\beta + \varepsilon$. The restricted least squares estimator is

$$\mathbf{b}_* = \mathbf{b} - (\mathbf{X}'\mathbf{X})^{-1}\mathbf{R}'[\mathbf{R}(\mathbf{X}'\mathbf{X})^{-1}\mathbf{R}'](\mathbf{Rb} - \mathbf{q}) \tag{8–31}$$

and its variance matrix is

$$\mathrm{Var}[\mathbf{b}_*] = \sigma^2[(\mathbf{X}'\mathbf{X})^{-1} - (\mathbf{X}'\mathbf{X})^{-1}\mathbf{R}'(\mathbf{R}(\mathbf{X}'\mathbf{X})^{-1}\mathbf{R}')^{-1}\mathbf{R}(\mathbf{X}'\mathbf{X})^{-1}]. \tag{8–32}$$

The variance matrix of $\mathbf{b}_*$ is equal to that of $\mathbf{b}$ minus a positive definite matrix, so it is smaller in the sense defined in Chapter 2. However, unless the restrictions are correct in the population, $\mathbf{b}_*$ is biased; $E[\mathbf{b}_*] = \beta - \mathbf{W}(\mathbf{R}\beta - \mathbf{q})$. It is still possible that the mean-squared-error of $\mathbf{b}_*$ is smaller than that of $\mathbf{b}$.

Since $\mathbf{b}$ is unbiased, its mean-squared-error matrix is its variance matrix:

$$\mathrm{MSE}[\mathbf{b}\,|\,\beta] = \sigma^2(\mathbf{X}'\mathbf{X})^{-1}.$$

To obtain the mean-squared-error matrix for $\mathbf{b}_*$, we can use (8–30) and the result preceding it:

$$\mathrm{MSE}[\mathbf{b}_*\,|\,\beta] = \mathrm{Var}[\mathbf{b}_*] + E[\mathbf{b}_* - \beta]E[\mathbf{b}_* - \beta]'$$
$$= \sigma^2(\mathbf{I} - \mathbf{WR})(\mathbf{X}'\mathbf{X})^{-1}(\mathbf{I} - \mathbf{WR})' + \mathbf{W}(\mathbf{R}\beta - \mathbf{q})(\mathbf{R}\beta - \mathbf{q})'\mathbf{W}.$$

[26] See, for example, Judge et al. (1985) and the many references cited therein.
[27] See, as well, the discussions in Judge et al. (1985, pp. 82–92) and Amemiya (1985, pp. 61–63).
[28] See the discussion of specification errors in the previous section.

It has been shown that $\mathbf{b}_*$ will be more precise in the sense that $\text{MSE}[\mathbf{b} \mid \boldsymbol{\beta}] - \text{MSE}[\mathbf{b}_* \mid \boldsymbol{\beta}]$ is a positive definite matrix if[29]

$$\lambda = \frac{(\mathbf{R}\boldsymbol{\beta} - \mathbf{q})'[\mathbf{R}(\mathbf{X}'\mathbf{X})^{-1}\mathbf{R}']^{-1}(\mathbf{R}\boldsymbol{\beta} - \mathbf{q})}{2\sigma^2} < \frac{1}{2}. \tag{8-33}$$

This is $J/2$ times the population analog to the F statistic that would be used to test the validity of the restrictions. *This implies that if the failure of the true parameters to satisfy the restrictions is not too severe, the biased estimator will be more precise in spite of its bias.*

Since λ depends on the unknown parameters we are trying to estimate, (8-33) cannot be computed. It is possible to test the inequality in (8-33) as a hypothesis, but not with the procedures we have used thus far. Under the hypothesis that $(\mathbf{R}\boldsymbol{\beta} - \mathbf{q}) = \mathbf{0}$,

$$\frac{2\hat{\lambda}}{J} = F = \frac{(\mathbf{Rb} - \mathbf{q})'[\mathbf{R}(\mathbf{X}'\mathbf{X})^{-1}\mathbf{R}']^{-1}(\mathbf{Rb} - \mathbf{q})/\sigma^2}{Js^2/\sigma^2} \tag{8-34}$$

has the familiar F distribution. But if the hypothesis is incorrect, the F distribution no longer applies. The difference arises because the numerator of (8-34) has a chi-squared distribution with J degrees of freedom only if $E[\mathbf{Rb} - \mathbf{q}] = \mathbf{0}$. If not, the numerator has a **noncentral chi-squared** distribution, and the ratio has a **noncentral** F distribution. These distributions arise as follows:

1. *Noncentral chi-squared distribution:* If z has a normal distribution with mean μ and standard deviation 1, the distribution of z^2 is *noncentral* chi-squared with parameters 1 and $\mu^2/2$. If μ equals zero, the familiar *central* chi-squared distribution results. An example is shown in Figure 8.5. The extensions that will enable us to deduce the distribution of F when the restrictions do not hold in the population are

   a. If $\mathbf{z} \sim N[\boldsymbol{\mu}, \boldsymbol{\Sigma}]$, with J elements, $\mathbf{z}'\boldsymbol{\Sigma}^{-1}\mathbf{z}$ has a noncentral chi-squared distribution with J degrees of freedom and noncentrality parameter $\boldsymbol{\mu}'\boldsymbol{\Sigma}^{-1}\boldsymbol{\mu}/2$, which we denote $\chi_*^2[J, \boldsymbol{\mu}'\boldsymbol{\Sigma}^{-1}\boldsymbol{\mu}/2]$.

   b. If $\mathbf{z} \sim N[\boldsymbol{\mu}, \mathbf{I}]$ and $\mathbf{M}$ is an idempotent matrix with rank J, then $\mathbf{z}'\mathbf{Mz} \sim \chi_*^2[J, \boldsymbol{\mu}'\mathbf{M}\boldsymbol{\mu}/2]$.

2. *Noncentral F distribution:* If X_1 has a noncentral chi-squared distribution with noncentrality parameter λ and degrees of freedom n_1, and X_2 has a central chi-squared distribution with degrees of freedom n_2 and is independent of X_1,

$$F_* = \frac{X_1/n_1}{X_2/n_2}$$

   has a noncentral F distribution with parameters n_1, n_2, and λ.[30] Note that in each of these cases the statistic and the distribution are the familiar ones, except that the effect of the nonzero mean, which induces the noncentrality, is to push the distribution to the right.

Thus, the distribution of the sample F statistic in (8-34) is noncentral F with degrees of freedom J and $n - K$ and noncentrality parameter λ, as given in (8-33). If the restrictions are valid, λ will be zero and the familiar central F distribution will result.

---

[29] See, for example, Fomby et al. (1984, pp. 98–100).

[30] The denominator chi-squared could also be noncentral, but we shall not use any statistics with doubly noncentral distributions.

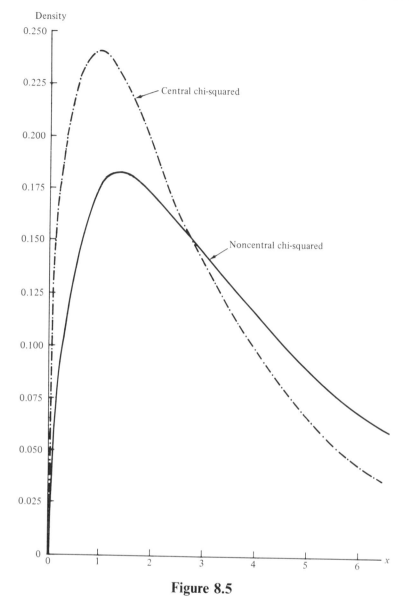

Figure 8.5

A test of the hypothesis that the mean-squared error of the restricted estimator is smaller than that of the unrestricted one can now be constructed. The test of $H_0: \lambda \leq \frac{1}{2}$ can be carried out by referring the sample F ratio to the noncentral F distribution with parameters J, $n - K$, and $\frac{1}{2}$. A value of F larger than the critical value in the table is taken as evidence that $\lambda > \frac{1}{2}$. Critical values for the noncentral F distribution have been tabulated by Wallace and Toro-Vizcarrondo (1969). Since this is a three-parameter distribution, the complete tabulation is a bit cumbersome. There is, however, a very simple and accurate approximation that requires only the central F tables given in the appendixes of most textbooks (including this one). The procedure is detailed in the following example.

EXAMPLE 8.7. Mean-Squared-Error Test (Hypothetical).   A Cobb–Douglas cost function of the form

$$\ln\left(\frac{C}{P_m}\right) = \beta_1 + \beta_2 \ln Q + \beta_3 \ln\left(\frac{P_k}{P_m}\right) + \beta_4 \ln\left(\frac{P_l}{P_m}\right) + \beta_5 \ln\left(\frac{P_e}{P_m}\right)$$

is estimated using 20 observations, where C is cost, Q is output, and P_k, P_l, P_e, and P_m are the unit prices of four factors of production: capital, labor, energy, and materials. The restriction that the function be homogeneous of degree zero in the prices is already imposed. The parameter β_2 is of primary interest. The F statistic for testing the hypothesis that $\beta_3 = \beta_4 = \beta_5 = 0$ is 4.17. Will the estimate of β_2 be improved by imposing the restriction? First, the critical value from the central F distribution for 5 percent significance is 3.29; so, outright, the restrictions are rejected by the familiar standard. But, for this test, we require the 5 percent critical value from the noncentral F distribution. This is C^* such that

$$\text{Prob}(F_*[3,\ \ 15,\ \tfrac{1}{2}] > C_*) = 0.05.$$

For degrees of freedom J and T, we can approximate the noncentral F critical values by using

$$C_* \simeq \left(1 + \frac{1}{J}\right)C,$$

where

$$\text{Prob}\left(F\left[J + \frac{1}{J+2},\ T\right] > C\right) = 0.05.$$

To find the critical value for noninteger degrees of freedom, it is necessary to interpolate in the F table, which is done using the reciprocals of the degrees of freedom. The neighboring values to the critical value for $F[3.2, 15]$ are 3.29 for $F[3, 15]$ and 3.06 for $F[4, 15]$. Therefore,

$$C = 3.29 - (3.29 - 3.06)\frac{(1/3.2 - 1/3)}{(1/4 - 1/3)} = 3.233,$$

so,

$$C_* = (1 + \tfrac{1}{3})3.233 = 4.310.$$

(The corresponding value from the Toro-Vizcarrondo and Wallace tables is 4.315.) Since the test statistic was 4.17, we would conclude that the restricted estimator is more precise, in spite of the earlier finding.

Because the critical points of the noncentral distribution are always to the right of those for the central distribution, it is worth emphasizing that this test can lead to retention of a set of restrictions when we might reject the restrictions themselves.

Should we use the restricted or the unrestricted estimator? This question is relevant in all of the settings we have considered thus far in this chapter. (That is, having tested a set of restrictions and failed to reject them, should we then impose them on the model and reestimate?) It is clear from the preceding that the answer depends on the precision of the estimator in a way that depends on some unknown parameters. Obviously, if we are sure that the restrictions are correct, we should impose them a priori and not concern ourselves with the unrestricted model. If we are sure that the restrictions are incorrect, it is unlikely that the earlier mean-squared-error test would favor the restricted estimator. It is the intermediate case, in which we are uncertain, that is at issue. Unfortunately, the problem becomes yet more complicated, because the process of sequential estimation implied here calls into question any further statistical inference that might be done.

8.5.2. Pretest Estimators

In dealing with the problem of multicollinearity,[31] one of the most tempting (and commonly used) strategies is simply to drop the variable(s) suspected of causing the problem. Consider the simplest case: that of a regression with two independent variables and no constant term. The regression is

$$y = \beta_1 x_1 + \beta_2 x_2 + \varepsilon.$$

Two competing estimators are the *short regression*,

$$b_1 = (x_1' x)^{-1} x_1' y$$

and the *long regression*,

$$b_{1.2} = (x_1' M_2 x_1)^{-1} x_1' M_2 y.$$

From our earlier results,

$$E[b_1] = \beta_1 + \beta_2 \frac{x_1' x_2}{x_1' x_1}$$

and

$$\text{Var}[b_1] = \frac{\sigma^2}{x_1' x_1},$$

while

$$E[b_{1.2}] = \beta_1$$

and

$$\text{Var}[b_{1.2}] = \frac{\sigma^2}{x_1' x_1 (1 - r_{12}^2)}.$$

Therefore, b_1 is biased but has a smaller variance. The estimators can be compared on the basis of their mean squared errors. Using the results of the previous section, we find that the short regression estimator is more precise if the population analog to the F statistic for testing $H_0: \beta_2 = 0$ is less than one. Since this is the square of the usual t ratio for this simple hypothesis, the basis for the mean-squared-error test of (8–33) is

$$\tau^2 = \frac{\beta_2^2}{\sigma^2/(S_{22}(1 - r_{12}^2))}. \tag{8–35}$$

The larger is β_2, the worse is the bias in b_1 and the less likely it is that λ will be less than $\frac{1}{2}$. Thus, b_1 will be a preferable estimator only if this bias is small, as measured by the earlier population t ratio. The test itself can be carried out by referring the square of the t ratio associated with b_2 to $F_*[1, n - K, \frac{1}{2}]$.

There are a few ways in which one might proceed at this point. If it is strongly believed that τ is close to zero, it makes sense to omit x_2 from the regression at the outset and use b_1. On the other hand, if one is convinced that x_2 is a significant influence in the regression, it

---

[31] This is the subject of Section 9.2 of the next chapter. For the present, we may view it as an imprecision in the estimation of the parameters that is caused by correlation between the independent variables in a multiple regression.

makes little sense even to consider b_1; $b_{1.2}$ is the better estimator. Unfortunately, most of the time, we shall be in neither situation. A third possibility (probably the one used most often) is to use a *sequential estimator*. We first compute the long regression and then choose the estimator on the basis of the t test, where we use t, the sample analog to τ, in

$$b_1^* = \begin{cases} b_1 & \text{if } t^2 < 1 \\ b_{1.2} & \text{if } t^2 \geq 1. \end{cases} \tag{8-36}$$

This is a "pretest" estimator because it is based on the preliminary regression.[32] It has been analyzed extensively, with some striking results.[33] Remember that b_1^* is a function not of the true τ but of the sample statistic, t. Therefore, its mean and variance depend on the value of t that is "drawn" in the sample. In particular,

$$E[b_1^*] = E[b_{1.2}] \operatorname{Prob}(t^2 \geq 1) + E[b_1] \operatorname{Prob}(t^2 < 1).$$

(Of course, t^2 can be less than one even if τ^2 is greater than one.) Since b_1^* is a weighted average of an unbiased estimator and a biased one, it must be biased. The larger is τ^2, the less likely it is that t^2 will be less than one, so this bias is a decreasing function of τ^2. The variance of b_1^* behaves similarly. The important thing to note is that this variance will not equal either of the variances of the two competing estimators unless τ^2 is zero or infinity.[34]

8.5.3. An Application—Inequality Restrictions

In many instances, prior information about the regression parameters is in the form of inequality restrictions. For example:

1. The price elasticities in a demand equation must be positive.
2. The marginal propensity to consume is between zero and one.
3. To rule out decreasing returns to scale, we would require that the sum of the output elasticities in a production function be greater than or equal to one.

Estimation subject to inequality restrictions is considerably more complicated than with equality restrictions. The estimation problem itself can be formulated as a quadratic programming problem in the framework of the Kuhn–Tucker problem:

$$\text{Minimize}_{\hat\beta} \ \tilde{L} = (\mathbf{y} - \mathbf{X}\hat\beta)'(\mathbf{y} - \mathbf{X}\hat\beta) + \lambda'(\mathbf{R}\hat\beta - \mathbf{q}).$$

The necessary conditions, in which we let $\tilde{\mathbf{b}}$ be the solution, are

$$\frac{\partial \tilde{L}}{\partial \tilde{\mathbf{b}}} = 2\mathbf{X}'\mathbf{X}\tilde{\mathbf{b}} - 2\tilde{\mathbf{b}}'\mathbf{X}'\mathbf{y} + \mathbf{R}'\lambda = 0$$

$$\frac{\partial \tilde{L}}{\partial \lambda} = \mathbf{R}\tilde{\mathbf{b}} - \mathbf{q} \geq 0$$

$$\lambda'(\mathbf{R}\tilde{\mathbf{b}} - \mathbf{q}) = 0$$

$$\lambda \leq 0.$$

[32] A related estimator suggested by Feldstein (1973) involves computing a weighted average of b_1 and $b_{1.2}$. He shows that the one with minimum mean-squared error is $b_1^{**} = wb_1 + (1 - w)b_{1.2}$, where $w = \tau^2/(1 + \tau^2)$. The sample statistic, t, is used instead of the unknown τ. Since b_1^{**} is a complicated function of t, little is known about its true distribution. Note, however, that b_1^{**} is not a sequential estimator. It is always based on both regressions.
[33] Pretest estimators are examined at length in Judge and Bock (1978 and 1983).
[34] It is a weighted average of the estimators plus a term that arises out of the noncentral distribution. See Bock et al. (1972).

As we have seen before, if $\mathbf{Rb} - \mathbf{q} = \mathbf{0}$, where $\mathbf{b} = (\mathbf{X'X})^{-1}\mathbf{X'y}$, then λ will equal zero, and this will be a solution. If not, some other solution will be required. Standard algorithms exist for solving the problem, and the computational aspects, while not simple, are at least straightforward.[35] The very difficult matter concerns the sampling properties of the estimator.[36] The following generalities have been obtained:

1. $\tilde{\mathbf{b}}$ is biased. It is, as always, a mix of an unbiased and a biased estimator.
2. $\text{Var}[\tilde{\mathbf{b}}]$ is always less than that of $\mathbf{b}$. This follows the arguments we have seen before; it is the value of the prior information.
3. $\text{MSE}[\tilde{\mathbf{b}} \mid \boldsymbol{\beta}]$ can be less than that of $\mathbf{b}$ but will sometimes be larger.

There will be some cases in which the solution can be written

$$\tilde{\mathbf{b}} = \mathbf{b} \qquad \text{if } \mathbf{Rb} - \mathbf{q} \geq \mathbf{0},$$

$$\tilde{\mathbf{b}} = \mathbf{b}_* \qquad \text{if } \mathbf{Rb} - \mathbf{q} < \mathbf{0},$$

where $\mathbf{b}_*$ is the equality restricted least squares estimator in (8–31). This will always be the case if there is only one constraint, which will be true in most instances analyzed in practice.[37] The estimator $\mathbf{b}$ fits directly into the pretest estimators we have discussed. The sampling distribution of the inequality restricted estimator is quite complicated, but it has been derived from some cases.[38]

EXAMPLE 8.8. Restricting a Coefficient to Be Positive. Suppose that the regression model is of the form[39]

$$y = \beta_1 + \beta_2 x + \varepsilon,$$

and the constraint is

$$\beta_2 \geq 0.$$

The inequality-constrained least squares estimator is

$$\tilde{b}_2 = 0 \qquad \text{if } b_2 < 0,$$

$$\tilde{b}_2 = b_2 \qquad \text{if } b_2 \geq 0.$$

Without restrictions, b_2 has the familiar normal distribution with mean β_2 and variance σ^2/S_{xx}, which, for convenience, we denote θ^2. Then $\tilde{b}_2$ is obviously biased unless β_2 equals zero:

$$E[\tilde{b}_2] = 0\,\text{Prob}[b_2 < 0] + \beta_2\,\text{Prob}[b_2 \geq 0],$$

which is between β_2 and 0. Let τ equal β_2/θ. This is the population t ratio that appeared earlier in (8–35), although here there is no other regressor. Since b_2 is normally distributed, we can use the standard normal distribution to obtain $\text{Prob}[b_2 \geq 0] = \Phi(-\tau)$. Let the

---

[35] See, for example, Fletcher (1980) and Bazara and Shetty (1979).

[36] An illustrative case in a relatively simple setting is analyzed by Thomson (1982). A recent study that employs some of these results is Goldberger (1986).

[37] If there are several constraints, it is still possible that the solution will appear as given earlier. However, it is also possible that only some of the constraints will be violated by the least squares estimator. Imposing only these particular constraints may induce failures of the other constraints, which previously were not violated. This complicates the analysis substantially. See Fomby et al. (1984, pp. 104–105) for a discussion.

[38] See Judge and Bock (1978) and Judge and Yancey (1981).

[39] Adding a set of additional regressors would complicate the algebra but would not materially change the solution we shall obtain.

density of the standard normal distribution evaluated at $-\tau$ be $\phi(-\tau)$, and denote $\phi(-\tau)/\Phi(-\tau) = \lambda(\tau)$. Thompson gives the following:[40]

$$\text{Bias}[\tilde{b}_2] = \beta_2 \Phi(-\tau)[\lambda(\tau) - \tau]$$

$$\text{MSE}[\tilde{b}_2] = \theta^2 + \theta^2 \Phi(-\tau)[\tau - 1 + \tau\lambda(\tau)].$$

The bias, as we have seen, is toward zero. The mean-squared error may be greater or lower than θ^2. Note the presence of $\tau - 1$ in the mean-squared error. If τ is greater than one, the mean-squared error of b_2 is greater than that of b_2, which is what we found earlier in a different problem. If $\tau < 1$, this mixed estimator may have a smaller mean-squared error than that of least squares.

To summarize, by using an estimator that depends on the outcome of a prior test based on the same data, we

1. obtained a biased estimator;
2. will, in all likelihood, base any subsequent inferences about the parameter on the wrong standard errors;
3. invalidate the usual inference procedures.

Exercises

1. Using the data in Table 7.1 (Section 7.2.4) to estimate the CES production function in Example 8.4, we obtain the following ordinary least squares regression results:

$$\ln Y = 1.4677 - 0.1115 \ln K + 1.1002 \ln L + 0.1522 \ln^2\left(\frac{K}{L}\right),$$

$$R^2 = 0.94677, \quad e'e = 0.8018, \quad n = 27,$$

0.1665			
−0.1009	0.1732		
0.08385	−0.1789	0.1885	
0.03164	−0.05192	0.05296	0.1622.

The full estimate of the covariance matrix for the parameters has already been given.[41]

(a) Compute the implied estimates of underlying parameters.
(b) Estimate the standard error of the estimate of ρ.
(c) Test the hypothesis that the coefficients on $\ln K$ and $\ln L$ sum to one.
(d) Test the hypothesis that ρ is zero. [**Hint:** Look closely at (8–15).]

2. Use (8–20) to derive the bias that results when the constant term in a regression is inappropriately omitted.

3. In Solow's classic (1957) study of technical change in the U.S. economy, he suggests the aggregate production function

$$q(t) = A(t)f[k(t)],$$

[40] Ibid. We have simplified Thomson's results a bit.
[41] Note that the functional form would be the same as that for the translog model, with constant returns to scale imposed if the second and third coefficients were made to sum to one. (See Problem 7.9.3.) This function, proposed by Kmenta (1967), is a precursor to the translog models that appeared in great number a few years later. The original source of the CES production function is Arrow et al. (1961). The paper is also reprinted in Zellner (1968).

where $q(t)$ is aggregate output per man-hour, $k(t)$ is the aggregate capital–labor ratio, and $A(t)$ is the technology index. Solow considered four static models:

$$\frac{q}{A} = \alpha + \beta \ln k,$$

$$\frac{q}{A} = \alpha - \frac{\beta}{k},$$

$$\ln\left(\frac{q}{A}\right) = \alpha + \beta \ln k,$$

$$\ln\left(\frac{q}{A}\right) = \alpha - \frac{\beta}{k}.$$

(He also estimated a dynamic model, $q(t)/A(t) - q(t-1)/A(t-1) = \alpha + \beta k$.)

(a) Sketch the four functions.

(b) Solow's data for the years 1909–1949 are listed here:

Year	q	k	A	Year	q	k	A	Year	q	k	A
1909	0.623	2.06	1.000	1923	0.809	2.61	1.196	1937	0.971	2.71	1.415
1910	0.616	2.10	0.983	1924	0.836	2.74	1.215	1938	1.000	2.78	1.445
1911	0.647	2.17	1.021	1925	0.872	2.81	1.254	1939	1.034	2.66	1.514
1912	0.652	2.21	1.023	1926	0.869	2.87	1.241	1940	1.082	2.63	1.590
1913	0.680	2.23	1.064	1927	0.871	2.93	1.235	1941	1.122	2.58	1.660
1914	0.682	2.20	1.071	1928	0.874	3.02	1.226	1942	1.136	2.64	1.665
1915	0.669	2.26	1.041	1929	0.895	3.06	1.251	1943	1.180	2.62	1.692
1916	0.700	2.34	1.076	1930	0.880	3.30	1.197	1944	1.265	2.63	1.812
1917	0.679	2.21	1.065	1931	0.904	3.33	1.226	1945	1.296	2.66	1.850
1918	0.729	2.22	1.142	1932	0.879	3.28	1.198	1946	1.215	2.50	1.769
1919	0.767	2.47	1.157	1933	0.869	3.10	1.211	1947	1.194	2.50	1.739
1920	0.721	2.58	1.069	1934	0.921	3.00	1.298	1948	1.221	2.55	1.767
1921	0.770	2.55	1.146	1935	0.943	2.87	1.349	1949	1.275	2.70	1.809
1922	0.788	2.49	1.183	1936	0.982	2.72	1.429				

(Op. cit., p. 314. Several variables are omitted.) Use these data to estimate the α and β of the four functions listed earlier. (Note that your results will not quite match Solow's. See the next problem for resolution of the discrepancy.) Sketch the functions, using your particular estimates of the parameters.

4. In the aforementioned study, Solow states:

A scatter of q/A against k is shown in Chart 4. Considering the amount of a priori doctoring which the raw figures have undergone, the fit is remarkably tight. Except, that is, for the layer of points which are obviously too high. These maverick observations relate to the seven last years of the period, 1943–1949. From the way they lie almost exactly parallel to the main scatter, one is tempted to conclude that in 1943 the aggregate production function simply shifted.

(a) Draw a scatter diagram of q/A against k. (Or obtain Solow's original study and examine his. An alternative source of the original paper is the volume edited by Zellner cited in Problem 1.)

(b) Estimate the four models you estimated in the previous problem, including a dummy variable for the years 1943–1949. How do your results change? (Note that these results match those reported by Solow, though he did not report the coefficient on the dummy variable.)

(c) Solow went on to surmise that, in fact, the data were fundamentally different in the years before 1943 than during and after. If so, one would guess that the regression should be different as well (though whether the change is merely in the data or in the underlying production function is not settled). Use a Chow test to examine the difference in the two subperiods, using your four functional forms. Note that with the dummy variable, you can do the test by introducing an interaction term between the dummy and whichever function of k appears in the regression. Use an F test to test the hypothesis.

5. Consider the two alternative regressions

$$(1) \quad y = \alpha_1 D_1 + \alpha_2 D_2 + \alpha_3 D_3 + \alpha_4 D_4 + \varepsilon,$$

$$(2) \quad y = \alpha + \alpha_2 D_2 + \alpha_3 D_3 + \alpha_4 D_4 + \varepsilon.$$

The variables are quarterly dummy variables (see (8–1)). There are equal numbers of observations in each quarter. By computing $(X'X)^{-1}X'y$ for the two models, obtain the precise formulas for the least squares coefficients in the two cases. Prove that if there were a term βx in the two equations, the least squares estimates of β would be identical.

6. What restriction on the parameters of (8–1) leads to the model in (8–2)? How would you test the restriction?

7. In a widely cited study of the American automobile market, Griliches (1961) reports the following regression results:

$$\ln Price = 6.4 + 0.056H + 0.249W + 0.023L + 0.010V$$

$$+ 0.023T + 0.090A + 0.088P + 0.109B + 0.157C$$

$$- 0.044D_1 - 0.015D_2 + 0.019D_3 + 0.44D_4 + 0.044D_5 + 0.023D_6,$$

where
H = advertised horsepower, in hundreds

W = shipping weight in thousands of pounds

L = overall length in tens of inches

$V = 1$ if the car has a V8 engine, 0 otherwise

$T = 1$ if the car is a hard top, 0 if a convertible

$A = 1$ if it has an automatic transmission, 0 if not

$P = 1$ if power steering is standard, 0 if not

$B = 1$ if power brakes are standard, 0 if not

$C = 1$ if the car is a compact, 0 if not

$D_1 = 1$ for 1955 model car, 0 otherwise

$D_2 = 1$ for 1956 model car, 0 otherwise

$D_3 = 1$ for 1957 model car, 0 otherwise

$D_4 = 1$ for 1958 model car, 0 otherwise

$D_5 = 1$ for 1959 model car, 0 otherwise

$D_6 = 1$ for 1960 model car, 0 otherwise

1954 is the base year.

(The value of 6.4 for the constant term is assumed here. The author did not report the constant terms in his results.)

The regression is estimated using a large sample of prices of cars for the years 1954–1960. Since the dependent variable is in logarithms and the coefficients are close to zero, they may be treated as percentage changes. For example, the model predicts that everything else held constant, an increase of 100 horsepower increased the cost of a car by 5.6 percent, while from 1954 to 1956, the price of a particular car fell by 1.5 percent.

(a) As a benchmark, suppose that an average car in 1954 had 141 horsepower, weighed 3452 pounds, and was 205 inches long (from Griliches, Table 1). Suppose, as well, that in 1954, 25 percent of the cars had V8's, 75 percent were hard tops, 20 percent had automatic transmission, 10 percent had power steering, 5 percent had power brakes, and 10 percent of the cars sold could be called compact. (All of these data are hypothetical; Griliches gives no figures for them.) What does the model predict for the median price of a car? (The prediction would not be the mean. See Example 5.9. Griliches reports a *geometric* mean of all prices for 1954 of $2360.)

(b) Everything else held constant, how much more would it cost to buy a car with a V8 and power steering in 1955 than without these two features in 1954?

(c) Everything else held constant, how much did the price of a car rise from 1956 to 1957? From 1956 to 1959?

(d) Suppose that putting a hard top on a car instead of manufacturing a convertible always added exactly 100 pounds to the weight of the car. How would this affect the interpretation of the coefficients on W and T in the regression?

(e) The R^2 in the previous regression was 0.922, using 570 observations. If the R^2 in the regression without $D_1,\ldots$ were 0.919, would the results support the hypothesis that variation in the mix of options and other features was entirely responsible for the variation in car prices in the 7-year period?

(f) Suppose that the preceding data had also been used to compute seven separate regressions, one for each year, with the following results:

	1954	1955	1956	1957	1958	1959	1960	All
Observations	65	55	87	95	103	87	78	570
e'e	104	88	206	144	199	308	211	1425

Test the hypothesis that the same coefficients apply in each year. (Note that the model with the pooled data allows a separate constant for each year. Note as well that you may need an approximate value for the F distribution with large degrees of freedom.)

8. Suppose that estimation of the model in (8–9) produced estimates of 0.34 for β and 0.1 for λ. The means of y and x are one and two respectively. What is the estimate of the elasticity, $(x/y)\partial E[y]/\partial x$? (For applications of the Box–Cox regression, see Section 11.7.)

9. Let $b_* = [X'X + kI]^{-1}X'y$. Prove that this is a biased estimator of β in the classical regression model. What is its mean squared error matrix? (This is a *ridge regression* estimator. It is discussed further in Section 9.2.4a.)

10. Given the results in part (e) of Problem 7, would the estimates of the other parameters in the model be sharpened if the six yearly dummy variables were dropped? Use the noncentral F test (see Example 8.7) to find out. Do this first assuming that there are 30 observations in total. Then use the chi-squared approximation to the distribution of JF.

11. Prove the result in (8–4).

12. *Reverse regression:* A common method of analyzing statistical data to detect discrimination in the workplace is to fit the following regression:

$$y = \alpha + \beta'x + \gamma d + \varepsilon, \tag{1}$$

where y is the wage rate and d is a dummy variable indicating either membership ($d = 1$) or nonmembership ($d = 0$) in the class toward which it is suggested the discrimination is directed. The regressors, x, include factors specific to the particular type of job, as well as indicators of the qualifications of the individual. The hypothesis of interest is $H_0: \gamma < 0$ versus $H_1: \gamma = 0$. The regression seeks to answer the question "In a given job, are individuals in the class ($d = 1$) paid less than equally qualified individuals not in the class ($d = 0$)?" Consider, however, the alternative possibility. Do individuals in the class in the same job as others, and receiving the same wage, uniformly have higher qualifications? If so, this might also be viewed as a form of discrimination. To analyze this question, Conway and Roberts (1983) suggested the following procedure:

(a) Fit (1) by ordinary least squares. Denote the estimates a, b, and c.

(b) Compute the set of *qualification indices*,

$$q = ai + Xb. \tag{2}$$

(Note the omission of cd from the fitted value.)

(c) Regress q on a constant, y, and d. The equation is

$$q = \alpha^*i + \beta^*y + \gamma^*d + \varepsilon^*. \tag{3}$$

The analysis suggests that if $\gamma < 0$, $\gamma^* > 0$.

(1) Prove that the theory notwithstanding, the least squares estimates, c and c^*, are related by

$$c^* = \frac{(\bar{y}_1 - \bar{y})(1 - R^2)}{(1 - P)(1 - r_{yd}^2)} - c, \tag{4}$$

where $\bar{y}_1$ is the mean of y for observations with $d = 1$

$\bar{y}$ is the mean of y for all observations

P is the mean of d

R^2 is the coefficient of determination for (1)

and

r_{yd}^2 is the squared correlation between y and d.

[**Hint:** The model contains a constant term. Thus, to simplify the algebra, assume that all variables are measured as deviations from the overall sample means and ignore the column of ones in your calculations. Second, in (2), use the fact that, based on the least squares results,

$$y = a\mathbf{i} + \mathbf{Xb} + c\mathbf{d} + \mathbf{e},$$

so

$$\mathbf{q} = \mathbf{y} - c\mathbf{d} - \mathbf{e}.$$

From here on, we drop the constant term.] Thus, in the regression in c, you are regressing $[\mathbf{y} - c\mathbf{d} - \mathbf{e}]$ on $\mathbf{y}$ and $\mathbf{d}$. Remember, all variables are in deviation form.

(2) Will the sample evidence necessarily be consistent with the theory? (**Hint:** Suppose that $c = 0$?)

  A symposium on the Conway and Roberts paper appeared in the *Journal of Business and Economic Statistics* in April 1984.

References

Aigner, D., A. Goldberger, and G. Kalton, "On the Explanatory Power of Dummy Variable Regressions," *International Economic Review*, 16, 2, 1975, pp. 503–509.

Akaike, H., "Information Theory and an Extension of the Maximum Likelihood Principle," in B. Petrov, and F. Csake, eds., *Second International Symposium on Information Theory*, Budapest: Akademiai Kiado, 1973.

Amemiya, T., *Advanced Econometrics*, Cambridge, Mass.: Harvard University Press, 1985.

Arrow, K., H. Chenery, B. Minhas, and R. Solow, "Capital–Labor Substitution and Economic Efficiency," *Review of Economics and Statistics*, 45, 1961, pp. 225–247.

Bazara, M., and C. Shetty, *Nonlinear Programming–Theory and Algorithms*, New York: Wiley, 1979.

Bock, M., T. Yancey, and G. Judge, "The Statistical Consequences of Preliminary Test Estimators in Regression," *Journal of the American Statistical Association*, 68, 1972, pp. 109–116.

Box, G., and D. Cox, "An Analysis of Transformations," *Journal of the Royal Statistical Society*, 1964 Series B, pp. 211–264.

Clark, C., *Mathematical Bioeconomics*, New York: Wiley, 1971.

Conway, D., and H. Roberts, "Reverse Regression, Fairness and Employment Discrimination," *Journal of Business and Economic Statistics*, 1, 1, 1983, pp. 75–85.

Draper, N., and H. Smith, *Applied Regression Analysis*, New York: Wiley, 1980.

Feldstein, M., "Multicollinearity and the MSE of Alternative Estimators," *Econometrica*, 41, 1973, pp. 337–346.

Fletcher, R., *Practical Methods of Optimization*, New York: Wiley, 1980.

Fomby, T., C. Hill, and S. Johnson, *Advanced Econometrics*, New York: Springer-Verlag, 1984.

Garber, S., and D. Poirier, "The Determinants of Aerospace Profit Rates," *Southern Economic Journal*, 41, 1974, pp. 228–238.

Goldberger, A., "One-Sided and Inequality Tests for a Pair of Means," University of Wisconsin–Madison: Social Science Research Institute, Number 8629, 1986.

Griliches, Z., "Hybrid Corn: An Exploration in the Economics of Technological Change," *Econometrica*, 25, 4, 1957, pp. 501–522.

Griliches, Z., "Hedonic Price Indexes for Automobiles: An Econometric Analysis of Quality Change," *Government Price Statistics, Hearings*, Washington, D.C.: U.S. Congress, Joint Economic Committee, January 24, 1961.

James, W., and C. Stein, "Estimation with Quadratic Loss," in J. Neyman, ed., *Proceedings of the Fourth Berkeley Symposium on Mathematical Statistics and Probability*, 1, 1961, pp. 361–379.

Johnston, J., *Econometric Methods*, New York: McGraw-Hill, 1984.

Judge, G., and M. Bock, *The Statistical Implications of Pre-Test and Stein Rule Estimators in Econometrics*, Amsterdam: North Holland, 1978.

Judge, G., and M., Bock, "Biased Estimation," in Intrilligator, M., and Griliches, Z., eds., *Handbook of Econometrics*, Vol. 1, Amsterdam: North Holland, 1983.

Judge, G., and T. Yancey, "Sampling Properties of an Inequality Restricted Estimator," *Economics Letters*, 4, 1981, pp. 327–333.

Judge, G., C. Hill, W. Griffiths, H. Lutkepohl, and T. Lee, *The Theory and Practice of Econometrics*, New York: Wiley, 1985.

Kmenta, J., "On Estimation of the CES Production Function," *International Economic Review*, 8, 1967, pp. 180–189.

Maddala, G., *Econometrics*, New York: McGraw-Hill, 1977.

McCullagh, P., and J. Nelder, *Generalized Linear Models*, London: Chapman and Hall, 1983, p. 137.

Nerlove, M., "Returns to Scale in Electricity Supply," in C. Christ, et al., eds., *Measurement in Economics: Studies in Mathematical Economics and Econometrics in Memory of Yehuda Grunfeld*, Stanford, Calif.: Stanford University Press, 1963.

Poirier, D., *The Econometrics of Structural Change*, Amsterdam: North Holland, 1974.

Ramsey, J., "Tests for Specification Errors in Classical Linear Least Squares Regression Analysis," *Journal of the Royal Statistical Society, Series B*, 31, 1969, pp. 350–371.

Solow, R., "Technical Change and the Aggregate Production Function," *The Review of Economics and Statistics*, 39, 1957, pp. 312–320.

Spitzer, J., "A Fast and Efficient Method for Estimation of Parameters in Models with the Box–Cox Transformation," *Journal of the American Statistical Association*, 77, 1982a, pp. 760–766.

Spitzer, J., "A Primer on Box–Cox Estimation," *The Review of Economics and Statistics*, 64, 1982b, pp. 307–313.

Suits, D., "Dummy Variables: Mechanics and Interpretation," *Review of Economics and Statistics*, 66, 1984, pp. 177–180.

Theil, H., *Principles of Econometrics*, New York: Wiley, 1977.

Thompson, M., "Some Results on the Statistical Properties of an Inequality Constrained Least Squares Estimator in a Linear Model with Two Regressors," *Journal of Econometrics*, 19, 1982, pp. 215–231.

Thursby, J., and P. Schmidt, "Some Properties of Tests for Specification Error in a Linear Regression Model," *Journal of the American Statistical Association*, 72, 1977, pp. 635–641.

Wallace, T. D., and V. Ashar, "Sequential Methods in Model Construction," *Review of Economics and Statistics*, 54, 1972, pp. 172–178.

Wallace, T. D., and C. Toro-Vizcarrondo, "Tables for the Mean Squared Error Test for Exact Linear Restrictions in Regression," *Journal of the American Statistical Association*, 64 1969, pp. 1649–1663.

Zarembka, P., "Transformations of Variables in Econometrics," in P. Zarembka, ed., *Frontiers in Econometrics*, New York: Academic Press, 1974.

Zellner, A., ed., *Readings in Economic Statistics and Econometrics*, Boston: Little Brown, 1968.

Chapter 9
Data Problems

9.1. Introduction

It is rare that the data one has in hand for estimating a regression model conform exactly to the theory underlying the model. Any number of problems will arise, even in the most carefully designed survey. The most prevalent of these are the following:

1. Multicollinearity: The measured variables are too highly intercorrelated to allow precise analysis of their individual effects.
2. Missing data: There are gaps in the data set.
3. Grouped data: The information contained in the original data has been masked or censored, so that the measured data are incomplete.
4. Measurement error: The measured data do not conform to the variables in the model, either because of poor measurement or because the variables in the model are inherently unmeasurable.

All of these factors cause problems in estimating and interpreting regression models. This chapter will survey some recent results in detecting and solving these problems.

9.2. Multicollinearity

In our analysis of the classical regression model, we have assumed that the matrix of independent variables, $\mathbf{X}$, has full rank, that is, there is no exact linear relationship among the independent variables. In order for $(\mathbf{X}'\mathbf{X})^{-1}$ to exist, $\mathbf{X}$ must have full column rank. Consider the case of just two explanatory variables and a constant. For either slope coefficient,

$$\text{Var}[b_k] = \frac{\sigma^2}{(1 - r_{12}^2)\sum_i(x_{ik} - \bar{x}_k)^2} = \frac{\sigma^2}{(1 - r_{12}^2)S_{kk}}, \qquad k = 1, 2. \qquad (9-1)$$

If the two variables are perfectly correlated, the variance is infinite. The case of an exact linear relationship among the regressors is a serious failure of the assumptions of the model, not of the data. The more common case is one in which the variables are highly but not perfectly correlated. In this instance, the regression model retains all of its assumed properties, although potentially severe statistical problems arise. We consider the two cases in turn.

9.2.1. Perfect Collinearity

We first considered the possibility of perfect collinearity when we laid out the assumptions of the regression model. In a consumption function,

$$C = \beta_1 + \beta_2 \text{nonlabor income} + \beta_3 \text{salary} + \beta_4 \text{income} + \varepsilon, \qquad (9\text{-}2)$$

it is not possible to separate individual effects of the components of income and total income. In particular, if we let N be nonlabor income, S be salary, and T be total income, then $T = N + S$ for every individual. According to the model,

$$E[C] = \beta_1 + \beta_2 N + \beta_3 S + \beta_4 T.$$

But if we let q be any nonzero value and let $\beta_2' = \beta_2 + q$, $\beta_3' = \beta_3 + q$, and $\beta_4' = \beta_4 - q$,

$$E[C] = \beta_1 + \beta_2' N + \beta_3' S + \beta_4' T$$

as well for a different set of parameters. Unlike the full rank case, this one allows the same value for $E[C]$ for many different values of the parameters.

It is worth emphasizing that this is a badly specified model, and its failure has nothing to do with the quality of the data involved. The parameters of this regression model are said to be **unidentified**. We shall return to this subject at several points later. In this example, we see the hallmark of what is known as the **identification problem**. For this model, as it is specified, there are an infinite number of possible parameter vectors that are consistent with the same expected value. Thus, no matter how much data we are able to obtain, we cannot estimate the parameters. The full rank assumption can be viewed as an identification assumption; it means that for a given vector $\mathbf{x}$, there is only one set of parameters consistent with a given value of $E(y)$.

In view of the preceding, we might ask whether anything can be salvaged. The answer is that, without additional information, very little. However, there is something that can be estimated in this model. In particular, for our example, regardless of the value of q, $\beta_1 + \beta_3$ will always equal $\beta_1' + \beta_3'$ and $\beta_2 + \beta_3$ will always equal $\beta_2' + \beta_3'$. It would appear that at least these combinations of the parameters can be estimated. A general result is that if $\mathbf{w}$ is a linear combination of the rows of $\mathbf{X}'\mathbf{X}$, then $\mathbf{w}'\boldsymbol{\beta}$ is a unique and estimable combination of the parameters.[1] Unfortunately, $\mathbf{w}'\boldsymbol{\beta}$ will rarely have any useful interpretation.

9.2.2. Near Multicollinearity

In the short-rank case, the regressor matrix has K columns but only rank $L < K$. It follows from the result given earlier that only L functions of the parameters can be estimated. The significance of this is that in the K columns of $\mathbf{X}$, there are only L independent sources of variation. Hence, the data permit only L estimable functions of the parameters. It is much more common for the variables to be correlated, but not perfectly so. The case of near collinearity or high intercorrelation among the variables is, in contrast, a statistical problem. The difficulty in estimation is not one of identification but of precision. The higher the correlation between the regressors becomes, the less precise our estimates will be.

---

[1] See, for example, Theil (1971) and Schmidt (1976, pp. 43–44).

9.2.3. The Symptoms of Multicollinearity

When the regressors are highly correlated, we often observe the following problems:

1. Small changes in the data can produce wide swings in the parameter estimates.
2. Coefficients may have very high standard errors and low significance levels in spite of the fact that they are jointly highly significant and the R^2 in the regression is quite high.
3. Coefficients will have the wrong sign or an implausible magnitude.

EXAMPLE 9.1. The Longley data analyzed in Section 7.3 are notorious for severe multicollinearity. Look, for example, at the last year of the data set. The last observation does not appear to be unusual. However, the results listed in Table 9.1, in which the earlier regression is reestimated without the last year of the data, suggest how severe the multicollinearity problem is in these data. The change in the results that occurs when one year of the data is dropped is dramatic. The last coefficient rises by 600 percent and the third rises by 800 percent. One might reach very different conclusions, depending on when the data were drawn.

In the inverse matrix, $(\mathbf{X'X})^{-1}$, the kth diagonal element (where we let k equal one for convenience) is

$$(\mathbf{x_1'M_2x_1})^{-1} = (\mathbf{x_1'x_1} - \mathbf{x_1'X_2(X_2'X_2)^{-1}X_2'x_1})^{-1}$$

$$= \left(\mathbf{x_1'x_1} \left(1 - \frac{\mathbf{x_1'X_2(X_2'X_2)^{-1}X_2'x_1}}{\mathbf{x_1'x_1}} \right) \right)^{-1} \qquad (9-3)$$

$$= \frac{1}{S_{11}(1 - R_{1.}^2)}.$$

$R_{1.}^2$ is the R^2 in the regression of $\mathbf{x_1}$ on the other independent variables in the regression. Therefore, in the multiple regression, the variance of b_1 is

$$\text{Var}[b_1] = \frac{\sigma^2}{(1 - R_{1.}^2)S_{11}}. \qquad (9-4)$$

We can envision a case in which we add a variable to the regression that is highly correlated with $\mathbf{x_1}$. S_{11} will not change at all, while R_1^2 will rise and $\text{Var}[b_1]$ will rise correspondingly.

The role of these $R_{k.}^2$'s is considerable. The simple correlations among the variables may not give an adequate indication of the problem. For a particular variable, Leamer (1978,

Table 9.1. Dependent Variable: Total Employment

	1947–1961	1947–1962
Constant	1459400	1169090
Year	−721.76	−576.464
GNP deflator	−181.12	−19.761
GNP	0.091068	0.064394
Armed forces	−0.074937	−0.010145

p. 179) suggests the following measure of the effect of multicollinearity:

$$c_2(b_k) = \left\{ \frac{[\sum_i (x_{ik} - \bar{x}_k)^2]^{-1}}{[(X'X)_{kk}^{-1}]} \right\}^{1/2}. \tag{9-5}$$

This measure is the square root of the ratio of the true variances of b_k when estimated with and without the other variables. If x_k were uncorrelated with the other variables, $c_2(b_k)$ would be 1. Otherwise, $c_2(b_k)$ is equivalent to $(1 - R_{k.}^2)^{1/2}$, which again suggests the usefulness of the auxiliary coefficients of determination. For example, our results thus far suggest that the coefficient on "armed forces" is being adversely affected by multicollinearity. However, the three simple correlations of this variable with "Year," "GNP deflator," and "GNP" are 0.417, 0.465, and 0.446, which are not particularly high. But, the corresponding R^2 in the regression of "armed forces" on these three variables is only 0.3562, so, evidently, yet more analysis is called for.[2]

We might observe that, regardless of the degree of multicollinearity, as long as X has full column rank, the least squares estimator continues to be *Best Linear Unbiased*. Therefore, the first effect noted earlier is, perhaps, of secondary concern. (We have done the best we can; it just doesn't happen to be very good.) Our primary concern might be the imprecision of our estimates. One rule of thumb that has been suggested is that we should be concerned about multicollinearity if the overall R^2 in the regression is less than any of the individual R_i^2's we have been considering.[3] The *estimated* variance of the kth coefficient (assuming that the constant term is the first) is

$$\text{Est. Var}[b_k] = \frac{s^2}{(1 - R_{k.}^2)S_{kk}} = \frac{(1 - R^2)S_{yy}}{(n - K)(1 - R_{k.}^2)S_{kk}}, \qquad k = 2, \ldots, K. \tag{9-6}$$

This shows the interaction of the two coefficients of determination. For our sample data, the overall R^2 is 0.97352, while the four coefficients of determination for the regressions of each independent variable on the other regressors are 0.99303, 0.98679, 0.99245, and 0.35616. On the basis of this criterion, we conclude that multicollinearity in these data is, indeed, a problem. The auxiliary R^2's of 0.99 for the first three variables are extremely high. Of course, this rule is only suggestive. It gives no indication of how to proceed. The second most volatile of the coefficients was that on "armed forces." But the R_i^2 for the "armed forces" variable is only 0.35616, so in spite of the obvious problem with this coefficient, the rule of thumb appears not to pick it up.

An alternative measure of multicollinearity has been suggested by Belsley et al. (1980). The condition number of a matrix is the square root of the ratio of the largest to the smallest characteristic root:

$$\gamma = \left(\frac{\lambda_{\max}}{\lambda_{\min}} \right)^{1/2}. \tag{9-7}$$

Belsley et al. suggest computing this ratio for the moment matrix, $X'X$. Since the roots are dependent on the scaling of the data, we first normalize the data by dividing each column in X by $\sqrt{x_1'x_i}$.[4] If the regressors are orthogonal (so that R_i^2 will be zero for all i), γ will be one. The

---

[2] The *multiple correlation* is the square root of this value, 0.5968.

[3] See, for example, Klein (1962).

[4] For computational purposes, the correct matrix is obtained by the product $S(X'X)S$, where S is a diagonal matrix with $1/\sqrt{x_i'x_i}$ on the diagonals.

greater the intercorrelation among the variables, the higher will be the condition number. Belsley et al. suggest that values in excess of 20 suggest potential problems.

EXAMPLE 9.2. Condition Number.   The characteristic roots of the normalized 5×5 matrix for the Longley data are

$$4.9199, \quad 0.045008, \quad 0.034928, \quad 0.0001253, \quad 0.0000387.$$

Thus, the condition number for these data is 356.6. This confirms what we have already suspected.

The results thus far suggest that the coefficient on "armed forces" is adversely affected by multicollinearity. But in the regression on the full data set (all 16 observations), the t ratio on the "armed forces" coefficient is -0.033, indicating that this coefficient is not significantly different from zero by any standard. A 95 percent confidence interval for the coefficient would be $[-0.6794, 0.6691]$, which is quite wide. Apparently, the range of variation we observed in this coefficient was simply due to the fact that it does not really have much explanatory power in the regression, and we merely observed sampling variation.

The point just noted has been the source of some confusion in the literature. It is tempting to conclude that a variable has a low t ratio, or is insignificant, because of multicollinearity. One might (some authors have) then conclude that if the data were not collinear, the coefficient would be significantly different from zero. Of course, this is not necessarily true. Sometimes a coefficient turns out to be insignificant because the variable does not have any explanatory power in the model. Moreover, in nonexperimental data, the suggestion that the results might be different if the data were not collinear has little practical value.

9.2.4.   Solutions to the Multicollinearity Problem

Several methods have been proposed for coping with multicollinearity. The obvious remedy (and surely the most frequently used) is to drop variables suspected of causing the problem from the regression. Of course, in so doing, one encounters the problems of specification analyzed in Section 8.4. A number of other approaches have been suggested. Before considering them, it is worth making a few observations about our predicament. Under the assumptions of the regression model, the least squares estimator (assuming that it exists) is the best unbiased estimator of the parameters. The problem with multicollinearity is that "best" is not very good.

One approach to the problem involves the incorporation of additional information. One might argue, however, that if such information were available at the outset, we ought to have used it before discovering the problem of multicollinearity. The situations in which such useful outside information is available are, unfortunately, rare in any event.

Another possibility for improvement within the confines of the model is to find a slightly biased estimator with a much smaller variance, that is, one with a smaller mean-squared error. Unfortunately, the distributions of such estimators, at least the ones that have been devised thus far, depend on unknown parameters. This puts us back where we started. Most of the "solutions" we shall discuss involve trading our unbiased estimator for a biased one about which our ability to make statistical inferences will be limited.[5]

---

[5] Nonetheless, this idea has produced a large and insightful literature. An up-to-date summary for econometrics appears in Judge et al. (1985).

9.2.4a. Ridge Regression

Two purely mechanical solutions have been proposed for dealing with the most obvious problem of multicollinearity, the large standard errors of the estimates. The ridge regression estimator is

$$\mathbf{b}_r = [\mathbf{X}'\mathbf{X} + k\mathbf{I}]^{-1}\mathbf{X}'\mathbf{y}, \tag{9-8}$$

where the scalar k is chosen arbitrarily.[6] In application, k is to be chosen in such a way that the resulting estimates are "stable," presumably with respect to small variations in k. The authors of the technique suggest that a small value be chosen at the outset, say 0.01, and then that successively larger values be tried until the coefficients stabilize. In its favor, it is easily shown that although the ridge estimator is biased,

$$E[\mathbf{b}_r] = [\mathbf{X}'\mathbf{X} + k\mathbf{I}]^{-1}\mathbf{X}'\mathbf{X}\beta,$$

its variance,

$$\text{Var}[\mathbf{b}_r] = \sigma^2[\mathbf{X}'\mathbf{X} + k\mathbf{I}]^{-1}(\mathbf{X}'\mathbf{X})[\mathbf{X}'\mathbf{X} + k\mathbf{I}]^{-1}, \tag{9-9}$$

is smaller than that of the ordinary least squares estimator.[7]

   EXAMPLE 9.4. Ridge Estimation.   Using the Longley data to pursue our example, we obtain the results given in Table 9.2 for the ridge estimator for various values of k (estimates of the constant term are omitted):

Table 9.2

	Year	Deflator	GNP	Armed Forces
$K = 0$ (OLS)	−576.46	−19.761	0.064394	−0.010145
$K = .0000001$	−564.21	−25.773	0.064439	−0.004397
$K = .000001$	−121.19	−81.751	0.048952	0.12188
$K = .00001$	−8.1198	−96.038	0.044999	0.15411
$K = .0001$	25.914	−100.34	0.043809	0.16381
$k = .001$	29.395	−100.78	0.043687	0.16480
$K = .01$	29.741	−100.77	0.043669	0.16488
$K = .1$	29.767	−100.49	0.043639	0.16477
$K = .2$	29.757	−100.10	0.043598	0.16460
$K = .3$	29.747	−99.768	0.043563	0.16445

Estimated Standard Errors of Estimates

OLS	433.48	138.89	0.01995	0.30856
Ridge	3.848	124.84	0.01323	0.28194

As expected, the estimates eventually do stabilize. However, the value of $k = 0.3$ is quite a bit higher than is typically found, and the final values, with the exception of the coefficient on "GNP," are quite unlike the original least squares values. The standard errors of the ridge

---

[6] See Hoerl and Kennard (1970) and extensive discussion in Judge et al. (1985, pp. 912–922).
[7] The proof is left as an exercise.

estimates based on $k = 0.3$ are not radically different from their OLS counterparts. (The original OLS value of s^2 is used to compute the variances for the ridge estimates.[8])

The ridge estimator may have a smaller mean-squared error than ordinary least squares.[9] Unfortunately, this mean-squared error is a function of the unknown parameters that we are trying to estimate (here, with a clear bias). Thus, this is unlikely to be a useful criterion. Economists have avoided use of this estimator, perhaps because of their aversion to biased estimators and partly because of the difficulty it presents for statistical inference. Unlike our earlier case of omitted variables, in this case, we have an unbiased estimate of σ^2, that obtained from the OLS regression with k equal to zero. Still, it is difficult to attach much meaning to hypothesis tests about an estimator that is biased in an unknown direction.

9.2.4b. Principal Components

A second approach that offers somewhat more intuitive appeal is that of principal componets. Referring back to our discussion of exact collinearity, we considered the problem that although the data matrix has K columns, it may have fewer than K truly independent sources of information, that is, variation. We can carry the same reasoning over to the full rank case. Even though the $\mathbf{X}$ matrix may have full rank, if there is substantial collinearity, we may still believe that there is only a limited number of independent sources of variation. The use of principal components is an attempt to extract from the $\mathbf{X}$ matrix a small number of variables that, in some sense, account for most or all of the variation in $\mathbf{X}$.

Algebraically, we may approach the calculation of principal components as a regression problem: "What linear function of the columns of $\mathbf{X}$ gives the best fit (highest R^2) when it is regressed on all of the columns of $\mathbf{X}$?" It can be shown that if this linear function is

$$\mathbf{z}_1 = \mathbf{Xc}_1,$$

the vector of coefficients, $\mathbf{c}_1$, is the characteristic vector of $\mathbf{X'X}$ associated with λ_1, the largest characteristic root. If the total variation in $\mathbf{X}$ is defined to be the trace of $\mathbf{X'X}$, the proportion of the variation in $\mathbf{X'X}$ explained by this variable is

$$w_1 = \frac{\lambda_1}{\sum_k \lambda_k}.$$

This exercise can be repeated by seeking a second linear combination of the columns of $\mathbf{X}$ with the same criterion, subject to the condition that this second variable be orthogonal to the first. There are K such variables, the kth computed using the characteristic vector corresponding to the kth largest characteristic root.

If we use all K principal components, we end up exactly where we started. This would amount to regressing $\mathbf{y}$ on K linear combinations of the columns of $\mathbf{X}$. The point of the exercise is to use a small number of principal components, so that the sum of their contributions is satisfactorily close to one.

---

[8] Why not use the sum of squares associated with the ridge estimator?

[9] Schmidt (1976, pp. 48–55) proves that there is always a k such that the trace of the mean-squared error matrix for the ridge estimator is smaller than that for least squares. Since this k depends on both β and σ^2, it is unlikely to be of much practical use.

EXAMPLE 9.5. **Principal Components.**   The decomposition of the $X'X$ matrix for the Longley data yields the following characteristic vectors associated with the characteristic roots (Table 9.3).

Table 9.3

	Characteristic Roots			
4.9199	0.045008	0.034928	0.0001253	0.0000387

	Characteristic Vectors = Weights in z_j			
Constant	0.0	0.00022015	0.000467	0.0	1.0000
Year	0.0047513	0.42607	0.90416	−0.030636	0.0
Deflator	0.0002533	0.013451	0.027528	0.99953	0.0
GNP	0.99997	−0.0079208	−0.0015258	−0.0001048	0.0
Armed forces	0.0065145	0.90456	−0.42630	−0.0004335	0.0

Fully 98.4 percent (4.9199/5) of the variation in this X is explained by the first principal component, which is, in fact, only trivially different from GNP. The second and third components are orthogonal combinations of "Year" and "Armed forces," while the fourth is the deflator. As might be predicted, the last component is the constant term. It is noteworthy (and a bit unusual) that, in these data, save for the second and third, the principal components are essentially the original variables.

Suppose that of the K columns of X, we use $L < K$ principal components. Thus, we regress y on $Z = XC_L$, where C_L is a $K \times L$ matrix containing L characteristic vectors of $X'X$. The estimator is

$$d = (Z'Z)^{-1}Z'y. \qquad (9\text{--}10)$$

From the definitions of characteristic roots and vectors,

$$Z'Z = C'_L X'X C_L = \Lambda_L,$$

where Λ_L is the $L \times L$ matrix that contains the L largest characteristic roots of $X'X$ on its diagonal. Also,

$$Z'y = C'_L X'y = C'_L X'Xb,$$

but

$$C'_L X'X = \Lambda_L C'_L.$$

Therefore, if we use L principal components, the resulting estimate is just a function of the OLS values.[10] By making the preceding substitutions,

$$d = C'_L b. \qquad (9\text{--}11)$$

That is, there is no need actually to compute the principal components z_1; we need only to decompose the moment matrix.

---

[10] Algebraically, one can do the entire analysis of principal components with just the results of ordinary least squares and the characteristic roots and vectors of $X'X$.

Like the ridge estimator, the principal components estimator is a biased estimator that may be more precise than its OLS counterpart. If we insert our estimate, $\mathbf{d}$, in the original formulation, we obtain the fitted values

$$\hat{\mathbf{y}} = \mathbf{Zd} = \mathbf{XC}_L\mathbf{d},$$

so we may view the principal components estimator of the full coefficient vector as

$$\mathbf{b}_p = \mathbf{C}_L\mathbf{d} = \mathbf{C}_L\mathbf{C}'_L\mathbf{b},$$

where $\mathbf{b}$ is the original OLS estimator. Since $\mathbf{b}$ is unbiased, this competing estimator is clearly biased.[11] However, its variance matrix is unambiguously smaller than the variance of $\mathbf{b}$.[12]

There are three problems with using this estimator. First, the results are quite sensitive to the scale of measurement in the variables. The obvious remedy is to standardize the variables, but, unfortunately, this has substantial effects on the computed results. Second, the principal components are not chosen on the basis of any relationship of the regressors to $\mathbf{y}$, the variable we are attempting to explain. Lastly, the calculation makes ambiguous the interpretation of the results. The principal components estimator is a mixture of all of the original coefficients. It is unlikely that we shall be able to interpret these combinations in any meaningful way.

9.3. Missing Observations

It is fairly common for a data set to have gaps, for a variety of reasons. Perhaps the most common occurrence of this problem is in survey data, in which it often happens that respondents simply fail to answer the questions. In a time series, the data may be missing because they do not exist at the frequency we wish to observe them; the model may specify monthly relationships, but some variables are observed only on a quarterly basis. There is a qualitative difference between the cross-section and time-series problems, and the solutions (to the extent that there are solutions) are quite different as well. We shall, therefore, treat the two issues separately.

There are two possible cases to consider, depending on why the data are missing. One is that the data are simply unavailable, for reasons unknown to the analyst and unrelated to the fact that other observations in the sample are complete. If this is the case, the complete observations in the sample constitute a usable data set, and the only issue is what possibly helpful information could be salvaged from the incomplete observations. Griliches (1986) calls this the *ignorable case* in that, for purposes of estimation, if we are not concerned with efficiency, we may simply ignore the problem. A second case, which has recently attracted a great deal of attention in the econometrics literature, is that in which the gaps in the data set are not benign but are systematically related to the phenomenon being modeled. This happens most often in surveys when the data are self-selected.[13] For example, if a survey were designed to study expenditure patterns and high-income individuals tended to withhold

---

[11] It is not biased if $\mathbf{C}_L\mathbf{C}'_L = \mathbf{I}$. Could this happen?

[12] Fomby et al. (1978) show that we can view the principal components estimator as a restricted least squares estimator with the property that its variance matrix has a smaller trace than that of any other restricted least squares estimator with the same number of restrictions. The small variance is, of course, a virtue, but because the estimator is biased, the relative size of its mean-squared error remains ambiguous.

[13] The vast surveys of Americans' opinions about sex by Ann Landers (*Chicago Tribune*, 1984, passim) and Hite (1987) constitute two celebrated studies that were surely tainted by a heavy dose of self-selection bias. The latter was pilloried in numerous publications for purporting to represent the population at large instead of the opinions of those strongly enough inclined to respond to the survey. The first was presented with much greater modesty.

information about their income, the gaps in the data set would represent more than just missing information. In this case, the complete observations would be qualitatively different. We treat this second case in Chapter 21, so we shall defer our discussion until later.

The early work on the subject of missing data concentrated primarily on the ignorable case.[14] The data in this instance may usefully be partitioned into three subsets:

$$y = X\beta + \varepsilon$$

for all observations, but the data are

$$y_A \, X_A \cdots n_A \text{ complete observations,}$$

$$-X_B \cdots n_B \text{ observations missing } y_B,$$

and

$$y_C - \cdots n_C \text{ observations missing } X_C.$$

In the third case, if X_C contains multiple regressors, we suppose that only some of the observations on some of the variables are missing. As noted, since this case is ignorable, the least squares regression of y_A on X_A produces estimates of β that have all of the usual properties. The various schemes for dealing with missing data concern how to fill the gaps in some way in order to use whatever information may be contained in the latter two sets. The question is solely one of efficiency and lost information.

Consider, first, case B, in which data on y are missing. Any method devised to utilize X_B will have to employ some predictor of y_B, so let $\hat{y}_B$ be that predictor. At this point, we leave unspecified just what that might be; some possibilities will be noted. The least squares slope vector in this "filled" data set is

$$b_f = \left[\begin{bmatrix} X_A \\ X_B \end{bmatrix}' \begin{bmatrix} X_A \\ X_B \end{bmatrix} \right]^{-1} \begin{bmatrix} X_A' y_A \\ X_B' \hat{y}_B \end{bmatrix}.$$

We can write this as

$$b_f = [X_A'X_A + X_B'X_B]^{-1}[X_A'y_A + X_B'\hat{y}_B].$$

Recall the normal equation for the multiple regression model,

$$X'Xb = X'y.$$

Let b_A be the least squares slopes in a regression that uses only the observations in group A, and define b_B likewise for the group B, using $\hat{y}_B$. Then we may write

$$b_f = [X_A'X_A + X_B'X_B]^{-1}[X_A'X_A b_A + X_B'X_B b_B] \tag{9-12}$$

$$= Fb_A + (I - F)b_B,$$

where

$$F = [X_A'X_A + X_B'X_B]^{-1}X_A'X_A.$$

This is a *matrix weighted average* of two least squares estimators. Now

$$E[b_f] = F\beta + (I - F)E[b_B], \tag{9-13}$$

---

[14] Afifi and Elashoff (1966, 1967, 1969), Haitovsky (1968), Anderson (1967), and Kelejian (1969) are a few of the major works.

which will equal β only if $\mathbf{b}_B$ is unbiased. A weighted average of an unbiased estimator and some other estimator can be unbiased only if the other estimator is unbiased as well. Therefore, we can draw a conclusion:

> Any scheme that purports to obtain an unbiased
> estimate by filling in missing values of the
> dependent variable must do so in such a way that
> a regression using only the filled observations
> would produce an unbiased estimator.[15]

This may be a tall order. Two schemes that have been suggested are as follows:

1. A *zero-order* regression: Replace the missing values in $\mathbf{y}_B$ with the mean of the complete observations in $\mathbf{y}_A$. Then the estimator using only the filled observations will be

$$\mathbf{b}_B = [\mathbf{X}_B'\mathbf{X}_B]^{-1}\mathbf{X}_B'\mathbf{i}\bar{y}_A,$$

where $\mathbf{i}$ is a column of n_B ones. But

$$\bar{y}_A = \bar{\mathbf{x}}_A'\boldsymbol{\beta} + \bar{\varepsilon}_A,$$

so

$$\mathbf{b}_B = [\mathbf{X}_B'\mathbf{X}_B]^{-1}\mathbf{X}_B'[\mathbf{i}\bar{\mathbf{x}}_A'\boldsymbol{\beta} + \bar{\varepsilon}_A\mathbf{i}].$$

The expected value of $\bar{\varepsilon}$ is zero. Also,

$$\mathbf{X}_B'\mathbf{i} = n_B\bar{\mathbf{x}}_B.$$

But

$$n_B[\mathbf{X}_B'\mathbf{X}_B]^{-1}\bar{\mathbf{x}}_B\bar{\mathbf{x}}_A' \neq \mathbf{I},$$

so this estimator fails the test.[16] There is another, perhaps more intuitive reason for this finding. Consider a simple regression with only a single regressor. If β is not zero, there is some covariation between y and x. Suppose that it is positive. Then high values of x are associated with high values of y. But if we replace every missing y_B with $\bar{y}_A$, high values of x_B do not imply higher values of these $\bar{y}$'s, even in expectation. Therefore, the higher the value of x_B, the larger is the disturbance at this observation. The regressor and the disturbance are, therefore, not independent for these observations. When this is the case, the least squares estimator is biased, which is what we found earlier.

2. A *first-order* regression: Use the A group to estimate β: then estimate $\mathbf{y}_B$ with $= \mathbf{X}_B\mathbf{b}_A$. This method passes the test of unbiasedness and appears to bring a gain in efficiency. But the gain in efficiency from using these fitted values may be illusory.[17] In finding the variance of the "mixed" estimator, we must account for the additional variation present in the predicted values.

Other suggestions have been made. In general, not much is known about the properties of estimators based on predicted values of y. Those results we do have are largely from

---

[15] If there are too few incomplete observations to compute the regression, it suffices for the expected value of each y_{Bi} to be $\mathbf{x}_i'\boldsymbol{\beta}$.

[16] The conclusion to the contrary drawn by Kmenta (1986, p. 385) is in error. In his ratio, even if the means are the same, there are different numbers of observations in the numerator and denominator. What he does show is that the estimator is biased toward zero, which makes sense in view of the next result.

[17] See Kosobud (1963) and Kelejian (1969).

simulation studies based on a particular data set or pattern of missing data. The results of these *Monte Carlo studies* are usually difficult to generalize. The overall conclusion seems to be that in a single-equation regression context, filling in missing values of y is not a good idea.

For the case of missing data in the regressors, it helps to consider the simple regression and multiple regression cases separately. In the first instance, X_C has two columns: the column of ones for the constant and a column of blanks where the missing data would be if we had them. As before, several schemes have been suggested for filling the blanks. The zero-order method of replacing each missing x in group C with $\bar{x}_A$ results in no changes and is equivalent to dropping the incomplete data. There are several ways to prove this, but the simplest is to observe that if each of the missing observations is equal to $\bar{x}_A$, then $\bar{x}$ for the full sample is equal to $\bar{x}_A$, and each term in $\Sigma(x - \bar{x})^2$ and $\Sigma(x - \bar{x})(y - \bar{y})$ that corresponds to one of these constructed observations is a zero. Therefore, the sample moments upon which the regression is computed are unchanged. Unfortunately, the R^2 will be lower, since even though the numerator in $b^2 S_{xx}/S_{yy}$ is unchanged, the denominator is increased by the new observations that have been brought into the sum. We conclude that there is no gain in the estimation of β, and the cost is to bring a poor fit for the constructed data. An alternative, *modified zero-order regression*, is to fill the second column of X_C with zeros and add a dummy variable that takes the value one for missing observations and zero for complete ones.[18] We leave it as an exercise to show that this is algebraically identical to simply filling the gaps with $\bar{x}_a$. Lastly, there is the possibility of computing fitted values for the missing x's by a regression of x on y in the complete data. The sampling properties of the resulting estimator are largely unknown, but what evidence there is suggests that this is not a beneficial way to proceed.[19]

Thus far, the picture is quite pessimistic. The best we have done is to present a case in which no harm was done. However, in a multiple regression, there is scope for culling some useful information from the incomplete observations. Consider a regression with just two regressors to illustrate the point.[20] The model is

$$y = \beta x + \gamma z + \varepsilon.$$

Suppose that it were valid to posit a linear relationship between x and z.[21] Then if, in addition

$$x = \delta z + u,$$

the model may be written in three equations:

$$y_A = \beta x_A + \gamma z_A + \varepsilon_A,$$

$$x_A = \delta z_A + u_A,$$

$$y_C = (\beta + \gamma\delta)z_C + \varepsilon_C + \beta u_C.$$

Each of the first two can be estimated by ordinary least squares. Let $\hat{x}_C$ be the predicted values of the missing x's obtained by using $\hat{\delta}_A$ and z_C. Consider combining the two data sets in one regression model:

$$\begin{bmatrix} y_A - \hat{\beta}_a x_A \\ y_C - \hat{\beta}_a \hat{x}_C \end{bmatrix} = \gamma \begin{bmatrix} z_A \\ z_C \end{bmatrix} + v.$$

---

[18] See Maddala (1977, p. 202).
[19] Afifi and Elashoff (1966) and Haitovsky (1968).
[20] This set of results is presented in much greater detail in Griliches (1986).
[21] In the case of nonstochastic regressors, this will only be descriptive; if the regressors are stochastic, it characterizes their joint distribution.

The compound disturbance, **v**, is a hodgepodge of the original disturbances and the sampling errors in estimation of β, γ, and δ. Assuming (correctly) that **v** and **z** are uncorrelated (at least asymptotically), γ can be estimated by least squares. At this point, the important thing to note is that although we have done nothing to the original estimate of β, some new information is being used to estimate γ in the second regression, which can be expected to provided added efficiency. Griliches provides additional results. The overall conclusion is that even though there may be a still more efficient way to use the same data, *there is some possibility that this estimator may outperform least squares, omitting group C*. In a multiple regression, there is information about the covariation between the regressors with complete data and the dependent variable that is not used if these observations are discarded. The problem is to use that information in such a way that the influence of the other variables is partialed out. The preceding illustrates one possibility.

We complete this discussion of the ignorable case with an observation about time-series data. In this setting, *interpolation* may be a more appropriate term than *filling*. It also suggests that, at least in some respects, the time-series case is a bit more promising. Suppose, for example, that we have a quarterly series and require monthly data. A common approach is simply to allocate the quarterly change in three parts to successive months so as to reproduce the movement in equal steps. There are, however, much more elaborate models, which fall under the heading of *ARIMA*, or *Box–Jenkins* (1982) models, that can be used for filling the adjacent unobserved data points. This may be done with the original series or with a parallel series, such as interpolating some components of an investment series with an aggregate value. The important element in this exercise is the continuity of some underlying process in adjacent observations that is missing in the cross-section case. In this instance, variants on the regression procedure we used are much more defensible.

9.4. Grouped Data

Reporting agencies often release only group mean data to preserve the anonymity of the constituents. Data are *censored* when a range of values that contains the actual value rather than the value itself is given. For example, rather than ask for income, surveys often request only the income category in which respondent falls. As a practical matter, to ease the burden of computation, it may make sense to analyze group means even if the original ungrouped data are available. There are two changes that generally occur as a result of this form of data aggregation:

1. The parameter estimates are less efficient, due to the loss of information.
2. The fit of the regression improves, sometimes dramatically.

Suppose that the usual regression model,

$$\mathbf{y} = \mathbf{X}\beta + \varepsilon, \tag{9-14}$$

applies to a full data set and that a preassigned grouping allocates the n observations into G groups, with $n_1, n_2, \ldots, n_G$ observations in them. For the n_g observations in group g, the same model applies, so for them, that is, for these particular rows of (9–14),

$$\mathbf{y}_g = \mathbf{X}_g\beta + \varepsilon_g. \tag{9-15}$$

These n_g observations are collapsed into a single observation, $[\bar{y}_g, \bar{x}_{1g}, \ldots, \bar{x}_{Kg}]$ by premultiplying by the $n_g \times 1$ vector, $(1/n_g)\mathbf{i}'$. Applying this to (9–15), we obtain

$$\frac{1}{n_g}\mathbf{i}'\mathbf{y}_g = \frac{1}{n_g}\mathbf{i}'\mathbf{X}_g\boldsymbol{\beta} + \frac{1}{n_g}\mathbf{i}'\boldsymbol{\varepsilon}_g,$$

which implies that

$$\bar{y}_g = \bar{\mathbf{x}}_g'\boldsymbol{\beta} + \bar{\varepsilon}_g. \tag{9–16}$$

The same regression model applies to each group mean as well. Assuming that G is larger than K, we can stack these observations in G rows in

$$\bar{\mathbf{y}} = \bar{\mathbf{X}}\boldsymbol{\beta} + \bar{\boldsymbol{\varepsilon}}.$$

Each element of $\bar{\boldsymbol{\varepsilon}}$ has mean zero, and it is easy to verify that the conditions necessary for least squares to be unbiased are met here. In principle, we need go no further. Least squares continues to be unbiased. Given the convenience of using the smaller number of observations, why not do this routinely?

Each element of $\bar{\boldsymbol{\varepsilon}}$ is $\bar{\varepsilon}_g = (1/n_g)(\varepsilon_{g1} + \varepsilon_{g2} + \cdots + \varepsilon_{gn_g})$, which has mean zero and variance σ^2/n_g. Therefore, one of the conditions of the classical regression model, equal variances across the disturbances, is not met here unless all of the groups have the same number of members. However, if we just multiply both sides of (9–16) by $\sqrt{n_g}$, the disturbance, say $\bar{\varepsilon}^* = \sqrt{n_g}\bar{\varepsilon}_g$, has variance σ^2 for all g. Therefore, a slightly modified model,

$$\bar{y}_g^* = \bar{\mathbf{x}}_g^{*\prime}\boldsymbol{\beta} + \bar{\varepsilon}_g^*, \tag{9–16'}$$

fits all of the assumptions of the classical regression model. Least squares regression of $\bar{y}_g^*$ on $\bar{\mathbf{x}}_g^*$ gives the best linear unbiased estimate of $\boldsymbol{\beta}$, given the data (i.e., the group means) in hand.[22] (We emphasize the qualification because, as we will show, we would do better yet if we had the original data.) Collecting the G observations in $\bar{\mathbf{X}}^*$ and $\bar{\mathbf{y}}^*$, the least squares estimator is

$$\mathbf{b}^* = [\bar{\mathbf{X}}^{*\prime}\bar{\mathbf{X}}^*]^{-1}[\bar{\mathbf{X}}^{*\prime}\bar{\mathbf{y}}^*] = \left[\sum_g n_g \bar{\mathbf{x}}_g \bar{\mathbf{x}}_g'\right]^{-1}\left[\sum_g n_g \bar{\mathbf{x}}_g \bar{y}_g\right]. \tag{9–17}$$

Note that the efficient estimator is obtained by multiplying each "observation" (i.e., group mean) by the respective group size. In effect, this replicates each group mean observation n_g times.

Obviously, the estimator in (9–17) is different from the one that would result if the original data were used. But it remains to be shown that any loss in efficiency has occurred. Let $\mathbf{H}$ be the $G \times n$ matrix that transforms the entire sample to $\bar{y}_g^*$ and $\bar{\mathbf{x}}_g^*$. $\mathbf{H}$ would appear

$$\mathbf{H} = \begin{bmatrix} \frac{1}{\sqrt{n_1}}(1 \; 1 \; \cdots \; 1) & (0 \; 0 \; \cdots \; 0) & \cdots & (0 \; 0 \; \cdots \; 0) \\ (0 \; 0 \; \cdots \; 0) & \frac{1}{\sqrt{n_2}}(1 \; 1 \; \cdots \; 1) & \cdots & (0 \; 0 \; \cdots \; 0) \\ & & \vdots & \\ (0 \; 0 \; \cdots \; 0) & (0 \; 0 \; \cdots \; 0) & \cdots & \frac{1}{\sqrt{n_G}}(1 \; 1 \; \cdots \; 1) \end{bmatrix}.$$

---

[22] This is an example of weighted least squares in a heteroscedastic regression model. The model is analyzed in greater detail in Chapter 14. This particular application is somewhat different from the usual case of heteroscedasticity in that the unequal variances arise as a consequence of the data construction rather than as a part of the structure of the model.

Since $\bar{X}^* = HX$ and the classical regression model applies to (9–16′), the variance matrix of b^* in (9–17) is

$$\text{Var}[b^*] = \sigma^2[X'H'HX]^{-1}. \tag{9-18}$$

To show that this is no smaller than $\sigma^2(X'X)^{-1}$, the variance matrix of the estimator for the ungrouped data, it is much easier to show that the inverse of the matrix in (9–18) is *no larger* than $X'X$. The difference is

$$X'X - X'H'HX = X'(I - H'H)X. \tag{9-19}$$

All that must be shown is that $(I - H'H)$ is positive semidefinite, which can easily be done by showing that $(I - H'H)$ is idempotent.[23] You can do this just by multiplying it out. The conclusion is that the best use of the group means will never be better than using the original data and may be worse.

The larger is the difference matrix in (9–19), the greater is the information loss in the grouped data. The kmth element of this difference matrix is

$$(X'(I - H'H)X)_{km} = \sum_{g=1}^{G}\left[\left(\sum_{i=1}^{n_g} x_{ik}x_{im}\right) - n_g \bar{x}_k \bar{x}_m\right]. \tag{9-20}$$

This is the within-groups variation in the language of the analysis of variance. It is no surprise that this is the result that emerges. The greater the variation within the groups that is discarded by replacing individual elements with group means, the greater will be the information loss.[24]

An interesting effect on the fit of the regression arises when group mean data are used. Cramer's classic (1964) study on the subject provides a good example. A subset of his results is given in Example 9.6.

EXAMPLE 9.6. Regressions Based on Group Mean Data. The results shown in Table 9.4 are reported in Cramer (op. cit.). The slope estimate is on income in an Engel curve.

Table 9.4

	Observations 278			
	Groups: six of 5, 26, 73, 106, 52, and 16			
	Slope		R^2	
Commodity	Ungrouped	Grouped	Ungrouped	Grouped
Oranges	16.87	16.84	0.242	0.968
Eggs	139.20	142.06	0.234	0.972
Apples	21.35	21.47	0.165	0.924
Butter	39.14	38.21	0.116	0.784
Cheese	29.01	30.00	0.105	0.876
Soap	3.73	3.55	0.099	0.949
Fish	14.31	15.40	0.036	0.868

[23] See result (2–116).
[24] Notice what happens to (9–20) if the observations in each group are already group averages.

There is a peculiar but potentially serious effect that can emerge if the scheme used to group the data is based on the dependent variable instead of the independent variable. Suppose, for example, that in fitting the expenditure equations, Cramer's grouping had been based on expenditure (the dependent variable) instead of income (the regressor). Then **H** would have been correlated with **y**, and hence ε. As a consequence, **HX** would have been correlated with **Hε**, and the usual biases that result when the regressor and disturbance are correlated would emerge. Example 9.7 demonstrates this result.

EXAMPLE 9.7. **The Other Regression—a Sampling Experiment.**   The following data are used to demonstrate the effect of an improper grouping scheme. They were produced with a random number generator from the standard normal distribution. The individual data conform to the model $y_i = 1 + x_i + \varepsilon_i$, where both x_i and ε_i are independent and $N[0, 1]$. The listed data are sorted keying on x and carrying y.

Table 9.5

			50 Observations on **x**				
−2.166	−2.111	−1.706	−1.664	−1.550	−1.547	−1.523	−1.322
−1.243	−1.193	−1.064	−0.793	−0.745	−0.508	−0.483	−0.322
−0.306	−0.305	−0.292	−0.174	−0.174	−0.154	−0.102	−0.057
−0.038	−0.017	−0.001	0.034	0.051	0.130	0.192	0.204
0.226	0.299	0.498	0.555	0.572	0.712	0.751	0.992
1.029	1.295	1.314	1.334	1.336	1.382	1.435	1.679
1.871	2.356						

			50 Observations on **y**				
−0.218	−3.350	−0.817	−0.870	−1.367	1.525	−1.121	1.379	−0.142
0.913	−0.242	−0.234	1.305	−2.323	−0.260	1.565	2.004	1.180
−0.987	−0.805	0.299	0.904	1.973	1.186	1.966	−0.181	0.191
2.347	1.452	1.717	2.105	1.939	3.115	2.788	2.625	2.138
3.426	2.312	1.063	3.547	1.723	2.656	1.409	3.184	3.711
2.148	2.982	0.660	2.228	2.837				

In regression 1, the data are grouped according to the values of x into five groups of 10 observations. The preceding data are sorted by the value of x, so the grouping scheme is observations 1–10, 11–20, and so on. In regression 2, the data were first sorted according to the value of y; then the same procedure was used to group them. The group means are

Table 9.6

	1	2	3	4	5
			Sorted on x		
$\bar{x}$	−1.602	−0.4999	−0.0328	0.4999	1.503
$\bar{y}$	−0.4068	0.1203	1.186	2.506	2.354

Table 9.6 (*Continued*)

	Sorted on y				
	1	2	3	4	5
$\bar{x}$	−1.107	−0.3312	−0.1775	0.4506	1.034
$\bar{y}$	−1.214	0.3256	1.444	2.116	3.087

Regression Results:	Constant	Slope	T Ratio	R^2
Individual data	1.179	1.026	6.714	0.488
1. Grouped on x	1.179	1.032	3.931	0.837
2. Grouped on y	1.204	2.002	8.153	0.957

If neither the individual data nor the grouping scheme were known, the second regression would be convincing. But given the known, true model, it is obviously far from correct.

9.5. *Measurement Error and Proxy Variables*

Thus far, it has been assumed (at least implicitly) that the data used to estimate the parameters of our models are true measurements on their theoretical counterparts. In practice, this happens only in the best of circumstances. All sorts of measurement problems creep into the data that must be used in our analyses. Even carefully constructed survey data do not always conform exactly to the variables the analysts have in mind for their regressions. Aggregate statistics such as GNP are only estimates of their theoretical counterparts, and some variables, such as depreciation, the services of capital, and *the* interest rate, do not even exist in an agreed-upon theory. At worst, there may be no physical measure corresponding to the variable in our model; intelligence, education, and permanent income are but a few examples. Nonetheless, all of them have appeared in very precisely defined regression models.

In this section, we examine some of the received results on regression analysis with badly measured data. The general assessment of the problem is not particularly optimistic. The biases introduced by measurement error can be rather severe. There are almost no known finite sample results for the models of measurement error; nearly all of the results that have been developed are asymptotic. The following presentation will use a few simple asymptotic results for the classical regression model. These are discussed in detail in the next chapter.[25] For purposes of the discussion, it is useful to summarize the essential result before proceeding.

The properties of the least squares estimator derived in the previous chapters have been obtained by analyzing the identity

$$\mathbf{b} = \boldsymbol{\beta} + [\mathbf{X'X}]^{-1}\mathbf{X'\varepsilon}. \tag{9–21}$$

---

[25] It may be useful to review the general results in Section 4.4 as well.

The unbiasedness property follows from the assumption that

$$\text{Cov}[\mathbf{X}, \varepsilon] = \mathbf{0}.$$

When this assumption is not met, it is clear that the second term in the previous equation will not be zero, and **b** will no longer estimate β. We have seen this at several points in our analysis:

1. In the analysis of specification errors in Chapter 7, the bias due to left-out variables can be cast in the framework of correlation between the included $\mathbf{X}_1$ and a disturbance consisting of $\varepsilon + \mathbf{X}_2\beta_2$.

2. In analyzing the effect of grouping, the "other regression" is a case of correlation between the regressor, y, and the disturbance.

3. The problem with certain schemes to fill in missing data on a regressor is that the filled-in data are correlated with the disturbance.

We may write (9–21) as

$$\mathbf{b} - \beta = \left[\frac{\mathbf{X}'\mathbf{X}}{n}\right]^{-1}\left[\frac{\mathbf{X}'\varepsilon}{n}\right].$$

Under most conditions, it will follow that

$$\text{plim}[\mathbf{b} - \beta] = \Sigma_{xx}\sigma_{x\varepsilon},$$

where Σ_{xx} is a positive definite matrix and $\sigma_{x\varepsilon}$ is a vector of covariances. If these covariances are not zero, least squares is inconsistent. The topics considered in this section are concerned with situations in which these covariances do not vanish even as $n \to \infty$. In the discussion, since only large-sample results are known, we assume that sample moments such as $\mathbf{X}'\mathbf{X}/n$ will converge in probability to population parameters such as Σ_{xx}. For convenience, results are cast in terms of the probability limits of sample moments. For example, we shall usually write "$\text{Cov}[x, y]$" when "the parameter estimated by $(1/n)\Sigma_i x_i y_i$" would be appropriate.

9.5.1.   One Badly Measured Variable

The simplest case to analyze is that of a regression model with a single regressor and no constant term. Although this is admittedly unrealistic, it illustrates the essential concepts, and we shall generalize it presently. Assume that the model

$$y^* = \beta x^* + \varepsilon \tag{9–22}$$

conforms to all of the assumptions of the classical normal regression model. If data on y^* and x^* were available, all of the apparatus of the classical model would apply. Suppose, however, that our observed data are only imperfectly measured versions of y^* and x^*. To put this in the context of an example, suppose that y^* is ln(output/labor) and x^* is ln(capital/labor). Neither factor input can be measured with precision, so the observed y and x contain errors of measurement. We assume that

$$y = y^* + v \qquad \text{with } v \sim N[0, \sigma_v^2] \tag{9–23a}$$

and

$$x = x^* + u \qquad \text{with } u \sim N[0, \sigma_u^2]. \tag{9–23b}$$

(We adhere to the widely used conventions of using *'s to indicate unobserved variables and omitting them on the measured variables.) Assume, as well, that u and v are independent of each other and of y^* and x^*. (As we shall see, adding these restrictions is not sufficient to rescue a bad situation.)

As a first step, insert (9–23a) in (9–22), assuming for the moment that only y^* is measured with error:

$$y = \beta x^* + \varepsilon + v$$
$$= \beta x^* + \varepsilon^*.$$

This conforms completely to the assumptions of the classical regression model. As long as the regressor is measured properly, measurement error on the dependent variable can be absorbed in the disturbance of the regression and ignored. To save some cumbersome notation, therefore, we shall henceforth assume that our measurement error problems concern only the independent variables in the model.

Consider, then, the regression of y on the observed x. By substituting (9–23b) in (9–22), we obtain

$$y = \beta x + [\varepsilon - \beta u] = \beta x + w. \tag{9–24}$$

Since x equals $x^* + u$, the regressor in (9–24) is obviously correlated with the disturbance:

$$\mathrm{Cov}[x, w] = \mathrm{Cov}[x^* + u, \varepsilon - \beta u] = -\beta \sigma_u^2. \tag{9–25}$$

Since this violates one of the central assumptions of the classical model, we can expect the least squares estimator,

$$b = \frac{(1/n) \sum xy}{(1/n) \sum x^2},$$

to be inconsistent. To find the probability limits, insert (9–22) and (9–23b) and use the Slutsky theorem:

$$\mathrm{plim}\, b = \frac{\mathrm{plim}(1/n) \sum (x^* + u)(\beta x^* + \varepsilon)}{\mathrm{plim}(1/n) \sum (x^* + u)^2}.$$

Since x^*, ε, and u are mutually independent, this reduces to

$$\mathrm{plim}\, b = \frac{\beta Q^*}{(Q^* + \sigma_u^2)} = \frac{\beta}{1 + \sigma_u^2/Q^*}, \tag{9–26}$$

where $Q^* = \mathrm{plim}(1/n)\sum x^{*2}$. As long as σ_u^2 is positive, b is inconsistent, with a persistent bias toward zero. Clearly, the greater the variability in the measurement error, the worse the bias. The effect of biasing the coefficient toward zero is called **attenuation**.

The result makes some sense in view of (9–24). In regressing y on x, we have omitted a variable, u, from the regression. Write (9–24) in a slightly different form:

$$y = \beta x + \theta u + \varepsilon. \tag{9–24'}$$

It so happens that θ equals $-\beta$, but neglect that for the moment. Were u an observed variable, the *multiple* regression of y on x and u would produce unbiased estimates of β and θ.[26] The important thing to note is that both x and u appear in the regression, and both affect y when they vary. In a model that contains only x, the effect of variation of u on y must be transmitted through variation in x. Viewed in this light, the omitted variable formula (8–20)

---

[26] They would not be efficient, as they neglect the constraint, $\theta = -\beta$, but they *are* unbiased nonetheless.

applies directly. In regressing y only on x, the coefficient we obtain is a mixture of that on x, that is, β, and that on u, that is, $-\beta$. Also, we know the sign on the coefficient on $-\beta$ in this mixture, since it is, in the notation of (8–20) and using plim's instead of expected values,

$$P_{1.2} = \frac{\text{plim}(\mathbf{x}'\mathbf{u}/n)}{\text{plim}(\mathbf{x}'\mathbf{x}/n)}.$$

(We use boldface letters here to indicate the vectors of observations.) Both parts are positive. If u were observed, we would estimate β using u and the fact that $\theta = -\beta$ by regressing y on $x - u$. But this is x^*, which puts us back where we started, with a classical regression model.

Before leaving this case, there is another facet to consider. As the model stands, β cannot be estimated. However, if the purpose of the analysis is only to establish whether or not β is zero, we could proceed by analyzing

$$\gamma = \frac{\beta}{(1 + \sigma_u^2/\mathbf{Q}^*)}$$

instead. Clearly, if γ equals zero, it must be because β does. We leave as an exercise a proof of the following (which is obtained by using the results of Section 8.4, especially (8–20):

In the classical errors in the variables model, (9–22) and (9–23b), the least squares slope estimator, b, has

$$\text{plim } b = \gamma = \beta\pi,$$

where $\pi = 1/(1 + \sigma_u^2/\mathbf{Q}^*)$ and

$$\sqrt{n}(b - \gamma) \xrightarrow{d} N(0, \sigma^2), \tag{9–27}$$

where

$$\sigma^2 = \frac{(\sigma_\varepsilon^2 + \sigma_u^2\beta^2\pi)}{(\mathbf{Q}^* + \sigma_u^2)}.$$

Notice that if $\sigma_u^2 = 0$, that is, there is no measurement error, then all of this reduces to the usual formulas for the classical regression model.

The point of this is that, even here, least squares estimates something. If all that is desired is a test of the hypothesis that β equals zero, the previous result implies that we can just apply a conventional t test (using the standard normal table for the critical point) to the slope in the regression of y on x.

The preceding result is obviously of only limited usefulness in practice. To this point, we have been unable to estimate β. The problem is one of identification. There are four "parameters" in the model—β, σ_ε^2, σ_u^2, and $\mathbf{Q}^*$—and only three pieces of information:

$$S_{yy}, \text{ which estimates plim } S_{yy} = \beta^2\mathbf{Q}^* + \sigma_\varepsilon^2,$$

$$S_{xx}, \text{ which estimates plim } S_{xx} = \mathbf{Q}^* + \sigma_u^2,$$

and

$$S_{xy}, \text{ which estimates plim } S_{xy} = \beta\mathbf{Q}^*.$$

Using the Slutsky theorem (i.e., the method of moments), we could, at this point, only manipulate our three estimators. As it stands, none of the parameters can be estimated. One approach to estimation is based on assuming that there is an additional known quantity or restriction. For example:

1. If σ_ε^2 were known, $(S_{yy} - \sigma_\varepsilon^2)/S_{xy}$ would be a consistent estimator of β, and the rest of the puzzle would unfold.

2. If σ_u^2 were known, $S_{xy}/(S_{xx} - \sigma_u^2)$ would be a consistent estimator of β.

3. If $\lambda = \sigma_u^2/Q^*$ were known, $(S_{xy}/S_{xx})(1 + \lambda)$ would be a consistent estimator of β.

Other combinations are possible; the logic is that any known function of the underlying parameters raises the number of known estimators to the number of unknown parameters. However, assuming that the unknown parameters are known is a bit utopian. Perhaps the third suggestion offers some hope; it is not unusual to have at least some information about the degree of error in a measured variable. Government statistics are often released with a range of error. Otherwise, the appeal of this approach is largely intellectual.

It has been pointed out that the preceding trap was set by locking ourselves into the normal distribution at the outset. If, for example, some other distribution were specified for ε and u, perhaps some higher moments, that is, the third moment of y or the product of y^2 and x, could be used to provide additional information about the parameters. It is known that this approach will be fruitless for the normal distribution, but almost any other symmetric distribution solves the identification problem.[27] Of course, assuming that some other particular distribution applies is also somewhat optimistic.

The approach stated in the preceding paragraph does, however, suggest a possibility in a time-series setting. The difficulty we face is that there is not enough information in the contemporaneous variances and covariances of the observed variables to identify the parameters of the model. To take a simple example, suppose that we add to the basic model of (9–22) and (9–23b) that x is a time series characterized by

$$x_t = x_t^* + u_t,$$

and

(9–23b′)

$$x_t^* = \rho x_{t-1}^* + v_t.$$

Then, because the disturbances and measurement errors are uncorrelated across observations, that is, across time,

$$\text{plim} \frac{1}{n} \sum x_{t-1} y_t = \text{plim} \frac{1}{n} \sum (\beta \rho x_{t-1}^* + \beta v_t + \varepsilon_t)(x_{t-1}^* + u_{t-1})$$

$$= \beta \rho Q^*$$

and

$$\text{plim} \frac{1}{n} \sum x_{t-1} x_t = \text{plim} \frac{1}{n} \sum (x_{t-1}^* + v_{t-1})(\rho x_{t-1}^* + v_t + u_t)$$

$$= \rho Q^*.$$

The ratio provides a consistent estimator of β, after which the remaining parameters can be derived.

---

[27] See Pal (1980). In a much earlier analysis, Riersol (1950) showed that the fundamental problem of identification in this model is peculiar to the bivariate normal distribution.

9.5.2.   Multiple Regression with Measurement Error

In a multiple regression model, matters only get worse. Suppose, to begin, we assume that

$$\mathbf{y} = \mathbf{X}^*\boldsymbol{\beta} + \boldsymbol{\varepsilon}$$

and

$$\mathbf{X} = \mathbf{X}^* + \mathbf{U},$$

allowing every observation on every variable to be measured with error. The extension of our earlier results is direct:

$$\text{plim}\,\frac{\mathbf{X}'\mathbf{X}}{n} = \mathbf{Q}^* + \boldsymbol{\Sigma}_{uu},$$

$$\text{plim}\,\frac{\mathbf{X}'\mathbf{y}}{n} = \mathbf{Q}^*\boldsymbol{\beta}.$$

Hence,

$$\text{plim}\,\mathbf{b} = [\mathbf{Q}^* + \boldsymbol{\Sigma}_{uu}]^{-1}\mathbf{Q}^*\boldsymbol{\beta} = \boldsymbol{\beta} - [\mathbf{Q}^* + \boldsymbol{\Sigma}_{uu}]^{-1}\boldsymbol{\Sigma}_{uu}\boldsymbol{\beta}. \tag{9-28}$$

This is a mixture of all of the parameters in the model. In the same fashion as before, bringing in outside information could lead to identification; however, the amount of information necessary is extremely large, and this approach is not particularly promising.

There are some particular cases of interest. It is common for only a single variable to be measured with error, and one might speculate that the problems would be isolated to the single coefficient. Unfortunately, this is not the case. For a single bad variable—assume that it is the first—the matrix $\boldsymbol{\Sigma}_{uu}$ is of the form

$$\boldsymbol{\Sigma}_{uu} = \begin{bmatrix} \sigma_u^2 & 0 & \cdots & 0 \\ 0 & 0 & \cdots & 0 \\ & & \vdots & \\ 0 & 0 & \cdots & 0 \end{bmatrix}.$$

It can be shown that for this special case

$$\text{plim}\,b_1 = \frac{\beta_1}{1 + \sigma_u^2 q^{*11}} \tag{9-29a}$$

(note the similarity of this result to the earlier one) and, for $k \neq 1$,

$$\text{plim}\,b_k = \beta_k - \beta_1 \left[\frac{\sigma_u^2 q^{*k1}}{1 + \sigma_u^2 q^{*11}} \right], \tag{9-29b}$$

where q^{*k1} is the k, 1th element in $\mathbf{Q}^{*-1}$.[28] Obviously, this depends on several unknowns and cannot be estimated. The coefficient on the badly measured variable is still biased toward zero. The other coefficients are all biased as well, though in unknown directions. A badly measured variable contaminates all of the least squares estimates.[29]

---

[28] Use (2–66) to invert $[\mathbf{Q}^* + \boldsymbol{\Sigma}_{uu}] = [\mathbf{Q}^* + (\sigma_u\mathbf{e}_1)(\sigma_u\mathbf{e}_1)']$, where $\mathbf{e}_1$ is the first column of a $K \times K$ identity matrix. The remaining results are then straightforward.

[29] This point is important to remember when the presence of measurement error is suspected. For example, notice that the marginal product of capital estimated in Example 8.3 is negative, which contradicts a firm theoretical result. Nerlove (1963) attributed this finding largely to measurement error in the variable used for the price of capital, but made no note of the likely effects on the other coefficients in the model.

If more than one variable is measured with error, there is very little that can be said.[30] Although expressions can be derived for the biases in a few of these cases, they generally depend on numerous parameters whose signs and magnitudes are unknown and, presumably, unknowable.

9.5.3. Forecasting with Measurement Error

It might seem, in view of the preceding discussion, that forecasting in this setting is as hazardous as estimation (even more so than usual). But this need not be the case. In Example 8.6, it was shown that omitting a variable from the regression does not necessarily bias the forecasts from that model. A like result is at work here. If either $\mathbf{X}^*$ is nonstochastic or $\mathbf{X}^*$ and $\mathbf{u}$ are normally distributed, forecasts produced from this model are unbiased in the sense that the forecast errors have zero means.

For a given vector of values $\mathbf{x}^0$, the forecast is

$$\hat{y}^0 = \mathbf{b}'\mathbf{x}^0,$$

where $\mathbf{b}$ is the least squares coefficient vector. The true value being forecasted is

$$y^0 = \boldsymbol{\beta}'\mathbf{x}^{*0} + \varepsilon^0.$$

The forecast error is then

$$y^0 - \hat{y}^0 = \boldsymbol{\beta}'\mathbf{x}^{*0} - \mathbf{b}'\mathbf{x}^0 + \varepsilon^0.$$

Since our results will be asymptotic, rather than the expected value, we insert plim $\mathbf{b}$ in the preceding before we consider the expected forecast error; thus, from this point, the equality in the results is only asymptotic. Our analysis amounts to asking, what is the expected forecast error in a large sample? Then, as we have shown,

$$\text{plim } \mathbf{b} = (\mathbf{Q}^* + \boldsymbol{\Sigma}_{uu})^{-1}\mathbf{Q}^*\boldsymbol{\beta}.$$

Inserting this in the forecast error gives

$$y^0 - \hat{y}^0 = \boldsymbol{\beta}'\mathbf{x}^{*0} - \boldsymbol{\beta}'(\mathbf{Q}^* + \boldsymbol{\Sigma}_{uu})^{-1}\mathbf{Q}^*\mathbf{x}^0$$

$$= \boldsymbol{\beta}'[\mathbf{x}^{*0} - (\mathbf{Q}^* + \boldsymbol{\Sigma}_{uu})^{-1}\mathbf{Q}^*\mathbf{x}^0) + \varepsilon^0.$$

Taking expectations, we find that the expected forecast error is

$$E[y^0 - \hat{y}^0] = \boldsymbol{\beta}'E[\mathbf{x}^{*0} - (\mathbf{Q}^* + \boldsymbol{\Sigma}_{uu})^{-1}\mathbf{Q}^*\mathbf{x}^0]. \qquad (9-30)$$

The pertinent question at this point is, what is the bracketed term? If $E[\mathbf{x}^{*0}|\mathbf{x}^0]$ is a linear function of $\mathbf{x}^0$, that is what appears in brackets. The proof relies on general results for multivariate distributions. In the joint multivariate distribution of $\mathbf{x}$ and $\mathbf{x}^*$, it is always true that

$$\text{Cov}[\mathbf{x}, \mathbf{x}^*] = \text{Cov}[\mathbf{x}, E(\mathbf{x}^*|\mathbf{x})].$$

If

$$E[\mathbf{x}^*|\mathbf{x}] = \boldsymbol{\Delta}\mathbf{x},$$

---

[30] Some firm analytic results have been obtained by Levi (1973), Theil (1961), Klepper and Leamer (1983), Garber and Klepper (1980), and Griliches (1986).

then

$$Cov[x, x^*] = Cov[x, \Delta x] = \Delta\, Var[x].$$

Multiplying by $(Var[x])^{-1}$ gives the desired result. Upon using the law of iterated expectations, it also follows (in all cases, linear or not) that

$$E[x^{*0} - E[x^{*0}|x^0]] = 0.$$

Assembling these, we conclude that the forecast is unbiased if $E[x^{*0}|x^0]$ is linear in x^0. If so, the expected value of the bracketed term in (9–30) is zero. It is if x^* and u are normally distributed and if x^* is nonstochastic.

This may be a counterintuitive result. The reason it occurs is the same as that in Example 8.6. In making our forecast of y based on x^0, we are implicitly including a forecast of u. Even though u has a zero unconditional mean, its mean given x^0 is not zero. In computing the regression, we obtain some information about the relationship between x and the measurement error; recall that whenever u moves, so does x. This information is incorporated in the forecast of y given x.

9.5.4. The Method of Instrumental Variables

An alternative set of results for estimation in this model (and numerous others) is built around the method of instrumental variables. To introduce it, consider once again the simple model

$$y = \beta x^* + \varepsilon, \qquad x = x^* + u.$$

The parameters, β, σ_ε^2, q^*, and σ_u^2, are not identified in terms of the moments of x and y. Suppose, however, that there exists a variable, z, such that z is correlated with x^* but not with u. For example, in surveys of families, income is notoriously badly reported, partly deliberately and partly because the respondent often neglects some minor sources. In fitting consumption functions based on these data, the regressor is thus subject to measurement error. Suppose, however, that one could determine the total amount of checks written by the head(s) of the household. It is quite likely that this z would be highly correlated with both consumption and income, but perhaps not significantly correlated with the errors of measurement. If $Cov[x^*, z]$ is not zero, the parameters of the model become estimable, as

$$\text{plim} \frac{(1/n)\sum yz}{(1/n)\sum xz} = \frac{\beta\, Cov[x^*, z]}{Cov[x^*, z]} = \beta. \tag{9–31}$$

It is not always clear where instrumental variables are to be found. For the simple errors in variables model we have discussed here, a few instruments have been devised based only on the data in hand:

$$z = 1 \text{ if } x > \text{median } x \text{ and } -1 \text{ if } x < \text{median } x$$
$$\text{(if } n \text{ is even, the middle observation is discarded)}[31]$$

or

$$z = \text{rank of } x.[32]$$

---

[31] This is sometimes called the *method of group averages*, as it amounts to passing a line between the group means of two groups of observations, one with small values of x and one with large values.

[32] To the extent that the ranking of x is determined by the size of the measurement error rather than by x^*, this instrument, like the one before it, will fail to satisfy the requirement that it be uncorrelated with the measurement error. The relevant quantity, as we have seen before, is σ_u^2/Q^*.

Notice, for instance, that in the time-series example of (9–23b'), the variable x_{t-1} is being used as an instrumental variable.

In a multiple regression framework, if only a single variable is measured with error, the preceding can be applied to that variable and the remaining variables can serve as their own instruments. If more than one variable is measured with error, the first preceding proposal will be cumbersome at best, while the second can be applied to each.

The preceding describes the application of the technique of instrumental variables to a particular problem. However, the technique is quite general and is used in numerous settings. Here we consider some general results. The consistency of least squares in the classical regression model,

$$\mathbf{y} = \mathbf{X}\boldsymbol{\beta} + \boldsymbol{\varepsilon},$$

hinges on

$$\text{plim}\left(\frac{1}{n}\right)\mathbf{X}'\boldsymbol{\varepsilon} = \mathbf{0}.$$

If this does not hold, least squares is not a consistent estimator of $\boldsymbol{\beta}$. Suppose, however, that there exists a matrix of K variables $\mathbf{Z}$ such that

$$\text{plim}\,\frac{1}{n}\mathbf{Z}'\boldsymbol{\varepsilon} = \mathbf{0}, \qquad \text{plim}\,\frac{1}{n}\mathbf{Z}'\mathbf{X} \neq \mathbf{0}.$$

Then the instrumental variable estimator

$$\mathbf{b}_{\text{IV}} = [\mathbf{Z}'\mathbf{X}]^{-1}\mathbf{Z}'\mathbf{y} \tag{9–32}$$

has

$$\text{plim}\,\mathbf{b}_{\text{IV}} = \text{plim}\left[\frac{1}{n}\mathbf{Z}'\mathbf{X}\right]^{-1}\text{plim}\left[\frac{1}{n}\mathbf{Z}'(\mathbf{X}\boldsymbol{\beta} + \boldsymbol{\varepsilon})\right]$$

$$= \boldsymbol{\beta} + \text{plim}\left[\frac{1}{n}\mathbf{Z}'\mathbf{X}\right]^{-1}\left[\frac{1}{n}\mathbf{Z}'\boldsymbol{\varepsilon}\right]$$

$$= \boldsymbol{\beta}.$$

To obtain the asymptotic covariance matrix for this estimator, we require

$$(\mathbf{b}_{\text{IV}} - \boldsymbol{\beta})(\mathbf{b}_{\text{IV}} - \boldsymbol{\beta})' = (\mathbf{Z}'\mathbf{X})^{-1}\mathbf{Z}'\boldsymbol{\varepsilon}\boldsymbol{\varepsilon}'\mathbf{Z}(\mathbf{X}'\mathbf{Z})^{-1},$$

from which it follows that the asymptotic covariance matrix is

$$\text{Asy. Var}[\mathbf{b}_{\text{IV}}] = \sigma^2[\mathbf{Z}'\mathbf{X}]^{-1}[\mathbf{Z}'\mathbf{Z}][\mathbf{X}'\mathbf{Z}]^{-1}. \tag{9–33}$$

Asymptotic normality of the estimator can be shown if some additional conditions are attached to the behavior of the columns of $\mathbf{Z}$. In general, if they are as well behaved as those of $\mathbf{X}$, which is likely, all of the necessary results can be obtained.[33]

It should be noted that the asymptotic variance of this estimator can be rather large if $\mathbf{Z}$ is not highly correlated with $\mathbf{X}$. Unfortunately, in most cases, there will not be much freedom in the choice of instruments. For any variables that are not correlated with the disturbances, as in the previous discussion, the column of $\mathbf{Z}$ can be the corresponding variable in $\mathbf{X}$. For the others, the choice of $\mathbf{Z}$ will usually be ad hoc.[34]

---

[33] White (1984) presents an extensive analysis.
[34] Results on "optimal instruments" appear in White (1984) and Hansen (1982).

There will be cases in which several variables are available to serve as instruments. Suppose, for example, that only one variable, x_j, is measured with error, and there are a set of L instrumental variables, $z_1, \ldots, z_L$ available. Another way to apply (9–32) is to use $\mathbf{Z} = \mathbf{X}$, where the columns of $\mathbf{X}$ are the fitted values in a regression of all of the columns of $\mathbf{X}$ on all of the columns in $\mathbf{X}$ *excluding* $\mathbf{X}_j$ plus all of the z's that are not already in $\mathbf{X}$. In this case, each of the included columns of $\mathbf{X}$ is replicated exactly, and x_j is replaced with the fitted value in the regression.[35] We can show that this procedure will satisfy the requirements for an instrumental variable estimator, provided that plim $z_l' \varepsilon / n = 0$ for all l.

9.5.5. Proxy Variables

There are situations in which the variable in a model simply has no observable counterpart. Education, intelligence, and like factors are perhaps the most common examples. In this instance, unless there is some observable indicator for the variable, the model will have to be treated in the framework of missing variables. Usually, however, such an indicator can be obtained; for the factors just given, years of schooling and test scores of various sorts are familiar examples. The usual treatment of such variables is in the measurement error framework. If, for example,

$$\text{Income} = \beta_1 + \beta_2 \text{Education} + \varepsilon$$

and

$$\text{Years of schooling} = \text{education} + u,$$

then the model of 9.5.1 applies directly. The only difference here is that the true variable in the model is "latent." No amount of improvement in reporting or measurement would bring the proxy closer to the variable for which it is proxying.

It is to be emphasized that a proxy variable is not an instrument (or the reverse). In the instrumental variables framework, this implies that we do not regress y on $\mathbf{Z}$ to obtain the estimates. To take an extreme example, suppose that the full model was

$$y = \mathbf{X}^* \boldsymbol{\beta} + \varepsilon,$$

$$\mathbf{X} = \mathbf{X}^* + \mathbf{U},$$

$$\mathbf{Z} = \mathbf{X}^* + \mathbf{W}.$$

That is, we happen to have two badly measured estimates of $\mathbf{X}^*$. The parameters of this model can be estimated without difficulty if $\mathbf{W}$ is uncorrelated with $\mathbf{U}$ and $\mathbf{X}^*$, *but not by regressing* y on $\mathbf{Z}$. The instrumental variables technique is called for.

When the model contains a variable such as education, the question naturally arises if interest centers on the other coefficients in the model, why not just discard the problem variable?[36] This produces the familiar problem of an omitted variable, compounded by the fact that the least squares estimator in the full model is inconsistent. Which estimator is worse? McCallum (1972) and Wickens (1972) show that the asymptotic bias (actually, degree of inconsistency) is worse if the proxy is omitted, even if it is a bad one (has a high proportion of measurement error). This neglects, however, the precision of the estimates. Aigner (1974) analyzed this aspect of the problem and found, as might be expected, that it could go either way. He concluded, however, that "there is evidence to broadly support use of the proxy."

---

[35] This is the method of two-stage least squares, which is discussed in Chapter 19.
[36] This discussion applies to the measurement error and latent variable problems equally.

9.5.6. A Specification Test for Measurement Error

Hausman (1978) has devised a test for the presence of errors of measurement. Under the hypothesis of no measurement error, both $\mathbf{b}$, the least squares estimator, and $\mathbf{b}_{IV}$, the instrumental variables estimator, are consistent estimators of β, although least squares is efficient, while the IV estimator is inefficient. But if the hypothesis is false, only $\mathbf{b}_{IV}$ is consistent. The test, then, examines the difference between $\mathbf{b}$ and $\mathbf{b}_{IV}$. Under the hypothesis of no measurement error, $\text{plim}(\mathbf{b} - \mathbf{b}_{IV}) = \mathbf{0}$, while if there is measurement error, this plim will be nonzero. We have done similar tests at many points before, using the Wald statistic, which is what Hausman suggests. The innovation of his study is to determine the appropriate covariance matrix to use. Let $\mathbf{V}_1$ be the estimated asymptotic covariance matrix for the IV estimator, and let $\mathbf{V}_0$ be $s^2(\mathbf{X}'\mathbf{X})^{-1}$, where s^2 is the estimate of σ^2 obtained using the IV estimator. We know that $\mathbf{V}_1$ is larger than $\mathbf{V}_0$ asymptotically, and our use of the same estimate of σ^2 will ensure this algebraically as well. Then the Wald statistic is simply

$$W = (\mathbf{b} - \mathbf{b}_{IV})'[\mathbf{V}_1 - \mathbf{V}_0]^{-1}(\mathbf{b} - \mathbf{b}_{IV}) \sim \chi^2[K]. \qquad (9-34)$$

As Hausman then shows, this may be referred to a chi-squared table.

The algebra simplifies a bit because the same estimate of σ^2 is used for both matrices. Inserting (9–33) and using $\mathbf{q} = \mathbf{b} - \mathbf{b}_{IV}$ reduces (9–34) to

$$W = \frac{\mathbf{q}'\{[\mathbf{X}'\mathbf{Z}(\mathbf{Z}'\mathbf{Z})^{-1}\mathbf{Z}'\mathbf{X}]^{-1} - (\mathbf{X}'\mathbf{X})^{-1}\}^{-1}\mathbf{q}}{s^2}$$

$$= \frac{\mathbf{q}'\{(\hat{\mathbf{X}}'\hat{\mathbf{X}})^{-1} - (\mathbf{X}'\mathbf{X})^{-1}\}^{-1}\mathbf{q}}{s^2}. \qquad (9-35)$$

Each column of $\hat{\mathbf{X}}$ is the set of fitted values when the corresponding column of $\mathbf{X}$ is regressed on all of the columns of $\mathbf{Z}$.

For the simple regression model with only a single regressor, the algebra simplifies even further. It can be shown that the test is equivalent to applying a standard test of significance to the coefficient on $\hat{u}$ in the least squares regression.

$$y = \beta_1 + \beta_2 x + \gamma \hat{u} + \tilde{\varepsilon},$$

where $\hat{u}$ is the vector of residuals obtained by regressing x on the instrumental variable, z. The results are valid only asymptotically, so the standard normal table is used instead of the t table.

9.6. Regression Diagnostics and Influential Data Points

Even in the absence of multicollinearity or other data problems, it is worthwhile to examine one's data and regression results closely for two reasons. First, the identification of outliers in the data is useful, particularly in relatively small cross sections in which the identity and perhaps even the ultimate source of the data point may be known. Second, it is possible to ascertain which, if any, particular observations are especially influential in the results obtained. As such, the identification of these data points may call for further study. It is worth emphasizing, though, that there is a certain danger in singling out particular observations for scrutiny or even elimination from the sample on the basis of statistical results that are based on those data. At the extreme, this may invalidate the usual inference procedures.[37]

Of particular importance in this analysis is the *hat matrix*:

$$\mathbf{H} = \mathbf{X}(\mathbf{X}'\mathbf{X})^{-1}\mathbf{X}'. \qquad (9-36)$$

This matrix appeared earlier as the matrix that projects any $n \times 1$ vector into the column space of $\mathbf{X}$; for any vector $\mathbf{y}$, $\mathbf{Hy}$ is the set of fitted values in the least squares regression of $\mathbf{y}$ on $\mathbf{X}$. The least squares residuals are

$$\mathbf{e} = \mathbf{My} = \mathbf{M\varepsilon} = (\mathbf{I} - \mathbf{H})\varepsilon,$$

so the variance matrix for the OLS residuals is

$$E[\mathbf{ee}'] = \sigma^2 \mathbf{M} = \sigma^2(\mathbf{I} - \mathbf{H}).$$

If one desires to identify which residuals are significantly large, they should be standardized by dividing by the appropriate standard error for that particular residual. Thus, we would use

$$\hat{e}_i = \frac{e_i}{(s^2(1 - h_{ii}))^{1/2}} = \frac{e_i}{(s^2 M_{ii})^{1/2}}. \qquad (9-37)$$

As a diagnostic tool, Belseley et al.[38] suggest going one step further. If the regression were estimated without the ith observation, the least squares coefficients would be

$$\mathbf{b}(i) = [\mathbf{X}(i)'\mathbf{X}(i)]^{-1}\mathbf{X}(i)'\mathbf{y}(i),$$

where the (i) notation indicates that the ith observation has been omitted. Using these coefficients, the modified residual would be

$$e_i(i) = y_i - \mathbf{b}(i)'\mathbf{x}_i$$
$$= \varepsilon_i + [\boldsymbol{\beta} - \mathbf{b}(i)]'\mathbf{x}_i.$$

Since the ith observation is not used in computing $\mathbf{b}(i)$, these two terms are independent. The appropriate variance is, therefore,

$$\text{Var}[e_i(i)] = \sigma^2[1 + h_{ii}(i)]$$
$$= \sigma^2[1 + \mathbf{x}_i(\mathbf{X}(i)'\mathbf{X}(i))^{-1}\mathbf{x}_i]. \qquad (9-38)$$

The estimate of σ^2 is $s^2(i)$. The standardized residual is approximately distributed as standard normal.[39] Values in excess of two suggest observations that deserve closer scrutiny. The calculation is repeated for each observation.[40]

This approach has some intuitive appeal. If the observation conforms to the model that is estimated with the other observations, this standardized residual should be small. If not, the particular observation may deserve scrutiny as perhaps not conforming to the model. It is worth emphasizing, though, that this interpretation is likely to be a bit problematic in a time-

---

[37] See the discussion of pretest estimators in Chapter 8.
[38] Op. cit.
[39] $e_i(i)$ is normally distributed, but in using s^2 instead of σ^2, we lose the normal distribution of the ratio. Nor is this distributed as t, since $e_i(i)$ is not independent of s^2.
[40] This does not require that the regression be recomputed n times. The rank one update formula can be used to do the computation recursively if desired. For each observation, the matrix $\mathbf{X}'\mathbf{X}$ is "updated" by subtracting an observation. If this exercise is to be performed on a large cross section involving many regressors, the economy provided by the updating formula may be worth exploiting.

Table 9.7

Obs.	Original	Standardized	Obs.	Original	Standardized
1	0.14096	0.32504	2	0.10774	0.24844
3	0.22574	0.52052	4	−0.045600	−0.10515
5	0.051204	0.11807	6	−0.14469	−0.33364
7	−0.077206	−0.17803	8	−0.018312	−0.042224
9	−0.027596	−0.063632	10	−0.11519	−0.26561
11	0.012476	0.028768	12	−0.29275	−0.67505
13	−0.20572	−0.47438	14	−0.031992	−0.073770
15	−0.27618	−0.63684	16	−0.002962	−0.006829
17	0.043139	0.099473	18	0.18614	0.42922
19	−0.12667	−0.29208	20	0.001627	0.0037520
21	0.10426	0.24042	22	0.47933	1.1053
23	−0.008710	−0.020084	24	0.00071	0.0016394
25	−0.21818	−0.50310	26	0.38916	0.89736
27	−0.15073	−0.34756			

series setting unless one is aware of some unusual event taking place at the time the observation in question was generated. The set of calculations is similar in spirit to the CUSUM and CUSUM-squared tests discussed earlier.

EXAMPLE 9.8. Influential Data Points. For the Cobb–Douglas production function of Example 7.1, the ordinary least squares and standardized residuals are listed in Table 9.7. In view of the value of R^2 for this regression, the absence of extreme data points is to be expected.

Exercises

1. The following sample moments were computed from 100 observations produced using a random number generator.

$$
\begin{array}{cccc}
\text{one} & \text{x1} & \text{x2} & \text{x3}
\end{array}
$$

$$
X'X = \begin{bmatrix} 100 & 123 & 96 & 109 \\ 123 & 252 & 125 & 189 \\ 96 & 125 & 167 & 146 \\ 109 & 189 & 146 & 168 \end{bmatrix}, \quad X'y = \begin{bmatrix} 460 \\ 810 \\ 615 \\ 712 \end{bmatrix}, \quad y'y = 3924,
$$

$$
(X'X)^{-1} = \begin{bmatrix} 0.03767 & & & \\ -0.06263 & 1.129 & & \\ -0.06247 & 1.107 & 1.110 & \\ 0.1003 & -2.192 & -2.170 & 4.292 \end{bmatrix}.
$$

The true model underlying these data is $y = x_1 + x_2 + x_3 + \varepsilon$.

(a) Compute the simple correlations among the regressors.

(b) Compute the ordinary least squares coefficients in the regression of y on a constant, x_1, x_2, and x_3.

(c) Compute the ordinary least squares coefficients in the regression of y on a constant, x_1, and x_2, on a constant, x_1, and x_3, and on a constant, x_2, and x_3.

(d) Compute Leamer's magnification factor [see (9–5)] associated with each variable.

(e) The regressors are obviously collinear. Which is the problem variable?

2. For the data in the previous exercise, compute the condition number for the moment matrix based on the constant, x_1, and x_2.

3. Prove that

$$E[\mathbf{b'b}] = \boldsymbol{\beta'}\boldsymbol{\beta} + \sigma^2 \sum_k \frac{1}{\lambda_k},$$

where $\mathbf{b}$ is the ordinary least squares estimator and λ_k is a characteristic root of $\mathbf{X'X}$.

4. What are the characteristic roots of the ridge estimator's moment matrix, $[\mathbf{X'X} + k\mathbf{I}]$?

5. Suppose that instead of choosing the principal components in (9–10) on the basis of the variation in $\mathbf{X}$, we compute all of the principal components and choose the one that is most highly correlated with $\mathbf{y}$. Show that the principal component, $\mathbf{z}_j = \mathbf{Xc}_j$, which is most highly correlated with $\mathbf{y}$, is the one that maximizes $\sqrt{\lambda_j}\mathbf{b'c}_j$, where $\mathbf{b}$ is the OLS estimator of $\boldsymbol{\beta}$, $\mathbf{c}_j$ is a characteristic vector of $\mathbf{X'X}$, and λ_j is the associated characteristic root.

6. Consider the simple regression $y = \alpha + \beta x + \varepsilon$. Assume that some of the observations on x are missing. Prove that filling these observations with zeros and adding a dummy variable to the regression that is one for each missing observation and zero otherwise is equivalent to dropping the incomplete observations.

7. The simple regression model

$$y_{ig} = \beta x_{ig} + \varepsilon_{ig},$$

$$E[\varepsilon_{ig}] = 0, \qquad \text{Var}[\varepsilon_{ig}] = \sigma^2$$

applies to observation i in group g. The observed data consist of group means. The following data are obtained from five groups:

Group	1	2	3	4	5	All
n_g	10	20	15	30	25	100
$\bar{y}_g$	2	4	3	1	5	—
$\bar{x}_g$	1	4	2	1	6	—

The following are three possible estimators of β:

$$\frac{\bar{y}}{\bar{x}} = \frac{\sum_g n_g \bar{y}_g / \sum_g n_g}{\sum_g n_g \bar{x}_g / \sum_g n_g},$$

$$\frac{\sum_g \bar{y}_g \bar{x}_g}{\sum_g \bar{x}_g^2} = \text{least squares},$$

and

$$\frac{\sum_g n_g \bar{x}_g \bar{y}_g}{\sum_g n_g \bar{x}_g^2} = \text{the estimator in (9–17).}$$

(a) Prove that all three estimators are unbiased.

(b) Derive the expression for the sampling variance of each estimator.

(c) Using the previous sample data, compute the three estimators and their sampling variances. Assume that $\sigma^2 = 1$. Which is the most efficient? The least efficient? (The difference you observe between the second and third estimators is that between the ordinary and generalized least squares estimator. This is the subject of Chapter 14.)

(d) Prove that the sampling variance of the third estimator is always less than that of the second.

8. For the model in (9–22) and (9–23), prove that when only x^* is measured with error, the squared correlation between y and x is less than that between y^* and x^*. (Note the assumption that $y^* = y$.) Does the same hold true if y^* is also measured with error?

9. *Reverse regression.* This and the next exercise continue the analysis of Exercise 12, Chapter 8. In the earlier exercise, interest centered on a particular dummy variable in which the regressors were accurately measured. Here we consider the case in which the crucial regressor in the model is measured with error. The paper by Kamlich and Polachek (1982) is directed to this issue.

Consider the simple errors in the variables model

$$y = \alpha + \beta x^* + \varepsilon,$$

$$x = x^* + u,$$

where u and ε are uncorrelated and x is the erroneously measured, observed counterpart to x^*.

(a) Assume that x^*, u, and ε are all normally distributed, with means μ^*, 0, and 0, variances σ_*^2, σ_u^2, and σ_ε^2, and zero covariances. Obtain the probability limits of the least squares estimates of α and β.

(b) As an alternative, consider regressing x on a constant and y, and then computing the reciprocal of the estimate. Obtain the probability limit of this estimate.

(c) Do the "direct" and "reverse" estimators bound the true coefficient?

10. *Reverse regression continued.* Suppose that the model in the preceding exercise is extended to

$$y = \beta x^* + \gamma d + \varepsilon,$$

$$x = x^* + u.$$

For convenience, we drop the constant term. Assume that x^*, ε, and u are independent and normally distributed, with zero means. Suppose that d is a random variable that takes the values one and zero, with probabilities π and $1 - \pi$ in the population, and is independent of all other variables in the model. To put this in context, the preceding model (and variants of it) have appeared in the literature on discrimination. We view y as a "wage" variable, x^* as "qualifications," and x as some imperfect measure such as education. The dummy variable, d, is membership ($d = 1$) or nonmembership ($d = 0$) in some protected class. The hypothesis of discrimination turns on $\gamma < 0$ versus $\gamma = 0$.

(a) What is the probability limit of c, the least squares estimator of γ, in the least squares regression of y on x and d? [**Hints:** The independence of x^* and d is important. Also, plim $\mathbf{d'd}/n = \text{Var}[d] + E^2[d] = \pi(1 - \pi) + \pi^2 = \pi$. This minor modification does not affect the model substantively, but it greatly simplifies the algebra.] Now, suppose that x^* and d are not independent. In particular, suppose that $E[x^*|d = 1] = \mu^1$ and $E[x^*|d = 0] = \mu^0$. Repeat the derivation with this assumption.

(b) Consider, instead, a regression of x on y and d. What is the probability limit of the coefficient on d in this regression? Assume that x^* and d are independent.

(c) Suppose that x^* and d are not independent, but γ is, in fact, less than zero. Assuming that both preceding equations still hold, what is estimated by $\bar{y}\mid d = 1 - \bar{y}\mid d = 0$? What does this quantity estimate if γ does equal zero?

11. A data set consists of n observations in $\mathbf{X}_n$ and $\mathbf{y}_n$. The least squares estimator based on these n observations is

$$\mathbf{b}_n = (\mathbf{X}_n'\mathbf{X}_n)^{-1}\mathbf{X}_n'\mathbf{y}_n.$$

Another observation, $\mathbf{x}_s$ and y_s, becomes available. Prove that the least squares estimator computed using this additional observation is

$$\mathbf{b}_{n,s} = \mathbf{b}_n + \frac{1}{1 + \mathbf{x}_s'(\mathbf{X}_n'\mathbf{X}_n)^{-1}\mathbf{x}_s}(\mathbf{X}_n'\mathbf{X}_n)^{-1}\mathbf{x}_s(y_s - \mathbf{x}_s'\mathbf{b}_n).$$

Note that the last term is e_s, the residual from the prediction of y_s, using the coefficients based on $\mathbf{X}_n$ and $\mathbf{y}_n$. Conclude that the new data change the results of least squares only if the new observation on y cannot be perfectly predicted using the information already in hand.

References

Afifi, T., and R. Elashoff, "Missing Observations in Multivariate Statistics," *Journal of the American Statistical Association*, September 1966, March 1967, and March 1969.

Aigner, D., "MSE Dominance of Least Squares with Errors of Observation," *Journal of Econometrics*, 2, 1974, pp. 365–372.

Anderson, T., "Maximum Likelihood Estimates for a Multivariate Normal Distribution When Some Observations Are Missing," *Journal of the American Statistical Association*, 62, 1967, pp. 126–129.

Belsley, D., E. Kuh, and R. Welsch, *Regression Diagnostics, Identifying Influential Data and Sources of Collinearity*, New York: Wiley, 1980.

Box, G., and G. Jenkins, *Times Series Analysis: Forecasting and Control*, San Francisco: Holden-Day, 1982.

Cramer, J. S., "Efficient Grouping, Regression and Correlation in Engel Curve Analysis," *Journal of the American Statistical Association*, 59, 1964, pp. 233–250.

Fomby, T., R. Hill, and S. Johnson, "An Optimal Property of Principal Components in the Context of Restricted Least Squares," *Journal of the American Statistical Association*, 73, 1978, pp. 191–193.

Garber, S., and S. Klepper, "Extending the Classical Normal Errors in Variables Model," *Econometrica*, 48, 1980, pp. 1541–1546.

Griliches, Z., "Economic Data Issues," in Z. Griliches and M. Intrilligator, eds., *Handbook of Econometrics*, Vol. 3, Amsterdam: North Holland, 1986.

Haitovsky, "Missing Data in Regression Analysis," *Journal of the Royal Statistical Society, Series B*, 1968, pp. 67–82.

Hansen, L. P., "Large Sample Results for Generalized Method of Moments Estimators," *Econometrica*, 50, 1982, pp. 1029–1054.

Hausman, J., "Specification Tests in Econometrics," *Econometrics*, 46, 1978, pp. 1251–1271.

Hite, S., *Women and Love*, New York: Alfred A. Knopf, 1987.

Hoerl, A., and R. Kennard, "Ridge Regression: Biased Estimation for Nonorthogonal Problems," *Technometrics*, 1970, 12, pp. 55–67.

Judge, G., C. Hill, W. Griffiths, T. Lee, and H. Lutkepohl, *The Theory and Practice of Econometrics*, New York: Wiley, 1985.

Kamlich, R., and S. Polachek, "Discrimination: Fact or Fiction? An Examination Using an Alternative Approach," *Southern Economic Journal*, 1982, 31, pp. 450–461.

Kelejian, H., "Missing Observations in Multivariate Regression—Efficiency of a First Order Method," *Journal of the American Statistical Association*, 1969, 64, pp. 1609–1616.

Klein, L., *An Introduction to Econometrics*, Englewood Cliffs, N.J.: Prentice-Hall, 1962.

Klepper, S., and E. Leamer, "Consistent Sets of Estimates for Regressions with Errors in All Variables," *Econometrica*, 52, 1983, pp. 163–184.

Kmenta, J., *Elements of Econometrics*, New York: Macmillan, 1986.

Kosobud, R., "A Note on a Problem Caused by the Assignment of Missing Data in Sample Surveys," *Econometrica*, 31, 1963, pp. 562–563.

Leamer, E., *Specification Searches*, New York: Wiley, 1978.

Levi, M., "Errors in Variables in the Presence of Correctly Measured Variables," *Econometrica*, 41, 1973, pp. 985–986.

Maddala, G., *Econometrics*, New York: McGraw-Hill, 1977.

McCallum, B., "Relative Asymptotic Bias from Errors of Omission and Measurement," *Econometrica*, 40, 1972, pp. 757–758.

Nerlove, M., "Returns to Scale in Electricity Supply," in *Measurement in Economics: Studies in Honor of Yehuda Grunfeld*, F. Christ, ed. Stanford, Calif: Stanford University Press, 1963.

Pal, M., "Consistent Moment Estimators of Regression Coefficients in the Presence of Errors in Variables," *Journal of Econometrics*, 14, 1980, pp. 666–668.

Riersol, O., "Identifiability of a Linear Relation Between Variables Which Are Subject to Error," *Econometrica*, 18, 1950, pp. 375–389.

Schmidt, P., *Econometrics*, New York: Marcel Dekker, 1976.

Theil, H., *Economic Forecasts and Policy*, Amsterdam: North Holland, 1961.

Theil, H., *Principles of Econometrics*, New York: Wiley, 1971.

White, H., *Asymptotic Theory for Econometricians*, New York, Academic Press, 1984.

Wickens, M., "A Note on the Use of Proxy Variables," *Econometrica*, 40, 1972, pp. 759–760.

Chapter 10

Large-Sample Results for the Classical Regression Model

10.1. Introduction

The discussion thus far has concerned *finite sample* properties of the least squares estimator. Under the assumptions of nonstochastic regressors and normally distributed disturbances, we know the exact distribution of the least squares estimator and several test statistics regardless of the sample size. However, these assumptions are rather limiting. The classical normal regression with nonstochastic regressors is a special case and does not include many of the most common applications, for example, models with lagged dependent variables. This chapter will generalize the classical regression model by relaxing these two important assumptions.[1] To do so, it is necessary to consider the asymptotic, or large-sample, properties of least squares.

10.2. The Finite-Sample Properties of Least Squares

The assumptions of the classical regression model are

    I. $y = \mathbf{X}\beta + \varepsilon$.

    II. $\mathbf{X}$ is a nonstochastic $n \times K$ matrix of rank K.

    III. $E[\varepsilon] = \mathbf{0}$.

    IV. $E[\varepsilon\varepsilon'] = \sigma^2 \mathbf{I}$.

The least squares estimators of the unknown parameters are

$$\hat{\beta} = \mathbf{b} = (\mathbf{X}'\mathbf{X})^{-1}\mathbf{X}'y$$

and

$$\hat{\sigma}^2 = s^2 = \frac{\mathbf{e}'\mathbf{e}}{n - K}.$$

By analyzing

$$\mathbf{b} = \beta + (\mathbf{X}'\mathbf{X})^{-1}\mathbf{X}'\varepsilon$$

---

[1] Much of this discussion will use standard results on asymptotic and limiting distributions. It may be helpful to review the related sections in Chapter 4 before proceeding.

and

$$s^2 = \frac{\varepsilon' \mathbf{M} \varepsilon}{n - K},$$

we obtained the following exact, finite-sample results:

1. $E[\mathbf{b}] = \beta$. (Least squares is unbiased.)
2. $\text{Var}[\mathbf{b}] = \sigma^2 (\mathbf{X}'\mathbf{X})^{-1}$.
3. The minimum variance linear unbiased estimator of any linear function $\mathbf{r}'\beta$ is $\mathbf{r}'\mathbf{b}$. This is the Gauss–Markov theorem.
4. $E[s^2] = \sigma^2$.
5. $\text{Cov}[\mathbf{b}, \mathbf{e}] = \mathbf{0}$.

For constructing confidence intervals and testing hypotheses, we derived the following additional results based on the normality assumption

V. $\varepsilon \sim N[\mathbf{0}, \sigma^2 \mathbf{I}]$.

6. $\mathbf{b}$ and $\mathbf{e}$ are statistically independent. It follows that $\mathbf{b}$ and s^2 are uncorrelated and statistically independent.
7. The exact distribution of $\mathbf{b}$ is $N[\beta, \sigma^2 (\mathbf{X}'\mathbf{X})^{-1}]$.
8. $(n - K)s^2/\sigma^2$ is distributed as $\chi^2[n - K]$. s^2 has mean σ^2 and variance $2\sigma^4/(n - K)$.
9. Based on results 6–8, the statistic

$$t[n - K] = \frac{(b_i - \beta_i)}{[s^2 (\mathbf{X}'\mathbf{X})_{ii}^{-1}]^{1/2}}$$

has a t distribution with $(n - K)$ degrees of freedom.

10. The test statistic for testing a set of J linear restrictions, $\mathbf{R}\beta = \mathbf{q}$,

$$\frac{(\mathbf{Rb} - \mathbf{q})'(\mathbf{R}(\mathbf{X}'\mathbf{X})^{-1}\mathbf{R}')^{-1}(\mathbf{Rb} - \mathbf{q})/J}{\mathbf{e}'\mathbf{e}/(n - K)} = (\mathbf{Rb} - \mathbf{q})'[\mathbf{R}(s^2(\mathbf{X}'\mathbf{X})^{-1})\mathbf{R}']^{-1}(\mathbf{Rb} - \mathbf{q})/J$$

has an F distribution with J and $n - K$ degrees of freedom.

Note the distinction between the properties of $\mathbf{b}$ established using I–IV and the additional inference results that are obtained with the further assumption of normality of the disturbances. The primary result in the first set is the Gauss–Markov theorem, which holds regardless of the distribution of the disturbances as long as assumptions I–IV are met. The normality assumption enables us to formulate inference tools but does not produce any additional finite sample optimality results. As we shall see, with normality, we obtain few large-sample properties that would not hold otherwise.

10.3. *Asymptotics for the Classical Regression Model*

For the basic model of assumptions I–IV, it is straightforward to derive the large-sample properties of the least squares estimator. We shall continue to assume that $\mathbf{X}$ is nonstochastic until Section 10.4. With assumption V (normality), the least squares estimator is normally distributed in every sample, so its asymptotic distribution must be normal as well. Nonetheless, it remains to demonstrate consistency and the appropriate asymptotic covariance matrix. It is useful, however, at the outset *not* to assume that the disturbances are normally distributed. An important result is that the consistency and the asymptotic normality of **b** can be established without assumption V. In Section 10.3.4., we shall reintroduce this assumption in order to consider the question of asymptotic efficiency.

10.3.1.   Consistency

The crucial elements in establishing the large-sample properties are the pair of assumptions made about (1) the variation in the columns of **X** and (2) the stochastic relationship (if any) between **X** and ε. We begin by assuming that

$$\lim_{n \to \infty} \frac{1}{n} \mathbf{X}'\mathbf{X} = \mathbf{Q}, \qquad \text{a positive definite matrix.} \tag{10-1}$$

If **X** is taken to be "fixed in repeated samples," or, equivalently, if the assumptions of this regression model are meant to apply only to the **X** matrix in hand, then (10–1) leads to $\mathbf{Q} = (1/n)\mathbf{X}'\mathbf{X}$. If, instead, **X** is taken to be nonstochastic, but not constant in repeated samples, then (10–1) is a statement about the means of choosing the sample data. The assumption implies, first of all, that the full rank condition assumed in Chapter 6 for the columns of **X** will always hold, regardless of how large the sample is. In addition, none of the samples on any of the variables will be dominated by infinitely large or very small values.

The least squares estimator may be written

$$\mathbf{b} = \beta + \left[\frac{1}{n}(\mathbf{X}'\mathbf{X}) \right]^{-1} \left[\frac{1}{n}\mathbf{X}'\varepsilon \right]. \tag{10-2}$$

Assuming that $\mathbf{Q}^{-1}$ exists, since the inverse is a continuous function of the original matrix, we obtain

$$\operatorname{plim} \mathbf{b} = \beta + \mathbf{Q}^{-1} \operatorname{plim} \left[\frac{1}{n}\mathbf{X}'\varepsilon \right].$$

[We have invoked result (4–23).] We now require the probability limit of the last term. Let

$$\bar{\mathbf{w}} = \frac{1}{n}\mathbf{X}'\varepsilon$$

$$= \frac{1}{n}\sum_i \mathbf{x}_i\varepsilon_i = \frac{1}{n}\sum_i \mathbf{w}_i.$$

Then

$$\mathbf{b} = \left(\frac{\mathbf{X}'\mathbf{X}}{n} \right)^{-1} \bar{\mathbf{w}}$$

and

$$\operatorname{plim} \mathbf{b} = \mathbf{Q}^{-1} \operatorname{plim} \bar{\mathbf{w}}.$$

Because **X** is a nonstochastic matrix,

$$E[\bar{\mathbf{w}}] = \frac{1}{n}\mathbf{X}'E[\varepsilon] = \mathbf{0}$$

and

$$\operatorname{Var}[\bar{\mathbf{w}}] = E[\bar{\mathbf{w}}\bar{\mathbf{w}}'] = \frac{1}{n}\mathbf{X}'E[\varepsilon\varepsilon']\mathbf{X}\frac{1}{n} = \frac{\sigma^2}{n}\left(\frac{\mathbf{X}'\mathbf{X}}{n} \right). \tag{10-3}$$

It follows, then, that

$$\lim_{n \to \infty} \text{Var}[\bar{\mathbf{w}}] = 0 \cdot \mathbf{Q} = \mathbf{0}. \tag{10-4}$$

Since the mean of $\bar{\mathbf{w}}$ is always zero and its variance converges to zero, $\bar{\mathbf{w}}$ converges in mean square to zero and plim $\bar{\mathbf{w}} = \mathbf{0}$. Consequently,

$$\text{plim } \mathbf{b} = \boldsymbol{\beta} + \mathbf{Q}^{-1} \cdot \mathbf{0} = \boldsymbol{\beta}. \tag{10-5}$$

This establishes that $\mathbf{b}$ is a consistent estimator of $\boldsymbol{\beta}$ in the classical regression model.

This way of proceeding is worthwhile in order to set the stage for the results derived in the next section. It is worth noting, though, that although (10-1) is a conventional assumption, it is a bit stronger than necessary and excludes one very common exception. If $\mathbf{X}$ contains a time trend, $(1/n)\mathbf{X}'\mathbf{X}$ will explode as n goes to infinity, not converge to a positive definite matrix. In this case, it would follow from the exact results

$$E[\mathbf{b}] = \boldsymbol{\beta}, \qquad \text{hence } \lim_{n \to \infty} E[\mathbf{b}] = \boldsymbol{\beta}$$

and

$$\text{Var}[\mathbf{b}] = \sigma^2 (\mathbf{X}'\mathbf{X})^{-1}, \qquad \text{hence } \lim_{n \to \infty} \text{Var}[\mathbf{b}] = \mathbf{0}$$

that $\mathbf{b}$ converges in mean square to $\boldsymbol{\beta}$. Indeed, this case is particularly favorable in that the difference between $\mathbf{b}$ and $\boldsymbol{\beta}$ converges to zero more rapidly than in the conventional case.[2]

Time-series settings that involve time trends and trending variables often pose cases in which the preceding assumptions are too restrictive.[3] A somewhat weaker set of assumptions about $\mathbf{X}$ that is broad enough to include most of these is the **Grenander conditions**:[4]

1. For each column of $\mathbf{X}$, $\mathbf{x}_k$, if $d_{nk}^2 = \mathbf{x}_k' \mathbf{x}_k$, $\lim_{n \to \infty} d_{nk}^2 = +\infty$. This means that $\mathbf{x}_k$ does not degenerate to a sequence of zeros.[5]

2. $\lim_{n \to \infty} x_{ik}^2 / d_{nk}^2 = 0$ for all $i = 1, \ldots, n$. This implies that no particular observation will ever dominate $\mathbf{x}_k' \mathbf{x}_k$, and as $n \to \infty$, individual observations will become less important.

3. Let $\mathbf{R}_n$ be the sample correlation matrix of the columns of $\mathbf{X}$, excluding the constant term if there is one. Then $\lim_{n \to \infty} \mathbf{R}_n = \mathbf{C}$, a positive definite matrix. This implies that the full rank condition will always be met.[6] We have already assumed that $\mathbf{X}$ has full rank in a finite sample, so this assumption ensures that the condition will never be violated.

The conditions ensure that the data matrix is "well behaved" in large samples in that no single observation dominates the sum of squares and sums of squares continue to grow as the sample size grows, but at a reasonable rate. This is a very weak assumption and is likely to be satisfied by almost any data set encountered in practice.[7]

---

[2] Further discussion of this case and several others is given in Schmidt (1976, pp. 85–88). White (1984) examines a number of other cases.

[3] These are sometimes labeled *asymptotically uncooperative regressors*. See, for example, Schmidt (1976, p. 85). An example is a regressor of the form λ^t, where t indexes the time series observation. A variable of precisely this form will figure prominently in our analysis of the geometric distributed lag model in Chapter 18. It turns out that consistency *cannot* be established in the presence of this type of variable unless $|\lambda| > 1$, which will cause other problems.

[4] Judge et al. (1985, p. 162).

[5] The regressor described in the earlier footnote violates this assumption.

[6] The formal statement of this condition in, for example, Judge et al. (1985) is a bit more involved. The preceding is equivalent.

[7] White (1984) continues this line of analysis. He also provides additional results on conditions that must be attached to *stochastic* regressors in order to establish the asymptotic properties of least squares.

10.3.2. Asymptotic Normality of the Least Squares Estimator

In order to derive the asymptotic distribution of the least squares estimator, we shall use the results of Section 4.4.2. First, it follows from (10–2) that

$$\sqrt{n}\,(\mathbf{b} - \boldsymbol{\beta}) = \left(\frac{\mathbf{X}'\mathbf{X}}{n}\right)^{-1}\left(\frac{1}{\sqrt{n}}\right)\mathbf{X}'\boldsymbol{\varepsilon}. \tag{10–6}$$

Since the inverse matrix is a continuous function of the original matrix, $\lim_{n \to \infty}(\mathbf{X}'\mathbf{X}/n)^{-1} = \mathbf{Q}^{-1}$. Therefore, if the limiting distribution exists, the limiting distribution of the statistic in (10–6) is the same as that of

$$\left[\lim_{n \to \infty}\left(\frac{\mathbf{X}'\mathbf{X}}{n}\right)^{-1}\right]\left(\frac{1}{\sqrt{n}}\right)\mathbf{X}'\boldsymbol{\varepsilon} = \mathbf{Q}^{-1}\left(\frac{1}{\sqrt{n}}\right)\mathbf{X}'\boldsymbol{\varepsilon}.^{[8]} \tag{10–7}$$

Thus, we must establish the limiting distribution of

$$\frac{1}{\sqrt{n}}\mathbf{X}'\boldsymbol{\varepsilon} = \sqrt{n}\,(\overline{\mathbf{w}} - E[\overline{\mathbf{w}}]), \tag{10–8}$$

where $E[\overline{\mathbf{w}}] = \mathbf{0}$. We can use the extension of the central limit theorem given in Section 4.4.2 to obtain the limiting distribution of $\sqrt{n}\,\overline{\mathbf{w}}$. Using that formulation,

$$\overline{\mathbf{w}} = \frac{1}{n}\sum_i \mathbf{x}_i\varepsilon_i$$

is the average of n independent random vectors, $\mathbf{x}_i\varepsilon_i$, with means $\mathbf{0}$ and variances

$$\text{Var}[\mathbf{x}_i\varepsilon_i] = \sigma^2\mathbf{x}_i\mathbf{x}_i' = \sigma^2\mathbf{Q}_i. \tag{10–9}$$

The variance of $\sqrt{n}\,\overline{\mathbf{w}}$ is

$$\begin{aligned}
\sigma^2\overline{\mathbf{Q}}_n &= \sigma^2\left(\frac{1}{n}\right)[\mathbf{Q}_1 + \mathbf{Q}_2 + \cdots + \mathbf{Q}_n] \\
&= \sigma^2\left(\frac{1}{n}\right)\sum_i \mathbf{x}_i\mathbf{x}_i' \\
&= \sigma^2\left(\frac{\mathbf{X}'\mathbf{X}}{n}\right).
\end{aligned} \tag{10–10)}$$

As long as the sum is not dominated by any particular term and the regressors are well behaved, which in this case means that (10–1) holds,

$$\lim_{n \to \infty} \sigma^2\overline{\mathbf{Q}}_n = \sigma^2\mathbf{Q}. \tag{10–11}$$

Therefore, we may apply the Central Limit Theorem to the vector $\sqrt{n}\,\overline{\mathbf{w}}$, as we did in Section 4.4.2 for the univariate case, $\sqrt{n}\,\overline{x}$.

Formal proofs of the following result, which is based on the Lindberg–Feller variant of the Central Limit Theorem, are given in Schmidt (1976) and White (1984). If

1. the disturbances all have the same distribution, with zero mean and finite variance, σ^2,

---

[8] This is a multivariate version of result (4–28).

2. the elements of $\mathbf{X}$ are bounded such that $|x_{tk}|$ is finite and $\operatorname{plim}(\mathbf{X}'\mathbf{X}/n) = \mathbf{Q}$, a finite positive definite matrix, then

$$\left(\frac{1}{\sqrt{n}}\right)\mathbf{X}'\boldsymbol{\varepsilon} \overset{d}{\to} N[(\mathbf{0}, \sigma^2\mathbf{Q})]. \qquad (10\text{--}12)$$

It follows then, that

$$\mathbf{Q}^{-1}\left(\frac{1}{\sqrt{n}}\right)\mathbf{X}'\boldsymbol{\varepsilon} \overset{d}{\to} N[\mathbf{Q}^{-1}\mathbf{0}, \mathbf{Q}^{-1}(\sigma^2\mathbf{Q})\mathbf{Q}^{-1}] \qquad (10\text{--}13)$$

or, combining terms,

$$\sqrt{n}(\mathbf{b} - \boldsymbol{\beta}) \overset{d}{\to} N[\mathbf{0}, \sigma^2\mathbf{Q}^{-1}]. \qquad (10\text{--}14)$$

Using the technique of Section 4.4.3, we then obtain the asymptotic distribution for $\mathbf{b}$:

$$\mathbf{b} \overset{a}{\to} N\left[\boldsymbol{\beta}, \frac{\sigma^2}{n}\mathbf{Q}^{-1}\right]. \qquad (10\text{--}15)$$

In practice, it is necessary to estimate $(1/n)\mathbf{Q}^{-1}$ with $(\mathbf{X}'\mathbf{X})^{-1}$ and σ^2 with $\mathbf{e}'\mathbf{e}/(n - K)$.

If ε is normally distributed, result (7), presented earlier, holds in every sample, so it holds asymptotically as well. The upshot of the preceding is that even if normality is not assumed, if the regressors are well behaved, it may still be assumed that the least squares estimator will be asymptotically normally distributed.

To complete the derivation, we can extend Theorem 4.4 directly to functions of the least squares estimator. Let $\mathbf{f}(\mathbf{b})$ be any set of J continuous, linear or nonlinear functions of the least squares estimates and

$$\mathbf{G} = \frac{\partial \mathbf{f}(\mathbf{b})}{\partial \mathbf{b}'}.$$

$\mathbf{G}$ is the $J \times K$ matrix whose jth row is the vector of derivatives of the jth function with respect to $\mathbf{b}$. Then

$$\mathbf{f}(\mathbf{b}) \overset{a}{\to} N\left[\mathbf{f}(\boldsymbol{\beta}), \mathbf{G}\left(\frac{\sigma^2}{n}\mathbf{Q}^{-1}\right)\mathbf{G}'\right]. \qquad (10\text{--}16)$$

If any of the functions are nonlinear, the property of unbiasedness that holds for $\mathbf{b}$ will *not* carry over to $\mathbf{f}(\boldsymbol{\beta})$. Nonetheless, it follows from (10–14) that $\mathbf{f}(\mathbf{b})$ is a *consistent* estimator of $\mathbf{f}(\boldsymbol{\beta})$, and the asymptotic covariance matrix is readily available. This result will greatly simplify hypothesis testing.

EXAMPLE 10.1. Log-Linear Model.   To estimate a log-linear model,

$$Y = AX^{\beta}e^{\varepsilon},$$

we first write

$$\ln Y = \ln A + \beta \ln X + \varepsilon$$

$$= \alpha + \beta x + \varepsilon$$

and then estimate the parameters by ordinary least squares. If we assume that ε has a normal distribution, the exact distribution of a, the estimator of α, is

$$a \sim N\left[\alpha, \frac{\sigma^2(1/n + \bar{x}^2)}{S_{xx}}\right].$$

The usual estimator of $A = e^{\alpha}$ will then be e^{a}. We can find the exact distribution of e^{a} by using the result:

If $a \sim N(\alpha, \theta^2)$, $e^{a} \sim$ lognormal with mean $e^{\alpha + \theta^2/2}$ and variance $e^{2\alpha + \theta^2}(e^{\theta^2} - 1)$.   (10–17)

By inserting the expression for the variance of a, we obtain the exact distribution of e^{a}. The exact, *finite sample distribution* is not normal, and e^{a} is a biased estimator of A. However, both the bias and the variance go to zero as $n \to \infty$, so e^{a} is consistent. Using our earlier results, the *asymptotic distribution* of e^{a} is normal, with mean A and variance $(e^{\alpha})^2\theta^2$, where

$$\theta^2 = \frac{1}{n} \lim_{n \to \infty} n \text{Var}[a].$$

We would estimate this with

$$T^2 = \frac{e^{2a}s^2(1/n + \bar{x}^2)}{S_{xx}}$$

$$= e^{2a}\text{Var}[a].$$

10.3.3.   Asymptotic Behavior of Some Test Statistics

Without normality of ε, the t, F, and chi-squared statistics given earlier do not have these distributions. We can appeal instead to the results of Section 4.3.4. We have shown that

$$\mathbf{b} \xrightarrow{a} N\left[\boldsymbol{\beta}, \frac{\sigma^2}{n}\mathbf{Q}^{-1}\right].$$

It follows that the asymptotic distribution of

$$\theta_k = \frac{(b_k - \beta_k)}{\left[\frac{\sigma^2}{n}Q_{kk}^{-1}\right]^{1/2}}$$

is standard normal. Since plim $s^2(\mathbf{X}'\mathbf{X}/n)^{-1} = \sigma^2\mathbf{Q}^{-1}$,

$$t_k = \frac{(b_k - \beta_k)}{[s^2(\mathbf{X}'\mathbf{X})_{kk}^{-1}]^{1/2}}$$

will have the same asymptotic distribution as θ_k. So, instead of the t distribution, we can refer the usual statistics for hypotheses about an element of $\boldsymbol{\beta}$ to the standard normal distribution.

The F statistic for testing a set of linear restrictions,

$$F = \frac{[\mathbf{e}'_*\mathbf{e}_* - \mathbf{e}'\mathbf{e}]/J}{\mathbf{e}'\mathbf{e}/(n - K)} = \frac{(\mathbf{Rb} - \mathbf{q})'[\mathbf{R}(s^2(\mathbf{X}'\mathbf{X})^{-1})\mathbf{R}']^{-1}(\mathbf{Rb} - \mathbf{q})}{J},$$

is no longer distributed as F because neither the numerator nor the denominator has the necessary chi-squared distribution. However, the Wald statistic, $JF[J, n - K]$, does have a chi-squared distribution asymptotically and can be used instead. This is the same result we have for the case of normally distributed disturbances. Under the usual assumptions, the Wald statistic may be used whether or not the disturbances are normally distributed. A proof of this important conclusion will be instructive.[9]

---

[9] See White (1984, p. 71).

Theorem. If $\sqrt{n}(\mathbf{b} - \boldsymbol{\beta}) \xrightarrow{d} N(0, \sigma^2\mathbf{Q}^{-1})$, and if $H_0: \mathbf{R}\boldsymbol{\beta} - \mathbf{q} = 0$ is true,

$$W = (\mathbf{Rb} - \mathbf{q})'[\mathbf{R}(s^2(\mathbf{X}'\mathbf{X})^{-1})\mathbf{R}']^{-1}(\mathbf{Rb} - \mathbf{q})$$

converges in distribution to a chi-squared variate with J degrees of freedom.

Proof: Since R is a matrix of constants,

$$\sqrt{n}\mathbf{R}(\mathbf{b} - \boldsymbol{\beta}) \xrightarrow{d} N[0, \mathbf{R}(\sigma^2\mathbf{Q}^{-1})\mathbf{R}'].\tag{1}$$

But $\mathbf{R}\boldsymbol{\beta} = \mathbf{q}$, so

$$\sqrt{n}(\mathbf{Rb} - \mathbf{q}) \xrightarrow{d} N[0, \mathbf{R}(\sigma^2\mathbf{Q}^{-1})\mathbf{R}'].\tag{2}$$

For convenience, write this as

$$\mathbf{z} \xrightarrow{d} N[0, \mathbf{P}].\tag{2'}$$

In Section 2.7.12, we defined the inverse square root of a positive definite matrix as another matrix, say, $\mathbf{T}$ such that $\mathbf{T}^2 = \mathbf{P}^{-1}$, and denoted $\mathbf{T}$ as $\mathbf{P}^{-1/2}$. Let $\mathbf{T}$ be the inverse square root of $\mathbf{P}$. Then, by the same reasoning as in (1) and (2),

$$\text{If } \mathbf{z} \xrightarrow{d} N[0, \mathbf{P}], \mathbf{P}^{-1/2}\mathbf{z} \xrightarrow{d} N[0, \mathbf{P}^{-1/2}\mathbf{PP}^{-1/2}] = N[0, \mathbf{I}].\tag{3}$$

We now invoke (4–31) for the limiting distribution of a function of a random variable. The sum of squares of uncorrelated (i.e., independent) standard normal variables is distributed as chi-squared. Thus, the limiting distribution of

$$(\mathbf{P}^{-1/2}\mathbf{z})'(\mathbf{P}^{-1/2}\mathbf{z}) = \mathbf{z}'\mathbf{P}^{-1}\mathbf{z} \xrightarrow{d} \chi^2(J).\tag{4}$$

Reassembling the parts from before, we have shown that the limiting distribution of

$$n(\mathbf{Rb} - \mathbf{q})[\mathbf{R}(\sigma^2\mathbf{Q}^{-1})\mathbf{R}']^{-1}(\mathbf{Rb} - \mathbf{q})\tag{5}$$

is chi-squared, with J degrees of freedom. Finally, if

$$\text{plim } s^2\left[\left(\frac{1}{n}\mathbf{XX}\right)^{-1}\right] = \sigma^2\mathbf{Q}^{-1},\tag{6}$$

the statistic obtained by replacing $\sigma^2\mathbf{Q}^{-1}$ by $s^2(\mathbf{XX}/n)^{-1}$ in (5) has the same limiting distribution. The n's cancel, and we are left with the Wald statistic from before. This completes the proof. The Wald statistic can be computed as J times the usual F statistic.

The implication of these asymptotic results is that if all the assumptions of the classical model with normal disturbances are not met, the significance levels assigned to the familiar test statistics will be inappropriate. The exact finite sample distribution of, for example, a t statistic will almost surely be intractable. But the same statistic will be asymptotically distributed as standard normal. Unfortunately, this leaves open the question of how to proceed in a moderately sized sample. If the sample is not large, the limiting distributions (e.g., standard normal instead of t) are likely to be overly optimistic. Conservativism may still argue in favor of using the finite sample distributions, t, F, or chi-squared.

10.3.4.   Asymptotic Efficiency—Maximum Likelihood Estimation

The Gauss–Markov theorem is an exact, finite-sample result. Least squares remains the minimum variance linear unbiased estimator of the coefficient vector, regardless of the sample size. However, we have not ruled out the possibility that some biased but consistent estimator has a smaller asymptotic variance. Thus far, we have only established the efficiency of least squares in a very restricted class of estimators. Without any further assumption about the distribution of ε, nothing more beyond the Gauss–Markov theorem can be said about the optimality of the least squares estimator. At this point, therefore, it is useful to assume once again that the disturbances in the regression have a normal distribution. We shall examine some alternative cases in Section 10.3.5.

Definition. An estimator is asymptotically efficient if it is consistent, asymptotically normally distributed, and has an asymptotic covariance matrix that is smaller than the asymptotic covariance matrix of any other consistent, asymptotically normally distributed estimator.[10]

Taken directly, asymptotic efficiency is likely to be extremely difficult to verify. There is, however, a valid indirect strategy. In any regular problem, the maximum likelihood estimator is asymptotically efficient by the previous definition.[11] Therefore, in order to establish that an estimator is asymptotically efficient, one need only show that the estimator in question either (1) *is* the maximum likelihood estimator or (2) has the same asymptotic properties as the maximum likelihood estimator. We shall use both of these approaches here, the first for the least squares estimator of β and the second for the least squares estimator of σ^2. As such, least squares has all of the desirable properties of maximum likelihood estimators, including asymptotic efficiency.[12]

The likelihood function for a sample of n independent, identically and normally distributed disturbances is

$$L = (2\pi\sigma^2)^{-n/2} e^{-\varepsilon'\varepsilon/(2\sigma^2)}. \tag{10-18}$$

The transformation from ε_i to y_i is $\varepsilon_i = y_i - \beta' x_i$, so the Jacobian for each observation, $|\partial\varepsilon_i/\partial y_i|$, is one.[13] Making the transformation, we find that the likelihood function for the n observations on the observed random variables is

$$L = (2\pi\sigma^2)^{-n/2} e^{(-1/(2\sigma^2))\Sigma_i(y_i - \beta' x_i)^2}$$

$$= (2\pi\sigma^2)^{-n/2} e^{(-1/(2\sigma^2))(y - X\beta)'(y - X\beta)}. \tag{10-19}$$

It is clear that to maximize this function with respect to β, it will be necessary to maximize the exponent or minimize the familiar sum of squares. Taking logs in (10–19), we obtain the log-likelihood function for the classical regression model:

$$\ln L = -\frac{n}{2}\ln 2\pi - \frac{n}{2}\ln \sigma^2 - \frac{1}{2\sigma^2}(y - X\beta)'(y - X\beta).$$

---

[10] *Smaller* is defined in the sense of Chapter 2: The covariance matrix of the less efficient estimator equals that of the efficient estimator plus a nonnegative definite matrix.

[11] By *regular*, we mean a likelihood function that satisfies the regularity conditions discussed in Sections 4.3.2 and 4.5.

[12] The general results are presented in Section 4.5.

[13] See (3–41) in Section 3.5.

The necessary conditions for maximizing this log-likelihood are

$$\frac{\partial \ln L}{\partial \boldsymbol{\beta}} = \frac{1}{\sigma^2} \mathbf{X}'(\mathbf{y} - \mathbf{X}\boldsymbol{\beta}) = \mathbf{0}, \tag{10-20}$$

$$\frac{\partial \ln L}{\partial \sigma^2} = -\frac{n}{2\sigma^2} + \frac{1}{2\sigma^4}(\mathbf{y} - \mathbf{X}\boldsymbol{\beta})'(\mathbf{y} - \mathbf{X}\boldsymbol{\beta}) = 0.$$

The values that satisfy these equations are

$$\hat{\boldsymbol{\beta}}_{ML} = (\mathbf{X}'\mathbf{X})^{-1}\mathbf{X}'\mathbf{y} = \mathbf{b}$$

$$\tag{10-21}$$

and

$$\hat{\sigma}^2_{ML} = \frac{\mathbf{e}'\mathbf{e}}{n}.$$

The slope estimator is the familiar one, while the variance estimator differs from the least squares value by the divisor of n instead of $n - K$.

The Cramér–Rao bound for the variance of an unbiased estimator is the negative inverse of the expectation of

$$\begin{bmatrix} \partial^2 \ln L/\partial \boldsymbol{\beta} \partial \boldsymbol{\beta}' & \partial^2 \ln L/\partial \boldsymbol{\beta} \partial \sigma^2 \\ \partial^2 \ln L/\partial \sigma^2 \partial \boldsymbol{\beta}' & \partial^2 \ln L/\partial (\sigma^2)^2 \end{bmatrix} = \begin{bmatrix} -(1/\sigma^2)\mathbf{X}'\mathbf{X} & -(1/(2\sigma^4))\mathbf{X}'\boldsymbol{\varepsilon} \\ -(1/(2\sigma^4))\boldsymbol{\varepsilon}'\mathbf{X} & n/(2\sigma^4) - \boldsymbol{\varepsilon}'\boldsymbol{\varepsilon}/\sigma^6 \end{bmatrix}. \tag{10-22}$$

In taking expected values, the off diagonal term vanishes. Thus, the Cramér–Rao variance bound is

$$-[\mathbf{I}(\boldsymbol{\beta}, \sigma^2)]^{-1} = \begin{bmatrix} \sigma^2(\mathbf{X}'\mathbf{X})^{-1} & \mathbf{0} \\ \mathbf{0}' & 2\sigma^4/n \end{bmatrix}. \tag{10-23}$$

The least squares slope estimator coincides with the maximum likelihood estimator for this problem. Therefore, it inherits all of the desirable asymptotic properties of maximum likelihood estimators. To reiterate:

1. It is *consistent*, which we showed earlier.
2. It is *asymptotically normally distributed*, with an asymptotic variance matrix equal to the Cramér–Rao bound for efficient estimation.
3. It is *asymptotically efficient*. No other consistent and asymptotically normally distributed estimator has a smaller asymptotic covariance matrix.
4. Maximum likelihood estimators are also *invariant*. The maximum likelihood estimator of any continuous function of $\boldsymbol{\beta}$ is that function of the maximum likelihood estimator. Whereas, by the Gauss–Markov theorem, we could assert that the most efficient linear unbiased estimator of $\mathbf{r}'\boldsymbol{\beta}$ is $\mathbf{r}'\mathbf{b}$, we now have a much broader result. At least asymptotically, the most efficient estimator of $\mathbf{f}(\boldsymbol{\beta})$, where $\mathbf{f}(\boldsymbol{\beta})$ is any set of continuous functions, is $\mathbf{f}(\mathbf{b})$. The asymptotic distribution of this continuous function of the maximum likelihood estimator is given by (10–16). Thus, the estimator of α in Example 10.1 is the maximum likelihood estimator.

We showed earlier that $s^2 = \mathbf{e}'\mathbf{e}/(n - K)$ is an unbiased estimator of σ^2. Therefore, the maximum likelihood estimator is biased toward zero:

$$E[\hat{\sigma}^2] = \frac{(n - K)}{n}\sigma^2 = \left(1 - \frac{K}{n}\right)\sigma^2 < \sigma^2. \tag{10-24}$$

In spite of its small-sample bias, the maximum likelihood estimator of σ^2 has all of the desirable asymptotic properties. We see in (10–24) that s^2 and $\hat{\sigma}^2$ differ only by a factor

$-K/n$, which vanishes in large samples. Nonetheless, it is instructive to formalize the asymptotic equivalence of the two. From (10–21) and (10–23), we know that

$$\sqrt{n}(\hat{\sigma}^2 - \sigma^2) \xrightarrow{d} N[0, 2\sigma^4].$$

It follows that the limiting distribution of

$$z_n = \left(1 - \frac{K}{n}\right)\sqrt{n}(\hat{\sigma}^2 - \sigma^2) + \frac{K}{\sqrt{n}}\sigma^2$$

is that of

$$\left(1 - \frac{K}{n}\right)N[0, 2\sigma^4] + \frac{K}{\sqrt{n}}\sigma^2.$$

But $K/\sqrt{n}$ and K/n vanish as $n \to \infty$, so the limiting distribution of z_n is also $N[0, 2\sigma^4]$. Since

$$z_n = \sqrt{n}(s^2 - \sigma^2),$$

we have shown that the asymptotic distribution of s^2 is the same as that of the maximum likelihood estimator.

We have not yet ruled out the possibility that there is some other *unbiased* estimator of σ^2 that is more efficient than $\mathbf{e}'\mathbf{e}/(n - K)$. We can invoke the results of Pitman and Rao–Blackwell to do so. The normal distribution is an exponential family of distributions.[14] Therefore, the most efficient unbiased estimator of the parameters of this distribution is the one that is a function of sufficient statistics (assuming that an unbiased estimator exists at all). It is easy to show that the means and sums of squares and cross-products in this distribution are the sufficient statistics. We conclude, therefore, since $\mathbf{b}$ and s^2 are functions of sufficient statistics, that

No other unbiased estimators of β or σ^2 in this
model have smaller variances than b and s^2.

With respect to β, this result extends the Gauss–Markov theorem a bit. Whereas Gauss–Markov applies to *linear* unbiased estimators, this result encompasses *all* unbiased estimators.

This completes the derivation of the properties of the least squares estimators in the classical *normal* regression model. It should be noted that at several points the unbiased estimator was used as a yardstick. As a burgeoning literature has investigated, there are many settings in which unbiasedness as an estimation criterion has very little to recommend it.[15] There will be cases in which it will make sense to accept a small amount of bias in trade for a more precise estimator. However, the asymptotic properties of least squares are unambiguously optimal.[16]

10.4. *Stochastic Regressors*

The assumption of nonstochastic **X**, while very useful from a theoretical standpoint, is inconsistent with most situations encountered in practice. For example, models that contain lagged values of the dependent variable among the regressors are quite common. If the

---

[14] See Kendall and Stuart (1972).
[15] A very good compendium on the subject is Judge et al. (1985).
[16] Even this must be qualified by the assumption of normality. Absent this assumption, least squares may become less attractive. We consider a specific example later.

results of our analysis are to have much generality, it will be necessary to relax this assumption. The overall conclusion reached in this section is that the essential results of Section 10.3 can be extended to an impressive array of far more general models.

10.4.1. Independent Observations on X and ε

We replace assumption II from Section 10.2 with the less restrictive one that the rows of **X** are drawn *independently* from some random process and that

1. Every element of ε is stochastically independent of every element of $\mathbf{X}$.[17]
2. $\operatorname{Plim} \bar{\mathbf{Q}}_n = (1/n)\mathbf{X}'\mathbf{X} = \mathbf{Q}$, where $\mathbf{Q}$ is a constant, positive definite matrix.

Assumption 2 amounts simply to replacing the ordinary limit in (10–1) with a probability limit (although it is a considerable change in the character of the model). If the rows of **X** are stochastic, then assumption 2 must be justified by a characterization of the random process generating the data. In this case, 2 is an assumption that the sample means of squares and cross-products give a consistent estimator of the matrix of expected squares and cross-products. One way to justifying this is to assume that the rows of **X** are a random sample drawn from a multivariate distribution with finite fourth moments.[18] In this case, a mean square convergence argument can be used to show that the sample second moment is consistent for the population second moment.[19] Now what becomes of our results if this new facet is added to the model?[20]

To begin, we shall obtain the finite sample properties of **b** and s^2. A convenient method of doing so is, first, to obtain the desired result conditional on the observed **X**.[21] This is equivalent to the nonstochastic regressors case. We then find the unconditional expectation or distribution by "averaging" (e.g., integrating over) the conditional distributions. The proof of unbiasedness to be shown provides a straightforward example.

The finite sample property of unbiasedness is intact, but the proof must be modified slightly. As before,

$$\mathbf{b} = \boldsymbol{\beta} + (\mathbf{X}'\mathbf{X})^{-1}\mathbf{X}'\boldsymbol{\varepsilon}. \tag{10–25}$$

So, conditioned on the observed **X**,

$$E[\mathbf{b}|\mathbf{X}] = \boldsymbol{\beta} + (\mathbf{X}'\mathbf{X})^{-1}\mathbf{X}'E[\boldsymbol{\varepsilon}|\mathbf{X}]. \tag{10–26}$$

A useful device is the law of iterated expectations:

$$E[\mathbf{b}] = E_{\mathbf{X}}[E[\mathbf{b}|\mathbf{X}]]$$
$$= \boldsymbol{\beta} + E_{\mathbf{X}}[(\mathbf{X}'\mathbf{X})^{-1}\mathbf{X}'E[\boldsymbol{\varepsilon}|\mathbf{X}]].$$

Applying this to (10–26), we find that if $E[\varepsilon|\mathbf{X}] = \mathbf{0}$, which it must be, given assumption (2'), then **b** is unbiased unconditionally as well. Thus,

$$E[\mathbf{b}] = E_{\mathbf{X}}[E[\mathbf{b}|\mathbf{X}]] = E_{\mathbf{X}}[\boldsymbol{\beta}] = \boldsymbol{\beta}. \tag{10–27}$$

---

[17] If one of the elements of **X** is a lagged value of y, this assumption will be violated.
[18] See, for example, (4–20). This is a multivariate generalization in which we might define $\mathbf{Q}_i = \mathbf{x}_i\mathbf{x}_i'$ and $\mathbf{X}'\mathbf{X}/n$ is then $(1/n)\Sigma_i\mathbf{Q}_i$. For **Q** to have a finite variance, **x** must have finite fourth moments.
[19] See, for example, (10–10) and (10–11).
[20] The assumptions also include the case in which some (or all) of the columns of **X** are nonstochastic.
[21] Doing this analysis conditionally on the observed **X** does not imply that the conditional results are necessarily of any interest. They are only a means to an end. The crux of the argument is that if we can establish results conditionally on an arbitrary **X**, we can average over the **X**'s to obtain an unconditional result.

The unbiasedness of OLS is robust to assumptions about the **X** matrix; it rests only on $E[\varepsilon|\mathbf{X}] = \mathbf{0}$.[22] The same logic shows that s^2 is still unbiased. We found that $E[s^2|\mathbf{X}] = \sigma^2$, so

$$E[s^2] = E_{\mathbf{X}}[E[s^2|\mathbf{X}]] = E[\sigma^2] = \sigma^2.$$

The variance of **b**, again conditional on **X**, is

$$\mathrm{Var}[\mathbf{b}|\mathbf{X}] = \sigma^2(\mathbf{X}'\mathbf{X})^{-1}.$$

For the exact variance, we use the decomposition of variance of (3–70):

$$\mathrm{Var}[\mathbf{b}] = E_{\mathbf{X}}[\mathrm{Var}[\mathbf{b}|\mathbf{X}]] + \mathrm{Var}_{\mathbf{X}}[E[\mathbf{b}|\mathbf{X}]].$$

From (10–27), the second term is zero, which leaves

$$\mathrm{Var}[\mathbf{b}] = E[\sigma^2(\mathbf{X}'\mathbf{X})^{-1}] = \sigma^2 E[(\mathbf{X}'\mathbf{X})^{-1}]. \tag{10–28}$$

Our earlier conclusion is altered slightly. We must replace $(\mathbf{X}'\mathbf{X})^{-1}$ with its expected value to get the appropriate finite sample variance.

   If we now invoke the normality assumption, we can obtain the counterparts to several of our earlier results. Since both

$$E[s^2|\mathbf{X}] = \sigma^2$$

and

$$\mathrm{Var}[s^2|\mathbf{X}] = \frac{2\sigma^4}{(n-K)}$$

are independent of **X**, the unconditional variance of σ^2 is $2\sigma^4/(n-K)$ as well. (See the preceding decomposition of $\mathrm{Var}[\mathbf{b}]$.) Finding the exact distributions of the estimators will be more complicated now. The exact distribution of $\mathbf{b}|\mathbf{X}$ is $N[\boldsymbol{\beta}, \sigma^2(\mathbf{X}'\mathbf{X})^{-1}]$. However, the unconditional, *exact, finite sample*, distribution of **b** will generally be impossible to obtain. Its precise form will be obtained by integrating **X** out of the joint density.

$$f[\mathbf{b}, \mathbf{X}] = f[\mathbf{b}|\mathbf{X}]g[\mathbf{X}],$$

where $g[\mathbf{X}]$ is the marginal distribution of the stochastic elements of **X**. Then

$$f[\mathbf{b}] = \int_{\mathbf{X}} f[\mathbf{b}|\mathbf{X}]g[\mathbf{X}]\,d\mathbf{X}$$

$$= \int_{\mathbf{X}} g[\mathbf{X}](2\pi\sigma^2)^{-K/2}|\mathbf{X}'\mathbf{X}|^{1/2}e^{-(\mathbf{b}-\boldsymbol{\beta})'\mathbf{X}'\mathbf{X}(\mathbf{b}-\boldsymbol{\beta})/(2\sigma^2)}\,d\mathbf{X}.$$

This will depend on the distribution of **X** and, except in the simplest possible cases, will be challenging, to say the least. It is precisely for this reason that we rely on the much simpler and *known* asymptotic distributions.

   It might seem that a similar conclusion should apply to s^2, but this would be unduly pessimistic. Conditioned on **X**, $(n-K)s^2/\sigma^2 \sim \chi^2[n-K]$. Since this distribution does not involve **X**, it is the unconditional distribution as well.[23] The distribution follows from the

---

[22] Note that this is stronger than $E[\varepsilon] = \mathbf{0}$. It is possible for $E[\varepsilon|\mathbf{X}]$ to be nonzero and $E[\varepsilon]$ to be zero if $E[\mathbf{X}] = \mathbf{0}$. To visualize a case, consider a regression line that is tilted through the point $(E[x] = 0, E[y])$. Disturbances left of $E[x]$ will tend to have one sign and those on the right the other. On average, they would be zero. We have ruled out this possibility with the strict independence of **X** and ε.

[23] We shall prove this proposition in the next section.

result that for any $\mathbf{X}$, stochastic or not, if $\varepsilon \sim N[\mathbf{0}, \sigma^2\mathbf{I}]$,

$$\left(\frac{\varepsilon}{\sigma}\right)'\mathbf{M}\left(\frac{\varepsilon}{\sigma}\right) \sim \chi^2[tr(\mathbf{M})].$$

It is worth reemphasizing that the result applies to *any* idempotent quadratic form in a standard normal vector, (ε/σ). It does not depend on the nature of the matrix in the quadratic form.

Finally, we have verified before that the covariance of $(\mathbf{b} - \boldsymbol{\beta}) = (\mathbf{X}'\mathbf{X})^{-1}\mathbf{X}'\varepsilon$ and $\mathbf{e} = \mathbf{M}\varepsilon$ is $\mathbf{0}$, conditioned on $\mathbf{X}$. The unconditional covariance is

$$\text{Cov}[(\mathbf{b} - \boldsymbol{\beta}), \mathbf{e}] = E_{\mathbf{X}}[\text{Cov}[(\mathbf{b} - \boldsymbol{\beta}), \mathbf{e}\,|\,\mathbf{X}]] + \text{Cov}_{\mathbf{X}}[E[(\mathbf{b} - \boldsymbol{\beta})\,|\,\mathbf{X}], E[\mathbf{e}\,|\,\mathbf{X}]].$$

Since all terms on the right-hand side are zero, we conclude that $\mathbf{b}$ and $\mathbf{e}$ are uncorrelated in this model. But because $\mathbf{b}$ and $\mathbf{e}$ are not joint normally distributed, *they are not necessarily independent*.[24]

EXAMPLE 10.2. Bivariate Normal Sampling.   Suppose that (y, x) are a sample of bivariate observations from a normal distribution with means zero. Then

$$y = \beta x + \varepsilon = E[y\,|\,x] + \varepsilon,$$

where

$$\beta = \frac{\text{Cov}[x, y]}{\text{Var}[x]} = \frac{\sigma_{xy}}{\sigma_{xx}},$$

$$\varepsilon \sim N[0, \sigma_{yy}(1 - \rho_{xy}^2)] = N[0, \sigma^2].$$

In the regression of y on x, $b = \mathbf{x}'\mathbf{y}/\mathbf{x}'\mathbf{x} = \beta + \mathbf{x}'\varepsilon/\mathbf{x}'\mathbf{x}$. As shown previously, the exact expectation of b is β. The exact variance is $\sigma^2 E[1/\mathbf{x}'\mathbf{x}]$. Since $\mathbf{x}$ is a sample of n independent observations from a normal distribution with a zero mean, $\mathbf{x}'\mathbf{x}$ is distributed as σ_{xx} times a chi-squared variable with n degrees of freedom. The expected value of the reciprocal of a squared variable can be derived from results for the gamma integral. The exact result is $1/(n - 2)$; hence, the exact variance of the least squares estimator in this model is $\sigma^2/[(n - 2)\sigma_{xx}]$. The exact distribution is intractable.

It is interesting that the asymptotic properties of the estimator in this model are the same as before. The simplest way to show this is to reconsider the log likelihood for the classical regression model. Using a basic result, (3–60), we obtain the joint distribution of y and $\mathbf{X}$:

$$f[\mathbf{y}, \mathbf{X}] = f[\mathbf{y}\,|\,\mathbf{X}]g[\mathbf{X}].$$

The log-likelihood function for the classical regression becomes

$$\ln L(\mathbf{y}, \mathbf{X}) = \ln[L(\mathbf{y}\,|\,\mathbf{X})g(\mathbf{X})] = \ln L(\mathbf{y}\,|\,\mathbf{X}) + \ln(g[\mathbf{X}])$$

$$= -\left(\frac{n}{2}\right)\ln 2\pi - \left(\frac{n}{2}\right)\ln \sigma^2 - \left(\frac{1}{2\sigma^2}\right)(\mathbf{y} - \mathbf{X}\boldsymbol{\beta})'(\mathbf{y} - \mathbf{X}\boldsymbol{\beta}) + \ln(g[\mathbf{X}]). \qquad (10\text{–}29)$$

As long as the probability distribution of $\mathbf{X}$ does not involve either $\boldsymbol{\beta}$ or σ^2, the least squares estimators of these parameters are still the maximum likelihood estimators. As such,

All of the asymptotic results of the model with nonstochastic regressors are retained in this extended model.

---

[24] The difference is explored in an example by Kelejian and Prucha (1985).

10.4.2. Test Statistics with Stochastic X and Normal ε

Finally, we consider the validity of our finite sample test statistics and inference procedures in this extended model. Consider, first, the conventional t statistic for testing $H_0: \beta_i = \beta_i^0$:

$$t\,|\,\mathbf{X} = \frac{(b_i - \beta_i^0)}{[s^2(\mathbf{X}'\mathbf{X})_{ii}^{-1}]^{1/2}}.$$

Conditional on $\mathbf{X}$, $t\,|\,\mathbf{X}$ has a t distribution with $(N - K)$ degrees of freedom. However, what interests us is the marginal, that is, the unconditional, distribution of t. As we saw, **b** is only normally distributed conditionally on $\mathbf{X}$; the marginal distribution is not normal. Similarly because of the presence of the stochastic $\mathbf{X}$, the denominator of the t statistic is not the square root of a chi-square divided by its degrees of freedom, again, except conditional on this $\mathbf{X}$. The surprising result, however, is that *in spite of these complications,*

The *marginal* distribution of t is still t, with $(n - K)$ degrees of freedom, regardless of the distribution of $\mathbf{X}$ or even of whether $\mathbf{X}$ is stochastic or nonstochastic!

The proof of this intriguing result is very simple:

Proof: $f(t\,|\,\mathbf{X}) = t[n - K]$. This is only a function of $n - K$ and not of $\mathbf{X}$. Let $g(\mathbf{X})$ be the joint density of all of the stochastic elements in $\mathbf{X}$. By definition, the joint distribution of t and all of the elements in $\mathbf{X}$, $f(t, \mathbf{X})$ is

$$f(t, \mathbf{X}) = f(t\,|\,\mathbf{X})g(\mathbf{X}).$$

We obtain the marginal distribution of t by integrating $\mathbf{X}$ out of the joint distribution:[25]

$$f(t) = \int_{\mathbf{X}} f(t, \mathbf{X})\,d\mathbf{X}$$

$$= \int_{\mathbf{X}} f(t\,|\,\mathbf{X})g(\mathbf{X})\,d\mathbf{X}.$$

But remember, $f(t\,|\,\mathbf{X})$ is not a function of $\mathbf{X}$, so we may move it outside the integral. What is left inside the integral is only $g(\mathbf{X})$, which integrates to one by definition. This completes the proof.

The same reasoning can be used to prove that the usual F ratio used for testing linear restrictions is valid whether $\mathbf{X}$ is stochastic or not. This is a quite powerful result. Its upshot is that

If the disturbances are normally distributed, we may carry out tests and construct confidence intervals for the parameters without making any change in our procedures, regardless of whether the regressors are stochastic, nonstochastic, or some mix of the two.

To summarize, surprisingly little is lost in extending the regression model to include stochastic regressors. In particular, what has changed is that the marginal distribution of **b** is no longer normal, and the exact finite sample variance of **b** is now $\sigma^2 E[\mathbf{X}'\mathbf{X}]^{-1}$. As before,

---

[25] We use a general notation for this nK-fold integral, allowing, as well that if any of the variables are discrete, integration for those variables is replaced with summation.

this is estimated by $s^2(\mathbf{X'X})^{-1}$. In contrast, the distribution of $(n-K)s^2/\sigma^2$ is $\chi^2[n-K]$ whether $\mathbf{X}$ is stochastic or not. All of the finite sample inference procedures and their asymptotic counterparts are exactly the same as before.

10.5. Further Implications of Nonnormal Disturbances

Most of the exact finite sample results obtained earlier no longer hold when the disturbances in the model are not normally distributed. In addition, any results that are established by showing that least squares is a maximum likelihood estimator will no longer be valid. At the same time, most asymptotic results will continue to be valid in spite of this generalization.

10.5.1   A Case in Which Least Squares Is Inefficient

Most of our procedures for the classical regression model are robust to nonnormality of the disturbances. As a result, we may leave the distribution unspecified and continue to use least squares and our familiar testing procedures. Rarely will it be appropriate to specify a particular alternative distribution for the disturbance, but if it is, alternatives to least squares may be more efficient. For example, Greene (1980) considers estimation in a regression model with an asymmetrically distributed disturbance,

$$y = \left(\alpha - \frac{\sqrt{P}}{\sigma}\right) + \beta'\mathbf{x} - \left(\varepsilon - \frac{\sqrt{P}}{\sigma}\right)$$
$$= \alpha^* + \beta'\mathbf{x} + \varepsilon^*,$$

(10-30)

where ε has the gamma distribution in Section 3.4.5 [see (3-39)] and $\sigma=\sqrt{P}/\lambda$ is the standard deviation of the disturbance. He shows that the covariance matrix of the least squares estimator of the slope coefficients (not including the constant term) is, as always,

$$\text{Var}[\mathbf{b}] = \sigma^2(\mathbf{X'M^0X})^{-1},$$

while for the maximum likelihood estimator (which is not the OLS estimator),

$$\text{Asy. Var}[\hat{\beta}_{ML}] \simeq \left[\frac{(P-2)}{P}\right]\sigma^2(\mathbf{X'M^0X})^{-1}.$$

But for the asymmetry parameter, this would be the same as the least squares estimator. We conclude that the estimator that accounts for the asymmetric disturbance distribution is more efficient asymptotically.

10.5.2.   Alternative Estimation Criteria

As a general rule, least squares treats negative and positive observations symmetrically and involves sums of observations that weight all observations equally. Maximum likelihood estimators make more explicit use of information about the shape of the disturbance distribution and, when appropriate, weight observations according to a more appropriate weighting scheme. To consider another example, if the disturbances were distributed according to the Laplace distribution,

$$f(\varepsilon) = \frac{1}{2\sigma}e^{-|\varepsilon|/2\sigma},$$

the maximum likelihood estimator of β would minimize the sum of absolute values of the residuals instead of the sum of squares.[26] The least squares estimator can be seriously distorted by outlying observations in a relatively small sample, while the minimum absolute deviations (MAD) estimator will be considerably less so.

The possibility of disturbance distributions with thicker tails than the normal, particularly in microeconomic data and in applications in finance, has led to the proposal of numerous robust estimators.[27] Most of these can be written in the form

$$S(\mathbf{b}) = \sum \eta \left[\frac{(y - \mathbf{b}'x)}{s} \right],$$

where $\eta[\cdot]$ is a weighting function designed to reduce the weight attached to extreme observations. Least squares and MAD are two we have already considered. Alternatives that have been suggested include $\eta(z) = |z|^p$ for alternative values of p between one and two and some discontinuous ones such as $\eta(z) = -\cos(z) - 1$ if $|z| \leq \pi$ and zero otherwise.[28] Koenker and Basset (1978) have proposed the following criterion function:

$$S(\mathbf{b}) = t \sum_{+} |(y - \mathbf{b}'x)| + (1 - t) \sum_{-} |(y - \mathbf{b}'x)|,$$

where t is a predetermined proportion. For certain thick-tailed distributions, this estimator has performed well in Monte Carlo studies. However, in practice, the choice of t is likely to be a problem. These estimators have found little use in econometrics, primarily because of the difficulty in implementing them and their largely ad hoc nature. Tinkering with the outlying observations amounts to letting the computer be the ultimate judge of the estimated relationship and diminishes the role of the underlying theory. Least squares remains by far the estimator of choice for the linear regression model.

10.5.3.   A Model for Asymmetric Disturbances

Attempts to fit "orthodox" frontier functions such as the gamma frontier have met with little success. There are two quite telling criticisms of the approach of the previous section. First, estimation is exceedingly difficult. The log likelihood involves logs of residuals, which are not necessarily positive even though their counterparts in the population are. More problematic is the fact that the model attributes all sources of the disturbance, including measurement error, to inefficiency, which seems unreasonable. A much more promising approach has been the use of *stochastic frontiers*. Even allowing for the definition of a production function, we acknowledge that many factors can intervene so that the frontier itself may not be fixed from firm to firm. Each firm's "efficient" frontier is unique to that firm.[29] A formulation that incorporates this reasoning is

$$y_i = \beta'\mathbf{x}_i + v_i - u_i.$$

We allow v_i to be normally distributed to reflect the random factors such as weather, and use a one-sided disturbance, u_i, to represent the inefficiency component. The compound disturbance is the sum of a symmetrically distributed variable and a one-sided one. Thus, it has a range of $-\infty$ to ∞, but is skewed to the right and has a nonzero mean (i.e., the mean of

---

[26] See Taylor (1974).

[27] An extensive survey may be found in Amemiya (1985, pp. 70–80).

[28] Andrews (1974).

[29] A producer's costs may be forced up by weather, other random and uncontrollable events, even a train wreck that causes supplies to be late. This can hardly be attributed to inefficiency.

$-u_i$). As before, the slopes can be estimated by least squares, though maximum likelihood is more efficient.

Several alternative models for u_i have been suggested; the absolute value of a normally distributed variable has proved most successful.[30] The density of a normally distributed variable minus the absolute value of another, independent normal variable has been shown to be

$$f(v - u) = f(\varepsilon) = \left(\frac{0.79745886}{\sigma}\right)\Phi\left(-\frac{\varepsilon\lambda}{\sigma}\right)\phi\left(\frac{\varepsilon}{\sigma}\right),$$

where $\Phi(.)$ is the standard normal cdf, $\phi(.)$ is the standard normal density, $\sigma = \sqrt{\sigma_v^2 + \sigma_u^2}$, and $\lambda = \sigma_u/\sigma_v$. Inserting $\varepsilon = y - x'\beta$, taking logs, and summing over the observations produces the log likelihood. Maximization is straightforward, as discussed in the aforementioned studies. This log likelihood has the interesting property that it may have two stationary points. The least squares estimates, with $\lambda = 0$, always satisfy the first-order conditions. If the residuals are skewed to the right (as are the true disturbances), there will be another stationary point at the maximum likelihood estimator.[31]

10.5.4. Detecting Nonnormality

In the stochastic frontier model, if there is no inefficiency, the disturbance will be symmetric (and normal). As such, the skewness of the disturbance distribution is informative about the amount of inefficiency. Since only the least squares constant term is biased, the residuals in the model are biased upward, but all by the same constant amount. Can we use the third moment of the least squares residuals to estimate the third moment of the true disturbances?[32] This section considers the more general problem of using the moments of the least squares residuals to make inference about the distribution of the true disturbances.

The natural estimator of

$$\mu_r = E[\varepsilon^r]$$

would be

$$m_r = \left(\frac{1}{n}\right)\sum_i e_i^r.$$

However, the least squares residuals are only imperfect estimates of the true disturbances:

$$e_i = \varepsilon_i - x_i'(b - \beta).$$

Since plim $b = \beta$, the larger the sample, the better an estimate this becomes. This is sometimes labeled *pointwise consistency*.[33] It can be shown that the sample of least squares residuals converges to the sample of true disturbances.[34] This implies that if

$$\hat{\mu}_r = \frac{1}{n}\sum_i \varepsilon_i^r$$

---

[30] See Aigner et al. (1977), Schmidt (1986), and Forsund et al. (1980).

[31] Waldman (1982).

[32] The fact that each residual is biased upward by the same amount is no problem, since it is a higher moment that interests us. If we knew the constant, say m, we would set each residual to $u_i = e_i - m$, but then use a central moment to calculate the skewness, thereby adding m once again.

[33] For an application of this result, see Greene (1980), where the result is used to show that "hanging" the estimated regression line on the highest data point will correct the bias in the constant term in the least squares estimates of (10–23).

[34] See, for example, Theil (1971).

is a consistent estimator of μ_r, then

$$m_r = \frac{1}{n} \sum_i e_i^r$$

is also.

The foregoing can be used to devise a test of normality. The normal distribution is symmetric and *mesokurtic*. The symmetry implies that the third moment, $E[\varepsilon^3]$, is zero. The standard measure of symmetry of a distribution is the skewness coefficient,

$$\sqrt{\beta_1} = \frac{E[\varepsilon^3]}{(\sigma^2)^{3/2}}.$$

Kurtosis is a measure of the thickness of the tails of a distribution. The normal distribution is the usual yardstick for this; the mesokurtic value is the kurtosis of the normal distribution, which is

$$\beta_2 = \frac{E[\varepsilon^4]}{(\sigma^2)^2} = 3.$$

Therefore, we might compare a distribution to the normal distribution by comparing its skewness to zero and its kurtosis to three. (In practice, the usual measure is the *degree of excess*, $(\beta_2 - 3)$.) The device we shall use is a Wald statistic. Under the hypothesis of normality, the test statistic would be

$$W = n\left[\frac{b_1}{6} + \frac{(b_2 - 3)^2}{24}\right] \sim \chi^2(2).$$

This is asymptotically distributed as chi-squared with two degrees of freedom. Feasible estimators of these parameters are computed using the least squares residuals.[35] The statistic can be referred to the standard chi-squared tables.

EXAMPLE 10.3. The data used in the aforementioned study of production frontiers by Aigner et al. are listed in Section 7.2.4. A central feature of the model is the asymmetry and nonnormality of the disturbance distribution. The results of a least squares regression of the log of output on a constant and the logs of capital and labor are given with the data. Although the OLS estimates are inefficient and the estimate of the constant term is inconsistent (at least within the assumptions of the frontier model), the least squares residuals are still informative about the skewness and excess of the true disturbances. For those least squares residuals, the three necessary sample moments are

$$m_2 = 0.03266, \qquad m_3 = 0.004482, \qquad \text{and} \qquad m_4 = 0.003801.$$

The skewness and excess coefficients are, therefore, 0.7597 and 0.5654. With 27 observations, the chi-squared statistic is 2.9251. The 5 percent critical value from the chi-squared table for two degrees of freedom is 5.99, which suggests that these residuals do not depart significantly from normality. Aigner et al. do not carry out this test specifically. But an indirect test is provided by their maximum likelihood estimates of the parameters. In the stochastic frontier model, the variance of u is the nonnormality parameter; if this is zero, the disturbance

---

[35] It is sometimes suggested that the residuals be transformed to remove their finite sample covariance before these testing procedures are performed. See, for example, Judge et al. (1985, p. 826). Since the tests are valid only asymptotically, when the residuals are uncorrelated anyway, this would not add to the validity of the test procedures. There is some evidence, for example, by Ramsey (1974), that using BLUS residuals [see Theil (1971)] makes matters worse instead of better.

becomes symmetric and normal. In their results, the authors present an estimate of σ_u^2 that is only 0.01 times as large as σ_v^2 and has an asymptotic t ratio of only 0.05.[36] Therefore, their results are consistent with these.

This test statistic has been derived as a Lagrange multiplier test in the context of the Pearson distributions by Bera and Jarque (1980a and 1980b).[37] It should be noted that the test is essentially nonconstructive. A finding of nonnormality does not necessarily suggest what to do next.[38] It might be indicative of the need for some robust estimator if the chi-squared statistic is extremely large, particularly if this is due to a large kurtosis component.

Exercises

1. Let e_i be the ith residual in the ordinary least squares regression of y on X in the clas-sical regression model, and let ε_i be the corresponding true disturbance. Prove that $\text{plim}(e_i - \varepsilon_i) = 0$.

2. For the simple regression model,

$$y_i = \mu + \varepsilon_i, \qquad \varepsilon_i \sim N(0, \sigma^2),$$

prove that the sample mean is consistent and asymptotically normally distributed. Now consider the alternative estimator

$$\hat{\mu} = \sum_i w_i y_i,$$

$$w_i = \frac{i}{(n(n+1)/2)} = \frac{i}{\sum_i i}.$$

Note that $\sum_i w_i = 1$. Prove that this is a consistent estimator of μ and obtain its asymptotic variance. [**Hint:** $\sum_i i^2 = n(n+1)(2n+1)/6$.]

3. Example 8.3 presents Nerlove's estimates of a generalized Cobb–Douglas cost function:

$$\log\left(\frac{C}{P_f}\right) = \alpha + \beta \log Q + \gamma \log^2 Y + \delta_k \log\left(\frac{P_k}{P_f}\right) + \delta_l \log\left(\frac{P_1}{P_f}\right) + \varepsilon.$$

(Nerlove used common, not natural, logarithms.) The purpose of the generalization was to produce a **U**-shaped average total cost curve. We are interested in the output at which the cost curve reaches its minimum. That is the point at which

$$\left.\frac{\partial \log C}{\partial \log Q}\right|_{Q=Q^*} = 1$$

or

$$Q^* = 10^{[(1-\beta)/(2\gamma)]}.$$

(You can simplify the analysis a bit by using the fact that $10^x = \exp(2.3026x)$. Thus,

$$Q^* = \exp\left(2.3026\left[\frac{(1-\beta)}{2\gamma}\right]\right).$$

---

[36] Aigner et al. (1977, p. 33).
[37] Additional results appear in Kiefer and Salmon (1983).
[38] Proceeding with estimation in the more general model of Pearson type 7 distributions is so cumbersome that empirical implementation is likely to be exceedingly difficult.

Using the estimates given in the example, compute the estimate of this *efficient scale*. Estimate the asymptotic distribution of this estimate, assuming that the estimate of the asymptotic covariance of $\hat{\beta}$ and $\hat{\gamma}$ is -0.00008.

4. Suppose that y_i is a discrete random variable whose distribution, given x_i, is

$$\text{Prob}[Y_i = y_i] = \frac{e^{-\beta x_i}(\beta x_i)^{y_i}}{y_i!}, \qquad y_i = 0, 1, \ldots$$

Thus, y_i has a Poisson distribution. We also assume that $x_i > 0$ for all i.

(a) Compute the maximum likelihood estimator of β and its asymptotic distribution. Using the result that the sum of Poisson variables y_i with parameters λ_i is distributed as Poisson with parameter $\sum_i \lambda_i$, it is possible to obtain the exact distribution of the maximum likelihood estimator. What is this?

(b) As shown in Chapter 3, $E[y_i | x_i] = \beta x_i$. Therefore, this is a linear regression model. It does not satisfy the assumptions of the classical model, however, since $\text{Var}[y_i | x_i] = \beta x_i$. Nonetheless, it can be shown that the OLS estimator is consistent. Do so. Obtain the asymptotic distribution of the estimator. What assumptions are necessary to ensure your result?

(c) Prove that the asymptotic variance of the maximum likelihood estimator is smaller than that of the OLS estimator. (**Hint:** The proof will hinge upon the assumption that x_i is strictly positive.)

5. For the principal components estimator in (9–11), prove that the variance estimator,

$$q^2 = \frac{(\mathbf{y} - \mathbf{Zd})'(\mathbf{y} - \mathbf{Zd})}{n},$$

is not a consistent estimator of σ^2. Obtain the probability limit of q^2. (**Hint:** $\mathbf{I} - \mathbf{C}_L\mathbf{C}'_L = \mathbf{C}_M\mathbf{C}'_M$, where $\mathbf{C}_M$ is the matrix of the other $K - L$ characteristic vectors of $\mathbf{X'X}$.)

6. For the classical regression model $\mathbf{y} = \mathbf{X\beta} + \boldsymbol{\varepsilon}$ with no constant term and K regressors, what is

$$\text{plim } F[K, n - K] = \text{plim}\frac{R^2/K}{(1 - R^2)/(n - K)},$$

assuming that the true value of β is zero? What is the exact expected value?

7. For the instrumental variables estimator of (9–32), prove that

$$\hat{\sigma}^2 = \frac{(\mathbf{y} - \mathbf{Xb}_{IV})'(\mathbf{y} - \mathbf{Xb}_{IV})}{n}$$

is a consistent estimator of σ^2.

8. The density function for the compound disturbance in the stochastic frontier model is given at the end of Section 10.5.3.

(a) Derive the log-likelihood function and its first derivatives to define the maximum likelihood estimators of β, σ, and λ. Note that a useful shortcut is $d\phi(x)/dx = -x\phi(x)$.

(b) Show how you would obtain estimates and standard errors for the underlying parameters, σ_v^2 and σ_u^2, given estimates of σ and λ and the appropriate estimate of their asymptotic covariance matrix.

References

Aigner, D., K. Lovell, and P. Schmidt, "Formulation and Estimation of Stochastic Frontier Production Models," *Journal of Econometrics*, 6, 1977, pp. 21–37.

Amemiya, T., *Advanced Econometrics*, Cambridge, Mass.: Harvard University Press, 1985.

Andrews, D., "A Robust Method for Multiple Linear Regression," *Technometrics*, 16, 1974, pp. 523–531.

Bera, A., and C. Jarque, "Model Specification Tests: A Simultaneous Approach," *Journal of Econometrics*, 20, 1980a, pp. 59–82.

Bera, A., and C. Jarque, "Efficient Tests for Normality, Heteroscedasticity, and Serial Independence of Regression Residuals," *Economics Letters*, 6, 1980b, pp. 255–259.

Forsund, F., K. Lovell, and P. Schmidt, "A Survey of Frontier Production and of their Relationship to Efficiency Measurement," *Journal of Econometrics*, 13, 1980, pp. 5–25.

Greene, W., "Maximum Likelihood Estimation of Econometric Frontier Functions," *Journal of Econometrics*, 13, 1980, pp. 27–56.

Judge, G., C. Hill, W. Griffiths, H. Lutkepohl, and T. Lee, *The Theory and Practice of Econometrics*, New York: Wiley, 1985.

Kelejian, H., and I. Prucha, "Independent or Uncorrelated Disturbances in Linear Regression: An Illustration of the Difference," *Economics Letters*, 19, 1985, pp. 35–38.

Kendall, A., and M. Stuart, *The Advanced Theory of Statistics*, Vol. 1, London: Griffin, 1972.

Kiefer, N., and M. Salmon, "Testing Normality in Econometric Models," *Economics Letters*, 11, 1983, pp. 123–128.

Koenker, R., and G. Bassett, "Regression Quantiles," *Econometrica*, 46, 1978, pp. 107–112.

Malinvaud, E., *Statistical Methods of Econometrics*, Amsterdam: North Holland, 1971.

Ramsey, J., "Classical Model Selection Through Specification Error Tests," in P. Zarembka, ed., *Frontiers in Econometrics*, New York: Academic Press, 1974.

Schmidt, P., *Econometrics*, New York: Marcel Dekker, 1976.

Schmidt, P., "Frontier Production Functions," *Econometric Reviews*, 4, 2, 1986, pp. 289–328.

Taylor, L., "Estimation by Minimizing the Sum of Absolute Errors," in P. Zarembka, *Frontiers in Econometrics*, New York: Academic Press, 1974.

Theil, H., *Principles of Econometrics*, New York: Wiley, 1971.

Waldman, D., "A Stationary Point for the Stochastic Frontier Likelihood," *Journal of Econometrics*, 18, 1982, pp. 275–279.

White, H., *Asymptotic Theory for Econometricians*, New York: Academic Press, 1984.

Chapter 11
Nonlinear Regression Models

11.1. Introduction

To this point, we have considered only linear models that can be estimated by ordinary least squares. Although the linear model is flexible enough to allow great variety in the shape of the regression, it still rules out many useful functional forms. In this chapter we shall examine models that are intrinsically nonlinear in their parameters. Although these models are often expensive and difficult to estimate, with the development of easy-to-use software, they have become quite common.

11.2. Nonlinear Models

A general form of the regression model is

$$y_i = h(\mathbf{x}_i, \boldsymbol{\beta}) + \varepsilon_i.^1 \qquad (11-1)$$

The linear model is obviously a special case, but this includes far more possibilities. For example,

$$y = \beta_1 + \beta_2 e^{\beta_3 x} + \varepsilon \qquad (11-2)$$

cannot be transformed to linearity. It would appear that

$$y = \beta_1 x_1{}^{\beta_2} x_2{}^{\beta_3} e^{\varepsilon}$$

is also nonlinear, but for the purposes of our discussion, this is a linear regression model, while the first is not. The second can be transformed to linearity by taking logarithms on both sides of the equation.

We shall require an operational definition to distinguish these cases. In the context of regression analysis, what will characterize (11–1) as a **nonlinear regression model** is the method used to estimate the parameters. In particular, we take as our benchmark the case

---

[1] In principle, it could be written in terms of $g(Y_i)$. But unless $g(Y_i)$ introduces new unknown parameters, as in the Box–Cox model, we can view this as determining the units of measurement of Y and retain the less cumbersome notation.

in which ε is normally distributed. Then, using the argument of Chapter 10, the values of the parameters that minimize the sum of squared deviations,

$$S(\tilde{\boldsymbol{\beta}}) = \sum_i \varepsilon_i^2 = \sum_i [y_i - h(\mathbf{x}_i, \tilde{\boldsymbol{\beta}})]^2 \qquad (11\text{-}3)$$

will be the maximum likelihood estimators, as well as the **nonlinear least squares** estimators. The first-order conditions for minimization of $S(\beta)$ are

$$\frac{\partial S(\tilde{\boldsymbol{\beta}})}{\partial \tilde{\boldsymbol{\beta}}} = -2 \sum_i [y_i - h(\mathbf{x}_i, \tilde{\boldsymbol{\beta}})] \frac{\partial h(\mathbf{x}_i, \tilde{\boldsymbol{\beta}})}{\partial \tilde{\boldsymbol{\beta}}} = \mathbf{0}. \qquad (11\text{-}4)$$

In the linear model of Chapter 6, this will be a set of linear equations, that is, the normal equations (6–11). But in this more general case, this will be a set of very nonlinear equations that do not admit an explicit solution. This will typically require an iterative procedure for solution.

EXAMPLE 11.1.   The first-order conditions for estimating the parameters of (11–2) by least squares are

$$\frac{\partial S(\beta)}{\partial \beta_1} = -2 \sum_i [y_i - \beta_1 - \beta_2 e^{\beta_3 x_i}] \qquad = 0,$$

$$\frac{\partial S(\beta)}{\partial \beta_2} = -2 \sum_i [y_i - \beta_1 - \beta_2 e^{\beta_3 x_i}] e^{\beta_3 x_i} = 0,$$

$$\frac{\partial S(\beta)}{\partial \beta_3} = -2 \sum_i [y_i - \beta_1 - \beta_2 e^{\beta_3 x_i}] x_i e^{\beta_3 x_i} = 0.$$

These equations do not have an explicit solution.

Conceding the potential for ambiguity, we define a nonlinear regression model at this point as follows:

Definition.   A nonlinear regression model is one for which the first-order conditions for least squares estimation of the parameters are nonlinear functions of the parameters.[2]

Thus, nonlinearity is defined in terms of the techniques needed to estimate the parameters, not the shape of the regression function. Later, we shall broaden our definition to include other techniques besides least squares.

11.3.   The Linearized Regression

The nonlinear regression model is

$$y = h(\mathbf{x}, \boldsymbol{\beta}) + \varepsilon.$$

(To save some notation, we have dropped the observation subscript.) Many of the results that have been obtained for nonlinear regression models are based on a linear Taylor series

---

[2] Judge et al. (1985, pp. 195–196) adopt a similar approach but take a somewhat broader view of estimation. In their framework, the nonlinearity of the model is defined by the optimization criterion used to define the estimator. Thus, least squares is but one of the possibilities they would consider. The broader definition will be useful when we analyze models for which maximum likelihood techniques are indispensable. But in this chapter, least squares will provide a satisfactory benchmark.

approximation to $h(\mathbf{x}, \boldsymbol{\beta})$ at a particular value for the parameter vector, $\boldsymbol{\beta}^0$:

$$h(\mathbf{x}, \boldsymbol{\beta}) \simeq h(\mathbf{x}, \boldsymbol{\beta}^0) + \sum_k \left. \frac{\partial h(\mathbf{x}, \boldsymbol{\beta})}{\partial \beta_k} \right|_{\boldsymbol{\beta} = \boldsymbol{\beta}^0} (\beta_k - \beta_k^0). \tag{11-5}$$

This is called the **linearized regression model**. By collecting terms, we obtain

$$h(\mathbf{x}, \boldsymbol{\beta}) \simeq h(\mathbf{x}, \boldsymbol{\beta}^0) - \sum_k \beta_k^0 \left. \frac{\partial h(\mathbf{x}, \boldsymbol{\beta})}{\partial \beta_k} \right|_{\boldsymbol{\beta} = \boldsymbol{\beta}^0} + \sum_k \beta_k \left. \frac{\partial h(\mathbf{x}, \boldsymbol{\beta})}{\partial \beta_k} \right|_{\boldsymbol{\beta} = \boldsymbol{\beta}^0}. \tag{11-6}$$

Let $\tilde{x}_k^0$ equal the kth partial derivative,[3] $\partial h(\mathbf{x}, \boldsymbol{\beta}^0)/\partial \beta_k^0$. For a given value of $\boldsymbol{\beta}^0$, this is a function only of the data, not of the unknown parameters. We now have

$$
\begin{aligned}
h(\mathbf{x}, \boldsymbol{\beta}) &\simeq [h^0 - \sum_k \tilde{x}_k^0 \beta_k^0] + \sum_k \tilde{x}_k^0 \beta_k \\
&= h^0 - \tilde{\mathbf{x}}^{0\prime} \boldsymbol{\beta}^0 + \tilde{\mathbf{x}}^{0\prime} \boldsymbol{\beta}
\end{aligned}
\tag{11-7}
$$

or

$$y \simeq h^0 - \tilde{\mathbf{x}}^{0\prime} \boldsymbol{\beta}^0 + \tilde{\mathbf{x}}^{0\prime} \boldsymbol{\beta} + \varepsilon.$$

By placing the known terms on the left-hand side of the equation, we obtain a regression model:

$$y - h^0 + \tilde{\mathbf{x}}^{0\prime} \boldsymbol{\beta}^0 = \tilde{\mathbf{x}}^{0\prime} \boldsymbol{\beta} + \varepsilon. \tag{11-8}$$

With a value of $\boldsymbol{\beta}^0$ in hand, we could compute $\tilde{y}$ and $\tilde{\mathbf{x}}$ and estimate the parameters of $(11-8)$ by linear least squares.

EXAMPLE 11.2 For the example given in $(11-2)$, the regressors in the linearized equation would be

$$\tilde{x}_1^0 = \frac{\partial h(.)}{\partial \beta_1} = 1,$$

$$\tilde{x}_2^0 = \frac{\partial h(.)}{\partial \beta_2} = e^{\beta_3^0 x},$$

$$\tilde{x}_3^0 = \frac{\partial h(.)}{\partial \beta_3} = \beta_2^0 x e^{\beta_3^0 x}.$$

With a set of values of the parameters, $\boldsymbol{\beta}^0$,

$$\tilde{y}^0 = y - h(x, \beta_1^0, \beta_2^0, \beta_3^0) + \beta_1^0 \tilde{x}_1^0 + \beta_2^0 \tilde{x}_2^0 + \beta_3^0 \tilde{x}_3^0$$

could be regressed on the three variables previously defined to estimate β_1, β_2, and β_3.

11.4. *Nonlinear Least Squares Estimation*

Least squares remains an attractive way to proceed for estimating the parameters. Numerous analytical results have been obtained for the estimator, for example, consistency and asymptotic normality.[4] However, we cannot be sure that nonlinear least squares is the most

---

[3] You should verify that for the linear regression model, these derivatives are the independent variables.
[4] A complete discussion of the subject can be found in Amemiya (1985). Other important references are Jennrich (1969) and Malinvaud (1970), and, especially, Goldfeld and Quandt (1972).

efficient estimator, except in the case of normally distributed disturbances. (This is the same conclusion we drew for the linear model.) Some examples that follow will illustrate the point.

Before continuing, it is necessary to make some assumptions about the regressors. The precise requirements are discussed in some detail in Judge et al. (1985) and Amemiya (1985). In the classical regression model, in order to obtain our asymptotic results, we assumed that the sample moment matrix, $(1/n)\mathbf{X}'\mathbf{X}$, converged to a positive definite matrix, $\mathbf{Q}$. By analogy, we impose the same condition on the "regressors" in the linearized model *when they are computed at the true parameter values*. Therefore, for the nonlinear regression model, the analog to (10–1) is

$$\operatorname{plim}\left(\frac{1}{n}\right)\tilde{\mathbf{X}}'\tilde{\mathbf{X}} = \operatorname{plim}\left(\frac{1}{n}\right)\sum_i \left[\frac{\partial h(\mathbf{x}_i, \boldsymbol{\beta}^0)}{\partial \boldsymbol{\beta}^0}\right]\left[\frac{\partial h(\mathbf{x}_i, \boldsymbol{\beta}^0)}{\partial \boldsymbol{\beta}^{0\prime}}\right] = \tilde{\mathbf{Q}}, \qquad (11\text{–}9)$$

where $\tilde{\mathbf{Q}}$ is a positive definite matrix. With this in hand, the asymptotic properties of the nonlinear least squares estimator have been derived. They are, in fact, much like those we have already seen for the linear model, except that in this case we place the derivatives in $\tilde{\mathbf{X}}$ in the role of the regressors.[5]

The requirement that the matrix in (11–9) converge to a positive definite matrix carries with it the condition that the columns of the regressor matrix, $\tilde{\mathbf{X}}$, be linearly independent. This is an identification condition analogous to the requirement that the independent variables in the linear model be linearly independent.

The nonlinear least squares criterion function is

$$S(\mathbf{b}) = \sum_i [y_i - h(\mathbf{x}_i, \mathbf{b})]^2, \qquad (11\text{–}10)$$

where we have inserted what will be the solution value, $\mathbf{b}$. The first-order conditions for a minimum are

$$\mathbf{g}(\mathbf{b}) = -2\sum_i [y_i - h(\mathbf{x}_i, \mathbf{b})]\frac{\partial h(\mathbf{x}_i, \mathbf{b})}{\partial \mathbf{b}} = 0. \qquad (11\text{–}11)$$

This is a standard problem in nonlinear optimization, which can be solved by a number of methods.[6] The method of Gauss–Newton is often used in this setting. Recall that in our discussion of the linearized regression model, if a value of $\boldsymbol{\beta}_0$ were available, the linear regression model shown there could be estimated by ordinary least squares. Once a parameter vector is obtained, it can play the role of a new $\boldsymbol{\beta}_0$ and the computation can be done again. The iteration can continue until the difference between successive parameter vectors is small enough to assume convergence. One of the main virtues of this method is that at the last iteration the estimate of $\tilde{\mathbf{Q}}^{-1}$ will, apart from the scale factor $\hat{\sigma}^2$, provide the correct estimate of the asymptotic covariance matrix for the parameter estimates.[7] A consistent estimate of σ^2 can be computed using the residuals:

$$\hat{\sigma}^2 = \left(\frac{1}{n}\right)\sum_i [y_i - h(\mathbf{x}_i, \mathbf{b})]^2. \qquad (11\text{–}12)$$

---

[5] This description is a bit informal. The specific results, and additional assumptions necessary to reach these conclusions, are spelled out in detail in Amemiya (1985). However, the overall assessment of that study is as follows: "[T]he practical consequence...is that all of the results for the linear regression model are asymptotically valid for the nonlinear regression model if we treat $\mathbf{G}$ as the regressor matrix" (p. 136).

[6] Chapter 12 includes some of these methods.

[7] There are some drawbacks to this method as well, including the possibility that the process may not converge at all. These problems are discussed in Chapter 12.

(A degrees of freedom correction, $1/(n-K)$, would have no virtue here, as all results are asymptotic in any event. The estimator in (11–12) is the maximum likelihood estimator.)

The nonlinear least squares estimator has been analyzed extensively. It has been shown[8] that

$$\mathbf{b} \overset{a}{\rightarrow} N\left(\beta, \frac{\sigma^2}{n}\mathbf{Q}^{-1}\right),$$

where

$$\mathbf{Q} = \text{plim}\left(\frac{\tilde{\mathbf{X}}'\tilde{\mathbf{X}}}{n}\right).$$

The sample estimate of the asymptotic covariance matrix is

$$\text{Est. Asy. Var}[\mathbf{b}] = \hat{\sigma}^2(\tilde{\mathbf{X}}'\tilde{\mathbf{X}})^{-1}. \tag{11–13}$$

Once these are in hand, inference and hypothesis tests can proceed in the same fashion as prescribed in Chapter 8. A minor problem can arise in evaluating the fit of the regression in that

$$R^2 = 1 - \frac{\sum e_i^2}{\sum (y_i - \bar{y})^2} \tag{11–14}$$

is no longer guaranteed to be in the range of zero to one. It does, however, provide a useful descriptive measure.

EXAMPLE 11.3. A Nonlinear Consumption Function. The linear consumption function analyzed at the beginning of Chapter 5 is a restricted version of the more general consumption function

$$C = \alpha + \beta Y^\gamma + \varepsilon,$$

in which γ equals one. With this restriction, the model is linear. However, if γ is free to vary, this becomes a nonlinear regression. The linearized model is

$$C - (\alpha^0 + \beta^0 Y^{\gamma^0}) + \alpha^0(1) + \beta^0(Y^{\gamma^0}) + \gamma^0(\beta^0 Y^{\gamma^0} \ln Y) = \alpha + \beta(Y^{\gamma^0}) + \gamma(\beta^0 Y^{\gamma^0} \ln Y) + \varepsilon.$$

After a bit of manipulation, the nonlinear least squares procedure reduces to iterated regression of

$$C^0 = C + \gamma^0\beta^0 Y^{\gamma^0} \ln Y$$

on

$$\frac{\partial h(.)}{\partial \alpha} = 1,$$

$$\frac{\partial h(.)}{\partial \beta} = Y^{\gamma^0},$$

$$\frac{\partial h(.)}{\partial \gamma} = \beta^0 Y^{\gamma^0} \ln Y.$$

[8] A comprehensive discussion may be found in Amemiya (1985).

The data on consumption and income that are shown in Table 11.1 are used to fit the consumption function.

Table 11.1.   Aggregate Income, Y, and Consumption, C

	1950	1951	1952	1953	1954	1955	1956	1957	1958
Y	791.8	819.0	844.3	880.0	894.0	944.5	989.4	1012.1	1028.8
C	733.2	748.7	771.4	802.5	822.7	873.8	899.8	919.7	932.9

	1959	1960	1961	1962	1963	1964	1965	1966	1967
Y	1067.2	1091.1	1123.2	1170.2	1207.3	1291.0	1365.7	1431.3	1493.2
C	979.4	1005.1	1025.2	1069.0	1108.4	1170.6	1236.4	1298.9	1337.7

	1968	1969	1970	1971	1972	1973	1974	1975	1976
Y	1551.3	1599.8	1688.1	1728.4	1797.4	1916.3	1896.6	1931.7	2001.0
C	1405.9	1456.7	1492.0	1538.8	1621.9	1689.6	1674.0	1711.9	1803.9

	1977	1978	1979	1980	1981	1982	1983	1984	1985
Y	2066.6	2167.4	2212.6	2214.3	2248.6	2261.5	2334.6	2468.4	2509.0
C	1883.8	1961.0	2004.4	2000.4	2024.2	2050.7	2145.9	2239.9	2312.6

Source: Data are from the *Economic Report of the President*, Government Printing Office, Washington, D.C., 1986.

In general, finding the initial values for a nonlinear procedure can be a problem.[9] Simply trying a convenient set of values can be unproductive. For example, for our model, the values of 1.0 for all three parameters seem reasonable but leads to divergence of the procedure after only two iterations. Similarly using the OLS values of α and β, and 0.5 instead of 1.0 for γ, while apparently reasonable, leads to almost immediate explosion of the predicted values. Unfortunately, there are no good rules for starting values, except that they should be as close to the final values as possible (not particularly helpful). When it is possible, an initial consistent estimator of β will be a good starting value. However, in many cases, the only consistent estimator available is the one we are trying to compute by least squares. For better or worse, trial and error is the most frequently used procedure. For the present model, a natural set of values can be obtained because a simple linear model is a special case. Thus, we can start α and β at the linear least squares values that would result in the special case of $\gamma = 1$ and use 1 for the starting value for γ.

The parameter estimates are stable to five digits after only six iterations (see Table 11.2).

The procedures outlined earlier are used at the last iteration to obtain asymptotic standard errors and an estimate of σ^2. It is illustrative to compare these to the estimates for the linear consumption function, as shown in Table 11.3.

For hypothesis testing and confidence intervals, the usual procedures can be used, with the proviso that all results are only asymptotic. As such, for testing a restriction, the chi-squared statistic rather than the F ratio is likely to be more appropriate. For example, for testing the hypothesis that γ is different from one, an asymptotic t test, based, of course, on the

[9] A lengthy discussion may be found in Draper and Smith (1981, pp. 473–474).

Table 11.2

	α	Iterations β	γ
1	11.1458	0.898534	1.0
2	209.825	−0.237125	1.15139
3	187.786	0.246078	1.14613
4	187.710	0.245692	1.15699
5	187.915	0.245968	1.15641
6	187.899	0.246004	1.15640

Table 11.3

	Linear			Nonlinear	
	Estimate	Std. Error		Estimate	Std. Error
α	11.1458	9.64	α	187.899	40.68
β	0.898530	0.00586	β	0.246004	0.08299
γ	1.00000	—	γ	1.15640	0.04101
$e'e$	12068		$e'e$	8420	
σ^2	18.309		σ^2	15.243	
R^2	0.99856		R^2	0.99899	

Estimated Asymptotic Covariance Matrix

	$\hat\alpha$	$\hat\beta$	$\hat\gamma$
$\hat\alpha$	1654.8		
$\hat\beta$	−3.3302	0.00677	
$\hat\gamma$	1.6412	−0.0034003	0.001681

standard normal distribution, is carried out, using

$$z = \frac{(1.1564 - 1)}{0.04101} = 3.813.$$

This is larger than the critical values of 1.96 for the 5 percent significance level, and we thus reject the linear model in favor of the nonlinear regression. We are also interested in the marginal propensity to consume. In this expanded model, $H_0: \gamma = 1$ is a test that the marginal propensity to consume is constant, not that it is one. (That would be a joint test of both $\gamma = 1$ and $\beta = 1$.) In this model, the marginal propensity to consume is

$$MPC = \frac{dc}{dY} = \beta\gamma Y^{\gamma-1},$$

which varies with Y. To test the hypothesis that this is one, we require a particular value of Y. Since it is the most recent value, we choose $Y_{1985} = 2509$. At this value, MPC is estimated as

0.9676. We estimate its standard error as the square root of

$$[\partial MPC/\partial b \quad \partial MPC/\partial c]\begin{bmatrix} \text{Var}(b) & \text{Cov}(b,c) \\ \text{Cov}(b,c) & \text{Var}(c) \end{bmatrix}\begin{bmatrix} \partial MPC/\partial b \\ \partial MPC/\partial c \end{bmatrix}$$

$$= [cY^{c-1} \quad bY^{c-1}(1 + c\ln Y)]\begin{bmatrix} 0.00677 & -0.00340 \\ -0.00340 & 0.00168 \end{bmatrix}\begin{bmatrix} cY^{c-1} \\ bY^{c-1}(1 + c\ln Y) \end{bmatrix}$$

$$= 0.00352,$$

which gives a standard error of 0.05933. For testing the hypothesis that in 1985 the MPC was equal to 1.0, we would refer

$$z = \frac{(0.9676 - 1)}{0.05933} = -0.5461$$

to a standard normal table. This is not statistically significant, so we would not reject the hypothesis.

11.5. A Specification Test for Nonlinear Regressions: Testing for Linear Versus Log-Linear Specification

MacKinnon et al. (1983) have extended the J test discussed in Chapter 7 to nonlinear regressions. Given the wide range of possible models one might consider in this setting, this is a particularly useful tool. One result of this analysis is a simple test for linearity versus log linearity.

The specific equations to be tested are

$$H_0: y = h^0(\mathbf{x}, \boldsymbol{\beta}) + \varepsilon_0,$$

versus

$$H_1: g(y) = h^1(\mathbf{z}, \gamma) + \varepsilon_1,$$

where $\mathbf{x}$ and $\mathbf{z}$ are regressor vectors and $\boldsymbol{\beta}$ and γ are the parameters. As the authors note, using y instead of, say, $j(y)$ in the first function is nothing more than an implicit definition of the units of measurement of the dependent variable.

An intermediate case is useful. If we assume that $g(y)$ is equal to y, but allow $h^0(.)$ and $h^1(.)$ to be nonlinear, the necessary modification of the J test is straightforward, albeit perhaps a bit more difficult to carry out. For this case, we form the compound model

$$y = (1 - \alpha)h^0(\mathbf{x}, \boldsymbol{\beta}) + \alpha h^1(\mathbf{z}, \gamma) + \varepsilon \qquad (11\text{-}15)$$
$$= h^0(\mathbf{x}, \boldsymbol{\beta}) + \alpha(h^1(\mathbf{z}, \gamma) - h^0(\mathbf{x}, \boldsymbol{\beta})) + \varepsilon.$$

Presumably, both $\boldsymbol{\beta}$ and γ could be estimated in isolation by nonlinear least squares. Suppose a nonlinear least squares estimate of γ has been obtained. One approach is to insert this in (11-15) and then estimate $\boldsymbol{\beta}$ and α by nonlinear least squares. The J test amounts to testing the significance of the estimate of α. Of course, the model is symmetric in $h^0(.)$ and $h^1(.)$, so their roles could be reversed. The same conclusions drawn earlier would apply here.

Davidson and MacKinnon (1981) propose what may be a simpler alternative. Given an estimate of β, say $\hat{\beta}$, approximate $h^0(\mathbf{x}, \beta)$ with a linear Taylor series at this point. The result is

$$h^0(\mathbf{x}, \beta) \simeq h^0(\mathbf{x}, \hat{\beta}) + \left[\frac{\partial h^0(.)}{\partial \hat{\beta}'}\right]\hat{\beta}$$

$$= \hat{h}^0 + \hat{\mathbf{H}}^0 \mathbf{b}.$$

Using this device, they replace (11–15) with

$$y - \hat{h}^0 = \hat{\mathbf{H}}^0 \mathbf{b} + \alpha(h^1(\mathbf{z}, \hat{\gamma}) - h^0(\mathbf{x}, \hat{\beta})) + \varepsilon, \qquad (11-16)$$

in which $\mathbf{b}$ and α can be estimated by linear least squares. As before, the J test amounts to testing the significance of $\hat{\alpha}$. If it is found that α is significantly different from zero, H_0 is rejected. For the authors' asymptotic results to hold, any consistent estimate of $\mathbf{b}$ will suffice for $\hat{\beta}$; the nonlinear least squares estimator that they suggest seems a natural choice.[10]

Now we can generalize the test to allow a nonlinear function, $g(y)$, in H_1. Davidson and MacKinnon require $g(y)$ to be monotonic, continuous, continuously differentiable, and not introduce any new parameters. (This excludes the Box–Cox model, which is considered in Section 11.7.) The compound model that forms the basis of the test is

$$(1 - \alpha)(y - h^0(\mathbf{x}, \beta)) + \alpha(g(y) - h^1(\mathbf{z}, \gamma)) = \varepsilon. \qquad (11-17)$$

Again, there are two approaches. As before, if $\hat{\gamma}$ is an estimate of γ, β and α can be estimated by maximum likelihood conditional on this estimate.[11] This promises to be extremely messy, and an alternative is proposed. Rewrite the preceding equation as

$$y - h^0(\mathbf{x}, \beta) = \alpha(h^1(\mathbf{z}, \gamma) - g(y)) + \alpha(y - h^0(\mathbf{x}, \beta)) + \varepsilon.$$

Now utilize the same linear Taylor series expansion for $h^0(\mathbf{x}, \beta)$ on the left-hand side, and replace both y and $h^0(\mathbf{x}, \beta)$ with $\hat{h}^0$ on the right. The resulting model is

$$y - \hat{h}^0 = \hat{\mathbf{H}}^0 \mathbf{b} + \alpha(\hat{h}^1 - g(\hat{h}^0)) + e. \qquad (11-18)$$

As before, with an estimate of β, this can be estimated by least squares.

This modified form of the J test is labeled the P_E test. As the authors discuss, it is probably not as powerful as any of the Wald, Lagrange multiplier, or likelihood ratio tests that we have considered. However, in their experience, it has sufficient power for applied research and is clearly simple to carry out.

The P_E test can be used to test a linear specification against a log-linear model. For this test, both $h^0(.)$ and $h^1(.)$ are linear, while $g(y) = \ln y$. Let the two competing models be denoted

$$H_0: y = \mathbf{x}'\beta + \varepsilon,$$

and

$$H_1: \ln y = \ln(\mathbf{x})'\gamma + \varepsilon.$$

(We stretch the usual notational conventions by using $\ln(\mathbf{x})$ for $(\ln x_1, \ldots, \ln x_K)$.) Now let $\mathbf{b}$ and $\mathbf{c}$ be the two linear least squares estimates of the parameter vectors. The P_E test for H_1 as

---

[10] This assumes that H_0 is correct, of course.

[11] Least squares will be inappropriate because of the transformation of y, which will translate to a Jacobian term in the log likelihood. See the later discussion of the Box–Cox model.

Table 11.4

Year	Interest r	Money M	GNP Y	Year	Interest r	Money M	GNP Y
1966	4.50	480.0	2208.3	1976	5.50	1163.6	2826.7
1967	4.19	524.3	2271.4	1977	5.46	1286.6	2958.6
1968	5.16	566.3	2365.6	1978	7.46	1388.9	3115.2
1969	5.87	589.5	2423.3	1979	10.28	1497.9	3192.4
1970	5.95	628.2	2416.2	1980	11.77	1631.4	3187.1
1971	4.88	712.8	2484.8	1981	13.42	1794.4	3248.8
1972	4.50	805.2	2608.5	1982	11.02	1954.9	3166.0
1973	6.44	861.0	2744.1	1983	8.50	2188.8	3277.7
1974	7.83	908.4	2729.3	1984	8.80	2371.7	3492.0
1975	6.25	1023.1	2695.0	1985	7.69	2563.6	3573.5

an alternative to H_0 is carried out by testing the significance of the coefficient $\hat{\alpha}$ in the model

$$y = \mathbf{x}'\boldsymbol{\beta} + \alpha[\ln y - \ln(\mathbf{x}'\mathbf{b})] + \varepsilon. \tag{11-19}$$

The second term is the difference between predictions of y obtained directly from the log-linear model and obtained as the log of the prediction from the linear model. We can also reverse the roles of the two formulas and test H_0 as the alternative. The compound regression is

$$\ln y = \ln(\mathbf{x})'\boldsymbol{\gamma} + \alpha(\hat{y} - e^{\ln(\mathbf{x})'\mathbf{c}}) + \varepsilon. \tag{11-20}$$

EXAMPLE 11.4. Money Demand. A large number of studies have estimated money demand equations, some linear and some log linear.[12] In Table 11.5 the results of a test of one versus the other are shown. The data are taken from the 1986 *Economic Report of the President*. The interest rate is the end of December value of the discount rate at the New York Federal Reserve Bank. The money stock is M2. The GNP is seasonally adjusted and stated in 1982 constant dollars.

Regressions of M on a constant, r, and Y, and $\ln M$ on a constant, $\ln r$, and $\ln Y$, produce the following results (standard errors are given in parentheses):

Linear $R^2 = 0.93526$

Standard error $= 175.73$

$$
\begin{array}{ccccc}
M = & a & + & b_r r & + & c_Y Y \\
& -3169.42 & & -14.9223 & & 1.58815 \\
& (310.8) & & (22.59) & & (0.1434)
\end{array}
$$

Log-linear $R^2 = 0.97578$

Standard error $= 0.0881$

$$
\begin{array}{ccccc}
\ln M = & a' & + & b_{\ln r} \ln r & + & c_{\ln Y} \ln Y \\
& -21.992 & & -0.03152 & & 3.65628 \\
& (1.648) & & (0.0967) & & (0.2255)
\end{array}
$$

[12] A comprehensive survey appears in Goldfeld (1973).

Table 11.5

	Estimate	Standard Error	t Ratio
Linear	-751.21	242.21	-3.102
Log linear	-0.0003426	0.0005063	-0.677

Both models appear to fit quite well,[13] and the pattern of significance of the coefficients is the same in both equations. After computing fitted values from the two equations, the estimates of α from the two models are as shown in Table 11.5. Referring these to a standard normal table, we reject the linear model in favor of the log-linear model.

11.6. *Parametric Transformations of the Dependent Variable*

Thus far, we have considered models in which the nonlinearity in the parameters was entirely on the right-hand side of the equation. There are models in which parameters appear nonlinearly in functions of the dependent variable as well. The Box–Cox transformation considered in the next section is one example. Another is given here.

EXAMPLE 11.5. A Generalized Production Function.   The Cobb–Douglas production function has often been used to study production. Among the assumptions of this model is that the average cost of production increases or decreases monotonically with increases in output. This is in direct contrast to the standard textbook treatment of a **U**-shaped average cost curve, as well as to a large amount of empirical evidence. In order to relax this assumption, Zellner and Revankar (1970) proposed a generalization of the Cobb–Douglas production function.[14] Their model allows economies of scale to vary with output, and to increase and then decrease as output rises:

$$\ln y + \theta y = \ln \gamma + \alpha(1 - \delta)\ln K + \alpha\delta \ln L + \varepsilon.$$

Note that the right-hand side of their model is intrinsically linear, according to the results of Section 8.3.3. However, the model as a whole is intrinsically nonlinear due to the transformation of y appearing on the left.

Suppose that, in general, the model is

$$g(y_i, \theta) = h(\mathbf{x}_i, \boldsymbol{\beta}) + \varepsilon_i. \tag{11-21}$$

One approach to estimation would be least squares, minimizing

$$S(\theta, \boldsymbol{\beta}) = \sum_i [g(y_i, \theta) - h(\mathbf{x}_i, \boldsymbol{\beta})]^2.$$

However, for this kind of regression model, maximum likelihood estimation is more efficient and generally not appreciably more difficult. For normally distributed disturbances, the

---

[13] The interest elasticity is in line with the received results. The income elasticity is quite a bit larger.
[14] An alternative approach is to model costs directly with a flexible functional form such as the translog model. This is examined in detail in Chapter 17.

density of y_i is

$$f(y_i) = \left| \frac{\partial \varepsilon_i}{\partial y_i} \right| (2\pi\sigma^2)^{-1/2} e^{-(g(y_i, \theta) - h(x_i, \beta))^2/(2\sigma^2)}.$$

The Jacobian of the transformation (see Section 3.6) is

$$J(y_i, \theta) = \left| \frac{\partial \varepsilon_i}{\partial y_i} \right| = \left| \frac{\partial g(y_i, \theta)}{\partial y_i} \right| = J_i.$$

Upon collecting terms, the log-likelihood function will be

$$\ln L = -\frac{n}{2}\ln 2\pi - \frac{n}{2}\ln \sigma^2 + \sum_i \ln J(y_i, \theta) - \frac{1}{2\sigma^2}\sum_i [g(y_i, \theta) - h(x_i, \beta)]^2. \quad (11\text{--}22)$$

Before proceeding, two aspects of the log likelihood should be noted. First, it is obvious that but for the Jacobians, nonlinear least squares would be maximum likelihood. However, if the Jacobian terms involve θ, *least squares is not maximum likelihood*. Second, as regards σ^2, this likelihood function is essentially the same as that for the simpler nonlinear regression model of (11–1). The maximum likelihood estimator of σ^2 will be

$$\hat{\sigma}^2 = \frac{1}{n}\sum_i [g(y_i, \hat{\theta}) - h(x_i, \hat{\beta})]^2$$

$$= \frac{1}{n}\sum_i e_i^2. \quad (11\text{--}23)$$

The likelihood equations for the unknown parameters are

$$\frac{\partial \ln L}{\partial \beta} = \frac{1}{\sigma^2}\sum_i \varepsilon_i \frac{\partial h(x_i, \beta)}{\partial \beta},$$

$$\frac{\partial \ln L}{\partial \theta} = \sum_i \frac{1}{J_i}\left(\frac{\partial J_i}{\partial \theta}\right) - \left(\frac{1}{\sigma^2}\right)\sum_i \varepsilon_i \frac{\partial g(y_i, \theta)}{\partial \theta}, \quad (11\text{--}24)$$

$$\frac{\partial \ln L}{\partial \sigma^2} = -\frac{n}{2\sigma^2} + \frac{1}{2\sigma^4}\sum_i \varepsilon_i^2.$$

These will usually be nonlinear, so a solution must be obtained iteratively. One special case that is common is a model in which θ is a single parameter. Given a particular value of θ, we would maximize (11–22) with respect to β by using nonlinear least squares. (It would be simpler yet if, in addition, $h(x_i, \beta)$ were linear, so that we could use ordinary linear least squares. See the following example.) Therefore, a way to maximize L for all of the parameters is to scan over values of θ for the one that, with the associated least squares estimates of β and σ^2, gives the highest value of L. (This requires, of course, that we know roughly what values of θ to examine.)

For more general models, a similar method could be used, but this will probably be much more difficult. If θ is a vector of parameters, direct maximization of L with respect to the full set of parameters may be preferable. (Methods of maximization are discussed in the next chapter.) There is an additional simplification that may be useful. Whatever values are ultimately obtained for the estimates of θ and β, the estimate of σ^2 will be given by (11–23). If we insert this solution in (11–22), we obtain the **concentrated log likelihood**,

$$\ln L_c = \sum_i \ln J(y_i, \theta) - \frac{n}{2}(1 + \ln(2\pi)) - \frac{n}{2}\ln\left[\frac{1}{n}\sum_i \varepsilon_i^2\right].$$

This is a function only of θ and β. We can maximize it with respect to θ and β, and obtain the estimate of σ^2 as a by-product.[15]

An estimate of the asymptotic covariance matrix of the maximum likelihood estimators can be obtained by inverting the estimated information matrix. However, it is quite likely that the Berndt et al. estimator will be much easier to compute. The log of the density for the ith observation is

$$\ln L_i = \ln J_i - \frac{1}{2}(\ln(2\pi) + \ln \sigma^2) - \frac{1}{2\sigma^2}[g(y_i,\theta) - h(x_i,\beta)]^2.$$

The derivatives of $\ln L_i$ with respect to the unknown parameters are

$$\mathbf{w}_i = \begin{bmatrix} \partial \ln L_i/\partial\beta \\ \partial \ln L_i/\partial\theta \\ \partial \ln L_i/\partial\sigma^2 \end{bmatrix} = \begin{bmatrix} (\varepsilon_i/\sigma^2)[\partial h(x_i,\beta)/\partial\beta] \\ (1/J_i)[\partial J_i/\partial\theta] - (\varepsilon_i/\sigma^2)[\partial g(y_i,\theta)/\partial\theta] \\ (1/2\sigma^2)[\varepsilon_i^2/\sigma^2 - 1] \end{bmatrix}. \qquad (11-25)$$

The covariance matrix for the maximum likelihood estimators is consistently estimated, using

$$\text{Est. Asy. Var}[\text{MLE}] = \left[\sum_i \mathbf{w}_i \mathbf{w}_i'\right]^{-1}.$$

EXAMPLE 11.5. Continued.   For Zellner and Revankar's production function, the Jacobian of the transformation from ε_i to y_i is $\partial\varepsilon_i/\partial y_i = (\theta + 1/y_i)$. Some simplification is achieved by writing this as $(1 + \theta y_i)/y_i$. The log likelihood is, then,

$$\ln L = \sum_i \ln(1 + \theta y_i) - \sum_i \ln y_i - \frac{n}{2}\ln(2\pi) - \frac{n}{2}\ln \sigma^2 - \frac{1}{2\sigma^2}\sum_i \varepsilon_i^2,$$

where

$$\varepsilon_i = (\ln y_i + \theta y_i - \beta_1 - \beta_2 \ln K_i - \beta_3 \ln L_i).$$

Estimation of this model is straightforward. For a given value of θ, β and σ^2 are estimated by ordinary least squares. Therefore, to estimate the full set of parameters, we can scan over the range of zero to one for θ. The value of θ that, with its associated least squares estimates of β and σ^2, maximizes the log-likelihood function provides the desired estimate. This is the procedure used by Zellner and Revankar. The data used for the study are listed in Table 11.6.[16]

In their model, Zellner and Revankar report the maximum likelihood estimates of the parameters listed in Table 11.7. For each estimate, three estimates of the asymptotic standard error are given. The authors report asymptotic standard errors based on the information matrix (1) and the (inappropriate) OLS standard errors (2). The third estimate is that obtained using the Berndt et al. estimator based on (11-25) instead of the second derivatives.

As usual, there is a problem in interpreting the coefficients in this nonlinear regression model. The slope coefficients of the regression are not the marginal effects. An approximation to the appropriate value can be obtained with

$$\frac{\partial E[y]}{\partial x_j} \simeq \left[\frac{\partial h(x,\beta)}{\partial x_j}\right]\frac{1}{g'(y)}. \qquad (11-26)$$

[15] A formal proof that this is a valid way to proceed is given by Amemiya (1985, pp. 125–127).
[16] Zellner and Revankar (1970, p. 249). Full descriptions of the variables are given in the study.

Table 11.6.   U.S. Annual Survey of Manufactures Data for the Transportation Equipment Industry, 1957

State	Value Added	Capital	Labor	Establishments
Ala.	126.148	3.804	31.551	68
Calif.	3201.486	185.446	452.844	1372
Conn.	690.670	39.712	124.074	154
Fla.	56.296	6.547	19.181	292
Ga.	304.531	11.530	45.534	71
Ill.	723.028	58.987	88.391	275
Ind.	992.169	112.884	148.530	260
Iowa	35.796	2.698	8.017	75
Kans.	494.515	10.360	86.189	76
Ky.	124.948	5.213	12.000	31
La.	73.328	3.763	15.900	115
Maine	29.467	1.967	6.470	81
Md.	415.262	17.546	69.342	129
Mass.	241.530	15.347	39.416	172
Mich.	4079.554	435.105	490.384	568
Mo.	652.085	32.840	84.831	125
N.J.	667.113	33.292	83.033	247
N.Y.	940.430	72.974	190.094	461
Ohio	1611.899	157.978	259.916	363
Pa.	617.579	34.324	98.152	233
Tex.	527.413	22.736	109.728	308
Va.	174.394	7.173	31.301	85
Wash.	636.948	30.807	87.963	179
W. Va.	22.700	1.543	4.063	15
Wis.	349.711	22.001	52.818	142

Source: A Zellner and N. Revankar, "Generalized Production Functions," *Review of Economic Studies, Ltd.,* 37, 1970, p. 249.
Notes: "Value Added," "Capital," and "Labor" are in millions of dollars. Data used for the regressions are per establishment.

In Table 11.7 the authors do not report the estimate of σ^2. It was computed using their data and estimates. The maximum likelihood estimates of the slope parameters are obtained by least squares regression of $\ln y + \theta y$ on a constant, $\ln K$, and $\ln L$. Using the preceding data and their estimate of θ, we find that the OLS slope estimates are, however, 3.0741, 0.36828, and 1.13455. There is no obvious reason for the discrepancy.[17]

Table 11.7.   Maximum Likelihood Estimates

	Estimate	SE(1)	SE(2)	SE(3)
β_1	3.0129	0.3854	0.1343	0.3438
β_2	0.333	0.1023	0.1022	0.1004
β_3	1.1551	0.1564	0.1228	0.1402
θ	0.134	0.0638	—	0.0609
σ^2	0.0485	0.0137	—	—

[17] The values shown in the table are those reported in the original study.

Elasticities are computed using

$$\frac{\partial \ln y}{\partial \ln x_j} \simeq \left[\frac{\partial h(\mathbf{x}, \boldsymbol{\beta})}{\partial x_j}\right]\left[\frac{x_j}{yg'(y)}\right]. \tag{11-27}$$

(Note the similarity to the form for the log-linear model. If $g(y) = \ln y$, then $yg'(y) = 1$ and we get the familiar result. These functions will vary with the data, so they must be computed at a particular data point. The predicted values and functions of them can be used in place of y and $g'(y)$ on the right-hand side of (11-26) and (11-27).

EXAMPLE 11.5. Continued. For Zellner and Revankar's generalized Cobb-Douglas production function, the elasticities are simple to compute using (11-27). First, we use the result

$$x_j\left[\frac{\partial h(\mathbf{x}, \boldsymbol{\beta})}{\partial x_j}\right] = \frac{\partial h(\mathbf{x}, \boldsymbol{\beta})}{\partial \ln x_j}.$$

Since $h(\mathbf{x}, \boldsymbol{\beta}) = \beta_1 + \beta_2 \ln K + \beta_3 \ln L$, these derivatives are the slope coefficients, β_2 and β_3. To compute a value for y, we insert the means of $\ln K$ and $\ln L$ on the right-hand side to obtain a prediction for $\ln y + \theta y = 1.1478$. The value of y for which $\ln y + 0.134y = 1.1478$ is 2.31. Finally, for this model,

$$g'(y) = \frac{1}{y} + \theta.$$

So,

$$\frac{\partial \ln y}{\partial \ln x_j} = \frac{\beta_j}{1 + \theta y}.$$

Assembling the terms, we obtain estimates of the output elasticities of

$$\text{Capital:} \quad \frac{0.333}{(1 + 0.134(2.31))} = 0.254,$$

$$\text{Labor:} \quad 1.551/(1 + 0.134(2.31)) = 0.882.$$

As a rough check on these values, consider a simple Cobb-Douglas function, which has $\theta = 0$. This can be efficiently estimated by ordinary least squares regression of $\ln y$ on a constant, $\ln K$, and $\ln L$. The slope coefficients in this regression, using the preceding data, are 0.279 and 0.927. Once again, the linear regression approximates the nonlinear regression surprisingly closely.

In this study, the parameter θ was of primary interest, so the result in the preceding paragraph is not necessarily a virtue. In the Cobb-Douglas model, the economies of scale parameter is the sum of the output elasticities. For these data, that would be 1.136, indicating a fair degree of economies of scale. (It can be shown that this parameter also corresponds to the ratio of average to marginal cost on the cost side, which indicates that average costs are declining throughout the range of y.) For the previous generalized production function, the economies of scale parameter is

$$\alpha = \frac{\beta_K + \beta_L}{1 + \theta y}.$$

Some representative values for their sample are listed in Table 11.8.

Table 11.8

State	Output	Economies of Scale
Florida	0.193	1.45
Louisiana	0.638	1.37
California	2.333	1.13
Maryland	3.219	1.04
Ohio	4.440	0.93
Michigan	7.182	0.76

11.7.   The Box–Cox Transformation

The Box–Cox transformation was introduced in Chapters 5 and 8 as a method of generalizing the linear model. The transformation is[18]

$$z^{(\lambda)} = \frac{z^{\lambda} - 1}{\lambda}.$$

As noted earlier, in a regression model the analysis could be done *conditionally*. For a given value of λ, the model

$$y = \alpha + \sum \beta_k x_k^{(\lambda)} + \varepsilon \qquad (11-28)$$

is a linear regression that can be estimated by least squares. Save for the complexity of the calculations, in principle, each regressor could be transformed by a different value of λ. In most applications, this level of generality becomes excessively cumbersome, and λ is assumed to be the same for all of the variables in the model.[19] At the same time, it is also possible to transform y by $y^{(\lambda)}$. However, this introduces new complications related to the allowable range of the dependent variable.

      EXAMPLE 11.6. Flexible Cost Function.   Caves et al. (1980) analyzed the costs of production for railroads providing freight and passenger service. Continuing a long line of literature on the costs of production in regulated industries, a translog cost function (see Example 7.3) would be a natural choice for modeling this multiple-output technology. However, several of the firms in the study produced no passenger service, which would preclude the use of the translog model. (This would require the log of zero.) An alternative is the Box–Cox transformation, which is computable for zero output levels. A constraint must still be placed on λ in their model, as $0^{(\lambda)}$ is defined only if λ is strictly positive. As shown in Example 11.8, a positive value of λ is not assured. A question does arise in this context (and other similar ones) as to whether zero outputs should be treated the same as nonzero outputs or whether an output of zero represents a discrete corporate decision distinct from other variation in the output levels.

11.7.1.   Transforming the Independent Variables

      If λ in (11–28) is taken to be an unknown parameter, the regression becomes nonlinear in the parameters. While no transformation will reduce it to linearity, nonlinear least squares

---

[18] Box and Cox (1964).
[19] See, for example, Seaks and Layson (1983).

is straightforward. In most instances, we can expect to find the least squares value of λ between -1 and 1. Typically, then, λ is estimated by scanning this range in increments of 0.1. If a minimum is found and greater precision is desired, the area to the right and left of the current optimum can be searched in increments of 0.01, and so on. Once the optimum value of λ is located, the least squares estimates, the mean squared residual, and this value of λ constitute the nonlinear least squares (and maximum likelihood) estimates of the parameters.

After determining the optimal value of λ, it is sometimes treated as if it were a *known* value in the least squares results.[20] However, $\hat{\lambda}$ is an estimate of an unknown parameter. It is not hard to show that the least squares standard errors will always underestimate the correct asymptotic standard errors.[21] To get the appropriate values, we need the derivatives of the right-hand side of (11–28) with respect to α, β, and λ. In the notation of (11–1), these are

$$\frac{\partial h(.)}{\partial \alpha} = 1,$$

$$\frac{\partial h(.)}{\partial \beta_k} = x_k^{(\lambda)},$$

$$\frac{\partial h(.)}{\partial \lambda} = \sum_k \beta_k \frac{\partial x_k^{(\lambda)}}{\partial \lambda}, \tag{11–29}$$

$$= \sum_k \beta_k \left[\frac{x_k^{\lambda}}{\lambda} \left(\ln x_k - \frac{1}{\lambda} \right) + \frac{1}{\lambda^2} \right].$$

We can now use (11–13) to estimate the asymptotic covariance matrix of the parameter estimates.

EXAMPLE 11.7. A More General Money Demand Equation. The estimates of the log-linear money demand equation in Example 11.4 are implicitly a Box–Cox model:

$$\ln M = \alpha + \beta_r r^{(\lambda)} + \beta_Y Y^{(\lambda)} + \varepsilon, \tag{11–30}$$

with λ equal to zero. Here we will allow λ to be a free parameter. For a given value of λ, the Box–Cox model is a linear regression model; we can compute $r^{(\lambda)}$ and $Y^{(\lambda)}$ and then obtain the remaining parameters by least squares. Maximum likelihood estimates of all of the parameters in the model are obtained by scanning over the range of λ from minus one to one. The sums of squared deviations, which we denote $S(\beta)$, for a range of values of λ are shown in Table 11.9.

At the optimal value of 0.47, the least squares results with the appropriate standard errors are as listed in Table 11.10.

It is important to remember that the coefficients in a nonlinear model are not equal to the slopes (i.e., here, the demand elasticities) with respect to the variables. In the simple Box–Cox model,[22]

$$\ln Y = \alpha + \beta \left[\frac{X^{\lambda} - 1}{\lambda} \right],$$

$$\frac{d \ln Y}{d \ln X} = \beta X^{\lambda}. \tag{11–31}$$

---

[20] That is, the least squares standard errors are computed conditionally upon this estimate.
[21] See Fomby et al. (1984, pp. 426–431).
[22] We have used the result $d \ln Y / d \ln X = X d \ln Y / dX$.

Table 11.9. Sums of Squared Deviations for Given λ

λ	$S(\beta)$	λ	$S(\beta)$	λ	$S(\beta)$
0.3	0.13016	0.44	0.12723	0.49	0.12721
0.4	0.12732	0.45	0.12721	0.50	0.12721
0.41	0.12729	0.46	0.12721	0.60	0.12753
0.42	0.12726	0.47	0.12720		
0.43	0.12724	0.48	0.12721		

Table 11.10

Variable	Coefficient	Standard Error	T Ratio
Constant	-0.543	8.78	0.062
$r^{(0.47)}$	-0.00607	0.0422	0.1438
$Y^{(0.47)}$	0.0867	0.8027	0.1080
λ	0.47	0.5467	0.8597

Inserting the means for r (7.273) and Y (2849.23), we obtain elasticities of -0.0154 and 3.6454, respectively. These are quite similar to our earlier results. Standard errors for these estimates could be obtained using (10–16). In the interest of brevity, the calculation is omitted here.

11.7.2.   Transforming the Model

It seems a natural generalization at this point to extend (11–28) to

$$y^{(\theta)} = \alpha + \sum \beta_k x_k^{(\lambda)} + \varepsilon$$

or

$$(11\text{–}32)$$

$$y^{(\theta)} = \beta' x^{(\lambda)} + \varepsilon.$$

This includes the linear and log-linear models as special cases. (This could form the basis of a test.)[23]

An issue has been raised concerning the values that y may take in this model. Take the simplest possible regression:

$$\frac{y^\theta - 1}{\theta} = \beta x + \varepsilon.$$

The transformation is valid only for nonnegative values of y, which means that

$$y \geq 0 \Rightarrow \beta x + \varepsilon \geq -\frac{1}{\theta}.$$

---

[23] Two useful references on this form of the model are Spitzer (1982a and 1982b).

It follows that

$$\varepsilon \geq -\left(\frac{1}{\theta} + \beta x\right).$$

Therefore, ε cannot be normally distributed; its range is not $-\infty$ to $+\infty$. Poirier and Melino (1978) and Poirier (1978) suggest that ε be treated as a truncated normal variable instead. This requires an extremely complicated maximum likelihood procedure and has generally not been adopted.[24] How serious the problem is likely to be depends on how serious the truncation is. If it is quite unlikely that ε would fall below $-(1/\theta) - (\beta'x)$, the resulting biases will be insignificant.[25] Draper and Cox (1969) argue that, as a practical matter, the Box–Cox transformation is likely to lead to the correct transformation at least approximately. The preceding, however, should be taken as a caveat.

Allowing θ to differ from λ is usually taken to be more cumbersome than necessary. The computational burden increases greatly with this level of generality. We shall assume that they are equal. If $\varepsilon \sim N[0, \sigma^2]$, the log-likelihood for a sample of n observations is

$$\ln L = -\frac{n}{2}\ln(2\pi) - \frac{n}{2}\ln\sigma^2 - \frac{1}{2\sigma^2}\sum_i \varepsilon_i^2.$$

Transforming from the distribution ε to that of y, we use the change of variable result

$$f_y(y) = \left|\frac{d\varepsilon}{dy}\right| f_\varepsilon(y).$$

From (11–32),

$$\varepsilon = y^{(\lambda)} - \mathbf{x}^{(\lambda)'}\boldsymbol{\beta}, \tag{11–33}$$

so the Jacobian is

$$\left|\frac{d\varepsilon}{dy}\right| = y^{\lambda - 1}.$$

Making the substitution and multiplying by the Jacobian, we obtain the log-likelihood function for the Box–Cox model:

$$\ln L = -\frac{n}{2}\ln(2\pi) - \frac{n}{2}\ln\sigma^2 + (\lambda - 1)\sum_i \ln y_i - \frac{1}{2\sigma^2}\sum_i (y_i^{(\lambda)} - \boldsymbol{\beta}'\mathbf{x}_i^{(\lambda)})^2. \tag{11–34}$$

As a first step, we "concentrate" the log likelihood. The maximum likelihood estimator of σ^2 will be the average squared residual. By inserting this result in (11–34), we see that at the maximum of the log likelihood, the last term will be $-n/2$. So the log likelihood will collapse to

$$\ln L_c = (\lambda - 1)\sum_i \ln y_i - \frac{n}{2}(\ln(2\pi) + 1) - \frac{n}{2}\ln\hat{\sigma}^2. \tag{11–35}$$

The maximum likelihood estimates of λ and $\boldsymbol{\beta}$ are computed by maximizing this function. The estimate of σ^2 will be a by-product and need not be considered separately. Now since there is still only one value of λ to be found, we can use the same one-dimensional grid search

---

[24] We examine the truncated regression model in Chapter 21. A useful reference on the subject is Hausman and Wise (1977).

[25] As discussed in Chapter 21, when the truncation problem is significant, it is likely that our estimates of the model coefficients will be biased toward zero.

used in Examples 11.5 and 11.7. However, it must be remembered that the criterion function is not $S(\boldsymbol{\beta} \mid \lambda)$ but

$$\ln L_c = (\lambda - 1) \sum_i \ln y_i - \frac{n}{2}(\ln(2\pi) + 1) - \frac{n}{2} \ln\left(\frac{S(\boldsymbol{\beta}, \lambda)}{n}\right).^{26} \qquad (11-36)$$

After searching for the appropriate λ, it is necessary to correct the least squares standard errors. The appropriate estimate of the asymptotic covariance matrix for the maximum likelihood estimates was presented in Chapter 4. For this model, the second derivatives of the log likelihood are quite cumbersome.[27] The estimator of the asymptotic covariance matrix for the maximum likelihood presented by Berndt et al. (1974) is much more convenient. The advantage of this estimator is that it only requires us to compute the first derivatives.[28] For the Box–Cox model,

$$\ln f(y, \theta) = (\lambda - 1)\ln y - \frac{1}{2}\ln 2\pi - \frac{1}{2}\ln \sigma^2 - \frac{1}{2\sigma^2}(y^{(\lambda)} - \boldsymbol{\beta}'\mathbf{x}^{(\lambda)})^2. \qquad (11-37)$$

Upon using

$$\varepsilon_i = y_i^{(\lambda)} - \boldsymbol{\beta}'\mathbf{x}^{(\lambda)},$$

the derivatives are

$$\frac{\partial \ln f(y_i)}{\partial \boldsymbol{\beta}} = \frac{\varepsilon_i}{\sigma^2}\mathbf{x}_i^{(\lambda)},$$

$$\frac{\partial \ln f(y_i)}{\partial \lambda} = \ln y_i - \frac{\varepsilon_i}{\sigma^2}\left(\frac{\partial y_i^{(\lambda)}}{\partial \lambda} - \sum_k \beta_k \frac{\partial x_k^{(\lambda)}}{\partial \lambda}\right), \qquad (11-38)$$

$$\frac{\partial \ln f(y_i)}{\partial \sigma^2} = \frac{1}{2\sigma^2}\left(\frac{\varepsilon_i^2}{\sigma^2} - 1\right).$$

For the second of these,

$$\frac{\partial([z^\lambda - 1]/\lambda)}{\partial \lambda} = \frac{\lambda z^\lambda \ln z - z^\lambda + 1}{\lambda^2}.$$

The various parts are reasonably simple to compute. If we then let

$$\mathbf{w}_i = \begin{bmatrix} \partial \ln f(y_i)/\partial \hat{\boldsymbol{\beta}} \\ \partial \ln f(y_i)/\partial \hat{\lambda} \\ \partial \ln f(y_i)/\partial \hat{\sigma}^2 \end{bmatrix}, \qquad (11-39)$$

the estimator of the asymptotic variance matrix for the maximum likelihood estimator is

$$\text{Est. Asy. Var}[\hat{\boldsymbol{\theta}}] = \left[\sum_i \mathbf{w}_i \mathbf{w}_i'\right]^{-1} = (\mathbf{W}'\mathbf{W})^{-1}, \qquad (11-40)$$

where each row of $\mathbf{W}$ is an observation $\mathbf{w}_i'$.

Note that the preceding differs from the procedure suggested in (11–29) in the inclusion of a row and column for σ^2 in the covariance matrix. The difference arises because in the

---

[26] A method of simplifying the search is suggested by Zarembka (1968).
[27] They are presented in full in Fomby et al. (1984, p. 429).
[28] See, as well, Spitzer (1984) and Blackley et al. (1984).

Table 11.11.   Estimated Money Demand Equation

	Estimate	Standard Error		T Ratio
Constant	−11.170	1.036	(0.7830)	−10.78
r	−0.005689	0.0212	(0.0159)	−0.268
Y	5.1437	0.3951	(0.2988)	13.02

model that transforms y as well as x (i.e., (11–32) versus (11–28)), the Hessian of the log likelihood is not block diagonal with respect to λ and σ^2. When y is transformed, the maximum likelihood estimates of λ and σ^2 are positively correlated, as both parameters reflect the scaling of the dependent variable in the model. This may seem a counterintuitive result. Consider the difference in the variance estimators that arises when a linear and a log-linear model are estimated. The variance of ln y around its mean is obviously different from that of y around its mean. These two models arise with different values of λ. By contrast, consider what happens when only the independent variables are transformed. The slope estimators vary accordingly, but in such a way that the variance of y around its conditional mean will stay constant.[29]

EXAMPLE 11.8. Money Demand Equation Continued.   The model of Example 11.7 treats y and x asymmetrically in that there $\theta = 0$, while the estimate of λ that was used was 0.45. By using the criterion in (11–36) instead and scanning over the range of minus one to plus one, we find the maximum likelihood estimate of λ to be −0.35. At this estimate, least squares regression gives the results shown in Table 11.11. The standard errors are computed using the Berndt et al. estimator.[30] For illustration, those computed (incorrectly) by least squares are also shown in parentheses.

In the more general model, the analog to the elasticity computed in Example 11.7 is, for the general case,

$$\frac{d \ln y}{d \ln x} = \beta \left(\frac{x}{y}\right)^{\lambda}. \tag{11-41}$$

In order to compute these values, we once again use the mean values of the regressors. For the values of y, we must compute a fitted value at these means. Using

$$\mathbf{b}'\bar{\mathbf{x}}^{(\lambda)} = y^{(\lambda)} = \frac{y^{\lambda} - 1}{\lambda},$$

we can then obtain the predicted value by inverting this function:

$$\hat{y} = [\lambda\{\mathbf{b}'\bar{\mathbf{x}}^{(\lambda)}\} + 1]^{1/\lambda}. \tag{11-42}$$

At the means of the independent variables, the two elasticities are −0.0257 for r and 2.8761 for Y, which, once again, are quite comparable to those obtained with the log-linear model.

11.7.3.   A Test for (Log-) Linearity

Given the unrestricted estimates of β, λ, and σ^2, a model that is linear ($\lambda = 1$) or log linear ($\lambda = 0$) is a simple parametric restriction and can be tested with a likelihood ratio

[29] See Seaks and Layson (1983).
[30] Fomby et al. (1984, p. 429) provide a complete list of the second derivatives of the log likelihood for the Box–Cox model.

statistic. The test statistic, as usual, is

$$\text{Chi-squared}(1) = -2(\ln L(\lambda = 1 \text{ or } 0) - \ln L(\lambda = \text{MLE})). \tag{11-43}$$

This will have a chi-squared distribution with one degree of freedom and can be referred to the standard table. Using the estimate of λ and its standard error, we could also carry out a t test (actually, a Wald test) of the hypothesis that $\lambda = 0$. An alternative Lagrange multiplier test is derived in Example 11.10.

It is not appropriate to test the linear model as an alternative to the log-linear model in this fashion. The models are not nested and neither estimate (zero or one) is an MLE. As such, this test is not a likelihood ratio test. (There is nothing to prevent the chi-squared statistic from being negative, which should suggest that there is something amiss with this "test.") It is tempting to use the two log likelihoods in a heuristic fashion to choose between them, but it should be remembered that except for the classical regression model, maximum likelihood is not a fitting criterion, that is, it doesn't maximize the fit. As such, choosing between estimators on this basis will not necessarily improve the model. This is one point at which Bayesian procedures offer an advantage; the *posterior odds ratio*, which is related to the ratio of the likelihoods, does provide a means of choosing between specifications.

EXAMPLE 11.9. Test for Linearity.   For the money demand data, the three relevant log-likelihood values are

$$\ln L(-0.35) = -116.51,$$

$$\ln L(0) = -118.07282,$$

$$\ln L(1) = -130.133.$$

With 20 observations, the two chi-squared test statistics are

$$\text{Linearity:} \quad -2(-130.133 - (-116.51)) = 27.25,$$

$$\text{Log linearity:} \ -2(-118.073 - (-116.51)) = 3.13.$$

Linearity is rejected, but the log linear model is not rejected at the 95 percent significance level.

11.8. *Hypothesis Testing and Parametric Restrictions*

In most cases, the sorts of hypotheses one would test in this context will involve fairly simple linear restrictions. The tests can be carried out using the usual formulas discussed in Chapter 7 and the asymptotic covariance matrix presented earlier. For more involved hypotheses and for nonlinear restrictions, the procedures are a bit less clear-cut. Three principal testing procedures were discussed in Chapter 4: the Wald, likelihood ratio, and Lagrange multiplier tests. In the linear model, it is simple to show that these are identical. In the nonlinear case, they are equivalent only asymptotically. We will work through each of these tests for the general case and then apply them to the example of the previous section.

The hypothesis to be tested is

$$H_0: \mathbf{R}(\boldsymbol{\beta}) = \mathbf{q}. \tag{11-44}$$

This may be any kind of restriction, linear or nonlinear. It is necessary, however, that they be **overidentifying restrictions**. This means, in formal terms, that if the original parameter vector has K free elements, the hypothesis $\mathbf{R}(\boldsymbol{\beta}) = \mathbf{q}$ must impose at least one functional relationship on the parameters. If there is more than one restriction, they must be functionally independent. These two conditions imply that the $J \times K$ matrix

$$\mathbf{G} = \frac{\partial \mathbf{R}(\boldsymbol{\beta})}{\partial \boldsymbol{\beta}'} \tag{11-45}$$

must have full row rank and that J, the number of restrictions, must be strictly less than K. (This is analogous to the linear model, in which $\mathbf{G}$ would be the matrix of coefficients in the restrictions.)

Let $\mathbf{b}$ be the unrestricted, nonlinear least squares estimator, and let $\mathbf{b}_*$ be the estimator obtained when the constraints of the hypothesis are imposed.[31] All of the test statistics to be considered here are the same asymptotically. Therefore, which test statistic one uses depends on how difficult the computations are. Unlike the linear model, the various testing procedures vary in complexity. For instance, in our example, the Lagrange multiplier is by far the simplest to compute. Of the four methods we will consider, only this test does not require us to compute a nonlinear regression.

11.8.1. An Asymptotically Valid F Test

The nonlinear analog to the familiar F statistic based on the fit of the regression (i.e., the sum of squared residuals) would be

$$F[J, n - K] = \frac{[S(\mathbf{b}_*) - S(\mathbf{b})]/J}{S(\mathbf{b})/(n - K)}. \tag{11-46}$$

This has the appearance of our earlier F ratio. However, in the nonlinear setting, neither the numerator nor the denominator has exactly the necessary chi-squared distribution, so the F distribution is only approximate. Note that this F statistic requires that both the restricted and unrestricted models be estimated.

11.8.2. Wald Test

The Wald test is based on the distance between $\mathbf{R}(\mathbf{b})$ and $\mathbf{q}$. If the unrestricted estimates fail to satisfy the restrictions, doubt is cast on the validity of the restrictions. The statistic is

$$W = (\mathbf{R}(\mathbf{b}) - \mathbf{q})'\{\text{Est. Asy. Var}[\mathbf{R}(\mathbf{b}) - \mathbf{q}]\}^{-1}(\mathbf{R}(\mathbf{b}) - \mathbf{q})$$
$$= (\mathbf{R}(\mathbf{b}) - \mathbf{q})'\{\mathbf{G}\hat{\mathbf{V}}\mathbf{G}'\}^{-1}(\mathbf{R}(\mathbf{b}) - \mathbf{q}), \tag{11-47}$$

where

$$\hat{\mathbf{V}} = \text{Est. Asy. Var}[\mathbf{b}].$$

This is a chi-squared statistic with J degrees of freedom. Under the null hypothesis that the restrictions are correct, the Wald statistic and J times the F statistic are asymptotically equivalent. The Wald statistic can be based on the estimated covariance matrix obtained earlier using the unrestricted estimates. This may provide a large saving in computing effort if the restrictions are nonlinear.

---

[31] This may be an extremely difficult computational problem in its own right, especially if the constraints are nonlinear. We defer until later consideration of this issue and assume here that the estimator has been obtained by whatever means is necessary.

11.8.3. Likelihood Ratio Test

The log likelihood for a sample of n observations, assuming normally distributed disturbances, is

$$\ln L = \text{Jacobian} - \frac{n}{2}\ln(2\pi\sigma^2) - \frac{\varepsilon'\varepsilon}{2\sigma^2}. \qquad (11-48)$$

Letting $\ln L^*$ be the log likelihood evaluated at the restricted estimates, the likelihood ratio statistic for testing the restrictions is

$$\lambda = -2(\ln L^* - \ln L). \qquad (11-49)$$

This statistic is asymptotically distributed as chi-squared with J degrees of freedom. For the present, assume that there is no Jacobian term in L. In each case, the maximum likelihood estimate of σ^2 is $e'e/n$, so the log likelihood computed at the least squares estimates is

$$\ln L = -\frac{n}{2}\left[1 + \ln(2\pi) + \ln\left(\frac{e'e}{n}\right)\right]. \qquad (11-50)$$

and likewise for the restricted estimates.[32] This is easily computed using only the sum of squared residuals. After collecting terms, the likelihood ratio statistic for a classical regression model (linear or nonlinear) is

$$\lambda = n(\ln\hat{\sigma}_*^2 - \ln\hat{\sigma}^2)$$
$$= n\ln\left(\frac{\hat{\sigma}_*^2}{\hat{\sigma}^2}\right). \qquad (11-51)$$

Like the earlier F statistic, the likelihood ratio statistic requires both restricted and unrestricted estimates.

11.8.4. Lagrange Multiplier Test

The Lagrange multiplier test is based on the decrease in the sum of squared residuals that would result if the restrictions in the restricted model were released. The formalities of the test are given in Section 4.7.3c. For the nonlinear regression model, the test has a particularly appealing form.[33] Let e_* be the vector of residuals, $y_i - h(x_i, b_*)$, computed using the restricted estimates. Recall that we defined $\tilde{X}$ as an $n \times K$ matrix of derivatives, computed at a particular parameter vector in (11-9). Let $\tilde{X}^*$ be this matrix *computed at the restricted estimates*. Then the Lagrange multiplier statistic for the nonlinear regression model is

$$\text{LM} = \frac{e^{*'}\tilde{X}^*[\tilde{X}^{*'}\tilde{X}^*]^{-1}\tilde{X}^{*'}e^*}{(e^{*'}e^*/n)} = n\tilde{R}_*^2. \qquad (11-52)$$

This is asymptotically distributed as a chi-squared statistic with J degrees of freedom. What is especially appealing about this approach is that it requires only the restricted estimates. This may provide some savings in computing effort if, as in our example, the restrictions result in a linear model. Note, also, that the Lagrange multiplier statistic is n times the uncentered R^2 in the regression of e^* on $\tilde{x}^*$. Many Lagrange multiplier statistics are computed in this fashion.

---

[32] This applies for all cases, both linear and nonlinear.
[33] This is derived in Judge et al. (1985).

EXAMPLE 11.10. Lagrange Multiplier Tests for the Box–Cox Model. For simplicity, we first consider the basic model

$$y = \beta_1 + \beta_2 \frac{x^\lambda - 1}{\lambda} + \varepsilon$$

$$= f(x, \beta_1, \beta_2, \lambda) + \varepsilon.$$

(For convenience, we have dropped the observation subscript.) We shall examine the more general forms of the model later. We consider a Lagrange multiplier test of the hypothesis that λ equals zero. The *pseudo-regressors* are

$$x_1^* = \frac{\partial f(.)}{\partial \beta_1} = 1,$$

$$x_2^* = \frac{\partial f(.)}{\partial \beta_2} = \frac{x^\lambda - 1}{\lambda},$$

$$x_3^* = \frac{\partial f(.)}{\partial \lambda} = \beta_2 \frac{\lambda(\ln x)x^\lambda - x^\lambda + 1}{\lambda^2}.$$

The test is carried out by first regressing y on a constant and $\ln x$ (i.e., the regressor evaluated at $\lambda = 0$) and then computing nR_*^2 in the regression of the residuals from this first regression on x_1^*, x_2^*, and x_3^*, also evaluated at $\lambda = 0$. The first and second of these are 1 and $\ln x$. To obtain the third, use

$$x_3^* = \beta_2 \left[\frac{\ln x \, x^\lambda}{\lambda} - \frac{x^\lambda - 1}{\lambda^2} \right].$$

By subtracting and then adding $(\ln x)/\lambda$ and rearranging the terms, we find that

$$x_3^* = \beta_2 \left[\ln x \left(\frac{x^\lambda - 1}{\lambda} \right) + \frac{\lambda \ln x - (x^\lambda - 1)}{\lambda^2} \right].$$

Now, to obtain the value of x_3^* at $\lambda = 0$, we consider separately the limits of the two terms in square brackets as λ goes to 0. The first obviously converges to $(\ln x)^2$. For the second, we apply l'Hopital's rule twice:

$$\lim_{\lambda \to 0} \frac{\lambda \ln x - (x^\lambda - 1)}{\lambda^2} = \lim_{\lambda \to 0} \frac{\ln x - \ln x(x^\lambda)}{2\lambda}$$

$$= \lim_{\lambda \to 0} \frac{-(\ln x)^2 x^\lambda}{2}$$

$$= -\frac{1}{2}(\ln x)^2.$$

Adding the two parts of x_3^*, then, we obtain

$$\lim_{\lambda \to 0} x_3^* = \beta_2 \left[\frac{1}{2}(\ln x)^2 \right].$$

Therefore, the Lagrange multiplier test is carried out in two steps. First, we regress $\ln y$ on a constant and $\ln x$ and compute the residuals. Second, we regress these residuals on a constant, $\ln x$, and $(b_2/2)(\ln x)^2$, where b_2 is the coefficient on $\ln x$ in the first regression. The Lagrange multiplier is nR^2 from the second regression. The generalization to several regressors is immediate. In the first regression, we would use the logs of all of the regressors. The additional regressor for the second regression would be

$$x_\lambda^* = \left(\frac{1}{2}\right) \sum_k b_k (\ln x_k)^2,$$

where the sum is taken over all of the variables that are transformed in the original model and the b_k's are the least squares coefficients in the first regression.

For an example, consider the Box–Cox model of Example 11.7. The model is

$$\ln M = \alpha + \beta_r r^{(\lambda)} + \beta_Y Y^{(\lambda)} + \varepsilon.$$

To carry out the Wald test, we use the square of the ratio of $\hat{\lambda}$ to its estimated standard error as a chi-squared statistic with one degree of freedom. This is $(0.47/0.5467)^2 = 0.7391$. For the likelihood ratio test, we use (11–51). With $\lambda = 0.47$, the sum of squared residuals is 0.1272. With $\lambda = 0$, we obtain the sum of squared residuals in the regression of $\ln M$ on a constant, $\ln r$, and $\ln Y$, which is 0.13196. Therefore, the likelihood ratio statistic is $20 \ln\{(0.13196/20)/(0.1272/20)\} = 0.7342$. Finally, for the Lagrange multiplier test, we first regress $\ln M$ on a constant, $\ln r$, and $\ln Y$ and compute the residuals, e_*. The R^2 in the regression of e_* on one, $\ln r$, $\ln M$, and $(1/2)(b_r(\ln r)^2 + b_Y(\ln Y)^2)$, is 0.04374, so the Lagrange multiplier test statistic is $20(0.04374) = 0.8748$. None of these are larger than the tabled critical value, so the hypothesis that $\lambda = 0$ is not rejected.

By extending this to the model of (11–32), we can devise a bona fide test of log linearity (against the more general model, not linearity).[34] The log likelihood for the model

$$\frac{y^\lambda - 1}{\lambda} = \beta_1 + \beta_2 \frac{x^\lambda - 1}{\lambda} + \varepsilon$$

is given in (11–34). The first derivatives are obtained in (11–37) to (11–39). Using the Berndt et al. estimator given in (11–40), we could construct the Lagrange multiplier statistic as

$$LM = \chi^2[1] = \left(\sum_i \mathbf{w}_i\right)' \left\{\sum_i \mathbf{w}_i \mathbf{w}_i'\right\}^{-1} \left(\sum_i \mathbf{w}_i\right),$$

where, for the preceding model, we would compute the various terms at $\lambda = 0$. Thus,

$$\hat{\varepsilon}_i = \ln y_i - \hat{\beta}_1 - \hat{\beta}_2 \ln x_i,$$

$\hat{\beta}_1$ and $\hat{\beta}_2$ computed by the OLS regression of y on a constant and x, and

$$\hat{\sigma}^2 = \frac{1}{n} \sum_i \hat{\varepsilon}_i^2.$$

Let

$$\hat{\varepsilon}_i^* = \frac{1}{2}(\ln y_i)^2 - \frac{\hat{\beta}_2}{2}(\ln x_i)^2.$$

[See (11–38).] Then,

$$\mathbf{w}_i = \begin{bmatrix} \hat{\varepsilon}_i/\hat{\sigma}^2 \\ (\ln x_i)\hat{\varepsilon}_i/\hat{\sigma}^2 \\ \ln y_i - \hat{\varepsilon}_i\hat{\varepsilon}_i^*/\hat{\sigma}^2 \\ (\hat{\varepsilon}_i^2/\hat{\sigma}^2 - 1)/(2\hat{\sigma}^2) \end{bmatrix}.$$

[34] This test was proposed by Davidson and MacKinnon (1985). They also suggested a test of linearity based on the same methodology by using $\lambda = 1$ instead of $\lambda = 0$ in the computations just described.

(If there are k regressors in the model, the second component in $\mathbf{w}_i$ will be a vector containing the logs of the variables, while $\hat{\varepsilon}_i^*$ in the third becomes

$$\hat{\varepsilon}_i^* = \frac{1}{2}(\ln y_i)^2 - \sum_k \frac{\hat{\beta}_k}{2}(\ln x_{ik})^2.$$

The usefulness of this approach for either of the models we have examined is that in testing the hypothesis, it is not necessary to compute the nonlinear, unrestricted, Box–Cox regression.

EXAMPLE 11.11. Hypotheses Tests in a Nonlinear Regression Model. For a second example, we test the hypothesis

$$H_0 : \gamma = 1$$

in the consumption function of Example 11.3.

1. *F statistic:*

$$F[1, 36 - 3] = \frac{(12{,}068 - 8{,}420)/1}{8{,}420/(36 - 3)}$$

$$= 14.297.$$

The critical value from the tables is 4.18, so the hypothesis is rejected.

2. *Wald statistic:* For our example, this is based on the distance of $\hat{\gamma}$ from one, and is simply the square of the asymptotic t ratio we computed at the end of the example.

$$W = \frac{(1.1564 - 1)^2}{0.001681} = 14.551.$$

The critical value from the chi-squared table is 3.84.

3. *Likelihood ratio:* For the example, $\mathbf{e}'\mathbf{e}$ is 8,420, while $\mathbf{e}_*'\mathbf{e}_*$ is 12,068. With $n = 36$, this yields

$$\lambda = 36(5.8147 - 5.4548) = 12.9548.$$

This is also larger than the tabled critical value. Note, however, that it is noticeably less than the Wald statistic. It is possible that the two different statistics could lead to different inferences. Unfortunately, this is a problem that can arise in a finite sample, and there is no formal result that mandates which is the better to choose.[35]

4. *Lagrange multiplier:* For our example, the elements in $\tilde{\mathbf{x}}_i$ are

$$\tilde{\mathbf{x}}_i = [1, Y^\gamma, \beta\gamma Y^\gamma \ln Y].$$

To compute this at the restricted estimates, we use the ordinary least squares estimates for α and β, and one for γ, so that

$$\tilde{\mathbf{x}}_i^* = [1, Y, \beta Y \ln Y].$$

The residuals are the ordinary least squares residuals computed from the linear regression. Inserting the values given earlier, we have

$$LM = \frac{3547.3}{12{,}068/36} = 10.582.$$

As expected, this statistic is also larger than the critical value from the chi-squared table.

---

[35] There is some evidence, though no prescription, on this problem in Berndt and Savin (1977).

There is a large and growing literature on the use of these tests in econometrics. The emerging results have documented many ways to extend beyond the conventional t and F tests, particularly in the area of nonnested models. The Lagrange multiplier test has been shown to be especially convenient in gathering under a broad umbrella an impressive variety of already familiar tests.[36]

Exercises

1. Describe how to obtain nonlinear least squares estimates of the parameters of the model

$$y = \alpha x^\beta + \varepsilon.$$

2. Use MacKinnon et al.'s P_E test to determine whether a linear or log-linear production model is more appropriate for the data in Table 7.1. (The test is described in Section 11.5 and Example 11.4.)

3. Example 8.4 discusses a method of estimating the parameters of the CES production function based on a linearization of the model around $\rho = 0$. An alternative way to proceed is by direct nonlinear least squares. For the model

$$\ln Y = \ln \gamma - \left(\frac{v}{\rho}\right)\ln[\delta K^{-\rho} + (1-\delta)L^{-\rho}] + \varepsilon,$$

derive the linearized model shown in (11–8). Describe in full how to obtain the nonlinear least squares estimates and how to compute the estimate of the asymptotic covariance matrix of these estimates.

4. Using the Box–Cox transformation, we may specify an alternative to the Cobb–Douglas model as

$$\ln Y = \alpha + \frac{\beta_k(K^\lambda - 1)}{\lambda} + \frac{\beta_l(L^\lambda - 1)}{\lambda} + \varepsilon.$$

Using Zellner and Revankar's data in Example 11.5, estimate α, β_k, β_l, and λ, using the scanning method suggested in Section 11.7.1. (Do not forget to scale Y, K, and L by the number of establishments.) Use (11–29) to compute the appropriate asymptotic standard errors for your estimates. Compute the two output elasticities, $\partial \ln Y/\partial \ln K$ and $\partial \ln Y/\partial \ln L$ at the sample means of K and L. (**Hint:** $\partial \ln Y/\partial \ln K = K\partial \ln Y/\partial K$.) How do these estimates compare to the values given in Example 11.5? Finally, compute the estimates of economies of scale for the states shown in Example 11.5 and compare your estimates to the values given there.

5. For the model in the previous problem, test the hypothesis that $\lambda = 0$, using a Wald test, a likelihood ratio test, and a Lagrange multiplier test. Note that the restricted model is the Cobb–Douglas log-linear model.

6. To extend Zellner and Revankar's model in a fashion similar to their's, we can use the Box–Cox transformation for the dependent variable as well. Use the method of Section 11.7.2 (with $\theta = \lambda$) to repeat the study of the previous two exercises. How do your results change?

7. Suppose that we wished to test the specification of Exercise 6 against that of Exercise 4. The models are not nested, so there is no obvious test. Indeed, they both use exactly the same parameters. One possibility is the following: Both models are special cases of

---

[36] Some useful references are Buse (1982), Pagan and Hall (1983), Engel (1984), and Breusch and Pagan (1980).

(11–32). In Problem 4 we assume that $\theta = 0$ while in Exercise 6 we impose $\theta = \lambda$. Thus, although it might seem otherwise, it is not obvious that Exercise 6 is a less restrictive or preferable model. One way to determine which model is preferable (albeit not a formal test) is to compare the log likelihoods under the two specifications. This can be done directly, using the results already obtained. Somewhat more evidence can be obtained by estimating the unrestricted model. This requires a two-dimensional search for θ and λ. Estimate the unrestricted model; then carry out an analysis of the sort done in Example 11.9.

References

Amemiya, T., *Advanced Econometrics*, Cambridge, Mass.: Harvard University Press, 1985.

Berndt, E., B. Hall, R. Hall, and J. Hausman, "Estimation and Inference in Nonlinear Structural Models," *Annals of Economic and Social Measurement*, 3/4, 1974, pp. 653–665.

Berndt, E., and E. Savin, "Conflict Among Criteria for Testing Hypotheses in the Multivariate Regression Model," *Econometrica*, 45, 1977, pp. 1263–1278.

Blackley, R., J. Follain, and J. Ondrich, "Box–Cox Estimation of Hedonic Models: How Serious Is the Iterative OLS Variance Bias?" *Review of Economics and Statistics*, 66, 1984, pp. 348–353.

Box, G., and D. Cox, "An Analysis of Transformations," *Journal of the Royal Statistical Society: Series B*, 26, 1964, pp. 211–243.

Breusch, T., and A. Pagan, "The LM Test and Its Applications to Model Specification in Econometrics," *Review of Economic Studies*, 47, 1980, pp. 239–254.

Buse, A., "The Likelihood Ratio, Wald, and Lagrange Multiplier Tests: An Expository Note," *The American Statistician*, 36, 1982, pp. 153–177.

Caves, D., L. Christensen, and M. Trethaway, "Flexible Cost Functions for Multiproduct Firms," *Review of Economics and Statistics*, 62, 1980, pp. 477–481.

Davidson, R., and J. MacKinnon, "Several Tests for Model Specification in the Presence of Alternative Hypotheses," *Econometrica*, 49, 1981, pp. 781–793.

Davidson, R., and J. MacKinnon, "Testing Linear and Loglinear Regressions Against Box–Cox Alternatives," *Canadian Journal of Economics*, 18, 1985, pp. 499–517.

Draper, N., and D. Cox, "On Distributions and Their Transformation to Normality," *Journal of the Royal Statistical Society, Series B*, 31, 1969, pp. 472–476.

Engel, R., "Wald, Likelihood Ratio, and Lagrange Multiplier Tests in Economics," in Z. Griliches and M. Intrilligator, eds., *Handbook of Economics*, Vol. 2, Amsterdam: North Holland, 1984.

Fomby, T., C. Hill, and S. Johnson, *Advanced Econometric Methods*, New York: Springer-Verlag, 1984.

Goldfeld, S., "The Demand for Money Revisited," *Brookings Papers on Economic Activity*, 3, 1973.

Goldfeld, S., and R. Quandt, *Nonlinear Methods in Econometrics*, Amsterdam: North Holland, 1972.

Hausman, J., and D. Wise, "Social Experimentation, Truncated Distributions, and Efficient Estimation," *Econometrica*, 45, 1977, pp. 919–938.

Jennrich, R. I., "The Asymptotic Properties of Nonlinear Least Squares Estimators," *The Annals of Statistics*, 2, 1969, pp. 633–643.

Judge, G., C. Hill, W. Griffiths, H. Lutkepohl, and T. Lee, *The Theory and Practice of Econometrics*, New York: Wiley, 1985.

MacKinnon, J., H. White, and R. Davidson, "Tests for Model Specification in the Presence of Alternative Hypotheses; Some Further Results," *Journal of Econometrics*, 21, 1, 1983, pp. 53–70.

Malinvaud, E., *Statistical Methods of Econometrics*, Amsterdam: North Holland, 1971.

Pagan, A., and A. Hall, "Diagnostic Tests as Residual Analysis," *Econometric Reviews*, 2, 1983, pp. 159–218.

Poirier, D., "The Use of the Box–Cox Transformation in Limited Dependent Variable Models," *Journal of the American Statistical Association*, 73, 1978, pp. 284–287.

Poirier, D., and A. Melino, "A Note on the Interpretation of Regression Coefficients within a Class of Truncated Distributions," *Econometrica*, 46, 1978, pp. 1207–1209.

Seaks, T., and L. Layson, "Box–Cox Estimation with Standard Econometric Problems," *Review of Economics and Statistics*, 65, 1983, pp. 160–164.

Spitzer, J., "A Primer on Box–Cox Estimation," *Review of Economics and Statistics*, 64, 1982a, pp. 307–313.

Spitzer, J., "A Fast and Efficient Algorithm for the Estimation of Parameters in Models with the Box and Cox Transformation," *Journal of the American Statistical Association*, 77, 1982b, pp. 760–766.

Spitzer, J., "Variance Estimates in Models with the Box–Cox Transformation: Implications for Estimation and Hypothesis Testing," *Review of Economics and Statistics*, 66, 1984, pp. 645–652.

White, H., "Using Least Squares to Approximate Unknown Regression Functions," *International Economic Review*, 21, 1980, pp. 149–170.

Zarembka, P., "Functional Form in the Demand for Money," *Journal of the American Statistical Association*, 63, 1968, pp. 502–511.

Zellner, A., and N. Revankar, "Generalized Production Functions," *Review of Economic Studies*, 37, 1970, pp. 241–250.

Chapter 12

An Introduction to Nonlinear Optimization[1]

12.1. Introduction

The nonlinear least squares regression discussed in Chapter 11 is an example of a nonlinear optimization problem. With the exception of the normal linear regression model, maximum likelihood estimation usually involves the solution of nonlinear equations as well. Nonlinear optimization is an intriguing practical problem. The theory provides few hard and fast rules, and there are relatively few cases in which it is obvious how to proceed. This chapter introduces some of the terminology and underlying theory of nonlinear optimization.[2] We begin with some general discussion on how to search for a solution to a nonlinear optimization problem and describe some specific commonly used methods. We then consider some practical problems that arise in optimization. An example is given in the final section.

12.2. Optimization Problems

Consider maximizing the quadratic function

$$F(\theta) = a + \mathbf{b}'\theta - \tfrac{1}{2}\theta'\mathbf{C}\theta, \tag{12-1}$$

where $\mathbf{C}$ is a positive definite matrix. The first-order condition for a maximum is

$$\frac{\partial F(\theta)}{\partial \theta} = \mathbf{b} - \mathbf{C}\theta = 0. \tag{12-2}$$

This set of *linear* equations has unique solution

$$\theta = \mathbf{C}^{-1}\mathbf{b}. \tag{12-3}$$

---

[1] The material of this chapter is somewhat advanced and may be skipped with no loss of continuity.
[2] There are numerous excellent references that offer a more complete exposition. Among these are Quandt (1983), Bazaraa and Shetty (1979), and Fletcher (1980).

This is a linear optimization problem. Note that it has a **closed-form solution**; for any a, b, and C, the solution can be computed directly.[3] In the more typical situation,

$$\frac{\partial F(\boldsymbol{\theta})}{\partial \boldsymbol{\theta}} = 0 \qquad (12-4)$$

is a set of nonlinear equations that cannot be solved explicitly for $\boldsymbol{\theta}$.[4] The techniques considered in this chapter provide systematic means of searching for a solution.

We consider the general problem of maximizing a function of several variables:

$$\text{Maximize}_{\boldsymbol{\theta}} \, F(\boldsymbol{\theta}), \qquad (12-5)$$

where $F(\boldsymbol{\theta})$ may be a log likelihood or some other function. Minimization of $F(\boldsymbol{\theta})$ is handled by maximizing $-F(\boldsymbol{\theta})$. Two special cases are

$$F(\boldsymbol{\theta}) = \sum_i f_i(\boldsymbol{\theta}), \qquad (12-6)$$

which is typical for maximum likelihood problems, and the **least squares problem**,[5]

$$f_i(\boldsymbol{\theta}) = -(y_i - f(\mathbf{x}_i, \boldsymbol{\theta}))^2. \qquad (12-7)$$

12.3. Grid Search

An obvious way to search for the $\boldsymbol{\theta}$ that maximizes $F(\boldsymbol{\theta})$ is by trial and error. If $\boldsymbol{\theta}$ has only a single element and it is known approximately where the optimum will be found, a **grid search** will be a feasible strategy. The Box–Cox model of Section 11.7 is usually estimated by scanning the range of -1 to 1 for the optimal value of λ.[6] Another example is a common time series problem, in which a one-dimensional search for a correlation coefficient is made in the interval $(-1, 1)$. The grid search can proceed in the obvious fashion, that is, $\ldots$, $-0.1, 0, 0.1$, $0.2, \ldots$, then $\hat{\theta}_{\text{max}} - 0.1$ to $\hat{\theta}_{\text{max}} + 0.1$ in increments of 0.01, and so on, until the desired precision is achieved. If $\boldsymbol{\theta}$ contains more than one parameter, a grid search is likely to be extremely costly, particularly if little is known about the parameter vector at the outset. Nonetheless, relatively efficient methods have been devised. Quandt (1983) and Fletcher (1980) contain further details.

12.4. General Characteristics of Algorithms

A more effective means of solving most nonlinear maximization problems is by an **iterative algorithm**:

Beginning from initial value θ_0, at entry to iteration t, if θ_t is not the optimal value for θ, compute direction vector, Δ_t, step size λ_t, then

$$\theta_{t+1} = \theta_t + \lambda_t \Delta_t. \qquad (12-8)$$

---

[3] Notice that the constant, a, is irrelevant to the solution. Many maximum likelihood problems are presented with the preface "neglecting an irrelevant constant." For example, the log likelihood for the normal linear regression model contains a term, $-(n/2)\ln(2\pi)$, that can be discarded.

[4] See, for example, the normal equations for the nonlinear least squares estimators of the previous chapter.

[5] Least squares is, of course, a minimization problem. The negative of the criterion is used to maintain consistency with the general formulation.

[6] It should be remembered, however, that nothing prevents λ from being outside this range. For example, if a Box–Cox model is fit to the production data of Example 7.1, two minima of the sum of squares can be found: a local minimum at 0.29 and a global minimum at 1.7.

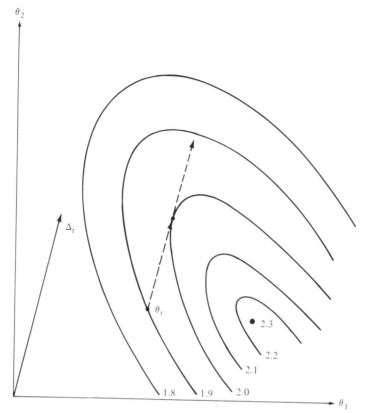

Figure 12.1   Iteration.

Figure 12.1 illustrates the structure of an iteration for a hypothetical function of two variables. The direction vector, $\mathbf{\Delta}_t$, is shown in the figure with $\boldsymbol{\theta}_t$. The dashed line is the set of points $\boldsymbol{\theta}_t + \lambda_t \mathbf{\Delta}_t$. Different values of λ_t lead to different contours; for this $\boldsymbol{\theta}_t$ and $\mathbf{\Delta}_t$, the best value of λ_t is about 0.5.

Notice in Figure 12.1 that for a given direction vector, $\mathbf{\Delta}_t$, and current parameter vector, $\boldsymbol{\theta}_t$, a secondary optimization is required to find the best λ_t. Translating from Figure 12.1, we obtain the form of this problem as shown in Figure 12.2. This subsidiary search is called a **line search**, as we search along the line $\boldsymbol{\theta}_t + \lambda_t \mathbf{\Delta}_t$ for the optimal value of $F(.)$. The formal solution to the line search problem would be the λ_t that satisfies

$$\frac{\partial F(\boldsymbol{\theta}_t + \lambda_t \mathbf{\Delta}_t)}{\partial \lambda_t} = \mathbf{g}(\boldsymbol{\theta}_t + \lambda_t \mathbf{\Delta}_t)' \mathbf{\Delta}_t \qquad (12\text{--}9)$$

$$= 0,$$

where $\mathbf{g}$ is the vector of partial derivatives of $F(.)$ evaluated at $\boldsymbol{\theta}_t + \lambda_t \mathbf{\Delta}_t$. In general, this will also be a nonlinear problem. In most cases, adding a formal search for λ_t will be too expensive, as well as unnecessary. Some approximate or ad hoc method will usually be chosen. It is worth emphasizing that finding the λ_t that maximizes $F(\boldsymbol{\theta}_t + \lambda_t \mathbf{\Delta}_t)$ at a given iteration does not generally lead to the overall solution in that iteration. This is clear in Figure 12.1, where the optimal value of λ_t leads to $F(.) = 2.0$, at which point we reenter the iteration.

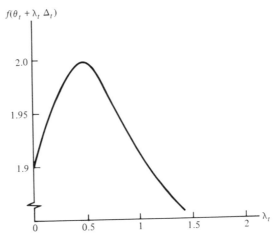

Figure 12.2   Line search.

12.5. *Gradient Methods*

The most commonly used algorithms are **gradient methods**, in which

$$\Delta_t = H_t g_t, \tag{12–10}$$

where H_t is a positive definite matrix and g_t is the **gradient** of $F(\theta_t)$:

$$g_t = g(\theta_t) = \frac{\partial F(\theta_t)}{\partial \theta_t}. \tag{12–11}$$

These methods are motivated partly by the following: Consider a linear Taylor series approximation to $F(\theta_t + \lambda_t \Delta_t)$ around $\lambda = 0$:

$$F(\theta_t + \lambda_t \Delta_t) \simeq F(\theta_t) + \lambda_t g(\theta_t)' \Delta_t. \tag{12–12}$$

Let $F(\theta_t + \lambda_t \Delta_t)$ equal F_{t+1}. Then

$$F_{t+1} - F_t \simeq \lambda_t g_t' \Delta_t.$$

If $\Delta_t = H_t g_t$,

$$F_{t+1} - F_t \simeq \lambda_t g_t' H_t g_t.$$

If g_t is not **0** and λ_t is small enough, $F_{t+1} - F_t$ must be positive. This means that if $F(\theta)$ is not already at its maximum, we can always find a stepsize such that a gradient-type iteration will lead to an increase in the function. (Recall that H_t is assumed to be positive definite.)

In the following, we will omit the iteration index, t, except where it is necessary to distinguish one vector from another. The following are some commonly used algorithms.[7]

---

[7] A more extensive catalog may be found in Judge et al. (1985, Appendix B). Those mentioned here are some of the more commonly used ones and are chosen primarily because they illustrate many of the important aspects of nonlinear optimization.

12.5.1. Steepest Ascent

The simplest algorithm to employ is the **steepest ascent** method, which uses

$$\mathbf{H} = \mathbf{I} \qquad \text{so that} \qquad \boldsymbol{\Delta} = \mathbf{g}. \tag{12–13}$$

As its name implies, the direction is the one of greatest increase of $F(.)$. Another virtue is that the line search has a straightforward solution; at least near the maximum, the optimal λ is

$$\lambda = \frac{-\mathbf{g}'\mathbf{g}}{\mathbf{g}'\mathbf{G}\mathbf{g}}, \tag{12–14}$$

where

$$\mathbf{G} = \frac{\partial^2 F(\boldsymbol{\theta})}{\partial \boldsymbol{\theta} \partial \boldsymbol{\theta}'}.$$

Therefore, the steepest ascent iteration is

$$\boldsymbol{\theta}_{t+1} = \boldsymbol{\theta}_t - \left(\frac{\mathbf{g}_t'\mathbf{g}_t}{\mathbf{g}_t'\mathbf{G}_t\mathbf{g}_t}\right)\mathbf{g}_t. \tag{12–15}$$

Computation of the second derivatives matrix may be extremely burdensome. Also, if $\mathbf{G}_t$ is not negative definite, which is likely if $\boldsymbol{\theta}_t$ is far from the maximum, the iteration may diverge. A systematic line search can bypass this problem. This algorithm usually converges very slowly, however, so other techniques are usually used.

12.5.2. Newton's Method

The basis for **Newton's method** is a linear Taylor series approximation. Expanding the first-order conditions (equation by equation)

$$\frac{\partial F(\boldsymbol{\theta})}{\partial \boldsymbol{\theta}} = \mathbf{0}$$

in a linear Taylor series around an arbitrary $\boldsymbol{\theta}^0$ yields

$$\frac{\partial F(\boldsymbol{\theta})}{\partial \boldsymbol{\theta}} \simeq \mathbf{g}^0 + \mathbf{G}^0(\boldsymbol{\theta} - \boldsymbol{\theta}^0) = \mathbf{0}, \tag{12–16}$$

where the superscript indicates that the term is evaluated at $\boldsymbol{\theta}^0$. Solving for $\boldsymbol{\theta}$ and then equating $\boldsymbol{\theta}$ to $\boldsymbol{\theta}_{t+1}$ and $\boldsymbol{\theta}^0$ to $\boldsymbol{\theta}_t$, we obtain the iteration

$$\boldsymbol{\theta}_{t+1} = \boldsymbol{\theta}_t - \mathbf{G}_t^{-1}\mathbf{g}_t. \tag{12–17}$$

Thus, for Newton's method,

$$\mathbf{H} = -\mathbf{G}^{-1}, \qquad \boldsymbol{\Delta} = -\mathbf{G}^{-1}\mathbf{g}, \qquad \text{and } \lambda = 1. \tag{12–18}$$

Newton's method will converge very rapidly in many problems. If the function is quadratic, this method will reach the optimum in one iteration from any starting point. [Consider, for example, the optimization problem posed in (12–1).] If the criterion function is globally concave, as it is in a number of problems that we shall examine later, it is probably the best algorithm available. This method is very well suited to maximum likelihood estimation.

12.5.3. Maximum Likelihood Estimation

For solving a maximum likelihood problem, the **method of scoring** replaces $\mathbf{H}$ with

$$\bar{\mathbf{H}} = -(E[\mathbf{G}(\theta)]^{-1}, \tag{12-19}$$

which will be recognized as the asymptotic variance of $\sqrt{n}$ times the maximum likelihood estimator. There is some evidence that where it can be used, this method performs better than Newton's method. However, the exact form of the expectation of the Hessian of the log likelihood is rarely known.[8] Newton's method, which uses actual instead of expected second derivatives, is generally used instead.

A particularly convenient variant of Newton's method is the **one-step maximum likelihood estimator**. It has been shown that if θ^0 is *any* consistent initial estimator of θ and $\mathbf{H}^*$ is $\mathbf{H}$ or $\bar{\mathbf{H}}$, or any other asymptotically equivalent estimator of $\mathrm{Var}[\sqrt{n}(\hat{\theta}_{\mathrm{MLE}} - \theta)]$,

$$\theta^1 = \theta^0 + \mathbf{H}^{*-1}\mathbf{g}^0 \tag{12-20}$$

is an estimator of θ that has the same asymptotic properties as the maximum likelihood estimator.[9] (Note that it is *not* the maximum likelihood estimator. As such, for example, it should not be used as the basis for likelihood ratio tests.)

12.5.4. Alternatives to Newton's Method

Newton's method is very effective in some settings, but it can perform very poorly in others. If the function is not approximately quadratic or the current estimate is very far from the maximum, it can cause wide swings in the estimates and even fail to converge at all. A number of means have been devised to improve upon Newton's method. An obvious one is to include a line search at each iteration rather than use $\lambda = 1$. However, two problems remain. At points distant from the optimum, the second derivatives matrix may not be negative definite, and, in any event, the computational burden of computing $\mathbf{G}$ may be excessive.

The **quadratic hill-climbing method** proposed by Goldfeld et al. (1966) deals directly with the first of these problems. In any iteration, if $\mathbf{G}$ is not negative definite, it is replaced with

$$\mathbf{G}_\alpha = \mathbf{G} - \alpha\mathbf{I}, \tag{12-21}$$

where α is a positive number chosen large enough to ensure the negative definiteness of $\mathbf{G}_\alpha$. Another suggestion is that of Greenstadt (1967), which uses, at every iteration,

$$\mathbf{G}_\pi = -\sum_i |\pi_i|\mathbf{c}_i\mathbf{c}_i', \tag{12-22}$$

where π_i is the ith characteristic root of $\mathbf{G}$ and $\mathbf{c}_i$ is its associated characteristic vector. Other proposals have been made to ensure the negative definiteness of the required matrix at each iteration.[10] However, the computational complexity of these methods remains a problem.

Two commonly used methods simultaneously simplify the calculation of $\mathbf{H}$ and solve the problem of definiteness. For maximum likelihood problems, the method of Berndt et al. (1974) replaces $\mathbf{H}$ with

$$\hat{\mathbf{H}} = \left[\sum_i \mathbf{g}_i\mathbf{g}_i'\right]^{-1}, \tag{12-23}$$

---

[8] Amemiya (1981) provides a number of examples.
[9] See, for example, Rao (1965).
[10] See, for example, Goldfeld and Quandt (1971).

where

$$g_i = \frac{\partial \ln f(\mathbf{x}_i, \boldsymbol{\theta})}{\partial \boldsymbol{\theta}}.$$

This is the third estimator for the variance of the maximum likelihood estimator that we considered in Chapter 4.[11] While $\hat{\mathbf{H}}$ and a consistent estimator of $-\mathbf{G}$ are asymptotically equivalent, $\hat{\mathbf{H}}$ has the additional virtues that it is always positive definite, and it is only necessary to differentiate the log likelihood once in order to compute it.

For the nonlinear least squares problem, the correct second derivatives matrix is

$$\mathbf{G} = -2\sum_i [\mathbf{g}_i \mathbf{g}_i' - (y_i - f_i)\mathbf{G}_i], \tag{12-24}$$

where $f_i = f(\mathbf{x}_i, \boldsymbol{\theta})$ and $\mathbf{g}_i$ and $\mathbf{G}_i$ are its first and second derivatives, respectively. This matrix can also fail to be positive definite at points different from the minimum. The **Gauss–Newton method** amounts simply to dropping the second term, which leaves a matrix that is always negative definite. Recall the linearized regression of Section 11.3:

$$f_i \simeq f_i^0 + \mathbf{g}_i^{0'}(\boldsymbol{\theta} - \boldsymbol{\theta}^0).$$

Inserting this in the sum of squares yields

$$F(\boldsymbol{\theta}) \simeq \sum_i [(y_i - f_i^0 + \mathbf{g}_i^{0'}\boldsymbol{\theta}^0) - \mathbf{g}_i^{0'}\boldsymbol{\theta}]^2$$

$$= \sum_i [y_i^0 - \mathbf{g}_i^{0'}\boldsymbol{\theta}]^2. \tag{12-25}$$

For a given value of $\boldsymbol{\theta}^0$, this is the linear least squares problem. The iterative solution to the minimization problem is, then,

$$\boldsymbol{\theta}_{t+1} = \left[\sum_i \mathbf{g}_i \mathbf{g}_i'\right]^{-1}\left[\sum_i \mathbf{g}_i(y_i - f_i + \mathbf{g}_i'\boldsymbol{\theta}_t)\right]$$

$$= \boldsymbol{\theta}_t + \left[\sum_i \mathbf{g}_i \mathbf{g}_i'\right]^{-1}\left[\sum_i \mathbf{g}_i(y_i - f_i)\right], \tag{12-26}$$

where all terms on the right-hand side are evaluated at $\boldsymbol{\theta}_t$.

This particular algorithm has some intuitive appeal. For each iteration, we update the previous parameter estimate by regressing the nonlinear least squares residuals, $(y_i - f_i)$, on the derivatives of the regression functions. As discussed in Chapter 11, the derivatives, $\mathbf{g}_i$, are in some respects analogous to the regressors, $\mathbf{x}_i$, in the linear model. Let $\tilde{\mathbf{X}}$ be the $n \times K$ matrix of derivatives and let $\tilde{\mathbf{e}}$ be the $n \times 1$ vector of residuals. Then the iteration in (12–27) is equivalent to

$$\boldsymbol{\theta}_{t+1} - \boldsymbol{\theta}_t = [\tilde{\mathbf{X}}'\tilde{\mathbf{X}}]^{-1}\tilde{\mathbf{X}}'\tilde{\mathbf{e}}.$$

The process will have converged (i.e., the update will be $\mathbf{0}$) when $\tilde{\mathbf{X}}'\tilde{\mathbf{e}}$ is close enough to $\mathbf{0}$.[12] This has a direct counterpart in the normal equations for the linear model,

$$\mathbf{X}'\mathbf{e} = \mathbf{0}.$$

In the same fashion as Newton's method, this algorithm can be improved by doing a line search at each iteration instead of using $\lambda = 1$.

---

[11] This is the estimator of the asymptotic covariance matrix used for the Box–Cox model in Example 11.8.
[12] It will not be exactly zero. See Section 12.6 for a discussion of convergence of nonlinear optimization algorithms.

12.5.5. Quasi-Newton Methods—Davidon, Fletcher, Powell (DFP)

A very effective class of algorithms has been developed that eliminates second derivatives altogether and has excellent convergence properties, even for ill-behaved problems. These are the **quasi-Newton methods**, which form

$$\mathbf{H}_{t+1} = \mathbf{H}_t + \mathbf{E}_t,$$

where $\mathbf{E}_t$ is a positive definite matrix.[13] As long as $\mathbf{H}_0$ is positive definite—$\mathbf{I}$ is commonly used—$\mathbf{H}_t$ will be positive definite at every iteration. In the **DFP method**, after a sufficient number of iterations, $\mathbf{H}_{t+1}$ will be an approximation to $-\mathbf{G}^{-1}$. Let

$$\delta_t = \lambda_t \Delta_t \qquad \text{and} \qquad \gamma_t = \mathbf{g}(\theta_{t+1}) - \mathbf{g}(\theta_t). \tag{12-27}$$

The DFP **variable metric algorithm** uses

$$\mathbf{H}_{t+1} = \mathbf{H}_t + \frac{\delta_t \delta_t'}{(\delta_t' \gamma_t)} + \frac{\mathbf{H}_t \gamma_t \gamma_t' \mathbf{H}_t}{(\gamma_t' \mathbf{H}_t \gamma_t)}. \tag{12-28}$$

Notice that in the DFP algorithm, the change in the first derivative vector is used in $\mathbf{H}$; an estimate of the inverse of the second derivatives matrix is being accumulated.

The variable metric algorithms are those that update $\mathbf{H}$ at each iteration while preserving its definiteness. For the DFP method, the accumulation of $\mathbf{H}_{t+1}$ is of the form

$$\mathbf{H}_{t+1} = \mathbf{H}_t + \mathbf{a}\mathbf{a}' + \mathbf{b}\mathbf{b}' = \mathbf{H}_t + [\mathbf{a}, \mathbf{b}][\mathbf{a}, \mathbf{b}]'.$$

The two-column matrix $[\mathbf{a}, \mathbf{b}]$ will have rank two; hence this is called a *rank two update* or *rank two correction*. Other methods, such as **Broyden's method**, involve a rank one correction instead. Any method that is of the form

$$\mathbf{H}_{t+1} = \mathbf{H}_t + \mathbf{Q}\mathbf{Q}'$$

will preserve the definiteness of $\mathbf{H}$, regardless of the number of columns in $\mathbf{Q}$.

The DFP algorithm is extremely effective and is among the most widely used gradient methods. An important practical consideration to keep in mind is that although $\mathbf{H}_t$ accumulates an estimate of the negative inverse of the second derivatives matrix, in maximum likelihood problems it rarely converges to a very good estimate of the variance matrix of the estimator and should generally not be used as one.

12.6. *Some Practical Considerations*

The reasons for the good performance of many algorithms, including DFP, are unknown. Moreover, different algorithms may perform differently in given settings. Indeed, for some problems, one algorithm may fail to converge, while another will succeed in finding a solution without great difficulty. In view of this, computer programs such as GQOPT[14] and Gauss[15] that offer a menu of different preprogrammed algorithms can be particularly useful. It is sometimes worth the effort to try more than one algorithm on a given problem.

Except for the steepest ascent case, an optimal line search is likely to be infeasible or to require more effort than it is worth in view of the potentially large number of function

---

[13] See Fletcher (1980).
[14] Goldfeld and Quandt (1972).
[15] Edlefson and Jones (1985).

evaluations required. In most cases, the choice of a stepsize is likely to be rather ad hoc. But within limits, the most widely used algorithms appear to be robust to inaccurate line searches. For example, one method used by the widely used TSP computer program[16] is the method of *squeezing*, which tries $\lambda = 1, \frac{1}{2}, \frac{1}{4}$, and so on, until an improvement in the function results. Although this is obviously a bit unorthodox, it appears to be quite effective when used with the Gauss–Newton method. A somewhat more elaborate rule is suggested by Berndt et al.[17] Choose an ε between 0 and $\frac{1}{2}$; then find a λ such that

$$\varepsilon < \frac{[F(\theta + \lambda\Delta) - F(\theta)]}{(\lambda g' \Delta)} < 1 - \varepsilon. \tag{12-29}$$

Of course, which value of ε to choose is still open, so the choice of λ remains ad hoc. Moreover, in neither of these cases is there any optimality to the choice; we merely find a λ that leads to a function improvement. Other authors have devised relatively efficient means of searching for a stepsize without doing the full optimization at each iteration.[18]

For certain functions, the programming of derivatives may be quite difficult. Numerical approximations can be used, although it should be borne in mind that analytic derivatives obtained by formally differentiating the functions involved are always to be preferred. With this as a caveat, first derivatives can be approximated by using

$$\frac{\partial F(\theta)}{\partial \theta_i} \simeq \frac{[F(\cdots\theta_i + \varepsilon\cdots) - F(\cdots\theta_i - \varepsilon\cdots)]}{2\varepsilon}. \tag{12-30}$$

The choice of ε is a remaining problem; extensive discussion may be found in Quandt (1983). The primary drawback to this means of computing the first derivatives is that it may require a tremendous number of function evaluations. Moreoever, it includes substantial rounding error, which can, in some cases, dramatically affect the optimization process. Second derivatives can also be computed numerically; however, in addition to the preceding problems, it is generally not possible to ensure negative definiteness of a Hessian computed in this manner. Unless the choice of ε is made extremely carefully, an indefinite matrix is a possibility. As a general proposition, the use of numerical derivatives should be avoided if possible.

Ideally, the iterative procedure should terminate when the gradient vector is zero. In practice, this will not be possible, primarily because of accumulated rounding error in the computation of the function and its derivatives. In view of this, a number of alternative convergence criteria are used. Most of them are based on the relative changes in the function or the parameters. There is considerable variation in those used in different computer programs. There are some pitfalls that should be avoided. A critical absolute value for the elements of the gradient vector or its norm will be affected by any scaling of the function, such as normalizing it by the sample size. Similarly, stopping on the basis of small absolute changes in the parameters can lead to premature convergence when the parameter vector approaches the maximum. It is probably best to use several criteria simultaneously, such as the change in both the function and the parameters. Belsley (1980) discusses a number of possible stopping rules. One that has proved useful and is immune to the scaling problem is to base convergence on $g'G^{-1}g$.

It is possible for a function to have several local extrema. Obviously, it is difficult to know a priori whether this is true of the one at hand. But if the function is not globally

---

[16] Hall (1982, p. 147).
[17] Op. cit.
[18] See, for example, Joreskog and Gruvaeus (1970), Powell (1964), Quandt (1983), and Hall (1982).

concave, it may be a good idea to attempt to maximize it from several starting points in order to ensure that the maximum obtained is the global one. Ideally, a starting value near the optimum can facilitate matters; in some settings, this can be obtained by using a consistent estimate of the parameter for the starting point. The method of moments, if available, is sometimes a convenient device for doing so.

Finally, it should be noted that in a nonlinear setting the iterative algorithm can break down, even in the absence of constraints, for at least two reasons. The first is that the problem being solved may be so numerically complex as to defy solution. The second possibility, which is often neglected, is that the proposed model may simply be inappropriate for the data. In a linear setting, a low R^2 or some other diagnostic test may suggest that the model and data are mismatched, but as long as the full rank condition is met by the regressor matrix, a linear regression can *always* be computed. Nonlinear models are not so forgiving. The failure of an iterative algorithm to find a maximum of the criterion function may be a warning that the model is not appropriate for this body of data.

12.7. Examples

To illustrate the use of gradient methods, we consider two simple problems.

EXAMPLE 12.1. Function of One Parameter.   Consider, first, maximizing a function of a single variable,

$$f(\theta) = \log(\theta) - \theta^2.$$

The first and second derivatives are

$$f'(\theta) = \frac{1}{\theta} - 2\theta$$

and

$$f''(\theta) = \frac{-1}{\theta^2} - 2$$

Equating f' to zero yields the simple solution $\theta = \sqrt{0.5} = 0.7071$. At the solution, $f'' = -4$, so this is indeed a maximum. To demonstrate the use of an iterative method, we solve this problem using Newton's method. Observe, first, that the second derivative is always negative for any admissable (positive) θ.[19] (The function resembles a parabola.) Therefore, it will not matter where we start the iterations; we shall eventually find the maximum. For a single parameter, Newton's method is

$$\theta_{t+1} = \theta_t - \frac{f'}{f''}.$$

The sequence of values that results when 5 is used as the starting value is given in Table 12.1.

---

[19] This is a problem in which an inequality restriction, $\theta > 0$, is required. However, as is common, for our first attempt we shall neglect the constraint.

Table 12.1

Iteration	θ	$f(\theta)$	$f'(\theta)$	$f''(\theta)$
0	5	−23.39	−9.80	−2.04
1	0.1961	−1.67	4.71	−28.01
2	0.3642	−1.14	2.02	−9.54
3	0.5746	−0.88	0.59	−5.02
4	0.6924	−0.85	0.06	−4.08
5	0.7070	−0.85	0.00	−4.00
6	0.7071			

If we begin from the starting values of 1, 25, and 0.001, the method requires 3, 8, and 12 iterations, respectively, to reach the same solution.

EXAMPLE 12.2. **Function of Two Parameters—the Gamma Distribution.** For random sampling from the gamma distribution,

$$f(y_i, \beta, \rho) = \left[\frac{\beta^\rho}{\Gamma(\rho)} \right] e^{-\beta y_i} y_i^{\rho-1}.$$

The log likelihood is

$$\ln L(\beta, \rho) = n\rho \ln \beta - n \ln \Gamma(\rho) - \beta \sum_i y_i + (\rho - 1) \sum_i \ln y_i.$$

It is often convenient to scale the log likelihood by the sample size. Suppose, as well, that we have a sample with

$$\bar{y} = 3,$$

$$\overline{\log y} = 1.$$

Then the function to be maximized is

$$F(\beta, \rho) = \rho \ln \beta - \ln \Gamma(\rho) - 3\beta + \rho - 1.$$

The derivatives are

$$\frac{\partial F}{\partial \beta} = \frac{\rho}{\beta} - 3,$$

$$\frac{\partial F}{\partial \rho} = \ln \beta - \frac{\Gamma'}{\Gamma},$$

$$\frac{\partial^2 F}{\partial \beta^2} = \frac{-\rho}{\beta^2},$$

$$\frac{\partial^2 F}{\partial \rho^2} = \frac{-(\Gamma\Gamma'' - \Gamma'^2)}{\Gamma^2},$$

$$\frac{\partial^2 F}{\partial \beta \partial \rho} = \frac{1}{\beta}.$$

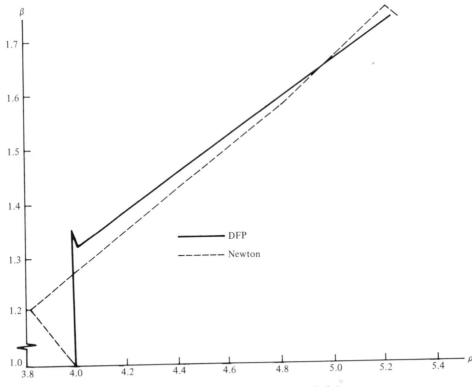

Figure 12.3   Iterations for trial 1.

Finding a good set of starting values is often a difficult problem. Here we choose three starting points somewhat arbitrarily:

	Trial			
				Correct
	1	2	3	Solution
ρ^0	4	8	2	5.230
β^0	1	3	7	1.743

The most commonly used methods are Newton's method and DFP. For the DFP method, we include a line search;[20] for Newton's method, $\lambda = 1$. The results for trials 1 and 2 are shown in Figures 12.3 and 12.4. Note the similarity between the two methods when beginning from a relatively good starting value, in trial 1, and the substantial difference between them when beginning from a somewhat poorer one. The third starting point shows the value of a line search. At this starting value, the Hessian is extremely large. The second value for the parameter vector with Newton's method is

$$\begin{bmatrix} \rho \\ \beta \end{bmatrix} = \begin{bmatrix} 2 \\ 7 \end{bmatrix} - \begin{bmatrix} 191.574 \\ 36.987 \end{bmatrix} = \begin{bmatrix} -189.574 \\ -29.987 \end{bmatrix},$$

---

[20] The one used is described in Joreskog and Gruvaeus (1970).

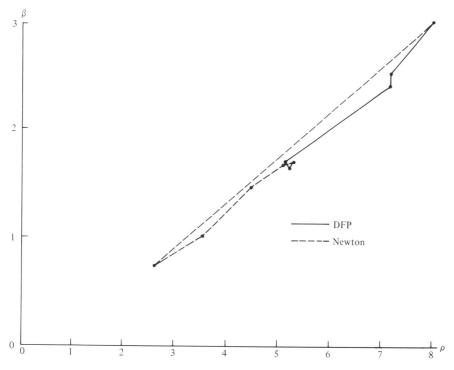

Figure 12.4   Iterations for trial 2.

at which point F cannot be computed and this method must be abandoned. Beginning with $\mathbf{H} = \mathbf{I}$ and using a line search, DFP reaches the point $(6.53, 2.14)$ at the first iteration, after which convergence occurs routinely in three more iterations.

We should note that there is another way we might have solved this problem. The first of the necessary conditions implies that at the solution, β equals $\rho/3$. Inserting this requirement in the second produces the alternative condition

$$\log \frac{\rho}{3} - \frac{\Gamma'(\rho)}{\Gamma(\rho)} = 0$$

or

$$\log \rho - \log 3 - \frac{\Gamma'(\rho)}{\Gamma(\rho)} = 0. \tag{12–31}$$

Therefore, we could just search for the ρ that satisfies $(12–31)$ and then find β equal to $\rho/3$.

Exercises

1. Show how to maximize the function

$$f(\beta) = \frac{1}{\sqrt{2\pi}} e^{-(\beta - c)^2/2}$$

with respect to β for a constant, c, using Newton's method. Show that maximizing $\ln f(\beta)$ leads to the same solution. Plot $f(\beta)$ and $\ln f(\beta)$.

2. Prove that Newton's method for minimizing the sum of squared residuals in the linear regression model will converge to the minimum in one iteration.

3. For the Poisson regression model,

$$\text{Prob}[Y_i = y_i \,|\, \mathbf{x}_i] = \frac{e^{-\lambda_i}\lambda_i^{y_i}}{y_i!},$$

where

$$\lambda_i = e^{\beta'\mathbf{x}_i},$$

the log-likelihood function is

$$\ln L = \sum_i \ln \text{Prob}[Y_i = y_i \,|\, \mathbf{x}_i].$$

(a) Insert the expression for λ_i to obtain the log-likelihood function in terms of the observed data.

(b) Derive the first-order conditions for maximizing this function with respect to β.

(c) Derive the second derivatives matrix of this criterion function with respect to β. Is this matrix negative definite?

(d) Define the computations for using Newton's method to obtain estimates of the unknown parameters.

(e) Write out the full set of steps in an algorithm for obtaining the estimates of the parameters of this model. Include in your algorithm a test for convergence of the estimates based on Belsley's suggested criterion.

(f) How would you obtain starting values for your iterations?

(g) The following data are generated by the Poisson regression model with

$$\ln \lambda = \alpha + \beta x:$$

y	6	7	4	10	10	6	4	7
x	1.5	1.8	1.8	2.0	1.3	1.6	1.2	1.9
y	2	3	6	5	3	3	4	
x	1.8	1.0	1.4	0.5	0.8	1.1	0.7	

Use your results from parts (a)–(f) to compute the maximum likelihood estimates of α and β. Also, obtain estimates of the asymptotic covariance matrix of your estimates.

References

Amemiya, T., "Qualitative Response Models: A Survey," *Journal of Economic Literature*, 19, 4, 1981, pp. 481–536.

Bazaraa, M., and C. Shetty, *Nonlinear Programming–Theory and Algorithms*, New York: Wiley, 1979.

Belsley, D. A., "On the Efficient Computation of the Nonlinear Full-Information Maximum Likelihood Estimator," Technical Report Number 5, Vol. II, Cambridge, Mass.: Center for Computational Research in Economics and Management Science, 1980.

Berndt, E., B. Hall, R. Hall, and J. Hausman, "Estimation and Inference in Nonlinear Structural Models," *Annals of Economic and Social Measurement*, 3/4, 1974, pp. 653–666.

Edlefson, L., and S. Jones, *Gauss*, Kent, Wash.: Aptech Systems, 1985.

Fletcher, R., *Practical Methods of Optimization*, New York: Wiley, 1980.

Goldfeld, S., R. Quandt, and H. Trotter, "Maximization by Quadratic Hill Climbing," *Econometrica,* 1966, 34 pp. 541–551.

Goldfeld, S., and R. Quandt, *Nonlinear Methods in Econometrics,* Amsterdam: North Holland, 1971.

Goldfeld, S., and R. Quandt, "GQOPT: A Package for Numerical Optimization of Functions," Princeton, N. J.: Princeton University Press, 1972.

Greenstadt, J., "On the Relative Efficiencies of Gradient Methods," *Mathematics of Computation,* 1967, pp. 360–367.

Hall, B., *TSP Version 4.0 Reference Manual,* Stanford, Calif.: TSP International, 1982.

Joreskog, K. G., "A General Method for Estimating a Linear Structural Equation System," in A. Goldberger, and O. Duncan, *Structural Equation Models in the Social Sciences,* New York: Academic Press, 1973.

Joreskog, G., and G. Gruvaeus, "A Computer Program for Minimizing a Function of Several Variables," Educational Testing Services, *Research Bulletin No. 70–14,* 1970.

Judge, G., C. Hill, W. Griffiths, T. Lee, and H. Lutkepohl, *The Theory and Practice of Econometrics,* New York: Wiley, 1985.

Powell, M., "An Efficient Method for Finding the Minimum of a Function of Several Variables Without Calculating Derivatives," *Computer Journal,* 1964, 7, pp. 165–172.

Quandt, R. E., "Computational Problems and Methods," in Z. Griliches and M. Intrilligator, eds., *Handbook of Econometrics,* Amsterdam: North Holland, 1983.

Rao, C. R., *Linear Statistical Inference and Its Applications,* New York: Wiley, 1965.

Part III

The Generalized Regression Model

Chapter 13

Nonspherical Disturbances

13.1. Introduction

In this chapter, we extend the multiple regression model to disturbances that violate the classical assumptions. The **generalized regression model** is

$$y = X\beta + \varepsilon,$$

$$E[\varepsilon] = 0, \tag{13-1}$$

$$E[\varepsilon\varepsilon'] = \sigma^2\Omega,$$

where Ω is a positive definite matrix.

Two cases we shall consider in detail are **heteroscedasticity** and **autocorrelation**. Disturbances are heteroscedastic when they have different variances. Heteroscedasticity usually arises in cross-section data where the scale of the dependent variable and the explanatory power of the model tend to vary across observations. Microeconomic data such as expenditure surveys are typical. The disturbances are still assumed to be uncorrelated across observations, so Ω would be

$$\sigma^2\Omega = \begin{bmatrix} \sigma_1^2 & 0 & \cdots & 0 \\ 0 & \sigma_2^2 & \cdots & 0 \\ & & \vdots & \\ 0 & 0 & \cdots & \sigma_n^2 \end{bmatrix}.$$

Autocorrelation is usually found in time-series data. Economic time series often display a "memory" in that variation is not independent from one period to the next. The seasonally adjusted price and quantity series published by government agencies are examples. The adjustment is done in order to smooth out unusual movements in data, and, as such, makes the current observation dependent on what was typical in the past. But a series of unusually high or low values will be carried forward to the adjustment of later data points as well. Time-series data are usually homoscedastic, so $\sigma^2\Omega$ might be

$$\sigma^2\Omega = \sigma^2 \begin{bmatrix} 1 & \rho_1 & \cdots & \rho_{n-1} \\ \rho_1 & 1 & \cdots & \rho_{n-2} \\ & & \vdots & \\ \rho_{n-1} & \rho_{n-2} & & 1 \end{bmatrix}.$$

The values that appear off the diagonal depend on the model used for the disturbance. In most cases, consistent with the notion of a fading memory, the values decline as we move away from the diagonal.

In recent studies, **panel data** sets, consisting of cross sections observed at several points in time, have presented both complications. We shall consider them in Chapter 16. This chapter presents some general results for this extended model. The next three chapters examine in detail specific types of generalized regression models.

Our earlier results for the classical model will have to be modified. We first consider the consequences of this more general formula for the least squares estimator. In subsequent sections, we will be interested in both appropriate estimation techniques and procedures for testing for the failure of the classical assumptions. We shall consider their general theoretical aspects in this chapter and then examine each topic in detail in Chapters 14 through 16.

13.2. *Consequences for Ordinary Least Squares*

The essential results for the classical model with **spherical** disturbances,

$$E[\varepsilon] = 0$$

and

(13–2)

$$E[\varepsilon\varepsilon'] = \sigma^2 I,$$

are presented in Chapters 5 through 10. To reiterate, we found that the ordinary least squares estimator,

$$b = (X'X)^{-1}X'y$$

$$= \beta + (X'X)^{-1}X'\varepsilon,$$

(13–3)

is best linear unbiased, consistent and asymptotically normally distributed (CAN), and, if the disturbances are normally distributed, asymptotically efficient among all CAN estimators. We now consider which of these properties continue to hold in the model of (13–1).

13.2.1. Finite-Sample Properties

By taking expectations on both sides of (13–3), we find that if $E[\varepsilon \,|\, X] = 0$,

$$E[b] = E_X[E[b \,|\, X]] = \beta.$$

(13–4)

If the regressors and disturbances are uncorrelated, the unbiasedness of least squares is unaffected by violations of assumption (13–2).

The sampling variance of the least squares estimator is

$$\text{Var}[b - \beta] = E[(b - \beta)(b - \beta)']$$

$$= E[(X'X)^{-1}X'\varepsilon\varepsilon'X(X'X)^{-1}]$$

$$= (X'X)^{-1}X'(\sigma^2\Omega)X(X'X)^{-1}$$

(13–5)

$$= \frac{\sigma^2}{n}\left(\frac{X'X}{n}\right)^{-1}\left(\frac{X'\Omega X}{n}\right)\left(\frac{X'X}{n}\right)^{-1}.$$

In (13–3), **b** is a linear function of ε. Therefore, if ε is normally distributed,

$$\mathbf{b} \sim N[\beta, \sigma^2(\mathbf{X'X})^{-1}(\mathbf{X'\Omega X})(\mathbf{X'X})^{-1}].$$

Since the variance of the least squares estimator is not $\sigma^2(\mathbf{X'X})^{-1}$, any inference based on $s^2(\mathbf{X'X})^{-1}$ is likely to be misleading. Not only is this the wrong matrix to be using, but s^2 may be a biased estimator of σ^2. There is usually no way to know whether $\sigma^2(\mathbf{X'X})^{-1}$ is larger or smaller than the true variance of **b**, so even with a good estimate of σ^2, the conventional estimator of Var[**b**] may not be particularly useful. Finally, since we have dispensed with the fundamental underlying assumption, the familiar inference procedures based on the F and t distributions will no longer be appropriate.

13.2.2.   Asymptotic Properties of Least Squares

If Var[**b**] converges to zero, **b** is consistent. With well-behaved regressors, $(\mathbf{X'X}/n)^{-1}$ will converge to a constant matrix (perhaps **0**), and the leading scalar, σ^2/n, will converge to 0. But $\mathbf{X'\Omega X}/n$ need not converge at all. If it does, ordinary least squares is consistent as well as unbiased. Therefore,

> If plim $(\mathbf{X'X}/n)$ and plim $(\mathbf{X'\Omega X}/n)$ are both
> finite positive definite matrices, **b** is   (13–6)
> consistent for β.

The conditions in (13–6) depend on both **X** and Ω. An alternative formula[1] that separates the two components is: Ordinary least squares is consistent in the generalized regression model if

1. The smallest characteristic root of $\mathbf{X'X}$ explodes as $n \to \infty$. This implies that $\text{plim}(\mathbf{X'X})^{-1} = 0$. If the regressors satisfy the Grenander conditions of Section 10.3.1, they will meet this requirement.

2. The largest characteristic root of Ω is finite for all n. For the heteroscedastic model, the variances are the characteristic roots, so this requires them to be finite. For models with autocorrelation, this requires that the elements of Ω be finite and that the off-diagonal elements not be too large relative to the diagonal elements.

EXAMPLE 13.1.   **A Model in Which Ordinary Least Squares Is Inconsistent.**   Suppose that the regression model is $y = \mu + \varepsilon$, where ε has a zero mean, constant variance, and equal-correlation ρ across observations. Then

$$\Omega = \begin{bmatrix} 1 & \rho & \rho & \cdots & \rho \\ \rho & 1 & \rho & \cdots & \rho \\ \rho & \rho & 1 & \cdots & \rho \\ & & \vdots & & \\ \rho & \rho & \rho & \cdots & 1 \end{bmatrix}.$$

The matrix **X** is a column of ones. The least squares estimator of μ is $\bar{y}$. Inserting this Ω into (13–5), we obtain

$$\text{Var}[\bar{y}] = \frac{\sigma^2}{n}(1 - \rho + n\rho). \tag{13–7}$$

---

[1] Amemiya (1985, p. 184).

The limit of this expression is $\rho\sigma^2$, not zero. Although ordinary least squares is unbiased, it is not consistent. For this model, $\mathbf{X'\Omega X}/n = 1 + \rho(n-1)$, which does not converge. Using (13–7) instead, $\mathbf{X}$ is a column of ones, so $\mathbf{X'X} = n$, a scalar, which satisfies condition (1). But the characteristic roots of $\mathbf{\Omega}$ are $(1-\rho)$ with multiplicity $n-1$ and $(1-\rho+n\rho)$, which does not satisfy condition (2). The difficulty with the model in this example is essentially that there is too much correlation across observations. In time-series settings, we shall generally require that the timewise correlation of observations fade as the distance between them grows. That condition is not met here. This gives some suggestion of what sort of require-ment we shall have to place upon the covariance matrix for autocorrelated disturbances discussed in the Introduction.

As an example of the preceding, consider a sample of profit rates of n industries, each observed in each of T periods. Suppose that in each period, although there are individual factors that are specific to each industry, the same macroeconomic "shock" hits them all. This is consistent with a model of the form

$$p_{it} = \pi + \varepsilon_{it} + \eta_t.$$

Now consider attempting to estimate the average rate of profit for the set of industries, using only the data from a single year. If ε_{it} and η_t are random disturbances, this is exactly the preceding model. The mean of the n observations in any year converges to $\pi + \eta_t$ as $n \to \infty$.

The OLS estimator is asymptotically normally distributed if the limiting distribution of

$$\sqrt{n}\,(\mathbf{b} - \boldsymbol{\beta}) = \left(\frac{\mathbf{X'X}}{n}\right)^{-1} \frac{1}{\sqrt{n}}\mathbf{X'}\boldsymbol{\varepsilon} \qquad (13\text{–}8)$$

is normal. If $\mathrm{plim}(\mathbf{X'X}/n) = \mathbf{Q}$, the limiting distribution of the right-hand side is the same as that of

$$\mathbf{v} = \mathbf{Q}^{-1}\frac{1}{\sqrt{n}}\mathbf{X'}\boldsymbol{\varepsilon}$$

$$\qquad (13\text{–}9)$$

$$= \mathbf{Q}^{-1}\frac{1}{\sqrt{n}}\sum_i \mathbf{x}_i \varepsilon_i,$$

where $\mathbf{x}'_i$ is a row of $\mathbf{X}$ (assuming, of course, that the limiting distribution exists at all). The question now is whether a central limit theorem can be applied directly to $\mathbf{v}$. If the dis-turbances are merely heteroscedastic and still uncorrelated, the answer is generally yes. In this case, it can easily be shown that as long as $\mathbf{X}$ is well behaved and the diagonal elements of $\mathbf{\Omega}$ are finite, the least squares estimator is asymptotically normally distributed, with the variance matrix given in (13–5).[2] For the most general case, the answer is no because the sums in (13–9) are not necessarily sums of independent or even uncorrelated random variables. Nonetheless, Amemiya (1985, p. 187) and Anderson (1971) have shown the asymptotic normality of $\mathbf{b}$ in a model of autocorrelated disturbances general enough to include most of the settings we are likely to meet in practice. We can conclude that, except in particularly unfavorable cases,

$$\begin{array}{cc} \mathbf{b} \text{ is asymptotically normally distributed, with} & (13\text{–}10) \\ \text{mean } \boldsymbol{\beta} \text{ and covariance matrix given in } (13\text{–}5). \end{array}$$

[2] The Lindeberg–Feller variant of the central limit theorem can be applied. See, for example, Schmidt (1976, pp. 57–65) or Greenberg and Webster (1983, pp. 17–22).

To summarize, ordinary least squares retains only some of its desirable properties in this model. It is unbiased, consistent, and asymptotically normally distributed. However, it will no longer be efficient—this remains to be verified—and the usual inference procedures are no longer appropriate.

13.3. *Efficient Estimation*

Efficient estimation of β in the general regression model requires knowledge of Ω. To begin, it is useful to consider cases in which Ω is a known, symmetric, positive definite matrix. This will occasionally be true, but in most models Ω will contain unknown parameters that must also be estimated. We shall examine this problem in Section 13.4.

13.3.1. Generalized Least Squares

Since Ω is a positive definite symmetric matrix, it can be factored into

$$\Omega = C\Lambda C', \tag{13-11}$$

where the columns of C are the characteristic vectors of Ω and the characteristic roots of Ω are arrayed in the diagonal matrix, Λ. Let $\Lambda^{1/2}$ be the diagonal matrix with ith diagonal element $\sqrt{\lambda_i}$, and let $T = C\Lambda^{1/2}$. Then $\Omega = TT'$. Also, let $P = C\Lambda^{-1/2}$, so

$$\Omega^{-1} = PP'.$$

It is useful to denote

$$P = \Omega^{-1/2}.$$

Premultiply the model in (13–1) by P to obtain

$$Py = PX\beta + P\varepsilon,$$

or

$$\tag{13-12}$$

$$y_* = X_*\beta + \varepsilon_*.$$

The variance of ε_* is

$$E(\varepsilon_*\varepsilon_*') = P\sigma^2\Omega P' = \sigma^2 I,$$

so that the classical regression model of Chapter 6 applies to this transformed model. Since Ω is known, y_* and X_* are observed data. In the classical model, ordinary least squares is efficient; hence

$$\hat{\beta} = (X_*'X_*)^{-1}X_*'y_* = (X'P'PX)^{-1}X'P'Py = (X'\Omega^{-1}X)^{-1}X'\Omega^{-1}y$$

is the efficient estimator of β. This is the **generalized least squares (GLS)** estimator of β. By appealing to the classical regression model in (13–12), we have the following, which are the generalized regression model analogs to our results of Chapter 6:

> *The GLS estimator $\hat{\beta}$ is unbiased if $E[\varepsilon_*|X_*] = 0$.*
> This is equivalent to $E[P\varepsilon|PX] = 0$, but since P
> is a matrix of known constants, we return to the
> familiar requirement $E[\varepsilon|X] = 0$. The requirement $\tag{13-13}$
> that the regressors and disturbances be uncorrelated
> is unchanged.

The GLS estimator is consistent if

$$\text{plim}\left(\frac{\mathbf{X}'_*\mathbf{X}_*}{n}\right) = \mathbf{Q}_*,$$

where $\mathbf{Q}_*$ is a finite positive definite matrix. Making the substitution, we see that this is

$$\text{plim}\left(\frac{\mathbf{X}'\mathbf{\Omega}^{-1}\mathbf{X}}{n}\right)^{-1} = \mathbf{Q}_*^{-1}. \tag{13-14}$$

We require the transformed data, $\mathbf{X}_* = \mathbf{PX}$, not the original data, $\mathbf{X}$, to be well behaved.[3]

Under the assumption in (13–14), *the GLS estimator is asymptotically normally distributed*, with mean β and sampling variance

$$\text{Var}[\hat{\beta}] = \sigma^2(\mathbf{X}'_*\mathbf{X}_*)^{-1} = \sigma^2(\mathbf{X}'\mathbf{\Omega}^{-1}\mathbf{X})^{-1}. \tag{13-15}$$

> *The GLS estimator $\hat{\beta}$ is the minimum variance linear*   (13–16)
> *unbiased estimator in the generalized regression model.*

This follows by applying the Gauss–Markov theorem to the model in (13–12). The result in (13–16) is Aitken's (1935) theorem, and $\hat{\beta}$ is sometimes called the *Aitken estimator*. This is a broad result that includes the Gauss–Markov theorem as a special case when $\mathbf{\Omega} = \mathbf{I}$.

For testing hypotheses, we can apply the full set of results in Chapter 7 to the transformed model in (13–12). For testing the J linear restrictions, $\mathbf{R}\beta = \mathbf{q}$, the appropriate statistic is

$$F[J, n - K] = \frac{(\mathbf{R}\hat{\beta} - \mathbf{q})'[\mathbf{R}(\hat{\sigma}^2(\mathbf{X}'_*\mathbf{X}_*)^{-1})\mathbf{R}']^{-1}(\mathbf{R}\hat{\beta} - \mathbf{q})}{J}$$

$$= \frac{(\hat{\varepsilon}'_c\hat{\varepsilon}_c - \hat{\varepsilon}'\hat{\varepsilon})/J}{\hat{\sigma}^2}, \tag{13-17}$$

where the residual vector is

$$\hat{\varepsilon} = \mathbf{y}_* - \mathbf{X}_*\hat{\beta}$$

and

$$\hat{\sigma}^2 = \frac{\hat{\varepsilon}'\hat{\varepsilon}}{(n - K)} = \frac{(\mathbf{y} - \mathbf{X}\hat{\beta})'\mathbf{\Omega}^{-1}(\mathbf{y} - \mathbf{X}\hat{\beta})}{(n - K)}.$$

The constrained GLS residuals, $\hat{\varepsilon}_c = \mathbf{y}_* - \mathbf{X}_*\hat{\beta}_c$, are based on

$$\hat{\beta}_c = \hat{\beta} - [\mathbf{X}'\mathbf{\Omega}^{-1}\mathbf{X}]^{-1}\mathbf{R}'[\mathbf{R}(\mathbf{X}'\mathbf{\Omega}^{-1}\mathbf{X})^{-1}\mathbf{R}']^{-1}(\mathbf{R}\hat{\beta} - \mathbf{q}).[4] \tag{13-18}$$

To summarize, all of the results for the classical model, including the usual inference procedures, apply to the model in (13–12).

There is no precise counterpart to R^2 in the generalized regression model. Alternatives have been proposed, but care must be taken when using them. For example, one choice is the R^2 in the transformed regression, (13–12). But this regression need not have a constant term, so the R^2 is not bounded by zero and one. Even if there is a constant term, the transformed regression is a computational device, not the model of interest. The fact that a good (or bad)

---

[3] Once again, in order to allow a time trend, we could weaken this assumption a bit.
[4] Note that this is the constrained OLS estimator using the transformed data.

fit is obtained in the model in (13–12) may be of no interest; the dependent variable in that model, y_*, is different from the one in the model as originally specified. The usual R^2 often suggests that the fit of the model is improved by a correction for heteroscedasticity and diminished by a correction for autocorrelation, but both changes can often be attributed to the computation of y_*. A more appealing fit measure might be based on the residuals from the original model once the GLS estimator is in hand, for example,

$$\tilde{R}^2 = 1 - \frac{(\mathbf{y} - \mathbf{X}\hat{\boldsymbol{\beta}})'(\mathbf{y} - \mathbf{X}\hat{\boldsymbol{\beta}})}{\sum(y - \bar{y})^2}.$$

However, like the earlier contender, this measure is not bounded in the unit interval. In addition, this measure cannot be reliably used to compare models. The generalized least squares estimator minimizes the generalized sum of squares,

$$\boldsymbol{\varepsilon}'_*\boldsymbol{\varepsilon}_* = (\mathbf{y} - \mathbf{X}\boldsymbol{\beta})'\boldsymbol{\Omega}^{-1}(\mathbf{y} - \mathbf{X}\boldsymbol{\beta}),$$

not $\varepsilon'\varepsilon$. As such, there is no assurance, for example, that dropping a variable from the model will result in a decrease in $\tilde{R}^2$, as it will in R^2. Other goodness of fit measures, designed primarily to be a function of the sum of squared residuals (raw or weighted by $\boldsymbol{\Omega}^{-1}$) and to be bounded by zero and one, have been proposed.[5] Unfortunately, all of them suffer from at least one of the previously noted shortcomings. The R^2-like measures in this setting are purely descriptive.

13.3.2. Maximum Likelihood Estimation

If the disturbances are multivariate normally distributed, the log-likelihood function for the sample is

$$\ln L = -\frac{n}{2}\ln(2\pi) - \frac{1}{2}\ln|\sigma^2\boldsymbol{\Omega}| - \frac{1}{2}\boldsymbol{\varepsilon}'(\sigma^2\boldsymbol{\Omega})^{-1}\boldsymbol{\varepsilon}.$$

Making the change of variable to $\mathbf{y} - \mathbf{X}\boldsymbol{\beta} = \varepsilon$, we obtain

$$L = -\frac{n}{2}\ln(2\pi) - \frac{n}{2}\ln\sigma^2 - \frac{1}{2\sigma^2}(\mathbf{y} - \mathbf{X}\boldsymbol{\beta})'\boldsymbol{\Omega}^{-1}(\mathbf{y} - \mathbf{X}\boldsymbol{\beta}) - \frac{1}{2}\ln|\boldsymbol{\Omega}|. \quad (13\text{--}19)$$

Since $\boldsymbol{\Omega}$ is a matrix of known constants, the maximum likelihood estimator of $\boldsymbol{\beta}$ is the vector that minimizes the *generalized sum of squares*,

$$S_*(\boldsymbol{\beta}) = (\mathbf{y} - \mathbf{X}\boldsymbol{\beta})'\boldsymbol{\Omega}^{-1}(\mathbf{y} - \mathbf{X}\boldsymbol{\beta}) \quad (13\text{--}20)$$

(hence the name *generalized least squares*). The necessary conditions for maximizing L are

$$\frac{\partial \ln L}{\partial \boldsymbol{\beta}} = \frac{1}{\sigma^2}\mathbf{X}'\boldsymbol{\Omega}^{-1}(\mathbf{y} - \mathbf{X}\boldsymbol{\beta}) = \frac{1}{\sigma^2}\mathbf{X}'_*(\mathbf{y}_* - \mathbf{X}_*\boldsymbol{\beta}) \quad (13\text{--}21)$$

and

$$\frac{\partial \ln L}{\partial \sigma^2} = -\frac{n}{2\sigma^2} + \frac{1}{2\sigma^4}(\mathbf{y} - \mathbf{X}\boldsymbol{\beta})'\boldsymbol{\Omega}^{-1}(\mathbf{y} - \mathbf{X}\boldsymbol{\beta})$$

$$= -\frac{n}{2\sigma^2} + \frac{1}{2\sigma^4}(\mathbf{y}_* - \mathbf{X}_*\boldsymbol{\beta})'(\mathbf{y}_* - \mathbf{X}_*\boldsymbol{\beta}). \quad (13\text{--}22)$$

---

[5] See, for example, Judge et al. (1985, p. 32) and Buse (1973).

The solutions are the OLS estimators using the transformed data:

$$\hat{\beta}_{ML} = (X'_* X_*)^{-1} X'_* y_* = (X'\Omega^{-1}X)^{-1} X'\Omega^{-1}y \qquad (13\text{–}23)$$

$$\hat{\sigma}^2_{ML} = \frac{(y_* - X_* \hat{\beta})'(y_* - X_* \hat{\beta})}{n} \qquad (13\text{–}24)$$

$$= \frac{(y - X\hat{\beta})'\Omega^{-1}(y - X\hat{\beta})}{n}.$$

This implies that with normally distributed disturbances, generalized least squares is also maximum likelihood. As in the classical regression model, the maximum likelihood estimator of σ^2 is biased. An unbiased estimator is

$$s^2 = \frac{(y - X\hat{\beta})'\Omega^{-1}(y - X\hat{\beta})}{n - K}. \qquad (13\text{–}25)$$

In order to obtain the asymptotic distribution for the maximum likelihood estimators, we can apply the results of Section 10.3.2 to the transformed model. The asymptotic distribution of $[\hat{\beta}_{ML}, \hat{\sigma}^2_{ML}]$ is, therefore,

$$\begin{bmatrix} \hat{\beta}_{ML} \\ \hat{\sigma}^2_{ML} \end{bmatrix} \xrightarrow{A} N \begin{bmatrix} \begin{bmatrix} \beta \\ \sigma^2 \end{bmatrix}, & \begin{bmatrix} \sigma^2(X'\Omega^{-1}X)^{-1} & 0 \\ 0' & 2\sigma^4/n \end{bmatrix} \end{bmatrix}. \qquad (13\text{–}26)$$

An alternative to (13–17) for testing a hypothesis about β is the likelihood ratio statistic. If we insert (13–23) and (13–24) in (13–19), we find, at the maximum likelihood estimators,

$$\ln \hat{L} = -\frac{n}{2}(1 + \ln(2\pi) + \ln \hat{\sigma}^2) - \frac{1}{2}\ln|\Omega|.$$

Therefore, the likelihood ratio test is based on

$$\lambda = -2(\ln \hat{L}_c - \ln \hat{L}) = n(\ln \hat{\sigma}^2_c - \ln \hat{\sigma}^2)$$

$$= n \ln\left(\frac{\hat{\sigma}^2_c}{\hat{\sigma}^2}\right).$$

The statistic is asymptotically distributed as chi-squared with J degrees of freedom, where J is the number of restrictions.

13.4. Estimation When Ω Is Unknown

In order to use the results of the previous section, Ω must be known. If Ω contains unknown parameters that must be estimated, generalized least squares is not feasible. But with an unrestricted Ω, there are $n(n + 1)/2$ additional parameters in $\sigma^2\Omega$. This is far too many to estimate with n observations. Obviously, some structure must be imposed on the model if we are to proceed.

13.4.1. Feasible Generalized Least Squares

The typical problem involves a small set of parameters, θ, such that $\Omega = \Omega(\theta)$. For example, the Ω in Example 13.1 has only one unknown parameter, ρ. Another commonly used formula is

$$
\Omega = \begin{bmatrix}
1 & \rho & \rho^2 & \rho^3 & \cdots & \rho^{n-1} \\
\rho & 1 & \rho & \rho^2 & \cdots & \rho^{n-2} \\
& & & \vdots & & \\
\rho^{n-1} & \rho^{n-2} & & & \cdots & 1
\end{bmatrix},
$$

which also involves only one additional unknown parameter. A commonly used model of heteroscedasticity that also has only one new parameter is

$$
\sigma_i^2 = \sigma^2 z_i^\alpha.
$$

Suppose, then, that $\hat{\theta}$ is a consistent estimator of θ. (We consider later how such an estimator might be obtained.) In order to make GLS estimation feasible, we shall use

$$
\hat{\Omega} = \Omega(\hat{\theta})
$$

instead of the true Ω. The issue we consider here is whether using $\Omega(\hat{\theta})$ requires us to change any of the results of the previous section.

It would seem that if plim $\hat{\theta} = \theta$, using $\hat{\Omega}$ is asymptotically equivalent to using the true Ω.[6] However, this need not be the case.[7] Let the **feasible generalized least squares** or **(FGLS)** estimator be denoted

$$
\hat{\hat{\beta}} = (X'\hat{\Omega}^{-1}X)^{-1}X'\hat{\Omega}^{-1}y.
$$

Conditions that imply that $\hat{\hat{\beta}}$ is asymptotically equivalent to $\hat{\beta}$ are

$$
\operatorname{plim} \frac{X'\hat{\Omega}^{-1}X}{n} = \operatorname{plim} \frac{X'\Omega^{-1}X}{n} \tag{13-27}
$$

and

$$
\operatorname{plim} \frac{1}{\sqrt{n}} X'\hat{\Omega}^{-1}\varepsilon = \operatorname{plim} \frac{1}{\sqrt{n}} X'\Omega^{-1}\varepsilon. \tag{13-28}
$$

If the transformed regressors in (13–12) are well behaved, the right-hand side of (13–28) has a limiting normal distribution. This is exactly the condition we used in Chapter 10 to obtain the asymptotic distribution of the least squares estimator. Therefore, (13–28) requires the same condition to hold when Ω is replaced with $\hat{\Omega}$.

These are conditions that must be verified on a case-by-case basis. Fortunately, in most familiar settings, they are met. If we assume that they are, the FGLS estimator based on $\hat{\theta}$ has the same asymptotic properties as the GLS estimator. This is an extremely useful result. Note, especially, the following:

> An asymptotically efficient FGLS estimation
> does not require that we have an efficient estimator
> of θ, only a consistent one.

---

[6] This is sometimes denoted plim $\hat{\Omega} = \Omega$. Since Ω is $n \times n$, it cannot have a probability limit. We use this term to indicate convergence element by element.

[7] Schmidt (1976, p. 69) constructs a counterexample.

Except for the simplest cases, the finite sample properties and exact distributions of FGLS estimators are unknown.[8] The asymptotic efficiency of FGLS estimators may not carry over to small samples because of the variability introduced by the estimated Ω. Some analyses for the case of heteroscedasticity are given by Taylor (1977). A model of autocorrelation is analyzed by Griliches and Rao (1969). In both studies, the authors find that over a broad range of parameters, FGLS is more efficient than least squares. But if the departure from the classical assumptions is not too severe, least squares may be more efficient than FGLS in a small sample.

13.4.2. Maximum Likelihood Estimation

For the moment, it is useful to treat Ω as an unrestricted matrix of unknown parameters. We shall impose the restrictions $\Omega = \Omega(\theta)$ later. It will simplify the computations if we estimate $\Gamma = \Omega^{-1}$ instead of Ω. Given the MLE of Γ, the MLE of Ω is $\hat{\Gamma}_{ML}^{-1}$.[9] We shall also use the results

$$\log|\Gamma| = -\log|\Omega|,^{10}$$

$$\frac{\partial \log|\Gamma|}{\partial \Gamma} = \Gamma^{-1},$$

and

$$\frac{\partial \varepsilon' \Gamma \varepsilon}{\partial \Gamma} = \varepsilon \varepsilon'.^{11}$$

Substituting Γ for Ω^{-1} in L, we obtain

$$\ln L = -\frac{n}{2}(\ln 2\pi + \ln \sigma^2) - \frac{1}{2\sigma^2}\varepsilon' \Gamma \varepsilon + \frac{1}{2}\ln|\Gamma|$$

$$\frac{\partial \ln L}{\partial \beta} = \frac{1}{\sigma^2}X'\Gamma(y - X\beta) \tag{13-29}$$

$$\frac{\partial \ln L}{\partial \sigma^2} = -\frac{n}{2\sigma^2} + \frac{1}{2\sigma^4}(y - X\beta)'\Gamma(y - X\beta) \tag{13-30}$$

$$\frac{\partial \ln L}{\partial \Gamma} = \frac{1}{2}\left[\Gamma^{-1} - \left(\frac{1}{\sigma^2}\right)\varepsilon\varepsilon'\right]$$

$$\tag{13-31}$$

$$= \frac{1}{2\sigma^2}[\sigma^2\Omega - \varepsilon\varepsilon'].$$

---

[8] The difficult part of most derivations is determining the exact distribution of functions of $\hat{\Omega}^{-1}$. There is one general, exact result that applies in several settings. If $\hat{\theta}$ is an *even function* of the true disturbances, the FGLS estimator is unbiased. The estimator, $\hat{\theta}$, is an even function of ε if the same numerical value would be obtained using $-\varepsilon$ instead. Consider, for example, the OLS estimator, $e'e/(n - K) = \varepsilon'M\varepsilon/(n - K) = (-\varepsilon)'M(-\varepsilon)/(n - K)$. The result was first reported by Kakwani (1967) for a multiple equation model. But it is straightforward to broaden the result to encompass the fuller generalized regression model we consider here. See, for example, Schmidt (1976, p. 72). Different conditions for the unbiasedness of the FGLS estimator are presented by Don and Magnus (1980) and Magnus (1978).

[9] The invariance principle is discussed in Section 4.5.1.

[10] The characteristic roots of Γ are the reciprocals of those of Ω. The determinants are the products of the characteristic roots, so the result follows immediately.

[11] See Section 2.9.1 for derivations of these results.

At the maximum of the likelihood function, the following are apparent:

1. We would use FGLS to obtain the MLE of β, using the maximum likelihood estimate of Ω.

2. Given the MLEs of β and Ω, the MLE of σ^2 would be $(1/n)(y - X\hat{\beta}_{ML})'\Omega_{ML}^{-1} \times (y - X\hat{\beta}_{ML})$.

The problem of too many parameters can be seen in the likelihood equation for Γ. At the solution, we would require the rank one matrix $\hat{\varepsilon}\hat{\varepsilon}'$ to equal the positive definite matrix $\hat{\sigma}^2\hat{\Omega}$, which is a contradiction. It might seem that we could simply use ee' to estimate $\sigma^2\Omega$, as prescribed by (13–31), but this matrix is singular and could not be used in (13–29) or (13–30).

Since Ω must be restricted in some way to make the estimation problem tractable, let us assume, once again, that $\Omega = \Omega(\theta)$, where θ is a vector of a small number of parameters and θ is not a function of any elements of β. With this assumption, there are two methods of obtaining estimates of the full set of parameters.

If it is straightforward to obtain estimates of θ that satisfy (13–31) for a given set of estimates of β and σ^2, the iterative two-step method proposed by Oberhofer and Kmenta (1974) will usually be the easiest way to proceed. (An example will be given.) Since the MLEs of β and σ^2 are the GLS estimates using the MLE of Ω, given an estimate $\hat{\theta}$, we use steps 1 and 2 to estimate β and σ^2. With the new estimates of β and σ^2, we then reestimate θ. Thereafter we repeat the iteration until satisfactory convergence has been achieved. If we assume that the initial $\hat{\theta}$ is a consistent estimator of θ, this estimator will be asymptotically efficient at every step. However, under certain conditions, the values to which β, σ^2, and Ω converge will also be the maximum likelihood estimates.[12] These include

1. The information matrix must be block diagonal, that is, Ω must not be a function of β.

2. The initial estimate of θ must be consistent.

3. At each step, the updated estimate of θ must be obtained by solving the first-order conditions for maximum likelihood estimates, given the present estimate of β.

The third condition is important to remember. There are cases, including one that we shall examine in detail in Section 15.6, in which there is more than one consistent estimate of θ given the current estimate of β.

If the method of Oberhofer and Kmenta is not usable, it may be necessary to maximize the log likelihood directly, for example, using one of the gradient methods described in Chapter 12. At the solution, regardless of how it is obtained, the MLEs of β and σ^2 will be the FGLS estimators. The difficult part of the problem is estimating θ. A complete analysis, including several applications, is presented by Magnus (1978). We shall examine some specific cases in the chapters to follow.

The information matrix for the maximum likelihood estimators of β, σ^2, and θ will be block diagonal of the form

$$-E\left[\frac{\partial^2 \ln L}{\partial\gamma\partial\gamma'}\right] = \begin{array}{c} \beta \\ \sigma^2 \\ \theta \end{array}\begin{array}{c}\overset{\beta'}{}\quad\overset{\sigma^2}{}\quad\overset{\theta'}{} \\ \left[\begin{array}{c|cc} (1/\sigma^2)X'\Omega^{-1}X & 0' & 0' \\ \hline 0 & n/(2\sigma^4) & \delta' \\ 0 & \delta & C \end{array}\right] \end{array}, \qquad (13\text{–}32)$$

[12] Note that the divisor in the estimator of σ^2 must be n, not $n - K$.

where γ is the full set of parameters. The inverse matrix will be block diagonal as well. Therefore, the asymptotic variance matrix of the maximum likelihood estimator is

$$\text{Asy. Var}[\hat{\boldsymbol{\beta}}_{\text{ML}}] = \sigma^2 (\mathbf{X}' \boldsymbol{\Omega}^{-1} \mathbf{X})^{-1}.$$

This is the same as that of the FGLS estimator. We conclude, therefore, that as long as the information is block diagonal, the GLS, FGLS, and ML estimators of $\boldsymbol{\beta}$ have the same asymptotic distributions. It follows that

> Exact knowledge of $\boldsymbol{\Omega}$ brings no gain in
> asymptotic efficiency in the estimation of $\boldsymbol{\beta}$.

This is not true if the information matrix is not block diagonal, nor is it true for estimation of σ^2:

$$\text{Asy. Var}[\hat{\sigma}^2_{\text{ML}}] = \left[\frac{n}{2\sigma^4} - \boldsymbol{\delta}' \mathbf{C}^{-1} \boldsymbol{\delta} \right]^{-1}$$

$$= \frac{2\sigma^4}{n} + \sum_{i=1}^{\infty} \left[\frac{2\sigma^4 \boldsymbol{\delta}' \mathbf{C}^{-1} \boldsymbol{\delta}}{n} \right]^i.$$

This is larger than $2\sigma^4/n$ unless $\boldsymbol{\delta} = \mathbf{0}$.

It is important to note that in this and many cases we shall examine later, having the same properties as the maximum likelihood estimator does not imply that the FGLS estimator *is* the maximum likelihood estimator. This means that likelihood ratio tests and Lagrange multiplier tests cannot be based on the FGLS estimator. By exploiting the asymptotic normality of the estimator, we can use the usual F statistic or an asymptotically equivalent chi-squared statistic to test a hypothesis about $\boldsymbol{\beta}$.

EXAMPLE 13.2. Groupwise Heteroscedasticity. A groupwise heteroscedastic regression is based on

$$y_i = \boldsymbol{\beta}' \mathbf{x}_i + \varepsilon_i, \qquad i = 1, \ldots, n$$

$$E[\varepsilon_i] = 0, \qquad i = 1, \ldots, n.$$

The n observations are grouped into G groups, each with n_g observations. The slope vector is the same in all groups, but within group g

$$\text{Var}[\varepsilon_{ig}] = \sigma^2_g, \qquad i = 1, \ldots, n_g.$$

The log-likelihood function is

$$\ln L = -\frac{n}{2} \ln(2\pi) - \frac{1}{2} \sum_g n_g \ln \sigma^2_g - \frac{1}{2} \sum_g \sum_{i=1}^{n_g} \frac{\varepsilon^2_{ig}}{\sigma^2_g}.$$

The MLE for $\boldsymbol{\beta}$ is generalized least squares, using the MLEs for σ^2_g. The **weighting matrix** is

$$\boldsymbol{\Omega} = \begin{bmatrix} \sigma^2_1 \mathbf{I} & 0 & \cdots & 0 \\ 0 & \sigma^2_2 \mathbf{I} & \cdots & 0 \\ & & \vdots & \\ 0 & 0 & \cdots & \sigma^2_G \mathbf{I} \end{bmatrix},$$

so the GLS estimator is

$$\hat{\boldsymbol{\beta}} = \left[\sum_g \frac{1}{\hat{\sigma}^2_g} \mathbf{X}'_g \mathbf{X}_g \right]^{-1} \left[\sum_g \frac{1}{\hat{\sigma}^2_g} \mathbf{X}'_g \mathbf{y}_g \right].$$

For each variance parameter, σ_g^2, the likelihood equation is

$$\frac{\partial \ln L}{\partial \sigma_g^2} = 0 = -\frac{n_g}{2\sigma_g^2} + \frac{1}{2\sigma_g^4}\sum_i \varepsilon_{ig}^2,$$

so that given the current value of $\hat{\beta}$,

$$\hat{\sigma}_g^2 = \frac{e_g' e_g}{n_g}.$$

To obtain this maximum likelihood estimator, a simple iterative procedure that satisfies the Oberhofer–Kmenta requirements is as follows:

1. Pool the data and estimate β by OLS.
2. Estimate the disturbance variances separately with $e_g' e_g / n_g$, where $e_g = y_g - X_g b$.
3. Compute $\hat{\beta}$.
4. If $\hat{\beta}$ has not converged, go to step 2; otherwise, exit.

The likelihood ratio test of Section 13.3.2 can be used to test a hypothesis about β or Ω. Once again, we insert the MLE for σ^2 in (13–24) in the likelihood function. At the maximum, we have

$$\ln \hat{L} = -\frac{n}{2}(1 + \ln(2\pi) + \ln \hat{\sigma}^2) - \frac{1}{2}\log|\hat{\Omega}|$$

$$= -\frac{n}{2}(1 + \ln(2\pi)) - \frac{1}{2}\ln|\hat{\sigma}^2\hat{\Omega}|.$$

Therefore, for testing constraints on β and/or Ω, the likelihood ratio statistic is

$$\lambda = \log|(\hat{\sigma}^2\hat{\Omega})_c| - \log|\hat{\sigma}^2\hat{\Omega}|.$$

The degrees of freedom for the chi-squared test is the number of parametric restrictions imposed. For the groupwise heteroscedastic model of Example 13.2, a likelihood ratio test of the hypothesis of homoscedasticity would be based on

$$\lambda = n \ln s^2 - \sum_g n_g \ln s_g^2,$$

where $n = \sum_g n_g$, s^2 is the pooled, least squares residual variance, $e'e/n$ (not $n - K$), and s_g^2 is defined in Example 13.2.

In general, maximum likelihood estimation of an unknown Ω greatly complicates the estimation problem. The likelihood equations for the unknown parameters in Ω are usually extremely involved and difficult to solve. In most cases, the asymptotically equivalent procedure of finding a consistent estimator for Ω and using FGLS is used instead. (Where it is convenient, analysts often use the Oberhofer–Kmenta procedure.) If θ contains any of the parameters in β, neither FGLS nor GLS is efficient. Full maximum likelihood estimation is likely to be extremely difficult in this case, but the maximum likelihood estimator that makes use of the information that β enters Ω as well as the regression will necessarily be more efficient.

Exercises

1. What is the covariance matrix of the GLS estimator and the difference between it and the OLS estimator?

$$\text{Cov}[\hat{\beta}, \hat{\beta} - b],$$

where

$$\hat{\beta} = (X'\Omega^{-1}X)^{-1}X'\Omega^{-1}y,$$

and

$$b = (X'X)^{-1}X'y.$$

The result plays a pivotal role in the development of specification tests in Hausman (1978).

2. For the Poisson model of Problem 4, Chapter 10, show that the maximum likelihood estimator is the GLS estimator. Show that the variances you derived in parts (a) and (b) are those in (13–5) and (13–15). (Note that this is an unusual case in that the GLS estimator is fully efficient even though the disturbance variances involve the parameters of the regression.)

3. This and the next two exercises are based on the test statistic usually used to test a set of J linear restrictions in the generalized regression model:

$$F[J, n - K] = \frac{(R\hat{\beta} - q)'[R(X'\Omega^{-1}X)^{-1}R']^{-1}(R\hat{\beta} - q)/J}{(y - X\hat{\beta})'\Omega^{-1}(y - X\hat{\beta})/(n - K)},$$

where $\hat{\beta}$ is the GLS estimator. Show that if Ω is known and the disturbances are normally distributed, this statistic is exactly distributed as F with J and $n - K$ degrees of freedom. What assumptions about the regressors are needed to reach this conclusion? Need they be nonstochastic?

4. Now suppose that the disturbances are not normally distributed, though Ω is still known. Proceeding along the lines of the proof in Section 10.4.2, show that the previous statistic is asymptotically distributed as $(1/J)$ times a chi-squared variable with J degrees of freedom. (**Hint:** The transformed model of (13–12) satisfies the assumptions of the theorem in Chapter 10.) Conclude that in the generalized regression model, the Wald statistic,

$$W = (R\hat{\beta} - q)'\{R\text{Est. Var}[\hat{\beta}]R'\}^{-1}(R\hat{\beta} - q),$$

tends asymptotically to a chi-squared statistic with J degrees of freedom, regardless of the distribution of the disturbances, so long as the data are otherwise well behaved. Note that in a finite sample the true distribution may be approximated with an $F[J, n - K]$ distribution. It is a bit ambiguous, however, to interpret this as implying that the statistic is asymptotically distributed as F with J and $n - K$ degrees of freedom, as the limiting distribution used to obtain our result is the chi-squared, not the F. In this instance, the $F[J, n - K]$ is a random variable that tends asymptotically to the chi-squared variate.

5. Finally, suppose that Ω must be estimated but that assumptions (13–27) and (13–28) are met by the estimator. What changes are required in the development of the previous problem?

6. An intriguing result is the following:

> In the generalized regression model, if the K columns of X are characteristic vectors of Ω, then ordinary least squares and generalized least squares are identical.

(The result is actually a bit broader; X may be any linear combination of exactly K characteristic vectors.)

(a) Prove the result directly, using matrix algebra.

(b) Prove that if **X** contains a constant term and if the remaining columns are in deviation form (so that the column sum is zero), the model of Example 13.1 is one of these cases. (The seemingly unrelated regressions model with identical regressor matrices, which is discussed in Chapter 17, is another.)

7. In the generalized regression model, suppose that Ω is known.

(a) What is the covariance matrix of the OLS and GLS estimators of β?

(b) What is the covariance matrix of the OLS residual vector, $\mathbf{e} = \mathbf{y} - \mathbf{Xb}$?

(c) What is the covariance matrix of the GLS residual vector, $\hat{\varepsilon} = \mathbf{y} - \mathbf{X}\hat{\beta}$?

(d) What is the covariance matrix of the OLS and GLS residual vectors?

8. Derive a general expression for the expected value of s^2, the OLS estimator of σ^2, in the context of the generalized regression model.

9. Suppose that y has the pdf

$$f(y\,|\,\mathbf{x}) = \left[\frac{1}{\beta'\mathbf{x}}\right]e^{-y/(\beta'\mathbf{x})}, \qquad y \geq 0.$$

Then $E[y\,|\,\mathbf{x}] = \beta'\mathbf{x}$ and $\text{Var}[y\,|\,\mathbf{x}] = (\beta'\mathbf{x})^2$. For this model, prove that the GLS and MLE are the same, even though this distribution, like the one in Exercise 2, involves the same parameters in the conditional mean function and the disturbance variance.

10. Consider estimation of σ^2 in the generalized regression model. There is a fundamental ambiguity in regard to this "parameter," as it is merely a scaling of $E[\varepsilon\varepsilon'] = \sigma^2\Omega$. Since both components are unknown, σ^2 cannot be regarded as an estimable parameter until some scaling of Ω is assumed to remove the indeterminacy. The most convenient assumption is

$$\text{tr}(\Omega) = n.$$

The classical regression model in which $\Omega = \mathbf{I}$ is one such case, so this provides a useful benchmark. Note that the second example in the Introduction embodies this assumption. Now consider the estimator $s^2 = \mathbf{e}'\mathbf{e}/(n - K)$, where $\mathbf{e}$ is the vector of least squares residuals.

(a) Prove that the exact expectation of s^2 is

$$E[s^2] = \frac{n\sigma^2}{(n - K)} - \frac{\sigma^2\,\text{tr}[\{\mathbf{X}'\mathbf{X}/(n - K)\}^{-1}\{\mathbf{X}'\Omega\mathbf{X}/(n - K)\}]}{(n - K)},$$

so that s^2 is biased. (**Hint:** As always, $\mathbf{e} = \mathbf{M}\varepsilon$. To obtain the expectation, use the same method as in Chapter 6.)

(b) Prove that if the assumptions in (13–6) hold,

$$\lim_{n \to \infty} E[s^2] = \sigma^2.$$

(c) To consider the issue of consistency, prove that

$$\text{plim } s^2 = \text{plim}\left(\frac{1}{n - K}\right)\sum_i \varepsilon_i^2.$$

[**Hint:** Expand $\mathbf{e}'\mathbf{e}/(n-K) = \varepsilon'\mathbf{M}\varepsilon/(n-K)$.] What are the exact mean and variance of the statistic on the right-hand side? Under what conditions is $\text{plim } s^2 = \sigma^2$?

References

Aitken, A. C., "On Least Squares and Linear Combinations of Observations," *Proceedings of the Royal Society*, 55, 1935, pp. 42–48.

Amemiya, T., *Advanced Econometrics*, Cambridge, Mass.: Harvard University Press, 1985.

Anderson, T., *The Statistical Analysis of Time Series*, New York: Wiley, 1971.

Buse, A., "Goodness of Fit in Generalized Least Squares Estimation," *The American Statistician*, 1973, pp. 106–108.

Don, F., and J. Magnus, "On the Unbiasedness of the Iterated GLS Estimator," *Communications in Statistics*, 1980, pp. 519–527.

Greenberg, E., and C. Webster, *Advanced Econometrics: A Bridge to the Literature*, New York: Wiley, 1983.

Griliches, Z., and P. Rao, "Small Sample Properties of Several Two Stage Regression Methods in the Context of Autocorrelated Errors," *Journal of the American Statistical Association*, 64, 1969, pp. 253–272.

Hausman, J., "Specification Tests in Econometrics," *Econometrica*, 46, 1978, pp. 1251–1271.

Judge, G., C. Hill, W. Griffiths, H. Lutkepohl, and T. Lee, *The Theory and Practice of Econometrics*, New York: Wiley, 1985.

Kakwani, N., "The Unbiasedness of Zellner's Seemingly Unrelated Regression Equation Estimators," *Journal of the American Statistical Association*, 62, 1967, pp. 141–142.

Magnus, J., "Maximum Likelihood Estimation of the Generalized Regression Model with Unknown Parameters in the Disturbance Covariance Matrix," *Journal of Econometrics*, 7, 1978, pp. 281–312.

Oberhofer, W., and J. Kmenta, "A General Procedure for Obtaining Maximum Likelihood Estimates in Generalized Regression Models," *Econometrica*, 42, 1974, pp. 579–590.

Schmidt, P., *Econometrics*, New York: Marcel Dekker, 1976.

Taylor, W. E., "Small Sample Properties of a Class of Two Stage Aitken Estimators," *Econometrica*, 45, 1977, pp. 497–508.

Chapter 14
Heteroscedasticity

14.1. Introduction

If the disturbance variance is not constant across observations, the regression is **hetero-scedastic**. In this case,

$$\text{Var}(\varepsilon_i) = \sigma_i^2, \qquad i = 1, \ldots, n.$$

We continue to assume that the disturbances are pairwise uncorrelated. Thus,

$$E[\varepsilon\varepsilon'] = \sigma^2\Omega = \begin{bmatrix} \sigma_1^2 & 0 & 0 & \cdots & 0 \\ 0 & \sigma_2^2 & 0 & \cdots & 0 \\ & & \vdots & & \\ 0 & 0 & 0 & \cdots & \sigma_n^2 \end{bmatrix}.$$

It will sometimes prove useful to write

$$\sigma_i^2 = \sigma^2\omega_i.$$

In any case, this is an arbitrary scaling. Thus, we shall use the normalization

$$tr(\Omega) = \sum_i \omega_i = n.$$

This makes the classical regression with homoscedastic disturbances a simple special case with $\omega_i = 1$. Intuitively, one might think of the ω's as weights that are scaled in such a way as to reflect only the variety in the disturbance variances. The scale factor, σ^2, then provides the overall scaling for the model of the disturbance process.

Heteroscedasticity arises in numerous applications, primarily in the analysis of cross-section data. For example, even after accounting for differences in firm sizes, we expect to observe greater variation in the profits of large firms than in those of small ones. The variance of profits might also depend upon product diversification, research and development expenditure, and industry characteristics, and thus might also vary across firms of similar sizes. In analyzing family spending patterns, we find that there is greater variation in expenditure on certain commodity groups among high-income families than low ones due to the greater discretion allowed by higher incomes.[1] Heteroscedasticity is sometimes a

[1] Prais and Houthakker (1955).

Table 14.1

State	Exp.	Income	State	Exp.	Income	State	Exp.	Income
Ala.	275	6247	Alaska	821	10851	Ariz.	339	7374
Ark.	275	6183	Calif.	387	8850	Colo.	452	8001
Conn.	531	8914	Del.	424	8604	D.C.	428	10022
Fla.	316	7505	Ga.	265	6700	Hawaii	403	8380
Idaho	304	6813	Ill.	437	8745	Ind.	345	7696
Iowa	431	7873	Kans.	355	8001	Ky.	260	6615
La.	316	6640	Maine	327	6333	Md.	427	8306
Mass.	427	8063	Mich.	466	8442	Minn.	477	7847
Miss.	259	5736	Mo.	274	7342	Mont.	433	7051
Nebr.	294	7391	Nev.	359	9032	N.H.	279	7277
N.J.	423	8818	N. Mex.	388	6505	N.Y.	447	8267
N.C.	335	6607	N. Dak.	311	7478	Ohio	322	7812
Okla.	320	6951	Oreg.	397	7839	Pa.	412	7733
R.I.	342	7526	S.C.	315	6242	S. Dak.	321	6841
Tenn.	268	6489	Tex.	315	7697	Utah	417	6622
Vt.	353	6541	Va.	356	7624	Wash.	415	8450
W. Va.	320	6456	Wis.	Missing	7597	Wyo.	500	9096

Table 14.2. Ordinary Least Squares Results

	Constant	Income	Income^2
Coefficient	832.91	−1834.2	1587.04
Standard error	(327.3)	(829.0)	(591.1)
t Ratio	2.545	−2.213	3.057
	$R^2 = 0.65534$		
	$s^2 = 3212.46$		

consequence of data aggregation. In Section 9.4, we found that the appropriate model for grouped data included a disturbance whose variance was σ^2/n_g, where n_g is the number of data points in the gth group. When we analyze group means, the greater precision of an average based on a larger sample implies that the disturbance variance in the regression model will vary inversely with the group size.

EXAMPLE 14.1. The data in Table 14.1 give per capita expenditure on public schools and per capita income by state in 1979.[2]

Least squares regression of spending on a constant, per capita income and the square of per capita income produces the results given in Table 14.2, with the estimated standard errors given in parentheses. (Income is scaled by 10^{-4} in these and all subsequent calculations.) Individually, the coefficients appear to be statistically significant different from zero by the usual t test. The joint test based on $F = [R^2/2]/[(1 - R^2)/47] = 44.68$ suggests that the coefficients are jointly significant as well. (The 1 percent critical value is 5.09.) A plot of the residuals against income for the 15 highest and 15 lowest values of income suggests that the disturbances in this regression are somewhat heteroscedastic (Figure 14.1).

[2] Data are from the United States Department of Commerce (1979, p. 157).

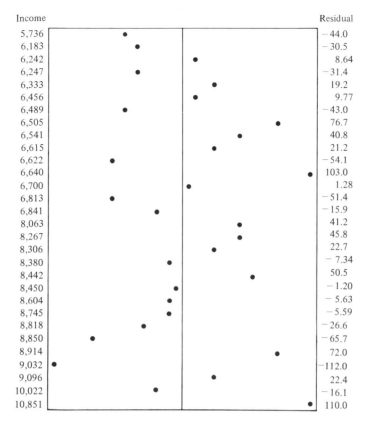

Income

	Residual
5,736	−44.0
6,183	−30.5
6,242	8.64
6,247	−31.4
6,333	19.2
6,456	9.77
6,489	−43.0
6,505	76.7
6,541	40.8
6,615	21.2
6,622	−54.1
6,640	103.0
6,700	1.28
6,813	−51.4
6,841	−15.9
8,063	41.2
8,267	45.8
8,306	22.7
8,380	−7.34
8,442	50.5
8,450	−1.20
8,604	−5.63
8,745	−5.59
8,818	−26.6
8,850	−65.7
8,914	72.0
9,032	−112.0
9,096	22.4
10,022	−16.1
10,851	110.0

Figure 14.1   Plot of residuals against income.

14.2.   *Ordinary Least Squares Estimation*

The results of Section 13.2 specialize for a heteroscedastic regression. Therefore, it follows immediately that

1. $\mathbf{b} = (\mathbf{X}'\mathbf{X})^{-1}\mathbf{X}'\mathbf{y}$ is unbiased.

If the disturbances are normally distributed,

2. Conditioned on $\mathbf{X}$, $\mathbf{b}$ is normally distributed with

$$E[\mathbf{b}] = \beta$$

and

$$\mathrm{Var}[\mathbf{b}] = \frac{\sigma^2}{n} \left(\frac{\mathbf{X}'\mathbf{X}}{n}\right)^{-1} \left(\frac{\mathbf{X}'\mathbf{\Omega}\mathbf{X}}{n}\right)\left(\frac{\mathbf{X}'\mathbf{X}}{n}\right)^{-1}$$

$$= \sigma^2(\mathbf{X}'\mathbf{X})^{-1}\left(\sum_i \omega_i \mathbf{x}_i \mathbf{x}_i'\right)(\mathbf{X}'\mathbf{X})^{-1}.$$

[See (13–3) and (13–5).] Assuming, as usual, that the regressors are well behaved, so that $(\mathbf{X}'\mathbf{X}/n)^{-1}$ converges to a positive definite matrix, we find that the mean square consistency of

b depends on the limiting behavior of the matrix

$$\mathbf{Q}_n^* = \frac{\mathbf{X}'\mathbf{\Omega}\mathbf{X}}{n} = \frac{1}{n}\sum_i \omega_i \mathbf{x}_i \mathbf{x}_i'. \tag{14-1}$$

If $\mathbf{Q}_n^*$ converges to a positive definite matrix as $n \to \infty$, **b** will converge to β in mean square. Under most circumstances, if σ^2 and ω_i are finite for all i, we would expect this to be true. Note that $\mathbf{Q}_n^*$ is a weighted sum of the squares and cross-products of **x** with weights ω_i/n, which sum to one. We have already assumed that another weighted sum, $\mathbf{X}'\mathbf{X}/n$, in which the weights are $1/n$, converges to a positive definite matrix, so it would be surprising if $\mathbf{Q}_n^*$ did not converge as well. In most cases, we would expect that

3. plim **b** $= \beta$, that is, **b** is consistent for β.

In addition, if the assumptions needed to ensure consistency are met, we can easily show that the least squares estimator is asymptotically normally distributed. The proof in Section 10.3.2 applies directly simply by defining $\mathbf{Q}_i$ to be $\omega_i \mathbf{x}_i \mathbf{x}_i'$ instead of $\mathbf{x}_i \mathbf{x}_i'$. If the ω_i's are not dominated by any particular element, the proof is identical. We conclude, then, that

4. $\mathbf{b} \xrightarrow{a} N\left[\beta, \frac{\sigma^2}{n}\mathbf{Q}^{-1}\mathbf{Q}^*\mathbf{Q}^{-1}\right],$

where

$$\mathbf{Q} = \text{plim}\frac{1}{n}\mathbf{X}'\mathbf{X}$$

and

$$\mathbf{Q}^* = \text{plim}\,\mathbf{Q}_n^*.$$

14.2.1.   Inefficiency of Least Squares

It follows from our earlier results that **b** is inefficient relative to the GLS estimator, though by how much depends on the setting.

EXAMPLE 14.2. Inefficiency of Ordinary Least Squares. Consider a very simple model,

$$y_i = \beta x_i + \varepsilon_i$$

$$\text{Var}[\varepsilon_i] = \sigma^2 x_i^2,$$

and assume that y and x are measured as deviations from their means. The variances of the OLS and GLS estimators of β are

$$\text{Var}[b] = \sigma^2[\mathbf{X}'\mathbf{X}]^{-1}[\mathbf{X}'\mathbf{\Omega}\mathbf{X}][\mathbf{X}'\mathbf{X}]^{-1} = \sigma^2\frac{\sum_i x_i^4}{(\sum_i x_i^2)^2}$$

and

$$\text{Var}[\hat{\beta}] = \sigma^2[\mathbf{X}'\mathbf{\Omega}^{-1}\mathbf{X}]^{-1} = \frac{\sigma^2}{n}.$$

The relative (in)efficiency of OLS is

$$k = \frac{n\sum_i x_i^4}{(\sum x_i^2)^2} = \frac{[\sum_i x_i^4/n]}{[\sum_i x_i^2/n]^2}. \tag{14-2}$$

This ratio must be greater than one. Let y_i equal x_i^2. Then

$$k = \frac{(1/n)\sum_i y_i^2}{[(1/n)\sum_i y_i]^2} = \frac{(1/n)\sum_i y_i^2}{\bar{y}^2}.$$

But

$$\frac{1}{n}\sum_i y_i^2 = \frac{1}{n}\sum_i (y_i - \bar{y})^2 + \bar{y}^2,$$

so

$$k = \frac{(1/n)\sum_i (y_i - \bar{y})^2}{\bar{y}^2} + 1 > 1.$$

Therefore, in this model, ordinary least squares is never as efficient as generalized least squares.

Suppose that the x's are drawn from a distribution with zero mean and finite fourth moment. Then, by applying the Slutsky theorem and Theorem 4.3 [with (4–20)], we obtain

$$\text{plim } k = \frac{E[x_i^4]}{E[x_i^2]^2} = \frac{\mu_4}{\sigma_x^4}.$$

This is the standardized measure of kurtosis that was discussed in Chapter 3 and Section 10.5.4. Its value depends on the distribution of x_i; it is three for the normal distribution. Theoretically, k can take any value greater than one, but for economic data, it is typically between two and four.[3] This example would suggest that the gain in efficiency from GLS over OLS can be substantial. A properly constructed confidence interval based on the OLS estimates would be over 70 percent wider than one based on GLS.

14.2.2.   The Estimated Covariance Matrix of b

If the type of heteroscedasticity is known with certainty, the ordinary least squares estimator is undesirable; we should use generalized least squares instead. However, the precise form of the heteroscedasticity is often unknown. In that case, generalized least squares is not usable, and we may need to salvage what we can from the results of ordinary least squares.

The conventionally estimated variance matrix for the least squares estimator, $\sigma^2(X'X)^{-1}$, is inappropriate; the appropriate matrix is $\sigma^2(X'X)^{-1}(X'\Omega X)(X'X)^{-1}$. It is unlikely that these two would coincide, so the usual estimators of the standard errors are likely to be erroneous. In this section, we consider how erroneous the conventional estimator is likely to be.

As usual,

$$s^2 = \frac{e'e}{n - K} = \frac{\varepsilon'M\varepsilon}{n - K},$$

where

$$M = I - X(X'X)^{-1}X'.$$

[3] Some examples: The logs of capital and labor in the example used in Chapter 7 have $k = 2.39$ and 2.64; the same variables for the data of Example 11.5 have $k = 2.72$ and 3.15; the kurtosis of the income data in Example 14.1 is 3.40.

Expanding this, we obtain

$$s^2 = \frac{\varepsilon'\varepsilon}{n-K} - \frac{\varepsilon'X(X'X)^{-1}X'\varepsilon}{n-K}. \tag{14-3}$$

Taking the two parts separately yields

$$E\left[\frac{\varepsilon'\varepsilon}{n-K}\right] = \frac{tr E[\varepsilon\varepsilon']}{n-K} = \frac{n\sigma^2}{n-K}. \tag{14-4}$$

(We have used the scaling, $tr(\Omega) = n$.) In addition,

$$E\left[\frac{\varepsilon'X(X'X)^{-1}X'\varepsilon}{n-K}\right] = \frac{tr[E[(X'X)^{-1}X'\varepsilon\varepsilon'X]]}{n-K}$$

$$= \frac{tr\left[\sigma^2\left(\dfrac{X'X}{n}\right)^{-1}\left(\dfrac{X'\Omega X}{n}\right)\right]}{n-K} \tag{14-5}$$

$$= \frac{\sigma^2}{n-K} tr\left[\left(\frac{X'X}{n}\right)^{-1} Q_n^*\right],$$

where Q_n^* is defined in (14-1). As $n \to \infty$, the term in (14-4) will converge to σ^2. The term in (14-5) will converge to zero if b is consistent, as both matrices in the product are finite. Therefore,

$$\text{If } b \text{ is consistent, } \lim_{n\to\infty} E[s^2] = \sigma^2.$$

It can also be shown—we leave it as an exercise—that if the fourth moment of every disturbance is finite and all of our other assumptions are met,

$$\lim_{n\to\infty} \text{Var}\left[\frac{e'e}{n-K}\right] = \lim_{n\to\infty} \text{Var}\left[\frac{\varepsilon'\varepsilon}{n-K}\right] = 0.$$

This implies, therefore, that

$$\text{If plim } b = \beta, \text{ then plim } s^2 = \sigma^2.$$

Before proceeding, it is useful to pursue this result. The normalization $tr(\Omega) = n$ implies that

$$\sigma^2 = \bar{\sigma}^2 = \frac{1}{n}\sum_i \sigma_i^2$$

and

$$\omega_i = \frac{\sigma_i^2}{\bar{\sigma}^2}.$$

Therefore, our previous convergence result implies that the least squares estimator, s^2, converges to plim $\bar{\sigma}^2$, that is, the probability limit of the average variance of the disturbances, *assuming that this probability limit exists.* Thus, some further assumption about these variances is necessary in order to obtain the result. For example, note the particular assumption that is needed in Example 14.2. (For another application, see Exercise 7, Chapter 16.)

The difference between the conventional estimator and the appropriate covariance matrix for b is

$$\text{Est. Var}[b] - \text{Var}[b] = s^2(X'X)^{-1} - \sigma^2(X'X)^{-1}(X'\Omega X)(X'X)^{-1}.$$

In a large sample, this is approximately equal to

$$\frac{\sigma^2}{n}\left(\frac{\mathbf{X}'\mathbf{X}}{n}\right)^{-1}\left[\frac{\mathbf{X}'\mathbf{X}}{n} - \frac{\mathbf{X}'\mathbf{\Omega}\mathbf{X}}{n}\right]\left(\frac{\mathbf{X}'\mathbf{X}}{n}\right)^{-1}.$$

The difference between the two matrices hinges upon

$$\Delta = \frac{\mathbf{X}'\mathbf{X}}{n} - \frac{\mathbf{X}'\mathbf{\Omega}\mathbf{X}}{n}$$

$$= \sum_i \left(\frac{1}{n}\right)\mathbf{x}_i\mathbf{x}_i' - \sum_i \left(\frac{\omega_i}{n}\right)\mathbf{x}_i\mathbf{x}_i',$$

(14–6)

where $\mathbf{x}_i$ is the ith row of $\mathbf{X}$. These are two weighted averages of the matrices $\mathbf{S}_i = \mathbf{x}_i\mathbf{x}_i'$, using weights $1/n$ for the first term and ω_i/n for the second. The scaling $tr(\mathbf{\Omega}) = n$ implies that $\sum_i(\omega_i/n) = 1$. Whether the weighted average based on ω_i/n differs much from the one using $1/n$ depends on the weights. If the weights are related to the values in $\mathbf{x}_i$, the difference can be considerable. However, if the weights are uncorrelated with $\mathbf{x}_i\mathbf{x}_i'$, the weighted average will tend to equal the unweighted average.[4]

Therefore, the comparison rests on whether the heteroscedasticity is related to any of x_i or x_ix_j. The (perhaps surprising) conclusion is that, in general, *if the heteroscedasticity is not correlated with the variables in the model, then, at least in large samples, the ordinary least squares computations, while not the optimal way to use the data, will not be misleading.*

EXAMPLE 14.3. In the heteroscedastic regression of Example 13.2, if the observations are grouped in the subsamples in a way that is unrelated to the variables in $\mathbf{X}$, then the usual OLS estimator of Var[$\mathbf{b}$] will, at least in large samples, provide a reliable estimate of the appropriate covariance matrix. It is worth remembering, however, that the least squares estimator will be inefficient, the more so the larger is the difference between the variances of the two groups.[5]

The preceding is a useful result, but we should not be overly optimistic. First, it remains true that ordinary least squares is demonstrably inefficient. Second, if the primary assumption of the analysis—that the heteroscedasticity is unrelated to the variables in the model, is incorrect—then the conventional standard errors may be quite far from the appropriate values. And our inferences may be very misleading. For example, it is not uncommon for the disturbance variance to be specified as $\sigma_i^2 = \sigma^2 x_i^2$.

14.2.3. Estimating the Appropriate Covariance Matrix for Ordinary Least Squares

It is clear from the preceding that heteroscedasticity has some potentially serious implications for inferences based on the results of least squares. However, the application of more appropriate estimation techniques requires a detailed formulation of $\mathbf{\Omega}$. It may well be that the form of the heteroscedasticity is unknown. White (1980) has shown that it is still

---

[4] Suppose, for example, that $\mathbf{X}$ contains a single column, and that both x_i and ω_i are independent and identically distributed random variables. Then $\mathbf{x}'\mathbf{x}/n$ converges to $E[\mathbf{x}_i^2]$, while $\mathbf{x}'\mathbf{\Omega}\mathbf{x}/n$ converges to $\text{Cov}[\omega_i, x_i^2] + E[\omega_i]E[x_i^2]$. $E[w_i] = 1$, so if ω and x^2 are uncorrelated, the sums have the same probability limit. An analogous argument is used earlier.

[5] Some general results, including analysis of the properties of the estimator based on estimated variances, are given in Taylor (1977).

Table 14.3

	Constant	Income	Income^2
Coefficient	832.91	−1834.2	1587.04
OLS standard error	(327.3)	(829.0)	(519.1)
White SE	(460.9)	(1243.0)	(830.0)
t ratio	1.807	−1.476	1.912

possible to obtain an appropriate estimator for the variance of the least squares estimator, even if the heteroscedasticity is related to the variables in $\mathbf{X}$.

The covariance matrix of $\mathbf{b}$ is $(\mathbf{X'X})^{-1}[\mathbf{X'}(\sigma^2\mathbf{\Omega})\mathbf{X}](\mathbf{X'X})^{-1}$. It would appear that in order to compute an estimate of this matrix, we need an estimate of $\sigma^2\mathbf{\Omega}$, which is unavailable. But what is actually required is an estimate of

$$\mathbf{\Sigma} = \frac{\sigma^2\mathbf{X'\Omega X}}{n} = \frac{1}{n}\sum_i \sigma_i^2 \mathbf{x}_i\mathbf{x}_i'. \tag{14-7}$$

White (1980) shows that under very general conditions, the matrix

$$\mathbf{S} = \frac{1}{n}\sum_i e_i^2 \mathbf{x}_i\mathbf{x}_i', \tag{14-8}$$

where e_i, the ith least squares residual, is a consistent estimator of $\mathbf{\Sigma}$.[6] Therefore,

$$\text{Est. Var}[\mathbf{b}] = n(\mathbf{X'X})^{-1}\mathbf{S}(\mathbf{X'X})^{-1} \tag{14-9}$$

can be used as an estimate of the true variance of the least squares estimator.

This is an extremely important and useful result.[7] It implies that without actually specifying the type of heteroscedasticity, we can still make appropriate inferences based on the results of least squares. This is especially useful if we are unsure of the precise nature of the heteroscedasticity (which is probably most of the time).

EXAMPLE 14.4. If the disturbances in the regression of Example 14.1 are heteroscedastic, as Figure 14.1 suggests, the ordinary least squares standard errors should be biased. Using the White estimator for the variance matrix of the least squares estimators produces the results given in Table 14.3. The corrected standard errors are considerably larger than the conventionally computed values. Indeed, neither of the slope coefficients appears to be statistically significant after the correction. The joint test of their significance can no longer be carried out with the F test used in Example 14.1, as it relies on homoscedasticity. We can, however, use a Wald test. The statistic is

$$W = \mathbf{Rb'}\{\mathbf{R}(\text{Est. Var}[\mathbf{b}])\mathbf{R'}\}^{-1}\mathbf{Rb},$$

where

$$\mathbf{R} = \begin{bmatrix} 0 & 1 & 0 \\ 0 & 0 & 1 \end{bmatrix}$$

---

[6] See also Eicker (1967).

[7] Further discussion and some refinements may be found in Cragg (1982). Cragg shows how White's observation can be extended to devise an estimator that improves on the efficiency of ordinary least squares.

and the covariance matrix is the White estimator. The statistic is asymptotically distributed as chi-squared with degrees of freedom equal to the number of slopes (here, two). (We use the last two elements of $\mathbf{b}$ and the lower 2×2 submatrix of the estimate of $\text{Var}[\mathbf{b}]$ for the test.) Using our previous results, we obtain $W = 49.5355$ which is highly significant, in spite of the previous results.

14.3. Generalized Least Squares When Ω Is Known

The GLS estimator is

$$\hat{\beta} = (\mathbf{X}'\Omega^{-1}\mathbf{X})^{-1}\mathbf{X}'\Omega^{-1}\mathbf{y}.$$

Consider the most general case,

$$\text{Var}[\varepsilon_i] = \sigma_i^2 = \sigma^2 \omega_i.$$

Then

$$\Omega = \begin{bmatrix} \omega_1 & 0 & 0 & \cdots & 0 \\ 0 & \omega_2 & 0 & \cdots & 0 \\ & & \vdots & & \\ 0 & 0 & 0 & \cdots & \omega_n \end{bmatrix},$$

so Ω^{-1} is a diagonal matrix whose ith diagonal element is $1/\omega_i$. The GLS estimator is obtained by regressing

$$\mathbf{Py} = \begin{bmatrix} y_1/\sqrt{\omega_1} \\ y_2/\sqrt{\omega_2} \\ \vdots \\ y_n/\sqrt{\omega_n} \end{bmatrix} \quad \text{on} \quad \mathbf{PX} = \begin{bmatrix} \mathbf{x}_1/\sqrt{\omega_1} \\ \mathbf{x}_2/\sqrt{\omega_2} \\ \vdots \\ \mathbf{x}_n/\sqrt{\omega_n} \end{bmatrix}.$$

Applying ordinary least squares to the transformed model, we obtain the **weighted least squares (WLS)** estimator,

$$\hat{\beta} = \left[\sum_i w_i \mathbf{x}_i \mathbf{x}_i' \right]^{-1} \left[\sum_i w_i \mathbf{x}_i y_i \right],$$

where

$$w_i = \frac{1}{\omega_i}.^8$$

The logic of the computation is that observations with smaller variances receive a larger weight in the computations of the sums and, therefore, have greater influence in the estimates obtained.

EXAMPLE 14.5. **Groupwise Heteroscedasticity.** Consider again the groupwise heteroscedastic regression model of Example 13.2. Assume that the variances are known. The GLS

---

[8] The weights are often denoted $w_i = 1/\sigma_i^2$. This is consistent with the equivalent $\hat{\beta} = [\mathbf{X}'(\sigma^2\Omega)^{-1}\mathbf{X}]^{-1}\mathbf{X}'(\sigma^2\Omega)^{-1}\mathbf{y}$. The σ^2's cancel, leaving the expression given previously.

estimator is

$$\hat{\beta} = \left[\sum_g \left(\frac{1}{\sigma_g^2} \right) X_g' X_g \right]^{-1} \left[\sum_g \left(\frac{1}{\sigma_g^2} \right) X_g' y_g \right].$$

Since $X_g' y_g = X_g' X_g b_g$, where b_g is the OLS estimator in the gth subset of observations,

$$\hat{\beta} = \left[\sum_g \left(\frac{1}{\sigma_g^2} \right) X_g' X_g \right]^{-1} \left[\sum_g \left(\frac{1}{\sigma_g^2} \right) X_g' X_g b_g \right]$$

$$= \left[\sum_g V_g \right]^{-1} \left[\sum_g V_g b_g \right].$$

This is a matrix weighted average—$\sum_g V_g = I$—of the G least squares estimators, where the weighting matrices are the inverses of the variances of the respective least squares estimators, times the sum of these inverses. The estimator with the smaller variance matrix therefore receives the larger weight.

Suppose, in addition, that X_g is the same in every group. This might occur in repeated sampling of experimental data. With a common X matrix, the GLS estimator reduces to

$$\hat{\beta} = \sum_g w_g b_g,$$

where

$$w_g = \frac{1/\sigma_g^2}{\sum_g 1/\sigma_g^2}.$$

Once again, the weights are larger for the estimators with the smaller variances. Since there are now no differences across the groups in the regressor matrices, only the disturbance variances are present in the weighting factors.

A common specification is that the variance is proportional to one of the regressors or its square. Our earlier example of family expenditures is one in which the relevant variable is usually income. Similarly, in studies of firm profits, the dominant variable is typically assumed to be firm size. If we assume that

$$\sigma_i^2 = \sigma^2 x_{ik}^2,$$

the transformed regression model for GLS is

$$\frac{y}{x_k} = \beta_k + \beta_1 \left[\frac{x_1}{x_k} \right] + \beta_2 \left[\frac{x_2}{x_k} \right] + \cdots + \frac{\varepsilon}{x_k}. \tag{14-10}$$

If the variance is proportional to x_k instead of x_k^2, the weight applied to each observation is $1/\sqrt{x_k}$ instead of $1/x_k$.

EXAMPLE 14.6.   Weighted least squares estimates of the model in Example 14.1 are given in Table 14.4. Estimated standard errors are shown in parentheses.

In (14-10), the coefficient on x_k becomes the constant term. But if the variance is proportional to any power of x_k other than two, the transformed model will no longer contain a constant, and we encounter the problem of interpreting R^2 mentioned earlier. For example, no conclusion should be drawn if the R^2 in the regression of y/z on $1/z$ and x/z is higher than that in the regression of y on a constant and x for any z, including x. The good fit of the weighted regression might be due to the presence of $1/z$ on both sides of the equality.

Table 14.4. WLS Results

	Constant	Income	Income^2
Least squares	832.91	-1834.20	1587.04
	(327.3)	(829.0)	(519.1)
Var$(\varepsilon) = \sigma^2$income	746.36	-1612.25	1447.46
	(328.2)	(844.8)	(537.7)
Var$(\varepsilon) = \sigma^2$income^2	644.58	-1399.28	1311.35
	(333.6)	(872.1)	(563.7)

14.4 *Estimation When Ω Contains Unknown Parameters*

The general form of the heteroscedastic regression model has too many parameters to estimate by ordinary methods. Typically, the model is restricted by formulating $\sigma^2\Omega$ as a function of a few parameters, as in $\sigma_i^2 = \sigma^2 x_i^a$ or $\sigma_i^2 = \sigma^2[\alpha' \mathbf{x}_i]^2$. GLS based on a consistent estimate of Ω is asymptotically equivalent to GLS, and FGLS based on a maximum likelihood of Ω is the maximum likelihood estimator if Ω does not contain any elements of β. As in the general case, however, the new problem introduced is that we must first find consistent estimates of the unknown parameters in Ω. Two methods are typically used for models of heteroscedasticity, two-step GLS and maximum likelihood.

14.4.1. Two-Step Estimation

For the heteroscedastic regression model, the GLS estimator is

$$\hat{\beta} = \left[\sum_i \left(\frac{1}{\sigma_i^2}\right)\mathbf{x}_i\mathbf{x}_i'\right]^{-1}\left[\sum_i \left(\frac{1}{\sigma_i^2}\right)\mathbf{x}_i y_i\right].$$

The two-step estimators are computed by first obtaining estimates $\hat{\sigma}_i^2$, usually by some function of least squares residuals, and then

$$\hat{\hat{\beta}} = \left[\sum_i \left(\frac{1}{\hat{\sigma}_i^2}\right)\mathbf{x}_i\mathbf{x}_i'\right]^{-1}\left[\sum_i \left(\frac{1}{\hat{\sigma}_i^2}\right)\mathbf{x}_i y_i\right].$$

The OLS estimates of β, while inefficient, are still consistent. As such, the least squares residuals,

$$e_i = y_i - \mathbf{x}_i'\mathbf{b}$$
$$= y_i - \mathbf{x}_i'\beta - \mathbf{x}_i'(\mathbf{b} - \beta) \tag{14-11}$$
$$= \varepsilon_i + v_i,$$

have the same limiting distribution as the true disturbances, ε_i. For the true ε_i's, $E[\varepsilon_i^2] = \sigma_i^2$. We can form a regression,

$$\varepsilon_i^2 = \sigma_i^2 + u_i, \tag{14-12}$$

where u_i is the difference between ε_i^2 and its expectation. For the least squares residual,

$$e_i^2 = \varepsilon_i^2 + (\mathbf{x}_i'(\mathbf{b} - \beta))^2 - 2\varepsilon_i\mathbf{x}_i'(\mathbf{b} - \beta).$$

The latter two terms will be negligible asymptotically, so that, at least approximately,[9]

$$e_i^2 = \sigma_i^2 + v_i. \tag{14-13}$$

A general procedure suggested by this is to treat the variance function as a regression model and use the squares of the least squares residuals as the dependent variable to estimate the parameters. If $\text{Var}(\varepsilon_i) = \sigma_i^2(\boldsymbol{\alpha}, \mathbf{z}_i)$, the (possibly nonlinear) regression of the squared residuals on $\mathbf{z}$ will provide a consistent estimate of $\boldsymbol{\alpha}$.[10] With estimates of the unknown parameters in $\boldsymbol{\Omega}$ in hand, we may then use FGLS.

To take a particularly straightforward case, suppose that

$$\sigma_i^2 = \boldsymbol{\alpha}' \mathbf{z}_i.^{[11]}$$

or

$$e_i^2 \simeq \boldsymbol{\alpha}' \mathbf{z}_i + v_i. \tag{14-14}$$

This is not a classical regression model; in a finite sample, v_i has a nonzero mean, is heteroscedastic, and is correlated across observations because each v_i is constructed from the same estimate of $\boldsymbol{\beta}$. However, as shown by Amemiya, the first and third of these difficulties are absent in large samples—v_i has a zero mean and is nonautocorrelated—so we can expect the ordinary least squares estimator of $\boldsymbol{\alpha}$ to be consistent. That is all that is required for the efficient estimation of $\boldsymbol{\beta}$ by FGLS using $\boldsymbol{\Omega}(\hat{\boldsymbol{\alpha}})$.

All of the general results obtained earlier apply directly. The small-sample properties of such an estimator are generally unknown. Because v_i is heteroscedastic, the OLS estimator of $\boldsymbol{\alpha}$ is inefficient. A more efficient estimator could be obtained in some cases.[12] The degree to which this would improve the sampling properties of the FGLS estimator remains to be determined. Asymptotically, it makes no difference, but the finite-sample properties remain uncertain.

EXAMPLE 14.7. In applying the preceding to the school expenditure data of Example 14.1, we find, first, that least squares regression of the squared residuals on a constant, income, and income squared produces the results shown in Table 14.5. The large difference between the OLS and White estimators of the standard errors is to be expected, given the heteroscedasticity in v_i. These estimates are then used to compute the elements of $\boldsymbol{\Omega}$.[13] We then obtain the GLS estimates in Table 14.6.

The preceding general results have been extended to other functional forms, most commonly

$$\text{Var}[\varepsilon_i] = \sigma^2 (\boldsymbol{\alpha}' \mathbf{z}_i)^2, \tag{14-15}$$

$$\text{Var}[\varepsilon_i] = \sigma^2 \exp(\boldsymbol{\alpha}' \mathbf{z}_i), \tag{14-16}$$

where $\mathbf{z}$ is a set of independent variables that may or may not coincide with $\mathbf{x}$.[14] In (14-15) the standard deviation, rather than the variance, is a linear function of the exogenous variables. In this case, a regression of the absolute values of the residuals on $\mathbf{z}$ provides the

---

[9] Formal analysis may be found in Amemiya (1985).
[10] Jobson and Fuller (1980) prove a somewhat more general version.
[11] This case is analyzed at length in Amemiya (1985, pp. 203–207, and 1977).
[12] See Fomby et al. (1984, pp. 177–186) and Amemiya (1985).
[13] This particular specification, unfortunately, does not preclude negative variances. For these data, none of the predicted variances were negative.
[14] An empirical study employing both of these models is Rutemiller and Bowers (1968).

Table 14.5. OLS Regression Using the Squared OLS Residuals

	Constant	Income	Income^2
Coefficient	59,218.80	161,960	113,663
Standard error	(22,790)	(58,190)	(36,440)
White's SE	(28,170)	(77,000)	(52,225)

Table 14.6. Generalized Least Squares Based on $\text{Var}[\varepsilon] = \sigma^2(\alpha'z)$

	Constant	Income	Income^2
Coefficient	709.05	-1506.40	1374.15
Standard error	(451.9)	(1199.0)	(790.8)

estimates of α required to compute the FGLS.[15] To estimate α in (14–16), we would regress $\ln(e^2)$ on a constant and z.

A special case of (14–14) is a model in which the variance is proportional to the square of the mean:

$$y = x'\beta + \varepsilon,$$
$$\text{Var}[\varepsilon] = \sigma^2[x'\beta]^2. \tag{14–17}$$

This differs from the earlier models in that no secondary regression of the residuals on x is required to estimate the parameters of the variance. We can use the fitted values from the least squares regression (or, if necessary, their absolute values) as the weights for weighted least squares. However, for this case, FGLS is not fully efficient, as β appears in Ω as well as the regression.[16]

EXAMPLE 14.8 Continuing our earlier example, weighted least squares using the absolute values of the fitted values from the first regression produces the results given in Table 14.7.

In model (14–16), if the variables in z are logs, the model is equivalent to

$$\sigma_i^2 = \sigma^2 \Pi_m z_{im}^{\alpha_m}.$$

A special case, with a single variable, is

$$\sigma_i^2 = \sigma^2 z_i^\alpha. \tag{14–18}$$

---

[15] The estimator was devised by Glesjer (1969). Harvey (1974) shows that this estimator is consistent for $c\alpha$, where c is a constant that depends on the distribution of ε_i. This implies that the matrix Ω is consistently estimated only up to the scale factor, c^2. Since this will fall out of the GLS estimator anyway, the scaling is of no consequence. Additional discussion may be found in Amemiya (1985).

[16] See Theil (1971), Prais and Houthakker (1955), and Amemiya (1973). Amemiya examines maximum likelihood estimation in a model in which FGLS is efficient in spite of this complication.

Table 14.7. WLS with the Variance
Proportional to the Square of the Mean

	Constant	Income	Income^2
Coefficient	591.08	−1195.15	1172.22
Standard error	(371.0)	(981.2)	(642.7)

Table 14.8. Regression of $\ln e^2$ on a
Constant, Income, Income^2

	Constant	Income	Income^2
Coefficient	21.858	−44.277	30.863
Standard error	(16.04)	(40.63)	(25.44)

Table 14.9. WLS Regression Based on
$\ln \sigma_i^2 = \ln \sigma^2 + \Sigma_m \alpha_m z_m$

	Constant	Income	Income^2
Coefficient	488.43	−912.69	980.71
Standard error	(529.1)	(1423.0)	(950.3)

If $\alpha = 0$, the disturbance is homoscedastic.[17] The models in Example 14.6 are special cases with α equal to one and two. For this model, the regression used to estimate the variances is

$$\log e_i^2 \simeq \log \sigma^2 + \alpha' z_i + v_i. \tag{14–19}$$

EXAMPLE 14.9. We use (14–19) to specify the variance of the disturbance in Example 14.1. The regression of the log of the squared residual on a constant, income, and income squared is given in Table 14.8.

Then the WLS regression, where estimated variances are the exponents of the fitted values from the previous regression, is shown in Table 14.9. With this specification, the estimated standard errors of the coefficients have become quite large. However, as before, although neither coefficient is statistically significant by the usual test, the Wald statistic for testing their joint significance is 39.291, which far exceeds the tabled critical value of 9.210 for a size of 1 percent.

14.4.2. Maximum Likelihood Estimation

The log-likelihood function for a sample of normally distributed observations would be

$$\ln L = -\frac{n}{2}\ln(2\pi) - \frac{1}{2}\sum_i \left[\ln \sigma_i^2 + \frac{1}{\sigma_i^2}(y_i - \beta' x_i)^2\right]. \tag{14–20}$$

---

[17] See Park (1966).

This can, in principle, be maximized directly, for example, using one of the methods discussed in Chapter 12. This is likely to be rather involved for most very general models. But if the variance function is relatively uncomplicated, a simple search procedure may simplify things considerably.

EXAMPLE 14.10.   Consider maximum likelihood estimation of the model in $(14-18)$.[18] In this case,

$$\sigma_i^2 = \sigma^2 z_i^\alpha$$

involves only a single new parameter whose value will probably fall in a reasonably small range, say, zero to three. For this model,

$$\ln L = -\frac{n}{2}[\ln(2\pi) + \ln \sigma^2] - \frac{\alpha}{2}\sum_i \ln z_i - \frac{1}{2\sigma^2}\sum_i \frac{\varepsilon_i^2}{z_i^\alpha}$$

$$\frac{\partial \ln L}{\partial \beta} = \sum_i \mathbf{x}_i \frac{\varepsilon_i}{\sigma^2 z_i^\alpha}$$

$$\frac{\partial \ln L}{\partial \sigma^2} = -\frac{n}{2\sigma^2} + \frac{1}{2\sigma^4}\sum_i \frac{\varepsilon_i^2}{z_i^\alpha}$$

$$\frac{\partial \ln L}{\partial \alpha} = -\frac{1}{2}\sum_i \ln z_i + \frac{1}{2\sigma^2}\sum_i \frac{\varepsilon_i^2 \ln z_i}{z_i^\alpha}.$$

For a given value of α, we estimate β and σ^2 by generalized least squares, using, as weights, z_i^α. The maximum of the likelihood function can be found by searching over values of α and choosing the one that, with the associated values of β and σ^2, maximizes the likelihood function.

For the school spending data, the values of the log likelihood for various values of α are as listed in Table 14.10. The maximum is found at $\alpha = 1.0$. (This is a bit surprising. Of course, the value is not invariant to the scaling of z, so this is not entirely accidental. If squared income is omitted from the regression and the entire process is repeated, the maximum

Table 14.10

α	L	
0.	-317.2168	
0.25	-316.7739	
0.50	-316.4442	
0.75	-316.1651	
0.85	-316.1919	
0.95	-316.1683	
0.99	-316.1653	
1.0	-316.1651	(!)
1.01	-316.1652	
1.05	-316.1677	

[18] A recent empirical study using this model is Lahiri and Egy (1981).

likelihood estimator of α is 4.3.) Denoting the full parameter vector by γ, we use

$$-E\left[\frac{\partial^2 \ln L}{\partial \gamma \partial \gamma'}\right]^{-1} = \begin{bmatrix} (1/\sigma^2)\sum_i x_i x_i'/z_i^\alpha & 0 & 0 \\ 0' & n/2\sigma^4 & (1/2\sigma^2)\sum_i \ln z_i \\ 0' & (1/2\sigma^2)\sum_i \ln z_i & (1/2)\sum_i(\ln z_i)^2 \end{bmatrix}^{-1}$$

to estimate the asymptotic covariance matrix for the maximum likelihood estimator. The sample estimate is

$$\begin{array}{llll} 107{,}714. & & & \\ -276{,}195. & 713{,}744. & & \\ 173{,}694. & -452{,}387. & 289{,}132. & \\ 0 & 0 & 0. & 1{,}714{,}030. \\ 0 & 0 & 0 & 1{,}771.33 \quad 2.24048. \end{array}$$

The square roots of the diagonal elements give the estimated asymptotic standard errors. The full set of maximum likelihood estimates is given in Table 14.11. This suggests that the optimal specification holds that the standard deviation of the disturbance is proportional to income.

We now consider more general models of heteroscedasticity. For simplicity, let

$$\sigma_i^2 = \sigma^2 f_i(\theta), \tag{14-21}$$

where θ is the vector of unknown parameters in Ω and $f_i(\theta)$ is indexed by i to indicate that it is a function of z_i. Assume, as well, that no elements of β appear in θ. The log-likelihood function becomes

$$\ln L = -\frac{n}{2}[\ln(2\pi) + \ln \sigma^2] - \frac{1}{2}\sum_i \ln f_i(\theta) - \frac{1}{2\sigma^2}\sum_i \left[\frac{1}{f_i(\theta)}\right](y_i - \beta'x_i)^2. \tag{14-22}$$

For convenience in what follows, substitute ε_i for $(y_i - \beta'x_i)$, denote $f_i(\theta)$ as just f_i and denote the vector of derivatives, $\partial f_i(\theta)/\partial \theta$, as g_i. Then the derivatives of the log-likelihood function are

$$\frac{\partial \ln L}{\partial \beta} = \sum_i x_i \frac{\varepsilon_i}{\sigma^2 f_i}$$

$$\frac{\partial \ln L}{\partial \sigma^2} = -\frac{n}{2\sigma^2} + \frac{1}{2\sigma^4}\sum_i \frac{\varepsilon_i^2}{f_i} \tag{14-23}$$

$$\frac{\partial \ln L}{\partial \theta} = -\frac{1}{2}\sum_i g_i \frac{1}{f_i} + \frac{1}{2\sigma^2}\sum_i g_i \frac{\varepsilon_i^2}{f_i^2}$$

$$= \frac{1}{2}\sum_i \left(\frac{\varepsilon_i^2}{\sigma^2 f_i} - 1\right)\frac{1}{f_i} g_i.$$

Since $E[\varepsilon_i] = 0$ and $E[\varepsilon_i^2] = \sigma^2 f_i$, it is clear that all derivatives have expectation zero, as required. The maximum likelihood estimators are those values of β, σ^2, and θ that simultaneously equate these derivatives to zero. The equations are generally highly nonlinear and will often require an iterative solution.

Note that the necessary conditions are identical to those for generalized least squares if θ is known. Likewise, for a given value of θ, the necessary condition for σ^2 gives the

Table 14.11

	Estimate	Standard Error	t Ratio
Constant	746.35	328.2	2.27
Income	-1612.25	844.8	-1.91
Income^2	1447.46	537.7	2.69
σ^2	2800.06	1307.8	2.14
α	1.0	1.496	0.669

familiar prescription, $1/n$ times the normalized sum of squared residuals. At the same time, conditioned on current values of β and σ^2, the third set of first-order conditions is a set of nonlinear equations whose solution will depend on the problem at hand. We consider two examples.

The information matrix for this model is obtained as follows:

$$E\left[\frac{\partial^2 \ln L}{\partial \beta \partial \beta'}\right] = E\left[-\sum_i \frac{1}{\sigma^2 f_i} x_i x_i'\right] = -\frac{1}{\sigma^2} X' \Omega^{-1} X,$$

$$E\left[\frac{\partial^2 \ln L}{\partial (\sigma^2)^2}\right] = E\left[\frac{n}{2\sigma^4} - \frac{1}{\sigma^6}\sum_i \frac{\varepsilon_i^2}{f_i}\right] = -\frac{n}{2\sigma^4}$$

$$E\left[\frac{\partial^2 \ln L}{\partial \sigma^2 \partial \beta}\right] = E\left[-\frac{1}{\sigma^4}\sum_i \frac{\varepsilon_i}{f_i} x_i\right] = 0$$

$$E\left[\frac{\partial^2 \ln L}{\partial \theta \partial \beta'}\right] = E\left[\sum_i \frac{-\varepsilon_i}{\sigma^2/f_i^2} g_i x_i'\right] = 0$$

$$E\left[\frac{\partial^2 \ln L}{\partial \sigma^2 \partial \theta}\right] = E\left[\frac{1}{2\sigma^4}\sum_i \frac{-\varepsilon_i^2}{f_i^2} g_i\right] = \frac{1}{2\sigma^2}\sum_i \frac{1}{f_i} g_i.$$

To obtain $E[\partial^2 \ln L/\partial \theta \partial \theta']$, let

$$\frac{\partial \ln L}{\partial \theta} = \frac{1}{2}\sum_i c_i r_i,$$

where

$$c_i = \left[\frac{\varepsilon_i^2}{\sigma^2 f_i} - 1\right]$$

and

$$r_i = \frac{1}{f_i} g_i.$$

Thus, $E[c_i] = 0$ and r_i is nonstochastic. Then

$$E\left[\frac{\partial^2 \ln L}{\partial \theta \partial \theta'}\right] = E\left[\frac{1}{2}\sum_i \left(c_i \frac{\partial r_i}{\partial \theta'} + r_i \frac{\partial c_i}{\partial \theta'}\right)\right].$$

The first term has expectation **0**, so

$$E\left[\frac{\partial^2 \ln L}{\partial\theta\partial\theta'}\right] = E\left[\frac{1}{2}\sum_i r_i \frac{\partial c_i}{\partial\theta'}\right]$$

$$= E\left[\frac{1}{2}\sum_i r_i \frac{\varepsilon_i^2}{\sigma^2}\left(\frac{-1}{f_i^2}g_i'\right)\right]$$

$$= -\frac{1}{2}\sum_i \frac{1}{f_i^2}g_i g_i'.$$

Let **G** be the $n \times M$ matrix whose ith row is $\partial f_i/\partial\theta'$, and let **i** be an $n \times 1$ column vector of ones. From (14–21), Ω is a diagonal matrix with ith diagonal element equal to f_i. The asymptotic covariance matrix for the maximum likelihood estimator in this model is, therefore,

$$-E\left[\frac{\partial^2 \ln L}{\partial\gamma\partial\gamma'}\right]^{-1} = \begin{bmatrix} (1/\sigma^2)X'\Omega^{-1}X & 0 & 0 \\ 0' & n/2\sigma^4 & (1/2\sigma^2)i'\Omega^{-1}G \\ 0' & (1/2\sigma^2)G'\Omega^{-1}i & (1/2)G'\Omega^{-2}G \end{bmatrix}^{-1}, \quad (14\text{–}24)$$

where $\gamma' = [\beta', \sigma^2, \theta']$. For computational purposes, an alternative estimator of the asymptotic covariance matrix for the MLE can be obtained using the Berndt et al. estimator.[19] For this model, we would insert our MLEs in

$$\hat{V} = \left[\sum_i \hat{\delta}_i \hat{\delta}_i'\right]^{-1}$$

where

$$\delta_i = \begin{bmatrix} x_i \dfrac{\varepsilon_i}{\sigma^2 f_i} \\[2ex] \dfrac{1}{2\sigma^2}\left(\dfrac{\varepsilon_i^2}{\sigma^2 f_i} - 1\right) \\[2ex] \dfrac{1}{2f_i}\left(\dfrac{\varepsilon_i^2}{\sigma^2 f_i} - 1\right)g_i \end{bmatrix}. \quad (14\text{–}25)$$

This may be a bit easier to compute than the Hessian. Both estimators are valid asymptotically.

A second method of maximizing the log likelihood is the procedure proposed by Oberhofer and Kmenta (1974). Solving the full set of likelihood equations simultaneously is likely to be extremely difficult. But, as we have seen, for given values of the variance parameters, the solutions for β and σ^2 are the GLS estimators. It may also be possible to solve the first-order conditions for θ for a given set of values for β and σ^2 relatively straightforwardly. In this model, this "zig-zag" procedure will be a valid means of finding maximum likelihood estimates.

EXAMPLE 14.11. Multiplicative Heteroscedasticity. Suppose that

$$\sigma_i^2 = \sigma^2 \exp(\alpha'z_i).[20] \quad (14\text{–}26)$$

---

[19] See Section 4.5.2, (4–52).
[20] This model is analyzed at length by Godfrey (1978).

Then the log likelihood is

$$\ln L = -\frac{n}{2}[\ln(2\pi) + \ln \sigma^2] - \frac{1}{2}\sum_i \ln(\exp(\alpha'z_i)) - \frac{1}{2\sigma^2}\sum_i \frac{\varepsilon_i^2}{\exp(\alpha'z_i)}. \tag{14-27}$$

With an estimate of α in hand, the efficient estimators of β and σ^2 are the usual GLS estimators. We can obtain a consistent estimate of α with which to begin the iterations by regressing the logs of the squared residuals on a constant and z.[21] The first iteration, then, is GLS based on these estimates.[22]

With estimates of β and σ^2 in hand, the likelihood equation for α is

$$\frac{\partial \ln L}{\partial \alpha} = \frac{-1}{2}\sum_i \left(\frac{\varepsilon_i^2}{\sigma^2 \exp(\alpha'z_i)} - 1\right)z_i = 0. \tag{14-28}$$

These equations, while nonlinear, are relatively straightforward to solve. One way to proceed would be to use Newton's method. Given the current value, α_t, find the next value by the iteration

$$\alpha_{t+1} = \alpha_t - H_t^{-1}g_t, \tag{14-29}$$

where g_t is $\partial \ln L/\partial \alpha$ and H is the Hessian:

$$H = \frac{-1}{2}\sum_i \left(\frac{\varepsilon_i^2}{\sigma^2 \exp(\alpha'z_i)}\right)z_i z_i'$$

$$= -\left(\frac{1}{2}\right)Z'AZ, \tag{14-30}$$

where

$$A = \mathrm{diag}\left[\frac{\varepsilon_i^2}{\sigma^2 \exp(\alpha'z_i)}\right].$$

Since H is always negative definite, the function is globally concave in α, given β and σ^2; Newton's method is guaranteed to find the solution. By this procedure, we find the α that maximizes the likelihood function for the given β and σ^2. Note that this is an iteration within an iteration. Having found the values for α, we can now recompute the GLS estimators and then reenter the iteration for the next α. We continue this back-and-forth procedure until β and α are no longer changing.

The OLS regression used at the outset to obtain the initial estimate of α does not provide a solution to (14-28) and hence will not converge to the MLE. There is, however, a related aspect of the problem that is revealing. An alternative to Newton's method is the *method of scoring*, which replaces H in (14-29) with $E[H]$. The expected value of the term in parentheses in (14-30) is one, so $E[H] = -(\frac{1}{2})Z'Z$. Therefore, the iteration in the method of scoring is

$$\alpha_{t+1} - \alpha_t = \Delta_t$$

$$= [Z'Z]^{-1}\left[\sum_i z_i\left(\frac{\varepsilon_i^2}{\sigma^2 \exp(\alpha'z_i)} - 1\right)\right] \tag{14-31}$$

$$= [Z'Z]^{-1}Z'w,$$

[21] The constant term in this regression is an estimate, unfortunately inconsistent, of σ^2. See Judge et al. (1985, pp. 439–441) and Godfrey (1978).

[22] Although it is not the maximum likelihood estimator, this two-step estimator is asymptotically efficient. We could stop here.

where $w_i = [\varepsilon_i^2/(\sigma^2 \exp(\mathbf{\alpha}'\mathbf{z}_i)) - 1]$.[23] Therefore, the iteration does involve a least squares regression. However, it is the correction factor that is obtained by least squares, and the dependent variable is not $\ln \varepsilon_i^2$ but $[\varepsilon_i^2/(\sigma^2 \exp(\mathbf{\alpha}'\mathbf{z}_i)) - 1]$. At the maximum of the likelihood function, the term $\mathbf{Z}'\mathbf{w}$ in Δ_t will be zero, as it is $\partial \ln L/\partial \mathbf{\alpha}$.

This model has been analyzed extensively by a number of authors. In spite of its analytic simplicity, the maximum likelihood estimators are still found to be more cumbersome than the FGLS estimators that have been proposed.[24]

14.5. Autoregressive Conditional Heteroscedasticity

Heteroscedasticity is usually associated with cross-sectional data, while time series are typically studied in the context of homoscedastic processes. In analyses of macroeconomic data, Engle (1982 and 1983) and Cragg (1982) have found evidence that for some phenomena the disturbance variances in time-series models are less stable than usually assumed.

Engle's results suggest that in analyzing models of inflation, large and small forecast errors appear to occur in clusters, suggesting a form of heteroscedasticity in which the variance of the forecast error depends on the size of the preceding disturbance. He has suggested the AutoRegressive, Conditionally Heteroscedastic, or ARCH, model as an alternative to the usual time-series process. A simple version of his model is

$$y_t = \mathbf{\beta}'\mathbf{x}_t + \varepsilon_t$$
$$\varepsilon_t = u_t[\alpha^0 + \alpha^1\varepsilon_{t-1}^2]^{1/2}, \tag{14-32}$$

where u_t is standard normal.[25] It follows that

$$E[\varepsilon_t | \varepsilon_{t-1}] = 0,$$

so

$$E[\varepsilon_t] = 0 \qquad \text{and} \qquad E[y_t] = \mathbf{\beta}'\mathbf{x}_t.$$

Also,

$$\begin{aligned} \text{Var}[\varepsilon_t | \varepsilon_{t-1}] &= E[\varepsilon_t^2 | \varepsilon_{t-1}] \\ &= E[u_t^2][\alpha^0 + \alpha^1\varepsilon_{t-1}^2] \\ &= \alpha^0 + \alpha^1\varepsilon_{t-1}^2 \\ &= \text{Var}[y_t | y_{t-1}]. \end{aligned}$$

Conditional on ε_{t-1}, ε_t is heteroscedastic. The *unconditional* variance of ε_t is[26]

$$\begin{aligned} \text{Var}[\varepsilon_t] &= E[\text{Var}[\varepsilon_t | \varepsilon_{t-1}]] \\ &= \alpha^0 + \alpha^1 E[\varepsilon_{t-1}^2] \\ &= \alpha^0 + \alpha^1 \text{Var}[\varepsilon_{t-1}]. \end{aligned}$$

---

[23] Harvey [1976, pp. 461–465, eq. (14)]. Harvey also presents some further refinements of this method.
[24] See Harvey (1974), Judge et al. (1985), and Just and Pope (1978).
[25] The assumption that u_t has unit variance is not a restriction. The scaling implied by any other variance would be absorbed by the other parameters.
[26] We are using the variance decomposition in (3–70). The variance of $E[\varepsilon_t | \varepsilon_{t-1}]$ is zero.

If the process generating the disturbances is **variance stationary**,[27] the unconditional variance is unchanging over time. Then,

$$
\begin{aligned}
\mathrm{Var}[\varepsilon_t] &= \mathrm{Var}[\varepsilon_{t-1}] \\
&= \alpha^0 + \alpha^1 \mathrm{Var}[\varepsilon_{t-1}] \\
&= \frac{\alpha^0}{1 - \alpha^1}.
\end{aligned}
\tag{14-33}
$$

Therefore, the model obeys the classical assumptions, and ordinary least squares is the most efficient *linear* estimator of β.

But there is a more efficient *nonlinear* estimator. The log-likelihood function for this model is given by Engle (1982). Conditioned on starting values y_0 and x_0, the log likelihood for observations $t = 1, \ldots, T$ is

$$
\ln L = -\frac{1}{2} \sum_t \ln(\alpha^0 + \alpha^1 \varepsilon_{t-1}^2) - \frac{1}{2} \sum_t \frac{\varepsilon_t^2}{\alpha^0 + \alpha^1 \varepsilon_{t-1}^2},
\tag{14-34}
$$

where

$$
\varepsilon_t = y_t - \beta' x_t.
$$

Maximization of $\ln L$ may be done by conventional methods. However, a simpler, four-step FGLS estimator is available.[28] Let the sample consist of y_t and x_t for $t = 0, 1, \ldots, T$, including the initial values.

1. Regress **y** on **X**, using least squares and all available observations to obtain **b** and **e**.
2. Regress e_t^2 on a constant and e_{t-1}^2 to obtain initial estimates of α^0 and α^1, using the T observations $t = 1, \ldots, T$. Notice that this is the same procedure we have used in several other FGLS procedures to estimate the variance parameters consistently. Denote the 2×1 estimated vector as $[a^0, a^1]' = \mathbf{a}$.
3. Compute $f_t = a^0 + a^1 e_{t-1}^2$ for $t = 1, \ldots, T$. Then compute the asymptotically efficient estimate

$$
\hat{\boldsymbol{\alpha}} = \mathbf{a} + \mathbf{d}_\alpha,
$$

where $\mathbf{d}_\alpha$ is the least squares coefficient vector in the regression of $[(e_t^2/f_t) - 1)]$ on $(1/f_t)$ and (e_{t-1}^2/f_t). The asymptotic covariance matrix for $\hat{\boldsymbol{\alpha}}$ is $2(\mathbf{Z}'\mathbf{Z})^{-1}$, where $\mathbf{Z}$ is the regressor matrix in this regression.[29]
4. Recompute f_t, using $\hat{\boldsymbol{\alpha}}$; then, for observations $t = 1, \ldots, T-1$, compute

$$
r_t = \left[\frac{1}{f_t} + 2\left(\frac{\hat{\alpha}^1 e_t}{f_{t+1}} \right)^2 \right]^{1/2}
$$

and

$$
s_t = \frac{1}{f_t} - \frac{\hat{\alpha}^1}{f_{t+1}} \left(\frac{e_{t+1}^2}{f_{t+1}} - 1 \right).
$$

---

[27] We shall treat this concept in more detail in Chapters 15 and 18.
[28] See Engle (1982) and Judge et al. (1985, pp. 441–444).
[29] This procedure is based on the method of scoring. Note the similarity of this step to the analogous step in Example 14.11.

Compute the estimate

$$\hat{\beta} = b + d_\beta,$$

where d_β is the least squares coefficient vector in the regression of $e_t s_t / r_t$ on $x_t r_t$. The asymptotic covariance matrix for $\hat{\beta}$ is $(W'W)^{-1}$, where W is the regressor matrix used in this regression.

This procedure is asymptotically equivalent to maximum likelihood. It is possible to iterate by returning to step 2 with new residuals calculated after step 4, but this brings no gains in efficiency and does not draw the procedure to the true maximum likelihood estimate. (Step 2 is not the solution to the likelihood equation for α.) One possible refinement of the model would be to add further lags in the ARCH process. The modification of the estimation process is minor; the regression in step 2 and the computation of f_t are extended by adding the additional lags of e_t^2.[30]

EXAMPLE 14.12. ARCH Process for the Rate of Inflation.   The annual percentage rate of increase in the U.S. Consumer Price Index by year from 1940 to 1986 is listed in Table 14.12.[31]

Table 14.12

1940	1.0	1950	5.8	1960	1.5	1970	5.5	1980	12.4
1941	9.7	1951	5.9	1961	0.7	1971	3.4	1981	8.9
1942	9.3	1952	0.9	1962	1.2	1972	3.4	1982	3.9
1943	3.2	1953	0.6	1963	1.6	1973	8.8	1983	3.8
1944	2.1	1954	-0.5	1964	1.2	1974	12.2	1984	4.0
1945	2.3	1955	0.4	1965	1.9	1975	7.0	1985	3.8
1946	18.2	1956	2.9	1966	3.4	1976	4.8	1986	1.1
1947	9.0	1957	3.0	1967	3.0	1977	6.8		
1948	2.7	1958	1.8	1968	4.7	1978	9.0		
1949	-1.8	1959	1.5	1969	6.1	1979	13.3		

We shall use these data and the four-step method outlined earlier to fit the ARCH model:

$$\Delta p_t = \beta_1 + \beta_2 \Delta p_{t-1} + \varepsilon_t$$

$$\varepsilon_t = u_t [\alpha^0 + \alpha^1 \varepsilon_{t-1}^2]^{1/2}.$$

Where appropriate, standard errors are given in parentheses below the estimates.

1. Regression of Δp_t on a constant and Δp_{t-1} for 1941–1986:

$$\Delta p_t = \underset{(0.8082)}{2.34625} + \underset{(0.1307)}{0.4968 \, \Delta p_{t-1}}$$

2. Regression of the squared residual on a constant and the lagged squared residual:

$$e_t^2 = 12.0453 - 0.031778 e_{t-1}^2$$

$$R^2 = 0.0014, \qquad T = 45.$$

---

[30] See Bollerslev (1986) for a discussion and some further generalizations.
[31] Data are from the 1987 *Economic Report of the President*, p. 312.

3. The correction to be applied to the preceding estimates is

$$\mathbf{d}_\alpha = [-0.02867, \quad 0.0019644],$$

which gives $\hat{\alpha}$. Then

$$e_t^2 = 12.0166 \ - \ 0.03374 e_{t-1}^2$$
$$(2.6248) - (0.03662).$$

4. The correction to the parameters, and updated values are

$$\mathbf{d}_\beta = [-0.034052, \quad -0.018355]$$

$$\Delta p_t = 2.31220 + 0.47844 \, \Delta p_{t-1}$$
$$(0.7553) + (0.1071).$$

The change that results from estimating according to the ARCH model is relatively small—compare step 4 to step 1. This was to be expected in view of the insignificant results at step 3.

Engle also presents a Lagrange multiplier test for the ARCH process against the null hypothesis that the disturbance is conditionally homoscedastic. The statistic is T times the R^2 in the regression at step 2. This is asymptotically distributed as chi-squared with one degree of freedom.[32] For the inflation data used in the example, the chi-squared value is 0.0468, which is far from statistically significant.

14.6. Testing for Heteroscedasticity

Heteroscedasticity poses potentially severe problems for inferences based on least squares. However, one can rarely be certain that the data are heteroscedastic (and, unfortunately, what form the heteroscedasticity takes if they are). As such, it is useful to be able to test for homoscedasticity and modify our procedures accordingly if necessary.[33] Several types of tests have been suggested. They can be roughly grouped in descending order in terms of their generality and, as might be expected, in ascending order in terms of their power.[34]

14.6.1. White's General Test

In order to formulate most of the available tests, it is necessary to specify, at least in rough terms, the nature of the heteroscedasticity. It would be desirable to be able to test a general hypothesis of the form

$$H_0: \sigma_i^2 = \sigma^2,$$

$$H_1: \text{Not } H_0.$$

---

[32] For a model with additional lags, the statistic would be based on the multiple regression and would have one degree of freedom for each lag.

[33] In Section 8.5, we considered the problems of pretest estimators. In the current context, the issue is the possibility that a preliminary test for heteroscedasticity will incorrectly lead us to use weighted least squares or fail to alert us to heteroscedasticity and lead us improperly to use least squares. The situation is rather more favorable here, as both estimators are consistent in both settings. Some limited results for the case of heteroscedasticity are given by Ohtani and Toyoda (1980). Their results suggest that it is best to test first for heteroscedasticity rather than merely to assume that it is present.

[34] A recent study that examines the power of several tests for heteroscedasticity is Ali and Giaccotto (1984).

In view of our earlier finding on the difficulty of estimation in a model with n unknown parameters, this is rather ambitious. Nonetheless, such a test has been devised by White (1980). The correct covariance matrix for the least squares estimator is

$$\text{Var}[\mathbf{b}] = \sigma^2 [\mathbf{X'X}]^{-1}(\mathbf{X'\Omega X})[\mathbf{X'X}]^{-1}, \tag{14-35}$$

which, as we have seen, can be estimated by

$$\text{Est. Var}[\mathbf{b}] = [\mathbf{X'X}]^{-1}\left[\sum_i e_i^2 \mathbf{x}_i \mathbf{x}_i'\right][\mathbf{X'X}]^{-1}. \tag{14-36}$$

The conventional estimator is

$$\mathbf{V} = s^2 [\mathbf{X'X}]^{-1}. \tag{14-37}$$

If there is no heteroscedasticity, (14–37) will give a consistent estimator of $\text{Var}[\mathbf{b}]$, while if there is, it will not. White has devised a statistical test based on this observation. A simple operational version of his test is carried out by obtaining nR^2 in the regression of e_i^2 on a constant and all unique variables in $\mathbf{x} \otimes \mathbf{x}$. The statistic is asymptotically distributed as chi-squared with $P - 1$ degrees of freedom, where P is the number of regressors in the regression.

EXAMPLE 14.13.   For the expenditure data of Example 14.1, the regression of the squares of the least squares residuals on a constant, income, and income squared, cubed, and to the fourth power produces an R^2 of 0.42314. The chi-squared statistic is, therefore, $50(0.42314) = 21.157$, which is highly significant.

This seems to be at odds with the maximum likelihood estimates of Example 14.10. Indeed, those results argue in favor of a homoscedastic model. One explanation may be that the simple specification of the example, which excludes income squared from the variance function, may be overly restrictive. The model of Example 14.11 may be more appropriate.

The White test is extremely general. In order to carry it out, we need not make any specific assumptions about the nature of the heteroscedasticity. Although this is a virtue, it is, at the same time, a potentially serious shortcoming. The test may reveal heteroscedasticity, but it may instead simply identify some other specification error (such as the omission of x^2 from a simple regression).[35] Except in the context of a specific problem, little can be said about the power of this test; it may be very low against some alternatives. In addition, unlike some of the other tests we shall discuss, the White test is *nonconstructive*. If we reject the hypothesis of homoscedasticity, the result of the test gives no indication of what to do next.

14.6.2. The Goldfeld–Quandt Test

By narrowing our focus somewhat, we can obtain a more powerful test. Two tests that are relatively general are the Goldfeld–Quandt (1965) test and the Breusch–Pagan (1979) Lagrange multiplier test.

For the Goldfeld–Quandt test, we assume that the observations can be divided into two groups in such a way that under the hypothesis of homoscedasticity, the disturbance variances would be the same in the two groups, while under the alternative, the disturbance variances would differ systematically. The most favorable case for this test would be the groupwise heteroscedastic model of Example 14.5 or a model such as $\sigma_i^2 = \sigma^2 x_i^2$ for some variable, x. By ranking the observations based on this x, we can separate the observations

---

[35] Thursby (1982) considers this issue in detail.

into those with high and low variances. The test is applied by dividing the sample into two groups with n_1 and n_2 observations. In order to obtain statistically independent variance estimators, the regression is then estimated separately with the two sets of observations. The test statistic is

$$F[n_1 - K, n_2 - K] = \frac{s_1^2}{s_2^2},$$

where we assume that the disturbance variance is larger in the first sample. (If not, reverse the subscripts.) Under the null hypothesis of homoscedasticity, this has an F distribution with $n_1 - K$ and $n_2 - K$ degrees of freedom. The sample value can be referred to the standard F table to carry out the test, with a large value leading to rejection of the null hypothesis.

In order to increase the power of the test, Goldfeld and Quandt suggest that a number of observations in the middle of the sample be omitted. However, the more observations are dropped, the smaller will be the degrees of freedom for estimation in each group, which will tend to diminish the power of the test. As a consequence, the choice of how many central observations to drop is largely subjective. Evidence by Harvey and Phillips (1974) suggests that no more than a third of the observations should be dropped. If the disturbances are normally distributed, the Goldfeld–Quandt statistic is exactly distributed as F under the null hypothesis, and the nominal size of the test is correct. If not, it will have an F distribution only in large samples.

EXAMPLE 14.14.   Goldfeld–Quandt Test.   We sort the expenditure data of Example 14.1 on the basis of income and then fit separate regressions for observations 1–17 and 35–51. The sums of squared residuals in the two regressions are 27096.50 and 52685.18, so the test statistic is

$$F[15, 15] = \frac{52,685.18/15}{27,096.50/15}$$

$$= 1.944.$$

The 5 percent critical value from the F table is 2.40, so we would not reject the hypothesis of homoscedasticity at this level of significance on the basis of this test. Based on a simple 25/25 split of the sample, the sums of squares are 44,598.68 and 85,526.35, giving an $F[22, 22]$ of 1.918. The 5 percent critical value is 2.048, so this is insignificant as well.

14.6.3.   The Breusch–Pagan/Godfrey Test

The Goldfeld–Quandt test has been found to be reasonably powerful when we are able to identify correctly the variable to use in the sample separation. However, this requirement does limit its generality. For example, several of the models we considered earlier allow the disturbance variance to vary with a set of regressors. [See (14–14) to (14–17).] Breusch and Pagan[36] have devised a Lagrange multiplier test of the hypothesis that $\sigma_i^2 = \sigma^2 f(\alpha^0 + \alpha' z_i)$, where z is a vector of exogenous variables. The model is homoscedastic if $\alpha = 0$.

The test can be carried out with a simple regression.

$$LM = \frac{1}{2} \text{explained sum of squares}$$

$$\text{in the regression of } \frac{e_i^2}{e'e/n} \text{ on } z. \tag{14–38}$$

---

[36] Op. cit.

Under the null hypothesis of homoscedasticity, LM is asymptotically distributed as chi-squared with degrees of freedom equal to the number of variables in **z**. This test can be applied to a variety of models, including, for example, those we examined earlier in (14–14) to (14–17).[37]

It has been argued that the Breusch–Pagan Lagrange multiplier test is quite sensitive to the assumption of normality. Koenkar (1981) and Koenkar and Basset (1982) suggest that the denominator in LM be replaced with a more robust estimator of the variance of ε_i^2,

$$V = \frac{1}{n}\sum_i \left(e_i^2 - \frac{e'e}{n}\right)^2.$$

(The variance of ε_i^2 is not necessarily equal to $2\sigma^4$ if ε_i is not normally distributed.) Under normality, this modified statistic will have the same asymptotic distribution as the Breusch–Pagan statistic, but absent normality, there is some evidence that it provides a more powerful test. Waldman (1983) has shown that if the variables in **z** are the same as those used for the White test described earlier, the two tests are algebraically the same.

EXAMPLE 14.15.   For the school spending data, the Breusch–Pagan Lagrange multiplier statistic and the corrected version of Koenkar and Basset are 18.912 and 7.916, respectively.[38] These are both statistically significant. The results thus far are mixed. Most of the tests strongly suggest that the disturbance is heteroscedastic, with the Goldfeld–Quandt test standing as an exception and the maximum likelihood estimates of Example 14.10 apparently arguing (though not particularly forcefully) against heteroscedasticity.

14.6.4.   Testing for Groupwise Heteroscedasticity

The more specific we can be about the form of the heteroscedasticity, the more powerful a test we can devise. For example, for the groupwise heteroscedasticity model of Example 14.5, under normality the likelihood ratio test will be a most powerful consistent test. The log-likelihood function, assuming homoscedasticity, is

$$\ln L_0 = -\frac{n}{2}(\ln(2\pi) + \ln \sigma^2) - \frac{1}{2\sigma^2}\sum_i \varepsilon_i^2,$$

where $n = \sum_g n_g$ is the total number of observations. Under the alternative hypothesis of heteroscedasticity,

$$\ln L_1 = -\frac{n}{2}\ln(2\pi) - \frac{1}{2}\sum_g n_g \ln \sigma_g^2 - \frac{1}{2}\sum_g \left(\frac{1}{\sigma_g^2}\sum_i \varepsilon_{ig}^2\right).$$

The maximum likelihood estimators of σ^2 and σ_g^2 are

$$s^2 = \frac{e'e}{n} \quad \text{and} \quad s_g^2 = \frac{e_g'e_g}{n_g},$$

respectively. The maximum likelihood estimator of β in Example 13.2 is to be used for the slope vector.[39] If we evaluate $\ln L_0$ and $\ln L_1$ at these estimates, the likelihood ratio test

---

[37] The model $\sigma_i^2 = \sigma^2 \exp(\alpha'z_i)$ is one of these cases. In analyzing this model specifically, Godfrey (1978) derived the same test statistic.

[38] Waldman's result does not apply here because **z** does not contain the third or fourth powers of income.

[39] It has been suggested that for convenience, we may use the OLS slope vectors within each group instead. If the sample is large enough, this will be valid. But in a small sample, if the information that the slope vector is the same in all groups is not used, the power of the test is likely to be reduced.

statistic for homoscedasticity is

$$-2(\ln L_0 - \ln L_1) = n \ln s^2 - \sum_g n_g \ln s_g^2.$$

Under the null hypothesis, the statistic is asymptotically distributed as chi-squared with $G - 1$ degrees of freedom.

In an analysis of variance context, when the only regressor in the model is a constant term and the mean is allowed to differ across groups, the model can be written as

$$y_{ig} = \mu_g + \varepsilon_{ig}.$$

For this specification, the statistics used for the likelihood ratio test are

$$s^2 = \frac{1}{n} \sum_g \sum_i (y_{ig} - \bar{y}_g)^2,$$

$$s_g^2 = \frac{1}{n_g} \sum_i (y_{ig} - \bar{y}_g)^2,$$

where

$$\bar{y}_g = \frac{1}{n_g} \sum_{i=1}^{n_g} y_{ig}.$$

14.6.5. Tests Based on Regressions—Glesjer's Test

Earlier, we considered three specific formulations in the class of models encompassed by the Lagrange multiplier test:

1. $\text{Var}[\varepsilon] = \sigma^2 [\alpha' z]$.
2. $\text{Var}[\varepsilon] = \sigma^2 [\alpha' z]^2$.
3. $\text{Var}[\varepsilon] = \sigma^2 \exp[\alpha' z]$.

In each case, a preliminary regression was computed to estimate α for use in an FGLS estimator of β. A joint test of the hypothesis that the slopes are all zero in each preceding case would be equivalent to a test of homoscedasticity. In particular, let w_i be e_i^2, $|e_i|$, or $\log|e_i|$. A Wald statistic can be used in each model to carry out the test. This would be

$$W = a' \{\text{Var}[a]\}^{-1} a.$$

Under the null hypothesis of homoscedasticity, W is asymptotically distributed as chi-squared with P degrees of freedom, where P is the number of variables in Z, excluding the constant term. The appropriate variance matrix to use will differ in the three models; however, an asymptotically valid expedient would be to use the White estimator in (14–9) (which will now involve the fourth powers of the residuals).[40] Each of these tests is likely to be more powerful than an omnibus test such as White's or Breusch–Pagan's *in the specific context of its regression model.*

EXAMPLE 14.16.   The preceding Wald statistics for the three specifications given, based on White's covariance matrix, are 9.692, 5.678, and 11.096. All are larger than the critical values from the table.

---

[40] See Fomby et al. (1984, pp. 176–187).

14.7. *General Conclusions*

It is rarely possible to be certain about the nature of the heteroscedasticity in a regression model. Still, this is a potentially serious problem that should be examined. With respect to FGLS estimation, the received statistical results are asymptotic, and there is some evidence that in small samples FGLS corrections for heteroscedasticity may do more harm than good. It is an important question whether, in a moderate-sized sample, ordinary least squares is preferable to a possibly incorrectly weighted least squares. In this connection, it sometimes seems that it makes little difference what weighting is used. Different weights seem to produce similar results. Unfortunately, counting on this in a given setting could be a bit risky. Consider the summary of the slope estimates for the school spending regressions that we have computed in the foregoing examples, which is shown in Table 14.13.

There is a large amount of variation in the coefficient estimates. But it is not as substantial as it might appear. If, instead of the coefficient values themselves, we were

Table 14.13

	Constant	Income	Income^2
Ordinary least squares (1)	832.91 (327.3)	−1834.2 (829.0)	1587.04 (519.1)
Weighted least squares Var(ε) = σ^2Income (2)	746.36 (328.2)	−1612.25 (844.8)	1447.46 (537.7)
Var(ε) = σ^2Income^2 (3)	644.58 (333.6)	−1399.28 (872.1)	1311.35 (563.7)
Generalized least squares based on Var[ε] = $\alpha'z$ (4)	709.05 (451.9)	−1506.40 (1199.0)	1374.15 (790.8)
Weighted least squares with the variance proportional to the square of the mean (5)	591.08 (371.0)	−1195.15 (981.2)	1172.22 (642.7)
Weighted least squares regression based on $\ln \sigma_i^2 = \ln \sigma^2 + \Sigma_m \alpha_m z_m$ (6)	488.43 (529.1)	−912.69 (1423.0)	980.71 (950.3)

Table 14.14

Model	γ
(1)	580.818
(2)	590.617
(3)	596.217
(4)	584.661
(5)	588.631
(6)	579.668

interested in

$$\gamma = \frac{\partial \text{Spending}}{\partial \text{Income}} = \beta_2 + 2\beta_3 \text{Income},$$

using mean income of 7608, we would find, for the six models previously estimated, the data listed in Table 14.14. Although there is tremendous variation in the coefficients, the marginal effects computed from the six models are essentially identical. The upshot, of course, is that whether the weighting used in computing the weighted least squares estimates makes a substantial difference or not depends, at least in part, on what we want to estimate.

Exercises

1. Suppose that the regression model is

$$y = \mu + \varepsilon,$$

where

$$E[\varepsilon \,|\, x] = 0, \qquad \text{but } \text{Var}[\varepsilon \,|\, x] = \sigma^2 x^2, \quad x > 0.$$

(a) Given a sample of observations on y and x, what is the most efficient estimator of μ? What is its variance?

(b) What is the OLS estimator of μ, and what is the variance of the ordinary least squares estimator?

(c) Prove that the estimator in part (a) is at least as efficient as the estimator in part (b).

2. For the model in the previous exercise, what is the probability limit of the following?

$$s^2 = \frac{1}{n-1} \sum_i (y_i - \bar{y})^2.$$

Note that this is the least squares estimate of the residual variance. It is also n times the conventional estimator of the variance of the OLS estimator,

$$\text{Est. Var}[\bar{y}] = s^2 (\mathbf{X}'\mathbf{X})^{-1} = \frac{s^2}{n}.$$

How does this compare to the true value you found in part (b) of the previous exercise? Does the conventional estimator produce the correct estimate of the true asymptotic variance of the least squares estimator?

3. Two samples of 50 observations each produce the following moment matrices. (In each case, $\mathbf{X}$ is a constant and one variable.)

	Sample 1	Sample 2
$\mathbf{X}'\mathbf{X}$	$\begin{bmatrix} 50 & 300 \\ 300 & 2100 \end{bmatrix}$	$\begin{bmatrix} 50 & 300 \\ 300 & 2100 \end{bmatrix}$
$\mathbf{y}'\mathbf{X}$	$[300 \quad 2000]$	$[300 \quad 2200]$
$\mathbf{y}'\mathbf{y}$	2100	2800

(a) Compute the least squares regression coefficients and the residual variances, s^2, for each data set. Compute the R^2 for each regression.

(b) Compute the OLS estimate of the coefficient vector, assuming that the coefficients and disturbance variances are the same in the two regressions. Also, compute the estimate of the asymptotic covariance matrix of the estimate.

(c) Test the hypothesis that the variances in the two regressions are the same without assuming that the coefficients are the same in the two regressions.

(d) Compute the two-step FGLS estimator of the coefficients in the regression, assuming that the constant and slope are the same in both regressions. Compute the estimate of the covariance matrix and compare it to the result of part (b).

4. Using the data in the previous exercise, use the Oberhofer–Kmenta method to compute the maximum likelihood estimate of the common coefficient vector.

5. This exercise is based on the following data set:

\multicolumn{9}{c}{50 observations on Y}								
−1.42	2.75	2.10	−5.08	1.49	1.00	0.16	−1.11	1.66
−0.26	−4.87	5.94	2.21	−6.87	0.90	1.61	2.11	−3.82
−0.62	7.01	26.14	7.39	0.79	1.93	1.97	−23.17	−2.52
−1.26	−0.15	3.41	−5.45	1.31	1.52	2.04	3.00	6.31
5.51	−15.22	−1.47	−1.48	6.66	1.78	2.62	−5.16	−4.71
−0.35	−0.48	1.24	0.69	1.91				

\multicolumn{9}{c}{50 observations on X_1}								
−1.65	1.48	0.77	0.67	0.68	0.23	−0.40	−1.13	0.15
−0.63	0.34	0.35	0.79	0.77	−1.04	0.28	0.58	−0.41
−1.78	1.25	0.22	1.25	−0.12	0.66	1.06	−0.66	−1.18
−0.80	−1.32	0.16	1.06	−0.60	0.79	0.86	2.04	−0.51
0.02	0.33	−1.99	0.70	−0.17	0.33	0.48	1.90	−0.18
−0.18	−1.62	0.39	0.17	1.02				

\multicolumn{9}{c}{50 observations on X_2}								
−0.67	0.70	0.32	2.88	−0.19	−1.28	−2.72	−0.70	−1.55
−0.74	−1.87	1.56	0.37	−2.07	1.20	0.26	−1.34	−2.10
0.61	2.32	4.38	2.16	1.51	0.30	−0.17	7.82	−1.15
1.77	2.92	−1.94	2.09	1.50	−0.46	0.19	−0.39	1.54
1.87	−3.45	−.88	−1.53	1.42	−2.70	1.77	−1.89	−1.85
2.01	1.26	−2.02	1.91	−2.23				

(a) Compute the ordinary least squares regression of Y on a constant, X_1, and X_2. Be sure to compute the conventional estimator of the asymptotic covariance matrix of the OLS estimator as well.

(b) Compute the White estimator of the appropriate asymptotic covariance matrix for the OLS estimates. [(See 14–9).]

(c) Test for the presence of heteroscedasticity, using White's general test. Do your results suggest the nature of the heteroscedasticity?

(d) Use the Breusch–Pagan Lagrange multiplier test to test for heteroscedasticity.

(e) Sort the data keying on X_1, and use the Goldfeld–Quandt test to test for heteroscedasticity. Repeat the procedure, using X_2. What do you find?

(f) Use one of Glesjer's tests to test for heteroscedasticity.

6. Using the data of the previous exercise, reestimate the parameters, using a two-step FGLS estimator. Try $(14-15)$, $(14-16)$, and $(14-17)$. Which one appears to be most appropriate?

7. For the model in Exercise 1, suppose that ε is normally distributed, with mean zero and variance $\sigma^2(1 + (\gamma x)^2)$. Show that σ^2 and γ^2 can be consistently estimated by a regression of the least squares residuals on a constant and x^2. Is this estimator efficient?

8. Derive the log-likelihood function, first-order conditions for maximization, and information matrix for the model

$$y = \boldsymbol{\beta}'\mathbf{x} + \varepsilon,$$

$$\varepsilon \sim N[0, \sigma^2(\gamma'\mathbf{z})^2].$$

References

Ali, M., and C. Giacotto, "A Study of Several New and Existing Tests for Heteroscedasticity in the General Linear Model," *Journal of Econometrics*, 26, 1984, pp. 355–374.

Amemiya, T., "Regression Analysis When the Variance of the Dependent Variable Is Proportional to the Square of Its Expectation," *Journal of the American Statistical Association*, 68, 1973, pp. 928–934.

Amemiya, T., "A Note on a Heteroscedastic Model," *Journal of Econometrics*, 6, 1977, pp. 365–370.

Amemiya, T., *Advanced Econometrics*, Cambridge, Mass.: Harvard University Press, 1985.

Bartlett, M. S., "Properties of Sufficiency and Statistical Tests," *Proceedings of the Royal Statistical Society, Series A*, 160, 1937, pp. 268–282.

Bollerslev, T., "Generalized Autoregressive Conditional Heteroscedasticity," *Journal of Econometrics*, 31, 1986, pp. 307–327.

Breusch, T., and A. Pagan, "A Simple Test for Heteroscedasticity and Random Coefficient Variation," *Econometrica*, 47, 1979, pp. 1287–1294.

Cragg, J., "Estimation and Testing in Testing in Time Series Regression Models with Heteroscedastic Disturbances," *Journal of Econometrics*, 20, 1982, pp. 135–157.

Cragg, J., "More Efficient Estimation in the Presence of Heteroscedasticity of Unknown Form," *Econometrica*, 51, 1983, pp. 751–763.

Eicker, F., "Limit Theorems for Regression With Unequal and Dependent Errors," in LeCam, L., and Neyman, J., *Proceedings of the Fifth Berkeley Symposium on Mathematical Statistics and Probability*, Berkeley: University of California Press, 1967, pp. 59–82.

Engle, R., "Autoregressive Conditional Heteroscedasticity with Estimates of the Variance of United Kingdom Inflations," *Econometrica*, 50, 1982, pp. 987–1008.

Engle, R., "Estimates of the Variance of U.S. Inflation Based on the ARCH Model," *Journal of Money, Credit, and Banking*, 15, 1983, pp. 286–301.

Fomby, T., C. Hill, and S. Johnson, *Advanced Econometric Methods*, New York: Springer Verlag, 1984.

Glesjer, H., "A New Test for Heteroscedasticity," *Journal of the American Statistical Association*, 64, 1969, pp. 316–323.

Godfrey, L., "Testing for Multiplicative Heteroscedasticity," *Journal of Econometrics*, 8, 1978, pp. 227–236.

Goldfeld, S., and R. Quandt, "Some Tests for Homoscedasticity," *Journal of the American Statistical Association*, 60, 1965, pp. 539–547.

Harvey, A. C., "Estimation of Parameters in a Heteroscedastic Regression Model," presented at the European Meetings of the Econometric Society, Grenoble, 1974.

Harvey, A. C., "Estimating Regression Models with Multiplicative Heteroscedasticity," *Econometrica*, 44, 1976, pp. 461–465.

Harvey, A., and G. Phillips, "A Comparison of the Power of Some Tests for Heteroscedasticity in the General Linear Model," *Journal of Econometrics*, 2, 1974, pp. 307–316.

Jobson, J., and W. Fuller, "Least Squares Estimation When the Covariance Matrix and Parameter

Vector Are Functionally Related," *Journal of the American Statistical Association*, 75, 1980, pp. 176–181.

Judge, G., C. Hill, W. Griffiths, H. Lutkepohl, and T. Lee, *The Theory and Practice of Econometrics*, New York: Wiley, 1985.

Just, R., and R. Pope, "Stochastic Specification of Production Functions and Economic Implications," *Journal of Econometrics*, 7, 1978, pp. 67–86.

Koenkar, R., "A Note on Studentizing a Test for Heteroscedasticity," *Journal of Econometrics*, 17, 1981, pp. 107–112.

Koenkar, R., and G. Basset, "Robust Tests for Heteroscedasticity Based on Regression Quantiles," *Econometrica*, 50, 1982, pp. 43–61.

Lahiri, K., and D. Egy, "Joint Estimation and Testing for Functional Form and Heteroscedasticity," *Journal of Econometrics*, 15, 1981, pp. 299–307.

Oberhofer, W., and J. Kmenta, "A General Procedure for Obtaining Maximum Likelihood Estimates in Generalized Regression Models," *Econometrica*, 42, 1974, pp. 579–590.

Ohtani, K., and T. Toyoda, "Estimation of Regression Coefficients After a Preliminary Test for Homoscedasticity," *Journal of Econometrics*, 12, 1980, pp. 151–159.

Park, R., "Estimation with Heteroscedastic Error Terms," *Econometrica*, 34, 1966, p. 888.

Prais, S., and H. Houthakker, *The Analysis of Family Budgets*, Cambridge: Cambridge University Press, 1955.

Rutemiller, H., and D. Bowers, "Estimation in a Heteroscedastic Regression Model," *Journal of the American Statistical Association*, 63, 1968, pp. 552–557.

Taylor, W. E., "Small Sample Properties of a Class of Two Stage Aitken Estimators," *Econometrica*, 45, 1977, pp. 497–508.

Theil, H., *Principles of Econometrics*, New York: Wiley, 1971.

Thursby, J., "Misspecification, Heteroscedasticity, and the Chow and Goldfeld–Quandt Tests," *Review of Economics and Statistics*, 64, 1982, pp. 314–321.

United States Department of Commerce, *Statistical Abstract of the United States*, Washington, D.C.: Government Printing Office, 1979.

United States Government Printing Office, *Economic Report of the President, 1987*, Washington, D.C., 1987.

Waldman, D., "A Note on the Algebraic Equivalence of White's Test and a Variant of the Godfrey/Breusch–Pagan Test for Heteroscedasticity," *Economics Letters*, 13, 1983, pp. 197–200.

White, H., "A Heteroscedasticity-Consistent Covariance Matrix Estimator and a Direct Test for Heteroscedasticity," *Econometrica*, 48, 1980, pp. 817–838.

Chapter 15
Autocorrelated Disturbances

15.1 Introduction

Heteroscedasticity is most commonly associated with cross-section data. In a time-series setting, the more common problem is autocorrelation, or serial correlation of the disturbances across periods. Consider, for example, the plot of the least squares residuals in the following example.

EXAMPLE 15.1. The data listed in Table 15.1 are used to fit an investment equation.[1] GNP and gross private domestic investment are in nominal terms in billions of dollars. The price index is the implicit price deflator for GNP. The interest rate is the average yearly discount rate charged by the New York Federal Reserve Bank. Variables used in the regressions reported in the examples to follow are real GNP and real investment, obtained by dividing the nominal figures by the price index. An approximation to the real interest rate is obtained by subtracting the rate of change in the price index from the discount rate.

Least squares regression of real investment on the real GNP and the real interest rate produces the results given in Table 15.2.

A plot of residuals is shown in Figure 15.1. The pattern in the residuals suggests that knowledge of the sign of a residual in one period is a fair indicator of the sign of the residual in the next period. This suggests that the effect of a given disturbance is carried, at least in part, across periods.[2]

One explanation for autocorrelation is that the factors omitted from the time-series regression, like those included, are correlated across periods.[2] Of course, this may be due to serial correlation in factors that should be in the regression model. Still, even after accounting for this possibility, it is reasonable to model most time series data as having some serial correlation. A second source of autocorrelation is the manner in which some published statistics are produced. For example, in seasonally adjusting variables such as the CPI and GNP, government agencies build autocorrelation into series that might otherwise be uncorrelated.

---

[1] The residuals also appear consistent with an ARCH process. But, the Lagrange multiplier test statistic is far from statistically significant (see Example 14.13).

[2] The classical regression does not require that the exogenous variables be nonautocorrelated, only the disturbances.

Table 15.1

Year	GNP	Investment	Price Index	Interest Rate
1963	596.7	90.9	0.7167	3.23
1964	637.7	97.4	0.7277	3.55
1965	691.1	113.5	0.7436	4.04
1966	756.0	125.7	0.7676	4.50
1967	799.6	122.8	0.7906	4.19
1968	873.4	133.3	0.8254	5.16
1969	944.0	149.3	0.8679	5.87
1970	992.7	144.2	0.9145	5.95
1971	1077.6	166.4	0.9601	4.88
1972	1185.9	195.0	1.0000	4.50
1973	1326.4	229.8	1.0575	6.44
1974	1434.2	228.7	1.1508	7.83
1975	1549.2	206.1	1.2579	6.25
1976	1718.0	257.9	1.3234	5.50
1977	1918.3	324.1	1.4005	5.46
1978	2163.9	386.6	1.5042	7.46
1979	2417.8	423.0	1.6342	10.28
1980	2631.7	401.9	1.7842	11.77
1981	2954.1	474.9	1.9514	13.42
1982	3073.0	414.5	2.0688	11.02

Source: Data are from the *Economic Report of the President*, Government Printing Office, Washington, D.C., 1984.

Table 15.2

Variable	Coefficient	Standard Error	
Constant	−12.5336	24.920	$R^2 = 0.81406$
Real Interest	−1.00144	2.369	
Real GNP	0.16914	0.02057	

EXAMPLE 15.2.   Suppose that x_t, $t = 1, \ldots, T$ is a random sample from a distribution with mean zero and variance σ^2.[3] Then $\text{Cov}[x_t, x_s] = 0$ if $t \neq s$. Let z_t be a "seasonally adjusted" series such that

$$z_t = \sum_{s=0}^{11} w_s x_{t-s},$$

where w_s is a monthly weight. Then

$$\text{Cov}[z_t, z_{t-s}] = w_0 w_s \sigma^2$$

for $s = 0, 1, \ldots, 11$ and zero for s greater than 11. The original series is uncorrelated, but the adjustment induces autocorrelation of 11 periods' duration.

---

[3] Since this chapter deals exclusively with time-series data, we shall use the t index for observations and T for the sample size throughout.

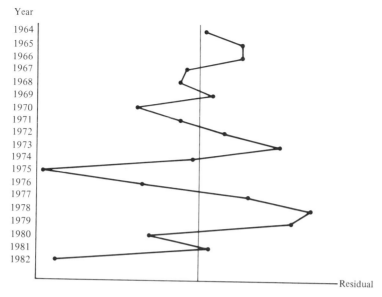

Figure 15.1   Plot of residuals.

The problems for estimation and inference caused by autocorrelation are similar to (though, unfortunately, more involved than) those caused by heteroscedasticity. As before, least squares is inefficient and inference based on the least squares estimates is adversely affected. Depending on the underlying process, however, GLS and FGLS estimators can be devised that circumvent these problems. We should emphasize that the models we shall examine here are quite far removed from the classical regression. The exact or small-sample properties of the estimators are rarely known, and only their asymptotic properties have been derived.

15.2. *Disturbance Processes*

In the usual time-series setting, the disturbances are assumed to be homoscedastic, but correlated across observations, so that

$$E[\boldsymbol{\varepsilon}\boldsymbol{\varepsilon}'] = \sigma^2 \boldsymbol{\Omega},$$

where $\sigma^2 \boldsymbol{\Omega}$ is a full, positive definite matrix with a constant $\sigma^2 = \text{Var}[\varepsilon_t]$ on the diagonal. As will be clear in the following discussion, we shall also assume that Ω_{ts} is a function of $|t - s|$, but not of t or s alone. This is a **stationarity** assumption, which we shall define more precisely. It implies that the covariance at lag s is a function of s, the distance apart in time of the observations, but not of t or s. We define the **autocovariances**,

$$\text{Cov}[\varepsilon_t, \varepsilon_{t-s}] = \text{Cov}[\varepsilon_{t+s}, \varepsilon_t] = \gamma_s.$$

Note that $\sigma^2 = \gamma_0$. The correlation between ε_t and ε_{t-s} is their **autocorrelation**,

$$\text{Corr}[\varepsilon_t, \varepsilon_{t-s}] = \frac{\text{Cov}[\varepsilon_t, \varepsilon_{t-s}]}{\sqrt{\text{Var}[\varepsilon_t]\text{Var}[\varepsilon_{t-s}]}} = \frac{\gamma_s}{\gamma_0} = \rho_s.$$

We can then write

$$E[\varepsilon\varepsilon'] = \gamma_0 \mathbf{R},$$

where $\mathbf{R}$ is an **autocorrelation matrix**:

$$\mathbf{R}_{ts} = \frac{\gamma_{|t-s|}}{\gamma_0}.$$

Different types of processes imply different patterns in $\mathbf{R}$. For example, the most frequently analyzed process is a **first-order autoregression** or AR(1) process,

$$\varepsilon_t = \rho\varepsilon_{t-1} + u_t,$$

for which we can verify that $\rho_s = \rho^s$. (We shall derive this formally later.) Higher-order **autoregressive processes** of the form

$$\varepsilon_t = \theta_1\varepsilon_{t-1} + \theta_2\varepsilon_{t-2} + \cdots + u_t$$

imply more involved patterns, including, for some values of the parameters, cyclical behavior of the autocorrelations.[4] Autoregressions are structured so that the influence of a given disturbance (or *innovation*, in the parlance of the more recent time series literature) fades as it recedes into the more distant past but vanishes only asymptotically. For example, for the AR(1), $\text{Cov}[\varepsilon_t, \varepsilon_{t-s}]$ is never zero, but does become negligible if ρ is less than one. *Moving average* processes such as the one in Example 15.2, conversely, have a short memory. For the MA(1) process,

$$\varepsilon_t = u_t - \lambda u_{t-1},$$

the memory in the process is only one period:

$$\gamma_0 = \sigma_u^2(1 + \lambda^2),$$

$$\gamma_1 = -\lambda\sigma_u^2,$$

but

$$\gamma_k = 0 \qquad \text{if } k > 1.$$

The memory in the MA(11) process of Example 15.2 is 11 periods.

Time-series processes such as the ones listed here can be characterized by their order, the values of their parameters, and the behavior of their autocorrelations.[5] We shall consider various forms at different points. The received empirical literature is overwhelmingly dominated by the AR(1) model. This is partly a matter of convenience. Processes more involved than this model are usually extremely difficult to analyze.[6] However, there is a more practical reason. It is very optimistic to expect to know precisely the correct form of the appropriate model for the disturbance in any given situation. The first-order autoregression has withstood the test of time and experimentation as a reasonable *model* for underlying processes that probably, in truth, are impenetrably complex. It is sometimes argued that models can be improved by more elaborate disturbance processes (we shall examine some of these in Chapter 18), but there is often a *j'e ne sais quoi* flavor to this exercise. The results are

[4] We shall take up this aspect in more detail in Chapter 18.
[5] See Box and Jenkins (1970) for an authoritative study.
[6] The literature on time series and autocorrelation is voluminous and enormously complex. For example, the bibliography in Judge et al. (1985) on the latter subject alone runs to 13 pages.

often highly sensitive to the specification chosen, and, in general, it is the data rather than an underlying theory that lead to the choice of the model, which is risky at best. As such, most researchers choose the simpler expedient of the AR(1) model in most cases.

15.3.   AR(1) Disturbances

The first-order autoregressive disturbance, or AR(1) process, is represented in the **autoregressive form** as

$$\varepsilon_t = \rho\varepsilon_{t-1} + u_t, \tag{15-1}$$

where

$$E[u_t] = 0,$$
$$E[u_t^2] = \sigma_u^2,$$

and

$$\mathrm{Cov}[u_t, u_s] = 0 \quad \text{if } t \neq s.$$

It will sometimes be convenient to assume that u_t is normally distributed, but that is not necessary at this point. By repeated substitution, we have

$$\varepsilon_t = u_t + \rho u_{t-1} + \rho^2 u_{t-2} + \cdots. \tag{15-2}$$

From the preceding **moving average form**, it is evident that each disturbance, ε_t, embodies the entire past history of the u's, with the most recent observations receiving greater weight than those in the distant past. Depending on the sign of ρ, the series will exhibit clusters of positive and then negative observations or, if ρ is negative, regular oscillations of sign.[7]
 Since the successive values of u_t are uncorrelated, the variance of ε_t is the variance of the right-hand side of (15–2):

$$\mathrm{Var}[\varepsilon_t] = \sigma_u^2 + \rho^2\sigma_u^2 + \rho^4\sigma_u^2 + \cdots. \tag{15-3}$$

In order to proceed, a restriction must be placed on ρ,

$$|\rho| < 1, \tag{15-4}$$

because otherwise (15–3) must explode. This is the stationarity assumption noted earlier. With (15–4), which implies that $\lim_{s \to \infty} \rho^s = 0$,

$$E[\varepsilon_t] = 0$$

$$\mathrm{Var}[\varepsilon_t] = \frac{\sigma_u^2}{1 - \rho^2} \tag{15-5}$$

$$= \sigma_\varepsilon^2.$$

With the stationarity assumption, there is an easier way to obtain the variance:

$$\mathrm{Var}[\varepsilon_t] = \rho^2 \, \mathrm{Var}[\varepsilon_{t-1}] + \sigma_u^2,$$

---

[7] Unless the data have been first differenced or otherwise manipulated in an unusual fashion, the case of negative autocorrelation is normally not relevant to economic data.

as $\text{Cov}[u_t, \varepsilon_s] = 0$ if $t > s$. With stationarity, $\text{Var}[\varepsilon_{t-1}] = \text{Var}[\varepsilon_t]$, which implies (15–5). Proceeding in the same fashion,

$$\begin{aligned}
\text{Cov}[\varepsilon_t, \varepsilon_{t-1}] &= E[\varepsilon_t \varepsilon_{t-1}] \\
&= E[\varepsilon_{t-1}(\rho \varepsilon_{t-1} + u_t)] \\
&= \rho \, \text{Var}[\varepsilon_{t-1}] \\
&= \frac{\rho \sigma_u^2}{1 - \rho^2}.
\end{aligned}$$

(15–6)

By repeated substitution in (15–1), we see that for any s,

$$\varepsilon_t = \rho^s \varepsilon_{t-s} + \sum_{i=0}^{s-1} \rho^i u_{t-i}$$

(15–7)

(e.g., $\varepsilon_t = \rho^3 \varepsilon_{t-3} + \rho^2 u_{t-2} + \rho u_{t-1} + u_t$). Therefore, since ε_s is not correlated with any u_t for which $t > s$ (i.e., any subsequent u_t), it follows that

$$\text{Cov}[\varepsilon_t, \varepsilon_{t-s}] = E[\varepsilon_t \varepsilon_{t-s}] = \frac{\rho^s \sigma_u^2}{1 - \rho^2}.$$

(15–8)

Dividing by $\gamma_0 = \sigma_u^2/(1 - \rho^2)$ provides the autocorrelations,

$$\text{Corr}[\varepsilon_t, \varepsilon_{t-s}] = \rho_s = \rho^s.$$

(15–9)

It is obvious that with the stationarity assumption, the autocovariances fade over time. Depending on the sign of ρ, they will either be declining in geometric progression or alternating in sign if ρ is negative. Collecting terms, we have

$$\sigma^2 \Omega = \frac{\sigma_u^2}{1 - \rho^2} \begin{bmatrix} 1 & \rho & \rho^2 & \rho^3 & \cdots & \rho^{T-1} \\ \rho & 1 & \rho & \rho^2 & \cdots & \rho^{T-2} \\ \rho^2 & \rho & 1 & \rho & \cdots & \rho^{T-3} \\ & & & \vdots & & \rho \quad \vdots \\ \rho^{T-1} & \rho^{T-2} & & & \cdots & 1 \end{bmatrix}.$$

(15–10)

15.4. *Least Squares Estimation*

Since Ω is not equal to $\mathbf{I}$, the now familiar problems will apply to least squares estimation. In general, least squares will continue to be unbiased; the earlier general proof includes autocorrelated disturbances. Whether least squares is consistent or not depends, as before, on the matrix

$$\mathbf{Q}_T^* = \frac{1}{T} \mathbf{X}' \Omega \mathbf{X}.$$

If this matrix converges to a matrix of finite elements, then, by our earlier reasoning, OLS is mean square consistent. We can expand this as

$$\mathbf{Q}_T^* = \frac{1}{T} \sum_t \sum_s \rho_{|t-s|} [\mathbf{x}_t \mathbf{x}_s' + \mathbf{x}_s \mathbf{x}_t'],$$

(15–11)

where $\mathbf{x}'_t$ and $\mathbf{x}'_s$ are rows of $\mathbf{X}$ and $\rho_{|t-s|}$ is the autocorrelation between ε_t and ε_s. Sufficient conditions for this matrix to converge are that the regressors be well behaved and the correlations between disturbances die off reasonably rapidly as the observations become further apart in time. For example, if the disturbances follow the AR(1) process described earlier, $\rho_k = \rho^k$ and $\mathbf{Q}_T^*$ will converge to a positive definite $\mathbf{Q}^*$ as $T \to \infty$.

Asymptotic normality of least squares is extremely difficult to establish for the general model, due, once again, to the complexity of (15–11). The results of Amemiya (1985) and Anderson (1971) noted in Chapter 13 do carry over to most of the familiar types of autocorrelated disturbances, so we shall assume that their analyses include the cases we examine here. We conclude, then, that ordinary least squares continues to be unbiased, consistent, asymptotically normally distributed, and, as before, inefficient.

15.4.1. OLS Estimation with Lagged Dependent Variables

There is an important exception to the results of the previous paragraph. If the regression contains any lagged values of the dependent variable, least squares will no longer be unbiased or consistent. To take the simplest case, suppose that

$$y_t = \beta y_{t-1} + \varepsilon_t$$
$$\varepsilon_t = \rho \varepsilon_{t-1} + u_t. \tag{15–12}$$

In this model, the regressor and the disturbance are correlated:

$$\begin{aligned} \text{Cov}[y_{t-1}, \varepsilon_t] &= \text{Cov}[y_{t-1}, \rho\varepsilon_{t-1} + u_t] \\ &= \rho\, \text{Cov}[y_{t-1}, \varepsilon_{t-1}] \\ &= \rho\, \text{Cov}[y_t, \varepsilon_t] \end{aligned}$$

by stationarity. But by repeated substitution in (15–12),

$$y_t = \sum_{i=0}^{\infty} \beta^i \varepsilon_{t-i},$$

so

$$\begin{aligned} \rho\, \text{Cov}[y_t, \varepsilon_t] &= \rho \sum_{i=0}^{\infty} \beta^i \text{Cov}[\varepsilon_t, \varepsilon_{t-i}] \\ &= \rho \sum_{i=0}^{\infty} \frac{\beta^i \rho^i \sigma_u^2}{1 - \rho^2} \tag{15–13} \\ &= \frac{\rho \sigma_u^2}{(1 - \beta\rho)(1 - \rho^2)}. \end{aligned}$$

(Note that this *is* zero if ρ is zero, regardless of β. This result is consistent with the observation that as long as the regressor is asymptotically uncorrelated with the disturbance, ordinary least squares is consistent even if the regressor is stochastic.) For the least squares estimator, we can use the general result

$$\text{plim } b = \beta + \frac{\text{Cov}[y_{t-1}, \varepsilon_t]}{\text{Var}[y_t]}. \tag{15–14}$$

But

$$\text{Var}[y_t] = \beta^2 \text{Var}[y_{t-1}] + \text{Var}[\varepsilon_t] + 2\beta \text{Cov}[y_{t-1}, \varepsilon_t].$$

Since the process is stationary, $\text{Var}[y_t] = \text{Var}[y_{t-1}]$. $\text{Var}[\varepsilon_t]$ is given in (15–5), while $\text{Cov}[y_{t-1}, \varepsilon_t]$ is given in (15–13). Collecting terms, we have

$$\text{Var}[y_t] = \frac{\sigma_u^2(1 + \beta\rho)}{(1 - \rho^2)(1 - \beta^2)(1 - \beta\rho)},$$

so

$$\text{plim } b = \beta + \frac{\rho(1 - \beta^2)}{1 + \beta\rho}. \tag{15–15}$$

Therefore, least squares is inconsistent unless ρ equals zero.

15.4.2. Efficiency of Least Squares

Since the model with autocorrelated disturbances is a generalized regression model, we should expect least squares to be inefficient. There are, however, few general results on how inefficient it is because knowledge of both the disturbance process and the process generating X is required. A few useful cases have been examined in detail.

First, suppose that the model is

$$y_t = \beta x_t + \varepsilon_t, \tag{15–16}$$

$$\varepsilon_t = \rho\varepsilon_{t-1} + u_t,$$

and x_t is also generated by an AR(1) process,

$$x_t = \delta x_{t-1} + v_t.$$

For convenience, let

$$\text{Var}[x_t] = \frac{\text{Var}[v_t]}{1 - \delta^2} \quad \text{and} \quad \text{Var}[\varepsilon_t] = \frac{\sigma_u^2}{1 - \rho^2}$$

$$= \sigma_x^2 \qquad\qquad\qquad = \sigma_\varepsilon^2.$$

With Ω given in (15–10),

$$\frac{1}{T}\mathbf{x}'\Omega\mathbf{x} = \frac{\sum_1^T x_t^2}{T} + 2\rho\frac{\sum_2^T x_t x_{t-1}}{T} + 2\rho^2\frac{\sum_3^T x_t x_{t-2}}{T} + \cdots \tag{15–17}$$

The autocovariances of x are $\sigma_x^2, \delta\sigma_x^2, \delta^2\sigma_x^2$, and so on. If T is large enough, the leading sums in (15–17) will approximate these, while if $|\delta| < 1$, the latter terms will be negligible. So,

$$\frac{1}{T}\mathbf{x}'\Omega\mathbf{x} \simeq \sigma_x^2 + 2\rho\delta\sigma_x^2 + 2\rho^2\delta^2\sigma_x^2 + \cdots$$

$$= 2\sigma_x^2\left(\sum_{i=0}^{\infty} (\rho\delta)^i\right) - \sigma_x^2$$

$$= \left(\frac{2\sigma_x^2}{1 - \rho\delta}\right) - \sigma_x^2$$

$$= \frac{\sigma_x^2(1 + \rho\delta)}{1 - \rho\delta}.$$

Collecting terms, we find that

$$\text{Var}[b] = \frac{\sigma_\varepsilon^2}{T}\left[\frac{\mathbf{x'x}}{T}\right]^{-1}\left[\frac{\mathbf{x'\Omega x}}{T}\right]\left[\frac{\mathbf{x'x}}{T}\right]^{-1}$$

is approximately

$$\text{Var}[b] \simeq \frac{\sigma_\varepsilon^2(1 + \rho\delta)}{T\sigma_x^2(1 - \rho\delta)}. \tag{15–18}$$

The variance of the GLS estimator is

$$\text{Var}[\hat\beta] = \left(\frac{\sigma_\varepsilon^2}{T}\right)\left[\frac{\mathbf{x'\Omega}^{-1}\mathbf{x}}{T}\right]^{-1},$$

for which we require

$$\mathbf{\Omega}^{-1} = \frac{1}{1 - \rho^2}\begin{bmatrix} 1 & -\rho & 0 & 0 & 0 & \cdots & \cdots & 0 \\ -\rho & 1 + \rho^2 & -\rho & 0 & 0 & \cdots & \cdots & 0 \\ 0 & -\rho & 1 + \rho^2 & -\rho & 0 & \cdots & \cdots & 0 \\ & & & \vdots & & & & \\ 0 & 0 & 0 & 0 & \cdots & -\rho & 1 + \rho^2 & -\rho \\ 0 & 0 & 0 & 0 & \cdots & 0 & -\rho & 1 \end{bmatrix}. \tag{15–19}$$

Then

$$\text{Var}[\hat\beta] = \frac{\sigma_\varepsilon^2}{T}\left[\frac{1}{1 - \rho^2}\left((1 + \rho^2)\frac{\sum_t x_t^2}{T} - \rho^2\frac{x_1^2 + x_T^2}{T} - 2\rho\frac{\sum_{t=2}^T x_t x_{t-1}}{T}\right)\right]^{-1}.$$

If the sample is large, the *end effect*, $(x_1^2 + x_T^2)/T$, will be negligible, so that

$$\text{Var}[\hat\beta] \simeq \frac{\sigma_\varepsilon^2(1 - \rho^2)}{T\sigma_x^2(1 + \rho^2 - 2\rho\delta)}. \tag{15–20}$$

The (in)efficiency of least squares relative to GLS is, therefore, approximately

$$\frac{\text{Var}[b]}{\text{Var}[\hat\beta]} = \frac{(1 + \rho\delta)/(1 - \rho\delta)}{(1 - \rho^2)/(1 + \rho^2 + 2\rho\delta)}. \tag{15–21}$$

Contours of the ratio are shown in Figure 15.2. The function is not monotonic in δ, but clearly, the least favorable cases are those with large values of ρ for any given δ. The efficiency of least squares relative to generalized least squares falls to less than 10 percent if ρ is close to one.

The preceding discussion gives a rather pessimistic conclusion, but it is derived under somewhat narrow assumptions. For models that involve relatively slowly changing variables, such as macroeconomic flows like consumption or output, the loss of efficiency in using least squares might not be quite so severe as this result suggests.[8]

15.4.3. Estimating the Variance of the Least Squares Estimator

As usual, $s^2(\mathbf{X'X})^{-1}$ is an inappropriate estimator of $\sigma^2(\mathbf{X'X})^{-1}(\mathbf{X'\Omega X})(\mathbf{X'X})^{-1}$, both because s^2 is a biased estimator of σ^2 and because the matrix is incorrect. With regard to σ^2,

---

[8] See Judge et al. (1982, p. 280).

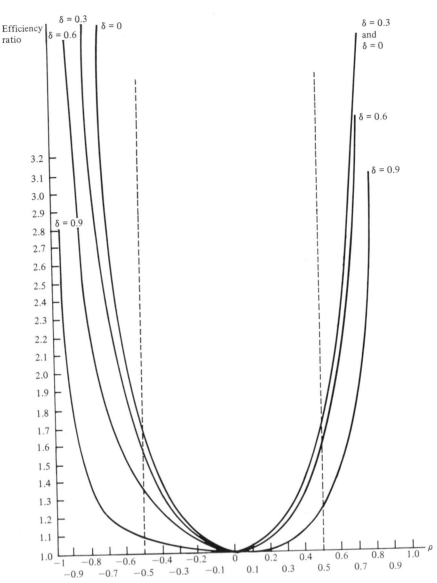

Figure 15.2   Variance ratio of OLS and GLS.

the analysis of Section 14.2.2 concerning heteroscedasticity is in general terms, and includes the current case as well. Thus, it is shown there that s^2 is a biased but consistent estimator of σ^2. Asymptotically, therefore, the difference between the estimated variance and the true variance of least squares hinges on the two matrices. For the model in (15–16),

$$\frac{(\mathbf{x}'\mathbf{x}/T)^{-1}}{(\mathbf{x}'\mathbf{x}/T)^{-1}(\mathbf{x}'\mathbf{\Omega}\mathbf{x}/T)(\mathbf{x}'\mathbf{x}/T)^{-1}} \simeq \frac{1 - \rho\delta}{1 + \rho\delta}. \tag{15-22}$$

If ρ and δ have the same sign, the ratio is less than one. Since, in most economic time series,

Table 15.3

Variable	OLS Estimate	OLS SE	Corrected SE
Constant	− 12.5336	24.92	18.96
Real GNP	0.16914	0.02057	0.01675
Real interest	− 1.00144	2.369	3.342

the autocorrelation is positive, this would seem to be the norm. As such, the standard errors conventionally estimated by least squares are likely to be too small.

   In view of this situation, if one is going to use least squares, it is desirable to have an appropriate estimator of the covariance matrix of the least squares estimator. There are two approaches. If the form of the autocorrelation is known, one can estimate the parameters of Ω directly and compute a consistent estimator. Of course, if so, it would be more sensible to use generalized least squares instead and not waste the sample information on an inefficient estimator. The second approach parallels the use of the White estimator for heteroscedasticity. Suppose that the form of the autocorrelation is unknown. Then a direct estimator of Ω or $\Omega(\theta)$ is not available. The problem in this setting is estimation of

$$\Sigma = \frac{1}{T} \sum_t \sum_s \rho_{|t-s|}[\mathbf{x}_t\mathbf{x}_s' + \mathbf{x}_s\mathbf{x}_t'].\tag{15–23}$$

Following White's suggestion for heteroscedasticity,[9] Newey and West (1987) have devised an estimator for autocorrelated disturbances with an unspecified structure:

$$\mathbf{S}_* = \frac{1}{T} \sum_{j=0}^{L} \sum_{t=j+1}^{T} w_j e_t e_{t-j}(\mathbf{x}_t\mathbf{x}_{t-j}' + \mathbf{x}_{t-j}\mathbf{x}_t'),\tag{15–24}$$

where

$$w_j = 1 - \frac{j}{L+1}.\tag{15–25}$$

   The result is surprisingly simple and relatively easy to implement. There is a final problem to be solved. It must be determined a priori how large L should be in order that autocorrelations at lags greater than L are small enough to ignore. For a moving average process, this can be expected to be a relatively small number. However, for autoregressive processes or mixtures, the autocorrelations are never zero, and the researcher must make a judgment as to how far back it is necessary to go. Unfortunately, the result is not so crisp as the White estimator for heteroscedasticity.

   EXAMPLE 15.3.   Using the investment data of Example 15.1, we find that the Newey–West estimator of the variance matrix of least squares based on $L = 4$ yields the results listed in Table 15.3.

---

[9] See Section 14.2.3.

15.5. *Efficient Estimation When Ω Is Known*

15.5.1. Generalized Least Squares

If the parameters of Ω are known, the GLS estimator,

$$\hat{\beta} = [X'\Omega^{-1}X]^{-1}[X'\Omega^{-1}y],$$

and its sampling variance,

$$\text{Var}[\hat{\beta}] = \sigma_\varepsilon^2[X'\Omega^{-1}X]^{-1},$$

can be computed directly. For the AR(1) process,

$$\Omega^{-1/2} = P = \begin{bmatrix} \sqrt{1-\rho^2} & 0 & 0 & 0 & \cdots & 0 & 0 \\ -\rho & 1 & 0 & 0 & \cdots & 0 & 0 \\ 0 & -\rho & 0 & 0 & \cdots & 0 & 0 \\ & & & \vdots & & & \\ 0 & & 0 & 0 & 0 & \cdots & -\rho & 1 \end{bmatrix}, \tag{15-26}$$

so the data for the transformed model are

$$y_* = \begin{bmatrix} \sqrt{1-\rho^2}\,y_1 \\ y_2 - \rho y_1 \\ y_3 - \rho y_2 \\ \vdots \\ y_T - \rho y_{T-1} \end{bmatrix}, \quad X_* = \begin{bmatrix} \sqrt{1-\rho^2}\,x_1 \\ x_2 - \rho x_1 \\ x_3 - \rho x_2 \\ \vdots \\ x_T - \rho x_{T-1} \end{bmatrix}. \tag{15-27}$$

(These transformations are sometimes labeled *quasi-differences* or *pseudo-differences*.) Note that in the transformed model, every observation except the first contains a constant term. What was the column of ones in X is transformed to $[\sqrt{1-\rho^2}, 1-\rho, 1-\rho,\ldots]$. Therefore, if the sample is relatively small, the problems noted earlier with measures of fit will reappear.

The variance of the transformed disturbance is

$$\text{Var}[\varepsilon_t - \rho\varepsilon_{t-1}] = \text{Var}[u_t] = \sigma_u^2.$$

[The variance of the first disturbance is also σ^2; see (15–5).]

Corresponding results have been derived for higher-order autoregressive processes. For the AR(2) model,

$$\varepsilon_t = \theta_1\varepsilon_{t-1} + \theta_2\varepsilon_{t-2} + u_t, \tag{15-28}$$

the transformed data for generalized least squares are obtained by

$$z_{*1} = \left[\frac{(1+\theta_2)[(1-\theta_2)^2 - \theta_1^2]}{1-\theta_2} \right]^{1/2} z_1,$$

$$z_{*2} = (1-\theta_2^2)^{1/2}z_2 - \frac{\theta_1(1-\theta_1^2)^{1/2}}{1-\theta_2}z_1, \tag{15-29}$$

$$z_{*t} = z_t - \theta_1 z_{t-1} - \theta_2 z_{t-2} \quad t > 2,$$

where z is used for y_t or x_t. The transformation becomes progressively more complex for higher-order processes.[10]

Note that in both the AR(1) and AR(2) models, the transformation to y_* and X_* involves "starting values" for the processes that depend only on the first one or two observations. We can view the process as having begun in the infinite past. However, since the sample contains only T observations, it is convenient to treat the first one or two (or P) observations as shown and consider them as "initial values." Whether we view the process as having begun at time $t = 1$ or in the infinite past is ultimately immaterial in regard to the asymptotic properties of our estimators. However, as we shall see, what we do with the initial values in a finite sample can make a substantial difference.

Higher-order MA processes and mixtures of AR and MA processes can be estimated by approximations to GLS.[11] (Full GLS is not well worked out for very many processes involving MA disturbances.) One would have to ask, however, how such a process might arise in the first place. Nicholls et al. (1975) describe some instances in which MA(1) disturbances might be expected, but as a general rule, they do not arise naturally. In the widely studied case of adjustment models that we examine in Chapter 18, the model does have an MA(1) disturbance, but it also contains a lagged dependent variable. As such, none of the apparatus developed earlier is applicable. The upshot is that MA and ARMA disturbances in econometric models should be applied with circumspection. A particular type of higher-order AR model has been advocated by Wallis (1972). In particular, for quarterly data, he suggests that the model

$$\varepsilon_t = \rho\varepsilon_{t-4} + u_t \tag{15-30}$$

is more appropriate than, say, an AR(1) model, because random effects are more likely to be correlated with the corresponding previous season than with the immediately preceding season. This process has a distinctive pattern of autocorrelations:

$$\text{Cov}[\varepsilon_t, \varepsilon_{t-i}] = \sigma_u^2 \frac{\rho^{i/4}}{(1-\rho^2)}, \qquad i = 0, 4, 8, \ldots$$

$$= 0 \text{ otherwise.}$$

Full GLS for this model is obtained using

$$X_{*t} = \sqrt{1-\rho^2}\, z_t, \qquad t = 1, 2, 3, 4, \ldots$$

$$= z_t - \rho z_{t-4}, \qquad t > 4.$$

15.5.2. Maximum Likelihood Estimation

If the parameters of the disturbance process are known, GLS and maximum likelihood estimation for the AR(1) model are equivalent. In order to obtain the likelihood function for normally distributed disturbances, we make use of

$$f(y_1, y_2, \ldots, y_T) = f(y_1)f(y_2|y_1)f(y_3|y_2)\cdots f(y_T|y_{T-1}).$$

---

[10] See Box and Jenkins (1976) and Fuller (1976).
[11] See, for example, Kmenta (1986, pp. 326–328) and Greenberg and Webster (1983) for moving average models.

Based on (15–27), we find that the transformed regression is

$$y_t^* = \boldsymbol{\beta}'\mathbf{x}_t^* + u_t,$$

so that in terms of the original data,

$$y_1 = \boldsymbol{\beta}'\mathbf{x}_1 + \frac{u_1}{\sqrt{1 - \rho^2}}$$

and

$$y_t \,|\, y_{t-1} = \rho y_{t-1} + \boldsymbol{\beta}'\mathbf{x}_t - \rho\boldsymbol{\beta}'\mathbf{x}_{t-1} + u_t$$

for $t = 2,\dots, T$. For the first observation, we use the change of variable formula from Chapter 3 to obtain

$$f(y_1) = |\sqrt{(1 - \rho^2)}|f_{u_1}\{\sqrt{(1 - \rho^2)}(y_1 - \boldsymbol{\beta}'\mathbf{x}_1)\}$$
$$= (1 - \rho^2)^{1/2}(2\pi\sigma^2)^{-1/2}e^{-[(1 - \rho^2)/(2\sigma_u^2)](y_1 - \boldsymbol{\beta}'\mathbf{x}_1)^2}.$$

The log-likelihood function is

$$\ln L = \ln f(y_1) + \sum_{t=2}^{T} \ln f(y_t \,|\, y_{t-1})$$

$$= -\frac{1}{2}[\ln(2\pi) + \ln\sigma_u^2 - \ln(1 - \rho^2)] - \frac{1 - \rho^2}{2\sigma_u^2}(y_1 - \boldsymbol{\beta}'\mathbf{x}_1)^2$$

$$-\frac{T - 1}{2}(\ln(2\pi) + \ln\sigma_u^2) \tag{15–31}$$

$$-\frac{1}{2\sigma_u^2}\sum_{t=2}^{T}[(y_t - \rho y_{t-1}) - \boldsymbol{\beta}'(\mathbf{x}_t - \rho\mathbf{x}_{t-1})]^2$$

$$= -\frac{T}{2}[\ln(2\pi) + \ln\sigma_u^2] + \frac{1}{2}\ln(1 - \rho^2) - \frac{1}{2\sigma_u^2}\sum_{t=1}^{T}[y_{*t} - \boldsymbol{\beta}'\mathbf{x}_{*t}]^2.$$

The sum of squares term is the residual sum of squares from the transformed, classical regression model in (15–27). *If ρ is known, the solution is least squares for $\boldsymbol{\beta}$ and σ^2, as usual, which is the GLS solution given in* (15–27). The derivatives of the log likelihood for a known $\boldsymbol{\Omega}$ were found earlier and apply here. The information matrix is

$$\mathbf{I}(\boldsymbol{\beta}, \sigma_u^2) = \begin{bmatrix} (1/\sigma_u^2)(\mathbf{X}'\boldsymbol{\Omega}^{-1}\mathbf{X}) & 0 \\ 0 & T/2\sigma_u^4 \end{bmatrix}.$$

15.6. *Estimation When $\boldsymbol{\Omega}$ Is Unknown*

15.6.1. AR(1) Disturbances

For an unknown $\boldsymbol{\Omega}$, there is, if anything, an embarrassment of riches of FGLS estimators. All have the same asymptotic properties, as we saw earlier for the general case, as long as the first-round estimators are consistent. But there is considerable variation in their small-sample properties.

Once again, the AR(1) model is the one most widely used and studied. The most common procedure is to begin FGLS with a natural estimator of ρ, the autocorrelation of the residuals. Since $\mathbf{b}$ is consistent, we can use

$$r = \frac{\sum_{t=2}^{T} e_t e_{t-1}}{\sum_{t=2}^{T} e_t^2}. \tag{15-32}$$

Two of the many other modifications that have been suggested are Theil's estimator.[12]

$$r^* = \left[\frac{T-K}{T-1}\right] r$$

and

$$r^{**} = 1 - \frac{d}{2},$$

where d is the Durbin–Watson statistic for testing the hypothesis that ρ equals zero.[13] The estimator suggested by Durbin (1960) is the coefficient on y_{t-1} in the least squares regression

$$y_t = \rho y_{t-1} + \boldsymbol{\beta}'\mathbf{x}_t - (\rho\boldsymbol{\beta})'\mathbf{x}_{t-1} + u_t. \tag{15-33}$$

(The coefficients are computed ignoring the constraint.) All of these are consistent estimators of ρ. Since ρ must be in the range minus one to one, another possibility is to search over this range and choose the value of ρ that leads to the smallest sum of squares.[14]

For the second step of FGLS, there are two possibilities:

1. Full FGLS. This is the Prais–Winsten (1954) estimator.
2. FGLS omitting the first observation. This was first suggested by Cochrane and Orcutt (1949).

In a large sample, the two are likely to be the same. However, the typical economic time series is not particularly long, and which one is chosen may make a great deal of difference. The question is not merely one of different numerical values. The efficiency of the FGLS estimator can be very adversely affected by discarding the initial observation(s) if the sample is relatively small and the regressors have a trend, which is common in economic data.[15]

It is possible to iterate these estimators to convergence. Since the estimator is efficient at every iteration, nothing is gained asymptotically by doing so. Moreover, unlike the heteroscedastic model, iterating when there is autocorrelation does not secure the maximum likelihood estimator. The iterated FGLS estimator does not account for the term $(\frac{1}{2})\ln(1-\rho^2)$ in the log-likelihood function [see (15–31)]. (None of the estimators discussed thus far satisfy $\partial \ln L/\partial \rho = 0$ for the current estimates of $\boldsymbol{\beta}$ and σ_u^2.)

Full maximum likelihood estimators can be obtained by maximizing the log likelihood in (15–31) with respect to $\boldsymbol{\beta}$, σ^2, and ρ. Apart from the constant term, the log-likelihood function may be written

$$\ln L = -\frac{\mathbf{u}'\mathbf{u}}{2\sigma_u^2} + \frac{1}{2}\ln(1-\rho^2) - \frac{T}{2}\ln\sigma_u^2 \tag{15-34}$$

[12] Theil (1971, p. 254).

[13] See, for example, Johnston (1984, p. 324). The Durbin–Watson statistic is discussed later.

[14] See Hildreth and Lu (1960).

[15] See Maeshiro (1979), Poirier (1978), and Park and Mitchell (1980).

(where, as before, the first observation is computed differently from the others). The likelihood equations can be derived from (15–34) and (15–31). From (15–34),

$$\frac{\partial \ln L}{\partial \beta} = \frac{1}{\sigma_u^2} \sum_{t=1}^{T} u_t \mathbf{x}_{*t},$$

where

$$u_1 = \sqrt{(1 - \rho^2)}(y_1 - \beta' \mathbf{x}_1),$$

$$u_t = (y_t - \rho y_{t-1}) - \beta'(\mathbf{x}_t - \rho \mathbf{x}_{t-1}) \qquad \text{for } t = 2, \ldots, T.$$

[Note that $\mathbf{x}_{*1} = \sqrt{1 - \rho^2}\, \mathbf{x}_1$ and $\mathbf{x}_{*t} = (\mathbf{x}_t - \rho \mathbf{x}_{t-1})$.] Also, from (15–34), we have

$$\frac{\partial \ln L}{\partial \sigma_u^2} = -\frac{T}{2\sigma_u^2} + \frac{1}{2\sigma_u^4} \sum_{t=1}^{T} u_t^2.$$

Turning now to the first part of (15–31), we find that

$$\frac{\partial \ln L}{\partial \rho} = \frac{1}{\sigma_u^2} \sum_{t=2}^{T} u_t \varepsilon_{t-1} + \frac{\rho \varepsilon_1^2}{\sigma_u^2} - \frac{\rho}{1 - \rho^2},$$

where $\varepsilon_t = y_t - \beta' \mathbf{x}_t$. For a given value of ρ, the maximum likelihood estimates of β and σ_u^2 are the usual ones, GLS and the mean squared residual using the transformed data. The problem is estimation of ρ. One possibility is to search the range $-1 < \rho < 1$ for the value that with the implied estimates of the other parameters, maximizes ln L. This is analogous to the Hildreth–Lu estimator.[16] Beach and MacKinnon (1978) argue that this is a very inefficient way to do the search and have devised a much faster algorithm. It is important to note that none of the two-step estimators described earlier will be the maximum likelihood estimator, even if iterated, because they do not account for the Jacobian term for the first observation.

The components of the information matrix are derived from

$$\frac{\partial^2 \ln L}{\partial \beta \partial \beta'} = -\frac{1}{\sigma_u^2} \sum_{t=1}^{T} \mathbf{x}_{*t} \mathbf{x}_{*t}' = -\frac{1}{\sigma_u^2} \mathbf{X}' \Omega^{-1} \mathbf{X},$$

$$\frac{\partial^2 \ln L}{\partial \beta \partial \sigma_u^2} = -\frac{1}{\sigma_u^4} \sum_{t=1}^{T} u_t \mathbf{x}_{*t},$$

$$\frac{\partial^2 \ln L}{\partial \beta \partial \rho} = \frac{1}{\sigma_u^2} \sum_{t=1}^{T} u_t \left(\frac{\partial \mathbf{x}_{*t}}{\partial \rho}\right),$$

$$\frac{\partial^2 \ln L}{\partial (\sigma_u^2)^2} = \frac{T}{2\sigma_u^4} - \frac{1}{\sigma_u^6} \sum_{t=1}^{T} u_t^2,$$

$$\frac{\partial^2 \ln L}{\partial \rho \partial \sigma_u^2} = -\frac{1}{\sigma_u^4} \left(\sum_{t=2}^{T} u_t \varepsilon_{t-1} + \rho \varepsilon_1^2\right),$$

$$\frac{\partial^2 \ln L}{\partial \rho^2} = -\frac{1}{\sigma_u^2} \sum_{t=2}^{T} \varepsilon_{t-1}^2 + \frac{\varepsilon_1^2}{\sigma_u^2} + \frac{1 + \rho^2}{(1 - \rho^2)^2}.$$

---

[16] An improvement on this is provided by Hildreth and Dent (1974).

(using $u_t = \varepsilon_t - \rho\varepsilon_{t-1}$). Taking the negative of the expected values produces the information matrix

$$
\mathbf{I}(\boldsymbol{\beta}, \sigma_u^2, \rho) = \begin{bmatrix} \dfrac{1}{\sigma_u^2}\mathbf{X}'\boldsymbol{\Omega}^{-1}\mathbf{X} & \mathbf{0} & \mathbf{0} \\[2ex] \mathbf{0}' & \dfrac{T}{2\sigma_u^4} & \dfrac{\rho}{\sigma_u^2(1-\rho^2)} \\[2ex] \mathbf{0}' & \dfrac{\rho}{\sigma_u^2(1-\rho^2)} & \dfrac{T-2}{(1-\rho^2)} - \dfrac{1+\rho^2}{(1-\rho^2)^2} \end{bmatrix}.
$$

The off-diagonal elements at the lower right result from the treatment of the first observation. If this observation is omitted, the calculations simplify a bit. Note that the other terms in the block are sums of $T - 1$ observations, so these "end effects" will be negligible asymptotically. Once again, their importance may be greater in a finite sample. Omitting the first observation produces the common approximation

$$
\mathbf{I}(\boldsymbol{\beta}, \sigma_u^2, \rho) = \begin{bmatrix} \dfrac{1}{\sigma_u^2}\mathbf{X}'\boldsymbol{\Omega}^{-1}\mathbf{X} & \mathbf{0} & \mathbf{0} \\[2ex] \mathbf{0}' & \dfrac{T}{2\sigma_u^4} & 0 \\[2ex] \mathbf{0}' & 0 & \dfrac{T-1}{1-\rho^2} \end{bmatrix}. \tag{15-35}
$$

It is common to drop the first observation from the previous calculations, arguing that it will be negligible asymptotically. Alternatively, one might do the analysis *conditionally* on the first observation (which appears unavoidably in the preceding sums.) From the point of view of the asymptotic properties of the estimators, it is certainly true that the first observation is inconsequential. But it must be remembered that the typical time series is not very long, and the numerical answers one obtains with and without explicit treatment of the first observation may be quite different. In such a case, the evidence suggests that retention is preferable.[17]

All of the foregoing estimators have the same asymptotic properties. The available evidence on their small-sample properties comes from Monte Carlo studies and is, unfortunately, only suggestive. Griliches and Rao (1969) find evidence that if the sample is relatively small and ρ is not particularly large, say, less than 0.3, least squares is as good as or better than FGLS. The problem is the additional variation introduced into the sampling variance by the variance of r (which increases as r decreases). A second fairly firm conclusion is that it can be far worse to omit the first observation than to keep it.[18] Beyond these, the results are rather mixed. Maximum likelihood seems to perform well in general, but the Prais–Winsten estimator is evidently nearly as efficient.

EXAMPLE 15.4. The various estimators described earlier give rather different results for the investment data of Example 15.1. First, some different estimates of ρ are given in Table 15.4.

Estimates of the regression parameters are shown in Table 15.5.

---

[17] See, for example, Maeshiro (1979) and Poirier (1978).
[18] See Harvey and McAvinchey (1979).

Table 15.4

r	0.3392
$1 - d/2$	0.3393
Theil	0.3015
Theil–Nagar	$0.3735\ [T^2(1 - d/2) + K^2/(T^2 - K^2)]$ [19]
Durbin	0.6385

Table 15.5

Estimator	Constant	GNP	Interest	ρ
OLS	−12.5336	0.16914	−1.00144	0
	(24.92)	(0.02057)	(2.369)	
Prais–Winsten				
Two-step	−15.6551	0.17073	−0.70394	0.3392
	(33.76)	(0.02791)	(2.816)	
Iterated	−15.673	0.17075	−0.70462	0.3527
(two iterations)	(33.84)	(0.02796)	(2.817)	
Cochrane–Orcutt				
Two-step	−18.3567	0.17286	−0.80775	0.3392
	(44.83)	(0.03633)	(3.102)	
Iterated	−18.3567	0.17286	−0.80775	0.3559
(two iterations)	(44.83)	(0.03633)	(3.102)	
Maximum likelihood	−14.4989	0.17006	−0.82422	0.27996
	(31.56)	(0.02608)	(2.718)	
Durbin	−26.787	0.21351	0.38499	0.6385
	(32.53)	(0.07050)	(3.824)	
Hildreth–Lu	−14.887	0.17029	−0.78936	0.3000
	(32.47)	(0.02681)	(2.754)	

(The search for r-included values:)

r	Sum of Squares
0.275	4428.3353
0.280	4427.5610
0.290	4426.5116
0.300	4426.1231
0.320	4427.3063
0.325	4428.0060
0.330	4428.8657

There are some distinctive results in Table 15.5. First, it would appear that the OLS standard errors are considerably biased downward. Second, comparing the Cochrane–Orcutt estimates to the Prais–Winsten estimates, the loss of efficiency from discarding the initial observation is substantial. Obtaining the maximum likelihood estimates by the method of Beach and MacKinnon required only three function evaluations, which is only one more than the iterated two-step estimators.

---

[19] Theil and Nagar (1961).

15.6.2. AR(2) Disturbance Processes

Maximum likelihood procedures for most other disturbance processes are exceedingly complex. Beach and MacKinnon (1978) have derived an algorithm for AR(2) disturbances. For higher-order autoregressive models, maximum likelihood estimation is presently impractical, but the two-step estimators can easily be extended. For models of the form

$$\varepsilon_t = \theta_1 \varepsilon_{t-1} + \theta_2 \varepsilon_{t-2} + \cdots + \theta_p \varepsilon_{t-p} + u_t, \tag{15-36}$$

a simple approach for estimation of the autoregressive parameters is to use either of the following methods:

1. An analog of Durbin's method. Regress y_t on $y_{t-1}, \ldots, y_{t-p}$, $\mathbf{x}$, $\mathbf{x}_{t-1}, \ldots$, and $\mathbf{x}_{t-p}$. The slopes on the lagged values of y give consistent estimates of the autoregressive parameters. If there are many regressors, this may involve an excessive number of variables.

2. By regressing e_t on $e_{t-1}, \ldots, e_{t-p}$, we also obtain consistent estimates of the autoregressive parameters.

With the estimates of $\theta_1, \ldots, \theta_p$ in hand, the Cochrane–Orcutt estimator can be obtained. If the model is an AR(2), the full FGLS procedure should be used instead.[20] The least squares computations for the transformed data provide (at least asymptotically) the appropriate estimates of σ^2 and the covariance matrix of $\hat{\beta}$. As before, iteration is possible but brings no gains in efficiency.

EXAMPLE 15.5. **Alternative Disturbance Processes.** The three models described earlier produce similar results for the parameters of the investment equation. For the AR(2) process, the first two autocorrelations are

$$\rho_1 = \frac{\theta_1}{1 - \theta_2},$$

and

$$\rho_2 = \theta_2 + \frac{\theta_1^2}{1 - \theta_2}.$$

The autoregressive parameters were estimated by regressing the OLS residuals on their lagged values. The full sets of estimates are given in Table 15.6.

Table 15.6

	AR(1)	AR(2)	MA(1)
β_1	−11.787 (29.37)	−16.176 (28.95)	−13.708 (32.73)
β_2	0.17173 (0.338)	0.17152 (0.0234)	0.16937 (0.0271)
β_3	−0.87506 (3.009)	−1.15662 (2.533)	−0.91063 (2.874)
ρ	0.2951		
θ_1	—	0.44327	—
θ_2	—	−0.45302	—
λ	—	—	0.3983
ρ_1	0.2951	0.30507	0.3438
ρ_2	0.08710	−0.31779	0

[20] Fuller (1976) gives expressions for general autoregressive processes, but these are rather cumbersome and are not yet in wide use.

Although the parameter estimates are similar, the autocorrelations of the disturbances are different. Some further evidence appears in Example 15.8, which suggests that the structure of the AR(1), that $\rho_2 = \rho_1^2$, may be overly restrictive.

15.6.3.   Estimation with a Lagged Dependent Variable

In Section 15.4.1, we considered the problem of estimation by least squares when the model contains both autocorrelation and lagged dependent variable(s). Since the OLS estimator is inconsistent, the residuals on which an estimator of ρ would be based are likewise inconsistent. Therefore $\hat{\rho}$ will be inconsistent as well. The consequence is that the FGLS estimators described earlier are not usable in this case. There is, however, an alternative way to proceed, based on the method of instrumental variables.

The method of instrumental variables was introduced in Section 9.5.4 in the context of measurement error in the classical regression model. To review, the general problem is that in the model

$$y = X\beta + \varepsilon,$$

if

$$\text{plim} \frac{1}{T} X'\varepsilon \neq 0,$$

the least squares estimator is not consistent. A consistent estimator is

$$b_{IV} = (Z'X)^{-1}(Z'y),$$

where Z is a set of K variables chosen such that

$$\text{plim} \frac{1}{T} Z'\varepsilon = 0$$

but

$$\text{plim} \frac{1}{T} Z'X \neq 0.$$

For the purpose of consistency only, any such set of z's will suffice. The relevance of that fact here is that the obstacle to consistent FGLS is, at least for the present, the lack of a consistent estimate of ρ. By using the technique of instrumental variables, we may estimate β consistently, obtain a consistent estimate of ρ, and proceed.

Hatanaka (1974) has devised an efficient two-step estimator based on this principle. To put the estimator in the current context, we consider estimation of the model

$$y_t = \beta'x_t + \gamma y_{t-1} + \varepsilon_t,$$

$$\varepsilon_t = \rho\varepsilon_{t-1} + u_t.$$

In order to get to the second step of FGLS, we require consistent estimates of the slope parameters. These can be obtained using an IV estimator, where the column of Z corresponding to y_{t-1} is the only one that need be different from that of X. An appropriate instrument can be obtained by using the fitted values in the regression of y_t on x_t and x_{t-1}.[21]

---

[21] One might use additional lags of x at this stage, perhaps to improve the small-sample properties of the estimator. Asymptotically, it is immaterial.

The residuals from this regression are then used to construct

$$\hat{\rho} = \frac{\sum_{t=3}^{T} \hat{\varepsilon}_t \hat{\varepsilon}_{t-1}}{\sum_{t=3}^{T} \hat{\varepsilon}_t^2},$$

where

$$\hat{\varepsilon}_t = y_t - \mathbf{b}_{IV}' \mathbf{x}_t - c_{IV} y_{t-1}.$$

FGLS estimates may now be computed by regressing

$$y_{*t} = y_t - \hat{\rho} y_{t-1}$$

on

$$\mathbf{x}_{*t} = \mathbf{x}_t - \hat{\rho} \mathbf{x}_{t-1},$$

$$y_{*t-1} = y_{t-1} - \hat{\rho} y_{t-2},$$

and

$$\hat{\varepsilon}_{t-1} = y_{t-1} - \mathbf{b}_{IV} \mathbf{x}_{t-1} - c_{IV} y_{t-2}.$$

Let d be the coefficient on $\hat{\varepsilon}_{t-1}$ in this regression. The efficient estimator of ρ is

$$\hat{\hat{\rho}} = \hat{\rho} + d.$$

Appropriate asymptotic standard errors for the estimators, including $\hat{\rho}$, are obtained from the $s^2 [\mathbf{X}_*' \mathbf{X}_*]^{-1}$ computed at the second step. Hatanaka shows that these estimates are asymptotically equivalent to maximum likelihood estimates.

15.7. *Testing for Autocorrelation*

15.7.1. The Durbin–Watson Test

Most of the available tests for autocorrelation are based on the principle that if the true disturbances are autocorrelated, this will be revealed through the autocorrelations of the least squares residuals. By far the most widely used test is the Durbin–Watson test.[22] The test statistic is

$$d = \frac{\sum_{t=2}^{T} (e_t - e_{t-1})^2}{\sum_{t=1}^{T} e_t^2}. \tag{15-37}$$

The statistic is closely related to the sample autocorrelation:

$$d = 2(1 - r) + \frac{e_1^2 + e_T^2}{\sum_{t=1}^{T} e_t^2}.$$

If the sample is reasonably large, the last term will be negligible, leaving

$$d \simeq 2(1 - r). \tag{15-38}$$

Values of d that differ significantly from two suggest autocorrelation of the disturbances. For testing for positive autocorrelation, the procedure would be to

Reject $H_0: \rho = 0$ if $d < d_*$,

---

[22] Durbin and Watson (1950) and (1951).

where d_* is the appropriate critical value for the distribution of d under H_0. (A test for negative autocorrelation can be based on $4 - d$.)

A serious shortcoming of the Durbin–Watson test is that the exact distribution of d depends on the data matrix. Durbin and Watson have provided a partial solution to this problem. They show that the true distribution of d lies between that of two other statistics, d_l (the lower bound) and d_u (the upper bound), such that the 5 percent critical value for the true distribution of d must lie to the right of that of d_l and to the left of that of d_u. The usefulness of the result is that the distributions of d_l and d_u depend only on T and K, and their 5 percent and 1 percent critical values have been tabulated.[23] Therefore, the test that may be carried out is

$$\text{Do not reject } H_0 \qquad \text{if } d > d_{*u},$$

$$\text{Reject } H_0 \qquad \text{if } d < d_{*l}.$$

No conclusion is drawn if $d_{*l} < d < d_{*u}$. An analogous test has been derived for quarterly data and fourth-order autocorrelation [see (15–30)] by Wallis (1972) based on

$$d_4 = \frac{\sum_{t=5}^{T}(e_t - e_{t-4})^2}{\sum_{t=1}^{T} e_t^2}. \tag{15-39}$$

Tables of the bounding distributions are given by Wallis.

EXAMPLE 15.6.   The Durbin–Watson statistic for the investment equation is 1.3083. The 5 percent critical values from the Savin–White (1977) tables are 1.074 and 1.536. Since the sample value falls in the inconclusive region, further analysis is called for.

The inconclusive region in the Durbin–Watson tables is a troubling problem. This area can be rather wide. For example, for $T = 19$ and $K = 3$ (i.e., our particular problem), the inconclusive region encompasses values of ρ from 0.218 to 0.463 (using $1 - d/2$). A great deal of research has been devoted to narrowing or eliminating this region. One approach is to deal specifically with certain kinds of regressors. For example, the critical values in the tables assume that the regression contains a constant term. If not, d_{*l} may be replaced with d_{*m}, where d_{*m} is greater than d_{*l}.[24] King (1981) presents an alternative set of bounds for regressions with quarterly seasonal dummy variables and trend variables. Giles and King (1978) present corresponding modifications for the Wallis test.

One could argue, on grounds of conservatism, that d_{*u} should always be used as the critical value. Failing to account for autocorrelation when it is present is almost surely worse than accounting for it when it is not. If the data are slowly changing, the correct critical value is more likely than not to be close to d_{*u}.[25] It is possible to calculate the correct percentage point for d for the particular data set, but this requires specialized software and is likely to be rather difficult. A number of authors have attempted to derive approximations to the appropriate critical values for the Durbin–Watson test. One that has been found to be quite accurate is also due to Durbin and Watson (1971).

The Durbin–Watson statistic can be written as

$$d = \frac{e'Ae}{e'e},$$

---

[23] See Savin and White (1977) or the appendix at the end of this book.
[24] See Farebrother (1980).
[25] See, for example, Theil and Nagar (1961) and Hannan and Terrell (1966).

where

$$
\mathbf{A} = \begin{bmatrix}
1 & -1 & 0 & 0 & \cdots & 0 \\
-1 & 2 & -1 & 0 & \cdots & 0 \\
0 & -1 & 2 & -1 & \cdots & 0 \\
0 & 0 & \cdots & -1 & 2 & -1 \\
0 & 0 & 0 & \cdots & -1 & 1
\end{bmatrix}.
$$

(15-40)

Since $\mathbf{e} = \mathbf{M}\boldsymbol{\varepsilon}$, where $\mathbf{M} = \mathbf{I} - \mathbf{X}(\mathbf{X}'\mathbf{X})^{-1}\mathbf{X}'$,

$$
d = \frac{(\boldsymbol{\varepsilon}/\sigma)'\mathbf{MAM}(\boldsymbol{\varepsilon}/\sigma)}{(\boldsymbol{\varepsilon}/\sigma)'\mathbf{M}(\boldsymbol{\varepsilon}/\sigma)}.
$$

(15-41)

The exact distribution of this statistic depends on $\mathbf{X}$. The approach is to approximate the true critical value, using

$$
\hat{d}_* = a + bd_{*u},
$$

where a and b are determined from

$$
E[d] = a + bE[d_u],
$$
$$
\mathrm{Var}[d] = b^2\mathrm{Var}[d_u].
$$

(15-42)

The expectations and variances are computed using the characteristic roots of $\mathbf{A}$:

$$
E[d_u] = \frac{1}{n}\sum_{j=K+1}^{T} \theta_j = \bar{\theta},
$$

$$
\mathrm{Var}[d_u] = \frac{2}{n(n+2)}\left[\sum_{j=K+1}^{T} \theta_j^2 - n\bar{\theta}^2\right],
$$

where $n = T - K$. We use the $T - K$ largest roots of $\mathbf{A}$. Then $E[d]$ and $\mathrm{Var}[d]$ are computed in the same manner, using the n nonzero characteristic roots of $\mathbf{MAM}$.

EXAMPLE 15.8. For our investment data, the characteristic roots, λ, of $\mathbf{MAM}$ are the following:

3.95633	3.87667	3.74689	3.55003	3.32671	3.08085
2.69580	2.48651	2.10701	1.81835	1.48363	1.18083
0.897094	0.644495	0.398000	0.209969	and three zeros.	

The 18 nonzero characteristic roots, θ, of $\mathbf{A}$ are the following:

3.97272	3.89163	3.75895	3.57828	3.35456	3.09390
2.80339	2.49097	2.16516	1.83484	1.50903	1.19661
0.906104	0.645437	0.421719	0.241052	0.108366	0.0272774

(The last is always zero.) Inserting these roots in the preceding equations gives $b = 0.9984689$ and $a = -0.0221681$. Therefore, the approximate value for d_* is 1.5115. This is consistent with our earlier observation in Example 15.5. Since the Durbin–Watson statistic for the regression is 1.3083, we would reject the hypothesis of no autocorrelation. Note that 1.3083 is squarely in the inconclusive region.

The characteristic roots of $\mathbf{A}$ are

$$\theta_i = 2 - 2\cos\left[\frac{\pi(i-1)}{T}\right],$$

so they can be computed easily. But if T is even moderately large, calculation of the characteristic roots of $\mathbf{MAM}$ is likely to be quite burdensome, assuming that the necessary software is available at all. ($\mathbf{MAM}$ is a $T \times T$ matrix.) An alternative calculation based only on $K \times K$ matrices is[26]

$$E[d] = \frac{P}{T-K},$$

where

$$P = 2(T-1) - tr[(\mathbf{X'AX})(\mathbf{X'X})^{-1}]$$

$$\mathbf{X'AX} = \sum_{t=2}^{T} \Delta\mathbf{x}_t\, \Delta\mathbf{x}'_t \qquad (15\text{–}43)$$

$$\Delta\mathbf{x}_t = \mathbf{x}_t - \mathbf{x}_{t-1}$$

and

$$\text{Var}[d] = \frac{2}{(T-K)(T-K+2)}(Q - PE[d]),$$

$$Q = 2(3T-4) - 2tr[(\mathbf{X'A^2X})(\mathbf{X'X})^{-1}] + tr[\{(\mathbf{X'AX})(\mathbf{X'X})^{-1}\}^2]$$

$$\mathbf{X'A^2X} = \sum_{t=3}^{T} \Delta^2\mathbf{x}_t\, \Delta^2\mathbf{x}'_t + \Delta\mathbf{x}_2\, \Delta\mathbf{x}'_2 + \Delta\mathbf{x}_T\, \Delta\mathbf{x}'_T,$$

$$\Delta^2\mathbf{x}_t = (\mathbf{x}_t - \mathbf{x}_{t-1}) - (\mathbf{x}_{t-1} - \mathbf{x}_{t-2}).$$

15.7.2. Other Testing Procedures

The Durbin–Watson test has been found to be quite powerful when compared to others for AR(1) processes. The test is not limited to testing for AR(1) disturbances, however. Regardless of the stochastic process,

$$\text{plim}\, d = 2 - 2\rho_1$$

where

$$\rho_1 = \text{Corr}[\varepsilon_t, \varepsilon_{t-1}].$$

Aside from the difficulty of the inconclusive region, however, there are two problems. First, it is strictly correct only when $\mathbf{X}$ is nonstochastic. Second, if the process is not an AR(1), ρ_1 may not be truly indicative of the pattern of autocorrelation.[27] Two alternative tests that are less restrictive have been devised.

The Breusch (1978)–Godfrey (1978) test is a Lagrange multiplier test of

$$H_0: \text{No autocorrelation,}$$

versus

$$H_1: \varepsilon_t = \text{AR}(P) \quad \text{or} \quad \varepsilon_t = \text{MA}(P).$$

---

[26] See Judge et al. (1982, pp. 468–469).
[27] See Example 15.10.

The same test is used for either structure. Operationally, the test can be carried out simply by regressing the ordinary least squares residuals, e_t, on $x_t, e_{t-1}, \ldots, e_{t-p}$ (filling in missing values for lagged residuals wih zeros) and referring TR^2 to the tabled critical value for the chi-squared distribution with P degrees of freedom. Since $X'e = 0$, the test is equivalent to regressing e_t on the part of the lagged residuals that is unexplained by X. There is, therefore, a compelling logic to it; if any fit is found, it is due to correlation between the current and lagged residuals. The test is a joint test of the first P autocorrelations of ε_t, not just the first.

An alternative though quite similar test is due to Box and Pierce. The Q test is carried out by referring

$$Q = T \sum_{j=1}^{L} r_j^2, \tag{15-44}$$

where

$$r_j^2 = \frac{\sum_{t=j+1}^{T} e_t e_{t-j}}{\sum_{t=1}^{T} e_t^2}$$

to the critical values of the chi-squared table with L degrees of freedom. A refinement suggested by Ljung and Box (1979) is

$$Q' = T(T+2) \sum_{j=1}^{L} \frac{r_j^2}{T-j}. \tag{15-44'}$$

This test has also been found to be reasonably powerful; however, it and the Breusch–Godfrey test have been criticized for the difficulty with the choice of L. It is worth noting that this problem of determining the depth of the lag to consider in these models of autocorrelation has reappeared at various points in our work here and pervades this literature.

EXAMPLE 15.9. The regression of the current residual on a constant, real GNP, the real interest rate, and four lags of the residual produces

$$e_t = -0.9840 - 0.000273\text{GNP} + 4.781\text{i} \qquad T = 19$$
$$\quad (17.57) \quad (0.01451) \qquad\quad (2.080) \qquad R^2 = 0.6352$$

$$-0.387e_{t-1} - 0.285e_{t-2} - 0.837e_{t-3} - 0.640e_{t-4}$$
$$\quad (0.308) \qquad (0.325) \qquad (0.342) \qquad (0.372)$$

The Breusch–Godfrey statistic is, thus, 12.068. The 5 percent critical value for the chi-squared distribution with four degrees of freedom is 9.488. The 1 percent critical value is 13.277. Therefore, the null hypothesis would be rejected at a significance level of 5 percent. The first four autocorrelations for the least squares residuals are

$$r_1 = 0.2507$$

$$r_2 = -0.2752$$

$$r_3 = -0.6605$$

$$r_4 = -0.3699$$

The Box–Pierce Q statistic is 13.5219, while the Ljung–Box statistic is 17.6895. Both are statistically significant at the 1 percent level. Both of these tests suggest that the insignificance of the Durbin–Watson test results from the fact that a significant autocorrelation appears at lag 3 but not at lag 1. Unfortunately, there is nothing in the construction of the data that would imply such a pattern of strong negative autocorrelation at lag 3. The small-sample size (19 observations) does imply that these results should be interpreted with caution.

The essential difference between the Godfrey–Breusch and the Box–Pierce tests is the use of partial correlations (controlling for $\mathbf{X}$ and the other variables) in the former and gross correlations in the latter. Since under the hypothesis that there is no autocorrelation in ε_t and no correlation between $\mathbf{x}_t$ and ε_s in any event, the two tests are asymptotically equivalent.

15.7.3. Testing in the Presence of Lagged Dependent Variables

The Durbin–Watson test is not likely to be valid when there is a lagged dependent variable in the equation.[28] The statistic will usually be biased toward a finding of no autocorrelation. Three alternatives have been devised.

The two tests described in the previous section can be used whether or not the regression contains a lagged dependent variable. As a simple alternative to the standard test, Durbin (1970) has derived a Lagrange multiplier test that is unaffected by the lagged dependent variable. The test may be carried out by referring

$$h = \left(1 - \frac{d}{2}\right) \sqrt{\frac{T}{1 - Ts_c^2}},\tag{15–45}$$

where s_c^2 is the estimated variance of the least squares regression coefficient on y_{t-1}, to the standard normal tables. Large values of h lead to rejection of H_0. The test has the virtues that it can be used even if the regression contains additional lags of y_t, and it can be computed using the standard results from the initial regression without any further regressions. However, if $s_c^2 > 1/T$, it cannot be computed. An alternative is to regress e_t on $\mathbf{x}_t$, $y_{t-1}, \ldots, e_{t-1}$, and any additional lags that are appropriate for e_t, and then testing the joint significance of the coefficient(s) on the lagged residual(s) with the standard F test. This is, of course, a modification of the Breusch–Godfrey test. Under H_0, the coefficients on the remaining variables will be zero, so the tests are the same asymptotically.

15.8. *Forecasting in the Presence of Autocorrelation*

For purposes of forecasting, we refer first to the transformed model,

$$y_{*t} = \boldsymbol{\beta}'\mathbf{x}_{*t} + \varepsilon_{*t}.$$

Suppose that the process governing ε_t is an AR(1), and ρ is known. Since this is a classical regression model, the results of Chapter 6 may be used directly. The optimal forecast of y_{*T+1}^0, given $\mathbf{x}_{T+1}^0$ and $\mathbf{x}_T$ (i.e., $\mathbf{x}_{*T+1}^0$), is

$$\hat{y}_{*T+1}^0 = \hat{\boldsymbol{\beta}}'\mathbf{x}_{*T+1}^0.$$

Disassembling $\hat{y}_{*T+1}^0$, we find

$$\hat{y}_{T+1}^0 - \rho y_T = \hat{\boldsymbol{\beta}}'\mathbf{x}_{T+1}^0 - \rho\hat{\boldsymbol{\beta}}'\mathbf{x}_T$$

or

$$\hat{y}_{T+1}^0 = \hat{\boldsymbol{\beta}}'\mathbf{x}_{T+1}^0 + \rho(y_T - \hat{\boldsymbol{\beta}}'\mathbf{x}_T)\tag{15–46}$$

$$= \hat{\boldsymbol{\beta}}'\mathbf{x}_{T+1}^0 + \rho e_T.$$

---

[28] This issue has been studied by Nerlove and Wallis (1966).

Thus, we carry forward a proportion ρ of the estimated disturbance in the preceding period. This can be justified by reference to

$$E[\varepsilon_{T+1} \mid \varepsilon_T] = \rho \varepsilon_T.$$

It can also be shown that to forecast n periods ahead, we would use

$$\hat{y}^0_{T+n} = \hat{\boldsymbol{\beta}}'\mathbf{x}^0_{T+n} + \rho^n e_t. \tag{15-47}$$

The extension to higher-order autoregressions is direct. For a second-order model, for example,

$$\hat{y}^0_{T+n} = \hat{\boldsymbol{\beta}}'\mathbf{x}^0_{T+n} + \theta_1 e_{T+n-1} + \theta_2 e_{T+n-2}. \tag{15-48}$$

For residuals that are outside the sample period, we use the recursion

$$\hat{e}_s = \theta_1 \hat{e}_{s-1} + \theta_2 \hat{e}_{s-2}, \tag{15-49}$$

beginning with the last two residuals within the sample.

Moving average models are somewhat simpler, as the autocorrelation lasts for only one period. For an MA(1) model, for the first postsample period,

$$\hat{y}^0_{T+1} = \hat{\boldsymbol{\beta}}'\mathbf{x}^0_{T+1} + \hat{\varepsilon}_{T+1},$$

where

$$\hat{\varepsilon}_{T+1} = \hat{u}_{T+1} - \lambda \hat{u}_T.$$

Therefore, a forecast of ε_{T+1} will use all previous residuals. One way to proceed is to accumulate $\hat{\varepsilon}_{T+1}$ from the recursion

$$\hat{u}_t = \hat{\varepsilon}_t + \lambda \hat{u}_{t-1}$$

with $\hat{u}_{t+1} = \hat{u}_0 = 0$ and $\hat{\varepsilon}_t = (y_t - \hat{\boldsymbol{\beta}}'\mathbf{x}_t)$. After the first postsample period, $\hat{\varepsilon}_{T+n} = \hat{u}_{T+n} - \lambda \hat{u}_{T+n-1} = 0$.

If the parameters of the disturbance process are known, the variances for the forecast errors can be computed using the results of Chapter 6. For an AR(1) disturbance, the estimated variance would be

$$s^2_f = \hat{\sigma}^2_\varepsilon [1 + (\mathbf{x}_t - \rho\mathbf{x}_{t-1})'\{\text{Est. Var}[\hat{\boldsymbol{\beta}}]\}(\mathbf{x}_t - \rho\mathbf{x}_{t-1})]. \tag{15-50}$$

For a higher-order process, it is only necessary to modify the calculation of $\mathbf{x}_{*t}$ accordingly. The forecast variances for an MA(1) process are somewhat more involved. Details may be found in Judge et al (1985). If the parameters of the disturbance process, ρ, λ, θ_j, and so on, are estimated as well, the forecast variance will be greater. For an AR(1) model, the necessary correction to the forecast variance of the n-period-ahead forecast error is $\hat{\sigma}^2_\varepsilon n^2 \rho^{2(n-1)}/T$. (For a one-period-ahead forecast, this merely adds a term, $1/T$, in the brackets in (15–50).) Higher-order AR and MA processes are analyzed in Baille.[29] Finally, if the regressors are stochastic, the expressions become more complex by another order of magnitude.

If ρ is known, (15–47) provides the best linear unbiased forecast of y_{t+1}.[30] If, however, ρ must be estimated, this assessment must be modified. There is information about ε_{t+1} embodied in e_t. However, having to estimate ρ implies that some or all of the value of this information is offset by the variation introduced into the forecast by including the stochastic

---

[29] Op. cit.
[30] See Goldberger (1962).

component $\hat{\rho} e_t$.[31] Whether (15–47) is preferable to the obvious expedient, $\hat{y}^0_{T+n} = \hat{\beta}' \mathbf{x}^0_{T+n}$, in a small sample when ρ is estimated remains to be settled.

For computational purposes, Pagan and Nicholls (1984) have extended Salkever's augmented regression (Section 6.8.1) to models of autocorrelation. The augmented regression for forecasting T^0 periods ahead, based on $\mathbf{X}^0$, would use

$$
\tilde{\mathbf{X}} = \begin{bmatrix} \mathbf{X} & \mathbf{0} \\ \mathbf{x}^0_{T+1} & 1 & 0 & 0 & \cdots \\ \mathbf{x}^0_{T+2} & \rho & 1 & 0 & \cdots \\ \mathbf{x}^0_{T+3} & \rho^2 & \rho & 1 & \cdots \end{bmatrix}, \quad \tilde{\mathbf{y}} = \begin{bmatrix} \mathbf{y} \\ \mathbf{y}^0 \end{bmatrix}.
$$

etc.

The authors have obtained general expressions for higher-order models and for mixtures of AR and MA models. There are two drawbacks, however. First, the unknown ρ must be replaced with the sample estimate. This is simple in principle. But it presents a practical difficulty not present in Salkever's computations. The classical regression is done in a single pass, so $\tilde{\mathbf{X}}$ and $\tilde{\mathbf{y}}$ can be constructed before the computations are begun. Pagan and Nicholls' augmented regressors must be constructed *after* the initial least squares regression. Most software does not relinquish control once the estimation of a model with autocorrelated disturbances is begun until all computations are finished. The second difficulty, also not present in Salkever's formulation, is that this augmented regression requires $\mathbf{y}^0$. Therefore, it can be used only for within-sample purposes (or for model validation based on partitioning of the sample).

Exercises

1. Does first differencing reduce autocorrelation? Consider the models

$$
y_t = \beta' \mathbf{x}_t + \varepsilon_t,
$$

where

$$
\varepsilon_t = \rho \varepsilon_{t-1} + u_t
$$

and

$$
\varepsilon_t = u_t - \lambda u_{t-1}.
$$

Compare the autocorrelation of ε_t in the original model to that of v_t in

$$
y_t - y_{t-1} = \beta'(\mathbf{x}_t - \mathbf{x}_{t-1}) + v_t,
$$

where

$$
v_t = \varepsilon_t - \varepsilon_{t-1}.
$$

2. Derive the disturbance covariance matrix for the model

$$
y_t = \beta' \mathbf{x}_t + \varepsilon_t,
$$

$$
\varepsilon_t = \rho \varepsilon_{t-1} + u_t - \lambda u_{t-1}.
$$

What parameter is estimated by the regression of the OLS residuals on their lagged values?

---

[31] See Baille (1979).

3. A least squares regression based on 24 observations produces the following results:

$$y_t = 0.3 + 1.21x_t \qquad R^2 = 0.982$$
$$\quad (0.1) \quad (0.2) \qquad DW = 1.31.$$

Test the hypothesis that the disturbances are not autocorrelated.

4. It can be shown in the regression model

$$y_t = \beta y_{t-1} + \varepsilon_t,$$

$$\varepsilon_t = \rho \varepsilon_{t-1} + u_t,$$

that

$$\operatorname{plim} r = \frac{\beta \rho (\beta + \rho)}{1 + \beta \rho},$$

where

$$r = \frac{\sum_{t=2}^{T} e_t e_{t-1}}{\sum_{t=2}^{T} e_t^2}.$$

Use this result to show that

$$\operatorname{plim} \frac{r}{b} = \beta \rho,$$

$$\operatorname{plim} b + r = \beta + \rho,$$

where b is the OLS estimator of β. If you were given only the ordinary least squares regression results and the Durbin–Watson statistic, could you estimate β and ρ? If so, how? If not, why not?

5. The appendix to Chapter 19 contains data for 1953 to 1984 on (among other variables) gross private domestic investment (I) and corporate profits (P). Estimate the efficiency ratio (15–21) for OLS estimation using the model

$$I_t = \alpha + \beta P_t + \varepsilon_t,$$

assuming that corporate profits satisfy the assumption made in that derivation.

6. Using the data and model of the previous problem, compute and plot the ordinary least squares residuals. Obtain the first and second autocorrelations of the OLS residuals. Now compute the GLS estimator, assuming that the disturbances are an AR(1) process. Use the Prais–Winsten estimator and then the Cochrane–Orcutt estimator. What differences do you observe? To estimate ρ, use any of the estimators discussed in the text.

7. The following regression is obtained by ordinary least squares, using 21 observations. (Estimated asymptotic standard errors are shown in parentheses.)

$$y_t = 1.3 + 0.97y_{t-1} + 2.31x_t, \qquad DW = 1.21.$$
$$\quad (0.3) \quad (0.18) \qquad (1.04)$$

Test for the presence of autocorrelation in the disturbances.

8. It is commonly asserted that the Durbin–Watson statistic is appropriate only for testing for first-order autoregressive disturbances. What combination of the coefficients of the model is estimated by the Durbin–Watson statistic in each of the following cases: AR(1), AR(2), MA(1), ARMA(1, 1)? In each case, assume that the regression model does not contain a lagged dependent variable. Comment on the impact on your results of relaxing this assumption.

References

Amemiya, T., *Advanced Econometrics*, Cambridge: Harvard University Press, 1985.

Anderson, T., *The Statistical Analysis of Time Series*, New York: Wiley, 1971.

Balestra, P., "A Note on the Exact Transformation Associated with the First-Order Moving Average Process," *Journal of Econometrics*, 14, 1980, pp. 381–394.

Baille, R., "The Asymptotic Mean Squared Error of Multistep Prediction from the Regression Model with Autoregressive Errors," *Journal of the American Statistical Association*, 74, 1979, pp. 175–184.

Beach, C., and J. MacKinnon, "A Maximum Likelihood Procedure for Regression with Autocorrelated Errors," *Econometrica*, 46, 1978, pp. 51–58.

Beach, J., and J. MacKinnon, "Full Maximum Likelihood Estimation of Second Order Autoregressive Error Models," *Journal of Econometrics*, 7, 1978, pp. 187–198.

Box, G., and G. Jenkins, *Time Series Analysis: Forecasting and Control*, San Francisco: Holden-Day, 1976.

Breusch, T., "Testing for Autocorrelation in Dynamic Linear Models," *Australian Economic Papers*, 17, 1978, pp. 334–355.

Cochrane, D., and G. Orcutt, "Application of Least Squares Regression to Relationships Containing Autocorrelated Error Terms," *Journal of the American Statistical Association*, 44, 1949, pp. 32–61.

Durbin, J., "Estimation of Parameters in Time-Series Regression Models," *Journal of the Royal Statistical Society, Series B*, 22, 1960, pp. 139–153.

Durbin, J., "Testing for Serial Correlation in Least Squares Regression When Some of the Regressors Are Lagged Dependent Variables," *Econometrica*, 38, 1970, pp. 410–421.

Durbin, J., and G. Watson, "Testing for Serial Correlation in Least Squares Regression—I," *Biometrika*, 37, 1950, pp. 409–428.

Durbin, J., and G. Watson, "Testing for Serial Correlation in Least Squares Regression—II," *Biometrika*, 38, 1951, pp. 159–178.

Durbin, J., and G. Watson, "Testing for Serial Correlation in Least Squares Regression—III," *Biometrika*, 58, 1971, pp. 1–42.

Farebrother, R., "The Durbin–Watson Test for Serial Correlation When There Is No Intercept in the Regression," *Econometrica*, 48, 1980, pp. 1553–1563.

Fuller, W., *Introduction to Statistical Time Series*, New York: Wiley, 1976.

Giles, D., and M. King, "Fourth Order Autocorrelation: Further Significance Points for the Wallis Test," *Journal of Econometrics*, 8, 1978, pp. 255–259.

Godfrey, L., "Testing Against General Autoregressive and Moving Average Error Models When the Regressors Include Lagged Dependent Variables," *Econometrica*, 46, 1978, pp. 1293–1302.

Goldberger, A., "Best Linear Unbiased Prediction in the Generalized Regression Model," *Journal of the American Statistical Association*, 57, 1962, pp. 369–375.

Griliches, Z., and P. Rao, "Small Sample Properties of Several Two Stage Regression Methods in the Context of Autocorrelated Errors," *Journal of the American Statistical Association*, 64, 1969, pp. 253–272.

Hannan, E., and R. Terrell, "Testing for Serial Correlation After Least Squares Regression," *Econometrica*, 54, 1966, pp. 646–660.

Harvey, A., and I. McAvinchey, "On the Relative Efficiency of Various Estimators of Regression Models with Moving Average Disturbances," in E. Charatsis, ed., *Proceedings of the Econometric Society European Meetings, Athens, 1979*, Amsterdam: North Holland, 1981.

Hatanaka, M., "An Efficient Estimator for the Dynamic Adjustment Model with Autocorrelated Errors," *Journal of Econometrics*, 2, 1974, pp. 199–220.

Hildreth, C., and W. Dent, "An Adjusted Maximum Likelihood Estimator," in W. Saelkert, ed., *Econometrics and Economic Theory: Essays in Honor of Jan Tinbergen*, London: Macmillan, 1974, pp. 3–25.

Hildreth, C., and J. Lu, "Demand Relations with Autocorrelated Disturbances," Technical Bulletin Number 276, Michigan State University Agricultural Experiment Station, 1960.

Johnston, J., *Econometric Methods*, New York: McGraw-Hill, 1984, pp. 138–140.

Judge, G., R. Hill, W. Griffiths, T. Lee, and H. Lutkepol, *Introduction to the Theory and Practice of Econometrics*, New York: Wiley, 1982.

Judge, G., R. Hill, W. Griffiths, and T. Lee, The Theory and Practice of Econometrics, New York: Wiley, 1985.

King, M., "The Durbin–Watson Test for Serial Correlation: Bounds for Regressions with Trend and/or Seasonal Dummy Variables," *Econometrica*, 49, 1981, pp. 1571–1581.

Kmenta, J., *Elements of Econometrics*, New York: Macmillan, 1986.

Ljung, T., and G. Box, "The Likelihood Function for a Stationary Autoregressive Moving Average Process," *Biometrika*, 66, 1979, pp. 265–270.

Maeshiro, A., "On the Retention of the First Observations in Serial Correlation Adjustment of Regression Models," *International Economic Review*, 20, 1979, pp. 259–265.

Nerlove, M., and K. Wallis, "Use of the Durbin–Watson Statistic in Inappropriate Situations," *Econometrica*, 34, 1966, pp. 235–238.

Newey, W., and K. West, "A Simple Positive Semi-Definite, Heteroscedasticity and Autocorrelation Consistent Covariance Matrix," *Econometrica*, 55, 1987, pp. 703–708.

Nicholls, D., A. Pagan, and R. Terrell, "The Estimation and Use of Models with Moving Average Disturbance Terms: A Survey," *International Economic Review*, 16, 1975, pp. 113–134.

Pagan, A., and D. Nicholls, "Estimating Prediction Errors and Their Standard Deviations Using Constructed Variables," *Journal of Econometrics*, 24, 1984, pp. 293–310.

Park, R., and B. Mitchell, "Estimating the Autocorrelated Error Model with Trended Data," *Journal of Econometrics*, 13, 1980, pp. 185–201.

Pesaran, M., "Exact Maximum Likelihood Estimation of a Regression Equation with a First-Order Moving-Average Error," *Review of Economic Studies*, 40, 1973, pp. 529–536.

Poirier, D., "The Effect of the First Observation in Regression Models with First-Order Autoregressive Disturbances," *Applied Statistics*, 27, 1978, pp. 67–68.

Prais, S., and C. Winsten, "Trend Estimation and Serial Correlation," Cowles Commission Discussion Paper Number 383, Chicago, 1954.

Savin, E., and K. White, "The Durbin–Watson Test for Serial Correlation with Extreme Sample Sizes or Many Regressors," *Econometrica*, 45, 1977, pp. 1989–1996.

Theil, H., *Principles of Econometrics*, New York: Wiley, 1971.

Theil, H., and A. Nagar, "Testing the Independence of Regression Disturbances," *Journal of the American Statistical Association*, 52, 1961, pp. 793–806.

Wallis, K., "Testing for Fourth Order Autocorrelation in Quarterly Regression Equations," *Econometrica*, 40, 1972, pp. 617–636.

White, H., *Asymptotic Theory for Econometricians*, New York: Academic Press, 1984.

Chapter 16

Models That Use Both Cross-Section and Time-Series Data

16.1. Introduction

Data sets that combine time series and cross sections are common in economics. For example, the published statistics of the OECD contain numerous series of economic aggregates observed yearly for many countries. Recently constructed *longitudinal* data sets contain observations on thousands of individuals or families, each observed at several points in time. Some empirical studies have analyzed time series data on several firms, states, or industries simultaneously. These data sets provide a rich source of information about the economy. However, modeling in this setting calls for some quite complex stochastic specifications. In this chapter, we survey the most commonly used techniques for time-series–cross-section data analyses.

16.2. Time-Series–Cross-Section Data

Many studies have analyzed data observed across countries or firms in which the number of cross-sectional units is relatively small and the number of time periods is (potentially) relatively large. The data set in Example 16.1 is an example, with five firms each observed for 20 years. In this setting, we can emphasize time series analysis. The data sets are typically "long" enough that we may study the disturbance terms in the context of stochastic processes. Heteroscedasticity is the effect of different processes applying to different cross-sectional units. The "narrow width" (i.e., smallness of the number of cross sections) of some of these data sets is not a serious concern.

Many recent studies have analyzed panel, or longitudinal, data sets. Two very famous ones are the National Longitudinal Survey of Labor Market Experience (NLS) and the Michigan Panel Study of Income Dynamics (PSID). In these data sets, very large cross sections, consisting of thousands of micro units, are followed through time. But the number of periods is often quite small. The PSID, for example, is a study of roughly 6000 families and 15,000 individuals who have been interviewed periodically from 1968 to the present. Another group of intensively studied panel data sets is those from the negative income tax experiments of the early 1970s, in which thousands of families were followed for 8 or 13 quarters. Constructing long, evenly spaced time series in this context would be prohibitively expensive, but for the purposes for which these data are typically used, this is unnecessary.

Time effects are often viewed as "transitions" or discrete changes of state. They are typically modeled as specific to the period in which they occur and are not carried across periods within a cross-sectional unit.[1] Panel data sets are more oriented toward cross-section analyses; they are wide but typically short. Heterogeneity across units is an integral part—indeed, often the central focus—of the analysis.

EXAMPLE 16.1. Investment Data. The following tables (16.1, 16.2, and 16.3) are part of the data used in a classic study of investment demand,[2] and are typical of the kinds of data that we would include in our first category. The data consist of time series of 20 yearly observations for 5 firms (of 10 in the original study) and 3 variables:

$$I_t = \text{gross investment,}$$

$$F_t = \text{market value of the firm at the end of}$$
$$\text{the previous year,}$$

$$C_t = \text{value of the stock of plant and equipment}$$
$$\text{at the end of the previous year.}$$

Table 16.1

	General Motors			Chrysler		
	I_t	F_t	C_t	I_t	F_t	C_t
1935	317.6	3078.5	2.80	40.29	417.5	10.5
1936	391.8	4661.7	52.60	72.76	837.8	10.2
1937	410.6	5387.1	156.9	66.26	883.9	34.7
1938	257.7	2792.2	209.2	51.60	437.9	51.8
1939	330.8	4313.2	203.4	52.41	679.7	64.3
1940	461.2	4643.9	207.2	69.41	727.8	67.1
1941	512.0	4551.2	255.2	68.35	643.6	75.2
1942	448.0	3244.1	303.7	46.80	410.9	71.4
1943	499.6	4053.7	264.1	47.40	588.4	67.1
1944	547.5	4379.3	201.6	59.57	698.4	60.5
1945	561.2	4840.9	265.0	88.78	846.4	54.6
1946	688.1	4900.9	402.2	74.12	893.8	84.8
1947	568.9	3526.5	761.5	62.68	579.0	96.8
1948	529.2	3254.7	922.4	89.36	694.6	110.2
1949	555.1	3700.2	1020.1	78.98	590.3	147.4
1950	642.9	3755.6	1099.0	100.66	693.5	163.2
1951	755.9	4833.0	1207.7	160.62	809.0	203.5
1952	891.2	4924.9	1430.5	145.00	727.0	290.6
1953	1304.4	6241.7	1777.3	174.93	1001.5	346.1
1954	1486.7	5593.6	2226.3	172.49	703.2	414.9

Source: I = gross investment*; F = value of the firm[†]; and C = stock of plant and equipment[‡].
    * *Moody's Industrial Manual* and Annual Reports of Corporations.
    [†] *Bank and Quotation Record* and *Moody's Industrial Manual.*
    [‡] *Survey of Current Business.*

---

[1] This has not prevented theorists from devising autocorrelation models applicable to panel data sets. See, for example, Lee (1978). As a practical matter, however, the empiricial literature in this field has tended to concentrate on the less intricate models. Time series modeling of the sort discussed in the previous chapter is somewhat unusual in the analysis of longitudinal data.
[2] Grunfeld (1958) and Grunfeld and Griliches (1960). The data were also used in Boot and deWitt (1960).

Table 16.2

	General Electric			Westinghouse		
	I_t	F_t	C_t	I_t	F_t	C_t
1935	33.1	1170.6	97.8	12.93	191.5	1.8
1936	45.0	2015.8	104.4	25.90	516.0	0.8
1937	77.2	2803.3	118.0	35.05	729.0	7.4
1938	44.6	2039.7	156.2	22.89	560.4	18.1
1939	48.1	2256.2	172.6	18.84	519.9	23.5
1940	74.4	2132.2	186.6	28.57	628.5	26.5
1941	113.0	1834.1	220.9	48.51	537.1	36.2
1942	91.9	1588.0	287.8	43.34	561.2	60.8
1943	61.3	1749.4	319.9	37.02	617.2	84.4
1944	56.8	1687.2	321.3	37.81	626.7	91.2
1945	93.6	2007.7	319.6	39.27	737.2	92.4
1946	159.9	2208.3	346.0	53.46	760.5	86.0
1947	147.2	1656.7	456.4	55.56	581.4	111.1
1948	146.3	1604.4	543.4	49.56	662.3	130.6
1949	98.3	1431.8	618.3	32.04	583.8	141.8
1950	93.5	1610.5	647.4	32.24	635.2	136.7
1951	135.2	1819.4	671.3	54.38	723.8	129.7
1952	157.3	2079.7	726.1	71.78	864.1	145.5
1953	179.5	2371.6	800.3	90.08	1193.5	174.8
1954	189.6	2759.9	888.9	68.60	1188.9	213.5

Source: See Table 16.1.

Table 16.3

	U.S. Steel		
	I_t	F_t	C_t
1935	209.9	1362.4	53.8
1936	355.3	1807.1	50.5
1937	469.9	2676.3	118.1
1938	262.3	1801.9	260.2
1939	230.4	1957.3	312.7
1940	261.6	2202.9	254.2
1941	472.8	2380.5	261.4
1942	445.6	2168.6	298.7
1943	361.6	1985.1	301.8
1944	288.2	1813.9	279.1
1945	258.7	1850.2	213.8
1946	420.3	2067.7	232.6
1947	420.5	1796.7	264.8
1948	494.5	1625.8	306.9
1949	405.1	1667.0	351.1
1950	418.8	1677.4	357.8
1951	588.2	2289.5	342.1
1952	645.2	2159.4	444.2
1953	641.0	2031.3	623.6
1954	459.3	2115.5	669.7

Source: See Table 16.1.

The variables F_t and I_t reflect anticipated profit and the expected amount of replacement investment required.[3]

The model to be estimated with these data is

$$I_{it} = \beta_1 + \beta_2 F_{it} + \beta_3 C_{it} + \varepsilon_{it}. \tag{16-1}$$

In the models we shall examine in this chapter, the data set consists of n cross-sectional units, denoted $i = 1, \ldots, n$, observed at each of T time periods, $t = 1, \ldots, T$.[4] We have a total of nT observations. Discussion of asymptotic properties will be couched in terms of $n \to \infty$ and/or $T \to \infty$. Which, if either, applies will make a difference in a particular context, and we will have to be specific in each case we examine. In the next section, the asymptotic results we obtain are with respect to $T \to \infty$. We assume that n is fixed, except where specifically noted otherwise.

16.3. Models of Several Time Series

The basic framework for this analysis is the generalized regression model:

$$y_{it} = \beta' x_{it} + \varepsilon_{it}. \tag{16-2}$$

It is useful to collect the n-time series,

$$y_i = X_i \beta + \varepsilon_i,$$

so that

$$\begin{bmatrix} y_1 \\ y_2 \\ \vdots \\ y_n \end{bmatrix} = \begin{bmatrix} X_1 \\ X_2 \\ \vdots \\ X_n \end{bmatrix} \beta + \begin{bmatrix} \varepsilon_1 \\ \varepsilon_2 \\ \vdots \\ \varepsilon_n \end{bmatrix}. \tag{16-3}$$

Each submatrix or subvector has T observations. In general terms,

$$V = E[\varepsilon \varepsilon'] = \begin{bmatrix} \sigma_{11}\Omega_{11} & \sigma_{12}\Omega_{12} & \cdots & \sigma_{1n}\Omega_{1n} \\ \sigma_{21}\Omega_{21} & \sigma_{22}\Omega_{22} & \cdots & \sigma_{2n}\Omega_{2n} \\ & & \vdots & \\ \sigma_{n1}\Omega_{n1} & \sigma_{n2}\Omega_{n2} & \cdots & \sigma_{nn}\Omega_{nn} \end{bmatrix} \tag{16-4}$$

For the present, we assume that the parameter vector β is the same for all i. A variety of models are obtained by varying the structure of V.

The classical regression model specifies that

$$E[\varepsilon_{it}] = 0,$$

$$\text{Var}[\varepsilon_{it}] = \sigma^2,$$

$$\text{Cov}[\varepsilon_{it}, \varepsilon_{js}] = 0 \qquad \text{if } t \neq s \text{ or } i \neq j.$$

---

[3] In the original study, the authors used the notation F_{t-1} and C_{t-1}. In order to avoid possible conflicts with the usual subscripting conventions used here, we have used the preceding notation instead.
[4] The requirement that each unit be observed the same number of periods is not necessary for much of this analysis.

Then

$$V = \begin{bmatrix} \sigma^2 I & 0 & \cdots & 0 \\ 0 & \sigma^2 I & \cdots & 0 \\ & \vdots & & \\ 0 & 0 & \cdots & \sigma^2 I \end{bmatrix}. \tag{16-5}$$

We can also stack the data in the pooled regression model in

$$y = X\beta + \varepsilon.$$

For this simple model, the GLS estimator reduces to pooled ordinary least squares.

EXAMPLE 16.2. Classical Regression.   By pooling all 100 observations and estimating the coefficients by ordinary least squares, we obtain

$$I_t = -48.0297 + 0.105085 F_t + 0.305366 C_t,$$
$$\quad\quad (21.48) \quad\quad (0.01138) \quad\quad (0.04351)$$
$$R^2 = 0.77886, \quad\quad s^2 = 16{,}194.67.$$

In this and the following examples, estimated standard errors for parameter estimates are shown in parentheses.

16.3.1.   Cross-Sectional Heteroscedasticity

The pooled regression model of (16-5) and Example 16.2 implies a number of restrictions on V. Examination of the data in the example suggests that the variance will be quite different in the five time series. If this were a cross-country comparison, we would expect tremendous variation in the scales of all variables in the model. We can relax the classical assumption by allowing σ^2 to vary across i. This results in the groupwise heteroscedastic model of Example 14.4:

$$V = \begin{bmatrix} \sigma_1^2 I & 0 & \cdots & 0 \\ 0 & \sigma_2^2 I & \cdots & 0 \\ & \vdots & & \\ 0 & 0 & \cdots & \sigma_n^2 I \end{bmatrix}. \tag{16-6}$$

The GLS estimator, as we saw earlier, is

$$\hat{\beta} = [X'V^{-1}X]^{-1}[X'V^{-1}y]$$
$$= \left[\sum_{i=1}^{n} \frac{1}{\sigma_i^2} X_i'X_i \right]^{-1} \left[\sum_{i=1}^{n} \frac{1}{\sigma_i^2} X_i'y_i \right].$$

Of course, the disturbance variances, σ_i^2, will rarely be known, so an alternative estimator will be required. The estimation procedure can be either two-step FGLS or, if maximum likelihood estimates are required, iterated two-step estimation.

EXAMPLE 16.3. Testing and Estimation with Groupwise Heteroscedasticity.   Using the OLS parameter estimates, we obtain the estimates of σ_i^2 listed in Table 16.4. These estimates suggest that the variance differs substantially across firms. We can use any of three possible tests for heteroscedasticity.

Table 16.4.   Residual Variances

(GM)	General Motors	9,410.91
(GE)	General Electric	32,488.49
(US)	U.S. Steel	33,455.51
(CH)	Chrysler	755.85
(WE)	Westinghouse	633.42
	Pooled	16,194,67

The Lagrange multiplier test is probably the most convenient test, since it does not require another regression after the pooled least squares regression. The log-likelihood function and its derivatives for the sample *without the restriction of equal variances* are

$$\ln L = -\frac{nT}{2}\ln(2\pi) - \frac{T}{2}\sum_i \ln \sigma_i^2 - \frac{1}{2}\sum_i \frac{\varepsilon_i'\varepsilon_i}{\sigma_i^2},$$

$$\frac{\partial \ln L}{\partial \beta} = \sum_i \frac{1}{\sigma_i^2}\mathbf{X}_i'(\mathbf{y}_i - \mathbf{X}_i\beta) = \sum_i \frac{1}{\sigma_i^2}\mathbf{X}_i'\varepsilon_i,$$

$$\frac{\partial \ln L}{\partial \sigma_i^2} = \frac{-T}{2\sigma_i^2} + \frac{1}{2\sigma_i^4}\varepsilon_i'\varepsilon_i, \qquad i = 1,\ldots,n,$$

$$\frac{\partial^2 \ln L}{\partial \beta \partial \beta'} = -\sum_i \frac{1}{\sigma_i^2}\mathbf{X}_i'\mathbf{X}_i,$$

$$\frac{\partial^2 \ln L}{\partial (\sigma_i^2)^2} = \frac{T}{2\sigma_i^4} - \frac{\varepsilon_i'\varepsilon_i}{\sigma_i^6}, \qquad i = 1,\ldots,n,$$

$$\frac{\partial^2 \ln L}{\partial \beta \partial \sigma_i^2} = -\sum_i \frac{1}{\sigma_i^4}\mathbf{X}_i'\varepsilon_i, \qquad i = 1,\ldots,n.$$

Under the null hypothesis of equal variances, the first derivatives are

$$\mathbf{g} = \begin{bmatrix} \partial \ln L/\partial \beta \\ \partial \ln L/\partial \sigma_i^2 \end{bmatrix} = \begin{bmatrix} (1/\sigma^2)\sum_i \mathbf{X}_i'\varepsilon_i \\ -T/(2\sigma^2) + \varepsilon_i'\varepsilon_i/(2\sigma^4) \end{bmatrix}$$

and the negative of the expected second derivatives matrix is

$$\mathbf{H}(\beta, \sigma^2) = \begin{bmatrix} (1/\sigma^2)\mathbf{X}'\mathbf{X} & \mathbf{0} \\ \mathbf{0}' & (T/2\sigma^4)\mathbf{I} \end{bmatrix}.$$

It is convenient to rewrite

$$\frac{\partial \ln L}{\partial \sigma_i^2} = \frac{T}{2\sigma^2}\left[\frac{\hat{\sigma}_i^2}{\sigma^2} - 1\right],$$

where $\hat{\sigma}_i^2$ is the ith unit-specific estimate of σ^2. The restricted maximum likelihood estimator of β is the pooled ordinary least squares estimator. At this restricted estimator, under the null hypothesis, $\partial \ln L/\partial \beta = \mathbf{0}$, as these are the OLS normal equations. The restricted maximum likelihood estimator of the common σ^2 is

$$s^2 = \frac{e'e}{nT}$$

$$= \frac{\sum_i e'_i e_i}{nT}$$

$$= \frac{1}{n}\sum_i s_i^2.$$

It is a simple average of the n consistent estimators. With this in hand, the Lagrange multiplier statistic, $g'H^{-1}g$ (computed at the pooled OLS estimates), reduces to

$$LM = \sum_i \left[\frac{T}{2s^2}\left(\frac{s_i^2}{s^2} - 1\right)\right]^2 \left[\frac{2s^4}{T}\right]$$

$$= \frac{T}{2}\sum_i \left[\frac{s_i^2}{s^2} - 1\right]^2.$$

The statistic has n degrees of freedom. Based on the preceding least squares results, $LM = 41.549$, which is highly significant.

The Lagrange multiplier statistic is simple to compute and asymptotically equivalent to a likelihood ratio test. It does assume normality. If this is not feasible, White's general test[5] is an alternative. To use White's test, we regress the squared OLS residual on a constant, F, C, F^2, C^2, and FC. The R^2 in this regression is 0.36854, so the chi-squared statistic is $(nT)R^2 = 36.584$, with five degrees of freedom. The 1 percent critical value from the table is 15.056, so we can reject the hypothesis of homoscedasticity on the basis of this test.

We can also carry out an approximate likelihood ratio test (these are not the maximum likelihood estimators), using the test statistic in Section 14.6.4. The appropriate likelihood ratio statistic is

$$-2\ln\lambda = (nT)\ln\hat\sigma^2 - \sum_i T\ln\hat\sigma_i^2,$$

where

$$\hat\sigma^2 = \frac{e'e}{nT} \qquad \text{and} \qquad \hat\sigma_i^2 = \frac{e'_i e_i}{T},$$

with all residuals computed using the maximum likelihood estimators. This chi-squared statistic has $n - 1$ degrees of freedom. (Iterated FGLS can be used to compute them.) If only least squares results are available, s^2 and s_i^2 may be used, possibly with some loss of power in small samples. For these data,

$$\chi^2 = 100\ln s^2 - \sum_i 20\ln s_i^2 = 108.54.$$

This far exceeds the tabled critical value.

We proceed to reestimate the regression, allowing for heteroscedasticity. The two estimators, FGLS and MLE, are given in Table 16.5.

---

[5] See Section 14.6.1.

Table 16.5

	FGLS	ML
$\hat{\beta}_1$	-36.2537 (6.1244)	-23.2583 (4.815)
$\hat{\beta}_2$	0.09499 (0.007409)	0.0943499 (0.006283)
$\hat{\beta}_3$	0.337813 (0.030225)	0.333702 (0.02204)

Variances $\hat{\sigma}_{ii}$		
GM	8,612.22	8,657.87
GE	36,562.89	40,211.13
US	32,903.13	29,824.92
CH	777.96	1,241.01
WE	409.20	175.78
Pooled	15,853.08	—

The likelihood ratio statistic for a test of homoscedasticity based on the MLEs is 123.96, which is extremely significant. With the unrestricted estimates as an alternative test procedure, we may use the Wald statistic. If we assume normality, the asymptotic variance of each variance estimator is $2\sigma_i^4/T$, and the variances are asymptotically uncorrelated. Therefore, the Wald statistic to test the hypothesis of a common variance, σ^2, would be

$$W = \sum_i (s_i^2 - \sigma^2)^2 \left(\frac{2\sigma_i^4}{T}\right)^{-1}.$$

Using s_i^2 to estimate σ_i^2 produces the sample statistic

$$W = \frac{T}{2} \sum_i \left(\frac{\sigma^2}{s_i^2} - 1\right)^2.$$

Note the similarity to the Lagrange multiplier statistic. The estimator of the common variance can be the pooled estimator from the first least squares regression or the total sum of squared GLS residuals divided by nT. Using the immediately preceding results, we find that the Wald statistic is 18,010.22. We observe the common occurrence of an extremely large Wald test statistic.

Returning to the least squares estimators, we should expect the OLS standard errors to be incorrect, given our findings. There are two possible corrections we can use, the White estimator and direct computation of the appropriate asymptotic covariance matrix. For ordinary least squares, these give the results shown in Table 16.6.

A Note on Computation. The computation of GLS estimators can involve very burdensome calculations and matrices of large orders. This might be of particular

Table 16.6

Coefficient	OLS SE	White	Correct
-48.0297	21.48	15.02	14.20
0.105085	0.01138	0.009146	0.009065
0.305366	0.04351	0.05911	0.040947

concern if one wishes to do these calculations on a microcomputer.[6] For the present model, the calculations are much simpler than they might appear. We require for the computations, computed only once at the outset of the iterations, $X'X$, $X'y$, and $y'y$ for the pooled data and for each cross-sectional unit. All OLS results are obtained using familiar results from Chapter 6, so we need not repeat the formulas here. For the FGLS and ML results, we are iterating between

$$1. \ \hat{\beta} = \left[\sum_i \frac{1}{s_i^2} X_i' X_i\right]^{-1} \sum_i \frac{1}{s_i^2} X_i' y_i$$

and

$$2. \ s_i^2 = \frac{e_i' e_i}{n_i}.$$

At the end of the iterations (or after the first), the inverse matrix in brackets ([ ]) provides the estimated asymptotic covariance matrix for the FGLS estimator. But

$$e_i = y_i - x_i \hat{\beta},$$

so

$$e_i' e_i = y_i' y_i + \hat{\beta}' X_i' X_i \hat{\beta} - 2 \hat{\beta}' X_i' y_i.$$

Therefore, all computations are based entirely on sample moments and simple manipulations of matrices that are only $K \times K$, $K \times 1$, or 1×1.

16.3.2. Cross-Sectional Correlation

In the example data, we have two automobile producers, two major suppliers to the electric utility industry, and one major supplier to all four of the others, U.S. Steel. It is very likely that the macroeconomic factors that affect these firms affect all of them to varying degrees. For the auto industry, the fates of GM and Chrysler are obviously tied both to the economy as a whole and to factors that are specific to the two firms. As such, it would seem reasonable to allow correlation of the disturbances across firms. The extension of the model for cross-sectional correlation is

$$E[\varepsilon_i \varepsilon_j'] = \sigma_{ij} I.$$

We continue to assume that observations are uncorrelated across time. With this generalization, we obtain

$$V = \begin{bmatrix} \sigma_{11} I & \sigma_{12} I & \cdots & \sigma_{1n} I \\ \sigma_{21} I & \sigma_{22} I & \cdots & \sigma_{2n} I \\ & \vdots & & \\ \sigma_{n1} I & \sigma_{n2} I & \cdots & \sigma_{nn} I \end{bmatrix}. \tag{16-7}$$

This model can also be estimated either by FGLS or MLE by iterating. As before, at step 1, we use OLS to obtain b and e_i. A consistent estimate of σ_{ij} can be obtained using the least squares residuals in

$$s_{ij} = \frac{e_i' e_j}{T}. \tag{16-8}$$

Some treatments use $T - K$ instead of T in the denominator of s_{ij}.[7] There is no problem created by doing so, but we should note that the resulting estimator is not unbiased regardless. With s_{ij} in hand, FGLS may be computed using $[\mathbf{X}'\hat{\mathbf{V}}^{-1}\mathbf{X}]^{-1}[\mathbf{X}'\hat{\mathbf{V}}^{-1}\mathbf{y}]$, where $\mathbf{X}$ and $\mathbf{y}$ are the stacked data matrices in (16-3).

Once again, in practical terms, this is a formidable computation. However, as before, things are simpler than they appear. $\mathbf{V}$ can be written as

$$\mathbf{V} = \Sigma \otimes \mathbf{I}, \tag{16-9}$$

where Σ is an $n \times n$ matrix, so

$$\mathbf{V}^{-1} = \Sigma^{-1} \otimes \mathbf{I}. \tag{16-10}$$

Let σ^{ij} denote the ijth element of Σ^{-1}. Then

$$\mathbf{V}^{-1} = \begin{bmatrix} \sigma^{11}\mathbf{I} & \sigma^{12}\mathbf{I} & \cdots & \sigma^{1n}\mathbf{I} \\ \sigma^{21}\mathbf{I} & \sigma^{22}\mathbf{I} & \cdots & \sigma^{2n}\mathbf{I} \\ & \vdots & & \\ \sigma^{n1}\mathbf{I} & \sigma^{n2}\mathbf{I} & \cdots & \sigma^{nn}\mathbf{I} \end{bmatrix}. \tag{16-11}$$

The usefulness of this is that

$$\mathbf{X}'\mathbf{V}^{-1}\mathbf{X} = \sum_i \sum_j \sigma^{ij}\mathbf{X}_i'\mathbf{X}_j \tag{16-12}$$

and

$$\mathbf{X}'\mathbf{V}^{-1}\mathbf{y} = \sum_i \sum_j \sigma^{ij}\mathbf{X}_i'\mathbf{y}_j,$$

so

$$\hat{\beta} = \left[\sum_i \sum_j \sigma^{ij}\mathbf{X}_i'\mathbf{X}_j \right]^{-1} \left[\sum_i \sum_j \sigma^{ij}\mathbf{X}_i'\mathbf{y}_j \right].$$

Therefore, to compute the FGLS estimators for this model, we first compute the full set of sample moments, $\mathbf{y}_i'\mathbf{y}_j$, $\mathbf{X}_i'\mathbf{X}_j$, and $\mathbf{X}_i'\mathbf{y}_j$, for all pairs of cross-sectional units. Maximum likelihood estimates can be obtained by iterating to convergence between

$$(1) \quad \hat{\beta} = [\mathbf{X}'\hat{\mathbf{V}}^{-1}\mathbf{X}]^{-1}[\mathbf{X}'\hat{\mathbf{V}}^{-1}\mathbf{y}]$$

and

$$(2) \quad s_{ij} = \frac{[\mathbf{y}_i'\mathbf{y}_j + \hat{\beta}'\mathbf{X}_i'\mathbf{X}_j\hat{\beta} - \hat{\beta}'\mathbf{X}_i'\mathbf{y}_j - \hat{\beta}'\mathbf{X}_j'\mathbf{y}_i]}{n}.$$

The computations are simple, using basic matrix algebra. Hypothesis tests about β may be done using the usual results. The appropriate asymptotic covariance matrix is the inverse matrix in brackets in (1).

EXAMPLE 16.4. Testing and Estimation with Groupwise Heteroscedasticity and Cross-Sectional Correlation. For the investment data, the FGLS and maximum likelihood estimates are listed in Table 16.7.

The estimated covariance matrix for the disturbances based on the FGLS estimates, with correlations placed in parentheses above the diagonal for purposes of the display, is

---

[7] See, e.g., Kmenta (1986, p. 620). Elsewhere, for example, in Fomby et al. (1984, p. 327), T is used instead.

Table 16.7

	β_1	β_2	β_3
FGLS	-14.7121	0.06368	0.18125
	(1.775)	(0.003418)	(0.02407)
MLE	-0.5099	0.02949	0.20844
	(2.053)	(0.004194)	(0.01495)

Table 16.8

	GM	GE	US	CH	WE
GM	80712.4	(-0.802)	(0.830)	(0.878)	(0.300)
GE	-19358.9	7227.61	(-0.834)	(-0.865)	(0.317)
US	61930.6	-18616.4	68975.2	(0.914)	(0.008)
CH	9959.13	-2934.52	9586.6	1593.39	(-0.208)
WE	-1016.74	321.312	25.2096	-99.021	142.309

given in Table 16.8. Note that the disturbance variances have changed dramatically. This is due in large part to the quite large off-diagonal elements. It is noteworthy that in spite of the great changes in Σ, the parameter estimates have not changed much from the earlier ones.

For testing the hypothesis that the off-diagonal elements of Σ are zero, that is, that there is no correlation across firms, there are two approaches. If we have obtained maximum likelihood estimates, we can use a likelihood ratio test. This test is based on the statistic

$$\lambda_{LR} = T\left(\sum_i \log \hat{\sigma}_i^2 - \log|\hat{\Sigma}|\right), \tag{16–13}$$

where $\hat{\sigma}_i^2$ are the estimates of σ_i^2 obtained from iterating the groupwise heteroscedastic treatment (see Example 16.3) and $\hat{\Sigma}$ is the maximum likelihood estimator in the unrestricted model, that is, this example. The large-sample distribution of the statistic is chi-squared with $n(n-1)/2$ degrees of freedom. The Lagrange multiplier test developed by Breusch and Pagan (1980) provides an alternative. The general form of the statistic is

$$\lambda_{LM} = T\sum_{i=1}^{M}\sum_{j=1}^{i-1} r_{ij}^2, \tag{16–14}$$

where r_{ij}^2 is the ijth residual correlation coefficient. If every firm had a different parameter vector, then, firm by firm, ordinary least squares would be efficient (and MLE), and we would compute r_{ij} from the OLS residuals. However, here we are assuming only a single parameter vector.[8] Therefore, the strictly appropriate basis for computing the correlations is the residuals from the iterated estimator in the groupwise heteroscedastic model, that is, the same residuals used to compute $\hat{\sigma}_i^2$ earlier. An asymptotically valid approximation to the test can be based on the FGLS residuals instead. The two test statistics based on the results

---

[8] The Breusch–Pagan result is based on this unrestricted specification. However, the same statistic emerges for the model with a common slope vector.

given previously are

$$\lambda_{LR} = 20(42.264 - 37.385) = 97.583$$

(the MLE of Σ is not shown) and

$$\lambda_{LM} = 92.31$$

based on the FGLS estimates given earlier. For 10 degrees of freedom, the critical value from the chi-squared table is 23.21, so both results lead to rejection of the hypothesis of a diagonal Σ. We conclude that the simple heteroscedastic model is not general enough for these data.

> *Postscript.* We shall examine the effect of assuming that all five firms have the same parameters in Chapter 17. For now, we note that one of the effects is to inflate the disturbance correlations. When the Lagrange multiplier statistic is recomputed with firm-by-firm separate regressions, the statistic falls to 29.04, which is still significant, but far less than what we found earlier. Based on the restricted model with diagonal Σ but common parameter vector, the Lagrange multiplier statistic is 26.66.

16.3.3. Autocorrelation

The preceding discussion dealt with heteroscedasticity and cross-sectional correlation. Through a simple modification of the procedures, it is possible to relax the assumption of nonautocorrelation as well.

Before proceeding, we note that problems are introduced by models that contain lagged dependent variables. These are the same ones we encountered in Chapter 15, and the remedies discussed there will apply here. In addition, because of the Jacobian term in the log-likelihood function pertaining to the initial observation(s), iterated FGLS will no longer give maximum likelihood estimates. Therefore, in what follows, we shall not iterate the FGLS estimators. In many settings, this is likely to be an important consideration, as the typical time series is relatively short. It is possible, however, to scan the admissable range of the autocorrelation parameters for the maximum likelihood estimators. Lastly, at various points, variance estimators are computed using $e'e/T$. One could use the degrees of freedom, $T - K$, instead. Either is appropriate, and the asymptotic properties are the same for both. However, because this is not a classical regression model, the degrees of freedom correction does not bring about an unbiased estimator in any event.

It is simplest to begin with assumption that

$$\text{Corr}[\varepsilon_{it}, \varepsilon_{js}] = 0 \qquad \text{if } i \neq j.$$

That is, the disturbances between cross-sectional units are uncorrelated. Now we can take the approach of Chapter 15 to allow for autocorrelation within the cross-sectional units. Suppose that, for each i,

$$E[\varepsilon_i \varepsilon_i'] = \sigma_i^2 \Omega_i,$$

where Ω_i is an autocorrelation matrix. With our earlier assumption, this produces

$$V = \begin{bmatrix} \sigma_1^2 \Omega_1 & 0 & \cdots & 0 \\ 0 & \sigma_2^2 \Omega_2 & \cdots & 0 \\ & & \vdots & \\ 0 & 0 & & \sigma_n^2 \Omega_n \end{bmatrix}. \tag{16-15}$$

The AR(1) model is the simplest to formulate. Generalizations along the lines discussed in Chapter 15 would be cumbersome but straightforward. Consider, in general, then, the model

$$\varepsilon_{it} = \rho_i \varepsilon_{it-1} + u_{it}$$

$$\mathrm{Var}[\varepsilon_{it}] = \sigma_i^2 = \frac{\sigma_{ui}^2}{1 - \rho_i^2}. \tag{16-16}$$

For FGLS estimation of the model, suppose that r_i is a consistent estimate of ρ_i. Then, if we take each time series $[\mathbf{y}_i, \mathbf{X}_i]$ separately, we can transform the data using the Prais–Winsten transformation,

$$\mathbf{y}_{*i} = \begin{bmatrix} \sqrt{1 - r_i^2} \, y_{i1} \\ y_{i2} - r_i y_{i1} \\ y_{i3} - r_i y_{i2} \\ \vdots \\ y_{iT} - r_i y_{iT-1} \end{bmatrix}, \quad \mathbf{X}_{*i} = \begin{bmatrix} \sqrt{1 - r_i^2} \, \mathbf{x}_{i1} \\ \mathbf{x}_{i2} - r_i \mathbf{x}_{i1} \\ \mathbf{x}_{i3} - r_i \mathbf{x}_{i2} \\ \vdots \\ \mathbf{x}_{iT} - r_i \mathbf{x}_{iT-1} \end{bmatrix}. \tag{16-17}$$

In terms of the transformed data, $\mathbf{y}_{*i}$ and $\mathbf{X}_{*i}$, the model is now only heteroscedastic; the transformation has removed the autocorrelation. As such, the groupwise heteroscedastic model of Section 16.3.1 applies to the transformed data. We may use weighted least squares, as described earlier. This requires a second least squares estimate. The first regression produces initial estimates of ρ_i. The transformed data are then used in a second least squares regression to obtain consistent estimates,

$$\hat{\sigma}_{ui}^2 = \frac{\mathbf{e}'_{*i} \mathbf{e}_{*i}}{T}. \tag{16-18}$$

With these estimates in hand, we may proceed to the calculation of the heteroscedastic regression. If needed, the computational procedure given in the preceding note can be used. At the end of the calculation, the moment matrix used in the last regression gives the correct asymptotic covariance matrix for $\hat{\boldsymbol{\beta}}$. If desired, a consistent estimate of $\sigma_{\varepsilon i}^2$ is obtained using

$$\hat{\sigma}_{\varepsilon i}^2 = \frac{\hat{\sigma}_{ui}^2}{1 - r_i^2}. \tag{16-19}$$

The remaining question is how to obtain the initial estimates, r_i. There are two possible structures to consider.

If the disturbances have a common stochastic process, with the same ρ_i, $\boldsymbol{\Omega}_i = \boldsymbol{\Omega}$ for all i. Three possible estimators of the common ρ, all of which are consistent, are

$$\bar{r} = \frac{1}{n} \sum_i r_i,$$

$$r = \frac{\sum_i \sum_t e_{it} e_{it-1}}{\sum_i \sum_t e_{it}^2}, \tag{16-20}$$

and

$$r^* = \text{sample Corr}[e_{i,t-1}, e_{it}].$$

Note that the first is an average of consistent but inefficient estimates.[9] The components r_i in $\bar{r}$ may be any of the estimators in Section 15.6.1 derived from the individual units. Since asymptotically each estimate has a variance of $(1 - \rho_i^2)/T$, a more efficient weighting would use the reciprocals of the variances, leading to

$$\bar{\bar{r}} = \sum_i w_i r_i,$$

$$w_i = \frac{1/(1 - r_i^2)}{\sum_i 1/(1 - r_i^2)}.$$

(16–21)

Since FGLS based on any of these estimators is asymptotically efficient, the choice of which to use is arbitrary. The small-sample properties are likely to be different, however.

The assumption of a common ρ is a restriction on the model, but not so severe a restriction as homoscedasticity. In Example 16.5, we shall see that the estimated autocorrelations of the first three firms are quite similar. Also, if the time series are short, this may be a necessary restriction in order to bring enough information to bear on the estimation of ρ to produce a reasonable estimate of β. Once again, the relevance is to the small-sample properties. If the time series are very short, it may be preferable to impose the restriction of a common ρ, even if it is violated in the population, in order to improve the small-sample performance of the estimator $\hat{\beta}$.[10]

If the processes are different across observational units, each time series may be analyzed separately. Any of the estimators described in Chapter 15 may be used; once again, the objective is consistency of the estimate. We note, both for this case and the previous one, that if there are lagged dependent variables in the model, the original least squares estimates will not yield consistent estimates of ρ_i. Instrumental variables or the method of Hatanaka may be used instead.

Last, one may wish to allow for cross-sectional correlation across units. Example 16.4 strongly suggests that this is appropriate for the investment data. The preceding has a natural generalization. If we assume that

$$\text{Cov}[u_{it}, u_{jt}] = \sigma_{uij},$$

we obtain the model of Section 16.3.2 in which the off-diagonal blocks of $\mathbf{V}$, $\sigma_{ij}\mathbf{I}$, are replaced by

$$\mathbf{\Omega}_{ij} = \frac{\sigma_{uij}}{1 - \rho_i \rho_j} \begin{bmatrix} 1 & \rho_j & \rho_j^2 & \cdots & \rho_j^{T-1} \\ \rho_i & 1 & \rho_j & \cdots & \rho_j^{T-2} \\ \rho_i^2 & \rho_i & 1 & \cdots & \rho_j^{T-3} \\ & & & \vdots & \\ \rho_i^{T-1} & \rho_i^{T-2} & \rho_i^{T-3} & \cdots & 1 \end{bmatrix}.$$

(16–22)

For estimation of this model, the technique of the preceding section needs only to be extended to the model of cross-sectional correlation in the obvious fashion. Initial estimates of ρ_i are required, as before. The Prais–Winsten transformation renders all of the blocks in $\mathbf{V}$ diagonal. Therefore, the model of cross-sectional correlation in Section 16.3.2 applies to the

---

[9] The consistency of $\bar{r}$ follows from the consistency of r_i in the dimension T, not from convergence in the dimension of n. An average of a fixed number of consistent estimators will be consistent, even if they are correlated. We continue to take n as fixed in this section.

[10] This is a point at which increasing n can play a role in the asymptotic properties of the estimates. Suppose that T is fixed and relatively small. Then, if $n \to \infty$, all of the estimators of ρ will still be consistent.

transformed data. The method of estimation described there may be used directly. Once again, the GLS moment matrix obtained at the last iteration (or the first, if no iterations are performed) provides the asymptotic covariance matrix for $\hat{\boldsymbol{\beta}}$. Estimates of $\sigma_{\varepsilon ij}$ can be obtained from the least squares residual covariances obtained from the transformed data:

$$\hat{\sigma}_{\varepsilon ij} = \frac{\hat{\sigma}_{uij}}{1 - r_i r_j}, \tag{16-23}$$

where

$$\hat{\sigma}_{uij} = \frac{\mathbf{e}'_{*i}\mathbf{e}_{*j}}{T}.$$

EXAMPLE 16.5. We now allow for different AR(1) processes for each firm. From the initial least squares estimates, the firm-specific autocorrelations and estimated variances of u_{it} and ε_{it} based on the transformed data are given in Table 16.9. The FGLS parameter estimates based on the transformed data are as shown in Table 16.10. Finally, the estimates are recomputed using the full model with cross-sectional covariances, giving the results shown in Table 16.11. The estimated variances using these estimates follow in Table 16.12.

Table 16.9

			Firm		
Estimate	GM	GE	US	CH	WE
r	0.53127	0.46395	0.54547	0.00798	0.29349
s_{ui}^2	6028.0	11929.3	12224.4	520.079	482.873
$s_{\varepsilon i}^2$	8398.4	15201.42	17402.3	520.112	528.386

Table 16.10

	$\hat{\hat{\beta}}_1$	$\hat{\hat{\beta}}_2$	$\hat{\hat{\beta}}_3$
FGLS	−23.9356	0.0858349	0.33292
	(7.6630)	(0.01042)	(0.03500)

Table 16.11

	$\hat{\hat{\beta}}_1$	$\hat{\hat{\beta}}_2$	$\hat{\hat{\beta}}_3$
FGLS	−4.33872	0.0460313	0.24783
	(2.364)	(0.004537)	(0.01571)

Table 16.12

Firm	GM	GE	US	CH	WE
s_{ui}^2	28,812.35	2991.33	21,231.69	1051.027	149.623

We observe rather large differences in the estimates when we allow correlation across firms, primarily in the constant term and the estimated disturbance variances. We can attribute this to the rather large off-diagonal elements in the estimated disturbance variance matrix. This leads to a very different weighting of individual estimates of β. The standard errors are also considerably smaller.

16.3.4.   A Random Coefficients Model

Thus far, the model $y_i = X_i\beta + \varepsilon_i$ has been analyzed within the familiar limits of heteroscedasticity and autocorrelation. Although the models in Sections 16.3.2 and 16.3.3 allow considerable flexibility, they do entail the not entirely plausible assumption that there is no parameter variation across firms (i.e., across the cross-sectional units). A fully general approach would combine all of the machinery of the previous sections with a model that allows β to vary across firms. We shall examine just such a model in the next chapter.

In an interesting (albeit fairly short) branch of literature, a number of authors have suggested that parameter heterogeneity can be reasonably viewed as due to stochastic variation.[11] Suppose that we write

$$y_i = X_i\beta_i + \varepsilon_i,$$

where

$$\beta_i = \beta + v_i, \qquad (16-24)$$
$$E[v_i] = 0,$$

and

$$E[v_i v_i'] = \Gamma.$$

Assume for now that there is no autocorrelation or cross-sectional correlation of the sort examined in the previous section. Then the β_i applying to a particular cross-sectional unit is the outcome of a random process with mean vector β and covariance matrix Γ. Combining terms, we obtain the model

$$y_i = X_i\beta + (\varepsilon_i + X_i v_i) \qquad (16-25)$$
$$= X_i\beta + w_i,$$

where

$$E[w] = 0$$

and

$$E[w_i w_i'] = \sigma_i^2 I + X_i \Gamma X_i'$$
$$= \Pi_i.$$

This model fits directly into our earlier framework of groupwise heteroscedasticity (although the matrix algebra is a bit more weighty). For the full sample of observations,

$$V = \begin{bmatrix} \Pi_1 & 0 & 0 & \cdots & 0 \\ 0 & \Pi_2 & 0 & \cdots & 0 \\ & & \vdots & & \\ 0 & 0 & 0 & & \Pi_n \end{bmatrix}.$$

[11] The most widely cited studies are Hildreth and Houck (1968), Swamy (1970, 1971, and 1974), and Hsiao (1975).

For purposes of estimation, let $\mathbf{b}_i$ be the ith ordinary least squares coefficient vector, and let $\mathbf{V}_i + \boldsymbol{\Gamma} = (\mathbf{X}'\mathbf{X})^{-1}\mathbf{X}'\boldsymbol{\Pi}_i\mathbf{X}(\mathbf{X}'\mathbf{X})^{-1}$ be the covariance matrix of $\mathbf{b}_i$ [see (13–5)], where

$$\mathbf{V}_i = \sigma_i^2[\mathbf{X}_i'\mathbf{X}_i]^{-1}. \tag{16–26}$$

It can be shown[12] that the GLS estimator in this groupwise heteroscedastic model may be written

$$\hat{\boldsymbol{\beta}} = \sum_i \mathbf{W}_i \mathbf{b}_i, \tag{16–27}$$

where

$$\mathbf{W}_i = \left\{\sum_{i=1}^n [\boldsymbol{\Gamma} + \mathbf{V}_i]^{-1}\right\}^{-1}[\boldsymbol{\Gamma} + \mathbf{V}_i]^{-1}.$$

This result shows (once again) the intuitive property that the GLS estimator is a matrix weighted average of the OLS estimators. (As in all such cases, $\sum_i \mathbf{W}_i = \mathbf{I}$.) The asymptotic covariance matrix for $\hat{\boldsymbol{\beta}}$ is the inverse matrix in braces in the previous expression.

The obstacle to the application of (16–27) is the unknown parameters in $\boldsymbol{\Gamma}$ and $\mathbf{V}_i$. Swamy (1971) has suggested a two-step approach. As always, it begins with ordinary least squares. Let $\mathbf{b}_i$ be the specific OLS coefficient vector, and let $\hat{\mathbf{V}}_i$ be the sample covariance matrix, $s_i^2(\mathbf{X}_i'\mathbf{X}_i)^{-1}$, where $s_i^2 = \mathbf{e}_i'\mathbf{e}_i/(T - K)$. Let

$$\bar{\mathbf{b}} = \frac{1}{n}\sum_i \mathbf{b}_i. \tag{16–28}$$

Then,

$$\hat{\boldsymbol{\Gamma}} = \mathbf{G} = \frac{1}{n-1}\left(\sum_i \mathbf{b}_i\mathbf{b}_i' - n\bar{\mathbf{b}}\bar{\mathbf{b}}'\right) - \frac{1}{n}\sum_i \hat{\mathbf{V}}_i. \tag{16–29}$$

A potential problem (which appears in our data) is that $\mathbf{G}$ may not be positive definite. The two matrices in $\mathbf{G}$ are of order 1 and $1/(nT)$. Therefore, in terms of the large-sample behavior of $\mathbf{G}$, the second matrix will be negligible. Swamy suggests various fixups for a non-positive definite $\mathbf{G}$, but a simple and asymptotically valid expedient is simply to drop the second part.[13]

EXAMPLE 16.6. A Random Coefficients Model for Investment. For our investment data, least squares for the five firms produces the estimates given in Table 16.13. (The last

Table 16.13

	b_1		b_2		b_3	
GM	− 149.782	(105.8)	0.11928	(0.02583)	0.37145	(0.03707)
GE	− 9.9563	(31.37)	0.02655	(0.01557)	0.15169	(0.02570)
US	− 30.3685	(157.0)	0.15657	(0.07889)	0.42386	(0.1552)
CH	− 6.18995	(13.51)	0.07795	(0.01997)	0.31572	(0.0288)
WE	− 0.50938	(8.015)	0.05289	(0.01571)	0.09241	(0.05610)
$\bar{b}$	− 39.3613		0.086649		0.271026	
$\tilde{b}$	− 2.05809		0.05372		0.21136	

[12] This uses a result due to Rao (1965, p. 29).
[13] We should note that $\mathbf{G}$ is not a matrix that converges to $\mathbf{0}$ asymptotically. It is the estimator of the variance of the process generating $\boldsymbol{\beta}_i$, not of a sampling distribution of an estimator.

Table 16.14

	β_1		β_2		β_3	
	OLS	Predicted	OLS	Predicted	OLS	Predicted
GM	−149.782	−71.629	0.11928	0.10278	0.37145	0.36785
GE	−9.9563	−12.033	0.02655	0.02794	0.15169	0.15083
US	−30.3685	−27.706	0.15657	0.14776	0.42386	0.45133
CH	6.18995	−9.8193	0.07795	0.08424	0.31572	0.30922
WE	−0.50938	3.2695	0.05289	0.04111	0.09241	0.14072

estimate, $\tilde{\mathbf{b}}$, is an alternative weighted average of the OLS estimates that is discussed in Examples 16.7 and 16.8.) As noted, $\hat{\boldsymbol{\Gamma}}$ in (16−29) is not positive definite. Using the simpler version, we obtain for the FGLS random coefficients estimator,

$$\hat{\beta} = [-23.5836\,(34.55)\quad 0.080765\,(0.02508)\quad 0.283988\,(0.06779)].$$

Finally, for comparison, the FGLS estimates from the least restrictive model of the previous section were

$$\text{FGLS} = [-4.33872\,(2.364)\quad 0.046031\,(0.004537)\quad 0.24783\,(0.01571)].$$

The standard errors of the random coefficient estimators are quite a bit larger than those of the FGLS estimator. This is to be expected. The variation of the estimates across firms is explicitly accounted for in the variance of the random coefficients model, while it is not in the generalized regression.

The FGLS procedure estimates the mean vector of the random process generating β_i. It may be useful to produce predictions of the individual parameter vectors as well. A best linear predictor for β_i would be

$$\hat{\beta}_i = [\boldsymbol{\Gamma}^{-1} + \mathbf{V}_i^{-1}][\boldsymbol{\Gamma}^{-1}\hat{\beta} + \mathbf{V}_i^{-1}\mathbf{b}_i] \tag{16−30}$$
$$= \mathbf{A}_i\hat{\beta} + [\mathbf{I} - \mathbf{A}_i]\mathbf{b}_i,$$

once again, a matrix weighted average.[14] In this case, the weights are the inverses of the variance matrices of $\hat{\beta}_i$ and $\mathbf{b}_i$. The forecast is made feasible by inserting our estimates $\mathbf{G}$ and $\hat{\mathbf{V}}_i$.

EXAMPLE 16.7. The forecasts and the OLS estimates for the investment data are listed in Table 16.14.

It has been suggested that a test of the random coefficients model can be based on the differences between the OLS estimates equation by equation and a weighted average of the OLS estimates. The test statistic suggested by Swamy (1971) is

$$\chi^2 = \sum_i [\mathbf{b}_i - \tilde{\mathbf{b}}]' \hat{\mathbf{V}}_i^{-1} [\mathbf{b}_i - \tilde{\mathbf{b}}], \tag{16−31}$$

where

$$\tilde{\mathbf{b}} = \left[\sum_i \hat{\mathbf{V}}_i^{-1}\right]^{-1} \sum_i \hat{\mathbf{V}}_i^{-1}\mathbf{b}_i.$$

---

[14] See Lee and Griffiths (1979).

The statistic is asymptotically distributed as chi-squared with $K(n-1)$ degrees of freedom under the null hypothesis of parameter constancy. It can be shown[15] that the statistic is algebraically the same as the standard F statistic for testing

$$H_0: \beta_1 = \beta_2 = \cdots = \beta_n$$

in the generalized model

$$
\begin{bmatrix} y_1 \\ y_2 \\ \vdots \\ y_n \end{bmatrix} = \begin{bmatrix} X_1 & 0 & \cdots & 0 \\ 0 & X_2 & \cdots & 0 \\ & & \vdots & \\ 0 & 0 & \cdots & X_n \end{bmatrix} \begin{bmatrix} \beta_1 \\ \beta_2 \\ \vdots \\ \beta_n \end{bmatrix} + \begin{bmatrix} \varepsilon_1 \\ \varepsilon_2 \\ \vdots \\ \varepsilon_n \end{bmatrix}
$$

$$E[\varepsilon_i \varepsilon_j'] = \sigma_i^2 I \qquad \text{if } i = j \text{ and } [0] \text{ if not.}$$

Which method is more convenient will depend on the format of the data and the available software.

EXAMPLE 16.8. For the investment data, the weighted average estimator, $\tilde{\tilde{b}}$, is given in Example 16.6. The chi-squared test statistic, with 12 degrees of freedom, is 603.99. This is statistically significant by any measure. Consequently, we would reject the hypothesis of parameter constancy (again).

This test is not strictly a test for the random coefficients model. It can be construed as such, but also simply as a test of constancy of the parameter vector across classical regression models. This raises an interesting question that reappears at various points in this literature. If the coefficients are found to differ across units, should we attribute this to random variation or to fixed parameters that simply are different? Unfortunately, the same data are consistent with both hypotheses. Conditioned on the data we have actually observed, it is little more than a matter of interpretation whether we attribute heterogeneity to random or fixed effects.

16.3.5. Summary

The preceding sections have suggested a variety of different specifications of the generalized regression model. Which ones apply in a given situation depends on the setting. Homoscedasticity will depend on the nature of the data and will often be directly observable at the outset. Uncorrelatedness across the cross-sectional units is a strong assumption, particularly in view of the fact that the model assigns the same parameter vector to all units. Autocorrelation is a qualitatively different property. Although it does appear to arise naturally in time-series data, as the following results suggest, one would want to look carefully at the data before assuming that it is present.

The properties of all of these estimators depend on an increase in T, so they are generally not well suited to the types of data sets described in the next section. The various models, in increasing order of their generality, produced the estimates for our sample data shown in Table 16.15.

Moving down the columns, we see that the gains in efficiency that result from relaxing the constraints in V are clearly visible in the first three models. Not surprisingly, the standard errors rise noticeably with the introduction of autocorrelation in the fourth model. The disturbance variance that previously contained only contemporaneous variation now

---

[15] See Johnston (1984, p. 415).

Table 16.15

	Parameter		
Model	β_1	β_2	β_3
Classical regression	−48.030	0.10508	0.30534
	(21.48)	(0.0114)	(0.0435)
Groupwise heteroscedastic	−36.254	0.09499	0.33781
	(6.124)	(0.0074)	(0.0302)
Groupwise heteroscedastic and cross-sectionally correlated	−14.712	0.06368	0.18125
	(1.775)	(0.0034)	(0.0241)
Groupwise heteroscedastic, cross-sectionally correlated, and within-group autocorrelated	−23.931	0.08584	0.33292
	(7.663)	(0.0104)	(0.0351)
Groupwise heteroscedastic, cross-sectionally correlated, within- and between-group autocorrelated	−4.3387	0.04603	0.24783
	(2.364)	(0.0045)	(0.0157)
Random coefficients	−23.484	0.08077	0.28399
	(34.55)	(0.0251)	(0.0678)

reflects the retention of lagged effects and their attendant variation in the current disturbance. This suggests that one might want to exercise some caution in extending a model to this level of generality. Nonautocorrelation is a testable restriction, and it is clear that there is some benefit to be gained if it is not present. (Of course, neglecting it when it *is* present is probably even worse.) The reduction in the standard errors of the estimates from the fourth to the fifth models reflects the same gain present in the difference between the second and third models. Allowing the off-diagonal elements of the contemporaneous disturbance covariance matrix to be nonzero introduces a large amount of new information into the estimator. [Compare the formula for $\hat{\beta}$ in the computational note after Example 16.3 to the more general form in (16–12).] Finally, the random coefficients model undoes some of the alleged efficiencies of the previous models by apportioning some of the cross-unit variation to the parameters instead of putting all of it in the disturbances.

16.4. *Longitudinal Data*

The analysis of panel or longitudinal data is the subject of one of the most active and innovative bodies of literature in econometrics. This is partly because panel data provide such a rich environment for the development of estimation techniques and theoretical results. In more practical terms, however, researchers have been able to use time-series cross-section data to examine issues that could not be studied in either cross-sectional or time-series setting alone. Two examples are as follows:

1. In a widely cited study of labor supply, Ben-Porath (1973) observes that at a certain point in time, in a cohort of women, 50 percent may appear to be working. It is ambiguous whether this finding implies that, in this cohort, one-half of the women on average will be working or that the same one-half will be working in every period. These have very different implications for policy and for the interpretation of any

statistical results. Cross-section data alone will not shed any light on the question. Panel data provide a revealing source of information.

2. A long-standing problem in the analysis of production functions has been the inability to separate economies of scale and technological change. Cross-section data provide information only about the former, while time-series data muddle the two effects, with no prospect of separation. It is common, for example, to assume constant returns to scale in order to reveal the technical change.[16] Of course, this assumes away the problem. A recent study by Greene (1983) examines the cost of electric power generation for a large number of firms, each observed in each of several years. The basic model, for the ith firm in year t,

$$\text{Cost}_{it} = C(Y_{it}, P_{it}, t),$$

where Y is output and $\mathbf{p}$ is a vector of factor prices, provides estimates of the rate of technological change,

$$\delta_t = \frac{-d \ln C}{dt}$$

and economies of scale,

$$\text{e.s.}_{it} = \frac{1}{d \ln C / d \ln y_{it}} - 1.[17]$$

In principle, the methods of the previous section can be applied to longitudinal data sets. However, in the typical panel, there are a large number of cross-sectional units and only a few periods. Thus, the time series methods discussed earlier may be somewhat problematic. Recent work has generally concentrated more on models better suited to these short and wide data sets. The techniques are focused on cross-sectional variation, or heterogeneity. In this section, we shall examine the two most widely used models and then look briefly at some of their most recent extensions.

16.4.1. A Basic Model of Heterogeneity

The basic framework for this discussion is a regression model of the form

$$y_{it} = \alpha_i + \boldsymbol{\beta}' \mathbf{x}_{it} + \varepsilon_{it}. \tag{16-32}$$

There are K regressors in $\mathbf{x}_{it}$, *not including the constant term*. The *individual effect is* α_i, which is taken to be constant over time, t, and specific to the individual cross-sectional unit, i. As it stands, this is a classical regression model. In particular, if we take the α_i's to be the same across units, ordinary least squares provides consistent and efficient estimates of α and $\boldsymbol{\beta}$.

EXAMPLE 16.9. Cost Function.   The data in Table 16.16 are taken from the study by Greene described earlier. Output in millions of kilowatt-hours and total generation cost in millions of dollars, consisting of fuel, labor, and capital costs, are observed for six firms in

---

[16] In a classic study of this issue, Solow (1957) states: "From time series of $\dot{Q}/Q$, w_K, $\dot{K}/K$, w_L and $\dot{L}/L$ or their discrete year-to-year analogues, we could estimate A/A and thence $A(t)$ itself. Actually an amusing thing happens here. Nothing has been said so far about returns to scale. But if all factor inputs are classified either as K or L, then the available figures always show w_K and w_L adding up to one. Since we have assumed that factors are paid their marginal products, this amounts to assuming the hypothesis of Euler's theorem. The calculus being what it is, we might just as well assume the conclusion, namely, that F is homogeneous of degree one."

[17] Different measures of economies of scale are used in different studies. For the one given, there are economies of scale if e.s.$_{it}$ is positive, constant returns to scale if it is zero, and diseconomies of scale if it is negative.

Table 16.16

Firm		t = 1 1955	t = 2 1960	t = 3 1965	t = 4 1970
			Time		
i = 1	Cost	3.154	4.271	4.584	5.849
	Output	214	419	588	1,025
i = 2	Cost	3.859	5.535	8.127	10.966
	Output	696	811	1,640	2,506
i = 3	Cost	19.035	26.041	32.444	41.180
	Output	3,202	4,802	5,821	9,275
i = 4	Cost	35.229	51.111	61.045	77.885
	Output	5,668	7,612	10,206	13,702
i = 5	Cost	33.154	40.044	43.125	57.727
	Output	6,000	8,222	8,484	10,004
i = 6	Cost	73.050	98.846	138.88	191.56
	Output	11,796	15,551	27,218	30,958

each of 4 years. For purposes of the example, we fit the simple regression

$$\ln C_{it} = \alpha + \beta \ln Y_{it} + \varepsilon_{it}.$$

Least squares regression produces

$$\ln C = -4.17478 + 0.887987 \ln Y \qquad R^2 = 0.9707$$
$$\quad\;\;(0.2769) \quad\;\;(0.0329) \qquad\qquad s^2 = 0.04614^{.}$$

16.4.2. Fixed Effects

A common formulation of the model assumes that differences across units can be captured in differences in the constant term.[18] Thus, in (16–32), each α_i is an unknown parameter to be estimated. Let y_i and X_i be the T observations for the ith unit, and let ε_i be the associated $T \times 1$ vector of disturbances. Then, we may write (16–32) as

$$y_i = i\alpha_i + X_i\beta + \varepsilon_i.$$

Collecting these, we have

$$
\begin{bmatrix} y_1 \\ y_2 \\ \vdots \\ y_n \end{bmatrix} =
\begin{bmatrix} i & 0 & \cdots & 0 \\ 0 & i & \cdots & 0 \\ & & \vdots & \\ 0 & 0 & \cdots & i \end{bmatrix}
\begin{bmatrix} \alpha_1 \\ \alpha_2 \\ \vdots \\ \alpha_n \end{bmatrix} +
\begin{bmatrix} X_1 \\ X_2 \\ \vdots \\ X_n \end{bmatrix} \beta +
\begin{bmatrix} \varepsilon_1 \\ \varepsilon_2 \\ \vdots \\ \varepsilon_n \end{bmatrix}
\qquad (16\text{--}33)
$$

or

$$y = [d_1, d_2 \cdots d_n \quad X] \begin{bmatrix} \alpha \\ \beta \end{bmatrix} + \varepsilon,$$

[18] It is also possible to allow the slopes to vary across i, but this introduces some new methodological issues, as well as considerable complexity in the calculations. A recent study on the topic is Cornwell and Schmidt (1984).

where $\mathbf{d}_i$ is a dummy variable indicating the ith unit. Let the $nT \times n$ matrix $\mathbf{D} = [\mathbf{d}_1, \mathbf{d}_2, \ldots, \mathbf{d}_n]$. Then, assembling all nT rows gives

$$\mathbf{y} = \mathbf{D}\boldsymbol{\alpha} + \mathbf{X}\boldsymbol{\beta} + \boldsymbol{\varepsilon}. \tag{16-34}$$

This is usually referred to as the *least squares dummy variable (LSDV)* model.

This is a classical regression model, so no new results are needed to analyze it. It is the same model examined in Sections 8.2.2 and 8.2.3 in our discussion of dummy variables. If n is small enough, the model can be estimated by ordinary least squares with K regressors in $\mathbf{X}$ and n columns in $\mathbf{D}$, as a multiple regression with $n + K$ parameters. Of course, if n is thousands, as is typical, this is likely to exceed the storage capabilities of any computer. But, as we found in Chapter 8, there is an easier way to proceed. Using familiar results for a partitioned regression,[19] we write the OLS estimator of $\boldsymbol{\beta}$ as

$$\mathbf{b} = [\mathbf{X}'\mathbf{M}_d\mathbf{X}]^{-1}[\mathbf{X}'\mathbf{M}_d\mathbf{y}], \tag{16-35}$$

where

$$\mathbf{M}_d = \mathbf{I} - \mathbf{D}(\mathbf{D}'\mathbf{D})^{-1}\mathbf{D}'.$$

This amounts to a least squares regression using the transformed data, $\mathbf{X}_* = \mathbf{M}_d\mathbf{X}$ and $\mathbf{y}_* = \mathbf{M}_d\mathbf{y}$. The structure of $\mathbf{D}$ is particularly convenient; its columns are orthogonal, so

$$\mathbf{M}_d = \begin{bmatrix} \mathbf{M}^0 & \mathbf{0} & \mathbf{0} & \cdots & \mathbf{0} \\ \mathbf{0} & \mathbf{M}^0 & \mathbf{0} & \cdots & \mathbf{0} \\ & & \vdots & & \\ \mathbf{0} & \mathbf{0} & \mathbf{0} & \cdots & \mathbf{M}^0 \end{bmatrix}.$$

Each matrix on the diagonal is

$$\mathbf{M}^0 = \mathbf{I}_T - \frac{1}{T}\mathbf{i}\mathbf{i}'.$$

Premultiplying any $T \times 1$ *vector*, $\mathbf{z}_i$, by $\mathbf{M}^0$ creates $\mathbf{M}^0\mathbf{z}_i = \mathbf{z}_i - \bar{z}\mathbf{i}$. (Note that the mean is taken over only the T observations for unit i.) Therefore, the regression of $\mathbf{M}_d\mathbf{y}$ on $\mathbf{M}_d\mathbf{X}$ is equivalent to the regression of $[y_{it} - \bar{y}_{i.}]$ on $[\mathbf{x}_{it} - \bar{\mathbf{x}}_{i.}]$, where $\bar{\mathbf{x}}_{i.}$ is the $K \times 1$ vector of means of $\mathbf{x}_{it}$ over the T observations. The dummy variable coefficients can be recovered from the other normal equation in the partitioned regression:

$$\mathbf{D}'\mathbf{D}\mathbf{a} + \mathbf{D}'\mathbf{X}\mathbf{b} = \mathbf{D}'\mathbf{y}$$

or

$$\mathbf{a} = [\mathbf{D}'\mathbf{D}]^{-1}\mathbf{D}'(\mathbf{y} - \mathbf{X}\mathbf{b}). \tag{16-36}$$

This implies that for each i,

$$a_i = \text{the mean residual in the } i\text{th group.} \tag{16-37}$$

Alternatively,

$$a_i = \bar{y}_{i.} - \mathbf{b}'\bar{\mathbf{x}}_{i.}.$$

The appropriate estimator of the variance matrix for $\mathbf{b}$ is

$$\text{Var}[\mathbf{b}] = s^2[\mathbf{X}'\mathbf{M}_d\mathbf{X}]^{-1}, \tag{16-38}$$

---

[19] See Section 6.3.4.

which uses the usual second moment matrix with $\mathbf{x}$'s, now expressed as deviations from their respective unit means. The disturbance variance estimator is

$$s^2 = \frac{\sum_i \sum_t (y_{it} - a_i - \mathbf{b}'\mathbf{x}_{it})^2}{nT - n - K}.$$

The itth residual is

$$e_{it} = y_{it} - a_i - \mathbf{b}'\mathbf{x}_{it}$$

$$= y_{it} - (\bar{y}_{i.} - \mathbf{b}'\bar{\mathbf{x}}_{i.}) - \mathbf{b}'\mathbf{x}_{it}$$

$$= (y_{it} - \bar{y}_{i.}) - \mathbf{b}'(\mathbf{x}_{it} - \mathbf{x}_{i.}).$$

Thus, the numerator in s^2 is exactly the sum of squared residuals from the regression in (16–35). But most computer programs will use $nT - K$ for the denominator in computing s^2, so a correction will be necessary. For the individual effects,

$$\text{Var}[a_i] = \frac{\sigma^2}{T} + \bar{\mathbf{x}}_{i.}'\text{Var}[\mathbf{b}]\bar{\mathbf{x}}_{i.}. \qquad (16\text{–}39)$$

so a simple estimator based on s^2 can be computed.

The usual t- ratio for α_i implies a test of the hypothesis that α_i equals zero. But typically this is not a useful hypothesis to test in a regression context. If we are interested in differences across groups, we can test the hypothesis that the constant terms are all equal with the usual F test. Under the null hypothesis, the efficient estimator is pooled least squares. The F ratio used for the test is

$$F(n - 1, nT - n - K) = \frac{(R_u^2 - R_p^2)/(n - 1)}{(1 - R_u^2)/(nT - n - K)}, \qquad (16\text{–}40)$$

where u indicates the unrestricted model and p indicates the pooled or restricted model with only a single overall constant term. (The sums of squared residuals may be used instead if that is more convenient.) It may be more convenient to estimate the model with an overall constant and $n - 1$ dummy variables instead. The other results will be unchanged, and, rather than estimate α_i, each dummy variable coefficient will be an estimate of $\alpha_i - \alpha_1$. The F test that the coefficients on the $n - 1$ dummy variables are zero is identical to the one above. It is important to keep in mind that although the statistical results are the same, the interpretation of the dummy variable coefficients in the two formulations is different.[20]

EXAMPLE 16.10. Cost Function with Firm Effects. Least squares estimation of the model in Example 16.9 with individual firm dummy variables produces

$$\ln C = 0.674279 \ln Y \qquad R^2 = 0.9924$$
$$\quad\quad (0.06113) \qquad\qquad s^2 = 0.0155$$

$$- 2.69353d_1 - 2.9117d_2 - 2.4400d_3$$
$$\quad (0.3828) \qquad (0.4396) \qquad (0.5287)$$

$$- 2.13449d_4 - 2.3108d_5 - 1.9035d_6$$
$$\quad (0.5588) \qquad (0.5532) \qquad (0.6081)$$

$$F[5, 17] = \frac{(0.9924 - 0.9707)/5}{(1 - 0.9924)/17} = 9.708.$$

---

[20] For a discussion of the differences, see Suits (1984).

The 1 percent critical value from the F table is 4.34, so the hypothesis that the firm effects are the same is rejected at the 1 percent significance level.

The least squares dummy variable approach can be extended to include a time-specific effect as well. The extended model is

$$y_{it} = \alpha_i + \gamma_t + \boldsymbol{\beta}'\mathbf{x}_{it} + \varepsilon_{it}. \tag{16-41}$$

This model is obtained from the preceding one by the addition of an additional $T - 1$ dummy variables. (One of the time effects must be dropped to avoid perfect collinearity.) If the number of variables is too large to handle by ordinary regression, this can also be estimated by using the partitioned regression. Least squares estimates of the slopes are obtained by regression of

$$y_{*it} = y_{it} - \bar{y}_{i.} - \bar{y}_{.t} + \bar{\bar{y}} \tag{16-42}$$

on

$$\mathbf{x}_{*it} = \mathbf{x}_{it} - \bar{\mathbf{x}}_{i.} - \bar{\mathbf{x}}_{.t} + \bar{\bar{\mathbf{x}}},$$

where

$$\bar{y}_{.t} = \frac{1}{n}\sum_i y_{it}$$

and

$$\bar{\bar{y}} = \frac{1}{nT}\sum_i\sum_t y_{it},$$

and likewise for $\bar{\mathbf{x}}_{.t}$ and $\bar{\bar{\mathbf{x}}}$. The dummy variable coefficients can be recovered from the normal equations as

$$a_i = (\bar{y}_{i.} - \bar{\bar{y}}) - \mathbf{b}'(\bar{\mathbf{x}}_{i.} - \bar{\bar{\mathbf{x}}}),$$
$$c_t = (\bar{y}_{.t} - \bar{\bar{y}}) - \mathbf{b}'(\bar{\mathbf{x}}_{.t} - \bar{\bar{\mathbf{x}}}). \tag{16-43}$$

(If one of n or T is small and the other is large, it will usually be simpler just to treat the smaller set as an ordinary set of variables and apply the previous results to the one-way fixed effects model defined by the larger set.) Although more general, this model is rarely used in practice. There are two reasons. First, the cost in terms of degrees of freedom is often not justified. Second, in those instances in which a model of the timewise evolution of the disturbance is desired, a more general model than the dummy variable formulation is usually used.

16.4.3.   Random Effects

The fixed effects model is a reasonable approach when we can be confident that the differences between units can be viewed as parametric shifts of the regression function. This model might be viewed as applying only to the cross-sectional units in the study, not to additional ones outside the sample. For example, an intercountry comparison may well include the full set of countries for which it is reasonable to assume that the model is constant. Likewise, in Greene's study cited earlier, the sample of 114 firms was nearly exhaustive of the investor-owned utilities in the United States. In other settings, it might be more appropriate to view individual specific constant terms as randomly distributed across cross-sectional units. This would be appropriate if we believed that sampled cross-sectional units were drawn from a large population. It would certainly be the case for the longitudinal data sets listed in the Introduction.[21]

Consider, then, a reformulation of the model

$$y_{it} = \alpha + \beta' x_{it} + u_i + \varepsilon_{it}, \tag{16-44}$$

where there are K regressors in addition to the constant term. The component u_i is the random disturbance characterizing the ith observation and is constant through time. In the analysis of families, we can view them as the collection of factors not in the regression that are specific to that family. We assume further that

$$E[\varepsilon_{it}] = E[u_i] = 0,$$

$$E[\varepsilon_{it}^2] = \sigma_\varepsilon^2,$$

$$E[u_i^2] = \sigma_u^2,$$

$$E[\varepsilon_{it} u_j] = 0 \qquad \text{for all } i, t, \text{ and } j \tag{16-45}$$

$$E[\varepsilon_{it} \varepsilon_{js}] = 0 \qquad \text{if } t \neq s \text{ or } i \neq j,$$

$$E[u_i u_j] = 0 \qquad \text{if } i \neq j.$$

As before, it is useful to view the formulation of the model in blocks of T observations for observations i, y_i, X_i, $u_i i$, and ε_i. For these T observations, let

$$w_{it} = \varepsilon_{it} + u_i$$

and

$$\mathbf{w}_i = [w_{i1}, w_{i2}, \dots, w_{iT}]'.$$

Then

$$E[w_{it}^2] = \sigma_\varepsilon^2 + \sigma_u^2,$$

$$E[w_{it} w_{is}] = \sigma_u^2.$$

For the T observations for unit i, let $\Omega = E[\mathbf{w}_i \mathbf{w}_i']$. Then

$$\Omega = \begin{bmatrix} \sigma_\varepsilon^2 + \sigma_u^2 & \sigma_u^2 & \sigma_u^2 & \cdots & \sigma_u^2 \\ \sigma_u^2 & \sigma_\varepsilon^2 + \sigma_u^2 & \sigma_u^2 & \cdots & \sigma_u^2 \\ & & \vdots & & \\ \sigma_u^2 & \sigma_u^2 & \sigma_u^2 & & \sigma_\varepsilon^2 + \sigma_u^2 \end{bmatrix} \tag{16-46}$$

$$= \sigma_\varepsilon^2 \mathbf{I} + \sigma_u^2 \mathbf{i} \mathbf{i}',$$

where $\mathbf{i}$ is a $T \times 1$ column vector of ones. Since observations i and j are independent, the disturbance covariance for the full nT observations is

$$V = \begin{bmatrix} \Omega & 0 & 0 & 0 \\ 0 & \Omega & 0 & 0 \\ & & \vdots & \\ 0 & 0 & 0 & \Omega \end{bmatrix} = \mathbf{I} \otimes \Omega. \tag{16-47}$$

This matrix has a particularly simple structure.

---

[21] This is not a hard and fast distinction; it is purely heuristic. We shall return to this issue later.

16.4.3a. *Generalized Least Squares*

For generalized least squares, we require $\mathbf{V}^{-1/2} = \mathbf{I} \otimes \mathbf{\Omega}^{-1/2}$. Therefore, we need only find $\mathbf{\Omega}^{-1/2}$, which is

$$\mathbf{\Omega}^{-1/2} = \mathbf{I} - \frac{\theta}{T} \mathbf{i} \mathbf{i}',$$

where

$$\theta = 1 - \frac{\sigma_\varepsilon}{(T\sigma_u^2 + \sigma_\varepsilon^2)^{1/2}}.$$

The transformation of $\mathbf{y}_i$ and $\mathbf{X}_i$ for GLS is, therefore,

$$\mathbf{\Omega}^{-1/2}\mathbf{y}_i = \begin{bmatrix} y_{i1} - \theta \bar{y}_{i.} \\ y_{i2} - \theta \bar{y}_{i.} \\ \vdots \\ y_{iT} - \theta \bar{y}_{i.} \end{bmatrix}, \tag{16-48}$$

and likewise for the rows of $\mathbf{X}_i$.[22] For the data set as a whole, generalized least squares is computed by the regression of these partial deviations in y_{it} on the same transformations of x_{it}. Note the similarity of this procedure to the computation in the LSDV model, which has $\theta = 1$.

An alternative formulation of the GLS estimator is illuminating. We could formulate the regression model in three ways: First, the original formulation is

$$y_{it} = \alpha + \boldsymbol{\beta}'\mathbf{x}_{it} + [\varepsilon_{it} + u_i]. \tag{16-49a}$$

In terms of deviations from the unit means,

$$y_{it} - \bar{y}_{i.} = \boldsymbol{\beta}'(\mathbf{x}_{it} - \bar{\mathbf{x}}_{i.}) + \varepsilon_{it} - \bar{\varepsilon}_{i.}, \tag{16-49b}$$

while in terms of the unit means,

$$\bar{y}_{i.} = \alpha + \boldsymbol{\beta}'\bar{\mathbf{x}}_{i.} + \bar{\varepsilon}_{i.} + u_i. \tag{16-49c}$$

All three are generalized regression models, and, in principle, all three could be estimated, at least consistently if not efficiently, by ordinary least squares. [Note that (16–49c) involves only n observations.] Consider, then, the matrices of sums of squares and cross-products that would be used in each case, where we focus only on estimation of $\boldsymbol{\beta}$. In (16–49a), the moments would be about the overall means, $\bar{\bar{y}}$ and $\bar{\bar{\mathbf{x}}}$, and we would use the *total* sums of squares and cross-products,

$$\mathbf{S}_{xx}^t = \sum_i \sum_t (\mathbf{x}_{it} - \bar{\bar{\mathbf{x}}})(\mathbf{x}_{it} - \bar{\bar{\mathbf{x}}})'$$

and

$$\mathbf{S}_{xy}^t = \sum_i \sum_t (\mathbf{x}_{it} - \bar{\bar{\mathbf{x}}})(y_{it} - \bar{\bar{y}}).$$

(The use of the superscript t indicates "total" and is unrelated to the time subscript.) For (16–49b), since the data are in deviations already, the means of $(y_{it} - \bar{y}_{i.})$ and $(\mathbf{x}_{it} - \bar{\mathbf{x}}_{i.})$ are

---

[22] This is a special case of the more general model treated in Nerlove (1971).

zero. The moment matrices are the *within-units* sums of squares and cross-products,

$$S_{xx}^w = \sum_i \sum_t (\mathbf{x}_{it} - \bar{\mathbf{x}}_{i.})(\mathbf{x}_{it} - \bar{\mathbf{x}}_{i.})'$$

and

$$S_{xy}^w = \sum_i \sum_t (\mathbf{x}_{it} - \bar{\mathbf{x}}_{i.})(y_{it} - \bar{y}_{i.}).$$

Finally, for (16–49c), the mean of unit means is the overall mean. The moment matrices are the *between-units* sums of squares and cross-products,

$$S_{xx}^b = \sum_i T(\bar{\mathbf{x}}_{i.} - \bar{\bar{\mathbf{x}}})(\bar{\mathbf{x}}_{i.} - \bar{\bar{\mathbf{x}}})'$$

and

$$S_{xy}^b = \sum_i T(\bar{\mathbf{x}}_{i.} - \bar{\bar{\mathbf{x}}})(\bar{y}_{i.} - \bar{\bar{y}}).$$

It is easy to verify that

$$S_{xx}^t = S_{xx}^w + S_{xx}^b$$

and

$$S_{xy}^t = S_{xy}^w + S_{xy}^b.$$

There are, therefore, three possible least squares estimators of β corresponding to the decomposition. The least squares estimator is

$$\mathbf{b}^t = [S_{xx}^t]^{-1} S_{xy}^t \tag{16–50}$$
$$= [S_{xx}^w + S_{xx}^b]^{-1} [S_{xy}^w + S_{xy}^b].$$

The *within-units* estimator is

$$\mathbf{b}^w = [S_{xx}^w]^{-1} S_{xy}^w. \tag{16–51}$$

This is the LSDV estimator computed earlier. (See (16–35).) An alternative estimator would be the *between-units* estimator,

$$\mathbf{b}^b = [S_{xx}^b]^{-1} S_{xy}^b. \tag{16–52}$$

This is the least squares estimator of (16–49c) based on the n sets of groups means. From the preceding expressions (and familiar previous results),

$$S_{xy}^w = S_{xx}^w \mathbf{b}^w$$

and

$$S_{xy}^b = S_{xx}^b \mathbf{b}^b.$$

Inserting these in (16–50), we see that the OLS estimator is a matrix weighted average of the within- and between-units estimators:

$$\mathbf{b}^t = \mathbf{F}^w \mathbf{b}^w + \mathbf{F}^b \mathbf{b}^b, \tag{16–53}$$

where

$$\mathbf{F}^w = [S_{xx}^w + S_{xx}^b]^{-1} S_{xx}^w = \mathbf{I} - \mathbf{F}^b.$$

Table 16.17

Firm	ln Cost	ln Output
1	1.47234	6.17826
2	1.88787	7.11813
3	3.35085	8.58816
4	3.99068	9.08403
5	3.75274	8.99269
6	4.76838	9.89485
Overall	3.20381	8.30935

EXAMPLE 16.11.   The OLS estimator for the cost data is given in Example 16.9. The LSDV estimator in Example 16.10 is the within-units estimator. For the six firms, the unit means are as listed in Table 16.17.

The three estimators for the slope are

$$b^t = 0.887987,$$

$$b^w = 0.674279,$$

$$b^b = 0.911073.$$

The weighting for the two estimators can be derived from

$$b^t = mb^w + (1 - m)b^b,$$

as

$$m = \frac{b^t - b^b}{b^w - b^b} = 0.09749.$$

Most of variation is between units. The data were chosen to include wide variation in output across firms, so this is not surprising. The steady but undramatic growth of the firms that provides the within-units variation is small compared to the differences across firms.

It can be shown that the GLS estimator is, likewise, a matrix weighted average of the within- and between-units estimators:

$$\hat{\beta} = \hat{F}^w b^w + (I - \hat{F}^w)b^{b},^{[23]}$$

(16–54)

where

$$\hat{F}^w = [S^w_{xx} + \lambda S^b_{xx}]^{-1} S^w_{xx},$$

$$\lambda = \frac{\sigma^2_\varepsilon}{\sigma^2_\varepsilon + T\sigma^2_u} = (1 - \theta)^2.$$

To the extent that λ differs from one, we see that the inefficiency of least squares will follow from an inefficient weighting of the two least squares estimators. In particular, compared

---

[23] An alternative form of this expression, in which the weighting matrices are proportional to the variance matrices of the two estimators, is given by Judge et al. (1985).

to generalized least squares, ordinary least squares places too much weight on the between-units variation. It includes it all in the variation in $\mathbf{X}$, rather than apportioning some of it to random variation across groups attributable to the variation in u_i across units.

There are some polar cases to consider. If λ equals one, generalized least squares is ordinary least squares. This would occur if σ_u^2 were zero, in which case a classical regression model would apply. If λ equals zero, the estimator is the dummy variable estimator we used in the fixed effects setting. There are two possibilities. If σ_ε^2 were zero, all variation across units would be due to the different u_i's, which, because they are constant across time, would be equivalent to the dummy variables we used in the fixed-effects model. The question of whether they were fixed or random would then become moot. They are the only source of variation across units once the regression is accounted for. The other case is $T \to \infty$. We can view it this way: If $T \to \infty$, the unobserved u_i becomes observable. Take the T observations for the ith unit. Our estimator of $[\alpha, \beta]$ is consistent in the dimensions T or n. Therefore,

$$y_{it} - \alpha - \beta'\mathbf{x}_{it} = u_i + \varepsilon_{it}$$

is observable. The individual means will provide

$$\bar{y}_{i.} - \alpha - \beta'\bar{\mathbf{x}}_{i.} = u_i + \bar{\varepsilon}_{i.}.$$

But $\bar{\varepsilon}_{i.}$ converges to zero, which reveals u_i to us. Therefore, if T goes to infinity, u_i becomes the d_i we used earlier. (The fact that it is not 1 is immaterial; it is nonzero only for unit i.)

16.4.3b   *Feasible Generalized Least Squares When Ω Is Unknown*

If the variance components are known, generalized least squares can be computed without much difficulty. Of course, this is not likely, so, as usual, we must first estimate the disturbance variances and then use an FGLS procedure. A heuristic approach to estimation of the components is as follows:

$$y_{it} = \alpha + \beta'\mathbf{x}_{it} + \varepsilon_{it} + u_i$$

and

$$\bar{y}_{i.} = \alpha + \beta'\bar{\mathbf{x}}_{i.} + \bar{\varepsilon}_{i.} + u_i. \tag{16-55}$$

Therefore, deviations from the unit means remove the heterogeneity:

$$y_{it} - \bar{y}_{i.} = \beta'[\mathbf{x}_{it} - \bar{\mathbf{x}}_{i.}] + [\varepsilon_{it} - \bar{\varepsilon}_{i.}]. \tag{16-56}$$

Since

$$E\left[\sum_t (\varepsilon_{it} - \bar{\varepsilon}_{i.})^2\right] = (T-1)\sigma_\varepsilon^2,$$

if β were observed, an unbiased estimator of σ_ε^2 based on T observations in unit i would be

$$\hat{\sigma}_{\varepsilon i}^2 = \frac{1}{T-1}\sum_t (\varepsilon_{it} - \bar{\varepsilon}_{i.})^2. \tag{16-57}$$

Since β must be estimated—we use the LSDV estimator in (16–35)—we make the usual degrees of freedom correction and use

$$s_{ei}^2 = \frac{\sum_t (e_{it} - \bar{e}_{i.})^2}{T-K-1}. \tag{16-58}$$

We have n such estimators, so we average them to obtain

$$\bar{s}_e^2 = \frac{1}{n} \sum_i s_{ei}^2$$

$$= \frac{1}{n} \sum_i \frac{\sum_t (e_{it} - \bar{e}_{i.})^2}{T - K - 1} \tag{16-59}$$

$$= \frac{1}{nt - nK - n} \sum_i \sum_t (e_{it} - \bar{e}_{i.})^2.$$

The degrees of freedom correction in $\bar{s}_e^2$ is excessive, as it assumes that α and β are reestimated for each i. The estimated parameters are the n means $\bar{y}_{i.}$ and the K slopes. Therefore, we propose the unbiased estimator

$$\hat{\sigma}_\varepsilon^2 = \frac{\sum_i \sum_t (e_{it} - \bar{e}_{i.})^2}{(nT - n - K)}. \,^{24} \tag{16-60}$$

For convenience, it is worth noting that this is just the usual variance estimator in the LSDV model in (16–60), appropriately corrected for degrees of freedom. The n means,

$$\varepsilon_{**i} = \bar{y}_{i.} - \alpha - \beta' \bar{x}_{i.}$$

$$= \bar{\varepsilon}_{i.} + u_i, \tag{16-61}$$

are independent and have variance

$$\text{Var}[\varepsilon_{**i}] = \sigma_{**}^2 = \frac{\sigma_\varepsilon^2}{T} + \sigma_u^2.$$

Incorporating the degrees of freedom correction for the estimate of β in the group means least squares regression of (16–55), we can use

$$\hat{\sigma}_{**}^2 = \frac{e_{**}' e_{**}}{n - K} \tag{16-62}$$

as an unbiased estimator of $\sigma_\varepsilon^2/T + \sigma_u^2$. This suggests the estimator

$$\hat{\sigma}_u^2 = \hat{\sigma}_{**}^2 - \frac{\hat{\sigma}_\varepsilon^2}{T}. \tag{16-63}$$

The estimator in (16–63) is unbiased but could be negative in a finite sample. Alternative estimators have been proposed.[25] Indeed, since we only require a consistent estimator of σ_u^2, *any* consistent estimate of β could be used in (16–62), including the original pooled OLS estimator. However, such a finding might cast some doubt on the appropriateness of the model, and before proceeding in this fashion, one might do well to reconsider the random effects specification.

Breusch and Pagan (1980) have devised a Lagrange multiplier test for the random effects model based on the OLS residuals. For

$$H_0: \sigma_u^2 = 0 \quad (\text{or } \text{Corr}[w_{it}, w_{is}] = 0),$$

$$H_0: \sigma_u^2 \neq 0,$$

---

[24] A formal proof of this proposition may be found in Maddala (1971) or in Judge et al. (1985, p. 551).
[25] See, for example, Wallace and Hussain (1969), Maddala (1971), Fuller and Battese (1974), and Amemiya (1971).

the test statistic is

$$LM = \frac{nT}{2(T-1)}\left[\frac{\sum_i(\sum_t e_{it})^2}{\sum_i\sum_t e_{it}^2} - 1\right]^2. \tag{16-64}$$

Under the null hypothesis, LM is distributed as chi-squared with one degree of freedom. A useful shortcut for computing LM is as follows: Let **D** be the matrix of dummy variables defined in (16–33), and let **e** be the OLS residual vector. Then

$$LM = \frac{nT}{2(T-1)}\left[\frac{\mathbf{e'DD'e}}{\mathbf{e'e}} - 1\right]^2. \tag{16-65}$$

EXAMPLE 16.12.   The least squares estimates for the cost data are given in Example 16.9. Based on the OLS residuals, we obtain a Lagrange multiplier test statistic of

$$\frac{6(4)}{2(4-1)}\left[\frac{2.24522}{1.01520} - 1\right]^2 = 5.87185.$$

The 5 percent and 1 percent critical values from the chi-squared distribution with one degree of freedom are 3.842 and 6.635, so the statistic is significant at the 5 percent level of significance but not at the 1 percent level. The evidence in favor of the error components model is present, but not compelling.

With the variance estimators in hand, FGLS can be used to estimate the parameters of the model. All of our earlier results for FGLS estimators apply here. It would also be possible to obtain the maximum likelihood estimator.[26] The likelihood function is complicated, but as we have seen repeatedly, the MLE of β will be GLS based on the maximum likelihood estimators of the variance components. It can be shown that the MLEs of σ_ε^2 and σ_u^2 are the unbiased estimators shown earlier, *without* their degrees of freedom corrections.[27] This model satisfies the requirements for the Oberhofer–Kmenta algorithm, so we could also use the iterated FGLS procedure to obtain the MLEs if desired. The initial consistent estimates could be based on least squares residuals. Still other estimators have been proposed. None will have better asymptotic properties than the MLE or FGLS estimators, but they may outperform them in a finite sample.[28]

EXAMPLE 16.13.   To compute the FGLS estimator, we require estimates of the variance components. As noted earlier, the unbiased estimator of σ_ε^2 is the residual variance estimator in the within-units (LSDV) regression. Thus,

$$\hat{\sigma}_\varepsilon^2 = \frac{0.264062}{17} = 0.015531.$$

The unit means are given in Example 16.11. The residual sum of squares in the unit means regression is 0.135202, so

$$\widehat{\frac{\sigma_\varepsilon^2}{T} + \sigma_u^2} + \frac{0.135202}{4} = 0.033801.$$

---

[26] See Hsiao (1986).
[27] See Berzeg (1979).
[28] See Maddala and Mount (1973).

Therefore,

$$\hat{\sigma}_u^2 = 0.033801 - \frac{0.015531}{4} = 0.0299178.$$

For purposes of FGLS,

$$\hat{\theta} = 1 - \left[\frac{0.015531}{4(0.033801)} \right]^{1/2} = 0.661074.$$

Finally, the FGLS regression produces

$$\ln C_{it} - \hat{\theta} \overline{\ln C_{i.}} = -3.41310 + 0.796321 (\ln Y_{it} - \hat{\theta} \overline{\ln Y_{i.}}).$$
$$\quad\quad\quad\quad\quad\quad\quad (0.3615) \quad (0.04256)$$

It is instructive to compare these to the OLS results we obtained earlier:

$$\ln C = -4.17478 + 0.887987 \ln Y.$$
$$\quad\quad (0.2769) \quad (0.0329)$$

The FGLS constant term is an estimate of $\alpha(1 - \theta)$, so the implied estimate of the constant term would be $-10.0703.$[29] Recall that we derived the implicit weighting between the within- and between-units estimators for OLS:

$$0.887987 = 0.09749\, b^w + 0.90251\, b^b,$$

where

$$b^w = 0.674279$$

and

$$b^b = 0.911073.$$

To do likewise for the FGLS estimator, we require the decomposition of the variance of $\ln Y$, which is

$$S_{xx}^t = 42.6346,$$

$$S_{xx}^b = 38.4754,$$

$$S_{xx}^w = 4.15626.$$

The weighting to be used would be

$$w_{GLS} = \frac{S_{xx}^w}{S_{xx}^w + (1 - \hat{\theta})^2 S_{xx}^b} = 0.4846.$$

Therefore, for the FGLS estimator,

$$0.796321 = 0.4846\, b^w + 0.5154\, b^b.$$

As expected, the weight attached to the between-units estimator is lower when we use FGLS.

None of the desirable properties of the estimators in the random effects model rely on T going to infinity.[30] Indeed, T is likely to be quite small. The maximum likelihood estimator of

---

[29] Since $\hat{\theta}$ is an estimated parameter, it is not obvious how one would obtain an appropriate standard error for this nonlinear function of two estimates. It is likely that the GLS constant term and $\hat{\theta}$ are correlated, and we have not derived the variance for $\hat{\theta}$. Therefore, we are unable to apply the usual linear approximation for a nonlinear function.
[30] See Nickell (1981).

σ_ε^2 is exactly equal to an average of n estimators, each based on the T observations for unit i. [See (16–59).] Each component in this average is, in principle, consistent. That is, its variance is of order $1/T$ or smaller. Since T is small, this may be relatively large; however, each term provides some information about the parameter. The average over the n cross-sectional units has a variance of order $1/(nT)$, which will go to zero if n increases, even if we regard T as fixed. The conclusion to draw is that nothing in this treatment relies on T growing large. Although it can be shown that some consistency results will follow for T increasing, the typical panel data set is based on data sets for which it does not make sense to assume that T increases without bound or, in some cases, at all.[31] As a general proposition, it is necessary to take some care in devising estimators whose properties hinge on whether T is large or not. The widely used conventional ones we have discussed here do not, but we have not exhausted the possibilities.

The LSDV model *does* rely on T increasing for consistency. To see this, we use the partitioned regression. The slopes are

$$\mathbf{b} = [\mathbf{X}'\mathbf{M}_d\mathbf{X}]^{-1}[\mathbf{X}'\mathbf{M}_d\mathbf{y}].$$

Since $\mathbf{X}$ is $nT \times K$, as long as the inverted moment matrix converges to a zero matrix, $\mathbf{b}$ is consistent as long as either n or T increases without bound. But the dummy variable coefficients are

$$a_i = \bar{y}_{i.} - \mathbf{b}'\bar{\mathbf{x}}_{i.}$$

$$= \frac{1}{T}\sum_t e_{it}.$$

We have already seen that $\mathbf{b}$ is consistent. Suppose, for the present, that $\bar{\mathbf{x}}_{i.} = \mathbf{0}$. Then $\mathrm{Var}[a_i] = \mathrm{Var}[y_{it}]/T$. Therefore, unless $T \to \infty$, the estimates of the unit-specific effects are not consistent. (They are, however, best linear unbiased.) This is worth bearing in mind when analyzing data sets for which T is fixed and there is no intention to replicate the study, and no logical argument that would justify the claim that it could have been replicated in principle.

The random effects model was developed by Balestra and Nerlove (1966). Their formulation included a time-specific component as well as the individual effect:

$$y_{it} = \alpha + \boldsymbol{\beta}'\mathbf{x}_{it} + \varepsilon_{it} + u_i + v_t.$$

The extended formulation is rather complicated analytically. In Balestra and Nerlove's study, it was made even more so by the presence of a lagged dependent variable that causes all of the problems discussed earlier in our discussion of autocorrelation. A full set of results for this extended model, including a method for handling the lagged dependent variable, has been developed.[32] However, the full model is rarely used. Most studies limit the model to the individual effects and, if needed, model the time effects in some other fashion.[33]

16.4.4. Fixed or Random Effects?

At various points, we have made the distinction between fixed and random effects models. An inevitable question is, which should be used? It has been suggested that the

---

[31] In this connection, Chamberlain (1983) has provided some innovative treatments of panel data that, in fact, take T as given in the model and that base consistency results solely on n increasing. We will consider one of his models in a later section. Some additional results for dynamic models are given by Bhargava and Sargan (1981).

[32] See Balestra and Nerlove (1966), Fomby et al. (1984), Judge et al. (1985), Hsiao (1986), Anderson and Hsiao (1982), and Nerlove (1971).

[33] See Macurdy (1982) and Beggs (1986).

distinction between fixed and random effects models is an erroneous interpretation. Mundlak (1978) argues that we should always treat the individual effects as random. The fixed effects model is simply analyzed conditionally on the effects present in the observed sample. One can argue that certain institutional factors or characteristics of the data argue for one or the other, but, unfortunately, this approach does not always provide much guidance. From a purely practical standpoint, the dummy variable approach is costly in terms of degrees of freedom lost, and in a wide, longitudinal data set, the random effects model has some intuitive appeal. On the other hand, the fixed effects approach has one considerable virtue. There is no justification for treating the individual effects as uncorrelated with the other regressors, as is assumed in the random effects model. The random effects treatment, therefore, may suffer from the inconsistency due to omitted variables. [34]

It is possible to test for orthogonality of the random effects and the regressors. The specification test devised by Hausman (1978)[35] has the same format as that for the errors in variables model discussed in Section 9.5.6. It is based on the idea that under the hypothesis of no correlation, both OLS in the LSDV model and GLS are consistent, but OLS is inefficient,[36] while under the alternative, OLS is consistent, but GLS is not. Therefore, under the null hypothesis, the two estimates should not differ systematically, and a test can be based on the difference. The other essential ingredient for the test is the variance of the difference vector, $[\mathbf{b} - \hat{\boldsymbol{\beta}}]$;

$$\text{Var}[\mathbf{b} - \hat{\boldsymbol{\beta}}] = \text{Var}[\mathbf{b}] + \text{Var}[\hat{\boldsymbol{\beta}}] - \text{Cov}[\mathbf{b}, \hat{\boldsymbol{\beta}}] - \text{Cov}[\mathbf{b}, \hat{\boldsymbol{\beta}}]'. \quad (16\text{--}66)$$

Hausman's essential result is that *the covariance of an efficient estimator with its difference from an inefficient estimator, is zero.* This implies that

$$\text{Cov}[(\mathbf{b} - \hat{\boldsymbol{\beta}}), \hat{\boldsymbol{\beta}}] = \text{Cov}[\mathbf{b}, \hat{\boldsymbol{\beta}}] - \text{Var}[\hat{\boldsymbol{\beta}}] = \mathbf{0},$$

or that

$$\text{Cov}[\mathbf{b}, \hat{\boldsymbol{\beta}}] = \text{Var}[\hat{\boldsymbol{\beta}}].$$

Inserting this in (16–66) produces the required variance matrix for the test,

$$\text{Var}[\mathbf{b} - \hat{\boldsymbol{\beta}}] = \text{Var}[\mathbf{b}] - \text{Var}[\hat{\boldsymbol{\beta}}] = \boldsymbol{\Sigma}. \quad (16\text{--}67)$$

The chi-squared test is based on the Wald criterion:

$$W = \chi^2(K) = [\mathbf{b} - \hat{\boldsymbol{\beta}}]'\hat{\boldsymbol{\Sigma}}^{-1}[\mathbf{b} - \hat{\boldsymbol{\beta}}]. \quad (16\text{--}68)$$

For $\hat{\boldsymbol{\Sigma}}$, we use the estimated variance matrices of the slope estimator in the LSDV model and the estimated variance matrix in the random effects model, excluding the constant term. Under the null hypothesis, W is asymptotically distributed with K degrees of freedom.

EXAMPLE 16.14. For the cost function example, the test is based on a single coefficient, so it simplifies to

$$W = \frac{(b - \hat{\beta})^2}{(\text{Var}[b] - \text{Var}[\hat{\beta}])},$$

which is asymptotically distributed as chi-squared with one degree of freedom. Alternatively, the square root of this statistic may be referred to the standard normal table.

---

[34] See Hausman and Taylor (1981) and Chamberlain (1978).
[35] Related results are given by Baltagi (1986).
[36] Referring to the GLS matrix weighted average given earlier, we see that the efficient weight uses θ, while OLS sets $\theta = 1$.

From Examples 16.10 and 16.13, we have

$$W = \frac{(0.674279 - 0.873586)^2}{(0.06113^2 - 0.03563^2)} = 16.099.$$

The hypothesis that the individual effects are uncorrelated with log Y should be rejected.

16.4.5.   Recent Developments

The study of longitudinal data has been one of the most active areas of econometric research in the past few years. Recent publications that contain descriptions of current developments include special issues of the *Journal of Econometrics* (Heckman and Singer (1985)) and the *Annals d'Insee* (Mazodier (1978), a symposium in *Econometric Reviews* (Hsiao (1985)), a recent monograph by Hsiao (1986), and a useful summary in the *Handbook of Econometrics* (Chamberlain (1983)). Many of the extensions in the recent literature involve forays into areas of limited dependent variables, duration models, and other highly nonlinear models.[37] However, research also continues into how better to formulate the linear model to take advantage of the wealth of information embodied in longitudinal data. We consider two examples.

Chamberlain has suggested that for small T, we may incorporate the T observations for observation i into the framework of Section 16.3.2, thereby allowing the covariance structure for the T disturbances to be unrestricted.[38] We take a case of $T = 2$ for illustration. The departure point, is, for y_i,

$$y_{i1} = \alpha_i + \beta' x_{i1} + \varepsilon_{i1}, \tag{16-69}$$

$$y_{i2} = \alpha_i + \beta' x_{i2} + \varepsilon_{i2},$$

where α_i are *unobserved* individual effects. In order to allow for possible correlation between the individual specific effects and the regressors, we consider the relationship between α_i and x_i. If the conditional mean, $E[\alpha_i | x_{i1}, x_{i2}]$, were known, we could simply incorporate it in the regression model. Since this is unlikely to be known, we approximate instead with the *projection*, or linear approximation,

$$\alpha_i = \mu + \alpha_1' x_{i1} + \alpha_2' x_{i2} + \omega_i.$$

If we insert this in (16-69), we can collect the various parts in

$$\begin{bmatrix} y_{i1} \\ y_{i2} \end{bmatrix} = \begin{bmatrix} 1 & x_{i1}' & x_{i2}' & 0 & 0 \\ 1 & 0 & 0 & x_{i1}' & x_{i2}' \end{bmatrix} \begin{bmatrix} \mu \\ \beta + \alpha_1 \\ \alpha_2 \\ \alpha_1 \\ \beta + \alpha_2 \end{bmatrix} + \begin{bmatrix} v_1 \\ v_2 \end{bmatrix} \tag{16-70}$$

or

$$\begin{bmatrix} y_{i1} \\ y_{i2} \end{bmatrix} = \begin{bmatrix} 1 & x_{*1} \\ 1 & x_{*2} \end{bmatrix} \begin{bmatrix} \mu \\ \beta_* \end{bmatrix} + \begin{bmatrix} v_1 \\ v_2 \end{bmatrix} \tag{16-71}$$

$$\text{Var}[v_1, v_2] = \Omega.$$

---

[37] See, for example, Chamberlain (1980) and the application in Chapter 20.

[38] His treatment is equivalent to this, although he casts it in somewhat different terms. See also Chamberlain (1982) and Kiefer (1980) for a related model.

Each pair of observations (or set of T) is stacked as shown here. If we allow v_1 and v_2 to be freely correlated, then, aside from the restrictions embodied in the parameter vector, this is the model of Section 16.3.2. We could estimate it using the method described there. Unfortunately, this will produce two (or T) different estimates of β. A restricted estimator is required to reconcile the estimates. To sum up, note that this approach preserves the parsimony of the random effects model but, at the same time, deals directly with the omitted variable problem that arises if the individual effects are correlated with the regressors. Issues that must be settled are the implications of approximating $E[\alpha_i | x_{i1}, x_{i2}]$ with the linear projection and the properties of the restricted estimator, given the structure of the constructed disturbances. Further discussion and a large number of extensions can be found in Chamberlain's papers.

A recurrent problem in using microeconomic data is errors of measurement. As we saw in Chapter 9, this is a thorny problem, and our conclusion there was a pessimistic one. Unless we can use some otherwise unknown parameters, the least squares estimates will be inconsistent, and little can be done to remedy the problem. Griliches and Hausman (1986) show that the picture brightens considerably when panel data are used.[39] Consider their first example:

$$y_{it} = \alpha_i + \beta x_{it}^* + \varepsilon_{it}$$
$$x_{it} = x_{it*} + u_{it}, \tag{16-72}$$

where x_{it}^* is the true but unobserved datum and x_{it} is the observed, badly measured counterpart. This is the "errors in variables" model of Section 9.5 with the addition of the individual effect. Unless α_i is constant across i, ordinary least squares regression of y_{it} on a constant and x_{it} will be biased and inconsistent for two reasons: correlation of x_{it} with the omitted individual effects and the familiar attenuation effect of measurement error. The authors suggest two approaches for getting rid of the first problem. The within-units estimator (LSDV estimator), that is, the regression of $[y_{it} - \bar{y}_{i.}]$ on $[x_{it} - \bar{x}_{i.}]$, sweeps out the effect of α_i. Because the measurement error remains, however, the estimator is still inconsistent. It can be shown that

$$\text{plim } b^w = \beta \left[1 - \frac{(T-1)\sigma_u^2}{T \text{Var}[x_{it} - \bar{x}_{i.}]} \right]. \tag{16-73}$$

A second possibility is the estimator based on first differences. By direct substitution,

$$(y_{it} - y_{i,t-1}) = \beta(x_{it} - x_{i,t-1}) + [(\varepsilon_{it} - \varepsilon_{i,t-1}) - \beta(u_{it} - u_{i,t-1})].$$

or

$$\Delta y_{it} = \beta[\Delta x_{it}] + \Delta(\varepsilon_{it} - \beta u_{it}). \tag{16-74}$$

Least squares remains inconsistent because of the measurement error:

$$\text{plim } b^d = \beta \left[1 - \frac{2\sigma_u^2}{\text{Var}[\Delta x]} \right]. \tag{16-75}$$

But since $\text{Var}[x_{it} - \bar{x}_{i.}]$ and $\text{Var}[\Delta x]$ are both estimable with sample statistics, these two results provide two equations in two unknowns. A consistent estimate of β is provided (as we have seen so many times before) by a weighted average of two estimators,

$$\hat{\beta} = g b^w + (1 - g) b^d, \tag{16-76}$$

---

[39] A precursor with some similar results is Chamberlain and Griliches (1975).

where

$$g = \frac{2/\text{Var}[\Delta x]}{2/\text{Var}[\Delta x] + \dfrac{T-1}{T}\text{Var}[x_{it} - \bar{x}_{i.}]}$$ (16–77)

and

$$\hat{\sigma}_u^2 = \frac{(\hat{\beta} - b^d)\text{Var}[\Delta x]}{2\hat{\beta}}.$$

The general observation is that with panel data we have several different possible estimators of the parameters. Although they may each be inconsistent, we can use the method of moments and invoke the Slutsky theorem to obtain consistent estimators. Hausman and Griliches proceed to a discussion of more general models including multiple regressions. The authors also provide a method of obtaining appropriate standard errors.

Exercises

1. The model

$$\begin{bmatrix} \mathbf{y}_1 \\ \mathbf{y}_2 \end{bmatrix} = \begin{bmatrix} \mathbf{x}_1 \\ \mathbf{x}_2 \end{bmatrix}\beta + \begin{bmatrix} \varepsilon_1 \\ \varepsilon_2 \end{bmatrix}$$

satisfies the groupwise heteroscedastic regression model of (16–3) and (16–6). All variables have zero means. The following sample second moment matrix is obtained from a sample of 20 observations:

	y_1	y_2	x_1	x_2
y_1	20	6	4	3
y_2	6	10	3	6
x_1	4	3	5	2
x_2	3	6	2	10

(a) Compute the two separate OLS estimates of β, their sampling variances, the estimates of σ_1^2 and σ_2^2, and the R^2's in the two regressions.

(b) Carry out the Lagrange multiplier test of the hypothesis that $\sigma_1^2 = \sigma_2^2$.

(c) Compute the two-step FGLS estimate of β and an estimate of its sampling variance. Test the hypothesis that β equals one.

(d) Carry out the Wald test of equal disturbance variances.

(e) Compute the maximum likelihood estimates of β, σ_1^2, and σ_2^2 by iterating the FGLS estimates to convergence.

(f) Carry out a likelihood ratio test of equal disturbance variances.

(g) Compute the two-step FGLS estimate of β, assuming that the model in (16–7) applies. [That is, allow for cross-sectional correlation.] Compare your results to those of part (c).

2. Suppose that in the model of Section 16.3.1 X_i is the same for all i. What is the generalized least squares estimator of β? How would you compute the estimator if it were necessary to estimate σ_i^2?

3. Repeat the previous exercise for the model of Section 16.3.2.

4. The following table presents a hypothetical panel of data:

	$i = 1$		$i = 2$		$i = 3$	
	y	x	y	x	y	x
$t = 1$	30.27	24.31	38.71	28.35	37.03	21.16
$t = 2$	35.59	28.47	29.74	27.38	43.82	26.76
$t = 3$	17.90	23.74	11.29	12.74	37.12	22.21
$t = 4$	44.90	25.44	26.17	21.08	24.34	19.02
$t = 5$	37.58	20.80	5.85	14.02	26.15	18.64
$t = 6$	23.15	10.55	29.01	20.43	26.01	18.97
$t = 7$	30.53	18.40	30.38	28.13	29.64	21.35
$t = 8$	39.90	25.40	36.03	21.78	30.25	21.34
$t = 9$	20.44	13.57	37.90	25.65	25.41	15.86
$t = 10$	36.85	25.60	33.90	11.66	26.04	13.28

(a) Estimate the groupwise heteroscedastic model of Section 16.3.1. Include an estimate of the asymptotic variance of the slope estimator. Use a two-step procedure, basing the FGLS estimator at the second step on residuals from the pooled least squares regression.

(b) Carry out the Wald, Lagrange multiplier, and likelihood ratio tests of the hypothesis that the variances are all equal. For the likelihood ratio test, use the FGLS estimates.

(c) Carry out a Lagrange multiplier test of the hypothesis that the disturbances are uncorrelated across individuals.

5. The following is a panel of data on investment (y) and profit (x) for $n = 3$ firms over $T = 10$ periods:

	$i = 1$		$i = 2$		$i = 3$	
	y	x	y	x	y	x
$t = 1$	13.32	12.85	20.30	22.93	8.85	8.65
$t = 2$	26.30	25.69	17.47	17.96	19.60	16.55
$t = 3$	2.62	5.48	9.31	9.16	3.87	1.47
$t = 4$	14.94	13.79	18.01	18.73	24.19	24.91
$t = 5$	15.80	15.41	7.63	11.31	3.99	5.01
$t = 6$	12.20	12.59	19.84	21.15	5.73	8.34
$t = 7$	14.93	16.64	13.76	16.13	26.68	22.70
$t = 8$	29.82	26.45	10.00	11.61	11.49	8.36
$t = 9$	20.32	19.64	19.51	19.55	18.49	15.44
$t = 10$	4.77	5.43	18.32	17.06	20.84	17.87

(a) Pool the data and compute the least squares regression coefficients of the model

$$y_{it} = \alpha + \beta x_{it} + \varepsilon_{it}.$$

(b) Estimate the fixed effects model of (16–33), and then test the hypothesis that the constant term is the same for all three firms.

(c) Estimate the random effects model of (16–44), and then carry out the Lagrange multiplier test of the hypothesis that the classical model without the common effect applies.

(d) Carry out Hausman's specification test for the random versus the fixed model.

6. Suppose that the model of (16–33) is formulated with an overall constant term and $n - 1$ dummy variables (dropping, say, the last one). Investigate the effect that this has on the set of dummy variable coefficients and on the least squares estimates of the slopes.

7. Derive the log-likelihood function for the model in (16–44), assuming that ε_{it} and u_i are normally distributed. [**Hints:** Write the log-likelihood function as

$$\ln L = \sum_{i=1}^{n} \ln L_i,$$

where $\ln L_i$ is the log-likelihood function for the T observations in group i. These T observations are joint normally distributed, with the covariance matrix given in (16–46). The log likelihood is the sum of the logs of the joint normal densities of the n sets of T observations,

$$\varepsilon_{it} + u_i = y_{it} - \alpha \pm \beta' x_{it}.$$

This will involve the inverse and determinant of Ω. Use (2–66) to prove that

$$\Omega^{-1} = \frac{1}{\sigma_\varepsilon^2}\left[I - \frac{\sigma_\varepsilon^2}{\sigma_\varepsilon^2 + T\sigma_u^2} ii'\right].$$

To find the determinant, use the product of the characteristic roots. Note first that

$$|\sigma_\varepsilon^2 I + \sigma_u^2 ii'| = (\sigma_\varepsilon^2)^T \left|I + \frac{\sigma_u^2}{\sigma_\varepsilon^2} ii'\right|.$$

The roots are determined by

$$\left[I + \frac{\sigma_\varepsilon^2}{\sigma_u^2} ii'\right] c = \lambda c$$

or

$$\frac{\sigma_\varepsilon^2}{\sigma_u^2} ii'c = (\lambda - 1)c.$$

Any vector whose elements sum to zero is a solution. There are $T - 1$ such independent vectors, so $T - 1$ characteristic roots are $(\lambda - 1) = 0$ or $\lambda = 1$. Premultiply the expression by i' to obtain the remaining characteristic root. (Remember to add 1 to the result.) Now collect terms to obtain the log likelihood.]

8. *Unbalanced design for random effects.* Suppose that the random effects model of Section 16.4.3. is to be estimated with a panel in which the groups have different numbers of observations. Let T_i be the number of observations in group i.

   (a) Show that the pooled least squares estimator in (16–44) is unbiased and consistent in spite of this complication.

   (b) Show that the estimator in (16–60) based on the pooled least squares estimator of β (or, for that matter, *any* consistent estimator of β) is a consistent estimator of σ_ε^2.

   (c) The group mean regression in (16–61) is heteroscedastic. Investigate the properties of the residual variance estimator. [**Hints:** For large-sample results, rely on $n \to \infty$, not T_i. Take T_i as potentially small and fixed for each i. This set of results will parallel the discussion of Section 14.2.2. What will you require to assert that the estimator based on (16–60) and (16–62),

$$\hat{\sigma}_u = \hat{\sigma}^2_{**} - Q\hat{\sigma}^2_\varepsilon,$$

where

$$Q = \left(\frac{1}{n}\right)\left(\frac{1}{T_1} + \frac{1}{T_2} + \cdots + \frac{1}{T_n}\right)$$

is a consistent estimator of σ^2_u?]

(d) What change is needed in (16–48) in order to implement an FGLS estimator?

Postscript: The term $(nt)/(2(T-1))$ in (16–64) must be replaced with $(\Sigma_i T_i)^2/(2\Sigma_i T_i(T_i - 1))$.

9. In estimating the random effects model, if $K + 1$ is greater than n, the group means regression cannot be computed. Comment on the suggestion that in this event, we use a generalized inverse by dropping enough columns (variables) to produce a non-singular moment matrix and then using the sum of squared residuals from this regression.

10. What are the probability limits of $(1/n)LM$, where LM is defined in (16.64) under the null hypotheses that $\sigma^2_u = 0$ and under the alternative that $\sigma^2_u \neq 0$?

11. The text proposes two possible residuals to use in the estimation of σ^2_{**} in (16–62): the least squares coefficient vector, including the constant term in the group means regression, and the full slope vector, including the constant term, in the pooled least squares estimator. Comment on the third alternative, $\bar{e}_{i.} = \bar{y}_{i.} - a_i - \mathbf{b}'\bar{\mathbf{x}}_{i.}$, based on the LSDV estimators.

12. *A two-way fixed-effects model.* Suppose that the fixed-effects model is modified to include a time-specific dummy variable, as well as an individual-specific variable. Then

$$y_{it} = \alpha_i + \gamma_t + \boldsymbol{\beta}'\mathbf{x}_{it} + \varepsilon_{it}.$$

At every observation, the individual- and time-specific dummy variables sum to one, so there are some redundant coefficients. The discussion following (16–41) shows one way to remove the redundancy. Another useful way to do this is to include an overall constant and to drop one of the time-specific *and* one of the time-dummy variables. The model is, thus,

$$y_{it} = \delta + (\alpha_i - \alpha_1) + (\gamma_t - \gamma_1) + \boldsymbol{\beta}'\mathbf{x}_{it} + \varepsilon_{it}.$$

(Note that the respective time- or individual-specific variable is zero when t or i equals one.) Ordinary least squares estimates of β can be obtained by regression of

$$y_{it} - \bar{y}_{i.} - \bar{y}_{.t} + \bar{y}_{..}$$

on

$$\mathbf{x}_{it} - \bar{\mathbf{x}}_{i.} - \bar{\mathbf{x}}_{.t} + \bar{\mathbf{x}}_{..}$$

Then $(\alpha_i - \alpha_1)$ and $(\gamma_t - \gamma_1)$ are estimated using the expressions in (16–43), while $d = \bar{y}_{..} - \mathbf{b}'\bar{\mathbf{x}}_{..}$. Using the following data, estimate the full set of coefficients for the least squares dummy variable model:

	$t = 1$	$t = 2$	$t = 3$	$t = 4$	$t = 5$	$t = 6$	$t = 7$	$t = 8$	$t = 9$	$t = 10$
y	21.7	10.9	33.5	22.0	17.6	16.1	19.0	18.1	14.9	23.2
x_1	26.4	17.3	23.8	17.6	26.2	21.1	17.5	22.9	22.9	14.9
x_2	5.79	2.60	8.36	5.50	5.26	1.03	3.11	4.87	3.79	7.24
					$i = 2$					
y	21.8	21.0	33.8	18.0	12.2	30.0	21.7	24.9	21.9	23.6
x_1	19.6	22.8	27.8	14.0	11.4	16.0	28.8	16.8	11.8	18.6
x_2	3.36	1.59	6.19	3.75	1.59	9.87	1.31	5.42	6.32	5.35
					$i = 3$					
y	25.2	41.9	31.3	27.8	13.2	27.9	33.3	20.5	16.7	20.7
x_1	13.4	29.7	21.6	25.1	14.1	24.1	10.5	22.1	17.0	20.5
x_2	9.57	9.62	6.61	7.24	1.64	5.99	9.00	1.75	1.74	1.82
					$i = 4$					
y	15.3	25.9	21.9	15.5	16.7	26.1	34.8	22.6	29.0	37.1
x_1	14.2	18.0	29.9	14.1	18.4	20.1	27.6	27.4	28.5	28.6
x_2	4.09	9.56	2.18	5.43	6.33	8.27	9.16	5.24	7.92	9.63

Test the hypotheses that (1) the "period" effects are all zero, (2) the "group" effects are all zero, and (3) both period and group effects are zero. Use an F test in each case.

13. *Two-way random-effects model.* We modify the random-effects model by the addition of a time-specific disturbance. Thus,

$$y_{it} = \alpha + \boldsymbol{\beta}'\mathbf{x}_{it} + \varepsilon_{it} + u_i + v_t,$$

where

$$E[\varepsilon_{it}] = E[u_i] = E[v_t] = 0,$$

$$E[\varepsilon_{it}u_j] = E[\varepsilon_{it}v_s] = E[u_iv_t] = 0 \qquad \text{for all } i, j, t, s,$$

$$\text{Var}[\varepsilon_{it}] = \sigma_\varepsilon^2, \quad \text{Cov}[\varepsilon_{it}, \varepsilon_{js}] = 0 \qquad \text{for all } t, j, t, s,$$

$$\text{Var}[u_i] = \sigma_u^2, \quad \text{Cov}[u_i, u_j] = 0 \qquad \text{for all } i, j,$$

$$\text{Var}[v_t] = \sigma_v^2, \quad \text{Cov}[v_t, v_s] = 0 \qquad \text{for all } t, s.$$

Write out the full covariance matrix for a data set with $n = 2$ and $T = 2$.

14. *Estimation of the full random effects model.* Fuller and Battese (1974) have developed a method of FGLS estimation of the two-way random-effects model.[40] Let

$$s_{i.}^2 = \text{residual variance in the regression of group}$$
means of y_{it} on a constant and the group means of x_{it}. (This is n observations.)

$$s_{.t}^2 = \text{residual variance in the regression of period}$$
means of y_{it} on a constant and the period means of x_{it}. (This is T observations.)

[40] See, as well, Judge et al. (1985, pp. 530–536).

s_a^2 = residual variance in the full dummy variable regression with both individual- and time-specific dummies. This can be computed using the method described in Exercise 12.

The following notation is that of Judge et al. (1985, p. 534).] Using the three preceding regressions, we can show that

$$(n - K - 1)s_{i.}^2 \text{ estimates } \sigma_1^2 = \sigma_\varepsilon^2 + T\sigma_u^2,$$

$$(T - K - 1)s_{.t}^2 \text{ estimates } \sigma_2^2 = \sigma_\varepsilon^2 + n\sigma_v^2,$$

$$s_a^2 \text{ estimates } \sigma_\varepsilon^2.$$

Then

$$(n - K - 1)s_{i.}^2 + (T - K - 1)s_{.t}^2 - s_a^2 \text{ estimates } \sigma_3^2 = \sigma_\varepsilon^2 + T\sigma_u^2 + n\sigma_v^2.$$

Let

$$\theta_1 = 1 - \frac{\sigma_\varepsilon}{\sigma_1},$$

$$\theta_2 = 1 - \frac{\sigma_\varepsilon}{\sigma_2},$$

$$\theta_3 = \theta_1 + \theta_2 - 1 + \frac{\sigma_\varepsilon}{\sigma_3}.$$

Generalized least squares is equivalent to ordinary least squares regression of

$$y_t^* = y_{it} - \theta_1 \bar{y}_{i.} - \theta_2 \bar{y}_{.t} + \theta_3 \bar{y}_{..}$$

on

$$x_t^* = x_{it} - \theta_1 \bar{x}_{i.} - \theta_2 \bar{x}_{.t} + \theta_3 \bar{x}_{..},$$

where x_t^* includes the constant term . This provides efficient estimates of the coefficients of the model. The usual estimator of the asymptotic covariance matrix of the estimated coefficient vector is appropriate. The sample estimates of θ_1, θ_2, and θ_3 are used when their population counterparts are unknown.

(a) Using the data from Problem 12, estimate the parameters of the two-way random effects model. [**Hint:** The variance estimators based on the group means lead to negative estimates of the variance components. But as shown in Problem 11, (16–62) can be based on any consistent estimator of the slopes. Use the pooled ordinary least squares estimates instead.]

(b) The extension of the Lagrange multiplier statistic of (16–64) to this model is

$$LM = \frac{nT}{2} \left[\frac{1}{T-1} \left[\frac{\sum_i (\sum_t e_{it})^2}{\sum_i \sum_t e_{it}^2} - 1 \right]^2 + \frac{1}{n-1} \left[\frac{\sum_t (\sum_i e_{it})^2}{\sum_i \sum_t e_{it}^2} - 1 \right]^2 \right].$$

This statistic is asymptotically distributed as chi-squared with two degrees of freedom. Carry out the Lagrange multiplier test of the two-way random effects model.

References

Amemiya, T., "The Estimation of Variances in a Variance-Components Model," *International Economic Review*, 12, 1971, pp. 1–13.

Anderson, T., and C. Hsiao, "Formulation and Estimation of Dynamic Models Using Panel Data," *Journal of Econometrics*, 18, 1982, pp. 67–82.

Balestra, P., and M. Nerlove, "Pooling Cross Section and Time Series Data in the Estimation of a Dynamic Model: The Demand for Natural Gas," *Econometrica*, 34, 1966, pp. 585–612.

Baltagi, B., "Pooling Under Misspecification, Some Monte Carlo Evidence on the Kmenta and Error Components Techniques," *Econometric Theory*, 2, 3, 1986, pp. 429–441.

Beggs, J., "Time Series Analysis in Pooled Cross Sections," *Econometric Theory*, 2, 1986, pp. 331–349.

Ben-Porath, Y., "Labor Force Participation Rates and Labor Supply," *Journal of Political Economy*, 81, 1973, pp. 697–704.

Berzeg, K., "The Error Components Model: Conditions for the Existence of Maximum Likelihood Estimates," *Journal of Econometrics*, 10, 1979, pp. 99–102.

Bhargava, A., and J. Sargan, "Estimating Dynamic Random Effects Models from Panel Data Covering Short Periods," *Econometrica*, 51, 1981, pp. 221–236.

Boot, J., and G. deWitt, "Investment Demand: An Empirical Contribution to the Aggregation Problem," *International Economic Review*, 1, 1960, pp. 3–30.

Breusch, T., and A. Pagan, "The Lagrange Multiplier Test and Its Applications to Model Specification in Econometrics," *Review of Economic Studies*, 47, 1980, pp. 239–253.

Chamberlain, G., "Omitted Variable Bias in Panel Data: Estimating the Returns to Schooling," *Annales de L'Insee*, 30/31, 1978, pp. 49–82.

Chamberlain, G., "Analysis of Covariance with Qualitative Data," *Review of Economic Studies*, 47, 1980, pp. 225–238.

Chamberlain, G., "Multivariate Regression Models for Panel Data," *Journal of Econometrics*, 18, 1982, pp. 5–46.

Chamberlain, G., "Panel Data," in Z. Griliches and M. Intrilligator, eds., *Handbook of Econometrics*, Amsterdam: North Holland, 1983.

Chamberlain, G., and Z. Griliches, "Unobservables with a Variance Components Structure: Ability, Schooling, and the Economic Success of Brothers," *International Economic Review*, 16, 1975, pp. 422–450.

Cornwell, C., and P. Schmidt, "Panel Data with Cross Sectional Variation in Slopes as Well as in Intercept," Michigan State University, Department of Economics, Econometrics Workshop Paper Number 8404, 1984.

Fomby, T., R. Hill, and N. Johnson, *Advanced Econometrics*, New York: Springer-Verlag, 1984.

Fuller, W., and G. Battese, "Estimation of Linear Models with Crossed-Error Structure," *Journal of Econometrics*, 2, 1974, pp. 67–78.

Greene, W., "Simultaneous Estimation of Factor Substitution, Economies of Scale, and Non-Neutral Technical Change," in A. Dogramaci, ed., *Econometric Analyses of Productivity*, Boston: Kluwer-Nijoff, 1983.

Griliches, Z., and J. Hausman, "Errors in Variables in Panel Data," *Journal of Econometrics*, 31, 1986, pp. 93–118.

Grunfeld, Y., "The Determinants of Corporate Investment," unpublished Ph.D. thesis, University of Chicago, 1958.

Grunfeld, Y., and Z. Griliches, "Is Aggregation Necessarily Bad?" *Review of Economics and Statistics*, 42, 1960, pp. 1–13.

Hausman, J., "Specification Tests in Econometrics," *Econometrica*, 46, 1978, pp. 69–85.

Hausman, J., and W. Taylor, "Panel Data and Unobservable Individual Effects," *Econometrica*, 49, 1981, pp. 1377–1398.

Heckman, J., and B. Singer, eds., "Econometric Analysis of Longitudinal Data," *Journal of Econometrics*, 32, 1985, pp. 1–195.

Hildreth, C., and J. Houck, "Some Estimators for a Linear Model with Random Coefficients," *Journal of the American Statistical Association*, 63, 1968, pp. 584–595.

Hsiao, C., "Some Estimation Methods for a Random Coefficient Model," *Econometrica*, 43, 1975, pp. 305–325.

Hsiao, C., "Benefits and Limitations of Panel Data," *Econometric Reviews*, 4, 1, 1985, pp. 121–174.

Hsiao, C., *Analysis of Panel Data*, Cambridge: Cambridge University Press, 1986.

Johnston, J., *Econometric Methods*, New York: McGraw-Hill, 1984, pp. 138–140.

Judge, G., R. Hill, W. Griffiths, T. Lee, and H. Lutkepohl, *The Theory and Practice of Econometrics*, New York: Wiley, 1985.

Kiefer, N., "Estimation of Fixed Effects Models for Time Series of Cross-Sections with Arbitrary Intertemporal Covariance," *Journal of Econometrics*, 14, 1980, pp. 195–202.

Kmenta, J., *Elements of Econometrics*, New York: Macmillan 1986.

Lee, L. F., "Estimation of Error Components Model with ARMA(p, q) Time Component—An Exact GLS Approach," University of Minnesota, Center for Economics Research, Number 78–104, 1978.

Lee, L., and W. Griffiths, "The Prior Likelihood and Best Linear Unbiased Prediction in Stochastic Coefficient Linear Models," University of New England Working Papers in Econometrics and Applied Statistics, Number 1, 1979.

Macurdy, T., "The Use of Time Series Processes to Model the Error Structure of Earnings in a Longitudinal Data Analysis," *Journal of Econometrics*, 18, 1, 1982, pp. 83–114.

Maddala, G., "The Use of Variance Components Models in Pooling Cross Section and Time Series Data," *Econometrica*, 39, 1971, pp. 341–358.

Maddala, G., and T. Mount, "A Comparative Study of Alternative Estimators for Variance Component Models," *Journal of the American Statistical Association*, 68, 1973, pp. 324–328.

Mazodier, P., ed., *Annales de L'Insee*, 30/31, 1978.

Mundlak, Y., "On the Pooling of Time Series and Cross Sectional Data," *Econometrica*, 46, 1978, pp. 69–86.

Nerlove, M., "Further Evidence on the Estimation of Dynamic Relations from a Time Series of Cross Sections," *Econometrica*, 39, 1971, pp. 359–382.

Nerlove, M., "A Note on Error Components Models," *Econometrica*, 39, 1971, pp. 383–396.

Nickell, S., "Biases in Dynamic Models with Fixed Effects," *Econometrica*, 49, 1981, pp. 1417–1426.

Rao, C., *Linear Statistical Inference and Its Applications*, New York: Wiley, 1965, p. 29.

Solow, R., "Technical Change and the Aggregate Production Function," *The Review of Economics and Statistics*, 39, 1957, pp. 312–320.

Suits, D., "Dummy Variables: Mechanics vs. Interpretation," *Review of Economics and Statistics*, 66, 1984, pp. 177–180.

Swamy, P., "Efficient Inference in a Random Coefficient Regression Model," *Econometrica*, 38, 1970, pp. 311–323.

Swamy, P., *Statistical Inference in Random Coefficient Regression Models*, New York: Springer-Verlag, 1971.

Swamy, P., "Linear Models with Random Coefficients," in P. Zarembka, ed., *Frontiers in Econometrics*, New York: Academic Press, 1974.

Wallace, T., and A. Hussain, "The Use of Error Components in Combining Cross Section with Time Series Data," *Econometrica*, 37, 1969, pp. 55–72.

Part IV

Topics in Econometrics

Chapter 17

Systems of Regression Equations

17.1. Introduction

There are many settings in which the models of the previous chapters apply to a group of related variables. In these contexts, it makes sense to consider the several models jointly. Some examples follow.

1. In the Grunfeld–Boot and de Witt investment model of Chapter 16, we have a set of firms each of which makes investment decisions based on variables that reflect anticipated profit and replacement of the capital stock. We specified

$$I_{it} = \beta_1 + \beta_2 F_{it} + \beta_3 C_{it} + \varepsilon_{it}.$$

Whether the parameter vector should be the same for all firms is a question that we shall study in this chapter. But the disturbances in the investment equations certainly include factors that are common to all of the firms, such as the perceived general health of the economy, as well as factors that are specific to the particular firm or industry. We discovered in our examples that considerable efficiency was gained by estimating the equations jointly (with the assumed common parameter vector) as a generalized regression. The hypothesis that the disturbances of the five companies were contemporaneously uncorrelated was strongly rejected by both likelihood ratio and Lagrange multiplier tests in Example 16.4.

2. In Chamberlain's analysis of a panel data model, a useful formulation involved treating the cross sections observed in the T periods as if a separate regression applied in each period. Constraints applied to the parameter vector and the correlation of the disturbances in these T equations imposed the common structure of the regression model.

3. The capital asset pricing model of Finance stipulates that for a given security,

$$r_{it} - r_{ft} = \alpha_i + \beta_i(r_{mt} - r_{ft}) + \varepsilon_{it},$$

where r_{it} is the return over period t on security i, r_{ft} is the return on a risk-free security, r_{mt} is the market return, and β_i is that security's beta coefficient. The disturbances are obviously correlated across securities. The knowledge that the return on security i exceeds the risk-free rate by a given amount gives some information about the excess return of security j, at least for some j's. It will be useful to estimate the previous M equations jointly rather than to ignore this connection.

4. In a model of production, the optimization conditions of economic theory imply that if a firm faces a set of factor prices $\mathbf{p}$, its set of cost-minimizing factor demands for producing

output Y will be a set of equations of the form $x_m = f_m(Y, \mathbf{p})$. Cast in the form of an econometric model, we have

$$x_1 = f_1(Y, \mathbf{p}:\boldsymbol{\theta}) + \varepsilon_1$$
$$x_2 = f_2(Y, \mathbf{p}:\boldsymbol{\theta}) + \varepsilon_2$$
$$\vdots$$
$$x_M = f_M(Y, \mathbf{p}:\boldsymbol{\theta}) + \varepsilon_M.$$

Once again, the disturbances should be correlated. In addition, the same parameters of the production technology will enter all of the demand equations, so the set of equations has cross-equation restrictions. Estimating the equations separately will waste the information that the same set of parameters appears in all of the equations.

5. In analyzing a sample of test scores, a common formulation holds that

$$y_1 = \beta_1 x_* + \varepsilon_1$$
$$y_2 = \beta_2 x_* + \varepsilon_2$$
$$\vdots$$
$$y_M = \beta_M x_* + \varepsilon_M$$
$$x_* = \gamma' \mathbf{x} + u,$$

where y_m is performance by the mth measure, x_* is latent talent or intelligence, and $\mathbf{x}$ is the vector of observables that are believed to feed into or affect the latent variable. Inserting the last equation into the first M, we find that the disturbance in the resulting equation is $v_m = \varepsilon_m + u$, which is obviously correlated across equations. Moreover, the parameter vector γ is also common to all of the equations. Estimating the equations separately would ignore both of these useful pieces of information.

All of these examples have a common multiple equation structure, which we may write as

$$\mathbf{y}_1 = \mathbf{X}_1 \boldsymbol{\beta}_1 + \boldsymbol{\varepsilon}_1$$
$$\mathbf{y}_2 = \mathbf{X}_1 \boldsymbol{\beta}_2 + \boldsymbol{\varepsilon}_2 \qquad\qquad (17\text{--}1)$$
$$\vdots$$
$$\mathbf{y}_M = \mathbf{X}_M \boldsymbol{\beta}_M + \boldsymbol{\varepsilon}_M.$$

There are M equations and T observations in the sample of data used to estimate them.[1] The five examples embody different types of constraints across equations and different structures of the disturbances. However, a basic set of principles will apply to all of them.

17.2.   The Seemingly Unrelated Regressions Model

All of the preceding examples and several of the models in Chapter 16 can be written in the form

$$\mathbf{y}_m = \mathbf{X}_m \boldsymbol{\beta}_m + \boldsymbol{\varepsilon}_m, \qquad\qquad (17\text{--}2)$$

---

[1] The use of T is not necessarily meant to imply any connection to time series. For instance, in Examples 4 and 5, the data might be cross-sectional.

where

$$\varepsilon = [\varepsilon_1', \varepsilon_2', \dots, \varepsilon_M']'$$

has

$$E[\varepsilon] = 0$$

and

$$E[\varepsilon\varepsilon'] = V.$$

We assume that a total of T observations are used in estimating the parameters of the M equations. Each equation involves K_m regressors, for a total of $K = \sum_m K_m$. The data are assumed to be well behaved, as described in Chapter 10, and we shall not treat the issue separately here. For the present, we also assume that disturbances are uncorrelated across observations. Therefore,

$$E[\varepsilon_{mt}\varepsilon_{ns}] = \sigma_{mn} \qquad \text{if } t = s \text{ and } 0 \text{ otherwise.}$$

(For present purposes, we use the subscript n to indicate the nth equation in the system, rather than the nth observation in a sample of n, as in previous chapters. The subscript m is used throughout to indicate the mth equation.) The disturbance formulation is, therefore,

$$E[\varepsilon_m\varepsilon_n'] = \sigma_{mn}\mathbf{I}$$

or

$$E[\varepsilon\varepsilon'] = \mathbf{V} = \begin{bmatrix} \sigma_{11}\mathbf{I} & \sigma_{12}\mathbf{I} & \cdots & \sigma_{1M}\mathbf{I} \\ \sigma_{21}\mathbf{I} & \sigma_{22}\mathbf{I} & \cdots & \sigma_{2M}\mathbf{I} \\ & & \vdots & \\ \sigma_{M1}\mathbf{I} & \sigma_{M2}\mathbf{I} & \cdots & \sigma_{MM}\mathbf{I} \end{bmatrix}. \tag{17-3}$$

17.2.1. Generalized Least Squares

Each equation is, by itself, a classical regression. Therefore, the parameters could be estimated consistently, if not efficiently, by ordinary least squares. The generalized regression model applies to the stacked regression,

$$\begin{bmatrix} \mathbf{y}_1 \\ \mathbf{y}_2 \\ \vdots \\ \mathbf{y}_M \end{bmatrix} = \begin{bmatrix} \mathbf{X}_1 & \mathbf{0} & \cdots & \mathbf{0} \\ \mathbf{0} & \mathbf{X}_2 & \cdots & \mathbf{0} \\ & & \vdots & \\ \mathbf{0} & \mathbf{0} & \cdots & \mathbf{X}_M \end{bmatrix} \begin{bmatrix} \boldsymbol{\beta}_1 \\ \boldsymbol{\beta}_2 \\ \vdots \\ \boldsymbol{\beta}_M \end{bmatrix} + \begin{bmatrix} \varepsilon_1 \\ \varepsilon_2 \\ \vdots \\ \varepsilon_M \end{bmatrix} \tag{17-4}$$

$$= \mathbf{X}\boldsymbol{\beta} + \varepsilon.$$

Therefore, the efficient estimator is generalized least squares. The model has a particularly convenient form. For the tth observation, the $M \times M$ covariance matrix of the disturbances is

$$\boldsymbol{\Sigma} = \begin{bmatrix} \sigma_{11} & \sigma_{12} & \cdots & \sigma_{1M} \\ \sigma_{12} & \sigma_{22} & \cdots & \sigma_{2M} \\ & & \vdots & \\ \sigma_{1M} & \sigma_{2M} & \cdots & \sigma_{MM} \end{bmatrix}, \tag{17-5}$$

so, in (17–2),

$$V = \Sigma \otimes I \tag{17-6}$$

and

$$V^{-1} = \Sigma^{-1} \otimes I. \tag{17-7}$$

Denoting the ijth element of Σ^{-1} by σ^{ij}, we find that the GLS estimator is

$$\hat{\beta} = [X'V^{-1}X]^{-1}X'V^{-1}y$$

$$= [X'(\Sigma^{-1} \otimes I)X]^{-1}X'(\Sigma^{-1} \otimes I)y$$

$$= \begin{bmatrix} \sigma^{11}X_1'X_1 & \sigma^{12}X_1'X_2 & \cdots & \sigma^{1M}X_1'X_M \\ \sigma^{12}X_2'X_1 & \sigma^{22}X_2'X_2 & \cdots & \sigma^{2M}X_2'X_M \\ \vdots & & & \vdots \\ \sigma^{1M}X_M'X_1 & \sigma^{2M}X_M'X_2 & \cdots & \sigma^{MM}X_M'X_M \end{bmatrix}^{-1} \begin{bmatrix} \sum_m \sigma^{1m}X_1'y_m \\ \sum_m \sigma^{2m}X_2'y_m \\ \vdots \\ \sum_m \sigma^{Mm}X_M'y_m \end{bmatrix}. \tag{17-8}$$

The asymptotic covariance matrix for the GLS estimator is the inverse matrix in (17–8). All of the results of Chapter 13 carry over to this model.

This is obviously different from ordinary least squares. At this point, however, the equations are linked only by their disturbances—hence the name *seemingly unrelated regressions model*—so it is interesting to ask just how much efficiency is gained by using generalized least squares instead of ordinary least squares. Dwivedi and Srivastava (1978) have analyzed some special cases in detail.

1. If the equations are actually unrelated, that is, $\sigma_{mn} = 0$, there is obviously no payoff to GLS. Indeed, GLS is OLS.
2. If the equations have identical explanatory variables, that is, $X_m = X_n$, it can be shown (we leave it as an exercise) that OLS and GLS are identical.[2]
3. If the regressors in one block of equations are a subset of those in another, GLS brings no efficiency gain in estimation of the smaller equations.[3]

In the more general case, with unrestricted correlation of the disturbances and different regressors in the equations, the results are complicated and dependent on the data. Two propositions that apply generally are as follows:

1. The greater the correlation of the disturbances, the greater the efficiency gain accruing to GLS.
2. The less correlation there is between the X matrices, the greater is the gain in using GLS.

17.2.2.   Feasible Generalized Least Squares

The preceding discussion assumes that Σ is known, which, as usual, is rarely the case. FGLS estimators have been devised, however.[4] The least squares residuals may be used (of course) to estimate consistently the elements of Σ with

$$\hat{\sigma}_{mn} = s_{mn} = \frac{e_m'e_n}{T}. \tag{17-9}$$

---

[2] An intriguing result, albeit probably of negligible practical significance, is that the result also applies if the X's are all nonsingular, and not necessarily identical, linear combinations of the same set of variables.

[3] We shall examine one such model in detail later. The result was analyzed by Goldberger (1970) and later by Revankar (1974) and Conniffe (1982).

[4] See Zellner (1962) and Zellner and Huang (1962).

The consistency of s_{mn} follows from that of $\mathbf{b}_m$. A degrees of freedom correction in the divisor is occasionally suggested.[5] Two possibilities are

$$s_{mn}^* = \frac{\mathbf{e}_m' \mathbf{e}_n}{[(T - K_m)(T - K_n)]^{1/2}}$$

and

$$s_{mn}^{**} = \frac{\mathbf{e}_m' \mathbf{e}_n}{[T - \max(K_m, K_n)]}.$$

The second is unbiased only if m equals n or K_m equals K_n, while the first is unbiased only if m equals n. Whether unbiasedness of the estimate of Σ used for FGLS is a virtue here is uncertain.[6] The asymptotic properties of $\hat{\boldsymbol{\beta}}$ do not rely on an unbiased estimator of Σ; all of our results from Chapter 13 for FGLS estimators carry over to this model, with no modification. It is worth noting that the matrix $\hat{\Sigma}$ based on the second correction is not necessarily positive definite. If the sample is large, it will be, but then the degrees of freedom correction is moot anyway. How the different estimators will behave in small samples is another question. Precise results are available only for some special cases, though suggestive results have been obtained in Monte Carlo studies.[7] We shall use (17–9) in what follows. With

$$\mathbf{S} = \begin{bmatrix} s_{11} & s_{12} & \cdots & s_{1M} \\ s_{12} & s_{22} & \cdots & s_{2M} \\ & & \vdots & \\ s_{1M} & s_{2M} & \cdots & s_{MM} \end{bmatrix} \tag{17–10}$$

in hand, FGLS can proceed as usual. Iterated FGLS will be maximum likelihood if it is based on (17–9).

Goodness of fit measures for the system have been devised. For instance, McElroy (1977) suggested the systemwide measure

$$R_*^2 = \frac{\hat{\boldsymbol{\varepsilon}}' \hat{\mathbf{V}}^{-1} \hat{\boldsymbol{\varepsilon}}}{\sum_m \sum_n \hat{\sigma}_{mn} [\sum_t (y_{mt} - \bar{y}_m)(y_{nt} - \bar{y}_n)]}. \tag{17–11}$$

where $\hat{\ }$ indicates the GLS estimate. The measure is bounded by zero and one and is related to the F statistic used to test the hypothesis that all of the slopes in the model are zero. Fit measures in this context have all of the shortcomings discussed in Chapter 13. An additional problem for this model is that overall fit measures such as (17–11) will obscure the variation in fit across the equations. In our investment example, comparing the overall fit of the unrestricted model to that of the restricted model of Chapter 16 may be interesting in its own right, but if we wish to test the hypothesis of equal-parameter vectors, we can do that directly. As for the fit of the model, it is unclear just how one should interpret an overall statistic that mixes the fits of all five equations. If it is desired to examine this aspect of the model, it is probably more useful to use one of the descriptive measures for each equation, of course with the usual set of caveats.

---

[5] See, for example, Theil (1972, p. 321) and Judge et al., (1985, p. 469).

[6] Kakwani's (1967) result applies to all three; the FGLS estimator of β is unbiased regardless of which divisor is used.

[7] Zellner (1963), Kmenta and Gilbert (1968), Conniffe (1982), and Revankar (1974).

Table 17.1. Parameter Estimates (Standard Errors in Parentheses).

			Seemingly Unrelated Regressions			
GM	GE	US	CH	WE	Pooled	GM by OLS
−162.36	−22.439	85.423	0.5043	1.0889	−14.712	−149.78
(89.46)	(25.52)	(111.9)	(11.51)	(6.259)	(1.775)	(105.8)
0.12049	0.03729	0.1015	0.06955	0.05701	0.06368	0.11928
(0.0216)	(0.0123)	(0.0547)	(0.0169)	(0.0114)	(0.00342)	(0.0258)
0.38275	0.13078	0.3999	0.3086	0.0415	0.1813	0.37145
(0.0328)	(0.0221)	(0.1278)	(0.0259)	(0.0412)	(0.0241)	(0.0371)

			Residual Covariance Matrix			
	GM	GE	US	CH		WE
GM	7216.04	(0.269)	(−0.329)	(−0.298)		(0.157)
US	605.337	700.456	(0.483)	(0.006)		(0.777)
GE	−2686.52	1224.41	9188.15	(0.384)		(0.699)
CH	−313.703	2.04737	455.089	152.849		(0.138)
WE	129.887	200.316	652.716	16.6606		94.9125

For testing a hypothesis about β, a statistic analogous to the F ratio in multiple regression analysis is

$$F[J, MT - K] = \frac{(\mathbf{R}\hat{\beta} - \mathbf{q})'[\mathbf{R}(\mathbf{X}'\mathbf{V}^{-1}\mathbf{X})^{-1}\mathbf{R}']^{-1}(\mathbf{R}\hat{\beta} - \mathbf{q})/J}{\hat{\varepsilon}'\mathbf{V}^{-1}\hat{\varepsilon}/(MT - K)}. \qquad (17\text{–}12)$$

The computation requires the unknown $\mathbf{V}$. If we insert the FGLS estimate, $\hat{\mathbf{V}}$ based on (17–9), the statistic reduces to

$$\hat{F} = \frac{1}{J}(\mathbf{R}\hat{\hat{\beta}} - \mathbf{q})'[\mathbf{R} \,\text{Vâr}[\hat{\hat{\beta}}]\mathbf{R}']^{-1}(\mathbf{R}\hat{\hat{\beta}} - \mathbf{q}). \qquad (17\text{–}13)$$

This can be referred to the standard F table. Because it uses the estimated Σ, the F distribution is only asymptotically valid. In general, the statistic $F[J, n]$ converges to $1/J$ times chi-squared (J) as $n \to \infty$. Therefore, an alternative test statistic that is asymptotically distributed as chi-squared with J degrees of freedom is

$$J\hat{F} = (\mathbf{R}\hat{\hat{\beta}} - \mathbf{q})'[\mathbf{R} \,\text{Vâr}[\hat{\hat{\beta}}]\mathbf{R}']^{-1}(\mathbf{R}\hat{\hat{\beta}} - \mathbf{q}). \qquad (17\text{–}14)$$

This can be recognized as a Wald statistic that measures the distance between $\mathbf{R}\hat{\hat{\beta}}$ and $\mathbf{q}$. Both statistics are valid asymptotically, but (17–13) may perform better in a small or moderately sized sample.[8] Once again, the divisor used in computing $\hat{\sigma}_{ij}$ will make a difference, and there is no general rule.

EXAMPLE 17.1. By relaxing the constraint that all five firms have the same parameter vector in Example 16.4, we obtain a five-equation, seemingly unrelated regressions model. The FGLS estimators for the system are given in Table 17.1, where we have included the equality constrained estimator of Example 16.4 for comparison, as well as the ordinary least

---

[8] See Judge et al. (1985, p. 476).

squares estimates of the GM equation. The variables are the constant terms F and C, respectively.

The correlations of the GLS residuals are given above the diagonal. It is worth noting that the assumption of equal-parameter vectors appears to have seriously distorted the earlier estimated correlations. A comparison with Example 16.4 shows that the elements in $\hat{\Sigma}$ are drastically inflated by the imposition of the constraint, as are the correlations across equations.

The F statistic for testing the hypothesis of equal-parameter vectors in all five equations is 1550.03 with 12 and $(100 - 15)$ degrees of freedom. This is obviously larger than the tabled critical value, so the hypothesis of parameter homogeneity should be rejected. We might have expected this result in view of the dramatic reduction in the diagonal elements of $\hat{\Sigma}$ compared to those of Example 16.4.

It may also be of interest to test whether Σ is a diagonal matrix. Two possible approaches were described in Example 16.4 [see (16–13) and (16–14)]. The unrestricted model is the one we are using here, while the restricted model is the groupwise heteroscedastic model of Chapter 16, without the restriction of equal-parameter vectors. As such, the restricted model reduces to separate regression models, estimable by ordinary least squares. The likelihood ratio statistic would be

$$\lambda_{LR} = T\left[\sum_m \ln s_m^2 - \ln|\hat{\Sigma}|\right], \tag{17–15}$$

where s_m^2 is $e_m'e_m/T$ from the individual least squares regressions and $\hat{\Sigma}$ is the maximum likelihood estimate of Σ. This statistic is asymptotically distributed as chi-squared with $M(M - 1)/2$ degrees of freedom.

The alternative suggested by Breusch and Pagan (1980) is the Lagrange multiplier statistic,

$$\lambda_{LM} = T\sum_{m=1}^{M}\sum_{n=1}^{m-1} r_{mn}^2, \tag{17–16}$$

where r_{mn}^2 is the estimated correlation, $s_{mn}/[s_{mm}s_{nn}]^{1/2}$. Note the similarity of this to the Box–Pierce statistic we encountered in Chapter 15. Asymptotically, this statistic is also distributed as chi-squared with $M(M - 1)/2$ degrees of freedom. This test has the advantage that it does not require computation of the maximum likelihood estimator of Σ, since it is based on the OLS residuals.

EXAMPLE 17.2. The sample correlations of the ordinary least squares residuals are shown below the diagonal in Table 17.2. For comparison, the estimates of the correlations using the GLS estimator of β are shown above the diagonal:

Table 17.2

	GM	GE	US	CH	WE
GM	—	0.269	-0.329	-0.298	0.157
US	0.279	—	0.483	0.006	0.777
GE	-0.278	0.373	—	0.384	0.699
CH	-0.273	-0.068	0.362	—	0.138
WE	0.158	0.729	0.615	0.115	—

Based on the OLS results, the Lagrange multiplier statistic is 29.046, with 10 degrees of freedom. The 1 percent critical value is 23.209, so the hypothesis that Σ is diagonal can be rejected.

17.2.3.   Maximum Likelihood Estimation

17.2.3a.   Iterated FGLS

The Oberhofer–Kmenta (1974) conditions are met for the seemingly unrelated regressions model, so maximum likelihood estimates can be obtained by iterating the FGLS procedure. We note, once again, that this presumes the use of (17–9) for estimation of σ_{ij} at each iteration. It is worth noting that maximum likelihood enjoys no advantages over FGLS in its asymptotic properties. Whether it would be preferable in a small sample is an open question whose answer will depend, unfortunately, on the particular data set.

EXAMPLE **17.3.** The maximum likelihood estimates of the parameters estimated by FGLS in Example 17.1 are given in Table 17.3. As might be expected, the differences are not substantial. (The estimates are, in fact, not radically different from the ordinary least squares estimates.)

17.2.3b.   Direct Maximum Likelihood Estimation

By simply inserting the special form of V in the log-likelihood function for the generalized regression model in (13–19), we can consider direct maximization instead of iterated FGLS. It is useful, however, to reexamine the model in a somewhat different formulation. This alternative construction of the likelihood function appears in many other related models in a number of literatures.

Consider one observation on each of the M dependent variables and their associated regressors. We wish to arrange this observation horizontally instead of vertically. The model for this observation can be written

$$[y_1 \quad y_2 \quad \cdots \quad y_M] = [\mathbf{x}_t^*]'[\boldsymbol{\beta}_1 \quad \boldsymbol{\beta}_2 \quad \cdots \quad \boldsymbol{\beta}_M] + [\varepsilon_1 \quad \varepsilon_2 \quad \cdots \quad \varepsilon_M], \quad (17\text{–}17)$$

Table 17.3.   Parameter Estimates (Standard Errors in Parentheses)

	GM	GE	US	CH	WE
l	−173.218	−16.6623	136.969	2.39111	4.37312
	(84.30)	(24.96)	(94.8)	(11.63)	(6.018)
F	0.122040	0.0371	0.08865	0.06741	0.05397
	(0.02025)	(0.01177)	(0.04542)	(0.01709)	(0.0103)
C	0.38914	0.11723	0.31246	0.30520	0.026930
	(0.03185)	(0.02173)	(0.118)	(0.02606)	(0.03708)

Residual Covariance Matrix

	GM	GE	US	CH	WE
GM	7309.16				
GE	548.604	742.032			
US	−2882.25	1412.30	9684.61		
CH	−330.738	11.5799	463.216	155.097	
WE	118.500	220.829	737.171	18.7949	103.384

where x_t^* is the full set of all K independent variables that appear in the model. The parameter matrix then has one column for each equation, but the columns are not the same as β_m in (17–2) unless every variable happens to appear in every equation. Otherwise, the ith equation will have a number of zeros in it, imposing an **exclusion restriction**.

EXAMPLE 17.4. Consider the GM and GE equations from the Boot–de Witt data we have used in the previous examples. The tth observation would be

$$[I_g \quad I_e] = [1 \quad F_g \quad C_g \quad F_e \quad C_e] \begin{bmatrix} \alpha_g & \alpha_e \\ \beta_{1g} & 0 \\ \beta_{2g} & 0 \\ 0 & \beta_{1e} \\ 0 & \beta_{2e} \end{bmatrix} + [\varepsilon_g \quad \varepsilon_e].$$

This is one observation. Let ε_t be the vector of M disturbances for this observation arranged, for now, in a column. Then, $E[\varepsilon\varepsilon'] = \Sigma$. The log of the joint normal density of these M disturbances is

$$\ln L_t = -\frac{M}{2}\ln(2\pi) - \frac{1}{2}\ln|\Sigma| - \frac{1}{2}\varepsilon_t'\Sigma^{-1}\varepsilon_t. \tag{17–18}$$

The log likelihood for a sample of T joint observations is the sum of these over t:

$$\ln L = \sum_t \ln L_t$$

$$= -\frac{MT}{2}\ln(2\pi) - \frac{T}{2}\ln|\Sigma| - \frac{1}{2}\sum_{t=1}^{T}\varepsilon_t'\Sigma^{-1}\varepsilon_t. \tag{17–19}$$

Denote the mnth element of Σ^{-1} as σ^{mn}. Then

$$\varepsilon_t'\Sigma^{-1}\varepsilon_t = \sum_{m=1}^{M}\sum_{n=1}^{M}\varepsilon_{tm}\varepsilon_{tn}\sigma^{mn}.$$

Summing these over T observations, we have

$$\sum_{t=1}^{T}\varepsilon_t'\Sigma^{-1}\varepsilon_t = \sum_{t=1}^{T}\sum_{m=1}^{M}\sum_{n=1}^{M}\varepsilon_{tm}\varepsilon_{tn}\sigma^{mn}.$$

Now reverse the order of summation and move σ^{mn} outside to obtain

$$\sum_{t=1}^{T}\varepsilon_t'\Sigma^{-1}\varepsilon_t = \sum_{m=1}^{M}\sum_{n=1}^{M}\sigma^{mn}\sum_{t=1}^{T}\varepsilon_{tm}\varepsilon_{tn}.$$

The innermost sum, $\sum_{t=1}^{T}\varepsilon_{tm}\varepsilon_{tn}$, is T times the mnth element of $\mathbf{W}$, where

$$\mathbf{W}_{mn} = \frac{1}{T}\sum_{t=1}^{T}\varepsilon_{tm}\varepsilon_{tn}.$$

Since this uses actual disturbances, $E[\mathbf{W}_{mn}] = \sigma_{mn}$; $\mathbf{W}$ is the $M \times M$ matrix we would use to estimate Σ if the ε's were actually observed. Returning to the derivation, we have, therefore,

$$\sum_{t=1}^{T}\varepsilon_t'\Sigma^{-1}\varepsilon_t = T\sum_{m=1}^{M}\sum_{n=1}^{M}\sigma^{mn}\mathbf{W}_{mn}.$$

Finally, the mth diagonal element of the matrix product $\Sigma^{-1}W$ is $\sum_n \sigma^{mn}W_{mn}$. The preceding sum is T times the sum of these, which is T times the trace of the product. Therefore,

$$\sum_{t=1}^{T} \varepsilon_t'\Sigma^{-1}\varepsilon_t = T tr(\Sigma^{-1}W). \tag{17-20}$$

Inserting this in the log likelihood, we have

$$\ln L = -\frac{MT}{2}\ln(2\pi) - \frac{T}{2}\ln|\Sigma| - \frac{T}{2}tr(\Sigma^{-1}W). \tag{17-21}$$

This is a particularly simple and useful formulation. Recall that W is the matrix of residual sums of squares and cross-products. We now consider maximum likelihood estimation of parameters of a model.

It has been shown[9] that

$$\frac{\partial \ln L}{\partial \Sigma} = -\frac{T}{2}\Sigma^{-1}(\Sigma - W)\Sigma^{-1}. \tag{17-22}$$

Equating this to a zero matrix, we see that given the maximum likelihood estimates of the slope parameters, the maximum likelihood estimator of Σ is W, the matrix of mean residual sums of squares and cross-products, that is, the matrix we have used for FGLS. (Notice that there is no correction for degrees of freedom; $\partial \ln L/\partial \Sigma = 0$ implies (17-9).)

We also know that because this is a generalized regression model, the maximum likelihood estimator of the parameter matrix, $[B]$, must be equivalent to the FGLS estimator we discussed earlier.[10] It is useful to go a step further. If we insert our solution for Σ in the likelihood function, we obtain the **concentrated log likelihood**,

$$\ln L_c = -\frac{MT}{2}(1 + \ln(2\pi)) - \frac{T}{2}\ln|W|. \tag{17-23}$$

We have shown, therefore, that the criterion for choosing the maximum likelihood estimator of β is

$$\hat{\beta}_{ML} = \text{Min}_\beta \frac{1}{2}\ln|W| \tag{17-24}$$

subject to the exclusion restrictions. This is an important result that reappears in many other models and settings. This minimization must be done subject to the constraints in the parameter matrix. In our two-equation example, there are two blocks of zeros in the parameter matrix. These must be present in the MLE as well.[11]

The results of Chapter 13 apply here, so we need not rederive the information matrix to obtain the correct asymptotic covariance matrix for the maximum likelihood estimates. They are the ones given earlier for GLS. It would rarely be used, but, if needed, the asymptotic covariance matrix for the maximum likelihood estimator of Σ is (with the elements stacked in an $M^2 \times 1$ vector)

$$\text{Asy. Var}[\hat{\Sigma}_{ML}] = \frac{2}{T}\Sigma \otimes \Sigma. \tag{17-25}$$

---

[9] See, for example, Joreskog (1973).

[10] This establishes the Oberhofer–Kmenta conditions.

[11] As we have seen, the maximum likelihood estimator can be obtained by iterated FGLS. The preceding is equivalent. However, direct maximization of the likelihood by Newton's method is quite straightforward and may be simpler, particularly for some types of constrained systems.

This can be estimated with $(2/T)\mathbf{W} \otimes \mathbf{W}$. It can be used, for example, to test the hypothesis that Σ is diagonal.

The likelihood ratio statistic is an alternative to the F statistic discussed earlier for testing hypotheses about β. The likelihood ratio statistic is

$$\lambda = -2(\ln L_r - \ln L_u) = T(\ln|\mathbf{W}_r| - \ln|\mathbf{W}_u|), \qquad (17\text{-}26)$$

where $\mathbf{W}_r$ and $\mathbf{W}_u$ are the residual sums of squares and cross-product matrices using the constrained and unconstrained estimators, respectively. The likelihood ratio statistic is asymptotically distributed as chi-squared with degrees of freedom equal to the number of restrictions.

EXAMPLE 17.5. The log determinant of the unrestricted maximum likelihood estimator of Σ given in Example 17.4 is 31.71986. The log likelihood is, therefore,

$$L_u = -\frac{20(5)}{2}(\ln(2\pi) + 1) - \frac{20}{2}31.71986$$

$$= -459.0925.$$

The restricted model with equal-parameter vectors and correlation across equations is discussed in Section 16.3.2, and the restricted MLEs are given in Example 16.4. (The MLE of Σ is not shown there.) The log determinant for the constrained model is 37.38471. The log likelihood for the constrained model is, therefore, -515.741. The likelihood ratio test statistic is 113.297. The 1 percent critical value from the chi-squared distribution with 12 degrees of freedom is 26.217, so the hypothesis of homogeneity is (once again) rejected.

17.2.4. Autocorrelation

The seemingly unrelated regressions model can be extended to allow for autocorrelation in the same fashion as in Chapter 16. To reiterate, suppose that

$$\mathbf{y}_m = \mathbf{X}_m\beta_m + \varepsilon_m,$$

$$\varepsilon_{mt} = \rho_m\varepsilon_{m,t-1} + u_{mt},$$

where u_{mt} is uncorrelated across observations. This will imply that the blocks in $\mathbf{V}$, instead of $\sigma_{mn}\mathbf{I}$, are $\sigma_{mn}\mathbf{\Omega}_{mn}$, where $\mathbf{\Omega}_{mn}$ is given in (16-22).

The treatment shown by Parks (1967) is the one we used earlier. This calls for a three-step approach:

1. Estimate each equation in the system by ordinary least squares. Use any of the consistent estimators of ρ described in Chapter 15. For that equation, transform the data by the Prais–Winsten transformation to remove the autocorrelation.[12] Note that there will not be a constant term in the transformed data, as there will be a column with $(1 - r_m^2)^{1/2}$ as the first observation and $(1 - r_m)$ for the remainder.
2. Using the transformed data, use ordinary least squares once more to estimate Σ.
3. Use FGLS based on the estimated Σ and the transformed data.

[12] There is a complication with the first observation, which is not treated quite correctly by this procedure. For details, see Judge et al. (1985), pp. 486–489. The strictly correct (and quite cumbersome) results are for the true GLS estimator, which assumes a known Ω. It is unlikely that in a finite sample anything is lost by using the Prais–Winsten procedure with the estimated Ω. One suggestion has been to use the Cochrane–Orcutt procedure and drop the first observation. But in a small sample, the cost of discarding the first observation is almost surely greater than that of neglecting to account properly for the correlation of the first disturbance with the other first disturbances. It is an issue that merits further study.

Table 17.4

	GM	GE	US	CH	WE
Durbin–Watson	0.9375	1.0721	0.9091	1.984	1.413
Autocorrelation	0.531	0.463	0.545	0.009	0.294

Residual Covariance Matrix $[\hat{\sigma}_{mn}/(1 - r_m r_n)]$

	GM	GE	US	CH	WE
GM	6679.5				
GE	483.79	684.59			
US	−1381.6	1484.1	8638.1		
CH	−220.97	43.7891	342.89	151.96	
WE	88.373	190.37	676.88	19.964	92.788

Parameter Estimates (Standard Errors in Parentheses)

	GM	GE	US	CH	WE
β_1	−51.337	−24.913	14.0207	−0.4536	4.7091
	(80.62)	(25.67)	(96.49)	(11.86)	(6.510)
β_2	0.094038	0.04271	0.16415	0.06847	0.05091
	(0.01733)	(0.01134)	(0.0386)	(0.0174)	(0.01060)
β_3	0.40723	0.10954	0.2006	0.32041	0.04284
	(0.04261)	(0.03012)	(0.1428)	(0.0258)	(0.04127)

There is no benefit to iteration. The estimator is efficient at every step, and iteration does not produce a maximum likelihood estimator. After the last step, Σ should be reestimated with the GLS estimates. The estimated covariance matrix for ε can then be reconstructed using

$$\hat{\sigma}_{mn}(\varepsilon) = \frac{\hat{\sigma}_{mn}}{1 - r_m r_n}. \tag{17-27}$$

EXAMPLE 17.6. Table 17.4 is a list of the autocorrelation-corrected estimates of the model of Example 17.1. The Durbin–Watson statistics for the five data sets given here, with the exception of Chrysler, strongly suggest that there is, indeed, autocorrelation in the disturbances. The differences between these and the uncorrected estimates given earlier are sometimes relatively large, as might be expected, given the fairly high autocorrelation and small sample size. The smaller diagonal elements in the disturbance covariance matrix compared to those of Example 17.1 reflect the improved fit brought about by introducing the lagged values into the equation.

An extension of the model with autocorrelated disturbances is the **vector autoregression**. If current disturbances depend on lagged values of the disturbances in other equations, the process might be formulated as

$$\varepsilon_t = \mathbf{R}\varepsilon_{t-1} + \mathbf{u}_t, \tag{17-28}$$

where ε_t is the $M \times 1$ vector of disturbances at time t. The analogous condition to $|\rho| < 1$ is that the characteristic roots of $\mathbf{R}$ must be less than one in absolute value. The roots need not be real, since $\mathbf{R}$ is not necessarily symmetric. This enhancement renders the model extremely cumbersome, although the theoretical details have been well worked out.[13] The autocorre-

---

[13] See Guilkey (1974) and Guilkey and Schmidt (1973).

lation matrix, **R**, can be estimated using the least squares residuals. Thereafter, neglecting complications of the first observation, the transformation to remove the autocorrelation would be accomplished as follows: We rearrange the observations so that for observation t we may write

$$
\begin{bmatrix} y_{1t} \\ y_{2t} \\ \vdots \\ y_{Mt} \end{bmatrix} = \begin{bmatrix} \mathbf{x}'_{1t} & \mathbf{0}' & \cdots & \mathbf{0}' \\ \mathbf{0}' & \mathbf{x}'_{2t} & \cdots & \mathbf{0}' \\ & & \vdots & \\ \mathbf{0}' & \mathbf{0}' & \cdots & \mathbf{x}'_{Mt} \end{bmatrix} \begin{bmatrix} \beta_1 \\ \beta_2 \\ \vdots \\ \beta_M \end{bmatrix} + \begin{bmatrix} \varepsilon_{1t} \\ \varepsilon_{2t} \\ \vdots \\ \varepsilon_{Mt} \end{bmatrix}
$$

or

$$
\mathbf{y}_t = \mathbf{X}_t \boldsymbol{\beta} + \boldsymbol{\varepsilon}_t.
$$

Then the autocorrelation is removed by

$$
\begin{aligned}
\mathbf{y}_{*t} &= \mathbf{y}_t - \mathbf{R}\mathbf{y}_{t-1}, \\
\mathbf{X}_{*t} &= \mathbf{X}_t - \mathbf{R}\mathbf{X}_{t-1}.
\end{aligned}
\tag{17-29}
$$

The treatment of the earlier sections can be applied to the transformed model. This transformation has the consequence that in the transformed model, every variable and lags of every variable will appear in every equation. As a practical matter, this is likely to be extremely cumbersome. Otherwise, the model is straightforward to estimate, using the methods developed earlier.

17.3. Systems of Demand Equations—Singular Systems

Most of the recent applications of the multivariate regression model have been in the context of systems of demand equations, either commodity demands or factor demands in studies of production.

EXAMPLE 17.7 Stone's expenditure system[14] is based on a set of logarithmic commodity demand equations,

$$
\ln q_m = \alpha_m + \eta_m \ln Y + \sum_n \eta_{mn} \ln p_n,
$$

where η_m is the total expenditure elasticity and η_{mn} is the cross-price elasticity. From the Slutsky equation (not the theorem from Chapter 3),

$$
\eta_{mn} = \eta_{mn}^* - \eta_m w_n,
$$

where η_{mn}^* is the compensated cross-price elasticity and w_n is the nth commodity's budget share. The underlying theory implies that demand equations must be homogeneous of degree zero in prices, so

$$
\sum_n \eta_{mn}^* = 0.
$$

---

[14] A very readable survey of the estimation of systems of commodity demands is Deaton and Muellbauer (1980). The example discussed here is taken from their Chapter 3 and the references to Stone's work cited therein.

Inserting these constraints in the demand equations, we obtain

$$\ln q_m = \alpha_m + \eta_m \ln\left(\frac{Y}{P}\right) + \sum_n \eta_{mn}^* \ln\left(\frac{p_n}{P}\right),$$

where P is a generalized (share-weighted) price index. We can interpret this as the demand equation in real expenditure and real prices. The resulting set of equations constitutes an econometric model in the form of a set of seemingly unrelated regressions. In estimation, we must account for a number of restrictions, namely, homogeneity of degree one in income, $\Sigma_m \eta_m = 1$, and symmetry of the matrix of compensated price elasticities, $\eta_{mn}^* = \eta_{nm}^*$.

Other examples include the systems of factor demands and factor cost shares from production, which we shall consider again later. In principle, each of these is merely a particular application of the model of the previous section. But some special problems arise in these settings. First, the parameters of the systems are generally constrained across equations. That is, the unconstrained model is inconsistent with the underlying theory.[15] The numerous constraints in the system of demand equations presented earlier give an example. A second intrinsic feature of many of these models is that the disturbance covariance matrix, Σ, is singular.

EXAMPLE 17.8. Cobb–Douglas Cost Function.   Consider a Cobb–Douglas production function,

$$Y = \alpha_0 \Pi_m x_m^{\alpha_m}.$$

Profit maximization calls for the firm to maximize output for a given cost level, C (or minimize costs for a given output, Y). The Lagrangean for the maximization problem is

$$\Lambda = \alpha_0 \Pi_m x_m^{\alpha_m} + \lambda(C - \mathbf{p}'\mathbf{x}),$$

where $\mathbf{p}$ is the vector of M factor prices. The necessary conditions for maximizing this are

$$\frac{\partial \Lambda}{\partial x_m} = \frac{\alpha_m Y}{x_m} - \lambda p_m = 0,$$

$$\frac{\partial \Lambda}{\partial \lambda} = C - \mathbf{p}'\mathbf{x} = 0.$$

The joint solution provides $x_m(Y, \mathbf{p})$ and $\lambda(Y, \mathbf{p})$. The total cost of production is

$$\sum_m p_m x_m = \sum_m \frac{\alpha_m Y}{\lambda p_m}.$$

---

[15] This does not imply that the theoretical restrictions are not testable or that the unrestricted model cannot be estimated. However, sometimes the meaning of the model is ambiguous without the restrictions. Statistically rejecting the restrictions implied by the theory, which were used to derive the econometric model in the first place, can put us in a rather uncomfortable position. For example, in a study of utility functions, Christensen et al. (1975), after rejecting the cross-equation symmetry of a set of commodity demands, stated: "With this conclusion we can terminate the test sequence, since these results invalidate the theory of demand" (p. 380).

The cost share allocated to factor the ith factor is

$$\frac{p_m x_m}{\sum_m p_m x_m} = \frac{\alpha_m}{\sum_m \alpha_m} = \beta_m.$$

(A simpler, more direct approach based on Shephard's lemma is used in the next section.) This provides the basis for a multivariate regression model. The full model is[16]

$$\ln C = \beta_0 + \beta_y \ln Y + \sum_m \beta_m \ln p_m + \varepsilon_c,$$

$$s_1 = \beta_1 + \varepsilon_1$$

$$s_2 = \beta_2 + \varepsilon_2 \qquad\qquad (17\text{--}30)$$

$$\vdots$$

$$s_M = \beta_M + \varepsilon_M.$$

By construction,

$$\sum_m \beta_m = 1$$

and

$$\qquad\qquad (17\text{--}31)$$

$$\sum_m s_m = 1.$$

The cost shares will also sum identically to one in the data. It follows, therefore, that

$$\sum_m \varepsilon_m = 0$$

at every data point, so the system is singular. For the moment, ignore the cost function. Let the $M \times 1$ disturbance vector from the shares be

$$\varepsilon = [\varepsilon_1, \varepsilon_2, \ldots, \varepsilon_M]'.$$

Since

$$\varepsilon'\mathbf{i} = 0 \qquad \text{(where } \mathbf{i} \text{ is a column of ones),}$$

it follows that

$$E[\varepsilon\varepsilon'\mathbf{i}] = \Sigma\mathbf{i} = 0.$$

This implies that Σ is singular.[17] Therefore, the methods of the previous sections cannot be used here.

The solution to the singularity problem appears to be to drop one of the equations, estimate the remainder, and solve for the last parameter from the other $M - 1$. The constraint in (17–31) is that the cost function must be homogeneous of degree one in the prices, a theoretical necessity. If we impose the constraint

$$\beta_M = 1 - \beta_1 - \beta_2 - \cdots - \beta_{M-1}, \qquad\qquad (17\text{--}32)$$

---

[16] We leave as an exercise the derivation of β_0, which is a mixture of all of the parameters and β_y, which equals $1/\sum_m \alpha_m$.

[17] You should verify that the *sample* covariance of least squares residuals will also be singular.

the system is reduced to a nonsingular one:

$$\ln\left(\frac{C}{p_M}\right) = \beta_0 + \beta_y \ln Y + \sum_{m=1}^{M-1} \beta_m \ln\left(\frac{p_m}{p_M}\right) + \varepsilon_c,$$

$$s_1 = \beta_1 + \varepsilon_1$$

$$s_2 = \beta_2 + \varepsilon_2$$

$$\vdots$$

$$s_{M-1} = \beta_{M-1} + \varepsilon_{M-1}.$$

This system provides estimates of β_0, β_y, and $\beta_1, \ldots, \beta_{M-1}$. The last parameter is estimated using (17–32).

In principle, it is immaterial which factor is chosen as the numeraire. Unfortunately, the FGLS parameter estimates in the now nonsingular system will depend on which one is chosen. Invariance is achieved by using maximum likelihood estimates instead of FGLS.[18] These can be obtained by iterating FGLS or by direct maximum likelihood estimation.[19]

EXAMPLE 17.9. Nerlove's (1963) study of the electric power industry described in Example 8.3 provides an example of the preceding Cobb–Douglas cost function model. His ordinary least squares estimates of the parameters were listed in the earlier example. Among the results are (unfortunately) a negative capital coefficient in three of the six regressions. Nerlove also found that the simple Cobb–Douglas model did not adequately account for the relationship between output and average cost. Christensen and Greene (1976) further analyzed the Nerlove data and augmented the data set with cost share data in order to estimate the complete demand system. Table 17.5 lists 20 of Nerlove's 145 observations with Christensen and Greene's cost share data. Cost is the total cost of generation in millions of dollars, output is in millions of kilowatt-hours, the capital price is an index of construction costs, the wage rate is in dollars per hour for production and maintenance, the fuel price is an index of the cost per BTU of fuel purchased by the firms, and the data reflect the 1955 costs of production.

The regression estimates are given in Table 17.6.

Least squares estimates of the Cobb–Douglas cost function are given in the first column.[20] As expected, the coefficient on capital is negative. In view of the fact that $\beta_m = \beta_y \partial \ln Y / \partial \ln x_m$, that is, a positive multiple of the output elasticity of the mth factor, this is a troubling finding. The third column gives the maximum likelihood estimates obtained in the constrained system. Two things to note are the dramatically smaller standard errors and the now positive (and reasonable) estimate of the capital coefficient. The estimates of economies of scale in the basic Cobb–Douglas model are $1/\beta_y = 1.11$ (column 1) and 1.05 (column 3), which suggests some increasing returns to scale. However, Nerlove had found evidence that at extremely large firm sizes, economies of scale diminished and eventually disappeared. In order to account for this (essentially a classical U-shaped average cost curve), he appended a quadratic term in log output in the cost function. The single equation and maximum likelihood multivariate regression estimates are given in the second and fourth columns.

---

[18] The invariance result is proved in Barton (1969).
[19] Some additional results on the method are given by Revankar (1976).
[20] Results based on Nerlove's full data set are given in Example 8.3.

Table 17.5. Cost Function Data

Firm	Cost	Output	Pk	Pl	Pf	Sk	Sl	Sf
1	0.423	39	164	2.30	23.6	0.4137	0.1702	0.4161
2	1.130	130	176	1.82	38.9	0.2779	0.1712	0.6049
3	1.565	197	183	2.19	29.1	0.4151	0.0692	0.5157
4	2.382	338	163	1.85	24.6	0.4799	0.0616	0.4585
5	4.580	484	176	1.75	42.8	0.2828	0.1009	0.6162
6	5.535	719	174	1.70	26.9	0.4946	0.0703	0.4351
7	6.754	984	158	1.76	26.9	0.2435	0.1083	0.6482
8	7.743	1,122	162	2.19	29.1	0.3744	0.0977	0.5279
9	8.488	1,215	164	2.19	29.1	0.4390	0.0695	0.4915
10	10.879	1,649	177	2.32	31.9	0.3991	0.0974	0.5035
11	15.437	2,023	163	2.11	24.4	0.3989	0.0808	0.5203
12	12.905	2,341	183	2.04	20.7	0.4165	0.0945	0.4890
13	11.320	2,870	167	1.76	10.3	0.5822	0.1333	0.2845
14	19.035	3,202	170	2.30	23.6	0.4974	0.0983	0.4043
15	29.845	4,764	195	2.19	29.1	0.3530	0.1328	0.5142
16	21.988	5,283	159	2.04	20.7	0.4491	0.0630	0.4879
17	40.594	7,193	162	2.12	28.6	0.3550	0.0729	0.5721
18	33.354	7,886	178	1.61	17.8	0.5835	0.0587	0.3578
19	67.120	11,477	151	2.24	26.5	0.3458	0.0670	0.5872
20	119.939	16,719	162	2.30	23.6	0.4340	0.0906	0.4754

Table 17.6. Regression Estimates (Standard Errors in Parentheses)

	Ordinary Least Squares		Multivariate Regression	
β_0	−6.034 (1.11)	−5.937 (1.13)	−9.468 (0.192)	−8.682 (0.563)
β_y	0.9045 (0.023)	0.7786 (0.172)	0.9521 (0.023)	0.7110 (0.166)
β_{yy}	—	0.0093 (0.013)	—	0.0175 (0.012)
β_k	−0.0026 (0.265)	0.0574 (0.263)	0.4077 (0.020)	0.4078 (0.020)
β_l	0.5946 (0.125)	0.5795 (0.129)	0.0933 (0.006)	0.0934 (0.006)
β_f	0.4080 (0.302)	0.3631 (0.312)	0.4990 (0.019)	0.4988 (0.019)
R^2	0.9921	0.9924	—	—
Log|W|	—	—	−15.718	−15.801

If $C(Y, \mathbf{p})$, the total cost function, has a **U**-shape; then the point of minimum average cost, or the bottom of the **U**, occurs at the output where marginal cost equals average cost, or at the Y such that

$$\frac{\partial C/\partial Y}{C/Y} = \frac{\partial \ln C}{\partial \ln Y} = 1.$$

This is the point at which economies of scale are exhausted. In Nerlove's expanded model, this is the solution to

$$\beta_y + 2\beta_{yy} \ln Y = 1.$$

Inserting the parameter estimates from the rightmost model in the preceding table, we obtain a value of Y of 3855. This is rather large in our subsample and larger than that of 120 of the

145 firms in the original sample. (Observation 20 here is the largest from Nerlove's sample.) The results suggest that economies of scale are exhausted well within the range of sample outputs.

17.4.   Flexible Functional Forms — Translog Production Function

The literatures on production and cost and on utility and demand have evolved in several directions. In the area of models of producer behavior, the classic paper by Arrow et al. (1963) called into question the inherent restriction of the Cobb–Douglas model that all elasticities of factor substitution are equal to one. Researchers have since developed numerous flexible functions that allow substitution to be unrestricted (i.e., not even constant).[21] Similar strands of literature have appeared in the analysis of commodity demands.[22] In this section, we examine in detail a model of production.

Suppose that production is characterized by a production function,

$$Y = f(\mathbf{x}).$$

The solution to the problem of minimizing the cost of producing a specified output rate given a set of factor prices produces the cost-minimizing set of factor demands

$$x_m = x_m(Y, \mathbf{p}).$$

The total cost of production is given by the cost function,

$$C = \sum_m p_m x_m(Y, \mathbf{p}) = C(Y, \mathbf{p}). \tag{17–33}$$

If there are constant returns to scale, it can be shown that

$$C = Yc(\mathbf{p}) \tag{17–34}$$

or

$$\frac{C}{Y} = c(\mathbf{p}),$$

where $c(\mathbf{p})$ is the unit or average cost function.[23] The cost-minimizing factor demands are obtained by applying Shephard's (1970) lemma, which states that if $C(Y, \mathbf{p})$ gives the minimum total cost of production, then the cost-minimizing set of factor demands is given by

$$x_m^* = \frac{\partial C(Y, \mathbf{p})}{\partial p_m}$$

$$= \frac{Y \partial c(\mathbf{p})}{\partial p_m}. \tag{17–35}$$

---

[21] See, in particular, Berndt and Christensen (1973). Two useful surveys of the topic are Jorgenson (1983) and Diewert (1974).

[22] See, for example, Christensen et al. (1975) and two surveys, Deaton and Muellbauer (1980) and Deaton (1983).

[23] The Cobb–Douglas function of the previous section gives an illustration. The restriction of constant returns to scale is $\beta_y = 1$, which is equivalent to $C = Yc(\mathbf{p})$. Nerlove's more general version of the cost function allows nonconstant returns to scale. See Christensen and Greene (1976) and Diewert (1974) for some of the formalities of the cost function and its relationship to the structure of production.

Alternatively, by differentiating logarithmically, we obtain the cost-minimizing factor cost shares:

$$S_m = \frac{\partial \ln C(Y, \mathbf{p})}{\partial \ln p_m}$$

$$= \frac{p_m x_m}{C}.$$

(17–36)

With constant returns to scale, $\ln C(Y, \mathbf{p}) = \ln Y + \ln c(\mathbf{p})$, so

$$S_m = \frac{\partial \ln c(\mathbf{p})}{\partial \ln p_m}.$$

(17–37)

In many empirical studies, the objects of estimation are the elasticities of factor substitution and the own price elasticities of demand. These are given by

$$\sigma_{mn} = \frac{c \partial^2 c / \partial p_m \partial p_n}{(\partial c / \partial p_m)(\partial c / \partial p_n)}$$

and

$$\eta_{mm} = S_m \sigma_{mm}.$$

By suitably parameterizing the cost function (17–34) and the cost shares (17–37), we obtain an M or $M + 1$ equation econometric model that can be used to estimate these quantities.[24]

The translog function is the most frequently used flexible function in empirical work.[25] By expanding $\ln c(\mathbf{p})$ in a second-order Taylor series about the point $\ln \mathbf{p} = 0$, we obtain

$$\ln c \simeq \beta_0 + \sum_m \left(\frac{\partial \ln c}{\partial \ln p_m} \right) \ln p_m + \frac{1}{2} \sum_m \sum_n \left(\frac{\partial^2 \ln c}{\partial \ln p_m \partial \ln p_n} \right) \ln p_m \ln p_n,$$

(17–38)

where all derivatives are evaluated at the expansion point. If we identify these derivatives as coefficients and impose the symmetry of the cross-price derivatives, the cost function becomes

$$\ln c = \beta_0 + \beta_1 \ln p_1 + \cdots + \beta_M \ln p_M$$

$$+ \frac{\delta_{11}(\ln p_1)^2}{2}$$

$$+ \delta_{12} \ln p_1 \ln p_2 + \frac{\delta_{22}(\ln p_2)^2}{2}$$

$$+ \qquad \vdots$$

$$+ \cdots \qquad + \frac{\delta_{MM}(\ln p_M)^2}{2}.$$

(17–39)

---

[24] The cost function is only one of several approaches to this study. See Jorgenson (1983) for a discussion.
[25] The function was developed as a means of approximating the CES production function by Kmenta (1967) and was introduced formally in a series of papers by Berndt, Christensen, Jorgenson, and Lau, including Berndt and Christensen (1973) and Christensen et al. (1973). The literature has produced something of a competition in the development of exotic functional forms. However, the translog function has remained the most popular, and by one account, Guilkey, et al. (1983) is the most reliable of several available alternatives.

This is the transcendental logarithmic, or translog, cost function. If δ_{mn} equals zero, it reduces to the Cobb–Douglas function we looked at earlier. The cost shares are given by

$$s_1 = \frac{\partial \ln c}{\partial \ln p_1} = \beta_1 + \delta_{11} \ln p_1 + \delta_{12} \ln p_2 + \cdots + \delta_{1M} \ln p_M,$$

$$s_2 = \frac{\partial \ln c}{\partial \ln p_2} = \beta_2 + \delta_{12} \ln p_1 + \delta_{22} \ln p_2 + \cdots + \delta_{2M} \ln p_M,$$

$$\vdots$$

$$s_M = \frac{\partial \ln c}{\partial \ln p_M} = \beta_M + \delta_{1M} \ln p_1 + \delta_{2M} \ln p_2 + \cdots + \delta_{MM} \ln p_M.$$

(17–40)

The cost shares must sum to 1, which requires, in addition to the symmetry restrictions already imposed,

$$\beta_1 + \beta_2 + \cdots + \beta_M = 1,$$

$$\sum_m \delta_{mn} = 0 \qquad \text{(column sums equal zero)},$$

$$\sum_n \delta_{mn} = 0 \qquad \text{(row sums equal zero)}.$$

(17–41)

The system of share equations provides a seemingly unrelated regressions model that can be used to estimate the parameters of the model.[26] To make the model operational, we must impose the restrictions in (17–41) and solve the problem of singularity of the disturbance covariance matrix of the share equations. The first is accomplished by dividing the first $M - 1$ prices by the Mth, thus eliminating the last term in each row and column of the parameter matrix. As in the Cobb–Douglas model, we obtain a nonsingular system by dropping the Mth share equation. We compute maximum likelihood estimates of the parameters in order to ensure invariance with respect to the choice of which share equation we drop. For the translog cost function, the elasticities of substitution are particularly simple to compute once the parameters have been estimated.

$$\sigma_{mn} = \frac{\delta_{mn} + s_m s_n}{s_m s_n},$$

$$\sigma_{mm} = \frac{\delta_{mm} + s_m(s_m - 1)}{s_m^2}.$$

(17–42)

These will differ at every data point. It is common to compute them at some central point such as the means of the data.[27]

EXAMPLE 17.10. A Cost Function for U.S. Manufacturing.   A number of recent studies utilizing the translog methodology have used a four-factor model, with capital, K, labor, L, energy, E, and materials, M, the factors of production. Berndt and Wood (1975) have

[26] The cost function may be included if desired. This will provide an estimate of β_0 but is otherwise inessential. However, absent the assumption of constant returns to scale, the cost function will contain parameters of interest that do not appear in the share equations. As such, one would want to include it in the model. See Christensen and Greene (1976) for an example.

[27] They will also be highly nonlinear functions of the parameters and the data. A method of computing asymptotic standard errors for the estimated elasticities is presented in Anderson and Thursby (1986).

estimated a translog cost function for the U.S. manufacturing sector. The three factor shares used to estimate the model are

$$s_K = \beta_K + \delta_{KK}\ln\left(\frac{p_K}{p_M}\right) + \delta_{KL}\ln\left(\frac{p_L}{p_M}\right) + \delta_{KE}\ln\left(\frac{p_E}{p_M}\right),$$

$$s_L = \beta_L + \delta_{KL}\ln\left(\frac{p_K}{p_M}\right) + \delta_{LL}\ln\left(\frac{p_L}{p_M}\right) + \delta_{LE}\ln\left(\frac{p_E}{p_M}\right),$$

$$s_E = \beta_E + \delta_{KE}\ln\left(\frac{p_K}{p_M}\right) + \delta_{LE}\ln\left(\frac{p_L}{p_M}\right) + \delta_{EE}\ln\left(\frac{p_E}{p_M}\right).$$

Berndt and Wood's data are reproduced in Table 17.7. Maximum likelihood estimates of the full set of parameters are given in Table 17.8.

The implied estimates of the elasticities of substitution and demand for 1959 (the central year in the data) are derived in Table 17.9 using the fitted cost shares. The departure from the Cobb–Douglas model with unit elasticities in substantial. For example, the results

Table 17.7

						Cost Shares			
Year	Total Input Cost[a]	K	L	E	M	P_k	P_1	P_e	P_m^*
1947	182.373	0.05107	0.24727	0.04253	0.65913	1.00000	1.00000	1.00000	1.00000
1948	183.161	0.05817	0.27716	0.05127	0.61340	1.00270	1.15457	1.30258	1.05525
1949	186.533	0.04602	0.25911	0.05075	0.64411	0.74371	1.15584	1.19663	1.06225
1950	221.710	0.04991	0.24794	0.04606	0.65609	0.92497	1.23535	1.21442	1.12430
1951	255.945	0.05039	0.25487	0.04482	0.64992	1.04877	1.33784	1.25179	1.21694
1952	264.699	0.04916	0.26655	0.04460	0.63969	0.99744	1.37949	1.27919	1.19961
1953	291.160	0.04728	0.26832	0.04369	0.64071	1.00653	1.43458	1.27505	1.19044
1954	274.457	0.05635	0.27167	0.04787	0.62411	1.08757	1.45362	1.30356	1.20612
1955	308.908	0.05258	0.26465	0.04517	0.63760	1.10315	1.51120	1.34277	1.23835
1956	328.286	0.04604	0.26880	0.04576	0.63940	0.99606	1.58186	1.37154	1.29336
1957	338.633	0.05033	0.27184	0.04820	0.62962	1.06321	1.64641	1.38010	1.30703
1958	323.318	0.06015	0.27283	0.04836	0.61866	1.15619	1.67389	1.39338	1.32699
1959	358.435	0.06185	0.27303	0.04563	0.61948	1.30758	1.73430	1.36756	1.30774
1960	366.251	0.05788	0.27738	0.04585	0.61889	1.25413	1.78280	1.38025	1.33946
1961	366.162	0.05903	0.27839	0.04640	0.61617	1.26328	1.81977	1.37630	1.34319
1962	390.668	0.05578	0.28280	0.04530	0.61613	1.26525	1.88531	1.37689	1.34745
1963	412.188	0.05601	0.27968	0.04470	0.61962	1.32294	1.93379	1.34737	1.33143
1964	433.768	0.05452	0.28343	0.04392	0.61814	1.32798	2.00998	1.38969	1.35197
1965	474.969	0.05467	0.27996	0.04114	0.62423	1.40659	2.05539	1.38635	1.37542
1966	521.291	0.05460	0.28363	0.04014	0.62163	1.45100	2.13441	1.40102	1.41878
1967	540.941	0.05443	0.28646	0.04074	0.61837	1.38617	2.20616	1.39197	1.42428
1968	585.447	0.05758	0.28883	0.03971	0.61388	1.49901	2.33869	1.43388	1.43481
1969	630.450	0.05410	0.29031	0.03963	0.61597	1.44957	2.46412	1.46481	1.53356
1970	623.466	0.05255	0.29755	0.04348	0.60642	1.32464	2.60532	1.45907	1.54758
1971	658.235	0.04675	0.28905	0.04479	0.61940	1.20177	2.76025	1.64689	1.54978

Source: E. Berndt and D. Wood, "Technology, Prices, and the Derived Demand for Energy," *Review of Economics and Statistics*, 57, 1975, pp. 376–384.
[a] Billions of current dollars.

Table 17.8.   Parameter Estimates[28]
(Standard Errors in Parentheses)

β_K	0.05803 (0.00138)	δ_{KM}	-0.02649 (0.01030)
β_L	0.2549 (0.00214)	δ_{LL}	0.07111 (0.00675)
β_E	0.04725 (0.00101)	δ_{LE}	-0.01068 (0.00301)
β_M	0.6398 (0.00354)	δ_{LM}	-0.05823 (0.01130)
δ_{KK}	0.03484 (0.00585)	δ_{EE}	-0.00087 (0.00326)
δ_{KL}	-0.002192 (0.00399)	δ_{EM}	0.01771 (0.00778)
δ_{KE}	-0.006159 (0.00360)	δ_{MM}	0.06702 (0.02477)

Table 17.9

	Capital	Labor	Energy	Materials
		Cost Shares for 1959		
Fitted share	0.05713	0.27451	0.044192	0.62416
Actual share	0.06185	0.27303	0.04563	0.61948

Implied Elasticities of Substitution

	Capital	Labor	Energy	Materials
Capital	-5.828			
Labor	0.8602	-1.699		
Energy	-1.440	0.1196	-22.07	
Materials	0.2572	0.6602	1.642	-0.4302

Implied Own Price Elasticities

Capital	Labor	Energy	Materials
-0.3330	-0.4666	-0.9755	-0.2685

suggest almost no substitutability between energy and labor[29] and some complementarity between capital and energy.

The preceding system has the symmetry restrictions already imposed. However, the three equations could be estimated without the restrictions. The unrestricted model (unlike the restricted one) is a case of identical regressors and is, therefore, efficiently estimated by least squares. As such, it is possible to test the symmetry restrictions. We should note, before doing so, that the model without the symmetry restrictions is somewhat ambiguous. The cost shares were obtained by differentiation, so if the cross-derivatives are the same in the cost function, which they must be if it is continuous, they must be the same in the share equations.

---

[28] These are not the same as those reported by Berndt and Wood. In order to purge their data of possible correlation with the disturbances, they first regressed the prices on 10 exogenous macroeconomic variables, such as U.S. population, government purchases of labor services, real exports of durable goods, and U.S. tangible capital stock, and then based their analysis on the fitted values. The estimates given here are, in general, quite close to those given by Berndt and Wood. For example, their estimates of the first five parameters are 0.0564, 0.2539, 0.0442, 0.6455, and 0.0254.

[29] Berndt and Wood's estimate of σ_{EL} for 1959 is 0.64.

Be that as it may, the log determinants of the residual covariance matrices are

$$\ln|\mathbf{W}| = -31.6232 \quad \text{with symmetry}$$

and

$$\ln|\mathbf{W}| = -35.9008 \quad \text{without symmetry.}$$

The likelihood ratio statistic is, therefore,

$$\lambda_{LR} = 25(35.9008 - 31.6232) = 106.94!$$

The appropriate critical value from the chi-squared distribution with three degrees of freedom is 13.277. The test, therefore, (unfortunately) rejects the symmetry restrictions. How one should proceed from this point is unclear, since the finding calls into question the entire formulation of the model. The example is presented to illustrate the possibility.

17.5. Models with Unobservable Variables

Most econometric models, with the exceptions of the errors in variables models and panel data models with unobserved heterogeneity, are cast in terms of measured variables. However, there are some cases in economics and many in other social sciences, particularly psychology, in which some of the variables in the model are unobserved and possibly unobservable. Friedman's (1957) permanent income model is a classic example. There has been considerable interest among economists in latent variables recently, though they have appeared in the literatures of other social sciences for a number of years.[30]

17.5.1. Regression with a Latent Variable

Consider a simple application, perhaps based on the permanent income hypothesis:

$$y = \delta z^* + \varepsilon \quad \text{(consumption function)}, \quad (17-43)$$

where the unobservable z^* has zero mean, unit variance, and is uncorrelated with ε and with any lagged or future values of itself. (Since neither δ nor z^* is observed, assuming the unit variance is not a restriction.) Obviously, δ cannot be estimated. The sample data are only a consistent estimate of the variance of y, $\delta^2 + \sigma_\varepsilon^2$.[31] Suppose, however, that a secondary equation,

$$z = z^* + u, \quad E[u\varepsilon] = 0 \quad \text{(measured income)}$$

$$z^* = \boldsymbol{\beta}'\mathbf{x} \quad \text{(determinants of permanent income)}, \quad (17-44)$$

is also postulated. (Permanent income might be determined by age, education, other socioeconomic factors, and so on.) The three equations (17–43) and (17–44) constitute a **structural model**.[32] They can be combined in a multivariate regression model, called the **reduced form**:

$$\begin{bmatrix} y \\ z \end{bmatrix} = \begin{bmatrix} X & 0 \\ 0 & X \end{bmatrix} \begin{bmatrix} \pi \\ \beta \end{bmatrix} + \begin{bmatrix} \varepsilon \\ u \end{bmatrix}.$$

[30] See Aigner and Goldberger (1977) and Aigner et al. (1983). An interesting historical reference on the subject is Goldberger's "Econometrics and Psychometrics: A Survey of Commonalities" (1971).
[31] A more formal treatment of this identification problem may be found in Judge et al. (1985, pp. 711–713). There are also settings in which higher moments of y might be informative. See Aigner et al. (1983) for discussion.
[32] See Goldberger (1972) and Zellner (1970).

This is a familiar multivariate regression, indeed somewhat simpler than those we are used to by now because Σ is diagonal. But there is a nonlinear restriction in that $\pi = \delta\beta$; the model contains only $K + 1$ slope parameters, not $2K$.

Estimation can proceed along two lines. Assuming normality, direct maximization of the log likelihood requires maximization of

$$\ln L = -T \ln 2\pi - \frac{T}{2}\ln\sigma_\varepsilon^2 - \frac{T}{2}\ln\sigma_u^2$$

$$-\frac{1}{2\sigma_\varepsilon^2}(\mathbf{y} - \mathbf{X}\delta\beta)'(\mathbf{y} - \mathbf{X}\delta\beta) \qquad (17\text{--}45)$$

$$-\frac{1}{2\sigma_u^2}(\mathbf{z} - \mathbf{X}\beta)'(\mathbf{z} - \mathbf{X}\beta)$$

with respect to δ, β, σ_ε^2, and σ_u^2. Goldberger[33] presents a method of obtaining the maximum likelihood estimates. An alternative two-step procedure was devised by Zellner. The second equation,

$$\mathbf{z} = \mathbf{X}\beta + \mathbf{u},$$

satisfies all of the requirements for the classical regression model. Therefore, β (and an appropriate asymptotic covariance matrix for the estimator) can be estimated by ordinary least squares. Then, based on the equation

$$\mathbf{y} = \delta(\mathbf{X}\beta) + \varepsilon,$$

he suggests computing $\hat{\mathbf{z}} = \mathbf{Xb}$ and using an OLS regression of $\mathbf{y}$ on $\mathbf{z}$ to estimate δ. In view of the reduced form, it would seem that this is a less efficient way to proceed. However, Pagan (1984) shows that, in fact, Zellner's method is consistent, as asymptotically efficient as full MLE, and far easier to carry out. There is a problem, however, in computing the correct asymptotic variance for $\hat{\delta}$. The least squares computations do not produce the correct asymptotic variance, but a simple remedy is to use

$$\text{Est. Var}[\hat{\delta}] = \frac{(\mathbf{y} - \mathbf{z}\hat{\delta})'(\mathbf{y} - \mathbf{z}\hat{\delta})}{T(\hat{\mathbf{z}}'\hat{\mathbf{z}})^{-1}}.$$

Pagan's result is an interesting outcome. By rearranging the model a bit, we can see why it comes about. Rewrite the structure as

$$\mathbf{y} = \delta\mathbf{z} + (\varepsilon - \delta\mathbf{u}),$$

$$\mathbf{z} = \mathbf{X}\beta + \mathbf{u}.$$

This structure is written entirely in terms of the observables, and it shows that, in fact, the relationship between $\mathbf{y}$ and $\mathbf{z}$ provides no information about β. That is all embodied in the regression equation. This structure cannot be estimated in the usual fashion because $\mathbf{z}$ is correlated with $(\varepsilon - \delta\mathbf{u})$. But we have used a well-established technique (which we shall discuss at length in Chapter 19) called *two-stage least squares* to remedy that problem. Instead of regressing $\mathbf{y}$ on $\mathbf{z}$, which is correlated with $(\varepsilon - \delta\mathbf{u})$, we use $\hat{\mathbf{z}}$, which (at least asymptotically) is not.[34]

---

[33] Ibid.
[34] Viewed from this perspective, this model is merely a conventional simultaneous equations model.

Before proceeding, it is worth reiterating the method of analysis we used earlier. The structure of the model involves a latent variable. However, by examining (1) the reduced form of the model in terms of the observable variables and (2) the relationships among the expected values of the moments (variances and covariances) of the observable variables and the structural parameters, we are able to estimate the structural parameters. This is a general method by which models involving latent variables are often estimated. (Direct maximum likelihood estimation is sometimes a preferable alternative.)

17.5.2. Multiple Indicators of a Latent Variable

An interesting problem in psychology is the analysis of batteries of test scores. Consider the following formulation: Suppose that we have a sample of single test scores, which we believe are largely determined by the innate ability or intelligence (however defined) of the students sampled.

$$y = \beta z^* + \varepsilon.$$

As we have seen, this model cannot be estimated. The sample data consist of one value (i.e., one estimate),

$$s_{yy} \text{ with plim } s_{yy} = \beta^2 + \theta^2,$$

where we denote the variance of ε as θ^2. Suppose, however, that we have three uncorrelated (except through z^*) test scores, all indicative of the same latent cause, z^*. Then

$$y_1 = \beta_1 z^* + \varepsilon_1,$$
$$y_2 = \beta_2 z^* + \varepsilon_2,$$
$$y_3 = \beta_3 z^* + \varepsilon_3.$$

If we assume that the disturbances are uncorrelated, then with six unknown parameters, β_1, θ_1^2, β_2, θ_2^2, β_3, and, θ_2^2, we also have six sample pieces of information (moments):

$$s_{11} \text{ with plim } s_{11} = \beta_1^2 + \theta_1^2$$
$$s_{22} \text{ with plim } s_{22} = \beta_2^2 + \theta_2^2$$
$$s_{33} \text{ with plim } s_{33} = \beta_3^2 + \theta_2^2$$
$$s_{12} \text{ with plim } s_{12} = \beta_1 \beta_2$$
$$s_{13} \text{ with plim } s_{13} = \beta_1 \beta_3$$
$$s_{23} \text{ with plim } s_{23} = \beta_2 \beta_3.$$

The method of moments provides a unique solution for the six unknowns in terms of the six observables:

$$\beta_1 = \left[\frac{s_{12} s_{13}}{s_{23}} \right]^{1/2}$$

$$\beta_2 = \left[\frac{s_{12} s_{23}}{s_{13}} \right]^{1/2}$$

$$\beta_3 = \left[\frac{s_{13} s_{23}}{s_{12}} \right]^{1/2}$$

$$\theta_m^2 = s_{mm} - \beta_m^2, \qquad m = 1, 2, 3.$$

Once again, it is not necessary to observe the unobservable variables in order to estimate the parameters of the model. The moments of the sampled data contain enough information to identify the structural parameters. Indeed, because this model is *exactly identified* (i.e., has exactly one solution), under normality these estimates are maximum likelihood, with all of their desirable properties.

Suppose, now, that we have M such indicators of z^*. The model is

$$y = \beta z^* + \varepsilon,$$

$$Var[y] = \Sigma = \beta\beta' + \Theta^2.$$

The model states that the $M \times M$ variance matrix of y is the sum of a rank one matrix, $\beta\beta'$, and a diagonal matrix, Θ^2. If M is greater than three, not only are there more unique sample variances and covariances $(M(M+1)/2)$ than unknown parameters $(2M)$, but it is impossible to express the sample covariance matrix, S_{yy}, exactly as the sum of a rank one matrix and a diagonal matrix. This model is said to be *overidentified*. This means that in order to estimate the parameters, we must find a way to reconcile possibly conflicting estimates of the same parameters. [For example, if M is four, both $[s_{14}s_{24}/s_{12}]^{1/2}$ and $[s_{14}s_{34}/s_{13}]^{1/2}$ provide estimates of β_1, but these will not be equal in the sample data.] Three approaches to estimation have been suggested:[35]

1. Maximum likelihood:

$$\text{Minimize } \ln|\Sigma| + tr(\Sigma^{-1}S_{yy}).$$

2. Least squares:

$$\text{Minimize } tr(S_{yy} - \Sigma)^2 = \sum_m \sum_n (S_{yy_{mn}} - \Sigma_{mn})^2.$$

3. Generalized least squares:

$$\text{Minimize } tr(S_{yy} - \Sigma)^2 S_{yy}^{-1}.$$

After estimation of the parameters, it might be useful to predict the values of z^*. This might seem like an attempt to observe the unobservable, but we can make a forecast. Assuming that z^* as well as ε is normally distributed, the conditional mean of $z^* | y$ is given by

$$E[z^* | y] = E[z^*] + Cov[y, z^*]'[Var[y]]^{-1}(y - E[y]).$$

(See (3–102a).) All means are zero, so this reduces to

$$E[z^* | y] = Cov[y, z^*]'[Var[y]]^{-1}y.$$

The required parts are

$$Var[y] = \beta\beta' + \Theta^2$$

and

$$Cov[y, z^*] = \beta.$$

Therefore, the prediction is

$$\hat{z}^* = \beta'[\beta\beta' + \Theta^2]^{-1}y.$$

---

[35] Aigner et al. (1983) provide details on estimation.

(We insert our estimates for the parameters.) This simplifies to an interesting form. Using the rank one update formula, we obtain the inverse

$$[\beta\beta' + \Theta^2]^{-1} = \Theta^{-2} - \frac{\Theta^{-2}\beta\beta'\Theta^{-2}}{1 + \beta'\Theta^{-2}\beta}.$$

Inserting this in $\hat{z}*$, we find that

$$\hat{z}* = \beta'\Theta^{-2}\left[\frac{1}{(1 + \beta'\Theta^{-2}\beta)}\right]y.$$

Finally, because of the diagonal form of Θ^{-2}, this is

$$\hat{z}* = \sum_m \lambda_m y_m,$$

where

$$\lambda_m = \frac{\beta_m/\theta_m^2}{[1 + \sum_m \beta_m^2/\theta_m^2]}.$$

17.5.3. Multiple Indicators and Multiple Causes

The combination of the two preceding models is called a **multiple indicators/multiple causes (MIMIC)** model.[36] The structural form is

$$y = \beta z* + \varepsilon,$$

$$z* = x'\alpha + u.$$

The reduced form is, once again, a multivariate regression model. It is most revealing to arrange it in the horizontal form we used earlier. For a single observation,

$$[y_1 \quad y_2 \quad \cdots \quad y_M] = x'[\alpha_1\beta \quad \alpha_2\beta \quad \cdots \quad \alpha_M\beta] + [w_1 \quad w_2 \quad \cdots \quad w_M],$$

where

$$w_m = \varepsilon_m + \beta_m u.$$

For a sample of n observations,

$$Y = X[\alpha\beta'] + W,$$

$$\Sigma = \beta\beta' + \Theta^2.$$

This is a multivariate regression with identical regressors. But it has two restrictions. First, the $K \times M$ parameter matrix has rank one; every column is a multiple of the first one. Second, the disturbance covariance matrix has the rank one plus diagonal format we saw in the previous model.

Estimation can be done using maximum likelihood, as described by Joreskog and Goldberger. Since this is a multivariate regression and W is uncorrelated with X, OLS estimates, equation by equation, will be consistent, albeit obviously inefficient. What consistency means in this setting is that in a large enough sample, the OLS parameter matrix, P, will, like the true parameter matrix, $\Pi = \alpha\beta'$, have rank one. However, in a finite sample, it will not.

---

[36] Joreskog and Goldberger (1975).

Chen (1981) has devised an elegant and surprisingly simple method for estimating the MIMIC model, based on what is known as the *EM algorithm*.[37] The structure of the model is

$$y_1 = \beta_1 z^* + \varepsilon_1$$

$$y_2 = \beta_2 z^* + \varepsilon_2$$

$$\vdots$$

$$y_M = \beta_M z^* + \varepsilon_M$$

$$z^* = x'\alpha + u.$$

If z^* were observed, the model could be estimated one equation at a time by ordinary squares. The EM algorithm proceeds essentially along this basis as follows: With z^* observed, by using the least squares estimates, we could estimate the variances θ_m^2 with the OLS residual variances. Suppose, then, at iteration l, we have in hand estimates $\hat{\alpha}$, $\hat{\beta}$, and $\hat{\theta}_m^2$. The conditional mean of $z^* \mid y$ is, as we saw before, a linear function of $\mathbf{y}$. Collecting the full set of observations in data matrices z, $\mathbf{X}$, and $\mathbf{y}$, for this model, we obtain

$$E[\mathbf{z}^* \mid \mathbf{X}, \mathbf{Y}] = (1 + \boldsymbol{\beta}'\boldsymbol{\Theta}^{-2}\boldsymbol{\beta})^{-1}(\mathbf{X}\boldsymbol{\alpha} + \mathbf{Y}\boldsymbol{\Theta}^{-2}\boldsymbol{\beta}).$$

This suggests that we might use a prediction of $\mathbf{z}^*$:

$$\hat{\mathbf{z}}^* = \frac{1}{1 + \hat{\boldsymbol{\beta}}'\hat{\boldsymbol{\Theta}}^{-2}\hat{\boldsymbol{\beta}}}(\mathbf{X}\hat{\boldsymbol{\alpha}} + \mathbf{Y}\hat{\boldsymbol{\Theta}}^{-2}\hat{\boldsymbol{\beta}}).$$

Then we can use equation-by-equation least squares. This is, in fact, an effective algorithm for obtaining maximum likelihood estimates in this model. We iterate between

1. Compute $\hat{\mathbf{z}}^*$ as shown earlier and
2. $\hat{\boldsymbol{\alpha}} = (\mathbf{X}'\mathbf{X})^{-1}\mathbf{X}'\hat{\mathbf{z}}^*$,
   $\hat{\boldsymbol{\beta}} = (\hat{\mathbf{z}}^{*\prime}\hat{\mathbf{z}}^*)^{-1}\hat{\mathbf{z}}^{*\prime}\mathbf{Y}$,
   $\hat{\theta}_m^2 = \dfrac{1}{T}(\mathbf{y}_m'\mathbf{y}_m - \hat{\beta}_m^2\hat{\mathbf{z}}^{*\prime}\hat{\mathbf{z}}^*).$

As Chen points, this entire set of computations is based on the sample moments $\mathbf{Y}'\mathbf{Y}$, $\mathbf{Y}'\mathbf{X}$, and $\mathbf{X}'\mathbf{X}$, which need be computed only once before entering the iterations. Therefore, the amount of computing effort needed after the moments are obtained is independent of the sample size.

EXAMPLE 17.12. Avery (1979) estimated a model in which monetary policy was treated as the latent z^* in a MIMIC model. The causes (presumably the variables that enter the Federal Reserve Board of Governors' decision process) included functions of (1) "foreign merchandise export surplus," (2) "unemployment rate," (3) "Federal Reserve Industrial Production Index," (4) "Consumer Price Index," (5) "time trend," and (6) a periodic cubic spline in the time trend with knots at March, June, and September. The indicators were first differences of (1) "borrowings of member banks from the Fed," (2) "net free reserves," (3) "end-of-month discount rate," (4) "federal funds rate," (5) "long-term government bond rate," and (6) "three-month Treasury bill rate." Based on the likelihood ratio tests, the first four groups of causes were all found individually to be highly significant. The trend and some

---

[37] Dempster et al. (1977). We shall encounter this method again in our treatment of limited dependent variables in Chapter 21. For another application, see Section 20.3.2c.

of the terms in the spline were not. One of the interesting problems in this model is interpreting the sign of the latent variable. It is, for example, not immediately obvious how to interpret a positive coefficient on indicator (4). Presumably, policy is either contractionary or expansionary. Avery deduced from the positive signs of the coefficients on the causal variables (α in the structure) that an increase in $z*$ is consistent with contractionary policy. The impact of changes in the causes is then deduced from the signs in the reduced form matrix, $\Pi = \alpha\beta'$.

Exercises

1. A sample of 100 observations produces the following sample data:

$$\bar{y}_1 = 1 \qquad \bar{y}_2 = 2$$
$$\mathbf{y}_1'\mathbf{y}_1 = 150 \qquad \mathbf{y}_2'\mathbf{y}_2 = 550$$
$$\mathbf{y}_1'\mathbf{y}_2 = 260.$$

The underlying bivariate regression model is

$$y_1 = \mu + \varepsilon_1,$$
$$y_2 = \mu + \varepsilon_2.$$

(a) Compute the OLS estimate of μ, and estimate the sampling variance of this estimator.

(b) Compute the FGLS estimate of μ and the sampling variance of your estimator.

2. Consider estimation of the following two-equation model:

$$y_1 = \beta_1 \qquad + \varepsilon_1,$$
$$y_2 = \beta_2 x + \varepsilon_2.$$

A sample of 50 observations produces the following moment matrix:

	1	y_1	y_2	x
1	50			
y_1	150	500		
y_2	50	40	90	
x	100	60	50	100

(a) Write the explicit formula for the GLS estimator of $[\beta_1, \beta_2]$. What is the asymptotic covariance matrix of the estimator?

(b) Derive the OLS estimator and its sampling variance in this model.

(c) Obtain the OLS estimates of β_1 and β_2, and estimate the sampling covariance matrix of the two estimates. Use n instead of $(n-1)$ as the divisor to compute the estimates of the disturbance variances.

(d) Compute the FGLS estimates of β_1 and β_2 and the estimated sampling covariance matrix.

(e) Test the hypothesis that $\beta_2 = 1$.

3. The model

$$y_1 = \beta_1 x_1 + \varepsilon_1,$$
$$y_2 = \beta_2 x_2 + \varepsilon_2,$$

satisfies all of the assumptions of the classical multivariate regression model. All variables have zero means. The following sample second moment matrix is obtained from a sample of 20 observations:

$$
\begin{array}{c}
\begin{array}{cccc} y_1 & y_2 & x_1 & x_2 \end{array} \\
\begin{array}{c} y_1 \\ y_2 \\ x_1 \\ x_2 \end{array}
\begin{bmatrix}
20 & 6 & 4 & 3 \\
6 & 10 & 3 & 6 \\
4 & 3 & 5 & 2 \\
3 & 6 & 2 & 10
\end{bmatrix}.
\end{array}
$$

(*Note:*   These are the data from Exercise 1, Chapter 16.)

(a) Compute the FGLS estimates of β_1 and β_2.

(b) Test the hypothesis that $\beta_1 = \beta_2$.

(c) Compute the maximum likelihood estimates of the model parameters.

(d) Use the likelihood ratio test to test the hypothesis in part (b).

4. Prove that in the model

$$y_1 = X_1\beta_1 + \varepsilon_1,$$

$$y_2 = X_2\beta_2 + \varepsilon_2.$$

Generalized least squares is equivalent to equation-by-equation ordinary least squares if $X_1 = X_2$. Does your result hold if it is also known that $\beta_1 = \beta_2$?

5. Consider the two-equation system

$$y_1 = \beta_1 x_1 \qquad\qquad + \varepsilon_1$$

$$y_2 = \qquad \beta_2 x_2 + \beta_3 x_3 + \varepsilon_2.$$

Assume that the disturbance variances and covariance are known. Now suppose that the analyst of this model applies GLS, but erroneously omits x_3 from the second equation. What effect does this specification error have on the consistency of the estimator of β_1?

6. Consider the system

$$y_1 = \alpha_1 + \beta x + \varepsilon_1$$

$$y_2 = \alpha_2 \qquad\quad + \varepsilon_2.$$

The disturbances are freely correlated. Prove that GLS applied to the system leads to the OLS estimates of α_1 and α_2 but to a mixture of the least squares slopes in the regressions of y_1 and y_2 on x as the estimator of β. What is the mixture? To simplify the algebra, assume (with no loss of generality) that $\bar{x} = 0$.

7. For the model

$$y_1 = \alpha_1 + \beta x + \varepsilon_1$$

$$y_2 = \alpha_2 \qquad\quad + \varepsilon_2$$

$$y_3 = \alpha_3 \qquad\quad + \varepsilon_3$$

assume that $y_{i2} + y_{i3} = 1$ at every observation. Prove that the sample covariance matrix of the least squares residuals from the three equations will be singular, thereby precluding computation of the FGLS estimator. How could you proceed in this case?

8. Derive the first-order conditions for maximizing the log likelihood in (17–45).

9. Continuing the analysis of Section 17.4.1, we find that a translog cost function for one output and three factor inputs that does not impose constant returns to scale is

$$\ln C = \alpha + \beta_1 \ln p_1 + \beta_2 \ln p_2 + \beta_2 \ln p_3$$

$$+ \delta_{11} \frac{(\ln^2 p_1)}{2} + \delta_{12} \ln p_1 \ln p_2 + \delta_{13} \ln p_1 \ln p_3$$

$$+ \delta_{22} \frac{(\ln^2 p_2)}{2} + \delta_{23} \ln p_2 \ln p_3$$

$$+ \delta_{33} \frac{(\ln^2 p_3)}{2}$$

$$+ \gamma_{y1} \ln Y \ln p_1 + \gamma_{y2} \ln Y \ln p_2 + \gamma_{y3} \ln Y \ln p_3$$

$$+ \beta_y \ln Y + \beta_{yy} \frac{(\ln^2 Y)}{2} + \varepsilon_c.$$

The factor share equations are

$$S_1 = \beta_1 + \delta_{11} \ln p_1 + \delta_{12} \ln p_2 + \delta_{13} \ln p_3 + \gamma_{y1} \ln Y + \varepsilon_1,$$
$$S_2 = \beta_2 + \delta_{12} \ln p_1 + \delta_{22} \ln p_2 + \delta_{23} \ln p_3 + \gamma_{y2} \ln Y + \varepsilon_2,$$
$$S_3 = \beta_3 + \delta_{13} \ln p_1 + \delta_{23} \ln p_2 + \delta_{33} \ln p_3 + \gamma_{y3} \ln Y + \varepsilon_3.$$

[See Christensen and Greene (1976) for analysis of this model.]

(a) The three factor shares must add identically to one. What restrictions does this place on the model parameters?

(b) Show that the adding-up condition in (17–41) can be imposed directly on the model by specifying the translog model in (C/p_3), (p_1/p_3), and (p_2/p_3) and dropping the third share equation. (See Example 17.10.) Notice that this reduces the number of free parameters in the model to 10.

(c) Continuing part (b), the model as specified, with the symmetry and equality restrictions, has 15 parameters. By imposing the constraints, you reduce this number to 10 in the estimating equations. How would you obtain estimates of the parameters not estimated directly?

The remaining parts of this exercise require specialized software. The TSP, Shazam, or ET programs noted in the Preface are three that could be used. All estimation is to be done using the data in Example 17.9.

(d) Estimate each of the three equations you obtained in part (b) by ordinary least squares. Do the estimates appear to satisfy the cross-equation equality and symmetry equations implied by the theory?

(e) Using the data in Example 17.9, estimate the full system of three equations (cost and the two independent shares), imposing the symmetry and cross-equation equality constraints.

(f) Using your parameter estimates, compute the estimates of the elasticities in (17–42) at the means of the variables.

(g) Use a likelihood ratio statistic to test the joint hypothesis that $\gamma_{yi} = 0$, $i = 1, 2, 3$. (**Hint:**   Just drop the relevant variables from the model.)

(h) At the end of Example 17.9, we computed the Y at which

$$\frac{\partial \ln C}{\partial \ln Y} = 1.$$

Repeat this computation using your results obtained here. Note that this derivative now involves the logs of the prices. Use the sample averages for your computations. How does your result compare to the one in the example? Note that, in the example, the model is specified with the term $\beta_{yy} \ln^2 Y$, so the derivative involves $2\beta_{yy} \ln Y$. In the preceding model, we used $\beta_{yy} \ln^2 Y/2$, so that the derivative would involve only $\beta_{yy} \ln Y$. (The computation of an asymptotic standard for this estimate of the efficient scale of production is examined in Exercise 3, Chapter 10.)

References

Aigner, D., and A. Goldberger, eds., *Latent Variables in Socioeconomic Models*, Amsterdam: North Holland, 1977.

Aigner, D., C. Hsiao, A. Kapteyn, and T. Wansbeek, "Latent Variable Models in Econometrics," in Z. Griliches, and M. Intrilligator, eds., *Handbook of Econometrics*, Vol. 3, Amsterdam: North Holland, 1983.

Anderson, R., and J. Thursby, "Confidence Intervals for Elasticity Estimators in Translog Models," *Review of Economics and Statistics*, 68, 1986, pp. 647–657.

Arrow, K., H. Chenery, B. Minhas, and R. Solow, "Capital–Labor Substitution and Economic Efficiency," *Review of Economics and Statistics*, 45, 1963, pp. 225–247.

Avery, R., "Modeling Monetary Policy as an Unobserved Variable," *Journal of Econometrics*, 10, 1979, pp. 291–311.

Barton, A., "Maximum Likelihood Estimation of a Complete System of Demand Equations," *European Economic Review*, 1, 1969, pp. 7–73.

Berndt, E., and L. Christensen, "The Translog Function and the Substitution of Equipment, Structures, and Labor in U.S. Manufacturing, 1929–1968," *Journal of Econometrics*, 2, 1973, pp. 81–114.

Berndt, E., and D. Wood, "Technology, Prices, and the Derived Demand for Energy," *Review of Economics and Statistics*, 57, 1975, pp. 376–384.

Breusch, T., and A. Pagan, "The LM Test and Its Applications to Model Specification in Econometrics," *Review of Economic Studies*, 47, 1980, pp. 239–254.

Chen, C., "The EM Approach to the Multiple Indicators and Multiple Causes Model Via the Estimation of the Latent Variable," *Journal of the American Statistical Association*, 76, 1981, pp. 704–708.

Christensen, L., and W. Greene, "Economies of Scale in U.S. Electric Power Generation," *Journal of Political Economy*, 84, 1976, pp. 655–676.

Christensen, L., D. Jorgenson, and L. Lau, "Transcendental Logarithmic Production Frontiers," *Review of Economics and Statistics*, 55, 1973, pp. 28–45.

Christensen, L., D. Jorgenson, and L. Lau, "Transcendental Logarithmic Utility Functions," *American Economic Review*, 65, 1975, pp. 367–383.

Christensen, L., and M. Manser, "Estimating U.S. Consumer Preferences for Meat with a Flexible Utility Function," *Journal of Econometrics*, 5, 1977, pp. 37–53.

Conniffe, D., "Covariance Analysis and Seemingly Unrelated Regression Equations," *The American Statistician*, 36, 1982, pp. 169–171.

Conniffe, D., "A Note on Seemingly Unrelated Regressions," *Econometrica*, 50, 1982, pp. 229–233.

Deaton, A., "Demand Analysis," in Z. Griliches, and M. Intrilligator, eds., *Handbook of Econometrics*, Amsterdam: North Holland, 1983.

Deaton, A., and J. Muellbauer, "An Almost Ideal Demand System," *American Economic Review*, 70, 1980, pp. 312–326.

Deaton, A., and J. Muellbauer, *Economics and Consumer Behavior*, Cambridge: Cambridge University Press, 1980.

Dempster. A., N. Laird, and D. Rubin, "Maximum Likelihood Estimation from Incomplete Data Via the EM Algorithm," *Journal of the Royal Statistical Society, Series B*, 39, 1977, pp. 1–38.

Diewert, E., "Applications of Duality Theory," in M. Intrilligator, and D. Kendrick, eds., *Frontiers in Quantitative Economics*, Amsterdam: North Holland, 1974.

Dwivedi, T., and K. Srivastava, "Optimality of Least Squares in the Seemingly Unrelated Regressions Model," *Journal of Econometrics*, 7, 1978, pp. 391–395.

Friedman, M., *A Theory of the Consumption Function*, Princeton, N.J.: Princeton University Press, 1957.

Goldberger, A., "Estimation of a Regression Coefficient Matrix Containing a Block of Zeroes," University of Wisconsin, SSRI, EME, Number 7002, 1970.

Goldberger, A., "Econometrics and Psychometrics: A Survey of Communalities," *Biometrika*, 36, 1971, pp. 83–107.

Goldberger, A., "Maximum Likelihood Estimation of Regressions Containing Unobservable Independent Variables," *International Economic Review*, 13, 1972, pp. 1–15.

Guilkey, D., "Alternative Tests for a First-Order Vector Autoregressive Error Specification," *Journal of Econometrics*, 2, 1974, pp. 95–104.

Guilkey, D., C. Lovell, and R. Sickles, "A Comparison of the Performance of Three Flexible Functional Forms," *International Economic Review*, 24, 1983, pp. 591–616.

Guilkey, D., and P. Schmidt, "Estimation of Seemingly Unrelated Regressions with Vector Autoregressive Errors," *Journal of the American Statistical Association*, 68, 1973, pp. 642–647.

Joreskog, K., "A General Method for Estimating a Linear Structural Equation System," in A. Goldberger, and O. Duncan, eds., *Structural Equation Methods in the Social Sciences*, New York: Seminar Press, 1973, pp. 85–112.

Joreskog, K., and A. Goldberger, "Estimation of a Model with Multiple Indicators and Multiple Causes of a Single Latent Variable," *Journal of the American Statistical Association*, 70, 1975, pp. 631–639.

Joreskog, K., and D. Sorbom, "LISREL V User's Guide," Chicago: National Educational Resources, 1981.

Jorgenson, D., "Econometric Methods for Modeling Producer Behavior," in Z. Griliches, and M. Intrilligator, *Handbook of Econometrics, Vol. 3*, Amsterdam: North Holland, 1983.

Kakwani, N., "The Unbiasedness of Zellner's Seemingly Unrelated Regression Equation Estimators," *Journal of the American Statistical Association*, 62, 1967, pp. 141–142.

King, B., "Market and Industry Factors in Stock Price Behavior," *Journal of Business*, 39, 1966, pp. 139–168.

Kmenta, J., "On Estimation of the CES Production Function," *International Economic Review*, 8, 1967, pp. 180–189.

Kmenta, J., and R. Gilbert, "Small Sample Properties of Alternative Estimators of Seemingly Unrelated Regressions," *Journal of the American Statistical Association*, 63, 1968, pp. 1180–1200.

Lluch, C., and R. Williams, "Consumer Demand Systems and Aggregate Consumption in the U.S.A.: An Application of the Extended Linear Expenditure System," *Canadian Journal of Economics*, 8, 1974, pp. 49–66.

McElroy, M., "Goodness of Fit for Seemingly Unrelated Regressions: Glahn's $R^2_{y.x}$ and Hooper's $\bar{r}^2$," *Journal of Econometrics*, 6, 1977, pp. 381–387.

Nerlove, M., "Returns to Scale in Electricity Supply," in C. Christ, ed., *Measurement in Economics*, Stanford, Calif.: Stanford University Press, 1963.

Oberhofer, W., and J. Kmenta, "A General Procedure for Obtaining Maximum Likelihood Estimates in Generalized Regression Models," *Econometrica*, 42, 1974, pp. 579–590.

Pagan, A., "Econometric Issues in the Analysis of Regressions with Generated Regressors," *International Economic Review*, 25, 1984, pp. 221–247.

Parks, R., "Efficient Estimation of a System of Regression Equations When Disturbances Are Both

Serially and Contemporaneously Correlated," *Journal of the American Statistical Association*, 62, 1967, pp. 500–509.

Revankar, N., "Some Finite Sample Results in the Context of Two Seemingly Unrelated Regression Equations," *Journal of the American Statistical Association*, 69, 1974, pp. 187–190.

Revankar, N., "Use of Restricted Residuals in SUR Systems: Some Finite Sample Results," *Journal of the American Statistical Association*, 71, 1976, pp. 183–188.

Shephard, R., *The Theory of Cost and Production*, Princeton, N.J.: Princeton University Press, 1970.

Stone, J., *The Measurement of Consumers' Expenditure and Behaviour in the United Kingdom*, 1920–1983, Cambridge: Cambridge University Press, 1954.

Theil, H., *Principles of Econometrics*, New York: Wiley, 1971.

Zellner, A., "An Efficient Method of Estimating Seemingly Unrelated Regressions and Tests of Aggregation Bias," *Journal of the American Statistical Association*, 57, 1962, pp. 500–509.

Zellner, A., "Estimators for Seemingly Unrelated Regression Equations: Some Exact Finite Sample Results," *Journal of the American Statistical Association*, 58, 1963, pp. 977–992.

Zellner, A., "Estimation of Regression Relationships Containing Unobservable Independent Variables," *International Economic Review*, 11, 1970, pp. 441–454.

Zellner, A., and D. Huang, "Further Properties of Efficient Estimators for Seemingly Unrelated Regression Equations," *International Economic Review*, 3, 1962, pp. 303–313.

Chapter 18

Models of Economic Time Series

18.1. Introduction

With the exception of our discussions of autocorrelation and the possibly deleterious effects of lagged dependent variables on ordinary least squares, the models considered thus far have given only a very limited role to time as an influencing factor. In this chapter, we consider a number of models in which time and relationships through time play an explicit part in the formulation. We begin with a discussion of distributed lag models. These are models that specifically include as independent variables earlier as well as contemporaneous values of the regressors. Time-varying parameter models, in contrast, are models in which the effect of time is embodied in the evolution of the parameters.

18.2. Distributed Lag Models[1]

Many events have effects that persist over time, and an appropriate model will include lagged variables.

> **EXAMPLE 18.1. The Demand for Energy.** In the typical household, electricity, heating fuels, and gasoline are demanded not for their own sake but for use in appliances, furnaces, and cars. The household's accumulated energy-using "capital stock" is determined by income, habits, and past prices of fuels. Consequently, in any period, the household's demand for energy is a function of the current price, which influences how intensively the stock of equipment is used, and past prices, which have influenced the size and composition of that stock. A simple structural model of these effects might be
>
> $$\text{Demand:} \quad Q_t = \alpha + \beta P_t + \gamma K_t + \varepsilon_t,$$
>
> $$\text{Equipment:} \quad K_t = \theta_0 + \theta_1 P_{t-1} + \theta_2 P_{t-2} + \cdots + \delta Y_t.$$
>
> Inserting the second equation in the first produces a **distributed lag model**,
>
> $$Q_t = \alpha_0 + \delta Y_t + \beta_0 P_t + \beta_1 P_{t-1} + \beta_2 P_{t-2} + \cdots + \varepsilon_t.$$

---

[1] Important references on distributed lag models are Dhrymes (1971), Hendry et al. (1984), Griliches (1967), Nerlove (1972), and Harvey (1981).

When the price of energy changes, its immediate impact will be to cause households to use their equipment less intensively. But it takes time to replace that equipment, so the full effect of a price change will not be felt for some time thereafter.

A general form of the distributed lag model is

$$y_t = \alpha + \sum_{i=0}^{\infty} \beta_i x_{t-i} + \varepsilon_t. \tag{18-1}$$

In this model, a one-time change in x_t at any point in time will affect $E[y_s]$ in every period thereafter. When it is believed that the duration of the lagged effects is extremely long, for example, in the analysis of monetary policy, *infinite lag* models that have effects that gradually fade over time are quite common. The assumption of infinite lags, even if their weights fade over time, may be excessive, and models are often constructed in which changes in x cease to have any influence after a finite number of periods. We shall consider these *finite lag* models first.

Marginal effects in the classical regression model are one-time events. The response of y to a change in x is assumed to be immediate and to be complete at the end of the period of measurement. In a distributed lag model, the counterpart to a marginal effect is the effect of a one-time change in x_t on the equilibrium of y_t. If the level of x_t has been unchanged for many periods prior to t, the equilibrium value of $E[y_t]$ (assuming that it exists) will be

$$\bar{y} = \alpha + \sum_{i=0}^{\infty} \beta_i \bar{x}$$

$$= \alpha + \bar{x} \sum_{i=0}^{\infty} \beta_i. \tag{18-2}$$

In order for this to be finite, we require

$$\left| \sum_{i=0}^{\infty} \beta_i \right| < +\infty. \tag{18-3}$$

Consider the effect of a unit change in x occurring in period s. To focus ideas, consider the earlier example of consumers' demand for electricity, and suppose that x_t is the unit price. Prior to the oil shock, demand had reached an equilibrium consistent with accumulated habits, experience with stable real prices, and the accumulated stocks of appliances. Now suppose that $\bar{x}$ rises to $\bar{x} + 1$ in period s. The path to the new equilibrium might appear as shown in Figure 18.1. The short-run effect is that which occurs in the same period as the change in x. This is β_0 in the figure.

Definition. $\beta_0 =$ **impact multiplier**
$\quad\quad\quad\quad = $ **short-run multiplier**.

The difference between the old equilibrium and the new one is the sum of the individual period effects. The **long-run multiplier** is this total effect.

Definition. $\sum_{i=0}^{\infty} \beta_i =$ **equilibrium multiplier**.

Since the lag coefficients are regression coefficients, their scale is determined by the scales of the variables in the model. As such, it is often useful to define the

Lag weights: $w_i = \dfrac{\beta_i}{\sum_i \beta_i}$

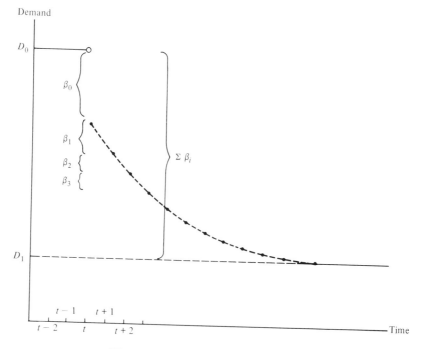

Figure 18.1   Lagged adjustment.

and to rewrite the model as

$$y_t = \alpha + \beta \sum_{i=0}^{\infty} w_i x_{t-i} + \varepsilon_t. \tag{18-4}$$

Two useful statistics, based on the lag weights, that characterize the period of adjustment to a new equilibrium are the

$$\textbf{Median lag} = \textbf{q}^* \qquad \text{such that} \qquad \sum_{i=0}^{q^*-1} w_i = 0.5 \tag{18-5}$$

and the

$$\textbf{Mean lag} = \sum_{i=0}^{\infty} i w_i.^2 \tag{18-6}$$

A convenient device for manipulating lagged variables is the lag operator,[3]

$$Lx_t = x_{t-1}.$$

It follows that

$$L^p x_t = x_{t-p}$$

and

$$L^q(L^p x_t) = L^{p+q} x_t = x_{t-p-q}.$$

---

[2] If the lag coefficients do not all have the same sign, these results may not be meaningful. In some contects, lag coefficients with different signs may be taken as an indication that there is a flaw in the specification of the model.
[3] Extensive discussion of this tool is given in Dhrymes (1978).

By definition,

$$L^0 = 1.$$

The distributed lag model can be written

$$y_t = \alpha + \sum_{i=0}^{\infty} \beta_i L^i x_t + \varepsilon_t \tag{18-7}$$

$$= \alpha + B(L)x_t + \varepsilon_t,$$

where $B(L)$ is a polynomial in L,

$$B(L) = \beta_0 + \beta_1 L + \beta_2 L^2 + \cdots$$

Two useful results are

$$B(1) = \beta_0 1^0 + \beta_1 1^1 + \beta_2 1^2 + \cdots \tag{18-8}$$

$$= \text{long-run multiplier}$$

and

$$B'(1) = \frac{dB(L)}{dL}\bigg|_{L=1} = \sum_{i=0}^{\infty} i\beta_i,$$

so that

$$\frac{B'(1)}{B(1)} = \text{mean lag.} \tag{18-9}$$

18.2.1. Finite Distributed Lag Models

An unrestricted finite distributed lag model would be specified as

$$y_t = \alpha + \sum_{i=0}^{q} \beta_i x_{t-i} + \varepsilon_t. \tag{18-10}$$

For the present, we assume that x_t is nonstochastic. The assumption that there are no other regressors is just a convenience. We also assume that ε_t is normally distributed, with mean zero and variance σ_ε^2. Unstructured models such as this, with long but finite lags, have been used in many recent macroeconomic analyses.[4]

If the lag length, q, is known, (18-10) is a classical regression model. Aside from questions about the properties of the independent variables, the usual estimation results apply.[5] Unfortunately, the appropriate length of the lag is rarely, if ever, known, so one must undertake a specification search, with all of its pitfalls. Worse yet, least squares is likely to be rather ineffective, as (1) the typical time series is fairly short, so (18-10) will consume an excessive number of degrees of freedom; (2) ε_t will usually be serially correlated; and (3) multicollinearity is likely to be quite severe.

Various procedures have been suggested for determining the appropriate lag length. The adjusted R^2 is one possibility. Another commonly used fit measure is **Akaike's** (1973)

---

[4] See, for example, Sims (1972) and the spate of subsequent related studies.
[5] The question of whether the regressors are well behaved or not becomes particularly pertinent in this setting, especially if one or more of them happen to be lagged values of the dependent variable. In what follows, we shall assume that the Grenander conditions discussed in Chapter 10 are met. We thus assume that the usual asymptotic results for the classical or generalized regression model will hold.

information criterion (AIC),

$$AIC(q) = \ln\left[\frac{e'e}{T}\right] + \frac{2q}{T}. \tag{18-11}$$

If some maximum, Q, is known, $q \leq Q$ can be chosen to minimize $AIC(q)$. $AIC(q)$ is similar in spirit to $\bar{R}^2$ in that it rewards good fit but penalizes the loss of degrees of freedom.[6] An alternative approach, also based on a known Q, is to do sequential F tests on the last $Q - q$ coefficients, stopping when the test rejects the hypothesis that the coefficients are jointly zero. Each of these criteria has flaws and virtues. The AIC criterion, for instance, retains a positive probability of leading to overfitting even as $T \to \infty$. It does, however, avoid the inference problems of sequential estimators. The sequential F tests require successive revision of the significance levels to be appropriate, but they do have a statistical underpinning.[7]

EXAMPLE 18.2. Finite Unstructured Distributed Lag Models. Does money matter? The received literature is ambivalent on whether or not a change in the money stock ultimately leads to a change in output.[8] In this example, we will estimate a distributed lag model for changes in M1 and changes in nominal GNP.

Table 18.1 presents quarterly data on M1 and nominal GNP from 1950 to 1983.[9] We first fit the distributed lag model,

$$\ln y_t = \alpha + \sum_{i=0}^{8} \beta_i \ln M_{t-i} + \varepsilon_t.$$

Ordinary least squares regression produces the results given in Table 18.2. (Asymptotic t ratios are given in parentheses below the coefficients.)

The extremely low t ratios and the very high F statistic suggest a problem of multicollinearity. The Durbin–Watson statistic also suggests a considerable amount of autocorrelation. The data were, therefore, first differenced to obtain the following results. The model estimated is

$$\Delta \ln Y_t = \alpha + \sum_{i=0}^{8} \beta_i (\Delta \ln M1)_{t-i} + \varepsilon_t.$$

(What is the implication of the nonzero constant term in this model?) Results for various lag lengths are given in Table 18.3. Observations for 1952–II through 1983–IV are used in all regressions. T ratios for the estimates are given in parentheses below the estimated coefficients.

There is no obvious interpretation of the persistent negative weights at lags of five and six quarters. It is intriguing to note that in their much more extensive study, which included several other variables in the regression, used levels instead of logarithms, and used data from a different period, Schmidt and Waud (1973) likewise found negative weights at lags of five and six quarters in regressions of nominal GNP on money. Excluding the model that includes no lagged values, the regressions all produce very similar estimates of the long-run multiplier. According to these results, a 1 percent increase in the growth of M1 ultimately leads to roughly a 0.85 percent increase in the growth rate of nominal GNP. Finally, we

---

[6] For further discussion and some alternative measures, see Geweke and Meese (1981), Amemiya (1985, pp. 146–147), and Judge et al. (1985, pp. 353–355).

[7] See Pagano and Hartley (1981) and Trivedi and Pagan (1979).

[8] See, for example, the recent survey by Blanchard (1987). An interesting study with a somewhat broader focus is Schmidt and Waud (1973).

[9] The data are from Gordon (1986, Appendix). The tables were compiled by R. Gordon and N. Balke.

Table 18.1. Money and Output Data

| | Nominal GNP | | | | M1 | | | |
	I	II	III	IV	I	II	III	IV
1950	267.6	277.1	294.8	306.3	110.20	111.75	112.95	113.93
1951	320.4	328.3	335.0	339.2	115.08	116.19	117.76	119.89
1952	341.9	342.1	347.8	360.0	121.31	122.37	123.64	124.72
1953	366.1	369.4	368.4	363.1	125.33	126.05	126.22	126.37
1954	362.5	362.3	366.7	375.6	126.54	127.18	128.38	129.72
1955	388.2	396.2	404.8	411.0	131.07	131.88	132.40	132.64
1956	412.8	418.4	423.5	432.1	133.11	133.38	133.48	134.09
1957	440.2	422.3	449.4	444.0	134.29	134.36	134.26	133.48
1958	436.8	440.7	453.9	467.0	133.72	135.22	136.64	138.48
1959	477.0	490.6	489.0	495.0	140.35	141.75	142.23	141.20
1960	506.9	506.3	508.0	504.8	140.83	140.83	142.00	141.98
1961	508.2	519.2	528.2	542.6	142.85	143.88	144.90	146.18
1962	554.2	562.7	568.9	574.3	147.18	147.95	147.90	148.93
1963	582.0	590.7	601.8	612.4	150.45	151.93	153.38	154.80
1964	625.3	634.0	642.8	648.8	155.85	157.20	159.75	161.63
1965	668.8	681.7	696.4	717.2	162.90	163.90	166.05	169.10
1966	738.5	750.0	760.6	774.9	171.95	172.98	172.80	173.33
1967	780.7	788.6	805.7	823.3	175.25	178.10	181.93	184.73
1968	841.2	867.2	884.9	900.3	187.15	190.63	194.30	198.55
1969	921.2	937.4	955.3	962.0	201.73	203.18	204.18	206.10
1970	972.0	986.3	1003.6	1009.0	207.90	209.78	212.78	216.08
1971	1049.3	1068.9	1086.6	1105.8	220.28	225.25	228.45	230.70
1972	1142.4	1171.7	1196.1	1233.5	235.60	239.38	244.55	250.70
1973	1283.5	1307.6	1337.7	1376.7	254.80	258.40	261.03	264.68
1974	1387.7	1423.8	1451.6	1473.8	268.77	271.23	273.73	276.73
1975	1479.8	1516.7	1578.5	1621.8	278.75	283.80	288.13	290.88
1976	1672.0	1698.6	1729.0	1772.5	295.18	299.53	303.35	309.35
1977	1834.8	1895.1	1954.4	1988.9	316.55	321.80	327.60	334.80
1978	2031.7	2139.5	2202.5	2281.6	341.13	348.70	335.45	361.38
1979	2335.5	2377.9	2454.8	2502.9	367.08	376.10	384.58	388.38
1980	2572.9	2578.8	2639.1	2736.0	394.30	390.00	405.50	416.10
1981	2875.8	2918.0	3009.3	3027.9	420.90	429.30	432.60	437.50
1982	3026.0	3061.2	3080.1	3109.6	448.80	451.30	458.20	475.70
1983	3173.8	3267.0	3346.6	3431.7	490.90	505.20	517.20	523.40

Table 18.2

β_0	β_1	β_2	β_3	β_4	β_5	β_6	β_7	β_8
0.105	0.042	0.182	0.313	0.103	0.103	−0.429	0.055	−0.020
(1.9)	(0.12)	(0.05)	(0.20)	(0.35)	(0.11)	(−0.47)	(0.06)	(−0.03)

$$R^2 = 0.9902, \qquad s = 0.0719, \qquad D - W = 0.0452, \qquad r = 0.98.$$

Table 18.3.   Distributed Lags

R^2	0.3190	0.3171	0.3159	0.3007	0.2970	0.2969	0.2892	0.2469	0.1404
$D-W$	1.446	1.449	1.454	1.479	1.463	1.462	1.469	1.452	1.367
AIC	-9.15	-9.16	-9.18	-9.17	-9.18	-9.20	-9.21	-9.17	-9.04
Sum	0.800	0.822	0.805	0.885	0.916	0.933	0.876	0.722	0.402
$t-0$	0.303	0.298	0.308	0.304	0.282	0.292	0.308	0.371	0.402
	(3.32)	(3.29)	(3.53)	(3.46)	(3.37)	(3.39)	(3.62)	(4.42)	(4.52)
$t-1$	0.350	0.337	0.338	0.314	0.313	0.310	0.337	0.351	
	(3.85)	(3.84)	(3.86)	(3.62)	(3.61)	(3.65)	(4.10)	(4.19)	
$t-2$	0.240	0.240	0.245	0.242	0.234	0.230	0.231		
	(2.68)	(2.69)	(2.77)	(2.72)	(2.65)	(2.70)	(2.70)		
$t-3$	0.136	0.131	0.131	0.114	0.101	0.101			
	(1.51)	(1.46)	(1.47)	(1.28)	(1.15)	(1.15)			
$t-4$	0.005	0.006	0.011	-0.017	-0.014				
	(0.05)	(0.06)	(0.13)	(-0.19)	(-0.16)				
$t-5$	-0.082	-0.088	-0.080	-0.073					
	(-0.88)	(-0.95)	(-0.88)	(-0.80)					
$t-6$	-0.136	-0.145	-0.148						
	(-1.5)	(-1.6)	(-1.6)						
$t-7$	0.039	0.043							
	(0.41)	(0.45)							
$t-8$	-0.055								
	(-0.57)								

strongly reject the hypothesis that all coefficients are zero, which suggests that increases in the growth of money *are* associated with subsequent increases in the growth of output. This might have been predicted on the basis of the *quantity theory*, but this theory is silent on how long the adjustment takes.

18.2.1a. *Misspecification of the Lag Length*

If the appropriate lag length is unknown, two potential problems can arise. If the model is overfit, the familiar results for the classical regression model apply. The coefficients on the superfluous lagged variables are consistent estimates of zero, while those on the appropriate lagged variables are consistent but inefficient estimates of the true parameters. By contrast, if the model is underfit, the estimates of the individual lag coefficients may be inconsistent. The results for omitted variables in regression discussed in Section 8.4.1 would apply.

In most cases involving long lags, such as the preceding one, the individual coefficients are of relatively little interest. The effects of incorrectly omitting the trailing lagged values of x_t on the estimates of the short- and long-run multipliers remain to be investigated. We consider the simple case in which x_t is an AR(1) process,

$$x_t = \rho x_{t-1} + w_t.$$

Suppose that the true model is

$$y_t = \beta_0 x_t + \beta_1 x_{t-1} + \beta_2 x_{t-2} + \varepsilon_t.$$

Assume, for convenience, that the data on x_t, x_{t-1}, and x_{t-2} are standardized and the data are well behaved, so that the sample moments have

$$\frac{1}{T} \sum_{t=1}^{T} x_t^2 = 1,$$

$$\text{plim} \frac{1}{T} \sum_{t=2}^{T} x_t x_{t-1} = \text{plim } r_1 = \rho_1,$$

$$\text{plim} \frac{1}{T} \sum_{t=3}^{T} x_t x_{t-2} = \text{plim } r_2 = \rho_2,$$

where ρ_1 and ρ_2 are the first and second autocorrelations of x_t. If y_t is regressed only on x_t and x_{t-1}, omitting x_{t-2}, the usual results for a left-out variable apply to the probability limits of the least squares estimates. *In general, b_0 and b_1 are biased and inconsistent estimates of β_1 and β_2.* But what of $b_0 + b_1$ as an estimate of the long-run multiplier, $\beta_0 + \beta_1 + \beta_2$? Applying the omitted-variable formula, we obtain

$$\text{plim} \begin{bmatrix} b_0 \\ b_1 \end{bmatrix} = \begin{bmatrix} \beta_0 \\ \beta_1 \end{bmatrix} + \text{plim} \begin{bmatrix} 1 & r_1 \\ r_1 & 1 \end{bmatrix}^{-1} \begin{bmatrix} r_2 \\ r_1 \end{bmatrix} \beta_2.$$

Adding the two estimates gives

$$\text{plim } b_0 + b_1 = \beta_0 + \beta_1 + \frac{\rho_1 + \rho_2}{\rho_1 + 1} \beta_2.$$

The larger is ρ_2; the smaller is the bias. For example, suppose that the three lag weights are 0.7, 0.2, and 0.1, and x_t is an AR(1) process with $\rho = \rho_1 = 0.9$. Then $\rho_2 = \rho_1^2 = 0.81$ and $\text{plim } b_0 + b_1 = 0.99$, while $\beta_0 + \beta_1 + \beta_2 = 1$.

Continuing, we maintain the assumption of an AR(1) process with parameter ρ for x_t and suppose that the correct model has q lags, but we estimate it with only $q - 1$. Let

$$\mathbf{X}_1 = [\mathbf{x}, \mathbf{x}_{-1}, \mathbf{x}_{-2}, \ldots, \mathbf{x}_{-q+1}]$$

and

$$\mathbf{X}_2 = \mathbf{x}_{-q}.$$

It is helpful to assume that the data are standardized,[10] so that

$$\text{plim} \frac{1}{T} \mathbf{X}_1' \mathbf{X}_1 = \Gamma_{11},$$

where Γ_{11} is the autocorrelation matrix in (15–10). Then

$$\text{plim} \frac{1}{T} \mathbf{X}_1' \mathbf{X}_2 = \Gamma_{12} = \rho \text{ times the last column of } \Gamma_{11}.$$

Thus,

$$\text{plim } \Gamma_{11}^{-1} \Gamma_{12} = [0, 0, 0, \ldots, \rho]'$$

(i.e., ρ times the last column of an identity matrix). Inserting this in the omitted variable formula, we obtain a striking result:

$$\text{plim } \mathbf{b} = \beta_0, \beta_1, \beta_2, \ldots, \beta_{n-1} + \rho\beta_q.$$

---

[10] The result to follow is not dependent on this condition.

Table 18.4. Distributed Lag Consumption Functions

Sum	0	1	2	3	4	5	6	7	8
					Lag				
0.910	0.641	0.231	0.097	−0.046	−0.114	−0.084	−0.025	0.140	0.070
0.910	0.652	0.225	0.096	−0.059	−0.118	−0.074	−0.008	0.192	
0.909	0.662	0.230	0.075	−0.068	−0.096	−0.028	0.133		
0.907	0.671	0.217	0.065	−0.055	−0.064	0.074			
0.907	0.667	0.211	0.072	−0.038	−0.006				
0.908	0.662	0.211	0.071	−0.042					
0.908	0.668	0.203	0.038						
0.908	0.675	0.232							
0.905	0.905								

Only the last coefficient is inconsistent. This provides two interesting results for estimation of the long- and short-run multipliers *when x_t is an AR(1) process:*

1. If any lags at all are included in the model, the impact multiplier is consistently estimated.

2. The long-run multiplier is underestimated by

$$\text{plim } \mathbf{i'b} - [\mathbf{i'}\boldsymbol{\beta} + \beta_n] = (1 - \rho)\beta_q.$$

Although the AR(1) model is a special case, it is a useful benchmark that is closely approximated by many observed series. If the lag is relatively long and a reasonably large number of lags are included, β_q and the bias in the long-run multiplier are likely to be quite small.[11]

EXAMPLE 18.3. Insufficient Lags with an AR(1) Regressor. The data used in the previous example obviously do not fit the assumptions made here. The first eight autocorrelations of $\Delta \ln M1_t$ are 0.0612, 0.2634, 0.1779, 0.0882, 0.2401, 0.0846, 0.3450, and 0.1586, which bear no resemblance to what an AR(1) process would produce. Consider, as an alternative, the consumption data used in Example 18.6. Estimation of some simple, unstructured distributed lag models produces the results shown in Table 18.4.

The stability of the long- and short-run multipliers is striking. The income data are, in fact, strongly autocorrelated, with the pattern of an AR(1) with the parameter close to one. (This may be largely due to a strong trend.) One other result is worth noting. In the eight lags, the *lowest* autocorrelation is 0.993, so these data are as nearly collinear as one is likely to encounter. In the preceding regressions, only the coefficient on current income is ever larger than 1.96 times its standard error, and of the remainder, only the one on Y_{t-1} is ever larger than 1.2 times its standard error. However, in the nine regressions, the estimated standard error of the sum ranges from 0.00398 in the last case to 0.00431 in the first, for *t* ratios of roughly 225. Even though only the impact multiplier can be estimated with any precision in the distributed lag models, the sum of the coefficients is estimable with great precision.

---

[11] An extension in which several lags are omitted is considered in the exercises.

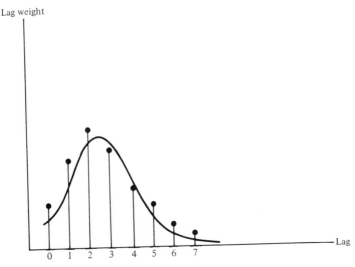

Lag weight

Lag

Figure 18.2 Polynomial approximation

18.2.1b. *Polynomial Distributed Lag Models*

In some settings, the necessary lag length may be extremely long. In principle, this merely extends (18–10), but the problem of multicollinearity is likely to become quite severe, especially in macroeconomic data. In such cases, it is common to impose some structure on the lag distribution, in effect reducing the number of parameters in the model. A model that is quite popular is the **polynomial distributed lag**, or *Almon* (1965) *lag*. The polynomial lag model is based on the assumption that the true distribution of lag coefficients can be well approximated by a polynomial of fairly low order,

$$\beta_i = \alpha_0 + \alpha_1 i + \alpha_2 i^2 + \cdots + \alpha_p i^p, \qquad i = 0, \ldots, q > p. \qquad (18\text{--}12)$$

Figure 18.2 shows the principle. The order of the polynomial, p, is usually taken to be quite low, rarely exceeding three or four.[12]

In addition to the $p + 1$ parameters of the polynomial, there are two unknowns to be determined: the length of the lag structure, q, and the degree of the polynomial, p. We shall return to these later and, for the present, take them as given. By substituting (18–12) in (18–10) and collecting terms, the model can be written

$$
\begin{aligned}
y_t = \alpha + \alpha_0 (x_t &+ x_{t-1} + x_{t-2} + x_{t-3} + \cdots + x_{t-q}) \\
+ \alpha_1 (&\quad x_{t-1} + 2x_{t-2} + 3x_{t-3} + \cdots + qx_{t-q}) \\
+ \alpha_2 (&\quad x_{t-1} + 4x_{t-2} + 9x_{t-3} + \cdots + q^2 x_{t-q}) \\
+ &\qquad\qquad\qquad \vdots \\
+ \alpha_p (&\quad x_{t-1} + 2^p x_{t-2} + 3^p x_{t-3} + \cdots + q^p x_{t-q}) \\
+ \varepsilon_t & \\
= \alpha + \alpha_0 z_{t0} &+ \alpha_1 z_{t1} + \alpha_2 z_{t2} + \cdots + \alpha_p z_{tp} + \varepsilon_t.
\end{aligned}
\qquad (18\text{--}13)
$$

---

[12] See Amemiya and Morimune (1974).

Each z_j is a linear combination of x and the n lagged variables. We can collect the relationships in (18–13) in $\beta = H\alpha$, where

$$
H = \begin{bmatrix}
1 & 0 & 0 & \cdots & 0 \\
1 & 1 & 1 & \cdots & 1 \\
1 & 2 & 4 & \cdots & 2^p \\
1 & 3 & 9 & \cdots & 3^p \\
  &   &   & \vdots & \\
1 & q & q^2 & \cdots & q^p
\end{bmatrix},
\tag{18–14}
$$

and write the full model as

$$
\begin{aligned}
Y &= XH\alpha + \varepsilon \\
&= Z\alpha + \varepsilon.
\end{aligned}
\tag{18–15}
$$

In this formulation, the model can be estimated by ordinary least squares or FGLS if the disturbances are autocorrelated. Once again, this a classical regression model, so no new tools are required. After

$$
\hat{\alpha} = [Z'Z]^{-1}Z'y
\tag{18–16}
$$

has been computed, estimates of the distributed lag coefficients may be recovered using

$$
\hat{\beta} = H\hat{\alpha}.
\tag{18–17}
$$

Asymptotic standard errors may be obtained using

$$
\text{Vâr}[\hat{\beta}] = H\{\text{Var}[\hat{\alpha}]\}H' = s^2 H(Z'Z)^{-1}H'.
\tag{18–18}
$$

It is occasionally suggested that the lag distribution should be "tied down" at its endpoints by imposing $\beta_{-1} = 0$ and $\beta_{q+1} = 0$.[13] Normally, it is inadvisable to impose these restrictions. The model does not pertain to the coefficients outside the interval $[0, \ldots, q]$, so the restrictions are not justifiable on theoretical grounds. But, more importantly, the endpoint restrictions will constrain all of the coefficients in the model, not just the head and tail, in ways that might not be desirable.[14]

EXAMPLE 18.4. Polynomial Distributed Lag Models.   In her pioneering study, Almon (1965) estimated a polynomial lag model for the relationship between appropriations and capital expenditure for "all manufacturing" and a large number of specific industries. The data used for this study are listed in Table 18.5.[15]

Almon's regressions were computed using a fourth-order polynomial and lags extending to seven periods. She also included seasonal dummy variables whose four coefficients were constrained to sum to zero and imposed both endpoint restrictions noted earlier. The results of several regressions are reported in Table 18.6.[16] The maximum likelihood estimates were

---

[13] The implied restrictions are

$$
\beta_{-1} = \alpha_0 - \alpha_1 + \alpha_2 - \cdots = 0,
$$

$$
\beta_{q+1} = \alpha_0 + \alpha_1(q + 1) + \alpha_2(q + 1)^2 + \cdots = 0.
$$

[14] See Schmidt and Waud (1973).

[15] The original study used quarterly data for 1953 to 1961. Longer series (through 1967) for the same variables may be found in Maddala (1977, p. 370) and Judge et al. (1982, p. 734) (through 1974). Those wishing to extend these results to more recent data sets might consider these sources and the original, National Industrial Conference Board, "Survey of Capital Appropriations," *Conference Board Business Record*, various years.

[16] The OLS results under the polynomial lag with $\beta_{-1} = \beta_8 = 0$ do not match those reported by Almon. It was not possible to reproduce her results with these data.

Table 18.5.   Capital Appropriations Data (in $Million)

	Expenditures				Appropriations			
	I	II	III	IV	I	II	III	IV
1953	2072	2077	2078	2043	1660	1926	2181	1897
1954	2062	2067	1964	1981	1695	1705	1731	2151
1955	1914	1991	2129	2309	2556	3152	3763	3903
1956	2614	2896	3058	3309	3912	3571	3199	3262
1957	3446	3466	3435	3183	3476	2993	2262	2011
1958	2697	2338	2140	2012	1511	1631	1990	1993
1959	2071	2192	2240	2421	2520	2804	2919	3024
1960	2639	2733	2721	2640	2725	2321	2131	2552
1961	2513	2448	2429	2516	2234	2282	2533	2517

Table 18.6.   Polynomial Distributed Lag Models

	Unrestricted Model		Polynomial Lag		Polynomial Lag with $\beta_{-1} = \beta_8 = 0$	
	OLS	MLE	OLS	MLE	OLS	MLE
Qtr. I	−2.97	1.01	−6.98	−5.95	−13.30	−7.96
Qtr. II	−5.54	−0.51	−8.76	−3.00	−7.02	−3.36
Qtr. III	−23.31	−14.81	−15.70	−6.41	−7.63	−4.16
Qtr. IV	31.84	14.31	31.44	15.36	27.95	15.48
$t − 0$	0.040	0.065	0.027	0.059	0.087	0.090
$t − 1$	0.110	0.090	0.144	0.131	0.123	0.133
$t − 2$	0.189	0.199	0.182	0.169	0.134	0.147
$t − 3$	0.223	0.218	0.165	0.170	0.137	0.148
$t − 4$	0.070	0.092	0.122	0.141	0.139	0.143
$t − 5$	0.064	0.074	0.085	0.102	0.139	0.134
$t − 6$	0.139	0.140	0.088	0.085	0.129	0.115
$t − 7$	0.146	0.113	0.168	0.133	0.092	0.076
Sum	0.981	0.991	0.981	0.990	0.980	0.986
R^2	0.9189	—	0.9177	—	0.9142	—
$D − W$	0.406	—	0.445	—	0.445	—
$\ln L$	—	−168.22	—	−169.49	—	−169.87

obtained using Beach and MacKinnon's method for AR(1) disturbances. For brevity, only the overall test statistics are reported.

Note the similarity of the polynomial lag coefficients to the unrestricted least squares estimates. The F test of the restrictions implied by the polynomial model is far from significant by any standard. Figure 18.3 shows the three lag distributions estimated by least squares. In principle, the sum of the lag coefficients should be one if all appropriations ultimately become expenditures within the length of time of the longest lag. Our results come quite close to this sum. (Almon's estimate of the long-run multiplier for this model was 0.922. She attributed the discrepancy to cancellations of past appropriations.)

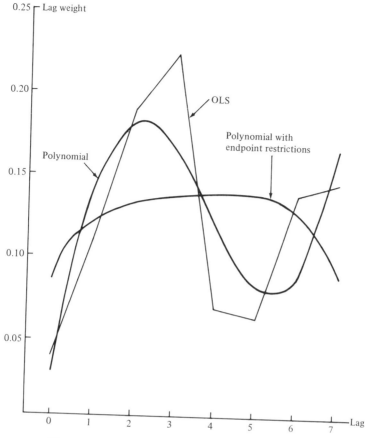

Figure 18.3   Polynomial lags for investment.

DETERMINING THE DEGREE OF THE POLYNOMIAL

If the appropriate lag length, q, is known, determining the right degree for the polynomial becomes a problem of testing nested hypotheses. It helps to note, first, that if we use a q-degree polynomial when the maximum lag is q, then $\mathbf{H}$ is square, and we simply have $\boldsymbol{\alpha} = \mathbf{H}^{-1}\boldsymbol{\beta}$. As a consequence, the $q + 1$ OLS estimates (including the coefficient on x_t) will fit exactly on the qth-order polynomial. The polynomial lag model thus places no restrictions on the coefficients. Successively lower-order polynomials do impose restrictions. A sequential testing procedure may be used by beginning with a high-order polynomial, say p^*—absent any knowledge about p^*, we might use $p^* = q$—and reducing its degree by one in successive regressions.[17] At each step, the F statistic for testing a polynomial of degree p against one of degree p^* is

$$F(p^* - p, T - p^* - 1) = \frac{[\mathbf{e'e}|p - \mathbf{e'e}|p^*]/(p^* - p)}{\mathbf{e'e}|p^*/(T - p^* - 1)}. \qquad (18\text{–}19)$$

[17] See Godfrey and Poskitt (1975).

(The denominator degrees of freedom is reduced if there are other coefficients, such as a constant term in the model.) The appropriate degree of the polynomial is assumed to be the lowest p for which the statistic in (18–19) is less than the appropriate critical value from the F table. It must be remembered, though, that at each step except the first, the true significance level differs from the nominal one because of the probability of a type 2 error at the previous step. Trivedi and Pagan[18] suggest that the appropriate significance level at the jth step is

$$\alpha'_j = 1 - (1 - \alpha_1)(1 - \alpha_2) \cdots (1 - \alpha_j). \tag{18–20}$$

If, as would be common, the same nominal significance level is used at each step, the true significance level would be

$$\alpha'_j = 1 - (1 - \alpha)^j.$$

For example, at the usual 5 percent significance level, we would have 5 percent, 9.75 percent, 14.26 percent, and so on, for the sequential tests. The practical implication is that at successively lower levels, we should require progressively higher F statistics to reject the restrictions at the same true significance level.

ESTIMATION BY RESTRICTED LEAST SQUARES

If there are n lags in the model, the polynomial lag model imposes $n - p$ constraints on the parameters. A pth-order polynomial lag structure implies the constraints

$$(1 - L)^{p+1} \beta_i = 0.[19]$$

For example, for a third-order polynomial, the restrictions would be

$$\beta_0 - 4\beta_1 + 6\beta_2 - 4\beta_3 + \beta_4 \quad\; = 0,$$
$$\beta_1 - 4\beta_2 + 6\beta_3 - 4\beta_4 + \beta_5 = 0,$$

and so on. Thus the polynomial distributed lag model can also be estimated using constrained least squares. Ignoring for the moment any other parameters (such as the constant term) that might appear in the model, the restrictions of the polynomial lag model may be written in the form

$$\mathbf{R}\boldsymbol{\beta} = \mathbf{0}. \tag{18–21}$$

The elements in $\mathbf{R}$ can be obtained from Pascal's triangle,

$$
\begin{array}{ccccccc}
 & & & 1 & & & \\
 & & 1 & & -1 & & \\
 & 1 & & -2 & & 1 & \\
1 & & -3 & & 3 & & -1 \\
\end{array}
\tag{18–22}
$$

$$
\begin{array}{cccccc}
1 & -4 & 6 & -4 & 1 \\
 & & \vdots & & \\
\end{array}
$$

and so on. Each value is the sum of the two nearest values above it, while the signs in each row alternate beginning with positive. For a pth-order polynomial, the relevant row is the

[18] Op. cit.
[19] See, for example, Fomby et al. (1984, pp. 375–377).

$p + $ 1st. Then the matrix for the restrictions is

$$
R = \begin{bmatrix} p' & 0 & 0 & \cdots & 0 \\ 0 & p' & 0 & \cdots & 0 \\ & & \vdots & & \\ 0 & 0 & 0 & \cdots & p' \end{bmatrix}.
\tag{18-23}
$$

There are two practical advantages to this approach. First, if the maximum lag length is known, the entire analysis of the polynomial lags may be based on the single unrestricted regression involving the full set of lagged variables. Second, considerable rounding error can accumulate in the calculation of the "scrambled variables" in (18–13), while the restricted regression is computed with the full precision of least squares. In a relatively low-order polynomial, the problem will be insignificant. But for higher-order models, particularly if the data are highly collinear, the differences can be quite large.[20]

DETERMINING THE LAG LENGTH

If the lag length is unknown, the problem of inference is compounded.[21] One possible procedure would be first to determine the lag length, using the OLS or GLS estimates and the procedures described in the previous section. Once the maximum lag is determined, we may then employ the method just described to determine the appropriate degree of the polynomial. Unfortunately, unless the test statistics are overwhelming, a large amount of caution must be exercised. The true significance levels in these tests remain to be derived, and the true distribution of the resulting estimator is unknown.

There has been extensive analysis of the consequences of misspecifying the lag length and order of the polynomial in the polynomial lag model. The generalities are what intuition would suggest. Assuming that there is a true polynomial and lag length, fitting a polynomial of insufficient order is equivalent to imposing invalid restrictions.[22] Overfitting the polynomial would lead only to inefficiency, since if the lag coefficients lie on a polynomial of order p, they will also lie on one of order $p + 1$, $p + 2$, and so on. The consequences of misspecifying the lag length are somewhat more complicated. Underestimating the lag length leads to the usual results. However, overfitting the lag may not be so harmless here. In an unrestricted model, the zero coefficients on superfluous variables would be consistently estimated by least squares. However, if we force the coefficients to lie on a polynomial, the restriction may force a coefficient that is truly zero to be nonzero in the model.[23]

18.2.1c.   Shiller's Smoothness Prior

Shiller (1973) has argued that one's prior beliefs about the shape of a lag distribution are unlikely to be as sharp as the polynomial lag model would suggest. (A less sympathetic view is that the restrictions of the polynomial model are motivated not by a prior theory but simply by a desire to obtain a pleasing shape for the lag distribution.) His suggestion is to make the restrictions in (18–21) stochastic rather than deterministic,

$$
R\beta + v = 0,
\tag{18-24}
$$

[20] See Cooper (1972).
[21] Frost (1975).
[22] This assumption may be a bit optimistic. See Schmidt and Sickles (1975).
[23] See, for instance, Schmidt and Waud (1973), Trivedi and Pagan (1979), Hendry et al. (1984), and Schmidt and Sickles (1975) for extensive discussion.

where v is an $(n - p)$ variate random vector. We can incorporate (18–24) in the model by writing

$$\begin{bmatrix} \mathbf{y} \\ \mathbf{0} \end{bmatrix} = \begin{bmatrix} \mathbf{X} \\ \mathbf{R} \end{bmatrix} \boldsymbol{\beta} + \begin{bmatrix} \boldsymbol{\varepsilon} \\ \mathbf{v} \end{bmatrix}. \tag{18–25}$$

Assume that the variance matrix of $\mathbf{v}$ is $\lambda^2 \mathbf{I}$. If λ^2 and σ^2 are known, (18–25) can be estimated using the procedure for groupwise heteroscedasticity discussed in Chapter 14. The GLS estimator of $\boldsymbol{\beta}$ would be

$$\hat{\boldsymbol{\beta}} = \left(\frac{1}{\sigma^2} \mathbf{X}'\mathbf{X} + \frac{1}{\lambda^2} \mathbf{R}'\mathbf{R} \right)^{-1} \left(\frac{1}{\sigma^2} \mathbf{X}'\mathbf{y} + \frac{1}{\lambda^2} \mathbf{R}'\mathbf{0} \right) \tag{18–26}$$

$$= [\mathbf{X}'\mathbf{X} + k\mathbf{R}'\mathbf{R}]^{-1} \mathbf{X}'\mathbf{y},$$

where

$$k = \frac{\sigma^2}{\lambda^2}. \,^{24}$$

If k is zero, $\hat{\boldsymbol{\beta}}$ is the unrestricted OLS estimator. Referring back to (18–21), we see that $\lambda^2 = 0$ corresponds to the exact restrictions of the Almon estimator.[25] In practice, σ^2 can be estimated using the unrestricted OLS residuals. Shiller suggests

$$\hat{\lambda}^2 = \frac{64 [\sum_i \beta_i]}{(q + 1)^4}. \tag{18–27}$$

For $\sum_i \beta_i$, one can use either the sum of the coefficients in the unrestricted regression—this could be justified by the presumed consistency of ordinary least squares—or one, on the presumption that any impulse into the system will ultimately be fully distributed if the model is correctly specified.

EXAMPLE 18.5. Shiller Smoothness Priors. Using the ordinary least squares results of Example 18.4 gives an estimate of σ^2 of 155.24^2. The sum of the weights is 0.982 and the lag length is 7, so Shiller's rule-of-thumb estimate of λ^2 is 0.1228^2. The estimate of k is, thus, 1,598,124. The estimated lag coefficients for the unrestricted model, the polynomial model with exact restrictions, and Shiller's smoothness prior are shown in Table 18.7. The similarity of the Shiller estimator to the Almon estimator has been widely observed, and follows from the fact that his rule-of-thumb estimator of λ often leads to a very tight prior for the variance of the restrictions.[26]

Table 18.7

Lag	0	1	2	3	4	5	6	7
OLS	0.040	0.110	0.189	0.223	0.070	0.064	0.139	0.146
Almon	0.026	0.144	0.182	0.165	0.123	0.085	0.087	0.168
Shiller	0.027	0.142	0.183	0.167	0.121	0.084	0.090	0.167

[24] This is an example of a *mixed estimator*. See Theil and Goldberger (1961) and Taylor (1974).
[25] For discussion, see Shiller (1973).
[26] See Maddala (1977) for discussion. Note that the discrepancy of the estimate of λ obtained here with Maddala's follows from his use of n^2 instead of $(n + 1)^4$ in the denominator.

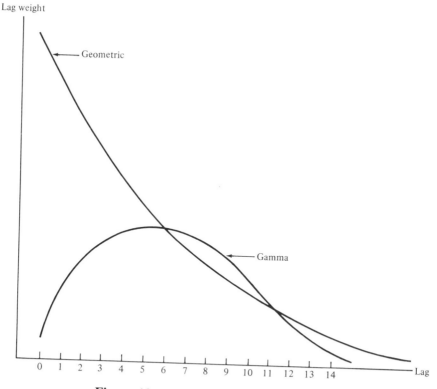

Lag weight

Figure 18.4   Infinite lag distributions.

18.2.2. Infinite Distributed Lag Models

Estimation of the unrestricted model of (18–10) will be difficult at best. The polynomial lag model reduces the problem, but even with Shiller's modification, it has some troubling limitations. Finding the right degree for the polynomial and the appropriate lag length presents difficult inference problems. The infinite lag model is often preferable but, obviously, some restrictions have to be placed on the parameters in order to make it estimable. These considerations have led researchers to formulate compact parametric models that allow infinite lags but require only a small number of parameters.

The similarity of the lag weights in a distributed lag model to discrete probabilities has suggested a number of formulations. The geometric lag model,

$$w_i = (1 - \lambda)\lambda^i, \qquad 0 \le \lambda < 1, \tag{18–28}$$

and the gamma lag model,[27]

$$w_i = (i + 1)^\gamma \lambda^i, \qquad 0 \le \lambda < 1, \qquad 0 < \gamma < 1, \tag{18–29}$$

shown in Figure 18.4, are two examples of infinite lag models. Both models incorporate infinite lags but assign arbitrarily small weights to the distant past. The geometric lag model is by far the most popular distributed lag model in the empirical literature, so we will examine it in detail. Some alternatives will be considered at the end of the section.

---

[27] Tsurumi (1971), Theil and Stern (1960), and Schmidt (1974b).

18.2.2a. Geometric Lag Models

There are many cases in which the distributed lag is a model of the accumulation of information. The formation of expectations is an example. In these instances, intuition suggests that the most recent past will receive the greatest weight in the process, and the influence of past observations will fade uniformly with the passage of time. The **geometric lag model** is a commonly used tool for these settings.

The geometric lag model is

$$\beta_i = \beta(1 - \lambda)\lambda^i. \tag{18-30}$$

Thus,

$$y_t = \alpha + \beta \sum_{i=0}^{\infty} (1 - \lambda)\lambda^i x_{t-i} + \varepsilon_t. \tag{18-31}$$

The mean lag is

$$\bar{w} = \frac{B'(1)}{B(1)}, \tag{18-32}$$

where

$$B(L) = \frac{1 - \lambda}{1 - \lambda L}.$$

Thus,

$$\bar{w} = \frac{\lambda}{1 - \lambda}.$$

The median lag is q^* such that

$$\sum_{i=0}^{q^*-1} w_i = 0.5. \tag{18-33}$$

We can solve for q^* by using the result

$$\sum_{i=0}^{q} \lambda^i = \frac{1 - \lambda^{q+1}}{1 - \lambda}.$$

Thus,

$$q^* = \frac{\ln. 5}{\ln \lambda}.$$

The impact multiplier is $\beta(1 - \lambda)$. The long-run multiplier is

$$\beta(1 - \lambda)\sum_i \lambda^i = \beta.^{28}$$

The model was initially associated with Koyck's (1954) study of investment. It also arises naturally in two familiar economic frameworks: models of expectations and models of partial adjustment. The **adaptive expectations model** consists of a regression equation,

$$y_t = \alpha + \beta x_t^* + \varepsilon_t, \tag{18-34}$$

---

[28] We should raise a warning flag here. The geometric lag model is often *written* with $\beta_i = \beta\lambda^i$. In this form, the *short-run* multiplier is β, while the long-run multiplier is $\dfrac{\beta}{1 - \lambda}$.

in the expectations variable, x_t^*, and a mechanism for the formation of the expectation based on the current observation, x_t,

$$x_t^* - x_{t-1}^* = (1 - \lambda)(x_t - x_{t-1}^*).$$ (18–35)

An example would be a demand equation based on an expected price. The expectation would be revised after observing the current outcome. This suggests a more intuitively appealing, equivalent form.

$$x_t^* = \lambda x_{t-1}^* + (1 - \lambda)x_t.$$ (18–36)

Thus, the currently formed expectation is a weighted average of the previous expectation and the most recent observation. The parameter λ is the adjustment coefficient. If λ equals one, the current datum is ignored and expectations are never revised. A value of zero characterizes a strict pragmatist. The model can be "solved" by writing (18–35) as

$$x_t^* = \lambda L x_t^* + (1 - \lambda)x_t$$

or

$$x_t^* = \frac{1 - \lambda}{1 - \lambda L} x_t$$ (18–37)

$$= (1 - \lambda)[x_t + \lambda x_{t-1} + \lambda^2 x_{t-2} + \cdots].$$

Inserting (18–37) in (18–34) leads to a regression with geometrically declining weights,

$$y_t = \alpha + \beta(1 - \lambda)(x_t + \lambda x_{t-1} + \lambda^2 x_{t-2} + \cdots) + \varepsilon_t.$$ (18–38)

(In this form, it would probably provide a suitable model for Example 18.1.)

It may be reasonable to treat ε_t in (18–38) as a spherical, serially independent disturbance, which makes (18–38) a classical regression. If, instead, ε_t is autocorrelated, it will be necessary to adapt a method of FGLS. In either case, the primary obstacle to estimation will be the infinite number of regressors.

The model in (18–38) is called the **moving average (MA)** form. (It is also called the **distributed lag** form.) The **autoregressive (AR)** form is an alternative that is often useful. We insert (18–37) in (18–34) to obtain

$$y_t = \alpha + \beta\left(\frac{1 - \lambda}{1 - \lambda L}\right)x_t + \varepsilon_t,$$

multiply through by $(1 - \lambda L)$, and collect terms in

$$y_t = \alpha(1 - \lambda) + \lambda y_{t-1} + \beta(1 - \lambda)x_t + (\varepsilon_t - \lambda \varepsilon_{t-1}).$$ (18–39)

The autoregressive form is commonly used in demand equations. If the variables are in logarithms, the short-run elasticity is $\beta(1 - \lambda)$ and the long-run elasticity is β. But for the (serious) complication of a lagged dependent variable appearing with an autocorrelated disturbance, the parameters could be estimated by ordinary least squares or two-step generalized least squares. Unfortunately, without some special assumptions, neither of these methods will provide consistent estimates.

The primary equation of the **partial adjustment** model describes the *desired* level of y_t:

$$y_t^* = \alpha + \beta x_t.$$ (18–40)

For example, this might describe a rule for the optimal inventory level as a function of sales. The adjustment of the actual level is a proportion of the difference between this period's desired level and last period's actual level:

$$y_t - y_{t-1} = (1 - \lambda)(y_t^* - y_{t-1}) + \varepsilon_t. \tag{18-41}$$

In the alternative form,

$$y_t = (1 - \lambda)y_t^* + y_{t-1} + \varepsilon_t,$$

the actual, current level is a weighted average of the desired level and last period's actual level. The adjustment parameter reflects the degree to which the input variable, x_t, will be incorporated in y_t. To continue the example, $\lambda = 0$ would reflect a fixed-inventory policy, while $\lambda = 1$ would make desired inventory a function only of current sales.

Inserting (18–40) in (18–41) produces the autoregressive form,

$$y_t = \alpha(1 - \lambda) + \lambda y_{t-1} + \beta(1 - \lambda)x_t + \varepsilon_t. \tag{18-42}$$

[Note the similarity to (18–39).] Alternatively, we may write (18–42) as

$$y_t(1 - \lambda L) = \alpha(1 - \lambda) + \beta(1 - \lambda)x_t + \varepsilon_t.$$

Dividing both sides by $[1 - \lambda L]$ and expanding produces the moving average form,

$$y_t = \alpha + \beta(1 - \lambda) \sum_{i=0}^{\infty} \lambda^i x_{t-i} + \sum_{i=0}^{\infty} \lambda^i \varepsilon_{t-i}. \tag{18-43}$$

The infinite moving average disturbance can be written as

$$u_t = \lambda u_{t-1} + \varepsilon_t. \tag{18-44}$$

Therefore, the moving average form of the partial adjustment model has an AR(1) disturbance with the same parameter as the lag weights. Note, again, that apart from the disturbance, the MA form of the partial adjustment model in (18–43) is the same as that of the adaptive expectations model in (18–38).

18.2.2b.   Stochastic Specifications in the Geometric Lag Model

The most efficient means of estimating the parameters of the geometric lag model will depend on the stochastic specification of the structural disturbance, ε_t, in (18–34) and (18–41). We typically consider two possibilities:

1. **White noise:** ε_t is homoscedastic and not autocorrelated.
2. **AR(1):** $\varepsilon_t = \rho \varepsilon_{t-1} + u_t$, where u_t is a white noise series.

The model can be estimated either in the moving average form or the autoregressive form. This might provide a useful test of the specification, since we should obtain the same estimates either way, apart from sampling variation.[29]

18.2.2c.   Estimating the MA Form of the Geometric Lag Model

The MA form of the geometric lag model is most convenient for the adaptive expectations model. If ε_t in (18–34) is white noise, the resulting MA form in (18–38) is a classical regression. Likewise, if ε_t is autocorrelated, (18–34) can, in principle, be estimated using the methods of Chapter 15. We consider these two possibilities in turn, with reference to the adaptive expectations model. We shall then consider the partial adjustment model.

---

[29] Estimation of the moving average form will, in general, be preferable, as it is more robust to misspecification of autocorrelation in the disturbance. See Maddala and Rao (1971).

UNCORRELATED DISTURBANCES

We may write (18–31) as

$$y_t = \alpha + \beta(1 - \lambda) \sum_{i=0}^{\infty} \lambda^i x_{t-i} + \varepsilon_t$$

$$= \alpha + \beta(1 - \lambda)(x_t + \lambda x_{t-1} + \cdots + \lambda^{t-1} x_1) \tag{18–45}$$

$$+ \beta(1 - \lambda)\lambda^t(x_0 + \lambda x_{-1} + \cdots) + \varepsilon_t.$$

The third term is

$$\mu^0 = E[y_0 - \alpha].$$

If we treat this *truncation remainder* as an unknown parameter, the model becomes

$$y_t = \alpha + \beta(1 - \lambda)x_t^* + \lambda^t \mu^0 + \varepsilon_t,$$

where
$$\tag{18–46}$$

$$x_t^* = x_t + \lambda x_{t-1} + \cdots + \lambda^{t-1} x_1.$$

This is a nonlinear regression model. The log likelihood is

$$\ln L(\alpha, \beta, \lambda, \mu^0, \sigma_\varepsilon^2) = -\frac{T}{2}(\ln(2\pi) + \ln \sigma_\varepsilon^2) - \frac{1}{2\sigma_\varepsilon^2} \sum_t \varepsilon_t^2, \tag{18–47}$$

where

$$\varepsilon_t = y_t - \alpha - \beta(1 - \lambda)x_t^* - \mu^0 \lambda^t.$$

Maximum likelihood estimates can be obtained by nonlinear least squares.[30] The maximum likelihood estimator of σ_ε^2 is the usual one,

$$\hat{\sigma}_\varepsilon^2 = \frac{1}{T} \sum_t \hat{\varepsilon}_t^2. \tag{18–48}$$

For a given value of λ, estimates of α, $k = \beta(1 - \lambda)$, and μ^0 can be obtained by a *linear* regression of y_t on a constant, x_t^*, and λ^t. Since λ is between zero and one, the estimates can be computed by searching over values of λ between zero and one and choosing as the set of estimates those associated with the value of λ that produces the smallest sum of squared residuals. In practice, x_t^* may be computed by the recursion

$$x_1^* = x_1,$$
$$\tag{18–49}$$
$$x_t^* = x_t + \lambda x_{t-1}^*.$$

The estimates of the standard errors of the parameters may be obtained from the inverse of the information matrix,

$$\mathbf{I}(\alpha, k, \mu^0, \lambda, \sigma_\varepsilon^2) = \frac{1}{\sigma_\varepsilon^2} \begin{bmatrix} T & & & & \\ \sum_t x_t^* & \sum_t x_t^{*2} & & & \\ \sum_t \lambda^t & \sum_t \lambda^t x_t^* & \sum_t (\lambda^t)^2 & & \\ \sum_t \Delta_t & \sum_t \Delta_t x_t^* & \sum_t \Delta_t \lambda^t & \sum_t \Delta_t^2 & \\ 0 & 0 & 0 & 0 & T/2\sigma_\varepsilon^2 \end{bmatrix}, \tag{18–50}$$

[30] See Dhrymes (1969).

where

$$\Delta_t = \frac{\partial(kx_t^* + \mu^0\lambda^t)}{\partial\lambda}$$

$$= k\frac{\partial x_t^*}{\partial\lambda} + \mu^0 t\lambda^{t-1}.$$

(18–51)

The sample values of $\partial x_t^*/\partial\lambda$ may also be computed by a recursion. Using (18–49), we obtain

$$\frac{\partial x_1^*}{\partial\lambda} = 0,$$

$$\frac{\partial x_2^*}{\partial\lambda} = x_1,$$

(18–52)

and

$$\frac{\partial x_t^*}{\partial\lambda} = \lambda\frac{\partial x_{t-1}^*}{\partial\lambda} + x_{t-1}^*, \qquad t = 3, \dots, T. \qquad (18–53)$$

Finally,

$$\hat{\beta} = \frac{\hat{k}}{1 - \hat{\lambda}}. \qquad (18–54)$$

The asymptotic standard error of this estimate may be estimated with

$$\text{Var}[\hat{\beta}] = \left(\frac{\partial\hat{\beta}}{\partial\hat{k}}\right)^2 \text{Var}[\hat{k}] + \left(\frac{\partial\hat{\beta}}{\partial\hat{\lambda}}\right)^2 \text{Var}[\hat{\lambda}] + 2\left(\frac{\partial\hat{\beta}}{\partial\hat{k}}\right)\left(\frac{\partial\hat{\beta}}{\partial\hat{\lambda}}\right)\text{Cov}[\hat{k}, \hat{\lambda}].^{31} \quad (18–55)$$

There is a question as to whether one need even bother with the truncation remainder. Asymptotically, it makes no difference. As $T \to \infty$, the column of values λ^t will be predominately zeroes.[32] Nonetheless, there is some evidence that it can make a considerable difference in a small sample. The available results suggest that it is better to keep the truncation remainder than to omit it.[33]

AUTOREGRESSIVE DISTURBANCES

If the disturbance in (18–31) is autocorrelated, with

$$\varepsilon_t = \rho\varepsilon_{t-1} + u_t,$$

the preceding may be applied to the transformed model,

$$[y_t - \rho y_{t-1}] = \alpha(1 - \rho) + k[x_t^* - \rho x_{t-1}^*] + \mu^0[\lambda^t - \rho\lambda^{t-1}] + [\varepsilon_t - \rho\varepsilon_{t-1}]. \quad (18–56)$$

For a given value of ρ, we would use the method of the previous paragraphs. A method for finding the full set of parameters would be a two-dimensional search over values of λ from zero to one and over ρ from minus one to one. The pair that, with the associated least squares estimates of the other parameters, produces the smallest sum of squared deviations gives the maximum likelihood estimates.[34] The inverse of the information provides an estimate of the

[31] See Section 4.4.4 and Theorem 4.4.
[32] Consequently, $\hat{\mu}^0$ is not consistent.
[33] See Schmidt (1975), Pesaran (1973), and Maddala and Rao (1971).
[34] This analysis is conditioned on the first observation. See Chapter 15 for an analysis of the unconditional approach.

asymptotic covariance matrix of the estimates. In (18–57), the operator δ is used to indicate the partial difference, as in $\delta x_t^* = x_t^* - \rho x_{t-1}^*$. The information matrix is

$$
\mathbf{I}
\begin{bmatrix}
\alpha \\
k \\
\mu^0 \\
\lambda \\
\sigma_u^2 \\
\rho
\end{bmatrix}
= \frac{1}{\sigma_u^2}
\begin{bmatrix}
T(1-\rho) \\
\Sigma_t \delta x_t^* & \Sigma_t (\delta x_t^*)^2 \\
\Sigma_t \delta \lambda^t & \Sigma_t \delta \lambda^t \delta x_t^* & \Sigma_t (\delta \lambda^t)^2 \\
\Sigma_t \delta \Delta_t & \Sigma_t \delta \Delta_t \delta x_t^* & \Sigma_t \delta \Delta_t \delta \lambda^t & \Sigma_t (\delta \Delta_t)^2 \\
0 & 0 & 0 & 0 & T/2\sigma_u^2 \\
0 & 0 & 0 & 0 & 0 & T\sigma_u^2/(1-\rho^2)
\end{bmatrix}.
\tag{18–57}
$$

EXAMPLE 18.6. Consumption Function.   In a widely cited study, Zellner and Geisel (1970) applied the foregoing results to estimation of a consumption function,

$$ C_t = \beta Y_t^* + \varepsilon_t, $$

where C_t is consumption and Y_t^* is normal real income. Normal income satisfies the adjustment model,

$$ Y_t^* = (1 - \lambda)Y_t + \lambda Y_{t-1}^*. $$

From (18–37), we obtain

$$ Y_t^* = (1 - \lambda)(Y_t + \lambda Y_{t-1} + \lambda^2 Y_{t-2} \cdots), $$

which, when inserted in the consumption function, produces the geometric lag model. This differs from the earlier treatment in the absence of a constant term. The authors estimated the model using quarterly data on U.S. consumption and disposable personal income for the years 1947 to 1960.[35] In this example, we shall reestimate the model using more recent data, and then compare our results to those of Zellner and Geisel.

Table 18.8 lists quarterly data for real consumption and real disposable income for the years 1953 to 1984.[36]

For the model with uncorrelated disturbances, the search over the values of λ produced the results shown in Table 18.9. The global minimum occurs at $\lambda = 0.25$. The full set of results based on $\hat{\lambda} = 0.25$ is shown in Table 18.10. It is useful to compare the implied lag coefficients to those obtained by unrestricted ordinary least squares. The OLS estimates are given in Example 18.3. For the first three periods, the OLS estimates are 0.668, 0.203, and 0.037.[37] The corresponding values for the geometric lag model are $\beta(1 - \lambda) = 0.682$, $\beta(1 - \lambda)\lambda = 0.171$, and $\beta(1 - \lambda)\lambda^2 = 0.043$.

In their study, Zellner and Geisel found two minima of the sum of squares function, a local minimum at $[\lambda, \beta] = [0.45, 0.937]$ and the global minimum at $[0.96, 1.129]$. The optimal value of β is implausible on theoretical grounds. The authors attributed the result to possible inadequacies of the model or the data. With the more recent data, $\hat{\beta}$ is between 0 and 1, as expected, and the likelihood function has a single maximum. The Durbin–Watson statistic based on the nonlinear least squares residuals is 0.5960. While the Durbin–Watson tables are not quite appropriate because this is not a linear regression model with nonstochastic regressors, a value this small is nonetheless compelling. The estimated

---

[35] Their data are listed in Griliches et al. (1962).

[36] The data are from the National Income and Product Accounts, U.S. Department of Commerce, Bureau of Economic Analysis, "Survey of Current Business: Business Statistics, 1984," Washington, D.C., 1984, pp. 205, 212, and 221. The data are normalized to 1972 dollars, using the implicit price deflator for personal consumption.

[37] After three periods, the OLS estimates become small and negative.

Table 18.8. Consumption and Income Data

	Consumption				Disposable Income			
Year	I	II	III	IV	I	II	III	IV
1953	362.8	364.6	363.6	362.6	395.5	401.0	399.7	400.2
1954	363.5	366.2	371.8	378.6	399.7	397.3	403.8	411.8
1955	385.2	392.2	396.4	402.6	414.7	423.8	430.8	437.6
1956	403.2	403.9	405.1	409.3	441.2	444.7	446.6	452.7
1957	411.7	412.4	415.2	416.0	452.6	455.4	457.9	456.0
1958	411.0	414.7	420.9	425.2	452.1	455.1	464.6	471.3
1959	424.1	439.7	443.3	444.6	474.5	482.2	479.0	483.1
1960	448.1	454.1	452.7	453.2	487.8	490.7	491.0	488.8
1961	454.0	459.9	461.4	470.3	493.4	500.7	505.5	514.8
1962	474.5	479.8	483.7	490.0	519.5	523.9	526.7	529.0
1963	493.1	497.4	503.9	507.5	533.3	538.9	544.4	552.5
1964	516.6	525.6	534.3	535.3	563.6	579.4	586.4	593.0
1965	546.0	550.7	559.2	573.9	599.7	607.8	623.6	634.6
1966	581.2	582.3	588.6	590.5	639.7	642.0	649.2	700.7
1967	594.8	602.4	605.2	608.2	665.0	671.3	676.5	682.0
1968	620.7	629.9	642.3	644.7	690.4	701.9	703.6	708.7
1969	651.9	656.2	659.6	663.9	710.4	717.0	730.1	733.2
1970	667.4	670.5	676.5	673.9	737.1	752.6	759.7	756.1
1971	687.0	693.3	698.2	708.6	771.3	779.7	781.0	785.5
1972	718.6	731.1	741.3	757.1	791.7	798.5	842.2	838.1
1973	768.8	766.3	769.7	766.7	855.0	862.1	868.0	873.4
1974	761.2	764.1	769.4	756.5	859.9	859.7	859.7	851.1
1975	763.3	775.6	785.4	793.3	845.1	891.3	878.4	884.9
1976	809.9	817.1	826.5	838.9	899.3	904.1	908.8	914.9
1977	851.7	858.0	867.3	880.4	919.6	934.1	951.9	965.9
1978	883.8	901.1	908.6	919.2	973.5	982.6	994.2	1005.0
1979	921.2	919.5	930.9	938.6	1011.1	1011.8	1019.7	1020.2
1980	938.3	919.6	929.4	940.0	1025.9	1011.8	1019.3	1030.2
1981	950.2	949.1	955.7	946.8	1044.0	1041.0	1058.4	1056.0
1982	953.7	958.9	964.2	976.3	1052.8	1054.7	1057.7	1067.5
1983	982.5	1006.2	1015.6	1032.4	1073.3	1082.2	1102.1	1124.4
1984	1044.1	1064.2	1065.9	1075.4	1147.8	1165.3	1176.7	1186.9

Table 18.9

λ	$e'e$	$\beta(1-\lambda)$	μ^0	λ	$e'e$	$\beta(1-\lambda)$	μ^0
0.05	11,284	0.86191	438.37	0.40	11,180	0.54718	365.48
0.10	11,114	0.81695	397.38	0.45	11,428	0.50222	364.05
0.15	10,991	0.77199	383.62	0.50	11,775	0.45725	362.85
0.20	10,915	0.72703	376.64	0.55	12,240	0.41228	361.83
0.21	10,906	0.71804	375.63	0.60	12,850	0.36730	360.97
0.22	10,899	0.70905	374.71	0.65	13,632	0.32231	360.28
0.23	10,894	0.70006	373.86	0.70	14,623	0.27732	359.78
0.24	10,891	0.69105	373.08	0.75	15,856	0.23232	359.48
0.25	10,890	0.68207	372.36	0.80	17,380	0.18732	359.36
0.26	10,892	0.67308	371.69	0.85	19,324	0.14232	359.32
0.30	10,922	0.63711	369.41	0.90	22,375	0.09736	359.14
0.35	11,015	0.59215	367.21	0.95	30,033	0.05252	359.31

Table 18.10

Parameter	Estimate	Standard Error
β	0.9094	0.00369
λ	0.25	0.0901
μ^0	364.13	36.33
σ_ε^2	85.08	7.52
$\lambda/(1-\lambda)$	0.3333	0.1602

Table 18.11

Parameter	Estimate	Std. Error	Zellner and Geisel Estimate	Zellner and Geisel Std. Error
λ	0.64	0.0080	0.66	0.085
β	0.9205	0.0451	0.94	0.46
μ^0	368.31	30.54	—	—
σ_u^2	26.58	2.359	8.07	—
ρ	0.87	0.044	0.69	0.076
σ_ε^2	110.24	16.24	—	—
$\lambda/(1-\lambda)$	1.78	0.062	1.94	0.735

autocorrelation given in the following table is 0.87. Zellner and Geisel's estimate of the same parameter is 0.69. Thus, there is considerable evidence of autocorrelation in both data sets.

A two-dimensional search over λ and ρ produced the results shown in Table 18.11; we present both our results and those of Zellner and Geisel for comparison. The estimate of σ_ε^2 is $\hat{\sigma}_u^2/(1-\hat{\rho}^2)$. The standard errors for $\hat{\sigma}_\varepsilon^2$ and $\hat{\lambda}/(1-\hat{\lambda})$ are estimated using the variance of a nonlinear function. Note the similarity of the estimates of λ and β for the two data sets.

ESTIMATING THE MA FORM OF THE PARTIAL ADJUSTMENT MODEL

The MA form of the partial adjustment model is exactly the second case we looked at earlier in (18–56) and (18–57), with the additional restriction that $\rho = \lambda$. [See (18–43) and (18–44).] Let us see what becomes of the estimator if we impose this restriction. Referring to (18–56), it is immediately apparent that the truncation remainder vanishes. In addition, in (18–49), if $\rho = \lambda$, then $(x_t^* - \rho x_{t-1}^*)$ equals x_t. This implies that the estimating equation (18–56) is

$$(y_t - \lambda y_{t-1}) = \alpha(1-\lambda) + kxt + u_t$$

or

$$y_t = \alpha(1-\lambda) + \beta(1-\lambda)x_t + \lambda y_{t-1} + u_t. \qquad (18-56')$$

Therefore, in the partial adjustment model with uncorrelated disturbances, efficient estimates of $\alpha(1-\lambda)$, $\beta(1-\lambda)$, and λ are obtained by linear least squares regression of y_t on a constant, x_t, and y_{t-1}.

18.2.2d. Estimation of the Autoregressive Form

The autoregressive model is

$$y_t = \alpha(1 - \lambda) + \beta(1 - \lambda)x_t + \lambda y_{t-1} + \varepsilon_t. \tag{18-58}$$

The lagged dependent variable removes this model from the classical regression framework. Depending on the initial formulation of ε_t, we find that the estimation may be further complicated by autocorrelation. For example, in the adaptive expectations model, the disturbance in this form is $\varepsilon_t - \lambda\varepsilon_{t-1}$. As we saw in Section 15.4.1, autocorrelation in the presence of a lagged dependent variable renders the usual two-step procedures ineffective, as the estimates at the first step are inconsistent.[38] The autoregressive form of the geometric model is best suited to estimation of the partial adjustment model. Thus, consistent with the earlier treatment, we analyze this model first and then return to the adaptive expectations model.

UNCORRELATED DISTURBANCES

Even if ε_t is not serially correlated, the classical assumption that ε_t is uncorrelated with $z_s = [1, x_s, y_{s-1}]$ *for all t and s* is violated. Since y_t embodies all *previous* values y_s, it follows that every ε_t is correlated with every *subsequent* y_s. The correlation does fade with increasing separation in time, however, with the consequence that, in spite of this complication and its stochastic regressor, (18–58) may be treated as a classical regression, at least asymptotically. The requirements

$$|\lambda| < 1$$

and

$$\text{plim} \frac{1}{T} \sum_t \begin{bmatrix} 1 \\ x_t \\ y_{t-1} \end{bmatrix} [1, x_t, y_{t-1}] = \mathbf{Q}, \tag{18-59}$$

where $\mathbf{Q}$ is a positive definite matrix, are sufficient to ensure that the OLS estimates retain their desirable *asymptotic* properties. (The exact finite sample properties are largely unknown.[39]) As we saw earlier, this is the efficient estimator for the partial adjustment model, assuming that the disturbance in (18–41) is not autocorrelated.

AUTOCORRELATED DISTURBANCES—INSTRUMENTAL VARIABLES

If ε_t is autocorrelated, OLS estimates of (18–58) are biased and inconsistent. (See Section 15.4.1 for a derivation of the precise result when there is no regressor.) There are, however, several ways to obtain consistent estimates.

The method of instrumental variables was introduced in Section 9.5.4, in connection with the errors in variables problem, and was used in Section 15.6.3 for precisely the problem facing us here. To reiterate, let

$$\mathbf{X} = [\mathbf{i}, \mathbf{x}, \mathbf{y}_{-1}].$$

The problem is that

$$\text{plim} \frac{1}{T} \mathbf{X}'\varepsilon \neq \mathbf{0}.$$

---

[38] For some overviews, see, for example, Grether and Maddala (1973) and Dhrymes (1969 and 1971).
[39] Doran and Griffiths (1978). See also Schmidt (1976, pp. 96–101).

The instrumental variable estimator,

$$\hat{\theta}_{IV} = (\mathbf{Z}'\mathbf{X})^{-1}\mathbf{Z}'\mathbf{y}, \tag{18-60}$$

will be consistent and asymptotically distributed as

$$\hat{\theta} \xrightarrow{a} N[\theta, \sigma_\varepsilon^2 (\mathbf{Z}'\mathbf{X})^{-1}(\mathbf{Z}'\mathbf{Z})(\mathbf{X}'\mathbf{Z})^{-1}],$$

provided that the matrix of instrumental variables satisfies the two requirements

$$\text{plim}\, \frac{1}{T}\mathbf{Z}'\varepsilon = \mathbf{0}$$

and

$$\text{plim}\, \frac{1}{T}\mathbf{Z}'\mathbf{X} \neq \mathbf{0}. \tag{18-61}$$

In the present context, the constant and $\mathbf{x}$ can serve as their own instruments. The usual choice for the instrumental variable for y_{t-1} is x_{t-1},[40] leading to

$$\mathbf{Z} = [\mathbf{i}, \mathbf{x}, \mathbf{x}_{-1}].$$

It is useful to note at this point that if the instrumental variables satisfy (18–61), $\hat{\theta}_{IV}$ is consistent *regardless of the type of autocorrelation in ε.*

AUTOREGRESSIVE DISTURBANCES—HATANAKA'S ESTIMATOR AND THE MAXIMUM LIKELIHOOD ESTIMATOR

An efficient estimator can be obtained if the specific form of the autocorrelation is known. Consider, first, an autoregressive disturbance. This would arise, for example, in the partial adjustment model if the structural disturbance in (18–41) were autoregressive.

Although the IV estimator is consistent, it is generally inefficient. Hatanaka (1976) showed that a second-round estimator using the IV estimator at the first step would have the same asymptotic properties as the maximum likelihood estimator for normally distributed disturbances. (However, he did raise some questions about the small-sample performance of the estimator.) The procedure, detailed in Section 15.6.3, is as follows:

1. Use the IV estimator to estimate the parameters; then compute ρ, using the residuals.
2. Regress $y_t - \hat{\rho}y_{t-1}$ on a constant, $x_t - \hat{\rho}x_{t-1}$, $y_{t-1} - \hat{\rho}y_{t-2}$, and $\hat{u}_{t-1}$.

The appropriate asymptotic covariance matrix is the conventional estimator computed at step 2.

For normally distributed disturbances, we may also compute a maximum likelihood estimator. If $\varepsilon_t = \rho\varepsilon_{t-1} + u_t$,

$$u_t = (y_t - \rho y_{t-1}) - \alpha(1-\lambda)(1-\rho) - \beta(1-\lambda)(x_t - \rho x_{t-1}) - \lambda(y_{t-1} - \rho y_{t-2}). \tag{18-62}$$

Conditioned on the initial observations, the estimates that minimize the sum of squares provide the maximum likelihood estimates. For a given value of ρ, this requires only a linear regression of δy_t on a constant, δx_t, and δy_{t-1}. [We use $\delta x_t = x_t - \rho x_{t-1}$. See (18–57).] Since the OLS estimates are inconsistent, the Cochrane–Orcutt method will not necessarily produce a consistent estimate, even if it is iterated.[41] A simple expedient is to scan the range

---

[40] Liviatan (1963).
[41] Betancourt and Kalejian (1981) and Fomby and Guilkey (1983).

of $-1 < \rho < 1$ for the value that produces the global minimum of $\Sigma_t u_t^2$. Alternatively, if the process is begun with a consistent estimator of ρ, such as the IV estimator, the second step (and subsequent) estimates will have the desirable properties of maximum likelihood estimates. Standard errors for the maximum likelihood estimates of $[\alpha(1 - \lambda), \beta(1 - \lambda), \lambda, \rho, \sigma_u^2]$ may be obtained from the inverse of the estimate of the information matrix,[42]

$$
\mathbf{I} = \frac{1}{\sigma_u^2}
\begin{bmatrix}
T(1 - \rho)^2 & & & & \\
(1 - \rho)\Sigma_t \delta x_t & \Sigma_t(\delta x_t)^2 & & & \\
(1 - \rho)\Sigma_t \delta y_{t-1} & \Sigma_t \delta x_t \delta y_{t-1} & \Sigma_t(\delta y_{t-1})^2 & & \\
0 & 0 & T\sigma_u^2/(1 - \lambda) & T\sigma^2/(1 - \rho^2) & \\
0 & 0 & 0 & 0 & T/2\sigma_u^2
\end{bmatrix}.
$$

$$(18-63)$$

Standard errors for the individual estimates of α and β are computed using the result for the variance of a nonlinear function. [See $(18-54)$ and $(18-55)$.[43]]

MA DISTURBANCES—THE ADAPTIVE EXPECTATIONS MODEL

The AR form of the adaptive expectations model is

$$
y_t = \alpha(1 - \lambda) + \beta(1 - \lambda)x_t + \lambda y_{t-1} + (\varepsilon_t - \lambda\varepsilon_{t-1}). \tag{18-64}
$$

This AR form has an MA(1) disturbance with the same parameter as the adjustment equation. Consistent estimates can be obtained by using the method of instrumental variables. As we saw earlier, efficient estimates can be computed by using the MA form and the truncation remainder. [See $(18-47)$ and the subsequent discussion.] The (only apparently) messy case, in which, in addition, $\varepsilon_t = \rho\varepsilon_{t-1} + u_t$, is exactly the model in $(18-56)$. In either case, no new results are needed. The upshot is that *efficient* estimates of the AR form with a moving average error are obtained simply by reverting back to the MA form.

EXAMPLE 18.7. Estimates of the AR Form.   Using the techniques described earlier, we obtain the following estimates of the autoregressive form of the consumption function (Table 18.12), with estimated asymptotic standard errors given in parentheses: (The grid search produced a single minimum of the sum of squared deviations. The sum of squares declined monotonically from 5384 at $\rho = -0.5$ to the minimum of 3500.04 at $\rho = 0.27$, and then increased monotonically to 4735 at $\rho = 0.9$.)

18.2.2e.   *Disturbance Specifications in the Geometric Lag Model*

The preceding discussion has analyzed numerous combinations of model formulation (adaptive expectation or partial adjustment), stochastic specification of the structural disturbance [white noise, AR(1), MA(1)], and estimating equation (MA or AR form). Given the number of possibilities, it might appear that one could merely pick one off the shelf and estimate the model with whatever form seems simplest to use (or produces the most agreeable

---

[42] The counterpart to the 4,3 element in Johnston (1984, p. 367) is in error. It is obtained here as $TE[(-\partial u_t/\partial\lambda)$ $(-\partial u_t/\partial\rho)]$. We use $(18-62)$ to find $-\partial u_t/\partial\lambda = y_{t-1} - \rho y_{t-2}$ and $u_t = \varepsilon_t - \rho\varepsilon_{t-1}$ to obtain $-\partial u_t/\partial\rho = \varepsilon_{t-1}$. Now write $(18-58)$ as $y_s = \alpha + \beta(1 - \lambda)x_s/(1 - \lambda L) + \varepsilon_s/(1 - \lambda L)$ for $s = t - 1$ and $t - 2$. Therefore, $E[\varepsilon_{t-1}y_{t-1}] = \sigma_\varepsilon^2/(1 - \lambda)$ and $\rho E[\varepsilon_{t-1}y_{t-2}] = \rho^2\sigma_\varepsilon^2/(1 - \lambda)$. Combining terms and imposing $\sigma_\varepsilon^2 = \sigma_u^2/(1 - \rho^2)$ leads to the previous result. For $\partial u_t/\partial\lambda$ note that $\alpha(1 - \lambda)$ and $\beta(1 - \lambda)$ are free parameters.
[43] In some models, α and β appear directly, so this step is unnecessary.

Table 18.12

	Least Squares	Instrumental Variables	Hatanaka Two-Step	AR(1) with Grid Search	Zellner–Geisel
$\beta(1 - \lambda)$	0.1767	0.4651	0.2863	0.2423	0.321
	(0.0451)	(0.1115)	(0.0560)	(0.0498)	—
λ	0.8119	0.4913	0.6901	0.7386	0.66
	(0.0502)	(0.1240)	(0.0623)	(0.0555)	(0.085)
β	0.9394	0.9142	0.9238	0.9269	0.94
	(0.0148)	(0.0122)	(0.0078)	(0.0067)	(0.46)
$\dfrac{\lambda}{1 - \lambda}$	4.32	0.966	2.27	2.83	1.94
	(1.419)	(0.4791)	(0.6487)	(0.8122)	(0.74)
ρ	0	0	0.3869	0.27	0.69
	—	—	(0.0805)	(0.0861)	(0.076)
$\dfrac{e'e}{T}$	29.26	31.41	28.38	27.78	—

Table 18.13. Estimates of Lag Coefficients

	0	1	2
MA form			
OLS	0.671	0.199	0.038
Nonlinear OLS	0.682	0.171	0.043
Nonlinear GLS	0.320	0.211	0.139
AR form			
OLS	0.177	0.144	0.117
Inst. variable	0.465	0.228	0.112
Hatanaka	0.286	0.197	0.136
Grid search	0.242	0.178	0.132

results). It is worth emphasizing that, particularly in the MA form, the answers one will obtain depend crucially on the stochastic assumption. For example, Table 18.13 gives the implied estimates of the first three lag coefficients for the several estimators computed in Examples 18.6 and 18.7. Such wide disparity might seem a bit surprising in a data set in which the R^2 in the simplest regression (C_t on Y_t) exceeds 0.998.

The residuals should be carefully examined in order to ascertain the appropriate stochastic specification. It is useful to note that for this purpose we have two robust estimators of the parameters. For the MA form, the nonlinear least squares estimator is consistent regardless of the form of autocorrelation. Likewise, in the AR form, the instrumental variables estimator is robust to different types of disturbances. We thus have two ways to obtain a set of usable residuals for our analysis. We consider the adaptive expectations model in detail. The partial adjustment model is left as an exercise.

The structural equations are

$$y_t = \alpha + \beta x_t^* + \varepsilon_t,$$
$$x_t^* = \lambda x_{t-1}^* + (1 - \lambda)x_t.$$

Table 18.14

	Moving Average Form	Autoregressive Form
I.	White noise*	$\Rightarrow$ MA(1)
II.	AR(1), parameter $= \rho^*$	$\Rightarrow$ ARMA(1, 1)
III.	AR(1), parameter $= \lambda$	$\Leftarrow$ White noise*
IV.	AR(2), parameters $= (\rho + \lambda)$, $-\rho\lambda$	$\Leftarrow$ AR(1)*

The two estimating equations are

$$\text{MA form: } y_t = \alpha + \beta(1 - \lambda)(x_t + \lambda x_{t-1} + \cdots) + \varepsilon_t. \tag{18-65}$$

$$\text{AR form: } y_t = \alpha(1 - \lambda) + \beta(1 - \lambda)x_t + \lambda y_{t-1} + \varepsilon_t - \lambda \varepsilon_{t-1}.$$

The relationships between the MA and AR disturbances under different assumptions are listed in the following table. The * indicates the usual assumption, so the arrow points in the direction of its implication.

Case I is obvious. Cases II and III arise as follows: Let v_t be the disturbance in the AR form. If

$$\varepsilon_t = \rho\varepsilon_{t-1} + u_t,$$

then

$$\varepsilon_t = \frac{u_t}{1 - \rho L}.$$

Therefore,

$$v_t = \varepsilon_t - \lambda\varepsilon_{t-1}$$

$$= \frac{u_t}{1 - \rho L} - \frac{\lambda u_{t-1}}{1 - \rho L}.$$

Multiplying by $(1 - \rho L)$ and collecting terms produces the ARMA(1, 1) disturbance of Case II,

$$v_t = \rho v_{t-1} + u_t - \lambda u_{t-1}.$$

If, however, $\rho = \lambda$, this may be written as

$$v_t[1 - \lambda L] = u_t[1 - \lambda L].$$

Dividing by the common factor produces $v_t = u_t$, which is Case III. This case is of particular interest. It implies that the AR form can be estimated consistently and efficiently by ordinary least squares. Zellner and Geisel (1970, p. 871) made particular note of this possibility and, indeed, the condition is nearly met by their sample estimates. (See Example 18.6.) Case IV shows what is required in order to obtain an AR(1) disturbance in the AR form equation. It follows directly by assuming that

$$\varepsilon_t - \lambda\varepsilon_{t-1} = \rho(\varepsilon_{t-1} - \lambda\varepsilon_{t-2}) + u_t.$$

(This is Zellner and Geisel's assumption IV.)

Which assumption is appropriate? If the sample is reasonably large, we should be able to discern the answer from the data. We consider several possibilities, using, at each step, the results of our consumption function in Examples 18.6 and 18.7.[44]

EXAMPLE 18.8. An Analysis of Stochastic Specification

Case I. White Noise in the MA Form.   Any of the Durbin–Watson, Box–Pierce, or Godfrey (1978) Lagrange multiplier tests may be used directly. We require a robust estimator of the parameters, which is provided by the nonlinear least squares estimator. The Durbin–Watson statistic is 0.5960, which is extremely low. The Box–Pierce chi-squared statistic with one degree of freedom would be $127(0.702)^2 = 65.6$. There seems little question that the hypothesis $\rho = 0$ can be rejected. As a further test, this hypothesis implies that the AR form disturbance is an MA(1), which has zero autocorrelation after one period. Using the IV estimator, the second autocorrelation of the residuals is 0.4619, using 127 observations. Under the hypothesis of white noise, the autocorrelation is approximately normally distributed with zero mean and standard deviation $1/\sqrt{T} = 0.089$. Thus, $(0.4619 - 0)/0.089 = 5.2$ is highly significant. *This effectively rules out Case I.* We consider Case III next, as it follows immediately.

Case III. White Noise in the AR Form.   The preceding result also rules out Case III. The AR form residuals based on the IV estimator should, apart from sampling variation, be white noise in Case III. The finding of a large and significant second autocorrelation suggests that they are not. We also have some direct tests.[45] Godfrey's Lagrange multiplier test, obtained by regressing the least squares residuals on Y_t, C_{t-1}, and the lagged residual, produces a t ratio on the lagged residual of 2.64. For Durbin's h test, we would refer

$$h = 0.218 \left[\frac{127}{(1 - 127(0.0502^2))} \right]^{1/2} = 2.979$$

to the standard normal table. *Both statistics are larger than the tabled critical value, so we would reject Case III.*

Case IV. AR(1) in the AR Form.   This implies a rather peculiar form of the MA form disturbance. We can analyze this case with a tool called the **partial autocorrelation function**. If

$$\varepsilon_t = \rho \varepsilon_{t-1} + u_t,$$

then, if we regress ε_t on ε_{t-1} and ε_{t-2} using a sample of observations, the coefficient on ε_{t-1} will be an estimate of ρ and the coefficient on ε_{t-2} will, apart from sampling error, be zero. A set of usable residuals is provided by the IV estimator. For the consumption data, the slopes in the regression are 0.315 and 0.322, with t ratios of 3.686 and 3.761, respectively. *We thus conclude that the data are not consistent with Case IV.*

Case II. AR(1) in the MA Form.   Case II implies an unrestricted first-order autoregression in the MA form, which can be analyzed in the same manner as we did for Case IV. In the regression of the nonlinear least squares residuals from the MA form on their first two lagged values, we obtain slopes of 0.632 and 0.165, with t ratios of 7.15 and 1.86.

---

[44] This is a relatively limited application. The four preceding cases encompass most of the empirical applications. The theory contains many more. Some generalities may be found in Judge et al. (1985, Chapter 10).
[45] See Maddala and Rao (1976).

The first is highly significant, while the second is not. These results are consistent with an AR(1) process, which suggests that the estimates obtained in Example 18.6, with the AR(1) correction, are the ones we should retain.

We should note, finally, that it is possible that none of the four cases just analyzed is correct. One can extend the disturbance specification to higher-order autoregressive and moving average models. But it should be borne in mind that mechanical application of these techniques will almost surely bring drastic swings in the results (often associated with surprisingly small changes in parameter values). They should be used with circumspection.

18.2.2f. Extensions

The polynomial lag model has the attractive feature that it allows a great deal of flexibility in the shape of the lag distribution. In contrast, the geometric lag model imposes a declining pattern of the lag weights that might be inconsistent with the data. However, unlike the geometric lag model, the polynomial model truncates the distribution at an arbitrarily chosen point and requires an estimate of the degree of the polynomial. The properties of the resulting estimator remain to be derived. Several alternatives to these two popular functional forms have been devised that combine the desirable features of both.[46]

A MODIFIED GEOMETRIC LAG MODEL

One approach addresses directly the limitation of the geometric model. Since the issue is whether the lag weights can reasonably be assumed to decline throughout their range, one possibility is to allow them to be unrestricted for a few periods and then impose the geometric structure only at the tail of the distribution. A revised specification that allows two unrestricted weights is

$$y_t = \alpha + \beta_0 x_t + \beta_1 x_{t-1} + \beta(1 - \lambda) \sum_{i=0}^{\infty} \lambda^i x_{t-2-i} + \varepsilon_t. \tag{18-66}$$

This can be estimated by using a slight modification of the procedure we used earlier. The sum in the last term may be written

$$\sum_{i=0}^{\infty} \lambda^i x_{t-2-i} = \sum_{i=0}^{t-3} \lambda^i x_{t-2-i} + \sum_{i=t-2}^{\infty} \lambda^i x_{t-2-i}$$

$$= x_{t-2}^* + \lambda^t \sum_{i=0}^{\infty} \lambda^{i-2} x_{-i}.$$

Once again, we treat the second part as a truncation remainder. Assembling the parts, we find that the estimating equation is

$$y_t = \alpha + \beta_0 x_t + \beta_1 x_{t-1} + \beta(1 - \lambda) x_{t-2}^* + \lambda^t \mu^0 + \varepsilon_t.$$

The recursion for computing x_{t-2}^* is

$$x_1^* = x_2^* = 0,$$

$$x_3^* = x_1,$$

$$x_s^* = \lambda x_{s-1}^* + x_{s-2}, \qquad s = 4, \ldots, T.$$

---

[46] The sources mentioned in the Introduction provide extensive summaries. Maddala (1977) also provides a concise catalog with many useful observations on the mechanics of estimation. There is a bit of gadgetry in some of the proposed lag distributions, but, unfortunately, economic theory is usually silent on what the lag distribution should look like. The data themselves and the resourcefulness of the analyst often provide most of the guidance.

Estimation is based on observations 3 through T, and is otherwise the same as before. Least squares with a search over $0 \leq \lambda < 1$ provides the maximum likelihood estimates. The information matrix is the same as (18–50), with two additional rows and columns for β_0 and β_1. Autocorrelation can be handled in the same fashion as before.

This is a useful way to extend the model, as it relaxes the constraints of the geometric lag model at precisely the points where they are most likely to be binding. However, unless a very few initial lags are satisfactory, the result will be a model encumbered with the multicollinearity problem that we sought to avoid in the first place. Consequently, a number of alternative lag distributions with more compact parametric representations have been designed. We consider a few of them.

PASCAL LAG MODEL

The Pascal lag model derived by Solow (1960) is a generalization of the geometric lag model. The lag coefficients in the infinite distributed lag form are

$$\beta_i = \beta(1 - \lambda)^r \lambda^i \binom{i + r - 1}{i} = \beta(1 - \lambda)^r \lambda^i \frac{(i + r - 1)!}{i!(r - 1)!}.$$

If $r = 1$, this is the geometric lag model. But for $r = 2, 3$, and so on, the lag distribution has the "hump" shape of the polynomial model in the early periods and then fades in the fashion of the geometric model at distant lags. This can be easily seen by use of the recursion

$$\beta_i = \frac{\lambda(i + r - 1)}{i} \beta_{i-1}, \qquad i = 1, 2, \ldots,$$

beginning with $\beta_0 = \beta(1 - \lambda)^r$. For large i, the ratio is essentially equal to λ, which is the relationship for the geometric lag model. An example will be given. The exponent, r, is to be estimated. Values of two, three, four, or five are typical. For a given value of r, the remaining parameters can be estimated with a search over λ, in a fashion similar to that for the geometric model. Extensive details are provided by Maddala and Rao (1971).

DISCOUNTED POLYNOMIAL LAG MODEL

Schmidt (1974a) has proposed a model that combines the polynomial and geometric lag models. The weights in the geometric lag model are reformulated as

$$\beta_i = (\alpha_0 + \alpha_1 i + \cdots + \alpha_p i^p)\lambda^i, \qquad 0 \leq \lambda < 1.$$

At the head end of the distribution, the lag weights can resemble those of the polynomial lag model, first rising then falling, while the tail end of the distribution will be dominated by the geometric lag structure. One immediate advantage is that this form eliminates the troublesome search for a truncation point. The degree of polynomial remains to be determined, but this can be analyzed with well-established techniques. If $\alpha_1 = \alpha_2 = \cdots = \alpha_p = 0$, the model reduces to the geometric lag model. The parameters can be estimated using an extension of the estimating equation for the geometric lag model. For a quadratic model,

$$y_t = \alpha + \alpha_0 z_{0t} + \alpha_1 z_{1t} + \alpha_2 z_{2t} + \mu_0^0 \lambda^t + \mu_1^0 t \lambda^t + \mu_2^0 t^2 \lambda^t + \varepsilon_t,$$

where

$$z_{0t} = \sum_{i=0}^{t-1} \lambda^i x_{t-1},$$

$$z_{1t} = \sum_{i=0}^{t-1} \lambda^i x_{t-1},$$

and

$$z_{2t} = \sum_{i=0}^{t-1} i^2 \lambda^i x_{t-1}.$$

Schmidt provides a compact expression for the information matrix. The extension to higher-order polynomials would continue the preceding pattern. The equation is nonlinear in λ but can be estimated by ordinary least squares by searching over values of λ from zero to one for the minimum sum of squared residuals.

It has been suggested that this model has the additional advantage over the polynomial lag model that the existence of *any* lagged effect is a testable restriction. To be sure, if $\lambda = 0$, the model *is* a simple regression, with no distributed lag. (The coefficient on x_t will be $\alpha_0 0^0 = \alpha_0$.) However, the implied test of this restriction has a curious ambiguity. If $\lambda = 0$, the model is the same regardless of p. Thus, it is unclear just what is being tested by a simple asymptotic t test based on the unrestricted model. To underscore the point, the model cannot be estimated with $\lambda = 0$ and a nonzero p, so a likelihood ratio test is impossible. The Lagrange multiplier test is likewise precluded. This problem is not present in the geometric or Pascal lag models. However, since the other restrictions of these models may not be acceptable, perhaps a better way to test the hypothesis of no lagged effects would be an F test based on a relatively long, unrestricted model (i.e., (18–10)).

RATIONAL LAG MODEL

A very general specification is Jorgenson's (1966) rational lag model,

$$y_t = \frac{B(L)}{C(L)} x_t + \varepsilon_t. \tag{18–67}$$

The ratio of two polynomials in the lag operator can produce essentially any desired shape of the lag distribution. The geometric lag model and numerous other models in the literature are special cases. The autoregressive form is

$$C(L)y_t = B(L)x_t + C(L)\varepsilon_t. \tag{18–68}$$

In this form, the model has both lagged variables and a moving average disturbance. As such, the OLS estimator is inconsistent. For low-order polynomials, Maddala and Rao (1971) have derived a fairly straightforward method of computing maximum likelihood estimates.[47] Extensive details may be found in their study, so we shall just sketch a simple case here.

Consider the case in which both $B(L)$ and $C(L)$ are quadratic. The model is, then,

$$y_t = \alpha + \frac{\beta_0 + \beta_1 L + \beta_2 L^2}{1 - \gamma_1 L - \gamma_2 L^2} x_t + \varepsilon_t \tag{18–69}$$

or

$$y_t = \alpha(1 - \gamma_1 - \gamma_2) + \beta_0 x_t + \beta_1 x_{t-1} + \beta_2 x_{t-2} + \gamma_1 y_{t-1} + \gamma_2 y_{t-2} + \varepsilon_t - \gamma_1 \varepsilon_{t-1} - \gamma_2 \varepsilon_{t-2}. \tag{18–70}$$

---

[47] Although most theoretical treatments are given in fully general terms, in practice, polynomials of order higher than one or two are rarely used. They quickly become extremely cumbersome, both to estimate and to interpret. Moreover, models with numerous lags of the dependent variables are distressingly sensitive to seemingly small parameter variation.

Define

$$x_t^* = \frac{1}{1 - \gamma_1 L - \gamma_2 L^2} x_t. \tag{18-71}$$

Then

$$x_t^* = x_t + \gamma_1 x_{t-1}^* + \gamma_2 x_{t-2}^*. \tag{18-72}$$

For given values of γ_1 and γ_2, x_t^* can be computed by a recursion. [Note the similarity to (18–49).] With x_t^* thus computed,

$$y_t = \alpha + \beta_0 x_t^* + \beta_1 x_{t-1}^* + \beta_2 x_{t-2}^* + \varepsilon_t, \tag{18-73}$$

and α, β_0, β_1, and β_2 can be estimated by ordinary least squares. Assuming normally distributed disturbances, a grid search over γ_1 and γ_2 for the minimum sum of squared deviations provides the maximum likelihood estimates. The range of values for which (18–70) is stable (see the Appendix for discussion) is the triangle bounded by the points $(\beta_1, \beta_2) =$ $(-2, -1)$, $(2, -1)$, and $(0, 1)$. Griliches (1967, pp. 27–28) shows that only positive values of β_1 are consistent with a positive set of lag weights. This will help to limit the necessary search.[48]

There is a troubling loose end. Where does one begin the recursion in (18–72)? The problem is that x_{-1}^* and x_0^* are unobserved. The logical choice is $x_{-1}^* = x_0^* = 0$. Then $x_1^* = x_1$, $x_2^* = \gamma_1 x_1 + x_2$, and (18–72) is used for x_3^* to x_T^*. Alternatively, one may treat x_0^* and x_{-1}^* as unknown parameters to be estimated. Unfortunately, this approach turns the linear estimation problem into a highly nonlinear one. As Maddala and Rao (1971) discovered, the treatment of these values can make a drastic difference in the results even in a sample as large as 60. They suggest a useful approach based on preliminary sample estimates of x_0^* and x_{-1}^*.

EXAMPLE 18.9. Distributed Lag Models. The Almon data have provided the canonical proving ground for the development of distributed lag techniques. In the interest of continuing that tradition, we display in Table 18.15 and Figure 18.5 several lag distributions estimated with the 1953–1967 version of these data.[49]

18.3. Models with Time-Varying Parameters

In constructing their models, forecasters often adjust the intercept term to improve the forecasts, for example, by shifting it so that the model predicts the last sample observation perfectly. This raises an issue addressed by Cooley and Prescott in their analysis of models with time-varying parameters (1973a and 1973b). Does the analyst believe that the intercept

---

[48] This does not guarantee that in a particular sample the parameter estimates will satisfy the restrictions. In particular, for the consumption data, the minimum sum of squares occurs at a point *outside* the stable range at roughly $(1.06, 0.1)$. Apropos footnote 47 the sum of squares is 9800 at this point and over 50,000 at $(1.09, 0.1)$.

[49] The original Almon study used the first 9 years. Many subsequent researchers have used the 60 observations spanning all 15 years, attributing the additional observations to Almon, whose study was first presented in 1963. Estimates from the rational lag and Pascal models appear in Maddala and Rao (1971). The unrestricted least squares estimates and the geometric and discounted polynomial models were computed using the full data set, which is listed in Maddala (1977, p. 370). Maddala and Rao also present estimates of Almon's polynomial lag model. However, these *are* taken from Almon's study, and are of a model with four seasonal dummy variables and a "backlog" variable that appears considerably to affect the results. See Almon (1965, pp. 186, 190). They are, therefore, not comparable to their other estimates. We have also reestimated the Almon models for this example.

Table 18.15. Lag Weights from Estimated Distributed Lag Models

Models: 1 = unrestricted regression
2 = geometric, $\lambda = 0.82$
3 = modified geometric, two free parameters
4 = polynomial, fourth order
5 = polynomial, same, with endpoint restrictions
6 = rational (2, 2)
7 = Pascal, $r = 3$
8 = discounted polynomial, $\lambda = 0.49$

Lag	1	2	3	4	5	6	7	8
0	0.081	0.180	0.394	0.049	0.097	0.021	0.085	0.063
1	0.92	0.148	−0.147	0.152	0.137	0.187	0.143	0.122
2	0.236	0.121	0.201	0.186	0.144	0.177	0.160	0.173
3	0.183	0.099	0.147	0.168	0.140	0.155	0.150	0.174
4	0.142	0.081	0.107	0.122	0.136	0.127	0.126	0.145
5	−0.042	0.067	0.078	0.077	0.129	0.100	0.099	0.109
6	0.137	0.055	0.057	0.074	0.117	0.075	0.074	0.076
7	0.058	0.045	0.042	0.157	0.082	0.055	0.053	0.051
8	0.147	0.037	0.030	0	0	0.039	0.037	0.032
9	−0.010	0.030	0.022	0	0	0.026	0.025	0.020
10	0.069	0.025	0.016	0	0	0.017	0.017	0.012
11	−0.045	0.020	0.012	0	0	0.010	0.011	0.007
12	0.081	0.017	0.009	0	0	0.006	0.007	0.004

Note: Estimates of models 6 and 7 are from Maddala and Rao (1971).

is fixed over time or not? The authors suggest that the model the forecaster truly has in mind does not have a fixed constant, but one that varies randomly in the sample period. They propose the **adaptive regression model** as one that incorporates this notion.

The adaptive regression model with a time-varying intercept is

$$y_t = \alpha_t + \beta' x_t + \varepsilon_t, \tag{18–74}$$

where

$$\alpha_t = \alpha_{t-1} + v_t.$$

The constant shifts up or down in each period in the fashion of a random walk. The disturbances ε_t and v_t are assumed to be independent of each other as well as across time, and normally distributed with zero means and variances

$$\text{Var}(\varepsilon_t) = \sigma_\varepsilon^2 = (1 - \gamma)\sigma^2$$

and

$$\text{Var}(v_t) = \sigma_v^2 = \gamma\sigma^2,$$

where

$$0 < \gamma < 1.$$

The parameter γ gives the relative importance of two sources of variation in y_t, random shocks and structural shift. The random shock, ε_t, is labeled the *transitory* part, as its

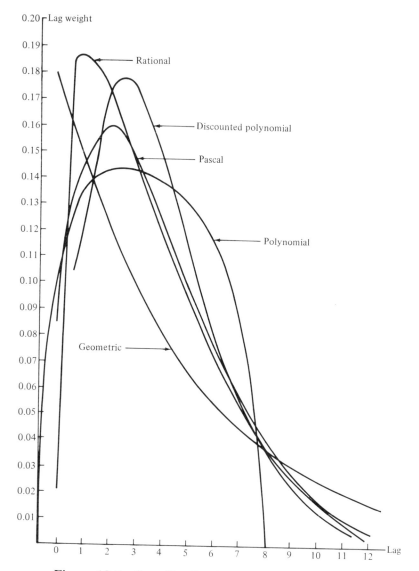

Figure 18.5   Lag distributions for the Almon data.

influence is confined to the current period. In contrast, since $v_t = \alpha_0 + \sum_{i=1}^{t-1} v_i$, every v_s appears in every subsequent y_t. As such, v_t is labeled the *permanent* random component.

Estimation of the model poses a problem because the constant term is a different random outcome in every period, not a parameter. The usual regression methods will not work here. But for forecasting purposes, we can identify the constant in the first postsample period as a parameter and construct an estimable equation. The path of α_t through the sample period is

$$\alpha_1 = \alpha_0 + v_1, \qquad \alpha_2 = \alpha_1 + v_2 = v_2 + v_1 + \alpha_0,$$

and so on, through

$$\alpha_t = \alpha_0 + v_1 + v_2 + \cdots + v_t$$

and

$$\alpha_T = \alpha_0 + \sum_{i=0}^{T} v_{T-i}.$$

In the first postsample period, then,

$$\alpha_{T+1} = \alpha_t + \sum_{i=t+1}^{T+1} v_i. \qquad (18-75)$$

Therefore,

$$\alpha_t = \alpha_{T+1} - \sum_{i=t+1}^{T+1} v_i. \qquad (18-76)$$

Insert this in the regression model to obtain

$$y_t = \alpha_{T+1} + \beta'x_t + \varepsilon_t - \sum_{i=t+1}^{T+1} v_i. \qquad (18-77)$$

The disturbances are

$$u_1 = \varepsilon_1 - v_1 - v_2 - \cdots - v_T - v_{T+1}.$$

$$u_2 = \varepsilon_2 \qquad - v_2 - \cdots - v_T - v_{T+1}$$

$$\vdots$$

$$u_{T-1} = \varepsilon_{T-1} \qquad\qquad - v_T - v_{T+1}$$

$$u_T = \varepsilon_T \qquad\qquad\qquad - v_{T+1}.$$

It follows that the covariance matrix for the disturbances is

$$\text{Var}[u] = \sigma^2\Omega = (1-\gamma)\sigma^2 I + \gamma\sigma^2 Q, \qquad (18-78)$$

where

$$Q = \begin{bmatrix} T & T-1 & T-2 & \cdots & 2 & 1 \\ T-1 & T-1 & T-2 & \cdots & 2 & 1 \\ T-2 & T-2 & T-2 & \cdots & 2 & 1 \\ & & & \vdots & & \\ 1 & 1 & 1 & & 1 & 1 \end{bmatrix}. \qquad (18-79)$$

For a sample of T observations, the log likelihood is

$$\ln L = -\frac{T}{2}\ln 2\pi - \frac{1}{2}\ln|\sigma^2\Omega|$$

$$-\frac{1}{2\sigma^2}(y - X\beta)'\Omega^{-1}(y - X\beta), \qquad (18-80)$$

where we have included a column of ones in X and the first element of β is α_{T+1}. For a given value of γ, Ω is known, so the maximum likelihood estimates of β and σ^2 would be the GLS estimators,

$$\hat{\beta} = [X'\Omega(\gamma)^{-1}X]^{-1}X'\Omega(\gamma)^{-1}y \qquad (18-81)$$

and

$$\hat{\sigma}^2 = s^2 = \frac{(y - X\hat{\beta})'\Omega(\gamma)^{-1}(y - X\hat{\beta})}{T}.$$

Of course, γ remains to be estimated. Inserting $\hat{\beta}$ and $\hat{\sigma}^2$ in (18–80) produces the *concentrated log likelihood*,

$$\ln L^* = -\frac{T}{2}(1 + \ln 2\pi) - \frac{1}{2}\ln|s^2\Omega(\gamma)|$$

$$= -\frac{T}{2}(1 + \ln 2\pi + \ln s^2) - \frac{1}{2}\ln|\Omega(\gamma)|. \tag{18–82}$$

Since γ must be between zero and one, we can obtain the maximum likelihood estimates by searching over this range. The complete set of estimates are those that maximize the concentrated log likelihood. The estimate of the asymptotic covariance matrix for $\hat{\beta}$ is the conventional one. Cooley and Prescott show that

$$\text{Asy. Var}(\hat{\gamma}) = \frac{2}{T(\text{Var}[c_t])^2}, \tag{18–83}$$

where the variance in the denominator is

$$\frac{1}{T}\sum_t (c_t - \bar{c})^2,$$

$$c_t = \frac{d_t - 1}{1 + \hat{\gamma}(d_t - 1)}, \tag{18–84}$$

and d_t is a characteristic root of the $\mathbf{Q}$ in (18–79).

If the sample size is large, repeated GLS will be extremely time-consuming and burdensome due to the repeated inversion of Ω. Cooley and Prescott have derived a useful transformation of the model that greatly simplifies the calculations. Let $\mathbf{P}$ be the matrix whose columns are the characteristic vectors of $\mathbf{Q}$. Thus, $\mathbf{P}'\mathbf{P} = \mathbf{I}$ and $\mathbf{P}'\mathbf{QP} = \mathbf{D}$, the diagonal matrix of characteristic roots of $\mathbf{Q}$ that appears in (18–84). As in Chapter 13, let

$$\mathbf{y}^* = \mathbf{P}'\mathbf{y}, \mathbf{X}^* = \mathbf{P}'\mathbf{X} \quad \text{and} \quad \mathbf{u}^* = \mathbf{P}'\mathbf{u}.$$

In terms of the starred variables, the model is

$$\mathbf{y}^* = \mathbf{X}^*\boldsymbol{\beta} + \mathbf{u}^*,$$

where

$$E[\mathbf{u}^*\mathbf{u}^{*\prime}] = \sigma^2\mathbf{P}'[(1 - \gamma)\mathbf{I} + \gamma\mathbf{Q}]\mathbf{P}$$

$$= \sigma^2[\mathbf{I} + \gamma(\mathbf{D} - \mathbf{I})].$$

By this simple device, we have transformed the model into one that is merely heteroscedastic:

$$\text{Var}[u_t^*] = \sigma^2[1 + \gamma(d_t - 1)],$$

$$\text{Cov}[u_t^*, u_s^*] = 0 \quad \text{if } t \neq s.$$

The concentrated log likelihood is reduced to

$$\ln L_c = -\frac{T}{2}(1 + \ln(2\pi) + \ln s_*^2) - \frac{1}{2}\ln|\Omega^*|, \tag{18–85}$$

where

$$s_*^2 = \frac{1}{T}\sum_t \frac{e_t^2}{1 + \gamma(d_t - 1)}$$

and

$$\ln|\Omega^*| = \sum_t \ln(1 + \gamma(d_t - 1)).$$

Estimation is now done using simple weighted least squares. As before, we search over γ for the value that maximizes the concentrated log likelihood. Computation of the characteristic roots and vectors of Q is not simple, especially if T is large, but it need only be done once, at the beginning of the estimation. They are not a function of γ. Given P, y^* and X^* are computed only once, and estimation of the model is otherwise routine.

EXAMPLE 18.10. **Adaptive Consumption Function.**   As an illustration of the foregoing, we estimate a consumption function using quarters 1979IV to 1984III of the data in Example 18.6. We thus leave the last quarter of the data set to be forecasted by our model. We use as our forecasting model a simple consumption function,

$$C_t = \alpha_t + \beta Y_t + \varepsilon_t.$$

The equation is first fit by ordinary least squares, ignoring the drift in the intercept. We then estimate the model using the method of Cooley and Prescott, with the transformation to heteroscedasticity. Estimates of the parameters with their estimated standard errors are given in Table 18.16.

The two fitted functions are shown in Figure 18.6. The first postsample observation is 1984IV, with $C_{1984IV} = 1075.4$ and $Y_{1984IV} = 1186.9$. The forecasts by the two models are 1083.5 for the least squares regression and 1074.8 for the adaptive regression. The actual data point is shown in the figure. The adaptive regression gives a considerably better forecast.

Cooley and Prescott have extended their model to variation in the slopes of the model as well as the intercept. The parameters are assumed to follow the specification

$$y_t = \beta_t' x_t,$$
$$\beta_t = \beta_t^p + u_t, \tag{18-86}$$
$$\beta_t^p = \beta_{t-1}^p + v_t.$$

The disturbance vectors u_t and v_t are independently normally distributed, with zero means vectors and covariance matrices

$$Var[u_t] = (1 - \gamma)\sigma^2 \Sigma_u$$

and

$$Var[v_t] = \gamma\sigma^2 \Sigma_v. \tag{18-87}$$

Table 18.16.   Estimated Consumption Functions

	Least Squares	Adaptive Regression
α	−7.2387 (39.44)	155.985 (125.0)
β	0.91898 (0.0368)	0.77410 (0.1071)
γ	—	0.82 (0.2616)

Figure 18.6   Estimated consumption functions.

Note that there is no disturbance in (18–86). We assume that the equation includes a constant term, so what would be the disturbance, ε_t in the earlier model, is just the first term in u_t. Similarly, the first element in $\mathbf{v}_t$ corresponds to v_t in (18–74).

To proceed, it is necessary to assume that $\boldsymbol{\Sigma}_u$ and $\boldsymbol{\Sigma}_v$ are known. The authors argue that it is reasonable to assume that they are diagonal and equal to each other. They also suggest that the results obtained with their model are relatively robust to misspecifications of these matrices. This is probably useful, since the underlying theory is unlikely to provide much guidance in what values to use.

Once again, attention is directed to the first postsample value. In terms of $\boldsymbol{\beta}_{T+1}$, the model is

$$y_t = \boldsymbol{\beta}'_{T+1}\mathbf{x}_t + \mathbf{x}'_t \mathbf{u}_t + \mathbf{x}'_t \sum_{i=t+1}^{T+1} \mathbf{v}_i$$

$$= \boldsymbol{\beta}'_{T+1}\mathbf{x}_t + \mathbf{w}_t.$$

(Note that with a constant term, if the only nonzero elements in $\boldsymbol{\Sigma}_u$ and $\boldsymbol{\Sigma}_v$ are in the upper left corner, the model with a time-varying intercept discussed earlier emerges.) The covariance matrix of the T compound disturbances is

$$\text{Var}[\mathbf{w}] = \sigma^2 \boldsymbol{\Omega} = \sigma^2[(1 - \gamma)\mathbf{R} + \gamma \mathbf{Q}^*],$$

where

$$R = \text{diag}[x'_t\Sigma_u x_t], \qquad t = 1, \ldots, T$$

and

$$q^*_{ij} = x'_i\Sigma_v x_j q_{ij},$$

where q_{ij} is given in (18–79).

Since the only unknown in Ω is γ, we can search over γ as before to obtain the maximum likelihood estimates. For a given value of γ, the maximum likelihood estimates of β and σ^2 are the GLS estimators in (18–81). The appropriate asymptotic covariance matrix for these estimates is the conventional one. The asymptotic variance of γ is given in (18–83), with the characteristic roots taken from the matrix $Q^{**} = q^*_{ij}/(r_{ii}r_{jj})^{1/2}$. Cooley and Prescott also extend the device used earlier to transform the model to a heteroscedastic regression. The computation is the same as the earlier one, where we apply it to $\tilde{y} = R^{-1/2}y$ and $\tilde{X} = R^{-1/2}X$. Thereafter, the results are exactly the same as the previous ones.

A further extension called a *state space model* allows the coefficients to evolve according to a *transition equation*, $\beta_t = \Gamma\beta_{t-1} + v_t$. Estimation by maximum likelihood has been derived and is greatly facilitated by a technique known as the **Kalman filter**. Models at this level of generality have been used only rarely in economics, primarily because of the lack of a theoretical justification.[50]

Exercises

1. Obtain the mean lag and the long- and short-run multipliers for the following distributed lag models:

   (a) $y_t = 0.55(0.02x_t + 0.15x_{t-1} + 0.43x_{t-2} + 0.23x_{t-3} + 0.17x_{t-4}) + \varepsilon_t$.

   (b) The model in Exercise 5.

   (c) The model in Exercise 8. (Do for either x or z.)

2. Explain how to estimate the parameters of the following model:

   $$y_t = \alpha + \beta x_t + \gamma y_{t-1} + \delta y_{t-2} + \varepsilon_t,$$

   $$\varepsilon_t = \rho\varepsilon_{t-1} + u_t.$$

   Is there any problem with ordinary least squares? Using the method you have described, fit the previous model to the data in Table 18.8. Report your results.

3. Show how to estimate a polynomial distributed lag model with lags of six periods and a third-order polynomial, using restricted least squares.

4. Using the data in the appendix to Chapter 19, fit a polynomial distributed lag model of the form

   $$\text{Investment}_t = \alpha + \beta\sum_i \delta_i \, \text{Profit}_{t-i} + \varepsilon_t.$$

   Attempt to determine the appropriate lag length and polynomial degree, using the methods discussed in the text.

---

[50] For an application, see Burmeister and Wall (1982).

5. Expand the rational lag model

$$y_t = \frac{0.6 + 2L}{1 - 0.6L + 0.5L^2} x_t + \varepsilon_t.$$

What are the coefficients on x_t, x_{t-1}, x_{t-2}, x_{t-3}, and x_{t-4}?

6. Suppose that the model of the previous problem were respecified as

$$y_t = \alpha + \frac{\beta + \gamma L}{1 - \delta_1 L + \delta_2 L^2} x_t + \varepsilon_t.$$

Describe a method of estimating the parameters. Is ordinary least squares consistent?

7. Derive equation (18–50).

8. Describe how to estimate the parameters of the model

$$y_t = \alpha + \beta \frac{x_t}{1 - \gamma L} + \delta \frac{z_t}{1 - \phi L} + \varepsilon_t,$$

where ε_t is a serially uncorrelated, homoscedastic, classical disturbance.

9. Using the results in Table 18.15, deduce the estimates of α_0, α_1, and α_2 in the discounted polynomial lag model.

Appendix: The Characteristic Equation of an Autoregressive Model

A characteristic of a dynamic model that is of particular interest, especially if it is to be used for forecasting, is its stability (or lack of stability). If the sum of the lag coefficients in

$$y_t = \alpha + \sum_{i=0}^{\infty} \beta_i x_{t-i} + \varepsilon_t$$

is finite, there is no question of stability of the equation, even if the lag length is infinite. We can postulate an equilibrium as we did earlier, disturb it by, for instance, increasing x by one unit in period s, and proceed to a new equilibrium, as we did in Figure 18.1. But equations such as this are rather clumsy, and it is common to reduce the number of terms by using autoregressive models, that is, those with a few lagged values of y_t. A common specification is a model with geometric lag weights,

$$y_t = \alpha + \beta x_t + \gamma y_{t-1} + \varepsilon_t,$$

or

$$(1 - \gamma L)y_t = \alpha + \beta x_t + \varepsilon_t.$$

After successive substitution, we see that this is a distributed lag model with an infinite lag structure,

$$y_t = \alpha \sum_{i=0}^{\infty} \gamma^i + \beta \sum_{i=0}^{\infty} \gamma^i x_{t-i} + \sum_{i=0}^{\infty} \gamma^i \varepsilon_{t-i}$$

$$= \alpha(1 + \gamma + \gamma^2 + \cdots) + (\beta x_t + \varepsilon_t)(1 + \gamma L + (\gamma L)^2 + \cdots).$$

It is no longer self-evident that this model is stable. The condition $|\gamma| < 1$ must be imposed, in which case

$$y_t = \frac{\alpha}{1 - \gamma} + \frac{\beta x_t}{1 - \gamma L} + \frac{\varepsilon_t}{1 - \gamma L}.$$

A more general model would be

$$C(L)y_t = \alpha + \beta x_t + \varepsilon_t$$

or

$$y_t = \gamma_1 y_{t-1} + \cdots + \gamma_p y_{t-p} + \alpha + \beta x_t + \varepsilon_t.$$

Once again, there is a question of the stability of the equation. However, successive substitution will quickly reveal that the necessary conditions are now considerably more complicated.

In autoregressive models, stability or, alternatively, the existence of an equilibrium turns on the roots of the **characteristic equation**,

$$C(z) = 1 - \gamma_1 z - \gamma_2 z^2 - \cdots = 0.$$

This is a polynomial in z, with (possibly) complex roots $z = a + bi$. Stability requires that all roots be outside the unit circle (i.e., have modulus, $a^2 + b^2$, greater than one.)[51]

There is an alternative form of the stability condition that provides a useful result. Consider a third-order autoregressive model as an example. The model is

$$y_t - \gamma_1 y_{t-1} - \gamma_2 y_{t-2} - \gamma_3 y_{t-3} = \alpha + \beta x_t + \varepsilon_t.$$

The characteristic equation is

$$1 - \gamma_1 z - \gamma_2 z^2 - \gamma_3 z^3 = 0.$$

We can write this as a first-order autoregressive model in a vector, $\mathbf{y}_t^*$. First,

$$y_t = \gamma_1 y_{t-1} + \gamma_2 y_{t-2} + \gamma_3 y_{t-3} + \alpha + \beta x_t + \varepsilon_t,$$

$$y_{t-1} = y_{t-1},$$

$$y_{t-2} = y_{t-2}.$$

We collect the three variables on the left-hand side in a vector, $\mathbf{y}_t^*$. The preceding is equivalent to

$$\mathbf{y}_t^* = \begin{bmatrix} \gamma_1 & \gamma_2 & \gamma_3 \\ 1 & 0 & 0 \\ 0 & 1 & 0 \end{bmatrix} \mathbf{y}_{t-1}^* + \mathbf{D}\mathbf{z}_t,$$

where $\mathbf{z}_t = [1, x_t, \varepsilon_t]'$ and

$$\mathbf{D} = \begin{bmatrix} \alpha & \beta & 1 \\ 0 & 0 & 0 \\ 0 & 0 & 0 \end{bmatrix}.$$

---

[51] If we interpret the root as the point (a, b) in a plane, with one axis the real part and the other the imaginary one, the condition is that all roots lie outside a circle with radius one and center at the origin.

This can also be written as

$$\mathbf{y}_t^* = \mathbf{C}L\mathbf{y}_t^* + \mathbf{D}\mathbf{z}_t$$

or

$$(\mathbf{I} - \mathbf{C}L)\mathbf{y}_t^* = \mathbf{D}\mathbf{z}_t.$$

Then, by successive substitution,

$$\mathbf{y}_t^* = \mathbf{D}\mathbf{z}_t + \mathbf{C}\mathbf{D}\mathbf{z}_{t-1} + \mathbf{C}^2\mathbf{D}\mathbf{z}_{t-2} + \cdots$$

There is, as yet, no assurance that $\mathbf{C}^i$ does not explode. For any square matrix, $\mathbf{C}$, we can write

$$\mathbf{C} = \mathbf{P}\Lambda\mathbf{Q},$$

where Λ is a diagonal matrix whose diagonal elements are the characteristic roots of $\mathbf{C}$, and $\mathbf{P}$ and $\mathbf{Q}$ are matrices such that $\mathbf{QP} = \mathbf{I}$.[52] Then $\mathbf{C}^i = \mathbf{P}\Lambda^i\mathbf{Q}$, and the question of stability now turns on the characteristic roots, Λ. But *the characteristic roots of* $\mathbf{C}$ *are the reciprocals of the roots of the characteristic equation.* The proof follows.

$$\mathbf{C} - \lambda\mathbf{I} = \begin{bmatrix} \gamma_1 - \lambda & \gamma_2 & \gamma_3 \\ 1 & -\lambda & 0 \\ 0 & 1 & -\lambda \end{bmatrix}.$$

The roots are determined by

$$|\mathbf{C} - \lambda\mathbf{I}| = \lambda^3 - \gamma_1\lambda^2 - \gamma_2\lambda - \gamma_3 = 0.$$

Let $z = 1/\lambda$ be a root. Multiplying both sides of the determinantal equation by z^3 produces the characteristic equation of the lag polynomial, which proves the result for this special case. (The general result can be proved by expanding the determinant along the first column and is left as an exercise.) Therefore, we reach the same condition as before.

References

Akaike, H., "Information Theory and an Extension of the Maximum Likelihood Principle," in B. Petrov, and F. Csake, eds., *Second International Symposium on Information Theory*, Budapest: Akademiai Kiado, 1973.

Almon, S., "The Distributed Lag Between Capital Appropriations and Expenditures," *Econometrica*, 33, 1965, pp. 178–196.

Amemiya, T., *Advanced Econometrics*, Cambridge, Mass.: Harvard University Press, 1985.

Amemiya, T., and K. Morimune, "Selecting the Optimal Order of Polynomial in the Almon Distributed Lag," *Review of Economics and Statistics*, 56, 1974, pp. 378–386.

Anderson, T., *The Statistical Analysis of Time Series*, New York: Wiley, 1971.

Betancourt, R., and H. Kalejian, "Lagged Endogenous Variables and the Cochrane–Orcutt Procedure," *Econometrica*, 49, 1981, pp. 1073–1078.

Blanchard, O., "Why Does Money Affect Output? A Survey," National Bureau of Economic Research, Working Paper Number 2285, 1987.

Box, G., and G. Jenkins, *Time Series Analysis: Forecasting and Control*, San Francisco: Holden-Day, 1982.

Burmeister, E., and K. Wall, "Kalman Filtering Estimation of Unobserved Rational Expectations with an Application to the German Hyperinflation," *Journal of Econometrics*, 20, 1982, pp. 255–284.

---

[52] See Section 2.7.9. The result differs slightly here, as $\mathbf{C}$ is not symmetric. Its characteristic roots and vectors may be complex pairs.

Chatfield, C., *The Analysis of Time Series: Theory and Practice*, London: Chapman and Hall, 1975.

Cooley, T., and E. Prescott, "Varying Parameter Regression: A Theory and Some Applications," *Annals of Economic and Social Measurement*, 2/4, 1973a, pp. 463–473.

Cooley, T., and E. Prescott, "An Adaptive Regression Model," *International Economic Review*, 14, 1973b, pp. 364–371.

Cooper, P., "Two Approaches to Polynomial Distributed Lag Estimation," *The American Statistician*, 26, 1972, pp. 32–35.

Dhrymes, P., "Efficient Estimation of Distributed Lags with Autocorrelated Errors," *International Economic Review*, 10, 1969, pp. 47–67.

Dhrymes, P., *Distributed Lags: Problems of Estimation and Formulation*, San Francisco: Holden-Day, 1971.

Dhrymes, P., *Mathematics for Econometrics*, New York: Springer-Verlag, 1978.

Dickey, D., and W. Fuller, "Distribution of the Estimators for Autoregressive Time Series with a Unit Root," *Journal of the American Statistical Association*, 74, 1979, pp. 427–431.

Dickey, D., and W. Fuller, "Likelihood Ratio Statistics for Autoregressive Time Series with a Unit Root," *Econometrica*, 49, 1981, pp. 1057–1072.

Doran, H., and W. Griffiths, "Inconsistency of the OLS Estimator of the Partial Adjustment—Adaptive Expectations Model," *Journal of Econometrics*, 6, 1978, pp. 133–146.

Fomby, T., and D. Guilkey, "An Examination of Two-Step Estimators for Models with Lagged Dependent Variables and Autocorrelated Errors," *Journal of Econometrics*, 22, 1983, pp. 291–300.

Fomby, T., C. Hill, and S. Johnson, *Advanced Econometric Methods*, New York: Springer-Verlag, 1984.

Frost, P., "Some Properties of the Almon Lag Technique When One Searches for Degree of Polynomial and Lag," *Journal of the American Statistical Association*, 70, 1975, pp. 606–612.

Fuller, W., *Introduction to Statistical Time Series*, New York: Wiley, 1976.

Geweke, J., and R. Meese, "Estimating Regression Models of Finite But Unknown Order," *International Economic Review*, 22, 1981, pp. 55–70.

Godfrey, L., "Testing Against General Autoregressive and Moving Average Error Models When the Regressors Include Lagged Dependent Variables," *Econometrica*, 46, 1978, pp. 1293–1302.

Godfrey, L., and D. Poskitt, "Testing the Restrictions of the Almon Lag Technique," *Journal of the American Statistical Association*, 70, 1975, pp. 105–108.

Gordon, R., ed., *The American Business Cycle*, Chicago: National Bureau of Economic Research, 1986.

Granger, C., *Forecasting in Business and Economics*, New York: Academic Press, 1980.

Granger, C., and P. Newbold, *Forecasting Economic Time Series*, New York: Academic Press, 1976.

Grether, D., and G. Maddala, "Errors in Variables and Serially Correlated Disturbances in Distributed Lag Models," *Econometrica*, 41, 1973, pp. 255–262.

Griliches, Z., "Distributed Lags: A Survey," *Econometrica*, 35, 1967, pp. 16–49.

Griliches, Z., G. Maddala, R. Lucas, and N. Wallace, "Notes on Estimated Aggregate Quarterly Consumption Functions," *Econometrica*, 30, 1962, pp. 491–500.

Harvey, A., *The Econometric Analysis of Time Series*, Oxford: Philip Allan, 1981.

Hatanaka, M., "Several Efficient Two-Step Estimators for the Dynamic Simultaneous Equations Model with Autoregressive Disturbances," *Journal of Econometrics*, 4, 1976, pp. 189–204.

Hendry, D., A. Pagan, and D. Sargan, "Dynamic Specification," in Z. Griliches, and M. Intrilligator, eds., *Handbook of Econometrics*, Vol. 2, Amsterdam: North Holland, 1984.

Johnston, J., *Econometric Methods*, New York: McGraw-Hill, 1984.

Jorgenson, D., "Rational Distributed Lag Functions," *Econometrica*, 34, 1966, pp. 135–149.

Judge, G., C. Hill, W. Griffiths, T. Lee, and H. Lutkepohl, *Introduction to the Theory and Practice of Econometrics*, New York: Wiley, 1982.

Koyck, L., *Distributed Lags and Investment Analysis*, Amsterdam: North Holland, 1954.

Liviatan, N., "Consistent Estimation of Distributed Lags," *International Economic Review*, 4, 1963, pp. 44–52.

Maddala, G., *Econometrics*, New York: McGraw-Hill, 1977.

Maddala, G., and A. Rao, "Maximum Likelihood Estimation of Solow's and Jorgenson's Distributed Lag Models," *Review of Economics and Statistics*, 53, 1971, pp. 80–88.

Maddala, G., and A. Rao, "Tests for Serial Correlation in Regression Models with Lagged Dependent Variables and Serially Correlated Errors," *Econometrica*, 41, 1976, pp. 761–774.

Nelson, C., and C. Plosser, "Trends and Random Walks in Macroeconomic Time Series: Some Evidence and Implications," *Journal of Monetary Economics*, 10, 1982, pp. 139–162.

Nerlove, M., "Lags in Economic Behavior," *Econometrica*, 40, 1972, pp. 221–251.

Pagano, M., and M. Hartley, "On Fitting Distributed Lag Models Subject to Polynomial Restrictions," *Journal of Econometrics*, 16, 1981, pp. 171–198.

Pesaran, H., "The Small Sample Problem of Truncation Remainders in the Estimation of Distributed Lag Models with Autocorrelated Errors," *International Economic Review*, 14, 1973, pp. 120–131.

Schmidt, P., "A Modification of the Almon Distributed Lag," *Journal of the American Statistical Association*, 69, 1974a, pp. 679–681.

Schmidt, P., "An Argument for the Usefulness of the Gamma Distributed Lag Model," *International Economic Review*, 15, 1974b, pp. 246–250.

Schmidt, P., "The Small Sample Effects of Various Treatments of Truncation Remainders in the Estimation of Distributed Lag Models," *Review of Economics and Statistics*, 57, 1975, pp. 387–389.

Schmidt, P., *Econometrics*, New York: Marcel-Dekker, 1976.

Schmidt, P., and R. Sickles, "On the Efficiency of the Almon Lag Technique," *International Economic Review*, 16, 1975, pp. 792–795.

Schmidt, P., and R. Waud, "The Almon Lag Technique and the Monetary versus Fiscal Policy Debate," *Journal of the American Statistical Association*, 68, 1973, pp. 11–19.

Shiller, R., "A Distributed Lag Estimator Derived from Smoothness Priors," *Econometrica*, 41, 1973, pp. 775–778.

Sims, C., "Money, Income, and Causality," *American Economic Review*, 62, 1972, pp. 540–552.

Solow, R., "On a Family of Lag Distributions," *Econometrica*, 28, 1960, pp. 393–406.

Taylor, W., "Smoothness Priors and Stochastic Prior Restrictions in Distributed Lag Estimation," *International Economic Review*, 15, 1974, pp. 803–804.

Theil, H., and A. Goldberger, "On Pure and Mixed Estimation in Economics," *International Economic Review*, 2, 1961, pp. 65–78.

Theil, H., and R. Stern, "A Simple Unimodal Lag Distribution," *Metroeconomica*, 12, 1960, pp. 111–119.

Trivedi, P., and A. Pagan, "Polynomial Distributed Lags: A Unified Treatment," *Economic Studies Quarterly*, 30, 1979, pp. 37–49.

Tsurumi, H., "A Note on Gamma Distributed Lags," *International Economic Review*, 12, 1971, pp. 317–324.

United States Department of Commerce, *National Income and Product Accounts*, Bureau of Economic Analysis, "Survey of Current Business: Business Statistics, 1984," Washington, D.C., 1984.

Zellner, A., and M. Geisel, "Analysis of Distributed Lag Models with Application to the Consumption Function," *Econometrica*, 38, 1970, pp. 865–888.

Chapter 19

Simultaneous-Equations Models

19.1. Introduction

Most of our work thus far has been in the context of single-equation models. But even a cursory look through almost any economics textbook shows that much of the theory is built upon sets, or *systems*, of relationships. Familiar examples include market equilibrium, models of the macroeconomy, and sets of factor or commodity demand equations. Whether one's interest is only in a particular part of the system or in the system as a whole, the interaction of the variables in the model will have important implications for both interpretation and estimation of the model's equations. The implications of simultaneity for econometric estimation were recognized long before the apparatus discussed in this chapter was developed.[1] The subsequent research in the subject, continuing to the present, is perhaps the most extensive in econometrics and, it could be argued, encompasses a large proportion of the field.[2]

This chapter considers the issues that arise in interpreting and estimating multiple-equations models. Section 19.2 describes the general framework used for analyzing systems of simultaneous equations and presents some examples. Most of the discussion of these models centers on problems of estimation. But before estimation can even be considered, the fundamental question of whether the parameters of interest in the model are even estimable must be resolved. This problem of identification is discussed in Section 19.3. Section 19.4 then discusses methods of estimation. Sections 19.5 and 19.6 are concerned with specification tests and forecasting with simultaneous equations models. In Section 19.6 the special characteristics of dynamic models are examined. Forecasting is considered in Section 19.7.

19.2. Fundamental Issues in Simultaneous-Equations Models

In this section we describe the basic terminology and statistical issues in the analysis of simultaneous-equations models. We begin with some simple examples and then present a general framework.

---

[1] See, for example, Working (1926) and Haavelmo (1943).

[2] The literature on simultaneous-equations models is enormous and continually expanding. Even constructing a complete and current bibliography is a considerable undertaking. Three recent surveys in the *Handbook of Econometrics*, Vol. I (Griliches and Intrilligator (1983)) by C. Hsiao on identification, J. Hausman on specification and estimation, and P. Phillips on small-sample properties of estimators provide a good overview of the literature. Other extensive sources include Judge et al. (1985) and Fomby et al. (1984). The latter half of Schmidt (1976) contains many useful theorems and results.

19.2.1. Illustrative Systems of Equations

A familiar example of a system of simultaneous equations is a model of market equilibrium, consisting of the following:

$$\text{Demand equation:} \quad q_d = \alpha_1 p + \alpha_2 y + \varepsilon_d,$$

$$\text{Supply equation:} \quad q_s = \beta_1 p \qquad + \varepsilon_s,$$

$$\text{Equilibrium condition:} \quad q_d = q_s = q.$$

These are **structural equations** in that they are derived from theory and each purports to describe a particular aspect of the economy.[3] Since the model is one of the joint determination of price and quantity, they are labeled **jointly dependent** or **endogenous** variables. Income, y, is assumed to be determined outside of the model, which makes it **exogenous**. The disturbances are added to the usual textbook description to obtain an **econometric model**. All three equations are needed to determine the equilibrium price and quantity, so the system is **interdependent**. Finally, since an equilibrium solution for price and quantity in terms of income and the disturbances is, indeed, implied (unless α_1 equals β_1), the system is said to be a **complete system of equations**.

Suppose that interest centers on estimating the demand elasticity, α_1. For simplicity, assume that ε_d and ε_s are well-behaved, classical disturbances with

$$E[\varepsilon_{dt}] = E[\varepsilon_{st}] = 0,$$

$$E[\varepsilon_{dt}^2] = \sigma_d^2, \qquad E[\varepsilon_{st}^2] = \sigma_s^2, \qquad E[\varepsilon_{dt}\varepsilon_{st}] = 0,$$

and

$$E[\varepsilon_{dt} y_t] = E[\varepsilon_{st} y_t] = 0.$$

All variables are mutually uncorrelated with observations at different time periods. Price, quantity, and income are measured in logarithms in deviations from their sample means. Solving the equations for p and q in terms of y, ε_d, and ε_s produces the **reduced form** of the model,

$$p = \frac{\alpha_2 y}{\beta_1 - \alpha_1} + \frac{\varepsilon_d - \varepsilon_s}{\beta_1 - \alpha_1} = \pi_1 y + v_1,$$

$$q = \frac{\beta_1 \alpha_2 y}{\beta_1 - \alpha_1} + \frac{\beta_1 \varepsilon_d - \alpha_1 \varepsilon_s}{\beta_1 - \alpha_1} = \pi_2 y + v_2.$$

(19–1)

(Note the "completeness" requirement that α_1 not equal β_1.)

It follows that $\text{Cov}[p, \varepsilon_d] = \sigma_d^2/(\beta_1 - \alpha_1)$, so the demand equation does not satisfy the assumptions of the classical regression model. The price elasticity cannot be consistently estimated by least squares regression of q on y and p. This result is characteristic of simultaneous-equations models. Because the endogenous variables are all correlated with the disturbances, least squares estimates of the parameters of equations with endogenous variables on the right-hand side are inconsistent.[4]

---

[3] The distinction between *structural* and *nonstructural* models is sometimes drawn on this basis. See, for example, Cooley and LeRoy (1985).

[4] This failure of least squares is sometimes labeled *simultaneous-equations bias*.

Suppose that α_1 could be consistently estimated, perhaps by some other method. Is it the desired elasticity? The usual definition holds that

$$\text{price elasticity} = \frac{d \ln Q}{d \ln P} \bigg| \text{ ceteris paribus.} \tag{19-2}$$

In the current setting, there is an inconsistency in this statement. If everything else is to be held constant, what shall induce the change in p? The quantity dq/dp has no content until we identify what caused p to change. There are three sources of change in the model: shifts in the demand curve due to changes in y or ε_d and shifts in the supply curve due to changes in ε_s. If income changes, inducing a shift of the demand curve,

$$\frac{dq}{dp} = \frac{(\partial q/\partial y)dy}{(\partial p/\partial y)dy} = \beta_1,$$

not α_1. Alternatively, if the supply curve shifts,

$$\frac{dq}{dp} = \frac{(\partial q/\partial \varepsilon_s)d\varepsilon_s}{(\partial p/\partial \varepsilon_s)d\varepsilon_s} = \alpha_1.$$

Under normal circumstances, β_1 and α_1 have different signs, so the meaning of (19-2) is a bit unclear. In a complete model such as this one, it makes no sense to speak of the change in one of the jointly determined variables "induced" by a change in another jointly determined variable without first specifying what was responsible for the changes.

Now let us return to the problem of estimation. For simplicity, consider the supply equation. Suppose that we have a sample of T observations on p, q, and y, such that

$$\text{plim} \frac{1}{T} \mathbf{y}'\mathbf{y} = \sigma_y^2.$$

Then the coefficient in a simple regression of q on p would have probability limit

$$\text{plim} \frac{\mathbf{p}'\mathbf{q}/T}{\mathbf{p}'\mathbf{p}/T} = \frac{[\beta_1(\alpha_2^2\sigma_y^2 + \sigma_d^2) + \alpha_1\sigma_s^2]/(\beta_1 - \alpha_1)^2}{[(\alpha_2^2\sigma_y^2 + \sigma_d^2) + \sigma_s^2]/(\beta_1 - \alpha_1)^2}$$

$$= \theta\alpha_1 + (1 - \theta)\beta_1,$$

where

$$0 \le \theta = \frac{\sigma_s^2}{(\alpha_2^2\sigma_{yy} + \sigma_d^2) + \sigma_s^2} \le 1.$$

The slope estimates a mixture of the slopes of the supply and demand curves. The constant, θ, is the proportion of the variance of p accounted for by shifts of the supply curve. This reflects, as we saw earlier, the fact that covariation of p and q arises through shifts of both curves.

Since least squares is inconsistent, we might instead use an **instrumental variable estimator.**[5] The only variable in the system not correlated with the disturbances is y. Consider, then, the IV estimator, $\hat{\beta}_1 = \mathbf{q}'\mathbf{y}/\mathbf{p}'\mathbf{y}$. This estimator has

$$\text{plim} \hat{\beta}_1 = \text{plim} \frac{\mathbf{q}'\mathbf{y}/T}{\mathbf{p}'\mathbf{y}/T} = \frac{\beta_1\alpha_2\sigma_y^2/(\beta_1 - \alpha_1)}{\alpha_2\sigma_y^2/(\beta_1 - \alpha_1)} = \beta_1.$$

---

[5] See Sections 9.5.4 and 18.2.2d for discussion if this is not familiar.

Evidently, the parameter of the supply curve can be estimated by using an instrumental variable estimator. There are two useful arrangements of this result. First, from (19–1), we see that

$$\hat{\beta}_1 = \frac{p_{11}}{p_{12}} = \frac{\text{slope in the regression of } q \text{ on } y}{\text{slope in the regression of } p \text{ on } y}.$$

Thus, the estimator is the ratio of the OLS estimates of π_1 and π_2. This technique is labeled **indirect least squares**. Second, in the least squares regression of **p** on **y**, the predicted values are

$$\hat{\mathbf{p}} = \left(\frac{\mathbf{p}'\mathbf{y}}{\mathbf{y}'\mathbf{y}}\right)\mathbf{y}.$$

It follows that in the instrumental variable regression the instrument is $\hat{\mathbf{p}}$. That is,

$$\hat{\beta}_1 = \frac{\hat{\mathbf{p}}'\mathbf{q}}{\hat{\mathbf{p}}'\mathbf{p}}.$$

Finally, since $\hat{\mathbf{p}}'\mathbf{p} = \hat{\mathbf{p}}'\hat{\mathbf{p}}$, $\hat{\beta}_1$ is also the slope in a regression of q on these predicted values. This interpretation defines the **two-stage least squares estimator**.

EXAMPLE 19.1. Supply Equation for Agricultural Goods. Yearly data on price and quantity for the U.S. agricultural sector and real per capita disposable income for U.S. consumers for the years 1960 to 1986 are listed in the appendix to this chapter. Ordinary least squares regression of Q on P produces

$$\hat{Q} = 54.13 + 0.4195P.$$

The instrumental variable estimator suggested earlier produces

$$\hat{Q} = 46.93 + 0.5038P,$$

a 20.1 percent difference in the estimated slope.

It would be desirable to use a similar device to estimate the parameters of the demand equation. But, unfortunately, we have exhausted the information in the sample. Not only does least squares fail to estimate the demand equation but, without some further assumptions, the sample contains no other information that can be used. This example illustrates the **problem of identification** alluded to in the Introduction.

A second example is the following simple model of income determination.

EXAMPLE 19.2. A Small Macroeconomic Model

(Consumption) $c_t = \alpha_0 + \alpha_1 y_t + \alpha_2 c_{t-1} + \varepsilon_{t1}$,

(Investment) $i_t = \beta_0 + \beta_1 r_t + \beta_2(y_t - y_{t-1}) + \varepsilon_{t2}$,

(Demand) $y_t = c_t + i_t + g_t$.

The model contains the autoregressive consumption function we examined in Chapter 18, an investment equation based on interest and the growth in output, and an equilibrium condition. The model determines the values of the three endogenous variables, c_t, i_t, and y_t. This is a **dynamic model**. In addition to the exogenous variables, r_t and g_t, it contains two **predetermined variables**, c_{t-1} and y_{t-1}. These are obviously not exogenous, but, as regards the current values of the endogenous variables, may be regarded as having already been determined. The deciding factor is whether or not they are uncorrelated with the current disturbances, which we might assume. The reduced form of this model is

$$\Delta c_t = \alpha_0(1 - \beta_2) + \beta_0\alpha_1 + \alpha_1\beta_1 r_t + \alpha_1 g_t$$
$$+ \alpha_2(1 - \beta_2)c_{t-1} - \alpha_1\beta_2 y_{t-1} + (1 - \beta_2)\varepsilon_{t1} + \alpha_1\varepsilon_{t2},$$
$$\Delta i_t = \alpha_0\beta_2 + \beta_0(1 - \alpha_1) + \beta_1(1 - \alpha_1)r_t + \beta_2 g_t$$
$$+ \alpha_2\beta_2 c_{t-1} - \beta_2(1 - \alpha_1)y_{t-1} + \beta_2\varepsilon_{t1} + (1 - \alpha_1)\varepsilon_{t2},$$
$$\Delta y_t = \alpha_0 + \beta_0 + \beta_1 r_t + g_t + \alpha_2 c_{t-1} - \beta_2 y_{t-1} + \varepsilon_{t1} + \varepsilon_{t2},$$

where

$$\Delta = 1 - \alpha_1 - \beta_2.$$

Note that the reduced form preserves the equilibrium condition.

This model is a generalization of the autoregressive models we examined in the previous chapter. By using the lag operator and substituting the second and third equations into the first, we can reduce it one of the form

$$c_t = \delta_{0t} + \delta_1 c_{t-1} + \delta_2 c_{t-2} + \delta_3 c_{t-3}.$$

As we saw in the previous chapter, a third-order difference equation such as this need not be stable or have an equilibrium. Since each equation in the model could be similarly manipulated, the stability and existence of equilibrium of the entire model are characteristics that we will want to examine.

The distinction between endogenous and exogenous variables in econometric models is occasionally controversial. In a model of supply and demand, there is little question as to what is and what is not determined within the market. But in macroeconomic models the issue is much more ambiguous. To take a common example, the estimation of consumption functions by least squares, as we did in Chapter 18, is usually treated as a respectable enterprise, in spite of the fact that most macroeconomic models (including the examples given here) depart from a consumption function in which income is endogenous. Nonetheless, the distinction is crucial.[6] *The completeness of the system requires that the number of equations equal the number of endogenous variables.* We observe that, as a general rule, it is not possible to estimate the parameters of incomplete systems.

The preceding two models illustrate systems in which there are **behavioral equations** and **equilibrium conditions**. The latter are distinct in that even in an econometric model, they have no disturbances. Another model, which illustrates nearly all of the concepts to be discussed in this chapter, is shown in the next example.

EXAMPLE 19.3. Klein's Model I. A widely used example of a simultaneous equations model of the economy is Klein's (1950) *Model I*. The model may be written

$$C_t = \alpha_0 + \alpha_1 P_t + \alpha_2 P_{t-1} + \alpha_3(W_t^p + W_t^g) + \varepsilon_{1t} \text{ (consumption)},$$

$$I_t = \beta_0 + \beta_1 P_t + \beta_2 P_{t-1} + \beta_3 K_{t-1} \qquad + \varepsilon_{2t} \quad \text{(investment)},$$

$$W_t^p = \gamma_0 + \gamma_1 X_t + \gamma_2 X_{t-1} + \gamma_3 A_t \qquad + \varepsilon_{3t} \text{ (private wages)},$$

$$X_t = C_t + I_t + G_t \qquad\qquad\qquad \text{(equilibrium demand)},$$

---

[6] The issue of "causality" discussed by a number of authors, for example, Sims (1972), is closely related. It makes sense that in a model of the determination of Y, if Y causes X, treating X as exogenous would be problematic, almost regardless of one's definition of causality.

$$P_t = X_t - T_t - W_t^p \qquad \text{(private profits)},$$

$$K_t = K_{t-1} + I_t \qquad \text{(capital stock)}.$$

[Other equivalent forms of this model have been reported in different places in the literature. See, for example, Goldberger (1964) and Kmenta (1986).] The endogenous variables are each on the left-hand side of an equation and labeled on the right. The exogenous variables are G = government spending, T = indirect business taxes plus net exports, W^g = government wage bill, A = time trend measured as years from 1931, and the constant term. There are also three predetermined variables: the lagged values of the capital stock, private profits, and total demand. The model contains three behavioral equations: an equilibrium condition and two accounting identities. This model provides an excellent example of a small, dynamic model of the economy. It has also been widely used as a test ground for simultaneous-equations estimators. Klein estimated the parameters using data for 1921 to 1941. The data are listed in the appendix.

19.2.2.   A General Notation for Simultaneous-Equations Models

The **structural form** of the model is[7]

$$\gamma_{11} y_{1t} + \gamma_{21} y_{2t} + \cdots + \gamma_{M1} y_{Mt} + \beta_{11} x_{1t} + \cdots + \beta_{K1} x_{Kt} = \varepsilon_{t1}$$

$$\gamma_{12} y_{1t} + \gamma_{22} y_{2t} + \cdots + \gamma_{M2} y_{Mt} + \beta_{12} x_{1t} + \cdots + \beta_{K2} x_{Kt} = \varepsilon_{t2}$$

$$\vdots \qquad\qquad (19\text{-}3)$$

$$\gamma_{1M} y_{1t} + \gamma_{2M} y_{2t} + \cdots + \gamma_{MM} y_{Mt} + \beta_{1M} x_{1t} + \cdots + \beta_{KM} x_{Kt} = \varepsilon_{tM}.$$

There are M equations and M endogenous variables, denoted $y_1, \ldots, y_M$. There are K exogenous variables, $x_1, \ldots, x_K$, which may include predetermined values of $y_1, \ldots, y_M$ as well. The first element of $\mathbf{x}_t$ will usually be the constant, one. Finally, $\varepsilon_{t1}, \ldots, \varepsilon_{tM}$ are the **structural disturbances**. The subscript, t, will be used to index observations, $t = 1, \ldots, T$.

In matrix terms, the system may be written

$$[y_1 \quad y_2 \quad \cdots \quad y_M]_t \begin{bmatrix} \gamma_{11} & \gamma_{12} & \cdots & \gamma_{1M} \\ \gamma_{21} & \gamma_{22} & \cdots & \gamma_{2M} \\ & & \vdots & \\ \gamma_{M1} & \gamma_{M2} & \cdots & \gamma_{MM} \end{bmatrix} + [x_1 \quad x_2 \quad \cdots \quad x_K]_t \begin{bmatrix} \beta_{11} & \beta_{12} & \cdots & \beta_{1M} \\ \beta_{21} & \beta_{22} & \cdots & \beta_{2M} \\ & & \vdots & \\ \beta_{K1} & \beta_{K2} & \cdots & \beta_{KM} \end{bmatrix}$$

$$= [\varepsilon_1 \quad \varepsilon_2 \quad \cdots \quad \varepsilon_M]_t$$

or

$$\mathbf{y}_t' \mathbf{\Gamma} + \mathbf{x}_t' \mathbf{B} = \boldsymbol{\varepsilon}_t'. \qquad (19\text{-}4)$$

Each column of the parameter matrices is the vector of coefficients in a particular equation, while each row applies to a specific variable.

The underlying theory will imply a number of restrictions on $\mathbf{\Gamma}$ and $\mathbf{B}$. One of the variables in each equation is labeled the *dependent* variable, so that its coefficient in the model will be 1. Thus, there will be at least one "1" in each column of $\mathbf{\Gamma}$. If there are any identities,

---

[7] For the present, it is convenient to ignore the special nature of lagged endogenous variables and treat them the same as the strictly exogenous variables.

the corresponding columns of Γ and $\mathbf{B}$ will be completely known, and there will be no disturbance for that equation. Since not all variables appear in all equations, some of the parameters will be zero. The theory may also impose other types of restrictions on the parameter matrices.

A special case of the preceding is worth noting before we proceed. If Γ is an upper triangular matrix, the system is said to be **triangular**. In this case, the model is of the form

$$y_{1t} = f_1(\mathbf{x}_t) + \varepsilon_{1t}$$

$$y_{2t} = f_2(y_{1t}, \mathbf{x}_t) + \varepsilon_{2t}$$

$$\vdots$$

$$y_{Mt} = f_M(y_{1t}, y_{2t}, \ldots, y_{M-1,t} \mathbf{x}_t) + \varepsilon_{Mt}.$$

The joint determination of the variables in this model is *recursive*. The first is completely determined by the exogenous factors. Then, given the first, the second is likewise determined, and so on. The temporal aspects of some processes in the economy suggest this form of model.

EXAMPLE 19.4. **Cobweb Model.** The cobweb model of market equilibrium may be written

$$Q_t = \alpha_0 + \alpha_1 P_{t-1} + \varepsilon_{1t} \qquad \text{(supply)},$$

$$P_t = \beta_0 + \beta_1 Q_t + \varepsilon_{2t} \qquad \text{(inverse demand)}.$$

The quantity supplied to the market is determined by last year's price, a bygone. Supply in the current period is perfectly inelastic. Demand responds to the usual forces and determines an equilibrium price, which feeds into next year's supply.

In essence, the endogenous variables are determined in turn, each one depending on the values of the logically preceding ones. Users of spreadsheet programs and those who fill out their own tax returns will recognize other familiar examples of recursive systems.

The solution of the system of equations determining y_t in terms of $\mathbf{x}_t$ and ε_t is the **reduced form** of the model,

$$\mathbf{y}_t' = -\mathbf{x}_t'\mathbf{B}\Gamma^{-1} + \varepsilon_t'\Gamma^{-1}$$

$$= \mathbf{x}_t'\Pi + \mathbf{v}_t'$$

$$= [x_1 \quad x_2 \quad \cdots \quad x_K]_t \begin{bmatrix} \pi_{11} & \pi_{12} & \cdots & \pi_{1M} \\ \pi_{21} & \pi_{22} & \cdots & \pi_{2M} \\ & & \vdots & \\ \pi_{K1} & \pi_{K2} & \cdots & \pi_{KM} \end{bmatrix} + [v_1 \quad \cdots \quad v_M]_t$$

where

$$\Pi = -\mathbf{B}\Gamma^{-1} \qquad\qquad (19-5)$$

and

$$\mathbf{v}_t' = \varepsilon_t'\Gamma^{-1}.$$

In order for this solution to exist, the model must satisfy the

Completeness condition: Γ is nonsingular.

EXAMPLE 19.5. Structure and Reduced Form.   For the small model in Example 19.2,

$$\mathbf{y}' = [c, i, y], \qquad \mathbf{x}' = [1, r, g, c_{-1}, y_{-1}]$$

$$\Gamma = \begin{bmatrix} 1 & 0 & -1 \\ 0 & 1 & -1 \\ -\alpha_1 & -\beta_2 & 1 \end{bmatrix}, \qquad \mathbf{B} = \begin{bmatrix} -\alpha_0 & -\beta_0 & 0 \\ 0 & -\beta_1 & 0 \\ 0 & 0 & -1 \\ -\alpha_2 & 0 & 0 \\ 0 & \beta_2 & 0 \end{bmatrix}$$

$$\Gamma^{-1} = \begin{bmatrix} (1-\beta_2)/(1-\alpha_1-\beta_2) & \beta_2/(1-\alpha_1-\beta_2) & 1/(1-\alpha_1-\beta_2) \\ \alpha_1/(1-\alpha_1-\beta_2) & (1-\alpha_1)/(1-\alpha_1-\beta_2) & 1/(1-\alpha_1-\beta_2) \\ \alpha_1/(1-\alpha_1-\beta_2) & \beta_2/(1-\alpha_1-\beta_2) & 1/(1-\alpha_1-\beta_2) \end{bmatrix}$$

$$\Pi' = \frac{1}{1-\alpha_1-\beta_2} \begin{bmatrix} \alpha_0(1-\beta_2+\beta_0\alpha_1) & \alpha_1\beta_1 & \alpha_1 & \alpha_2(1-\beta_2) & -\beta_2\alpha_1 \\ \alpha_0\beta_2+\beta_0(1-\alpha_1) & \beta_1(1-\alpha_1) & \beta_2 & \alpha_2\beta_2 & -\beta_2(1-\alpha_1) \\ \alpha_0+\beta_0 & \beta_1 & 1 & \alpha_2 & -\beta_2 \end{bmatrix}$$

The completeness condition is that α_1 and β_2 do not sum to one.

The structural disturbances are assumed to be randomly drawn from an M-variate distribution with

$$E[\varepsilon_t] = 0 \qquad \text{and} \qquad E[\varepsilon_t \varepsilon_t'] = \Sigma. \tag{19-6}$$

For the present, we assume that

$$E[\varepsilon_t \varepsilon_s'] = 0 \qquad \text{for all } t \neq s.$$

Later, we will drop this assumption in order to allow for autocorrelation. It will occasionally be useful to assume that ε_t has a multivariate normal distribution, but we shall postpone this assumption until it becomes necessary. It may be convenient to retain the identities without disturbances as separate equations. If so, one way to proceed with the stochastic specification is to place rows and columns of zeros in the appropriate places in Σ.

It follows that the **reduced-form disturbances**,

$$\mathbf{v}_t' = \varepsilon_t' \Gamma^{-1} \tag{19-7}$$

have

$$E[\mathbf{v}_t] = (\Gamma^{-1})'0 = 0, \tag{19-8}$$
$$E[\mathbf{v}_t \mathbf{v}_t'] = (\Gamma^{-1})' \Sigma \Gamma^{-1} = \Omega.$$

This implies that

$$\Sigma = \Gamma' \Omega \Gamma.$$

The preceding formulation describes the model as it applies to an observation $[\mathbf{y}', \mathbf{x}', \varepsilon']_t$ at a particular point in time or in a cross section. In a sample of data, each joint observation will be one row in a data matrix,

$$[\mathbf{Y} \quad \mathbf{X} \quad \mathbf{E}] = \begin{bmatrix} \mathbf{y}_1' & \mathbf{x}_1' & \varepsilon_1' \\ \mathbf{y}_2' & \mathbf{x}_2' & \varepsilon_2' \\ \vdots \\ \mathbf{y}_T' & \mathbf{x}_T' & \varepsilon_T' \end{bmatrix}.$$

In terms of the full set of T observations, the structure is

$$\mathbf{Y\Gamma + XB = E,}$$ (19–9)

with

$$E[\mathbf{E}] = \mathbf{0} \quad \text{and} \quad E\left[\frac{\mathbf{E'E}}{T}\right] = \mathbf{\Sigma}.$$

Under general conditions, we can strengthen this to

$$\text{plim}\left[\frac{\mathbf{E'E}}{T}\right] = \mathbf{\Sigma}.$$ (19–10)

An important assumption, comparable to the one made in Chapter 10 for the classical regression model, is

$$\text{plim}\,\frac{\mathbf{X'X}}{T} = \mathbf{Q}, \quad \text{a finite positive definite matrix.}$$ (19–11)

Once again, an important exception, which appears in our primary example in this chapter, is a time trend. The same consideration is made here; formally, what we require is for $\text{plim}[\mathbf{X'X}]^{-1}$ to vanish. If $\mathbf{x}$ contains lagged values of $\mathbf{y}$, the assumption places a number of restrictions on the process generating the data, primarily that any autocorrelation in the variables fades sufficiently rapidly with distance in time that the preceding probability limit exists. Some discussion appears in Chapter 10. Schmidt[8] gives some additional results.

We also assume that

$$\text{plim}\,\frac{\mathbf{X'E}}{T} = \mathbf{0}.$$ (19–12)

This is what distinguishes the predetermined from the endogenous variables. If the rows of $\mathbf{X}$ are nonstochastic, (19–12) will obviously hold, but in realistic settings, that is unlikely. For stochastic x's, we assume that if there is autocorrelation, it is sufficiently weak that (19–12) holds. The assumption in (19–11) hinges on the same condition.

The reduced form is

$$\mathbf{Y = X\Pi + V,}$$

where

$$\mathbf{V = E\Gamma^{-1}.}$$

With the earlier assumptions, we also have

$$\text{plim}\,\frac{\mathbf{V'V}}{T} = (\mathbf{\Gamma^{-1}})'\mathbf{\Sigma\Gamma^{-1}} = \mathbf{\Omega,}$$

$$\text{plim}\,\frac{\mathbf{Y'Y}}{T} = \mathbf{\Pi'Q\Pi} + \mathbf{\Omega,}$$ (19–13)

$$\text{plim}\,\frac{\mathbf{X'V}}{T} = \mathbf{0,}$$

and

$$\text{plim}\,\frac{\mathbf{X'Y}}{T} = \mathbf{Q\Pi.}$$

[8] Op. cit.

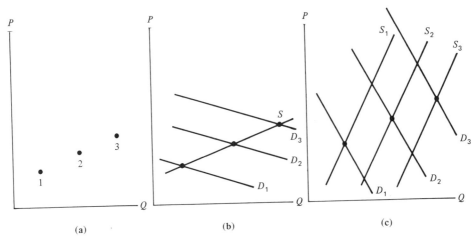

Figure 19.1 Market equilibria.

19.3. *The Problem of Identification*

Solving the problem to be considered here, the identification problem, logically precedes estimation. We ask at this point whether there is *any* way to obtain estimates of the parameters of the model. We have in hand a certain amount of information upon which to base any inference about its underlying structure. If more than one theory is consistent with the same "data," they are said to be **observationally equivalent**, and there is no way of distinguishing them. The structure is said to be *unidentified.*[9]

EXAMPLE 19.6. **Observational Equivalence.**   The *observed* data consist of the market outcomes shown in Figure 18.1a. We have no knowledge of the conditions of supply and demand beyond our belief that the data represent *equilibria*. Unfortunately, Figures 19.1b and 19.1c both show *structures*, that is, true underlying supply and demand curves, which are consistent with the data in Figure 19.1a. With only the data in Figure 19.1a, we have no way of determining which of theories 19.1b or 19.1c is the right one. Thus, the structure underlying the data in Figure 19.1a is unidentified.[10] To suggest where our discussion is headed, suppose that we add to the preceding the known fact that the conditions of supply were unchanged during the period over which the data were drawn. This rules out 19.1.c and identifies 19.1b as the correct structure. This is precisely the scenario underlying Example 19.1 and the surrounding discussion.

The identification problem is not one of sampling properties or the size of the sample. To focus ideas, it is even useful to suppose that we have at hand an infinite-sized sample of observations on the variables in the model. Now, with this and our prior theory, what information do we have?

In the reduced form,

$$\mathbf{y}_t' = \mathbf{x}_t'\mathbf{\Pi} + \mathbf{v}_t', \qquad E[\mathbf{v}_t\mathbf{v}_t'] = \mathbf{\Omega},$$

---

[9] A useful survey of this issue is Hsiao (1983).
[10] This example paraphrases the classic argument of Working (1926).

the predetermined variables are uncorrelated with the disturbances. Thus, we can "observe"

$$\text{plim}\,\frac{\mathbf{X}'\mathbf{X}}{T} = \mathbf{Q} \qquad [\text{assumed; see } (19\text{--}11)],$$

$$\text{plim}\,\frac{\mathbf{X}'\mathbf{Y}}{T} = \text{plim}\,\frac{\mathbf{X}'(\mathbf{X}\boldsymbol{\Pi} + \mathbf{V})}{T} = \mathbf{Q}\boldsymbol{\Pi},$$

and

$$\text{plim}\,\frac{\mathbf{Y}'\mathbf{Y}}{T} = \text{plim}\,\frac{(\boldsymbol{\Pi}'\mathbf{X}' + \mathbf{V}')(\mathbf{X}\boldsymbol{\Pi} + \mathbf{V})}{T} = \boldsymbol{\Pi}'\mathbf{Q}\boldsymbol{\Pi} + \boldsymbol{\Omega}.$$

Therefore, $\boldsymbol{\Pi}$, the matrix of reduced-form coefficients, is observable:

$$\boldsymbol{\Pi} = \left[\text{plim}\left(\frac{\mathbf{X}'\mathbf{X}}{\mathbf{T}}\right)\right]^{-1}\left[\text{plim}\left(\frac{\mathbf{X}'\mathbf{Y}}{\mathbf{T}}\right)\right].$$

This is simply the equation-by-equation least squares regression of $\mathbf{Y}$ on $\mathbf{X}$. Since $\boldsymbol{\Pi}$ is observable, $\boldsymbol{\Omega}$ is also:

$$\boldsymbol{\Omega} = \text{plim}\,\frac{\mathbf{Y}'\mathbf{Y}}{T} - \text{plim}\left[\frac{\mathbf{Y}'\mathbf{X}}{T}\right]\left[\frac{\mathbf{X}'\mathbf{X}}{T}\right]^{-1}\left[\frac{\mathbf{X}'\mathbf{Y}}{T}\right].$$

This should be recognizable as the matrix of least squares residual variances and covariances. Therefore,

> $\boldsymbol{\Pi}$ and $\boldsymbol{\Omega}$ can be estimated consistently by
> ordinary least squares regression of $\mathbf{Y}$ on $\mathbf{X}$.

The information in hand, therefore, consists of $\boldsymbol{\Pi}$, $\boldsymbol{\Omega}$, and whatever other nonsample information we have about the structure.

We have not necessarily shown that this is *all* of the information in the sample. What we have, in general, is knowledge of the joint distribution of the elements of $\mathbf{y}_t$ conditioned on $\mathbf{x}_t$, which is the likelihood function for the reduced form. With normally distributed disturbances, the likelihood function depends only on $\boldsymbol{\Pi}$ and $\boldsymbol{\Omega}$. [See Section 19.4.5b, (19–100).] So, in this case, $\boldsymbol{\Pi}$ and $\boldsymbol{\Omega}$ are all of the information forthcoming. With other distributions, it is possible that higher (or other) moments of $\mathbf{y}\,|\,\mathbf{x}$ might provide additional information.[11] Of course, the assumption of some other particular joint distribution would have to be justified.

Now, can we deduce the structural parameters from the reduced form? Consider the following example:

EXAMPLE 19.7. Identification.   Consider the following market in which q is a quantity of Q, p is price, and z is the price of Z, a related good. We assume that z enters both the supply and demand equations. For example, Z might be a crop that is purchased by consumers and that will be grown by farmers instead of Q if its price rises enough relative to p. Thus, we would expect $\alpha_2 > 0$ and $\beta_2 < 0$.

---

[11] See, for example, Goldberger (1964, p. 311) and Hausman (1983, pp. 402–403). To see that this not trivial, consider that Riersol (1950) showed that the simple errors in the variables model of Section 9.5.1 is unidentified *only* because of the assumption of normality.

$$q_d = \alpha_0 + \alpha_1 p + \alpha_2 z + \varepsilon_1 \text{ (demand)},$$

$$q_s = \beta_0 + \beta_1 p + \beta_2 z + \varepsilon_2 \text{ (supply)},$$

$$q_d = q_s = q \qquad \text{(equilibrium)}.$$

The reduced form is

$$q = \frac{\alpha_1 \beta_0 - \alpha_0 \beta_1}{\alpha_1 - \beta_1} + \frac{\alpha_1 \beta_2 - \alpha_2 \beta_1}{\alpha_1 - \beta_1} z + \frac{\alpha_1 \varepsilon_2 - \alpha_2 \varepsilon_1}{\alpha_1 - \beta_1}$$

$$= \pi_{11} + \pi_{21} z + v_q,$$

$$p = \frac{\beta_0 - \alpha_0}{\alpha_1 - \beta_1} + \frac{\beta_2 - \alpha_2}{\alpha_1 - \beta_1} z + \frac{\varepsilon_2 - \varepsilon_1}{\alpha_1 - \beta_1}$$

$$= \pi_{12} + \pi_{22} z + v_p.$$

With only four reduced form coefficients and six structural parameters, it is obvious that there will not be a solution. Suppose, though, that it is known that $\beta_2 = 0$ (farmers do not substitute the alternative crop for this one). Then the solution for β_1 is π_{22}/π_{21}. After a bit of manipulation, we also obtain $\beta_0 = \pi_{11} - \pi_{12}\pi_{22}/\pi_{21}$. The restriction identifies two of the five parameters. Unfortunately, this is as far as we can go.

The correspondence between the structural and reduced-form parameters is the relationships

$$\Pi = -\mathbf{B}\Gamma^{-1} \qquad \text{and} \qquad \Omega = E[\mathbf{vv}'] = (\Gamma^{-1})'\Sigma\Gamma^{-1}. \tag{19-14}$$

If Γ were known, we could deduce $\mathbf{B}$ as $-\Pi\Gamma$ and Σ and $\Gamma'\Omega\Gamma$. It would appear, therefore, that our problem boils down to obtaining Γ. This makes sense. If Γ were known, we could rewrite (19–3), collecting the endogenous variables times their respective coefficients on the left-hand side of a regression, and estimate the remaining unknown coefficients on the predetermined variables by ordinary least squares.[12] While this is correct, unfortunately, it makes the problem appear simpler than it is.

Suppose that the true structure is $[\Gamma, \mathbf{B}, \Sigma]$. Now consider an imposter,

$$\mathbf{y}'\tilde{\Gamma} + \mathbf{x}'\tilde{\mathbf{B}} = \tilde{\varepsilon}',$$

obtained by postmultiplying the first structure by some nonsingular matrix, $\mathbf{F}$. Thus,

$$\tilde{\Gamma} = \Gamma\mathbf{F}, \tilde{\mathbf{B}} = \mathbf{B}\mathbf{F} \qquad \text{and} \qquad \tilde{\varepsilon}' = \varepsilon'\mathbf{F}.$$

The reduced form that corresponds to this structure is

$$\tilde{\Pi} = -\tilde{\mathbf{B}}\tilde{\Gamma}^{-1} = \mathbf{B}\mathbf{F}\mathbf{F}^{-1}\Gamma^{-1} = \Pi,$$

and, in the same fashion, $\tilde{\Omega} = \Omega$. The false structure looks just like the true one, at least in terms of the information we have. Statistically, there is no way we can tell them apart. The structures are observationally equivalent.

Since $\mathbf{F}$ was chosen arbitrarily, we conclude that *any* nonsingular transformation of the original structure has the same reduced form. Any reason for optimism that we might have had should be abandoned. As the model stands, there is no means by which the structural parameters can be deduced from a reduced form. It does not follow, though, that identification is hopeless. We have not used any of our theoretical information. Before formalizing the notion, it is useful to consider another example.

---

[12] This is precisely the approach of the LIML estimator. See Section 19.4.4d.

EXAMPLE 19.8. An Identified Model.   Suppose that in the earlier example income, y, rather than z, appears in the demand equation. The revised model is

$$q = \alpha_0 + \alpha_1 p + \qquad \alpha_2 y + \varepsilon_1,$$

$$q = \beta_0 + \beta_1 p + \beta_2 z \qquad + \varepsilon_2.$$

The structure is now

$$[q \quad p]\begin{bmatrix} 1 & 1 \\ -\alpha_1 & -\beta_1 \end{bmatrix} + [1 \quad y \quad z]\begin{bmatrix} -\alpha_0 & -\beta_0 \\ -\alpha_2 & 0 \\ 0 & -\beta_2 \end{bmatrix} = [\varepsilon_1 \quad \varepsilon_2].$$

The reduced form is

$$[q \quad p] = [1 \quad y \quad z]\begin{bmatrix} (\alpha_1\beta_0 - \alpha_0\beta_1)/\Delta & (\beta_0 - \alpha_0)/\Delta \\ -\alpha_2\beta_1/\Delta & -\alpha_2/\Delta \\ \alpha_1\beta_2/\Delta & \beta_2/\Delta \end{bmatrix} + [v_1 \quad v_2]$$

where

$$\Delta = (\alpha_1 - \beta_1).$$

Every false structure has the same reduced form. But in the coefficient matrix,

$$\tilde{\mathbf{B}} = \mathbf{BF} = \begin{bmatrix} \alpha_0 f_{11} + \beta_0 f_{12} & \alpha_0 f_{12} + \beta_0 f_{22} \\ \alpha_3 f_{11} & \alpha_3 f_{12} \\ \beta_2 f_{21} & \beta_2 f_{22}e \end{bmatrix},$$

if f_{12} is not zero, the imposter will have income appearing in the supply equation, which our theory has ruled out. Likewise, if f_{21} is not zero, z will appear in the demand equation, which is also ruled out by our theory. Thus, while all false structures have the same reduced form as the true one, the only one that is consistent with our theory (i.e., is **admissible**) and has coefficients of 1 on q in both equations (examine $\Gamma\mathbf{F}$) is $\mathbf{F} = \mathbf{I}$. This just produces the original structure.

The unique solutions for the structural parameters in terms of the reduced form parameters are

$$\alpha_0 = \pi_{11} - \pi_{12}\left(\frac{\pi_{31}}{\pi_{32}}\right), \qquad \beta_0 = \pi_{11} - \pi_{12}\left(\frac{\pi_{21}}{\pi_{22}}\right),$$

$$\alpha_1 = \frac{\pi_{31}}{\pi_{32}}, \qquad \beta_1 = \frac{\pi_{21}}{\pi_{22}},$$

$$\alpha_2 = \pi_{22}\left(\frac{\pi_{21}}{\pi_{22}} - \frac{\pi_{31}}{\pi_{32}}\right), \qquad \beta_2 = \pi_{32}\left(\frac{\pi_{31}}{\pi_{32}} - \frac{\pi_{21}}{\pi_{22}}\right).$$

The preceding discussion has considered two equivalent methods of establishing identifiability. If it is possible to deduce the structural parameters from the known reduced-form parameters, the model is identified. Alternatively, if it can be shown that no false structure is admissible, that is, satisfies the theoretical restrictions, then the model is identified.[13]

---

[13] Amemiya (1985, p. 230) suggests the equivalent, *existence of a consistent estimator*. While this criterion is, indeed, equivalent, it is not necessarily operational. In practice, one must still appeal to the conventional rules. To see why, consider Example 19.13. The two-stage least squares estimator used there looks like a consistent estimator. It is not. A related paper is Gabrielsen (1978).

It is useful to summarize what we have determined thus far. The unknown structural parameters consist of

$$\Gamma = \text{an } M \times M \text{ nonsingular matrix,}$$

$$\mathbf{B} = \text{a } K \times M \text{ parameter matrix,}$$

and

$$\Sigma = \text{an } M \times M \text{ symmetric positive definite matrix.}$$

The known, reduced-form parameters are

$$\Pi = \text{the } K \times M \text{ reduced-form coefficients}$$

and

$$\Omega = \text{the } M \times M \text{ reduced-form covariance matrix.}$$

Simply counting parameters in the structure and reduced forms yields an excess of

$$l = M^2 + KM + \frac{M(M + 1)}{2} - KM - \frac{M(M + 1)}{2}$$

$$= M^2,$$

which is, as might be expected from the earlier results, the number of unknown elements in Γ. Without further information, identification is clearly impossible. The additional information comes in several forms.

1. *Normalizations.* In each equation, one variable has a coefficient of one. This normalization is a necessary scaling of the equation that is logically equivalent to putting one variable on the left-hand side of a regression. For purposes of identification (and some estimation methods), the choice among the endogenous variables is arbitrary. But at the time the model is formulated, each equation will usually have some natural dependent variable. The normalization does not identify the dependent variable in any formal or causal sense. For example, in a model of supply and demand, both the "demand" equation, $Q = f(P, \mathbf{x})$, and the "inverse demand" equation, $P = g(Q, \mathbf{x})$, are appropriate specifications of the relationship between price and quantity. We note, though, the following:

> With the normalizations there are $M(M - 1)$, not
> M^2, undetermined values in Γ, and this many
> indeterminacies in the model to be resolved
> through nonsample information.

2. *Identities.* In some models, variable definitions or equilibrium conditions imply that all of the coefficients in a particular equation are known. In the preceding market example, there are three equations, but the third is the equilibrium condition $Q_d = Q_s$. Klein's Model I (Example 19.3) contains six equations, including two accounting identities and the equilibrium condition. There is obviously no question of identification with respect to identities. They may be carried as additional equations in the model, as we do with Klein's Model I in several later examples, or built into the model a priori, as is typical in models of supply and demand.

The substantive nonsample information that will be used in identifying the model will consist of the following:

3. *Exclusions.* The omission of variables from an equation places zeros in $\mathbf{B}$ and Γ. In

the previous example, the exclusion of income from the supply equation served to identify its parameters.

4. *Linear restrictions.* Restrictions on the structural parameters may also serve to rule out false structures. For example, a long-standing problem in the estimation of production models using time series data is the inability to disentangle the effects of economies of scale from those of technological change. In some treatments, the solution is to assume that there are constant returns to scale, thereby identifying the effects due to technological change. (See Section 16.4 and footnote 16 in Chapter 16.)

5. *Restrictions on the disturbance covariance matrix.* In the identification of a model, these are similar to restrictions on the slope parameters. For example, if the previous market model were to apply to a microeconomic setting, it would probably be reasonable to assume that the structural disturbances in the supply and demand equations are uncorrelated. Example 19.12 shows a case in which a covariance restriction identifies an otherwise unidentified model.

6. *Nonlinearities.* In many models, the variables and/or the parameters enter nonlinearly. For example, a variable may appear in both levels and logarithms. Or there may be nonlinear restrictions on the coefficients. Although this will usually greatly complicate the analysis, nonlinearities can aid in identification. Exercise 4 considers such a case.

To formalize the identification criteria, we require a notation for a single equation. The coefficients of the jth equation are contained in the jth columns of Γ and $\mathbf{B}$. The jth equation is

$$\mathbf{y}'\Gamma_j + \mathbf{x}'\mathbf{B}_j = \varepsilon_j. \tag{19-15}$$

(*For convenience, we have dropped the observation subscript.*) In this equation, we know that (1) one of the elements in Γ_j is one and (2) some variables that appear elsewhere in the model are excluded from this equation. Table 19.1 defines the notation used to incorporate these restrictions in (19–15).

The number of equations is $M_j + M_j^* + 1 = M$.
The number of exogenous variables is $K_j + K_j^* = K$.
The coefficient on y_j in equation j is one.
*'s will always be associated with excluded variables.

Equation j may be written

$$y_j = \mathbf{Y}_j'\gamma_j + \mathbf{Y}_j^{*'}\gamma_j^* + \mathbf{x}_j'\beta_j + \mathbf{x}_j^{*'}\beta_j^* + \varepsilon_j.$$

The exclusions imply that $\gamma_j^* = \mathbf{0}$ and $\beta_j^* = \mathbf{0}$. Thus,

$$\Gamma_j' = [1 \quad -\gamma_j' \quad \mathbf{0}'] \quad \text{and} \quad \mathbf{B}_j' = [-\beta_j' \quad \mathbf{0}'].$$

(Note the sign convention.)

Table 19.1. Components of Equation j (Dependent Variable $= y_j$)

	Endogenous Variables	Exogenous Variables
Included	$\mathbf{Y}_j = M_j$ variables	$\mathbf{x}_j = K_j$ variables
Excluded	$\mathbf{Y}_j^* = M_j^*$ variables	$\mathbf{x}_j^* = K_j^*$ variables

For this equation, we partition the reduced-form coefficient matrix in the same fashion:

$$
[y_j \quad Y_j' \quad Y_j^{*\prime}] = [x_j' \quad x_j^{*\prime}]
\begin{array}{c}
(1) \quad (M_j) \quad (M_j^*) \\
\begin{vmatrix} \pi_j & \underline{\Pi}_j & \bar{\Pi}_j \\ \pi_j^* & \Pi_j^* & \bar{\Pi}_j^* \end{vmatrix}
\end{array}
+ [v_j \quad V_j' \quad V_j^{*\prime}]
\begin{array}{c} [K_j \text{ rows}] \\ [K_j^* \text{ rows}] \end{array}
\tag{19-16}
$$

The reduced-form coefficient matrix is

$$
\Pi = -\mathbf{B}\Gamma^{-1},
$$

which implies that

$$
\Pi\Gamma = -\mathbf{B}.
$$

The jth column of this matrix equation applies to the jth equation,

$$
\Pi\Gamma_j = -\mathbf{B}_j.
$$

Inserting the parts from Table 19.1 yields

$$
\begin{bmatrix} \pi_j & \underline{\Pi}_j & \bar{\Pi}_j \\ \pi_j^* & \Pi_j^* & \bar{\Pi}_j^* \end{bmatrix}
\begin{bmatrix} 1 \\ -\gamma_j \\ 0 \end{bmatrix}
= \begin{bmatrix} \beta_j \\ 0 \end{bmatrix}.
$$

Now extract the two subequations,

$$
\pi_j - \underline{\Pi}_j\gamma_j = \beta_j \qquad (K_j \text{ equations}) \tag{19-17}
$$

$$
\pi_j^* - \Pi_j^*\gamma_j = 0 \qquad (K_j^* \text{ equations}) \tag{19-18}
$$

$$
(1) \qquad (M_j)
$$

The solution for **B** in terms of Γ that we observed at the beginning of this discussion is in (19–17). Equation (19–18) may be written

$$
\Pi_j^*\gamma_j = \pi_j^*. \tag{19-19}
$$

This is K_j^* equations in M_j unknowns. If they can be solved for γ_j, (19–17) gives the solution for β_j and the equation is identified. In order for there to be a solution, there must be at least as many equations as unknowns, which leads to the following condition.

Order Condition for Identification of Equation j

$$
K_j^* > M_j. \tag{19-20}
$$

The number of exogenous variables excluded from equation j must be at least as large as the number of endogenous variables included in equation j.

The order condition is only a counting rule. It is a necessary, but not sufficient condition for identification. It ensures that (19–19) has at least one solution, but it does not ensure that it has only one solution. The sufficient condition for uniqueness follows.

Rank Condition for Identification

$$
\text{rank}[\pi_j^*, \Pi_j^*] = \text{rank}[\Pi_j^*] = M_j. \tag{19-21}
$$

This imposes a restriction on a submatrix of the reduced-form coefficient matrix.

The rank condition ensures that there is one solution for the structural parameters given the reduced-form parameters. Our alternative approach to the identification problem was to use the prior restrictions on $[\mathbf{\Gamma}, \mathbf{B}]$ to eliminate all false structures. An equivalent condition based on this approach is simpler to apply and has more intuitive appeal. We first rearrange the structural coefficients in the matrix

$$\mathbf{A} = \begin{bmatrix} \mathbf{\Gamma} \\ \mathbf{B} \end{bmatrix} = \begin{bmatrix} 1 & \mathbf{A}_1 \\ -\gamma_j & \mathbf{A}_2 \\ 0 & \mathbf{A}_3 \\ -\beta_j & \mathbf{A}_4 \\ 0 & \mathbf{A}_5 \end{bmatrix} = [\mathbf{a}_j \quad \mathbf{A}_j]. \tag{19-22}$$

The jth column in a false structure $[\mathbf{\Gamma F}, \mathbf{BF}]$ (i.e., the imposter for our equation j) would be $[\mathbf{\Gamma f}_j, \mathbf{Bf}_j]$, where $\mathbf{f}_j$ is the jth column of $\mathbf{F}$. This new jth equation is to be built up as a linear combination of the old one and the other equations in the model. Thus, partitioning as previously,

$$\tilde{\mathbf{a}}_j = \begin{bmatrix} 1 & \mathbf{A}_1 \\ -\gamma_j & \mathbf{A}_2 \\ 0 & \mathbf{A}_3 \\ -\beta_j & \mathbf{A}_4 \\ 0 & \mathbf{A}_5 \end{bmatrix} \begin{bmatrix} f^0 \\ \mathbf{f}^1 \end{bmatrix} = \begin{bmatrix} 1 \\ \tilde{\gamma}_j \\ 0 \\ \tilde{\beta}_j \\ 0 \end{bmatrix}. \tag{19-23}$$

If this hybrid is to have the same variables as the original, it must have nonzero elements in the same places, which can be ensured by taking $f^0 = 1$, and zeroes in the same positions as the original $\mathbf{a}_j$. Extracting the third and fifth rows, if $\tilde{\mathbf{a}}_j$ is to be admissible, it must meet the requirement

$$\begin{bmatrix} \mathbf{A}_3 \\ \mathbf{A}_5 \end{bmatrix} \mathbf{f}^1 = \mathbf{0}. \tag{19-24}$$

This is not possible if the preceding $(M_j^* + K_j^*) \times (M - 1)$ matrix has full column rank, so we have the equivalent rank condition,

$$\text{rank} \begin{bmatrix} \mathbf{A}_3 \\ \mathbf{A}_5 \end{bmatrix} = M - 1. \tag{19-25}$$

The corresponding order condition is that the preceding matrix have at least as many rows as columns. Thus $M_j^* + K_j^* > M - 1$. But since $M = M_j + M_j^* + 1$, this is the same as the order condition in (19-20). The equivalence of the two rank conditions is pursued in the exercises.

The preceding provides a simple method for checking the rank and order conditions. We need only arrange the structural parameters in a tableau and examine the relevant sub-matrices; one at a time; $\mathbf{A}_3$ and $\mathbf{A}_5$ are the structural coefficients in the other equations on the variables that are excluded from equation j.

EXAMPLE 19.9. Rank and Order Conditions.   The structural coefficients in the model of Example 19.7 may be written in the preceding form as

	q	p	1	z
Demand	1	$-\alpha_1$	$-\alpha_0$	$-\alpha_2$
Supply	1	$-\beta_1$	$-\beta_0$	$-\beta_2$

Neither A_3 nor A_5 has any rows, so $[A_3', A_5']$ cannot have rank $M - 1 = 1$. Neither equation is identified. The alternative in Example 19.8 is

	q	p	1	y	z
Demand	1	$-\alpha_1$	$-\alpha_0$	$-\alpha_2$	0
Supply	1	$-\beta_1$	$-\beta_0$	0	$-\beta_2$

For the demand equation,

$$[A_3', A_5'] = -\beta_2,$$

which has rank $M - 1 = 1$ unless $\beta_2 = 0$. The supply equation is also identified unless $\alpha_2 = 0$. Now suppose that z appears in the demand equation but not in the supply equation. Then the structure is

	q	p	1	y	z
Demand	1	$-\alpha_1$	$-\alpha_0$	$-\alpha_2$	$-\alpha_3$
Supply	1	$-\beta_1$	$-\beta_0$	0	0

For the demand equation, $[A_3', A_5']$ has no rows, so the equation is not identified. But, for the supply equation,

$$[A_3', A_5'] = [-\alpha_2 \quad -\alpha_3],$$

which has rank one, so the supply equation is identified. This example illustrates the possibility that a model may be *partially identified*.

There is a rule of thumb that is sometimes useful in checking the rank and order conditions of a model:

If every equation has its own predetermined   (19–26)
variable, the entire model is identified.

The proof is simple and is left as an exercise. For a final example, we consider a somewhat larger model.

EXAMPLE 19.10. Identification of Klein's Model I.   The structural coefficients in the consumption function of Klein's Model I (transposed and multiplied by minus one for convenience) are listed in Table 19.2.

Identification requires that the matrix shown in Table 19.3 have rank five. None of the columns marked by x's can be formed as linear combinations of the others, so the rank condition is met. Verification of the rank and order conditions for the other two equations is left as an exercise.

It is unusual for a model to pass the order but not the rank condition. (But see Example 19.13 for a case in the literature.) Generally, either the conditions are obvious or the model is so large and has so many predetermined variables that the conditions are met trivially. In practice, for a small model it is simple to check both conditions. For a large model, frequently only the order condition is verified. We distinguish three cases:

1. *Underidentified:* $K_j^* < M_j$ or rank condition fails.
2. *Exactly identified:* $K_j^* = M_j$ and rank condition is met.
3. *Overidentified:* $K_j^* > M_j$ and rank condition is met.

Table 19.2

	C	I	W^p	X	P	K	1	W^g	G	T	A	P_{-1}	K_{-1}	X_{-1}
C	-1	0	α_3	0	α_1	0	α_0	α_3	0	0	0	α_2	0	0
I	0	-1	0	0	β_1	0	β_0	0	0	0	0	β_2	β_3	0
W^p	0	0	-1	γ_1	0	0	γ_0	0	0	0	γ_3	0	0	γ_2
X	1	1	0	-1	0	0	0	0	1	0	0	0	0	0
P	0	0	-1	1	-1	0	0	0	0	-1	0	0	0	0
K	0	1	0	0	0	-1	0	0	0	0	0	0	1	0

Table 19.3

	I	X	K	G	T	A	K_{-1}	X_{-1}
Eq.		$\mathbf{A}'_3$				$\mathbf{A}'_5$		
I	-1	0	0	0	0	0	β_3	0
Wp	0	γ_1	0	0	0	γ_3	0	γ_2
X	1	-1	0	1	-1	0	0	0
P	0	1	0	0	0	0	0	0
X	1	0	-1	0	0	0	1	0
	x	x		x	x	x		

For an example of the last case, consider the third model of Example 19.9. The reduced form is

$$q = \pi_{11} + \pi_{21}y + \pi_{31}z + v_1,$$
$$p = \pi_{12} + \pi_{22}y + \pi_{32}z + v_2,$$

where

$$\pi_{21} = \frac{\beta_1\alpha_2}{\beta_1 - \alpha_1} \qquad \pi_{31} = \frac{\beta_1\alpha_3}{\beta_1 - \alpha_1},$$

$$\pi_{22} = \frac{\alpha_2}{\beta_1 - \alpha_1} \qquad \pi_{32} = \frac{\alpha_3}{\beta_1 - \alpha_1}.$$

There are two solutions for β_1 in terms of the elements of $\mathbf{\Pi}$. In the theoretical structure, they would be identical. In a finite sample, estimates of them would differ and it would be necessary to find a way to reconcile the conflicting results.

There are a number of other types of nonsample information that can produce identification of a model.

LINEAR RESTRICTIONS ON COEFFICIENTS

In order to obtain a general rule for identification in the presence of linear restrictions on the parameters, it is useful to employ an alternative formulation of the rank condition due to Fisher (1976). If we write the jth equation as

$$y_j = \mathbf{Y}'_j\gamma_j + \mathbf{Y}^{*'}_j\gamma^*_j + \mathbf{x}'_j\beta_j + \mathbf{x}^{*'}_j\beta^*_j + \varepsilon_j$$

(already imposing the normalization), then the exclusion restrictions are

$$\gamma_j^* = 0 \qquad \text{and} \qquad \beta_j^* = 0.$$

Collect the full set of parameters in

$$\mathbf{a}_j = \begin{bmatrix} 1 \\ \gamma_j \\ \gamma_j^* \\ \beta_j \\ \beta_j^* \end{bmatrix}. \qquad (19\text{--}27)$$

Each restriction on the coefficient vector is in the form

$$\boldsymbol{\phi}_i' \mathbf{a}_j = 0. \qquad (19\text{--}28)$$

The full set of exclusion restrictions can be written

$$\boldsymbol{\Phi} \mathbf{a}_j = 0, \qquad (19\text{--}29)$$

where

$$\boldsymbol{\Phi} = \begin{bmatrix} 0 & 0 & \mathbf{I} & 0 & 0 \\ 0 & 0 & 0 & 0 & \mathbf{I} \end{bmatrix} \qquad \begin{matrix} (M_j^* \text{ rows}) \\ (K_j^* \text{ rows}). \end{matrix}$$

Each row of $\boldsymbol{\Phi}$ is the coefficients of a linear restriction on $\mathbf{a}_j$. We may now impose more general linear restrictions simply by adding rows to $\boldsymbol{\Phi}$. For example, consider the model

$$
\begin{aligned}
y_1 + \gamma_{21} y_2 + \beta_{11} x_1 + \beta_{21} x_2 \qquad\qquad + \beta_{41} x_4 &= \varepsilon_1 \\
\gamma_{12} y_1 + \qquad y_2 + \beta_{12} x_1 + \beta_{22} x_2 + \beta_{32} x_3 + \beta_{42} x_4 &= \varepsilon_2,
\end{aligned}
\qquad (19\text{--}30)
$$

with the restriction $\beta_{11} + \beta_{21} = 0$. The restrictions on the first equation are

$$\begin{bmatrix} 0 & 0 & 0 & 0 & 1 & 0 \\ 0 & 0 & 1 & 1 & 0 & 0 \end{bmatrix} \begin{bmatrix} 1 \\ \gamma_{21} \\ \beta_{11} \\ \beta_{21} \\ \beta_{31} \\ \beta_{41} \end{bmatrix} = \begin{bmatrix} 0 \\ 0 \end{bmatrix}.$$

Suppose that there are

$$n_j = M_j^* + K_j^* + R_j \qquad (19\text{--}31)$$

restrictions in total. Then $\boldsymbol{\Phi}$ is $n_j \times (M + K)$. Let the full matrix of structural parameters with the equation of interest placed in the first column be

$$\mathbf{A} = \begin{bmatrix} \boldsymbol{\Gamma} \\ \mathbf{B} \end{bmatrix} = \begin{bmatrix} 1 & \mathbf{A}_1 \\ \gamma & \mathbf{A}_2 \\ \gamma^* & \mathbf{A}_3 \\ \beta & \mathbf{A}_4 \\ \beta^* & \mathbf{A}_5 \end{bmatrix} = [\mathbf{a}_j \quad \mathbf{A}_j]. \qquad (19\text{--}32)$$

As in (19–23), the jth equation in a false structure would be

$$\tilde{\mathbf{a}}_j = \mathbf{a}_j f^0 + \mathbf{A}_j \mathbf{f}^1.$$

If $\tilde{\mathbf{a}}_j$ is to satisfy the restrictions of (19–29),

$$\mathbf{\Phi}\tilde{\mathbf{a}}_j = \mathbf{\Phi}\mathbf{a}_j f^0 + \mathbf{\Phi}\mathbf{A}_j \mathbf{f}^1 = \mathbf{0}. \tag{19–33}$$

Since $\mathbf{\Phi}\mathbf{a}_j = \mathbf{0}$, this requires

$$(\mathbf{\Phi}\mathbf{A}_j)\mathbf{f}^1 = \mathbf{0}. \tag{19–34}$$

This is not possible if $\mathbf{\Phi}\mathbf{A}_j$ has full column rank. Since $\mathbf{\Phi}\mathbf{A}_j$ has $M - 1$ columns, with (19–29), we have the necessary and sufficient condition for the identification of the jth equation:

$$\text{rank}(\mathbf{\Phi}\mathbf{A}) = \text{rank}(\mathbf{0} \quad \mathbf{\Phi}\mathbf{A}_j) = M - 1. \tag{19–35}$$

If the only restrictions are exclusions, then, by multiplying it out, we see that this condition is, once again, (19–25). Corresponding to this, we have a modified order condition,

$$n_j \geq M - 1. \tag{19–36}$$

This states that the total number of restrictions on the parameters of each equation must be at least as large as the number of equations minus one. For the entire model to be identified, this must be true for each of the M equations, so the total number of restrictions imposed on the structure must be at least $M(M - 1)$. Recall that after imposing the normalization rule, we found that $M(M - 1)$ was the number of indeterminacies in the model, so this was to be expected.

EXAMPLE 19.11. Identification with Linear Restrictions.   By the rank and order conditions of (19–25), the second equation in (19–30) is not identified. Nothing is excluded from it. However, if we impose the restriction

$$\beta_{32} + \beta_{42} = 0,$$

then

$$\mathbf{\Phi} = [0 \quad 0 \quad 0 \quad 1 \quad 1]$$

and, for the second equation,

$$\mathbf{\Phi}\mathbf{A} = 0 + \beta_{41} = \beta_{41}.$$

This has rank one, so the restriction identifies the second equation.

We verified in Example 19.10 that the consumption function in Klein's Model I is identified using only the exclusion restrictions. But there is also a linear restriction in the equation; the coefficients on W^p and W^g are equal. Using the ordering of variables in Example 19.10, this would add the row $\phi_9 = [0, 0, 1, 0, 0, 0, 0, -1, 0, 0, 0, 0, 0, 0]$. The resulting tableau would have another column, $[0, -1, 0, -1, 0]'$. Of course, since the equation is already identified, this column is superfluous.

RESTRICTIONS ON THE STRUCTURAL COVARIANCE MATRIX

The observant reader will have noticed that no mention of $\mathbf{\Sigma}$ is made in the preceding discussion. To this point, that is because all of the information contained $\mathbf{\Omega}$ is used in the estimation of $\mathbf{\Sigma}$—for given $\mathbf{\Gamma}$, the relationship between $\mathbf{\Omega}$ and $\mathbf{\Sigma}$ is one to one. Recall that $\mathbf{\Sigma} = \mathbf{\Gamma}'\mathbf{\Omega}\mathbf{\Gamma}$. But if restrictions are placed on $\mathbf{\Sigma}$, there is more information in $\mathbf{\Omega}$ than is needed for estimation of Σ. This is useful because the excess information can be used, instead, to help infer the elements in Γ. A useful case is that of zero covariances across the disturbances.[14] Once again, it is most convenient to consider this case in terms of a false structure. In particular, if the structure is $[\Gamma, B, \Sigma]$, a false structure would have parameters

$$[\tilde{\Gamma}, \tilde{B}, \tilde{\Sigma}] = [\Gamma F, BF, F'\Sigma F]. \tag{19–37}$$

If any of the elements in Σ are zero, in order to be admissible, the false structure must preserve those restrictions. For example, suppose that we specify that $\sigma_{12} = 0$. Then it must also be true that $\tilde{\sigma}_{12} = f_1'\Sigma f_2 = 0$, where f_1 and f_2 are columns of F. As such, there is a restriction on F that may identify the model.

EXAMPLE 19.12. Identification with a Covariance Restriction.   Consider the model in Example 19.1,

$$q = \alpha_0 + \alpha_1 p + \alpha_2 y + \varepsilon_1,$$
$$q = \beta_0 + \beta_1 p \qquad\quad + \varepsilon_2.$$

It is obvious from the preceding that the demand equation is unidentified. The parameter matrices in the true structure are

$$\Gamma = \begin{bmatrix} 1 & 1 \\ -\alpha_1 & -\beta_1 \end{bmatrix}, \quad B = \begin{bmatrix} -\alpha_0 & -\beta_0 \\ -\alpha_2 & 0 \end{bmatrix}, \quad \Sigma = \begin{bmatrix} \sigma_{11} & \sigma_{12} \\ \sigma_{12} & \sigma_{22} \end{bmatrix}.$$

Using the transformation matrix

$$F = [f_1 \quad f_2] = \begin{bmatrix} f_{11} & f_{12} \\ f_{21} & f_{22} \end{bmatrix},$$

the condition that y not appear in the second equation implies that the lower right element in

$$BF = \begin{bmatrix} -\alpha_0 f_{11} - \beta_0 f_{21} & -\alpha_0 f_{21} - \beta_0 f_{22} \\ -\alpha_2 f_{11} & -\alpha_2 f_{12} \end{bmatrix}$$

is zero. Thus, $f_{12} = 0$. The covariance in the false structure is

$$f_1'\Sigma f_2 = f_{11} f_{12} \sigma_{11} + f_{21} f_{22} \sigma_{22} = 0.$$

But we already know that $f_{12} = 0$, so either f_{22} or f_{21} must be zero. If $f_{22} = 0$, the false structure has no second equation. Thus, $f_{21} = 0$, and the only admissable F matrix is a diagonal one. With the normalization, $F = I$ and both equations are identified.
    The reduced form of this model is

$$-B\Gamma^{-1} = \Pi = \begin{bmatrix} (\alpha_1\beta_0 - \alpha_0\beta_1)/(\alpha_1 - \beta_1) & (\beta_0 - \alpha_0)/(\alpha_1 - \beta_1) \\ -\beta_1\alpha_2/(\alpha_1 - \beta_1) & -\alpha_2/\beta_1 \end{bmatrix}$$

$$= \begin{bmatrix} \pi_{11} & \pi_{12} \\ \pi_{21} & \pi_{22} \end{bmatrix}.$$

The parameters of the supply equation are

$$\beta_1 = \frac{\pi_{21}}{\pi_{22}}.$$

---

[14] More general cases are discussed in Hausman (1983) and Judge et al. (1985).

and

$$\beta_0 = \pi_{11} - \beta_1 \pi_{12} = \pi_{11} - \pi_{12}\left(\frac{\pi_{21}}{\pi_{22}}\right).$$

For the demand equation, the off-diagonal element of $\Sigma = \Gamma'\Omega\Gamma$ is zero. This is

$$[1 - \alpha_1]\begin{bmatrix} \omega_{11} & \omega_{12} \\ \omega_{12} & \omega_{22} \end{bmatrix}\begin{bmatrix} 1 \\ -\beta_1 \end{bmatrix} = 0$$

or

$$\omega_{11} - \alpha_1\omega_{12} - \beta_1\omega_{12} + \alpha_1\beta_1\omega_{22} = 0.$$

Given the solution for β_1 already obtained, we find that

$$\alpha_1 = \frac{\omega_{11} - \beta_1\omega_{12}}{\omega_{12} - \beta_1\omega_{22}}.$$

The remaining parameters are

$$\alpha_2 = \pi_{22}(\beta_1 - \alpha_1)$$

and

$$\alpha_0 = \pi_{12}(\beta_1 - \alpha_1) + \beta_0.$$

Continuing Example 19.1, we obtain the following estimates of the reduced form using the agricultural data:

$$\mathbf{P} = \begin{bmatrix} 5.718 & -81.81 \\ 0.00987 & 0.0196 \end{bmatrix}, \qquad \mathbf{W} = \begin{bmatrix} 46.02 & 37.66 \\ 37.66 & 247.88 \end{bmatrix}.$$

If we assume that the disturbances are uncorrelated, the complete set of estimates of the structural parameters is

(Demand) $\hat{q} = -19.66 - 0.3102p + 0.01595y,$ $s_d^2 = 93.24$

(Supply) $\hat{q} = 46.93 + 0.5037p,$ $s_s^2 = 70.97$

The OLS estimates of the demand equation are

$$\hat{q} = 18.14 + 0.1519p + 0.00691y, \qquad s_d^2 = 40.29.$$

THE FULLY RECURSIVE MODEL

The fully recursive model is an important special case of the preceding result. A triangular model is

$$y_1 = \boldsymbol{\beta}_1'\mathbf{x} + \varepsilon_1$$

$$y_2 = \gamma_{12}y_1 + \boldsymbol{\beta}_2'\mathbf{x} + \varepsilon_2 \tag{19-38}$$

$$\vdots$$

$$y_M = \gamma_{1M}y_1 + \gamma_{2M}y_2 + \cdots + \gamma_{M-1,M}y_{M-1} + \boldsymbol{\beta}_M'\mathbf{x} + \varepsilon_M.$$

We place no restrictions on **B**. The first equation is identified, since it is already in reduced form. But for any of the others, linear combinations of it and the ones above it involve the same variables. Thus, we conclude that *without some identifying restrictions, only the parameters of the first equation in a triangular system are identified.* But suppose that Σ is diagonal. Then the entire model is identified, as we now prove. As usual, we attempt to find a false structure that satisfies the restrictions of the model.

The jth column of $\mathbf{F}$, $\mathbf{f}_j$, is the coefficients in a linear combination of the equations that will be an imposter for equation j. Many $\mathbf{f}_j$'s are already precluded.

1. $\mathbf{f}_1$ must be the first column of an identity matrix. The first equation is identified and normalized on y_1.
2. In all remaining columns of $\mathbf{F}$, all elements below the diagonal must be zero, since an equation can only involve the y's in it or the equations above it.

Unfortunately, without further restrictions, any upper triangular $\mathbf{F}$ is an admissible transformation. But with a diagonal Σ, we have more information. Consider the second column. Since $\tilde{\Sigma}$ must be diagonal, $\mathbf{f}_1' \Sigma \mathbf{f}_2 = 0$. But given $\mathbf{f}_1$ above,

$$\mathbf{f}_1' \Sigma \mathbf{f}_2 = \sigma_{11} f_{12} = 0,$$

so $f_{12} = 0$. The second column of $\mathbf{F}$ is now complete and is equal to the second column of $\mathbf{I}$. Continuing in the same manner, we find that

$$\mathbf{f}_1' \Sigma \mathbf{f}_3 = 0 \quad \text{and} \quad \mathbf{f}_2' \Sigma \mathbf{f}_3 = 0$$

will suffice to establish that $\mathbf{f}_3$ is the third column of $\mathbf{I}$. In this fashion, it can be shown that the only admissable $\mathbf{F}$ is $\mathbf{F} = \mathbf{I}$, which was to be shown.

With Γ upper triangular, $M(M-1)/2$ unknown parameters remained. That is exactly the number of restrictions placed on Σ when it was assumed to be diagonal.

NONLINEARITIES

Another even more complex problem arises in models that are nonlinear in the endogenous variables. They arise fairly frequently, for example, in models in which variables appear both in levels and in logarithms, and in macroeconomic models in which the price level and real and nominal variables all appear. For some reasonably general cases, a number of results have been obtained.[15] A very useful, simple result has been obtained for the common case in which the model involves the endogenous variables and nonlinear functions of them that each involve a single variable.[16] For these models, the fundamental rank condition,

$$\text{rank}[\mathbf{\Phi A}] = M - 1,$$

is extended by simply adding the nonlinear functions to the system as additional endogenous variables (but without increasing the number of equations). The following example illustrates the use of this criterion.

EXAMPLE 19.13. A Model of Industry Structure.   The following model of industry structure and performance was estimated by Strickland and Weiss (1976). Note that the square of the endogenous variable, C, appears in the first equation.

---

[15] See Brown (1983).
[16] See Fisher (1976, pp. 127–167, especially pp. 147–148).

Table 19.4

	Γ				B						
	A/S	C	C^2	M	l	Cd/S	Gr	D	MES/S	K/S	Gd
Advt.	-1	α_3	α_4	α_1	α_0	α_2	α_5	α_6	0	0	0
Conc.	β_1	-1	0	0	β_0	0	0	0	β_2	0	0
Margin	γ_5	γ_3	0	-1	γ_0	0	0	γ_2	γ_6	γ_1	γ_4

$$\frac{A}{S} = \alpha_0 + \alpha_1 M + \alpha_2 \left(\frac{Cd}{S}\right) + \alpha_3 C + \alpha_4 C^2 + \alpha_5 Gr + \alpha_6 D + \varepsilon_1,$$

$$C = \beta_0 + \beta_1 \left(\frac{A}{S}\right) + \beta_2 \left(\frac{MES}{S}\right) + \varepsilon_2,$$

$$M = \gamma_0 + \gamma_1 \left(\frac{K}{S}\right) + \gamma_2 Gr + \gamma_3 C + \gamma_4 Gd + \gamma_5 \left(\frac{A}{S}\right) + \gamma_6 \left(\frac{MES}{S}\right) + \varepsilon_3.$$

A = advertising $\qquad M$ = price cost margin

S = industry sales $\qquad D$ = durable goods industry (0/1)

C = concentration $\qquad Gr$ = industry growth rate

Cd = consumer demand $\qquad K$ = capital stock

MES = efficient scale $\qquad Gd$ = geographic dispersion.

Since the only restrictions are exclusions, we may use the rule $\text{rank}[\mathbf{A}'_3, \mathbf{A}'_5] = M - 1$ discussed in the first part of this section. The augmented coefficient matrix (with all signs reversed) is shown in Table 19.4. Identification of the first equation requires

$$[\mathbf{A}'_3, \mathbf{A}'_5] = \begin{bmatrix} \beta_2 & 0 & 0 \\ \gamma_6 & \gamma_1 & \gamma_4 \end{bmatrix}$$

to have rank two, which it does unless $\beta_2 = 0$. Thus, the first equation is identified by the presence of the scale variable in the second equation. It is easily seen that the second equation is overidentified. But for the third,

$$[\mathbf{A}'_3, \mathbf{A}'_5] = \begin{bmatrix} \alpha_4 & \alpha_2 & \alpha_6 \\ 0 & 0 & 0 \end{bmatrix} (!),$$

which has rank one, not two. The third equation is not identified. It passes the order condition but fails the rank condition.[17]

---

[17] The failure of the third equation is obvious on inspection. There is no variable in the second equation that is not in the third. The reader who has already studied this topic may wonder at this point how the authors were able to obtain their two-stage least squares estimates of this equation. This question is considered in Section 19.4.4.f.

19.4. *Methods of Estimation*

It is possible to estimate the reduced-form parameters, Π and Ω, consistently by ordinary least squares. But except for forecasting $\mathbf{y}$ given $\mathbf{x}$, these are generally not the parameters of interest; Γ, $\mathbf{B}$, and Σ are. OLS estimates of the structural parameters are inconsistent, ostensibly because the included endogenous variables in each equation are correlated with the disturbances. Still, it is at least of passing interest to examine what, in particular, is estimated by ordinary least squares, particularly in view of its widespread use (in spite of its inconsistency). Since the proof of identification was based on solving for Γ, $\mathbf{B}$, and Σ from Π and Ω, one way to proceed is to apply our finding to the sample estimates, $\mathbf{P}$ and $\mathbf{W}$. This **indirect least squares approach** is feasible but inefficient. Worse, there will usually be more than one possible estimator, and no obvious means of choosing among them. There are two approaches for direct estimation, both based on the principle of instrumental variables.[18] It is possible to estimate each equation separately, using a **limited information** estimator. But the same principle that suggests that joint estimation brings efficiency gains in the seemingly unrelated regressions setting is at work here, so we shall also consider **full information** or system methods of estimation.

19.4.1. Ordinary Least Squares (OLS)

For all T observations, the nonzero terms in the jth equation are

$$\mathbf{y}_j = \mathbf{Y}_j\gamma_j + \mathbf{X}_j\beta_j + \varepsilon_j$$

$$= \mathbf{Z}_j\delta_j + \varepsilon_j. \qquad (19\text{--}39)$$

The M reduced form equations are

$$\mathbf{Y} = \mathbf{X}\Pi + \mathbf{V}.$$

For the included endogenous variables, $\mathbf{Y}_j$, the reduced forms are the M_j appropriate columns of Π and $\mathbf{V}$, written

$$\mathbf{Y}_j = \mathbf{X}\Pi_j + \mathbf{V}_j. \qquad (19\text{--}40)$$

[Note that Π_j is the middle part of Π shown in (19–16).] Likewise, $\mathbf{V}_j$ is M_j columns of $\mathbf{V} = \mathbf{E}\Gamma^{-1}$. The least squares estimator is

$$\mathbf{d}_j = [\mathbf{Z}_j'\mathbf{Z}_j]^{-1}\mathbf{Z}_j'\mathbf{y}_j \qquad (19\text{--}41)$$

$$= \delta_j + \begin{bmatrix} \mathbf{Y}_j'\mathbf{Y}_j & \mathbf{Y}_j'\mathbf{X}_j \\ \mathbf{X}_j'\mathbf{Y}_j & \mathbf{X}_j'\mathbf{X}_j \end{bmatrix}^{-1} \begin{matrix} \mathbf{Y}_j'\varepsilon_j \\ \mathbf{X}_j'\varepsilon_j. \end{matrix}$$

None of the terms in the inverse matrix converge to $\mathbf{0}$. Although $\text{plim}(1/T)\mathbf{X}_j'\varepsilon_j = \mathbf{0}$,

$$\text{plim}\frac{\mathbf{Y}_j'\varepsilon_j}{T} = \omega_j - \Omega_{jj}\gamma_j,$$

where ω_j and Ω_{jj} are parts of Ω. Therefore, both parts of $\mathbf{d}_j$ are inconsistent. We can write

$$\mathbf{y}_j = E[\mathbf{y}_j \,|\, \mathbf{Y}_j, \mathbf{x}_j] + \mathbf{u}_j.$$

---

[18] For other examples, see Section 9.5.4 on measurement error and Section 18.2.2d on estimating the geometric lag model.

If this function is linear,

$$y_j = Y'_j \eta_j + x'_j \theta_j + u_j.$$

(If both ε and x are multivariate normally distributed, this result will follow, but multivariate normality is stronger than necessary.) Least squares regression of y_j on Y_j and X_j consistently estimates η_j and θ_j. However, these are a mixture of all of the parameters in the model, including Σ as well as Γ and B. The formalities are pursued in the exercises. The following gives a simple example.

EXAMPLE 19.14. Regression Function.   The model of Example 19.7 is

$$q = \alpha_1 p + \alpha_2 z + \varepsilon_1 \qquad \text{(demand)},$$

$$q = \beta_1 p + \beta_2 z + \varepsilon_2 \qquad \text{(supply)}.$$

The reduced form is

$$q = \frac{\alpha_1 \beta_2 - \alpha_2 \beta_1}{\alpha_1 - \beta_1} z + v_1 = \pi_1 z + v_1,$$

$$p = \frac{\beta_2 - \alpha_2}{\alpha_1 - \beta_1} z + v_2 = \pi_2 z + v_2.$$

It is convenient to assume that $\text{Var}(z) = \Sigma_{zz} = 1$. Based on this, we may derive the quantities.

$$\text{Var}[q] = \pi_1^2 + \omega_{11} \qquad\qquad \text{Cov}[q, z] = \pi_1,$$

$$\text{Var}[p] = \pi_2^2 + \omega_{22} \qquad\qquad \text{Cov}[p, z] = \pi_2,$$

$$\text{Cov}[q, p] = \pi_1 \pi_2 + \omega_{12}.$$

If we compute the OLS regression of q on p and z, using a sample of observations, the slope vector, d, will estimate

$$\text{plim} \begin{bmatrix} p'p/T & p'x/T \\ z'p/T & z'z/T \end{bmatrix}^{-1} \begin{bmatrix} p'q/T \\ z'q/T \end{bmatrix} = \begin{bmatrix} \text{Var}[p] & \text{Cov}[p, z] \\ \text{Cov}[z, p] & \text{Var}[z] \end{bmatrix}^{-1} \begin{bmatrix} \text{Cov}[p, q] \\ \text{Cov}[z, q] \end{bmatrix}.$$

After some tedious algebra (including the computation of $\Omega = (\Gamma^{-1})' \Sigma \Gamma^{-1}$), this reduces to

$$\text{plim } d = \theta \begin{bmatrix} \alpha_1 \\ \alpha_2 \end{bmatrix} + (1 - \theta) \begin{bmatrix} \beta_1 \\ \beta_2 \end{bmatrix},$$

where

$$\theta = \frac{\sigma_{11} - \sigma_{12}}{\sigma_{11} + \sigma_{22} - 2\sigma_{12}}.$$

Therefore, least squares estimates a mixture of the supply and demand curves, where the weights are proportional to the sources of variation. The effect is even clearer if it is assumed that σ_{12} is zero, which may not be unreasonable.

The preceding example illustrates a general result. The least squares estimates are inconsistent estimates of a structural equation precisely because they are consistent estimates of a mixture of all of the equations in the model.[19]

---

[19] The distinction between structures and regressions, or conditional mean functions that we have explored here, is the subject of some interesting commentary in the literature. See, for example, Working (1926), Haavelmo (1943), and Waugh (1961). Waugh argued for the use of least squares, offering as justification the example in which hog farmers would be interested in knowing the expected price given a year's output.

19.4.1a. *Estimation of Triangular Systems*

An intuitively appealing form of simultaneous equations model is the **triangular system**,

$$
\begin{aligned}
(1)\ \ y_1 &= x'\beta_1 &&+ \varepsilon_1, \\
(2)\ \ y_2 &= x'\beta_2 + \gamma_{12}y_1 &&+ \varepsilon_2, \\
(3)\ \ y_3 &= x'\beta_3 + \gamma_{13}y_1 + \gamma_{23}y_2 + \varepsilon_3,
\end{aligned}
\qquad\qquad (19\text{-}42)
$$

and so on. If Γ is upper triangular and Σ is diagonal, so that the disturbances are uncorrelated, the system is a **fully recursive model**. (No restrictions are placed on **B**.) It is easy to see that in this case the entire system may be estimated consistently (and, as we shall show later, efficiently) by ordinary least squares. The first equation is a classical regression model. In the second equation, $\text{Cov}(y_1, \varepsilon_2) = \text{Cov}(x'\beta_1 + \varepsilon_1, \varepsilon_2) = 0$, so it too may be estimated by ordinary least squares. Proceeding in the same fashion to (3), it is clear that y_1 and ε_3 are uncorrelated. Likewise, if we substitute (1) in (2) and then the result for y_2 in (3), we find that y_2 is also uncorrelated with ε_3. Continuing in this way, we find that in every equation the full set of right-hand variables is uncorrelated with the respective disturbance. The result is that *the fully recursive model may be consistently estimated using equation-by-equation ordinary least squares.*

   In the more general case, in which Σ is not diagonal, the preceding argument does not apply. Consistent and efficient estimates can be obtained using the methods to be discussed. This model does have an interesting feature, however. Although *ordinary* least squares is inconsistent, *generalized* least squares estimation of the entire system, in the manner of the seemingly unrelated regressions model, *ignoring the simultaneity*, produces both consistent and efficient estimates.[20] Since Σ^{-1} is positive definite, it can be factored into TT' where T is an upper triangular matrix. The modified system,

$$
y'(\Gamma T) + x'(BT) = \varepsilon'T,
$$

has an upper triangular Jacobian, ΓT—the product of upper triangular matrices is upper triangular—and a diagonal disturbance covariance matrix,

$$
E[T'\varepsilon\varepsilon'T] = T'\Sigma T = T'(T')^{-1}T^{-1}T = I.
$$

Therefore, the argument of the previous paragraph applies to estimation of (ΓT) and (BT). But the sum of squares is

$$
\sum_t (\varepsilon'T)(\varepsilon'T)' = \sum_t \varepsilon'TT'\varepsilon
$$

$$
= \sum_t (y'_t\Gamma + x'_tB)\Sigma^{-1}(y'_t\Gamma + x'_tB)',
$$

which is the minimand for generalized least squares estimation of Γ and **B**. If Σ must be estimated, which will almost always be the case, Lahiri and Schmidt find that full efficiency in estimation requires an *efficient* estimate of Σ. This is in contrast to the seemingly unrelated regressions model, which requires only a *consistent* estimate of Σ. (See Section 17.2.2.) Iterating via the Oberhofer and Kmenta (1974) method produces the desired estimates. (See Section 17.2.3a.)

---

[20] This intriguing result is due to Lahiri and Schmidt (1978).

19.4.2. Indirect Least Squares (ILS)

In obtaining the rank and order conditions for identification, we implicitly defined an estimator for the structural parameters. For the jth equation,

$$\pi_j - \underline{\Pi}_j\gamma_j = \beta_j \quad (K_j \text{ equations}),$$
$$\pi_j^* - \Pi_j^*\gamma_j = 0 \quad (K_j^* \text{ equations}). \tag{19-43}$$

By analogy, then, if P is the OLS estimate of Π, the ILS estimator of β_j would be

$$b_j = p_j - \underline{P}_j c_j. \tag{19-44}$$

It remains to find c_j, the ILS estimator of γ_j. In the second equation, there are K_j^* equations and M_j unknown parameters to be determined. There are three possibilities:

1. $K_j^* < M_j$. Then the equation is unidentified, and no solution can be obtained.
2. $K_j^* = M_j$. The equation is exactly identified. In this case, we may compute

$$c_j = [P_j^*]^{-1}p_j^*. \tag{19-45}$$

3. $K_j^* > M_j$. The equation is overidentified. There is more than one solution.

EXAMPLE 19.15. ILS Estimation of an Overidentified Model. Suppose that the model of Example 19.1 is expanded to

$$(\text{Demand}) \quad q = \alpha_0 + \alpha_1 p + \alpha_2 y + \alpha_3 t + \varepsilon_1,$$
$$(\text{Supply}) \quad q = \beta_0 + \beta_1 p + \beta_2 z + \varepsilon_2, \tag{19-46}$$

where y, t, and z are income, a time trend, and an input cost, respectively. The reduced form is

$$q = \frac{\alpha_1\beta_0 - \beta_1\alpha_0}{\Delta} - \frac{\alpha_2\beta_1}{\Delta}y - \frac{\alpha_3\beta_1}{\Delta}t + \frac{\alpha_1\beta_2}{\Delta}z + v_1,$$

$$p = \frac{\beta_0 - \alpha_0}{\Delta} - \frac{\alpha_2}{\Delta}y - \frac{\alpha_3}{\Delta}t + \frac{\beta_2}{\Delta}z + v_2,$$

where $\Delta = \alpha_1 - \beta_1$. There are two solutions for β_1. Using the data in the appendix to this chapter for the U.S. agricultural market, the estimated reduced form is

$$\hat{q} = 6170 \ + 0.0172y - 3.17t + 0.372z, \quad s^2 = 36.12,$$
$$\hat{p} = 17{,}875 + 0.0387y - 9.23t + 1.17z, \quad s^2 = 98.80.$$

The demand equation is exactly identified, while the supply equation is overidentified. The two ILS estimates of β_1 are 0.444 and 0.343. There is no obvious way to reconcile them.

19.4.3. Estimation by Instrumental Variables (IV)

In the next several sections, we will discuss the various methods of consistent and efficient estimation. As will be evident quite soon, there is a surprisingly long menu of choices. It a useful result that all of the methods in general use can be placed under the umbrella of **instrumental variable (IV) estimators**.

Returning to the structural form, we first consider direct estimation of the jth equation,

$$y_j = Y_j\gamma_j + X_j\beta_j + \varepsilon_j$$
$$= Z_j\delta_j + \varepsilon_j. \tag{19-47}$$

As we saw above, estimates of δ_j are inconsistent because of the correlation of Z_j and ε_j. A general method of obtaining consistent estimates is the method of instrumental variables. Let W_j be a $T \times (M_j + K_j)$ matrix that satisfies the requirements for an IV estimator,

$$\text{plim} \frac{W_j'Z_j}{T} = \Sigma_{wz} = \text{a finite nonsingular matrix,} \tag{19-48.1}$$

$$\text{plim} \frac{W_j'\varepsilon_j}{T} = 0, \tag{19-48.2}$$

$$\text{plim} \frac{W_j'W_j}{T} = \Sigma_{ww} = \text{a positive definite matrix.} \tag{19-48.3}$$

Then the IV estimator,

$$\hat{\delta}_{j,\text{IV}} = [W_j'Z_j]^{-1}W_j'y_j, \tag{19-49}$$

will be consistent and have asymptotic covariance matrix

$$\text{Asy. Var}[\hat{\delta}_{j,\text{IV}}] = \frac{\sigma_{jj}}{T} \text{plim} \left[\frac{W_j'Z_j}{T}\right]^{-1}\left[\frac{W_j'W_j}{T}\right]\left[\frac{Z_j'W_j}{T}\right]^{-1} \tag{19-50}$$

$$= \frac{\sigma_{jj}}{T}[\Sigma_{wz}^{-1}\Sigma_{ww}\Sigma_{zw}^{-1}].$$

Proof: $\hat{\delta}_{j,\text{IV}} = \delta_j + \left[\dfrac{W_j'Z_j}{T}\right]^{-1}\dfrac{W_j'\varepsilon_j}{T}.$

Consistency follows from (19–48.1) and (19–49). For the asymptotic distribution, we consider the limiting distribution of

$$\sqrt{T}(\hat{\delta}_{j,\text{IV}} - \delta_j) = \left[\frac{W_j'Z_j}{T}\right]^{-1}\left[\frac{W_j'\varepsilon_j}{\sqrt{T}}\right].$$

If the limiting distribution exists, it is the same as that of

$$z_j = \Sigma_{wz}^{-1}\left[\frac{W_j'\varepsilon_j}{\sqrt{T}}\right].$$

It can be shown that the limiting distribution of z_j is normal, with mean zero and covariance matrix equal to T times the matrix in (19–50). This gives the asymptotic distribution as shown earlier. The assumption that the limiting distribution exists need not be met, but the same assumptions that underlie the entire analysis of this chapter will be sufficient.
A consistent estimate of σ_{jj} is obtained using

$$\hat{\sigma}_{jj} = \frac{(Y_j - Z_j\hat{\delta}_{j,\text{IV}})'(Y_j - Z_j\hat{\delta}_{j,\text{IV}})}{T}. \tag{19-51}$$

This is the familiar sum of squares of the estimated disturbances. A degrees of freedom correction for the denominator, $T - M_j - K_j$, is sometimes suggested. Asymptotically, the correction is immaterial. Whether it is beneficial in a small sample remains to be settled. The resultant estimator is not unbiased in any event, as it would be in the classical regression model. (Only) in the interest of simplicity, we shall omit the degrees of freedom correction in what follows.

The various estimators that have been developed for simultaneous-equations models are all IV estimators. They differ in the choice of instruments and in whether the equations are estimated one at a time or jointly. We divide them into two classes, **limited information** or **full information**, on this basis.

19.4.4. Single-Equation Instrumental Variable Methods

Estimation of the system one equation at a time has the benefit of computational simplicity. But because these methods neglect information contained in the other equations, they are labeled *limited-information methods*.

19.4.4a. Estimating an Exactly Identified Equation

A useful departure point is an exactly identified equation. Identification of equation j requires that K_j^*, the number of excluded exogenous variables, be at least as large as M_j, the number of included endogenous variables in $\mathbf{Y}_j$. If the equation is exactly identified, $K_j^* = M_j$. Consider, then, the IV estimator based on

$$\mathbf{W}_j = [\mathbf{X}_j^* \quad \mathbf{X}_j] = \mathbf{X}. \tag{19–52}$$

There is an excluded exogenous variable available to serve as an instrument for each included endogenous variable. The estimator is

$$\hat{\boldsymbol{\delta}}_{j,\text{ILS}} = [\mathbf{X}'\mathbf{Z}_j]^{-1}\mathbf{X}'\mathbf{y}_j = \begin{bmatrix} \mathbf{c}_j \\ \mathbf{b}_j \end{bmatrix}. \tag{19–53}$$

This is the ILS estimator. The estimated reduced form is

$$\mathbf{P} = (\mathbf{X}'\mathbf{X})^{-1}\mathbf{X}'[\mathbf{y}_j \quad \mathbf{Y}_j \quad \mathbf{Y}_j^*]. \tag{19–54}$$

We do not require the last M_j^* columns. For the remainder, after premultiplying by $\mathbf{X}'\mathbf{X}$ and partitioning $\mathbf{X}$ as $\mathbf{W}_j$ shown, we have

$$\begin{bmatrix} \mathbf{X}_j^{*\prime}\mathbf{X}_j^* & \mathbf{X}_j^{*\prime}\mathbf{X}_j \\ \mathbf{X}_j'\mathbf{X}_j^* & \mathbf{X}_j'\mathbf{X}_j \end{bmatrix}\begin{bmatrix} \mathbf{p}_j^* & \mathbf{P}_j^* \\ \mathbf{p}_j & \mathbf{P}_j \end{bmatrix} = \begin{bmatrix} \mathbf{X}_j^{*\prime}\mathbf{y}_j & \mathbf{X}_j^{*\prime}\mathbf{Y}_j \\ \mathbf{X}_j'\mathbf{y}_j & \mathbf{X}_j'\mathbf{Y}_j \end{bmatrix}. \tag{19–55}$$

Recall the equations that defined the ILS estimator, (19–43). Using $\mathbf{P}$ instead,

$$\begin{bmatrix} \mathbf{p}_j^* & \mathbf{P}_j^* \\ \mathbf{p}_j & \mathbf{P}_j \end{bmatrix}\begin{bmatrix} 1 \\ -\mathbf{c}_j \end{bmatrix} = \begin{bmatrix} \mathbf{0} \\ \mathbf{b}_j \end{bmatrix}. \tag{19–56}$$

Postmultiplying both sides of (19–55) by $[1 \quad -\mathbf{c}_j']'$ produces

$$\begin{bmatrix} \mathbf{X}_j^{*\prime}\mathbf{X}_j^* & \mathbf{X}_j^{*\prime}\mathbf{X}_j \\ \mathbf{X}_j'\mathbf{X}_j^* & \mathbf{X}_j'\mathbf{X}_j \end{bmatrix}\begin{bmatrix} \mathbf{0} \\ \mathbf{b}_j \end{bmatrix} = \begin{bmatrix} \mathbf{X}_j^{*\prime}\mathbf{y}_j & \mathbf{X}_j^{*\prime}\mathbf{Y}_j \\ \mathbf{X}_j'\mathbf{y}_j & \mathbf{X}_j'\mathbf{Y}_j \end{bmatrix}\begin{bmatrix} 1 \\ -\mathbf{c}_j \end{bmatrix}. \tag{19–57}$$

Upon collecting terms, this defines the ILS estimator according to the equations

$$\begin{bmatrix} \mathbf{X}_j^{*\prime}\mathbf{X}_j & \mathbf{X}_j^{*\prime}\mathbf{Y}_j \\ \mathbf{X}_j'\mathbf{X}_j & \mathbf{X}_j'\mathbf{Y}_j \end{bmatrix}\begin{bmatrix} \mathbf{b}_j \\ \mathbf{c}_j \end{bmatrix} = \begin{bmatrix} \mathbf{X}_j^{*\prime}\mathbf{y}_j \\ \mathbf{X}_j'\mathbf{y}_j \end{bmatrix}. \tag{19–58}$$

By premultiplying (19–53) by $\mathbf{X}'\mathbf{Z}_j$, we obtain exactly this expression, so the two are equivalent. To reiterate the result, for an exactly identified equation, we may obtain consistent estimates by using the excluded exogenous variables as instruments for the included endogenous variables. The appropriate asymptotic covariance matrix can be computed using (19–50) and (19–51).

19.4.4b.   Two-Stage Least Squares (2SLS)

For the exactly identified equation, ILS provides a consistent (and, we shall show, efficient) estimate. In the usual case, however, the equation to be estimated will be overidentified, so $\mathbf{X}'\mathbf{Z}_j$ will have more rows than columns and cannot be inverted. As such, the ILS/IV estimator cannot be used. The method of two-stage least squares is the usual alternative.[21]

Since we have an excess of exogenous variables in $\mathbf{X}_j^*$ to choose from, it might make sense just to choose M_j from the set. Indeed, you can easily show that we could just use any M_j independent linear combinations of them,

$$\hat{\mathbf{Y}} = \mathbf{X}_j^*\mathbf{D}, \tag{19-59}$$

for some matrix $\mathbf{D}$ with full column rank. A natural candidate would be the predicted values from a set of regressions of the variables in $\mathbf{Y}_j$ on $\mathbf{X}_j^*$. We leave as an exercise the proof that this would provide a consistent estimator. However, it would not be efficient. In our discussion of IV estimators in Section 9.5.4, we obtained the qualitative result that the greater the correlation of the instruments with the included variables, the smaller the asymptotic variance matrix. Now from the reduced form (19–40), we know that $\mathbf{Y}_j = \mathbf{X}\boldsymbol{\Pi}_j + \mathbf{V}_j$, so, by regressing $\mathbf{Y}_j$ only on a subset of the x's, we neglect the information about $\mathbf{Y}_j$ contained in the remainder. The **two-stage least squares** (2SLS) method consists of using as the instruments for $\mathbf{Y}_j$ the predicted values in a regression of $\mathbf{Y}_j$ on *all* of the x's:

$$\hat{\mathbf{Y}}_j = \mathbf{X}[(\mathbf{X}'\mathbf{X})^{-1}\mathbf{X}'\mathbf{Y}_j] = \mathbf{X}\mathbf{P}_j. \tag{19-60}$$

(It can be shown that this is the most efficient IV estimator that can be formed using only the columns of $\mathbf{X}$.) Note the emulation of $E[\mathbf{Y}_j] = \mathbf{X}\boldsymbol{\Pi}_j$ in the result. The 2SLS estimator is, thus,

$$\hat{\boldsymbol{\delta}}_{j,\,2\text{SLS}} = \begin{bmatrix} \hat{\mathbf{Y}}_j'\mathbf{Y}_j & \hat{\mathbf{Y}}_j'\mathbf{X}_j \\ \mathbf{X}_j'\mathbf{Y}_j & \mathbf{X}_j'\mathbf{X}_j \end{bmatrix}^{-1} \begin{bmatrix} \hat{\mathbf{Y}}_j'\mathbf{y}_j \\ \mathbf{X}_j'\mathbf{y}_j \end{bmatrix}. \tag{19-61}$$

Before proceeding, it is important to emphasize the role of the identification condition in this result. In the matrix $[\hat{\mathbf{Y}}_j, \mathbf{X}_j]$, which has $M_j + K_j$ columns, all columns are linear functions of the K columns of $\mathbf{X}$. There exist, at most, K linearly independent combinations of the columns of $\mathbf{X}$. If the equation is not identified, $M_j + K_j$ is greater than K, and $[\hat{\mathbf{Y}}_j, \mathbf{X}_j]$ will not have full column rank. In this case, the 2SLS estimator cannot be computed. If, however, the order condition but not the rank condition is met, then although the 2SLS estimator can be computed, it is not a consistent estimator. See Example 19.13 for a case in point.

There are a few useful simplifications. First, since

$$\mathbf{X}(\mathbf{X}'\mathbf{X})^{-1}\mathbf{X}' = (\mathbf{I} - \mathbf{M})$$

is idempotent,

$$\hat{\mathbf{Y}}_j'\mathbf{Y}_j = \hat{\mathbf{Y}}_j'\hat{\mathbf{Y}}_j.$$

Second,

$$\mathbf{X}_j'\mathbf{X}(\mathbf{X}'\mathbf{X})^{-1}\mathbf{X}' = \mathbf{X}_j',$$

---

[21] Since this method leads to indirect least squares if the equaton is exactly identified, the two cases need not be considered separately.

implies

$$X'_j Y_j = X'_j \hat{Y}_j.$$

Thus, (19–61) can also be written

$$\hat{\delta}_{j, \text{2SLS}} = \begin{bmatrix} \hat{Y}'_j \hat{Y}_j & \hat{Y}'_j X_j \\ X'_j \hat{Y}_j & X'_j X_j \end{bmatrix}^{-1} \begin{bmatrix} \hat{Y}'_j y_j \\ X'_j y_j \end{bmatrix}. \tag{19–62}$$

The 2SLS estimator is obtained by ordinary least squares regression of y_j on $\hat{Y}_j$ and X_j. Thus, the name stems from the two regressions in the procedure:

1. Stage 1: Obtain the ordinary least squares predictions from regression of Y_j on X.
2. Stage 2: Estimate δ_j by ordinary least squares regression of y_j on $\hat{Y}_j$ and X_j.

A direct proof of the consistency of the 2SLS estimator requires only that we establish that it is a valid IV estimator. For (19–48.1) we require

$$\text{plim} \begin{bmatrix} \hat{Y}'_j Y_j / T & \hat{Y}'_j X_j / T \\ X'_j Y_j / T & X'_j X_j / T \end{bmatrix} = \text{plim} \begin{bmatrix} P'_j X'(X\Pi_j + V_j)/T & P'_j X'X/T \\ X'(X\Pi_j + V_j)/T & X'_j X_j / T \end{bmatrix}$$

to be a finite nonsingular matrix. We have used (19–40) for Y_j. This is a continuous function of P_j, which has plim $P_j = \Pi_j$. The Slutsky theorem thus allows us to substitute Π_j for P_j in the probability limit. That the parts converge to a finite matrix follows from (19–11) and (19–13). It will be nonsingular if Π_j has full column rank, which, in turn, will be true if the equation is identified.[22] For (19–48.2), we require

$$\text{plim} \frac{1}{T} \begin{bmatrix} \hat{Y}'_j \varepsilon_j \\ X'_j \varepsilon_j \end{bmatrix} = \begin{bmatrix} 0 \\ 0 \end{bmatrix}.$$

The second part is assumed in (19–12). For the first, by direct substitution,

$$\text{plim} \frac{1}{T} Y'_j X (X'X)^{-1} X' \varepsilon_j = \text{plim} \left(\frac{Y'_j X}{T} \right) \left(\frac{X'X}{T} \right)^{-1} \left(\frac{X' \varepsilon_j}{T} \right).$$

The third part on the right converges to zero, while the other two converge to finite matrices, which confirms the result. Since $\hat{\delta}_{j, \text{2SLS}}$ is an IV estimator, we can appeal to the earlier results for the asymptotic distribution. A proof of asymptotic efficiency requires the establishment of the benchmark, which we shall do in the discussion of the k class of estimators. Finally, by a (rather involved) application of the central limit theorem, it can be shown that if the data are well behaved, the two-stage least squares estimator is asymptotically normally distributed.

As a final shortcut that is useful for programming purposes, we note that if X_j is regressed on X, a perfect fit is obtained, so $\hat{X}_j = X_j$. Using the idempotent matrix $(I - M)$, we can thus write (19–62) as

$$\hat{\delta}_{j, \text{2SLS}} = \begin{bmatrix} Y'_j(I - M)Y_j & Y'_j(I - M)X_j \\ X'_j(I - M)Y_j & X'_j(I - M)X_j \end{bmatrix}^{-1} \begin{bmatrix} Y'_j(I - M)y_j \\ X'_j(I - M)y_j \end{bmatrix}. \tag{19–63}$$

Thus,

$$\hat{\delta}_{j, \text{2SLS}} = [\hat{Z}'_j \hat{Z}_j]^{-1} \hat{Z}'_j y_j$$

$$= [(Z'_j X)(X'X)^{-1}(X'Z_j)]^{-1}(Z'_j X)(X'X)^{-1} X' y_j, \tag{19–64}$$

---

[22] Schmidt (1976, pp. 150–151) provides a proof of this result.

Table 19.5

	Constant	Profits	Lagged Profits	Wages
OLS	16.2 (1.30)	0.193 (0.091)	0.090 (0.091)	0.796 (0.040)
IV	16.1 (1.34)	0.061 (0.140)	0.165 (0.122)	0.825 (0.041)
2SLS	16.6 (1.32)	0.017 (0.118)	0.216 (0.107)	0.810 (0.040)

where all columns of $\hat{\mathbf{Z}}_j$ are obtained as predictions in a regression of the corresponding column of $\mathbf{Z}_j$ on $\mathbf{X}$. This also results in a useful simplification of the estimated asymptotic covariance matrix,

$$\text{Est. Asy. Var}[\hat{\boldsymbol{\delta}}_{j,\,2SLS}] = \hat{\sigma}_{jj}[\hat{\mathbf{Z}}_j'\hat{\mathbf{Z}}_j]^{-1}. \tag{19-65}$$

It is important to note that σ_{jj} is estimated by

$$\hat{\sigma}_{jj} = \frac{(\mathbf{y}_j - \mathbf{Z}_j\hat{\boldsymbol{\delta}}_j)'(\mathbf{y}_j - \mathbf{Z}_j\hat{\boldsymbol{\delta}}_j)}{T}, \tag{19-66}$$

using the original data, not $\hat{\mathbf{Z}}_j$.

EXAMPLE 19.16. Consumption Function. The three behavioral equations of Klein's Model I (see Example 19.3 and the appendix) are all overidentified. OLS, 2SLS, and IV estimates that use only the lagged dependent variables and the time trend (omitting G, T, and W^g) are listed in Table 19.5. Estimated standard errors are given in parentheses.[23]

It can also be shown that 2SLS applied to an exactly identified equation is the same as ILS. If the equation is exactly identified, $\mathbf{Z}_j'\mathbf{X}$ is square and has an inverse. Thus, the inverse in brackets in (19-64) may be expanded to obtain

$$\hat{\boldsymbol{\delta}}_{2SLS} = (\mathbf{X}'\mathbf{Z}_j)^{-1}(\mathbf{X}'\mathbf{X})(\mathbf{Z}_j'\mathbf{X})^{-1}(\mathbf{Z}_j'\mathbf{X})(\mathbf{X}'\mathbf{X})^{-1}\mathbf{X}'\mathbf{y}_j.$$

Eliminating the products of inverses leaves (*for the exactly identified case only*)

$$\hat{\boldsymbol{\delta}}_{j,\,2SLS} = (\mathbf{X}'\mathbf{Z}_j)^{-1}\mathbf{X}'\mathbf{y}_j,$$

which is (19-53).

19.4.4c.   The k Class of Estimators

There is a useful alternative way to express the 2SLS estimator. Since $\hat{\mathbf{Y}}_j$ is the set of predicted values from a least squares regression,

$$\hat{\mathbf{Y}}_j = \mathbf{Y}_j - \hat{\mathbf{V}}_j, \tag{19-67}$$

where $\hat{\mathbf{V}}_j$ are least squares residuals. It follows that

$$\hat{\mathbf{Y}}_j'\hat{\mathbf{V}} = \mathbf{0}.$$

Thus, we may also write the 2SLS estimator as

$$\hat{\boldsymbol{\delta}}_{j,\,2SLS} = \begin{bmatrix} \mathbf{Y}_j'\mathbf{Y}_j - \hat{\mathbf{V}}'\hat{\mathbf{V}} & \mathbf{Y}_j'\mathbf{X}_j \\ \mathbf{X}_j'\mathbf{Y}_j & \mathbf{X}_j'\mathbf{X}_j \end{bmatrix}^{-1} \begin{bmatrix} (\mathbf{Y}_j - \hat{\mathbf{V}}_j)'\mathbf{y}_j \\ \mathbf{X}_j'\mathbf{y}_j \end{bmatrix} \tag{19-68}$$

$$= [\mathbf{W}_j'\mathbf{Z}_j]^{-1}\mathbf{W}_j'\mathbf{y}_j,$$

[23] The IV estimates are presented in Brundy and Jorgenson (1971 and 1974).

where

$$W'_j = [(Y_j - \hat{V}_j) \quad X_j].$$

The k class of estimators is defined by estimators of the form

$$\hat{\delta}_{j,k} = \begin{bmatrix} Y'_j Y_j - k\hat{V}'_j \hat{V}_j & Y'_j X_j \\ X'_j Y_j & X'_j X_j \end{bmatrix}^{-1} \begin{bmatrix} (Y_j - k\hat{V}_j)' y_j \\ X'_j y_j \end{bmatrix}. \qquad (19\text{--}69)$$

This will qualify as an IV estimator with

$$W_j = [Y_j - k\hat{V}_j \quad X_j]$$

if we can show that

$$\operatorname{plim} \frac{1}{T} \frac{W'_j \varepsilon_j}{T} = 0.$$

Since $\operatorname{plim}(1/T)X'_j\varepsilon_j = 0$, it suffices to show that

$$\operatorname{plim} \frac{1}{T}(Y_j - k\hat{V}_j)'\varepsilon_j = 0.$$

To do so, we use

$$Y_j - k\hat{V}_j = Y_j - V_j + (V_j - k\hat{V}_j)$$
$$= X\Pi_j + V_j - kMV_j,$$

where $M = I - X(X'X)^{-1}X'$ and V_j are the true disturbances estimated by $\hat{V}_j$. Since $\operatorname{plim} \Pi'_j X'\varepsilon_j/T = 0$ by assumption, the k-class estimator is consistent if and only if

$$\operatorname{plim}(V_j - kMV_j)'\varepsilon_j/T = \operatorname{plim}[(1 - k)V_j + kX(X'X)^{-1}X'V_j]'\varepsilon_j/T$$

equals zero. The second term does by assumption. The first term is $\operatorname{plim}(1 - k)$ times part of $\operatorname{plim} V'E/T = (\Gamma^{-1})'\Sigma$. Since this is not zero, the result is obtained if and only if

$$\operatorname{plim} k = 1. \qquad (19\text{--}70)$$

We have thus established that all members of the k class with $\operatorname{plim} k = 1$ are consistent. This includes two-stage least squares. Of course, not all members of the k class are consistent, since ordinary least squares is a member with $k = 0$.

It has also been shown [24] that all k-class estimators for which

$$\operatorname{plim} \sqrt{T}(k - 1) = 0 \qquad (19\text{--}71)$$

have the same asymptotic covariance matrix as the 2SLS estimator. This is usually computed as

$$\text{Est. Asy. Var}[\hat{\delta}_{j,k}] = \hat{\sigma}_{jj} \begin{bmatrix} Y'_j Y_j - k\hat{V}'_j \hat{V}_j & Y'_j X_j \\ X'_j Y_j & X'_j X_j \end{bmatrix}^{-1}. \qquad (19\text{--}72)$$

For computational purposes,

$$\hat{V}'_j \hat{V}_j = Y'_j Y_j - Y'_j X(X'X)^{-1}X'Y_j,$$

and

$$\hat{V}'_j y_j = Y'_j y_j - Y'_j X(X'X)^{-1}X'y_j.$$

[24] See, for example, Schmidt (1976, pp. 166–169).

This enables us to draw an important conclusion. For normally distributed disturbances, it has been shown that the limited information maximum likelihood estimator is a member of the k class that satisfies (19–71). Since the maximum likelihood estimator is asymptotically efficient among limited-information estimators, it follows that the 2SLS estimator is also fully efficient in the class of limited-information estimators. (This is in addition to the earlier proposition that 2SLS is efficient among limited-information IV estimators.)

19.4.4d.   Limited Information Maximum Likelihood (LIML)

The **limited information maximum likelihood (LIML) estimator** is based on a single equation. With normally distributed disturbances, LIML is efficient among single-equation estimators. To construct the log-likelihood function for the jth equation, we consider the joint distribution of the endogenous variables, y_j and Y_j. The reduced form for these $M_j + 1$ variables is

$$[y_j \quad Y_j] = [X_j \quad X_j^*] \begin{bmatrix} \pi_j & \Pi_j \\ \pi_j^* & \Pi_j^* \end{bmatrix} + [v_j \quad V_j]$$

or

$$Y_j^0 = X\Pi_j^0 + V_j^0. \tag{19–73}$$

The $(M_j + 1) \times (M_j + 1)$ reduced-form covariance matrix is

$$\Omega_j^0 = \begin{bmatrix} \omega_{jj} & \omega_j' \\ \omega_j & \Omega_{jj} \end{bmatrix}. \tag{19–74}$$

The log of the joint density is, therefore,

$$\ln L_j^0 = -\frac{T}{2}[(M_j + 1)\ln(2\pi) + \ln|\Omega_j^0|] - \frac{1}{2}\sum_t [Y_{jt}^0 - x_t'\Pi_j^0]'\Omega_j^{0-1}[Y_{jt}^0 - x_t'\Pi_j^0]. \tag{19–75}$$

The LIML estimator maximizes this log likelihood, subject to the constraints that relate the structure to the reduced form,

$$\pi_j - \Pi_j \gamma_j = \beta_j, \tag{19–76}$$
$$\pi_j^* - \Pi_j^* \gamma_j = 0.$$

The first of these just shows how to obtain β_j given γ_j. The second shows the restrictions on Π. There are three cases to consider:

1. The equation is unidentified. No estimation is possible.
2. The equation is exactly identified. There are no restrictions: $\gamma_j = \Pi_j^{*-1}\Pi_j^*$.
3. The equation is overidentified. The restrictions in (19–76) are substantive.

Absent any restrictions, (19–75) is the log-likelihood function for the seemingly unrelated regressions model analyzed in Chapter 17. As such, since all equations have the same regressors, ordinary least squares, equation by equation, is consistent and efficient. Before proceeding, therefore, we obtain the following useful result:

> If the equation is exactly identified, the LIML estimator is the ILS estimator. Moreover, it is also equal to the 2SLS, as was proved earlier.

If the equation is overidentified, the likelihood function is to be maximized with respect to all of its unknown parameters. The analytical solution to the resulting problem is extremely lengthy and involved. Fortunately, this is one of those unusual cases in which the practical application is far simpler than the formal solution.

The jth structural equation may be written

$$\mathbf{y}_j - \mathbf{Y}_j \gamma_j = \mathbf{X}_j \boldsymbol{\beta}_j + \boldsymbol{\varepsilon}_j$$

or

$$\mathbf{Y}_j^0 \gamma_j^0 = \mathbf{X}_j \boldsymbol{\beta}_j + \boldsymbol{\varepsilon}_j,$$

where

$$\gamma_j^0 = \begin{bmatrix} 1 \\ -\gamma_j \end{bmatrix}. \tag{19-77}$$

If γ_j^0 were known, $\boldsymbol{\beta}_j$ could be estimated by a least squares regression of

$$\mathbf{y}_j^0 = \mathbf{Y}_j^0 \gamma_j^0 \tag{19-78}$$

on $\mathbf{X}_j$. The sum of squared residuals in this regression would be

$$\mathbf{e}_j^{0\prime} \mathbf{e}_j^0 = \mathbf{y}_j^{0\prime} (\mathbf{I} - \mathbf{X}_j (\mathbf{X}_j' \mathbf{X}_j)^{-1} \mathbf{X}_j') \mathbf{y}_j^0 = \mathbf{y}_j^{0\prime} \mathbf{M}_j \mathbf{y}_j^0.$$

If, instead, the full set of regressors were used, the sum of squared residuals would be

$$\mathbf{e}_j^{1\prime} \mathbf{e}_j^1 = \mathbf{y}_j^{0\prime} (\mathbf{I} - \mathbf{X} (\mathbf{X}' \mathbf{X})^{-1} \mathbf{X}') \mathbf{y}_j^0 = \mathbf{y}_j^{0\prime} \mathbf{M} \mathbf{y}_j^0.$$

Since adding variables to a regression never decreases the sum of squared residuals, the variance ratio

$$\lambda_j = \frac{\mathbf{e}_j^{0\prime} \mathbf{e}_j^0}{\mathbf{e}_j^{1\prime} \mathbf{e}_j^1} \tag{19-79}$$

is never less than one. Making the substitution for $\mathbf{y}_j^0$ and using the basic result for the least squares residuals, (6-16), we have

$$\lambda_j = \frac{\gamma_j^{0\prime} \mathbf{Y}_j^{0\prime} \mathbf{M}_j \mathbf{Y}_j^0 \gamma_j^0}{\gamma_j^{0\prime} \mathbf{Y}_j^{0\prime} \mathbf{M} \mathbf{Y}_j^0 \gamma_j^0}. \tag{19-80}$$

The vector γ_j^0 that minimizes λ_j is the **least variance ratio** estimator of γ_j^0. Anderson and Rubin (1949) showed that this estimator is equivalent to the limited-information maximum likelihood estimator.

In the numerator of λ_j, the mnth element of $\mathbf{Y}_j^{0\prime} \mathbf{M}_j \mathbf{Y}_j^0 = \mathbf{W}_j^0$ is the sum of squares or cross-products of the least squares residuals from the regression of the mth and nth variables in $\mathbf{Y}_j^0$ on $\mathbf{X}_j$. The corresponding matrix in the denominator is $\mathbf{W}_j^1$, defined likewise with respect to regressions on all of $\mathbf{X}$. Thus, the function to be minimized is

$$\lambda_j = \frac{\gamma_j^{0\prime} \mathbf{W}_j^0 \gamma_j^0}{\gamma_j^{0\prime} \mathbf{W}_j^1 \gamma_j^0}. \tag{19-81}$$

Multiplying the necessary condition, $\partial \lambda_j / \partial \hat{\gamma}_j^0 = \mathbf{0}$, by $\hat{\gamma}_j^{0\prime} \mathbf{W}_j^1 \hat{\gamma}_j^0 / 2$ produces the solution,

$$[\mathbf{W}_j^0 - \lambda_j \mathbf{W}_j^1] \hat{\gamma}_j^0 = \mathbf{0}. \tag{19-82}$$

For a nonzero solution to exist, the matrix in brackets must be singular, so λ_j is defined by the determinantal equation,

$$|\mathbf{W}_j^0 - \lambda_j \mathbf{W}_j^1| = 0. \tag{19-83}$$

The polynomial has $\mathbf{M}_j + 1$ roots. Since the root is the original function, we seek the smallest one.[25] Once λ_j is obtained, $\hat{\gamma}_j$ can be computed using (19-82),

$$\begin{bmatrix} w_{jj}^0 - \lambda w_{jj}^1 & \mathbf{w}_j^{0\prime} - \lambda \mathbf{w}_j^{1\prime} \\ \underline{\mathbf{w}}_j^0 - \lambda \underline{\mathbf{w}}_j^1 & \mathbf{W}_{jj}^0 - \lambda \mathbf{W}_{jj}^1 \end{bmatrix} \begin{bmatrix} 1 \\ -\hat{\gamma}_j \end{bmatrix} = 0$$

or

$$\hat{\gamma}_{j,\,\text{LIML}} = [\mathbf{W}_{jj}^0 - \lambda \mathbf{W}_{jj}^1]^{-1}(\underline{\mathbf{w}}_j^0 - \lambda \underline{\mathbf{w}}_j^1). \tag{19-84}$$

With $\hat{\gamma}_j$ in hand, $\hat{\mathbf{y}}_j^0$ can be computed and β_j can be estimated by ordinary least squares regression of $\hat{\mathbf{y}}_j^0$ on $\mathbf{X}_j$. As usual, σ_{jj} may be estimated using (19-51).

There are several useful theoretical aspects of this estimator. First, the LIML estimator is a member of the k class with $k = \lambda_j$.[26] As a consequence, an equivalent computational method is to compute the root and then use (19-69) to compute the slopes. It has also been shown that

$$\text{plim}\,\sqrt{T}\,(\lambda_j - 1) = 0, \tag{19-85}$$

which implies that the LIML estimator is consistent and has the same asymptotic covariance matrix as the 2SLS estimator. Since LIML is efficient, this confirms our earlier observation that 2SLS is asymptotically efficient as well. Finally, if the equation is exactly identified, $\lambda = 1$, so that LIML = 2SLS, which we have already shown equals ILS as well.

Since the determinant of $\mathbf{W}_j^1$ is nonzero, λ_j in (19-83) is also defined by

$$|(\mathbf{W}_j^1)^{-1}\mathbf{W}_j^0 - \lambda \mathbf{I}| = 0. \tag{19-86}$$

Thus, λ_j is the smallest characteristic root of $(\mathbf{W}_j^1)^{-1}\mathbf{W}_j^0$. A practical obstacle is that $(\mathbf{W}_j^1)^{-1}\mathbf{W}_j^0$ is an asymmetric matrix. Most widely used econometric software[27] contains easily used routines for computing characteristic roots and vectors for symmetric matrices. But there are relatively few counterparts for asymmetric matrices. We can also bypass this difficulty, since the roots of $(\mathbf{W}_j^1)^{-1}\mathbf{W}_j^0$ are the same as those of the symmetric matrix, $(\mathbf{W}_j^1)^{-1/2}\mathbf{W}_j^0(\mathbf{W}_j^1)^{-1/2}$, which are real.

EXAMPLE 19.17. LIML Estimation of Klein's Consumption Function.   For the consumption function in Klein's model I,

$$\mathbf{X}_c = [1, P_{-1}] \qquad \text{and} \qquad \mathbf{X} = [1, G, T, A, W^g, P_{-1}, K_{-1}, X_{-1}].$$

The included endogenous variables are

$$Y_c^0 = [C \quad P \quad (W^p + W^g)].$$

The residual sums of squares and cross-product matrices in the regressions of Y_c^0 on $\mathbf{X}_c$ and $\mathbf{X}$ are

$$\mathbf{W}_c^0 = \begin{bmatrix} 541.16 & & \\ 123.82 & 145.49 & \\ 672.21 & 120.26 & 758.59 \end{bmatrix}, \qquad \mathbf{W}_c^1 = \begin{bmatrix} 58.099 & & \\ 58.628 & 61.950 & \\ 43.661 & 41.576 & 40.072 \end{bmatrix}.$$

---

[25] All roots are greater than one. For a proof, see Schmidt (1976).
[26] See Schmidt (1976, pp. 173–174).
[27] For example, TSP, RATS, SHAZAM, LIMDEP, and SAS.

Using (2–105), we obtain

$$(\mathbf{W}_c^1)^{-1/2} = \begin{bmatrix} 0.785645 & & \\ -0.490974 & 0.523609 & \\ -0.266918 & 0.053884 & 0.355695 \end{bmatrix}.$$

The characteristic roots of $(\mathbf{W}_c^1)^{-1/2}\mathbf{W}_c^0(\mathbf{W}_c^1)^{-1/2}$ are 186.161, 7.61756, and 1.49874. Using (19–84), we obtain

$$\hat{\gamma} = [-.2225, \quad 0.8226].$$

Finally, the least squares regression of

$$y_c^0 = C + 0.2225P - 0.8226(W^p + W^g)$$

on 1 and P_{-1} produces estimates of 17.477 and 0.396027. (Note that the coefficient on P has the wrong sign. The full information maximum likelihood estimator does also.)

The preceding discussion shows how to compute the LIML estimator by decomposing two residual covariance matrices. Taking λ_j into (19–84) is an alternative method, as is using λ_j in the k-class estimator of (19–69). There is a third approach to the computation. For the endogenous variables in equation j, we have $M_j + 1$ equations

$$\begin{aligned} \mathbf{y}_j &= \mathbf{Y}_j\gamma_j + \mathbf{X}_j\beta_j + \varepsilon_j, \\ \mathbf{Y}_j &= \mathbf{X}\Pi_j^0 \qquad + \mathbf{V}_j. \end{aligned} \tag{19–87}$$

Pagan (1979) has shown that the LIML estimator may be computed by treating the preceding as a seemingly unrelated regressions model, ignoring both the constraints on the reduced form and the correlation between $\mathbf{Y}_j$ and ε_j, and using the iterative GLS method discussed in Chapter 17.[28]

19.4.4e. Two-Stage Least Squares with Autocorrelation

If the equation being estimated does not contain any lagged endogenous variables, the treatment of autocorrelation is a simple extension of the methods of Chapter 15. Suppose that the autocorrelation is a first-order autoregression,

$$\varepsilon_{t,j} = \rho_j\varepsilon_{t-1,j} + u_{t,j}. \tag{19–88}$$

In the absence of lagged endogenous variables, the problems caused by autocorrelation concern efficiency and the inappropriateness of the usual estimators of the standard errors of the estimates, not consistency. Making the usual transformation, we have

$$y_{t,j} - \rho_j y_{t-1,j} = (\mathbf{Y}'_{t,j} - \rho_j\mathbf{Y}'_{t-1,j})\gamma_j + (\mathbf{x}'_{t,j} - \rho_j\mathbf{x}'_{t-1,j})\beta_j + u_{t,j}. \tag{19–89}$$

If ρ_j were known, the simultaneous-equations estimation problem would carry over in the familiar fashion to this modified equation. A consistent estimate of ρ_j can be obtained by using

$$\hat{\rho}_j = \frac{\sum_t \hat{\varepsilon}_{t,j}\hat{\varepsilon}_{t-1,j}}{\sum_t \hat{\varepsilon}_{t,j}^2}, \tag{19–90}$$

---

[28] For Klein's Model I, this procedure took over 80 iterations to converge for the consumption function and over 100 for the investment equation. In view of the rather small number of computations that succeed the extraction of the smallest root, the iterative SURE procedure is rather inefficient. See, as well, Hausman (1983, p. 426).

where $\hat{\varepsilon}_{j,t}$ is an estimated disturbance based on any consistent estimate of δ_j. The obvious choice is the 2SLS estimator. With $\hat{\rho}_j$ in hand, (19–89) can be estimated by an IV estimator. The asymptotic properties of the resulting estimator are the same as if the true ρ_j were used, so the only issue remaining concerns the choice of the instrumental variables.[29] Since only $Y_{t,j}$ is correlated with $u_{t,j}$, a consistent estimator is obtained by using $\hat{Y}_j = XP_j$ as usual. This estimator is asymptotically efficient as well if the disturbances are normally distributed.[30] The model may be estimated by a three-step procedure:

1. Estimate Π with $(X'X)^{-1}X'Y$ and compute $\hat{Y}_j = XP_j$.
2. Compute $\hat{\delta}_j$ using 2SLS; then estimate ρ_j as shown earlier.
3. Using $\hat{Y}_{t,j}$ based on x_t, compute FGLS estimates based on the modified structural equation (19–89).

It is also possible to iterate step 3, but the benefit of doing so remains to be verified. Asymptotically, it makes no difference, since the estimator is efficient at the first repetition.

If the equation contains lagged endogenous variables, neither the reduced-form estimates at the first step nor $\hat{\rho}_j$ at the second will be consistent. By repeating the transformation of (19–89), we see that in terms of temporally uncorrelated disturbances, the full reduced form includes x_t, x_{t-1}, Y_{t-1}, and Y_{t-2}, which is likely to be an inordinately large number of variables.[31] With a moderately sized sample, it may even be impossible to compute the estimated reduced form. But at the first step, we only require a consistent estimate of ρ, not an efficient one. A simple expedient is to treat the lagged endogenous variables as if they were current endogenous variables, and include only the current and lagged values of the strictly exogenous variables among the predetermined variables at step 1. The regression at step 2, then, is consistent but not efficient. A consistent set of residuals is produced that can be used in (19–90) to compute $\hat{\rho}$. FGLS estimates based on this $\hat{\rho}$ and the "purged" endogenous variables, $\hat{Y}_j$ and $\hat{Y}_{-1,j}$, are then computed at step 3.

Step 3 almost surely brings gains in asymptotic efficiency, though, as always, the issue as regards a small sample is less clear. We should note, though, that even with normally distributed disturbances, the estimator is not fully efficient for two reasons. First, as suggested by Brundy and Jorgenson, full efficiency would require an estimate of the full reduced form.[32] Second, unlike the previous case, this estimator requires an efficient estimator of ρ. This can be achieved by iterating over ρ at step 3. Another approach that is also fully efficient involves an extension of Hatanaka's method.[33]

19.4.4f. Two-Stage Least Squares in Nonlinear Models (NL2SLS)

The analysis of simultaneous equations becomes considerably more complicated when the equations are nonlinear. Amemiya presents a general treatment of nonlinear models.[34] A case that is broad enough to include many practical applications is the one analyzed by Kelejian (1971),

$$y_j = \gamma_{1j}f_{1j}(y, x) + \gamma_{2j}f_{2j}(y, x) + \cdots + X_j\beta_j + \varepsilon_j. \tag{19–91}$$

---

[29] See Section 13.4.

[30] See, for example, Fomby et al. (1984, pp. 582–583). This is a useful simplification in view of the fact that (19–89) implies that the full reduced form and the strictly correct set of instruments includes all of Y_{t-1}, x_t, and x_{t-1}. Related discussion appears in Sargan (1961) and Fair (1972). Fair also considers higher-order autocorrelation.

[31] Fair (1970).

[32] See, as well, Fair (1972).

[33] See Section 15.6.3 and Hatanaka (1976).

[34] Amemiya (1985, pp. 245–265).

This is the direct extension of (8–7). Ordinary least squares will be inconsistent for the same reasons as before, but an IV estimator, if one can be devised, should have the usual properties. Because of the nonlinearity, it may not be possible to solve for the reduced-form equations (assuming that they exist), $h_{ij}(\mathbf{x}) = E[f_{ij} \mid \mathbf{x}]$. Kelejian shows that 2SLS based on a Taylor series approximation to h_{ij}, using linear terms, higher powers, and cross-products of the variables in $\mathbf{x}$, will be consistent. The analysis of 2SLS presented earlier, then, applies to the $\hat{\mathbf{Z}}_j$ consisting of $[\hat{\mathbf{f}}_{1j}, \hat{\mathbf{f}}_{2j}, \dots, \mathbf{X}_j]$.[35]

EXAMPLE 19.18. Nonlinear Two-Stage Least Squares.   The model of Example 19.13 contains three endogenous variables, A/S, C, and M. The first equation also involves C^2. Fitted values for 2SLS were obtained by regressing all four endogenous functions on a constant, the exogenous variables and their squares, and all distinct cross-products. A much larger nonlinear model (42 equations in total, including 16 behavioral equations) was estimated by Rice and Smith (1977). They used linear approximations for the reduced forms.

In a linear model, if an equation fails the order condition, it cannot be estimated by 2SLS. This is not true of Kelejian's approach, however, since taking higher powers of the regressors creates many more linearly independent instrumental variables. If an equation in a linear model fails the rank condition but not the order condition, the 2SLS estimates can be computed in a finite sample but will fail to exist asymptotically because $\mathbf{X}\Pi_j$ will have short rank. Unfortunately, to the extent that Kelejian's approximation never exactly equals the true reduced form unless it happens to be the polynomial in $\mathbf{x}$ (unlikely), this built-in control need not be present, even asymptotically. As such, there is an interesting (and open) question of just what is estimated by the estimator if the model is not identified. Thus, as we saw earlier, although the model in Example 19.13 is unidentified, computation of Kelejian's NL2SLS estimator appears to be routine. Amemiya's methods are more general and, in principle, would break down (asymptotically) in an unidentified model. But they are somewhat more difficult to apply. The upshot, of course, is that one should ensure that the model is identified before embarking on the estimation step.

19.4.5.   System Methods of Estimation

We may formulate the full system of equations as

$$
\begin{bmatrix} \mathbf{y}_1 \\ \mathbf{y}_2 \\ \vdots \\ \mathbf{y}_M \end{bmatrix} = \begin{bmatrix} \mathbf{Z}_1 & \mathbf{0} & \cdots & \mathbf{0} \\ \mathbf{0} & \mathbf{Z}_2 & \cdots & \mathbf{0} \\ \vdots & \vdots & \vdots & \vdots \\ \mathbf{0} & \mathbf{0} & \cdots & \mathbf{Z}_M \end{bmatrix} \begin{bmatrix} \delta_1 \\ \delta_2 \\ \vdots \\ \delta_M \end{bmatrix} + \begin{bmatrix} \varepsilon_1 \\ \varepsilon_2 \\ \vdots \\ \varepsilon_M \end{bmatrix} \tag{19-92}
$$

or

$$ \mathbf{y} = \mathbf{Z}\delta + \varepsilon, $$

where

$$ E[\varepsilon] = \mathbf{0} $$

and

$$
E[\varepsilon\varepsilon'] = \bar{\Sigma} = \begin{bmatrix} \sigma_{11}\mathbf{I} & \sigma_{12}\mathbf{I} & \cdots & \sigma_{1M}\mathbf{I} \\ \sigma_{21}\mathbf{I} & \sigma_{22}\mathbf{I} & \cdots & \sigma_{2M}\mathbf{I} \\ & & & \\ \sigma_{M1}\mathbf{I} & \sigma_{M2}\mathbf{I} & \cdots & \sigma_{MM}\mathbf{I} \end{bmatrix} = \Sigma \otimes \mathbf{I}.
$$

[35] The alternative approach of directly computing fitted values for $\mathbf{y}$ appears to be inconsistent. See Kelejian (1971) and Goldfeld and Quandt (1968).

The least squares estimator,

$$\mathbf{d} = [\mathbf{Z}'\mathbf{Z}]^{-1}\mathbf{Z}'\mathbf{y},$$

which is equation-by-equation ordinary least squares, is inconsistent. But even if ordinary least squares were consistent, we know from our results for the seemingly unrelated regressions model that it would be inefficient compared to an estimator that makes use of the cross-equation correlations of the disturbances. For the first issue, we turn once again to an IV estimator. For the second, as we did in Chapter 17, we use a generalized least squares approach. Thus, assuming that $\bar{\mathbf{W}}$ satisfies the requirements for an IV estimator, a consistent though inefficient estimator would be

$$\hat{\delta}_{IV} = [\bar{\mathbf{W}}'\mathbf{Z}]^{-1}\bar{\mathbf{W}}'\mathbf{y}. \tag{19-93}$$

Analogous to the seemingly unrelated regressions model, a more efficient estimator would be based on the generalized least squares principle,

$$\hat{\delta}_{IV,\,GLS} = [\bar{\mathbf{W}}'(\Sigma^{-1} \otimes \mathbf{I})\mathbf{Z}]^{-1}\bar{\mathbf{W}}'(\Sigma^{-1} \otimes \mathbf{I})\mathbf{y} \tag{19-94}$$

or

$$\hat{\delta}_{IV,\,GLS} = \begin{bmatrix} \sigma^{11}\mathbf{W}'_1\mathbf{Z}_1 & \sigma^{12}\mathbf{W}'_1\mathbf{Z}_2 & \cdots & \sigma^{1M}\mathbf{W}'_1\mathbf{Z}_M \\ \sigma^{21}\mathbf{W}'_2\mathbf{Z}_1 & \sigma^{22}\mathbf{W}'_2\mathbf{Z}_2 & \cdots & \sigma^{2M}\mathbf{W}'_2\mathbf{Z}_M \\ & & \vdots & \\ \sigma^{M1}\mathbf{W}'_M\mathbf{Z}_1 & \sigma^{M2}\mathbf{W}'_M\mathbf{Z}_2 & \cdots & \sigma^{MM}\mathbf{W}'_M\mathbf{Z}_M \end{bmatrix}^{-1} \begin{bmatrix} \sum_j \sigma^{1j}\mathbf{W}'_1\mathbf{y}_j \\ \sum_j \sigma^{2j}\mathbf{W}'_2\mathbf{y}_j \\ \vdots \\ \sum_j \sigma^{Mj}\mathbf{W}'_M\mathbf{y}_j \end{bmatrix}. \tag{19-95}$$

Two techniques are generally used for joint estimation of the entire system of equations: three-stage least squares and maximum likelihood.

19.4.5a.   Three-Stage Least Squares (3SLS)

Consider the IV estimator formed from

$$\bar{\mathbf{W}} = \hat{\mathbf{Z}} = \begin{bmatrix} \mathbf{X}(\mathbf{X}'\mathbf{X})^{-1}\mathbf{X}'\mathbf{Z}_1 & 0 & \cdots & 0 \\ 0 & \mathbf{X}(\mathbf{X}'\mathbf{X})^{-1}\mathbf{X}'\mathbf{Z}_2 & \cdots & 0 \\ & & \vdots & \\ 0 & 0 & & \mathbf{X}(\mathbf{X}'\mathbf{X})^{-1}\mathbf{X}'\mathbf{Z}_M \end{bmatrix}$$

$$= \begin{bmatrix} \hat{\mathbf{Z}}_1 & 0 & \cdots & 0 \\ 0 & \hat{\mathbf{Z}}_2 & \cdots & 0 \\ & & \vdots & \\ 0 & 0 & \cdots & \hat{\mathbf{Z}}_M \end{bmatrix}. \tag{19-96}$$

The IV estimator

$$\hat{\delta}_{IV} = [\hat{\mathbf{Z}}'\mathbf{Z}]^{-1}\hat{\mathbf{Z}}'\mathbf{y}$$

is nothing more than equation-by-equation 2SLS. We have already established the consistency of 2SLS. However, by analogy with the seemingly unrelated regressions model of Chapter 17, we would expect this estimator to be less efficient than a GLS estimator. A natural candidate would be

$$\hat{\delta}_{3SLS} = [\hat{\mathbf{Z}}'(\Sigma^{-1} \otimes \mathbf{I})\mathbf{Z}]^{-1}\hat{\mathbf{Z}}'(\Sigma^{-1} \otimes \mathbf{I})\mathbf{y}. \tag{19-97}$$

In order for this to be a valid IV estimator, we must establish that

$$\text{plim} \frac{1}{T} \hat{\mathbf{Z}}'(\boldsymbol{\Sigma}^{-1} \otimes \mathbf{I})\boldsymbol{\varepsilon} = \mathbf{0}.$$

This is M sets of equations of the form

$$\text{plim} \frac{1}{T} \sum_j \sigma^{ij} \hat{\mathbf{Z}}'_j \boldsymbol{\varepsilon}_j.$$

Each is the sum of vectors all of which converge to zero, as we saw in the development of the 2SLS estimator. The second requirement that

$$\text{plim} \frac{1}{T} \hat{\mathbf{Z}}(\boldsymbol{\Sigma} \otimes \mathbf{I})\mathbf{Z} \neq \mathbf{0}$$

and that the matrix be nonsingular can be established along the lines of its counterpart for 2SLS. Identification of every equation by the rank condition is sufficient.[36]

Once again using the idempotency of $\mathbf{I} - \mathbf{M}$, we may also interpret this as a GLS estimator of the form

$$\hat{\boldsymbol{\delta}}_{3SLS} = [\hat{\mathbf{Z}}'(\boldsymbol{\Sigma}^{-1} \otimes \mathbf{I})\hat{\mathbf{Z}}]^{-1} \hat{\mathbf{Z}}'(\boldsymbol{\Sigma}^{-1} \otimes \mathbf{I})\mathbf{y}. \tag{19-98}$$

The appropriate asymptotic covariance matrix for the estimator is

$$\text{Asy. Var}[\hat{\boldsymbol{\delta}}_{3SLS}] = [\bar{\mathbf{Z}}'(\boldsymbol{\Sigma}^{-1} \otimes \mathbf{I})\bar{\mathbf{Z}}]^{-1}, \tag{19-99}$$

where $\bar{\mathbf{Z}} = \text{diag}[\mathbf{XII}_j, \mathbf{X}_j]$. This would be estimated with the inverse matrix in (19-98).

Using sample data, we find that $\bar{\mathbf{Z}}$ may be estimated with $\hat{\mathbf{Z}}$. The remaining difficulty is to obtain an estimate of $\boldsymbol{\Sigma}$. In estimation of the multivariate regression model, for efficient estimation (that remains to be shown), any consistent estimate of $\boldsymbol{\Sigma}$ will do. The designers of the 3SLS method, Zellner and Theil (1962), suggest the natural choice arising out of the two-stage least estimates. The **three-stage least squares estimator** is thus defined as follows:

1. Estimate $\boldsymbol{\Pi}$ by ordinary least squares and compute $\hat{\mathbf{Y}}_j$ for each equation.
2. Compute $\boldsymbol{\delta}_{j, 2SLS}$ for each equation; then

$$\hat{\sigma}_{ij} = \frac{(\mathbf{y}_i - \mathbf{Z}_i \hat{\boldsymbol{\delta}}_i)'(\mathbf{y}_j - \mathbf{Z}_j \hat{\boldsymbol{\delta}}_j)}{T}.$$

3. Compute the GLS estimator according to (19-98) and an estimate of the asymptotic covariance matrix according to (19-99), using $\hat{\mathbf{Z}}$ and $\hat{\boldsymbol{\Sigma}}$.

It is also possible to iterate the 3SLS computation. However, unlike the seemingly unrelated regressions estimator, this does not provide the maximum likelihood estimator, nor does it improve the asymptotic efficiency.

By showing that the 3SLS estimator satisfies the requirements for an IV estimator, we have established its consistency. The question of asymptotic efficiency remains. Now it can be shown that among all IV estimators that use only the sample information embodied in the system, 3SLS is asymptotically efficient.[37] For normally distributed disturbances, it can be also shown that 3SLS has the same asymptotic distribution as the full-information

---

[36] A formal proof is given by Schmidt (1976, pp. 205–207).
[37] See Schmidt (1976) for a proof of its efficiency relative to 2SLS.

maximum likelihood estimator, which is asymptotically efficient among all estimators. A direct proof based on the information matrix is possible, but we shall take a much simpler route by simply exploiting a handy result due to Hausman in the next section.

19.4.5b.   Full-Information Maximum Likelihood Estimation (FIML)

Because of their simplicity and asymptotic efficiency, 2SLS and 3SLS are used almost exclusively (when ordinary least squares is not used) for the estimation of simultaneous-equations models. Nonethelesss, it is occasionally useful to obtain maximum likelihood estimates directly. The **full-information maximum likelihood (FIML) estimator** is based on the entire system of equations. With normally distributed disturbances, FIML is efficient among all estimators.

The FIML estimator treats all equations and all parameters jointly. To formulate the appropriate log-likelihood function, we begin with the reduced form,

$$\mathbf{Y} = \mathbf{X\Pi} + \mathbf{V},$$

where each row of $\mathbf{V}$ is assumed to be multivariate normally distributed, with mean $\mathbf{0}$ and covariance matrix, $E[\mathbf{v}_t \mathbf{v}'_t] = \mathbf{\Omega}$. The log likelihood for this model is precisely that of the seemingly unrelated regressions model of Chapter 17. For the moment, we can ignore the relationship between the structural and reduced-form parameters. Thus, from (17–21),

$$\ln L = -\frac{T}{2}[M \ln(2\pi) + \ln|\mathbf{\Omega}| + tr(\mathbf{\Omega}^{-1}\mathbf{W})], \qquad (19\text{–}100)$$

where

$$\mathbf{W}_{ij} = \frac{(\mathbf{y}_i - \mathbf{X}\pi_i^0)'(\mathbf{y}_j - \mathbf{X}\pi_j^0)}{T}$$

and

$$\pi_j^0 = j\text{th column of } \mathbf{\Pi}.$$

This is to be maximized subject to all of the restrictions imposed by the structure. Make the substitutions

$$\mathbf{\Pi} = -\mathbf{B\Gamma}^{-1} \qquad \text{and} \qquad \mathbf{\Omega} = (\mathbf{\Gamma}^{-1})'\mathbf{\Sigma\Gamma}^{-1},$$

so that

$$\mathbf{\Omega}^{-1} = \mathbf{\Gamma}\mathbf{\Sigma}^{-1}\mathbf{\Gamma}'.$$

Thus,

$$\ln L = -\frac{MT}{2}\ln(2\pi) - \frac{T}{2}\ln|(\mathbf{\Gamma}^{-1})'\mathbf{\Sigma\Gamma}^{-1}|$$

$$-\frac{T}{2}tr\left(\frac{\mathbf{\Gamma}\mathbf{\Sigma}^{-1}\mathbf{\Gamma}'(\mathbf{Y} + \mathbf{XB\Gamma}^{-1})'(\mathbf{Y} + \mathbf{XB\Gamma}^{-1})}{T}\right). \qquad (19\text{–}101)$$

This can be simplified. First,

$$-\frac{T}{2}\ln|(\mathbf{\Gamma}^{-1})'\mathbf{\Sigma\Gamma}^{-1}| = -\frac{T}{2}\ln|\mathbf{\Sigma}| + T\ln|\mathbf{\Gamma}|.$$

Second, $\boldsymbol{\Gamma}'(\mathbf{Y} + \mathbf{XB}\boldsymbol{\Gamma}^{-1})' = \boldsymbol{\Gamma}'\mathbf{Y}' + \mathbf{B}'\mathbf{X}'$. By permuting $\boldsymbol{\Gamma}$ from the beginning to the end of the trace and collecting terms,

$$tr(\boldsymbol{\Omega}^{-1}\mathbf{W}) = tr\left[\frac{\boldsymbol{\Sigma}^{-1}(\mathbf{Y}\boldsymbol{\Gamma} + \mathbf{XB})'(\mathbf{Y}\boldsymbol{\Gamma} + \mathbf{XB})}{T}\right]. \qquad (19\text{--}102)$$

Therefore, the log likelihood is

$$\ln L = -\frac{MT}{2}\ln(2\pi) + T\ln|\boldsymbol{\Gamma}| - \frac{T}{2}tr(\boldsymbol{\Sigma}^{-1}\mathbf{S}), \qquad (19\text{--}103)$$

where

$$s_{ij} = \frac{(\mathbf{Y}\boldsymbol{\Gamma}_i + \mathbf{XB}_i)'(\mathbf{Y}\boldsymbol{\Gamma}_j + \mathbf{XB}_j)}{T}.$$

[In terms of nonzero parameters, s_{ij} is $\hat{\sigma}_{ij}$ of (19–51).]

In maximizing $\ln L$, it is necessary to impose all of the additional restrictions on the structure. It is useful, therefore, to note that the trace may be written in the form

$$tr(\boldsymbol{\Sigma}^{-1}\mathbf{S}) = \frac{\sum_i\sum_j\sigma^{ij}(\mathbf{y}_i - \mathbf{Y}_i\boldsymbol{\gamma}_i - \mathbf{X}_i\boldsymbol{\beta}_i)'(\mathbf{y}_j - \mathbf{Y}_j\boldsymbol{\gamma}_j - \mathbf{X}_j\boldsymbol{\beta}_j)}{T}. \qquad (19\text{--}104)$$

Maximizing $\ln L$ subject to the exclusions in (19–104) and any other restrictions, if necessary, produces the FIML estimator. This has all of the desirable asymptotic properties of maximum likelihood estimators and, therefore, is asymptotically efficient among estimators of the simultaneous-equations model. The asymptotic covariance matrix for the FIML estimator is the same as that for the 3SLS estimator.

The computation of FIML estimates, except for the special cases noted subsequently, is extremely complicated. A useful interpretation of the estimator is provided by Hausman (1975 and 1983). He shows that the FIML estimator of $\boldsymbol{\delta}$ is a fixed point in the equation.

$$\hat{\boldsymbol{\delta}}_{\text{FIML}} = [\hat{\mathbf{Z}}(\hat{\boldsymbol{\delta}})'(\hat{\boldsymbol{\Sigma}}^{-1}\otimes\mathbf{I})\mathbf{Z}]^{-1}[\hat{\mathbf{Z}}(\hat{\boldsymbol{\delta}})(\hat{\boldsymbol{\Sigma}}^{-1}\otimes\mathbf{I})\mathbf{y}] = [\hat{\bar{\mathbf{Z}}}'\mathbf{Z}]^{-1}\hat{\bar{\mathbf{Z}}}'\mathbf{y}, \qquad (19\text{--}105)$$

where

$$\hat{\mathbf{Z}}(\hat{\boldsymbol{\delta}})(\hat{\boldsymbol{\Sigma}}^{-1}\otimes\mathbf{I}) = \begin{bmatrix} \hat{\sigma}^{11}\hat{\mathbf{Z}}_1 & \hat{\sigma}^{12}\hat{\mathbf{Z}}_1 & \cdots & \hat{\sigma}^{1M}\hat{\mathbf{Z}}_1 \\ \hat{\sigma}^{21}\hat{\mathbf{Z}}_2 & \hat{\sigma}^{22}\hat{\mathbf{Z}}_2 & \cdots & \hat{\sigma}^{2M}\hat{\mathbf{Z}}_2 \\ & & & \\ \hat{\sigma}^{M1}\hat{\mathbf{Z}}_M & \hat{\sigma}^{M2}\hat{\mathbf{Z}}_M & \cdots & \hat{\sigma}^{MM}\hat{\mathbf{Z}}_M \end{bmatrix} = \hat{\bar{\mathbf{Z}}}$$

and

$$\hat{\mathbf{Z}}_j = [\mathbf{X}\hat{\boldsymbol{\Pi}}_j \quad \mathbf{X}_j].$$

$\hat{\boldsymbol{\Pi}}$ is computed from the structural estimates

$$\hat{\boldsymbol{\Pi}}_j = M_j \text{ columns of } -\hat{\mathbf{B}}\hat{\boldsymbol{\Gamma}}^{-1}$$

and

$$\hat{\sigma}_{ij} = \frac{(\mathbf{y}_i - \mathbf{Z}_i\hat{\boldsymbol{\delta}}_i)'(\mathbf{y}_j - \mathbf{Z}_j\hat{\boldsymbol{\delta}}_j)}{T},$$

$$\hat{\sigma}^{ij} = (\hat{\boldsymbol{\Sigma}}^{-1})_{ij}.$$

This result implies that the FIML estimator is also an IV estimator. The asymptotic covariance matrix for the FIML estimator follows directly from its form as an IV estimator. Since this is the same as that of the 3SLS estimator, we conclude that with normally distributed disturbances, 3SLS has the same asymptotic distribution as maximum likelihood. The practical usefulness of this important result has not gone unnoticed by practitioners. The 3SLS estimator is far easier to compute than the FIML estimator. The benefit in computational cost comes at no cost in asymptotic efficiency.

As Hausman notes, although this is an interesting interpretation, it does not necessarily provide an efficient means of computing the FIML estimator. The implied iteration is

$$\hat{\delta}_{s+1} = [\hat{Z}(\hat{\delta}_s)'Z]^{-1}\hat{Z}(\hat{\delta}_s)'y, \qquad (19\text{--}106)$$

starting, say, at the 2SLS or 3SLS estimates. However, this is likely to converge very slowly, if at all. The matrix of the calculation is not necessarily positive definite, and the difference, $\hat{\delta}_{s+1} - \hat{\delta}_s$, need not point toward increases in the log likelihood even for very small steps.

Finally, there are two special cases worth noting. First, for the fully recursive model,

1. Γ is upper triangular, with ones on the diagonal. Therefore, $|\Gamma| = 1$ and $\ln|\Gamma| = 0$.
2. Σ is diagonal, so $\ln|\Sigma| = \Sigma_j \ln \sigma_{jj}$ and the trace in the exponent becomes

$$tr(\Sigma^{-1}S) = \sum_j \frac{1}{\sigma_{jj}} \frac{(y_j - Y_j\gamma_j - X_j\beta_j)'(y_j - Y_j\gamma_j - X_j\beta_j)}{T}. \qquad (19\text{--}107)$$

The log likelihood reduces to $\ln L = \sum_{j=1}^M \ln L_j$, where

$$\ln L_j = -\frac{T}{2}[\ln(2\pi) + \ln \sigma_{jj}] - \frac{1}{2\sigma_{jj}}(y_j - Y_j\gamma_j - X_j\beta_j)'(y_j - Y_j\gamma_j - X_j\beta_j). \qquad (19\text{--}108)$$

Therefore, the FIML estimator for this model is just equation-by-equation least squares. We found earlier that ordinary least squares was consistent in this setting. We now find that it is asymptotically efficient as well.

The second case is that of the exactly identified model. If every equation is exactly identified, there is a one-to-one correspondence between $[\Gamma, B]$ and $[\Pi]$. Since Π is unrestricted in the exactly identified case, FIML is obtained by estimating Π by OLS. Without going further, we may simply appeal to the general invariance result of MLEs. In an exactly identified model, ILS is also the FIML estimator.

19.4.6. Comparison of Methods

The preceding has described a large number of estimators for simultaneous-equations models. For practical purposes, it is appropriate to consider which is to be preferred. As an example, Table 19.6 presents limited- and full-information estimates for Klein's Model I based on the original data for 1921 to 1941. (For those who wish to update these results, the appendix to this chapter contains yearly data from 1953 to 1984 on the variables in Klein's Model I, as well as several other macroeconomic variables.)

EXAMPLE 19.19. Estimates of Klein's Model I.   It might seem, in light of the entire discussion, that one of the structural estimators, which have been described previously, should always be preferred to ordinary least squares, which, alone among the estimators considered here, is inconsistent. Unfortunately, the issue is not so clear. First, it is often found that the OLS estimator is surprisingly close to the structural estimator. It can be shown that at least in some cases, OLS has a smaller variance about its mean than does 2SLS about its

Table 19.6. Estimates of Klein's Model I (Estimated Asymptotic Standard Errors in Parentheses)

	Limited-Information Estimates				Full-Information Estimates			
	2SLS				3SLS			
C	16.6	0.017	0.216	0.810	16.4	0.125	0.163	0.790
	(1.32)	(0.118)	(0.107)	(0.040)	(1.30)	(0.108)	(0.100)	(0.038)
I	20.3	0.150	0.616	−0.158	28.2	−0.103	0.756	−0.195
	(7.54)	(0.173)	(0.162)	(0.036)	(6.79)	(0.162)	(0.153)	(0.038)
Wp	1.50	0.439	0.147	0.130	1.80	0.400	0.181	0.150
	(1.15)	(0.036)	(0.039)	(0.029)	(1.12)	(0.032)	(0.034)	(0.028)
	LIML				FIML			
C	17.5	−0.222	0.396	0.823	17.8	−0.214	0.351	0.853
	(1.93)	(0.212)	(0.182)	(0.058)	(2.12)	(0.96)	(0.101)	(0.047)
I	22.6	0.075	0.680	−0.168	17.2	0.130	0.613	−0.136
	(6.89)	(0.275)	(0.205)	(0.049)	(6.47)	(0.137)	(0.140)	(0.038)
Wp	1.53	0.434	0.151	0.132	1.41	0.498	0.087	0.403
	(1.08)	(0.057)	(0.141)	(0.169)	(0.943)	(0.018)	(0.015)	(0.021)
	OLS				3SLS			
C	16.2	0.193	0.090	0.796	16.6	0.165	0.177	0.766
	(1.30)	(0.091)	(0.091)	(0.040)	(1.22)	(0.096)	(0.090)	(0.035)
I	10.1	0.480	0.333	−0.112	42.9	−0.356	1.01	−0.260
	(5.47)	(0.097)	(0.101)	(0.027)	(10.6)	(0.260)	(0.249)	(0.051)
Wp	1.48	0.439	0.146	0.130	2.62	0.375	0.194	0.168
	(1.27)	(0.032)	(0.037)	(0.032)	(1.20)	(0.031)	(0.032)	(0.029)

mean, leading to the possibility that OLS might be more precise in a mean squared error sense.[38] But this result must be tempered by the finding that the OLS standard errors are, in all likelihood, not useful for inference purposes.[39] In spite of this, OLS appears to be the most frequently used estimator. Obviously this discussion is relevant only to finite samples. Asymptotically, 2SLS must dominate OLS and, in a correctly specified model, any full-information estimator must dominate any limited-information one. The finite-sample properties are of crucial importance. Most of what we know is asymptotic properties, but nearly all applications are based on rather small or moderate-sized samples.

Intuition would surely suggest that systems methods, 3SLS and FIML, are to be preferred to single-equation methods, 2SLS and LIML. Indeed, since the advantage is so transparent, why would one ever choose a single-equation estimator? The proper analogy is to the use of single-equation OLS versus GLS in the SURE model of Chapter 17. An obvious practical consideration is the computational simplicity of the single-equation methods. But the current state of available software has all but eliminated this advantage. However, several related aspects make the choice less clear-cut.

Although the systems methods are asymptotically better, they have two problems. First, any specification error in the structure of the model will be propagated throughout the

[38] See Goldberger (1964, pp. 359–360).
[39] Cragg (1967).

system by 3SLS or FIML. The limited-information estimators will, by and large, confine a problem to the particular equation in which it appears. Second, in the same fashion as the SURE model, the finite-sample variation of the estimated covariance matrix is transmitted throughout the system. Thus, the finite-sample variance of 3SLS may well be as large as or larger than that of 2SLS. Although they are only estimates, the previous results for Klein's Model I give a striking example. The upshot would appear to be that the advantage of the systems estimators in finite samples may be more modest than the asymptotic results would suggest. Monte Carlo studies of the issue have tended to reach the same conclusion.[40]

Since asymptotic comparisons are unambiguous, the remaining considerations are based primarily on small-sample behavior. Unfortunately, there are few usable general results. What results there are come from two sources: extensive analysis of very small models and Monte Carlo studies.[41] In the main, these studies tend to reinforce what intuition would suggest.

19.5. *Specification Tests*

In a strident criticism of structural estimation, Liu (1960) argued that all simultaneous-equations models of the economy were truly unidentified and that only reduced forms could be estimated.[42] While his criticisms may have been exaggerated (and never gained wide acceptance), modelers have been interested in testing the restrictions that overidentify an econometric model.

The first procedure for testing the overidentifying restrictions in a model was developed by Anderson and Rubin (1950). Their likelihood ratio test statistic is a by-product of LIML estimation:

$$\text{LR} = \chi^2[K_j^* - M_j] = T(\lambda_j - 1), \qquad (19\text{--}109)$$

where λ_j is the smallest root of the determinantal equation used to find the LIML estimator. [See (19–81).] The statistic is asymptotically distributed as chi-squared with degrees of freedom equal to the number of overidentifying restrictions. A large value is taken as evidence that there are exogenous variables in the model that have been inappropriately omitted from the equation being examined. If the equation is exactly identified, $K_j^* - M_j = 0$, but, at the same time, the root will be one. In later work, Basmann (1960) found that the Anderson–Rubin statistic rejected the null hypothesis too often. He suggested two alternatives. First,

$$F'[K_j^* - M_j, T - K] = \frac{T - K}{K_j^* - M_j}(\lambda_j' - 1), \qquad (19\text{--}110)$$

where λ_j' is computed by evaluating (19–81) at the 2SLS estimator instead of the LIML estimator. Second, he suggested computing F' at the LIML estimator. Both are approximately distributed as $F[K_j^* - M_j, T - K]$ under the null hypothesis of exact identification.[43] An alternative statistic based on the Lagrange multiplier principle was proposed by Hausman (1983, p. 433). Operationally, the test requires only the calculation of TR^2,

---

[40] See Cragg (1967) and the many related studies listed by Judge et al. (1985, pp. 646–653).

[41] See, for example, Greenberg and Webster (1983, pp. 243–280) and Phillips (1983).

[42] Since (he felt that) the primary objective of modeling was for forecasting purposes, this posed no problem. See Section 19.7.

[43] Malinvaud (1970) proposes $T(\lambda_j' - 1)$ as yet another alternative. Obviously, all of these are equivalent asymptotically.

Table 19.7.   Test Statistics

	λ	λ'	LR	TR^2	F	F'	$K_j^* - M_j$
Consumption	1.499	1.716	9.98	8.77	1.08	1.55	6
Investment	1.086	1.095	1.72	1.81	0.223	0.247	5
Wages	2.466	2.469	29.3	12.49	3.81	3.82	5

Table 19.8

	$F[5, 13]$	$F[6, 13]$	$\chi^2[5]$	$\chi^2[6]$	$\chi^2[16]$
5%	3.03	2.92	11.07	12.59	26.30
1%	4.86	4.62	15.09	16.81	32.00

where the R^2 is the uncentered R^2 in the regression of

$$\hat{\varepsilon}_j = \mathbf{y}_j - \mathbf{Z}_j \hat{\delta}_j$$

on all of the predetermined variables in the model. The estimated parameters may be computed using 2SLS, LIML, LIVE, or any other *efficient* limited-information estimator. The statistic is asymptotically distributed as chi-squared with $K_j^* - M_j$ degrees of freedom.

Finally, a systemwide statistic may be based on the restrictions imposed on Π by the structure. If the entire system is exactly identified, the reduced form estimated by OLS is fully efficient. If not, an efficient estimate of Π that embodies the restrictions is $\hat{\Pi} = -\hat{\mathbf{B}}\hat{\Gamma}^{-1}$, where the latter are *any efficient full-information estimators* (say, 3SLS or FIML). The log likelihood for the reduced form is given in (19–100). By concentrating over Ω, we obtain, at the maximum,

$$\ln L = -\frac{MT}{2}(1 + \ln 2\pi) - \frac{T}{2}\ln|\mathbf{W}|, \tag{19–111}$$

where

$$\mathbf{W} = \frac{1}{T}(\mathbf{Y} - \mathbf{X}\hat{\Pi})'(\mathbf{Y} - \mathbf{X}\hat{\Pi}).^{44}$$

Therefore, the likelihood ratio statistic based on the two estimators of Π is simply

$$LR = -2(\ln L_r - \ln L_u) = T(\ln|\mathbf{W}_{FI}| - \ln|\mathbf{W}_{OLS}|). \tag{19–112}$$

This statistic is asymptotically distributed as chi-squared with degrees of freedom equal to the total number of overidentifying restrictions:

$$d = \sum_j K_j^* - M_j.$$

EXAMPLE 19.20. Testing Overidentifying Restrictions.   For Klein's Model I, the test statistics for the overidentifying restrictions for the three equations are given in Table 19.7. The likelihood ratio statistic for the entire system is 77.441. Critical values for the chi-squared and F distributions are listed in Table 19.8. There are 21 observations used to estimate the

---

[44] For a system containing identities, $\mathbf{W}$ is computed by assembling $\hat{\Pi}$ for the full system first and then discarding columns corresponding to the identities. Doing the same for $\mathbf{Y}$, we then compute $\mathbf{W} = (\mathbf{Y}'\mathbf{Y} - \mathbf{Y}'\mathbf{X}\hat{\Pi} - \hat{\Pi}'\mathbf{X}'\mathbf{Y} + \hat{\Pi}'\mathbf{X}'\mathbf{X}\hat{\Pi})/T$.

model and 8 predetermined variables. The overidentifying restrictions for the wage equation are rejected by all single-equation tests. There are two possibilities. The equation may well be misspecified. Or, as Liu suggests, in a dynamic model, if there is autocorrelation of the disturbances, the treatment of lagged endogenous variables as if they were exogenous is a specification error.

The preceding tests are nonconstructive. It is unclear, for example, how we should proceed after our finding about the wage equation in the example.[45]

Another specification error occurs if the variables assumed to be exogenous in the system are not, in fact, uncorrelated with the structural disturbances. Since all of the asymptotic properties claimed earlier rest on this assumption, this specification error would be quite serious. Several authors have studied this issue.[46] The specification test devised by Hausman that we used in Section 9.5.4 in the errors in variables model and Section 16.4.4 in analyzing cross-section/time-series models provides a method of testing for exogeneity in a simultaneous-equations model.[47] Suppose that the variable x^* is in question. The test is based on the existence of two estimators, say $\hat{\delta}$ and $\hat{\delta}^*$, such that

Under H_0: (x^* is exogenous), both $\hat{\delta}$ and $\hat{\delta}^*$ are consistent
and $\hat{\delta}^*$ is asymptotically efficient.

Under H_1: (x^* is endogenous), $\hat{\delta}$ is consistent, but $\hat{\delta}^*$ is
inconsistent.

Hausman bases his version of the test on $\hat{\delta}$ being the 2SLS estimator and $\hat{\delta}^*$ being the 3SLS estimator. A shortcoming of the procedure is that it requires an arbitrary choice of some equation that does not contain x^* for the test. For instance, in the next example, to pursue the finding of Example 19.20, we consider the exogeneity of X_{-1} in the third equation of Klein's Model I. To apply this test, we must use one of the other two equations.

A single-equation version of the test has been devised by Spencer and Berk (1981). We now suppose that x^* appears in equation j, so that

$$\mathbf{Y}_j = \mathbf{Y}_j\gamma_j + \mathbf{X}_j\beta_j + x^*\theta + \varepsilon_j$$
$$= [\mathbf{Y}_j \quad \mathbf{X}_j \quad x^*]\delta_j + \varepsilon_j.$$

Then $\hat{\delta}^*$ is the 2SLS estimator, treating x^* as an exogenous variable in the system, while $\hat{\delta}$ is the IV estimator based on regressing $\mathbf{y}_j$ on $\hat{\mathbf{Y}}_j$, $\mathbf{X}_j$, and $\hat{x}^*$, where the least squares fitted values are based on all of the remaining exogenous variables, excluding x^*. The test statistic is then

$$w = (\hat{\delta}^* - \hat{\delta})\{\text{Est. Var}[\hat{\delta}] - \text{Est. Var}[\hat{\delta}^*]\}^{-1}(\hat{\delta}^* - \hat{\delta}). \qquad (19\text{--}113)$$

This is the Wald statistic based on the difference of the two estimators. The statistic has one degree of freedom. (The extension to a set of variables is direct.) A convenient way to carry out the test is to test the significance of the coefficient(s) α_j in the least squares regression

$$\mathbf{y}_j = \hat{\mathbf{Z}}_j\delta_j + [\hat{\mathbf{Y}}_j\hat{x}^*]\alpha_j + \varepsilon_j^*, \qquad (19\text{--}114)$$

where $\hat{\mathbf{Z}}_j$ is the usual 2SLS set of instrumental variables and $\hat{\mathbf{Y}}_j$ and $\hat{x}^*$ are predicted values based on the reduced set of exogenous variables. Note, finally, that the theory underlying the

---

[45] Once again, Liu offers some commentary on this problem.
[46] Wu (1973), Durbin (1954), Hausman (1978), and Nakamura and Nakamura (1981).
[47] We should note that this test is related to but much less ambitious than the causality tests noted in the previous chapter.

conventional F statistic no longer applies, though the F distribution may be approximately correct. The Wald statistic,

$$w = \hat{\alpha}_j' \{ \text{Est. Var}[\hat{\alpha}_j] \}^{-1} \hat{\alpha}_j, \qquad (19\text{--}115)$$

will be asymptotically distributed as chi-squared with degrees of freedom equal to the number of elements in α_j. (The variance matrix in brackets is a submatrix of the full covariance matrix produced by the regression.)

EXAMPLE 19.21. Exogeneity Test.   The previous example suggested a specification problem in the third equation of Klein's Model I. To pursue that finding, we now apply the preceding to test the exogeneity of X_{-1}. This is roughly equivalent to a test of autocorrelation, albeit a bit indirect (and probably not too powerful), since if the disturbances are autocorrelated, lagged endogenous variables may no longer be treated as predetermined. The two estimated parameter vectors are

$$\hat{\delta}^* = [1.5003, \quad 0.43886, \quad 0.14667, \quad 0.13040] \qquad \text{(i.e., 2SLS)}$$

and

$$\hat{\delta} = [1.2524, \quad 0.42277, \quad 0.16714, \quad 0.13062].$$

Using the Wald criterion, the chi-squared statistic is 1.3977. Thus, the hypothesis (such as it is) is not rejected. The alternative computation based on (19–114) could not be carried out. The predicted values of X based on all predetermined variables and all predetermined variables excluding the lagged value of X were virtually identical.

19.6.   *Properties of Dynamic Models*

Models with lagged endogenous variables may be viewed as generalizations of the auto-regressive distributed lag models we examined in the previous chapter. In these models, the entire previous time path of the exogenous variables and disturbances, not just their current values, determines the current value of the dependent variables. As we saw earlier, the intrinsic dynamic properties of the autoregressive model, such as stability and the existence of an equilibrium value, are embodied in their autoregressive parameters. In this section, we extend the analysis of Chapter 18 to multiple equations. As before, we are interested in long- and short-run multipliers, stability properties, and simulated time paths of the dependent variables.

19.6.1.   **Dynamic Models and Their Multipliers**

The structural form of a dynamic model is

$$\mathbf{y}_t' \mathbf{\Gamma} + \mathbf{x}_t' \mathbf{B} + \mathbf{y}_{t-1}' \mathbf{\Lambda} = \mathbf{\varepsilon}_t.\text{[48]} \qquad (19\text{--}116)$$

The reduced form is

$$\mathbf{y}_t' = \mathbf{x}_t' \mathbf{\Pi} + \mathbf{y}_{t-1}' \mathbf{\Delta} + \mathbf{v}_t', \qquad (19\text{--}117)$$

---

[48] The model may also contain lagged exogenous variables but, for present purposes, these need not be treated separately. If there are additional lags of the endogenous variables in the model, it can still be written in the preceding form by using an extension of the technique detailed in the appendix to the previous chapter. No generality is lost by assuming that only one lagged value of $\mathbf{y}_t$ appears in the model.

where

$$\Pi = -B\Gamma^{-1}$$

and

$$\Delta = -\Lambda\Gamma^{-1}.$$

EXAMPLE 19.22. The 2SLS estimates of the structure and reduced form of Klein's Model I are given in Table 19.9. (Only the nonzero rows of $\hat{\Lambda}$ and $\hat{\Delta}$ are shown.)

In order to obtain the long- and short-run multipliers, it is useful to revert briefly to a single-equation case. In the geometric distributed lag model,

$$y_t = \alpha + \beta x_t + \delta y_{t-1} + v_t,$$

the impact or short-run multiplier is

$$\frac{\partial E[y_t]}{\partial x_t} = \beta.$$

The lag coefficients,

$$\beta_i = \beta\delta^i = \frac{\partial E[y_t]}{\partial x_{t-i}}, \quad i = 0, 1, \ldots,$$

are the lagged effects on $E[y_t]$ of a change in x that occurred i periods previously. In the current context, these would be labeled the *dynamic multipliers* or the *delay i multipliers*. If x_t

Table 19.9

Variable		C	I	W^p	X	P	K
				Equation			
$\hat{\Gamma} =$	C	1	0	0	-1	0	0
	I	0	1	0	-1	0	-1
	W^p	-0.810	0	1	0	1	0
	X	0	0	-0.439	1	-1	0
	P	-0.017	-0.15	0	0	1	0
	K	0	0	0	0	0	1
$\hat{B} =$	1	-16.555	-20.278	-1.5	0	0	0
	W^g	-0.810	0	0	0	0	0
	T	0	0	0	0	1	0
	G	0	0	0	-1	0	0
	t	0	0	-0.13	0	0	0
$\hat{\Lambda} =$	X_{-1}	0	0	-0.147	0	0	0
	P_{-1}	-0.216	-0.616	0	0	0	0
	K_{-1}	0	0.158	0	0	0	-1
$\hat{\Pi} =$	1	42.80	25.83	31.63	68.63	37.00	25.83
	W^g	1.35	0.124	0.646	1.47	0.825	0.125
	T	-0.128	-0.176	-0.133	-0.303	-1.17	-0.176
	G	0.663	0.153	0.797	1.82	1.02	0.153
	t	0.159	-0.007	0.197	0.152	-0.045	-0.007
$\hat{\Delta} =$	X_{-1}	0.179	-0.008	0.222	0.172	-0.051	-0.008
	P_{-1}	0.767	0.743	0.663	1.51	0.848	0.743
	K_{-1}	-0.105	-0.182	-0.125	-0.287	-0.161	0.818

were fixed at, say, $\bar{x}$ until period t, then changed to $\bar{x} + 1$ and held at that level thereafter, the immediate effect on y_t would be β. Neglecting the disturbances, the change in the value of y_{t+1} given the permanent increase in x_t is

$$(y_{t+1}|\bar{x} + 1) - (y_{t+1}|\bar{x}) = \beta(1 + \delta).$$

Also, in subsequent periods, the differences would be

$$(y_{t+2}|\bar{x} + 1) - (y_{t+2}|\bar{x}) = \beta(1 + \delta + \delta^2)$$

and

$$(y_{t+s}|\bar{x} + 1) - (y_{t+s}|\bar{x}) = \sum_{i=0}^{s-1} \beta\delta^i.$$

These are *cumulated multipliers*. They give the sequence of effects of a permanent change in the fixed level of x_t. The s-period cumulated multipliers can be obtained by use of the identity

$$\beta(1 + \delta + \cdots + \delta^{s-1}) = \frac{\beta(1 - \delta^s)}{1 - \delta}.$$

If x_t were permanently fixed at $\bar{x}$, the equilibrium for y_t (assuming it exists), would then be $\bar{y}$ such that

$$\bar{y} = y_t = y_{t-1}$$

$$= \frac{\alpha}{1 - \delta} + \frac{\beta\bar{x}}{1 - \delta}.$$

The necessary condition for the equilibrium to exist is $|\delta| < 1$. The equilibrium, or long-run, multiplier is the effect on $\bar{y}$ of a permanent unit change in $\bar{x}$,

$$\frac{\partial \bar{y}}{\partial \bar{x}} = \frac{\beta}{1 - \delta}.$$

The "last" (or infinite) cumulative multiplier is the equilibrium multiplier.

We now extend these multipliers to the model of (19–116). From the reduced form,

$$\frac{\partial y_{t,m}}{\partial x_{t,k}} = \Pi_{km}. \tag{19–118}$$

The short-run effects are the coefficients on the current x's, so Π is the matrix of **impact multipliers**. By substituting for $\mathbf{y}_{t-1}$ in (19–116), we obtain

$$\mathbf{y}_t' = \mathbf{x}_t'\Pi + \mathbf{x}_{t-1}'\Pi\Lambda + \mathbf{y}_{t-2}'\Lambda^2 + (\mathbf{v}_t' + \mathbf{v}_{t-1}'\Lambda^2). \tag{19–119}$$

Continuing this for the full t periods, we obtain

$$\mathbf{y}_t' = \sum_{s=0}^{t-1} [\mathbf{x}_{t-s}'\Pi\Lambda^s] + \mathbf{y}_0'\Lambda^t + \sum_{s=0}^{t-1} \mathbf{v}_{t-s}'\Lambda^s. \tag{19–120}$$

This shows how the **initial conditions**, y_0, and the subsequent time path of the exogenous variables and disturbances completely determine the current values of the endogenous variables. The coefficient matrices in the bracketed sum are the **dynamic multipliers**,

$$\frac{\partial y_{t,m}}{\partial x_{t-s,k}} = (\Pi\Lambda^s)_{km}. \tag{19–121}$$

The **cumulated multipliers** are obtained by adding the matrices of dynamic multipliers. If we let s go to infinity in (19–120), we obtain the **final form** of the model,[49]

$$\mathbf{y}'_t = \sum_{s=0}^{\infty} [\mathbf{x}'_{t-s} \mathbf{\Pi} \mathbf{\Delta}^s] + \sum_{s=0}^{\infty} [\mathbf{v}'_{t-s} \mathbf{\Delta}^s]. \tag{19–122}$$

This is analogous to the moving average form of the distributed lag model in (18–38).

Assume for the present that $\lim_{t \to \infty} \mathbf{\Delta}^t = \mathbf{0}$. Then the matrix of cumulated multipliers in the final form is

$$\mathbf{\Pi}[\mathbf{I} + \mathbf{\Delta} + \mathbf{\Delta}^2 + \cdots] = \mathbf{\Pi}[\mathbf{I} - \mathbf{\Delta}]^{-1}. \tag{19–123}$$

These coefficient matrices are the long-run or **equilibrium multipliers.** Analogous to our single-equation case, we can also obtain the cumulated multipliers for s periods as

$$\text{Cumulated multipliers} = \mathbf{\Pi}[\mathbf{I} - \mathbf{\Delta}]^{-1}[\mathbf{I} - \mathbf{\Delta}^s]. \tag{19–124}$$

Suppose that the values of $\mathbf{x}$ were permanently fixed at $\bar{\mathbf{x}}$. Then the final form shows that if there are no disturbances, the equilibrium value of $\mathbf{y}_t$ would be

$$
\begin{aligned}
\bar{\mathbf{y}} &= \sum_{s=0}^{\infty} [\bar{\mathbf{x}} \mathbf{\Pi} \mathbf{\Delta}^s] \\
&= \bar{\mathbf{x}} \sum_{s=0}^{\infty} \mathbf{\Pi} \mathbf{\Delta}^s \\
&= \bar{\mathbf{x}} \mathbf{\Pi}[\mathbf{I} - \mathbf{\Delta}]^{-1}.
\end{aligned}
\tag{19–125}
$$

Therefore, the equilibrium multipliers are

$$\frac{\partial \bar{y}_m}{\partial \bar{x}_k} = [\mathbf{\Pi}(\mathbf{I} - \mathbf{\Delta})^{-1}]_{km}. \tag{19–126}$$

Some examples will now be shown for Klein's Model I.

EXAMPLE 19.23. Dynamic Multipliers.   For a particular variable or group of variables, the various multipliers are submatrices of the multiplier matrices. The dynamic multipliers for the fiscal policy variables, T and G, corresponding to the estimates in Example 19.22, are given in Table 19.10 for several lags.[50]

The model has the interesting feature that the long-run multipliers of both policy variables for investment are both zero. This is intrinsic to the model. We shall return to this point in the later discussion of equilibrium. The estimated long-run *balanced-budget multiplier* for equal increases in spending and taxes (an anachronism?) is $2.10 + (-1.48) = 0.62$.

19.6.2. Stability

It remains to be shown that the matrix of multipliers in the final form converges. In order for the analysis to proceed, it is necessary for the matrix $\mathbf{\Delta}^t$ to converge to a zero matrix. Although $\mathbf{\Delta}$ is not a symmetric matrix, it will still have a spectral decomposition of the form

$$\mathbf{\Delta} = \mathbf{C} \mathbf{\Lambda} \mathbf{C}^{-1}, \tag{19–127}$$

---

[49] In some treatments, (19–120) is labeled the final form instead. Both forms eliminate the lagged values of the dependent variables from the current value. The dependence of the first form on the initial values may be simpler to interpret.

[50] A method of computing asymptotic standard errors for the estimates of the dynamic multipliers is given by Schmidt (1973).

Table 19.10

| | Taxes | | | | Spending | | | |
| | Investment | | Output | | Investment | | Output | |
Lag	Period	Cum.	Period	Cum.	Period	Cum.	Period	Cum.
0	−0.760	−0.760	−1.30	−1.30	0.153	0.153	1.82	1.82
1	−0.834	−1.59	−1.74	−3.04	0.715	0.868	1.06	2.88
2	−0.507	−2.10	−1.27	−4.31	0.383	1.25	1.01	3.89
3	−0.122	−2.22	−0.502	−4.81	0.061	1.31	0.334	4.22
4	0.192	−2.03	0.198	−4.61	−0.184	1.13	−0.225	4.00
5	0.388	−1.64	0.682	−3.93	−0.328	0.800	−0.590	3.41
6	0.462	−1.18	0.914	−3.02	−0.374	0.426	−0.748	2.66
7	0.434	−0.749	0.921	−2.10	−0.342	0.084	−0.731	1.93
8	0.338	−0.411	0.764	−1.33	−0.258	−0.174	−0.591	1.34
9	0.210	−0.201	0.519	−0.814	−0.154	−0.328	−0.387	0.952
10	0.082	−0.119	0.253	−0.561	−0.052	−0.380	−0.173	0.779
11	−0.023	−0.142	0.019	−0.542	0.030	−0.350	0.009	0.788
12	−0.095	−0.237	−0.152	−0.694	0.083	−0.267	0.138	0.926
13	−0.129	−0.366	−0.247	−0.941	0.106	−0.161	0.206	1.13
14	−0.131	−0.497	−0.271	−1.21	0.104	−0.057	0.218	1.35
15	−0.109	−0.606	−0.241	−1.45	0.085	0.028	0.189	1.54
16	−0.075	−0.681	−0.178	−1.63	0.056	0.084	0.134	1.67
17	−0.037	−0.718	−0.101	−1.73	0.025	0.109	0.072	1.75
18	−0.003	−0.721	−0.023	−1.76	−0.007	0.102	0.015	1.76
19	0.021	−0.700	0.028	−1.73	−0.019	0.083	−0.028	1.73
20	0.035	−0.665	0.064	−1.67	−0.029	0.054	−0.054	1.68
∞	0	0	0	−1.48	0	0	0	2.10

where Λ is a diagonal matrix containing the characteristic roots of A and each column of C is a right characteristic vector,

$$\Delta c_m = \lambda_m c_m.\text{[51]}$$ (19–128)

Since A is not symmetric, the elements of Λ (and C) may be complex. Nonetheless, (2–105) continues to hold:

$$A^2 = CAC^{-1}CAC^{-1} = CA^2C^{-1}$$

and

$$A^t = CA^tC^{-1}.$$ (19–129)

It is apparent that whether or not A^t vanishes as $t \to \infty$ depends on its characteristic roots. The condition, is $|\lambda_m| < 1$. For the case of a complex root,

$$|\lambda_m| = |a + bi| = \sqrt{a^2 + b^2}.$$

For a given model, the stability may be established with reference to the largest or **dominant root**. Since it is ultimately a function of the sample estimates of the parameters, the estimate

[51] For discussion, see Rao (1965, pp. 43–44).

of the dominant root of the model is a sample statistic for which an estimate of its asymptotic sampling variance can be computed.[52]

With many endogenous variables in the model but only a few lagged variables, Δ is a large but sparse matrix. Finding the characteristic roots of large, asymmetric matrices is a rather complex computation problem (although there exists specialized software for doing so). There is a way to make the problem a bit more compact. To put this in the context of an example, in Klein's Model I, Δ is 6×6, but with three rows of zeros, it has only rank three and three nonzero roots. The following partitioning is useful. Let y_{t1} be the set of endogenous variables that appear in both current and lagged form, and let y_{t2} be those that appear only in current form. Then the model may be written

$$[y_{t1}' \quad y_{t2}'] = x_t'[\Pi_1 \quad \Pi_2] + y_{t-1,1}'y_{t-1,2}'\begin{bmatrix} \Delta_1 & \Delta_2 \\ 0 & 0 \end{bmatrix} + v_{t1}'v_{t2}'. \qquad (19\text{-}130)$$

The characteristic roots of Δ are defined by the characteristic polynomial, $|\Delta - \lambda I| = 0$. For the partitioned model, this is

$$\begin{vmatrix} \Delta_1 - \lambda I & \Delta_2 \\ 0 & -\lambda I \end{vmatrix} = 0.$$

We may use (2–73) to obtain

$$|\Delta - \lambda I| = (-\lambda)^{M_2}|\Delta_1 - \lambda I| = 0,$$

where M_2 is the number of variables in y_2. Consequently, we need only concern ourselves with the submatrix of Δ that defines explicit autoregressions. The part of the reduced form defined by

$$y_{t2}' = x_t'\Pi_2 + y_{t-1,1}'\Delta_2$$

is not directly relevant.

EXAMPLE 19.24. Model Stability.   For the 2SLS estimates of Klein's Model I, the relevant submatrix of $\hat{\Delta}$ is

	X	P	K	
	0.172	-0.051	-0.008	X_{-1}
$\hat{\Delta}_1 =$	1.511	0.848	0.743	P_{-1}
	-0.287	-0.161	0.818	K_{-1}

The characteristic roots of this matrix are 0.2995 and the complex pair $0.7692 \pm 0.3494i$. The moduli of the complex roots are 0.8448, so we conclude that the model is stable.

19.6.3.   Adjustment to Equilibrium

The adjustment of a dynamic model to an equilibrium involves the following conceptual experiment: We assume that the exogenous variables, x_t, have been fixed at a level, $\bar{x}$, for a long enough time that the endogenous variables have fully adjusted to their equilibrium, $\bar{y}$ [defined in (19–125)]. In some arbitrarily chosen period, labeled period 0, an exogenous one-time shock hits the system, so that in period $t = 0$, $x_t = x_0 \neq \bar{x}$. Thereafter, x_t returns to its

[52] The computations are detailed in Theil and Boot (1962). An alternative approach is given by Kmenta and Oberhofer (1973). Schmidt (1974b) shows that (as might be expected) the Theil–Boot formula based on the reduced form and the Oberhofer–Kmenta formula based on the structural form give the same result.

former value, $\bar{\mathbf{x}}$, and $\mathbf{x}_t = \bar{\mathbf{x}}$ for all $t > 0$. We know from the expression for the final form that, if disturbed, $\mathbf{y}_t$ will ultimately return to the equilibrium. That is ensured by the stability condition. Here we consider the time path of the adjustment. Since our only concern at this point is with the exogenous shock, we will ingore the disturbances in the analysis.

At time 0,

$$\mathbf{y}_0' = \mathbf{x}_0'\mathbf{\Pi} + \mathbf{y}_{-1}'\mathbf{\Delta}.$$

But prior to time 0, the system was in equilibrium, so

$$\mathbf{y}_0' = \mathbf{x}_0'\mathbf{\Pi} + \bar{\mathbf{y}}'\mathbf{\Delta}.$$

The initial displacement due to the shock to $\bar{\mathbf{x}}$ is

$$\mathbf{y}_0' - \bar{\mathbf{y}}' = \mathbf{x}_0'\mathbf{\Pi} - \bar{\mathbf{y}}'(\mathbf{I} - \mathbf{\Delta}).$$

Substituting $\bar{\mathbf{x}}'\mathbf{\Pi} = \bar{\mathbf{y}}'(\mathbf{I} - \mathbf{\Delta})$ produces

$$\mathbf{y}_0' - \bar{\mathbf{y}}' = (\mathbf{x}_0' - \bar{\mathbf{x}})'\mathbf{\Pi}. \tag{19-131}$$

As might be expected, the initial displacement is determined entirely by the exogenous shock occurring in that period. Since $\mathbf{x}_t = \bar{\mathbf{x}}$ after period 0, (19–120) implies that

$$\mathbf{y}_t' = \sum_{s=0}^{t-1} \bar{\mathbf{x}}'\mathbf{\Pi}\mathbf{\Delta}^s + \mathbf{y}_0'\mathbf{\Delta}^t$$

$$= \bar{\mathbf{x}}'\mathbf{\Pi}(\mathbf{I} - \mathbf{\Delta})^{-1}(\mathbf{I} - \mathbf{\Delta}^t) + \mathbf{y}_0'\mathbf{\Delta}^t$$

$$= \bar{\mathbf{y}}' - \bar{\mathbf{y}}'\mathbf{\Delta}^t + \mathbf{y}_0'\mathbf{\Delta}^t$$

$$= \bar{\mathbf{y}}' + (\mathbf{y}_0' - \bar{\mathbf{y}}')\mathbf{\Delta}^t.$$

Thus, the entire time path is a function of the initial displacement. By inserting (19–131), we see that

$$\mathbf{y}_t' = \bar{\mathbf{y}}' + (\mathbf{x}_0' - \bar{\mathbf{x}})'\mathbf{\Pi}\mathbf{\Delta}^t. \tag{19-132}$$

Since $\lim_{t \to \infty} \mathbf{\Delta}^t = \mathbf{0}$, this defines the path back to the equilibrium subsequent to the exogenous shock $(\mathbf{x}_0 - \bar{\mathbf{x}})$. The stability condition imposed on $\mathbf{\Delta}$ ensures that if the system is disturbed at some point by a one-time shock, barring further shocks or disturbances, it will return to its equilibrium. Since $\mathbf{y}_0$, $\bar{\mathbf{x}}$, $\mathbf{x}_0$, and $\mathbf{\Pi}$ are fixed for all time, the shape of the path is completely determined by the behavior of $\mathbf{\Delta}^t$, which we now examine.

In the previous section, in (19–127) to (19–130), we used the characteristic roots of $\mathbf{\Delta}$ to infer the (lack of) stability of the model. The spectral decomposition of $\mathbf{\Delta}^t$ given in (19–129) may be written

$$\mathbf{\Delta}^t = \sum_{m=1}^{M} \lambda_m^t \mathbf{c}_m \mathbf{d}_m', \tag{19-133}$$

where $\mathbf{c}_m$ is the mth column of $\mathbf{C}$ and $\mathbf{d}_m'$ is the mth row of $\mathbf{C}^{-1}$.[53] Inserting this in (19–132), we have

$$(\mathbf{y}_t - \bar{\mathbf{y}})' = [(\mathbf{x}_0 - \bar{\mathbf{x}})'\mathbf{\Pi}] \sum_{m=1}^{M} \lambda_m^t \mathbf{c}_m \mathbf{d}_m'$$

$$= \sum_{m=1}^{M} \lambda_m^t [(\mathbf{x}_0 - \bar{\mathbf{x}})'\mathbf{\Pi}\mathbf{c}_m \mathbf{d}_m'] = \sum_{m=1}^{M} \lambda_m^t \mathbf{g}_m. \tag{19-134}$$

---

[53] See Section 2.7.9.

(Note that this may involve fewer than M terms, since some of the roots may be zero. For Klein's model I, $M = 6$, but there are only three nonzero roots.) Since $\mathbf{g}_m$ depends only on the initial conditions and the parameters of the model, the behavior of the time path of $(\mathbf{y}_t - \bar{\mathbf{y}})$ is completely determined by Λ^t. In each period, the deviation from the equilibrium is a sum of M terms of powers of λ_m times a constant. (Each variable has its own set of constants.) The

Table 19.11

	C	I	W^p	P	K	X
Initial	69.7	4.9	53.3	23.5	209.4	88.4
Equilibrium	70.5	0	52.2	20.5	227.7	84.3

Table 19.12.   Deviations from Equilibrium

Year	C	I	W_p	X	P	K
1941	−0.5	4.9	1.1	4.1	3.0	−18.3
1942	5.0	5.5	5.2	10.5	5.3	−12.8
1943	7.3	6.2	7.4	13.5	6.0	−6.6
1944	7.7	5.6	7.8	13.3	5.5	−1.0
1945	6.7	4.2	6.7	10.8	4.1	3.1
1946	4.8	2.4	4.8	7.2	2.5	5.5
1947	2.6	0.8	2.5	3.4	0.8	6.3
1948	0.6	−0.6	0.5	0.0	−0.5	5.7
1949	−1.0	−1.4	−1.0	−2.4	−1.3	4.3
1950	−1.9	−1.8	−2.0	−3.7	−1.7	2.6
1951	−2.2	−1.7	−2.3	−3.9	−1.7	0.9
1952	−2.1	−1.4	−2.1	−3.4	−1.4	−0.5
1953	−1.6	−0.9	−1.6	−2.5	−0.9	−1.4
1954	−1.0	−0.4	−1.0	−1.4	−0.4	−1.8
1955	−0.4	0.0	−0.3	−0.3	0.0	−1.8
1956	0.1	0.3	0.2	0.5	0.3	−1.4
1957	0.5	0.5	0.5	1.0	0.5	−0.9
1958	0.6	0.5	0.6	1.1	0.5	−0.4
1959	0.6	0.4	0.6	1.1	0.4	0.0
1960	0.5	0.3	0.5	0.8	0.3	0.3
1961	0.4	0.2	0.3	0.5	0.2	0.5
1962	0.2	0.0	0.2	0.2	0.0	0.5
1963	0.0	0.0	0.0	0.0	−0.0	0.5
1964	−0.1	−0.1	−0.1	−0.2	−0.1	0.3
1965	−0.2	−0.1	−0.2	−0.3	−0.1	0.2
1966	−0.2	−0.1	−0.2	−0.3	−0.1	0.0
1967	−0.2	−0.1	−0.2	−0.3	−0.1	−0.0
1968	−0.1	−0.0	−0.1	−0.2	0.0	−0.1
1969	0.0	0.0	0.0	0.0	0.0	−0.2
1970	0.0	0.0	0.0	0.0	0.0	−0.1
1971	0.0	0.0	0.0	0.0	0.0	−0.1
1972	0.0	0.0	0.0	0.0	0.0	0.0

terms in the sum behave as follows:

$$\lambda_m \text{ real} > 0, \qquad \lambda_m^t \text{ adds a damped exponential term,}$$

$$\lambda_m \text{ real} < 0, \qquad \lambda_m^t \text{ adds a damped sawtooth term,}$$

$$\lambda_m \text{ complex}, \qquad \lambda_m^t \text{ adds a damped sinusoidal term.}$$

If we write the complex root $\lambda_m = a + bi$ in polar form,

$$\lambda = A[\text{Cos } B + i \text{ Sin } B]$$

where

$$A = [a^2 + b^2]^{1/2}$$

and

$$B = \text{Arccos } \frac{a}{A} \qquad \text{(in radians),}$$

the sinusoidal components each have amplitude A^t and period $2\pi/B$.[54]

EXAMPLE 19.25. Adjustment of Klein's Model I.   We start the model at the conditions of the last data point, 1941. The initial and equilibrium values for the six endogenous variables are given in Table 19.11. The equilibrium is based on $W^g = 8.5$, $G = 13.8$, $T = 11.6$, and $A = 10$.) The equilibrium of zero for investment might seem a bit peculiar. But note that the model imposes $K_t - K_{t-1} = I_t$, and both K and I are endogenous. If K_t is in equilibrium, there is no investment. The path to the new equilibrium for the six endogenous variables is shown in Table 19.12.

Note the cyclical behavior in Table 19.12. The complex roots are $0.8448[\text{Cos } 0.4263 \pm i \text{ Sin } 0.4263]$. The period for the oscillations is, thus, $2\pi/0.4263 = 14.73$.

19.7. Forecasting

For forecasting purposes, we are interested in $\hat{\mathbf{y}}_f = \mathbf{x}_f' \hat{\Pi}$ for some specified values of the exogenous variables. Thus, the parameters of interest are the reduced form. There are two approaches. The obvious one is simply to ignore the structure and estimate Π by ordinary least squares. Much of our work thus far has rested on the consistency of this estimator. The alternative is to use the work invested in the previous sections and compute the *derived reduced form*.

$$\hat{\Pi} = -\hat{\mathbf{B}} \hat{\Gamma}^{-1}.$$

As long as $\hat{\Gamma}$ and $\hat{\mathbf{B}}$ are consistent, the Slutsky theorem implies that $\hat{\Pi}$ will be also. The question of which approach to take reduces to one of efficiency. One special case is simple to resolve. If the entire model is exactly identified, then all structural estimators reduce to ILS, so the preceding computation simply undoes the calculation. Of course, few models are exactly identified, so the equation remains.

If the structural estimator is the FIML or 3SLS estimator, there is no question that the indirect approach is the preferred one. But, if 2SLS or LIML has been used to estimate the

---

[54] Goldberger (1964, p. 378).

structure, it may well be that the OLS estimates of the reduced form are more precise. This counterintuitive result may be explained by noting that the limited information estimators do not use the information provided by the cross equation correlations of the structural disturbances. Thus, both the direct OLS estimator, which ignores any overidentifying restrictions, and the indirect limited information estimators neglect some relevant information. Which has the smaller asymptotic variance will be unclear, and the matter is even more muddled in a small sample.

For computing forecast intervals, an appropriate asymptotic covariance matrix for $\hat{\Pi}$ will be required. If the direct least squares estimator is used, we may use the formula in Chapter 17. The estimated asymptotic covariance matrix of the ith and jth columns of $\hat{\Pi} = P$ is

$$\hat{\Theta}_{ij} = \text{Est. Asy. Var.}[\hat{\pi}_i^0, \hat{\pi}_j^0] = \hat{\omega}_{ij}(\mathbf{X}'\mathbf{X})^{-1}$$

For the derived reduced form, since $\hat{\Pi}$ is a nonlinear function of $\hat{\Gamma}$ and $\hat{B}$, the computation is much more involved. A full derivation is presented by Goldberger.[55] Let the $(M + K) \times (M + K)$ matrix

$$\hat{Q}_{jj} = \text{Est. Asy. Var.}[\hat{a}_j],$$

where

$$\hat{a}_j = j\text{th column of } \begin{bmatrix} \hat{\Gamma} \\ \hat{B} \end{bmatrix}.$$

Many (probably most) of the elements in $\hat{a}_j$ are zero or one, so $\hat{Q}_{jj}$ will have numerous rows and columns of zeros. Likewise, let

$$\hat{Q}_{ij} = \text{Est. Asy. Cov.}[\hat{a}_i, \hat{a}_j].$$

If FIML or 3SLS were used for estimation, the nonzero elements of $\hat{Q}_{ij}$ will be part of the standard results. But, if a limited information estimator such as 2SLS or LIML is used, $\hat{Q}_{ij}$ must be constructed. The nonzero elements for the 2SLS estimator are given by

$$\text{Est. Asy. Cov.}[\hat{\delta}_i, \hat{\delta}_j] = \hat{\sigma}_{ij}[\hat{Z}_i'\hat{Z}_i]^{-1}[\hat{Z}_i'\hat{Z}_j][\hat{Z}_j'\hat{Z}_j]^{-1},$$

where (19–103) may be used to compute $\hat{\sigma}_{ij}$. Of course, $\hat{Q}_{ij}$ will also contain many zeros. With the relevant matrices assembled, the estimated asymptotic covariance matrix of the ith and jth columns of the derived reduced form estimator is

$$\hat{\Theta}_{ij} = [\hat{\Pi}\ \mathbf{I}]\left[\sum_{l=1}^{M}\sum_{m=1}^{M}\hat{\gamma}^{il}\hat{\gamma}^{jm}\hat{Q}_{lm}\right]\begin{bmatrix} \hat{\Pi} \\ \mathbf{I} \end{bmatrix}.$$

Computation of the forecasts and appropriate forecast intervals is done with the methods developed in Chapter 6. The set of forecast errors is

$$e_{fj} = \hat{y}_{fj} - y_{fj} = \mathbf{x}_f'(\hat{\pi}_j^0 - \pi_j^0) - \varepsilon_{fj}, \qquad j = 1, \dots, M.$$

Assuming that $\mathbf{x}$ is strictly exogenous and nonstochastic, the estimated covariance matrix of the forecast errors is

$$\text{Est. Asy. Cov.}[e_{fi}, e_{fj}] = \mathbf{x}_f'\hat{\Theta}_{ij}\mathbf{x}_f + \hat{\omega}_{ij}, \qquad i, j = 1, \dots, M.$$

There are two additional considerations. First, if $\mathbf{x}_f$ is stochastic, the variance given above is too small.[56] Matters become substantially more complicated in a dynamic model. If

---

[55] Op. cit., pp. 364–371. See, as well, Dhrymes (1973), Schmidt (1976, pp. 236–243), and Fomby, et al. (1984, pp. 512–525).

[56] See, e.g., Fomby, et al., op. cit., pp. 522–524.

the forecast involves y_{f-1}, then obviously the results for stochastic regressors must be invoked. Yet another aspect of the problem is the manner in which y_{f-1} is obtained. Whether the previously observed data or a simulated value from the model is to be used is a decision of some importance. The relevant asymptotic covariance matrix in the latter case is likely to be quite complicated.[57]

Exercises

1. Consider the following two-equation model:

$$y_1 = \gamma_1 y_2 + \beta_{11} x_1 + \beta_{21} x_2 + \beta_{31} x_3 + \varepsilon_1,$$

$$y_2 = \gamma_2 y_1 + \beta_{12} x_1 + \beta_{22} x_2 + \beta_{32} x_3 + \varepsilon_1.$$

(a) Verify that, as stated, neither equation is identified.

(b) Establish whether or not the following restrictions are sufficient to identify (or partially identify) the model:

(1) $\beta_{21} = \beta_{32} = 0,$

(2) $\beta_{12} = \beta_{22} = 0,$

(3) $\gamma_1 = 0,$

(4) $\gamma_1 = \gamma_2$ and $\beta_{32} = 0,$

(5) $\sigma_{12} = 0$ and $\beta_{31} = 0,$

(6) $\gamma_1 = 0$ and $\sigma_{12} = 0,$

(7) $\beta_{21} + \beta_{22} = 1,$

(8) $\sigma_{12} = 0, \beta_{21} = \beta_{22} = \beta_{31} = \beta_{32} = 0,$

(9) $\sigma_{12} = 0, \beta_{11} = \beta_{21} = \beta_{22} = \beta_{31} = \beta_{32} = 0.$

2. Verify the rank and order conditions for identification of the second and third behavioral equations in Klein's Model I. (**Hint:** See Example 19.10.)

3. Check the identifiability of the parameters of the following model:

$$[y_1 \ y_2 \ y_3 \ y_4] \begin{bmatrix} 1 & \gamma_{12} & 0 & 0 \\ \gamma_{21} & 1 & \gamma_{23} & \gamma_{24} \\ 0 & \gamma_{32} & 1 & \gamma_{34} \\ \gamma_{41} & \gamma_{42} & 0 & 1 \end{bmatrix}$$

$$+ [x_1 \ x_2 \ x_3 \ x_4 \ x_5] \begin{bmatrix} 0 & \beta_{12} & \beta_{13} & \beta_{14} \\ \beta_{21} & 1 & 0 & \beta_{24} \\ \beta_{31} & \beta_{32} & \beta_{33} & 0 \\ 0 & 0 & \beta_{43} & \beta_{44} \\ 0 & \beta_{52} & 0 & 0 \end{bmatrix}$$

$$= [\varepsilon_1 \ \varepsilon_2 \ \varepsilon_3 \ \varepsilon_4].$$

[57] See, e.g., Schmidt (1974 and 1978).

4. Examine the identifiability of the following supply and demand model:

$$\ln Q = \beta_0 + \beta_1 \ln P + \beta_2 \ln \text{Income} + \varepsilon_1 \quad \text{(demand)},$$

$$Q = \gamma_0 + \gamma_1 P \quad + \gamma_2 \text{Input cost} + \varepsilon_2 \quad \text{(supply)}.$$

5. Obtain the reduced form for the model in Exercise 1 under each of the assumptions made in parts (a) and (b1), (b6), and (b9).

6. The following model is specified:

$$y_1 = \gamma_1 y_2 + \beta_{11} x_1 \qquad\qquad + \varepsilon_1,$$

$$y_2 = \gamma_2 y_1 + \beta_{22} x_2 + \beta_{32} x_3 + \varepsilon_2.$$

All variables are measured as deviations from their means. The sample of 25 observations produces the following matrix of sums of squares and cross-products:

	y_1	y_2	x_1	x_2	x_3
y_1	20	6	4	3	5
y_2	6	10	3	6	7
x_1	4	3	5	2	3
x_2	3	6	2	10	8
x_3	5	7	3	8	15

(a) Estimate the two equations by OLS.

(b) Estimate the parameters of the two equations by 2SLS. Also, estimate the asymptotic covariance matrix of the 2SLS estimates.

(c) Obtain the LIML estimates of the parameters of the first equation.

(d) Estimate the two equations by 3SLS.

(e) Estimate the reduced-form coefficient matrix by OLS and indirectly by using your structural estimates from part (b).

7. For the model

$$y_1 = \gamma_1 y_2 + \beta_{11} x_1 + \beta_{21} x_2 + \varepsilon_1,$$

$$y_2 = \beta_2 y_1 + \beta_{32} x_3 + \beta_{42} x_4 + \varepsilon_2,$$

show that there are two restrictions on the reduced-form coefficients. Describe a procedure for estimating the model while incorporating the restrictions.

8. What are the ILS estimates of the parameters of the demand equation in Example 19.15? Which parameters are overidentified and what are the conflicting estimates?

9. Show that (19–59) produces a consistent estimate for any D with rank M_j.

10. An updated version of Klein's Model I was estimated with the data in the appendix to this chapter. Using the 2SLS estimates, the relevant submatrix of Λ (see (19–129)) is

$$\Lambda_1 = \begin{matrix} -0.1899 & -0.9471 & -0.8991 \\ 0 & 1.0287 & 0 \\ -0.0656 & -0.0791 & 0.0952 \end{matrix}$$

Is the model stable?

11. Prove that

$$\text{plim}\,\frac{Y'_j\varepsilon_j}{T} = \underline{\omega}_j - \Omega_{jj}\gamma_j.$$

12. Prove that an underidentified equation cannot be estimated by 2SLS.

13. The full set of data necessary for updating Klein's Model I is given in Table 19.14 in the appendix to this chapter.

   (a) Reestimate the three structural equations of Klein's Model I, using 2SLS and the 1953–1984 data.

   (b) Reestimate the system, using 3SLS.

   (c) Compare your results to those obtained in the text for the earlier period.

Appendix: Yearly Data on the U.S. Economy

The data used to estimate Klein's Model I are listed in Table 19.13. Variable definitions are given in Example 19.3. All estimates are computed using the 1921–1941 data because of the lagged values of P and X.

The data used for the updated version of Klein's Model I are listed in Tables 19.14–19.17. Several other variables are also listed for those who wish to estimate different specifications or alternative models. For constructing more extensive data sets, the following sources also contain quarterly data on these and numerous other variables.[58] All flow variables (e.g., consumption, investment, imports) are seasonally adjusted annual rates in constant (1972) dollars. The variables in the tables are as follows:

$$P^c = \text{implicit price deflator for personal consumption } (1972 = 100)$$

$$P^g = \text{implicit price deflator for GNP } (1972 = 100)$$

$$C = \text{personal consumption, total}$$

$$Y^d = \text{disposal personal income}$$

$$\text{GNP} = \text{gross national product}$$

$$G = \text{federal government purchases of goods and services}$$

$$T = \text{indirect business taxes}$$

$$\text{M1} = \text{money stock}$$

$$I = \text{gross private domestic investment}$$

$$K = \text{capital stock} = K_{-1} + I;\ K_{1952} = 655.7$$

$$P = \text{corporate profits}$$

$$E = \text{exports}$$

$$M = \text{imports}$$

---

[58] A pitfall to avoid: The data in the national income and product accounts are annual rates. Thus, direct application of $K_t = K_{t-1} + I_t$ overestimates the capital stock by a factor of almost four. The investment series must be converted to a quarterly rate.

r = 6-month commercial paper rate

X = total product = $C + I + G + X - M$

W^g = federal government compensation of employees

W^p = private wages = $X - P - W^g$

W = total wages = $W^p + W^g$

U = civilian rate of unemployment

Table 19.13.   Data for Klein's Model I

Year	C	P	W^p	I	K_{-1}	X	W^g	G	T
1920	39.8	12.7	28.8	2.7	180.1	44.9	2.2	2.4	3.4
1921	41.9	12.4	25.5	−0.2	182.8	45.6	2.7	3.9	7.7
1922	45.0	16.9	29.3	1.9	182.6	50.1	2.9	3.2	3.9
1923	49.2	18.4	34.4	5.2	184.5	57.2	2.9	2.8	4.7
1924	50.6	19.4	33.9	3.0	189.7	57.1	3.1	3.5	3.8
1925	52.6	20.1	35.4	5.1	192.7	61.0	3.2	3.3	5.5
1926	55.1	19.6	37.4	5.6	197.8	64.0	3.3	3.3	7.0
1927	56.2	19.8	37.9	4.2	203.4	64.4	3.6	4.0	6.7
1928	57.3	21.1	39.2	3.0	207.6	64.5	3.7	4.2	4.2
1929	57.8	21.7	41.3	5.1	210.6	67.0	4.0	4.1	4.0
1930	55.0	15.6	37.9	1.0	215.7	61.2	4.2	5.2	7.7
1931	50.9	11.4	34.5	−3.4	216.7	53.4	4.8	5.9	7.5
1932	45.6	7.0	29.0	−6.2	213.3	44.3	5.3	4.9	8.3
1933	46.5	11.2	28.5	−5.1	207.1	45.1	5.6	6.7	5.4
1934	48.7	12.3	30.6	−3.0	202.0	49.7	6.0	4.0	6.8
1935	51.3	14.0	33.2	−1.3	199.0	54.4	6.1	4.4	7.2
1936	57.7	17.6	36.8	2.1	197.7	62.7	7.4	2.9	8.3
1937	58.7	17.3	41.0	2.0	199.8	65.0	6.7	4.3	6.7
1938	57.5	15.3	38.2	−1.9	201.8	60.9	7.7	5.3	7.4
1939	61.6	19.0	41.6	1.3	199.9	69.5	7.8	6.6	8.9
1940	65.0	21.1	45.0	3.3	201.2	75.7	8.0	7.4	9.6
1941	69.7	23.5	53.3	4.9	204.5	88.4	8.5	13.8	11.6

Table 19.14

	P^c	P^g	C	Y^d	GNP	G	T
1953	63.2	58.8	363.4	399.1	623.6	114.7	19.0
1954	63.7	59.6	370.0	403.6	616.1	96.1	17.0
1955	64.4	60.8	394.1	427.0	657.5	88.2	18.1
1956	65.6	62.8	405.4	446.5	671.6	86.8	18.5
1957	67.8	64.9	413.8	455.2	683.8	90.6	18.8
1958	69.2	66.0	418.0	461.0	680.9	93.4	18.0
1959	70.6	67.6	440.4	479.3	721.7	91.4	18.6

Source: With two exceptions, all data have been obtained from the U.S. Department of Commerce, Bureau of Economic Analysis, *Business Statistics 1984,* Supplement to the *Survey of Current Business.* The exceptions are M1, K_{1952}, and r, which were obtained from Gordon (1986), and T, which was obtained from various issues of the *Survey of Current Business.*

Table 19.14 (*Continued*)

	P^c	P^g	C	Y^d	GNP	G	T
1960	71.9	68.7	452.0	489.6	737.2	90.4	20.1
1961	72.6	69.3	461.4	503.9	756.6	95.3	20.2
1962	73.7	70.6	482.0	524.8	800.3	102.8	21.5
1963	74.8	71.7	500.5	542.7	832.5	101.8	22.6
1964	75.9	72.8	528.0	580.5	876.4	100.2	22.5
1965	77.2	74.4	557.5	616.3	929.3	100.3	22.5
1966	79.4	76.7	585.7	647.0	984.8	112.6	20.7
1967	81.4	79.1	602.7	673.1	1011.4	125.1	21.0
1968	84.6	82.5	634.4	701.4	1058.1	128.1	21.8
1969	88.4	86.8	657.9	722.7	1087.6	121.8	21.7
1970	92.5	91.5	672.1	751.7	1085.6	110.6	21.1
1971	96.5	96.0	696.8	779.1	1122.4	103.7	21.1
1972	100.0	100.0	737.1	810.3	1185.9	101.7	19.9
1973	105.7	105.8	767.9	865.2	1254.3	95.9	19.9
1974	116.4	115.1	762.8	857.7	1246.3	96.6	18.9
1975	125.3	125.8	779.4	874.8	1231.6	97.4	11.3
1976	131.7	132.3	823.1	906.9	1298.2	96.8	17.7
1977	139.3	140.0	864.3	943.3	1369.7	100.4	17.8
1978	149.1	150.4	903.2	988.6	1438.6	100.3	18.7
1979	162.5	163.4	927.6	1015.5	1479.4	102.1	18.4
1980	179.0	178.4	931.8	1021.7	1475.0	106.4	22.8
1981	194.5	195.6	950.5	1049.7	1512.2	110.3	31.3
1982	206.0	207.8	963.3	1058.5	1480.0	117.0	24.1
1983	213.6	215.3	1009.2	1095.5	1534.7	116.2	24.3
1984	220.4	223.4	1062.4	1169.1	1639.3	122.5	24.8

Table 19.15

	M1	K	I	P	E	M	r
1953	125.99	655.7	85.3	70.0	26.6	21.8	2.52
1954	127.95	738.8	83.1	65.0	27.8	20.9	1.59
1955	132.00	842.6	103.8	80.9	30.7	23.4	2.19
1956	133.51	945.2	102.6	79.0	35.3	25.2	3.31
1957	134.10	1042.2	97.0	74.1	38.0	26.1	3.82
1958	136.02	1129.7	87.5	63.4	33.2	27.6	2.47
1959	141.38	1237.7	108.0	77.8	33.8	31.1	3.96
1960	141.41	1342.4	104.7	72.5	38.4	30.7	3.85
1961	144.45	1446.3	103.9	71.7	39.3	30.9	2.96
1962	147.99	1563.9	117.6	77.9	41.8	34.3	3.26
1963	152.64	1689.0	125.1	83.2	44.8	35.4	3.56
1964	158.61	1822.0	133.0	91.4	50.3	37.5	3.96
1965	165.49	1973.9	151.9	103.8	51.7	41.6	4.38
1966	172.76	2136.9	163.0	108.1	54.4	47.9	5.55
1967	180.00	2291.8	154.9	100.8	56.7	51.3	5.11
1968	192.66	2453.4	161.6	107.2	61.2	59.3	5.90
1969	203.79	2624.8	171.4	99.9	65.0	64.1	7.83
1970	211.63	2783.3	158.5	82.4	70.5	66.6	7.71
1971	226.17	2957.2	173.9	90.4	71.0	69.3	5.11
1972	242.56	3152.2	195.0	100.6	77.5	76.7	4.73
1973	259.73	3369.7	217.5	118.8	97.3	81.8	8.15

Table 19.15 (*Continued*)

	M1	K	I	P	E	M	r
1974	272.61	3565.2	195.5	118.8	108.5	80.7	9.84
1975	285.39	3720.0	154.8	105.0	103.5	71.4	6.32
1976	301.85	3904.5	184.5	125.7	110.1	84.7	5.34
1977	325.19	4118.7	214.2	139.0	112.9	90.9	5.61
1978	351.66	4355.4	236.7	152.3	126.7	102.7	7.99
1979	379.03	4591.7	236.3	154.6	146.2	109.0	10.91
1980	401.48	4800.2	208.5	131.5	159.1	108.8	12.29
1981	430.08	5031.1	230.9	113.1	160.2	116.4	14.76
1982	458.50	5225.4	194.3	79.6	147.6	118.0	11.89
1983	509.18	5446.4	221.0	94.4	139.5	126.9	8.81
1984	547.30	5736.3	289.9	105.5	146.0	161.1	10.16

Table 19.16

	W^g	W^p	W	X	U
1953	49.6	429.5	479.1	578.2	3.9
1954	47.2	427.0	474.1	556.1	4.1
1955	45.9	448.6	494.4	593.4	4.0
1956	45.6	461.8	507.4	604.9	4.1
1957	45.8	474.6	520.4	613.3	4.3
1958	44.5	478.5	523.0	604.5	6.9
1959	44.5	501.5	546.0	642.5	5.5
1960	45.2	517.0	562.2	654.8	5.5
1961	46.2	530.9	577.1	669.0	6.7
1962	48.3	562.2	610.5	699.9	5.5
1963	48.2	582.8	631.0	736.8	5.7
1964	48.5	611.6	660.1	774.0	5.2
1965	48.7	644.8	693.5	819.8	4.5
1966	53.0	686.0	739.0	867.8	3.8
1967	57.2	709.1	766.3	888.1	3.8
1968	58.0	739.0	797.0	926.0	3.6
1969	58.2	772.2	830.4	954.0	3.5
1970	55.2	786.3	841.5	965.1	4.9
1971	52.5	812.0	864.5	976.1	5.9
1972	50.1	864.0	914.1	1034.6	5.6
1973	48.2	910.0	958.2	1096.8	4.9
1974	48.5	896.6	945.1	1082.7	5.6
1975	48.4	899.0	947.4	1063.7	8.5
1976	48.5	938.0	986.5	1129.8	7.7
1977	48.6	995.4	1044.0	1200.8	7.1
1978	49.3	1043.9	1093.2	1264.2	6.1
1979	49.0	1081.2	1130.2	1303.2	5.8
1980	49.6	1093.2	1142.8	1297.0	7.1
1981	50.0	1141.1	1191.1	1335.5	7.6
1982	50.5	1150.0	1200.5	1304.2	9.7
1983	51.3	1189.0	1240.3	1359.0	9.6
1984	51.9	1277.5	1329.4	1459.7	7.5

Table 19.17

Year	Output	Price Index	Land Value	Input Cost	CPI	Income
1960	72	51	24	46	88.7	6,036
1961	70	52	25	46	89.6	6,113
1962	71	54	26	47	90.6	6.271
1963	74	55	27	47	91.7	6,378
1964	72	55	29	47	92.9	6,727
1965	76	53	31	48	94.5	7,027
1966	73	55	33	50	97.2	7,280
1967	77	52	35	50	100.0	7,513
1968	79	52	38	50	104.2	7,728
1969	80	50	40	52	109.8	7,891
1970	77	52	42	54	116.3	8,134
1971	86	56	43	57	121.3	8,322
1972	87	60	47	61	125.3	8,562
1973	92	91	53	73	133.1	9,042
1974	84	117	66	83	147.7	8,867
1975	93	105	75	91	161.2	8,944
1976	92	102	86	97	170.5	9,175
1977	100	100	100	100	181.5	9,381
1978	102	105	109	108	195.4	9,735
1979	113	116	125	125	217.4	9,829
1980	101	125	145	138	246.8	9,722
1981	117	134	158	148	272.4	9,769
1982	117	121	157	150	289.1	9,725
1983	88	128	148	153	298.4	9,930
1984	111	139	146	155	311.1	10,421
1985	117	120	128	151	322.2	10,563
1986	108	106	112	146	328.4	10,780

Source: Economic Report of the President, 1987.

The data used for estimating the model of the agricultural sector are listed in Table 19.17. Output, the agricultural price, land values, input costs, and the consumer price index are all index numbers. Income is real (1982) per capita disposable income. Some variables not used in the text are listed for readers who are interested in estimating different forms of the model.

References

Abramovitz, M., and I. Stegun, *Handbook of Mathematical Functions*, New York: Dover Press, 1965.

Adelman, F., and I. Adelman, "The Dynamic Properties of the Klein–Goldberger Model," *Econometrica*, 27, 1959, pp. 596–625.

Amemiya, T., *Advanced Econometrics*, Cambridge, Mass.: Harvard University Press, 1985.

Anderson, T., and H. Rubin, "Estimation of the Parameters of a Single Equation in a Complete System of Stochastic Equations," *Annals of Mathematical Statistics*, 20, 1949, pp. 46–63.

Anderson, T., and H. Rubin, "The Asymptotic Properties of Estimators of the Parameters of a Single Equation in a Complete System of Stochastic Equations," *Annals of Mathematical Statistics*, 21, 1950, pp. 570–582.

Basmann, R., "On Finite Sample Distributions of Generalized Classical Linear Identifiability Test Statistics," *Journal of the American Statistical Association*, 55, 1960, pp. 650–659.

Bowden, R., "The Theory of Parametric Identification," *Econometrica*, 41, 1973, pp. 1069–1074.

Brown, R., "The Identification Problem in Systems Nonlinear in the Variables," *Econometrica*, 51, 1983, pp. 175–196.

Brundy, J., and D. Jorgenson, "Consistent and Efficient Estimation of Systems of Simultaneous Equations by Means of Instrumental Variables," *Review of Economics and Statistics*, 53, 1971, pp. 207–224.

Brundy, J., and D. Jorgenson, "Consistent and Efficient Estimation of Systems of Simultaneous Equations by Means of Instrumental Variables," in P. Zarembka, ed., *Frontiers in Econometrics*, New York: Academic Press, 1974.

Chemical Rubber Company, *Standard Mathematical Tables*, Cleveland, 1972.

Cooley, T., and S. LeRoy, "Atheoretical Macroeconomics: A Critique," *Journal of Monetary Economics*, 16, 1985, pp. 283–308.

Cragg, J., "On the Relative Small-Sample Properties of Several Structural-Equation Estimators," *Econometrica*, 35, 1967, pp. 89–110.

Durbin, J., "Errors in Variables," *Review of the International Statistical Institute*, 22, 1954, pp. 23–32.

Dhrymes, P., "Restricted and Unrestricted Reduced Forms: Asymptotic Distribution and Relative Efficiency," *Econometrica*, 41, 1973, pp. 119–134.

Fair, R., "The Estimation of Simultaneous Equations Models with Lagged Endogenous Variables and First Order Serially Correlated Errors," *Econometrica*, 38, 1970, pp. 507–516.

Fair, R., "Efficient Estimation of Simultaneous Equations with Autoregressive Errors by Instrumental Variables," *Review of Economics and Statistics*, 54, 1972, pp. 444–449.

Fisher, F., *The Identification Problem in Econometrics*, New York: Krieger, 1976.

Fomby, T., C. Hill, and S. Johnson, *Advanced Econometric Methods*, New York: Springer-Verlag, 1984.

Gabrielsen, A., "Consistency and Identifiability," *Journal of Econometrics*, 8, 1978, pp. 261–263.

Goldberger, A., *Impact Multipliers and Dynamic Properties of the Klein–Goldberger Model*, Amsterdam: North Holland, 1959.

Goldberger, A., *Econometric Theory*, New York: Wiley, 1964.

Goldfeld, S., and R. Quandt, "Nonlinear Simultaneous Equations: Estimation and Prediction," *International Economic Review*, 9, 1968, pp. 113–136.

Gordon, R. J., *The American Business Cycle*, Chicago: National Bureau of Economic Research, 1986.

Greenberg, E., and C. Webster, *Advanced Econometrics: A Bridge to the Literature*, New York: Wiley, 1983.

Griliches, Z., and M. Intrilligator, eds. *Handbook of Econometrics*, Amsterdam: North Holland, 1983.

Haavelmo, T., "The Statistical Implications of a System of Simultaneous Equations," *Econometrica*, 11, 1943, pp. 1–12.

Hatanaka, M., "Several Efficient Two-Step Estimators for the Dynamic Simultaneous Equations Model with Autoregressive Disturbances," *Journal of Econometrics*, 4, 1976, pp. 189–204.

Hausman, J., "An Instrumental Variable Approach to Full-Information Estimators for Linear and Certain Nonlinear Models," *Econometrica*, 43, 1975, pp. 727–738.

Hausman, J., "Specification Tests in Econometrics," *Econometrica*, 46, 1978, pp. 1251–1271.

Hausman, J., "Specification and Estimation of Simultaneous Equations Models," in Z. Griliches and M. Intrilligator, eds., *Handbook of Econometrics*, Amsterdam: North Holland, 1983.

Hsiao, C., "Identification," in Z. Griliches and M. Intrilligator, eds., *Handbook of Econometrics*, Amsterdam: North Holland, 1983.

Johnston, J., *Econometric Methods*, New York: McGraw-Hill, 1984.

Judge, G., C. Hill, W. Griffiths, and T. Lee, *The Theory and Practice of Econometrics*, New York: Wiley, 1985.

Kelejian, H., "Two-Stage Least Squares and Econometric Systems Linear in Parameters But Nonlinear in the Endogenous Variables," *Journal of the American Statistical Association*, 66, 1971, pp. 373–374.

Kelly, J., "Linear Cross Equation Constraints and the Identification Problem," *Econometrica*, 43, 1975, pp. 125–140.

Klein, L., *Economic Fluctuations in the United States 1921–1941*, New York: Wiley, 1950.

Kmenta, J., *Elements of Econometrics*, New York: Macmillan, 1986.

Kmenta, J., and W. Oberhofer, "Estimation of Standard Errors of the Characteristic Roots of a Dynamic Econometric Model," *Econometrica*, 41, 1973, pp. 171–177.

Lahiri, K., and P. Schmidt, "On the Estimation of Triangular Structural Systems," *Econometrica*, 46, 1978, pp. 1217–1221.

Liu, T., "Underidentification, Structural Estimation, and Forecasting," *Econometrica*, 28, 1960, pp. 855–865.

Malinvaud, E., *Statistical Methods of Econometrics*, Amsterdam: North Holland, 1970.

Nakamura, A., and M. Nakamura, "On the Relationships Among Several Specification Error Tests Presented by Durbin, Wu, and Hausman," *Econometrica*, 49, 1981, pp. 1583–1588.

Oberhofer, W., and J. Kmenta, "A General Procedure for Obtaining Maximum Likelihood Estimates in Generalized Regression Models," *Econometrica*, 42, 1974, pp. 579–590.

Pagan, A., "Some Consequences of Viewing LIML as an Iterated Aitken Estimator," *Economics Letters*, 3, 1979, pp. 369–372.

Phillips, P., "Exact Small Sample Theory in the Simultaneous Equations Model," in Z. Griliches and M. Intrilligator, eds., *Handbook of Econometrics*, Amsterdam: North Holland, 1983.

Rao, C. R., *Linear Statistical Inference and Its Applications*, New York: Wiley, 1965.

Rice, P., and K. Smith, "An Econometric Model of the Petroleum Industry," *Journal of Econometrics*, 6, 1977, pp. 263–287.

Riersol, O., "Identifiability of a Linear Relation Between Variables Which Are Subject to Error," *Econometrica*, 18, 1950, pp. 375–389.

Sargan, J., "The Maximum Likelihood Estimation of Economic Relationships with Autoregressive Residuals," *Econometrica*, 29, 1961, pp. 414–426.

Schmidt, P., "The Asymptotic Distribution of Dynamic Multipliers," *Econometrica*, 41, 1973, pp. 161–164.

Schmidt, P., "The Asymptotic Distribution of Forecasts in the Dynamic Simulation of an Econometric Model," *Econometrica*, 42, 1974a, pp. 303–310.

Schmidt, P., "The Algebraic Equivalence of the Oberhofer–Kmenta and Theil–Boot Formulae for the Asymptotic Variance of a Characteristic Root of a Dynamic Econometric Model," *Econometrica*, 42, 1974b, pp. 591–592.

Schmidt, P., *Econometrics*, New York: Marcel Dekker, 1976.

Schmidt, P., "A Note on Dynamic Simulation Forecasts and Stochastic Forecast-Period Exogenous Variables," *Econometrica*, 46, 1978, pp. 1227–1230.

Sims, C., "Money, Income, and Causality," *American Economic Review*, 62, 1972, pp. 540–555.

Spencer, D., and K. Berk, "A Limited Information Specification Test," *Econometrica*, 49, 1981, pp. 1079–1085.

Strickland, A., and L. Weiss, "Advertising, Concentration, and Price Cost Margins," *Journal of Political Economy*, 84, 1976, pp. 1109–1121.

Theil, H., and J. Boot, "The Final Form of Econometric Equation Systems," *Review of the International Statistical Institute*, 30, 1962, pp. 136–152.

Waugh, F., "The Place of Least Squares in Econometrics," *Econometrica*, 29, 1961, pp. 386–396.

Working, E., "What Do Statistical Demand Curves Show?," *Quarterly Journal of Economics*, 41, 1926, pp. 212–235.

Wu, D., "Alternative Tests of Independence Between Stochastic Regressors and Disturbances," *Econometrica*, 41, 1973, pp. 733–750.

Zellner, A., and H. Theil, "Three Stage Least Squares: Simultaneous Estimation of Simultaneous Equations," *Econometrica*, 30, 1962, pp. 63–68.

Chapter 20

Models with Discrete
Dependent Variables

20.1. *Introduction*

There are many settings in which the phenomenon we seek to model is discrete rather than continuous. Consider, for example, modeling labor force participation, the decision of whether or not to make a major purchase, or the decision of which candidate to vote for in an election. For the first of these, intuition would suggest that factors such as age, education, marital status, number of children, and other economic factors would be relevant in explaining whether an individual chooses to seek work or not in a given period. But something is obviously lacking if this is treated as the same sort of regression model we used to analyze consumption or the costs of production. In this chapter, we shall examine a variety of what have come to be known as *qualitative response (QR)* models. There are numerous different types that apply in different situations. What they have in common is that they are models in which the dependent variable is a discrete outcome, such as a "yes or no" decision, so that conventional regression methods are inappropriate.

This chapter is a lengthy but far from complete survey of topics in estimating QR models. The topics in each section are arranged so that they become progressively more advanced. For a short course, Sections 20.1, 20.2, and introduction to 20.3, 20.3.2 through part (b), and 20.4 through 20.4.1 will probably suffice. Those interested in a more advanced treatment can choose among the remaining sections. Almost none of these models can be estimated with linear regression methods. Therefore, readers interested in the mechanics of estimation may want to review the material in Chapter 12 before continuing. In nearly all cases, the method of estimation is maximum likelihood. The various properties of maximum likelihood estimators were discussed in Chapters 4 and 10. We shall assume throughout this chapter that the necessary conditions behind the optimality properties of maximum likelihood estimators are met and, therefore, will not derive or establish these properties specifically for the QR models. Detailed proofs for most of these models can be found in surveys by Amemiya (1985), McFadden (1984), Maddala (1983), and Dhrymes (1984).

20.2. *Discrete Choice Models*

The general class of models we shall consider are those for which the dependent variable takes values $0, 1, 2, \ldots$ In a few cases, the values will themselves be meaningful, as in the following:

1. Number of patents: $y = 0, 1, 2, \ldots$ These are *count* data.

But in most of the cases we shall study, the values taken by the dependent variable are merely a coding for some qualitative outcome. Some examples are as follows:

2. Labor force participation: We equate "no" with zero and "yes" with one. These are qualitative choices. The zero/one coding is a mere convenience.

3. Opinions of a certain type of legislation: Let zero represent "strongly opposed," one "opposed, " two "neutral," three "support," and four "strongly support." These are *rankings*, and the values chosen are not quantitative but merely an ordering. The difference between the outcomes represented by one and zero is not necessarily the same as that between two and one.

4. The occupational field chosen by an individual: Let zero be clerk, one engineer, two lawyer, three politician, and so on. These are merely categories, giving neither a ranking nor a count.

5. A consumer chooses among several shopping areas in deciding where to shop on a given day. This has the same characteristics as (4) but, as we shall see, the appropriate model is a bit different.

None of these situations lend themselves readily to regression analysis. Nonetheless, in each case, we can construct models that link the decision or outcome to a set of factors, at least in the spirit of regression. Our approach will be to analyze each of them in the general framework of probability models:

$$\text{Prob[event } j \text{ occurs]} = \text{Prob}[Y = j] = F[\text{relevant effects: parameters}]. \quad (20\text{--}1)$$

It is convenient for our purposes to group the models into two broad categories, binomial and multinomial, depending on whether the outcome is the choice between two or more than two alternatives. The great majority of recent empirical work in economics has used binomial models. As such, most of the material of this chapter will be devoted to them. The multinomial cases involve some new issues but are, for the most part, extensions of the binomial models. Within the multinomial models, we further divide the settings into unordered outcomes, such as those in examples (4) and (5), and ordered outcomes, such as those in examples (1) and (3). The latter have some of the familiar characteristics of regression models but involve some new complications as well. They are considered in the final section.

20.3. Models for Binomial Outcomes—Probit and Logit Models

To focus ideas, consider a model of labor force participation.[1] The *respondent* either works or seeks work ($Y = 1$) or doesn't ($Y = 0$) in the period in which our survey is taken. We believe that a set of factors, such as age, marital status, education, work history, and so on, gathered in a vector, **x**, explain the decision, so that

$$\text{Prob}[Y = 1] = F(\mathbf{x}, \beta),$$
$$\text{Prob}[Y = 0] = 1 - F(\mathbf{x}, \beta). \quad (20\text{--}2)$$

[1] Models for qualitative dependent variables can now be found in most disciplines in economics. However, their most frequent use is in labor economics in the analysis of micro-level data sets.

The set of parameters β reflect the impact of changes in $\mathbf{x}$ on the probability. For example, among the factors that might interest us is the marginal effect of marital status on the probability of labor force participation. The problem at this point is to devise a suitable model for the right-hand side of the equation.

One possibility is a linear regression,

$$F(\mathbf{x}, \beta) = \beta'\mathbf{x}.$$

Since $E[y] = F(\mathbf{x}, \beta)$, we can construct the regression model,

$$y = E[y] + (y - E[y])$$
$$= \beta'\mathbf{x} + \varepsilon. \tag{20-3}$$

But the **linear probability model** has a number of shortcomings. A minor complication is presented by the fact that ε is heteroscedastic in a way that depends on β. Since $\beta'\mathbf{x} + \varepsilon$ must equal zero or one, ε equals either $\beta'\mathbf{x}$ or $1 - \beta'\mathbf{x}$, with probabilities $1 - F$ and F, respectively. Thus, you can easily show that

$$\text{Var}[\varepsilon] = \beta'\mathbf{x}(1 - \beta'\mathbf{x}). \tag{20-4}$$

Of course, absent any other problems, we could manage this with an FGLS estimator in the fashion of Chapter 14. For our purposes, though, a more serious flaw is that without some ad hoc tinkering with the disturbances, we cannot be assured that the predictions from this model will truly look like probabilities. We cannot constrain $\beta'\mathbf{x}$ to the zero–one interval. This produces both nonsense probabilities and negative variances.[2] In view of this, and given the ready availability of convenient software for estimation, the linear model is becoming less frequently used except as a basis for comparison to some other more appropriate models.

Our requirement, then, is a model that will produce predictions consistent with the underlying theory in (20–1). For a given regressor vector, we would expect

$$\lim_{\beta'\mathbf{x} \to +\infty} \text{Prob}[Y = 1] = 1,$$

and

$$\lim_{\beta'\mathbf{x} \to -\infty} \text{Prob}[Y = 1] = 0. \tag{20-5}$$

See Figure 20.1. In principle, any proper, continuous probability distribution defined over the real line will suffice. The normal distribution has been used in many analyses, giving rise to the **probit** model,

$$\text{Prob}[Y = 1] = \int_{-\infty}^{\beta'\mathbf{x}} \phi(t)\, dt.$$
$$= \Phi(\beta'\mathbf{x}). \tag{20-6}$$

---

[2] The linear model is not beyond redemption. Aldrich and Nelson (1984) analyze the properties of the model at length. Judge et al. (1985) and Fomby et al. (1984) give interesting discussions of the ways we may modify the model to force internal consistency. But the fixes are sample dependent, and the resulting estimator, such as it is, may have no known sampling properties. Still, the linear model and linear regression are useful devices. See Aldrich and Nelson for a discussion and Section 20.3.4e for an alternative interpretation of linear regression in this context.

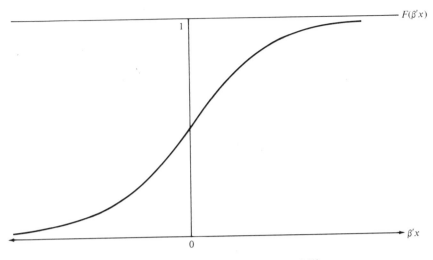

Figure 20.1   Model for a probability.

The function $\Phi(.)$ is a commonly used notation for the standard normal distribution. Partly because of its mathematical convenience, the logistic distribution,

$$\text{Prob}[Y = 1] = \frac{e^{\boldsymbol{\beta}'\mathbf{x}}}{1 + e^{\boldsymbol{\beta}'\mathbf{x}}} \tag{20-7}$$

$$= \Lambda(\boldsymbol{\beta}'\mathbf{x}),$$

has also been used in many applications. We shall use the notation $\Lambda(.)$ to indicate the logistic cumulative distribution function. This model is called the **logit** model for reasons we shall discuss in the next section. Other distributions have been suggested,[3] but in econometric applications the probit and logit models have been used almost exclusively.

The probability model is a regression:

$$E[y] = 0[1 - F(\boldsymbol{\beta}'\mathbf{x})] + 1[F(\boldsymbol{\beta}'\mathbf{x})] \tag{20-8}$$

$$= F(\boldsymbol{\beta}'\mathbf{x}).$$

Whatever distribution is used, it is important to note that the parameters of the model, like those of any nonlinear regression model, are not necessarily the marginal effects we are accustomed to analyzing. In general,

$$\frac{\partial E[y]}{\partial \mathbf{x}} = \left\{ \frac{\partial F(\boldsymbol{\beta}'\mathbf{x})}{\partial(\boldsymbol{\beta}'\mathbf{x})} \right\} \boldsymbol{\beta} \tag{20-9}$$

$$= f(\boldsymbol{\beta}'\mathbf{x})\boldsymbol{\beta},$$

where $f(.)$ is the density function that corresponds to the cumulative distribution, $F(.)$. For the normal distribution, this is

$$\frac{\partial E[y]}{\partial \mathbf{x}} = \phi(\boldsymbol{\beta}'\mathbf{x})\boldsymbol{\beta}, \tag{20-10}$$

[3] See, for example, Maddala (1983, pp. 27–32) and Aldrich and Nelson (1984).

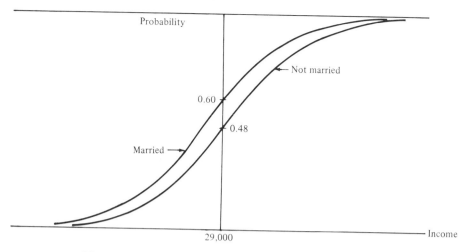

Figure 20.2   Effect of marital status on predicted probabilities.

where $\phi(t)$ is the standard normal density. For the logistic distribution,

$$\frac{d\Lambda[\beta'x]}{d(\beta'x)} = \frac{e^{\beta'x}}{(1 + e^{\beta'x})^2} \qquad (20\text{--}11)$$

$$= \Lambda(\beta'x)(1 - \Lambda(\beta'x)),$$

which is particularly convenient. Thus, in the logit model,

$$\frac{\partial E[y]}{\partial x} = \Lambda(\beta'x)(1 - \Lambda(\beta'x))\beta. \qquad (20\text{--}12)$$

It is obvious that these will vary with the values of **x**. In interpreting the estimated model, it will be useful to calculate this at, say, the means of the regressors and, where necessary, other pertinent values. For convenience, it is worth noting that the same scale factor applies to all of the slopes in the model.

The computation of partial derivatives is useful when the variable in question is continuous. However, most applications contain at least one dummy variable, for which a partial derivative is not meaningful. For such models, it is more informative to compute the probabilities over the range of $\beta'x$ (using the sample estimates, of course) and the two values of the binary variable. Example 20.1 and Figure 20.2 illustrate for a hypothetical study.

EXAMPLE 20.1.   Suppose that a study produces the following estimated probit model: $Y = 1$ if the respondent purchased a car in the year of the survey and $Y = 0$ if not.

$$\text{Prob}[Y = 1] = \Phi(-1.5 + 0.05\text{Income} + 0.3\text{Married}).$$

Income in the sample ranges from \$16,000 to \$40,000 and averages \$29,000. The marginal effect of a \$1000 change in income on the probability of purchase is given by

$$\text{Married: } \phi(-1.5 + 0.05I + 0.3)0.05 = \phi(-0.4)0.05 \quad = 0.018 \text{ at } I = 16,000$$

$$= \phi(0.25)0.05 \quad = 0.019 \text{ at } I = 29,000$$

$$= \phi(0.8)0.05 \quad = 0.015 \text{ at } I = 40,000$$

Not married: $\qquad = \phi(-0.7)0.05 \quad = 0.016$ at $I = 16{,}000$

$\qquad = \phi(-0.05)0.05 = 0.020$ at $I = 29{,}000$

$\qquad = \phi(0.5)0.05 \quad = 0.018$ at $I = 40{,}000$

The effect of marital status on the probabilities is shown in Figure 20.2, with income held at the sample average.

The question of which distribution to use is a natural one. Figure 20.3 shows the standard normal and standardized logistic distributions. The variance of the logistic distribution in (20–7) is $\pi^2/3 \simeq 3.29$, not 1. To make the comparison, we have plotted the standardized distribution, $F((\sqrt{3}/\pi)z)$. The logistic distribution is similar to the normal except in the tails, which are considerably heavier. (It more closely resembles a t distribution with seven degrees of freedom.) Therefore, for intermediate values of $\beta'x$ (say, between -1.2 and $+1.2$), the two distributions tend to give similar probabilities. The logistic distribution tends to give larger probabilities to $y = 0$ when $\beta'x$ is extremely small (and smaller probabilities to $y = 0$ when $\beta'x$ is very large) than the normal distribution. It is difficult to provide practical generalities on this basis, however, since they would require knowledge of β. However, we should expect different predictions from the two models if our sample contains (1) very few responses (y's equal to one) or very few nonresponses (y's equal to zero) and (2) very wide variation in an important independent variable, particularly if (1) is also true. There are practical reasons for favoring one or the other in some cases for mathematical convenience, but it is difficult to justify the choice of one distribution or another on theoretical grounds. Amemiya (1981) discusses a number of related issues, but as a general proposition, the question is unresolved. In most applications, it seems not to make much difference. However, this is not true in the multiple-outcome cases of Section 20.4.

20.3.1. Analysis of Proportions Data

Data for the analysis of binary response models will be in one of two forms, *individual* or *grouped*. Individual data are typically gathered from surveys and, for each individual, consist of the regressors, x_i, and the actual response, y_i, equal to zero or one. Grouped data are

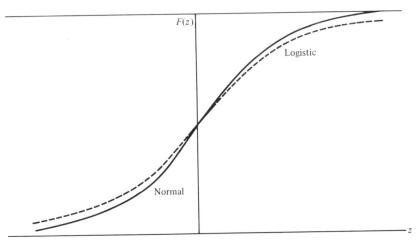

Figure 20.3 Normal and logistic CDFs.

typified by the sorts of laboratory results that were often used in the earliest applications of probit analysis.[4] For example, in a study of the effectiveness of an insecticide, a dosage level, x_t, is administered to a group of n_t subjects. The proportion that respond (by dying) is P_t. The data to be analyzed consist of $[n_t, \mathbf{x}_t, P_t]$ for T different dosage levels. Most economic applications involve individual data. Nonetheless, it is instructive to work through some aspects of the analysis of grouped data. In keeping with the origins of the technique, we pursue an example from a bioassay. (With a suitable change of names, we could put the exercise in an economic context.)

20.3.1a.   Theoretical Foundation

Suppose that our study is on the effectiveness of a certain insecticide. We assume that each subject possesses its own tolerance, x^*, to the insecticide. The tolerance is normally distributed across individuals, with means zero and variance one.[5] The level of "stimulation" is related to the dosage level, x, by the relation

$$s = \alpha + \beta x.^6$$

The unknown parameters, α and β, are presumably characteristic of the particular species of insect and its reaction to this insecticide and are, thus, of primary interest. For any particular subject i receiving dosage level x_t, if the stimulus exceeds the tolerance, the insect will succumb. Denoting this by $y_{it} = 1$, we obtain

$$
\begin{aligned}
\text{Prob}[y_{it} = 1] &= \text{Prob}[x_{it}^* < s_t] \\
&= \text{Prob}[x_{it}^* < \alpha + \beta x_t] \\
&= \Phi(\alpha + \beta x_t) \\
&= \pi_{t.}^{\ 7}
\end{aligned}
\tag{20-13}
$$

If we administer the same dosage level, x_t, to n_t subjects, a proportion, P_t, will die. Since x_t is constant, this P_t is an estimate of the true probability, π_t. By varying x_t across groups, we can observe the variation in P_t and, in principle, deduce the relationship between π_t and x_t.

The purpose of the experiment is to ascertain the response rates and, in particular, to learn about certain lethal dosage levels, for example, LD50, the dosage level, x, at which we can expect 50 percent of the sample in the laboratory (or the population in the field) to respond (perish). Similarly, LD95 and LD99 are interesting quantities in connection with the minimal application necessary to achieve a satisfactory extermination program.

20.3.1b.   Estimation Using Proportions Data

Based on the normal distribution, for each P_t,

$$P_t \simeq \Phi(\alpha + \beta x_t) = \int_{-\infty}^{\beta x_t} \phi(z)\, dz. \tag{20-14}$$

---

[4] An important survey is Finney (1971). Another useful reference is Cox (1970).
[5] We shall justify this normalization later. The assumption of normality has a long history in the biological sciences and can be justified by invoking the central limit theorem for the additive effect of many factors.
[6] Finney (ibid.) suggests that $\ln x$ may be more appropriate in some settings.
[7] If we had not assumed that $\mu = 0$ and $\sigma = 1$, this probability would be $\Phi((\alpha + \beta x - \mu)/\sigma) = \Phi((\alpha - \mu)/\sigma + (\beta/\sigma)x) = \Phi(\alpha' + \beta' x)$, which is what we have in (20–13). The parameters μ and σ are, therefore, not separately estimable.

Since the cdf is a monotonic function, we can obtain an estimate of $\alpha + \beta x_t$ with

$$z_t = \Phi^{-1}(P_t) = \alpha + \beta x_t. \qquad (20\text{–}15)$$

We can compute these *normits* (normal equivalent deviates) just by reading the normal table backward from the body to the margin.[8] The proportions will usually range from, say, 0.01 to 0.99, so these values will be in the range -3 to $+3$.[9] A simple plot of these normits against x will suggest the placement of $\alpha + \beta x$, whereupon a well-placed ruler will, with some minor calculations, provide estimates of α and β. Having obtained the parameters of the line, we are now in a position to solve the original problem. We require solutions x such that $z = \alpha + \beta x$ has $\Phi(z) = 0.5$ (this is LD_{50}), $\Phi(z) = 0.95$, and $\Phi(z) = 0.99$. The requisite z's are 0, 1.645, and 2.33, so the solutions for x are $LD_{50} = -\alpha/\beta$, $LD_{95} = (1.645 - \alpha)/\beta$, and $LD_{99} = (2.330 - \alpha)/\beta$.

EXAMPLE 20.2.   Suppose that the experiment produces the following data:

Sample size	1000	1000	1000	1000	1000	1000
Dosage level	0.1	0.5	0.75	1.0	1.5	2.0
Response rate	0.075	0.308	0.411	0.540	0.854	0.919
Normit	-1.439	-0.501	-0.224	0.101	1.054	1.399

We shall use these data to estimate α, β, and LD_{50}, LD_{95}, and LD_{99}. The values of z corresponding to these proportions are the normits given here. A plot of the normits against the dosages is given in Figure 20.4. The line nearest all six points is approximately

$$\text{Normit} \simeq -1.4 + 1.5x.$$

The solutions to the initial problem are

$$LD_{50} = 0.93, \qquad LD_{95} = 2.03, \qquad LD_{99} = 2.48.$$

There are several ways to improve on the preceding method. We can, of course, allow for multiple influences. In addition, ordinary least squares regression of the normits on **x** will probably be an improvement, but this will neglect heteroscedasticity in the implied regression. For the moment, we leave the distribution unspecified. The model implies that

$$\pi_t = \text{Prob}[Y_t = 1] = F(\boldsymbol{\beta}'\mathbf{x}_t). \qquad (20\text{–}16)$$

The sample proportion, P_t, is an estimate of π_t, so that

$$P_t = \pi_t + \varepsilon_t,$$

where ε_t is the sampling error of the sampling proportion. The variance of the sample proportion in random sampling is

$$\text{Var}[\varepsilon_t] = \text{Var}[P_t] = \frac{\pi_t(1 - \pi_t)}{n_t}. \qquad (20\text{–}17)$$

---

[8] The inverse function must be approximated if it is desired to do this with a computer. A number of approximating formulas may be found in Abramovits and Stegun (1972).

[9] In the earliest days, the need to manipulate negative numbers was a complication of some magnitude. Researchers used the probit = normit + 5 instead.

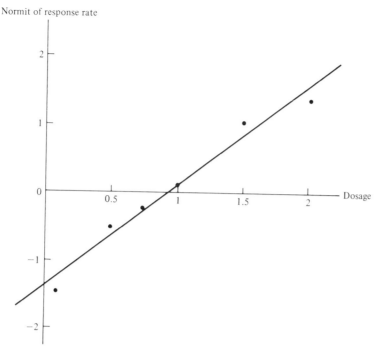

Figure 20.4   Probit analysis.

We obtained our working observation by using

$$F^{-1}(P_t) = z_t = \alpha + \beta x_t + u_t, \tag{20-18}$$

where u_t is the sampling error $F^{-1}(P_t) - F^{-1}(\pi_t)$. Ordinary least squares regression of z_t on a constant and $\mathbf{x}_t$ would be consistent but, in view of (20–17), inefficient. The precise variance of u_t remains to be determined, but the variance of P_t is seen to depend on both n_t and π_t. To obtain z_t, we used

$$F^{-1}(P_t) = F^{-1}(\pi_t + \varepsilon_t). \tag{20-19}$$

Expanding this in a linear Taylor series around $\varepsilon_t = 0$ gives

$$F^{-1}(P_t) \simeq F^{-1}(\pi_t) + \left[\frac{dF^{-1}(\pi_t)}{d\pi_t}\right]\varepsilon_t. \tag{20-20}$$

Since $F(.)$ is monotonic,

$$\frac{dF^{-1}(\pi_t)}{d\pi_t} = \frac{1}{\{dF(F^{-1}(\pi_t))/dF^{-1}(\pi_t)\}}$$

$$= \frac{1}{dF(\beta'\mathbf{x})/d(\beta'\mathbf{x})}$$

$$= \frac{1}{f(\beta'\mathbf{x})},$$

where $f(\boldsymbol{\beta}'\mathbf{x})$ is the density function. Thus,

$$F^{-1}(P_t) \simeq \pi_t + \frac{\varepsilon_t}{f(\boldsymbol{\beta}'\mathbf{x}_t)}. \tag{20-21}$$

To save some notation, let $f_t = f(\boldsymbol{\beta}'\mathbf{x}_t)$ and $F_t = F(\boldsymbol{\beta}'\mathbf{x}_t)$. The disturbance in (20-18) is heteroscedastic with variance

$$\mathrm{Var}\left[\frac{\varepsilon_t}{f_t}\right] = \frac{F_t(1 - F_t)}{(n_t f_t^2)}. \tag{20-22}$$

The weights for weighted least squares regression based on the normal distribution would be

$$w_t = \frac{n_t \phi_t^2}{\Phi_t(1 - \Phi_t)}. \tag{20-23}$$

One of the primary virtues of the logistic distribution is that its inverse function has a closed form. If

$$F_t = \Lambda_t = \frac{e^{\boldsymbol{\beta}'\mathbf{x}_t}}{(1 + e^{\boldsymbol{\beta}'\mathbf{x}_t})}, \tag{20-24}$$

then

$$\ln\left(\frac{F_t}{1 - F_t}\right) = \boldsymbol{\beta}'\mathbf{x}_t. \tag{20-25}$$

This function is called the *logit* of F_t (hence the name *logit analysis*). Weighted least squares regression of the logits of the observed proportions on $\mathbf{x}_t$ provides efficient estimates of the parameters. For the logit model,

$$f_t = \Lambda_t(1 - \Lambda_t)$$

[see (20-11)], so

$$\mathrm{Var}\left[\frac{\varepsilon_t}{f_t}\right] = \frac{1}{(n_t \Lambda_t(1 - \Lambda_t))}. \tag{20-26}$$

There is a remaining complication. The variance functions involve the unknown parameters we are estimating. The solution in Chapter 14 was first to use ordinary least squares to estimate the unknown parameters consistently, though not efficiently, and then to estimate the variances and compute the FGLS based on these weights.[10] The same procedure can be used here.

It would seem natural to invoke the results of Chapter 14 for the asymptotic properties of the FGLS estimator. This is fine, except that the generalized regression is an approximation based on the Taylor series in (20-20), not the actual underlying model. Moreover, the disturbances are functions of the parameters of the regression. Fortunately, the conclusion, if not the argument, is correct. Amemiya (1985, pp. 275-280) shows that in spite of these complications, the weighted least squares estimator has the same asymptotic distri-

---

[10] Intuition might suggest using the sample proportions, P_t, for F_t in computing the weights. However, that would be analogous to using y_i^2 instead of an estimate of σ_i^2 in the heteroscedastic regression. The incorrect weights are surely correlated with the correct ones, which means that this improperly weighted least squares estimator will be inefficient and its asymptotic covariance matrix will not be estimated consistently. Both the fitted probabilities and, if we are using the probit model, the densities should be computed using the estimated parameter values.

bution as the maximum likelihood estimator.[11] Hypothesis tests may proceed along the lines developed for the heteroscedastic regression. All results are asymptotic, so we use the chi-squared distribution instead of the F distribution. A straightforward way to proceed is to base tests of restrictions on

$$\chi^2 = \frac{\text{restricted sum of squared residuals minus}}{\text{unrestricted sum of squared residuals,}} \quad (20\text{–}27)$$

where the degrees of freedom is the number of restrictions being imposed.

EXAMPLE 20.3. The vote counts, by state, in the 1976 U.S. presidential election are listed in Table 20.1. "Dem." and "Rep." are the counts, in thousands, of the votes for the Democratic and Republican parties. (The small proportion of the total vote for other parties is omitted from these data.) "Income" is the 1975 median family income. "School" is the median number of years of school completed by persons 18 years of age or older. "Urban" is the percentage of the population living in a Standard Metropolitan Statistical Area as defined by the Census Bureau.[12] "Region" is defined (somewhat arbitrarily) as 1 for the Northeast, 2 for the Southeast, 3 for the Midwest and Middle South, and 4 for the West and Mountain states.

Weighted least squares regressions based on the proportion of voters who voted Democratic are given in Table 20.2.

In the full regressions, none of the variables included appear to be significant determinants of the voting pattern. We are interested in whether the region is significant in explaining the vote. The chi-squared statistic is quite small and suggests strongly that it is not. It is interesting that with the regional indicators omitted, schooling appears to be a significant influence. The data suggest that schooling and region are highly correlated, so perhaps this was to be expected.

These data are quite closely bunched in the intermediate area of the distributions. As such, we should expect similar results from the probit and logit models. One indicator is a comparison of the coefficients. In view of the different variances of the distributions, 1 for the normal and $\pi^2/3$ for the logistic, we should obtain comparable estimates by multiplying the probit coefficients by $\pi/\sqrt{3} = 1.8$. Amemiya (1981) suggests the scaling factor 1.6 instead.[13] Multiplying the preceding probit coefficients by 1.6 does, indeed, produce a surprisingly close approximation to the logit coefficients.

20.3.2. Analysis of Individual Data

Recent work in economics has been based primarily on individual data. With individual responses, in principle, every respondent has a different $\mathbf{x}$ vector, and P_i is either zero or one for every observation. Therefore, the regression approach of the previous section cannot be used.

---

[11] There is a side condition. The sample P_i's must converge to the population π_i's. Thus, these asymptotic properties are based on every n_t increasing without bound.

[12] All of these variables are extracted from the *Statistical Abstract of the United States*, Washington, D.C.: Department of Commerce, 1980.

[13] The normalization 1.8 is suggested in order to equate the variances of the logistic and normal variables. However, he found by trial and error that 1.6 works better. The result in (20–9) may suggest why. The index, $\boldsymbol{\beta}'\mathbf{x}$, is not the random variable. (See the discussion in the next section.) The marginal effect in the probit model for, say, x_k is $\phi(\boldsymbol{\beta}_p'\mathbf{x})\beta_{pk}$, while that for the logit is $\Lambda(1-\Lambda)\beta_{lk}$. (The subscripts p and l are for probit and logit.) Amemiya suggests that his approximation works best at the center of the distribution, where $F = 0.5$, or $\boldsymbol{\beta}'\mathbf{x} = 0$ for either distribution. Suppose that it is. Then $\phi(0) = 0.3989$ and $\Lambda(0)[1 - \Lambda(0)] = 0.25$. If the marginal effects are to be the same, $0.3989\beta_{pk} = 0.25\beta_{lk}$ or $\beta_{lk} = 1.6\beta_{pk}$, which is the regularity observed by Amemiya.

Table 20.1

State	Dem.	Rep.	Income	School	Urban	Region
Ala.	659	504	11,785	12.2	61.8	2
Alaska	44	72	22,432	12.7	43.7	4
Ariz.	296	419	13,569	12.6	74.7	4
Ark.	499	268	10,106	12.2	38.4	3
Calif.	3742	3882	15,069	12.7	92.7	4
Colo.	460	584	14,992	12.8	80.6	4
Conn.	648	719	16,244	12.6	88.2	1
Del.	123	110	15,732	12.5	68.5	1
D.C.	138	28	15,002	12.6	100.0	1
Fl.	1636	1470	12,205	12.4	85.9	2
Ga.	979	484	12,441	12.3	56.8	2
Hawaii	147	140	17,770	12.7	80.5	4
Idaho	127	204	12,844	12.6	16.9	4
Ill.	2271	2364	16,032	12.5	81.3	3
Ind.	1015	1184	14,411	12.4	67.8	3
Iowa	620	663	14,464	12.5	37.4	3
Kans.	430	503	13,412	12.6	46.2	3
Ky.	616	532	11,019	12.1	45.1	3
La.	661	587	12,576	12.3	63.2	2
Maine	232	236	11,839	12.5	23.3	1
Md.	760	673	17,556	12.6	84.8	1
Mass.	1429	1030	15,531	12.6	86.1	1
Mich.	1697	1894	15,385	12.5	81.3	3
Minn.	1070	819	14,740	12.5	63.9	3
Miss.	381	367	9,999	12.1	26.6	2
Mo.	998	927	13,011	12.4	63.5	3
Mont.	149	174	13,608	12.6	24.4	4
Nebr.	234	360	14,209	12.6	44.6	3
Nev.	92	101	14,961	12.6	81.3	4
N.H.	148	186	14,258	12.6	36.6	1
N.J.	1445	1510	16,432	12.4	92.1	1
N. Mex.	201	211	11,798	12.5	33.6	4
N.Y.	3390	3101	15,288	12.5	88.4	1
N.C.	927	742	11,834	12.2	45.2	2
N. Dak.	136	153	13,626	12.5	22.7	4
Ohio	2012	2001	14,822	12.4	79.8	3
Okla.	532	546	12,172	12.4	55.6	4
Oreg.	490	492	13,854	12.7	59.9	4
Pa.	2329	2206	14,153	12.4	80.4	1
R.I.	228	181	14,530	12.4	92.2	1
S.C.	451	346	12,188	12.2	48.3	2
S. Dak.	147	152	12,051	12.5	27.9	4
Tenn.	826	634	11,341	12.2	63.0	3
Tex.	2082	1953	12,672	12.4	79.4	4
Utah	182	338	14,329	12.8	78.7	4
Vt.	81	102	12,415	12.5	0.0	1
Va.	814	837	14,579	12.4	65.6	1
Wash.	717	778	14,962	12.7	71.1	4
W.V.	436	315	12,007	12.1	36.1	1
Wis.	1040	1005	15,064	12.5	63.0	3
Wyo.	62	93	14,784	12.6	0.0	4

Table 20.2.   (Standard errors are given in parentheses.)

	Probit		Logit	
Constant	2.30119	4.62209	3.63631	7.37955
	(2.174)	(1.524)	(3.512)	(2.460)
Income	−0.0000238	−0.0000150	−0.0000384	−0.0000239
	(0.000019)	(0.000014)	(0.000030)	(0.000024)
School	−0.160899	−0.361341	−0.253518	−0.576929
	(0.1886)	(0.1308)	(0.3047)	(0.2111)
Urban	0.001488	0.001691	0.002389	0.002705
	(0.00108)	(0.00105)	(0.00175)	(0.00169)
Southeast	0.018437	—	0.029336	—
	(0.06251)		(0.1011)	
Midwest	−0.049975	—	−0.080529	—
	(0.04007)		(0.06467)	
West	−0.090739	—	−0.146445	—
	(0.05780)		(0.09338)	
Sum of squared residuals	0.511516	0.562563	1.33273	1.46512
Chi-squared	0.05105		0.13239	

20.3.2a.   *Index Function and Random Utility Models*

Discrete dependent-variable models are often cast in the form of *index function models*. We view the outcome of a discrete choice as a reflection of an underlying regression. As an often cited example, consider the decision to make a large purchase. The theory states that the consumer makes a marginal benefit–marginal cost calculation. Since marginal benefit is obviously not observable, we model the difference between benefit and cost as an unobserved variable, y^*, such that

$$y^* = \boldsymbol{\beta}'\mathbf{x} + \varepsilon.$$

We assume that ε has a normal or logistic distribution with mean zero and variance one. We do not observe the net benefit of the purchase, only whether it is made or not. Therefore, our observation is

$$y = 1 \quad \text{if } y^* > 0,$$

$$y = 0 \quad \text{if } y^* \le 0.$$

In this formulation, $\boldsymbol{\beta}'\mathbf{x}$ is called the *index function*.

Two aspects of this construction merit our attention. First, the assumption of unit variance is an innocent normalization. Suppose that we assume that the variance is σ^2 instead and likewise multiply the coefficients by σ^2. Our observed data will be unchanged; y is zero or one, depending only on the sign of y^*, not on its scale. Second, the assumption of zero for the threshold is likewise innocent if the model contains a constant term.[14] Now the probability that $y = 1$ is

$$\text{Prob}[y^* > 0] = \text{Prob}[\boldsymbol{\beta}'\mathbf{x} + \varepsilon > 0]$$

$$= \text{Prob}[\varepsilon > -\boldsymbol{\beta}'\mathbf{x}].$$

---

[14] Unless there is some compelling reason, binomial probability models should not be estimated without constant terms.

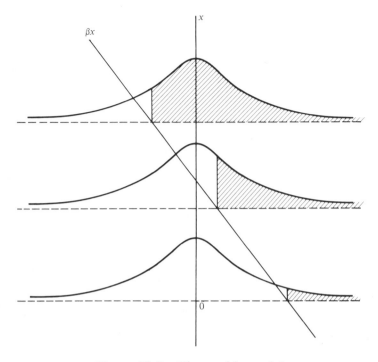

Figure 20.5   The probit model.

If the distribution is symmetric, as are the normal and logistic,

$$\text{Prob}[y^* > 0] = \text{Prob}[\varepsilon < \boldsymbol{\beta}'\mathbf{x}]$$
$$= F(\boldsymbol{\beta}'\mathbf{x}).$$

This, therefore, provides an underlying structural model for our probability. Figure 20.5 shows the connection between the latent regression and the probability.

EXAMPLE 20.4. Structural Equations for a Probit Model.   Nakosteen and Zimmer (1980) analyze a model of migration based on the following structure:[15]
For individual i, the market wage they can earn at their present location is

$$y_p^* = \boldsymbol{\beta}'\mathbf{x}_p + \varepsilon_p.$$

Variables in the equation include age, sex, race, growth in employment, and growth in per capita income. If the individual migrates to a new location, his market wage would be

$$y_m^* = \boldsymbol{\gamma}'\mathbf{x}_m + \varepsilon_m$$

However, migration entails costs that are related both to the individual and to the labor market,

$$C^* = \boldsymbol{\alpha}'\mathbf{z} + u.$$

---

[15] A number of other studies have also used variants of this basic formulation. Some important examples are Willis and Rosen (1979) and Robinson and Tomes (1982). The study by Tunali examined in Example 20.7 is another example.

Costs of moving are related to whether the individual is self-employed and whether the individual recently change their industry of employment. The individual migrates if the benefit, $y_m^* - y_p^*$, is greater than the cost, C^*. The net benefit of moving is

$$M^* = y_m^* - y_p^* - C^*$$

$$= \gamma' \mathbf{x}_m - \beta' \mathbf{x}_p - \alpha' \mathbf{z} + (\varepsilon_m - \varepsilon_p - u)$$

$$= \delta' \mathbf{w} + \varepsilon.$$

We could use an ordinary regression but for the fact that M^* is unobservable. The individual either moves or does not. After the fact, we observe only y_m^* if the individual has moved or y_p^* if he or she has not. But we do observe that $M = 1$ for a move and $M = 0$ for no move. If the disturbances are normally distributed, this produces the probit model we analyzed earlier. Logistic disturbances produce the logit model instead.

An alternative interpretation of data on individual choices is provided by the *random utility* model. Suppose that, in the Nakosteen–Zimmer framework, y_m and y_p represent the individual's utility of two choices, which we might denote U^a and U^b. For another example, U^a might be the utility of rental housing and U^b that of home ownership. The observed choice between the two reveals which one provides the greater utility, but not the unobservable utilities. Hence, the observed indicator equals one if $U^a > U^b$ and zero if $U^a < U^b$. For two choices, this is essentially the same model. The extension to more than two choices involves some additional issues, which we consider in Section 20.4.

20.3.2b.   *Estimation with Individual Data*

Individual data cannot be analyzed with the regression methods used for proportions data. An alternative approach is based on the method of maximum likelihood. We treat each observation as a single draw from a Bernoulli distribution (binomial with one draw). The model with probabilities $F(\beta' \mathbf{x}_i)$ and independent observations leads to the joint probability, or likelihood function,

$$\text{Prob}[Y_1 = y_1, Y_2 = y_2, \ldots, \quad Y_n = y_n] = \Pi_{y=0}\{1 - F(\beta' \mathbf{x}_i)\} \Pi_{y=1}\{F(\beta' \mathbf{x}_i)\}. \quad (20\text{–}28)$$

This can be conveniently written as

$$L = \Pi_i [F(\beta' \mathbf{x}_i)]^{y_i} [1 - F(\beta' \mathbf{x}_i)]^{1-y_i}. \quad (20\text{–}29)$$

This is the likelihood for a sample of n observations. Taking logs, we obtain

$$\ln L = \sum_i [y_i \ln F(\beta' \mathbf{x}_i) + (1 - y_i) \ln(1 - F(\beta' \mathbf{x}_i))]. \quad (20\text{–}30)$$

The first-order conditions for maximization require

$$\frac{\partial \ln L}{\partial \beta} = \sum_i \left[\frac{y_i f_i}{F_i} + (1 - y_i) \frac{-f_i}{(1 - F_i)} \right] \mathbf{x}_i = \mathbf{0}. \quad (20\text{–}31)$$

(In (20–31) and later, we use the subscript i to indicate that the function has an argument $\beta' \mathbf{x}_i$.) The choice of a particular form for F_i leads to the empirical model.

Unless we are using the linear probability model, the equations in (20–31) will be highly nonlinear and require an iterative solution. But both of the models we have looked at thus far are relatively straightforward to analyze. For the logit model, by inserting (20–7) and

(20–11) in (20–31), we get, after a bit of manipulation, the necessary conditions

$$\frac{\partial \ln L}{\partial \boldsymbol{\beta}} = \sum_i (y_i - \Lambda_i)\mathbf{x}_i. \qquad (20\text{–}32)$$

Note that if $\mathbf{x}_i$ contains a constant term, the first-order conditions imply that the average of the predicted probabilities must equal the proportion of ones in the sample. This also bears some similarity to the least squares normal equations if we view the term $y_i - \Lambda_i$ as a residual.[16]

For the normal distribution, the log likelihood is

$$\ln L = \sum_{y=0} \ln(1 - \Phi_i) + \sum_{y=1} \ln \Phi_i. \qquad (20\text{–}33)$$

The first-order conditions for maximizing L are

$$\frac{\partial \ln L}{\partial \boldsymbol{\beta}} = \sum_{y=0} \frac{-\phi_i}{1 - \Phi_i}\mathbf{x}_i + \sum_{y=1} \frac{\phi_i}{\Phi_i}\mathbf{x}_i. \qquad (20\text{–}34)$$

The interpretation is not quite so neat as that for the logistic, but it is interesting in its own right. We shall return to both of them later.

For both models, Newton's method is a straightforward way to estimate the parameters.[17] Standard errors for the estimated parameters may be obtained from the inverse of the estimated information matrix. (See Section 20.3.2c.)

EXAMPLE 20.5.   In this example, the election data of Example 20.3 are reexamined, using the probit and logit models. Instead of the proportions of the total vote, we use for the dependent variable $y = 1$ if more voters voted for the Democratic candidate (Jimmy Carter) than the Republican candidate (Gerry Ford). Summary statistics for the two models appear first in Table 20.3, followed by Table 20.4.

The scale factor listed with the coefficients is the scalar multiple in (20–9) evaluated at the means of the regressors. Multiplying the coefficients on the continuous variables by this value gives the marginal effect of changes in these variables on the predicted probability.

The results are essentially the same as those obtained in the grouped data regressions. The predictions in the tables suggest that in spite of the paucity of significant effects, either model predicts y considerably better than the naive model, which always assigns a one (Democrat) to y. As before, we are interested in the hypothesis that the region is important in explaining the vote. The test statistics for the joint hypothesis that the last three coefficients are zero are

$$\text{Likelihood ratio} = 2.9498$$

$$\text{Wald (significance)} = 0.7022$$

---

[16] The same result holds for the linear probability model. Although regularly observed in practice, the result has not been verified for the probit model. A general result for the distributions for which the mean predicted probability will equal the sample proportion is given in Hein (1987).

[17] If the sample contains grouped instead of individual data, maximum likelihood estimates of the parameters can be computed using the preceding results after replacing y_i with $n_i P_i$ and $(1 - y_i)$ with $n_i(1 - P_i)$ in (20–29) to (20–33). This will not provide more efficient estimates but, given the format of the available software, it may be easier to compute.

Table 20.3

	Probit	Logit
Log likelihood	−18.125	−18.210
Restricted (slopes = 0) log − L	−35.262	−35.262
Chi-squared [6]	34.274	34.104

Predicted Versus Actual Outcomes

Probit

		Predicted 0	Predicted 1	Total
Actual	0	21	5	26
	1	3	22	25
Total		24	27	51

Correct predictions   43

Logit

		Predicted 0	Predicted 1	Total
Actual	0	21	6	27
	1	3	21	24
Total		24	27	51

Correct predictions   42

Table 20.4.   Parameter Estimates

	Probit			Logit		
Variable	Coefficient	Standard Error	t	Coefficient	Standard Error	t
Scale factor	0.37953			0.13236		
Constant	61.555	30.55	2.02	100.42	55.791	1.80
Income	−0.0000092	0.00023	−0.040	−0.000058	0.00044	−0.130
School	−5.0864	2.608	−1.95	−8.2583	4.8016	−1.72
Urban	0.031845	0.01610	1.98	0.05926	0.02863	1.92
SE	4.8724	906.1	0.005	16.570	3352.9	0.005
MW	−0.08983	0.5816	−0.155	−0.22668	1.0022	−0.226
WE	−0.59325	0.7263	−0.817	−1.1785	1.3284	−0.887

20.3.2c.   Statistical Inference in Binomial Response Models Estimating the Asymptotic Covariance Matrices

Asymptotic covariance matrices for the logit or probit estimates can be obtained by inverting any of three estimators of the information matrix:

1. The negative of the Hessian of the log-likelihood function, evaluated at the observed data,

$$-\mathbf{H} = \left[\frac{-\partial^2 \ln L}{\partial \hat{\beta} \partial \hat{\beta}'}\right] = \sum_i h_i \mathbf{x}_i \mathbf{x}_i'. \tag{20-35}$$

2. The negative of the expected value of the Hessian,

$$-E[\mathbf{H}] = \sum_i E[h_i] \mathbf{x}_i \mathbf{x}_i'. \tag{20-36}$$

3. The Berndt et al. estimator, which is the summed outer product of the first derivatives,

$$\mathbf{B} = \sum_i g_i^2 \mathbf{x}_i \mathbf{x}_i'. \tag{20-37}$$

Amemiya (1981) shows that

$$-E[h_i] = \frac{f_i^2}{F_i(1 - F_i)}. \tag{20-38}$$

For the logit model,

$$h_i = E[h_i] = \hat{\Lambda}_i(1 - \hat{\Lambda}_i), \tag{20-39}$$
$$g_i^2 = (y_i - \hat{\Lambda}_i)^2.$$

The expressions are somewhat more complicated for the probit model. We can simplify things by defining the functions

$$\lambda(y_i, \mathbf{x}_i, \boldsymbol{\beta}) = \lambda_{0i} = \frac{-\phi_i}{1 - \Phi_i} \qquad \text{if } y_i = 0,$$

$$= \lambda_{1i} = \frac{\phi_i}{\Phi_i} \qquad \text{if } y_i = 1, \tag{20-40}$$

$$= \lambda_i.$$

(Note that λ_i is a function of y_i.) This is the scalar term in the derivatives, so that

$$\frac{\partial L}{\partial \boldsymbol{\beta}} = \sum_i \lambda_i \mathbf{x}_i \tag{20-41}$$

and the Berndt et al. estimator is

$$\mathbf{B} = \sum_i \lambda_i^2 \mathbf{x}_i \mathbf{x}_i'. \tag{20-42}$$

Using (20-38), we obtain

$$-E[\mathbf{H}] = \sum_i \left[\frac{\phi_i^2}{\Phi_i(1 - \Phi_i)} \right] \mathbf{x}_i \mathbf{x}_i'. \tag{20-43}$$

The actual Hessian for the probit model is somewhat complicated. A useful result is

$$\frac{d\phi(z_i)}{dz_i} = -z_i \phi(z_i).$$

After some fairly tedious algebra, we find that the second derivative has a surprisingly simple form,

$$h_i = \lambda_i^2 + (\boldsymbol{\beta}' \mathbf{x}_i) \lambda_i. \tag{20-44}$$

The estimator for the variance matrix is, therefore,

$$-\mathbf{H} = \sum_i \{\lambda_i^2 + \hat{\boldsymbol{\beta}}' \mathbf{x}_i \lambda_i\} \mathbf{x}_i \mathbf{x}_i'. \tag{20-45}$$

TESTING HYPOTHESES

For testing hypotheses about the coefficients, the full menu of procedures is available. The simplest method for a single restriction would be based on the usual t tests, using the standard errors from the information matrix. Using the normal distribution of the estimator, we would use the standard normal table rather than the t table for critical points. For more involved restrictions, it is possible to use the Wald test. For a set of restrictions $\mathbf{R}\boldsymbol{\beta} = \mathbf{q}$, the statistic is

$$W = (\mathbf{R}\hat{\boldsymbol{\beta}} - \mathbf{q})'\{\mathbf{R}(\text{Est. Asy. Var}[\hat{\boldsymbol{\beta}}])\mathbf{R}'\}^{-1}(\mathbf{R}\hat{\boldsymbol{\beta}} - \mathbf{q}).$$

EXAMPLE 20.6. Wald Test for a Subset of Coefficients.   In Example 20.5, we tested the hypothesis that a subset of the coefficients were equal to zero. For the Wald test,

$$\mathbf{R} = [\mathbf{0} \,|\, I_3]$$

and $\mathbf{q} = \mathbf{0}$. Collecting terms, we find that the statistic is

$$W = \hat{\boldsymbol{\beta}}_r' \mathbf{V}_r^{-1} \hat{\boldsymbol{\beta}}_r, \tag{20-46}$$

where the subscript r indicates the subvector or submatrix corresponding to the regional variables and $\mathbf{V}$ is the estimated asymptotic covariance matrix of $\boldsymbol{\beta}$.

Likelihood ratio and Lagrange multiplier statistics can also be computed. The likelihood ratio statistic is

$$\text{LR} = -2[\ln \hat{L}_r - \ln \hat{L}], \tag{20-47}$$

where $\hat{L}_r$ and $\hat{L}$ are the log-likelihood functions evaluated at the unrestricted and restricted estimates, respectively. The Lagrange multiplier test statistic is $\text{LM} = \mathbf{g}'\mathbf{V}\mathbf{g}$, where $\mathbf{g}$ is the first derivatives of the unrestricted model evaluated at the restricted parameter vector and $\mathbf{V}$ is any of the three estimators of the asymptotic covariance matrix of the maximum likelihood estimator. Davidson and MacKinnon (1984) find evidence that $E[\mathbf{H}]$ is the best of the three estimators to use, which gives

$$\text{LM} = \left(\sum_i g_i \mathbf{x}_i\right)'\left\{\sum_i E[h_i]\mathbf{x}_i\mathbf{x}_i'\right\}^{-1}\left(\sum_i g_i \mathbf{x}_i\right). \tag{20-48}$$

For the logit model, this has a particularly convenient form,

$$\text{LM} = nR^2,$$

where R^2 is the uncentered coefficient of determination in the regression of $(y_i - P)$ on $\mathbf{x}_i$ and P is the proportion of ones in the sample. All of the statistics listed here are asymptotically equivalent, and are asymptotically distributed as chi-squared with degrees of freedom equal to the number of restrictions being tested. We consider some examples later.

ASYMPTOTIC VARIANCES FOR PREDICTIONS AND MARGINAL EFFECTS

The predicted probabilities, $F(\hat{\boldsymbol{\beta}}'\mathbf{x}) = \hat{F}$, and the estimated marginal effects, $f(\hat{\boldsymbol{\beta}}'\mathbf{x}) \times \hat{\boldsymbol{\beta}} = \hat{f}\hat{\boldsymbol{\beta}}$, are nonlinear functions of the parameter estimates. To compute standard errors, we can use the linear approximation approach discussed in Chapter 4. For the predicted probabilities,

$$\text{Asy. Var}[\hat{F}] = \left(\frac{\partial \hat{F}}{\partial \hat{\boldsymbol{\beta}}}\right)'\mathbf{V}\left(\frac{\partial \hat{F}}{\partial \hat{\boldsymbol{\beta}}}\right),$$

where

$$\mathbf{V} = \text{Asy. Var}[\hat{\boldsymbol{\beta}}].$$

The estimated asymptotic variance matrix of $\hat{\beta}$ can be any of the three described earlier. Let $z = \mathbf{x}'\hat{\beta}$. Then the derivative vector is

$$\frac{\partial \hat{F}}{\partial \hat{\beta}} = \left(\frac{d\hat{F}}{dz}\right)\left(\frac{\partial z}{\partial \hat{\beta}}\right) = \hat{f}\mathbf{x}.$$

Combining terms gives

$$\text{Asy. Var}[\hat{F}] = \hat{f}^2\mathbf{x}'\mathbf{V}\mathbf{x}.$$

This depends, of course, on the particular $\mathbf{x}$ vector used.

For the marginal effects, let $\hat{\gamma} = \hat{f}\hat{\beta}$. Then

$$\text{Asy. Var}[\hat{\gamma}] = \left[\frac{\partial\hat{\gamma}}{\partial\hat{\beta}'}\right]\mathbf{V}\left[\frac{\partial\hat{\gamma}}{\partial\hat{\beta}'}\right]'.$$

The matrix of the derivatives is

$$\hat{f}\left(\frac{\partial\hat{\beta}}{\partial\hat{\beta}'}\right) + \hat{\beta}\left(\frac{d\hat{f}}{dz}\right)\left(\frac{\partial z}{\partial\hat{\beta}'}\right) = \hat{f}\mathbf{I} + \left(\frac{d\hat{f}}{dz}\right)\hat{\beta}\mathbf{x}'.$$

For the probit model, $d\hat{f}/dz = -z\hat{\phi}$, so,

$$\text{Asy. Var}[\hat{\gamma}] = \hat{\phi}^2[\mathbf{I} - \hat{\beta}\mathbf{x}']\mathbf{V}[\mathbf{I} - \hat{\beta}\mathbf{x}']'.$$

For the logit model, $\hat{f} = \hat{\Lambda}(1 - \hat{\Lambda})$, so

$$\frac{d\hat{f}}{dz} = (1 - 2\hat{\Lambda})\left(\frac{d\hat{\Lambda}}{dz}\right) = (1 - 2\hat{\Lambda})\hat{\Lambda}(1 - \hat{\Lambda}).$$

Collecting terms, we obtain

$$\text{Asy. Var}[\hat{\gamma}] = (\hat{\Lambda}(1 - \hat{\Lambda}))^2[\mathbf{I} + (1 - 2\hat{\Lambda})\hat{\beta}\mathbf{x}']\mathbf{V}[\mathbf{I} + (1 - 2\hat{\Lambda})\hat{\beta}\mathbf{x}']'.$$

This is a rather involved computation. As before, the value obtained will depend on the $\mathbf{x}$ vector used.[18]

THE HESSIANS FOR THESE MODELS ARE NEGATIVE DEFINITE

The effectiveness of some computing algorithms and the question of whether the likelihood function has more than one maximum depend on whether the Hessian of the log likelihood (not its expected value) is negative definite. This is immediately apparent for the logit model, since $-F_i(1 - F_i)$ must be negative for all i. (See (20–39).) Whether the same holds true for the probit model is less obvious. To show that the probit Hessian is negative definite, it suffices to show that h_i in (20–44) is always positive for both $y = 0$ and $y = 1$. The literature contains a number of proofs,[19] but the simplest one is based on a result now widely used in the literature on sample selection.[20] Suppose that ε is distributed as $N[0, 1]$. The following are true:

$$0 < \text{Var}(\varepsilon \mid \varepsilon < -z) = 1 - z\lambda_0(z) - \lambda_0(z)^2 < 1$$

and   (20–49)

$$0 < \text{Var}(\varepsilon \mid \varepsilon > -z) = 1 - z\lambda_1(z) - \lambda_1(z)^2 < 1,$$

---

[18] For an application, see the study by Cecchetti discussed in Example 20.9.
[19] See, for example, Amemiya (1985, pp. 273–274) and Maddala (1983, p. 63).
[20] See Section 21.4.

where the functions λ_0 and λ_1 are defined in (20–40). These are the variances of the *truncated normal* distribution.[21] Then h_i is just one minus these variances evaluated at $z_i = \boldsymbol{\beta}'\mathbf{x}_i$. Since these are between zero and one for both λ_0 and λ_1 and for all z_i, this completes the proof.

EM ESTIMATION OF THE PROBIT MODEL

Another aspect of the probit model is useful for the results in Chapter 21. Suppose that the unobserved index variable, y^*, were observable. Then we could estimate the parameters by ordinary least squares. The EM method, which we encountered in the estimation of the MIMIC model, provides a strategy for estimation based on this logic. In particular,

$$E[y^*\,|\,\mathbf{x}, y] = E[\boldsymbol{\beta}'\mathbf{x} + \varepsilon\,|\,\mathbf{x}, y].$$

It might seem that this is just $\boldsymbol{\beta}'\mathbf{x}$, but that would ignore some information. If we know that y equals one, we know that $\varepsilon > -\boldsymbol{\beta}'\mathbf{x}$. Therefore,

$$E[y^*\,|\,\mathbf{x}, y = 1] = \boldsymbol{\beta}'\mathbf{x} + E[\varepsilon\,|\,\varepsilon > -\boldsymbol{\beta}'\mathbf{x}]. \tag{20–50}$$

The latter term is one we have not encountered previously, but we used it previously, and it will reappear repeatedly in the next chapter. The now standard result[22] is

$$E[\varepsilon\,|\,\varepsilon > -\boldsymbol{\beta}'\mathbf{x}] = \frac{\phi(-\boldsymbol{\beta}'\mathbf{x})}{1 - \Phi(-\boldsymbol{\beta}'\mathbf{x})}$$

$$= \frac{\phi(\boldsymbol{\beta}'\mathbf{x})}{\Phi(\boldsymbol{\beta}'\mathbf{x})} \tag{20–51}$$

$$= \lambda_1(\boldsymbol{\beta}'\mathbf{x}).$$

(The fact that this term happens to be the derivative that appears in the likelihood function is a striking and very convenient result. That the second derivative is the conditional variance is also extremely convenient.) The analog for the $y = 0$ values is, as might be expected,

$$E[\varepsilon\,|\,\varepsilon < -\boldsymbol{\beta}'\mathbf{x}] = \frac{-\phi(-\boldsymbol{\beta}'\mathbf{x})}{\Phi(-\boldsymbol{\beta}'\mathbf{x})}$$

$$= \frac{-\phi(\boldsymbol{\beta}'\mathbf{x})}{1 - \Phi(\boldsymbol{\beta}'\mathbf{x})} \tag{20–52}$$

$$= \lambda_0(\boldsymbol{\beta}'\mathbf{x}).$$

Therefore, an alternative strategy, in the same spirit as the one for the MIMIC model, is

(1) Given $\hat{\boldsymbol{\beta}}$, an estimate of $\boldsymbol{\beta}$, compute

$$\hat{y}^* = \hat{\boldsymbol{\beta}}'\mathbf{x} + \lambda_1(\hat{\boldsymbol{\beta}}'\mathbf{x}) \qquad \text{if } y = 1,$$

or

$$\hat{y}^* = \hat{\boldsymbol{\beta}}'\mathbf{x} + \lambda_0(\hat{\boldsymbol{\beta}}'\mathbf{x}) \qquad \text{if } y = 0. \tag{20–53}$$

(2) Compute the new $\hat{\boldsymbol{\beta}}$ by least squares regression of $\hat{y}^*$ on x.

---

[21] See Johnson and Kotz (1971). We shall make repeated use of this distribution in the next chapter.
[22] See, for example, Heckman (1979).

We repeat the interaction until satisfactory convergence occurs. The repeated least squares aspect of this calculation is an interesting interpretation of the maximization process.[23]

20.3.2d.   Goodness of Fit Measures

There have been numerous attempts to derive fit measures for the QR models.[24] At a minimum, one would want to report the maximized value of the log-likelihood function, $\ln \hat{L}$. Since the hypothesis that all of the slopes in the model are zero is often interesting $\ln L_0$, the log likelihood computed with only a constant term, should also be reported. You can easily show that for either the logit or the probit model (or, for that matter, any other),

$$\ln L_0 = n[P \ln P + (1 - P) \ln(1 - P)], \qquad (20-54)$$

where P is the proportion of observations with $y = 1$ in the sample.

A number of proposals have been made for defining a measure analogous to R^2 in a conventional regression model. One suggested measure is the likelihood ratio index,

$$\text{LRI} = 1 - \frac{\ln \hat{L}}{\ln L_0}. \qquad (20-55)$$

The measure has an intuitive appeal in that it is bounded by zero and one. If all of the slope coefficients are zero, it equals zero. There is no way to make it equal one, however, though we can come close. If F_i is always one when y equals one and zero when y equals zero, $\ln \hat{L}$ equals zero (the log of one) and LRI equals one. It has been suggested that this latter finding would be indicative of a "perfect fit" and that LRI increases as the fit of the model improves. Unfortunately, values between zero and one have no natural interpretation. If F_i is a proper pdf, then even with many regressors, the model cannot fit perfectly unless $\beta' x_i$ explodes to $-\infty$ or $+\infty$. As a practical matter, this sometimes happens, and it is indicative not of a good fit, as such, but of a flaw in the specification of the model.

> If one of the regressors contains a value, say x^*,
> such that whenever this x is greater than x^*, y
> equals one, and vice versa, and whenever this x is
> less than this x^*, y equals zero and vice versa,
> the model will be a *perfect predictor*. This
> also holds if the sign of $\beta' x$ gives a perfect
> predictor of y for some β.[25]

For example, careless researchers sometimes include as regressors dummy variables that are identical to the dependent variable. In this case, the maximization procedure will break down precisely because $\beta' x$ is exploding during the iterations. Of course, this is not at all what we have in mind for a good fit.

A useful summary of the predictive ability of the model is a 2×2 table of the hits and misses of the prediction rule

$$\hat{y} = 1 \text{ if } \hat{F} > 0.5 \text{ and } 0 \text{ otherwise.} \qquad (20-56)$$

---

[23] It appears to have been first reported by Hartley (1976). The method itself was later formalized by Dempster et al. (1977). It has since been analyzed by a number of economists in the context of *missing-data* models.

[24] See, for example, Cragg and Uhler (1970), Maddala (1983), Amemiya (1981), and McFadden (1974).

[25] See McFadden (1984). If this condition holds, gradient methods *will* find that β.

However, it is important not to place too much emphasis on this measure of goodness of fit. Consider, for example, the naive predictor

$$\hat{y} = 1 \text{ if } P > 0.5 \text{ and } 0 \text{ otherwise,} \tag{20-57}$$

where P is the proportion of ones in the sample. (Note that (20–57) is the same as (20–56) for the restricted model with all slopes equal to zero.) This rule will always predict correctly $100P$ percent of the observations, which means that the naive model does not have zero fit. In fact, if the proportion of ones in the sample is very high, it is possible to construct examples in which the second model will generate more correct predictions than the first![26] Once again, this is not a flaw in the model; it is a flaw in the fit measure.

EXAMPLE 20.7. Tunali (1986) estimated a probit model in a study of migration, subsequent remigration, and earnings for a large sample of observations of male members of households in Turkey. Among his results, he reports the following summary for a probit model:

		Predicted		
		$D = 0$	$D = 1$	Total
Actual	$D = 0$	471	16	487
	$D = 1$	183	20	203
	Total	654	36	690

The estimated model is highly significant, with a likelihood ratio test of the hypothesis that the coefficients (16 of them) are zero based on a chi-squared value of 69 with 16 degrees of freedom.[27] The model predicts 491 of 690, or 71.2 percent, of the observations correctly, though the likelihood ratio index is only 0.083. A naive model, which always predicts that $y = 0$ because $P < 0.5$, predicts 487 of 690, or 70.6 percent, of the observations correctly. This is hardly suggestive of no fit. The maximum likelihood estimator produces several significant influences on the probability but makes only four more correct predictions than the naive predictor.[28]

The likelihood ratio index is obviously related to the likelihood ratio statistic for testing the hypothesis that the coefficient vector is zero. Other similar fit measures have been proposed. Although they are suggestive, whether they have any relationship to maximizing any type of fit in the more familiar sense is a question that needs to be studied.[29] The maximum likelihood estimator is *not* chosen in order to maximize a fitting criterion based on prediction of y, as it is in the classical regression (which maximizes R^2). It is chosen to maximize the joint density of the observed dependent variables. It remains an interesting question for research whether fitting y well or obtaining good parameter estimates is a preferable estimation criterion. Evidently, they are not necessarily compatible.

[26] Amemiya (1981) discusses this issue at length.
[27] This actually understates slightly the significance of his model, as the preceding predictions are based on a bivariate model. However, the likelihood ratio tests fails to reject the hypothesis that a univariate model applies.
[28] It is also noteworthy that nearly all of the correct predictions of the maximum likelihood estimator are the zeroes. It hits only 10 percent of the ones in the sample.
[29] Manski (1975) has devised an estimator that is related to the predictive ability of (20–56). However, the procedure is quite cumbersome and has not yet found its way into the mainstream of applied research.

20.3.3.   Specification Tests in Binary Choice Models

In the classical regression model, we considered two important specification problems, the effect of omitted variables and the effect of heteroscedasticity. In the classical model, $y = X_1\beta_1 + X_2\beta_2 + \varepsilon$ when least squares estimates b_1 are computed, omitting X_2.

$$E[b_1] = \beta_1 + [X_1'X_1]^{-1}X_1'X_2\beta_2.$$

Unless X_1 and X_2 are orthogonal, b_1 is biased. If we ignore heteroscedasticity, although the least squares estimator is still unbiased and consistent, it is inefficient and the usual estimate of its sampling covariance matrix is inappropriate. Yatchew and Griliches (1984) have examined these same issues in the setting of the probit and logit models. Their general results are far more pessimistic. In the context of a binary choice model, they find the following:

1. If x_2 is omitted from a model containing x_1 and x_2,

   $$\text{plim }\hat{\beta}_1 = c_1\beta_1 + c_2\beta_2,$$

   where c_1 and c_2 are complicated functions of the unknown parameters. The implication is that even if the omitted variable is uncorrelated with the included one, the coefficient on the included variable will be inconsistent.

2. If the disturbances in the underlying regression are heteroscedastic, the maximum likelihood estimators are inconsistent and the variance matrix is inappropriate.

The second result finding is particularly troubling in view of the fact that the probit model is most often used with microeconomic data, which are frequently heteroscedastic.

Any of the three methods of hypothesis testing can be used to analyze these specification problems. The Lagrange multiplier test has the advantage that it can be carried out using the estimates from the restricted model, which sometimes brings a large saving in computational effort. This is especially true for the test for heteroscedasticity.[30]

To reiterate, the Lagrange multiplier statistic is computed as follows: Let the null hypothesis, H_0, be a specification of the model, and let H_1 be the alternative. For example, H_0 might specify that only variables x_1 appear in the model, while H_1 might specify that x_2 appears in the model as well. The statistic is

$$\text{LM} = g_0'V_0^{-1}g_0,$$

where g_0 is the vector of derivatives of the log likelihood as specified by H_1, but evaluated at the maximum likelihood estimator of the parameters assuming that H_0 is true, and V_0^{-1} is any of the three consistent estimators of the variance matrix of the maximum likelihood estimator under H_1, also computed using the maximum likelihood estimators based on H_0. The statistic is asymptotically distributed as chi-squared with degrees of freedom equal to the number of restrictions.

20.3.3a.   Testing for Omitted Variables

The hypothesis to be tested is

$$\begin{aligned} H_0: y^* &= \beta_1'x_1 + \quad\quad + \varepsilon, \\ H_1: y^* &= \beta_1'x_1 + \beta_2'x_2 + \varepsilon, \end{aligned} \tag{20-58}$$

---

[30] The results in this section are based on Davidson and MacKinnon (1984) and Engle (1983).

so the test is of the hypothesis that $\beta_2 = 0$. We carried out this test earlier in the voting example (Example 20.5) for the regional dummy variables, using a conventional significance (Wald) test and a likelihood ratio test. The Lagrange multiplier test would be carried out as follows:

1. Estimate the model in H_0 by maximum likelihood. The restricted coefficient vector is $[\hat{\beta}, 0]$.

2. Let $\mathbf{x}$ be the compound vector, $[\mathbf{x}_1, \mathbf{x}_2]$.

The statistic is then computed according to (20–48). It is possible to show that this is equivalent to nR^2 in the regression of

$$r_i = y_i \left[\frac{1 - F_i}{F_i} \right]^{1/2} + (y_i - 1) \left[\frac{F_i}{1 - F_i} \right]^{1/2} \qquad (20-59)$$

on

$$\mathbf{x}_i^* = \frac{f_i}{[F_i(1 - F_i)]^{1/2}} \mathbf{x}_i.$$

Given the simplicity of (20–48), the appeal of this solution may be largely aesthetic. It is noteworthy, though, that in this case as in many others, the Lagrange multiplier is the coefficient of determination in a regression.[31]

20.3.3b. Testing for Heteroscedasticity

We use the general formulation analyzed by Godfrey,

$$\text{Var}[\varepsilon] = \exp(\gamma'z).[32]$$

As noted by Davidson and Mackinnon, this test is not well suited to the logit model, so we will derive it specifically for the probit model. The model is

$$y^* = \beta'\mathbf{x} + \varepsilon,$$
$$\text{Var}[\varepsilon] = e^{\gamma'z}. \qquad (20-60)$$

The log likelihood is

$$\ln L = \sum_i y_i \ln F\left(\frac{\beta'\mathbf{x}_i}{\exp(\gamma'z_i)} \right) + (1 - y_i) \ln\left[1 - F\left(\frac{\beta'\mathbf{x}_i}{\exp(\gamma'z_i)} \right) \right]. \qquad (20-61)$$

In order to be able to estimate all of the parameters, z cannot have a constant term. The derivatives are

$$\frac{\partial \ln L}{\partial \beta} = \sum_i \left[\frac{f_i(y_i - F_i)}{F_i(1 - F_i)} \right] \exp(-\gamma'z_i)\mathbf{x}_i,$$

$$\frac{\partial \ln L}{\partial \gamma} = \sum_i \left[\frac{f_i(y_i - F_i)}{F_i(1 - F_i)} \right] \exp(-\gamma'z_i)z_i(-\beta'\mathbf{x}_i). \qquad (20-62)$$

---

[31] The denominator in R^2 is *uncentered*. We use $\mathbf{r}'\mathbf{r}$, which equals n in (20–59).
[32] See Chapter 14 for details.

This is a difficult log likelihood to maximize. But if the model is estimated assuming that $\gamma = 0$, we can easily test for homoscedasticity. Let

$$\mathbf{w}_i = \begin{bmatrix} \mathbf{x}_i \\ (-\hat{\boldsymbol{\beta}}'\mathbf{x}_i)\mathbf{z}_i \end{bmatrix} \tag{20-63}$$

computed at the maximum likelihood estimator, assuming that $\gamma = 0$. Then (20–48) can be used as usual for the Lagrange multiplier statistic.

Davidson and MacKinnon carried out a Monte Carlo study to examine the true sizes and power functions of these tests. As might be expected, the test for omitted variables is relatively powerful. However, the test for heteroscedasticity may well pick up some other form of misspecification, including perhaps the simple omission of z from the index function, so its power may be problematic. It is perhaps not surprising that the same problem arose earlier in our tests for heteroscedasticity in the linear regression model.[33]

EXAMPLE 20.8.   For the voting data in Example 20.6, using the probit model, the two preceding tests give the following results:

1. For the hypothesis that the regional variables can be omitted from the model,

$$LM = 2.396.$$

Recall that the likelihood ratio and Wald test statistics were

$$LR = 2.9498$$

and

$$W = 0.7022.$$

None of these are larger than the critical value of chi-squared with three degrees of freedom, 7.815, for a test of size 0.05.

2. The Lagrange multiplier test statistic for the hypothesis that the disturbance variance is unrelated to the regressors in the model is 6.208, which is also insignificant. We conclude that the data are consistent with a homoscedastic disturbance.

20.3.4.   Recent Developments

Qualitative response models have been a growth industry in econometrics. The recent literature, particularly in the area of panel data analysis, has produced a number of new techniques and methods. We shall now consider a sample of them.[34]

20.3.4a.   *A Logit Model for Panel Data*

Consider a logit model for a panel of data of the form

$$\text{Prob}[y_{it} = 1] = \frac{e^{\boldsymbol{\beta}'\mathbf{x}_{it}}}{1 + e^{\boldsymbol{\beta}'\mathbf{x}_{it}}}. \tag{20-64}$$

---

[33] These and a number of related issues are analyzed in a recent symposium on the subject of specification tests in discrete choice models, Blundell (1987).

[34] There have been several recent symposia on the subject of qualitative (and limited) dependent-variable models, including Manski and McFadden (1981), and two in the *Journal of Econometrics*, Duncan (1986) and Blundell (1987). Useful compendia on the general topic of qualitative dependent variables are Maddala (1983), Aldrich and Nelson (1984), Amemiya (1981 and 1985, chapters 9 and 10), and McFadden (1984). Research continues on the subject, and this list is far from exhaustive.

For precisely the same reasons as in the linear regression model, if there is heterogeneity across units, the estimated parameters from this model will be inconsistent.[35] A fixed-effects logit model that accounts for heterogeneity is

$$\text{Prob}[y_{it} = 1] = \frac{e^{\alpha_i + \beta' x_{it}}}{1 + e^{\alpha_i + \beta' x_{it}}}. \tag{20-65}$$

This model is likely to present some extremely difficult estimation problems. First, if there are a large number of cross-sectional units, say thousands, the number of unknown parameters that must be estimated will quickly become intractable. In this nonlinear setting, it is not possible to sweep out the heterogeneity by taking deviations from group means. In addition, as we saw in the linear regression case, even if we can estimate the parameters, any desirable asymptotic properties for the individual effects depend on T increasing. This will not be the case in the typical panel data set, in which T is very small, sometimes less than 10. This will be particularly problematic for maximum likelihood estimators, whose only desirable properties are asymptotic.

Chamberlain (1980) has proposed a means of estimating a logit model with unobserved heterogeneity in panel data sets with large n and small T.[36] His suggestion is that we consider the set of T observations for observational unit i as a group. The unconditional likelihood function for the nT observations is

$$L = \Pi_i \Pi_t (F_{it})^{y_{it}} (1 - F_{it})^{1 - y_{it}}. \tag{20-66}$$

He suggests, instead, that we maximize the conditional likelihood function,

$$L^c = \Pi_i \text{Prob}\left[Y_{i1} = y_{i1}, Y_{i2} = y_{i2}, \ldots, Y_{iT} = y_{iT} \left| \sum_t y_{it} \right. \right]. \tag{20-67}$$

That is, the likelihood for each set of T observations is conditioned on the number of ones in the set. It is useful to consider an example. Suppose that the sample consists of a large number of cross-sectional units, each observed in two periods, 1 and 2. The unconditional likelihood is, therefore,

$$L = \Pi_i \text{Prob}[Y_{i1} = y_{i1}] \text{Prob}[Y_{i2} = y_{i2}]. \tag{20-68}$$

(The observations are independent, so the likelihood function is just the product of the probabilities.) For each pair of observations, we have the following possibilities:

1. $y_{i1} = 0$ and $y_{i2} = 0$. Prob(0 and 0 | sum = 0) = 1.
2. $y_{i1} = 1$ and $y_{i2} = 1$. Prob(1 and 1 | sum = 2) = 1.

The ith term in L^c for either such pair is just one, so they contribute nothing to the conditional likelihood function. When we take logs, these terms (and these observations) will drop out. But suppose that the two observations are zero and one. Then

$$\text{Prob}(0 \text{ and } 1 \,|\, \text{sum} = 1) = \frac{\text{Prob}(0 \text{ and } 1 \text{ and sum} = 1)}{\text{Prob}(\text{sum} = 1)}$$

$$= \frac{\text{Prob}(0 \text{ and } 1)}{\text{Prob}(0 \text{ and } 1) + \text{Prob}(1 \text{ and } 0)}.$$

---

[35] See the discussion of Section 20.3.3.

[36] In principle, his technique is not limited to small T. However, the amount of computation rises geometrically with T and becomes excessive for T larger than about five or six.

Therefore, for this pair of observations, the conditional probability is

$$\frac{\dfrac{1}{1+e^{\alpha_i+\beta'\mathbf{x}_{i1}}}\dfrac{e^{\alpha_i+\beta'\mathbf{x}_{i2}}}{1+e^{\alpha_i+\beta'\mathbf{x}_{i2}}}}{\dfrac{1}{1+e^{\alpha_i+\beta'\mathbf{x}_{i1}}}\dfrac{e^{\alpha_i+\beta'\mathbf{x}_{i2}}}{1+e^{\alpha_i+\beta'\mathbf{x}_{i2}}}+\dfrac{e^{\alpha_i+\beta'\mathbf{x}_{i1}}}{1+e^{\alpha_i+\beta'\mathbf{x}_{i1}}}\dfrac{1}{1+e^{\alpha_i+\beta'\mathbf{x}_{i2}}}}=\frac{e^{\beta'\mathbf{x}_{i2}}}{e^{\beta'\mathbf{x}_{i1}}+e^{\beta'\mathbf{x}_{i2}}}. \qquad (20\text{--}69)$$

By conditioning on the sum of the two observations, we have been able to remove the heterogeneity. Therefore, we can construct the conditional likelihood function as the product of these terms for the pairs of observations for which the two observations are (0, 1). Pairs of observations with one and zero are included analogously. The product of the terms such as the preceding, for those observation sets for which the sum is not zero or T, constitutes the conditional likelihood. Maximization of the resulting function is straightforward and may be done by conventional methods.[37]

As in the linear regression model, it is of some interest to test whether there is, indeed, heterogeneity. With homogeneity ($\alpha_i = \alpha$), there is no unusual problem, and the model can be estimated, as usual, as a logit model. However, it is not possible to test the hypothesis using the likelihood ratio test, because the two likelihoods are not comparable. (The conditional likelihood is based on a restricted data set.) None of the usual tests of restrictions can be used because the individual effects are never actually estimated. However, Hausman's (1978) specification test is a natural one to use here. Under the null hypothesis of homogeneity, both Chamberlain's conditional maximum likelihood estimator (CMLE) and the usual maximum likelihood estimator are consistent, but Chamberlain's is inefficient. (It fails to use the information that $\alpha_i = \alpha$, and it may not use all of the data.) Under the alternative hypothesis, the unconditional maximum likelihood estimator is inconsistent, while Chamberlain's estimator is consistent and efficient. The Hausman test can be based on the chi-squared statistic

$$\chi^2 = (\hat{\beta}_{ML} - \hat{\beta}_{CML})'(\text{Var}[CML] - \text{Var}[ML])^{-1}(\hat{\beta}_{ML} - \hat{\beta}_{CML}). \qquad (20\text{--}70)$$

The estimated variance matrices are those computed by the usual methods for the two maximum likelihood estimators. For the maximum likelihood estimator, the row and column corresponding to the constant term are dropped. A large value will cast doubt on the hypothesis of homogeneity. (There are K degrees of freedom for the test.) It is possible that the variance matrix for the maximum likelihood estimator will be larger than that for the conditional maximum likelihood estimator. If so, the difference matrix in brackets is assumed to be a zero matrix, and the chi-squared statistic is therefore zero.

EXAMPLE 20.9.   Cecchetti (1986) applied Chamberlain's model in a study of the frequency of the price changes for a sample of 38 magazines observed over a 27-year period. The constant term for each magazine was allowed to change every 3 years, implying a total of 318 free parameters. The data were analyzed in 9-year subperiods, so a cross-section unit in our earlier notation consists of $T = 3$ periods. Since a price change could occur in any period, the sums of y_{it} were zero, one, two, or three. The model included as regressors (1) the time since the last price change, (2) inflation since the last price change, (3) the size of the last price change, (4) current inflation, (5) industry sales growth, and (6) a measure of sales volatility. The most important determinants of the probability of a price change were found

---

[37] The log likelihood is globally concave, and Newton's method is quite effective.

Table 20.5. (Asymptotic t ratios are given in parentheses; slopes are computed at regressor means.)

	Coefficient	Marginal Effect
Time since last change	0.79 (2.68)	0.13 (0.94)
Inflation since last change	24.18 (2.94)	3.98 (1.07)
Previous change	−6.33 (1.50)	−1.04 (1.40)
Current inflation	−27.60 (1.97)	−4.54 (1.14)
Industry sales growth	7.93 (2.23)	1.30 (0.98)
Sales volatility	0.15 (1.45)	0.024 (0.74)

to be (1), (2), and (5). In none of Cecchetti's models was the Hausman statistic less than 40, indicating that the data did exhibit heterogeneity.

Among his results, Cecchetti reports the data listed in Table 20.5. The model suggests that the most important determinant of the probability of a price increase is the path of inflation. An increase in the current inflation rate of 5 percent reduces the probability of a price increase in this period by 0.028. [This is 0.05 times 3.98 + (−4.54).] But in the following year, if there is no additional inflation, the effect of the previous year's 5 percent increase in inflation will be to raise the probability by 0.05(3.98) = 0.199.

20.3.4b. *Bivariate Outcomes—The Bivariate Probit Model*

In Chapter 17, we analyzed a number of different multiple-equation extensions of the classical and generalized regression. A natural extension of the probit model would be to allow more than one equation, with correlated disturbances, in the same spirit as the seemingly unrelated regressions model. The general specification for a two-equation model would be

$$y_1^* = \boldsymbol{\beta}_1' \mathbf{x}_1 + \varepsilon_1, \qquad y_1 = 1 \text{ if } y_1^* > 0, 0 \text{ otherwise,}$$

$$y_2^* = \boldsymbol{\beta}_2' \mathbf{x}_2 + \varepsilon_2, \qquad y_2 = 1 \text{ if } y_2^* > 0, 0 \text{ otherwise,}$$

$$E[\varepsilon_1] = E[\varepsilon_2] = 0,$$

$$\text{Var}[\varepsilon_1] = \text{Var}[\varepsilon_2] = 1, \qquad (20\text{--}71)$$

$$\text{Cov}[\varepsilon_1, \varepsilon_2] = \rho.$$

A multivariate model would extend this in an obvious fashion.

In principle, this model can be estimated using familiar maximum likelihood techniques. The problem is made extremely difficult, however, by the integrals of the bivariate and multivariate normal distributions. Reasonably efficient approximations have been devised for the bivariate normal distribution. Some progress has been made on trivariate integrals, but existing results are not sufficient to allow accurate and efficient evaluation for more than two variables in a sample of even moderate size. Therefore, applications of the model have been limited to two equations.

EXAMPLE 20.10.   Greene (1984) reports estimates of a model of voter behavior in two decisions, whether to send at least one child to public school and whether to vote in favor of a school budget.[38] Regressors in the model were "income," "taxes" = property taxes paid, and

---

[38] Data for the study are given in Pindyck and Rubinfeld (1981) and Rubinfeld (1977).

Table 20.6

	Single Equation	Bivariate
	Public School	
Constant	−4.972 (3.996)	−4.764 (4.009)
Income	0.1537 (0.4495)	0.1149 (0.5958)
Taxes	0.6440 (0.5654)	0.6699 (0.7226)
	School Budget	
Constant	−0.6862 (4.009)	−0.3066 (3.850)
Income	0.9961 (0.4404)	0.9895 (0.4863)
Taxes	−1.2646 (0.5672)	−1.3080 (0.6748)
Years	−0.01644 (0.0147)	−0.0176 (0.0136)
Correlation	0.0	0.317 (0.2303)
Log likelihood	−40.0830 + −58.5006	−97.4117

"years" of residence in the community. The results in Table 20.6 were obtained using 95 observations.

Bivariate normal probabilities are a bit cumbersome to specify. We shall employ a useful shorthand. First, define

$$q_1 = 2y_{i1} - 1$$

and

$$q_2 = 2y_{i2} - 1.$$

Thus, $q_j = 1$ if $y_{ij} = 1$ and -1 if $y_j = 0$ for $j = 1$ and 2.[39] The bivariate normal cdf is

$$\text{Prob}[X_1 < x_1, X_2 < x_2] = \int_{-\infty}^{x_2} \int_{-\infty}^{x_1} \phi_2(z_1, z_2, \rho)\, dz_1\, dz_2,$$

which we denote $\Phi_2(x_1, x_2, \rho)$. The density (which was given in Chapter 3) is

$$\phi_2(x_1, x_2, \rho) = \frac{e^{-1/2(x_1^2 + x_2^2 - 2\rho x_1 x_2)/(1 - \rho^2)}}{2\pi(1 - \rho^2)^{1/2}}. \tag{20-72}$$

Now let

$$z_1 = \boldsymbol{\beta}_1' \mathbf{x}_{i1}, \qquad w_1 = q_1 z_{i1},$$

$$z_2 = \boldsymbol{\beta}_2' \mathbf{x}_{i2}, \qquad w_2 = q_2 z_{i2},$$

$$\rho_* = q_1 q_2 \rho.$$

In addition:

Note the notational convention. The subscript 2 is used to indicate the bivariate normal density, ϕ_2 and cdf, Φ_2. In all other cases, the subscript 2 indicates the variables in the second equation in (20–71). As before, ϕ and Φ denote the univariate density and cdf.

[39] To save some notation, we have dropped the observation subscript.

We can now construct the log likelihood to use for parameter estimation. The probabilities that enter the likelihood function are

$$\text{Prob}[y_1 = y_1, y_2 = y_2] = \Phi_2(w_1, w_2, \rho_*). \tag{20-73}$$

(This accounts for all of the necessary sign changes needed to compute probabilities for y's equal to zero and one.) Thus,

$$\ln L = \sum_i \ln \Phi_2(w_1, w_2, \rho_*). \tag{20-74}$$

The derivatives of the bivariate distribution are rather complicated. But, using the previous simplifications, they reduce to

$$\frac{\partial \ln L}{\partial \beta_1} = \sum_i \left(\frac{q_1 g_1}{\Phi_2}\right) \mathbf{x}_1$$

$$\frac{\partial \ln L}{\partial \beta_2} = \sum_i \left(\frac{q_2 g_2}{\Phi_2}\right) \mathbf{x}_2 \tag{20-75}$$

$$\frac{\partial \ln L}{\partial \rho} = \sum_i \frac{q_1 q_2 \phi_2}{\Phi_2},$$

where

$$g_1 = \phi(w_1)\Phi\left[\frac{w_2 - \rho_* w_1}{(1 - \rho_*^2)^{1/2}}\right],$$

$$g_2 = \phi(w_2)\Phi\left[\frac{w_1 - \rho_* w_2}{(1 - \rho_*^2)^{1/2}}\right]. \tag{20-76}$$

Note that the derivatives are functions of the univariate normal distribution and are, therefore, simple to compute.[40] The derivative with respect to ρ is also surprisingly simple. Before considering the Hessian, it is useful to note what becomes of the preceding if $\rho = 0$. For $\partial \ln L/\partial \beta_1$, if $\rho = \rho_* = 0$, g_1 reduces to $\phi(w_1)\Phi(w_2)$, ϕ_2 is $\phi(w_1)\phi(w_2)$, and $\Phi_2 = \Phi(w_1)\Phi(w_2)$. Inserting these in (20-75) with q_1 and q_2 produces (20-34). Since $\Phi_2 = \Phi(w_1)\Phi(w_2)$ is not a function of ρ, $\partial \ln L/\partial \rho$ is zero.

The maximum likelihood estimates are obtained by simultaneously setting the three derivatives to zero. The second derivatives are relatively straightforward but tedious. Some simplifications are useful. Let

$$\delta = \frac{1}{\sqrt{1 - \rho_*^2}},$$

$$v_1 = \delta(w_2 - \rho_* w_1), \quad \text{so} \quad g_1 = \phi(w_1)\Phi(v_1),$$

$$v_2 = \delta(w_1 - \rho_* w_2), \quad \text{so} \quad g_2 = \phi(w_2)\Phi(v_2).$$

By multiplying it out, you can show that

$$\phi(w_1)\phi(v_1) = \phi(w_2)\phi(v_2) = \phi_2.$$

---

[40] This suggests that a trivariate model could be estimated, since the derivatives of the trivariate normal distribution are functions of the bivariate normal integrals. In obtaining the parameters, gradient methods need not actually compute the log-likelihood function. The function itself is needed only for hypothesis testing. A study that uses this result is Hausman and Wise (1978).

Then

$$\frac{\partial^2 \ln L}{\partial \boldsymbol{\beta}_1 \partial \boldsymbol{\beta}_1'} = \sum_i \mathbf{x}_1 \mathbf{x}_1' \left[\frac{-w_1 \phi(w_1)\Phi(v_2) - \rho_* \delta \phi_2}{\Phi_2} - \frac{g_1^2}{\Phi_2^2} \right],$$

$$\frac{\partial^2 \ln L}{\partial \boldsymbol{\beta}_1 \partial \boldsymbol{\beta}_2'} = \sum_i q_1 q_2 \mathbf{x}_1 \mathbf{x}_2' \left[\frac{\delta \phi_2}{\Phi_2} - \frac{g_1 g_2}{\Phi_2^2} \right],$$

$$\frac{\partial^2 \ln L}{\partial \boldsymbol{\beta}_1 \partial \rho} = \sum_i q_2 \mathbf{x}_1 \phi_2 \delta^2 \left[\rho_* \delta (w_2 - \rho_* w_1) - \frac{w_1}{\delta} \right],$$

$$\frac{\partial^2 \ln L}{\partial \rho^2} = \sum_i \frac{\phi_2}{\Phi_2} \left[\rho_* + \delta^2 (1 + \rho_*^2) w_1 w_2 - \frac{\phi_2^2}{\Phi_2^2} \right].$$

(For $\boldsymbol{\beta}_2$, change the subscripts in $\partial^2 \ln L/\partial \boldsymbol{\beta}_1 \partial \boldsymbol{\beta}_1'$ and $\partial^2 \ln L/\partial \boldsymbol{\beta}_1 \partial \rho$ accordingly.) The complexity of the second derivatives for this model makes it an excellent candidate for the Berndt et al. estimator of the variance matrix of the maximum likelihood estimator.

Even though it is (almost) impossible to estimate higher-dimensional models, it is possible to test for correlation among the equations. The Lagrange multiplier test is a natural device in this setting. Under the null hypothesis that ρ equals zero, the model consists of independent probit equations, which can be estimated separately. Moreover, in the multivariate model, all of the bivariate (or multivariate) densities and probabilities factor into the products of the marginals if the correlations are zero. This makes construction of the test statistic a simple matter of manipulating the results of the independent probits. The Lagrange multiplier statistic for testing $H_0: \rho = 0$ in a bivariate probit model is[41]

$$\text{LM} = \frac{g^2}{h}, \tag{20-77}$$

where

$$g = \sum_i q_1 q_2 \frac{\phi(w_1)\phi(w_2)}{\Phi(w_1)\Phi(w_2)}$$

and

$$h = \sum_i \frac{[\phi(w_1)\phi(w_2)]^2}{\Phi(w_1)\Phi(-w_1)\Phi(w_2)\Phi(-w_2)}.$$

EXAMPLE 20.11.   Continuing the preceding example, we find that there are three ways in which we may test the hypothesis that ρ equals zero. A simple t test is equivalent to the Wald test. The square of the t ratio is the Wald statistic. Under the null hypothesis, the log likelihood is the sum of the log likelihoods for the two independent probits. The Lagrange multiplier statistic is computed as shown earlier, using only the two independent probits. The results are

Wald statistic	1.8947,
Likelihood ratio	2.3438,
Lagrange multiplier	2.0581.

All three statistics suggest that the hypothesis that ρ equals zero cannot be rejected.

---

[41] This is derived in Kiefer (1982).

Table 20.7

	Coefficients			Ratios		
	Linear	Probit	Logit	Lg./Pr.	Ln./Lg.	Ln./Pr.
Const.	−1.498	−7.4523	−13.02	—	—	—
GPA	0.4639	1.6258	2.826	1.74	0.164	0.285
PSI	0.3786	1.4263	2.379	1.67	0.159	0.265
TUCE	0.0105	0.0517	0.095	1.84	0.110	0.203

20.3.4c. Linear Regression

In his survey of qualitative response models, Amemiya (1981) reports the following widely cited approximations for the linear probability (LP) model: Over the range of probabilities of 30 to 70 percent,

$$\hat{\beta}_{LP} \simeq 0.4\hat{\beta}_{probit} \text{ for the slopes}^{42} \tag{20-78}$$

and

$$\hat{\beta}_{LP} \simeq 0.25\hat{\beta}_{logit} \text{ for the slopes.} \tag{20-79}$$

Aside from confirming our intuitive belief that least squares approximates the nonlinear model and providing a quick comparison for the three models involved, the practical usefulness of the formula is somewhat limited. Still, it is a striking result.[43] A recent series of papers has focused on reasons why the least squares estimates should be proportional to the probit and logit models. A related question concerns the problems associated with assuming that a probit model applies when, in fact, a logit model is appropriate, or vice versa.[44] The approximations would seem to suggest that with this type of misspecification, we would, once again, obtain a scaled version of the correct coefficient vector.[45]

EXAMPLE 20.12. Aldrich and Nelson (1984) report the estimates listed in Table 20.7 for a model of the effect of a teaching method known as PSI on the performance of students in a macroeconomics course.[46] The dependent variable is "Grade," an indicator of whether the students' grades on exams in the class improved after exposure to PSI. The regressors are a constant; "GPA," their grade point average; "TUCE," a pretest score indicating entering knowledge of the material; and "PSI," a dummy variable indicating whether they had the new teaching method or not.

A number of authors have analyzed the conditions under which projections of y on $\mathbf{x}$ (i.e., linear regressions) estimate scaled versions of the true coefficient vector. The approach taken by Greene (1983)[47] is to assume that the probit model is correct and, in addition, that

---

[42] An additional 0.5 is added for the constant term in both models.

[43] This does not imply that it is useful to report 2.5 times the linear probability estimates with the probit estimates for comparability. The linear probability estimates are already in the form of marginal effects, while the probit estimates must be scaled *downward*. If the sample proportion happens to be close to 0.5, the right scale factor will be roughly $\phi[\Phi^{-1}(0.5)] = \phi[0] = 0.3989$. But the density falls rapidly as P moves away from 0.5, so the 0.4 scale factor will be inappropriate.

[44] See Ruud (1986).

[45] Amemiya also reports the widely observed relationship $\hat{\beta}_{logit} \simeq 1.6\hat{\beta}_{probit}$. See Example 20.1 for a clear example and Example 20.3 for discussion.

[46] The source of their example is Spector and Mazzeo (1980).

[47] This builds on earlier work by Goldberger, especially (1981).

the regressors are themselves multivariate normally distributed. He then derives the probability limit of the least squares estimator. Not surprisingly, under these assumptions,

$$\text{plim } \mathbf{b} = c\beta, \tag{20-80}$$

where c is a scalar that depends on some population parameters. That is, under the assumption of multinormality of the regressors, the proportionality result is to be expected. As a side result, Greene finds that c is estimable using the sample data, so a "moment" estimator of the true β can be obtained by dividing the least squares coefficients by $\hat{c}$. The method is detailed in Example 20.13.

EXAMPLE 20.13. Unscaling the Probit Coefficients.   The correction factors are based on the following least squares statistics:

$$a = \text{constant term}$$

$$\mathbf{b} = \text{coefficient vector}$$

$$R^2 = \text{coefficient of determination}$$

$$P = \text{sample proportion of ones.}$$

Necessary preliminary calculations are

$$d = \Phi^{-1}(P), \tag{20-81}$$

$$f = \phi(d).$$

Then,

$$\hat{c} = f\left[1 - \frac{R^2 P(1-P)}{f^2}\right]^{1/2}.$$

The slope coefficients are estimated by

$$\hat{\beta} = \frac{\mathbf{b}}{\hat{c}}, \tag{20-82}$$

while the constant term is estimated with

$$\hat{\alpha} = \frac{a}{\hat{c}} - \frac{P + fd}{\hat{c}}. \tag{20-83}$$

Aldrich and Nelson report that $P = \frac{11}{32} = 0.34375$ and $R^2 = 0.4159$. Therefore, $d = \Phi^{-1}(0.34375) = -0.402$ and $f = \phi(-0.402) = 0.368$. Inserting the relevant parts, $\hat{c} = 0.20397$. For the results given earlier, we have the data given in Table 20.8. The corrected least squares results are reasonably close to the maximum likelihood estimates. The approxi-

Table 20.8

	OLS	Probit MLE	Corrected	Amemiya
Constant	-1.498	-7.4523	-8.3043	-4.995
GPA	0.4639	1.6258	2.2744	1.1598
PSI	0.3786	1.4263	1.8562	0.9465
TUCE	0.0105	0.0517	0.0515	0.0263

mation is slightly more cumbersome than Amemiya's. It will frequently perform better because it makes use of the sample proportion of ones, which, as he notes, will affect the accuracy of the computation.

The side result that assumes that the regressors are joint normally distributed is useful only for the same purpose as Amemiya's quick correction. Multivariate normality is obviously quite inconsistent with most applications. In the example, for instance, PSI is a dummy variable. However, Cheung and Goldberger (1984) have shown that much weaker conditions than joint normality will achieve the same proportionality result. For a probit model, they require only that $E[\mathbf{x} \mid y^*]$ be linear in y^*. Several authors have built on these observations to pursue the issue of what circumstances will lead to proportionality results such as these. Stoker (1986) has extended these results to a very wide class of models that goes well beyond those of Cheung and Goldberger.[48]

20.4.   Models for Multiple Choices

Some recent studies of multiple-choice settings include the following:

1. Hensher (1986), McFadden (1974), and many others have analyzed the travel mode of urban commuters.
2. Schmidt and Strauss (1975a and 1975b) and Boskin (1974) have analyzed occupational choice among multiple alternatives.
3. Terza (1985) has studied the assignment of bond ratings to corporate bonds as a choice among multiple alternatives.

These are all distinct from the multivariate probit model we examined earlier. In that setting, there were several decisions, each between two alternatives. Here there is a single decision among two or more alternatives. We will examine two broad types of choice sets, *ordered* and *unordered*. The choice among means of getting to work, by car, bus, train, or bicycle, is clearly unordered. However, a bond rating is, by design, a ranking—that is its purpose. As we shall see, quite different techniques are used for the two types of models.

20.4.1.   Unordered Multiple Choices

Unordered-choice models can be motivated by a random utility model. For the ith consumer faced with J choices, suppose that the utility of choice j is

$$U_{ij} = \boldsymbol{\beta}' \mathbf{z}_{ij} + \varepsilon_{ij}. \qquad (20-84)$$

If the consumer makes choice j in particular, we assume that U_{ij} is the maximum among the J utilities. Hence, the statistical model is driven by the probability that choice j is made, which is

$$\text{Prob}[U_{ij} > U_{ik}] \qquad \text{for all other } k \neq j. \qquad (20-85)$$

The model is made operational by a particular choice of distribution for the disturbances. As before, two models have been considered, logit and probit. As in the multivariate probit case, because of the need to evaluate multiple integrals of the normal distribution, the probit

---

[48] It is noteworthy that his results specifically exclude dummy variables, but it is those for which the proportionality result seems to be most robust. See the Example 20.13 and Greene (1981).

model has found rather limited use in this setting. Let Y_i be a random variable indicating the choice made. McFadden (1973) has shown that if (and only if) the J disturbances are independent and identically distributed with Weibull distribution,

$$F(\varepsilon_{ij}) = e^{-e^{-\varepsilon_{ij}}}, \tag{20-86}$$

then

$$\text{Prob}[Y_i = j] = \frac{e^{\boldsymbol{\beta}'\mathbf{z}_{ij}}}{\sum_j e^{\boldsymbol{\beta}'\mathbf{z}_{ij}}}. \tag{20-87}$$

This leads to what is called the *conditional logit model*.[49]

Utility depends on $\mathbf{x}_{ij}$, which includes aspects specific to the individual as well as to the choices. It is useful to distinguish them. Let $\mathbf{z}_{ij} = [\mathbf{x}_{ij}, \mathbf{w}_i]$. Then $\mathbf{x}_{ij}$ varies across the choices and possibly across the individuals as well. (The components of $\mathbf{x}_{ij}$ are typically called the **attributes** of the choices.) But $\mathbf{w}_i$ contains the characteristics of the individual and is, therefore, the same for all choices. If we incorporate this in the model, (20–87) becomes

$$\text{Prob}[Y_i = j] = \frac{e^{\boldsymbol{\beta}'\mathbf{z}_{ij} + \boldsymbol{\alpha}'\mathbf{w}_i}}{\sum_j e^{\boldsymbol{\beta}'\mathbf{z}_{ij} + \boldsymbol{\alpha}'\mathbf{w}_i}}. \tag{20-88}$$

Terms that do not vary across alternatives, that is, those specific to the individual, fall out of the probability. Evidently, if the model is to allow individual specific effects, it must be modified. One method is to create a set of dummy variables for the choices and multiply each of them by the common $\mathbf{w}$. We then allow the coefficient to vary across the choices instead of the characteristics.

EXAMPLE 20.14.   A model of shopping center choice by individuals might specify that the choice depends on attributes of the shopping centers such as number of stores and distance from the central business district, both of which are the same for all individuals, and income, which varies across individuals. Suppose that there were three choices. The three regressor vectors would be as follows:

Choice 1: Stores Distance Income   0   0

Choice 2: Stores Distance   0   Income   0

Choice 3: Stores Distance   0   0   Income

The parameter vector is β_1, β_2, α_1, α_2, and α_3. However, we have isolated the third income variable. To avoid the dummy variable trap in this model, we must drop the third (last) dummy variable. [If we fail to do this, the Hessian, (either actual or expected), will be singular the first time it is computed, and the model will be inestimable.] The normalization we would use here is α_3 (α_J) = 0.

The data sets typically analyzed by economists do not contain mixtures of individual- and choice-specific attributes. Such data would be far too costly to gather for most purposes. When they do, the preceding framework can be used. For the present, it is useful to examine the two types of data separately and consider aspects of the model that are specific to the two types of applications.

---

[49] It is occasionally labeled the *multinomial logit model*, but this conflicts with the usual name for the model discussed in the next section, which differs slightly.

20.4.1a.   The Multinomial Logit Model

To set up the model that applies when data are individual specific, it will help to consider an example.

EXAMPLE 20.15.   Schmidt and Strauss (1975a and 1975b) estimated a model of occupational choice based on a sample of 1000 observations drawn from the Public Use Samples for three years, 1960, 1967, and 1970.[50] For each sample, the data for each individual in the sample consist of the following:

1. Occupation: $1 =$ menial, $2 =$ blue   collar, $3 =$ craft, $4 =$ white   collar, $5 =$ professional.

2. Regressors: Constant, Education, Experience, Race, Sex.

Schmidt and Strauss coded the outcomes 1, 2, 3, 4, and 5. For consistency with our earlier models, we will relabel them 0, 1, 2, 3, and 4. The model for occupational choice is, then,

$$\text{Prob}(Y = j) = \frac{e^{\beta'_j x_i}}{\sum_{k=0}^{4} e^{\beta'_k x_i}}. \tag{20-89}$$

The model in (20–89) is the **multinomial logit model**.[51] The estimated equations provide a set of probabilities for the $J + 1$ choices for a decision maker with characteristics x_i. Before proceeding, we must remove an indeterminacy in the model. If we define $\beta^*_j = \beta_j + q$ for any nonzero vector q, the identical set of probabilities result, as the terms involving q all drop out. A convenient normalization that solves the problem is to assume that $\beta_0 = 0$.[52] The probabilities are, therefore,

$$\text{Prob}(Y = j) = \frac{e^{\beta'_j x_i}}{1 + \sum_{k=0}^{4} e^{\beta'_k x_i}} \qquad \text{for } j = 1, 2, \ldots, J.$$

$$\text{Prob}(Y = 0) = \frac{1}{1 + \sum_{k=0}^{4} e^{\beta'_k x_i}}. \tag{20-90}$$

The binomial case examined in Section 20.3 is now the special case with $J = 1$.

The coefficients in this model are difficult to interpret. By differentiating (20–90), we find that the marginal effects of the regressors on the probabilities are

$$\frac{\partial P_j}{\partial x} = P_j \left[\beta_j - \sum_k P_k \beta_k \right]. \tag{20-91}$$

These can be computed from the parameter estimates. (See the following example.) Standard errors can be estimated using the results of the last section but are likely to be exceedingly complex.[53] The model implies that we can compute J log-odds ratios

$$\ln \left[\frac{P_{ij}}{P_{io}} \right] = \beta'_j x_i. \tag{20-92}$$

[50] U.S. Bureau of the Census (1970).
[51] Nerlove and Press (1973).
[52] The alternative, $\sum_{j=0}^{J} \beta_j = 0$, has been suggested, for example, by Nerlove and Press.
[53] The literature contains relatively few studies in which the marginal effects and *their* standard errors are presented. The usual focus is on the coefficient estimates. Equation (20–91) suggests that there is at least some potential for confusion. Note, for example, that for any particular x_k, $\partial P_j / \partial x_k$ need not have the same sign as β_{jk}.

We could normalize on any other probability as well and obtain

$$\ln\left[\frac{P_{ij}}{P_{ik}}\right] = \mathbf{x}_i'(\boldsymbol{\beta}_j - \boldsymbol{\beta}_k).^{54}$$

From the point of view of estimation, it is useful that the odds ratio, P_j/P_k, does not depend on the other choices. This follows from the independence of disturbances in the original model. From a behavioral viewpoint, this is not so attractive. We shall return to this problem later.

Estimation of the multinomial logit model is straightforward. Newton's method will normally find a solution very readily unless the data are badly conditioned. The log likelihood can be derived by defining, for each individual, $d_{ij} = 1$ if alternative j is chosen by individual i, and 0 if not, for the $J + 1$ possible outcomes. Then, for each i, one and only one of the d_{ij}'s is one. The log likelihood is a generalization of that for the binomial probit or logit model:

$$\ln L = \sum_i \sum_{j=0}^{J} d_{ij} \ln \text{Prob}[Y_i = j]. \tag{20-93}$$

The derivatives have the characteristically simple form

$$\frac{\partial \ln L}{\partial \boldsymbol{\beta}_j} = \sum_i [d_{ij} - P_{ij}]\mathbf{x}_i \qquad \text{for } j = 1, \ldots, J. \tag{20-94}$$

The exact second derivatives matrix has J^2 blocks, each $K \times K$.

The jth diagonal block is $\sum_i - P_{ij}(1 - P_{ij})\mathbf{x}_i\mathbf{x}_i'.$

$$\tag{20-95}$$

The jkth off-diagonal block is $\sum_i (P_{ij}P_{ik})\mathbf{x}_i\mathbf{x}_i'.$

Since the Hessian does not involve d_{ij}, these are the expected values, and Newton's method is equivalent to the method of scoring. The Berndt et al. method can be used instead by summing the outer products of the first derivatives. However, this will rarely be an improvement because of the very simple form and global concavity of the log likelihood. It is worth noting that the number of parameters in this model proliferates with the number of choices. This is unfortunate, as the typical cross section sometimes involves a fairly large number of regressors.

Finding adequate fit measures in this setting presents the same difficulties as in the binomial models. As before, it is useful to report the log likelihood. The hypothesis that all of the slope coefficients are zero is simple to test *if the regressor vector includes a constant term.* If so, the restricted log likelihood is

$$\ln L_0 = \sum_{j=0}^{J} n_j \ln P_j,$$

where P_j is the sample proportion of observations that make choice j. If desired, the likelihood ratio index can also be reported. A useful table will give a listing of hits and misses of the prediction rule "predict $Y_j = j$ if P_j is the maximum of the predicted probabilities."[55]

---

[54] Schmidt and Strauss present the 10 unique possible pairings for their model.
[55] Unfortunately, it is common for this rule to predict all observations with the same value in an unbalanced sample or a model with little explanatory power.

20.4.1b. *The Conditional Logit Model*

When the data consist of choice-specific attributes instead of individual-specific characteristics, the appropriate model is that of (20–87):

$$\text{Prob}[Y_i = j] = \frac{e^{\beta' z_{ij}}}{\sum_j e^{\beta' z_{ij}}}. \tag{20–96}$$

Here, we let $j = 1, 2, \ldots, J$ for a total of J alternatives. The model is otherwise essentially the same as the multinomial logit. However, even more care will be required in interpreting the parameters. Once again, an example will help to focus ideas.

EXAMPLE 20.16. Hensher (1986) estimated a model of mode choice for urban travel for a sample of Sydney commuters. The four choices were Car/Driver (C/D), Car/Passenger, Train, and Bus. For a basic model, the attributes were (1) a Car/Driver dummy, (2) a Car/Passenger dummy, (3) a Train dummy, (4) In-Vehicle Time (in minutes), (5) Waiting Time (in minutes), (6) Walking Time (in minutes), (7) In-Vehicle Costs, (8) Parking Cost, (9) Number of Household Business Vehicles Required, and (10) Percentage of Travel Cost Covered by a Nonhousehold Source ((9) and (10) for C/D only). The sample consists of 1455 observations. A summary of the data is given in Table 20.9.

Hensher reports the results listed in Table 20.10.

At the sample means given here, the four predicted probabilities and predicted frequencies are given in Table 20.11.

Table 20.9. Summary Statistics for Model Structure

	In-Veh. Cost	In-Veh. Time	Walk Time	Wait Time	Number Choosing
C/D	64.56	28.65	0.76	0.15	953
C/P	4.37	28.32	0.71	2.89	78
Train	98.23	43.84	10.50	8.37	279
Bus	81.61	38.15	7.47	7.11	145

C/D only: Parking cost = 26.59
         Household business vehicles = 0.186
         Percent travel cost paid for = 17.58

Source: Hensher (ibid., p. 14). Standard deviations given by Hensher are omitted.

Table 20.10. Parameter Estimates. (*t* values are in parentheses.)

(1)	0.8973 (4.86)	(2)	−2.2154 (−10.36)
(3)	1.3286 (9.10)	(4)	−0.0227 (−4.70)
(5)	−0.1336 (−6.68)	(6)	−0.0672 (−5.44)
(7)	−0.0063 (−5.03)	(8)	−0.0086 (−5.05)
(9)	0.4524 (1.83)	(10)	0.0119 (3.71)

Log likelihood at $\beta = 0$ = −2017.1
Log likelihood (sample shares) = −1426.6
Log likelihood at convergence = −598.2

Table 20.11

	C/D	C/P	Train	Bus
Probability	0.88625	0.03799	0.01390	0.06186
Predicted N	1290	55	20	90
Actual N	953	78	279	145

Elasticities of Probabilities
with Respect to In-vehicle Cost

Attribute Level of:

Mode	CD	CP	Train	Bus
CD	−0.077	0.253	0.253	0.253
CP	0.002	−0.013	0.002	0.002
Train	0.098	0.098	−0.231	0.098
Bus	0.042	0.042	0.042	−0.292

In this model, the coefficients are not directly tied to the marginal effects. The marginal effects for continuous variables can be obtained by differentiating (20–96) with respect to $\mathbf{x}$ to obtain

$$\frac{\partial P_j}{\partial \mathbf{x}_j} = P_j(1 - P_j)\boldsymbol{\beta},$$

$$\frac{\partial P_j}{\partial \mathbf{x}_k} = -P_j P_k \boldsymbol{\beta}. \tag{20-97}$$

(To avoid cluttering the notation, we have dropped the observation subscript.) It is clear that through its presence in P_j and P_k, every attribute set $\mathbf{x}_j$ affects all of the probabilities. Hensher suggests that one might prefer to report elasticities of the probabilities. These would be

$$\frac{\partial \ln P_j}{\partial \ln x_{jm}} = \beta_m x_{jm}(1 - P_j),$$

$$\frac{\partial \ln P_j}{\partial \ln x_{km}} = -\beta_m x_{km} P_j. \tag{20-98}$$

Since there is no ambiguity about the scale of the probability itself, whether one should report the derivatives or the elasticities is largely a matter of taste. Some of Hensher's elasticity estimates are presented in the previous example.

Estimation of the conditional logit model is simplest by Newton's method or the method of scoring. The log likelihood is the same as for the multinomial logit model. Once again, we define $d_{ij} = 1$ if $Y_i = j$ and 0 otherwise. Then

$$\ln L = \sum_i d_{ij} \ln \text{Prob}[d_{ij} = 1]. \tag{20-99}$$

Because of the simple form of L, the gradient and Hessian have particularly convenient forms:

$$\frac{\partial \ln L}{\partial \beta} = \sum_i \sum_j P_{ij}(\mathbf{x}_{ij} - \bar{\mathbf{x}}_i) \tag{20--100}$$

$$\frac{\partial^2 \ln L}{\partial \beta \partial \beta'} = -\sum_i \sum_j P_{ij}(\mathbf{x}_{ij} - \bar{\mathbf{x}}_i)(\mathbf{x}_{ij} - \bar{\mathbf{x}}_i)', \tag{20--101}$$

where

$$\bar{\mathbf{x}}_i = \sum_j P_{ij}\mathbf{x}_{ij}.$$

Once again, Newton's method and the method of scoring are equivalent and should converge readily. In this setting, the size of the estimation problem is independent of the number of choices. It is feasible to estimate a model for up to 100 or more alternatives. (Whether it is reasonable to model consumer choices with this many alternatives is a different question.) A data set constructed with more than a few choices is likely to be quite cumbersome. In this context, it is the data that proliferate with the number of choices, and far faster than the number of parameters did in the previous model. Every new choice added to the set adds a new row to the data set for every observation. For the example, the four-outcome model requires $4 \times 1455 = 5820$ rows. Adding only one more alternative would add another 1455 rows of data.

The usual problems of fit measures appear here. The log-likelihood ratio and tabulation of actual versus predicted choices will be useful. There are two possible constrained log likelihoods. Since the model cannot contain a constant term, the constraint $\beta = 0$ renders all probabilities equal to $1/J$. The constrained log likelihood for this constraint is then $L_0 = -n \ln J$. Of course, it is unlikely that this hypothesis would fail to be rejected. Alternatively, we could fit the model with only the $J - 1$ choice-specific dummy variables. This makes the constrained log likelihood the same as in the multinomial logit model, $\ln L_0^* = \sum_j n_j \ln P_j$.

20.4.1c. *The Independence of Irrelevant Alternatives*

We noted earlier that the odds ratios in the multinomial logit or conditional logit models are independent of the other alternatives. This is a convenient property as regards estimation, but it is not a particularly appealing restriction to place on consumer behavior. The property of the logit model whereby P_j/P_k is independent of the remaining probabilities is termed the **independence of irrelevant alternatives**. An example of the problem is suggested by Hensher's data. The model allocates 89 percent of the passengers to cars as drivers. Thus, the odds ratio between cars as drivers and buses is 0.89/0.06, or about 14.8 to 1. Suppose that we differentiate by type of car, domestic and foreign, and it happens to be an even split. We would expect the 89 percent of the population who drive to work to divide themselves evenly and the others to continue as they did before. Unfortunately, if they do, the odds between each car type and bus will fall to 7.4 to 1. In order to preserve the 14.8 to 1 odds ratio between cars and buses, half of the bus riders will be switched either to the train or to cars as passengers.

The independence assumption follows from the initial assumption that the disturbances are independent.[56] Two tests have been developed for testing the validity of the assumption.

---

[56] Albright et al. (1977).

Hausman and McFadden (1984) suggest that if a subset of the choice set truly is irrelevant, omitting it from the model altogether will not change parameter estimates systematically. Inclusion of these choices will be inefficient but will not lead to inconsistency. But if the remaining odds ratios are not truly independent of these alternatives, the parameter estimates obtained when these choices are eliminated will be inconsistent. This is the usual basis for Hausman's specification test. The statistic is

$$\chi^2 = (\hat{\boldsymbol{\beta}}_s - \hat{\boldsymbol{\beta}}_f)'[\hat{\mathbf{V}}_s - \hat{\mathbf{V}}_f]^{-1}(\hat{\boldsymbol{\beta}}_s - \hat{\boldsymbol{\beta}}_f), \qquad (20\text{--}102)$$

where s indicates the estimators based on the restricted subset, f indicates the estimator based on the full set of choices, and $\hat{\mathbf{V}}_s - \hat{\mathbf{V}}_f$ are the respective estimates of the asymptotic covariance matrices. The statistic is asymptotically distributed as chi-squared with K degrees of freedom.[57]

EXAMPLE 20.17.   In the previous example, are the odds ratios CD to Bus and CD to Train really independent of the presence of the CP alternative? To use the Hausman test, we would eliminate choice 2, CP, from the choice set and estimate a three-choice model. Since 78 respondents chose this mode, we would lose 78 observations. In addition, for every data vector left in the sample, the second attribute, which is the CP dummy, would always be zero. Thus, this parameter could not be estimated. We would drop this variable. The test would be based on the two estimators of the nine remaining parameters.

If the independence of irrelevant alternatives test fails, an alternative to the multinomial logit model may be needed. The natural alternative is a multivariate probit model:

$$U_j = \boldsymbol{\beta}'\mathbf{x}_j + \varepsilon_j, \qquad j = 1, \ldots J.$$
$$[\varepsilon_1, \varepsilon_2, \ldots, \varepsilon_J] \sim N[0, \boldsymbol{\Sigma}]. \qquad (20\text{--}103)$$

We had considered this model earlier but found that as a general model of consumer choice, its failing was the practical difficulty of computing the multinormal integral. Hausman and Wise (1978) point out that for a model of consumer choice, the probit model may not be so impractical as it might seem. First, for J choices, the comparisons implicit in $U_j > U_k$ for $k \neq j$ involve the $J - 1$ differences, $\varepsilon_j - \varepsilon_k$. Thus, starting with a J-dimensional problem, we need only consider $J - 1$ order probabilities. Second, as we saw earlier, the derivatives of the L-variate normal distribution involve only $L - 1$ variate probabilities. It is not necessary to compute the log-likelihood function in order to maximize it, only its derivatives. Therefore, to come to a concrete example, a model with four choices requires only the evaluation of bivariate normal integrals, which is well within the received technology.

Other procedures have been suggested that show some promise of raising the four-choice limit. Lerman and Manski (1981) suggest a sampling approach to the calculation of normal probabilities. In brief, if we desire the probability of a certain event from $N[0, \boldsymbol{\Sigma}]$, we can simulate draws from this distribution and tabulate the relative proportion of draws that fall in the desired range. Given the enormous number of draws needed to achieve a satisfactory degree of accuracy and the fact that the process would have to be repeated three times for every parameter for each observation each time the vector of derivatives is needed, which typically would be three times per iteration, it is unlikely that this procedure could be efficiently employed except in an extremely small data set with very few parameters. (The authors reach a similar conclusion.) Another procedure, suggested by Clark (1961), offers some potential. The approach is based on the distribution of the maximum in a subset of a set

---

[57] McFadden (1987) shows how this hypothesis can also be tested using a Lagrange multiplier test.

of random variables. Daganzo et al. (1977) have analyzed this method and suggest that it is, indeed, efficient enough to be practical. But Maddala (1983, p. 64) has seriously questioned the accuracy of the method in models general enough to be used for consumer choice. This leaves us, of course, back where we were before, with either the multinomial logit model or a four-choice multinomial probit model.

20.4.2. Ordered Data

Some multinomial-choice variables are inherently ordered. Examples that have appeared in the literature are the following:

1. Bond ratings.
2. Results of taste tests.
3. Opinion surveys.
4. The assignment of military personnel to job classifications by skill level.
5. Voting outcomes on certain programs.
6. The level of insurance coverage taken by a consumer: none, part, or full.
7. Employment: unemployed, part time, or full time.

In each of these cases, although the outcome is discrete, the multinomial logit or probit models would fail to account for the ordinal nature of the dependent variable.[58] However, ordinary regression analysis would err in the opposite direction. Take the outcome of an opinion survey. If the responses are coded $0, 1, 2, 3$, or 4, linear regression would treat the difference between a 4 and a 3 the same as that between a 3 and a 2, while in fact they are only a ranking.

The ordered probit and logit models have come into fairly wide use as a framework for analyzing such responses (Zavoina and McElvey, 1975). The model is built around a latent regression in the same manner as the binomial probit model. We begin with

$$\mathbf{y}^* = \boldsymbol{\beta}'\mathbf{x} + \varepsilon. \tag{20-104}$$

As usual, y^* is unobserved. What we do observe is

$$
\begin{aligned}
y &= 0 && \text{if } y^* \le 0, \\
&= 1 && \text{if } 0 \le y^* < \mu_1, \\
&= 2 && \text{if } \mu_1 \le y^* < \mu_2, \\
&\;\;\vdots \\
&= J && \text{if } \mu_{J-1} \le y^*.
\end{aligned}
\tag{20-105}
$$

This is a form of censoring. The μ's are unknown parameters to be estimated with β. Consider, for example, an opinion survey. The respondents have their own intensity of feeling, which depends on certain measurable factors, $\mathbf{x}$, and certain unobservable factors, ε. In principle, they could respond to the questionnaire with their own y^* if asked to do so.

---

[58] In two recent papers, Beggs, et al. (1981) and Hausman and Ruud (1986), the authors have begun to explore the possibility of using a richer specification of the logit model when respondents provide their rankings of the full set of alternatives in addition to the identity of the most preferred choice. This application falls somewhere between the conditional logit model and the ones we shall discuss here, in that rather than provide a single choice among J either unordered or ordered alternatives, the consumer chooses one of the $J!$ possible orderings of the set of unordered alternatives.

Given only, say, five possible answers, they choose the cell that most closely represents their own feelings on the question.

As before, we assume that ε is normally distributed across observations. For the same reasons as in the binomial probit model (which is the special case here of $J = 1$), we normalize the mean and variance of ε to zero and one. (The model can also be estimated with a logistically distributed disturbance. This is a trivial modification of the formulation and appears to make virtually no difference in practice.) With the normal distribution, we have the following probabilities:

$$\text{Prob}[y = 0] = \Phi(-\beta'x),$$

$$\text{Prob}[y = 1] = \Phi(\mu_1 - \beta'x) - \Phi(-\beta'x),$$

$$\text{Prob}[y = 2] = \Phi(\mu_2 - \beta'x) - \Phi(\mu_1 - \beta'x), \qquad (20\text{--}106)$$

$$\vdots$$

$$\text{Prob}[y = J] = 1 - \Phi(\mu_{J-1} - \beta'x).$$

In order for all of the probabilities to be positive, we must have

$$0 < \mu_1 < \mu_2 < \cdots < \mu_{J-1}.$$

Figure 20.6 shows the implications of the structure. It is evident that this is a generalization of the probit model we looked at earlier. The log-likelihood function and its derivatives can be obtained readily, and optimization can be done by the usual means.

As usual, the marginal effects of the regressors, $\mathbf{x}$, on the probabilities are not equal to the coefficients. It is helpful to consider a simple example. Suppose that there are three categories. This implies only one unknown threshold parameter. The three probabilities are

$$\text{Prob}[y = 0] = 1 - \Phi(\beta'x),$$

$$\text{Prob}[y = 1] = \Phi(\mu - \beta'x) - \Phi(-\beta'x),$$

$$\text{Prob}[y = 2] = 1 - \Phi(\mu - \beta'x).$$

For the three probabilities, the marginal effects of changes in the regressors are

$$\frac{\partial \text{Prob}[y = 0]}{\partial \mathbf{x}} = -\phi(\beta'x)\beta,$$

$$\frac{\partial \text{Prob}[y = 1]}{\partial \mathbf{x}} = (\phi(-\beta'x) - \phi(\mu - \beta'x))\beta,$$

$$\frac{\partial \text{Prob}[y = 2]}{\partial \mathbf{x}} = \phi(\mu - \beta'x)\beta.$$

Figure 20.7 illustrates the effect. The probability distributions of y and y^* are shown in the solid curve. Increasing one of the $\mathbf{x}$'s while holding β and μ constant is equivalent to shifting the distribution slightly to the right, which is shown as the dashed curve. The effect of the shift is unambiguously to shift some mass out of the leftmost cell. Assuming that β is positive (for this $\mathbf{x}$), this means that $\text{Prob}[y = 0]$ must decline. Alternatively, from the previous expression, it is obvious that the derivative of $\text{Prob}[y = 0]$ has the opposite sign from β. By a similar logic, the change in $\text{Prob}[y = 2]$ (or $\text{Prob}[y = J]$ in the general case) must have the same sign as β. Assuming that the particular β is positive, we are shifting some probability into the rightmost cell. But what happens to the middle cell is ambiguous. It depends on the

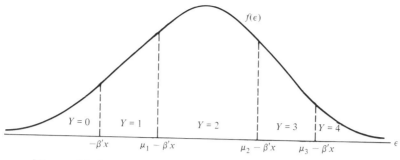

Figure 20.6 Probabilities in the ordered probit model.

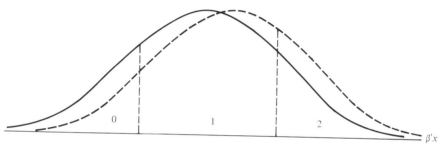

Figure 20.7 Effects of change in x on predicted probabilities.

two densities. In the general case, relative to the signs of the coefficients, only the signs of the changes in $\text{Prob}[y = 0]$ and $\text{Prob}[y = J]$ are unambiguous! The upshot is that we must be very careful in interpreting the coefficients in this model. This is the least obvious of all of the models we have considered. Indeed, without a fair amount of extra calculation, it is quite unclear how the coefficients in the ordered probit model should be interpreted.[59]

EXAMPLE 20.18. Rating Assignments Marcus and Greene (1985) estimated an or-dered probit model for the job assignments of new Navy recruits. The Navy attempts to direct recruits into job classifications in which they will be most productive. The broad classifications the authors analyzed were technical jobs with three clearly ranked skill ratings: "medium skilled," "highly skilled," and "nuclear qualified/highly skilled." Since the assignment is partly based on the Navy's own assessment and needs and partly on factors specific to the individual, an ordered probit model was used with the following determinants: (1) ENSPE = a dummy variable indicating that the individual entered the Navy with an "A school" (technical training) guarantee, (2) EDMA = educational level of the entrant's mother, (3) AFQT = score on the Air Force Qualifying Test, (4) EDYRS = years of education completed by the trainee, (5) MARR = a dummy variable indicating that the

---

[59] This point seems uniformly to be overlooked in the received literature. Authors routinely report coefficients and t ratios, occasionally with some commentary about significant effects, but rarely suggest upon what or in what direction those effects are exerted.

individual was married at the time of enlistment, and (6) AGEAT = trainee's age at the time of enlistment. The sample size was 5641. The results are reported in Table 20.12. The extremely large t ratio on the AFQT score is to be expected, since it is a primary sorting device used to assign job classifications. In order to obtain the marginal effects of the continuous variables, we require the standard normal density evaluated at $-\beta'x = -0.8479$ and $\mu - \beta'x = 0.9421$. Inserting the mean values for the regressors produces -0.8479 and 0.9421, so the predicted probabilities are $\Phi(-0.8479) = 0.198$, $\Phi(0.9421) - \Phi(-0.8479) = 0.628$, and $1 - \Phi(0.9421) = 0.173$. (The actual frequencies were 0.25, 0.52, and 0.23.) The two densities are $\phi(-0.8479) = 0.278$ and $\phi(0.9421) = 0.255$. Therefore, the derivatives of the three probabilities with respect to AFQT, for example, are:

$$\frac{\partial P_0}{\partial AFQT} = (-0.278)0.039 \qquad = -0.01084,$$

$$\frac{\partial P_1}{\partial AFQT} = (0.278 - 0.255)0.039 = 0.0009,$$

$$\frac{\partial P_2}{\partial AFQT} = 0.255(0.039) \qquad = 0.00995.$$

Note that the marginal effects sum to zero; this follows from the requirement that the probabilities add to one. This approach is not appropriate for evaluating the effect of a dummy variable. We can analyze a dummy variable by comparing the probabilities that result when the variable takes its two different values with those that occur with the other variables held at their sample means. For example, for the MARR variable, we have the results given in Table 20.13.

Table 20.12

Variable	Estimate	t Ratio	Mean of Variable
Constant	−4.34	—	—
ENSPA	0.057	1.7	0.66
EDMA	0.007	0.8	12.1
AFQT	0.039	39.9	71.2
EDYRS	0.190	8.7	12.1
MARR	−0.48	−9.0	0.08
AGEAT	0.0015	0.1	18.8
μ	1.79	80.8	—

Table 20.13

	$-\hat{\beta}'x$	$\hat{\mu} - \hat{\beta}'x$	Prob[$y = 0$]	Prob[$y = 1$]	Prob[$y = 2$]
MARR = 0	−0.8863	0.9037	0.187	0.629	0.184
MARR = 1	−0.4063	1.3837	0.342	0.574	0.084
Change			0.155	−0.055	−0.100

Table 20.14

	A	B	C	D	E	60–64	65–69	70–74	75–79	Service	Actual	Fitted
	Ship Type					**Year Constructed**				**Accidents**		
1	1	0	0	0	0	1	0	0	0	127	0	3.12
2	1	0	0	0	0	0	1	0	0	63	4	4.63
3	1	0	0	0	0	0	0	1	0	1,095	18	14.70
4	1	0	0	0	0	0	0	0	1	2,244	11	10.54
5	0	1	0	0	0	1	0	0	0	17,176	29	23.05
6	0	1	0	0	0	0	1	0	0	20,370	53	54.38
7	0	1	0	0	0	0	0	1	0	13,099	44	52.85
8	0	1	0	0	0	0	0	0	1	7,117	18	13.71
9	0	0	1	0	0	1	0	0	0	1,179	1	0.55
10	0	0	1	0	0	0	1	0	0	676	1	0.76
11	0	0	1	0	0	0	0	1	0	1,948	2	2.50
12	0	0	1	0	0	0	0	0	1	274	1	1.20
13	0	0	0	1	0	1	0	0	0	251	0	1.44
14	0	0	0	1	0	0	1	0	0	288	0	2.16
15	0	0	0	1	0	0	0	1	0	1,208	11	6.76
16	0	0	0	1	0	0	0	0	1	2,051	4	4.64
17	0	0	0	0	1	1	0	0	0	45	0	1.84
18	0	0	0	0	1	0	1	0	0	789	7	3.06
19	0	0	0	0	1	0	0	1	0	2,161	12	10.19
20	0	0	0	0	1	0	0	0	1	542	1	4.92

20.4.3. A Poisson Regression Model for Count Data

The data on ship accidents analyzed in Example 8.2 are typical of count data. (They are reproduced in Example 20.19.) In principle, we could analyze them using multiple linear regression, as we did in Example 8.2. But the preponderance of zeroes and small values and the clearly discrete nature of the dependent variable suggest that we could improve on least squares with a model that accounts for these characteristics. The Poisson regression model has been widely used to study such data.

EXAMPLE 20.19.   The number of accidents for a sample of ships are listed in Table 20.14. The ships are one of five types constructed in one of four periods. Service is an indicator of the amount of service the ship has seen.[60]

The Poisson regression model has been used by a number of authors to analyze count data. The model stipulates that each y_i is drawn from a Poisson distribution with parameter λ_i, which is related to the regressors, $\mathbf{x}_i$. The primary equation of the model is

$$\text{Prob}(Y_i = y_i) = \frac{e^{-\lambda_i}\lambda_i^{y_i}}{y_i!}, \qquad y_i = 0, 1, 2, \ldots$$

The most common formulation for λ_i is

$$\ln \lambda_i = \boldsymbol{\beta}'\mathbf{x}_i.$$

[60] Data are from McCullagh and Nelder (1983). See Example 8.2 for details.

It is easily shown that

$$E[y_i \mid \mathbf{x}_i] = \operatorname{Var}[y_i \mid \mathbf{x}_i] = \lambda_i$$
$$= e^{\boldsymbol{\beta}'\mathbf{x}_i},$$

so

$$\frac{\partial E[y \mid \mathbf{x}]}{\partial \mathbf{x}} = \lambda_i \boldsymbol{\beta}.$$

With the parameter estimates in hand, this can be computed using any data vector desired.

In principle, the Poisson model is simply a nonlinear regression. But it is far easier to estimate the parameters with maximum likelihood techniques. The log-likelihood function is

$$\ln L = \sum_i [-\lambda_i + y_i \boldsymbol{\beta}'\mathbf{x}_i - \ln y_i!].$$

The likelihood equations are

$$\frac{\partial \ln L}{\partial \boldsymbol{\beta}} = \sum_i (-\lambda_i + y_i)\mathbf{x}_i = \mathbf{0}.$$

The Hessian is

$$\frac{\partial^2 \ln L}{\partial \boldsymbol{\beta} \partial \boldsymbol{\beta}'} = -\sum_i \lambda_i \mathbf{x}_i \mathbf{x}_i'.$$

The Hessian is negative definite for all $\mathbf{x}$ and $\boldsymbol{\beta}$. Newton's method is a simple algorithm for this model and will usually converge rapidly. At convergence, $[\sum_i \hat{\lambda}_i \mathbf{x}_i \mathbf{x}_i']^{-1}$ provides an estimate of the asymptotic covariance matrix for the parameter estimates. Given the estimates, the prediction for observation i is $\hat{\lambda}_i$. A standard error for the prediction interval can be formed by using a linear Taylor series approximation. The estimated variance of prediction will be $\lambda_i^2 \mathbf{x}_i' \mathbf{V} \mathbf{x}_i$, where $\mathbf{V}$ is the estimated asymptotic covariance matrix for $\boldsymbol{\beta}$.

EXAMPLE 20.20.   A Poisson regression model is shown in Table 20.15.

Table 20.15

	Unrestricted		Restricted
Log likelihood	−46.799		−69.931
Scale factor for slopes	0.11207		0.08540
Restricted (slopes = 0) log L		−199.899	
Mean dependent variable		10.85	

Variable	Coefficient	Asy. t Ratio	Coefficient	Asy. t Ratio
Constant	1.1211	4.0890	2.0433	11.680
Type = B	−0.43206	−0.98213	0.41778	1.2278
Type = C	−1.8946	−3.9455	−1.8960	−3.9509
Type = D	−0.79328	−2.5474	−0.79275	−2.5458
Type = E	−0.51914	−1.8295	−0.50046	−1.7661
65–69	0.40292	1.6845	—	—
70 – 74	1.4109	6.1860	—	—
75 – 79	0.91409	3.1294	—	—
Service	0.0001426	4.6418	0.00007340	3.9668

The hypothesis that the year of construction is not a significant factor in explaining the number of accidents is strongly rejected by the likelihood ratio test.

$$\chi^2 = -2[-69.931 - (-46.799)] = 46.264.$$

The Poisson regression model has been criticized because of its implicit assumption that the variance equals the mean. Some extensions that relax this assumption may be found in McCullagh and Nelder (1983), Cameron and Trivedi (1986), and Hausman et al. (1984).

Exercises

1. A binomial probability model is to be based on the following index function model:

$$y^* = \alpha + \beta d + \varepsilon,$$
$$y = 1 \quad \text{if } y^* > 0,$$
$$y = 0 \quad \text{otherwise.}$$

The only regressor, d, is a dummy variable. The data consist of 100 observations that have the following:

	y	
	0	1
d = 0	24	28
d = 1	32	16

Obtain the maximum likelihood estimators of α and β, and estimate the asymptotic standard errors of your estimates. Test the hypothesis that β equals zero by using a Wald test (asymptotic t test) and a likelihood ratio test. Use the probit model and then repeat, using the logit model. Do your results change? (**Hint:** Formulate the log likelihood in terms of α and $\delta = \alpha + \beta$.)

2. Compute the marginal effects and interpret the estimated coefficients presented in Example 20.5. For the income variable, what would be the effect on the predicted probability of a 1 percent increase in the median family income at the average of $13,963?

3. Suppose that a linear probability model is to be fit to a set of observations on a dependent variable, y, which takes values zero and one, and a single regressor, x, which varies continuously across observations. Obtain the exact expressions for the least squares slope in the regression in terms of the mean(s) and variance of x, and interpret the result.

4. Given the following data set,

$$Y: \quad 1 \ 0 \ 0 \ 1 \ 1 \ 0 \ 0 \ 1 \ 1 \ 1,$$
$$X: \quad 9 \ 2 \ 5 \ 4 \ 6 \ 7 \ 3 \ 5 \ 2 \ 6,$$

estimate a probit model, and test the hypothesis that X is not influential in determining the probability that Y equals one.

5. Construct the Lagrange multiplier statistic for testing the hypothesis that all of the slopes (but not the constant term) equal zero in the binomial logit model. Prove that the Lagrange multiplier statistic is nR^2 in the regression of $(y_i - P)$ on the x's, where P is the sample proportion of ones.

6. We are interested in the ordered probit model of (10–104) and (20–105). Our data consist of 250 observations, of which the responses are

$$Y = 0 \quad 1 \quad 2 \quad 3 \quad 4$$

$$n \quad 50 \quad 40 \quad 45 \quad 80 \quad 35$$

Using the preceding data, obtain maximum likelihood estimates of the unknown parameters of the model. (**Hint:**   Consider the probabilities as the unknown parameters.)

7. Prove (20–38).

8. The following hypothetical data give the participation rates in a particular type of recycling program and the number of trucks purchased for collection by 10 towns in a small mid-Atlantic state:

Town	Trucks	Participation (%)
1	160	11
2	250	74
3	170	8
4	365	87
5	210	62
6	206	83
7	203	48
8	305	84
9	270	71
10	340	79

The town of Eleven is contemplating initiating a recycling program but wishes to achieve a 95 percent rate of participation. Using a probit model for your analysis,

(a) How many trucks would the town expect to have to purchase in order to achieve their goal? Use (20–14), (20–15), and (20–23). Note that in (20–23) you will use $n_t = 1$.

(b) If trucks cost $20,000 each, is a goal of 90 percent reachable within a budget of $6.5 million? (That is, should they *expect* to reach the goal?)

(c) According to your model, what is the marginal value of the 301st truck in terms of the increase in the percentage participation?

References

Abramovitz, M., and I. Stegun, *Handbook of Mathematical Functions*, New York: Dover Publications, 1972.

Albright, R., S. Lerman, and C. Manski, "Report on the Development of an Estimation Program for the Multinomial Probit Model," Washington, D.C.: Federal Highway Administration, 1977.

Aldrich, J., and F. Nelson, *Linear Probability, Logit, and Probit Models*, Beverly Hills, Calif.: Sage, 1984.

Amemiya, T., "Qualitative Response Models: A Survey," *Journal of Economic Literature*, 19, 1981, pp. 1483–1536.

Amemiya, T., *Advanced Econometrics*, Cambridge, Mass.: Harvard University Press, 1985.

Beggs, S., S. Cardell, and J. Hausman, "Assessing the Potential Demand for Electric Cars," *Journal of Econometrics*, 17, 1981, pp. 1–19.

Blundell, R., ed., "Specification Testing in Limited and Discrete Dependent Variable Models," *Journal of Econometrics*, 34, 1/2, 1987, pp.1–274.

Boskin, M., "A Conditional Logit Model of Occupational Choice," *Journal of Political Economy*, 82, 1974, pp. 389–398.

Butler, J., and R., Moffitt, "A Computationally Efficient Quadrature Procedure for the One Factor Multinomial Probit Model." *Econometrica*, 50, 1982, pp. 761–764.

Cameron, A., and P. Trivedi, "Econometric Models Based on Count Data: Comparisons and Applications of Some Estimators and Tests," *Journal of Applied Econometrics*, 1, 1986, pp. 29–54.

Cecchetti, S., "The Frequency of Price Adjustment: A Study of the Newsstand Prices of Magazines," *Journal of Econometrics*, 31, 1986, pp. 255–274.

Chamberlain, G., "Analysis of Covariance with Qualitative Data," *Review of Economic Studies*, 47, 1980, pp. 225–238.

Chamberlain, G., "Asymptotic Efficiency in Semi-Parametric Models with Censoring," *Journal of Econometrics*, 32, 1986, pp. 189–218.

Cheung, C., and A. Goldberger, "Proportional Projections in Limited Dependent Variable Models," *Econometrica*, 52, 1984, pp. 531–534.

Clark, C., "The Greatest of a Finite Set of Random Variables," *Operations Research*, 9, 1961, pp. 145–162.

Cox, D., *Analysis of Binary Data*, London: Methuen, 1970.

Cragg, J., and R., Uhler, "The Demand for Automobiles," *Canadian Journal of Economics*, 3, 1970, pp. 386–406.

Daganzo, C., F. Bouthelier, and Y. Sheffi, "Multinomial Probit and Qualitative Choice—A Computationally Efficient Algorithm," *Transportation Science*, 11, 1977, pp. 338–358.

Davidson R., and J. MacKinnon, "Convenient Specification Tests for Logit and Probit Models," *Journal of Econometrics*, 25, 1984, pp. 241–262.

Dempster, A., N. Laird, and D. Rubin, "Maximum Likelihood Estimation from Incomplete Data via the EM Algorithm" *Journal of the Royal Statistical Society, Series B*, 39, 1977, pp. 1–38.

Dhrymes, P., "Limited Dependent Variables," in Z. Griliches and M. Intrilligator, eds., *Handbook of Econometrics*, Vol. 2, Amsterdam: North Holland, 1984.

Duncan, G., ed., "Continuous/Discrete Econometric Models with Unspecified Error Distribution," *Journal of Econometrics*, 32, 1, 1986, pp. 1–187.

Engle, R., "Wald, Likelihood Ratio, and Lagrange Multiplier Tests in Econometrics," in Z. Griliches and M. Intrilligator, eds., *Handbook of Econometrics*, Amsterdam: North Holland, 1983.

Finney, D., *Probit Analysis*, Cambridge: Cambridge University Press, 1971.

Fomby, T., R. Hill, and N. Johnson, *Advanced Econometrics*, New York, Springer-Verlag, 1984.

Goldberger, A., "Linear Regression After Selection," *Journal of Econometrics*, 15, 1981, pp. 357–366.

Goldberger, A., "Abnormal Selection Bias," in S. Karlin, T. Amemiya, and L. Goodman, eds., *Studies in Econometrics, Time Series, and Multivariate Statistics*, New York: Academic Press, 1983.

Greene, W., "On the Asymptotic Bias of the Ordinary Least Squares Estimator of the Tobit Model," *Econometrica*, 49, 1981, pp. 505–514.

Greene, W., "Estimation of Limited Dependent Variable Models by Ordinary Least Squares and the Method of Moments," *Journal of Econometrics*, 21, 1983, pp. 195–212.

Greene, W., "Estimation of the Correlation Coefficient in a Bivariate Probit Model Using the Method of Moments," *Economics Letters*, 16, 1984, pp. 285–291.

Hartley, M., "The Tobit and Probit Models: Maximum Likelihood Estimation by OLS," State University of New York, Buffalo, Department of Economics, Working Paper Number 375, 1976.

Hausman, J., "Specification Tests in Econometrics," *Econometrica*, 46, 1978, pp. 1251–1271.

Hausman, J., B. Hall, and Z. Griliches, "Econometric Models for Count Data with an Application to the Patents–R&D Relationship," *Econometrica*, 52, 1984, pp. 909–938.

Hausman, J., and D. McFadden, "A Specification Test for the Multinomial Logit Model," *Econometrica*, 52, 1984, pp. 1219–1240.

Hausman, J., and P. Ruud, "Specifying and Testing Econometric Models for Rank Ordered Data with an Application to the Demand for Mobile and Portable Telephones," University of California, Berkeley, Department of Economics, Working Paper 8605, 1986.

Hausman, J., and D. Wise, "A Conditional Probit Model for Qualitative Choice: Discrete Decisions

Recognizing Interdependence and Heterogeneous Preferences," *Econometrica*, 46, 1978, pp. 403–426.

Heckman, J., "Sample Selection Bias as a Specification Error," *Econometrica*, 47, 1979, pp. 153–161.

Heckman, J., and R. Willis, "Estimation of a Stochastic Model of Reproduction: An Econometric Approach," in N. Terleckyj, ed., *Household Production and Consumption*, National Bureau of Economic Research, New York, 1976.

Hein, D., "Predicted and Actual Frequencies in Binomial Response Models," *Economics Letters*, 23, 1987, pp. 104–108.

Hensher, D., "Simultaneous Estimation of Hierarchical Logit Mode Choice Models," Macquarie University, School of Economic and Financial Studies, Working Paper Number 24, 1986.

Johnson, N., and S., Kotz, *Distributions is Statistics: Continuous Univariate Distributions*, New York: Wiley, 1971.

Kiefer, N., "Testing for Independence in Multivariate Probit Models," *Biometrika*, 69, 1982, pp. 161–166.

Lerman, R., and C. Manski, "On the Use of Simulated Frequencies to Approximate Choice Probabilities," in C. Manski and D. McFadden, eds., *Structural Analysis of Discrete Data with Econometric Applications*, Cambridge, Mass.: MIT Press, 1981.

Maddala, G., *Limited Dependent and Qualitative Variables in Econometrics*, Cambridge: Cambridge University Press, 1983.

Manski, C., "The Maximum Score Estimation of the Stochastic Utility Model of Choice," *Journal of Econometrics*, 3, 1975, pp. 313–333.

Manski, C, "Semiparametric Analysis of Discrete Response: Asymptotic Properties of the Maximum Score Estimator," *Journal of Econometrics*, 27, 1985, pp. 313–333.

Manski, C., and D. McFadden, *Structural Analysis of Discrete Data with Econometric Applications*, Cambridge, Mass.: MIT Press, 1981.

Marcus, A., and W. Greene, "The Determinants of Rating Assignment and Performance," Center for Naval Analyses, Working Paper CRC528, 1985.

McCullagh, P., and J. Nelder, *Generalized Linear Models*, London: Chapman and Hall, 1983, p. 137.

McFadden, D., "Conditional Logit Analysis of Qualitative Choice Behavior," in P. Zarembka, ed., *Frontiers in Econometrics*, New York: Academic Press, 1973.

McFadden, D., "The Measurement of Urban Travel Demand," *Journal of Public Economics*, 3, 1974, pp. 303–328.

McFadden, D., "Econometric Analysis of Qualitative Response Models," in Z. Griliches and M. Intrilligator, eds., *Handbook of Econometrics*, Vol. 2, Amsterdam: North Holland, 1984.

McFadden, D., "Regression Based Specification Tests for the Multinomial Logit Model," *Journal of Econometrics*, 34, 1987, pp. 63–82.

Nakosteen, R., and M. Zimmer, "Migration and Income: The Question of Self-Selection," *Southern Economic Journal*, 46, 1980, pp. 840–851.

Nerlove, M., and S. Press, "Univariate and Multivariate Log-Linear and Logistic Models," RAND—R1306-EDA/NIH, Santa Monica, Calif., 1973.

Pindyck, R., and D. Rubinfeld, *Econometric Models and Economic Forecasts*, New York: McGraw-Hill, 1981.

Poirier, D., "Partial Observability in Bivariate Probit Models," *Journal of Econometrics*, 12, 1980, pp. 209–217.

Robinson, C., and N. Tomes, "Self Selection and Interprovincial Migration in Canada," *Canadian Journal of Economics*, 15, 1982, pp. 474–502.

Rubinfeld, D., "Voting in a Local School Election: A Micro Analysis," *Review of Economics and Statistics*, 59, 1977, pp. 30–42.

Ruud, P., "Specification Errors in Limited Dependent Variable Models," Ph.D. thesis, Department of Economics, Massachusetts Institute of Technology, Cambridge, 1981.

Ruud, P., "Consistent Estimation of Limited Dependent Variable Models Despite Misspecification of the Distribution," *Journal of Econometrics*, 32, 1986, pp. 157–187.

Schmidt, P., and R. Strauss, "The Prediction of Occupation Using Multiple Logit Models," *International Economic Review*, 16, 1975a, pp. 471–486.

Schmidt, P., and R. Strauss, "Estimation of Models with Jointly Dependent Qualitative Variables: A Simultaneous Logit Approach," *Econometrica*, 43, 1975b, pp. 745–755.

Spector, L., and M. Mazzeo, "Probit Analysis and Economic Education," *Journal of Economic Education*, 11, 1980, pp. 37–44.

Stoker, T., "Consistent Estimation of Scaled Coefficients," *Econometrica*, 54, 1986, pp. 1461–1482.

Terza, J., "Ordinal Probit: A Generalization," *Communications in Statistics*, 14, 1985, pp. 1–12.

Tunali, I., "Geographic Mobility, Earnings, and Selectivity: From Theory to Fact—Evidence from Turkey, 1963–1973," Ph.D. thesis, Department of Economics, University of Wisconsin, Madison, 1985.

Tunali, I., "A General Structure for Models of Double Selection and an Application to a Joint Migration/Earnings Process with Remigration," *Research in Labor Economics*, 8, 1986, pp. 235–282.

U.S. Bureau of the Census, *Public Use Samples of Basic Records from the 1970 Census*, Washington, D.C.: U.S. Government Printing Office, 1972.

Willis, R., and S. Rosen, "Education and Self-Selection," *Journal of Political Economy*, 87, 1979, pp. S7–S36.

Wynand, P., and M. Bernard, "The Demand for Deductibles in Private Health Insurance: A Probit Model with Sample Selection," *Journal of Econometrics*, 17, 1981, pp. 229–252.

Yatchew, A. and Z. Griliches, "Specification Error in Probit Models," *Review of Economics and Statistics*, 66, 1984, pp. 134–139.

Zavoina, T., and W. McElvey, "A Statistical Model for the Analysis of Ordinal Level Dependent Variables," *Journal of Mathematical Sociology*, Summer 1975, pp. 103–120.

Chapter 21

Limited Dependent Variable Models

21.1. Introduction

This chapter is concerned with truncation and censoring.[1] The effect of truncation occurs when sample data are drawn from a subset of a larger population of interest. For example, studies of income based on incomes above or below some poverty line may be of limited usefulness for inference about the whole population. This is essentially a characteristic of the distribution from which the sample data are drawn. Censoring is a more common problem in recent studies. To continue the example, suppose that instead of being unobserved, incomes below the poverty line are reported as if they were *at* the poverty line. The censoring of a range of values of the variable of interest introduces a distortion into conventional statistical results similar to that of truncation. Unlike truncation, however, censoring is essentially a defect in the sample data. Presumably, if they were not censored, the data would be a representative sample from the population of interest.

This chapter deals with three broad topics: truncation, censoring, and a form of truncation called the *sample selection problem*. Although most of the recent empirical work in this area involves censoring rather than truncation, we shall study the simpler model of truncation first. It provides most of the theoretical tools we need to analyze models of censoring and sample selection. In each section, we present some important distribution theory, describe methods of regression analysis, and, finally, consider some related topics and applications. A number of results are collected in an appendix.

21.2. Truncation

In this section, we are concerned with inferring the characteristics of a population from a sample drawn from a restricted part of that population.

> **EXAMPLE 21.1.** "The typical 'upper affluent American'... makes $142,000 per year.... The people surveyed had household incomes of at least $100,000."[2] Does this statistic tell

---

[1] Four recent surveys of these topics are Dhrymes (1984), Maddala (1983), Maddala (1984), and Amemiya (1984). The last is part of a symposium on censored and truncated regression models.
[2] *New York Post* (1987).

us anything about the "typical American"? As it stands, probably not (popular impressions notwithstanding). The article goes on to state, "If you're in that category, pat yourself on the back—only 2 percent of American households make the grade, according to the survey."

21.2.1. Truncated Distributions

For our purposes, a truncated distribution is the part of an untruncated distribution that is above or below some specified value. For instance, in Example 21.1, we are given a characteristic of the distribution of incomes above $100,000. This is, of course, only a part of the full distribution.

Theorem 21.1. Density of a Truncated Random Variable. If a continuous random variable, x, has pdf $f(x)$ and a is a constant,

$$f(x\,|\,x > a) = \frac{f(x)}{\text{Prob}[x > a]}.^3 \tag{21-1}$$

The proof follows from the definition of conditional probability. This amounts to scaling the density so that it integrates to one over the range above a.

EXAMPLE 21.2.   If x has a uniform distribution, $U(0, 1)$,

$$f(x) = 1, \qquad 0 \le x \le 1.$$

Consider truncation at $x = \frac{1}{3}$. From (21–1),

$$f\left(x\,\Big|\,x > \frac{1}{3}\right) = \frac{f(x)}{\text{Prob}[x > \frac{1}{3}]}$$

$$= \frac{1}{\left(\frac{2}{3}\right)}$$

$$= \frac{3}{2}, \qquad \frac{1}{3} < x \le 1.$$

Most recent applications use the **truncated normal distribution**. If z has a normal distribution with mean μ and standard deviation σ,

$$\text{Prob}[z > a] = 1 - \Phi\left(\frac{a - \mu}{\sigma}\right) \tag{21-2}$$

$$= 1 - \Phi(\alpha),$$

where

$$\alpha = \frac{(a - \mu)}{\sigma}$$

and

$$\Phi(.) \text{ is the standard normal cdf.}$$

---

³ The case of truncation from above instead of below is handled in an analogous fashion and does not require any new results.

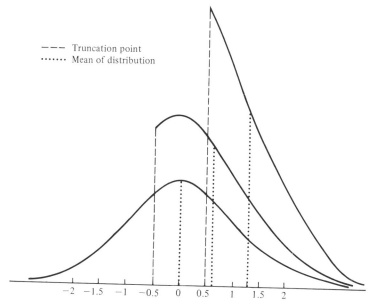

Figure 21.1   Truncated normal distributions.

The truncated normal distribution is, then,

$$
\begin{aligned}
f(z \mid z > a) &= \frac{f(z)}{1 - \Phi(\alpha)} \\
&= \frac{(2\pi\sigma^2)^{-1/2} e^{-(z-\mu)^2/2\sigma^2}}{1 - \Phi(\alpha)} \qquad (21-3) \\
&= \frac{(1/\sigma)\phi((z-\mu)/\sigma)}{1 - \Phi(\alpha)},
\end{aligned}
$$

where $\phi(.)$ is the standard normal pdf. The **truncated standard normal distribution**, with $\mu = 0$ and $\sigma = 1$, is illustrated for $a = -0.5$, 0, and 0.5 in Figure 21.1. For convenience in what follows, we shall call a random variable whose distribution is truncated a **truncated random variable**.

21.2.2.   Moments of Truncated Distributions

We are usually interested in the mean and variance of the truncated random variable. These would be obtained in the usual fashion:

$$
E[x \mid x > a] = \int_a^\infty x f(x \mid x > a)\, dx \qquad (21-4)
$$

for the mean, and likewise for the variance.

EXAMPLE 21.3.   For the uniformly distributed random variable in Example 21.2,

$$
E[x \mid x > \tfrac{1}{3}] = \int_{1/3}^1 x(\tfrac{3}{2})\, dx = \tfrac{2}{3}.
$$

For a variable distributed uniformly between L and U, the variance is $(U - L)^2/12$. Thus,

$$\text{Var}[x \mid x > \tfrac{1}{3}] = \tfrac{1}{27}.$$

The mean and variance of the untruncated distribution are $\tfrac{1}{2}$ and $\tfrac{1}{12}$, respectively.

Example 21.3 illustrates two results.

1. If the truncation is from below, the mean of the truncated variable is greater than the mean of the original one. If the truncation is from above, the mean of the truncated variable is smaller than the mean of the original one.
2. Truncation reduces the variance compared to the variance in the untruncated distribution.

Henceforth, we shall use the terms **truncated mean** and **truncated variance** to refer to the mean and variance in the truncated distribution.

For the truncated normal distribution, we have the following theorem:[4]

Theorem 21.2. Moments of the Truncated Normal Distribution. If $z \sim N[\mu, \sigma^2]$ and a is a constant,

$$E[z \mid \text{truncation}] = \mu + \sigma\lambda(\alpha) \tag{21-5}$$

$$\text{Var}[z \mid \text{truncation}] = \sigma^2(1 - \delta(\alpha)), \tag{21-6}$$

where $\alpha = (a - \mu)/\sigma$ and

$$\lambda(\alpha) = \frac{\phi(\alpha)}{1 - \Phi(\alpha)} \qquad \text{if truncation is } x > a, \tag{21-7a}$$

$$\lambda(\alpha) = \frac{-\phi(\alpha)}{\Phi(\alpha)} \qquad \text{if truncation is } x < a, \tag{21-7b}$$

$$\delta(\alpha) = \lambda(\alpha)(\lambda(\alpha) - \alpha).[5] \tag{21-8}$$

An important result is

$$0 < \delta(\alpha) < 1, \qquad \text{for all values of } \alpha. \tag{21-9}$$

This implies (2) earlier. A convenient result that follows from

$$\frac{d\phi(\alpha)}{d\alpha} = -\alpha\phi(\alpha)$$

is

$$\delta(\alpha) = \frac{d\lambda(\alpha)}{d\alpha}. \tag{21-10}$$

The function $\lambda(\alpha)$ is called the **inverse Mills ratio**. The case in (21–7a) is also the **hazard function** for the distribution. The mean of the truncated standard normal distribution is shown in Figure 21.2 as a function of the truncation point, a.

The effects of changes in the truncation point, a, on the truncated mean and variance are clear in Figure 21.2. A useful way to view these effects is in terms of the probability that

---

[4] Details may be found in Johnson and Kotz (1970, p. 81).
[5] Note that the functions $\lambda(\alpha)$ are the ones that appeared in (20–40) in our earlier discussion of the probit model. See the discussion of the EM method in Section 20.3.2c, especially (20–51).

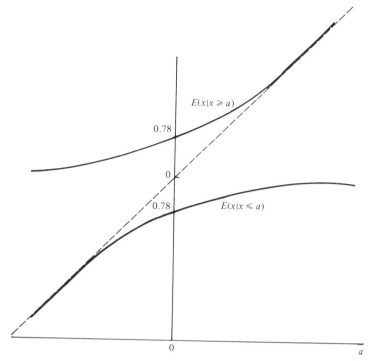

Figure 21.2 Mean of the truncated normal distribution.

z is less than a, which we shall call the **degree of truncation**.[6] This is an increasing function of a. As this probability rises, a greater proportion of the distribution is being discarded, and the mean rises accordingly. Figure 21.3 shows the relationship between $E[z \mid z > a]$ and $\text{Prob}[z > a]$ for the standard normal distribution.

EXAMPLE 21.4. Continuing Example 21.1, Figure 21.2 suggests that since the degree of truncation in the sample is 98 percent, the $142,000 is probably quite far from the mean in the full population.

Suppose that incomes in the population are lognormally distributed. Then the log of income has a normal distribution with, say, mean μ and standard deviation σ. Let $y = \ln z$. Two useful numbers for this example are $\ln 100 = 4.605$ and $\ln 142 = 4.956$. Suppose that the survey is large enough for us to treat the sample average as the true mean. The article states that

$$E[y \mid y > 4.605] = 4.956.$$

It also tells us that $\text{Prob}[y > 4.605] = 0.02$. From Theorem 21.2,

$$E[y \mid y > 4.605] = \mu + \frac{\sigma\phi(\alpha)}{1 - \Phi(\alpha)},$$

[6] Some authors use a itself as the degree of truncation. We prefer $\Phi(\alpha)$, as a has no natural base or units, while $\Phi(\alpha)$ is a probability.

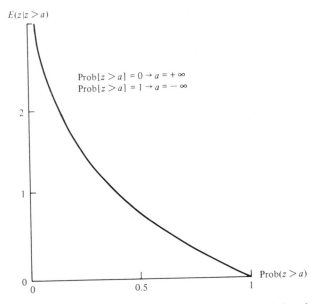

Figure 21.3 Conditional mean as a function of the degree of truncation.

where

$$\alpha = \frac{(4.605 - \mu)}{\sigma}.$$

But we know that $\Phi(\alpha) = 0.98$, so $\alpha = \Phi^{-1}(0.98) = 2.054$. Continuing, then,

(a) $2.054\sigma = 4.605 - \mu$.

In addition, given $\alpha = 2.054$, $\phi(\alpha) = \phi(2.054) = 0.0484$. From (21–5), then,

$$4.956 = \mu + \sigma\left(\frac{0.0484}{0.02}\right)$$

or

(b) $4.956 = \mu + 2.420\sigma$.

The solutions to (a) and (b) are

$$\mu = 2.635 \quad \text{and} \quad \sigma = 0.959.$$

To obtain the mean income, we use the result

$$\text{If } z \sim N[\mu, \sigma^2], \qquad E[e^z] = e^{\mu + \sigma^2/2}.$$

Inserting our values for μ and σ gives $E[z] = \$22,087.$[7]

---

[7] The 1987 *Statistical Abstract of the United States* lists average household income across all groups for the United States as about \$25,000.

21.2.3. The Truncated Regression Model

In the model of the earlier examples, we now assume that

$$\mu = \beta' x_i,$$

the deterministic part of the classical regression model. Then

$$y_i = \beta' x_i + \varepsilon_i,$$

where

$$\varepsilon_i \sim N[0, \sigma^2],$$

so that

$$y_i | x_i \sim N[\beta' x_i, \sigma^2].$$

We are interested in the distribution of y_i given that y_i is greater than the truncation point, a. This is precisely the model described in Theorem 21.2. It follows that

$$E[y_i | y_i > a] = \beta' x_i + \sigma \frac{\phi((a - \beta' x_i)/\sigma)}{1 - \Phi((a - \beta' x_i)/\sigma)}. \qquad (21\text{--}11)$$

The conditional mean is therefore a nonlinear function of x and β.

The marginal effects in this model *in the subpopulation* can be obtained by writing

$$E[y_i | y_i > a] = \beta' x + \sigma \lambda(\alpha_i), \qquad (21\text{--}12)$$

where now $\alpha_i = (a - \beta' x_i)/\sigma$. Then

$$\frac{\partial E[y | y > a]}{\partial x} = \beta + \sigma \left(\frac{d\lambda_i}{d\alpha_i} \right) \frac{\partial \alpha_i}{\partial x}$$

$$= \beta + \sigma(\lambda_i^2 - \alpha_i \lambda_i) \left(-\frac{\beta}{\sigma} \right) \qquad (21\text{--}13)$$

$$= \beta(1 - \lambda_i^2 + \alpha_i \lambda_i)$$

$$= \beta(1 - \delta(\alpha_i)).$$

Note the appearance of the truncated variance. Since the truncated variance is between zero and one, we conclude that for every element of x, the marginal effect is less than the corresponding coefficient. There is a similar attenuation of the variance. In the subpopulation $y_i > a$, the regression variance is not σ^2 but

$$\text{Var}[y_i | y_i > a] = \sigma^2(1 - \delta(\alpha_i)).$$

Whether the marginal effect in (21–13) or the coefficient β itself is of interest depends on the intended inferences of the study. If the analysis is to be confined to the subpopulation, (21–13) is of interest. However, if the study is intended to extend to the entire population, it is the coefficients β that are actually of interest.

EXAMPLE 21.5. Hausman and Wise (1977) estimated an earnings equation for low-income families.[8] The truncation in their model is from above, with thresholds at poverty

---

[8] A similar set of results is presented in Crawford (1975).

levels defined as a function of family size. Their model links the log of earnings to education, a score on an intelligence test, a union membership dummy variable, the number of months in vocational training, a dummy variable equal to one if the individual reported having an illness that limited the ability to work, and age. The assumption implicit in the model is that there is a linear equation connecting these variables in the full population that we seek to study, using data drawn from the subpopulation of people with incomes below the poverty levels. The discussion of the estimates in the article appears to indicate particular attention to the group from which the sample is drawn, not the population at large. (A set of estimates is presented in Example 21.6.)

21.2.3a.   Least Squares Estimation

We now consider estimation of the parameters of the truncated regression. One's first inclination might be to use ordinary least squares. For the subpopulation from which the data are drawn, we could write (21–12) in the form

$$y_i | y_i > a = E[y_i | y_i > a] + u_i$$
$$= \beta'x_i + \sigma\lambda_i + u_i, \tag{21-14}$$

where u_i is y_i minus its conditional expectation. By construction, u_i has a zero mean, but it is heteroscedastic,

$$\text{Var}[u_i] = \sigma^2(1 - \lambda_i^2 + \lambda_i\alpha_i), \tag{21-15}$$

which is a function of x_i. If we estimate (21–14) by ordinary least squares regression of **y** on **X**, we have omitted a variable, the nonlinear term λ_i. All of the biases that arise because of an omitted variable can be expected.

Without some knowledge of the distribution of **x**, it is not possible to determine how serious the bias is likely to be. A result obtained by Cheung and Goldberger (1984) is broadly suggestive. If $E[x | y]$ in the full population is a linear function of y,

$$\text{plim } \mathbf{b} = \beta\tau \tag{21-16}$$

for some proportionality constant, τ. This is consistent with the widely observed (albeit rather rough) proportionality relationship between least squares estimates of this model and consistent maximum likelihood estimates.[9] The proportionality result appears to be quite general. In applications, it is usually found that, compared to consistent maximum likelihood estimates, the OLS estimates are biased toward zero. (See Example 21.6.)

21.2.3b.   Maximum Likelihood Estimation

As specified in Theorem 2.1,

$$f(y_i) = \frac{\frac{1}{\sigma}\phi((y_i - \beta'x_i)/\sigma)}{1 - \Phi((a - \beta'x_i)/\sigma)}. \tag{21-17}$$

---

[9] See, as well, the appendix in Hausman and Wise (1977).

The log likelihood is the sum of logs of these densities,

$$\ln L = -\frac{n}{2}(\ln(2\pi) + \ln \sigma^2) - \frac{1}{2\sigma^2} \sum_i (y_i - \boldsymbol{\beta}'\mathbf{x}_i)^2$$

$$- \sum_i \ln \left[1 - \Phi\left(\frac{a - \boldsymbol{\beta}'\mathbf{x}_i}{\sigma}\right) \right]. \tag{21-18}$$

Maximization, while rather involved because of the extreme nonlinearity of the function, is straightforward in principle using the methods of Chapter 12. After a small amount of manipulation, the necessary conditions for maximizing (21–18) reduce to

$$\frac{\partial \ln L}{\partial \boldsymbol{\beta}} = \sum_i \left[\frac{y_i - \boldsymbol{\beta}'\mathbf{x}_i}{\sigma^2} - \frac{\lambda_i}{\sigma} \right] \mathbf{x}_i = \mathbf{0},$$

$$\frac{\partial \ln L}{\partial \sigma^2} = \sum_i \left[-\frac{1}{2\sigma^2} + \frac{(y_i - \boldsymbol{\beta}'\mathbf{x}_i)^2}{2\sigma^4} - \frac{\alpha_i \lambda_i}{2\sigma^2} \right] = 0, \tag{21-19}$$

where

$$\alpha_i = \frac{(a - \boldsymbol{\beta}'\mathbf{x}_i)}{\sigma}$$

and

$$\lambda_i = \frac{\phi(\alpha_i)}{1 - \Phi(\alpha_i)}. [10]$$

The Hessian for this model is quite involved [see Olsen (1978) for a simplification.] Hausman and Wise suggest using the Berndt et al. estimator during the iterations and to obtain the standard errors instead. This involves summing the outer product of the vectors in (21–19), which are written by individual observation to suggest the computation involved.

EXAMPLE 21.6. Hausman and Wise report the estimates listed in Table 21.1 for the study described in the previous example. Standard errors are given in parentheses. The authors used 684 observations. The marginal effects are computed using (21–13), with an assumed income cutoff of $5002. In the study, this was used for a family of four. The scale factor is 0.2456. Since the dependent variable is measured in logarithms, the effects are given in percentages. The authors did not present these marginal effects.

The authors note, for example, that "If we interpret the coefficient on education as the rate of return to a year of education, we find that it is quite low, approximately 1.6 percent" (p. 926). (The coefficient 0.0165 is reported for a model with a different specification for the age variable.) The surrounding discussion is obviously directed at the low-income people in the sample, for which, in view of (21–13), their observation rather understates the case. Their estimate of the return to a year of education *for the low-income people in their sample* is closer to about 0.4 percent.

21.2.4. Summary

The truncated regression model is the least common of the three forms of limited dependent-variable models we shall consider. We have analyzed it in detail because the other

---

[10] A useful shortcut in the derivation is $\partial \alpha_i / \partial \sigma^2 = -\alpha_i/(2\sigma^2)$.

Table 21.1

	Least Squares	Maximum Likelihood	Mean of X	Marginal Effect (%)
Constant	8.2030	9.1023	1.00	
	(0.0910)	(0.0255)		
Education	0.0095	0.0146	8.76	0.36
	(0.0057)	(0.0070)		
IQ	0.0016	0.0061	33.5	0.14
	(0.0016)	(0.0048)		
Training	0.0022	0.0065	3.27	0.14
	(0.0016)	(0.0031)		
Union	0.0900	0.2463	0.56	
	(0.0305)	(0.0887)		
Illness	−0.0761	−0.2259	0.21	
	(0.0378)	(0.1069)		
Age	−0.0030	−0.0162	36.7	−0.39
	(0.0018)	(0.0053)		
σ	0.391	0.618	$\sigma_{y|x} = 0.306$	

models are built upon this one and use the same principles. We now consider two extensions. In the censored regression model, rather than discard the truncated portion of the distribution, we mask it by assigning all values in that range the same value. The problem of selection, broadly speaking, is one of *incidental truncation*. Our observed distribution is conditioned on some other random variable being in a particular part of its distribution.

21.3. *Censored Data*

A very common problem in microeconomic data is censoring of the dependent variable. When the dependent variable is censored, values in a certain range are all transformed to (or reported as) a single value.

EXAMPLE 21.7.   We are interested in the number of tickets demanded for events at a certain arena. Our only measure is the number actually sold. However, whenever an event sells out, we know that the actual number demanded is larger than the number sold. The number of tickets demanded is censored when it is transformed to obtain the number sold.

Some other examples that have appeared in the empirical literature are as follows:[11]

1. Household purchases of durable goods.[12]
2. The number of extramarital affairs.[13]
3. The number of hours worked by a woman in the labor force.[14]
4. The number of arrests after release from prison.[15]
5. Household expenditure on various commodity groups.[16]

[11] More extensive listings may be found in Amemiya (1984) and Maddala (1983).
[12] Tobin (1958).
[13] Fair (1978).
[14] Quester and Greene (1982).
[15] Witte (1980).
[16] Jarque (1987).

Each of these studies analyzes a dependent variable that is zero for a significant fraction of the observations. Conventional regression methods fail to account for the qualitative difference between *limit* (zero) observations and *nonlimit* (continuous) observations.

21.3.1. The Censored Normal Distribution

The relevant distribution theory for a censored variable is similar to that for a truncated one. Once again, we focus on the normal distribution, as nearly all of the received work has been based on an assumption of normality. We also assume that the censoring point is zero, though this is only a convenient normalization.

In a truncated distribution, only the part of distribution above $y = 0$ is relevant to our computations. To make the distribution integrate to one, we scale it up by the probability that an observation in the untruncated population falls in the range that interests us. When data are censored, the distribution *that applies to the sample data* is a mixture of discrete and continuous distributions. Figure 21.4 shows the effects.

To analyze this distribution, we define a new random variable, y, transformed from the original one, y^*, by

$$y = 0 \qquad \text{if } y^* \leq 0,$$

$$y = y^* \qquad \text{if } y^* > 0.$$

The distribution that applies if $y^* \sim N[\mu, \sigma^2]$ is

$$\text{Prob}[y = 0] = \text{Prob}[y^* \leq 0]$$

$$= \Phi(-\mu/\sigma)$$

$$= 1 - \Phi(\mu/\sigma)$$

and if $y^* > 0$, y has the density of y^*.

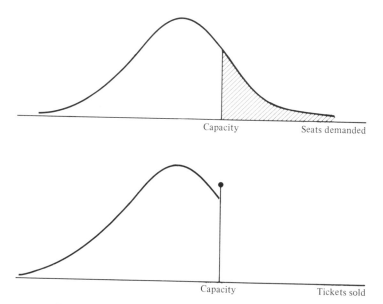

Figure 21.4 Partially censored distribution.

This distribution is a mixture of discrete and continuous parts. The total probability is one, as required, but instead of scaling the second part, we simply assign the full probability in the censored region to the censoring point, in this case, zero.

The expected value of the censored random variable can be obtained by using the laws of probability,

$$E[y] = 0 \text{ Prob}[y = 0] + E[y^*|y^* > 0] \text{ Prob}[y^* > 0].$$

Theorem 21.2 provides the necessary results. Because of the symmetry of the normal distribution, $1 - \Phi[-\mu/\sigma] = \Phi[\mu/\sigma]$, so

$$E[y] = \Phi\left(\frac{\mu}{\sigma}\right)(\mu + \sigma\lambda),$$

where

$$\lambda = \frac{\phi(\mu/\sigma)}{\Phi(\mu/\sigma)}.$$

(21–20)

The variance is a bit more complicated and is given in Theorem 21.3.

Theorem 21.3. Moments of the Censored Normal Variable.

$$E[y] = (\mu + \sigma\lambda)\Phi = \sigma(\alpha + \lambda)\Phi, \qquad (21-21)$$

$$\text{Var}[y] = \sigma^2[(1 - \delta) + (\alpha + \lambda)^2\Phi](1 - \Phi), \qquad (21-22)$$

where $\delta = \lambda^2 + \alpha\lambda$.

EXAMPLE 21.8. To continue Example 21.7, suppose that the arena in question has 20,000 seats and, in a recent season, sold out 25 percent of the time. If the average attendance, including sellouts, was 18,000, what are the mean and standard deviation of the demand for seats? According to Theorem 21.3, the 18,000 is an estimate of

$$E[\text{Demand}] = 20,000(1 - \Phi) + [\mu + \sigma\lambda]\Phi.$$

Since this is truncation from above, rather than below,

$$\lambda = \frac{-\phi(\alpha)}{\Phi(\alpha)}.$$

The argument of Φ, ϕ and λ is

$$\alpha = \frac{(20,000 - \mu)}{\sigma}.$$

If 25 percent of the events are sellouts, $\Phi = 0.75$. Inverting the standard normal at 0.75 gives $\alpha = 0.675$. In addition, if $\alpha = 0.675$, then $-\phi(0.675)/0.75 = \lambda = -0.424$. This provides a pair of equations in μ and σ,

$$18,000 = 0.25(20,000) + 0.75(\mu - 0.424\sigma)$$

and

$$0.675\sigma = 20,000 - \mu.$$

The solutions are $\sigma = 2426$ and $\mu = 18,362$.

For comparison, suppose that we were told that the mean of 18,000 applies only to the events that were *not* sold out and that, on average, the arena sells out 25 percent of the time.

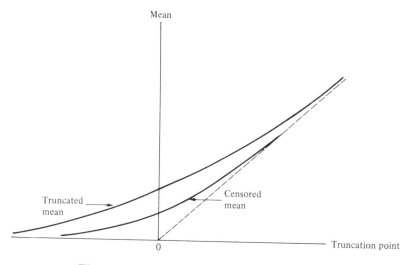

Figure 21.5 Conditional mean functions.

Now our estimates would be obtained from the equations

$$18,000 = \mu - 0.424\sigma$$

and

$$0.675\sigma = 20,000 - \mu.$$

The solution is $\sigma = 1820$ and $\mu = 18,772$.

The mean of the censored distribution is similar to the truncated mean; indeed, it is a weighted average of zero and the truncated mean. As such, it must lie between the truncated mean and the truncation point. A comparison of the two functions is shown in Figure 21.5.

21.3.2. The Censored Regression Model—Tobit Analysis

The regression model based on the preceding discussion is referred to as the **censored regression model** or the **Tobit model**.[17] The regression is obtained by making the mean in the preceding correspond to a classical regression model. The general formulation is usually given in terms of an index function,

$$y^* = \beta'x + \varepsilon,$$
$$y = 0 \qquad \text{if } y^* \le 0, \tag{21–23}$$
$$y = y^* \qquad \text{if } y^* > 0.$$

There are potentially three conditional mean functions to consider, depending on the purpose of the study. For the index variable, sometimes called the *latent variable*, $E[y^*]$ is $\beta'x$. However, if the data are always censored, this will usually not be useful. Consistent with

---

[17] This is in reference to Tobin (1958), where the model was first proposed.

Theorem 21.3, for an observation randomly drawn from the population, which may or may not be censored,

$$E[y_i \mid x_i] = \Phi\left(\frac{\beta' x_i}{\sigma}\right)(\beta' x_i + \sigma \lambda_i), \qquad (21-24)$$

where

$$\lambda_i = \frac{\phi(\beta' x_i/\sigma)}{\Phi(\beta' x_i/\sigma)}.$$

Finally, if we intend to confine our attention to uncensored observations, the results of the previous section apply.[18] It is an unresolved question which of these functions should be used for computing predicted values from this model. Intuition suggests that $E[y \mid x]$ is correct, but authors differ on this point. For the setting in Example 21.8, for predicting the number of tickets sold, say, in order to plan for an upcoming event, the censored mean is obviously the relevant quantity. On the other hand, if the objective is to study the need for a new facility, the mean of the latent variable, y^*, would be more interesting.

There are differences in the marginal effects in the models as well. For the index variable,

$$\frac{\partial E[y^* \mid x]}{\partial x} = \beta.$$

But for y, given the censoring, the marginal effect is only

$$\frac{\partial E[y \mid x]}{\partial x} = \beta \Phi\left(\frac{\beta' x}{\sigma}\right). \qquad [19] \qquad (21-25)$$

Once again, which one is relevant depends on the purpose of the estimates. Although it is used less frequently, the censored standard deviation in (21–23) is also very different from its uncensored counterpart. Nearly all of the received empirical studies that present estimated Tobit coefficients, including those that present the marginal effects in (21–26), present the estimate of σ as if it were the conditional standard deviation of the dependent variable. In view of Theorem 21.3, this is obviously not so.

EXAMPLE 21.9.   In a study of the number of hours worked in a survey year by a large sample of wives, Quester and Greene (1982) were interested in whether wives whose marriages were statistically more likely to dissolve hedged against that possibility by spending, on average, more time working.[20] They reported the Tobit estimates given in Table 21.2. The last figure in the table implies that a very large proportion of the women surveyed reported zero hours, so least squares regression would be inappropriate.

The figures in parentheses are the ratio of the coefficient estimate to the estimated asymptotic standard error. The dependent variable is hours worked in the survey year. "Small Kids" is a dummy variable indicating whether there were children in the household. The "Education Difference" and "Relative Wage" variables compare husband and wife on these two dimensions. The wage rate used for wives was predicted using a previously estimated regression model and is thus available for all individuals, whether working or not.

---

[18] This does not mean that limit observations should be discarded. We will consider this issue later.

[19] McDonald and Moffit (1980) present a useful decomposition of this effect.

[20] In a not completely unrelated study done at roughly the same time, Fair (1978) applied the Tobit methodology to a model of the allocation of leisure time between spouse and paramour.

Table 21.2. Tobit Estimates of an Hours-Worked Equation

	White Wives		Black Wives	
	Coefficient	Slope	Coefficient	Slope
Constant	−1803.13		−2753.87	
	(−8.64)		(−9.68)	
Small kids	−1324.84	−385.89	−824.19	−376.53
	(−19.78)		(−10.14)	
Education difference	−48.08	−14.00	22.59	10.32
	(−4.77)		(1.96)	
Relative wage	312.07	90.90	286.39	130.93
	(5.71)		(3.32)	
Second marriage	175.85	51.51	25.33	11.57
	(3.47)		(0.41)	
Mean divorce probability	417.39	121.58	481.02	219.75
	(6.52)		(5.28)	
High divorce probability	670.22	195.22	578.66	264.36
	(8.40)		(5.33)	
σ	1559	618	1511	826
Sample size	7459		2798	
Proportion working	0.29		0.46	

"Second Marriage" is a dummy variable. Divorce probabilities were produced by a large microsimulation model presented in another study.[21] The variables used here were dummy variables indicating "Mean" if the predicted probability was between 0.01 and 0.03 and "High" if it was greater than 0.03. The "slopes" are the marginal effects described earlier.

Note the marginal effects compared to the Tobit coefficients. Likewise, the estimate of σ is quite misleading as an estimate of the standard deviation of hours worked.

The effects of the divorce probability variables were as expected, and were quite large. One of the questions raised in connection with this study was whether the divorce probabilities could reasonably be treated as independent variables. It might be that for these individuals, the number of hours worked was a significant determinant of the probability.

21.3.3. Estimation

Estimation of this model is very similar to that of truncated regression. Some new issues do arise, but they are almost entirely theoretical. In practical terms, the Tobit model has become so routine, and been incorporated in so many computer packages, that in spite of formidable obstacles in years past, estimation is now essentially on the level of ordinary regression.[22]

21.3.3a. Ordinary Least Squares

The conditional mean function is highly nonlinear, so ordinary least squares is obviously inconsistent. We could write

$$E[y \mid \mathbf{x}] = \boldsymbol{\beta}'\mathbf{x}_i + \sigma(\lambda_i - (1 - \Phi_i)\alpha_i). \qquad (21-26)$$

[21] Orcutt et al. (1976).
[22] See Hall (1984).

Table 21.3

Variable	MLE	Marginal Effect	Least Squares	Scaled Least Squares
Small kids	−824.19	−376.53	−352.63	−766.59
Education difference	22.59	10.32	11.47	24.93
Relative wage	286.39	130.93	123.95	269.46
Second marriage	25.33	11.57	13.14	28.57
Mean divorce probability	481.02	219.75	219.22	476.57
High divorce probability	578.66	264.36	244.17	530.80

As in the truncated regression model, then, least squares regression of $\mathbf{y}$ on $\mathbf{X}$ neglects a regressor. Once again, it is difficult to obtain results on the direction of the bias without specific information about $\mathbf{x}$. Almost without exception, empirical researchers find that the OLS estimates are biased toward zero compared to the maximum likelihood estimator. For multinormal regressors, Greene (1981) has extended Goldberger's (1981) results for the truncated regression to the Tobit model. He shows that for OLS slopes,

$$\text{plim } \mathbf{b} = \beta \Phi\left(\frac{\mu}{\sigma_*}\right),$$

where

$$\Phi\left(\frac{\mu}{\sigma_*}\right) = \text{Prob}[y > 0].$$

The bias depends on the amount of censoring. (Here the degree of censoring is $1 - \Phi$.) The proportionality factor in this special case is consistently estimated by the proportion of nonlimit observations in the sample. Although this is not a general result because of the restrictive assumption of multinormality, its empirical regularity is rather striking. Researchers often find that by scaling the least squares estimates by the reciprocal of the proportion of nonlimit observations in the sample, they obtain an estimate that is surprisingly close to the maximum likelihood estimate.

EXAMPLE 21.10. Least Squares Versus Maximum Likelihood.   For their second regression in Example 21.9, Quester and Greene also obtained the least squares results listed in Table 21.3.[23]

The marginal effects in the model are obtained by scaling the maximum likelihood estimates by $\hat{\Phi} = 0.4568 = \Phi(\hat{\beta}'\bar{\mathbf{x}}/\hat{\sigma})$. The scale factor for the least squares estimates is $1/P$, where P is the proportion of nonlimit observations in the sample, 0.4601. There are two things to note. First, as expected, even though the regressors are not multinormally distributed, the scaled least squares coefficients closely resemble the consistent maximum likelihood estimates.[24] Second, the marginal effects estimated for the Tobit model rather

---

[23] The following are taken from Greene (1981).
[24] This does not imply that the corrected OLS results are consistent. That depends on the distribution of $\mathbf{x}$.

closely resemble the least squares estimates. We recall the discussion of nonlinear regression models in Chapter 11. The slopes of the highly nonlinear conditional mean function in this model appear to be approximated rather well by the OLS estimates.

It is often suggested that one should discard the limit observations and apply least squares to the nonlimit data. The set of nonlimit observations corresponds to the truncated regression model of Section 21.2, so this only trades one inconsistent estimator for another. Which is worse? Unfortunately, it is impossible to tell. The results of Goldberger and Greene weigh slightly in favor of not discarding the limit observations. But this decision considers only the degree of inconsistency and requires a special assumption about the regressors. Questions of precision and, ultimately, mean squared error in a more general model remain to be explored. Of course, this compares two inconsistent estimators. It is simple to show that in terms of the MLEs it is *always* better to keep the limit observations.

21.3.3b.   *Some Consistent Estimators*

It is feasible to use nonlinear least squares or nonlinear weighted least squares to obtain the estimates of the Tobit or truncated regression models.[25] However, this is inefficient and far more burdensome than maximum likelihood estimation, and the approach has not been used in practice. Also, Amemiya's (1973) instrumental variables estimator, while interesting in its own right, is, in practical terms, not especially useful given the availability of efficient methods of obtaining maximum likelihood estimates. An ingenious two-step approach that has revealed much about the structure of the Tobit and related models has been proposed by Heckman (1976 and 1979).

The data set for the censored regression analysis contains two bodies of information. For each observation, we have

$$x_i = \text{regressors},$$

$$y_i = \text{measured dependent variable}$$

$$= \beta' x_i + \varepsilon_i \quad \text{if } \beta' x_i + \varepsilon_i > 0 \text{ and 0 if not,}$$

$$z_i = \text{censoring indicator}$$

$$= 1 \quad \text{if } y_i > 0 \text{ and 0 if not.}$$

Consider the conditional mean from the truncated regression model,

$$E[y \mid x_i, z_i = 1] = \beta' x_i + \sigma \lambda_i. \tag{21-27}$$

If λ_i were an observed variable, β and σ could be estimated consistently, if not efficiently (the disturbance is heteroscedastic), by ordinary least squares. Of course, λ_i involves unknown parameters—see (21-25)—so this is not feasible. But consider the censoring indicator. The model implies that

$$\text{Prob}[z_i = 1] = \text{Prob}[y^* > 0] = \Phi\left(\frac{\beta' x_i}{\sigma}\right),$$

$$\text{Prob}[z_i = 0] = \text{Prob}[y^* \leq 0] = 1 - \Phi\left(\frac{\beta' x_i}{\sigma}\right).$$

---

[25] For discussion, see Amemiya (1985, Chapter 10).

Now let $\gamma = \boldsymbol{\beta}/\sigma$. Then

$$1. \ \text{Prob}[z_i = 1] = \Phi(\gamma' \mathbf{x}_i)$$

$$\text{Prob}[z_i = 0] = 1 - \Phi(\gamma' \mathbf{x}_i)$$

and

$$2. \ \lambda_i = \phi \frac{(\gamma' \mathbf{x}_i)}{\Phi(\gamma' \mathbf{x}_i)}.$$

The model in (1) is exactly the univariate probit model of the previous chapter. Therefore, even ignoring y, γ can be efficiently estimated using the probit estimator discussed in Chapter 20, based on $\mathbf{z}$ and $\mathbf{X}$. Once this is done, we can compute estimates of ϕ_i, Φ_i, and λ_i by using the estimated probit coefficients. Then $\boldsymbol{\beta}$ and σ can be estimated by regressing the nonlimit observations on y on the associated values of $\mathbf{x}$ and the predicted values of λ. Indeed, with the probit coefficients in hand, there are two other similar estimators. Based on (21–26), we might use the probit coefficients to compute an estimate of $t_i = (\lambda_i - (1 - \Phi_i)\alpha_i)$ for every observation in the sample, both nonlimit and limit, and then regress $\mathbf{y}$ on $\mathbf{X}$ and $\mathbf{t}$. Second, based on (21–24), which implies that

$$E[y_i | \mathbf{x}_i] = \boldsymbol{\beta}'(\Phi_i \mathbf{x}_i) + \sigma \phi_i,$$

we could regress $\mathbf{y}$ on $\Phi_i \mathbf{x}_i$ and ϕ_i as well.[26] The following questions remain:

1. Are these estimators consistent? [Yes; see Heckman (1979).]
2. Are these estimators efficient? [No; see Paarsch (1984) and Nelson (1984).]
3. Are the estimated standard errors produced by this least squares regression appropriate? [No; see Heckman (1979) and Greene (1981).]

We shall pursue these issues in Section 21.4.

21.3.3c. Maximum Likelihood Estimation

The log likelihood for the censored regression model is

$$\ln L = -\frac{n_1}{2}(\ln(2\pi) + \ln \sigma^2) - \frac{1}{2\sigma^2}\sum_1 (y_i - \boldsymbol{\beta}'\mathbf{x}_i)^2$$

$$+ \sum_0 \ln\left[1 - \Phi\left(\frac{\boldsymbol{\beta}'\mathbf{x}_i}{\sigma}\right)\right]. \tag{21-28}$$

The two parts correspond to the classical regression for the nonlimit observations and the relevant probabilities for the limit observations. This is not the usual type of likelihood, and the maximum likelihood estimator is somewhat more difficult to analyze than those we have seen thus far. In a seminal paper Amemiya (1973) showed that in spite of the complications, proceeding in the usual fashion to maximize L would produce an estimator with all of the desirable properties.

An interesting method of obtaining the maximum likelihood estimates is the EM method proposed by Hartley (1976). The method is based essentially on the estimation of the

---

[26] The second of these procedures is analyzed at length in Stapleton and Young (1981) and Wales and Woodland (1980). The first appears to be new.

missing data. For the observations that are censored,

$$E[y_i | \mathbf{x}_i, y_i \text{ was censored}] = \boldsymbol{\beta}'\mathbf{x}_i + \sigma\lambda_i, \qquad (21-29)$$

where now,

$$\lambda_i = -\frac{\phi_i}{1 - \Phi_i}.^{27}$$

If the censored data were actually observed (i.e., not censored), efficient estimates of $\boldsymbol{\beta}$ would be obtained by ordinary least squares. The EM method is essentially based on predicting the missing observations using (21–29), then using least squares based on the predicted data and the complete observations. Another approach that is similar to this one was devised by Fair (1977).[28]

21.3.4.   Some Issues in Specification

Two issues that commonly arise in microeconomic data, heteroscedasticity and nonnormality, have been analyzed at length in the Tobit setting.[29] Among the questions raised about the Tobit model has been whether it is reasonable to treat the probability of a limit observation and the nonlimit dependent variable as being generated by the same normal distribution.

21.3.4a.   Heteroscedasticity

Maddala and Nelson (1975), Hurd (1979), Arabmazar and Schmidt (1982), and Brown and Moffitt (1982) all have varying degrees of pessimism regarding how inconsistent the maximum likelihood estimator will be when heteroscedasticity occurs. Not surprisingly, the degree of censoring is the primary determinant. Unfortunately, all of the analyses have been carried out in the setting of very specific models, for example, involving only a single dummy variable or one with groupwise heteroscedasticity, so the primary lesson is the very general conclusion that heteroscedasticity emerges as an obviously serious problem.

One can approach the heteroscedasticity problem directly. Petersen and Waldman (1981) present the computations needed to estimate a Tobit model with heteroscedasticity of several types. Replacing σ with σ_i in the log-likelihood function and including σ_i^2 in the summations produces the needed generality. Specification of a particular model for σ_i provides the empirical model for estimation.

EXAMPLE 21.11.   Petersen and Waldman analyzed the volume of short interest in a cross section of common stocks. The regressors included a measure of the market component of heterogeneous expectations as measured by the firm's *BETA* coefficient; a company-specific measure of heterogeneous expectations, *NONMARKET*; the *NUMBER* of analysts making earnings forecasts for the company; the number of common shares to be issued for the acquisition of another firm, *MERGER*; and a dummy variable for the existence of *OPTION*s. They report the results listed in Table 21.4 for a model in which the variance is assumed to be of the form $\sigma_i^2 = \exp(\boldsymbol{\alpha}'\mathbf{x}_i)$. The values in parentheses are the ratio of the coefficient to the estimated asymptotic standard error.

---

[27] See (21–7b.) Here $\alpha = (0 - \boldsymbol{\beta}'\mathbf{x})/\sigma$, so $\Phi(-\boldsymbol{\beta}'\mathbf{x}/\sigma) = [1 - \Phi(\alpha)]$.
[28] See also Maddala (1983) for a useful discussion.
[29] Two recent symposia that contain numerous results on these subjects are Blundell (1987) and Duncan (1986).

Table 21.4. Estimates of a Tobit Model

	Homoscedastic	Heteroscedastic	
	β	β	α
Constant	-18.28	-4.11	-0.47
	(5.10)	(3.28)	(0.60)
BETA	10.97	2.22	1.20
	(3.61)	(2.00)	(1.81)
NONMARKET	0.65	0.12	0.08
	(7.41)	(1.90)	(7.55)
NUMBER	0.75	0.33	0.15
	(5.74)	(4.50)	(4.58)
MERGER	0.50	0.24	0.06
	(5.90)	(3.00)	(4.17)
OPTION	2.56	2.96	0.83
	(1.51)	(2.99)	(1.70)
Log L.	-547.30	-466.27	
Sample size	200	200	

The effect of heteroscedasticity on the estimates is extremely large. A test of the hypothesis that $\alpha = 0$ (except for the constant term) can be based on the likelihood ratio statistic. For these results, the statistic is $-2(-547.3 - (-466.27)) = 162.06$. This is asymptotically distributed as chi-squared with five degrees of freedom. The sample value exceeds the critical value in the table, so the hypothesis can be rejected.

In the preceding example, we carried out a likelihood ratio test against the hypothesis of homoscedasticity. This requires estimation of the heteroscedastic model. Although estimation of the homoscedastic model is routine, estimation of the heteroscedastic model is anything but that. It would be desirable to be able to carry out the test without having to estimate the unrestricted model. A Lagrange multiplier test can be used for that purpose. Consider the heteroscedastic Tobit model in which we specify that

$$\sigma_i^2 = \sigma^2 e^{\alpha' w_i}.$$

This is a fairly general model that includes many familiar ones as special cases. The null hypothesis of homoscedasticity is $\alpha = 0$. After some algebra, the necessary conditions for maximization of the log likelihood *under the null hypothesis* reduce to the following, in which subscripts are used to indicate partial differentiation of the log likelihood:

$$\ln L_\beta = \sum_i a_i x_i,$$

$$\ln L_{\sigma^2} = \sum_i b_i, \qquad (21-30)$$

$$\ln L_\alpha = \sum_i \sigma^2 b_i w_i,$$

where

$$a_i = z_i \left(\frac{\varepsilon_i}{\sigma^2} \right) + \frac{(1 - z_i)(-\phi_i/(1 - \Phi_i))}{\sigma},$$

$$b_i = \frac{z_i(\varepsilon_i^2/\sigma^2 - 1)}{2\sigma^2} + \frac{(1 - z_i)(\beta' x_i \phi_i/(1 - \Phi_i))}{2\sigma^3}.$$

The sums are taken over all observations, and all functions involving unknown parameters $(\varepsilon, \phi, \boldsymbol{\beta}'\mathbf{x}_i, \text{etc.})$ are evaluated at the restricted (homoscedastic) maximum likelihood estimates. To construct the Lagrange multiplier statistic, we use the Berndt et al. estimator for the information matrix. Under the null hypothesis, at the maximum likelihood estimates, L_β and L_{σ^2} are both zero. Therefore, the statistic can be computed as

$$\text{LM} = \ln L_\alpha' \mathbf{Q}_{\alpha\alpha'} \ln L_\alpha,$$

where $\ln L_\alpha$ is as above and $\mathbf{Q}_{\alpha\alpha'}$ is the lower right block in

$$\mathbf{Q} = \sum_i \left[\begin{array}{ccc} a_i^2 \mathbf{x}_i \mathbf{x}_i' & a_i b_i \mathbf{x}_i & \sigma^2 a_i b_i \mathbf{x}_i \mathbf{w}_i' \\ a_i b_i \mathbf{x}_i' & b_i^2 & \sigma^2 b_i^2 \mathbf{w}_i' \\ \sigma^2 a_i b_i \mathbf{w}_i \mathbf{x}_i' & \sigma^2 b_i^2 \mathbf{w}_i & \sigma^4 b_i^2 \mathbf{w}_i \mathbf{w}_i' \end{array} \right]^{-1} \tag{21-31}$$

Unfortunately, this does not reduce to an elegant nR^2, as it would in the classical regression model. (If there were no limit observations, it would reduce to the Breusch–Pagan statistic discussed in Chapter 14.) But given the maximum likelihood estimates of the Tobit model coefficients, it is quite simple to compute. The statistic is asymptotically distributed as chi-squared with degrees of freedom equal to the number of variables in $\mathbf{w}_i$.

21.3.4b. *Nonnormality*

Nonnormality is an especially difficult problem in this setting. It has been shown that if the underlying disturbances are not normally distributed, the usual estimator is inconsistent. Research is ongoing both on alternative estimators and on methods for testing for this type of misspecification.[30]

One approach to the estimation is use an alternative distribution. Kalbfleisch and Prentice[31] present a unifying treatment that includes several distributions such as the exponential, lognormal, and Weibull. (Their primary focus is on survival analysis in a medical statistics setting. This is an interesting convergence of the techniques in very different disciplines.) Of course, assuming some other specific distribution does not necessarily solve the problem and may make it worse. A preferable alternative would be to devise an estimator that is robust to changes in the distribution. Powell's (1981) least absolute deviations estimator appears to offer some promise. The main drawback to its use is its computational complexity. Research on robust methods is ongoing.[32]

Although estimation in the nonnormal case is quite difficult, testing for this failure of the model is worthwhile in order to assess the estimates obtained by the conventional methods. The tests that have been developed are of two types, Lagrange muliplier tests[33] and Hausman tests. The latter, were developed by Nelson (1981). In the usual case, to employ a Hausman test, we require an estimator that is consistent and efficient under the null hypothesis but inconsistent under the alternative—the usual Tobit estimator with normality—and an estimator that is consistent under both hypotheses but inefficient under the null hypothesis. For estimation of β, this requires a robust estimator of β, which restores the difficulties of the previous paragraph. However, Nelson simplifies the problem by considering, instead of β, $\text{Prob}[y > 0]$ from the marginal distribution of y and $E[(1/n)\mathbf{X}'\mathbf{y}]$, both of which can be estimated using sample moments.

---

[30] See Duncan (1983) and Goldberger (1983).
[31] Kalbfleisch and Prentice (1980).
[32] See Duncan (1986) for a symposium on the subject and Amemiya (1984).
[33] Bera et al. (1982).

21.3.4c.   *Misspecification of* Prob[$y^* < 0$]

In an early study in this literature, Cragg (1971) proposed a somewhat more general model in which the probability of a limit observation is independent of the regression model for the nonlimit data. One can imagine, for instance, the decision on whether or not to purchase a car as being different from the decision on how much to spend on the car, having decided to buy one. A related problem raised by Fin and Schmidt (1984) is that in the Tobit model, a variable that increases the probability of an observation being a nonlimit observation also increases the mean of the variable. They cite as an example loss due to fire in buildings. Older buildings might be more likely to have fires, so that $\partial \operatorname{Prob}[y > 0]/\partial \operatorname{age}$ > 0, but, because of the value of newer buildings, incur smaller losses when they do, so that $\partial E[y \mid y > 0]/\partial \operatorname{age} < 0$. This would require the coefficient on age to have different signs in the two functions, which is impossible in the Tobit model because they are the same coefficient.

A more general model that accommodates these objections is

1. Decision equation:

$$\operatorname{Prob}[y_1^* > 0] = \Phi(\gamma' x_i), \qquad z_i = 1 \text{ if } y_1^* > 0, \tag{21-32}$$
$$\operatorname{Prob}[y_1^* \le 0] = 1 - \Phi(\gamma' x_i), \qquad z_i = 0 \text{ if } y_1^* \le 0.$$

2. Regression equation for nonlimit observations:

$$E[y_i \mid z_i = 1] = \beta' x_i + \sigma \lambda_i, \tag{21-33}$$

according to Theorem 21.2.

This is a combination of the truncated regression model of Section 21.2 and the univariate probit model of Chapter 20, which suggests a method of analyzing it. The Tobit model of this section arises if $\gamma = \beta/\sigma$. The parameters of the decision equation can be estimated using the probit estimator of Chapter 20. The parameters of the regression equation can be estimated independently using the truncated regression model of Section 21.2.

Schmidt and Fin considered testing the restriction of the Tobit model. Based on only the Tobit model, they devised a Lagrange multiplier statistic that, while a bit cumbersome algebraically, can be computed without great difficulty. If one is able to estimate the truncated regression model, the Tobit model, and the probit models separately, there is a simpler way to test the hypothesis. The Tobit log likelihood is the sum of log likelihoods for the truncated regression and probit models.[34] Therefore, a likelihood ratio statistic can easily be computed using

$$\lambda = -2[\ln L_T - (\ln L_P + \ln L_{TR})], \tag{21-34}$$

where

$$\ln L_T = \text{log likelihood from the Tobit model}$$
$$\text{with the same coefficients in (1) and (2),}$$

$$\ln L_P = \text{log likelihood from estimating (1),}$$

$$\ln L_{TR} = \text{log likelihood from estimating (2).}$$

---

[34] To show this, add and subtract $\sum_0 \ln \Phi\left(\dfrac{\beta' x}{\sigma}\right)$ in (21–28). This produces (21–18) plus the log likelihood for the probit model following (21–27).

21.3.5. Variations and Extensions

The empirical literature contains many extensions of the Tobit model. One that has proved useful is a model with more than one region censored.

EXAMPLE 21.12. **Doubly Censored Regression.** Nakamura and Nakamura (1983) have extended the Tobit model to a setting in which the sampled data contain three types of observations.[35] Where y is hours worked, they have

$$y = 0 \qquad \text{if not working}$$

$$y = \text{hours} \qquad \text{if working part time}$$

$$y = 1400 \qquad \text{if working full time (hours} \geq 1400)$$

If we define an index variable, $y^* = \beta'x + \varepsilon$, the preceding defines a doubly censored regression model. The appropriate log-likelihood function would be

$$\ln L = \begin{aligned} &\sum_0 \ln \text{Prob}[y^* \leq 0] + \sum_{1400} \ln \text{Prob}[y^* \geq 1400] \\ &+ \sum_i \left(-\frac{1}{2}\ln(2\pi) - \frac{1}{2}\ln \sigma^2 - \frac{1}{2\sigma^2}(y_i - b'x_i)^2 \right). \end{aligned} \qquad (21\text{-}35)$$

The third term is the sum over the middle set of observations. Estimation of the parameters can be done in the usual fashion and is not appreciably more difficult than the usual Tobit problem. (Instead of maximum likelihood, Nakamura and Nakamura used a variant of the Heckman method described in Section 21.3.3b.)

The marginal effects in this model are similar to those of the singly censored Tobit model. It is instructive to derive them in order to demonstrate a set of calculations that is recurrent in this literature. The model in general terms with lower limit, L, and upper limit point, U, is

$$y^* = \beta'x + \varepsilon, \qquad \varepsilon \sim N[0, \sigma^2],$$

$$y = L \qquad \text{if } y^* \leq L,$$

$$y = y^* \qquad \text{if } L < y^* < U,$$

$$y = U \qquad \text{if } y^* \geq U.$$

Therefore,

$$E[y] = L\,\text{Prob}[y = L] + U\,\text{Prob}[y = U] + E[y^*\,|\,L < y < U]\,\text{Prob}[L < y^* < U].$$

Let

$$l = \frac{L - \beta'x}{\sigma}, \qquad u = \frac{U - \beta'x}{\sigma},$$

$$\phi_l = \phi(l), \qquad \phi_u = \phi(u), \qquad \Phi_l = \Phi(l), \qquad \Phi_u = F(u).$$

---

[35] The model discussed here was also analyzed earlier by Rosett and Nelson (1975). These authors also examined a special case of the model discussed in the next example.

Then,

$$E[y] = L\Phi_l + U(1 - \Phi_u) + \left\{ \boldsymbol{\beta}'\mathbf{x} + \sigma \frac{\phi_l - \phi_u}{\Phi_u - \Phi_l} \right\} (\Phi_u - \Phi_l)$$

$$= U + L\Phi_l - U\Phi_u + (\Phi_u - \Phi_l)\boldsymbol{\beta}'\mathbf{x} + \sigma(\phi_l - \phi_u).$$

To differentiate with respect to $\mathbf{x}$, we make use of the result

$$\frac{d\Phi(z)}{dz} = \phi(z) \quad \text{and} \quad \frac{d\phi(z)}{dz} = -z\phi(z).$$

Then

$$\partial E[y]/\partial \mathbf{x} = L\left(\frac{-\boldsymbol{\beta}}{\sigma}\right)\phi_l - U\left(\frac{-\boldsymbol{\beta}}{\sigma}\right)\phi_u + (\Phi_u - \Phi_l)\boldsymbol{\beta}$$

$$+ \boldsymbol{\beta}'\mathbf{x}\left[\left(\frac{-\boldsymbol{\beta}}{\sigma}\right)\phi_u - \left(\frac{-\boldsymbol{\beta}}{\sigma}\right)\phi_l\right] + \sigma\left[-l\left(\frac{-\boldsymbol{\beta}}{\sigma}\right)\phi_l - (-u)\left(\frac{-\boldsymbol{\beta}}{\sigma}\right)\phi_u\right]$$

$$= \left(\frac{-\boldsymbol{\beta}}{\sigma}\right)[(L - \boldsymbol{\beta}'\mathbf{x}) - \sigma l]\phi_l - \left(\frac{-\boldsymbol{\beta}}{\sigma}\right)[(U - \boldsymbol{\beta}'\mathbf{x}) - \sigma u]\phi_u + (\Phi_u - \Phi_l)\boldsymbol{\beta}$$

$$= (\Phi_u - \Phi_l)\boldsymbol{\beta} = (\text{Prob}[L < y^* < U])\boldsymbol{\beta}.$$

This is the parameter vector scaled by the probability in the uncensored region. This is the same as (21–25).

The logical limit of this extension is a case in which the dependent variable is always censored.[36] For example, income or earnings are often reported only in the form of a bracket.

EXAMPLE 21.13. Grouped Data Regression.   Stewart (1983) analyzed earnings data for a United Kingdom sample of manufacturing workers in which the dependent variable was reported as

$$
\begin{aligned}
y &= 0 && \text{if income} \leq a_1, \\
y &= 1 && \text{if } a_1 < \text{income} \leq a_2, \\
&\;\;\vdots \\
y &= J && \text{if } a_J < \text{income}.
\end{aligned}
\tag{21-36}
$$

Ordinary regression would be problematic here, since the coded values of income are not even of the same scale as income. As before, we can define an index function and a transformation,

$$
\begin{aligned}
y^* &= \boldsymbol{\beta}'\mathbf{x} + \varepsilon, \\
y^* &\sim N[\boldsymbol{\beta}'\mathbf{x}, \sigma^2], \\
y &= j && \text{if } a_j < \text{income} \leq a_{j+1}.
\end{aligned}
\tag{21-37}
$$

For consistency, we define $a_0 = -\infty$ and $a_{J+1} = +\infty$. This variable corresponds exactly to Figure 3.5. What sets this model apart from the other ones we have discussed in this chapter is

---

[36] This type of random variable was discussed in Section 3.6. See Figure 3.5 for an illustration.

that the dependent variable is now discrete, not continuous. The appropriate modeling framework is, therefore, the discrete dependent variable models of Chapter 20.

A maximum likelihood estimator can be obtained by maximizing

$$\ln L = \sum_0 \ln \text{Prob}[y = 0] + \sum_1 \ln \text{Prob}[y = 1] + \cdots + \sum_J \ln \text{Prob}[y = j]. \quad (21-38)$$

For an observation whose dependent variable takes the value j, the appropriate probability is

$$\text{Prob}[y_i = j] = \Phi\left(\frac{a_{j+1} - \boldsymbol{\beta}'\mathbf{x}}{\sigma}\right) - \Phi\left(\frac{a_j - \boldsymbol{\beta}'\mathbf{x}}{\sigma}\right). \quad (21-39)$$

(Figure 20.6 for the ordered probit model shows how these arise. In this model, the unknown μ_j's in that figure are replaced with the known bracket limits, a_j.) Summing the logs of these limits provides the maximand for estimation. Once again, maximization is quite similar to the Tobit model.

A practical problem in Stewart's analysis was the exceedingly large size of his sample— over 5000 observations. Given this size, conventional methods of maximization were likely to be excessively expensive. In the spirit of the EM method, we observe that if the data were not censored, the efficient estimator would be ordinary least squares. Within a particular range, $(a_j, a_{j+1}]$,

$$E[y^* \mid y = j] = \boldsymbol{\beta}'\mathbf{x} + \sigma \frac{\phi(\alpha_j) - \phi(\alpha_{j+1})}{\Phi(\alpha_{j+1}) - \Phi(\alpha_j)}, \quad (21-40)$$

where

$$\alpha_k = \frac{(a_k - \boldsymbol{\beta}'\mathbf{x})}{\sigma}.$$

At entry to an iteration, if estimates of $\hat{\boldsymbol{\beta}}$ and $\hat{\sigma}$ are in hand, we can compute $\hat{y}^*$ according to (21-40) and then use ordinary least squares. This is the EM method. Stewart provides further details and a set of estimates.

This model might seem to be the same as the ordered probit model of Chapter 20. But a peculiar difference emerges in that the parameter σ is estimable here, whereas in the ordered probit model it was necessary to normalize σ to one. The difference in this setting is that the censoring limits, a_j, provide the information about the scale of the dependent variable here, whereas there is no such information for the ordered probit model.

21.4. *Selection—Incidental Truncation*

The topic of sample selection, or *incidental truncation,* has been the subject of an enormous recent literature, both theoretical and applied.[37] This analysis combines both of the previous topics.

EXAMPLE 21.14. Incidental Truncation.   In the high-income survey discussed in Examples 21.1 and 21.4, respondents were also included in the survey if their net worth, not including their homes, was at least \$500,000. Suppose that the survey of incomes was based *only* on people whose net worth was at least \$500,000. This is a form of truncation, but not

[37] The four surveys noted in the Introduction provide fairly extensive, though far from exhaustive, lists of the studies.

quite the same as in Section 21.2. This selection criterion does not necessarily exclude individuals whose incomes at the time might be quite low. Still, one would expect that, on average, individuals with a high net worth would have a high income as well. Thus, the average income in this subpopulation would, in all likelihood, also be misleading as an indication of the income of the typical American. The data in such a survey would be incidentally truncated, or nonrandomly selected.

Recent econometric studies of nonrandom sampling have analyzed the deleterious effects of sample selection on the properties of conventional estimators such as least squares; have produced a variety of alternative estimation techniques; and, in the process, have yielded a rich crop of empirical models. In some cases, the analysis has led to a reinterpretation of earlier results.

21.4.1.   Incidental Truncation in a Bivariate Distribution

Suppose that y and z have a bivariate distribution with correlation ρ. We are interested in the distribution of y given that z exceeds a particular value. Intuition suggests that if y and z are positively correlated, the truncation of z should push the distribution of y to the right. As before, we are interested in (1) the form of the incidentally truncated distribution and (2) the mean and variance of the incidentally truncated random variable. Since it has dominated the empirical literature, we will focus on the bivariate normal distribution.

The truncated *joint* density of y and z is

$$f(y, z \mid z > a) = \frac{f(y, z)}{\mathrm{Prob}[z > a]}. \tag{21–41}$$

To obtain the incidentally truncated marginal density for y, we would then integrate z out of this expression.[38] Figure 21.6 shows a particular case in which y and z are bivariate standard normal with correlation 0.7 and truncation of $z > 0$.

The moments of the incidentally truncated normal distribution are given in Theorem 21.4.[39]

Theorem 21.4. Moments of the Incidentally Truncated Bivariate Normal Distribution. If y and z have a bivariate normal distribution with means μ_y and μ_z, standard deviations σ_y and σ_z, and correlation ρ, then

$$E[y \mid z > a] = \mu_y + \rho\sigma_y \lambda(\alpha_z) \tag{21–42}$$

$$\mathrm{Var}[y \mid z > a] = \sigma_y^2 (1 - \rho^2 \delta(\alpha_z)), \tag{21–43}$$

where

$$\alpha_z = \frac{a - \mu_z}{\sigma_z},$$

$$\lambda(\alpha_z) = \frac{\phi(\alpha_z)}{1 - \Phi(\alpha_z)},$$

$$\delta(\alpha_z) = \lambda(\alpha_z)(\lambda(\alpha_z) - \alpha_z).$$

---

[38] The precise form for a bivariate normal distribution is given in Maddala (1983, pp. 266–267).

[39] Much more general forms of the result that apply to multivariate distributions are given in Johnson and Kotz (1974).

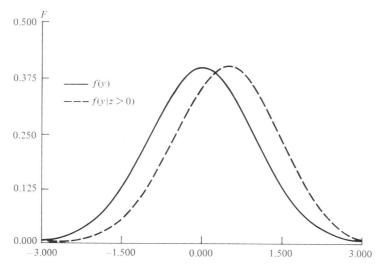

Figure 21.6   Incidental truncation.

Note that the expressions involving z are precisely the moments of the truncated distribution of z given in Theorem 21.2. If the truncation is $z < a$, we make the replacement

$$\lambda(\alpha_z) = \frac{-\phi(\alpha_z)}{\Phi(\alpha_z)}.$$

As expected, the truncated mean is pushed in the direction of the correlation if the truncation is from below and in the opposite direction if it is from above. In addition, the incidental truncation reduces the variance, as both $\delta(\alpha)$ and ρ^2 are between zero and one. However, as might be expected, the variance is reduced less by incidental truncation than by direct truncation.

21.4.2.   Regression in a Model of Selection

To motivate a regression model that corresponds to the results in Theorem 21.4, we consider two examples.

EXAMPLE 21.15. A Model of Labor Supply.   A simple model of female labor supply that has been examined in many studies[40] consists of two equations:

Wage equation: The difference between a person's *market wage*, what they could command in the labor market, and their *reservation wage*, the wage rate necessary to make them choose to participate in the labor market, is a function of characteristics such as age and education, as well as, for example, number of children and where they live.

---

[40] See, for example, Heckman (1976). This strand of literature begins with an exchange by Gronau (1974) and Lewis (1974).

Hours equation: The desired number of labor hours supplied depends on the wage, home characteristics such as whether there are small children present, marital status (see Example 21.9), and so on.

The problem of truncation surfaces when we account for the fact that the second equation describes desired hours, but an actual figure is observed only if the individual is working. We infer from this that the market wage exceeds the reservation wage. Thus, the hours variable in the second equation is incidentally truncated.

EXAMPLE 21.16. A Migration Model. Example 20.4 presents a model of migration analyzed by Nakosteen and Zimmer. That model fits precisely into the framework described earlier. Briefly, the equations of the model are

$$\text{Net benefit of moving:} \qquad M^* = \gamma'w + u,$$

$$\text{Income if moves:} \qquad I_1 = \beta_1'x_1 + \varepsilon_1,$$

$$\text{Income if stays:} \qquad I_0 = \beta_0'x_0 + \varepsilon_0.$$

One of the components of the net benefit is the market wage individuals could achieve if they move, compared to what they could obtain if they stay. Therefore, among the determinants of the net benefit are factors that also affect the income received in either place. An analysis of income in a sample of migrants must account for the incidental truncation of the mover's income on a positive net benefit. Likewise, the income of the stayer is incidentally truncated on a nonpositive net benefit. The model implies an income after moving for all observations, but we observe it only for those who actually do move.

To put the preceding examples in a general framework, let the equation that determines the sample selection be

$$z^* = \gamma'w + u^{41} \tag{21-44}$$

and let the equation of primary interest be

$$y = \beta'x + \varepsilon. \tag{21-45}$$

The sampling rule is that y is observed only when z^* is greater than zero. Suppose, as well, that ε and u have a bivariate normal distribution with zero means and correlation ρ. Then we may insert these in Theorem 21.4 to obtain the model *that applies to the observations in our sample*:

$$
\begin{aligned}
E[y \,|\, y \text{ is observed}] &= E[y \,|\, z^* > 0] \\
&= E[y \,|\, u > -\gamma'w] \\
&= \beta'x + E[\varepsilon \,|\, u > -\gamma'w] \tag{21-46} \\
&= \beta'x + \rho\sigma_\varepsilon \lambda(\alpha_u) \\
&= \beta'x + \beta_\lambda \lambda(\alpha_u),
\end{aligned}
$$

---

[41] Unfortunately, the literature contains great variation in the specification of this part of the model. Some authors enter u in this equation with a negative sign instead of a positive one. This has no effect on the structure of the model, but the negative sign now pervades the remaining results. Although this does not change the model substantively, it has been a source of some confusion. Readers should be alert to this possibility before beginning their foray into the received studies.

where

$$\alpha_u = \frac{-\gamma' \mathbf{w}}{\sigma_u} \tag{21-47}$$

and

$$\lambda(\alpha) = \frac{\phi(\gamma' \mathbf{w}/\sigma_u)}{\Phi(\gamma' \mathbf{w}/\sigma_u)}. \tag{21-48}$$

So

$$y \mid z^* > 0 = \boldsymbol{\beta}'\mathbf{x} + \beta_\lambda \lambda(\alpha_u) + v. \tag{21-49}$$

Least squares regression using the observed data—for instance, OLS regression of hours on its determinants, using only data for women who are working—produces inconsistent estimates of $\boldsymbol{\beta}$. Once again, we can view the problem as an omitted variable. Least squares regression of y on $\mathbf{x}$ *and* λ would produce consistent estimates, but if λ is omitted, the specification error of an omitted variable is committed. Note, finally, that the second part of Theorem 21.4 implies that even if λ were observed, least squares would be inefficient. The disturbance, v, is heteroscedastic.

The marginal effect of the regressors on y *in the observed sample* consists of two components. There is the direct effect on the mean of y, which is $\boldsymbol{\beta}$. In addition, for a particular independent variable, if it appears in the probability that z^* is positive, it will influence y through its presence in λ. The full effect of changes in a regressor that appears in both $\mathbf{x}$ and $\mathbf{w}$ on y is

$$\frac{\partial E[y \mid z^* > 0]}{\partial x_k} = \beta_k - \gamma_k \left(\frac{\rho \sigma_\varepsilon}{\sigma_u} \right) \delta(\alpha_u), \tag{21-50}$$

where

$$\delta = \lambda^2 + \alpha\lambda.^{42}$$

Suppose that ρ is positive and $E[y]$ is greater when z^* is positive than when it is negative. Since $0 < \delta < 1$, the additional term serves to reduce the marginal effect. The change in the probability affects the mean of y in that the mean in the group $z^* > 0$ is higher. The second term in the derivative compensates for this effect, leaving only the marginal effect of a change *given that $z^* \geq 0$ to begin with.* Consider Example 21.16, and suppose that education affects both the probability of migration and the income in either state. If we suppose that the income of migrants is higher than that of otherwise identical people who do not migrate, the marginal effect of education has two parts, one due to its influence in increasing the probability of the individual's entering a higher income group and one due to its influence on income within the group. As such, the coefficient on age in the regression overstates the marginal effect of the education of migrants and understates it for nonmigrants. The sizes of the various parts depend on the setting. It is quite possible that the magnitude, sign, and statistical significance of the effect might all be different from those of the estimate of $\boldsymbol{\beta}$, a point that appears usually to be overlooked in empirical studies.

In most cases, the selection variable z^* is not observed. Rather, we oberve only its sign. To consider our two examples, we typically observe only whether a woman is working or not working, or whether an individual migrated or not. We can infer the sign of z^*, but not its magnitude, from such information. Since there is no information on the scale of z^*, the

---

[42] We have reversed the sign of α_u in (21–43) since $a = 0$, and $\alpha = \gamma' \mathbf{w}/\sigma_u$ is somewhat more convenient. Also, as such, $\partial \lambda / \partial \alpha = -\delta$.

disturbance variance in the selection equation cannot be estimated. (We encountered this problem in Chapter 20 in connection with the probit model.) Thus, we reformulate the model as follows:

$$\textbf{\textit{Selection Mechanism}}$$

$$z^* = \gamma'\mathbf{w} + u, \qquad u \sim N[0, 1],$$

$$z = 1 \qquad \text{if } z^* > 0,$$

$$z = 0 \qquad \text{if } z^* \leq 0, \tag{21-51}$$

$$\text{Prob}[z = 1] = \Phi(\gamma'\mathbf{w}),$$

$$\text{Prob}[z = 0] = 1 - \Phi(\gamma'\mathbf{w}).$$

$$\textbf{\textit{Regression Model}}$$

$$y = \boldsymbol{\beta}'\mathbf{x} + \varepsilon, \qquad \text{observed only if } z = 1,$$

$$(u, \varepsilon) \sim \text{bivariate normal } [0, 0, 1, \sigma_\varepsilon, \rho].$$

Suppose that, as in many of these studies, z_i and $\mathbf{w}_i$ are observed for a random sample of individuals, but y_i is observed only when $z_i = 1$. This is precisely the model we examined earlier, with

$$E[y_i \mid z_i = 1] = \boldsymbol{\beta}'\mathbf{x} + \rho\sigma_\varepsilon\lambda(\gamma'\mathbf{w}). \tag{21-52}$$

21.4.3.   Estimation

The parameters of the sample selection model can be estimated by maximum likelihood. However, this is quite cumbersome, and an alternative procedure due to Heckman (1979) is usually used instead. Heckman's two-step estimation procedure is as follows:

1. Estimate the probit equation by maximum likelihood to obtain estimates of γ. For each observation in the selected sample compute

$$\hat{\lambda}_i = \frac{\phi(\hat{\gamma}'\mathbf{w}_i)}{\Phi(\hat{\gamma}'\mathbf{w}_i)}. \tag{21-53}$$

We shall also require

$$\hat{\delta}_i = \hat{\lambda}_i(\hat{\lambda}_i + \hat{\gamma}'\mathbf{w}_i). \tag{21-54}$$

(If the selection is on $z_i = 0$, it is only necessary to replace $\hat{\lambda}_i$ with $-\phi/(1 - \Phi)$ and change $+$ to $-$ in the definition of $\hat{\delta}_i$.)

2. Estimate $\boldsymbol{\beta}$ and $\beta_\lambda = \rho\sigma_\varepsilon$ by least squares regression of y on $\mathbf{x}$ and $\hat{\lambda}$.

EXAMPLE 21.17. The Migration Model Continued.   Nakosteen and Zimmer (1980) applied the model of Example 21.16 to a sample of 9223 individuals with data for 2 years (1971 and 1973) sampled from the Social Security Administration's Continuous Work History Sample. Over the period, 1078 individuals migrated and the remaining 8145 did not. The independent variables in the migration equation were as follows:

SE = self-employment dummy variable; 1 if yes,

ΔEMP = rate of growth of state employment,

ΔPCI = growth of state per capita income,

AGE, RACE (nonwhite = 1), SEX (female = 1),

ΔSIC = 1 if individual changes industry.

Table 21.5

	Migration	Migrant Earnings	Nonmigrant Earnings
Constant	−1.509	9.041	8.593
SE	−0.708	−4.104	−4.161
	(−5.72)	(−9.54)	(−57.71)
ΔEMP	−1.488	—	—
	(−2.60)		
ΔPCI	1.455	—	—
	(3.14)		
AGE	−0.008	—	—
	(−5.29)		
RACE	−0.065	—	—
	(−1.17)		
SEX	−0.082	—	—
	(−2.14)		
ΔSIC	0.948	−0.790	−0.927
	(24.15)	(−2.24)	(−9.35)
λ	—	0.212	.863
		0.50)	2.84)

The earnings equations included ΔSIC and SE. The authors reported the results given in Table 21.5. The figures in parentheses are asymptotic t ratios.

Since the variables in the earnings equations are both dummy variables, we cannot obtain marginal effects for them. One noteworthy feature of these results is that they contain two conflicting tests of the hypothesis that ρ equals zero. Both coefficients on λ are estimates of $\rho\sigma_\varepsilon$. We may take it as self-evident that σ_ε is not zero, as if it were, the regression would give a perfect fit. Unfortunately, the tests suggest that ρ is and is not equal to zero.

It is also possible to obtain consistent estimates of the individual parameters ρ and σ_ε. At each observation, the true variance of the disturbance would be

$$\sigma_i^2 = \sigma_\varepsilon^2(1 - \rho^2\delta_i). \tag{21–55}$$

The average variance for the sample would converge to

$$\operatorname{plim}\frac{1}{n}\sum_i \sigma_i^2 = \sigma_\varepsilon^2 - \sigma_\varepsilon^2\rho^2\bar{\delta}. \tag{21–56}$$

This is what is estimated by the least squares residual variance, $e'e/n$. For the square of the coefficient on λ, we have

$$\operatorname{plim} b_\lambda^2 = \rho^2\sigma_\varepsilon^2,$$

while based on the probit results, we have

$$\operatorname{plim}\frac{1}{n}\sum_i \hat{\delta}_i = \bar{\delta}.$$

Then we can obtain a consistent estimator of σ_ε^2 using

$$\hat{\sigma}_\varepsilon^2 = \frac{e'e}{n} + \bar{\delta}b_\lambda^2. \tag{21–57}$$

Finally, an estimate of ρ^2 is obtained as

$$\hat{\rho}^2 = \frac{b_\lambda^2}{\hat{\sigma}_\varepsilon^2}. \qquad (21-58)$$

This provides a complete set of estimates of the model's parameters.

In order to test hypotheses, an estimate of the asymptotic covariance matrix of $[\mathbf{b}', b_\lambda]$ is needed. We have two problems to contend with. First, we can see in Theorem 21.4 that the disturbance term in

$$(y_i \mid z_i = 1) = \boldsymbol{\beta}'\mathbf{x}_i + \rho\sigma_\varepsilon\lambda_i + v_i \qquad (21-59)$$

is heteroscedastic:

$$\text{Var}[v_i] = \sigma_\varepsilon^2(1 - \rho^2\delta_i). \qquad (21-60)$$

Suppose that we assume for the moment that λ and δ are known (i.e., we do not have to estimate γ). For convenience, let $\mathbf{x}_i^* = [\mathbf{x}_i, \lambda_i]$ and let $\mathbf{b}^*$ be the least squares coefficient vector in the regression of y on $\mathbf{x}^*$ in the selected data. Then, using the appropriate form of the variance of ordinary least squares in a heteroscedastic model, from Chapter 14, we would have to estimate

$$\text{Var}[\mathbf{b}^*] = \sigma^2[\mathbf{X}_*'\mathbf{X}_*]^{-1}\left[\sum_i(1 - \rho^2\delta_i)\mathbf{x}_i^*\mathbf{x}_i^{*'}\right][\mathbf{X}_*'\mathbf{X}_*]^{-1}$$

$$= \sigma^2[\mathbf{X}_*'\mathbf{X}_*]^{-1}[\mathbf{X}_*'(\mathbf{I} - \rho^2\boldsymbol{\Delta})\mathbf{X}_*][\mathbf{X}_*'\mathbf{X}_*]^{-1}, \qquad (21-61)$$

where $\mathbf{I} - \rho^2\boldsymbol{\Delta}$ is a diagonal matrix with $(1 - \rho^2\delta_i)$ on the diagonal. Without any other complications, this could be computed fairly easily using $\mathbf{X}$, the sample estimates of σ^2 and ρ^2, and the assumed known values of λ_i and δ_i.

EXAMPLE 21.18. Lee (1978) applied the framework of Example 21.16 to a model of earnings in union and nonunion employment. In order to compute standard errors for the two-step least squares estimates, he used the approximation in (21–61). However, for his data, he found that the estimates of $\sigma^2(1 - \rho^2\delta_i)$ varied only from 0.070 to 0.085, with $\mathbf{e}'\mathbf{e}/n$ equal to 0.078 for the union equation and 0.100 to 0.1168 for the nonunion equation, with $\mathbf{e}'\mathbf{e}/n$ equal to 0.1112. Thus, the least squares standard errors were used as a reasonable approximation. Lee also attempted to use a weighted least squares estimator, with weights $w_i = 1/(\sigma^2(1 - \rho^2\delta_i))$, but found that the correlation between $1/w_i$ and λ_i/w_i was too high to allow estimation.

As Lee noted, matters are more complicated than (21–61). The parameters in γ do have to be estimated using the probit equation. Rewrite (21–59) as

$$(y_i \mid z_i = 1) = \boldsymbol{\beta}'\mathbf{x}_i + \beta_\lambda\lambda_i + v_i + \beta_\lambda(\hat{\lambda}_i - \lambda_i). \qquad (21-62)$$

In this form, we see that in the preceding expression, we have ignored both an additional source of variation in the compound disturbance and correlation across observations; the same estimate of γ is used to compute $\hat{\lambda}$ for every observation. Heckman has shown that the earlier variance matrix can be appropriately corrected by adding a term inside the brackets,

$$\mathbf{Q} = \hat{\rho}^2(\mathbf{X}_*'\,\boldsymbol{\Delta}\mathbf{W})\,\text{Est.}\,\text{Var}[\hat{\boldsymbol{\gamma}}](\mathbf{W}'\,\boldsymbol{\Delta}\mathbf{X}_*) = \hat{\rho}^2\mathbf{F}\hat{\mathbf{V}}\mathbf{F}', \qquad (21-63)$$

where $\hat{\mathbf{V}} = \text{Est.}\,\text{Asy.}\,\text{Var}[\hat{\boldsymbol{\gamma}}]$, the estimator of the asymptotic covariance of the probit coefficients. Any of (20–35) to (20–37) may be used to compute $\hat{\mathbf{V}}$. The complete expression is[43]

$$\text{Var}[\mathbf{b}, b_\lambda] = \hat{\sigma}_\varepsilon^2 [\mathbf{X}_*' \mathbf{X}_*]^{-1} [\mathbf{X}_*'(\mathbf{I} - \hat{\rho}^2 \hat{\Lambda})\mathbf{X}_* + \mathbf{Q}][\mathbf{X}_*' \mathbf{X}_*]^{-1}. \tag{21-64}$$

There is one additional complication. Suppose, once again, that λ is known. Then (21–61) would be the appropriate covariance matrix. The matrix in (21–61) is obviously positive definite, as both ρ^2 and δ are between zero and one. But note how ρ^2 is estimated in (21–58). It is a ratio of two other estimates, not a squared correlation. As such, in a finite sample, the estimate of ρ^2 could be larger than one. If it is too large, $(1 - \hat{\rho}^2 \hat{\delta}_i)$ could be less than zero, even though $(1 - \rho^2 \delta)$ could not. If it were less than one, it is possible that the sample estimate of the matrix in (21–61) might not be positive definite, and we could not compute standard errors. The effect would be at least partially offset by $\mathbf{Q}$ in the computation of (21–64), but this might not be sufficient, especially if the sample used to estimate the probit equation is very large and the selected subset is relatively small. This is a fairly common problem in the estimation of this model. It is unfortunate that if this happens, one cannot then report the usual least squares estimates, confident that they are smaller than the correct values. They might not be.[44]

21.4.4. Some Extensions

The basic model of selectivity outlined earlier has been extended in an impressive variety of directions.[45] Here we consider two interesting applications that have found wide use.

21.4.4a. The Mismeasured Treatment Effect

An earnings equation that accounts for the value of a college education is

$$\text{Earnings} = \boldsymbol{\beta}'\mathbf{x} + \delta C + \varepsilon, \tag{21-65}$$

where C is a dummy variable indicating whether or not the individual attended college. The same format has been used in any number of other analyses of programs, experiments, and treatments. The question is, does δ measure the value of a college education (assuming that the rest of the regression model is correctly specified)? The answer is no if the typical individual who chooses to go to college would have relatively high earnings whether or not he or she went to college. The problem is one of self-selection. If our observation is correct, least squares estimates of δ will actually overestimate the treatment effect. The same observation applies to estimates of the treatment effects in other settings in which the individuals themselves decide whether or not they will receive the treatment.

To put this in a more familiar context, suppose that we model program participation (e.g., whether or not the individual goes to college) as

$$C^* = \gamma'\mathbf{w} + u$$

$$C = 1 \quad \text{if } C^* > 0, 0 \text{ otherwise.}$$

We also suppose that, consistent with our previous conjecture, u and ε are correlated. Coupled with our earnings equation, we find that

$$E[y \mid C = 1] = \boldsymbol{\beta}'\mathbf{x} + \delta + E[\varepsilon \mid C = 1]$$
$$= \boldsymbol{\beta}'\mathbf{x} + \delta + \rho\sigma_\varepsilon \lambda(\gamma'\mathbf{w}) \tag{21-66}$$

[43] This formulation is derived in Greene (1981).
[44] Ibid.
[45] For a survey, see Maddala (1983).

once again. Evidently, a viable strategy for estimating this model is to use the two-step estimator discussed earlier. The net result will be a different estimate of δ that will account for the self-selected nature of program participation. For nonparticipants, the counterpart to (21–66) is

$$E[y\,|\,C = 0] = \boldsymbol{\beta}'\mathbf{x} + \rho\sigma_{\varepsilon}\left[\frac{-\phi(\boldsymbol{\gamma}'\mathbf{w})}{1 - \Phi(\boldsymbol{\gamma}'\mathbf{w})}\right]. \tag{21–67}$$

The difference in expected earnings between participants and nonparticipants is, then,

$$E[y\,|\,C = 1] - E[y\,|\,C = 0] = \delta + \rho\sigma_{\varepsilon}\left\{\frac{\phi^2}{\Phi(1 - \Phi)}\right\}. \tag{21–68}$$

If the selectivity correction, λ, is omitted from the least squares regression, this difference is what is estimated by the least squares coefficient on the treatment dummy variable. But since (by assumption) all terms are positive, we see that least squares overestimates the treatment effect. Note, finally, that simply estimating separate equations for participants and nonparticipants does not solve the problem. In fact, this would be equivalent to estimating the two regressions of Example 21.16 by least squares, which, as we have seen, would lead to inconsistent estimates of both sets of parameters.

There are many variations of this model in the recent empirical literature. They have been applied to the analysis of education,[46] the Headstart program,[47] and a host of other settings.[48] This is a particularly important strand of literature, as the use of dummy variable models to analyze treatment effects and program participation has a long history in empirical economics. This analysis has called into question the interpretation of a number of received studies.

21.4.4b.   Switching Regressions—Markets in Disequilibrium

The usual assumption in analysis of markets is that the observed price and quantity represent an equilibrium, the intersection of supply and demand. But there are many markets out of equilibrium at any time. Numerous methods have been developed for analyzing markets in disequilibrium. Two recent surveys that examine these models in detail are the monograph by Maddala and a review by Quandt (1982).

A simple approach to the modeling of a market out of equilibrium might begin with

$$
\begin{aligned}
\text{Supply:} \quad & Q_s = \mu P + \boldsymbol{\beta}'_s\mathbf{x}_s + \varepsilon_s, \\
\text{Demand:} \quad & Q_d = \pi P + \boldsymbol{\beta}'_d\mathbf{x}_d + \varepsilon_d, \\
\text{Observed:} \quad & Q = \text{Min}[Q_d, Q_s].
\end{aligned}
\tag{21–69}
$$

Let

$$
\begin{aligned}
Z^* &= Q_s - Q_d \\
&= (\mu - \pi)P + \boldsymbol{\beta}'_s\mathbf{x}_s - \boldsymbol{\beta}'_d\mathbf{x}_d + (\varepsilon_s - \varepsilon_d).
\end{aligned}
\tag{21–70}
$$

[46] Willis and Rosen (1979).
[47] Goldberger (1972).
[48] A useful summary of the issues is Barnow, Cain, and Goldberger (1981). See, as well, Maddala (1983) for a long list of applications.

The presumption in the third equation is the familiar one in microeconomics that if the market is in a state of adjustment, the "short side" of the market is always the one we observe. Suppose, for the present, that it is valid to treat P as an exogenous variable. If ε_d and ε_s are uncorrelated, the variance of $(\varepsilon_s - \varepsilon_d)$ is $(\sigma_s^2 + \sigma_d^2)$. Neglecting, for the present, whether or not we know which equation applies at any given time, the model implies that

$$Z^* = \gamma'w + u, \tag{21-71}$$

where

$$w = [P, x_s U x_d],$$

$$\gamma = \frac{(\mu - \pi, \theta)}{\sqrt{\sigma_s^2 + \sigma_d^2}},$$

and θ has three parts. Any variable x_{sk} only in x_s has coefficient β_{sk}, any x_{dk} only in x_d has coefficient $-\beta_{dk}$, and any variable in both has coefficient $(\beta_{sk} - \beta_{dk})$. Let $Z = 1$ if $Z^* > 0$. Then this is precisely the model of the previous section. In this case, data for each of the regressions (regimes) represents a selected sample. For example, if Z^* is positive and we are on the demand equation, we have

$$E[Q \mid \text{demand}] = \pi P + \beta_d' x_d + \rho \sigma_{\varepsilon_s} \lambda(\alpha_d). \tag{21-72}$$

Here we know a bit more about the parameters. In particular,

$$\rho = \text{corr}(\varepsilon_s, \varepsilon_s - \varepsilon_d) = \frac{\sigma_s}{\sqrt{\sigma_s^2 + \sigma_d^2}}, \tag{21-73}$$

$$\alpha_s = \frac{\gamma'w}{\sqrt{\sigma_s^2 + \sigma_d^2}},$$

and, of course,

$$\lambda(\alpha_s) = \frac{\phi(\alpha_s)}{\Phi(\alpha_s)}.$$

The counterpart for the supply equation is defined similarly.

There are two issues to consider. First, is it reasonable to treat P as an exogenous variable? In most cases, it is not, so a least squares–based approach, even one with the previous selection correction, leads to inconsistent estimates. Maximum likelihood estimation would be a valid approach, assuming, however, that we can deal with the second issue.[49] How do we know which equation is the right one at any given observation? The many switching regression models that have been developed differ primarily in their handling of this problem. Two solutions that have been proposed are labeled the **directional method** and the **quantitative method**. In the first, the sign of Z^* is implied by the direction of movement in price in the last period. If $(P_t - P_{t-1})$ is positive, there must be excess demand, which puts us on the supply curve for this period. A negative direction implies the demand curve instead.[50] Thus, we are able to deduce Z and, thereafter, apply our familiar two-step

---

[49] See Maddala (1983, chapter 10).
[50] The model is due to Fair and Jaffee (1972).

estimator. The quantitative method adds another structural equation,

$$P_t - P_{t-1} = \delta[Q_d - Q_s].$$

This might seem to imply that we could just use the directional method, as δ would surely be positive. The new difficulty is that with this formulation, we can no longer treat P_t as an exogenous variable. Once again, maximum likelihood methods have been developed.

The assumption of the directional method is a bit strong. Unfortunately, it or something like it is needed to legitimize the Heckman estimator for the switching regression model. Even if this is possible, we should note that there is yet another layer of inefficiency in this treatment. There are no parameters in the selection equation that are not in the regression equations. Therefore, the use of a maximum likelihood estimator is likely to be far more efficient. Most of the literature in this field, both applied and theoretical, focuses on maximum likelihood estimators.

We note, finally, that one remaining possibility is to assume that the sample separation is, in fact, not known. The model can still be estimated by maximum likelihood, if not by two-step least squares. However, this is one of the more difficult problems of maximum likelihood estimation, and as might be expected when we ask this much of a single data set, the estimates one obtains by this procedure are often highly unstable.[51]

21.4.5. Postscript

Recent research has cast some skepticism on the selection model based on the normal distribution. [See, e.g., Goldberger (1983).] Among the findings are that the parameter estimates are surprisingly sensitive to the distributional assumption that underlies the model. Of course, this in itself does not invalidate the normal model, but it does call its generality into question. On the other hand, the received evidence is compelling that sample selection, on its own, raises very serious problems. The most recent literature [Duncan (1986), for example] has suggested some promising approaches in the area of robust estimators, though the two-step approaches based on Heckman's results continue to dominate the applied literature.

Exercises

1. The following 20 observations are drawn from a censored normal distribution:

3.8396	7.2040	0.00000	0.00000	4.4132	8.0230
5.7971	7.0828	0.00000	0.80260	13.0670	4.3211
0.00000	8.6801	5.4571	0.00000	8.1021	0.00000
1.2526	5.6016				

The applicable model is

$$y_i^* = \mu + \varepsilon_i$$

$$y_i = y_i^* \quad \text{if } \mu + \varepsilon_i > 0, 0 \text{ otherwise.}$$

$$\varepsilon_i \sim N[0, \sigma^2].$$

All exercises in this section are based on the preceding. The OLS estimator of μ in the context of this Tobit model is simply the sample mean. Compute the mean of all 20

---

[51] An interesting literature has appeared on this issue, including Quandt and Ramsey (1978) and Kiefer (1979).

observations. Would you expect this estimator to over- or underestimate μ? If we consider only the nonzero observations, the truncated regression model applies. The sample mean of the nonlimit observations is the least squares estimator in this context. Compute it and then comment on whether this should be an overestimate or an underestimate of the true mean.

2. We now consider the Tobit model that applies to the full data set.

   (a) Formulate the log likelihood for this very simple Tobit model.

   (b) Reformulate the log likelihood in terms of $\theta = 1/\sigma$ and $\gamma = \mu/\sigma$. Then derive the necessary conditions for maximizing the log likelihood with respect to θ and γ.

   (c) Discuss how you would obtain the values of θ and γ to solve the problem in part (b).

   (d) Obtain the maximum likelihood estimators of μ and σ.

3. Using only the nonlimit observations, repeat the previous exercise in the context of the truncated regression model.

4. Estimate μ and σ by using the method of moments estimator outlined in Example 21.4. Compare your results to those in the previous exercises.

5. Continuing to use the data in Exercise 1, consider, once again only the nonzero observations. Suppose that the sampling mechanism is as follows: y^* and another normally distributed random variable, z, have population correlation 0.7. The two variables, y^* and z, are sampled jointly. When z is greater than zero, y is reported. When z is less than zero, both z and y are discarded. Exactly 35 draws were required in order to obtain the preceding sample. Estimate μ and σ. (**Hint:** Use Theorem 21.4.)

References

Abowd, J., and H. Farber, "Job Queues and Union Status of Workers," *Industrial and Labor Relations Review*, 35, 1982, pp. 354–367.

Amemiya, T., "Regression Analysis When the Dependent Variable Is Truncated Normal," *Econometrica*, 41, 1973, pp. 997–1016.

Amemiya, T., "Tobit Models: A Survey," *Journal of Econometrics*, 24, 1984, pp. 3–63.

Amemiya, T., *Advanced Econometrics*, Cambridge, Mass.: Harvard University Press, 1985.

Arabmazar, A., and P. Schmidt, "An Investigation into the Robustness of the Tobit Estimator to Nonnormality," *Econometrica*, 50, 1982a, pp. 1055–1063.

Arabmazar, A., and P. Schmidt, "Further Evidence on the Robustness of the Tobit Estimator to Heteroscedasticity," *Journal of Econometrics*, 17, 1982b, pp. 253–258.

Barnow, B., G. Cain, and A. Goldberger, "Issues in the Analysis of Selectivity Bias," in E. Stromsdorfer, and G. Farkas, eds., *Evaluation Studies Review Annual*, Vol. 5, Beverly Hills, Calif.: Sage, 1981.

Bera, A., C. Jarque, and L. Lee, "Testing for the Normality Assumption in Limited Dependent Variable Models," mimeo, Department of Economics, Department of Economics, University of Minnesota, 1982.

Blundell, R., ed., "Specification Testing in Limited and Discrete Dependent Variable Models," *Journal of Econometrics*, 34, 1987, pp. 1–274.

Brown, C., and R. Moffitt, "The Effect of Ignoring Heteroscedasticity on Estimates of the Tobit Model," mimeo, University of Maryland, Department of Economics, June 1982.

Catsiapis, G., and C. Robinson, "Sample Selection Bias with Multiple Selection Rules: An Application to Student Aid Grants," *Journal of Econometrics*, 18, 1982, pp. 351–368.

Cheung, C.-F., and A. Goldberger, "Proportional Projections in Limited Dependent Variable Models," *Econometrica*, 52, 1984, pp. 531–534.

Cragg, J., "Some Statistical Models for Limited Dependent Variables with Application to the Demand for Durable Goods," *Econometrica*, 39, 1971, pp. 829–844.

Crawford, D., "Estimating Earnings Functions from Truncated Samples," Discussion Paper 287–75, Institute for Research on Poverty, University of Wisconsin–Madison, 1975.

Dhrymes, P., "Limited Dependent Variables," in Z. Griliches, and M. Intrilligator, eds., *Handbook of Econometrics*, Amsterdam: North Holland, 1984.

Duncan, G., "Sample Selectivity as a Proxy Variable Problem: On the Use and Misuse of Gaussian Selectivity Corrections," *Research in Labor Economics*, Supplement 2, 1983, pp. 333–345.

Duncan, G., ed., "Continuous/Discrete Econometric Models with Unspecified Error Distribution," *Journal of Econometrics*, 32, 1, 1986, pp. 1–187.

Fair, R., "A Note on Computation of the Tobit Estimator," *Econometrica*, 45, 1977, pp. 1723–1727.

Fair, R., "A Theory of Extramarital Affairs," *Journal of Political Economy*, 86, 1978, pp. 45–61.

Fair, R., and D. Jaffee, "Methods of Estimation for Markets in Disequilibrium," *Econometrica*, 40, 1972, pp. 497–514.

Fin, T., and P. Schmidt, "A Test of the Tobit Specification Against an Alternative Suggested by Cragg," *Review of Economics and Statistics*, 66, 1984, pp. 174–177.

Goldberger, A., "Selection Bias in Evaluating Treatment Effects: Some Formal Illustrations," Discussion Paper 123–72, Institute for Research on Poverty, University of Wisconsin–Madison, 1972.

Goldberger, A., "Linear Regression After Selection," *Journal of Econometrics*, 15, 1981, pp. 357–366.

Goldberger, A., "Abnormal Selection Bias," in S. Karlin, T. Amemiya, and L. Goodman, eds., *Studies in Econometrics, Time Series, and Multivariate Statistics*, Stamford: Academic Press, 1983.

Greene, W., "On the Asymptotic Bias of the Ordinary Least Squares Estimator of the Tobit Model," *Econometrica*, 49, 1981, pp. 505–513.

Greene, W., "Sample Selection Bias as a Specification Error: Comment," *Econometrica*, 49, 1981, pp. 795–798.

Greene, W., "Estimation of Limited Dependent Variable Models by Ordinary Least Squares and the Method of Moments, "*Journal of Econometrics*, 21, 1983, pp. 195–212.

Griliches, Z., and M. Intrilligator, *Handbook of Econometrics* Amsterdam: North Holland, 1983.

Gronau, R., "Wage Comparisons: A Selectivity Bias," and Lewis, H., "Comments on Selectivity Biases in Wage Comparisons," *Journal of Political Economy*, 82, 1974, pp. 1119–1155.

Hall, B., "Software for the Computation of Tobit Model Estimates," *Journal of Econometrics*, 24, 1984, pp. 215–222.

Hartley, M., "The Tobit and Probit Models: Maximum Likelihood Estimation by OLS," Working Paper Number 375, State University of New York, Buffalo, Department of Economics, 1976.

Hausman, J., and D. Wise, "Social Experimentation, Truncated Distributions, and Efficient Estimation," *Econometrica*, 45, 1977, pp. 919–938.

Heckman, J., "The Common Structure of Statistical Models of Truncation, Sample Selection, and Limited Dependent Variables and a Simple Estimator for Such Models, "*The Annals of Economic and Social Measurement*, 5, 1976, pp. 475–492.

Heckman, J., "Sample Selection Bias as a Specification Error," *Econometrica*, 47, 1979, pp. 153–161.

Hurd, M., "Estimation in Truncated Samples When There Is Heteroscedasticity," *Journal of Econometrics*, 11, 1979, pp. 247–258.

Jarque, C., "An Application of LDV Models to Household Expenditure Analysis in Mexico," *Journal of Econometrics*, 36, 1987, pp. 31–54.

Johnson, N., and S. Kotz, *Distributions in Statistics: Continuous Univariate Distributions–1*, New York: Wiley, 1970, p. 81.

Johnson, N., and A. Kotz, *Distributions in Statistics—Continuous Multivariate Distributions*, New York: Wiley, 1974.

Kalbfleisch, J., and R. Prentice, *The Statistical Analysis of Failure Time Data*, New York: Wiley, 1980, pp. 42–58.

Kiefer, N., "On the Value of Sample Separation Information," *Econometrica*, 47, 1979, pp. 997–1003.

Lee, L., "Unionism and Wage Rates: A Simultaneous Equations Model with Qualitative and Limited Dependent Variables," *International Economic Review*, 19, 1978, pp. 415–433.

Lewis, H., "Comments on Selectivity Biases in Wage Comparisons," *Journal of Political Economy*, 82, 1974, pp. 1119–1155.

Maddala, G., *Limited-Dependent and Qualitative Variables in Econometrics*, Cambridge: Cambridge University Press, 1983.

Maddala, G., "Disequilibrium, Self-Selection, and Switching Models," in Z. Griliches and M. Intrilligator, eds., *Handbook of Econometrics*, Amsterdam: North Holland, 1984.

Maddala, G., and F. Nelson, "Specification Errors in Limited Dependent Variable Models," National Bureau of Economic Research, Working Paper 96, Cambridge, 1975.

McDonald, J., and R. Moffitt, "The Uses of Tobit Analysis," *Review of Economics and Statistics*, 62, 1980, pp. 318–321.

Nakamura, A., and M. Nakamura, "Part-Time and Full-Time Work Behavior of Married Women: A Model with a Doubly Truncated Dependent Variable," *Canadian Journal of Economics*, 16, 1983, pp. 201–218.

Nakosteen, R., and M. Zimmer, "Migration and Income: The Question of Self-Selection," *Southern Economic Journal*, 46, 1980, pp. 840–851.

Nelson, F., "A Test for Misspecification in the Censored Normal Model," *Econometrica*, 49, 1981, pp. 1317–1329.

Nelson, F., "Efficiency of the Two-Step Estimator for Models with Endogenous Sample Selection," *Journal of Econometrics*, 24, 1984, pp. 181–196.

New York Post, "America's New Big Wheels of Fortune," May 22, 1987, p. 3.

Olsen, R., "Note on the Uniqueness of the Maximum Likelihood Estimator of the Tobit Model," *Econometrica*, 46, 1978, pp. 1211–1215.

Olsen, R., "Approximating a Truncated Normal Regression with the Method of Moments," *Econometrica*, 48, 1980, pp. 1099–1106.

Orcutt, G., S. Caldwell, and R. Wertheimer, *Policy Exploration Through Microanalytic Simulation*, Washington, D.C.: Urban Institute, 1976.

Paarsch, H., "A Monte Carlo Comparison of Estimators for Censored Regression Models," *Journal of Econometrics*, 24, 1984, pp. 197–214.

Petersen, D., and D. Waldman, "The Treatment of Heteroscedasticity in the Limited Dependent Variable Model," mimeo, Chapel Hill: University of North Carolina, November 1981.

Poirier, D., "Partial Observability in Bivariate Probit Models," *Journal of Econometrics*, 12, 1980, pp. 209–217.

Powell, J., "Least Absolute Deviations Estimation for Censored and Truncated Regression Models," IMSSS, Technical Report 356, Stanford University, 1981.

Quandt, R., "Econometric Disequilibrium Models," *Econometric Reviews*, 1, 1982, pp. 1–63.

Quandt, R., and J. Ramsey, "Estimating Mixtures of Normal Distributions and Switching Regressions," *Journal of the American Statistical Association*, 73, 1978, pp. 730–752.

Quester, A., and W. Greene, "Divorce Risk and Wives' Labor Supply Behavior," *Social Science Quarterly*, 63, 1982, pp. 16–27.

Rosett, R., and F. Nelson, "Estimation of the Two-Limit Probit Regression Model," *Econometrica*, 43, 1975, pp. 141–146.

Stapleton, D., and D. Young, "Censored Normal Regression with Measurement Error on the Dependent Variable," Discussion Paper 81–30, Department of Economics, University of British Columbia, 1981.

Stewart, M., "On Least Squares Estimation When the Dependent Variable Is Grouped," *Review of Economic Studies*, 50, 1983, pp. 141–149.

Tobin, J., "Estimation of Relationships for Limited Dependent Variables," *Econometrica*, 26, 1958, pp. 24–36.

Wales, T., and A. Woodland, "Sample Selectivity and the Estimation of Labor Supply Functions," *International Economic Review*, 21, 1980, pp. 437–468.

Willis, R., and S. Rosen, "Education and Self-Selection," *Journal of Political Economy*, 87, 1979, pp. S7–S36.

Witte, A., "Estimating an Economic Model of Crime with Individual Data," *Quarterly Journal of Economics*, 94, 1980, pp. 57–84.

Appendix Tables

Table 1. Cumulative Normal Distribution: Table Entry Is Prob$[Z \leq z]$

z	.00	.01	.02	.03	.04	.05	.06	.07	.08	.09
0.0	.5000	.5040	.5080	.5120	.5160	.5199	.5239	.5279	.5319	.5359
0.1	.5398	.5438	.5478	.5517	.5557	.5596	.5636	.5675	.5714	.5753
0.2	.5793	.5832	.5871	.5910	.5948	.5987	.6026	.6064	.6103	.6141
0.3	.6179	.6217	.6255	.6293	.6331	.6368	.6406	.6443	.6480	.6517
0.4	.6554	.6591	.6628	.6664	.6700	.6736	.6772	.6808	.6844	.6879
0.5	.6915	.6950	.6985	.7019	.7054	.7088	.7123	.7157	.7190	.7224
0.6	.7257	.7291	.7324	.7357	.7389	.7422	.7454	.7486	.7517	.7549
0.7	.7580	.7611	.7642	.7673	.7704	.7734	.7764	.7794	.7823	.7852
0.8	.7881	.7910	.7939	.7967	.7995	.8023	.8051	.8078	.8106	.8133
0.9	.8159	.8186	.8212	.8238	.8264	.8289	.8315	.8340	.8365	.8389
1.0	.8413	.8438	.8461	.8485	.8508	.8531	.8554	.8577	.8599	.8621
1.1	.8643	.8665	.8686	.8708	.8729	.8749	.8770	.8790	.8810	.8830
1.2	.8849	.8869	.8888	.8907	.8925	.8944	.8962	.8980	.8997	.9015
1.3	.9032	.9049	.9066	.9082	.9099	.9115	.9131	.9147	.9162	.9177
1.4	.9192	.9207	.9222	.9236	.9251	.9265	.9279	.9292	.9306	.9319
1.5	.9332	.9345	.9357	.9370	.9382	.9394	.9406	.9418	.9429	.9441
1.6	.9452	.9463	.9474	.9484	.9495	.9505	.9515	.9525	.9535	.9545
1.7	.9554	.9564	.9573	.9582	.9591	.9599	.9608	.9616	.9625	.9633
1.8	.9641	.9649	.9656	.9664	.9671	.9678	.9686	.9693	.9699	.9706
1.9	.9713	.9719	.9726	.9732	.9738	.9744	.9750	.9756	.9761	.9767
2.0	.9772	.9778	.9783	.9788	.9793	.9798	.9803	.9808	.9812	.9817
2.1	.9821	.9826	.9830	.9834	.9838	.9842	.9846	.9850	.9854	.9857
2.2	.9861	.9864	.9868	.9871	.9875	.9878	.9881	.9884	.9887	.9890
2.3	.9893	.9896	.9898	.9901	.9904	.9906	.9909	.9911	.9913	.9916
2.4	.9918	.9920	.9922	.9925	.9927	.9929	.9931	.9932	.9934	.9936
2.5	.9938	.9940	.9941	.9943	.9945	.9946	.9948	.9949	.9951	.9952
2.6	.9953	.9955	.9956	.9957	.9959	.9960	.9961	.9962	.9963	.9964
2.7	.9965	.9966	.9967	.9968	.9969	.9970	.9971	.9972	.9973	.9974
2.8	.9974	.9975	.9976	.9977	.9977	.9978	.9979	.9979	.9980	.9981
2.9	.9981	.9982	.9982	.9983	.9984	.9984	.9985	.9985	.9986	.9986
3.0	.9987	.9987	.9987	.9988	.9988	.9989	.9989	.9989	.9990	.9990
3.1	.9990	.9991	.9991	.9991	.9992	.9992	.9992	.9992	.9993	.9993
3.2	.9993	.9993	.9994	.9994	.9994	.9994	.9994	.9995	.9995	.9995
3.3	.9995	.9995	.9995	.9996	.9996	.9996	.9996	.9996	.9996	.9997
3.4	.9997	.9997	.9997	.9997	.9997	.9997	.9997	.9997	.9997	.9998

Table 2.   Ordinates of the Standard Normal Density. Table Entry is $f(z)$.

z	.00	.01	.02	.03	.04	.05	.06	.07	.08	.09
0.0	.3989	.3989	.3989	.3988	.3986	.3984	.3982	.3980	.3977	.3973
0.1	.3970	.3965	.3961	.3956	.3951	.3945	.3939	.3932	.3925	.3918
0.2	.3910	.3902	.3894	.3885	.3876	.3867	.3857	.3847	.3836	.3825
0.3	.3814	.3802	.3790	.3778	.3765	.3752	.3739	.3725	.3712	.3697
0.4	.3683	.3668	.3653	.3637	.3621	.3605	.3589	.3572	.3555	.3538
0.5	.3521	.3503	.3485	.3467	.3448	.3429	.3410	.3391	.3372	.3352
0.6	.3332	.3312	.3292	.3271	.3251	.3230	.3209	.3187	.3166	.3144
0.7	.3123	.3101	.3079	.3056	.3034	.3011	.2989	.2966	.2943	.2920
0.8	.2897	.2874	.2850	.2827	.2803	.2780	.2756	.2732	.2709	.2685
0.9	.2661	.2637	.2613	.2589	.2565	.2541	.2516	.2492	.2468	.2444
1.0	.2420	.2396	.2371	.2347	.2323	.2299	.2275	.2251	.2227	.2203
1.1	.2179	.2155	.2131	.2107	.2083	.2059	.2036	.2012	.1989	.1965
1.2	.1942	.1919	.1895	.1872	.1849	.1826	.1804	.1781	.1758	.1736
1.3	.1714	.1691	.1669	.1647	.1626	.1604	.1582	.1561	.1539	.1518
1.4	.1497	.1476	.1456	.1435	.1415	.1394	.1374	.1354	.1334	.1315
1.5	.1295	.1276	.1257	.1238	.1219	.1200	.1182	.1163	.1145	.1127
1.6	.1109	.1092	.1074	.1057	.1040	.1023	.1006	.0989	.0973	.0957
1.7	.0940	.0925	.0909	.0893	.0878	.0863	.0848	.0833	.0818	.0804
1.8	.0790	.0775	.0761	.0748	.0734	.0721	.0707	.0694	.0681	.0669
1.9	.0656	.0644	.0632	.0620	.0608	.0596	.0584	.0573	.0562	.0551
2.0	.0540	.0529	.0519	.0508	.0498	.0488	.0478	.0468	.0459	.0449
2.1	.0440	.0431	.0422	.0413	.0404	.0396	.0387	.0379	.0371	.0363
2.2	.0355	.0347	.0339	.0332	.0325	.0317	.0310	.0303	.0297	.0290
2.3	.0283	.0277	.0270	.0264	.0258	.0252	.0246	.0241	.0235	.0229
2.4	.0224	.0219	.0213	.0208	.0203	.0198	.0194	.0189	.0184	.0180
2.5	.0175	.0171	.0167	.0163	.0158	.0154	.0151	.0147	.0143	.0139
2.6	.0136	.0132	.0129	.0126	.0122	.0119	.0116	.0113	.0110	.0107
2.7	.0104	.0101	.0099	.0096	.0093	.0091	.0088	.0086	.0084	.0081
2.8	.0079	.0077	.0075	.0073	.0071	.0069	.0067	.0065	.0063	.0061
2.9	.0060	.0058	.0056	.0055	.0053	.0051	.0050	.0048	.0047	.0046
3.0	.0044	.0043	.0042	.0040	.0039	.0038	.0037	.0036	.0035	.0034
3.1	.0033	.0032	.0031	.0030	.0029	.0028	.0027	.0026	.0025	.0025
3.2	.0024	.0023	.0022	.0022	.0021	.0020	.0020	.0019	.0018	.0018
3.3	.0017	.0017	.0016	.0016	.0015	.0015	.0014	.0014	.0013	.0013
3.4	.0012	.0012	.0012	.0011	.0011	.0010	.0010	.0010	.0009	.0009

Table 3. Percentiles of the Student's t Distribution.
Table Entry Is x Such That $\text{Prob}[t_n \le x] = P$.

n \ P	.750	.900	.950	.975	.990	.995
1	1.000	3.078	6.314	12.71	31.82	63.66
2	0.817	1.886	2.920	4.303	6.965	9.925
3	0.766	1.638	2.354	3.182	4.541	5.841
4	0.741	1.533	2.132	2.777	3.747	4.604
5	0.727	1.476	2.015	2.571	3.365	4.032
6	0.718	1.440	1.943	2.447	3.143	3.708
7	0.711	1.415	1.895	2.365	2.998	3.500
8	0.706	1.397	1.860	2.306	2.897	3.355
9	0.703	1.383	1.833	2.262	2.822	3.250
10	0.700	1.372	1.813	2.228	2.764	3.169
11	0.698	1.363	1.796	2.201	2.718	3.106
12	0.696	1.356	1.782	2.179	2.681	3.055
13	0.694	1.350	1.771	2.161	2.650	3.012
14	0.693	1.345	1.762	2.145	2.624	2.977
15	0.691	1.341	1.753	2.132	2.602	2.947
16	0.691	1.337	1.746	2.120	2.584	2.921
17	0.689	1.333	1.740	2.110	2.567	2.898
18	0.688	1.330	1.734	2.101	2.552	2.879
19	0.688	1.328	1.729	2.093	2.539	2.861
20	0.687	1.326	1.725	2.086	2.528	2.845
21	0.687	1.323	1.721	2.080	2.518	2.831
22	0.686	1.321	1.717	2.074	2.508	2.819
23	0.686	1.319	1.714	2.069	2.500	2.807
24	0.686	1.318	1.711	2.064	2.492	2.797
25	0.685	1.316	1.708	2.060	2.485	2.787
26	0.684	1.315	1.706	2.056	2.479	2.779
27	0.684	1.314	1.704	2.052	2.473	2.771
28	0.683	1.313	1.701	2.048	2.467	2.763
29	0.683	1.311	1.699	2.045	2.462	2.756
30	0.683	1.311	1.697	2.042	2.457	2.750
35	0.682	1.307	1.690	2.030	2.438	2.724
40	0.681	1.303	1.684	2.021	2.423	2.705
45	0.680	1.301	1.680	2.014	2.412	2.690
50	0.680	1.299	1.676	2.009	2.403	2.678
60	0.679	1.296	1.671	2.000	2.390	2.660
70	0.679	1.294	1.667	1.994	2.381	2.648
80	0.679	1.292	1.664	1.990	2.374	2.639
90	0.678	1.291	1.662	1.987	2.368	2.632
100	0.677	1.290	1.660	1.984	2.364	2.626
∞	0.674	1.282	1.645	1.960	2.326	2.576

Table 4.   Percentiles of the Chi-Squared Distribution.
Table Entry Is c Such That $\text{Prob}[\chi_n^2 \le c] = P$.

P \\ n	.005	.010	.025	.050	.100	.250	.500	.750	.900	.950	.975	.990	.995
1	.00004	.0002	.001	.004	0.02	0.10	0.46	1.32	2.71	3.84	5.02	6.63	7.89
2	0.01	0.02	0.05	0.10	0.21	0.58	1.39	2.77	4.61	5.99	7.38	9.21	10.60
3	0.07	0.12	0.22	0.35	0.59	1.21	2.37	4.11	6.25	7.82	9.35	11.34	12.84
4	0.21	0.30	0.49	0.71	1.06	1.92	3.36	5.39	7.78	9.49	11.14	13.28	14.86
5	0.41	0.56	0.83	1.15	1.61	2.68	4.35	6.63	9.24	11.07	12.83	15.09	16.75
6	0.68	0.87	1.24	1.64	2.21	3.46	5.35	7.84	10.64	12.59	14.45	16.81	18.55
7	0.99	1.24	1.69	2.17	2.83	4.25	6.35	9.04	12.02	14.07	16.01	18.48	20.28
8	1.35	1.65	2.18	2.73	3.49	5.07	7.34	10.22	13.36	15.51	17.54	20.09	21.96
9	1.74	2.09	2.70	3.33	4.17	5.90	8.34	11.39	14.68	16.92	19.02	21.67	23.59
10	2.16	2.56	3.25	3.94	4.87	6.74	9.34	12.55	15.99	18.31	20.48	23.21	25.19
11	2.60	3.05	3.82	4.57	5.58	7.59	10.34	13.70	17.28	19.68	21.92	24.72	26.76
12	3.07	3.57	4.40	5.23	6.30	8.44	11.34	14.85	18.55	21.03	23.34	26.22	28.30
13	3.57	4.11	5.01	5.89	7.04	9.30	12.34	15.98	19.81	22.36	24.74	27.69	29.82
14	4.07	4.66	5.63	6.57	7.79	10.17	13.34	17.12	21.07	23.69	26.12	29.14	31.32
15	4.60	5.23	6.26	7.26	8.55	11.04	14.34	18.25	22.31	25.00	27.49	30.58	32.80
16	5.14	5.81	6.91	7.96	9.31	11.91	15.34	19.37	23.54	26.30	28.85	32.00	34.27
17	5.70	6.41	7.57	8.67	10.09	12.79	16.34	20.49	24.77	27.59	30.19	33.41	35.72
18	6.26	7.01	8.23	9.39	10.86	13.68	17.34	21.61	25.99	28.87	31.53	34.81	37.16
19	6.84	7.63	8.91	10.12	11.65	14.56	18.34	22.72	27.20	30.14	32.85	36.19	38.58
20	7.43	8.26	9.59	10.85	12.44	15.45	19.34	23.83	28.41	31.41	34.17	37.57	40.00
21	8.03	8.90	10.28	11.59	13.24	16.35	20.34	24.93	29.62	32.67	35.48	38.93	41.40
22	8.64	9.54	10.98	12.34	14.04	17.24	21.34	26.04	30.81	33.93	36.78	40.29	42.80
23	9.26	10.20	11.69	13.09	14.85	18.14	22.34	27.14	32.01	35.17	38.08	41.64	44.18
24	9.89	10.86	12.40	13.85	15.66	19.04	23.34	28.24	33.20	36.42	39.37	42.98	45.56
25	10.52	11.52	13.12	14.61	16.47	19.94	24.34	29.34	34.38	37.65	40.65	44.32	46.93
26	11.16	12.20	13.84	15.38	17.29	20.84	25.34	30.44	35.56	38.89	41.92	45.64	48.29
27	11.81	12.88	14.57	16.15	18.11	21.75	26.34	31.53	36.74	40.11	43.19	46.96	49.65
28	12.46	13.56	15.31	16.93	18.94	22.66	27.34	32.62	37.92	41.34	44.46	48.28	50.99
29	13.12	14.26	16.05	17.71	19.77	23.57	28.34	33.71	39.09	42.56	45.72	49.59	52.34
30	13.79	14.95	16.79	18.49	20.60	24.48	29.34	34.80	40.26	43.77	46.98	50.89	53.67
31	13.70	15.04	17.11	19.01	21.31	25.46	30.50	36.00	41.33	44.70	47.73	51.38	53.94
32	14.37	15.74	17.87	19.80	22.15	26.37	31.50	37.08	42.49	45.91	48.98	52.67	55.26
33	15.05	16.45	18.62	20.59	22.99	27.29	32.50	38.17	43.65	47.12	50.22	53.96	56.59
34	15.73	17.16	19.38	21.39	23.83	28.21	33.50	39.25	44.81	48.32	51.46	55.25	57.90
35	16.42	17.88	20.14	22.19	24.68	29.13	34.50	40.33	45.97	49.52	52.70	56.53	59.21
36	17.11	18.60	20.91	22.99	25.52	30.05	35.50	41.41	47.12	50.71	53.94	57.81	60.52
37	17.81	19.33	21.68	23.80	26.37	30.97	36.50	42.49	48.27	51.91	55.17	59.08	61.83
38	18.51	20.06	22.45	24.61	27.22	31.89	37.50	43.57	49.42	53.10	56.39	60.35	63.13
39	19.22	20.79	23.22	25.42	28.08	32.81	38.50	44.65	50.57	54.29	57.62	61.62	64.42
40	19.92	21.53	24.00	26.23	28.93	33.73	39.50	45.72	51.71	55.47	58.84	62.88	65.71
41	20.64	22.27	24.78	27.05	29.79	34.66	40.50	46.80	52.86	56.66	60.06	64.14	67.00
42	21.35	23.01	25.57	27.87	30.65	35.58	41.50	47.87	54.00	57.84	61.28	65.40	68.29
43	22.07	23.76	26.35	28.69	31.51	36.51	42.50	48.95	55.14	59.02	62.49	66.65	69.57
44	22.79	24.51	27.14	29.51	32.37	37.44	43.50	50.02	56.27	60.19	63.70	67.91	70.84
45	23.52	25.26	27.93	30.34	33.23	38.37	44.50	51.09	57.41	61.37	64.91	69.15	72.12
46	24.25	26.02	28.72	31.16	34.10	39.29	45.50	52.16	58.55	62.54	66.12	70.40	73.39
47	24.98	26.77	29.52	31.99	34.96	40.22	46.50	53.23	59.68	63.72	67.32	71.64	74.66
48	25.71	27.53	30.32	32.82	35.83	41.15	47.50	54.30	60.81	64.89	68.53	72.88	75.92
49	26.45	28.30	31.12	33.65	36.70	42.08	48.50	55.37	61.94	66.05	69.73	74.12	77.19
50	27.19	29.06	31.92	34.49	37.57	43.02	49.50	56.44	63.07	67.22	70.92	75.35	78.45

Table 5.   95th Percentiles of the F Distribution.
Table Entry Is f Such That $\text{Prob}[F_{n_1,n_2} \leq f] = 0.95$.

n_2	1	2	3	4	5	6	7	8	9	10	12	15	20	30	40	50	60	∞
							n_1 = Degrees of Freedom for the Numerator											
1	161.	200.	216.	225.	230.	234.	237.	239.	241.	242.	244.	246.	248.	250.	251.	251.	252.	254.
2	18.5	19.0	19.2	19.2	19.3	19.3	19.4	19.4	19.4	19.4	19.4	19.4	19.5	19.5	19.5	19.5	19.5	19.5
3	10.1	9.55	6.54	9.12	5.89	8.94	5.63	8.85	5.49	8.79	8.74	5.32	8.66	8.62	8.59	8.58	8.57	8.83
4	7.71	6.94	6.59	6.39	6.26	6.16	6.09	6.04	6.00	5.97	5.91	5.86	5.80	5.75	5.72	5.70	5.69	5.63
5	6.61	5.79	5.41	5.19	5.05	4.95	4.88	4.82	4.77	4.74	4.68	4.62	4.56	4.50	4.46	4.44	4.43	4.37
6	5.99	5.14	4.76	4.53	4.39	4.28	4.21	4.15	4.10	4.06	4.00	3.94	3.88	3.81	3.78	3.75	3.74	3.67
7	5.59	4.74	4.35	4.12	3.97	3.87	3.79	3.73	3.68	3.64	3.58	3.51	3.45	3.38	3.34	3.32	3.31	3.23
8	5.32	4.46	4.07	3.84	3.69	3.58	3.50	3.44	3.39	3.35	3.28	3.22	3.15	3.08	3.04	3.02	3.01	2.93
9	5.12	4.26	3.86	3.63	3.48	3.37	3.29	3.23	3.18	3.14	3.07	3.01	2.94	2.86	2.83	2.80	2.79	2.71
10	4.96	4.10	3.71	3.48	3.33	3.22	3.14	3.07	3.02	2.98	2.91	2.85	2.78	2.70	2.66	2.64	2.62	2.54
11	4.84	3.98	3.59	3.36	3.20	3.10	3.01	2.95	2.90	2.85	2.79	2.72	2.65	2.57	2.53	2.51	2.49	2.40
12	4.75	3.89	3.49	3.26	3.11	3.00	2.91	2.85	2.80	2.75	2.69	2.62	2.54	2.47	2.43	2.40	2.39	2.30
13	4.67	3.81	3.41	3.18	3.03	2.92	2.83	2.77	2.72	2.67	2.60	2.53	2.46	2.38	2.34	2.31	2.30	2.21
14	4.60	3.74	3.34	3.11	2.96	2.85	2.77	2.70	2.65	2.60	2.54	2.46	2.39	2.31	2.27	2.24	2.22	2.13
15	4.54	3.68	3.29	3.06	2.90	2.79	2.71	2.64	2.59	2.54	2.48	2.40	2.33	2.25	2.21	2.18	2.16	2.07
16	4.49	3.63	3.24	3.01	2.85	2.74	2.66	2.59	2.54	2.49	2.43	2.35	2.28	2.19	2.15	2.12	2.11	2.01
17	4.45	3.59	3.20	2.97	2.81	2.70	2.62	2.55	2.50	2.45	2.38	2.31	2.23	2.15	2.10	2.08	2.06	1.96
18	4.41	3.56	3.16	2.93	2.77	2.66	2.58	2.51	2.46	2.41	2.34	2.27	2.19	2.11	2.06	2.04	2.02	1.92
19	4.38	3.52	3.13	2.90	2.74	2.63	2.54	2.48	2.42	2.38	2.31	2.24	2.16	2.07	2.03	2.00	1.98	1.88
20	4.35	3.49	3.10	2.87	2.71	2.60	2.52	2.45	2.39	2.35	2.28	2.20	2.13	2.04	1.99	1.97	1.95	1.84
21	4.32	3.47	3.07	2.84	2.69	2.57	2.49	2.42	2.37	2.32	2.25	2.18	2.10	2.01	1.97	1.94	1.92	1.81
22	4.30	3.44	3.05	2.82	2.66	2.55	2.46	2.40	2.34	2.30	2.23	2.15	2.07	1.99	1.94	1.91	1.89	1.78
23	4.28	3.42	3.03	2.80	2.64	2.53	2.44	2.38	2.32	2.28	2.20	2.13	2.05	1.96	1.91	1.89	1.87	1.76
24	4.26	3.40	3.01	2.78	2.62	2.51	2.42	2.36	2.30	2.26	2.18	2.11	2.03	1.94	1.89	1.86	1.84	1.73
25	4.24	3.39	2.99	2.76	2.60	2.49	2.41	2.34	2.28	2.24	2.17	2.09	2.01	1.92	1.87	1.84	1.82	1.71
26	4.23	3.37	2.98	2.74	2.59	2.48	2.39	2.32	2.27	2.22	2.15	2.07	1.99	1.90	1.85	1.82	1.80	1.70
27	4.22	3.36	2.96	2.73	2.57	2.46	2.37	2.31	2.25	2.21	2.13	2.06	1.97	1.89	1.84	1.81	1.79	1.68
28	4.20	3.34	2.95	2.72	2.56	2.45	2.36	2.29	2.24	2.19	2.12	2.04	1.96	1.87	1.82	1.79	1.77	1.66
29	4.18	3.33	2.94	2.70	2.55	2.43	2.35	2.28	2.22	2.18	2.11	2.03	1.95	1.86	1.81	1.78	1.75	1.65
30	4.17	3.32	2.92	2.69	2.53	2.42	2.34	2.27	2.21	2.17	2.09	2.02	1.93	1.84	1.79	1.76	1.74	1.62
35	4.12	3.27	2.88	2.64	2.49	2.37	2.29	2.22	2.16	2.12	2.04	1.96	1.88	1.79	1.74	1.70	1.68	1.57
40	4.08	3.23	2.84	2.61	2.45	2.34	2.25	2.18	2.13	2.08	2.00	1.92	1.84	1.75	1.69	1.66	1.64	1.51
45	4.06	3.21	2.81	2.58	2.42	2.31	2.22	2.15	2.10	2.05	1.98	1.90	1.81	1.71	1.66	1.63	1.60	1.48
50	4.05	3.18	2.79	2.56	2.40	2.29	2.20	2.13	2.07	2.03	1.95	1.87	1.79	1.69	1.63	1.60	1.58	1.45
60	4.00	3.15	2.76	2.53	2.37	2.26	2.17	2..0	2.04	1.99	1.92	1.84	1.75	1.65	1.60	1.56	1.54	1.39
70	3.98	3.13	2.74	2.50	2.35	2.23	2.14	2.07	2.02	1.97	1.89	1.81	1.72	1.62	1.57	1.53	1.51	1.36
80	3.96	3.11	2.72	2.49	2.33	2.22	2.13	2.06	2.00	1.95	1.88	1.79	1.70	1.60	1.55	1.51	1.48	1.34
90	3.95	3.10	2.71	2.47	2.32	2.20	2.11	2.04	1.99	1.94	1.86	1.78	1.69	1.59	1.53	1.49	1.47	1.32
100	3.94	3.09	2.70	2.46	2.31	2.19	2.10	2.03	1.98	1.93	1.85	1.77	1.68	1.57	1.52	1.48	1.45	1.30
∞	3.84	3.00	2.60	2.37	2.21	2.10	2.01	1.94	1.88	1.83	1.75	1.67	1.57	1.46	1.39	1.34	1.31	1.00

Table 6.   99th Percentiles of the F Distribution.

Table Entry Is f Such That $\text{Prob}[F_{n_1,n_2} \leq f] = 0.99$.

n_2	$n_1 = $ Degrees of Freedom for the Numerator																	
	1	2	3	4	5	6	7	8	9	10	12	15	20	30	40	50	60	∞
1	4052	5000	5403	5625	5724	5859	5928	5982	6023	6056	6106	6157	6209	6261	6287	6302	6313	6366
2	98.5	99.0	99.2	99.3	99.3	99.3	99.4	99.4	99.4	99.4	99.4	99.4	99.5	99.5	99.5	99.5	99.5	99.5
3	34.1	30.8	21.3	28.7	19.0	27.9	27.7	27.5	27.3	27.2	27.1	26.9	26.7	26.5	26.4	26.4	26.3	26.1
4	21.2	18.0	16.7	16.0	15.5	15.2	15.0	14.8	14.7	14.6	14.4	14.2	14.0	13.8	13.8	13.7	13.6	13.5
5	16.3	13.3	12.1	11.4	11.0	10.6	10.5	10.3	10.2	10.1	9.89	9.72	9.55	9.38	9.29	9.24	9.20	9.02
6	13.7	10.9	9.78	9.15	8.75	8.47	8.26	8.10	7.98	7.88	7.72	7.56	7.40	7.23	7.14	7.09	7.06	6.88
7	12.2	9.55	8.45	7.85	7.46	7.19	6.99	6.84	6.72	6.62	6.47	6.31	6.16	5.99	5.91	5.86	5.82	5.65
8	11.3	8.65	7.59	7.01	6.63	6.37	6.18	6.03	5.91	5.81	5.67	5.52	5.36	5.20	5.12	5.07	5.03	4.86
9	10.6	8.02	6.99	6.42	6.06	5.80	5.61	5.47	5.35	5.26	5.11	4.96	4.81	4.65	4.57	4.52	4.48	4.31
10	10.0	7.56	6.55	6.00	5.64	5.39	5.20	5.06	4.94	4.85	4.71	4.56	4.41	4.25	4.17	4.12	4.08	3.91
11	9.65	7.21	6.22	5.67	5.32	5.07	4.89	4.74	4.63	4.54	4.40	4.25	4.10	3.94	3.86	3.81	3.78	3.60
12	9.33	6.93	5.95	5.41	5.06	4.82	4.64	4.50	4.39	4.30	4.16	4.01	3.86	3.70	3.62	3.57	3.54	3.36
13	9.07	6.70	5.74	5.21	4.86	4.62	4.44	4.30	4.19	4.10	3.96	3.82	3.67	3.51	3.43	3.38	3.34	3.17
14	8.86	6.51	5.56	5.04	4.69	4.46	4.28	4.14	4.03	3.94	3.80	3.66	3.51	3.35	3.27	3.22	3.18	3.00
15	8.68	6.36	5.42	4.89	4.56	4.32	4.14	4.01	3.90	3.81	3.67	3.52	3.37	3.22	3.13	3.08	3.05	2.87
16	8.53	6.23	5.29	4.77	4.44	4.20	4.03	3.89	3.78	3.69	3.55	3.41	3.26	3.10	3.02	2.97	2.93	2.75
17	8.40	6.11	5.18	4.67	4.34	4.10	3.93	3.79	3.68	3.59	3.46	3.31	3.16	3.00	2.92	2.87	2.84	2.65
18	8.29	6.01	5.09	4.58	4.25	4.01	3.84	3.71	3.60	3.51	3.37	3.23	3.08	2.92	2.84	2.79	2.75	2.57
19	8.19	5.93	5.01	4.50	4.17	3.94	3.77	3.63	3.52	3.43	3.30	3.15	3.00	2.85	2.76	2.71	2.68	2.49
20	8.10	5.85	4.94	4.43	4.10	3.87	3.70	3.57	3.46	3.37	3.23	3.09	2.94	2.78	2.70	2.64	2.61	2.42
21	8.02	5.78	4.88	4.37	4.04	3.81	3.64	3.51	3.40	3.31	3.17	3.03	2.88	2.72	2.64	2.58	2.55	2.36
22	7.95	5.72	4.82	4.31	3.99	3.76	3.59	3.45	3.35	3.26	3.12	2.98	2.83	2.67	2.58	2.53	2.50	2.31
23	7.88	5.66	4.76	4.26	3.94	3.71	3.54	3.41	3.30	3.21	3.08	2.93	2.78	2.62	2.54	2.48	2.45	2.26
24	7.82	5.61	4.72	4.22	3.90	3.67	3.50	3.36	3.26	3.17	3.03	2.89	2.74	2.58	2.49	2.44	2.40	2.21
25	7.77	5.57	4.68	4.18	3.86	3.63	3.46	3.32	3.22	3.13	2.99	2.85	2.70	2.54	2.45	2.40	2.36	2.17
26	7.72	5.53	4.64	4.14	3.82	3.59	3.42	3.29	3.18	3.10	2.96	2.82	2.66	2.50	2.42	2.36	2.33	2.13
27	7.68	5.49	4.60	4.11	3.79	3.56	3.39	3.26	3.15	3.06	2.93	2.78	2.63	2.47	2.38	2.33	2.29	2.10
28	7.64	5.45	4.57	4.07	3.75	3.53	3.36	3.23	3.12	3.03	2.90	2.75	2.60	2.44	2.35	2.30	2.26	2.06
29	7.60	5.42	4.54	4.04	3.73	3.50	3.33	3.20	3.09	3.01	2.87	2.73	2.58	2.41	2.33	2.27	2.24	2.03
30	7.56	5.39	4.51	4.02	3.70	3.47	3.31	3.17	3.07	2.98	2.84	2.70	2.55	2.39	2.30	2.25	2.21	2.01
35	7.41	5.27	4.40	3.91	3.59	3.37	3.20	3.07	2.96	2.88	2.74	2.60	2.45	2.28	2.19	2.14	2.10	1.91
40	7.31	5.18	4.31	3.83	3.51	3.29	3.12	2.99	2.89	2.80	2.67	2.52	2.37	2.20	2.12	2.06	2.02	1.81
45	7.23	5.11	4.25	3.77	3.46	3.23	3.07	2.94	2.83	2.74	2.61	2.47	2.31	2.15	2.06	2.00	1.96	1.75
50	7.17	5.06	4.20	3.72	3.41	3.19	3.02	2.89	2.79	2.70	2.56	2.42	2.27	2.10	2.01	1.95	1.91	1.68
60	7.08	4.98	4.13	3.65	3.34	3.12	2.95	2.82	2.72	2.63	2.50	2.35	2.20	2.03	1.94	1.88	1.84	1.60
70	7.01	4.92	4.07	3.60	3.29	3.07	2.91	2.78	2.67	2.59	2.45	2.31	2.15	1.98	1.89	1.83	1.79	1.53
80	6.96	4.88	4.04	3.56	3.26	3.04	2.87	2.74	2.64	2.55	2.42	2.27	2.12	1.94	1.85	1.79	1.75	1.49
90	6.93	4.85	4.01	3.54	3.23	3.01	2.85	2.72	2.61	2.53	2.39	2.25	2.09	1.92	1.82	1.76	1.72	1.48
100	6.90	4.82	3.98	3.51	3.21	2.99	2.82	2.70	2.59	2.50	2.37	2.22	2.07	1.89	1.80	1.74	1.69	1.43
∞	6.63	4.61	3.78	3.32	3.02	2.80	2.64	2.51	2.41	2.32	2.18	2.04	1.88	1.70	1.57	1.51	1.46	1.00

Table 7. Durbin-Watson statistic: 1 percent significance points of dL and dU[a]

n	k'=1 dL	dU	k'=2 dL	dU	k'=3 dL	dU	k'=4 dL	dU	k'=5 dL	dU	k'=6 dL	dU	k'=7 dL	dU	k'=8 dL	dU	k'=9 dL	dU	k'=10 dL	dU
6	0.390	1.142	----	----	----	----	----	----	----	----	----	----	----	----	----	----	----	----	----	----
7	0.435	1.036	0.294	1.676	----	----	----	----	----	----	----	----	----	----	----	----	----	----	----	----
8	0.497	1.003	0.345	1.489	0.229	2.102	----	----	----	----	----	----	----	----	----	----	----	----	----	----
9	0.554	0.998	0.408	1.389	0.279	1.875	0.183	2.433	----	----	----	----	----	----	----	----	----	----	----	----
10	0.604	1.001	0.466	1.333	0.340	1.733	0.230	2.193	0.150	2.690	----	----	----	----	----	----	----	----	----	----
11	0.653	1.010	0.519	1.297	0.396	1.640	0.286	2.030	0.193	2.453	0.124	2.892	----	----	----	----	----	----	----	----
12	0.697	1.023	0.569	1.274	0.449	1.575	0.339	1.913	0.244	2.280	0.164	2.665	0.105	3.053	----	----	----	----	----	----
13	0.738	1.038	0.616	1.261	0.499	1.526	0.391	1.826	0.294	2.150	0.211	2.490	0.140	2.838	0.090	3.182	----	----	----	----
14	0.776	1.054	0.660	1.254	0.547	1.490	0.441	1.757	0.343	2.049	0.257	2.354	0.183	2.667	0.122	2.981	0.078	3.287	----	----
15	0.811	1.070	0.700	1.252	0.591	1.464	0.488	1.704	0.391	1.967	0.303	2.244	0.226	2.530	0.161	2.817	0.107	3.101	0.068	3.374
16	0.844	1.086	0.737	1.252	0.633	1.446	0.532	1.663	0.437	1.900	0.349	2.153	0.269	2.416	0.200	2.681	0.142	2.944	0.094	3.201
17	0.874	1.102	0.772	1.255	0.672	1.432	0.574	1.630	0.480	1.847	0.393	2.078	0.313	2.319	0.241	2.566	0.179	2.811	0.127	3.053
18	0.902	1.118	0.805	1.259	0.708	1.422	0.613	1.604	0.522	1.803	0.435	2.015	0.355	2.238	0.282	2.467	0.216	2.697	0.160	2.925
19	0.928	1.132	0.835	1.265	0.742	1.415	0.650	1.584	0.561	1.767	0.476	1.963	0.396	2.169	0.322	2.381	0.255	2.597	0.196	2.813
20	0.952	1.147	0.863	1.271	0.773	1.411	0.685	1.567	0.598	1.737	0.515	1.918	0.436	2.110	0.362	2.308	0.294	2.510	0.232	2.714
21	0.975	1.161	0.890	1.277	0.803	1.408	0.718	1.554	0.633	1.712	0.552	1.881	0.474	2.059	0.400	2.244	0.331	2.434	0.268	2.625
22	0.997	1.174	0.914	1.284	0.831	1.407	0.748	1.543	0.667	1.691	0.587	1.849	0.510	2.015	0.437	2.188	0.368	2.367	0.304	2.548
23	1.018	1.187	0.938	1.291	0.858	1.407	0.777	1.534	0.698	1.673	0.620	1.821	0.545	1.977	0.473	2.140	0.404	2.308	0.340	2.479
24	1.037	1.199	0.960	1.298	0.882	1.407	0.805	1.528	0.728	1.658	0.652	1.797	0.578	1.944	0.507	2.097	0.439	2.255	0.375	2.417
25	1.055	1.211	0.981	1.305	0.906	1.409	0.831	1.523	0.756	1.645	0.682	1.766	0.610	1.915	0.540	2.059	0.473	2.209	0.409	2.362
26	1.072	1.222	1.001	1.312	0.928	1.411	0.855	1.518	0.783	1.635	0.711	1.759	0.640	1.889	0.572	2.026	0.505	2.168	0.441	2.313
27	1.089	1.233	1.019	1.319	0.949	1.413	0.878	1.515	0.808	1.626	0.738	1.743	0.669	1.867	0.602	1.997	0.536	2.131	0.473	2.269
28	1.104	1.244	1.037	1.325	0.969	1.415	0.900	1.513	0.832	1.618	0.764	1.729	0.696	1.847	0.630	1.970	0.566	2.098	0.504	2.229
29	1.119	1.254	1.054	1.332	0.988	1.418	0.921	1.511	0.855	1.611	0.788	1.718	0.723	1.830	0.658	1.947	0.595	2.068	0.533	2.193
30	1.133	1.263	1.070	1.339	1.006	1.421	0.941	1.511	0.877	1.606	0.812	1.707	0.748	1.814	0.684	1.925	0.622	2.041	0.562	2.160
31	1.147	1.273	1.085	1.345	1.023	1.425	0.960	1.510	0.897	1.601	0.834	1.698	0.772	1.800	0.710	1.906	0.649	2.017	0.589	2.131
32	1.160	1.282	1.100	1.352	1.040	1.428	0.979	1.510	0.917	1.597	0.856	1.690	0.794	1.788	0.734	1.889	0.674	1.995	0.615	2.104
33	1.172	1.291	1.114	1.358	1.055	1.432	0.996	1.510	0.936	1.594	0.876	1.683	0.816	1.776	0.757	1.874	0.698	1.975	0.641	2.080
34	1.184	1.299	1.128	1.364	1.070	1.435	1.012	1.511	0.954	1.591	0.896	1.677	0.837	1.766	0.779	1.860	0.722	1.957	0.665	2.057
35	1.195	1.307	1.140	1.370	1.085	1.439	1.028	1.512	0.971	1.589	0.914	1.671	0.857	1.757	0.800	1.847	0.744	1.940	0.689	2.037
36	1.206	1.315	1.153	1.376	1.098	1.442	1.043	1.513	0.988	1.588	0.932	1.666	0.877	1.749	0.821	1.836	0.766	1.925	0.711	2.018
37	1.217	1.323	1.165	1.382	1.112	1.446	1.058	1.514	1.004	1.586	0.950	1.662	0.895	1.742	0.841	1.825	0.787	1.911	0.733	2.001
38	1.227	1.330	1.176	1.388	1.124	1.449	1.072	1.515	1.019	1.585	0.966	1.658	0.913	1.735	0.860	1.816	0.807	1.899	0.754	1.985
39	1.237	1.337	1.187	1.393	1.137	1.453	1.085	1.517	1.034	1.584	0.982	1.655	0.930	1.729	0.878	1.807	0.826	1.887	0.774	1.970
40	1.246	1.344	1.198	1.398	1.148	1.457	1.098	1.518	1.048	1.584	0.997	1.652	0.946	1.724	0.895	1.799	0.844	1.876	0.789	1.956
45	1.288	1.376	1.245	1.423	1.201	1.474	1.156	1.528	1.111	1.584	1.065	1.643	1.019	1.704	0.974	1.768	0.927	1.834	0.881	1.902
50	1.324	1.403	1.285	1.446	1.245	1.491	1.205	1.538	1.164	1.587	1.123	1.639	1.081	1.692	1.039	1.748	0.997	1.805	0.955	1.864
55	1.356	1.427	1.320	1.466	1.284	1.506	1.247	1.548	1.209	1.592	1.172	1.638	1.134	1.685	1.095	1.734	1.057	1.785	1.018	1.837
60	1.383	1.449	1.350	1.484	1.317	1.520	1.283	1.558	1.249	1.598	1.214	1.639	1.179	1.682	1.144	1.726	1.108	1.771	1.072	1.817
65	1.407	1.468	1.377	1.500	1.346	1.534	1.315	1.568	1.283	1.604	1.251	1.642	1.218	1.680	1.186	1.720	1.153	1.761	1.120	1.802
70	1.429	1.485	1.400	1.515	1.372	1.546	1.343	1.578	1.313	1.611	1.283	1.645	1.253	1.680	1.223	1.716	1.192	1.754	1.162	1.792
75	1.448	1.501	1.422	1.529	1.395	1.557	1.368	1.587	1.340	1.617	1.313	1.646	1.284	1.682	1.256	1.714	1.227	1.748	1.199	1.785
80	1.466	1.515	1.441	1.541	1.416	1.568	1.390	1.595	1.364	1.624	1.338	1.653	1.312	1.683	1.285	1.714	1.259	1.745	1.232	1.777
85	1.482	1.528	1.458	1.553	1.435	1.578	1.411	1.603	1.386	1.630	1.362	1.657	1.337	1.685	1.312	1.714	1.287	1.743	1.262	1.773
90	1.496	1.540	1.474	1.563	1.452	1.587	1.429	1.611	1.406	1.636	1.383	1.661	1.360	1.687	1.336	1.714	1.312	1.741	1.288	1.769
95	1.510	1.552	1.489	1.573	1.468	1.596	1.446	1.618	1.425	1.642	1.403	1.666	1.381	1.690	1.358	1.715	1.336	1.741	1.313	1.767
100	1.522	1.562	1.503	1.583	1.482	1.604	1.462	1.625	1.441	1.647	1.421	1.670	1.400	1.693	1.378	1.717	1.357	1.741	1.335	1.765
150	1.611	1.637	1.598	1.651	1.584	1.665	1.571	1.679	1.557	1.693	1.543	1.708	1.530	1.722	1.515	1.737	1.501	1.752	1.486	1.767
200	1.664	1.684	1.653	1.693	1.643	1.704	1.633	1.715	1.623	1.725	1.613	1.735	1.603	1.746	1.592	1.757	1.582	1.768	1.571	1.779

n	k'=11 dL	dU	k'=12 dL	dU	k'=13 dL	dU	k'=14 dL	dU	k'=15 dL	dU	k'=16 dL	dU	k'=17 dL	dU	k'=18 dL	dU	k'=19 dL	dU	k'=20 dL	dU
16	0.060	3.446	----	----	----	----	----	----	----	----	----	----	----	----	----	----	----	----	----	----
17	0.084	3.286	0.053	3.506	----	----	----	----	----	----	----	----	----	----	----	----	----	----	----	----
18	0.113	3.146	0.075	3.358	0.047	3.557	----	----	----	----	----	----	----	----	----	----	----	----	----	----
19	0.145	3.023	0.102	3.227	0.067	3.420	0.043	3.601	----	----	----	----	----	----	----	----	----	----	----	----
20	0.178	2.914	0.131	3.109	0.092	3.297	0.061	3.474	0.038	3.639	----	----	----	----	----	----	----	----	----	----
21	0.212	2.817	0.162	3.004	0.119	3.185	0.084	3.358	0.055	3.521	0.035	3.671	----	----	----	----	----	----	----	----
22	0.246	2.729	0.194	2.909	0.148	3.084	0.109	3.252	0.077	3.412	0.050	3.562	0.032	3.700	----	----	----	----	----	----
23	0.281	2.651	0.227	2.822	0.178	2.991	0.136	3.155	0.100	3.311	0.070	3.459	0.046	3.597	0.029	3.725	----	----	----	----
24	0.315	2.580	0.260	2.744	0.209	2.906	0.165	3.065	0.125	3.218	0.092	3.363	0.065	3.501	0.043	3.629	0.027	3.747	----	----
25	0.348	2.517	0.292	2.674	0.240	2.829	0.194	2.982	0.152	3.131	0.116	3.274	0.085	3.410	0.060	3.538	0.039	3.657	0.025	3.766
26	0.381	2.460	0.324	2.610	0.272	2.758	0.224	2.906	0.180	3.050	0.141	3.191	0.107	3.325	0.079	3.452	0.055	3.572	0.036	3.682
27	0.413	2.409	0.356	2.552	0.303	2.694	0.253	2.836	0.208	2.976	0.167	3.113	0.131	3.245	0.100	3.371	0.073	3.490	0.051	3.602
28	0.444	2.363	0.387	2.499	0.333	2.635	0.283	2.772	0.237	2.907	0.194	3.040	0.156	3.169	0.122	3.294	0.093	3.412	0.068	3.524
29	0.474	2.321	0.417	2.451	0.363	2.582	0.313	2.713	0.266	2.843	0.222	2.972	0.182	3.098	0.146	3.220	0.114	3.338	0.087	3.450
30	0.503	2.283	0.447	2.407	0.393	2.533	0.342	2.659	0.294	2.785	0.249	2.909	0.208	3.032	0.171	3.152	0.137	3.267	0.107	3.379
31	0.531	2.248	0.475	2.367	0.422	2.487	0.371	2.609	0.322	2.730	0.277	2.851	0.234	2.970	0.196	3.087	0.160	3.201	0.128	3.311
32	0.558	2.216	0.503	2.330	0.450	2.446	0.399	2.563	0.350	2.680	0.304	2.797	0.261	2.912	0.221	3.026	0.184	3.137	0.151	3.246
33	0.585	2.187	0.530	2.296	0.477	2.408	0.426	2.520	0.377	2.633	0.331	2.746	0.287	2.858	0.246	2.969	0.209	3.078	0.174	3.184
34	0.610	2.160	0.556	2.266	0.503	2.373	0.452	2.481	0.404	2.590	0.357	2.699	0.313	2.808	0.272	2.915	0.233	3.022	0.197	3.126
35	0.634	2.136	0.581	2.237	0.529	2.340	0.478	2.444	0.430	2.550	0.383	2.655	0.339	2.761	0.297	2.865	0.257	2.969	0.221	3.071
36	0.658	2.113	0.605	2.210	0.554	2.310	0.504	2.410	0.455	2.512	0.406	2.614	0.364	2.717	0.322	2.818	0.282	2.919	0.244	3.019
37	0.680	2.092	0.628	2.186	0.578	2.282	0.528	2.379	0.480	2.477	0.434	2.576	0.389	2.675	0.347	2.774	0.306	2.872	0.268	2.969
38	0.702	2.073	0.651	2.164	0.601	2.256	0.552	2.350	0.504	2.445	0.458	2.540	0.414	2.637	0.371	2.733	0.330	2.828	0.291	2.923
39	0.723	2.055	0.673	2.143	0.623	2.232	0.575	2.323	0.528	2.414	0.482	2.507	0.438	2.600	0.395	2.694	0.354	2.787	0.315	2.879
40	0.744	2.039	0.694	2.123	0.645	2.210	0.597	2.297	0.551	2.386	0.505	2.476	0.461	2.566	0.418	2.657	0.377	2.748	0.338	2.838
45	0.835	1.972	0.790	2.044	0.744	2.118	0.700	2.193	0.655	2.269	0.612	2.346	0.570	2.424	0.528	2.503	0.488	2.582	0.448	2.661
50	0.913	1.925	0.871	1.987	0.829	2.051	0.787	2.116	0.746	2.182	0.705	2.250	0.665	2.318	0.625	2.387	0.586	2.456	0.548	2.526
55	0.979	1.891	0.940	1.945	0.902	2.002	0.863	2.059	0.825	2.117	0.786	2.176	0.748	2.237	0.711	2.298	0.674	2.359	0.637	2.421
60	1.037	1.865	1.001	1.914	0.965	1.964	0.929	2.015	0.893	2.067	0.857	2.120	0.822	2.173	0.786	2.227	0.751	2.283	0.716	2.338
65	1.087	1.845	1.053	1.889	1.020	1.934	0.986	1.980	0.953	2.027	0.919	2.075	0.886	2.123	0.852	2.172	0.819	2.221	0.786	2.272
70	1.131	1.831	1.099	1.870	1.068	1.911	1.037	1.953	1.005	1.995	0.974	2.038	0.943	2.082	0.911	2.127	0.880	2.172	0.849	2.217
75	1.170	1.819	1.141	1.856	1.111	1.893	1.082	1.931	1.052	1.970	1.023	2.009	0.993	2.049	0.964	2.090	0.934	2.131	0.905	2.172
80	1.205	1.810	1.177	1.844	1.150	1.878	1.122	1.913	1.094	1.949	1.066	1.984	1.039	2.022	1.011	2.057	0.983	2.097	0.955	2.135
85	1.236	1.803	1.210	1.834	1.184	1.866	1.158	1.898	1.132	1.931	1.106	1.965	1.080	1.999	1.053	2.033	1.027	2.068	1.000	2.104
90	1.264	1.798	1.240	1.827	1.215	1.856	1.191	1.886	1.166	1.917	1.141	1.948	1.116	1.979	1.091	2.012	1.066	2.044	1.041	2.077
95	1.290	1.793	1.267	1.821	1.244	1.848	1.221	1.876	1.197	1.905	1.174	1.934	1.150	1.963	1.126	1.993	1.102	2.023	1.079	2.054
100	1.314	1.790	1.292	1.816	1.270	1.841	1.248	1.868	1.225	1.895	1.203	1.922	1.181	1.949	1.158	1.977	1.136	2.006	1.113	2.034
150	1.473	1.783	1.458	1.799	1.444	1.814	1.429	1.830	1.414	1.847	1.400	1.863	1.385	1.880	1.370	1.897	1.355	1.913	1.340	1.931
200	1.561	1.791	1.550	1.801	1.539	1.813	1.528	1.824	1.518	1.836	1.507	1.847	1.495	1.860	1.484	1.871	1.474	1.883	1.462	1.896

Source: N. E. Savin and K. J. White, The Durbin-Watson Test for Serial Correlation with Extreme Sample Sizes of Many Regressors, *Econometrica*, Vol. 45, no. 8, Nov. 1977, pp. 1992-1995.

[a] k' is the number of regressors excluding the intercept.

Table 7 (continued): 5 percent significance of points of dL and dU

n	k'=1 dL	k'=1 dU	k'=2 dL	k'=2 dU	k'=3 dL	k'=3 dU	k'=4 dL	k'=4 dU	k'=5 dL	k'=5 dU	k'=6 dL	k'=6 dU	k'=7 dL	k'=7 dU	k'=8 dL	k'=8 dU	k'=9 dL	k'=9 dU	k'=10 dL	k'=10 dU
6	0.610	1.400	----	----	----	----	----	----	----	----	----	----	----	----	----	----	----	----	----	----
7	0.700	1.356	0.467	1.896	----	----	----	----	----	----	----	----	----	----	----	----	----	----	----	----
8	0.763	1.332	0.559	1.777	0.368	2.287	----	----	----	----	----	----	----	----	----	----	----	----	----	----
9	0.824	1.320	0.629	1.699	0.455	2.128	0.296	2.588	----	----	----	----	----	----	----	----	----	----	----	----
10	0.879	1.320	0.697	1.641	0.525	2.016	0.376	2.414	0.243	2.822	----	----	----	----	----	----	----	----	----	----
11	0.927	1.324	0.758	1.604	0.595	1.928	0.444	2.283	0.316	2.645	0.203	3.005	----	----	----	----	----	----	----	----
12	0.971	1.331	0.812	1.579	0.658	1.864	0.512	2.177	0.379	2.506	0.268	2.832	0.171	3.149	----	----	----	----	----	----
13	1.010	1.340	0.861	1.562	0.715	1.816	0.574	2.094	0.445	2.390	0.328	2.692	0.230	2.985	0.147	3.266	----	----	----	----
14	1.045	1.350	0.905	1.551	0.767	1.779	0.632	2.030	0.505	2.296	0.389	2.572	0.286	2.848	0.200	3.111	0.127	3.360	----	----
15	1.077	1.361	0.946	1.543	0.814	1.750	0.685	1.977	0.562	2.220	0.447	2.472	0.343	2.727	0.251	2.979	0.175	3.216	0.111	3.438
16	1.106	1.371	0.982	1.539	0.857	1.728	0.734	1.935	0.615	2.157	0.502	2.388	0.398	2.624	0.304	2.860	0.222	3.090	0.155	3.304
17	1.133	1.381	1.015	1.536	0.897	1.710	0.779	1.900	0.664	2.104	0.554	2.318	0.451	2.537	0.356	2.757	0.272	2.975	0.198	3.184
18	1.158	1.391	1.046	1.535	0.933	1.696	0.820	1.872	0.710	2.060	0.603	2.257	0.502	2.461	0.407	2.667	0.321	2.873	0.244	3.073
19	1.180	1.401	1.074	1.536	0.967	1.685	0.859	1.848	0.752	2.023	0.649	2.206	0.549	2.396	0.456	2.589	0.369	2.783	0.290	2.974
20	1.201	1.411	1.100	1.537	0.998	1.676	0.894	1.828	0.792	1.991	0.692	2.162	0.595	2.339	0.502	2.521	0.416	2.704	0.336	2.885
21	1.221	1.420	1.125	1.538	1.026	1.669	0.927	1.812	0.829	1.964	0.732	2.124	0.637	2.290	0.547	2.460	0.461	2.633	0.380	2.806
22	1.239	1.429	1.147	1.541	1.053	1.664	0.958	1.797	0.863	1.940	0.769	2.090	0.677	2.246	0.588	2.407	0.504	2.571	0.424	2.734
23	1.257	1.437	1.168	1.543	1.078	1.660	0.986	1.785	0.895	1.920	0.804	2.061	0.715	2.208	0.628	2.360	0.545	2.514	0.465	2.670
24	1.273	1.446	1.188	1.546	1.101	1.656	1.013	1.775	0.925	1.902	0.837	2.035	0.751	2.174	0.666	2.318	0.584	2.464	0.506	2.613
25	1.288	1.454	1.206	1.550	1.123	1.654	1.038	1.767	0.953	1.886	0.868	2.012	0.784	2.144	0.702	2.280	0.621	2.419	0.544	2.560
26	1.302	1.461	1.224	1.553	1.143	1.652	1.062	1.759	0.979	1.873	0.897	1.992	0.816	2.117	0.735	2.246	0.657	2.379	0.581	2.513
27	1.316	1.469	1.240	1.556	1.162	1.651	1.084	1.753	1.004	1.861	0.925	1.974	0.845	2.093	0.767	2.216	0.691	2.342	0.616	2.470
28	1.328	1.476	1.255	1.560	1.181	1.650	1.104	1.747	1.028	1.850	0.951	1.958	0.874	2.071	0.798	2.188	0.723	2.309	0.650	2.431
29	1.341	1.483	1.270	1.563	1.198	1.650	1.124	1.743	1.050	1.841	0.975	1.944	0.900	2.052	0.826	2.164	0.753	2.278	0.682	2.396
30	1.352	1.489	1.284	1.567	1.214	1.650	1.143	1.739	1.071	1.833	0.998	1.931	0.926	2.034	0.854	2.141	0.782	2.251	0.712	2.363
31	1.363	1.496	1.297	1.570	1.229	1.650	1.160	1.735	1.090	1.825	1.020	1.920	0.950	2.018	0.879	2.120	0.810	2.226	0.741	2.333
32	1.373	1.502	1.309	1.574	1.244	1.650	1.177	1.732	1.109	1.819	1.041	1.909	0.972	2.004	0.904	2.102	0.836	2.203	0.769	2.306
33	1.383	1.508	1.321	1.577	1.258	1.651	1.193	1.730	1.127	1.813	1.061	1.900	0.994	1.991	0.927	2.085	0.861	2.181	0.795	2.281
34	1.393	1.514	1.333	1.580	1.271	1.652	1.208	1.728	1.144	1.808	1.080	1.891	1.015	1.979	0.950	2.069	0.885	2.162	0.821	2.257
35	1.402	1.519	1.343	1.584	1.283	1.653	1.222	1.726	1.160	1.803	1.097	1.884	1.034	1.967	0.971	2.054	0.908	2.144	0.845	2.236
36	1.411	1.525	1.354	1.587	1.295	1.654	1.236	1.724	1.175	1.799	1.114	1.877	1.053	1.957	0.991	2.041	0.930	2.127	0.868	2.216
37	1.419	1.530	1.364	1.590	1.307	1.655	1.249	1.723	1.190	1.795	1.131	1.870	1.071	1.948	1.011	2.029	0.951	2.112	0.891	2.198
38	1.427	1.535	1.373	1.594	1.318	1.656	1.261	1.722	1.204	1.792	1.146	1.864	1.088	1.939	1.029	2.017	0.970	2.098	0.912	2.180
39	1.435	1.540	1.382	1.597	1.328	1.658	1.273	1.722	1.218	1.789	1.161	1.859	1.104	1.932	1.047	2.007	0.990	2.085	0.932	2.164
40	1.442	1.544	1.391	1.600	1.338	1.659	1.285	1.721	1.230	1.786	1.175	1.854	1.120	1.924	1.064	1.997	1.008	2.072	0.945	2.149
45	1.475	1.566	1.430	1.615	1.383	1.666	1.336	1.720	1.287	1.776	1.238	1.835	1.189	1.895	1.139	1.958	1.089	2.002	1.038	2.088
50	1.503	1.585	1.462	1.628	1.421	1.674	1.378	1.721	1.335	1.771	1.291	1.822	1.246	1.875	1.201	1.930	1.156	1.986	1.110	2.044
55	1.528	1.601	1.490	1.641	1.452	1.681	1.414	1.724	1.374	1.768	1.334	1.814	1.294	1.861	1.253	1.909	1.212	1.959	1.170	2.010
60	1.549	1.616	1.514	1.652	1.480	1.689	1.444	1.727	1.408	1.767	1.372	1.808	1.335	1.850	1.298	1.894	1.260	1.939	1.222	1.984
65	1.567	1.629	1.536	1.662	1.503	1.696	1.471	1.731	1.438	1.767	1.404	1.805	1.370	1.843	1.336	1.882	1.301	1.923	1.266	1.964
70	1.583	1.641	1.554	1.672	1.525	1.703	1.494	1.735	1.464	1.768	1.433	1.802	1.401	1.837	1.369	1.873	1.337	1.910	1.305	1.948
75	1.598	1.652	1.571	1.680	1.543	1.709	1.515	1.739	1.487	1.770	1.458	1.801	1.428	1.834	1.399	1.867	1.369	1.901	1.339	1.935
80	1.611	1.662	1.586	1.688	1.560	1.715	1.534	1.743	1.507	1.772	1.480	1.801	1.453	1.831	1.425	1.861	1.397	1.893	1.369	1.925
85	1.624	1.671	1.600	1.696	1.575	1.721	1.550	1.747	1.525	1.774	1.500	1.801	1.474	1.829	1.448	1.857	1.422	1.886	1.396	1.916
90	1.635	1.679	1.612	1.703	1.589	1.726	1.566	1.751	1.542	1.776	1.518	1.801	1.494	1.827	1.469	1.854	1.445	1.881	1.420	1.909
95	1.645	1.687	1.623	1.709	1.602	1.732	1.579	1.755	1.557	1.778	1.535	1.802	1.512	1.827	1.489	1.852	1.465	1.877	1.442	1.903
100	1.654	1.694	1.634	1.715	1.613	1.736	1.592	1.758	1.571	1.780	1.550	1.803	1.528	1.826	1.506	1.850	1.484	1.874	1.462	1.898
150	1.720	1.746	1.706	1.760	1.693	1.774	1.679	1.788	1.665	1.802	1.651	1.817	1.637	1.832	1.622	1.847	1.608	1.862	1.594	1.877
200	1.758	1.778	1.748	1.789	1.738	1.799	1.728	1.810	1.718	1.820	1.707	1.831	1.697	1.841	1.686	1.852	1.675	1.863	1.665	1.874

n	k'=11 dL	k'=11 dU	k'=12 dL	k'=12 dU	k'=13 dL	k'=13 dU	k'=14 dL	k'=14 dU	k'=15 dL	k'=15 dU	k'=16 dL	k'=16 dU	k'=17 dL	k'=17 dU	k'=18 dL	k'=18 dU	k'=19 dL	k'=19 dU	k'=20 dL	k'=20 dU
16	0.098	3.503	----	----	----	----	----	----	----	----	----	----	----	----	----	----	----	----	----	----
17	0.138	3.378	0.087	3.557	----	----	----	----	----	----	----	----	----	----	----	----	----	----	----	----
18	0.177	3.265	0.123	3.441	0.078	3.603	----	----	----	----	----	----	----	----	----	----	----	----	----	----
19	0.220	3.159	0.160	3.335	0.111	3.496	0.070	3.642	----	----	----	----	----	----	----	----	----	----	----	----
20	0.263	3.063	0.200	3.234	0.145	3.395	0.100	3.542	0.063	3.676	----	----	----	----	----	----	----	----	----	----
21	0.307	2.976	0.240	3.141	0.182	3.300	0.132	3.448	0.091	3.583	0.058	3.705	----	----	----	----	----	----	----	----
22	0.349	2.897	0.281	3.057	0.220	3.211	0.166	3.358	0.120	3.495	0.083	3.619	0.052	3.731	----	----	----	----	----	----
23	0.391	2.826	0.322	2.979	0.259	3.128	0.202	3.272	0.153	3.409	0.110	3.535	0.076	3.650	0.048	3.753	----	----	----	----
24	0.431	2.761	0.362	2.908	0.297	3.053	0.239	3.193	0.186	3.327	0.141	3.454	0.101	3.572	0.070	3.678	0.044	3.773	----	----
25	0.470	2.702	0.400	2.844	0.335	2.983	0.275	3.119	0.221	3.251	0.172	3.376	0.130	3.494	0.094	3.604	0.065	3.702	0.041	3.790
26	0.508	2.649	0.438	2.784	0.373	2.919	0.312	3.051	0.256	3.179	0.205	3.303	0.160	3.420	0.120	3.531	0.087	3.632	0.060	3.724
27	0.544	2.600	0.475	2.730	0.409	2.859	0.348	2.987	0.291	3.112	0.238	3.233	0.191	3.349	0.149	3.460	0.112	3.563	0.081	3.658
28	0.578	2.555	0.510	2.680	0.445	2.805	0.383	2.928	0.325	3.050	0.271	3.168	0.222	3.283	0.178	3.392	0.138	3.495	0.104	3.592
29	0.612	2.515	0.544	2.634	0.479	2.755	0.418	2.874	0.359	2.992	0.305	3.107	0.254	3.219	0.208	3.327	0.166	3.431	0.129	3.528
30	0.643	2.477	0.577	2.592	0.512	2.708	0.451	2.823	0.392	2.937	0.337	3.050	0.286	3.160	0.238	3.266	0.195	3.368	0.156	3.465
31	0.674	2.443	0.608	2.553	0.545	2.665	0.484	2.776	0.425	2.887	0.370	2.996	0.317	3.103	0.269	3.208	0.224	3.309	0.183	3.406
32	0.703	2.411	0.638	2.517	0.576	2.625	0.515	2.733	0.457	2.840	0.401	2.946	0.349	3.050	0.299	3.153	0.253	3.252	0.211	3.348
33	0.731	2.382	0.668	2.484	0.606	2.588	0.546	2.692	0.488	2.796	0.432	2.899	0.379	3.000	0.329	3.100	0.283	3.198	0.239	3.293
34	0.758	2.355	0.695	2.454	0.634	2.554	0.575	2.654	0.518	2.754	0.462	2.854	0.409	2.954	0.359	3.051	0.312	3.147	0.267	3.240
35	0.783	2.330	0.722	2.425	0.662	2.521	0.604	2.619	0.547	2.716	0.492	2.813	0.439	2.910	0.388	3.005	0.340	3.099	0.295	3.190
36	0.808	2.306	0.748	2.398	0.689	2.492	0.631	2.586	0.575	2.680	0.520	2.774	0.467	2.868	0.417	2.961	0.369	3.053	0.323	3.142
37	0.831	2.285	0.772	2.374	0.714	2.464	0.657	2.555	0.602	2.646	0.548	2.738	0.495	2.829	0.445	2.920	0.397	3.009	0.351	3.097
38	0.854	2.265	0.796	2.351	0.739	2.438	0.683	2.526	0.628	2.614	0.575	2.703	0.522	2.792	0.472	2.880	0.424	2.968	0.378	3.054
39	0.875	2.246	0.819	2.329	0.763	2.413	0.707	2.499	0.653	2.585	0.600	2.671	0.549	2.757	0.499	2.843	0.451	2.929	0.404	3.013
40	0.896	2.228	0.840	2.309	0.785	2.391	0.731	2.473	0.678	2.557	0.626	2.641	0.575	2.724	0.525	2.808	0.477	2.892	0.430	2.974
45	0.988	2.156	0.938	2.225	0.887	2.296	0.838	2.367	0.788	2.439	0.740	2.512	0.692	2.586	0.644	2.659	0.598	2.733	0.553	2.807
50	1.064	2.103	1.019	2.163	0.973	2.225	0.927	2.287	0.882	2.350	0.836	2.414	0.792	2.479	0.747	2.544	0.703	2.610	0.660	2.675
55	1.129	2.062	1.087	2.116	1.045	2.170	1.003	2.225	0.961	2.281	0.919	2.338	0.877	2.396	0.836	2.454	0.795	2.512	0.754	2.571
60	1.184	2.031	1.145	2.079	1.106	2.127	1.068	2.177	1.029	2.227	0.990	2.278	0.951	2.330	0.913	2.382	0.874	2.434	0.836	2.487
65	1.231	2.006	1.195	2.049	1.160	2.093	1.124	2.138	1.088	2.183	1.052	2.229	1.016	2.276	0.980	2.323	0.944	2.371	0.908	2.419
70	1.272	1.986	1.239	2.026	1.206	2.066	1.172	2.106	1.139	2.148	1.105	2.189	1.072	2.232	1.038	2.275	1.005	2.318	0.971	2.362
75	1.308	1.970	1.277	2.006	1.247	2.043	1.215	2.080	1.184	2.118	1.153	2.156	1.121	2.195	1.090	2.235	1.058	2.275	1.027	2.315
80	1.340	1.957	1.311	1.991	1.283	2.024	1.253	2.059	1.224	2.093	1.195	2.129	1.165	2.165	1.136	2.201	1.106	2.238	1.076	2.275
85	1.369	1.946	1.342	1.977	1.315	2.009	1.287	2.040	1.260	2.073	1.232	2.105	1.205	2.139	1.177	2.172	1.149	2.206	1.121	2.241
90	1.395	1.937	1.369	1.966	1.344	1.995	1.318	2.025	1.292	2.055	1.266	2.085	1.240	2.116	1.213	2.148	1.187	2.179	1.160	2.211
95	1.418	1.929	1.394	1.956	1.370	1.984	1.345	2.012	1.321	2.040	1.296	2.068	1.271	2.097	1.247	2.126	1.222	2.156	1.197	2.186
100	1.434	1.923	1.416	1.948	1.393	1.974	1.371	2.000	1.347	2.026	1.324	2.053	1.301	2.080	1.277	2.108	1.253	2.135	1.229	2.164
150	1.579	1.892	1.564	1.908	1.550	1.924	1.535	1.940	1.519	1.956	1.504	1.972	1.489	1.989	1.474	2.006	1.458	2.023	1.443	2.040
200	1.654	1.885	1.643	1.896	1.632	1.908	1.621	1.919	1.610	1.931	1.599	1.943	1.588	1.955	1.576	1.967	1.565	1.979	1.554	1.991

Table 8.   Five Percent Significance Point of $d_{4,L}$ and $d_{4,U}$ for Regressions Without Quarterly Dummy Variables ($k = k' + 1$)

n	$k' = 1$		$k' = 2$		$k' = 3$		$k' = 4$		$k' = 5$	
	$d_{4,L}$	$d_{4,U}$	$d_{4,L}$	$d_{4,U}$	$d_{4,L}$	$d_{4,U}$	$d_{4,L}$	$d_{4,U}$	$d_{4,L}$	$d_{4,U}$
16	0.774	0.982	0.662	1.109	0.549	1.275	0.435	1.381	0.350	1.532
20	0.924	1.102	0.827	1.203	0.728	1.327	0.626	1.428	0.544	1.556
24	1.036	1.189	0.953	1.273	0.867	1.371	0.779	1.459	0.702	1.565
28	1.123	1.257	1.050	1.328	0.975	1.410	0.898	1.487	0.828	1.576
32	1.192	1.311	1.127	1.373	1.061	1.443	0.993	1.511	0.929	1.587
36	1.248	1.355	1.191	1.410	1.131	1.471	1.070	1.532	1.013	1.598
40	1.295	1.392	1.243	1.442	1.190	1.496	1.135	1.550	1.082	1.609
44	1.335	1.423	1.288	1.469	1.239	1.518	1.189	1.567	1.141	1.620
48	1.369	1.451	1.326	1.493	1.281	1.537	1.236	1.582	1.191	1.630
52	1.399	1.475	1.359	1.513	1.318	1.554	1.276	1.595	1.235	1.639
56	1.426	1.496	1.389	1.532	1.351	1.569	1.312	1.608	1.273	1.648
60	1.449	1.515	1.415	1.548	1.379	1.583	1.343	1.619	1.307	1.656
64	1.470	1.532	1.438	1.563	1.405	1.596	1.371	1.629	1.337	1.664
68	1.489	1.548	1.459	1.577	1.427	1.608	1.396	1.639	1.364	1.671
72	1.507	1.562	1.478	1.589	1.448	1.618	1.418	1.648	1.388	1.678
76	1.522	1.574	1.495	1.601	1.467	1.628	1.439	1.656	1.411	1.685
80	1.537	1.586	1.511	1.611	1.484	1.637	1.457	1.663	1.431	1.691
84	1.550	1.597	1.525	1.621	1.500	1.646	1.475	1.671	1.449	1.696
88	1.562	1.607	1.539	1.630	1.515	1.654	1.490	1.677	1.466	1.702
92	1.574	1.617	1.551	1.639	1.528	1.661	1.505	1.684	1.482	1.707
96	1.584	1.626	1.563	1.647	1.541	1.668	1.519	1.690	1.496	1.712
100	1.594	1.634	1.573	1.654	1.552	1.674	1.531	1.695	1.510	1.717

Source: K. F. Wallis, "Testing for Fourth Order Autocorrelation in Quarterly Regression Equations," *Econometrica*, Vol. 40, no. 4, July 1972, p. 623.

Author Index

---

* Asterisks indicate citations in chapter reference lists.

Subject Index